S0-EAO-840

WORK WITH DISPLAY UNITS 86

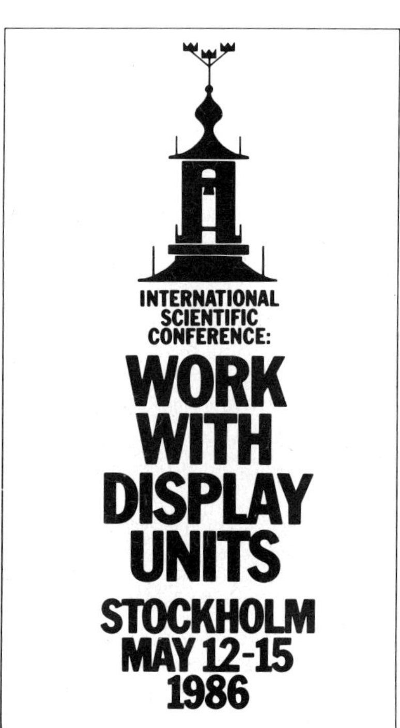
INTERNATIONAL
SCIENTIFIC
CONFERENCE:
WORK
WITH
DISPLAY
UNITS
STOCKHOLM
MAY 12-15
1986

WORK WITH DISPLAY UNITS 86

Selected Papers from the International Scientific Conference on Work with Display Units Stockholm, Sweden, May 12-15, 1986

edited by

BENGT KNAVE

Swedish National Board of Occupational Safety and Health Research Department

PER-GUNNAR WIDEBÄCK

Swedish Agency for Administrative Development

Co-editors:

Åsa Kilbom
Gunnela Westlander
Kjell Hansson Mild

Swedish National Board of Occupational Safety and Health Research Department

Yvonne Waern

University of Stockholm

Ove Franzén

University of Uppsala

1987

NORTH-HOLLAND
AMSTERDAM · NEW YORK · OXFORD · TOKYO

ISBN: 0 444 70171 0

Publishers:
ELSEVIER SCIENCE PUBLISHERS B.V.
P.O. Box 1991
1000 BZ Amsterdam
The Netherlands

Sole distibutors for the U.S.A. and Canada:
ELSEVIER SCIENCE PUBLISHING COMPANY, INC.
52 Vanderbilt Avenue
New York, N.Y. 10017
U.S.A.

PRINTED IN THE NETHERLANDS

PREFACE

This book will ensure the scientific heritage of the first International Scientific Conference: WORK WITH DISPLAY UNITS, Stockholm May 12-15, 1986.The Conference gathered 300 contributions by authors from 30 countries and altogether 1200 attendees from 35 countries. The programme of 60 oral paper presentation sessions (with interactive poster sessions and a parallel exhibition) was a good interdisciplinary start for the attendees with a professional interest in Occupational Health, Occupational Hygiene, Image Quality and Vision, Work Physiology, Work Place Design, Work Organisation or Human Computer Interaction. The attendees may by this book continue their penetration - disciplinary and interdisciplinary - on the subject WORK WITH DISPLAY UNITS, stressing health and well-being aspects. For the non-attendee this book is an opportunity to keep in touch with the topic area. And for all of us the book will serve as a preparation for the Second International Scientific Conference in 1989: WWDU 89 in Montréal September 11-14.

A BRIEF HISTORY OF THE CONFERENCE

After all the Welcomes in the worldwide spread Bulletins, in the Final Programme, in the Invitation to Exhibitors etc we would like to summarize the scope of the Conference but let us first recall the tense atmosphere during these May days in Stockholm through the Presidential Address.

Dear Conference Participants,

Three years ago, we were a group of Swedish delegates on our way to an international VDU standardization meeting in Manchester. It was on that trip the idea of having a conference in Stockholm grew into a decision: let´s have a conference that covers all aspects of health and well-being at Work With Display Units; there you have WWDU 1986. There had been some earlier ergonomic meetings (in Milan 1980 and Turin 1983), arranged by one of the pioneers in the field, professor Etienne Grandjean in Zürich. The meetings had been very successful and since we all knew professor Grandjean well it was quite natural for us to ask him for advice and to be the International Honorary Coordinator of our Conference. Professor Grandjean is retired since some years, and nowadays - and rightly so - he prefers sunny May days in Toscany together with his wife - to cloudy conference days at Stockholm. Anyway, our sincere thanks are given to professor Grandjean for all his help, and to all the other regional coordinators, who are present here today: without your help we hadn´t been where we are today. Thank you very much.

When we announced our Conference at that time (i.e. in 1983), some people said: 1986, why do you wait until 1986 - most probably there will be no problems with the VDUs then! Today we really know that a lot of problems still exist and that new ones have been added - problems to be discussed this week during the Conference days.

Early reactions from operators: Eye discomfort

My own experience goes back to 1972. I was called upon from an assurance company here in town where they just had equipped an office with VDUs, and it didn't take long time until complaints from the operators were brought forward to the company health physician - complaints indicating eye strain. The work place at that time was not especially good: dark screens, bright windows, reflexes in the screen etc. Ladies and gentlemen, some of these problems we still have in many work places and which we will deal with also at this Conference, 14 years later! But what I like to point out here is that those were the hardware problems dominating in the 1970'ies. Included were also discussions on keyboard design. As a matter of fact even radiation was drawn attention to because of some reports on cataracts (opacities of the lens in the eye) among operators. Vision ergonomics and image quality problems were the main issues, as I said. So, ergonomic measures were taken and the screen was improved - but still operators were not at ease, still there were complaints and subjective symptoms.

Work posture, stress, monotony and work organization

So, around 1980 or so, the interest was more directed towards work posture, towards work organization, stress and monotony. It became clear that there was postural discomfort, mainly from the neck, shoulders and upper part of the back, from VDU work, and that neck-back disorders in a way could be related to line of vision (or viewing axis), head position and furniture height. And the situation was not improved by the physical inactivity characteristic of VDT operators, on the contrary this was found to worsen discomfort. Add to this aspects from a work psychology view point: you come to your work place in the morning at 8 o'clock or so, you start a data entry work in front of the VDU, and you sit there all day (8 hours), you do this 5 days a week, 48 weeks a year, year after year... For many operators this is their work life. Of course this is unsatisfactory and will increase all types of symptoms and discomfort. And how odd it may sound there is also a stress component in this type of job. Let me quote from the program one title of the "Mental Load" Session later this afternoon: "Data entry tasks on VDU: Underload or overload". For instance the time you have to wait for an answer at the screen may be stressful, the same if the system breaks down when you least of all want it to break down ... As you can conclude from the extensive work psychology program of this Conference the psychologists know much more of these problems today than a couple of years ago. And what is most important, they have ideas of how to implement the new technique without damage to the work force. This is beneficial not only for the employees, the operators, but also for the employers, the management, as well. Results of investigations will give evidence of this.

Alternative displays

And of course we are eagerly waiting for the light, mobile, alternative VDUs (liquid cristal displays, electroluminiscent displays etc), because the use of these would alleviate the work a lot for the operators (for physiological postural and psychological reasons) on condition that the image quality is good. Unfortunately, the vision ergonomics of the new alternative screens today are inferior to most CRT screens and most often not acceptable in the work place. The technical development is rapid, however, so the future may not be so dark after all in this respect. We will hear more about this in the Thursday morning session on alternative VDU technologies.

Hardware and software

It was also in the first years of the 1980'ies that ergonomists and psychologists found another area of interest, namely software ergonomics, or man-machine dialogue, or human-computer-interaction in a more limited perspective. This grew into an important field along with the increasing popularity of personal computers. Are the programs used of a kind that is compatible with human function, or human brain and sensory functions? New concepts appeared: in addition to visibility, legibility, readability, the human-computer-interaction people talked about understandability, usability, userfriendliness, learnability. It is easy to realize that here are connections to the hardware image quality aspect of VDU work, as well as to work psychology problems in a broader sense. And the scientific interest in these questions increased: hardware was "out" and software "in" for some years...

Electromagnetic fields

But something new has come into the picture, again directing interest towards "hardware" - do the CRT based VDUs emit electromagnetic fields dangerous to health? Is there any relation between skin disorders and electrostatic fields of the operators? And is there a link between the electric charge of the operators and that of the VDUs? And, even more in focus: What are the results of the epidemiological studies on adverse pregnancy outcome and VDU work? What are the results of the experimental animal studies on magnetic fields and embryonic development? Well, much has been said in the news media and many statements and interpretations have been made. For the first time, ladies and gentlemen, we will now hear from the scientists themselves, we will have the possibility to take part of the scientific debate. What do the scientists themselves think of the results; of their own results and those of their colleagues? In the Organizing Committee we really appreciate that practically all scientists actively engaged in this research area have responded to our call for papers. All investigations in this area will be presented or commented upon during the sessions "Electromagnetic Fields", "Pregnancy Outcome" and "Skin Disorders". And of course the results, or the consequences of the results, will be touched upon also in some other sessions, e.g. in the "Information and Education" session to-day and in the "Recommendations and Regulations" session on Thursday.

Busy participants

Over 300 papers, in 60 sessions, to be presented orally as well as in special poster sessions - this means that all the the topic areas are well covered: "Ergonomics", "Image Quality and Vision", "Electromagnetic Fields", "Human Computer Interaction", "Work Organization" and "Occupational Health". To this we now have added sessions and demonstrations on "Functional disabilities and the new technique", an area of growing concern because of the widespread use of VDUs in work life and society. All this, Dear Participants, means that you are going to be very busy during the Conference days! Let me also remind you of the Exhibition next door and the Work Place Visits on Wednesday afternoon... and the Post Conference Tutorials on Friday... Really, it's a full time job to attend the VDU Conference in Stockholm.

Expectations

What can you expect from a Conference like this? Well, one thing is certain: we will not be able to solve all the problems which today are connected with Work With Display Units. The research process always takes a long time before you have a consensus among scientists and officials. But during the Conference days we will have the opportunity to discuss new findings and contradictory results. We will get a state of the art - and we will get the basis of an action programme for future research. There are problems that urgently need to be solved on a scientific basis. Otherwise standards and recommendations will be based on unreliable, soft grounds. As I said good research takes time - and for that reason, among other things - I am glad that there is a continuation of our Conference. As you all know by now the IRSST in Canada (Institut de Recherche en Santé et en Sécurité du Travail du Québec) will organize the Second International WWDU Conference in Montreal in 1989. I believe that it is not until then we will have a proper perspective to judge the results of WWDU 1986.

Welcome

So, the Presidential Address has come to an end. Dear Conference Participants, representing the Organizing Committee I have said it earlier in the Bulletins. Now it's a great pleasure for me to say it directly to you: Welcome to the International Scientific Conference "Work With Display Units" 1986!

So, the scope of the WWDU Conferences was to concentrate efforts to gather knowledge to make it possible to state and to solve problems; to inspire research within special fields as well as inter-disciplinary attacks. It is our forecast that the rich presentation and discussion of results from large field studies enlightened by research in the experimental field and by people in real life situations will appear also for future Conferences.

Now, it is time to think over the Papers and accept the challenge for a better understanding of health, comfort and effectiveness when working with new technology embodied in the display units. The history is also the pressure on the Conference during the last months before May 11 to release the Extended Abstracts. The electromagnetic fields had been hot stuff in Sweden. By accident two Extended Abstracts from Poland were conquered and used in Swedish press. The leak was fastly stopped up and the planning went on.

THE SELECTION OF PAPERS

You will find the two mentioned abstracts as full papers. You will have the same chance to read a Swedish paper that was used in the debate around the world.

Those Extended Abstracts with strong impact on the Conference have interested us when we selected the contributions. Our over all target is of course to reflect the whole conference. Because of the large numbers of good appearances we have favoured the high quality papers more central to the theme of the Conference.

The last task for the Scientific Organizing Committee has been to act in the selection of papers. The persons responsible in the Committee for a scientific area proposed - after discussions with other scholars in their field - a list of selections which were discussed with the editors. We want to thank the Scientific Organizing Committee for its job but we do not intend to evade our responsibility for the selection. Finally, we offered 120 contributions to come into the book. We calculated that some authors would not respond because of lack of time and other ways of publication. We have reprinted one Extended Abstract: The results of the important session on Pregnancy Outcome would not be understandable without the Canadian study.

THE BOOK - SOME COMMENTS

If you perchance compare the sessions of the Conference with the content of this volume you will find that many sessions are not represented by any paper. The lack of special scientific merits of the contributions has left out sessions like the more real life oriented sessions as Alternative VDU technologies and technical procurement and Recommendations and regulations. From a similar session, Information and Education, we have selected three papers. For the Human Computer Interaction area you will find an overview in the last paper of the book. The choice not to select about ten very qualified contributions has been founded on the fact that these papers would be published in a book together with similar papers of another conference under the name of Macinter (North-Holland). We do recommend this other book in a fastly developing area which is growing more central to future WWDU conferences.

The contributions to this book are ordered so that two overview and position papers on VDUs and health come first together with some papers reporting field studies on health. Then we have tried to follow a logic line up to the last paper.

We are aware that it takes time to state and evaluate scientific progress, sometimes it takes a very long time. The evaluation of contributions has a strong tendency to accept established ideas and reject fresh ideas without a fair penetration. So, what we might have missed of innovation in the selection of papers will probably be enlightened later on.

Anyway, many studies reported postural discomfort, eye discomfort and stress manifestations and in the discussions which followed here recommendations were often put forward on more research in the work organization area. There were also demands on continued research in other areas: Pregnancy Outcome, Skin Disorders, Alternative Technologies, Software Ergonomics and the broader Human Computer Interaction. We really regret that we only got one contribution each in the fields of Age and new technology, Culture and new technology and Effect of computers on thinking (and well-being). We hope for a better future response for these important areas.

To summarize, we think that all the important results of the Conference are gathered in this book and now it is up to you, Dear Reader, to evaluate and further discuss these results.

Bengt KNAVE
President WWDU 86

National Board of Occupational Safety and Health
Research Department
S-171 84 SOLNA, Sweden

Per-Gunnar WIDEBÄCK
Secretary General WWDU 86

Swedish Agency for Administrative Development
S-100 26 STOCKHOLM, Sweden

INTERNATIONAL SCIENTIFIC CONFERENCE: WORK WITH DISPLAY UNITS

Organized by the Swedish National Board of Occupational Safety and Health Research Department and Supported by the Swedish Agency for Administrative Development.

Scientific Organizing Committee

President	Bengt Knave
Secretary General	Per-Gunnar Widebäck
Secretary	Maud Werner
General Advisors	Tomas Berns, Lennart Möller, Tom Stewart
Members	Ove Franzén, Ph.D. (Image quality and vision) Kjell Hansson Mild, Ph.D. (Technical hygiene) Åsa Kilbom, M.D. (Ergonomics) Bengt Knave, M.D. (Occupational Health) Yvonne Waern, Ph.D. (Human-computer interaction) Gunnela Westlander, Ph.D. (Work organization)

Sponsors

Major Sponsors	Ericsson, IBM, Philips, Swedish Post Office, Swedish Telecommunications Administration.
Other Sponsors	Datapoint, Folksam Group, National Corporation of Swedish Pharmacies, Nokia, Scandinavian Airline System, Skandinaviska Enskilda Banken, SPP-AMFp, Teli Teleindustrier AB, Trygg-Hansa Mutual Insurance Companies.

International Coordinators

Honorary Coordinator
Prof. Etienne Grandjean
Switzerland

Regional Coordinators

Dr. Wolfgang Bachmann
Zentralinstitut für Arbeitsmedizin der DDR, Berlin

Dr. Diane Berthelette
IRSST
Montréal, Québec
Canada

Prof. N. Stuart Kirk
Univ. of Technology
Loughborough, United Kingdom

Prof. Kageyu Noro
Univ. OEH School of Medicine
Kitakyushu
Japan

Prof. Dr. Heinz Schmidtke
Institut für Ergonomi
München, Federal Republic of Germany

Prof. Michael Smith
Univ. of Wisconsin, Madison, USA

Prof. Jeanne M. Stellman
Columbia University, New York, USA

Prof. Alain L. Wisner
Conservatoire National des Arts et Métiers
Paris, France

CONTENTS

1. HEALTH

REVIEWS AND FIELD STUDIES

WORK WITH DISPLAY UNITS 86
B. Knave and P.-G. Widebäck (eds.)

VDT'S AND HEALTH
FACT OR FANCY?

J.A. Bonnell
Chief Medical Officer, CEGB, London

I would like to make a few brief comments on working with display units from the view point of the occupational health physician. Occupational medicine can be defined as a study of "the effects of health on work" and "the effect of work on health". I am therefore concerned with regarding the worker as a whole person; in general terms people spend 1/3 of their time at work, 1/3 of their time at home and 1/3 of their time asleep. It is important therefore to take account of activities during the time when a person is both at home as well as at work i.e. the total environment.

The introduction of new working systems is frequently accompanied by suspicion and anxiety and quoting from a very balanced leading article by Professor W.R. Lee in the British Medical Journal in October 1985 discussing work with VDU's "is likely to arouse instinctive caution on the part of organised labour".

The first action that has to be taken is that of assessing the physical working environment which exists in the vicinity of the display unit or terminal.

Fears have been expressed about the possible effects of radiation (both ionising and non ionising) which could be associated with VDU operation and also about electric and magnetic fields. I do not propose to reiterate what has been said already, but I would like to endorse what David Sliney said on Tuesday viz; let us at least go away from Stockholm convinced that there are no hazardous emanations arising from VDU's

Having hopefully dealt with the machine itself I should now like to examine the many different uses of VDU's; they are many and varied. Shorthand typists and secretaries use word processors instead of typewriters in many office situations and their use is obviously increasing at a great rate. These machines may be used intermittently as compared with their operation in, for example, mail-order situations and are different again in power station control rooms or in aviation control. In other words it is not enough merely to refer to VDU operators, but rather to various jobs in which the display unit is no more than a tool for a specific purpose. When investigating problems associated with VDU usage the total job must be taken into account. If the individual has to stand on his head to read a display screen he may develope a headache, but that is because he is standing on his head. Which brings me to the one point of real concern namely the ergonomic situation: proper workplace design is a necessary pre-requisite for persons whose job requires them to spend considerable periods of time interogating a display system. Much has already been said on this subject during the conference.

There are four problems relating to the use of VDU's which I would like to mention.

(a) Visual Problems - much has been written about this. It should be borne in mind that about 25% of the population do not have perfect vision, but only some of these people may require assistance for reading visual display screens. They can be relied upon to come forward if they know that assistance will be made available e.g. the provision of special refraction spectacles if it is necessary. I believe it is wrong and a waste of time (and money) to undertake prolonged and complicated eye screening tests on a routine basis. There are a number of other situations in industry in which this type of visual assistance may be required. In a recent study there was no significant difference in respect of frequency of eye strain or pain between full time typists and VDU users (Reading and Weale 1986, Lancet).

(b) Facial skin rash - these have been described and may be due to electrostatic deposition of charged dust particles on the face. Some VDU screens can develop an electrostatic potential of 10kV and the operator one of -0.6kV, poor ventilation can cause the deposition of dust on the face. Proper ventilation and antistatic devices or mats on carpets will alleviate the problem or even well watered potted plants. This is not a widespread problem but is largely confined to isolated reports describing individual cases.

(c) More recently the emotive question of reproductive effects or adverse pregnancy outcome has been raised as being associated with VDU use. I hope that the extensive study reported by Professor Alison Macdonald at this conference will have provided the reassurance required. This is a serious problem since in many countries pregnant women continue working well into their pregnancy. It is therefore highly desirable that the anxiety engendered by reports of increasing abortions and malformations should be considered sympathetically by employers. The fact that 20% of pregnancies never reach term is not a very convincing argument to put to a young woman in her first pregnancy. A point eloquently made by Ricardo Edstrom earlier this afternoon. Very much a case of the effect of health on work. There is no evidence to incriminate the emanations arising from VDU's as a possible cause of abnormal infants or of premature pregnancy terminations and it is the duty of investigators to make this point clearly to all concerned.

(d) Finally the question of "Repetitive Strain Syndrome" or "Repetition Strain Injuries" a group of conditions, also known as cumulative trauma disorders, affecting tendons and muscles of the hands, wrists arms and shoulders. Included in this group are carpal tunnel syndrome, tendinitis, tenosynovitis, de Quervans stenosing tenovaginitis, epicondylitis and cervical brachial disorders.

There are a wide variety of causes, including various occupations and many leisure and sporting acitivities e.g. playing musical instruments and tennis elbow, golf, electronic games, knitting, solving Rubic's cube, and even marathon running. In other words almost any activity involving rapid and repeated movements which can set up traumatic inflammation in tendons and muscles. Other factors including posture, muscular load, leverage and personality characteristics all play an important role.

Occupations include food packers, printed circuit board assemblers and keyboard operators including typists and more recently VDU users. The condition is commoner in women than men (2-10 times).

The actual incidence of this disease in a community is difficult to assess because of a lack of uniformity in diagnosis and semantics. Many cases are reminiscent of an old fashioned diagnosis of "writers cramp" in which there was a strong psychological overlay. The condition seems to be particularly common in Australia where there has been a 220% increase in claims of workers compensation over a 10 year period - 1344 claims in 1979-80 as opposed to 605 claims in 1970-71 in New South Wales alone.

The prevalance of the condition in those whose job includes VDU operation requires careful assessment in particular the question of leisure activities and out of work pursuits.

There is no doubt that work with VDU's has given rise to many questions for which answers must be found, in particular the anxiety engendered by reports of adverse pregnancy outcome. It is clear that ergonomic factors are fundamentally important which suggests that the majority of the problems can be readily solved with a little thought and the expenditure of moderate sums of money.

I would like to end at the point which I started with the British Medical Journal of 12th October 1985. Doctors are left "to reflect with Mark Twain that there is something fascinating about science as one gets such wholesome returns of conjectures out of such trifling investment of fact".

References

Lee, W.R. (1985) Brit. Med. J. 291:989

Reading, V.M., Weale, R.A. (1986) Lancet 1:905

Sliney, D.M., Wolbersht, M.L. This Conference *(not included).*

McDonald, Alison This Conference *(page 94, this volume).*

WORK WITH DISPLAY UNITS 86
B. Knave and P.-G. Widebäck (eds.)

HEALTH IMPACT OF WORK WITH VISUAL DISPLAY TERMINALS

Michael J. SUESS

Regional Officer for Environmental Health Hazards, WHO Regional Office for Europe, 8 Scherfigsvej, 2100 Copenhagen, Denmark*

A group of experts organized by the Regional Office for Europe of the World Health Organization was convened in Geneva, Switzerland, 21-23 May 1985, to review the health impact of visual display terminals (VDTs). Issues related to vision, ergonomics and radiation emissions were critically reviewed; other health considerations were also discussed. Health scientists recognize the existence of both physical and psychological influences on workers' health. While this review concentrates on the physical aspects, the difficulty is acknowledged of isolating the degree of physical causation from the confounding effect of psychosocial elements. However, the degrees to which the real physical problems exist are strongly dependent on the work environment and the intensity and duration of use of the equipment. (The psychosocial aspects of VDTs are the subject of a separate review, now under way).

1. VISUAL FACTORS

Workers and their organizations have expressed concern for some years about the possibly harmful effects of VDTs on the eyes. A critical review concluded that recent studies could not show elevated rates of ocular pathology in VDT users when compared to non-users [1]. Yet, in a number of surveys, a high incidence of complaints related to the eyes was reported. The most common symptom described and reported has been "eyestrain", more properly called visual fatigue. However, eyestrain is not recognized by ophthalmologists to be a clinical condition. There is evidence that visual acuity plays a comparatively minor part in the generation of symptoms. The causes of visual complaints may arise from the VDT itself, the indoor climatic conditions, or the operator's vision.

2. THE VIDEO DISPLAY

The WHO group of experts limited itself to review issues and data concerning VDTs based on cathode ray tubes (CRTs), even though other display forms exist. Factors discussed concerning the video display include: display characteristics, image quality, resolution, display stability, colour, display polarity, luminance and contrast, and hard copy quality. These subjects have been discussed well elsewhere [e.g., 1,2].

3. LIGHTING CONDITIONS

These conditions are affected by reflections, glare and workplace lighting, and

* The views expressed in this paper are those of the author and the WHO group of experts and do not necessarily represent the decisions or the stated policy of the World Health Organization.

various recommendations have been made in the full report concerning these factors.

4. THE OPERATOR'S VISION

No matter how well the display is designed and how optimal the lighting conditions are, if the operator is unable to see properly all is to no avail. The ability to see clearly depends upon a number of factors. They include especially visual acuity, or the ability to resolve objects in close proximity to each other; accommodation, or the ability to bring objects into focus at varying distances; and to a lesser extent, muscle balance, or the ability to direct both eyes simultaneously at the same object.

4.1. Visual acuity

A recent study failed to find any meaningful relationship between adequacy of refraction and the reporting of work-associated symptoms [3]. This somewhat surprising finding, however, would require much more extensive and detailed investigations and confirmation before one could dismiss totally any relationship between visual acuity and either performance or symptoms. It has been stated that a large proportion of the general population does not have adequately corrected vision [2]. This includes both persons who have never had their vision corrected and those whose previous corrections are no longer appropriate. Although some workers who use VDTs may have little or no problem even with a less-than-optimal correction of their visual acuity, it is felt that such a comparatively simple measure should be carried out before the cause of symptoms is sought elsewhere.

4.2. Accommodation

The loss of the power of accommodation is the disability of the eye lens to change shape enough to bring near objects into focus. This occurs in certain segments of the population, including many persons over the age of 40, an age at which most people begin to have problems. This defect can be corrected by suitable spectacles which, in turn, will limit distant focussing ability very much. Some VDT users may need a lens prescribed specifically for the VDT working distance. Other conditions of the eye may also affect the ability to see the screen clearly; chief among these are the phorias, or eye muscle imbalances. Within limits, these may be compensated for by subconscious muscular effort. This, however, may result in a degree of unacceptable muscular fatigue. Adequate correction by lenses is usually, although not always, possible.

5. INDOOR CLIMATE

5.1. Temperature

Whilst ambient temperature requirements for VDT operators do not differ in any way from those of other office workers, the VDT itself may be a significant source of heat. The heat generated by a VDT is usually in the range of 100-400 W, compared with 35-50 W from an electric typewriter and about 100 W from a human body. Thermal loading may be 30-150% greater compared with a working environment without VDTs. This obviously depends on a number of variables such as the type of VDT in use, the number and density of VDTs in a given area and the capability of the air handling system. Clearly, therefore, some account must be taken of thermal load before VDTs are introduced into a workplace, and engineering advice should be sought.

5.2. Relative humidity

It is not apparent that any unusual attention should be paid to relative humidity. However, wherever possible, at least 30% relative humidity and preferably higher, should be maintained when VDTs are in use. Higher humidity eliminates electrostatic charge accumulation, which might be responsible for skin rashes.

6. WORK STATION DESIGN AND LAYOUT

The VDT is a tool, and the work station must be designed around the kind of work the user is doing. It is necessary to consider space immediately in front of the VDT; attention must be given to keyboard and terminal adjustments; and there is a need for a work station design to satisfy the small and the tall, the chair being the most important item involved. However, it will sometimes be inevitable to make compromises between the operator's comfort and financial constraints. In view of all that is already known concerning the wide range of preferences of position on the part of operators, furniture design should be such as to allow the maximum of adjustability about already-known human dimensions.

7. RADIATION EMISSIONS

Radiation emissions were one of the issues critically reviewed. This issue, in particular, has frequently been misunderstood and dealt with on an emotional rather than on a rational level. Two types of radiation are associated with VDTs, namely, electromagnetic radiation - both ionizing and nonionizing - and acoustic radiation. The potential sources of the former radiation are the cathode ray tube (CRT), which may produce X-rays, ultraviolet (UV), optical and infrared (IR) radiations; and the horizontal deflection system, coils, transformers and other electronic circuitry, which may produce emissions at radiofrequencies (RF) and at extremely low frequencies (ELF). Acoustic emissions result from the mechanical vibrations generated in the core of the flyback transformer in the horizontal deflection system.

7.1. X-ray radiation

VDTs usually operate at a relatively low CRT voltage (about 12 kV) for monochrome units, and up to about 25 kV for colour units), and X-rays produced are absorbed by the glass of the CRT. Under these conditions emissions of X-rays are well below the natural background. Furthermore, designs of modern VDTs are such that a significant increase of the CRT voltage, which would result in an increased production of X-rays, is very unlikely. In monochrome CRTs, the display becomes unusable at about 15 kV. In colour CRTs (as those used in colour TV sets), where higher voltages are used, control circuitry is employed which causes the VDT to cease operation when the CRT voltage exceeds a set level.

A large scale study of X-ray radiation from VDTs and TV receivers, performed in the USA, indicated that the emissions under normal and severe test conditions are 26 nC/kgh or less [4]. Numerous tests of VDTs in use showed that X-ray emissions were below the natural background, i.e. about 2.6 nC/kgh [e.g., 5,6]. In a few cases, reports of excessive levels of X-rays were found after investigation to have been the result of faulty measurements [6]. Some models of colour TV monitors, which in pre-market testing under severe overload conditions were found to produce X-rays above 129 nC/kgh, were not allowed onto the market [4]. Finally, tests performed for nearly 70 different models in a low-background facility with extremely low background radiation showed that X-ray emissions were less than 7.7×10^{-8} nC/kgh. This was the background level in the test facility employed, and it can be considered as extremely low (approximately 1/1000 of the normal background). No X-rays could be attributed to operation of the VDT since the measured radiation levels were the same whether or not power to the test VDT was switched on or off [7]. In view of these results, the conclusions and recommendations of various government agencies (as reviewed in [6]) are well justified.

7.2. Ultraviolet, optical and infrared radiation

Measurements of emissions from VDTs in these parts of the electromagnetic spectrum have been reported [5,8,9]. Exposure limits are recommended in several countries. From making a comparison, it is apparent that UV, optical and IR emissions are about 100 or more times below the recommended limits.

7.3. Radiofrequency radiation

RF fields are characterized by the electric and magnetic fields. Extensive measurements at the frequency range 10 kHz-10 GHz have indicated that the main sources of emission are the flyback transformer and the horizontal deflection coil, which are parts of the electronic circuitry responsible for moving the electron beam horizontally on the screen. This movement usually occurs at a frequency of 15-22 kHz. In some VDTs, the main source of emissions is the high-voltage secondary wiring. Because of the complex waveform of the scanning signal, up to ten harmonics of the fundamental frequency 15-220 kHz are present [4,10,11]. Outside this frequency range, the emissions are very low. Some emissions may be present at frequencies of digital clocks and other digital circuits. Their range is 3-300 MHz, and the electric field strength is below 0.2 V/m at the VDT surface [6,11]. RF fields around VDTs at frequencies of 15-220 kHz are very low for many models. Various measurements showed that only some VDT models produce measurable emissions [4,8]. A small scale statistical sampling showed that in only about 35% of VDT models was the electric field strength in excess of 1 V/m at the operator's position. None of the measured emissions results in hazardous exposures.

A decrease in the field strengths is observed with increasing distance from the screen. At 0.3 m from the screen, the maximum electric field strength was 15 V/m and the maximum magnetic field strength was 0.17 A/m. These maximum values were obtained after testing 203 different models of VDTs. Some older models may produce stronger fields.

At a distance of 0.3 m from the VDT surface, close to the location of the flyback transformer or other source of emission, the maxima of the field strengths may reach 50 V/m and 1.1 A/m for the electric and magnetic fields, respectively; values of 15 V/m and 0.5 A/m are more typical [8,11]. These fields are localized. Still higher field strengths have been found in proximity to the VDT surface but the accuracy of measurement of these fields is suspect [6].

A comparison of the reported VDT operator exposures with these limits leads to the conclusion that unless the operator is within less than 1 m from the side or the back of another VDT which happens to produce high emissions, even the highest exposures are within the most stringent standards for the general population. In nearly 65% of cases exposures are below these limits by a factor of 10 (i.e., the electric field strength is below 1.5 V/m). Since some VDTs produce higher field strengths at the side or the back, it is a good practice, in order to maintain low levels of operator exposure to RF fields, to arrange the sitting of VDT operators so that they are 1 m or more from the side and/or back of adjacent VDTs. This recommendation does not apply if it is known that the adjacent VDTs emit only very low level RF radiation (e.g., at 0.3 m the electric field strength is not more than 10 V/m).

When the exposure of the VDT operator is compared with both the available scientific data on health effects and the recommended exposure limits, it can be concluded that it is very unlikely that the RF fields are of any health significance.

7.4. Extremely low frequencies

VDTs, like any other electric or electronic system and device, produce stray electric and magnetic fields at powerline frequencies (50 or 60 Hz) and its harmonics. Only a few VDT models have been tested, yielding measurements of the electric field strength of up to 10 V/m, and of the magnetic field strength up to 0.56 A/m [11]. The ELF fields around VDTs are not much different from ambient levels in laboratories and homes (typically, 1-10 V/m and 0.01-1 A/m), and they are weaker than the fields around other electric devices, such as household appliances, which reach up to 250 V/m and 23 A/m at a distance of 0.3 m [11,12]. Yet, there is substantial scientific evidence that a much higher ELF field strength is required to cause potentially hazardous biologic effects [12]. Biologic effects of weak ELF fields are of interest to basic science and medical applications. However, these interactions are not likely to affect human health.

7.5. Electrostatic fields

An electrostatic field (varying very slowly with time) is produced by the electric charge on the CRT Screen. The field's strength decreases rapidly with distance from the screen. The charge depends on display brightness, number of characters on the screen, the rate at which the writing beam is turned on and off, the design and operating history of the unit, and indoor climate conditions (e.g., humidity) [10]. Measurements performed on 54 units comprising 27 different models showed typical electrostatic field strengths at a distance of 0.3 m from the screen of between -150 V/m and +150 V/m, with a high of 1500 V/m [11], and in another study up to 30 kV/m.

The strength of the electrostatic field near VDTs can be compared with natural environmental fields. The average electrostatic field at ground level and in fair weather is about 130 V/m, but varies widely with elevation, temperature and humidity. Much stronger fields, up to 3000 V/m, are produced before and during thunderstorms. Furthermore, people can be charged to a high potential, depending on their clothing, floor surface and ambient conditions [13]; values of ±10 kV/m around charged persons are not unusual.

The available scientific data do not suggest any harmful biologic effects from electrostatic fields produced by VDTs, or from currents passing through the body when the person touches the VDT. Also, changes in the air ion balance due to a VDT, though more difficult to assess, are not expected to be large enough to produce biologic effects.

7.6. Acoustic radiation

Acoustic radiation with respect to VDTs includes both sound and ultrasound. In most practical situations, VDTs and affiliated equipment contribute little to the normal noise level in a workplace environment [14]. Depending on their scanning frequency, the acoustic emissions are sonic in the range of 15-20 kHz, or ultrasonic in the range of 20-32 kHz [4]. Measurements performed on 25 models of VDTs showed that maximum levels at the operator position were from 30 to 68 dB. These levels are below the recommended upper limits of 75 dB [15] or 80 dB [16]. However, some people are sensitive to lower levels of sound or ultrasound and may find this annoying [14]. Although this greater sensitivity does not imply the existence of physiological damage, acoustic shielding or modification of the CRT monitor may be in order to reduce annoyance.

8. OTHER HEALTH CONSIDERATIONS

8.1. Abnormal outcomes of pregnancy

In the past, the popular press published a number of reports on high rates of miscarriage or birth defect among groups of VDT users. Few of these reports have been the subject of detailed investigation, but where this has been done, either no cause attributable to VDTs has been found or it has been calculated that unusually high rates of such conditions can be expected on the basis of chance alone, particularly in view of the small size of the groups concerned. A number of epidemiological studies have been undertaken since the appearance of these reports although some have been criticized on methodological grounds [e.g., 13]. In a recent study, the analysed data covered 108 pairs of mothers from the Finnish national register of congenital malformations. All the mothers had worked with VDTs for at least 4 h/d during early pregnancy. The analysis led to the conclusion that exposure to VDTs does not cause birth defects [17]. In another study, data obtained from official Swedish statistical reports were examined with the conclusion that there was no evidence that work with VDTs had any effect on miscarriage rates or on rates of infant malformation [18].

8.2. The VDT as a potential cause

Is there anything inherent in the VDT itself that might make it a cause of spontaneous abortion, birth defects or any other unwanted complication of pregnancy? The most obvious possible factor is radiation. However, radiation of all kinds, whether alone or in combination, exists only at levels well below those known to have any biologic effect in man. Other potential factors include ergonomic conditions and occupational stress. Yet, ergonomic factors that may be related to fetal distress or reduced fetal growth are associated with hard physical activity at work and not with the sedentary type of activity of VDT workers. Occupational stress takes into account the kind of work being done, the organization of work, demands on work productivity and interpersonal relationships in the workplace. To these must be added stress that occurs outside the workplace and the emotions that may be brought about by the pregnancy itself. Therefore, VDT cannot be isolated as a single cause of stress. More likely, it would be the office environment rather than the apparatus itself, that would be a contributing factor.

8.3. Cataracts

Although only one report was made about the association between cataracts and use of VDT, the subject has received considerable publicity. Of 10 cases reported, 6 had inconsequential opacities not appreciably reducing visual acuity; in the 4 remaining cases there was either known pre-existing disease or exposure to a cataractogenic agent [1]. The causes of lenticular opacities are many, and the vast majority of visually disabling cataracts are associated with aging. Also Bergqvist, surveying a number of studies, concluded that there exist neither epidemiological nor experimental data to support the suggestion that VDT exposure could lead to cataract formation [17]. This is supported by the indication that none of the radiations alone, or all of them cumulatively, at levels associated with VDTs, are capable of inducing cataracts.

8.4. Skin rashes

One report discussed 10 cases of facial rashes, described as dermatitis, which were encountered among VDT operators [19]. The condition subsided rapidly when the individuals were away from VDT work. In one case, it was possible to reproduce the condition by the use of an electrostatic generator. Raising the relative humidity of the workplace and anti-static treatment of carpeting apparently cured the condition. Similar conditions have been reported by other authors. Although VDTs may contribute to some extent to the electrostatic load, it cannot be entirely separated from other indoor climate factors. To reduce the build-up of static charges, the relative air humidity should be raised wherever practicable (problems are caused in this respect by very low outdoor temperatures). Also, measures should be taken to reduce the electrostatic generation from carpeting and other materials.

8.5. Repetition strain injuries

Some reports indicate that there is an increased incidence of this sort in users of electronic keyboards and, in particular, VDTs. A comprehensive survey of repetition strain injuries was made in Australia, citing keyboard operation in occupations concerned with information and data processing as appearing to carry an increased risk of injury [20]. In some users, the condition has become so severe as to require clinical treatment, including surgical intervention. (Classification difficulties, and especially the loose and often incorrect use of the term "tenosynovitis", have made interpretation of reports difficult [21]). Further studies are required to describe the precise musculoskeletal conditions in relation both to keyboard design and, more generally, to workstation layout, so that preventive measures may be taken by equipment designers and manufacturers.

8.6. Photosensitive epilepsy

Some 1-3% of the epileptic population (5-15 per 100 000 of the total population) is subject to seizures provoked by visual stimuli, but the incidence falls off quite rapidly after the age of 16-18 years. The optimum flash frequencies to induce convulsions are between 10 and 25 Hz, although one study showed that convulsions could be produced at frequencies between 10 and 43 Hz by patterned stimulation [2]. However, it is unlikely that anyone will experience photosensitive epilepsy for the first time while operating a VDT. Modern displays do not flicker at the most troublesome (epileptogenic) frequencies and the lines of text on a VDT screen are, at the usual working distances, considerably coarser than the 3 per degree of arc stripes most likely to provoke seizures. There are no known reports of VDT-caused convulsions. It seems reasonable, however, to recommend that any known epileptic who is sensitive to visual stimuli should consult a physician before undertaking work with VDTs.

8.7. Polychlorinated biphenyls (PCBs)

In a few cases, emissions of PCBs have been attributed to VDTs. However, it was concluded as a result of several investigations that PCBs were deposited onto the VDTs from the contaminated ambient air and did not arise from the electrical components in the units [22].

8.8. Medical surveillance

No scientifically valid evidence was found which would suggest that the use of VDTs per se causes harm to the visual system, in the sense of anatomical or physiological damage [1]. A mandatory programme of ophthalmological examinations cannot, therefore, be justified. Working with VDTs is only one of many types of occupations which require a continuous near-visual effort but otherwise, no specific attention. Individuals who do complain of ocular discomfort or of difficulty in reading displays should seek medical advice, and such advice may include periodic surveillance.

9. CONCLUSIONS AND RECOMMENDATIONS

A critical review of the available data leads to a conclusion that the various factors discussed can be divided into three categories: factors which may lead to possible health problems, and which can be eliminated by taking preventive measures; unresolved issues, which may or may not prove to be significant; and factors of concern which have become issues, but have not proved to be such on the basis of scientific evidence.

Visual and musculoskeletal problems remain the two commonest areas of concern. They are usually a direct result of a lack of sufficient attention to ergonomics in terms of work place design and layout, and perhaps also due to problems with visual accommodation. They can be eliminated, or at least greatly limited.

Ionizing and nonionizing radiation, ocular pathology (including cataracts), epilepsy and PCBs, all have been frequently cited in nonscientific publications as problems, but in reality this has not been proven. The three latter issues have not even been shown to be directly associated with work on VDTs.

Adverse pregnancy outcomes, repetitive strain injuries and skin problems have not been fully resolved and require further investigations. The evidence on effects of work with VDTs on pregnancy outcomes is somewhat inconclusive and rather indicative of a lack of relationship. Because of the importance, there is a need to establish, with as high a level of confidence as possible, whether work with VDTs does or does not have any adverse effect on the pregnant woman or the fetus. Skin problems have been reported only in a very small number of cases, and are likely to be remedied easily through better control of the general workplace environment. Consequently, the WHO group of experts endorsed the following:

1. VDT workers, similarly to other workers whose jobs pose high visual demands, should have their vision corrected by proper spectacles, if needed.

2. The design of VDTs should be such as to ensure high image quality. (Essential factors are resolution, display stability, display polarity, luminance and contrast).

3. Lighting conditions are critical in eliminating visual discomfort. Specific measures must be taken to eliminate reflections and glare. The lighting of the workplace should be properly adapted to the task to be performed.

4. Modern VDT displays have the glass surface specially treated to ensure low reflectivity, no external filters are then needed. Use of glare filters on older VDTs, while it may eliminate reflections, at the same time may degrade the luminance of the display and its resolution, resulting in an increase in visual fatigue. Elimination of sources of reflection is the desired solution.

5. Because of the work demands put on VDT operators, it is important that environmental factors such as temperature, humidity and noise level are kept within limits that are at the least in the acceptable range and are preferably as near optimal as possible.

6. One of the most critical issues is the design and layout of the workstation so as to eliminate sources of operator postural problems. This is not only a very critical requirement but also a challenging and difficult one, as there are many different types of work and vast anatomical differences between VDT operators. There are already many well-established ergonomic principles that should be followed, but further research in this field is still required.

7. Ophthalmological examinations should be carried on for VDT operators who experience visual problems while working with VDTs.

8. Where VDT operators experience skin rashes, indoor climate factors (e.g., humidity), and static electricity should be measured, with proper controls implemented where required.

9. There is no need for periodic checks of VDTs for X-ray radiation, as there is no inherent factor which may cause X-ray emissions to increase with aging of a VDT.

10. There is no valid reason for VDT operators to wear a lead or any other metal apron, independently of whether they are pregnant or not.

11. It is very unlikely that radiofrequency fields are of any health significance, when exposure of the VDT operator is compared with available scientific data on health effects of these fields, and when this exposure is compared against recommended exposure limits. Nevertheless, it is good practice to avoid exposure to nonionizing radiation by spacing operators at least 1 m from other VDTs, unless the emissions from the equipment have been measured and found to be low.

12. There are no scientifically-established physical factors that could justify the transfer of a pregnant VDT operator to a job in which VDTs are not used.

ACKNOWLEDGEMENT

The final complete report, authored by I.A. Marriott and M.A. Stuchly, will be published in September 1986 in the Journal of Occupational Medicine. This paper is based on that report.

REFERENCES

[1] National Research Council Committee on Vision. Video Displays, Work, and Vision, Washington DC, National Academy Press, 1983.
[2] Cakir, A., Hart, D.J. & Stewart, T.F.M. Visual Display Terminals. Toronto, John Wiley and Sons, 1980.
[3] Smith, A.B., Tanaka, S., Halperin, W. & Richards, R.D. Correlates of Ocular and Somatic Symptoms among Video Display Terminal Users. Human Factors, 26: (2), 143 (1984).
[4] An Evaluation of Radiation Emission from Video Display Terminals. Rockville, MD, Bureau of Radiological Health, US Department of Health and Human Services, 1981. (Publication FDA 81-8153).
[5] Potential Health Hazards of Video Display Terminals. Washington, DC, National Institute for Occupational Safety and Health, US Department of Health and Human Services, 1981. (NIOSH Research Report, Publication 81-129).
[6] Investigation of Radiation Emissions from Video Display Terminals. Ottawa, Environmental Health Directorate, Health and Welfare Canada, 1983. (Publication 83-EHD-91).
[7] Pomroy, C & Noel, L. Low-background Radiation Measurements on Video Display Terminals. Health Physics, 46: 413-417 (1984).
[8] Electromagnetic Emissions from Video Display Terminals (VDTs). Yallambie, Victoria, Australian Radiation Laboratory, Commonwealth Department of Health, 1984.
[9] Weiss, M.M. The Video Display Terminals - is there a Radiation Hazard? Journal of Occupational Medicine, 25: 98-100 (1983).

[10] Harvey, S.M. Electric-field Exposure of Persons Using Video Display Units. Bioelectromagnetics, 5: 1-12 (1984).
[11] Video Display Units - Characterization of Electric and Magnetic Fields, Ontario Hydro Research Division, 1984. (Report No. 82-528-K).
[12] Stuchly, M.A., Lecuyer, D.W. & Mann, R.D. Extremely Low Frenquency Electromagnetic Emissions from Video Display Terminals and Other Devices. Health Physics, 45: 713-722 (1983).
[13] Bergqvist, U.O.V. Video Display Terminals. Scandinavian Journal of Work Environment & Health, 10: (suppl. 2), 1-87 (1984).
[14] Chatterjee, D.S. & Crookes, A.J. VDU's and Relative Annoyance from High Frequency Noise. Journal of Occupational Medicine, 26: 552-553 (1984).
[15] Hill, C.R. & ter Haar, G. Ultrasound. In: Suess, M.J., ed. Nonionizing Radiation Protection. Copenhagen, WHO Regional Office for Europe, 1982, pp. 199-228 (WHO Regional Publications, European Series No. 10).
[16] Ultrasound. Geneva, World Health Organization, 1982. (Environmental Health Criteria 16).
[17] Kurppa, K., Holmberg, P.C., Rantala, K. & Nurminen, T. Letter to the Editor. Lancet, ii, 1339 (1984).
[18] Källen, B. Dataskärmsarbete och graviditet [Data on Screen Work and Pregnancies]. Läkartidningen, 82: 1339-1342, (1985) (in Swedish).
[19] Linden, V. & Rolfsen, S. Video Computer Terminals and Occupational Dermatitis. Scandinavian Journal of Work, Environment & Health, 7: 62-67 (1981).
[20] Browne, C.D., Nolan, B.M. & Faithfull, D.K. Occupational Repetition Strain Injuries, Guidelines for Diagnosis and Management. Medical Journal of Australia, 140: 329 (1984).
[21] McPhee, B. Deficiencies in the Ergonomic Design of Keyboard Work and Upper Limb and Neck Disorders in Operators. Journal of Human Ergology, 11: 31-36 (1982).
[22] Benoit, F.M., LeBel, G.L. & Williams, D.T. Are Video Display Terminals a Source of Increased PCB Concentration in the Working Atmosphere? One Answer. International Archives of Occupational and Environmental Health, 53: 261 (1984).

WORK WITH DISPLAY UNITS 86
B. Knave and P.-G. Widebäck (eds.)

DETERMINANTS OF THE VDU OPERATOR'S WELL-BEING

Frank POT (1), Pieter PADMOS (2), Alfred BROUWERS (1)

(1) TNO Institute for Preventive Health Care,
P.O. Box 124, 2300 AC Leiden, The Netherlands
(2) TNO Institute for Perception, Soesterberg, The Netherlands

Patterns of complaints of VDU operators have been studied in relation to work organization, workplace ergonomics and operators' eye quality. Most subjects worked on data entry and word processing. The percentage of working day with VDU (VDUTIME) varied widely among subjects. The relations found were generally weak. Eye fatigue appeared to be related to eye quality and to visual ergonomics. Musculo-skeletal complaints were related to postural ergonomics. An interactive relation was found between health complaints on the one hand and VDUTIME and the work pressure and work atmosphere experienced on the other. Operators' satisfaction with ergonomic features often correlated reasonably with our quality assessments. Many operators want more work variation and miss opportunity for choice in their VDU tasks.

1. AIM AND LAY-OUT OF THE RESEARCH

This study was performed by order of the Netherlands' Ministry of Social Affairs. The aim of the field study was to investigate patterns of complaints by VDU operators and to relate types of complaints to many specific elements of the working conditions. First, relations were established between type of work, percentage VDU work, visual-and postural ergonomic characteristics on the one hand and health complaints on the other. Second, it was determined whether or not these relations are influenced by eye properties, work pressure, work atmosphere and autonomy. Third, operators' opinions were sought with regard to ergonomic aspects and to favourable and unfavourable aspects of the task. It is intended that results of this study enable the Labour Inspectorate to complete or adapt existing government recommendations.

The study included 222 VDU operators in many different office departments of primarily banking or insurance companies and government. The following types of work were selected: word processing, data entry, and simple retrieval and checking. According to our previous literature review [1] complaints are most frequent for these types of work. Operators were also selected on the basis of the mean percentage of the working day spent in VDU work. All operators were employed for at least 32 hours per week and had at least three months of experience with their present type of VDU work.

For each operator-workplace combination the following research methods were applied:

- detailed measurements of visual and postural ergonomic conditions at the workplace (160 items);
- detailed optometric measurements (60 items);
- a standardized interview on health complaints, ergonomic problems, task structure, working hours and job satisfaction (250 items).

The following sections cover respectively: variables and model of analysis (2), analysis results (3), reflections on improving the quality of VDU work (4). For a complete account of this study see reference [2].

2. VARIABLES AND MODEL OF ANALYSIS

For the purpose of the analysis a number of items from the measurements and the questionnaire were combined to new variables. As a first step a qualification "good" or "bad" was attached to each relevant ergonomic and optometric item. If the value of an item did not meet a criterion established a priori then it received the label "bad". Next, groups of items that might be relevant to the various complaints were composed, and from each group the items that showed at least a tendency towards a correlation with the corresponding health complaint (visual and optometric items with eye fatigue; postural ergonomic items with musculo-skeletal complaints) were selected in order to compose "sumvariables". For each operator-workplace combination the value of a particular sumvariable consisted of the number of scores "bad", summed over its constitutive items. Because of this method of selection, the correlations found between these sumvariables and health complaints must be interpreted with some caution. Studies of other samples of VDU operators should prove the more general predictive value of the ergonomic and optometric items selected.

These compilations and selections resulted in the construction of the following sumvariables:
- SUMVIS (Table 1), summation of scores "bad" for visual conditions;
- SUMPOST (Table 2), summation of scores "bad" for work posture;
- SUMEYE (Table 3), summation of scores "bad" for optometric properties;
- 23 sumvariables (specified in ref. [2]) for ergonomic items that might correlate with operators' answers to 23 questions regarding satisfaction with ergonomic conditions.

Table 1. Items making up SOMVIS

general VDU legibility
(line spacing)/(line width) VDU
line separation of wide tables VDU
VDU characters sharp, 50 cm distance
contrast character-screen background
contrast reflection-screen background
handwritten manuscript
viewing angle screen-keyboard
glare from light source
effectivity daylight screening

Table 2. Items making up SUMPOST

chair height minus lower leg length
footrest stability
footrest slope < 15 degree
trunk torsion
chair stability
head rotation
viewing angle screen-keyboard
foot space
footrest dimension
VDU movable
VDU tiltable

Table 3. Items making up SUMEYE

red eyes
often squinting, blinking, frowning
contact lens wearer
binocular visual acuity, distance
largest effective myopia
near visual performance index [3]
visual acuity, close
accommodation amplitude
instability lateral balance
positive relative convergence
positive fusional reserve
negative relative convergence
positive relative accommodation
negative relative accommodation
half, bi- or multi-focal spectacles

Table 4. Items making up SUMPRESS

recording of individual work output
mentally strenuous work
working under time pressure
work often too fatiguing
frequent overtime

Table 5. Items making up SUMSPHER

pleasant working room
work requires personal contacts
sufficient informal contact
well organized work
good relations among each other
good direct management
briefed about changes
advance deliberation about changes
appreciated sufficiently
pay according to work
job sufficiently secure
good promotion possibilities

Table 6. Items making up SUMAUTON

optional sequence VDU tasks
optional lay-out screen
optional command modes VDU
informal work breaks possible

Items from the questionnaire were also processed. To describe the tasks of the operators the following variables were constructed. The percentage of working time engaged in VDU work (VDUTIME) was divided into four classes (1-39%, 40-60%, 61-80%, 81-100%). There are three types of VDU work (VDUTASK), viz. word processing, data entry and retrieval/checking of data. Moreover, several questionnaire answers applying to work pressure or work atmosphere or autonomy were grouped and converted into sumvariables by counting the scores "bad" per operator and per group. This resulted in the following sumvariables:

- SUMPRESS (Table 4), summation of scores "bad" concerning work pressure,
- SUMSPHER (Table 5), summation of scores "bad" concerning work atmosphere,
- SUMAUTON (Table 6), summation of scores "bad" concerning autonomy.

Health complaints were grouped in a different way. Questions were posed concerning frequency of complaints (hardly ever, certain periods of the year, some days per month, some days per week, almost daily). For the analysis the answers "some days per week" and "almost daily" were taken together and denoted as "often". The other scores were denoted as "never/sometimes" Several complaints appeared to occur together, e.g. various complaints on eye fatigue. Therefore it was decided to define the occurrence of a compound complaint if an operator indicated having "often" one or more constitutive complaints. This resulted in the following variables for compound health complaints:

- EYECOM, often having (or not) one or more of the five complaints on eye fatigue asked about;
- MUSKECOM, often having (or not) one or more of the five musculo-skeletal complaints asked about;
- HEADCOM, often having (or not) headache;
- SKINCOM, often having (or not) one or both of the two complaints on skin rash asked about;
- NERFACOM, often having (or not) one or more of the six complaints on general fatigue and nervousness asked about.

Including the newly constructed (sum)variables, univariate analyses (relations between two variables) and multivariate analyses (relations among several variables) were performed subsequently. A summary of the statistical operations is presented in Figure 1.

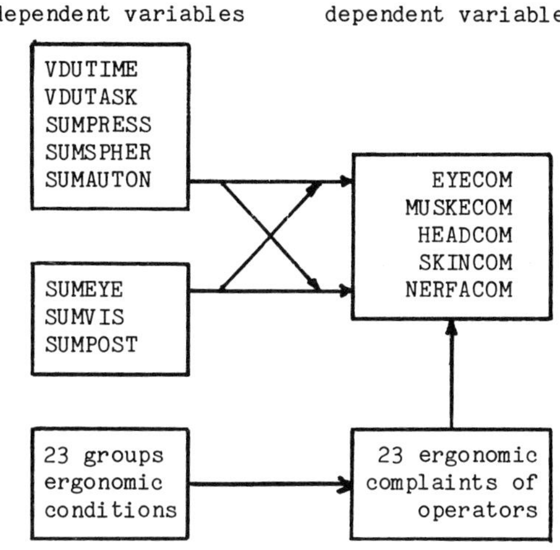

FIGURE 1
Main variables and analyses

3. RELATIONS AMONG VARIABLES, CONCLUSIONS

3.1 Frequencies of health complaints

Table 7 presents an overview of the percentage of VDU operators with one or more complaints reported "often", for each compound health complaint.

Table 7. Frequencies of compound health complaints.

Compound health complaint	Percentage	Number of items per compound complaint	Average % complaints per item
EYECOM	37	5	15
MUSKECOM	37	5	12
HEADCOM	20	1	20
NERFACOM	50	6	16
SKINCOM	17	2	10

In the category eye fatigue (EYECOM) the highest score is found in the item "fatigued eyes, painful feeling in or at the backside of the eyes" (28%). In the category of musculo-skeletal complaints (MUSKECOM) the highest frequency occurs in "shoulders, neck" (23%), and for complaints of general fatigue and nervousness (NERFACOM) the highest frequency occurs in "habitually waking up tired" (36%).

In comparison to the studies mentioned in our literature review [1], the percentages of health complaints reported here are relatively low. We assume that this is caused by the fact that our data refer to complaints reported "often", i.e. some days per week or almost daily. In several other studies no clear distinction has been made between complaints reported to occur often or sometimes. If, in the present study, the categories "often" and "sometimes" are combined, the results still yield somewhat lower frequencies compared with other studies.

Such comparisons between studies should be made with caution. Studies differ in their focus of research, methods of measurement and composition of samples (in particular types of VDU task).

3.2 Multivariate analysis

In univariate analysis many relations have been found between independent and dependent variables. But there are also mutual relations, between independent variables as well as between dependent variables. Therefore possible interactions and partial relations were investigated. The relations that remained of importance after this analysis, are presented in Table 8. For reasons of overview the variables VDUTASK and SUMAUTON are also included in Table 8, although these variables were not implicated in the multivariate analysis. From preliminary analysis both variables appeared to be unrelated to health complaints. Complaints on skin rash are not presented in the table. There is a separate discussion on this issue in paragraph 3.3.

Table 8. Relations between independent variables and health complaints.

	EYECOM	MUSKECOM	HEADCOM	NERFACOM
VDUTASK	o	o	o	o
VDUTIME, SUMPRESS, SUMSPHER (interaction)	+ +	+ +	+ +	+ +
SUMAUTON	o	o	o	o
SUMEYE	+ +	o	o	+
SUMVIS	+	o	+	o
SUMPOST	o	+ +	+	o

Relations are very weak (+) to weak (++), but significant.

The interactions between % time in VDU work (VDUTIME), work pressure (SUMPRESS) and atmosphere (SUMSPHER) find expression more specifically in Table 9, where the average number of health complaints per VDU operator is presented (computed over the four compound health complaints). The number of operators is indicated between brackets.

Table 9. Average number of health complaints per operator for work pressure, work atmosphere and % time in VDU work.

	SUMPRESS low		SUMPRESS high	
	VDUTIME		VDUTIME	
SUMSPHER	low	high	low	high
low	0.8 (88)	1.2 (24)	1.3 (34)	2.0 (22)
high	1.8 (12)	2.3 (4)	1.6 (7)	3.1 (26)

The following conclusions can be derived from these tables:
Headaches, eye fatigue, musculo-skeletal complaints and complaints on general fatigue and nervousness are related to a combination of a high value of VDUTIME, substantial work pressure and a poor work atmosphere.

The average number of health complaints per operator increases with the extent to which high VDUTIME, high work pressure and poor work atmosphere occur simultaneously. To some degree, headache complaints are also related to poor visual conditions and a bad work posture. Complaints of eye fatigue are also related to suboptimal optometric properties and, to a lesser extent, to bad visual conditions. Musculo-skeletal complaints are also related to a bad work posture. Complaints on general fatigue and nervousness are also slightly related to poor quality of eyes and spectacles.

With regard to the finding that the variables VDUTASK and SUMAUTON are not related to health complaints, it should be reminded that in this sample all of the tasks studied involve simple VDU work with little autonomy. This applies in particular to data-entry tasks.

3.3 Complaints on skin rash

In Table 8 there are no data on complaints of skin rash (SKINCOM). Weak relations have been found between skin rash on one side and work pressure, work atmosphere, work posture and a few complaints on ergonomic conditions on the other. However, none of these relations could be interpreted unequivocally.
A relation between skin rash and VDU work would imply a correlation between VDUTIME and SKINCOM. However, such a relation has not been found. In our previous literature review [1] we concluded that skin rash has to be considered as a serious complaint in VDU work. From our field study data we arrive at the same conclusion. But with regard to a possible relation with VDU work little can be concluded from the data collected here. To that purpose a study more specifically oriented on skin rash would be needed.

3.4 Ergonomic aspects

Significant relations have been found between ergonomic aspects and health complaints. However, these relations are weaker than expected from the data of our literature review. Several explanations may account for this finding.
It is possible that at present VDU's are of a better ergonomic quality and that companies are more aware of the importance of ergonomic working conditions in general. In this respect the situation differs from 1980 when the first generation of VDU effect studies was carried out. In the present field study we found very few truly bad workplaces. Negative scores on ergonomic conditions are more or less evenly distributed. This also caused a difficulty in constructing adequately differentiating measurement scales for visual conditions and physical work posture. Nevertheless a number of indications can be found for relations between ergonomic conditions and health complaints. A few examples concerning ergonomic items will be mentioned here. EYECOM is related to blurred VDU characters, MUSKECOM to a too steep slope of the footrest, instability of the chair, strong head rotation and lack of space for the legs. HEADCOM is related to insufficient daylight screening and strong head rotation.
In paragraph 2 it was stated that the relations between the sumvariables and health complaints have to be interpreted with some caution. This has to be realized in considering the weak relations that have been found between SUMVIS and EYECOM and between SUMPOST and MUSKECOM.

Furthermore, it appears that with regard to separate aspects of ergonomic conditions substantial improvements are still possible. For example, we found relatively often a high contrast between screen and close surroundings and between screen and manuscript, disturbing screen reflections, or VDU's positioned near windows in combination with ineffective daylight screening. Other bottlenecks regarding physical work posture, are the absence of manuscript holders and the difficult or even absent height-adjustability of VDU's and keyboards, such in combination with lacking footrests and thick keyboards. The main drawback of the working rooms is the too low air humidity.

3.5 Complaints on ergonomic conditions

There appeared to be distinct relations between operator complaints on ergonomic conditions and corresponding measurements and quality assessments of the research team. These relations provide a wealth of data on experienced comfort, on the basis of which an adjustment of various a-priori ergonomic quality criteria may be possible. For example, we found that the legibility of the manuscript (often handwritten) is much more problematic than the legibility of the VDU text. Furthermore the following questions were often answered positively: humidity too low, temperature too high, too low, screen reflections, glaring direct light, many changes of eye fixation, often bothered by draught, lack of possibilities to vary posture, irritating noises. The relevance of these finding was confirmed through meaningful relations found between complaints about ergonomic aspects and health complaints.

In the field study it appeared that most companies do employ some experts on ergonomic aspects of VDU work (physician, ergonomist). However, this expertise does not always spread through all branches and departments. It happened that operators requested specific improvements, such as manuscript holders or lighting adjustments. Those requests were not always met by the local management or the buying department.

3.6 Aspects of tasks

The percentage of the working day spent on VDU work (VDUTIME) appears to be related to a lesser extent to health complaints than was expected in the first instance. However, VDUTIME in combination with those aspects of the work that are expressed in the sumvariables on work pressure and work atmosphere, is related to health complaints. It is unlikely that aspects of pressure and atmosphere are specifically connected with VDU work. In other types of work these aspects can also contribute to workload. In our literature review it has been stated that in VDU work the number of, and the time available for, "natural breaks" is less in comparison to traditional office work. The resulting uninterrupted periods of intensive keyboard work may induce a greater taskload, in particular in central departments for data-entry and word processing. Moreover, in such departments the work is hardly ever interrupted by functional contacts. For more than 50% of the operators the work does not include regular contacts with colleagues. Most respondents were satisfied with the possibilities for informal contacts.

Although most operators have acceptable work-rest schedules, the breaks are obviously insufficient to recover from the load of a monotonous task, performed under high work pressure in a deteriorated work atmosphere. In our literature review we have already pointed out that work-rest schedules only offer a temporary solution. A preventive approach of health complaints includes the creation of varied and interesting work. Operators' opinions suggest the same conclusion. For many, the VDU work is too simple and they would like to alternate the VDU work with other tasks. In general, in our sample, a more positive opinion is expressed on non-VDU tasks (lower taskload, more contacts and choice opportunities) compared with the VDU tasks in the jobs.

Half of the workers regularly performs their work under time pressure. Also half of the operators judges their work to be mentally strenuous. Approximately 25% of the workers usually is insufficiently informed about changes in the work.

From the aforementioned it cannot be concluded that operators dislike their VDU work. There is an almost overall positive appreciation of the possibilities for swift, efficient and proper work. It is the monotony and simplicity of the work that is judged negatively by operators with a high percentage of time on VDU work. Taken together, the appreciation of VDU operators of their work (-situation) is a mixture of positive and negative experiences.
Providing interesting and varied jobs would imply that delimitation of a maximum of VDU working hours per day is not necessary. In two companies in this field study it was a management aim to create such interesting and varied work. In another company monotony was only reduced by replacing full-time workers by part-time workers.

There were almost no complaints on the information presentation and the operation of the computer systems. Most operators received on-the-job training. Well over half of the operators has no general knowledge of how computers work. There is a habitual delay in work speed by waiting time after commands, lack of computer capacity and occurrence of system break-downs. One-way traffic in man-machine interaction in data processing is seen as disagreeable by operators in data processing, because this results in lack of control on their performance.

3.7 Quality of eyes and spectacles

The measurement and analysis methods developed provide a detailed and standardized outline of the eye qualities of the operators. From the lack of relation between SUMEYE and VDUTIME it can be concluded that there is no indication that eye quality deteriorates through (more) VDU work.
Poor quality of eyes and spectacles clearly influence complaints of eye fatigue and, to a lesser extent, complaints of general fatigue and nervousness. The following separate items of SUMEYE are most clearly related to EYECOM: binocular visual acuity at a distance, negative relative convergence, and positive fusional reserve. However, the relation with this latter quantity had a different direction than that which has sometimes been assumed in the literature, in the sense that relatively more complaints occur for large values of the item. In follow-up studies it might be verified whether the "imperfection index" SUMEYE can be used as a predictor of eye fatigue.

In a minority of companies where the field study took place, operators appeared to have been recently submitted to eye examination. However, in such examinations the variables just mentioned, which are most relevant for eye fatigue, are not checked.

Concerning the use for VDU work of bifocal or multifocal spectacles for near vision disorders such as presbyopia, this research offers no conclusion as these spectacles and disorders were too rare in the sample. The relations found between complaints and scores "bad" of relevant items nevertheless indicate that in prescribing spectacles for near vision, attention should be paid not only to accommodative behaviour, but also to the relation between accommodation and convergence.

4. TOWARDS AN INTEGRATED APPROACH

In summary, we arrive at the following conclusions. The combination of prolonged monotonous, simple VDU work and a deteriorated work atmosphere and a high work pressure appears to be most strongly related to health complaints. This applies in particular to data-entry and word processing tasks, part of which is located in central departments. Here the monotonous VDU work is coupled with time pressure, lack of autonomy, few functional contacts, lack of consultations, lack of promotion possibilities and little variation in work posture. Relations between bad ergonomic conditions and health problems are less obvious. This may be caused by the fact that genuine bad workplaces (or rather worker-workplace combinations, from the ergonomic point of view) are rare. There is, however, independent of other variables, a distinct relation between optometric properties and complaints of eye fatigue.

Nature and extent of health complaints do justify adequate improvements of the work situations. Complaints on aspects of tasks and ergonomic conditions also give cause to such improvements. In view of the data and conclusions of this study an integrated approach of aspects of ergonomic conditions and tasks is recommended.
Problems that are specific for VDU work in offices are among others: luminance ratios, aspects of (arrangement of) equipment and furniture that relate to visual conditions, a deficit of natural breaks during the working day and the possibility of electronic monitoring of individual performance.
Problems that are less specifically connected with VDU work are: first, the prolonged execution of monotonous, simple tasks in combination with a deteriorated work atmosphere and high work pressure; second, the other bottlenecks in the visual conditions, physical work posture and working room. Therefore many of the aforementioned problems apply to office work in general; only a few are specific to office work carried out with a visual display unit.

These conclusions lead to the following reflection. The jobs and VDU tasks investigated typically belong to an early stage in the process of automation of information processing, in which separate information processing systems for specific tasks or departments are designed. At this stage there is a partial automation of information; the work is standardized; man-machine communication is often not interactive. However, most companies are working out a higher degree of automation of information processing. In this advanced stage departments are united, information systems connected, the man-machine communication is more of an interactive nature: integrated automation of information processing. There are inviting possibilities for an integration of data and word processing and for data processing and clerical and commercial jobs. Such possibilities can be used whenever automation is not purely viewed upon as a technical process. It should also be looked upon as a process of organizational changes, among others aimed at an improvement of the quality of work. Middle management and operators should be involved.

Such an integration of tasks in the framework of an integrated automation, may turn out to be disadvantageous for the women who in our study appeared to work in unfavourable conditions. Their monotonous work will probably disappear as a consequence of automation and organizational changes. The question is whether they will be considered as candidates for the "new" integrated jobs. Their present work hardly offers possibilities to obtain the necessary clerical, commercial or organizational qualifications. For those women a specific training program would be necessary. If not, the cynical situation emerges that for these women the problem of their workload is solved by becoming unemployed.

REFERENCES

[1] Padmos, P., Pot, F.D., Vos, J.J., and de Vries-de Mol, E.C., Gezondheid en welbevinden bij het werken met beeldschermen. I. Verslag van een vooronderzoek (Health and well-being in VDU operators. I. A state-of-the-art report). Ministry of Social Affairs report nr. 8412139, The Hague, 1985.
[2] Pot, F.D., Padmos, P., and Brouwers, A., Achter de schermen. Samenhangen tussen funktie-inhoud, ergonomische kondities, gezondheid en welbevinden bij beeldschermwerk op kantoren (Behind the screens. Relations between task content, ergonomic conditions, health and well-being in VDU work in offices). Ministry of Social Affairs report, The Hague, 1986.
[3] Vos, J.J., and Boogaard, J., De TNO-priegeltest (The TNO-pernickity test). T. Soc. Gezondheidszorg 62 (1984) 531-534.

APPENDIX: SEPARATE ASPECTS AND BOTTLENECKS

Health complaints and quality of work are, of course, the combined result of many factors in the working situation. Nevertheless, tangible improvements should also take place with regard to separate aspects of work and working conditions. Below are summarized the main separate aspects either for which many "bads" were scored (ergonomic conditions) or about which there were many complaints (task properties and ergonomics).

Ergonomic conditions
(20 most frequent scores "bad")

item	% bad
viewing angle mid keyboard-horizon	93
height adjustability VDU	91
manuscript holder present	86
height flat part of lumbal support	85
viewing angle mid manuscr.-horizon	79
contrast VDU-distant surroundings	76
contrast VDU-manuscript	74
contrast manuscr.-dist. surround.	74
handwritten manuscript	72
height-adjustability keyboard	72
angle manuscript-line of sight	65
contrast reflection-screen backgr.	63
contrast VDU-close surroundings	63
total eye movements per minute	59
space between characters VDU	57
contrast workplace-close surround.	55
contrast reflection-characters VDU	52
number of persons working in room	45
eye movement rate VDU-manuscript	44
tiltability VDU	44

Ergonomic complaints (items with more than 15% answers "yes")

item	% yes
often too dry	71
poor manuscript legibility	58
too little movement during work	58
often too hot	53
disturbing screen reflections	49
often too cold	45
glare from lighting or window	41
many changes of eye fixation	41
often bothered by draught	35
little possibil. of posture change	32
often irritating noise	32
often electrostatic shocks	32
uncomfortable chair	29
too little leg space	29
working room unpleasant	28
workplace often too bright	27
often bothered by smoke, odours	27
table height uncomfortable	21
position manuscript uncomfortable	19
fluttering, flickering screen	19
uncomfortable screen position	18
uncomfortable keyboard position	17

Autonomy

item	% no
optional lay-out screen	64
optional command modes VDU	57
informal work breaks possible	38
optional sequence VDU tasks	36

Work pressure (items with more than 15% answers "yes")

item	% yes
working under time pressure	51
mentally strenuous work	51
work often too fatiguing	18
recording of individ. work output	16

Work atmosphere (items with more than 15% answers "no")

item	% no
advance deliberation about changes	65
good promotion possibilities	59
work requires personal contacts	56
appreciated sufficiently	31
pay according to work	28
briefed about changes	24
good direct management	23
well organized work	17
good relations among each other	17

Diversity

item	% yes
(more) alternation with non-VDU work wanted	46
VDU work too simple	39
(more) variety of VDU work wanted	35

Man-machine interaction (items with more than 15% answers "no")

item	% no
"help" key present	65
general knowledge of computer	62
skipping operation stages possible	60
waiting time rare commands <2 sec	41
waiting time frequent commands predictable	22
waiting time frequent commands <2 sec	18

WORK WITH DISPLAY UNITS 86
B. Knave and P.-G. Widebäck (eds.)

ENVIRONMENTAL STRESSORS AND PERCEIVED HEALTH SYMPTOMS AMONG OFFICE WORKERS

Bradley D. Prezant and Goldy D.Kleinman
University of Washington
Department of Environmental Health
4132 Stone Way North
Seattle, Washington 98103

ABSTRACT

A questionnaire study of office workers at a large University was conducted with the cooperation of a union health and safety committee. Daily exposure to, and perceived health problems from various chemical and ergonomic/physical stressors were obtained from 655 of the 2800 employees. Sitting, uncomfortable furniture, and the use of video display terminals contributed the majority of reported musculoskeletal symptoms. Noise and crowding of people and equipment contributed the majority of mental/emotional symptoms. The effect of these stressors on VDT operators as compared with non-VDT operators was examined. VDT operators experienced significantly more ergonomic/physical stressors resulting in 1 or more health symptoms than non-VDT operators.

I. INTRODUCTION

In recent years, office workers have increasingly been calling attention to their health and safety concerns, especially those arising from the introduction of new technologies, e.g. video display terminals. In the United States, as the economy orientation has shifted from manufacturing to service, the number of employed persons engaged in occupations involving information processing and other office work has increased. In 1984, nearly 17 million people (about 80 percent women) were reported in the category "Administrative Support, including Clerical." This category includes almost all information processing and clerical personnel [1]. It is from among this 17 million that complaints arise of chemical exposures and ergonomic problems in the office. The sheer size of this group compels attention to their concerns.

2. BACKGROUND

Research on office workers has shown that they perceive a relationship between the physical environment and health. In the Steelcase National Study of Office Environments, conducted in 1980, 1004 office workers were queried on this relationship [2]. Seven of ten workers cited two factors which affected their personal comfort a great deal: good lighting and a comfortable chair. Temperature and air circulation were most frequently reported as items which office workers would change. Seventy-one percent of respondents said that improvements in the temperature and circulation of air would contribute to productivity. Sixty-seven percent indicated the need for quieter environment, while 46 percent felt that a more comfortable chair with good back support would contribute to their productivity. Approximately 25 percent of the office workers experienced back strain which they related to an uncomfortable office chair. Lack of privacy, crowding, and the need for more office space were identified as important environmental factors.

The BOSTI study [3] focused on architectural and environmental elements as part of overall office design. The impact of these elements on productivity and job satisfaction of office workers was evaluated using a questionnaire completed by more than 5000 public and private sector employees both before and twice after moving into new offices. Although data were gathered on job satisfaction and job performance, no information on health symptoms as they relate to various physical and chemical exposures was presented. Their results supported the need for a high degree of enclosure which could be satisfied in open plan offices provided that there was a fair amount of enclosure for each individual.

The importance of the architectural layout was investigated by Hedge, et. al. in a study of 649 employees working in five floors of open plan offices [4], [5]. This survey, while primarily designed to determine employee reactions to open-plan offices, queried office workers about job characteristics, job satisfaction, and the ambient environment in these offices, including temperature, ventilation, lighting, and static electricity. The authors stated, in [4], that 55 percent of employees found their offices too stuffy while 54 percent, 68 percent and 76 percent, respectively, of employees on floors one to three felt that the temperature was too hot. Forty six percent of employees on the ground floor found their work environment too cold, as did 59 percent of the employees on the fourth floor. Seventy-one percent of respondents responded yes to a question asking their agreement to a "distinct lack of privacy."

In a factor analysis, eight factors explaining 75 percent of the variance in attitudes toward the working environment were identified. First was a factor of "privacy and disturbances," second, one described as "health" which included somatic symptoms combined with adverse environmental conditions, and third was a factor describing problems with thermal comfort. The authors concluded that of those items emerging as health factors in the factor analysis, problems of ventilation were most prominent.

Stellman, et. al. reported the results of a cross-sectional survey of office workers at four office sites in the U.S. and Canada [6]. Multiple item scales were constructed to measure indoor air quality and ergonomic (physical) factors characteristic of these work environments. Respondent reports of air quality stressors were shown to be related to self-reported symptoms; reports of ergonomic stressors were related to the incidence and severity of musculoskeletal symptoms. The authors concluded that the concordance of stressors with their logical symptoms, as well as the reports of ergonomic stressors which were consistent with prior knowledge of the conditions in the buildings, added strength to the associations observed.

Measured environmental conditions including ventilation, temperature, and humidity, correlated poorly with symptom prevalence in a descriptive questionnaire study conducted at Las Terrasses de la Chaudiere, a massive office complex in Quebec, by McDonald et. al. [7]. The most frequent environmental complaints cited concerned ventilation, with noise and lighting also mentioned. Health symptoms which employees related to their work were mainly associated with irritations of the nose, throat, eyes and skin, often accompanied by an impaired sense of well-being. While efforts to identify non-uniform environmental factors which could explain the symptoms observed were generally unsuccessful, some small systematic differences were noted which suggested "some correlation" between building illness and temperature and ventilation. The authors concluded that there was a tendency for those working in cubicles to have suffered more than those in open areas or closed offices, and that imperfect ventilation together with periods of high temperature and low humidity were contributory factors.

The importance of considering the biological, chemical, physical and social agents responsible for health complaints among persons working in offices was emphasized by Baker in his review of indoor air epidemiology [8]. Likewise, Lindvall emphasized the importance of subtle medical effects, sensory reactions, and stress reactions in understanding building illness [9]. Understanding the work-related health problems of office workers requires a model which considers all the above factors and their interrelationships.

3. METHODOLOGY

In order to better understand the impact of various specific chemical and ergonomic/physical stressors present in offices on thehealth of office workers, 2800 office workers at the University of Washington were surveyedat the request of the Union which represents them. Development, distribution and collection of a self-administered questionnaire were done in conjunction with the Union, Classified Staff Association, SEIU 925, representing these workers.

The respondents worked in areas ranging from large offices to small outbuildings, as one might expect on a typical college campus. Because of this wide variety in layout, age, and office configuration, and the consequent difficulties of characterizing each specific worksite, no efforts were made to describe or measure architectural attributes.

The questionnaire was designed by employee representatives based upon their experiences with employee complaints with assistance from members of the Department of Environmental Health of the School of Public Health at the University of Washington. The questionnaire instructed employees to indicate their daily extent of exposure, in hours, to each of 31 stressors, if any health symptoms were felt to be associated with such exposures, and what those symptoms were. Specific symptoms were later grouped into nine categories.

Questionnaires were returned by 655 workers, yielding a response rate of 23 percent. One reason for the low response rate concerned the method of questionnaire distribution and collection. It is likely that this introduced a bias into the results, in that persons actively involved in Union activities, and/or supportive of such activities preferentially completed and returned the questionnaire. Given these constraints, the usefulness of the data is improved by considering respondents as a selected group.

Responses were coded, the data corrected for typographical errors, and analyzed using SPSS and SPSS-PC statistical packages. Exposures were characterized as either chemical or ergonomic/physical based upon logical criteria. Twelve chemical and 18 ergonomic/physical exposures were included in these categories (Tables 1 and 2).

4. RESULTS

Respondents had the following demographic characteristics: Eighty-nine percent of respondents were female. The average age was 40 years old. The majority had been employed at the University from 2 to 5 years, with 16 percent employed 6 to 10 years and 6 percent over ten years.

Reported health symptoms were grouped into categories. Based upon other investigations, and to allow specific exposure-symptom relationships to be explored, categories which included respiratory, nausea or other gastrointestinal, eye irritation or fatigue, skin irritation, headache, musculo-skeletal, circulatory, and mental/emotional symptoms were chosen. Symptoms which were not included in the above categories (approximately 10 percent of responses) were designated as other.

The 13 chemical and 19 ergonomic/physical stressors are listed in Tables 1 and 2. For each of the chemical stressors, Table 1 indicates the exposure frequency, and the percentage of exposed persons experiencing 1 or more health symptoms which they attribute to that exposure. Table 2 displays the same information for the ergonomic/physical stressors.

Table 1 shows that for some chemical stressors, such as whiteout typewriter correction fluid, a high prevalence of exposure but a low prevalence of associated health complaints (78 percent exposed, 6 percent of exposed reporting 1 or more associated health complaints) was reported. For other chemical stressors, such as "office fumes" (predominantly reflecting complaints asociated with cigarette smoking), a low prevalence of exposure but a high percentage of those exposed attributing health symptoms to the exposure was reported (23 percent exposed, 67 percent of exposed reporting 1 or more associated health complaints).

Table 3 ranks the chemical and ergonomic/physical stressors by the total number of all symptoms reported by respondents. Considered as an index of discomfort, a ranking of stressors by number of reported symptoms, as in Table 3, indicates their relative contribution to office discomfort. Of the chemical stressors, "office fumes" had the greatest number of symptoms, 103. Sitting (249), video display terminals (181), and noise (161) were the three most symptomatic ergonomic/physical stressors. Note the higher numbers of reported symptoms for the ergonomic/physical versus the chemical stressors.

The majority of respondents (65 percent) did not experience any of the chemical stressors as symptomatic, while 30 percent experienced 1 or 2 of the chemical stressors as symptomatic. Only a small number of individuals (5 percent) experienced 3 or more as symptomatic. For the ergonomic/physical stressors, the distribution was quite different. Figure 1 indicates that 28 percent of the respondents did not experience any ergonomic/physical stressors as symptomatic, 29 percent experienced 1 or 2 as symptomatic, and 43 percent experienced 3 or more as symptomatic.

This difference can be further illustrated by comparing the average number of symptomatic exposures. Table 4 permits a comparison between the chemical and ergonomic/physical stressors for the mean number of exposures per person resulting in 1 or more health symptoms. For the ergonomic/physical stressors, the mean number of symptomatic exposures (and 95 percent confidence levels) are 2.6 (2.4, 2.8). For the chemical stressors, the mean number of symptomatic exposures are 0.5 (0.5, 0.6) The confidence levels do not overlap; the differences are significant at the .01 level.

No statistically significant differences in the mean number of exposures per person resulting in 1 or more health symptoms were seen by duration of employment or by sex (see Table 4).

Table 5 shows the mean number of exposures per person resulting in 1 or more health symptoms by age. Persons greater than 55 years of age had fewer symptomatic ergonomic/physical stressors than younger respondents. The values for persons greater than 55 were 1.9 (1.4, 2.4) versus 2.7 (2.4, 3.0) for persons 30-55 years old and 2.8 (2.3, 3.2) for persons younger than 30 years old. This difference was of borderline significance.

Table 6 lists the number of symptoms attributed to stressors by respondents, rank ordered by category. Musculoskeletal symptoms were the most prevalent symptoms reported by respondents, followed by mental/emotional, headache, and eye irritation or fatigue. Sitting, uncomfortable furniture, and using video display terminals contributed the majority of reported musculoskeletal symptoms. Noise and crowding of people and equipment contributed the majority of mental/emotional symptoms. VDTs, "office fumes," and noise contributed the majority of headache symptoms. VDTs, too bright lighting, and too dim lighting contributed the majority of eye irritation or fatigue symptoms.

The frequency distributions of health symptoms attributed to sitting, noise, and the use of video display terminals were examined in more detail. These results are presented in Figures 2 through 4. The symptoms reported for each of these categories are consistent with expectations.

Sitting contributed the largest number of reported symptoms, as illustrated in Table 3. This is consistent with the observation that 84 percent of the respondents sat for greater than 1 hour daily (70 percent for greater than four hours daily). Of those persons reporting one or more symptoms due to sitting, musculoskeletal symptoms (reported by 78 percent) and circulatory symptoms (reported by 26 percent) were the symptoms most frequently reported. Small numbers of mental/emotional and headache symptoms were also reported. This can be seen in Figure 2. Figure 3 indicates that 75 percent of persons reporting one or more symptoms due to noise cited mental/emotional symptoms. Twenty-eight percent reported headache symptoms associated with their noise exposures. In the case of symptoms attributed to use of VDT (Figure 4), the results indicate 77 percent of respondents experienced eye irritation or fatigue, 39 percent experienced musculoskeletal symptoms, and 24 percent experienced mental/emotional symptoms. These are consistent with logical expectations, and in the case of video display terminals, with the published literature.

Of the 655 respondents, 382, or 58 percent, operated a video display terminal one or more hours daily. VDT operators are compared with non-VDT operators in Tables 7 through 10. Table 7, a 2 x 2 table of presence or absence of sitting symptoms by use of VDT, indicates an odds ratio of 1.5 (chi square = 6.64, $p < .01$) for the presence of sitting symptoms in VDT operators. Table 8 indicates an odds ratio of 1.6 (chi square = 5.01, $.01 < p < .05$) for the presence of uncomfortable furniture as perceived by VDT operators. VDT operators are therefore more likely to experience sitting symptoms and experience uncomfortable furniture than non-VDT operators. Since a larger percentage of VDT operators than non-operators spent more than four hours per day sitting, this may explain the observed relationship. While 26 percent of non-VDT operators reported crowding of equipment, a larger number (43 percent, $p < .001$) of VDT operators responded that their office areas were too crowded. A high prevalence for crowding of people was experienced by VDT operators (42 percent) and non-operators (37 percent) alike. There was no relationship seen between VDT operators and the perception of or number of symptoms due to uncomfortable temperatures.

Significantly more VDT operators than non-operators experienced their workplaces as noisy (50 percent vs. 30 percent, $p < .001$). This can probably be explained by the use of printers without sound hoods.

Despite the high prevalence of eye irritation or fatigue among VDT operators, as seen in Figure 4, lighting levels were not perceived by respondents as responsible. VDT operators did not report significantly more symptoms due to low or high lighting than non-VDT workers. In particular, high lighting levels and the associated glare have been thought to contribute to visual stress. It is not clear whether these results are due to a lack of recognition by respondents of the contribution of ambient lighting to visual difficulties or a perception that characteristics of the terminal display, such as resolution or flicker, are responsible for the higher level of perceived discomfort seen for VDT operators.

VDT operators experienced significantly more ergonomic/physical stressors resulting in 1 or more health symptoms than non-operators, as can be seen in Table 9. While this relationship is unaffected by duration of employment or sex, it is partly confounded by age, since VDT operators tended to be younger than non-operators (see Table 10) and older persons tended to experience fewer ergonomic/physical stressors as symptomatic (see Table 5).

Figure 5 indicates the percentages and numbers of video display terminals equipped with various desired features. It is noteworthy to consider the high levels of perceived discomfort associated with VDT use by respondents despite the high prevalence of various features. There was no relationship between the number or type of features and the number or type of health symptoms.

5. CONCLUSIONS

The results of this study indicated the importance, in terms of the number of self-reported symptoms, of many of the ergonomic/physical stressors relative to the chemical stressors for office workers. While the majority of respondents (65 percent) reported no symptoms from any of the chemical stressors, only 28 percent reported being free from symptoms from the ergonomic/physical stressors. Based upon these results, intervention strategies to improve the health and safety of office workers should begin with improving factors relating to these ergonomic/physical stressors, especially musculoskeletal stress. Sitting was identified as the most frequent source of health symptoms by VDT operators and non-operators alike. This corroborates the Steelcase study results, which indicated the chair to be an important factor affecting office workers' personal comfort. Much more attention has been devoted to workstation and chair design for VDT operators than non-operators; the results of this study indicate the importance of such factors for all office workers.

In these results, as in many of the studies reviewed above, crowding of people was identified as an important factor influencing job satisfaction and health. Crowding of equipment perhaps is a reflection of the introduction of new office technologies, as VDT operators reported this more frequently than non-VDT users. An all too familiar scenario for the introduction of VDTs is to simply move aside the telephone, typewriter and calculator and place the new display terminal, keyboard and printer on the work surface. Space is known to be a problem in all University facilities, perhaps independently of architectural configuration. Crowding of people and equipment could be better addressed in office architecture and during the planning process.

VDT operators were distinguished from non-VDT operators by significantly more health symptoms due to ergonomic/physical stressors (but not chemical stressors) and an increased perception of their workplaces as noisy, most probably due to computer printers without sound hoods.

Ventilation-associated symptoms tended to assume less prominence when compared with problems such as sitting and noise in this study than in the studies by McDonald, Hedge, and Stellman. One explanation would be that in both of those cases, the buildings were so-called "problem buildings" with pre-existing complaints of poor indoor air quality.

While ergonomic/physical problems are reported more frequently than chemical problems, the long-term consequences of office chemical problems, such as indoor air quality, are not understood at this time. This study did not address these long-term issues; these are appropriate topics for other studies.

REFERENCES

[1] U.S. Bureau of Census. Statistical Abstract of the United States: 1986 (106th addition), Washington, D.C., 1985, p. 402.
[2] Steelcase, Inc., Comfort and Productivity in the Office of the 80s: The Steelcase National Study of Office Environments, No. II (Steelcase, Grand Rapids,1980).
[3] BOSTI, Using Office Design to Increase Productivity (Westinghouse Furniture Systems, Grand Rapids, 1985).
[4] Hedge, A. J Arch Plan Res, I (1984) 163-174.
[5] Hedge, A., Environment and Behavior, Vol. 14 No. 5 (September 1982) 519-542.
[6] Stellman, J. M. et al., Am. Ind. Hyg. Assoc. J, 46 (May 1985) 286-293.
[7] McDonald, J.C. et al., Building Illness in a Large Office Complex, in: Walkinshaw, D.S., (ed.), Indoor Air Quality in Cold Climates: Hazards and Abatement Measures (Air Pollution Control Association, Pittsburgh, 1986) pp. 7-22.
[8] Baker, D.B., Epidemiologic Investigation of Office Environmental Problems, in: Evaluating Office Environmental Problems: Annals of The American Conference of Governmental Industrial Hygienists, Vol. 10 (American Conference of Governmental Industrial Hygienists, Cincinnati, 1984) pp. 37-44.
[9] Lindvall, T.I., Exposure Limits for Office Environments, in: Annals of The American Conference of Governmental Industrial Hygienists, Vol. 12 (American Conference of Governmental Industrial Hygienists, Cincinnati, 1985) pp. 99-108.

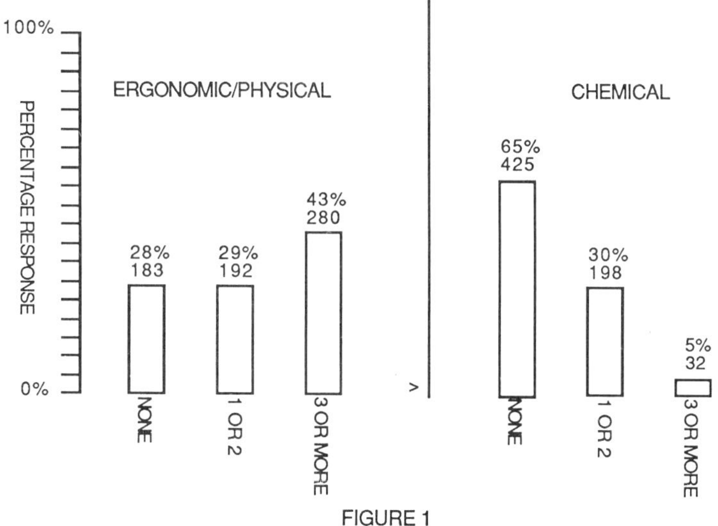

FIGURE 1

DISTRIBUTION OF RESPONDENTS BY NUMBER OF STRESSORS PER RESPONDENT RESULTING IN 1 OR MORE HEALTH SYMPTOM

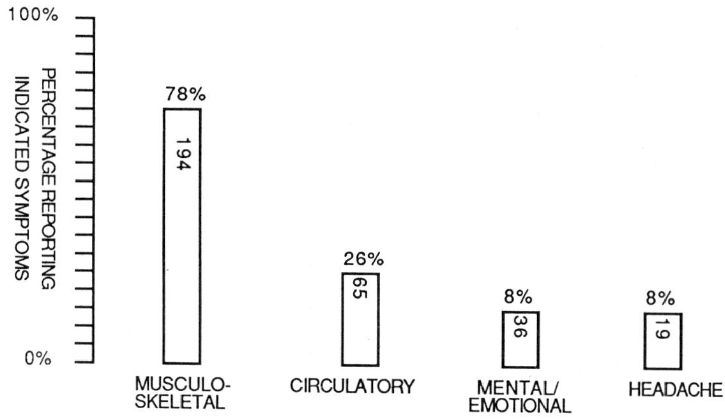

FIGURE 2

FREQUENCY DISTRIBUTION OF HEALTH SYMPTOMS ATTRIBUTED TO SITTING (550 EXPOSURES, 249 SYMPTOMS)

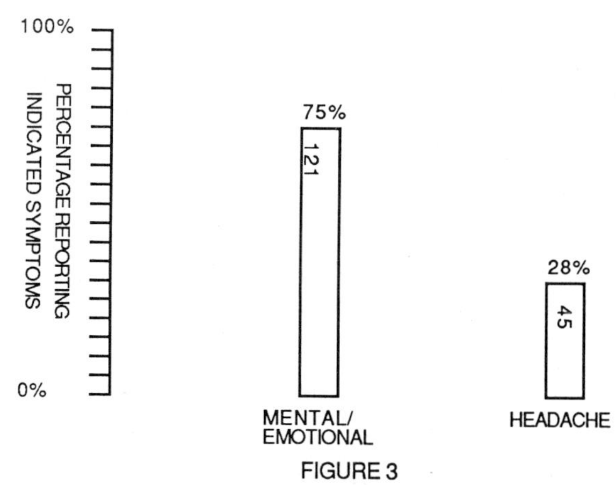

FIGURE 3

FREQUENCY DISTRIBUTION OF HEALTH SYMPTOMS ATTRIBUTED TO NOISE (267 EXPOSURES, 161 SYMPTOMS)

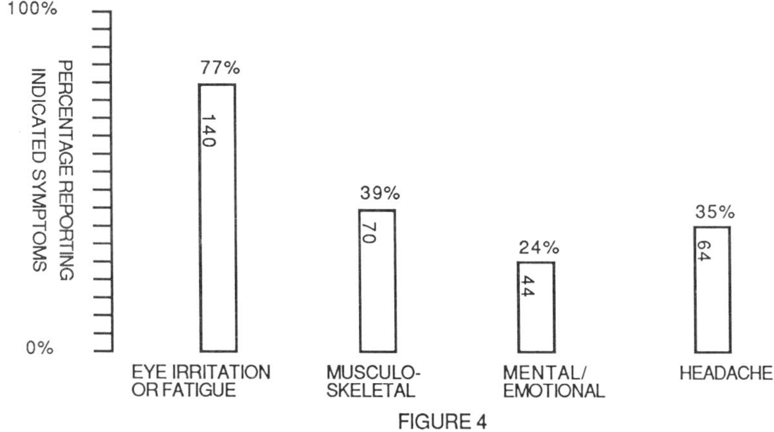

FIGURE 4

FREQUENCY DISTRIBUTION OFHEALTH SYMPTOMS ATTRIBUTED TO USE OF VDT 382 EXPOSURES, 181 SYMPTOMS)

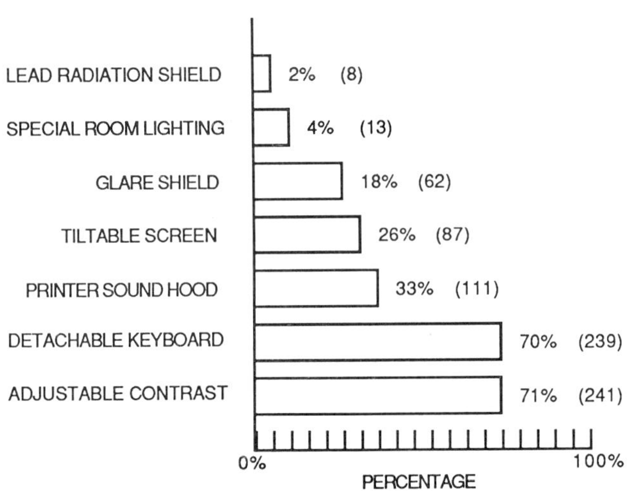

FIGURE 5

PERCENTAGE OF VDT'S EQUIPPED WITH:

TABLE 1
CHEMICAL STRESSORS, EXPOSURE FREQUENCY, AND PERCENTAGE OF EXPOSED ≥1 SYMPTOM

	PERCENTAGE EXPOSED >1 HR DAILY	NUMBER PERSONS EXPOSED >1 HR DAILY	PERCENTAGE OF EXPOSED EXPERIENCING 1 OR MORE HLTH SYMPTOMS
WHITEOUT FLUID	78.0	513	6.0
PHOTOCOPY MACHINES	69.0	453	13.0
CARBONLESS COPY PAPER	60.0	391	21.0
"OFFICE FUMES"	23.0	153	67.0
SPIRIT DUPLICATOR	17.0	110	25.0
STENCIL CORR. FLUID	14.0	90	20.0
MIMEOGRAPH MACHINES	14.0	90	12.0
"LABORATORY FUMES"	8.0	52	40.0
ELECT. STENCIL MAKER	8.0	52	18.0
OTHER "CHEMICAL FUMES"	7.0	43	72.0
ASBESTOS	4.0	26	41.0
OTHER DUP. MACHINES	3.0	19	28.0
"TOXIC WASTE FUMES"	2.0	13	60.0

TABLE 2
ERGONOMIC/PHYSICAL STRESSORS, EXPOSURE FREQUENCY, AND PERCENTAGE OF EXPOSED ≥1 SYMPTOM

	PERCENTAGE EXPOSED >1 HR DAILY	NUMBER PERSONS EXPOSED >1 HR DAILY	PERCENTAGE OF EXPOSED EXPERIENCING 1 OR MORE HLTH SYMPTOMS
SITTING	84.0	550	45.0
USE OF TYPEWRITER	80.0	526	17.0
USE OF VDT	58.0	382	47.0
STANDING	48.0	312	10.0
TEMP. TOO COLD	42.0	278	51.0
NOISE	41.0	267	60.0
CROWDING OF PEOPLE	37.0	243	54.0
STUFFY VENTILATION	37.0	240	45.0
CROWDING OF EQUIPMENT	32.0	210	41.0
LIFTING	30.0	195	29.0
TEMP. TOO HOT	29.0	193	37.0
USE OF DICTATION EQUIP.	28.0	182	20.0
UNCOMF. FURNITURE	27.0	177	78.0
DRAFTY VENTILATION	22.0	146	23.0
LIGHTING TOO HIGH	20.0	129	76.0
LIGHTING TOO LOW	14.0	91	28.0
RADIATION	6.0	41	37.0
OTHER OFFICE MACHINES	6.0	38	24.0
UNSAFE FURNITURE	4.0	23	7.0

TABLE 3
RANK ORDER OF STRESSORS BY SEVERITY

		FOR THOSE EXPOSED EXPERIENCING 1 OR MORE HEALTH SYMPTOMS	
		PERCENTAGE	NUMBER
ERG/PHY	SITTING	45.0	249
ERG/PHY	USE OF VDT	47.0	181
ERG/PHY	NOISE	60.0	161
ERG/PHY	TEMP. TOO COLD	51.0	142
ERG/PHY	UNCOMF. FURNITURE	78.0	138
ERG/PHY	CROWDING OF PEOPLE	54.0	132
ERG/PHY	STUFFY VENTILATION	45.0	108
CHEM	"OFFICE FUMES"	67.0	103
ERG/PHY	LIGHTING TOO HIGH	76.0	99
ERG/PHY	USE OF TYPEWRITER	17.0	89
ERG/PHY	CROWDING OF EQUIPMENT	41.0	86
CHEM	CARBONLESS COPY PAPER	21.0	82
ERG/PHY	TEMP. TOO HOT	37.0	71
ERG/PHY	DRAFTY VENTILATION	23.0	70
ERG/PHY	LIFTING	29.0	57
CHEM	PHOTOCOPY MACHINES	13.0	57
ERG/PHY	USE OF DICTATION EQUIP.	20.0	36
ERG/PHY	STANDING	10.0	33
CHEM	OTHER "CHEMICAL FUMES"	72.0	31
CHEM	WHITEOUT FLUID	6.0	28
CHEM	SPIRIT DUPLICATOR	25.0	27
ERG/PHY	LIGHTING TOO LOW	28.0	25
CHEM	"LABORATORY FUMES"	40.0	21
CHEM	STENCIL CORR. FLUID	20.0	18
ERG/PHY	RADIATION	37.0	15
CHEM	ASBESTOS	41.0	12
CHEM	MIMEOGRAPH MACHINES	12.0	11
ERG/PHY	OTHER OFFICE MACHINES	24.0	9
CHEM	ELECT. STENCIL MAKER	18.0	9
CHEM	"TOXIC WASTE FUMES"	60.0	9
CHEM	OTHER DUP. MACHINES	28.0	5
ERG/PHY	UNSAFE FURNITURE	7.0	2

NOTE: THE FIRST NUMBER IS THE % OF THOSE EXPOSED WITH SYMPTOMS, THE SECOND NUMBER IS THE ACTUAL NUMBER OF PERSONS WITH ONE OR MORE SYMPTOMS ATTRIBUTED TO THE DESIGNATED CATEGORY. IT CAN BE SEEN THAT ERGONOMIC/PHYSICAL STRESSORS WERE GREATER CONTRIBUTORS TO THE NUMBER OF REPORTED SYMPTOMS THAN WERE CHEMICAL STRESSORS.

TABLE 4
MEAN NUMBER OF STRESSORS PER INDIVIDUAL
RESULTING IN ≥1 HEALTH SYMPTOM,
BY SEX AND BY STRESSOR CLASSIFICATION

	ERGONOMIC/PHYSICAL		CHEMICAL	
	MEAN	CONF. INT.	MEAN	CONF. INT.
OVERALL	2.6	(2.4, 2.8)	0.5	(0.5, 0.6)
MALES	2.1	(1.5, 2.6)	0.4	(0.2, 0.6)
FEMALES	2.6	(2.4, 2.9)	0.6	(0.5, 0.7)

NOTE: THE CONFIDENCE INTERVALS FOR THE AVERAGE NUMBER OF SYMPTOMATIC STRESSORS PER INDIVIDUAL DIFFER SIGNIFICANTLY FOR ERGONOMIC/PHYSICAL VERSUS CHEMICAL EXPOSURES. NO SIGNIFICANT DIFFERENCE CAN BE SEEN FOR MALES VERSUS FEMALES.

TABLE 5
MEAN NUMBER OF STRESSORS PER INDIVIDUAL
RESULTING IN ≥1 HEALTH SYMPTOM,
BY AGE AND BY STRESSOR CLASSIFICATION

	ERGONOMIC/PHYSICAL		CHEMICAL	
	MEAN	CONF. INT.	MEAN	CONF. INT.
<30 YEARS	2.8	(2.3, 3.2)	0.6	(0.4, 0.7)
30-55 YRS	2.7	(2.4, 3.0)	0.6	(0.5, 0.7)
>55 YEARS	1.9	(1.4, 2.4)	0.5	(0.3, 0.7)

NOTE: OLDER INDIVIDUALS TENDED TO HAVE FEWER SYMPTOMATIC STRESSORS PER RESPONDENT.

TABLE 6
NUMBER OF SYMPTOMS ATTRIBUTED
TO STRESSORSBY RESPONDENTS,
RANK ORDERED BY CATEGORY

MUSCULOSKELETAL	552
MENTAL/EMOTIONAL	522
HEADACHE	427
EYE IRRITATION OR FATIGUE	399
OTHER	278
RESPIRATORY	210
SKIN	117
NAUSEA	42

TABLE 7
ODDS RATIO FOR PRESENCE
OF ≥1 SITTING SYMPTOM
VDT OP'S VERSUS NON-OP'S

	SITTING SYMPTOMS ≥1 +	-
VDT OP'S	161	221
NON-OP'S	88	185

(TOTAL = 655)

ODDS RATIO = 1.5
CHI SQUARE = 6.64, $p < .01$

TABLE 8
ODDS RATIO FOR PRESENCE
OF ≥1 UNCOMF. FURN. SYMPTOM
VDT OP'S VERSUS NON-OP'S

	UNCOMF. FURN. SYMPTOMS ≥1 +	-
VDT OP'S	92	290
NON-OP'S	46	227

(TOTAL = 655)

ODDS RATIO = 1.6
CHI SQUARE = 5.01, $.01 < p < .05$

TABLE 9
MEAN NUMBER OF STRESSORS RESULTING IN
≥1 HEALTH SYMPTOM BY USE OF VDT
AND BY STRESSOR CLASSIFICATION

	ERGONOMIC/PHYSICAL		CHEMICAL	
	MEAN	CONF. INT.	MEAN	CONF. INT.
VDT OP'S	2.9	(2.7, 3.3)	0.6	(0.5, 0.7)
NON-OP'S	2.1	(1.8, 2.4)	0.5	(0.4, 0.7)

NOTE: VDT OPERATORS WERE MORE LIKELY TO HAVE A GREATER NUMBER OF SYMPTOMATIC STRESSORS THAN NON-VDT OPERATORS.

TABLE 10
MEAN AGE OF VDT OPERATORS
VERSUS NON-VDT OPERATORS

VDT OP'S	39.3*	(38.2, 40.4)
NON-VDT OP'S	42.0	(40.6, 43.5)

*$p < .05$

WORK WITH DISPLAY UNITS 86
B. Knave and P.-G. Widebäck (eds.)

REPETITION STRAIN INJURY IN AUSTRALIAN VDU USERS

Susan Rowe, Maurice Oxenburgh and David Douglas
Health, Safety & Environment Services
CSR Limited, GPO Box 483
SYDNEY 2001 AUSTRALIA

INTRODUCTION

The results of a two year study of Repetition Strain Injury (RSI) or Occupational Cervico-brachial Disorders (OCD) occurring among workers in a Sydney Office are presented. Forty-five RSI cases reported during 1984 (Year I) were investigated and compared with a control group in similar jobs but who did not report symptoms or signs of RSI. Investigation included workstation inspection and workload analysis. Causative factors were identified and company management strategies determined. These included education programs, workstation assessment and refurbishing, workload restrictions, treatment and rehabilitation.

Forty cases of RSI reported in 1985 (Year II) were then investigated and compared with the original forty- five cases. Comparison of the two cohorts demonstrated clearly that the second group were less severely injured and required less time off work and less alternative work. However the overall incidence among clerical staff remained the same.

METHODS

The data used for the case comparison was collected by the Occupational Health Centre staff, the Workers' Compensation Department and from the VDU Survey by Oxenburgh (1).

Symptoms were classified according to severity as described by Brown et al (2). Stage One being the least severe and Stage Three the most severe form. Some Year II cases in which the symptoms were discomfort rather than tiredness or aching, were classified as Stage One.

Assessment and management of cases was carried out by company occupational health practitioners supported with referral to medical practitioners, specialists and other physical therapists as required.

RESULTS

Job Categories

Eighty-nine percent of Year I were clerical workers; this had dropped to 63% in Year II. The major increase was in people who had neither trained as typists nor attended the ergonomics and VDU training courses (eg accountants, computer programmers).

Injury Description

There has been little or no change in the anatomical site or side of the body with time. However, there was a significant change in the structures involved. In Year I, tendon and muscle symptoms were approximately equally represented, 45% and 41% respectively. In Year II, the majority of symptoms were in the muscles (71%).

Incidence Rates

Comparison was made of the incidence rates for clerical workers only. The first year the incidence rate was 0.17 (40/238) and for the second year the incidence rate was 0.14 (25/184) showing only a small change over this period.

Absence and Rehabilitation

Table A below indicates the mean number of days lost from work per person for Year I and Year II cases. Also shown are the periods spent back at work but on a rehabilitation program. Rehabilitation included an alternative work regime where work was modified e.g. repetitive work such as typing restricted or eliminated and in some cases hours of work reduced.

For cases occurring in Year I, the mean number of days absent from work was 33.9 days per person (total of 1527 days) for 75% of the cases, the remaining 25% were not absent.

For cases occurring in Year II, the mean number of days absent from work was 3.4 days per person (total of 135 days) and only 20% of cases were absent from work. The other 80% remained at work usually on alternative duties.

Table A
Absence and Alternative Duties

	Year I (earlier cases)		Year II (later cases)	
	average days	standard deviation	average days	standard deviation
absent from work	33.9	44.6	3.4	8.3
alternative work	91.0	90.4	31.5	30.6
	124.9		34.9	

There was a similar reduction in days on alternative work. In Year I the mean of 91.0 days per person (total of 4087 days) and in Year II it was 31.5 days per person (total of 1258 days). Thus the average time that a VDU operator reporting symptoms and not fully productive has been reduced from 124.8 days in Year I to 34.9 days in Year II; a reduction of 71%.

The work capabilities of all cases are shown in Table B

Table B
Return to work

	Year I (earlier cases)		Year II (later cases)	
	number	percent	number	percent
Fully fit for their original work	18	40	25	63
Still on alternative work or retrained for another job	27	60	15	38
	45	100	40	101

This was the situation 15 months after the end of the period for Year I and 3 months after the end of the period for Year II.

DISCUSSION

A comparison of cases over the two years was used to measure the effectiveness of control strategies. Following the analysis of Year I cases it was clear that the prevention strategy required greater emphasis to be placed on the importance of work organisation and control of workload. VDU guidelines were set out in brochure form and widely disseminated to managers and VDU users. A comparison of cases over the two years has been used to further evaluate the effectiveness of control strategies.

In Year I symptoms were classified according to severity, as described by Brown et al (2). Many of the cases in Year II were difficult to classify as the symptoms were vague and ill-defined. The anatomical sites of reported discomfort were the same for both years, discomfort was also believed to be work related. However, it is doubtful that Repetition Strain Injury is an accurate diagnosis. A better description maybe "muscular fatigue related to working conditions". Whilst controversy exists over an agreed medical definition we have continued to call these cases "RSI".

If these fatigue symptoms are taken not to be RSI (23% of all cases for Year II) then the incidence rate in Year II for clerical workers is reduced from 0.14 to 0.10 (18/184). This is a reduction in the incidence rate between Years I and II of 40%.

Analysis of these factors shows that there has been a marked reduction in the severity of musculoskeletal symptoms reported by VDU users in this organisation. This is confirmed by the reduction in time lost from work. Less time was also required on alternative work prior to being able to perform the full scope of the job.

In addition, in Year II there was an increase in the proportion of those who had completely recovered and an improved rate of recovery.

CONCLUSION

The reduction in costs in physical, psychological and in monetary terms has been substantial. These results indicate the value of a positive approach to prevention and rehabilitation for occupational health issues.

The important lessons from this study concern those factors which are more difficult to quantify. It is very clear that RSI results from many factors. The workplace and the workload can directly cause muscle and tendon fatigue leading to pain. However, the indirect causes, i.e. the psycho-social factors in the person's work and external environment, are the factors which contribute significantly to an person's response to pain, reponse to treatment, and ultimate return to full productive work. The interaction between physical and psycho-social factors therefore needs to be addressed if prevention of RSI is to be successful.

References

1. OXENBURGH, M.S. (1984) Musculoskeletal Injuries occurring in Word Processor Operators. Proceedings of the 21st Annual Conference, Ergonomics Society of Australia and New Zealand, Sydney pp 137-143.

2. BROWN C.D. NOLAN B.M. and FAITHFULL D.K. (1984) Occupational Repetition Strain Injuries, Medical Journal of Australia, 140: pp 329-332.

WORK WITH DISPLAY UNITS 86
B. Knave and P.-G. Wideb盲ck (eds.)

EYE FATIGUE AMONG VDU USERS AND NON-VDU USERS

Finn Levy & Ingrid Greger Ramberg. Institute of Occupational Health. POBox 8149-Dep, N-0033 Oslo 1, Norway.*

In a cross-sectional questionnaire study among VDU users and non-VDU users the prevalence of eye fatigue is shown to increase with time spent using the VDU and in particular among those performing full time data entry work. Men reported less complaints than women, but the work tasks were not identical. Eye fatigue was insignificantly less common among women aged 40 than among those aged under 40 years.

1. INTRODUCTION

Use of visual display units (VDUs) is reported to increase eye and musculo-skeletal problems among VDU users as reported by Knave [1], Evans [2,3] and L盲ubli [4] among others. Ergonomic and other factors of the work environment may interfere with reported health complaints as reviewed by Grandjean [5].

Whilst the general aim of this study was to compare health complaints related to office work with VDUs for different working hours to those of traditional office tasks, this presentation will mainly concentrate on eye fatigue (eye strain, visual fatigue) among VDU users and non-VDU users.

2. MATERIAL AND METHODS

2.1. Study population

This study was designed as a cross-sectional field survey in 18 small private and 7 large governmental enterprises, which use VDUs. Employees in the same offices not using VDUs served as a control group. There was no matching for age or gender.

TABLE 1. Study population according to main job category搂

Main job category	All N	Women N	Women %	Men N	Men %	No response N	No response %
Secretarial	101	99	98	1	1	1	1
Data entry	91	89	98	2	2	0	0
Office routine	247	220	89	27	11	0	0
Executive officers	121	77	64	43	36	1	1
Customer service	34	24	71	10	29	0	0
Telephone service	71	68	96	3	4	0	0
Other jobs	145	43	30	101	71	1	1
All women respondents	810	620	76.5	187	23	3	0.5

搂 For definition of job category see Appendix 1.

* The investigation was financed by The Norwegian Ministry of Labour and Municipal Affairs, (=Kommunal- og arbeidsdepartementet).

2.2. Questionnaire

A questionnaire was distributed by occupational health personnel and collected the same evening. It was completed by 810 out of 866 male and female VDU and non-VDU users aged 17-71 years, a response rate of 93.5%. The main job categories are shown in Table 1. Some use of VDUs was reported by 393 women (48.5%) and 123 men (15%) . The most common age groups were 20-29 years for women (33%) and 30-39 years for men (29%). 39% of women and 28% of men were less than 30 years of age.

In addition to 34 questions on health issues, we covered other issues including job type, equipment used, time spent with different equipment, work environment, work content, smoking habits etc.

Four questions were specifically related to eye symptoms during work: eye-fatigue; soreness and irritation; blurring of vision and redness of the eyes.

The frequency of health complaints was registered as "daily", "more than one day a week", "occationally", "seldom or never". Respondents without health complaints did not usually answer these questions.

The questionaire also asked if respondents felt that the work had contributed to their health problems, (in the tables "work reported as a concomitant cause") and whether the symptoms were present in their leisure hours. The latter will not be further reported in this paper.

2.3. Statistics

Pearson's correlation coefficient and chi-square tests with one degree of freedom using Yates correction for continuity were performed.

3. RESULTS AND DISCUSSION

3.1. Health complaints among office employees, (women and men).

TABLE 2. Health complaints (work reported as a concomitant cause).

Complaints	All respondents N=810	(100%)	Women § n=620	(100%)	Men § n=187	(100%)	Chi-square
Eye fatigue	255	31.5	204	32.9	49	26.2	n.s
Frontal headache	192	23.7	157	25.3	35	18.7	n.s
Stiff neck	312	38.5	258	41.6	53	28.3	xx
Shoulder complaints	260	32.1	225	36.3	33	17.6	xxx
Muscle/joint compl.	215	26.5	182	29.4	33	17.6	xx
Increased fatigue for longer periods	159	19.6	122	19.7	37	19.8	n.s
Irritability	108	13.3	82	13.2	26	13.9	n.s
Nervous complaints, anxiety, depression	50	6.2	38	6.1	12	6.4	n.s

Chi-square with Yates correction (df=1): Significance levels for differences in reporting complaints between women and men:
n.s.= p>0.05, *= 0.05>p>0.01, **= 0.01>p>0.001, *** = p<0.001.
§ 3 persons omitted due to lack of information on gender.

The following results are calculated only for the 810 respondents (100%): 620 (76.5 %) women, 187 (23%) men, and the 3 non responders on the questions of gender. These three are omitted from the tables showing distribution according to gender. The reasons for no response by 7.5% have not been further investigated since the overall response rate was high.

Selected symptoms where work was reported as a probable cause, and the statistical significance between male and female workers in reporting symptoms, are shown in Table 2.

Eye fatigue is not reported with a significant difference between women and men in the total population, neither is frontal headache nor fatigue or nervous complaints.

3.2. Musculo-skeletal complaints

In contrast to eye fatigue, musculo-skeletal complaints are significantly reported more often among women. "Stiff neck" and "shoulder complaints" were the most common musculo-skeletal symptoms, statistically occurring more often among women than men.

3.3. Intercorrelations between symptoms

That eye fatigue is not only a symptom of visual load is indicated by the correlation with other reported symptoms as well as to VDU use (Table 3). There was a fairly good correlation between eye fatigue and most other symptoms, with p-values of <0.001 and correlation coefficients of 0.588 to 0.315, as well as intercorrelation between most other health complaints. The results are in accordance with those reported by Knave [1]. The correlation with use of VDU is lower than that for most of the health complaints, but still significant.

TABLE 3. Correlation of eye fatigue with other parameters

Symptom	Number of respondents§	Pearson's "r" correlation coefficient	p-value
Eye irritation	467	.588	<0.001
Stiff neck	497	.417	<0.001
Frontal headache	490	.409	<0.001
Shoulder complaints	500	.401	<0.001
Occipital headache	469	.389	<0.001
Fatigue, general	510	.379	<0.001
Muscle/joint pain	512	.350	<0.001
Back pain	470	.316	<0.001
Irritability	502	.315	<0.001
Use of VDUs	254	.234	<0.001
Cutaneous irritation	462	.158	=0.001

Correlation between the symptom "eye fatigue" and some other parameters among the 810 responding office employees (620 women, 187 men, 3 gender not stated).

§ Number of respondents = number of respondents to the question, reporting complaints "daily", "more than one day a week", "occationally", "seldom or never".

3.4. Eye complaints and job category

Eye fatigue was the most commonly reported eye symptom for both sexes. Among the 620 women employees, 33% (204) complained of eye fatigue, 17% of soreness and irritation of the eyes, 10% of blurring of vision, and 9% of red eyes. Further details regarding women in different jobs are given in Table 4.

TABLE 4. Eye complaints and job category among women

		EYE-SYMPTOMS			
Main job category	Number of women 100%	Eye fatigue %	Irritation %	Blurring %	Redness %
1. Secretarial	99	22.2	8.1	6.1	5.1
2. Data entry	89	51.7	28.1	21.3	19.1
3. Office routine	220	30.5	13.6	9.1	6.4
4. Executive officers	77	23.4	10.4	6.5	3.9
5. Customer service	24	20.8	8.3	4.2	4.2
6. Telephone service	68	42.6	29.4	10.3	14.7
7. Other jobs	43	34.9	23.3	14.0	11.6
All women respondents	620	32.9	16.6	10.3	8.9

Eye complaints related to job category, among women office employees (n=620) in percent of women respondents. Symptoms attributed to present work. For definition of main job categories, see Appendix 1.

Data entry dominated the list of jobs connected with high rate of complaints.

Eye irritation, blurring of vision and redness were most common among data entry employees (operators) and the telephone service personnel (Table 4).

The difference between eye fatigue among women with data entry work and mixed office routines is significant (chi-square=11.4, df=1, $p<0.001$).

Women with glasses prescribed for use at work with VDUs, reported slightly more complaints from eye fatigue than those not using glasses, but the difference was not statistically significant.

3.5. Time spent with equipment

Differences in reported health complaints will depend upon the employees work load, work tasks, equipment design, time used in front of VDUs or other equipment, job content, work environment etc.

The eye complaints reported by women in different jobs are previously shown (Table 4). Eye fatigue is the most commonly reported eye complaint. It may be used as an indicator of intensive visual work, and is as such supposed to increase with increasing time spent at work, and the more visually demanding the job.

Employees in a modern office often use more than one type of equipment, and it is almost impossible to quantify the time used at VDUs in a large scale survey. The estimations given by the employees are those most easily obtainable and in surveys they are used, although they may be inaccurate.

Figure 1 shows how the reported frequency of eye fatigue increases with increased time using data entry terminals or standard size VDU terminals from 1 hour and on, whilst the increase when using a typewriter is registered only after 6-8 hours of work. The seemingly higher prevalence of complaints in short-time manual office routine and typewriter work than in VDU work, is a result of the 4-8 hours work with data entry or VDUs the rest of the day.

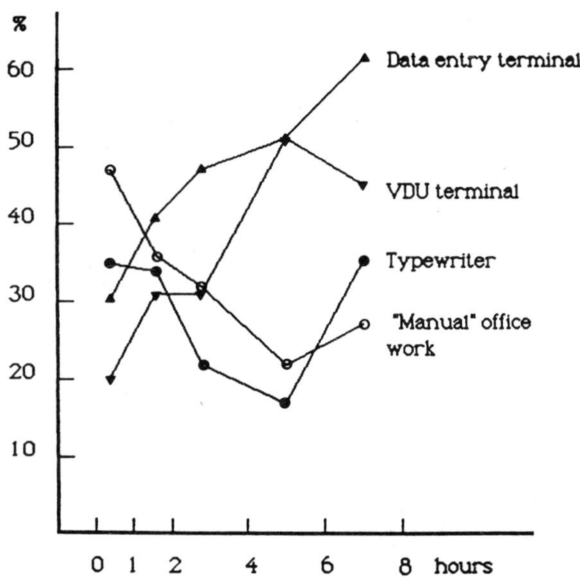

Hours spent with different equipment

FIGURE 1

Percentage of 810 employees reporting eye fatigue occurring daily or some days a week, in relation to length of time spent with office equipment: data entry VDU terminals using a small VDU screen; standard size VDU terminal; typewriter or "work without VDU, microfiche, typewriter or calculator" ("manual office work").

Eye fatigue was reported by about 20% of those using VDU's less than 1 hour daily, increasing to 50% between 4-6 hours, (the figures for women is 25% and 57% respectively). The increase in eye fatigue with increased hours working at VDUs is also described by Knave [1], Evans [2] and Ekenes [6] among others.

The prevalence of eye fatigue (as well as muscular pain and headache) was reported by up to about 50% after more than 4 hours daily work at the VDU, as well as with micro-fiche readers. Eye fatigue decreased with increase in time sp with a minimum at about 4-6 hours.

Our results indicate that the best compromise between VDU/non-VDU work and eye fatigue seems to be about 2-4 hours of VDU work combined with typing and "manual" office routines.

3.6. Equipment used more than 4 hours a day

Since an employee often uses more than one type of office equipment, the best estimate of effects may be the reported complaints in jobs when more than 50% of the day (ie. more than 4 hours), is spent at the same device.

Symptoms from eyes, head, and muscles of the upper extremities were more common among employees using data entry terminals with a small text-window, (upper line) more than 4 hours a day, than among VDU users with a normal sized screen in the total population (Figure 2).

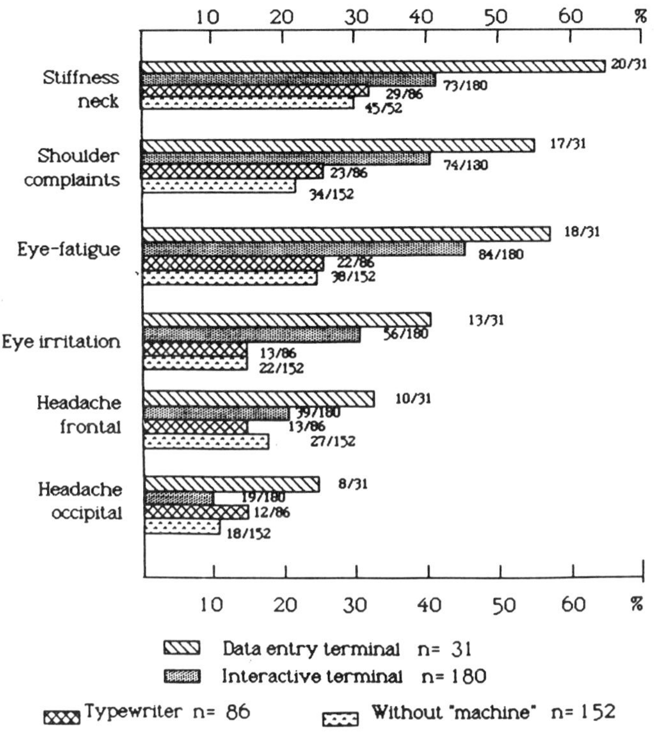

FIGURE 2

Symptoms reported to occur more than one day a week among office workers (n=810), women (n=620) and men (n=187), when working 4 hours or more per day with and without VDUs.

Employees using typewriters or who were working without special equipment, - consistently reported less eye complaints after 4 hours or more work, than did VDU users, but more symptoms at shorter time of use, due to more use of VDUs and data entry terminals when time with typewriter etc. is short.

One can question if this is caused by the VDU screens or by other factors connected with the job. The skilled data entry operators usually only throw a quick glance at the screen and looked mainly at the text documents (vouchers etc). The difference in complaints is probably due to a higher intensity of visual work than the use of data entry terminals in themselves. The picture is somewhat different if we exclude the male employees and look at the main job categories for women and the use of VDUs.

Table 5 shows how visually intensive work results in a very high incidence of eye fatigue irrespective of job category compared to work without display units. Secretarial work full day both with VDU (word processor) and typewriter must in this respect be regarded as visually intensive.

TABLE 5 Eye fatigue among women in different job categories related to VDU use/non-VDU use more than 4 hours a day

Job category	Equipment used	Number of women	Eye fatigue N	Eye fatigue %
1. Secretarial	VDU	12	10	83
	Typewriter	19	10	53
	None	7	1	14
2. Data entry	VDU	31	27	87
	Small VDU	27	14	52
	None	15	5	33
3. Office routine	VDU	44	28	64
	Small VDU	7	1	14
	Typewriter	54	7	13
4. Telephone service	VDU	8	5	63
	Micro-fiche	21	19	90
	None	39	5	13

Eye fatigue among women in different job categories related to VDU use/non VDU use. - N = number of women reporting eye fatigue.
VDU = Normal sized VDU terminal (24 lines or more).
Small VDU = data entry terminal, (usually less than 12 lines).
Micro-fiche = optic reader with projection from behind screen.
None = none of the above mentioned alternatives.

We find that the use of micro-fiche readers seems to cause as much eye fatigue as does intensive VDU use in telephone operators. Starr [7] did not find any difference between VDU use and non-VDU use in telephone enquiry personel, but the frequency of complaints was high in both groups.

Our results are in general accordance with reports by Knave [1], Dainoff [8] and Evans [2] in that eye symptoms are more prevalent among those with intensive visual work. In our study this seems to be valid for most VDU work and for the use of micro-fiche readers. In contrast to this, Böös et al. [9] showed that there was no difference between VDU users and references or between men and women in a subesequent ofthalmologic examination.

3.7. Job content

Data entry jobs and word processing were almost exclusively performed by women, while scientific or other interactive use of VDUs was most frequent among men. There was a minor correlation between reported eye fatigue and low degree of variation in job ($p<0.01$).

3.8. Intervals and intensity of VDU use

As the equipment used is strongly connected to the tasks performed, eye fatigue may be correlated to the patterns of VDU use. Table 6 shows how reported intensity and duration of work with display units is associated with inreased complaints of eye fatigue.

Women consistently reported more eye fatigue than men, but among the subgroups the difference is not statistically significant (p>0.05).

The difference between intensive/regular VDU use (50)% and "occasional use" with reports of 26.5% eye fatigue, is statistically significant (p<0.001) both for women and men.

Women employees using VDUs (172/393), reported nearly twice as much eye fatigue as did non-VDU users (52/227). The difference is significant (p<0.001), as is also the difference in eye fatigue between all male and female screen users (table 6), but not between non-screen users.

The difference between symptoms in male VDU (29/123) and male non-VDU (8/64) users was not significant at the 5% level, (chi-square=2.59).

TABLE 6. Eye fatigue and intensity of screen work

Pattern of visually intensive work	Eye fatigue daily or some days a week						
	Women			Men			Chi-
	total	cases	%	total	cases	%	square
Intensive/regular	186	94	50.5	31	13	41.9	n.s.
Intensive/periods	65	28	43.1	40	9	22.5	n.s.
Moderate/regular	86	35	43.1	26	5	19.2	n.s.
Occasional use	49	13	26.5	22	2	9.1	n.s.
Varying/other	7	2	28.6	4	0	-	n.s.
Mean:							
Screen use	393	172	43.8	123	29	23.6	***
Non screen users	227	52	22.9	64	8	12.5	n.s.
Mean, all employed	620	224	36.1	187	37	20.0	***

Eye fatigue related to intensity of work with VDUs and microfiche. The table includes all office workers that answered the question, irrespective of tasks in addition to use of VUDs, (micro-fiche users not excluded). Three persons where gender is not stated are omitted. Statistical difference between women and men: Chi-square with Yates corrction (df.=1): n.s.: p>0.05, ***: p<0.001. Total = number of persons. Cases = persons with eye fatigue.

Differences in work tasks may explain some of the differences in complaints between women and men, and between women workers,(see Table 1, Table 5).

Differences in reporting eye fatigue is significant between male and female screen users, as previously reported by Knave [1] among others. Our study indicates that a possible explanation may be differences in work tasks. The significant difference in eye fatigue between female screen users and non screen users supports the assumption that factors connected to screen use cause increased frequency of eye fatigue.

Indoor climate may play an important role in reports on health complaints among office workers. Hedge [10] pointed out that eye symptoms only occurred in excess when open-plan offices were air-conditioned. We have unfortunately no data on this.

Lighting of offices, together with the clarity and readability of screen are reported by Nishiyama [11] and Smith [12] to be important factors.

Long working hours without sufficient rest pauses is probably a main cause of problems in most VDU related work (Ekenes [6]), as is the design of the work station, as reviewed by Grandjean [4].

3.9. Age differences in eye fatigue among women

Table 7 shows the difference in eye fatigue and stiff neck in women less than or more than 40 years of age.

Women less than 40 years of age using VDUs more than 4 hours daily, reported slightly more eye fatigue (53%) than did typists (34%) or non-VDU/non-typewriting personel ("manual" office work) (37%). The difference was not significant (Chi-square test, p>0.05).

Eye fatigue might be expected to occur frequently among the higher age groups for office work. Our results do not support this. One explanation may be differences in visually demanding tasks, the more monotonous jobs being performed by the younger.

TABLE 7: Eye fatigue and stiff neck at ages below or above 40 years

VDU use:	Health complaints	< 40 years n=106	> 40 years n=28	Chi-square.
	Eye fatigue	56 (52.8%)	13 (46.6%)	n.s.
	Stiff neck	66 (62.3%)	8 (28.6%)	**
Typewriting:		< 40 years n=41	> 40 years n=38	
	Eye fatigue	14 (34.1%)	8 (21.1%)	n.s.
	Stiff neck	20 (48.8%)	6 (15.9%)	*
Manual office work:		< 40 years n=57	> 40 years n=43	
	Eye fatigue	21 (36.8%)	12 (27.9%)	n.s.
	Stiff neck	24 (42.1%)	13 (30.2%)	n.s.

Eye fatigue and "stiff neck" attributed to work and occurring more than once a week among women office employees (n=620) at less than and more than 40 years of age. Chi-square for differences between age groups (df=1) with Yates correction: n.s.= p>0.05, *=p<0.05, **=p<0.01

There was a statistically significant decrease in time spent with VDUs with increasing age (p<0.001), but there was no significant difference in eye fatigue between those less than 40 and those more than 40 years of age (p>0.05). The younger group reported, however, significantly more "stiff neck" both among those using typewriters and among VDU users (Table 7).

3.10. Additional observations

Smokers reported significantly more eye fatigue than non-smokers ($p<0.001$), but not eye irritation ($p>0.05$). No significant correlation was found between eye fatigue and smoking in the office. Smoking was most common in monotonous routine jobs such as telephone directory service and data entry.

5. CONCLUSIONS

Women generally reported more health complaints than men. In the total population of office workers the difference was significant only for musculoskeletal symptoms.

VDU users reported significantly more eye fatigue as well as symptoms from muscles in the neck and shoulder, compared both to those working with typewriters, and those using neither screens nor typewriters.

The increase in complaints connected with work is closely related to duration - and high intensity use of VDU with more than 4 hours spent with equipment.

Data entry work seems to give most adverse health effects. The slightly greater frequency of eye fatigue reported in younger women may be explained by their overrepresentation in these job categories.

Eye fatigue did not seem to be an age-related symptom among the women.

The total office environment must be taken into account when investigating and evaluating the health complaints related to VDU use.

Intense daily work with optic (micro-fiche) and electronic (VDU)screens for long periods is an important cause of eye symptoms among office employees and sufficient variation with other work tasks is therefore highly recommended.

ACKNOWLEDGEMENTS. We wish to thank Asbjørn Ekenes and colleagues at The Norwegian Computing Centre for preparing the questionnaire, and for registration of data for computer analysis at The Oslo University Computing Centre. This part of the study was financed by a grant from the Norwegian Ministry of Labour and Municipal Affairs. Thanks to The Occupational Health Services in the participating enterprises and to Dr. Elise Kloumann Bækken at The Institute of Social Medicine, The University of Tromsø for collecting data from local enterprises. To Berit Larssen for typing the manuscript and Anne-Lise Nordhagen and Ingrid Botnen for preparing the printed figures. To Professor Tor Norseth and my colleagues at our Medical Department, for valuable comments and to Adam Balfour for revising the English manuscript.

APPENDIX 1.

The main job categories used in this report comprises:

1. Secretarial: reception, secretarial work with and without word processing.

2. Data entry: data entry onto a VDU with completed forms/text, often using a small screen.

3. Office routines: usual variety of office work, data aquisition, some use of calculator, typewriter, fotocopier, filing, etc.

4. Executive officers: including senior and junior executive officers, and some departmental leaders in both governmental and private enterprises.

5. Customer service: sales, counter work, personal customer contact.

6. Telephone service: telephone directory enquiry operators with telephone directory listings registered on microfiche (n=21) or in a database (VDU screen); switchboard service and ticket reservation.

7. Other jobs: programming, control room personel, engineers, instructors, researchers etc. No responses (n=17) included. - Most persons in this category is men (n=105), women (n=43).

REFERENCES.

[1] Knave,B.G., Wibom,R.I., Voss,M., Hedström,L.D. and Bergquist,U.O.V., Work with video display terminals among office employees. I. Subjective symptoms and discomfort. Scand J Work Environ Health (1985) 11, 457-466.

[2] Evans, J., VDU operators display health problems. Health & Safety at Work, Nov. 1985, 33-37.

[3] Evans,J., Office conditions influence VDU operators' health. Health & Safety at Work. Dec. 1985, 34-36.

[4] Grandjean,E., Ergonomics of VDUs: review of present knowledge, in: Grandjean,E., Vigliani,E., Ergonomic Aspects of Visual Display Terminals (Taylor & Francis Ltd, London 1980) 1-12.

[5] Läubli,T., Hünting,W. and Grandjean,E., Visual impairments in VDU operators related to environmental conditions, in: Grandjean,E. (ed.), Ergonomic Aspects of Visual Display Terminals , (Taylor & Francis, London 1980), 85-94.

[6] Ekenes,A. and Thoresen,K., Arbeidsforhold med dataskjerm. (Work with VDU) Norwegian Computing Center, Oslo, Norway 1980. (In Norwegian).

[7] Starr,S.J., Thompson,C.R. and Shute,S.J.; Effects of Video Display Terminals on Telephone Operators. Human Factors (1982), 24(6), 699-711.

[8] Dainoff,M.J., Visual fatigue in VDT operators, in: Grandjean,E., Vigliani,E., Ergonomic Aspects of Visual Display Terminals (Taylor & Francis Ltd, London 1980) 95-99.

[9] Böös,S.R. Calissendorf, B.M., Knave, B.G., Nyman, K.G. and Voss, M., Work with video display terminals among office employees. III. Ofthalmologic factors. Scand J Work Environ Health (1985) 11, 475-481.

[10] Hedge,A., Ill Health Among Office Workers: an Examination of the Relationship Between Office Design and Employee Well-Being, in, Grandjean, E., Vigliani,E., Ergonomic Aspects of Visual Display Terminals (Taylor & Francis Ltd., London 1980) 46-51.

[11] Nishiyama,K., Nakaseko,M. and a,T., Health Aspects of VDT Operators in the Newspaper Industry, in: Grandjean,E. (ed.), Ergonomics and Health in Modern Offices (Taylor & Francis, London 1984), 113-118.

[12] Smith, A.B., Tanaka,S., Halperin,W.and Richards, R.D. Correlates of Ocular and Somatic Symptoms among Video Display Terminal Users. Human Factors (1984) 26(2), 143-156.

WORK WITH DISPLAY UNITS 86
B. Knave and P.-G. Wideback (eds.)

INTRAOCULAR PRESSURE DURING VDT WORK

Grignolo F.M.*, Di Bari A.*, Brogliatti B.*, Maina G.**

* Istituto di Clinica Oculistica, Universita' di Torino, V. Juvarra 19, 10100-Turin, Italy
** Istituto di Medicina del Lavoro, Universita' di Torino, V. Zuretti 29, 10128-Turin, Italy

ABSTRACT- About 200 VDU's operators, employed in the same factory and in similar work condition, were submitted to intraocular pressure measurement directly on the working site, during usual VDT work. A questionnaire was given to all the operators in order to ascertain their clinical history and subjective ocular complaints; they also underwent a visual examination. The intraocular pressure values, the results of visual examination,the ocular complaints and several VDT-working parameters have been studied and compared.

1. INTRODUCTION

Tonometric mass screenings do not usually take into account the relation between intraocular pressure (IOP), and different jobs, therefore few data are available in literature (1).
A study was made by Segal and coll. on about 16000 factory and office workers. In office workers, a higher incidence of glaucoma and ocular hypertension was found compared to the group of factory workers (2).
In another study made by Helm over a ten year period the incidence of glaucoma and ocular hypertension was found clearly higher in office workers (3).
Recent data show that about 4% of the world population suffers from ocular hypertension , but more than 65% of these subjects is not aware of this condition (1,4,5,6,7).

Our research was, firstly directed at identifying subjects with ocular hypertension among VDT workers. Secondly, to study whether or not any difference in intra ocular pressure values could be found as a function of VDT working time. Thirdly, to investigate the possible correlation between eye-discomfort and IOP values. We were also interested in testing the reliability of the Non-contact Tonometer (NCT), in industrial tonometric mass-screeening.

IOP can be affected physiologically by accomodation, pupillary reflexes and psychophysical stress. All these factors can be found in VDT work. Accomodation produces an increase of lens thickness, the iris is pushed forward and the amplitude of the anterior chamber angle is reduced. This can result in an IOP increase in predisposed subjects.
Pupillary reflexes can also increase IOP by impairing the aqueous flow from the posterior to the anterior chamber.
Boles Carenini and other studies have also proved the influence of psychophysical stress on IOP (8,9).

2. MATERIALS AND METHODS

181 VDT workers were examined, 168 females and 13 males, all being telephone operators.

A questionnaire was given to all the operators, in order to ascertain their clinical history and subjective ocular complaints.

All subjects were submitted to an extensive medical check-up by an occupational medicine specialist. They also underwent a visual screening test (visiotest), in order to obtain measures of visual acuity, stereopsis and to detect heterophorias (at both near and far optical distances) (10).
Corrective lenses were worn for the visual examination if used during work.

Ocular tonometry was taken directly on the working site, in the morning after about 2 hours of habitual VDT work.
In order to make the IOP measurement more acceptable, a Non-contact air-puff tonometer was used. This instrument works on the same principle as the Goldmann: applanation is produced by a controlled air-pulse of linearly increasing force impinging on the cornea; the interval of time required to produce applanation is proportional to IOP. This system may be used without topical anesthesia; there is no risk of microbiological contamination, and repeated measurements produce no significant alteration in corneal integrity or IOP (11)

The IOP was measured in 362 eyes : three readings were taken on the same eye and their mean value was calculated. A few minutes after the non-contact recordings a single Goldmann applanation measurement was taken, on some of the operators, with use of local surface anesthesia. All measurements were taken by differents ophthalmologists.

3. RESULTS

3.1 SAMPLE ANALYSIS

The mean age of the group was 32.8 years (s.d.=8.3), ranging from 23 to 60 years.
The mean working months at VDT were 90.5 (s.d.=49.7),ranging from 1 to 168 months of work.
The mean daily working hours at VDT were 4.1 (s.d.=0.9), ranging from 1 to 8 hours, with most operators working betweeen 2 and 4 hours.
The mean reading distance was 59.8 cm. (s.d.= 5.8), ranging from 25 to 110 cm. with the majority (52%) of the operators working more than 60 cm. away from the VDT.
The division into classes distribution is shown in Table 1.

Table 1: DISTRIBUTION CLASSES

AGE (years)			
<31	31–40	41–50	>50
18.2%	35.4%	39.8%	6.6%

WORK AT VDT (months)			
<19	19–48	48–96	>96
9.9%	19.3%	22.1%	48.6%

DAILY WORK AT VDT (hours)		
<2 hours	2–4 hours	>4 hours
2.8%	92.8%	4.4%

VDT READING DISTANCE (cm)		
<40 cm.	40–60 cm.	>60 cm.
13.8%	34.3%	51.9%

3.2 TONOMETERS COMPARISON

Data on 250 eyes was collected for the comparison between the two tonometers. The findings are shown in figure 1. The data from the two instruments closely agree, with a high coefficient of correlation (r= 0.85, slope= 1.10).

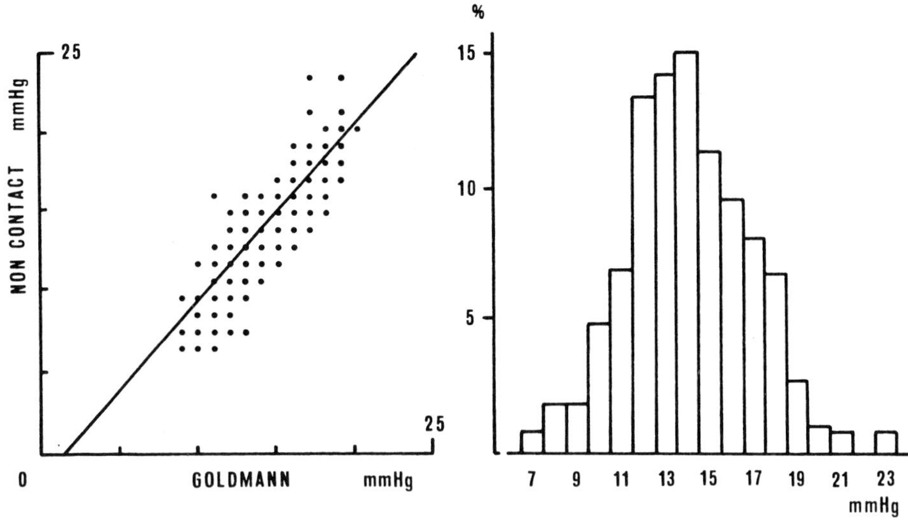

Fig. 1 TONOMETERS COMPARISON

Fig. 2 IOP VALUES DISTRIBUTION

3.2 TONOMETRIC VALUES

The Figure 2 shows the distribution of tonometric values. The mean IOP of the sample was 14.0 mmHg (s.d.=2.76),ranging from 7 to 23 mmHg.
Out of the 362 examined eyes, 4 (0.9%) had an IOP value higher than 20 mmHg (two 21 mmHg and two 23 mmHg readings). Table 2 shows these border-line values which were found in subjects more than 35 years old, with no relations to working months at vdt, daily working hours or VDT reading distance.

Table 2: BORDER LINE IOP VALUES

IOP (mmHg)	AGE	MONTHS AT VDT	VDT DAILY HOURS	VDT READING DISTANCE
21	37	90	2-4	< 40 cm.
21	48	120	2-4	> 60 cm.
23	38	138	2-4	40-60 cm.
23	36	108	2-4	40-60 cm.

Table 3: VISUAL EXAMINATIONS

SPECTACLE WEARERS	41.1%
CONTACT LENS WEARERS	3.9%
MYOPIA	19.5%
HYPEROPIA	37.2%
EMMETROPIA	43.3%
HETEROPHORIAS (>5Δ)	7.3%
IMPAIRED STEREOPSIS	6.2%

3.3 VISUAL PARAMETERS

Visual examination results are shown in Table 3.
No relationship was found between IOP and ametropias as shown in Figure 3 the same was found between IOP values and visual acuity.
In spectacle wearers the mean IOP resulted higher, but non significant, than in non wearers. On the contrary the IOP decrease in contact lens wearers appears statistically significant (Figure 4).
A significant increase in IOP (about 1 mmHg) was found in subjects with heterophorias higher than 5 prism diopters (Figure 5) and in subjects with deficit in stereopsis higher than 400 sec. (Figure 6). The correlation between ocular motility and binocular vision suggests that these two increases are related.

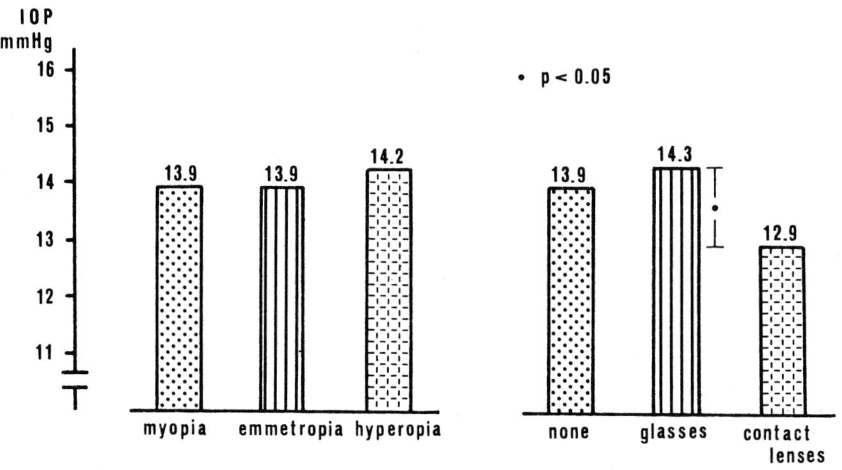

Fig. 3 IOP AND AMETROPIAS

Fig. 4 IOP AND CORRECTIVE LENSES

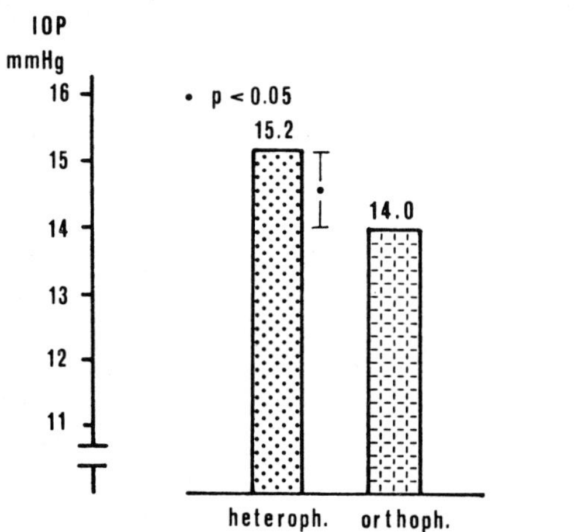

Fig. 5 IOP AND PHORIAS

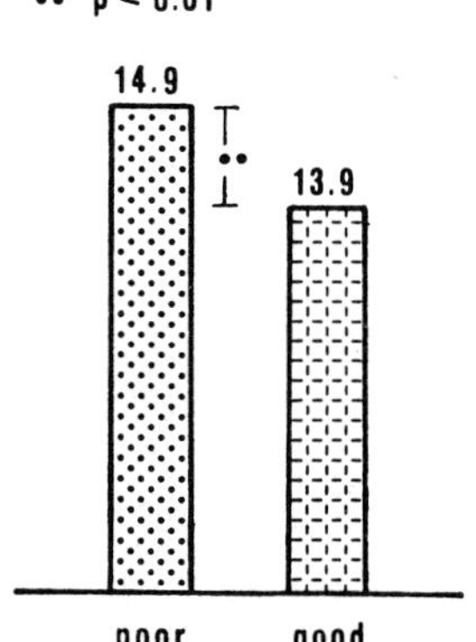

Fig. 6 IOP AND STEREOPSIS

3.4 AGE AND WORK PARAMETERS

The Figure 7 shows a small increase in IOP values as age advances. This result is statistically significant in the comparison between the group of subjects more than 40 years old and the younger group.
The Figure 8 shows that no relationship appears between mean tonometric values and VDT working months classes. Subjects who had worked at VDT for less than 18 months had slighty lower IOP values; however this difference is scarcely significant (p<0.1).
The analysis of pressure values shows a significant trend to an increase in IOP in those operators who used VDT for more than 2 hours per day, compared to the reference group who used the VDT for less than 2 hours (Figure 9).

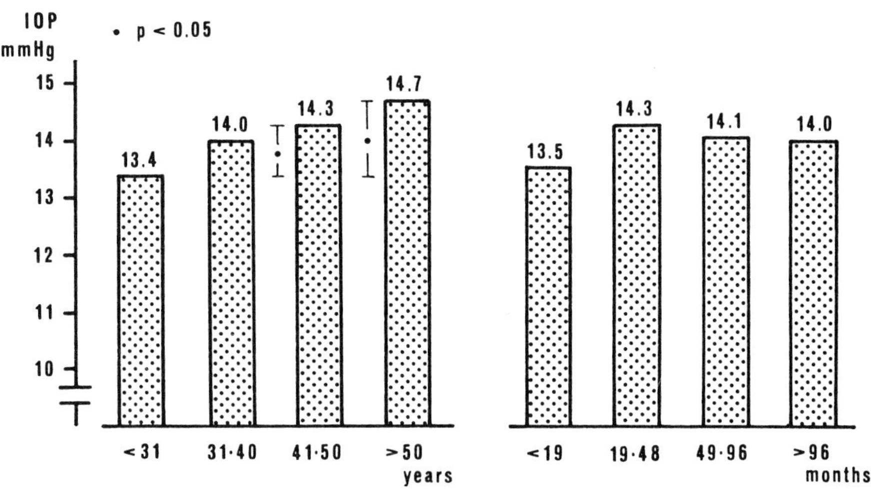

Fig. 7 IOP AND AGE

Fig. 8 IOP AND VDT WORKING MONTHS

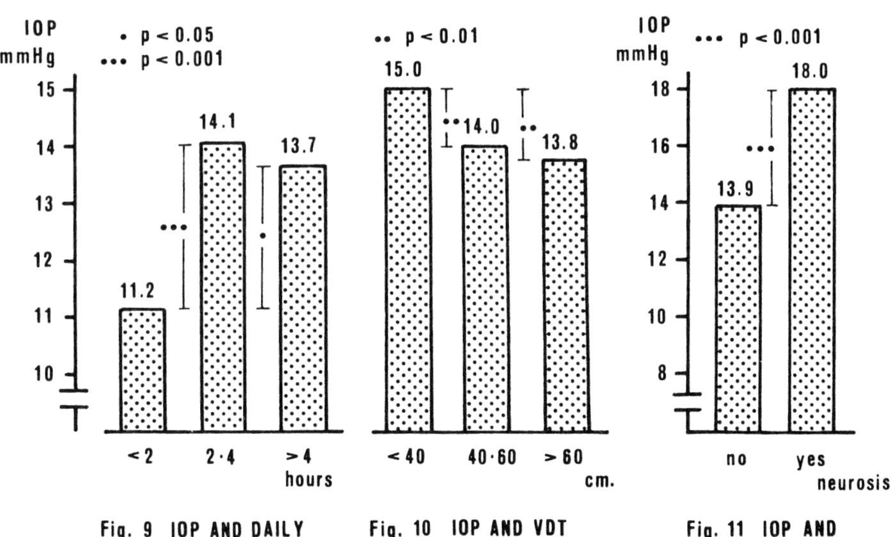

Fig. 9 IOP AND DAILY WORK AT VDT

Fig. 10 IOP AND VDT READING DISTANCE

Fig. 11 IOP AND NEUROSIS

The Figure 10 suggests a correlation between IOP values and VDT reading distances. The IOP shows an increase as reading distance decreases and therefore accomodation work increases. This trend was found to be statistically significant for distances less than 40 cm..

3.5 TONOMETRY RELATED TO NEUROSIS

A highly significant relationship was found between clinical diagnosed neurosis and increased IOP as shown in figure 11.
However the small number of subjects, 8, with sure diagnosis of neurosis must be taken into account.

3.6 OCULAR SYMPTOMATOLOGY

Table 4 shows the frequence of the operators' ocular complaints and the IOP variations related to the presence or absence of ocular complaints. The most frequent symptoms were eye strain, burning eyes, headache and blinking.
No relationship was found, however a small increase (less than 1mmHg) was found in subjects who complained of either double vision ($p<0.1$), blurred vision ($p<0.05$) or eye ache ($p<0.1$).
A small, but significant decrease was also found in subjects who complained of eye strain.

Table 4: CORRELATION BETWEEN OCULAR COMPLAINTS AND IOP

OCULAR COMPLAINTS	FREQUENCE	MEAN IOP VALUE (mmHg) Yes	No	DIFFERENCE (Y-N) mmHg
EYE STRAIN	71.7%	13.9	14.5	-0.6 *
BURNING EYE	65.5%	14.0	14.0	-
HEADACHE	59.4%	14.0	14.1	-0.1
BLINKING	53.8	13.9	14.1	-0.2
REDNESS	46.1	13,9	14,1	-0.2
BLURRED VISION	36.1	14.4	13.8	-0.6 *
TEARING	27.7	14.0	14.0	-
EYE ACHE	25.0%	14.4	13.9	+0.5
DOUBLE VISION	16.1%	14.4	14.0	+0.4

* $p < 0.05$

4. CONCLUSION

The high reliability of the Non-contact tonometer for mass-screening is confirmed. Our results suggest that VDT work does not increase the incidence of ocular hypertension in operators.
Mean tonometric values are not affected significantly by working months or by

daily working hours at VDT, except for the operators group who work for a short time at VDT. In these subjects the IOP values appear to be significantly lower.
A short VDT reading distance, as in the reading test which is used in the diagnosis of glaucoma, can result in IOP increase. In our study, however, the IOP values were always in the normal range.
It should be noted that the VDT operators' work condition can be highly stressing; that could be related to IOP increase which was found in subjects with signs of neurosis.
A weak correlation appears between variation in IOP values and eye discomfort. The small but significant variation related to subjects' complaints of blurred vision and visual strain, appears difficult to explain.

We intend to investigate further the effects of VDT work on IOP, also using a specific sample of glaucomatous subjects in order to ascertain possible variation in IOP in eyes with impaired aqueous hydrodynamics.

ACKNOWLEDGEMENTS

We would like to thank the SIP (Societa' Italiana per l'esercizio telefonico) and Mr. F. Moruzzi for their kind help during this study.

REFERENCES

(1) Boles Carenini B., Bauchiero L., Rolandi G., Epidemiologia del glaucoma cronico semplice, in: L'attendibilita' dei mezzi semeiologici nella diagnosi del glaucoma cronico semplice, (LVIII Congresso Soc. Oftalmol. Ital., Roma, 1977).
(2) Segal and coll., Mass screening of adults for glaucoma, Ophthalmologica 153 (1967) 336.
(3) Helm A. and coll., Ergbnisse einer 10 jahrigen Glaukome Dispensaire-Sprechstunde, Deutsch. Gesundh. Wes. 24 (1969) 83.
(4) Mc Donald J.E. and coll., Glaucoma screening in offices of general practitioners and internist a study of 10.000 patients, Am. J. Ophthalmol. 59 (1965) 875.
(5) Bankes J.L.K. and coll., Bedford glaucoma survey, Brit. Med. J. 1 (1968) 791.
(6) Grignolo F.M., Lega M., Zanotti M., Pesce F., Nuzzi R., The hypertensive eyes incidence: an epidemiological research, Paper presented at Glaucoma Society Meeting, 11-14 may 1986, Turin, Italy.
(7) Hitchings R.A., Ocular hypertension - a problem in prophylaxis, Paper presented at Glaucoma Society Meeting, 11-14 may 1986, Turin, Italy.
(8) Boles Carenini B., Grignolo F.M., Bongiovanni C., Der intraokulare Druck bei Psychischei Stress, Klin. Mbl. Augenheilk. 170 (1977) 562.
(9) Uno Y., Consideration of the variation of ocular tension in relation to stress, Acta Soc. Ophthalmol. Jpn. 68 (1964) 1055.
(10) Belicard P., Leonhardt-Jambon C., Le Visiotest. Depistage sommaire des defauts visuels, J. Fr. Ophtalmol. 1.3 (1978) 217.
(11) Forbes M., Pico G. Jr., Grolman B., A Non-contact Applanation Tonometer: Description and Clinical Evaluation, Arch. Ophthalmol. 91 (1974) 134.
(12) Bergquist U. OV., Video display terminals and health, Scand. J. Work Environ. Health 10 (1984) suppl. 2.
(13) Boos S.R., Calissendorf B., Knave B.G., Nyman K., Voss M., Work with video display terminals among office employees III. Ophthlmologic factors, Scand. J. Work Environ. Health 11 (1985) 475.
(14) Dainoff M.J., Happ A.,Crane P., Visual fatigue and occupational stress in VDT operators, Human Factors 23 (1981) 421.

2. RADIATION

PHYSICAL BACKGROUNDS

WORK WITH DISPLAY UNITS 86
B. Knave and P.-G. Wideback (eds.)

RADIATION EMISSIONS FROM VDUs

Lars-Erik PAULSSON

National Institute of Radiation Protection
S-104 01 Stockholm, Sweden

This paper describes various types of radiation from CRT-based VDUs, the radiation sources and the relevant measurement techniques. Results of surveys and original work of the author are summarized and compared with safety levels when such levels exist. Radiation emission from various non-CRT-based VDUs is breifly discussed. Special emphasis is placed on the emission of low frequency magnetic fields, since they have been of great concern lately.

1. INTRODUCTION

Typical CRT-based VDUs emit, or can under certain circumstances emit, several types of radiation or give rise to radiation related phenomena, eg. X-rays, UV, visible light, electromagnetic fields in the ELF to VHF bands, electrostatic fields and acoustical noise. Many of the alleged health problems with VDUs have been attributed to these variuos types of radiation, although most of the radiations are practically nonexistant or are emitted at very low levels. This paper presents the most important types of radiation from VDUs and their sources. It is based partly on measurements made by the author himself |1| and partly on the numerous similar studies reported in the literature. For an excellent review see |2| pp 13-27. No attempt is made to evaluate the possible biological effects of the different radiation phenomena. However comparisons with recommended safety levels are made when such levels exist.

2. SOURCES

The traditional VDU is based on the cathode ray tube, CRT. All radiation sources are situated inside this tube or in the electrical circuits driving it. Optical radiation (visible light and ultraviolet radiation) and X-rays are emitted when the electron beam strikes the phosphor on the inside of the screen. A static electric field is generated by the high potential on the accelerating electrode, which is a metalization covering the inside of the screen. Low frequency electric fields are generated mainly by the circuits connected to the accelerating electrode. Low frequency magnetic fields are generated mainly by the deflection coils used for scanning the the electron beam vertically and horizontally over the screen. Other sources are the circuits driving these coils. Extremely low frequency fields are generated by the transformers and circuits in the power supply. Electromagnetic fields of medium, high and very high frequencies are generated by the electronic circuits in the display unit. Acoustical noise is generated by fans and by components in the high tension and horizontal deflection system.

3. OPTICAL RADIATION

Visible light is in most investigations found to be at least two orders of magnitude below accepted limit values. A detailed spectral analysis on three VDUs with a positive image polarity shows that the radiance on these screens was less than 1/800 of the ACGIH TLV |3| for retinal injury, when weighted with the so called blue-light weighting factors. The VDUs selected for the study were visually examined for high levels of blue light. The ultraviolet part of the spectrum was also measured spectroradiometrically. The irradiance close to the screeen was found to be less than 25 mW/m2 in the UVA range and less than 0,01 mW/m2 in the actinic UVB-UVC range. Continuous exposure during working hours would result in a skin dose of about 1/100 of the accepted hygienic limit value. Considerably higher levels are found naturally outdoors or in modern office lighting. The result shows clearly that the increased light output from positive screens should be of no concern with regard to eye or skin injuries.

4. X-RAYS

Several radiation surveys, with a total number of tested units exceding 3000, have not revealed any X-ray emission from normally operating VDUs exceeding the industry emission standard for CRTs at 4.4 uGy/h. A few cases have been reported where this value was exceeded during testing at intended fault conditions. During the latest 10 years of tests of colour TV sets the Swedish institute for testing and approval of electrical equipment has only had a few such cases. Measurements in our own laboratory on about 150 VDUs have indicated that the VDU actually shields background radiation. It should be emphazised that the emission of X-rays from VDUs should be of no concern for the normal user, and that there is no reason for the use of lead-glass shields or lead-rubber aprons in VDU-work. Manufacturers of colour VDUs should however be aware of that the post accelerating voltage on the CRT should not be allowed to rise above a certain critical level (approximately 30kV) during fault conditions.

5. RADIOFREQUENCY ELECTROMAGNETIC RADIATION

In the frequency range of MHz and above very low levels of electric or magnetic fields are generated by ordinary VDUs. In surveys conducted with instruments used for hygienic purposes, eg. Narda, Holaday, Raham etc, no such radiation is ever detected. Some investigators have reported readings on these instruments which afterwards have been shown to be caused by signals outside the operational frequency range of the instrument and entering directly into the electronics of it. The weak radiofrequency fields that do exist however often carry digital information which it is possible to pic up with specialized equipment at a distance. The emission of radiowaves from VDUs is therefore of interest for information security in military and industrial systems but not for hygienic reasons. In urban areas, the field strength from radio and TV broadcast transmitters exceeds the levels found from VDUs. There is definitely no need to carry aprons or dresses made of microwave reflecting metalized fabric. The marketing of such products relies only on ignorance and misinformation of VDU users.

6. LOW FREQUENCY ELECTRIC AND MAGNETIC FIELDS

Both electric and magnetic fields with frequency components in the range of 50Hz to 0.5MHz are generated by ordinary VDUs. The time domain caracteristics of these fields are very complicated which leads to difficulties when using ordinary broadband measurements or frequency analysis when characterizing them 4 . In the surveys conducted at our laboratories, we have paid much attention to time domain analysis based on oscilloscope measurements of the magnetic fields and their time derivatives. Similar studies on the electric field have been reported in 5 . The main source emitting low frequency magnetic field pulses is the deflection coils. These coils generate sawtooth shaped magnetic fields used for deflecting the beam over the screen. In the most commonly used deflection coil, the toroid-saddle coil, the vertical magnetic field (used for horizontal deflection) is generated by an air-wound coil, while the horizontal field (used for vertical deflection) is generated by a coil wound on a toroid shaped core of magnetic material. The external field from such a coil has a dominant vertical component with time caracteristics of the horizontal deflection signal. The repetition frequency of this sawtooth shaped signal is in the range 15-60 kHz for ordinary VDUs. The sawtooth signal increases its amplitude at a steady rate during 85-95% of the period time when the beam scans over the screen and generates one line. During the remaining 5-15% of the period, the fly-back time, the beam is rapidly moved to the starting position of a new line. One way of measuring such a field is to use an electrically shielded test coil with a self resonant frequency well above the frequency range of interest and measuring the induced voltage in the coil with an oscilloscope. The induced voltage is proportional to the time derivative of the magnetic flux in the coil area and the number of turns. The time derivative of the magnetic flux density, dB/dt can thus be calculated from the voltage measurements. The magnetic field strength which is proportional to the flux density can subsequently be calculated by integrating the dB/dt. The integration can be performed by computer when using digital oscilloscopes or by means of operational amplifier techniques.

We have in our laboratories tested about 150 different types of CRT based VDUs. The magnetic field was measured in three orthogonal directions at two different test positions, 30cm and 70cm, in front of the screen. Wide variations in time characteristics, amplitudes and polarizations were found. However for most of the tested VDUs the vertical component of the field dominates and the dB/dt signal is composed of narrow pulses with a length equal to the fly-back time. In some cases this situation is disturbed by field components generated by the fly-back transformer etc. In the case of clean pulses a 1/r3 dependence is observed, where r is the distance from the deflection coil to the test point. If multiple sources exist this relation is disturbed. At the distance of 30cm the dominating component of dB/dt amounted to between 4 and 345 mT/s,peak to peak, (for details se table 1). Similar measurements were also performed on some non-CRT VDUs. For two plasma displays dB/dt was in the range 11-25mT/s and B in the range 28-40nT. A portable PC with an EL-display gave 30 mT/s and 50nT, while a portable PC with a LC-display showed very low values 2mT/s and 2nT. A conclusion from table 1 is that modern VDUs with high demands on visual quality and compact construction tend to emit higher levels of pulsed low frequency magnetic fields than older units. The division of the material in two groups according to linefrequency is thought to be an effective way of sorting older TV-like VDUs from more modern types constructed exclusively for data display purposes.

Table 1. Statistical distribution of B and dB/dt: strongest component at 30cm for 134 VDUs divided in two groups according to line frequency 25%=lower quartile, 50%=median and 75% upper quartile

fraction of total number	0%	25%	50%	75%	100%	0%	25%	50%	75%	100%
	time derivative of flux density mT/s					magnetic flux density nT				
f<20kHz	5	28	38	59	112	23	74	128	198	570
f>20kHz	4	35	91	145	345	42	125	283	530	1040

In order to further analyse this situation all tested VDUs with f>30kHz, totally 28, where grouped according to the dB/dt value. The median value for this group was 175mT/s. The distribution is graphically shown in fig 2 and could be compared with the distribution for the total number of units tested, which is shown in fig 1. The highest values shown in fig 2. are found around VDUs using a deflection unit of the saddle-saddle type eg. without a toroidal magnetic core.

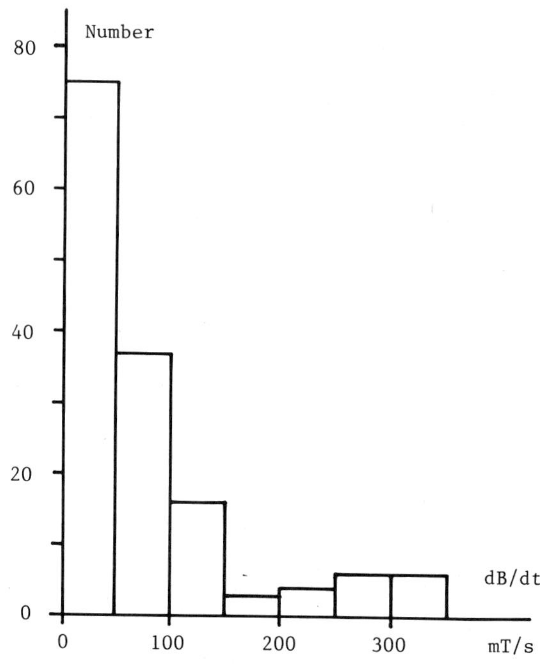

FIGURE 1
Statistical distribution of magnetic induction (dB/dt) for 147 different types of VDUs

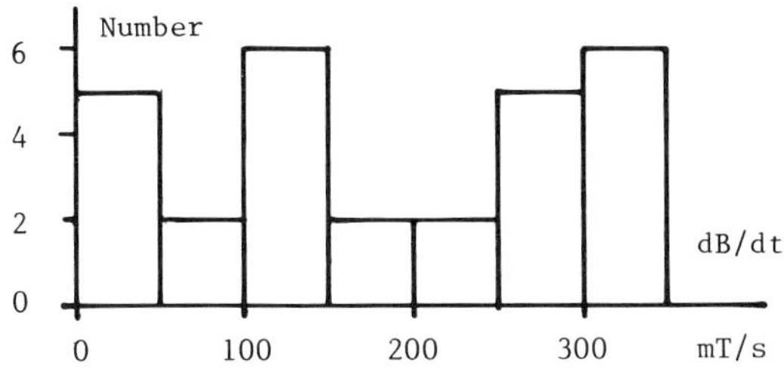

FIGURE 2
Statistical distribution of magnetic induction (dB/dt) for 28 different types of VDUs with a horizontal frequency in the range 30-65 kHz

7. ELECTROSTATIC FIELDS

The accelerating electrode in the CRT is a powerful source of the electrostatic field in front of the VDU due to its high electric potential. The field strength at the operator's position can be estimated as the potential difference divided by the distance. In most cases, the surface potential of the screen differs from the potential of the accelerating electrode due to physical properties of the glass and to charges accumulated on or within the glass. When performing measurements it is of the outmost . importance to strictly adhere to some defined procedure. The one found in |5| has been used extensively at our laboratory. It is furthermore essential that the disturbance of the field by the measuring equipment is understood and specified. In our measurements the instrument, a field mill, was placed in a hole in the center of a large metal plate, which was placed 30cm in front of the screen. With this arrangement it was possible to get reliable readings, useful when comparing different VDUs. However, the actual field strength on the face of the operator can only be found by actual measurements using fantoms with field sensors situated on the surface. With the measurement procedure outlined above values between 0 and 50kV/m are found. The statistical distribution of 147 different VDUs are shown in fig 3.

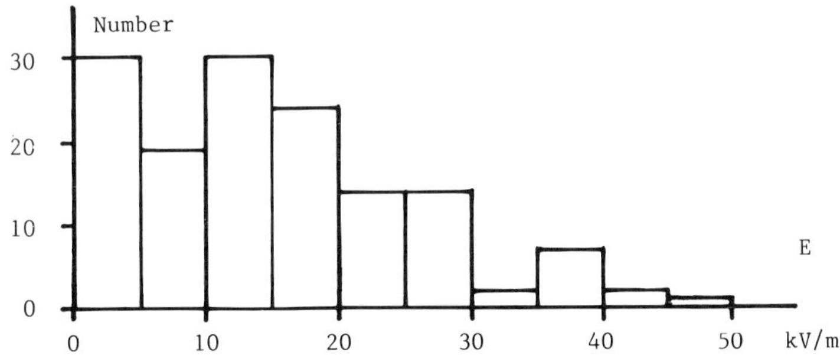

FIGURE 3
Statistical distribution of the electrostatic field for 147 different types of VDUs

REFERENCES

|1| Paulsson L.E. et al: Strålning från dataskärmar, Report a84-08 from the National institute of radiation protection, Stockholm (1984)(in Swedish)

|2| Berqvist U.O.V.: Video display terminals and health, Scandinavian J of Work, Environment & Health, 10, suppl.2(1984)

|3| American Conference of Governmental Industrial Hygienists. TLVs, threshold limit values for chemical substances in the work environment: adopted by ACGIH for 1983-1984. Cincinnati,OH (1983).

|4| Guy A.W.: Health hazards assessment of radio frequency electromagnetic fields emitted by video display terminals. This conference(1986)

|5| Harvey S.M.: Electric-field exposure of persons using video display units, Bioelectromagnetics 5: 1-12 (1984)

WORK WITH DISPLAY UNITS 86
B. Knave and P.-G. Wideбäck (eds.)

HEALTH HAZARDS ASSESSMENT OF RADIO FREQUENCY ELECTROMAGNETIC FIELDS EMITTED BY VIDEO DISPLAY TERMINALS

Arthur W. Guy

Bioelectromagnetics Research Laboratory, Center for Bioengineering, University of Washington, Seattle, WA 98195, USA

Abstract

Video display terminals emit three types of electromagnetic fields; static electric, extra low frequency, and very low to low frequency. The latter frequency range is the most important from the standpoint of inducing the maximum levels of current in the body of a person exposed to the device. The induced current is directly proportional to the time derivative of the exposure fields which consist of the pulsed waveform electric field from the fly back transformer lead and the saw tooth waveform magnetic field from the deflection yoke of the VDT. The electric field (E) which may be as high as several thousand V/m at the surface of the VDT and less than 10 V/m (rms) at the normal viewing distance, induces monophasic current pulses while the magnetic field (H) which is less than 5 A/m at the surface the VDT and of less than 0.1 A/m at the normal viewing distance induces biphasic current pulses in exposed tissues. Though the maximum exposure levels at the surface of the terminals may exceed some maximum recommended exposure levels, the exposures at normal viewing distance are below the most conservative safety levels. The maximum E field induced body currents are less than 70 μA for surface contact and less than 6 μA for exposure at normal viewing distances and the calculated maximum H field induced body current densities never exceed 20 μA/square centimeter rms. The equivalent whole body environmental exposure field for inducing the currents and current density levels typical of VDT exposures vary from 0.06 to 4.0 V/m for the E field and 0.6 to 10 mA/m for the H field. These exposure levels are significantly less than the maximum permitted exposure standards of the world.

1. INTRODUCTION

Most of the emphasis of the previous studies and surveys concerning nonionizing electromagnetic field (NEMF) emissions from video display terminals has been to relate the possible exposure field strengths to various safety standards and exposures known to produce biological effects as reported in the literature. Very little attention, however, has been directed toward the dosimetry aspects of the problem; the quantitation of the actual induced currents and absorbed energy in persons operating the devices. It is important to account for the highly localized near field nature of the emissions, the poor coupling of the energy to the body of the VDT user, and the relationship of the absorbed energy or the induced current density in the body to that known to be of biological significance as determined from research on animals and various biological preparations. It is the purpose of this paper to quantitatively analyze the exposure of VDT operators in terms of true biological significance as related to human exposure standards and biological effects reported in the literature. In achieving this it is necessary to 1) measure levels of exposure fields, 2) determine the rate of absorbed energy (SAR), induced current (I), or current density (J), in the exposed subject, and 3) compare values of SAR, I, or J with known thresholds for biological effects or levels equivalent to maximum permitted exposure levels.

2. SOURCE AND NATURE OF NEMF FROM VDTs

There are 3 major NEMF sources associated with the VDT. One is the extra low frequency (ELF) emissions resulting from the 120 or 240 V, 50 or 60 Hz ac input power and the vertical sweep circuits. These vertical sweep circuits, along with the wiring, power transformers and ac rectifiers within the display terminal emit both electric (E) and magnetic (H) fields of 50 to 60 Hz fundamental frequency and associated harmonics of diminishing magnitudes. The ubiquitous 50 to 60 Hz fields are not unique to the VDT, but occur often at much higher levels near other devices operating from the 120 or 240 V ac house or office electric supply system, as well as near the electric wiring itself. These devices include incandescent and flourescent lighting, electric tools, cooking devices, radio, TV, high fidelity sets, electric blankets, heating pads and other appliances. The second and strongest source of NEMF from the VDT, covering the very low frequency (VLF) to the low frequency (LF) range of approximately 15 - 200 kHz is the horizontal deflection system designed to sweep the electron beam in the cathode ray tube (CRT) rapidly back and forth across the flourescent screen. The electronic sweep circuits of the VDT send electric current pulses through the primary winding of what is called the "flyback" transformer and the magnetic coils surrounding the neck of the CRT. These pulses produce magnetic fields in the coils which cause the CRT electron beam to deflect linearly across the screen to the right and then rapidly back to the left side of the screen. This gives rise to high voltage pulses in the transformer occuring at the a rate of from 15,000 to 30,000 times per second. The flyback voltage pulses are stepped up to a level of 15,000 to 25,000 volts by the flyback transformer secondary winding. These pulses are rectified to produce a dc voltage for accelerating the electrons emitted by the cathode of the CRT to the high speeds necessary for visible light to be produced upon their striking the fluorescent screen. This dc voltage is the second major source of electric field from the VDT. The pulsatile high voltage associated with the flyback transformer secondary winding and the current through the magnetic deflection coils give rise to the third source of electric and magnetic fields with strengths that decay very rapidly (approximately inverse cube) with distance. Due to the pulsatile nature of the fields their peak values are high compared to their average values. They are characterized by a fundamental frequency of 15 - 30 kHz with significant harmonics up to approximately 200 kHz. The energy above 200 kHz becomes negligibly small with increasing frequency so that most of the emitted energy of the VDT can be considered to fall in the 15 - 200 kHz range.

The major source of H field originating from the VDT is the magnetic deflection coil while the major source of the E field is the high voltage winding and high voltage output lead of the flyback transformer which has a potential of 15 - 25 kV with respect to ground. The E field pattern of the VDT is shown in Figure 1 and the H field pattern is shown in Figure 2. The figures show the field configuration at a particular instant in time. The fields denated by lines with density proportional to strength and arrows indicating direction, change back and forth at a rate corresponding to the fundamental frequency of the emitted energy. The strength of the electric fields outside of the body of the VDT will depend on the position of the flyback transformer and on the amount of metal or conductive shielding between it and the cover of the VDT. The strength of the magnetic field is dependent on distance from the deflection magnetic coils. The electric fields from VDTs with metal or conductive cases will be considerably lower than those with

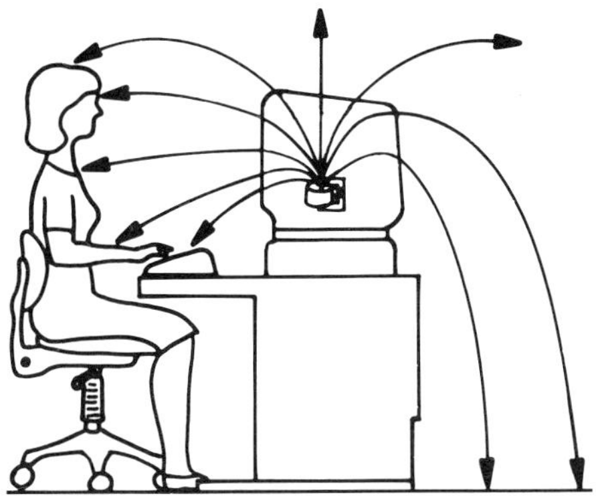

FIGURE 1
Emitted E field from VDT

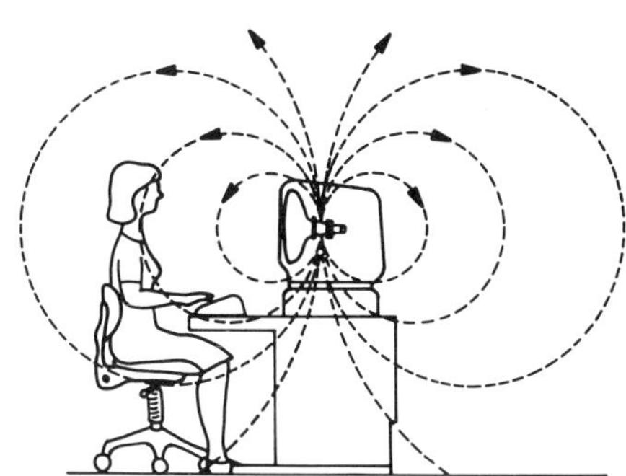

FIGURE 2
Emitted H field from VDT

plastic covers. The waveshapes of the electric and magnetic fields recorded at the surface of the screen of a typical VDT (AT&T-45) are shown in Figure 3. The magnetic field has a sawtooth waveshape with a relatively long (38 microseconds) linear increase in amplitude followed by a rapid change (8

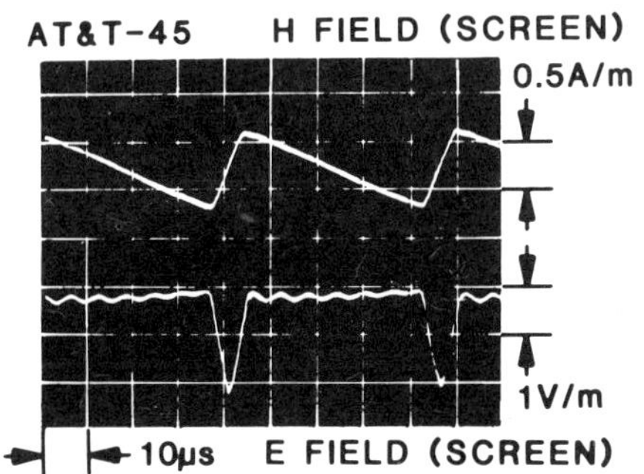

FIGURE 3
Recorded E and H fields at screen of AT&T model 45 VDT.

microseconds) in the opposite polarity. The pattern is in synchronism with the flyback transformer primary and the CRT coil current. The coil current produces the magnetic field necessary to cause the CRT electron beam to sweep to the right followed by rapid return to the left. The slow rise corresponds to the linear sweep and the fast decay corresponds to the return or "flyback" of the beam. The rapid 8 microsecond change in magnetic field generates a strong voltage pulse giving rise to the electric field shown in Figure 3.

The pattern of the electric field in the presence of a user shown in Figure 1 will be highly dependent on the position, posture, size and possibly the type of footwear of the user as well as the conductivity of the furniture and floor. The electric field vectors originating from the high voltage side of the flyback transformer winding and associated wiring will tend to terminate perpendicular to the surface of any conducting object. The fields will be strongest at the surface of an exposed user when the person is grounded. The fields will capacitively couple to the body and terminate perpendicularly at its surface, inducing internal currents, fields and energy absorption with magnitudes dependent on the exposed surface area and the impedance of the body to ground. The latter is dependent on many factors.

Figure 2 illustrates the configuration of magnetic field outside of the VDT which is independent of the location of the user. These fields will remain essentially the same with or without the presence of the VDT user. Since the human body does not contain any magnetic material and the induced currents in the tissues are relatively weak it is virtually transparent to the magnetic field. Thus, these fields can be accurately measured even with individuals in the vicinity of the device, since their bodies will not disturb the pattern or strength of the fields.

3. METHODS FOR MEASURING NEMF EMISSIONS FROM VDTs

Based on the pictoral sketch in Figure 1, it is clear that the most important electric field component in terms of the magnitude of induced currents will be that which is perpendicular to the surface of the exposed body. In fact, this field can increase substantially with decreasing distance between the user and the VDT. The magnetic field shown in Figure 2, on the other hand, will not be significantly perturbed by the body. Most field survey instruments fail in one way or another in quantifying the fields that exist under actual exposure conditions. Since the human body is highly conductive at the frequencies where the major emitted energy lies, the significant fields will be perpendicular to the body surface and have magnitudes that vary according to the shape and position of the body with respect to the source. The exposed body which has approximately 100 pf of capacitance to space (floor and walls of the room) can be considered part of an electric circuit which is capacitively coupled to the flyback transformer's high potential wiring. The displacement current flows to the surface of the body in the pattern corresponding to the fields perpendicular to its surface. This is balanced by an equal flow to displacement current out of the body through its capacitance to space. In addition, these currents can also return to ground through the capacitance and conductivity of the shoes or through parts of the body in contact with conducting surfaces of office furniture and equipment. Thus, the closer the measuring instrument comes to quantifying these perpendicular fields under actual exposure conditions the more accurately one can quantitate the internal fields and current flow within the body. An ideal instrument would be a sensor that could be put on the surface of the body to sense the perpendicular fields at various locations on its surface. Such a technique was developed by Kaune and Phillips [1], for measuring the induced current experimentally in phantom models of rats and pigs exposed to 60 Hz high voltage power lines. The author has previously developed a sensor for measuring VLF-LF electric fields normal to a large flat surface. The sensor was developed for measuring fields perpendicular to the ground for assessing hazards of VLF-LF frequencies [2]. The device is relatively simple and takes advantage of the versatility and portability of a Fluke 8060A multimeter. The microprocessor controlled meter covers the entire frequency range of the significant emission frequencies of the VDT and has a built-in digital counter that will read the fundamental frequency of the flyback transformer fields. The meter will also measure true root mean squared (rms) voltages and currents required to quantify the unique pulsatile VDT emissions for comparison with safe exposure standards.

Figure 4 illustrates the use of the sensor in measuring VDT electric fields.

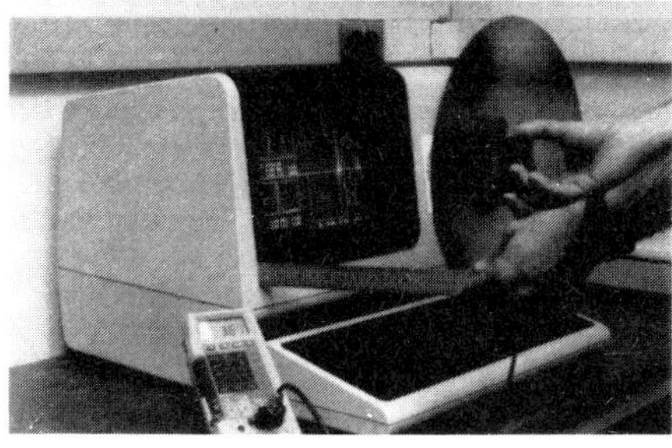

FIGURE 4
Measurement of electric field 30 cm from front of VDT

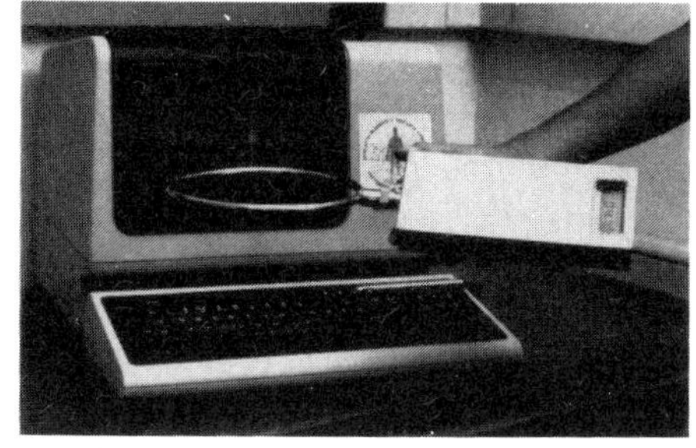

FIGURE 5
Measurement of magnetic field near screen of VDT

The operation of the electric field sensor is based on the amount of displacement current intercepted by a known area. The sensor consists of a double-back circuit board with an annular ring cut to isolate a 4 inch diameter disk from the rest of the conducting top surface. The relationship between the charging current, I, grounded through the input of the operational amplifier and the electric field, E, is given by equation

$$I = 2\pi\varepsilon_0 fES \tag{1}$$

where S is the area of the 4 inch diameter disk, ε_0 is the permittivity of free space, f is the frequency and E is the electric field strength. Through the use of a capacitive feed back loop on the amplifier, the output voltage will be given by

$$V_0 = I/2\pi fC = \varepsilon_0 ES/C. \tag{2}$$

The capacitor C is adjusted so that the operational amplifier output is 1 V when a current is applied to the disk that corresponds to the displacement current produced by 1 kV/m electric field strength. The output of the device is coupled by an RG 58 coaxial cable to the Fluke 8060A multimeter capable of providing accurate true rms voltage readings up to 200 kHz. The microprocessor controlled meter is also able to operate in a frequency counter mode so that the fundamental frequency of the applied signal can be easily determined. The operational amplifier and two 9 volt power supply batteries are shielded by means of a metal case with a removable bottom cover.

Guy and Chou [3] developed a broadband loop sensor capable of measuring the true rms value of a complex magnetic field waveshape. Figure 5 illustrates its use in measuring VDT magnetic field emissions.

Figure 6 illustrates the electric field as a function of distance from the front of the typical VDT as measured by the electric field sensor. Table 1 is a summary of the data on field emissions measured from a total of 24 video display terminals located in a typical office. For multiple terminals of the same type both the means and standard deviation are shown. The table illustrates the fields measured by the electric field sensor at the location of maximum intensity usually nearest the flyback transformer, at the face of the VDT screen and at a distance of 30 cm from the front of the VDT screen. Figure 7 illustrates the magnetic field as measured as a function of distance from the front of a typical VDT using the magnetic loop sensor shown in Figure 5. Table 2 illustrates the measured magnetic field strengths of various

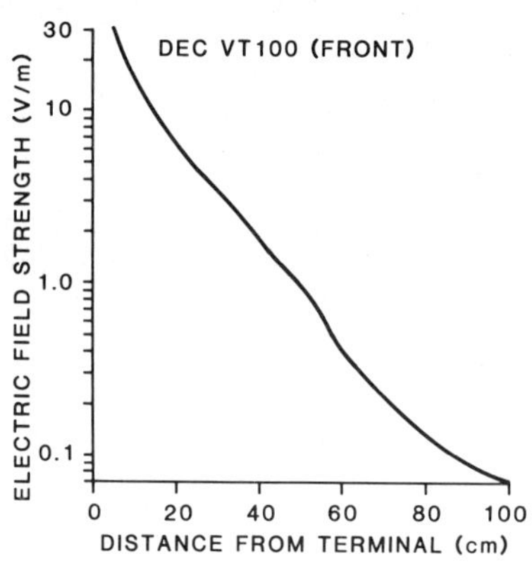

FIGURE 6
Electric field as function of distance from front of DEC VT100

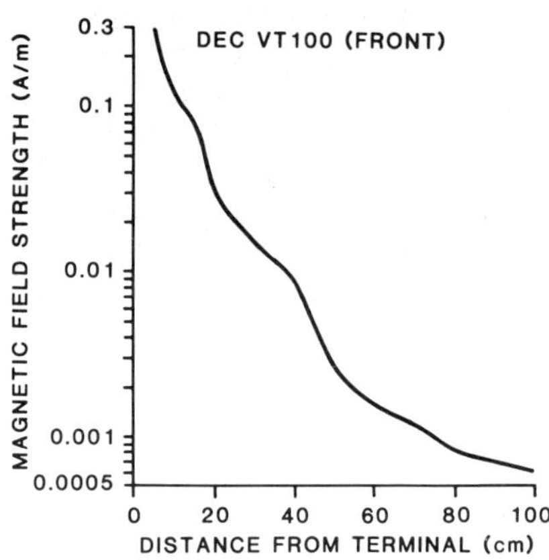

FIGURE 7
Magnetic field as function of distance from front of DEC VT100

locations near 24 different VDT terminals used in a typical office. Note that the strongest magnetic fields are at the top of the terminal varying from 2 to 10 times more than the levels measured from the front of the terminal.

TABLE 1. MEASURED VDT E FIELDS

VDT TYPE	FLYBACK FREQ (kHz)	E FIELD (V/m) MAX	SCREEN	30 cm
AT&T 45	21.78	1887* ±400	569 ±132	6.86 ±2.09
AT&T PC	25.87	52	1098	7.7
Tab 132/15	23.52	1775 ±318	80.6 ±13.4	6.86 ±2.09

*45.7 ±43.4 for 3 shielded units

TABLE 2. MEASURED VDT H FIELDS

VDT TYPE	FLYBACK FREQ (kHz)	H FIELD (A/m) MAX	SCREEN	30 cm
AT&T 45	21.78	2.50 ±0.232	0.506 ±0.0594	0.0493 ±0.0045
AT&T PC	25.87	1.67	0.17	0.003
Tab 132/15	23.52	1.49 ±0.0424	0.719 ±0.0163	0.0495 ±0.0332

However, because of the finite diameter of the loop, the plane of the loop may be placed much closer to the magnetic deflection coils at the top of the terminal. In general, the fields measured by the electric field disc sensor will change depending on grounding conditions of the equipment and of the person holding the sensor, as well as the total outside diameter of the sensor unit. Most accurate measurement of fields would require that the outside conducting surface have the same shape or size as the human body exposed to the VDT. Harvey [4] used a measuring system similar to the above with the same size 100 cm^2 sensor area, but represented the VDT user by a 30 x 120 cm flat copper foil surface. In using the apparatus, Harvey [4] measured VLF field strengths and obtained levels consistent with those obtained by the author.

4. DOSIMETRY AND QUANTITATIVE METHODS OF EVALUATING ABSORPTION OF VDT EMISSIONS IN EXPOSED SUBJECTS

It is now widely recognized by researchers that knowledge of the amount of energy absorbed by the tissues of subjects exposed to electromagnetic fields is essential for analyzing the biological effect on the organism. However, safe exposure standards are developed and enforced based on the rms magnitude of the exposure fields. Establishment of the relationship between the exposure fields and the fields or absorbed energy in the body is a fundamental requirement for the setting of exposure standards. Though it has been customary to quantify or express the internal absorbed energy in terms of specific absorption rate with units of watts per kilogram, other quantities may become more important in the VLF-LF bands. There are weak currents induced in the tissues of subjects exposed to VDTs, so in addition to SAR, the electric current density, J, and the total current, I, in the body resulting from exposure while in contact with objects or in free space are of interest. Exposures of the human body to even the highest fields in the environment of the VDT at frequencies of 50 Hz through 200 kHz, the significant range of VDT emissions, result in relatively low amounts of absorbed energy. Fortunately, since most exposed objects or subjects are small compared to a wavelength of VLF-MF frequencies, the analysis of energy coupling to the body and the internal current distribution is considerabley simplified since they are amenable to quasi-static analysis. Also, the analysis of field to subject interaction in this frequency range is easy, since work done at one frequency within the range is directly applicable to all frequencies within the range. Thus, one can fall back on the considerable amount of theoretical and experimental work done for the 50 - 60 Hz frequency range which is directly applicable to dosimetry problems in the VLF-MF range.

Well-quantified measurements by Deno [5] of currents induced in human bodies by high voltage transmission line electric fields form the most complete and accurate basis for analyzing field interactions with the human body. Deno measured body currents in hollow metal mannequins exposed to 60 Hz high electric fields and developed empirical equations for predicting total body current in various parts of the body, such as the neck, torso, waist, crotch, knees, and feet. He also did measurements for various positions in relation to transmission towers, for various distances from the ground, and with hands by the side, outstretched, or overhead. He also measured the unperturbed field enhancement at various locations in the body of the mannequin.

The results of Deno [5] are applicable only to whole body environmental exposures to relatively uniform electric fields so they don't apply to the highly localized exposures to divergent electric fields from the video display terminal. The electric field vectors terminating perpendicular to the surface of the exposed subject will induce weak current in the tissues. Since this current will be maximum when the exposed subject is in contact with a grounded object, such as a metal desk or other conducting furniture, a measurement of the short circuit body to ground current, I_{sc} will provide a worst case body current level that is easy to relate to safety standards. This current can be directly measured with a broadband rms microammeter connected between the subject and ground as shown in Figure 8. The wave shape of the current observed on an oscilloscope is directly related to the time derivative dE/dt or the rate of change of the exposure field with time $\Delta E/\Delta t$, hence there is a difference in waveshapes of the exposure field and the induced current as shown in Figure 9. The induced current varies considerably with the position of the subject with respect to the VDT reaching maximum levels when the hand is placed on the screen or on the surface of the terminal nearest the high voltage flyback transformer. The maximum measured induced currents for the exposure conditions given in Tables 1 and 2 are shown in Table 3. Maximum current for normal operating conditions is obtained when the finger is placed on the screen, typical of a user pointing at a line of text. However, this value can increase substantially if the hand is placed flat against the screen resulting in approximately 163 microamps rms average current for one class of terminals as shown in Table 3.

FIGURE 8
Measurement of body-to-ground current due to exposure to VDT electric field

TABLE 3. INDUCED CURRENTS FROM E FIELD

VDT TYPE	FLYBACK FREQ (kHz)	INDUCED CURRENT (uA) MAX	SCREEN	30 cm
AT&T 45	21.78	61.7 ±8.5	21.33* ±5.67	2.94 ±1.49
AT&T PC	25.87	5.0	8.9	0.9
Tab 132/15	23.52	36.3 ±5.3	----	3.40 ±2.26

*VALUE FOR FINGER POINTING AT VDT SCREEN INCREASES TO 163.3 ±34.8 FOR HAND ON SCREEN

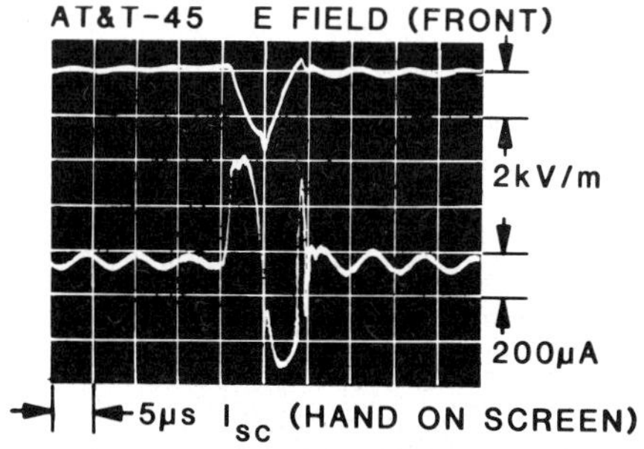

FIGURE 9
Comparison of measured E field and body-to ground current waveshape

The induced currents from the magnetic fields are impossible to measure in an exposed human subject, so one must resort to mathematical calculations. The magnetic exposure field may be expressed in terms of magnetic field strength H with the units for A/m as given in Figure 3 or Table 2 or it may be expressed in terms of magnetic flux density $B = \mu H$ with units of tesla (T) where μ is a constant equal to $4\pi \times 10^{-7}$. The circulating eddy currents induced in the body due to the magnetic field exposure are difficult to measure, but they can be approximated theoretically by modeling the exposed body as an equivalent spheroidal or ellipsoidal tissue geometry. The latter has been used extensively for determining induced currents or absorbed energy due to uniform magnetic field exposure. However, the magnetic fields from a video display terminal, are highly divergent so the classical theoretical models are not suitable. Hence, it is necessary to use a numerical approach by modeling the body as an equivalent electrical impedance or admittance network and solving for the internal currents numerically by a computer. These methodologies have been discussed by Armitage et al. [6],and Gandhi et al. [7]. Based on the magnetic field configuration shown in Figure 2, it appears that the maximum induced current due to the VDT magnetic fields would be in the torso of the exposed subject. The maximum current induced in the torso can be determined from a simple two-dimensional model as shown in Figure 10. In this model a section of the torso is shown along with the diverging magnetic fields from

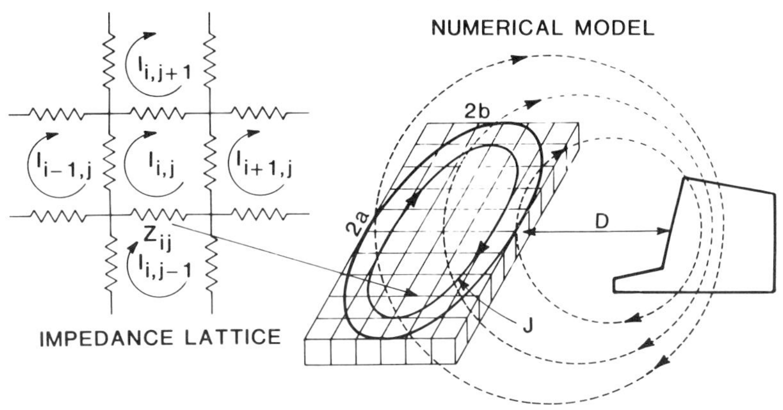

FIGURE 10
Determination of maximum induced current in human torso by numerical method using a two-dimensional impedance model

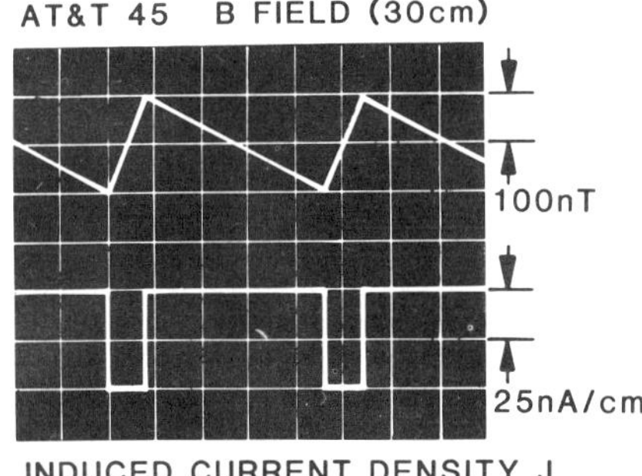

FIGURE 11
Estimated induced maximum current densities in human torso due to VDT field exposure

TABLE 4. MAXIMUM B FIELD AND INDUCED CURRENT DENSITY IN TORSO AT 30 cm FROM FRONT OF VDT

VDT TYPE	B rms (nT)	B p-p (nT)	dB/dt (mT/s)	J (nA/cm2) (p-p)	rms
AT&T 45	62.0 ±5.66	206. ±18.8	25.8 ±2.35	53.4 ±4.86	15.4 ±1.40
AT&T PC	3.77	13.5	2.25	4.65	1.16
Tab 132/15	62.2 ±41.7	202. ±136.	40.4 ±27.2	83.3 ±56.2	16.3 ±11.0

the VDT assuming the torso boundary is an ellipse with semi-axes a and b. The model is assumed to have the dielectric properties of a high water content tissue. Based on the dielectric properties of the tissue the impedance elements within the elliptical boundary may be determined and the impedance of air is assumed in defining the elements outside the elliptical boundary. The distribution of the current density J, may then be calculated where maximum current density is found at the periphery of the elliptical boundry and the ends of the minor axis. As for the case of the E field exposures the currents are proportional to the time derivative dB/dt or rate of change of magnetic exposure field with time $\Delta B/\Delta t$. The typical exposure fields and estimated current densities expressed in the time domain are shown in Figure 11. In this figure the magnetic field is expressed in units of nanotesla (nT) and the induced current density is expressed in units of nanoamperes per square centimeter (nA/cm^2). Table 4 illustrates the measured amplitudes and time derivatives of the magnetic exposure fields for the VDTs discussed above and the maximum calculated current densities in the torso of an exposed female at a distance of 30 cm from the front of the terminal. The table gives both the means and the standard deviations of the measured fields and calculated current densities. The maximum mean current density is found to be approximately 83 nA/cm^2.

5. EQUIVALENT ENVIRONMENTAL FIELD EXPOSURES

Since VDT emissions decrease very rapidly with distance from the unit only a portion of the user's body closest to the unit is exposed to the fields described above. Therefore, the induced current and current density in the body will be considerably less than encountered for whole body exposures on which exposure standards are based. Figure 12 illustrates how the total current induced in the body by a uniform electric field is proportional to the time rate of change of field strength multiplied by the permittivity of free space $\varepsilon_0 = 8.854 \times 10^{-9}$ and an equivalent exposed surface area of the body.

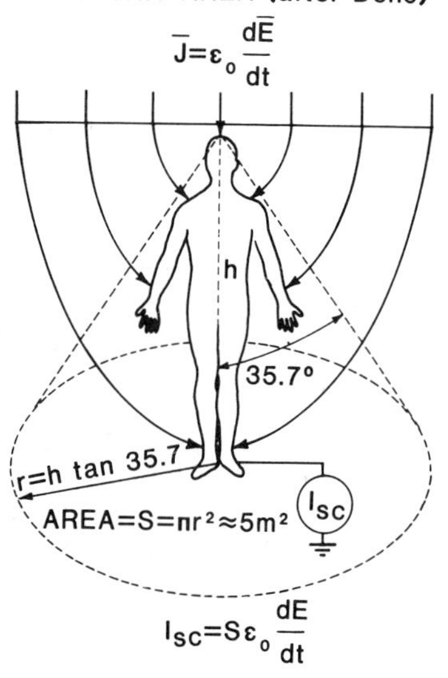

FIGURE 12
Equvalent surface area and induced human exposure to current for uniform VLF eletric field

TABLE 5. EQUIVALENT ENVIRONMENTAL WHOLE BODY E AND H FIELD EXPOSURE

VDT TYPE	FLYBACK FREQ (kHz)	EQUIVALENT MAX	EQUIVALENT SCREEN	E (V/m) 30 cm	H (A/m) 30 cm
AT&T 45	21.78	3.63 ±0.5	1.25* ±0.333	0.173 ±0.088	9.16 ±0.836
AT&T PC	25.87	0.294	0.523	0.0529	0.556
Tab 132/15	23.52	2.13 ±0.312	-----	0.199 ±0.133	9.16 6.15

*Value is 9.60 ±2.03 with hand on screen

The equivalent surface area of the body was found by Deno to be the same as that for the base of the cone shown in Figure 12. The equivalent area is 5 m^2 for a 1.75 m tall subject. Based on the measured currents due to VDT E field exposure given in Table 2, we can calculate the equivalent environmental whole body exposure E field strength that would induce the same current. This equivalent field will allow the partial-body exposure to be realistically compared to safety standards. The equivalent environmental H field exposures in terms of induced current density may be calculated from the impedance model shown in Figure 10 or from classical equations. For the maximum induced current due to environmental exposures where the entire body may be exposed, we assume an elliptical section corresponding to the area of the frontal plane of the body exposed to a uniform B field of magnitude sufficient to produce the same maximum current density as calculated for the VDT exposures. The frontal plane is used for this case, since this would be the maximum exposed cross section of the body that would result in the maximum induced current. The value of maximum induced current can be derived directly for an elliptical geometry exposed to a uniform B field from the equation

$$J = \sigma[a^2b/(a^2+b^2)]dB/dt \qquad (3)$$

where J is the current density, σ is the electrical conductivity of the tissue, a and b are the major and minor semi-axes of the equivalent ellipse and dB/dt is the time derivative of the environmental field. Table 5 illustrates the calculated equivalent whole body environmental E and H fields under the exposure conditions characterized in the previous tables and figures of this paper. Thus, under the worst case conditions the E field exposures correspond to a maximum environmental electric field exposure of .199 V/m, whereas the magnetic field exposures are equivalent to a maximum environmental magnetic field exposure of .009 A/m.

6. CONCLUSIONS

Table 6 summarizes typical exposure standards used in the United States and other countries. It is clear from the above analysis that the equivalent environmental field exposure levels, due to VDT emissions are less than the world's maximum safety exposure guidelines listed in Table 6. These guidelines result from scientific consensus on exposure levels for deleterious health effects and have incorporated safety factors of 10 or more.

TABLE 6. ELECTRIC AND MAGNETIC FIELD EXPOSURE STANDARDS (0.01-1.0 MHz)

	NATO	ANSI	ACGIH	USAF
FREQ (MHz)	0.01 - 1.0	0.3 - 3.0	0.01 - 3.0	0.01 -3.0
E (V/m)	1000	632	632	434
H (mA/m)	2600	1580	1580	1150
	IRPA	**MASS.**	**USSR(OCC)**	**USSR(GP)**
FREQ (MHz)	0.3 - 3.0	0.3 - 3.0	0.06 - 1.5	0.03 - 0.3
E (V/m)	307 - 205	275	50	20
H (mA/m)	814 - 295	729	5000	

ACKNOWLEDGEMENTS

This work was supported in part by IBM Corporation and in part by the National Institute of Occupational Safety and Health.

REFERENCES

[1] Kaune, W.T., and Phillips, R.D., "Comparison of The coupling of Grounded Humans, swine and Rats to Vertical, 60 Hz Electric Fields", Bioelectromagnetics, 1:117-129, 1980

[2] Guy, A.W., and Chou, C.K., "Hazard Analysis: Very Low Frequency Through Medium Frequency Range", Final Report Contract F33615-78-D-0617, Task 0065 South Eastern Center for Electrical Engineering Education Prepared for USAF School of Aerospace Medicine, Aerospace Medical Division (AFSC), Brooks Air Force Base, Texas 78235, 1982

[3] Guy, A.W., and Chou, C.K., "Very Low Frequency Hazard Study", Final Report Part 1 May 1985, Contract No F33615-83-C-0625 Prepared for USAF School of Aerospace Medicine, Brooks Air Force Base, Texas 78235, 1985

[4] Harvey, S.M., "Electric Field Exposure of Persons Using Video Display Units", Bioelectromagnetics, 5:1-12,1984

[5] Deno, D.W., "Currents Induced In The Human Body By High-Voltage Transmission Line Electric Field-Measurement and Calculation of Distribution and Dose", IEEE Trans. Power Apparatus and Systems, PAS #5 Sep./Oct., 96:1517-1527, 1977

[6] Armitage, D.W., Leveen, H.H. and R.Pethig, "Radio-Frequency-Induced Hyperthermia; Computer Simulation of Specific Absorption Rate Distributions Using Realistic Anatomic Models", Phy. Med. Biol., 28:1:31-42, 1983

[7] Gandhi, O.P., Deford, J.F. and Kanai, H. "Impedance Method for Calculation of Power Deposition Patterns In Magnetically Induced Hyperthermia", IEEE Tran. BME, 31:10:644-651, 1984

WORK WITH DISPLAY UNITS 86
B. Knave and P.-G. Wideback (eds.)

VIDEO DISPLAY TERMINALS
ELECTROMAGNETIC RADIATION AND HEALTH

Bernhard Frankenhaeuser

The Nobel Institute for Neurophysiology. Karolinska Institutet.
S-104 01 Stockholm Sweden

Video display terminals (VDT) have been blamed to cause a number of ill effects on health. The claimed effects on health cover a large variety of symptoms such as eye strain, headache, stress, epilepsy, skin rashes, spontaneous abortions, birth defects etc.

These health effects have been claimed to be caused by the VDT through the emission of: (1) an electrostatic field, alternatively (2) a magnetic field, or (3) ultra violet radiation from the screen, or (4) gamma radiation, or (5) through an electrostatic accummulation of radon daughters or charged particles on the skin, etc.

The electrostatic fields in the vicinity of the VDT:s have been measured [3, 8]. The magnetic fields have similarly been measured [8]. Measurements have also been made of the ultraviolet (UV) radiation [7, 8] and the gamma ray radiations [8] from the VDT:s.

The electrostatic fields in the vicinity of VDT-operators have further been measured [3]. The precipitation of small (i.e. 0.1 to 1 µm) particles on charged surfaces has been observed [3] and the mobility of these particles in an electric field [3] has been measured.

Reference is here given, for complementary information, to a comprehensive review by Bergqvist [1] of the technical measurements of the missions from the video display terminals and the possible effects of these emissions on the human body.

ELECTROSTATIC FIELDS

The elelectrostatic fields in the surrounding air in the vicinity of VDT:s have been measured with so called "field mills" [3, 8]. These are high impedance instruments for measurements of relatively homogeneous fields and charges within air or other very high impedance gases. These measurements require information about the resistivity of air for estimates of the currents flowing between a VDT-screen and a human body. Further, it is clear that information is required about how the human body is connected electrically to the surrounding. Note that the resistance, between the body and the surrounding may be much lower than the resistance between the video screen and the body. In situations of this kind it is commonly hopeless to make reasonable estimates of the current density in the body caused by the screen.

The ordinary VDT:s, of the cathode ray tube type, have an accelerator anode at the back surface of the front glass. This accelerator is charged to some 20 to 30 kV DC. The resistivity of air is about 5 GΩm or 500 GΩcm, which is high compared to the resistivity of the front glass. The latter can therefore be neglected, as being low impedance compared to the air, in a calculation of the current flowing between the screen and a grounded human body in front of the screen. Such approximative calculations indicate that the order of size of this current is about 1 μA. If we assume that this current of 1 μA enters the head and flows through the neck, the neck is chosen as a narrow part in the current flow path, in order to select conditions throughout giving too high calculated current densities and too high potential gradients. Then we find that the current density is <50 $\mu A/m^2$or <5 nA/cm^2. This gives a potential gradient of <200 μV/m or <2 μV/cm.

Below it will be considered whether or not potential gradients or current densities of this order of size, applied to the human body can have any ill effects on the human.

Measurements of the electric fields in the vicinity of the operators indicate that about 50% of these fields are negative [3]. This finding is strong support for the view that the charge of the operators has nothing whatsoever to do with the VDT:s, but are the result of friction electricity. Positive net charges, not negative, can be caused by the positive accelerator anode of the VDT.

MAGNETIC FIELDS

The body tissues are highly transparent to magnetic fields, and consequently very insensitive to them. Changes in the magnetic fields induce, however, currents in conductors within the fields. The effects can consequently be treated as the effects of these electric currents. Strong high frequency fields induce heat in the tissues [9].

Magnetic fields and changes of magnetic fields in the vicinity of VDT:s have been measured [8]. The estimates have as a rule been made through observations of the electric potential changes developed across coils of known dimensions placed at various known sites relative to the video display terminal. The technique is well known and reliable, it needs no further comments here.

Various body tissues are sensitive to electric currents. Calculations or measurements are consequently required of the currents caused within the body by the changes in the magnetic field in the surrounding. The human body is quite complex for such calculations. A number of approximations are clearly required for the calculations. One of the common approximations has been to do the calculations for one sphere [8] (=the whole body) or two spheres [2] (=one for the head and one for the main body). The equation used for such calculations [8] is the equation for an isolated conducting loop in a changing magnetic field. However, the short circuit of the bulk conductor has then entirely been neglected. The calculated current densities are thus clearly larger than the real densities.

The current densities, calculated as described above on the basis of measured rates of changes in the magnetic fields, are then at the periphery of the body a few mA/m^2 (or a few hundred nA/cm^2. As pointed out above this value is, due to the neglected short circuit higher than the real value, and it applies to the periphery only. In the center of the body the current density equals zero, according to the equation.

SENSITIVITY OF BIOLOGICAL TISSUES TO ELECTRIC CURRENTS

The tissues in the body are sensitive to the currents through them and to the potential gradients across the tissues, and especially to the potential across the cell membranes. They are very insensitive to the potential of the whole body, relative to the surrounding air, a collection of charged dust on the skin from the surrounding air may be an exception, provided that this dust causes skin irritation.

How do these potential gradients in the body, caused by the electrostatic fields of <200 μV/m (or <2 μV/cm), and the current densities of <50 $\mu A/m^2$ (or <5 nA/cm^2), and those correspondingly caused by the magnetic fields of <<40 mV/m (or <<about 400 μV/cm) respectively <<2 $mA7m^2$ (or <<200 na/cm^2, compare with the normal biological potential gradients and current densities within the body.

Cells in the body are as a rule polarized so that the inside of the cell is some 50 to 100 mV negative relative to the outside. Electrically excitable cells, like nerve fibres and muscle fibres discharge an impulse when the membrane is polarized some 20 mV from its resting value. The membrane potential changes then about 100 mV during the impulse, and the peak membrane current density during the impulse is about -60 A/m^2 (or -6 mA/cm^2). Compare this value with the current densities caused by VDT:s of << few mA/m^2.

The lowest suprathreshold field in the medium outside a thick myelinated nerve fibre is some 100 mV/cm when the nerve fibre is placed optimally as sharply bent (180 degrees) in the field [4, 5] i.e. the potential gradients in the body caused by VDT:s are less than two orders of size smaller than those required to excite a nerve fibre with low threshold and the longest known characteristic lenght in the mammalian body. Here it should be noted, that the currents calculated, not measured, to be elicited in the body are calculated as based on assumptions giving too high calculated values. The major currents caused by the changes in the magnetic fields are in a high frequency region where the biological tissues are extremely insensitive to the currents.

The characteristic length at these frequensies is shorter than at lower frequensies and the biological responses are slow. Changes in magnetic fields of several kT/s are required for local threshold stimulation of the human brain [6].

The heart, the muscles and the brain tissues produce during their normal activity local current densities and local electric potential gradients on neighbouring inactive cells which are orders of size larger than the current densities and potential gradients causec by the VDT:s.

Consequently I must conclude that I am convinced that the currents normally transmitted from a video display terminal to a human body can have no ill effects on the human body. The electric fields from the normal biological activity dominate heavily in the brain, in the thorax and in the abdomen over the fields caused by emissions from the VDT:s.

REFERENCES

1 Bergqvist, U.O.V, Video display terminals and helath, Scandinavian Journal of Work, Environment & Health 1984; 10; Suppl 2; 1-87.

2 Bernhardt, J., The direct influence of electromagnetic fields on nerve- and muscle cells of man within the frequency range of 1 Hz to 30 MHz Radiation and Environmental Biophysics 1979; 16; 309-323.

3 Cato Olsen, W., Electric field enhanced aerosol exposure in visual display unit environments. The Chr Michelsen Institute. Bergen, Norway. 1981; p 1-40.
4 Frankenhaeuser, B., Computed action potential in nerve from Zenopus laevis. Journal of Physiology 1965; 180; 780-787.
5 Frankenhaeuser, B., and Huxley, A.F., The action potential in the myelinated nerve fibre of Xenopus laevis as computed on the basis of voltage clamp data. Journal of Physiology 1964; 171; 302-315.
6 Hess, C.W., Mills, K.R. and Murray, N.M.F., Magnetic stimulation of the human brain: the effects of voluntary muscle activity. Journal of Physiology. In the press 1986.
7 Knave, B.g., Wibom, R., Bergqvist, U.O.V., Carlsson, L.L.W, Levin, M.I.B. and Nylén, P.R., Work with video display terminals among office employies: II physical exposure factors. Scandinavian Journal of Work, Environment & Health 1985; 11; 467-474.
8 Paulsson, L-E., Kristiansson, I. and Malmström, I., Strålning från dataskärmar. Report a84-08 from National Institute of Radiation Protection, Stockholm 1984 (Swedish).
9 Saunders, R.P. and Smith, H., Safety aspects of NMR clinical imaging. British Medical Bulletin 1984; 40; 148-154.

3. PREGNANCY OUTCOME

EPIDEMIOLOGICAL AND EXPERIMENTAL STUDIES

WORK WITH DISPLAY UNITS 86
B. Knave and P.-G. Wideбäck (eds.)

PREGNANCY AND VDT WORK - AN EVALUATION OF THE STATE OF THE ART

Ulf Bergqvist

Occupational Neuromedicine
National Board of Occupational Safety and Health
S-171 52 Solna, Sweden

The question of an effect of VDT work on pregnancy is reviewed. The reported clusters, while by itself unusual events, are not less common than expected, considering the large number of VDT workers. Hitherto, no VDT-specific factor has been shown to have an effect on foetal developments. Epidemiological studies have not shown any significant increase in adverse pregnancy outcomes due to VDT work. Thus, there is no evidence for a risk for adverse pregnancy outcome in VDT operators.

1. INTRODUCTION

The suggestion that VDT work may affect the outcome of pregnancies originated with observations during 1979-1980 of groups (*clusters*) of pregnant VDT workers with unusual frequencies of adverse pregnancy outcomes. Since then, a considerable volume of research has been performed to investigate this possibility.

This review will cover available results up to August 1986, and is performed in three steps; First, the cluster phenomenon is investigated, discussing what conclusion can be made from their existence. Secondly, possible VDT work related factors for adverse pregnancy outcome are discussed, predominantly but not exclusively centered on electromagnetic emissions from the VDTs. Thirdly, results of performed epidemiological studies are described. Finally, an evaluation of these data is presented.

Outcomes under discussion are by and large limited to spontaneous abortion in recognized pregnancies and to serious congenital defects, and the possible relationships between these and the mothers´ work at VDTs. In a few epidemiological studies, other outcomes such as perinatal death and low birth weights have also been recorded. Some limited data exist on pregnancy outcomes of wives of male VDT operators.

2. THE CLUSTER PHENOMENON

A number of clusters, i. e. groups of pregnant VDT workers with unusually high occurrences of spontaneous abortions and/or congenital defects, have been reported. From available reports, it appears that the highest frequency of these clusters occurred during 1979-1980, with 7 groups in USA and Canada (6 included unusual spontaneous abortion frequencies and 3 were also concerned with congenital defects). The average miscarriage rate of these clusters was 52% among (average) 12 pregnancies, compared to a "normal" rate of some 10-20%. Malformations occurred in 35% of (average) 10 pregnancies. (There may be some discrepancies in comparing these 35% to "normal" 1-4% of serious malformations, since diagnosis may differ.) It is nevertheless clear that these clusters represent unusual events. Additional clusters have since been recorded, both in North America and elsewhere.

A number of these occurring clusters have been investigated, without the identification of any suggestive causative factor. In some investigations (e. g. of the Runcorn cluster (1) and the Sears-Roebuck cluster (2)), the population under study was expanded beyond the cluster.

Some reviewers have computed the probability of these clusters appearing by chance alone (2, 3, 4). They all concluded that there was a very high probability of these clusters occurring under the assumption that adverse pregnancy outcome among VDT operators in general was the same as in the general population.

The author used the following data: 1/ assuming some 350 000 pregnant women working with VDTs in the year 1979/1980, 2/ dividing these into groups of 12 and 3/ assuming "normal" rates of occurrence among these 350 000 women (12.6%). The outcome was that 55 groups would be expected to have a spontaneous abortion rate in excess of 52%. Similar calculations were performed for congenital defects. Variations in all numerical assumptions stated above were then made, in order to find the "worst possible combination" (3).

Thus, the existence of these clusters is by itself no evidence of an adverse effect of VDT work on pregnancy outcomes. They do represent unusual events, but in a very large number of groups, also unusual events are due to occur. (An analogy: when rolling dice, 4 sixes in row would be highly unusual (probability 0.0008), but if tried 10 000 times, it would be expected to occur in some 7-8 attempts.)

3. THE POSSIBILITY OF CAUSATIVE FACTORS DUE TO VDT WORK

A number of factors related to the VDT itself or to VDT work has in the debate been suggested as possible causative factors for increased spontaneous abortion or congenital defects. Among these factors are PCB emission, ultraviolet radiation in combination with vitamin A, changes in light air ion concentrations, ultrasound, and X-ray or microwave radiation. None of these suggestions are viable, since the factors involved do not occur due to VDT or VDT work, or occur only at insignificant levels or changes. However, some other suggested factors merits a further discussion; viz. pulsed magnetic fields and stress reactions.

3.1 Pulsed magnetic fields

Since the publication of the work by Delgado and coworkers (5, 6), considerable attention has been given the possible effects of pulsed magnetic fields on embryo development. In these and subsequent experiments, square pulses of primarily 100 Hz and various field strengths have been investigated for effects, mostly on chicken embryos (5, 6, 7, 8), but also on pregnant mice (9, 10). The original studies (5, 6) have been found to be seriously flawed in terms of what exposure conditions were used, and attempts to replicate these studies have been unsuccesful. (To the authors awareness, two more unsuccesful attempts have been made to replicate the Delgado results. However, these studies have not been published.) In neither the original data by Ubeda et al (6) nor in the one study that has claimed some success in replication (8), has reported dB/dt values been found to correlate with the noted effects. This is noteworthy, since dB/dt is the factor that has been suggested as a link between these studies and VDT-type exposure situations.

The recently available preliminary data by Tribukait et al (9) on the effects of VDT-like exposure (sawtooth pulses) on pregnant mice have been given considerable attention. In the first report of January 1986, an increase in malformed foetuses from 2 (0.6%) (control) to 7 (3.0%) (group IV, higher level of VDT-like pulses) were noted. However, 5 (1.5%) dead foetuses were found among controls compared to none in the high exposure group. (All percentages are related to the total number of implants.) These data have thus been subject to a number of interpretations (11). Further data were presented at the conference (10). The added material (since January 1986) failed to show any differences regarding malformations or foetal deaths between the controls and group IV. Some questions do still remain on the occurrence of certain malformations. In the author's opinion, while these data should definitely be followed up by further studies (one such is in progress in Uppsala, Sweden), presently available data are not sufficient in themselves to suggest a risk to VDT operators due to these magnetic fields.

3.2 Stress reactions

Stress reactions as well as "excessive worry" have also been suggested as causative factors for primarily spontaneous abortion (12, 13). It appears however that the literature on this relationship is not decisive; at present the relationship can be considered suggestive but by no means established.

Regarding stress reactions in VDT work, the WHO working group on VDTs found "considerable evidence of an abundance of stress factors associated with VDT work", but "little consistent evidence of abnormal levels of stress related disorders" among VDT workers. It appears that other determinants of work (than whether work was performed with VDTs or not) were primarily associated with stress related disorders (14). (It should be noted, that the question of the debate on pregnancy outcome among VDT operators, serving as a cause of strong worry among some pregnant operators, may be regarded as a VDT-specific stress factor in these respects.) Should a relationship between stress reactions and miscarriage indeed be true, then this is obviously of concern in many other situations than only VDT work.

4. PERFORMED EPIDEMIOLOGICAL STUDIES

A number of epidemiological studies have been performed in the last few years, investigating the possibility of differences in frequencies of (primarily) spontaneous abortion and serious malformation. Those reviewed by the author are listed in table 1. (An additional study, by Bjerkedahl, was presented at the WWDU conference. Furthermore, the design of two more ongoing studies were also described.)

TABLE 1. Performed epidemiological studies (14)

Study	Pregnancies Year	Pregnancies Number	Spont abort excess? a/	Malformation excess? b/
		Cohort studies c/		
Canadian Labour Congress	<1982	108 d/	No/N	No/N
Newspaper Guild	1977-82e/	? d, f/	Not eval	Not eval
Montreal (*first previous*)g/	<1982	14700	No/C	No/C
" (*past*) g/	<1982	3863	No/C	No/C
" (*current*)g/	1981-82	3799	Not eval	No/C
Osaka	<1984	50	No/N	
Nat'l Insurance	1980-83 h/	4347	No/N	No/N
North Carolina i/	<1985	? d,i/	No/i/	
		Case-control within cohort studies		
South Australia	1960-78	90	No	
Swedish Registry	1980-81	1447	No	No
		Case-control studies		
Finnish Registry	1976-83	2950		No
		Other studies		

In addition, other studies have been performed. Some of these were cluster investigations or being extended around a cluster (e g the Runcorn study), while others were surveys, without a formal designation of a study population.

Explanations: a/, b/ For exact definition, see resp study. No = no significant difference could be shown. Not eval. = the outcome could/has not been evaluated, for various reasons.
c/ For these studies, comparison groups have been noted. /C = compared with control group, /N = compared with expected based on national average etc.
d/ Includes data from wives of VDT working men.
e/Further pregnancies from e g 1940-ies also included.
f/ Not given, guess is about 150
g/ Various reported subcohorts from the study.
h/ Miscarriages from 1980-81 only.
i/ Full report not available, e g no information on number of pregnancies. In the study, VDT workers with more than 50% VDT working time are compared with others (less than 50% or no VDT work).

All studies hitherto performed are retrospective, most being cohort studies. As such, they are beset by a number of possible bias problems. Some important factors that have been taken into considerations when evaluating these studies are: response rate and size of study, whether impact of possible confounding factors has been analyzed for, and administrative aspects of the data sources . Four of these studies stand up reasonably well to this scrutiny: the Montreal study, the Swedish and the Finnish Registry studies, and the Nat´l Insurance study.

However, regardless of whether only these four studies are used for evaluation, or all studies are included, the outcome is the same: No study has demonstrated any significant increase in spontaneous abortion or (serious) congenital defects among VDT operators compared to respective controls. Furthermore, while some studies do have nonsignificant increases in frequencies among VDT operators compared to controls (e g the Swedish Registry study), other comparisons (e g the Finnish study) show a nonsignificant decrease among VDT operators compared to controls.

Some comments are warranted on "exposure". In these comparisons, the "exposure" factor is work at VDT during pregnancy (in some studies during the first trimester of the pregnancy). A number of studies also present data on number of hours worked. Such data are however prone to bias in a retrospective study. It is noteworthy that two studies or subcohorts that depend on subjective reporting of working hours from (largely) years back (Swedish Registry and Montreal/past) do show some increase in malformations with increasing working hours, while the two other studies that either does not depend on subjective reporting (Finnish Registry) or is based on data from recent pregnancies (Montreal/current) do not show such an increase in malformation.

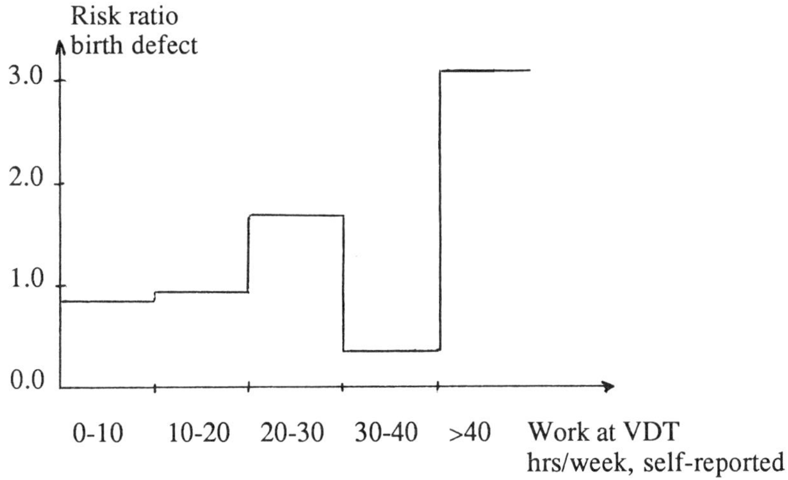

FIGURE 1
Risk ratio for birth defect (significant malformation, perinatal death ,very low birth weight) in relation to self-reported VDT working hours during pregnancy (15).

For the Swedish Registry study, more detailed data as to reported working hours are available (15), and are presented in Figure 1. (It should be noted that this analysis was not part of the study protocol, which called for examinations of wider time intervals only.) Nevertheless, the data do suggest the existence of a recall bias (as a viable explanation for the variations).

Other exposure factors have not been included in the studies. This is due to a combination of practical difficulties in obtaining such data in retrospective studies, and to the lack of known factors to test for. (In one planned study, gathering of such data - in regards to nonionizing radiation - will be attempted.)

5. AN EVALUATION AND SOME COMMENTS

Based on available data, an evaluation is possible, and demonstrates that VDT work has not been shown to constitute a risk of adverse pregnancy outcomes. Formally, this is not the same as stating that no risks occur. The statement contains two possibilities; a/ that no risks occur, or b/ that a risk may occur, but is too small to have been detected. In principle these two possibilities will always remain. (In the author's opinion, resolving this issue into a practical declaration of risk/no risk is basically not a scientific problem, but a political one.)

Further studies, both epidemiological and experimental, are in progress, and will be evaluated when available. Additional research is warranted on some aspects reviewed in this paper. These include possible relationships between magnetic fields and teratogenic or teratotoxic effects, and the possibility of effects on pregnancy outcomes of stress reactions. Both of these research areas should include, but should by no means be limited to condition during VDT work only.

The discussion on pregnancy and VDT work has resulted in a widespread concern and worry among VDT operators. It is possible, as suggested in (12), that such worry may be an emerging "real" risk factor. Because of this, a number of actions have been taken, concerning information, alternative work and attempts to decrease the magnetic fields around VDTs. It should also be stressed that good working conditions (in terms of absence of stress factors and good ergonomics), while of importance for all workers, may be especially important for a pregnant woman.

6. REFERENCES

1. Lee BV, McNamee R. Reproduction and work with visual display units - a pilot study. In: Proceedings of an International Meeting to Examine the Allegations of Reproductive Hazards from VDUs. London November 29-30 1984, pp 41-47.
2. Landrigan PJ, Melius JM, Rosenberg MJ, Coye MJ, Binkin NJ. Reproductive hazards in the workplace. Scand J Work Environ Health 9 (1983) 83-86.
3. Bergqvist UOV. Video display terminals and health. Scand J Work Environ Health 10 (1984) suppl 2.
4. Purdham J. Adverse pregnancy outcome amongst VDT operators - the cluster phenomenon. In: Proceedings of an International Meeting to Examine the Allegations of Reproductive Hazards from VDUs. London November 29-30 1984, pp 27-40.
5. Delgado JMR, Leal J, Monteagudo JL, Gracia MG. Embryological changes induced by weak, extremely low frequency electromagnetic fields. J Anat 134 (1982) 533-551.
6. Ubeda A, Leal J, Trillo MA, Jimenez MA, Delgado JMR. Pulse shape of magnetic fields influences chick embryogenesis. J Anat 137 (1983) 513-536.
7. Maffeo S, Miller MW, Carstensen EL. Lack of effects of weak low frequency electromagnetic fields on chick embryogenesis. J Anat 139 (1984) 613-618.
8. Juutilainen J, Harri M, Saali K, Lahtinen T. Effects of 100-Hz magnetic fields with various waveforms on the development of chick embryous. Radiat Environ Biophys 25 (1986) (in press).
9. Tribukait B, Cekan E, Paulsson L-E. Effects of pulsed magnetic fields on embryonic development in mice. Extended abstract, submitted in January to the conference on Work With Display Units, Stockholm May 12-15 1986
10. Tribukait B, Cekan E, Paulsson L-E. Effects of pulsed magnetic fields on embryonic development in mice. Data presented at the conference on Work With Display Units, Stockholm May 12-15 1986.
11. Electromagnetic radiation and fields at visual display terminals (VDTs). Memorandum by the National Swedish Board of Occupational Safety and Health, February 13th, 1986.
12. Björseth Å, Warncke M, Ursin H. Stress hos gravide: Konsekvenser for mor og barn (Stress in pregnant women: Consequences for mother and child, in Norwegian) Dept of Physiological Psychology, University of Bergen 1985.
13. MacKay C. Visual display unit operation: possible reproductive effects. In: Proceedings of an International Meeting to Examine the Allegations of Reproductive Hazards from VDUs. London November 29-30 1984, pp 137-159.
14. The use of visual display terminals. WHO 1986 (in press)
15. Data from the Swedish Registry study, presented by Malker H at the Swedish Government Hearing, 9th April 1985.

WORK WITH DISPLAY UNITS 86
B. Knave and P.-G. Wideback (eds.)

BIRTH DEFECT, SPONTANEOUS ABORTION AND WORK WITH VDUs

Alison D. McDONALD

Institut de Recherche en Santé et en Sécurité du Travail du Québec, 505 ouest, de Maisonneuve Montréal, Québec, H3A 3C2 Canada*

The findings of the study give no indication that the use of a VDU in pregnancy increases the risk of congenital defect and are insufficient to reject the null hypothesis with regard to spontaneous abortion.

1. METHODS

In a study designed to investigate possible reproductive hazards in the workplace, women were interviewed in hospital immediately after a pregnancy. In 2 years (11 May 1982 - 10 May 1984) 51,885 women who had just had a delivery (~90% of births in Montreal) and 4,127 who had received treatment for a spontaneous abortion were questioned on occupational, personal and social factors in the present and all previous pregnancies - a total of 104,620. Medical records were reviewed for pregnancy and pediatric information and further enquiries made about suspected birth defects.

Analyses to examine the possible effects on pregnancy of VDU use, which was one of many questions on work, were carried out in 17,632 pregnancies in which the women was employed full-time at the start of pregnancy in defined occupations with substantial VDU use. Current and previous pregnancies were analyzed separately because for spontaneous abortions the proportions were very different and for birth defects, age at ascertainment differed.

2. FINDINGS

Birth defects: In current pregnancies congenital defects were found in 3.3% of VDU users and 3.7% of non-users and in previous pregnancies in 3.8% of users and 3.6% of non-users. There was no important difference between users and non-users in rates of specific defects.

Spontaneous abortion: In current pregnancies, after correction by logistic regression for five confounding variables (age, pregnancy order, history of abortion, educational status and smoking habit) as compared with all working women, the ratio of observed to expected abortion was 1.21 for VDU users ($p=0.002$) and 0.89 for non-users ($p=0.03$). However, risk was not related to amount of VDU use; the ratio for those who used a VDU for more than 30 hours a week was 1.12 ($p=0.10$) whereas for those who used it for shorter periods it was 1.25 ($p=0.02$).

---

* This paper is a reprint from the Proceedings of WWDU 86. A full paper is submitted (March 1986) to the Journal of Occupational Medicin.

In previous pregnancies, the proportion of spontaneous abortions was high because women were interviewed at termination of a pregnancy. If a women conceived twice within 9 months, the first pregnancy could only have ended in abortion. VDU use was increasing rapidly during the period studied; in conceptions before 1977, 7.8% of women had used a VDU for 15 or more hours a week - by 1982 the rate was 37.2%. The simultaneous increase in both rates of abortion and VDU use in previous pregnancies indicated the desirability of analysis by year of conception.

After correction for the confounding variables specified above, but not for year of conception, the ratio of observed to expected abortions was 1.12 for users (p=0.03) and 0.95 for non-users (p=0.04). However, analysis by year of conception gave equal proportions of spontaneous abortions in users and non-users: - for 1982-3, 78.7% in users and 89.7% in non-users, for 1981, 35.7% and 35.5%; and before 1981, 15.0% in users and 15.8% in non-users.

Because of the discrepant results in current and previous pregnancies a further analysis was made of all 57,276 women employed at the start of pregnancy classified into 42 occupational groups. This was done to remove the possibility that the recorded use of VDUs by women immediately after an abortion might not be comparable with that by women after a full term delivery. The 42 groups were ranked according to the percentage use of a VDU for 15 or more hours a week in current and in previous pregnancies based on data for all women regardless of the outcome of their pregnancies. The percentage frequencies ranged widely from less than 5% to more than 45%. Observed to expected abortion ratios showed no association with VDU use. In current pregnancies the ratio of observed to expected abortions in occupations in which less than 5% of women used a VDU for 15 or more hours a week was 1.02; with 5-24% use, 0.99 and with 45% or more use, 1.03. In previous pregnancies the ratios were as follows: occupations with less than 5% use 0.98, 5-24% use 0.97, 25-44% use 1.03 and 45% or more use 1.02.

3. DISCUSSION

Clearly there was no evidence of an association between VDU use and congenital defects in either previous or current pregnancies. The same was true of spontaneous abortions in previous, but not in current pregnancies. However, in a retrospective study in which the outcome of pregnancy is known both by the women and the interviewer the possibility of bias in the responses of women immediately after abortion as compared to a term pregnancy could not be excluded. There were two main reasons to suspect this possibility: -

1. The period for recall of work at the time of conception is 6-7 months shorter after an abortion than a term pregnancy.

2. Knowledge of the outcome might well lead to under-reported VDU use after term pregnancy and over-reported use after abortion.

We believe that bias may well have been responsible for the findings in current pregnancies, for three reasons: 1) the ratio of observed to expected abortions in <u>non-users</u> was significantly lower than in all working women; 2) the exposure response relationship was, if anything, inverse and; 3) occupations ranging widely in VDU use had the same risk of abortion.

WORK WITH DISPLAY UNITS 86
B. Knave and P.-G. Wideback (eds.)

BIRTH DEFECTS, COURSE OF PREGNANCY, AND WORK WITH VIDEO DISPLAY UNITS. A FINNISH CASE-REFERENT STUDY

Kari Kurppa, MD, Peter C Holmberg, MD, Kaarina Rantala, MSc (Chem Eng), Tuula Nurminen, MSc, Lauri Saxén, MD PhD, Sven Hernberg, MD

Institute of Occupational Health, Topeliuksenkatu 41 a A, 00250 Helsinki, Finland; Department of Pathology, University of Helsinki, Finland

In a test of the allegation that exposure to video display units (VDUs) causes birth defects interview forms of Finnish mothers of 1,475 children with orofacial clefts, defects of the central nervous system, skeletal defects, or cardiovascular malformations and the same number of their paired referents were studied. The scrutiny revealed 490 mothers with occupational titles mostly in office work indicating potential VDU exposure. 235 of them were case mothers and 255 referent mothers. Thus, office work as such was unrelated to the occurrence of congenital malformations. Then, unaware of the case-referent status, mothers' descriptions of work day activities were perused for information indicating exposure to VDUs. Work with such units in the 1st trimester was ascertained for 111 mothers. Of these, 51 were case mothers and 60 were referents. The comparison of the mothers exposed to VDUs in the 1st trimester with those not exposed at all showed a crude odds ratio point estimate of 0.9 with 95% confidence limits of 0.6 and 1.2. Adjustment for potential confounders by multivariate logistic regression methods did not materially affect the risk estimates. The results did not indicate a teratogenic risk for VDU operators.

1. INTRODUCTION

According to newspaper stories working with video display units (VDUs) has resulted in increased rates of adverse pregnancy outcomes including congenital malformations. Such news have elicited much excitement among women. A high labor administrator in North America, insisting he did not want to create panic, has drawn a comparison between video display terminals (VDT) and the pesticide DDT and reminded that it had taken the best scientists a generation to discover the health effects of the latter [1]. In some countries the news have led to administrative recommendations or orders to ban working with VDUs during pregnancy and to setting of hygienic limits for electromagnetic fields near VDUs. Fears have also spread to Finland. Some secretaries now wear leaded aprons for protection against assumed radiation risk. Scientific justification for such worries has not been much [2].

We have analyzed the associations between VDU work during pregnancy and selected major congenital malformations. The data derives from a Finnish matched-pair study on 1,475 birth defects in which mothers of infants with birth defects and an equal number of their time-area matched referent mothers were interviewed after delivery. Special attention was paid to the work day description of the mother. The present paper is an extended version of the report that was published in 1985 [3]. We have recently exploited the series of the 1,475 referent mothers to survey for associations between VDU work, the course of pregnancy, and its outcome.

2. SUBJECTS AND METHODS

The Finnish Register of Congenital Malformations is a national surveillance system which must be notified of all birth defects found in stillborn infants or during the first year of life. A pathologist trained in teratology checks the reports for the validity of diagnosis. Selected groups of defects are more thoroughly investigated. The mother whose delivery immediately preceded that of the case mother in the same Maternity Care District was taken as a referent. The case mothers and their time-area matched referents were personally interviewed by midwives approximately three months after delivery (particulars of previous pregnancies, diseases, drug consumption, etc.). The retrieval rate of the questionnaires has been of the order of 97%. The validity of the present approach has been previously discussed [4,5].

The data covers a time-period from June 1976 until December 1982. Altogether 1,475 pairs of case and referent mothers were personally interviewed. Included were 365 consecutive defects of the central nervous system, 581 consecutive orofacial clefts, 360 consecutive structural defects of the skeleton, and 169 consecutive cardiovascular malformations. More than 95% of the mothers approached agreed to participate in this special study.

Gathering thorough information on mothers' work attendance and exposures at work is not a Register routine. Therefore, the standard procedure was supplemented by interviews on detailed occupational exposures during pregnancy. Two specially trained interviewers from the Institute of Occupational Health of Helsinki collected data on occupational and leisure time exposures by using a specially designed questionnaire [6,7]. They personally interviewed all case and referent mothers. Most mothers were interviewed at their Maternity Care Centres during the first postnatal visit some three months after delivery while a few interviews took place at home.

Mother's work attendance during pregnancy was recorded. The interviews included pro forma questions on certain chemical and physical exposures at work or at home. No pro forma questions covering VDU work were included. An open question of the interview requested the mother to describe her ordinary work day with all different work phases in detail. The description was recorded as such. The main function of the open question was to give the industrial hygienist a basis for estimating the possible exposures and work processes. The work description enabled us to study the VDU question.

Occupational titles [8] were utilized to pick up mothers with potential VDU exposure. In the selection process we used occupational titles that had been corrected, when necessary, to conform with the actual work description given by the mother [9]. The interview forms of the mothers with potential exposure were then scrutinized for VDU information by an industrial hygienist together with experts in occupational medicine, all unaware of the case-referent status. The interview forms of the pairs of the potentially exposed mothers were similarly studied as well as 100 randomly selected forms of mothers "not potentially VDU exposed" by occupational title. In none of these last instances was a probable VDU work detected.

The exposure during the 1st trimester was classified according to whether VDU was explicitly mentioned in the work description (75 mothers), VDU work, though not actually mentioned in writing, seemed obvious (31 mothers), VDU use was considered highly probable (5 mothers), or VDU exposure was improbable or could not be estimated (379 mothers).

Exposure time in the 1st trimester was categorized as an average of 4 hours or more daily for 5 days a week (62 mothers), less than 4 hours but at least 1 hour a day (17 mothers), or less than 1 hour daily on a weekly basis (32 mothers).

Confidence limits for the crude odds ratios were calculated using the test-based method [10]. The data were also analyzed by multivariate logistic regression methods for matched case-referent studies [11]. After looking at various associations with birth defects in bivariate analysis eleven potential confounders were included in the logistic analysis. (The variables controlled (contrasting any exposure to VDT to no exposure) were: maternal age _35/ 35 years: adjusted odds ratio 0.9, 95 % confidence interval 0.7-1.3; birth order greater than three/three or less: 1.0, 0.7-1.5; previous miscarriages: yes/no 1.0, 0.8-1.3; previous stillbirths with premature fetus: yes/no 1.4, 0.5-3.7; previous children with malformations: yes/no 3.0, 1.6-5.6; two or more induced abortions: yes/no 1.5, 0.8-2.9; common cold or fever in the 1st trimester: yes/no 1.8, 1.4-2.2; intake of analgetics/antipyretics in the 1st trimester: yes/no 1.8, 1.3-2.6; intake of sedatives/soporifics in the 1st trimester: yes/no 1.6, 0.8-3.4; alcohol intake during pregnancy: yes/no 1.0, 0.9-1.2; smoking during pregnancy: yes/no 1.4, 1.1-1.8.)

Power calculations for detecting an increased malformation risk were conducted by methods for pair-matched studies according to Schlesselman [12].

Table 1. Case and referent mothers by occupational titles representing potential VDT exposure

Occupations		Central nervous system defects	Orofacial clefts	Skeletal defects	Cardiovascular defects	Total
Journalists, editors, advertising copywriters	Cases	1	-	-	-	1
	Referents	1	1	-	-	2
Automated data processing directors, analysts, programmers; computer and keyboard operators	Cases	2	3	4	2	11
	Referents	4	4	2	3	13
Clerical workers, including bookkeepers and bank, post office and other office cashiers	Cases	5	8	4	3	20
	Referents	10	9	12	5	36
Secretaries and typists	Cases	8	12	13	4	37
	Referents	7	15	6	4	32
Office clerical workers, including office, bank, insurance, and travel agency clerks	Cases	43	59	44	20	166
	Referents	45	69	36	22	172
Total	Cases	59	82	65	29	235
	Referents	67	98	56	34	255

3. RESULTS

Altogether 490 mothers with potential VDU exposure according to occupational title were discerned (table 1). 235 of them were case mothers and 255 referent mothers. Most of the exposed mothers had worked in offices. The scrutiny of table 1 does not suggest an association between office occupations and congenital malformations.

The study of the interview forms of the 490 mothers in office occupations indicated that 120 mothers had had an obvious exposure to VDU during pregnancy. Exposure during the 1st trimester was evident in 111 of these.

Table 2 shows that the VDU exposure was similar among the case and referent mothers. There were 51 case mothers and 60 referent mothers working with VDU in the 1st trimester. For them the unadjusted odds ratio point estimate was 0.9 with 95% confidence interval 0.6-1.2. Thirty-one case mothers and 31 referents had continuously worked with VDU at least 20 hours a week in the 1st trimester. Adjusting for potential confounders did not materially affect the risk estimates. The adjusted odds ratio point estimate (for all malformations pooled) was 0.9 (with 95 % confidence interval 0.6-1.3) when mothers exposed to VDU in the 1st trimester were contrasted with those not exposed at all.

Table 2. Case and referent mothers for types of congenital malformations and estimates of unadjusted odds ratios (and the associated 95% confidence limits) contrasting exposure to VDT to no exposure.

Type of malformation	Exposed member of discordant pair	Exposure time per day: Less than 4 hours	4 hours or more	Total: Any ascertained exposure		
		N	N	N	OR	95 % limits
Central nervous system defects	Case	2	6	8	0.4	(0.2 - 1.0)
	Referent	4	14	18		
Orofacial clefts	Case	7	13	20	0.9	(0.5 - 1.7)
	Referent	17	5	22		
Skeletal defects	Case	3	7	10	0.8	(0.4 - 1.9)
	Referent	5	7	12		
Cardiovascular defects	Case	8	5	13	1.6	(0.7 - 3.9)
	Referent	3	5	8		
Total	Case	20	31	51	0.9	(0.6 - 1.2)
	Referent	29	31	60		

The number of discordant pairs in the present study (all birth defects pooled) is sufficient to detect a two-fold risk with 98% chance (assuming $\alpha = 0.05$ and a one-sided test) if working with VDUs were associated with the birth defects under study. Similarly, there would be a 68% chance of detecting a 1.5-fold risk.

Demographic characteristics, maternal habits, maternal medical histories, and outcomes of the last and previous pregnancies by categories of VDU work during last pregnancy, other office work (potential VDU exposure), and probable non-VDU work of the referent mothers are shown in table 3. In our study VDU work

Table 3. Demographic characteristics, maternal habits, maternal medical history, and present and previous (unadjusted) pregnancy outcome of the 1,475 referent mothers.

	VDU work (1st trimester)	Potential VDU work	Non-VDU work
		Office work	Other work
	(N 60)	(N 195)	(N 1220)
Maternal age (years; mean ±SD)	28±5	27±4	27±5
Maternal age ≥ 35 years (%)	8.4	10.0	6.7
Paternal age ≥ 35 years (%)	16.7	10.8	14.6
Alcohol consumption during pregnancy (%)	56.7	44.6	39.8
Smoking during pregnancy (%)	23.3	20.0	17.3
Irregular menses (%)	8.6	9.3	8.6
Previous miscarriage(s) (%)	13.3	16.4	15.4
Previous child with congenital malformation (%)	-	1.0	1.5
Birth order > 1 (%)	56.7	45.1	58.9
Length of gestation (days; mean ±SD)	283±13	281±12	281±14
Gestation > 37 weeks (%)	6.8	2.6	3.6
Abortus imminens (%)	21.7	21.5	20.3
Placental weight (g; mean ±SD)	606±116	620±124	618±130
Placental weight ≤ 400 g (%)	1.9	3.3	3.9
Birth weight (g; mean ±SD)	3548±550	3548±461	3557±528
Birth weight < 2500 g (%)	5.0	1.0	2.3
Maternal systolic BP (mmHg; mean ±SD)	120±11	121±12	120±12
Maternal diastolic BP (mmHg; mean ±SD)	71±10	73±8	72±10

was not associated with the risk of threatened abortion, length of gestation, birth weight of the infant, placental weight, or maternal systolic or diastolic blood pressure at the end of pregnancy. The frequency (unadjusted) of previous miscarriages or of irregular menses was similar for groups of mothers stratified according to the VDU work during the latest pregnancy.

4. CONCLUSIONS

The main conclusion to be drawn from this study is that the results yielded no evidence to suggest that VDU exposure would be associated with the occurrence of orofacial clefts, major structural malformations of the central nervous system, skeleton, or the heart and large vessels. According to the results of previous hygienic measurements and available biological knowledge, the possibility that VDU exposure would result in birth defects had a low prior probability before the present study. The a posteriori credibility for such a causal association was not increased by the results.

ACKNOWLEDGEMENTS

We thank Tuula Suomela and Ritva Vesanto-Paavola for their skillful technical assistance, and the Finnish Work Environment Fund for the financial support.

NOTES AND REFERENCES

NOTE

The main results have been published earlier (3); they are reprinted by permission of the Editor in Chief of the Scandinavian Journal of Work, Environment and Health.

REFERENCES

[1] NIOSH to probe births to VDT users; panel recommends 5-hour VDT-day. The Guild Reporter (Official Publication of the Newspaper Guild (AFL-CIO, CLC), Washington, DC) 1982 November 12 (vol XLIX, no 20).

[2] Bergvist UOV. Video display terminals and health. A technical and medical appraisal of the state of the art. Scand J Work Environ Health 1984;10(suppl 2):1-27.

[3] Kurppa K, Holmberg PC, Rantala K, Nurminen T, Saxén L. Birth defects and video display terminal exposure during pregnancy: A Finnish case-referent study. Scand J Work Environ Health 1985;11:353-6.

[4] Saxén L, Klemetti A, Härö AS. A matched-pair register for studies of selected congenital defects. Am J Epidemiol 1974;100:297-306.

[5] Saxén L. Twenty years of study of the etiology of congenital malformations in Finland. In: H Kalter ed. Issues and reviews in teratology. Volume 1. Plenum Publishing Corporation, 1983, 73-110.

[6] Holmberg PC, Nurminen M. Congenital defects of the central nervous system and occupational factors during pregnancy. A case-referent study. Am J Ind Med 1980;1:167-76.

[7] Kurppa K, Holmberg PC, Hernberg S, Rantala K, Riala R, Nurminen T. Screening for occupational exposures and congenital malformations. Preliminary results from a nation-wide case-referent study. Scand J Work Environ Health 1983;9:89-93.

[8] Classification of Occupations. Central Statistical Office of Finland. Handbook no 14, Helsinki 1981.

[9] Holmberg PC, Kurppa K, Hernberg S. Occurrence of congenital malformations in different occupational activities. XXI International Congress on Occupational Health, 1984, Dublin, Ireland, Abstracts, IE Eustace (ed), p 54.

[10] Miettinen OS. Estimability and estimation in case-referent studies. Am J Epidemiol 1976;103:226-235.

[11] Breslow NE, Day NE. Statistical methods in cancer research. The analysis of case-control studies. Lyon, IARC, 1980.

[12] Schlesselman JJ. Case-Control Studies. Design, Conduct, Analysis. Oxford University Press, New York, 1982.

WORK WITH DISPLAY UNITS 86
B. Knave and P.-G. Wideback (eds.)

PREGNANCY OUTCOME AND VDU-WORK IN A COHORT OF INSURANCE CLERKS

Peter Westerholm,
Swedish Trade Union Confederation, Stockholm, Sweden

Anders Ericson,
National Board of Health and Welfare (NBHW), Stockholm, Sweden

INTRODUCTION

The present study on pregnancies and births among social insurance clerks in Sweden was undertaken with the objective to contribute to the ongoing public debate on alleged pregnancy hazards caused by work with visual display units (VDU's). Clusters of abnormal pregnancy outcomes in a group of women working with VDU's have been described in the non-scientific press. These reports have been reviewed by Bergqvist in 1984 (1). The observations of Delgado et al in 1982 (2) of developmental disturbancies in chick embryos exposed to magnetic fields have also been important for the perception of VDU-work as a pregnancy hazard. Reasons for our study were, beside the health concerns among the public, access to information on a reasonably large study population through a centralized computer base. An important prerequisite for carrying out this study successfully was full cooperation at all stages of work with the employer and trade union concerned. The study was performed as an extension of an earlier study by Ericson and Källen in 1986 (3, 4) in which census information on the study population, completed with questionnaire investigation were used as primary sources of information. The epidemiologic cohort design was chosen for the present study.

STUDY POPULATION

The study population consisted of female clerks at social security bureaus in the whole country, retrieved from the computerized personnel records of the employer. The whole study population ever employed during the years 1980 – 1983 generated 4117 full term pregnancies.

Table 1.

Total study population. Pregnancies by year of birth.
Exposure groups.

Year of birth	Exposure groups				
	A	B	C	D	E
1980	728	109	2	84	190
1981	713	122	3	64	166
1982	683	109	3	73	155
1983	624	72	1	69	147
Total	2748	412	9	290	658

Whole study population: 4117

OUTCOME VARIABLES UNDER STUDY

Abortion rate (hospitalized miscarriages only), congenital malformations, birth weight, perinatal mortality.

INFORMATION SOURCES

The computerized personnel records on the study population were explored to identify persons with work involving the use of VDU equipment. The computer bases containing information on outcome variables - the hospitalized miscarriages register, the register of medical birth information and the register of congenital malformations are kept and operated by the National Board of Health and Welfare - were used with the aid of record linkage operations to obtain information on members of the study cohort.

The exposure classification was made jointly by the trade union and the employer for each type of work. The primary material for the classification consisted of detailed occupational categorization and the occupational coding used in the personnel records. The scheme of classification is shown in table 2.

Table 2.

Classification of exposure

A. "Extensive" VDU-exposure.
Not more than 15 hrs/wk.

B. Moderately extensive VDU exposure.
Not more than 10 hrs/wk.

C. Small extent of VDU-exposure.

D. Variable exposure, i.e. periodic programming, wordprocessor work etc.

E. No VDU work.

As can be seen in table 2, the study population has been, at the most, only moderately exposed to work with VDU's.

RESULTS

The stillbirts and perinatal deaths are shown in table 3. Expected numbers were calculated using national reference rates with correction made for the mothers' age and number of previous births.

Table 3.

Stillbirths and perinatal mortality

		Total group	Subgroup A
Stillbirths	Obs	7	5
	Exp	16,1	10,7
Perinatal deaths	Obs	13	9
	Exp	14,1	9,4

As shown in the table there was no deviation from what could be expected in the study population as regards stillbirts and perinatal mortality.

As to birth weights no deviation from expected distribution - using national rates for reference - could be observed. Correction was made for the sex of child and the mothers age and previous number of births.

Table 4 summarizes the observations of congenital malformations.

Table 4. **Congenital malformations**

		Exp. group				
		A	B	C	D	E
Births		2748	412	9	290	658
Any malformation		137 (5,0%)	24 (5,8%)	2 (22%)	14 (4,8%)	37 (5,6%)
Significant malformation	Obs	43	14	0	4	5
	Exp	46	7	0	5	11

The term "Any malformation" refers to the observations retrieved from the register of medical birth information, i.e. all observations reported. The term "Significant malformation" is a term used at the National Board of Health and Welfare referring to a selection of malformations which are judged to have a reasonably stable reporting rate. This means that minor aberrations of development are excluded. Examples of such excluded types of malformations are preauricular appendices, hip subluxations, postaxial polydactylism, minor positional foot defects and naevi.

As is shovn in table 4 there is in group A (most exposed subgroup) no deviation from expected values. In group B there is a two-fold rate of significant malformations.

In the combined groups A + B the ratio observed/expected was 57/53 whereas in the combined group C + D + E the same ratio was 9/16. The rate of these two ratios A + B/C + D + E could thus be calculated as 1,9 (0,9 - 3,8 in 95 % confidence intervals). This deviation from unity is primarly explained by the low observed/-expected rate in the combined group C + D + E.

When focusing attention on one particular type of congenital malformations and using the above method of comparison within the whole study population it appeared that the combined groups A+ B had twelve observed malformations of the heart versus between 8 and 9 expected and the combined C + D + E group had none observed versus two to three expected.

In studying malformations of the heart a recently establised register, the register of heart defects, was used as a complementary source of information. This register is based on reports from the regional pediatric cardiology hospital units and has been operated from 1981 onwards. It includes also heart defects diagnosed after the perinatal period, most commonly during the first year of life. For these reasons we have preferred to assess the expected numbers of heart defects rather than to give them an exact numerical value.

In figure 1 are shown the findings of spontaneous hospitalized miscarriages. Comparison groups were extracted from the population census of 1980. After standardization for age the risk ratio for spontaneous abortion in study population was calculated as 1,1 (0,8-1,4 95 % C I). As can be seen in figure 1 there are no impressive differences between the index group and the groups selected for comparison with regard to hospitalized miscarriage rate.

Figure 1

Quotient between numbers of spontaneous abortions and pregnancies (legal abortions not included) among women 1980-1981 with different occupations (A-D) or without occupation (E).
* Represents women of study group (insurance clerks). Bars give 95% confidence intervals.

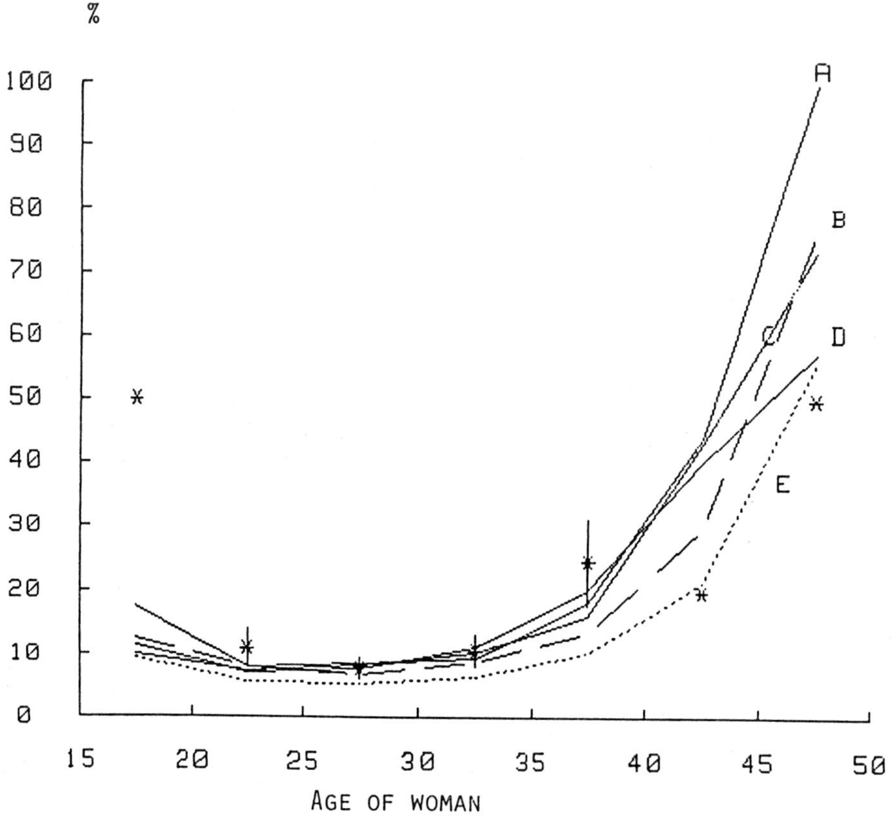

A = Commercial work

B = Natural sciences, technical work and medical and health services

C = Manufacturing

D = Transport and communication

E = Not occupationally employed

In part of our study population we had access to questionnaire responses of the women on the extent of their VDU work. This subgroup had been part of the study population used by Källen and Ericson (3,4) and which had been approached by them with a mailed questionnaire. The information obtained was thus in addition to the information we already had in the exposure classification made up by employer and trade union. In table 5 these two sources of information are shown for the subgroup concerned. As can be seen from the table there is good concordance between the information obtained through the questionnaires and from the job classification. It is not complete however. There is in exposure group a significant number of persons who have very little exposure (less than 5 hours a week). There are also in the supposedly none-exposed group E persons who say that they are exposed.

Table 5. Assessment of exposure

- Questionnaire responses VS joint employer/Trade union assessment.

Questionnaire information	Exposure group A	B	C	D	E
Exposed during pregnancy	302	50	-	27	42
< 5 hrs/wk	93	18	-	15	31
5 - 14 hrs/wk	165	27	-	9	9
15 + hrs/wk	41	5	-	3	2

In summary then, our study fails to demonstrate convincing deviations from what is to be expected with regard to pregnancy outcome in the group under study. It is not possible to judge whether the apparent increases of congenital malformations of the heart in two subgroups of the study population is to be regarded as a random or a non-random event. The reader is reminded that the study group must be characterized as having a low grade exposure. It should also be borne in mind that a study choosing hospitalized miscarriages as a health end-point is incomplete in the sence that abortions which are not hospitalized are left out of account.

Regarding messaures of exposure we wish to bring to the readers attention that the concept of exposure has to be handled with care in studies of environmental factors and pregnancy outcome. Job classification schemes and individual responses to questionnaires have a good but not complete concordance.

CONCLUSION

In this study we have not found any deviations from normal as regards pregnancy outcomes in the study group which we are willing to explain as an effect of VDU exposure.

REFERENCES

1. Bergqvist U (1984)
Video Display Terminals. A technical and medical appraisal of the state of the art.
Scand.J. Work Environ. Health 10, Suppl 2.

2. Delgado JMR, Leal J, Monteoagudo JL, Gracia MG (1982)
Embryological changes by weak, extremely low frequency electromagnetic fields.
J Anat. 134:533-551.

3. Ericson A, Källen B (1986)
An Epidemiological Study of Work with Video Screens and pregnancy Outcome. - I. A Registry Study.
Am. J. Industrial Med. 9:447-457.

4. Ericson A, Källen B (1986)
An Epidemiological Study of Work with Video Screens and pregnancy Outcome. - II. A Case-Control Study.
Am. J. Industrial Med. 9:459-475.

WORK WITH DISPLAY UNITS 86
B. Knave and P.-G. Wideback (eds.)

VIDEO DISPLAY TERMINALS AND BIRTH DEFECTS

A study of pregnancy outcomes of employees of the Postal-Giro-Center, Oslo, Norway

Tor Bjerkedal and John Egenæs
Department of Preventive Medicine, University of Oslo, Norway

1. BASIS FOR THE STUDY

A national birth defects monitoring or surveillance system was established in Norway 1970 (1). This system is based on mandatory notification of all births of 16 weeks of gestation and more. Notifications, giving detailed information on each pregnancy and its outcome, are processed centrally within two months of birth and computerized records of all births with the unique identificationnumber of the mother, father and the newborn are kept accessible in the Medical Birth Registry (2).

A very useful extension of the present surveillance system would be the ability to suvey or monitor pregnancy outcomes of employees in various industries. Unfortunately, information on mothers' and fathers' occupation is not presently collected as part of medical birth registration. This information, therefore, must be added to the record of the Medical Birth Registry through record linkage. In Norway, as in the other Nordic countries, record linkage is greatly facilitated by the use of the unique identification number alloted to each resident of the country.

The methodology of linking employment data and medical birth records has been developed and has been used in a number of studies of pregnancy outcomes of employees in various industries (3-5). It is used also in the present study of pregnancy outcomes of employees of the Postal-Giro-Center in Oslo.

At the Postal-Giro-Center the first video display terminal - VDT was introduced in 1976, however, extensively in use only since 1980. This "exposure"-situation at the Postal-Giro-Center and the fact that access to medical birth records goes back to 1967 offered the opportunity to design a study using historical controls, i.e. pregnancy outcomes of employees working in a changing work environment with a gradient over time in terms of exposure to VDT-s. For this purpose three 6-years periods are defined; 1967-1972, 1973-1978 and 1979-1984.

A comparison can be made also between outcomes of pregnancies related to employment at the Postal-Giro-Center and outcomes of pregnancies that took place before or after such employment.

The Portal-Giro-Center produced employment data for 2910 female employees and these data were linked to the Medical Birth Registry for the years 1967-1984. A total of 1820 birth records were identified. Reviewing the employment data identified 990 of these births as outcomes of pregnancies related to employment at the Postal-Giro-Center, while the pregnancies resulting in the remaining 830 births had taken place either before or after employment at the Postal-Giro-Center.

The number of pregnancy outcomes in the various subgroups of the total material of 1820 births are presented in Table 1.

Table 1

NUMBER OF BIRTHS DURING THE YEARS 1967-1984 OF FEMALE EMPLOYEES OF THE POSTAL-GIRO-CENTER, OSLO, NORWAY, ACCORDING TO YEAR OF BIRTH AND THE RELATION OF PREGNANCY TO EMPLOYMENT

Year of birth	Total Births	The relation of pregnancy to employment:		
		Before/after	During	
	Number	Number	Number	Percent of total births
1967 - 1972	327	232	95	29.1
1973 - 1978	467	119	348	74.5
1979 - 1984	1026	479	547	53.3
Total	1820	830	990	54.4

2. CHANGES FROM 1967 TO 1984 IN CERTAIN TYPES OF PREGNANCY OUTCOMES OF WOMEN WHO WERE PREGNANT WHILE EMPLOYED AT THE POSTAL-GIRO-CENTER.

The types of pregnancy outcomes analysed are: stillbirth, first week death, perinatal death, birth weight, preterm birth, multiple birth, and births with congenital malformations. These outcomes for the three 6-years periods are summarized in Table 2. It may be appreciated that the perinatal death rate has been substantially reduced from the first 6-years period to the last period, from 63.2 to 16.5 per 1000. Low birth weight i.e. less than 2500 grams, is reduced from 8.4 to 3.3 per cent, however, the percentage of very low birth weight (<1500 grams) is the same in all three 6-years periods. The same is true for the prevalence at birth of congenital malformations.

These trends, except for congenital malformations, are similar (though more marked) to those observed for pregnancy outcomes in the same period of women with residence in the Oslo-area. Congenital malformations on the other hand are seen to be registered more frequently over the years in births of the resident women.

3. COMPARISON OF PREGNANCY OUTCOMES ACCORDING TO EMPLOYMENT STATUS AT THE POSTAL-GIRO-CENTER (DATA FROM THE LAST 6-YEARS PERIODE (1979-1984).

The same pregnancy outcomes as dealt with in section 2 are analysed and results summarized in Table 3. First, it may be noticed that among the women giving birth while employed at the Postal-Giro-Center, there is a higher proportion of very young (<20 years of age), and relatively more primiparae. Pregnancy outcomes "under employment" can be seen to be generally slightly less favourable, with a higher perinatal mortality (16.5 vs. 8.4 per 1000), somewhat higher proportion of very low birth weight (1.1 vs. 0.8 per cent), preterm birth (9.0 vs. 6.5 per cent) and more births with congenital malformations (6.2 vs. 5.2 per cent). This same pattern is seen in each of the three 6-years periods, as well as in the total material.

Table 2
PREGNANCY OUTCOMES DURING THE YEARS 1967-1984 OF WOMEN EMPLOYED AT THE POSTAL-GIRO-CENTER IN OSLO, NORWAY

Pregnancy Outcome	Births 1967-1972		Births 1973-1978		Births 1979-1984		Births Total 1967-1984	
	Number	Rate	Number	Rate	Number	Rate	Number	Rate
Total number	95		348		547		990	
First births	64	67,4 %	275	79,0 %	352	64,4 %	691	69,8 %
Sex:								
Boys	44	46,3 %	193	55,5 %	271	49,5 %	508	51,3 %
Mortality:								
Stillbirths	3	31,6 ‰	5	14,4 ‰	9	16,5 ‰	17	17,2 ‰
1st week deaths*	3	32,6 ‰	5	14,6 ‰	0		8	8,2 ‰
Perinatal deaths	6	63,2 ‰	10	28,7 %	9	16,5 ‰	25	25,3 ‰
Birth weight:								
<2500 gram	8	8,4 %	20	5,7 %	18	3,3 %	46	4,6 %
<2000 gram	4	4,2 %	8	2,3 %	10	1,8 %	22	2,2 %
<1500 gram	1	1,0 %	3	0,9 %	6	1,1 %	10	1,0 %
Mean weight (grams)	3888		3429		3461		3443	
Pre term births:								
<38 weeks	16	16,8 %	33	9,5 %	49	9,0 %	97	9,8 %
Multiple births	2	2,1 %	2	0,6 %	12	2,2 %	16	1,6 %
Congenital Malformations								
Births with malformations	6	6,3 %	25	7,2 %	34	6,2 %	65	6,6 %
Diagnoses of malformations	6	63,2 ‰	28	80,5 ‰	37	67,6 ‰	71	71,7 ‰

Table 3
PREGNANCY OUTCOMES DURING 1979-1984 OF WOMEN WHILE EMPLOYED AT POSTAL-GIRO-CENTER, OSLO, NORWAY AND PREGNANCY OUTCOMES OF WOMEN BEFORE AND/OR AFTER EMPLOYMENT

Pregnancy outcome	Under employment		Before/after employment	
	Number	Rate	Number	Rate
Total number	547		479	
Mother's age:				
<20 years	53	9,7 %	11	2,3 %
35 +	5	0,9 %	5	1,0 %
Mean age (years)	24,0		24,6	
Firstbirths	352	64,4 %	277	57,9 %
Sex:				
Boys	271	49,5 %	252	52,6 %
Mortality:				
Stillbirths	9	16,5 ‰	2	4,2 ‰
1st week deaths*	0	-	2	4,2 ‰
Perinatal deaths	9	16,5 ‰	4	8,4 ‰
Birth weight:				
<2500 gram	18	3,3 %	29	6,1 %
<2000 gram	10	1,8 %	12	2,5 %
<1500 gram	6	1,1 %	4	0,8 %
Mean weight (grams)	3461		3414	
Pre term births:				
<38 weeks	49	9,0 %	31	6,5 %
Multiple births	12	2,2 %	10	2,1 %
Congenital Malformations:				
Births with malformations	34	6,2 %	25	5,2 %
Diagnoses of malformations	37	67,6 ‰	27	56,4 ‰

* Rate per 1000 livebirths

4. DISCUSSION AND CONCLUSION

Experience has shown that it is extremely difficult to select proper controls for the study of occupational effects on pregnancy outcomes. Historical controls may be no better, no worse, than other controls.

The use of historical controls assumes that personnel at the Postal-Giro-Center are recruited from the same segment (relatively speaking) of the population over the years and that those employed have a similar pattern of reproduction. It can easily be shown that age at employment and residence of those employed vary in the three 6-years periods. There are indications also of an increase in educational level of the employees. These changes would tend to reduce the frequency of adverse pregnancy outcomes, as also observed. Whether this reduction should have been even greater, which, if true, would suggest an effect of VDT on pregnancy outcome, cannot be answered on the basis of the information available, however, it is unlikely.

The comparison of pregnancy outcomes "during" and "before/after" employment reveals a somewhat higher frequency of adverse outcomes of pregnancies during employment. This is in agreement with earlier findings of a higher frequency of adverse pregnancy outcomes among economically active women compared to economically inactive (3). Also, the fact that the differences are of the same order of magnitude in all three 6-years periods, makes the introduction of VDT-s per se an unlikely cause.

It may be concluded therefore that the study do not indicate that introduction of VDT-s in the working environment of the Postal-Giro-Center has led to any increase in adverse pregnancy outcomes among the female employees.

It might be useful if this conclusion could be confirmed in a study of the actual exposure to VDT of cases (women with a defined adverse pregnancy outcome) and matched controls (women of same age and parity with "normal" pregnancy outcomes) drawn from the cohort of employees of the Postal-Giro-Center.

REFERENCES

(1) Bjerkedal, T., Bakketeig, L.S. & Lillestøl, J.: Changes in prevalences at birth of congenital malformations, prematurity and stillbirth. A surveillance system based on the medical birth registration in Norway. (In Norwegian) University of Bergen, Norway, 1971

(2) Bjerkedal, T.: The medical birth registry in Norway. In: Prospective Longitudinal Research. An empirical basis for the primary prevention of psychosocial disorders. Ed. Mednich, A., Baert, A.E. Oxford University Press, 1981.

(3) Bjerkedal, T.: Ouccupation and outcome of pregnancy. Report 80/9, Central Bureau of Statistics, Oslo, Norway, 1980.

(4) Bjerkedal, T.: Occupation and outcome of pregnancy. A population-based study in Norway. In: Prevention of Physical and Mental Congenital Defects, Ed. Marois, M. Alan R. Liss, New York, 1985.

(5) Bjerkedal, T.: Use of Medical Registration of Birth in the study of occupational hazards to human reproduction. Ed. Hemminki, K., Sorsa, M. and Vainio, H, Hemisphere Publishing Corporation, Washington, New York, London, 1985.

WORK WITH DISPLAY UNITS 86
B. Knave and P.-G. Wideback (eds.)

TASK-LOAD AND ENDOCRINOLOGICAL RISK FOR PREGNANCY IN WOMEN VDU OPERATORS*

H. Mikołajczyk, J. Indulski, T. Kameduła, M. Pawlaczyk, L. Walicka and E. Bieńkowska-Januszko

Institute of Occupational Medicine, 90-950 Łódź, Poland

Environmental investigations and questionnaire medical survey in women VDU operators or clerks were carried out in two business centers. The broadband electromagnetic field of intensity up to 10 V/m was found around VDUs and at the work places of their operators. Significantly higher incidence of spontaneous miscarriages was noted among pregnant VDU operators performing stressing tasks than in pregnant women working as clerks.

1. INTRODUCTION

For several years both harmful and harmless effects of VDU electromagnetic (e-m) fields on the early pregnancy have been reported [3, 5, 9, 12, 14, 18]. The degree of mental load due to the kind of task-work of VDU operators seems to be responsible for such discrepencies.
Since 1975 we have received information from several computer centers about incidence of unexplained spontaneous miscarriages in early stages of pregnancy in young women VDU operators. Since 1981 this Institute has been recommending to consider the employment of pregnant women at VDU as contraindicated. As far as we know the majority of computer centers respects this recommendation. Since few years we have no extra information about incidence of unexplained spontaneous miscarriages in women VDU operators in such centers.
In the work place at VDUs, the following environmental factors and mental loads have been recognized [2, 7, 8, 13, 15, 16, 19]: 1) Broadband pulse-modulated e-m fields of 1 kHz - 1 GHz with 95% energy within 10 - 125 kHz, and with intensities of an order 0.1 - 10 V/m for E field, and 80 - 200 uA/m for H field. 2) Constant magnetic field of 0.05 - 0.2 mT. 3) Static electric field of intensity 500 - 5000 V/m. 4) Chlorinated biphenyls at concentration about 80 $\mu g/m^3$. 5) Light pulsation from the screen. 6) Inappropriate position of an operator viewing the screen and inappropriate arrangement of display units. 7) Different degree of mental load depending on the task-work: a) simple introduction of data into memory systems; b) verification of data and their correction; c) simultaneous link with computer and direct or indirect (e.g. by phone) contacts with clients e.g. in the case of booking and reservation service. The last task-work is obviously more stressing than the first and second one. This paper presents the results of e-m fields measurement around VDUs and the results of question-

*This study was implemented within the project CPBR 11.1.04 coordinated by Central Institute of Labour Safety, Poland.

naire survey among women VDU operators or clerks in two different business centers.

2. MATERIALS AND METHODS

This Institute has been asked for consultation because of incidence of unexplained spontaneous miscarriages among pregnant women being VDU operators in the Polish Airlines Booking Office (PA-BO). Before final consultation it was necessary to carry out: 1) General ergonomic evaluation of work places at VDUs and of their arrangement. 2) Assessment of e-m fields using the broadband universal e-m meter MEH-1a with the broad-band probe SMPE-4 having linear characteristic for frequency range 10 kHz to 30 MHz. Thus it covers the main energetic range 10 - 125 kHz of VDUs e-m fields and at this frequency range it measures rms intensity of E field within the range of 0.05 - 10 V/m (Wrocław Technical University, Poland). 3) Narrowband E field was measured with interference meters LMZ-3 for 0.14 - 30 MHz and ULMZ-4/50 for 30 - 300 MHz (INCO, Poland). Both these meters do not cover the main energetic range 10 - 125 kHz of VDUs e-m fields. 4) Static electric field before the screen of VDUs was measured with meter VD-11 with probe having rotating electrode connected to the meter by lightguide (Glivice Technical University, Poland) 5) Induction of steady and low frequency magnetic fields was measured with Teslameter TH-26 with hallotrone probe (ASPAN, Poland). 6) 50 Hz electric field due to bulb and glim lamps situated in the close vicinity of VDU operators was measured with ME-2 meter (Wrocław Technical University, Poland). The respective measurements were performed also at VDUs used in the Building Construction Bureau (BC-B).
The questionnaire medical survey was carried out among women employed in both business centers at VDUs or as clerks. The questionnaire included personal data, actual occupation, questions concerning general health status, menstruations, pregnancies and deliveries, artificial and spontaneous abortions, and health of children (newborns, babies, small children). Such questionnaires were filled in by women-physicians, co-authors of this paper, providing medical care for personnel of the investigated business centers. The information on spontaneous abortions was verified by inspection of health registers in the out-patient departments at these centers. The questionnaire data enabled to make a comparative analysis for any period of the actual occupation of the investigated women. This paper presents the questionnaire information for the whole period of the actual occupation of these women i.e. 1 - 12 years, skipping the data on women aged over 40. Both environmental investigations and questionnaire medical survey were performed in 1984.

3. RESULTS

In PA-BO two types of VDUs i.e. Raytheon PTS-100 and Westighouse W1625 have been used for more than 15 years and in BC-B one type of VDU i.e. MERA 7950 has been used for some 10 years. In PA-BO all VDUs were grouped in four small rooms but in few other rooms single VDUs were used too. Non-ergonomic arrangement of VDUs was found in two rooms (Fig. 1a) and their more proper arrangement, like in the other two rooms, has been recommended (Fig. 1b). VDUs in BC-B were arraged more properly in large room.
The intensity of broadband e-m field was higher around the Raytheon and MERA VDUs than around the Westighouse VDUs. Consequently,

the intensity of e-m field was differentiated respectively at the work posts of VDU operators (Table 1).
The static electricity measured above the keyboard before screen i.e. 1 m above ground and 40 cm before screen was of the range 160 - 800 V at Raytheon PTS-100, 0 - 60 V at Westinghouse W1625, and 100 - 600 V at MERA 7950 VDUs. The static magnetic field measured 2 cm above the keyboard showed the induction of about 0.03 mT at Raytheon and about 0.13 mT at Westinghouse VDUs. To ensure sufficient light in the work-environment in PA-BO, because of a.m. and p.m. work shifts, numerous bulb and glim lamps were hanged quite near the VDU operators and the measurment of 50 Hz electric field revealed its intensity of the range 270 - 400 V/m at the distance of 10 cm from the lamps.

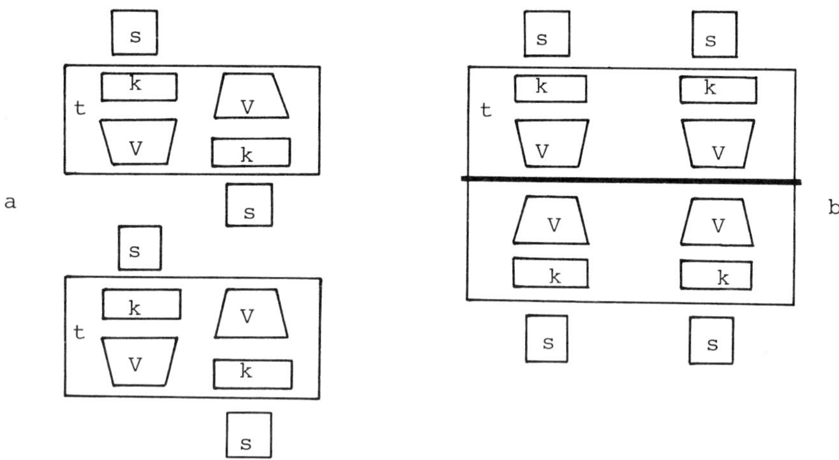

FIGURE 1
Arrangement of VDUs in PA-BO: a) non-ergonomic, b) recommended.
s - sit, k - keyboard, V - VDU, t - table

TABLE 1
Intensities of broadband E field in V/m at the distance of 30 cm around three types of VDUs and around operator's body.

	E in V/m at VDUs and at operator		
	Raytheon PTS-100	Westinghouse W1625	MERA 7950
1. above keyboard before screen	2.1 - >10	0.18 - 0.6	0.8 - 2.3
2. above VDU	7.6 - >10	~0 - 4.8	3.8 - >10
3. to the left side of VDU	1.3 - >10	~0 - 1.3	3.0 - >10
4. to the right side of VDU	0.6 - >10	~0 - 0.6	1.0 - >10
5. to the back side of VDU	9.2 - >10	~0 - 0.2	2.8 - >10
6. before operator's head	0.6 - 8.1	0.04 - 0.9	0.4 - 2.0
7. before operator's chest	0.6 - >10	0.04 - 0.6	0.5 - 2.0
8. before operator's abdomen	0.2 - 3.8	~0 - 0.3	0.2 - 1.7

>higher intensity than 10 V/m being an upper range of meter,
~intensity below the detectable range of meter.

The results of questionnaire survey indicate significantly higher incidence of spontaneous miscargiages, mostly in early stages of pregnancy, in young women employed during pregnancy at VDU in PA-BO than in women being clerks (Table 2). The frequency of spontaneous miscarriages was comparable in women being clerks in BC-B but there were no miscarriages in women employed during pregnancy at VDU in this bureau (Table 3). Women employed at VDUs, contrary to clerk women, in both business centers suffered more often from menstrual troubles, headaches and general indisposition.

TABLE 2
Results of questionnaire survey of women in PA-BO

Kind of information	Age groups of women (years)			
	VDU operators			
	21-30a	31-40b	21-30c	31-40d
1. number of investigated women	43	36	16	10
2. number of artificial abortions	12	19	2	7
(and an index ratio)	0.3	0.53	0.13	0.7
3. number of pregnant women artif. abortion excluded	20	30	7	9
4. number of pregnancies (excluding those terminated by artificial abortion)	20	38	9	16
5. number of spontan. abortions	8	12	2	3
6. percent ratio (5:4)	40	32	22	19
7. number of alive newborns	5	26	7	13
8. percent of women suffering from menstrual troubles	50	60	44	40

a) one women suffered from infertility, one delivered twice premature stillborn foetuses, one case of extrauterine pregnancy, 6 actually pregnant women (10 weeks to 8 months) were moved to clerk work; b) one woman delivered a newborn with accrania defect and another delivered premature alive newborn and second alive newborn with enzymatic defect; c) one woman delivered premature stillborn foetus; d) one newborn died 24 hrs after birth.

TABLE 3
Results of questionnaire survey of women in BC-B

Kind of information	Age groups of women (years)		
	VDU operators		Clerks
	21-30	31-40a	31-40b
1. number of surveyed women	12	13	12
2. number of artificial abortions	0	0	0
3. number of pregnant women	5	3	7
4. number of pregnancies	5	6	10
5. number of spontan. abortions	0	0	2
6. percent ration (5:4)	0	0	17
7. number of alive newborns	5	6	10
8. percent of women suffering from menstrual troubles	25	31	8

a) one woman suffering from infertility have been treated for 10 years, employed as VDU operator for 12 years; b) one woman suffers from infertility.

4. DISCUSSION

Environmental and work conditions were significantly different in the investigated centers. In PA-BO the majority of two types of VDUs were placed non-ergonomically in small rooms and there were two shifts of work (a.m. and p.m.). The VDU operators in this center were under stressing task-load because of direct or indirect (by phone) contact with clients. In BC-B the VDUs were properly arranged in a large room and the VDU operators were employed on one a.m. shift performing simple data operations. In both centers the VDU operators have few regular 10-15 minutes braks during work shift for meal or recreation. Clerk women have single 15 minute break for meal during 7 hrs work-shift.

Relatively high incidence of spontaneous miscarriages among women VDU operators in PA-BO seems to be related both to unfavourable environmental conditions including complex e-m fields and to stressing task-load. The experimental results on rats exposed to broadband e-m fields of television sets or to selected low frequency e-m fields indicate also the unfavourable influence of such fields on endocrine system and on pregnancy [11].

This paper does not predicate the definite pathology in pregnant women being the operators of VDUs nor it demonstrates evidence of disturbances at any level of endocrine system. However, it is necessary to pay attention to the critical period between 1st and 2nd trimester of pregnancy when the hypothalamo-hypophyseal-gonadal-placental relationships are highly non-stabile. At that period there is a very high risk for pregnancy maintenance because a number of internal and external factors could be responsible, directly or indirectly, for significantly higher incidence of miscarriages than in all other periods of normal pregnancy. Normal pregnancy changes the physiological status of woman organism, which depends on a progressive functional and anatomical adaptation of the endocrine regulatory system. The adaptative processes in this system start with the fecundation and proceed throughout the whole duration of pregnancy. The physiology of pregnancy recognizes that between 1st and 2nd trimester there are the lowest levels of hormones (HCG, progesterone, estrogens) and that various kinds of stress factors may be effective in inducing serious disorders responsible for inevitable abortion. Such disorders may include quantitative and qualitative changes of HCG in the blood of mather. It has been found that at threatening abortion in the 1st trimester, the doubling time of HCG concentration is significantly slower than in early normal pregnancy [6]. The results of experimental investigations show the effect of e-m fields on endocrine system in male and in nonpregnant females. The secretory function of the anterior pituitary gland, controlled by hypothalamic releasing hormones (TSH-RH, ACTH-RH, LH-RH, GH-RH), depends on Ca^{++} and K^{+} channels at the cellular level [17]. On the other hand, there are confirmed evidence that modulated low frequency e-m fields of low intensities disequilibrate the intake and/or release of Ca^{++} at the cellular level within the brain [1]. LF e-m nonmodulated fields also induce changes of Na^{+} and K^{+} contents in the brain of rats [11]. Moreover, the production and secretion of LH and FSH in the anterior pituitary gland starts only after pulsatile mode (square-wave) of LH-RH delivery. The amounts of LH and FSH depend on LH-RH pulse frequency i.e. slower LH-RH pulse frequencies elicit a greater FSH/LH release ratio whereas increased frequencies result in a greater LH/FSH ratio [4]. The investigations carried out in experimental animals demonstrated that e-m fields even of low intensity influence the gonadotropic function of an anterior pituitary gland [10]. Further investigations showed that the extract from hypothalamus of irradiated rats were more effective in releasing of FSH from anterior pituitary gland than extracts from hypothalamus of control rats [10]. Thus, it can be concluded that electromagnetic radiation affects anterior pituitary gland through the hypothalamus which seems to be the most sensitive tissue of the endocrine system to e-m radiation. The existing standards are referred to simple e-m fields and the comparison of broad-band modulated e-m fields emitted by VDUs with these standards is groundless. The specific nature of e-m fields from VDUs should be a subject of separate approach to standardization, taking into consideration other environmental and work factors. However, there are no satisfactory data concerning both with physical assessment and biological effects of VDU e-m fields to propose limitation of exposure. To reduce the risk of spontaneous miscarriages it can be recommended, on the basis of the above presented reasons, to consider the employment of pregnant women at VDU as contraindicated.

5. CONCLUSIONS

Assessment of e-m fields around VDUs and of questionnaire medical survey among women VDU operators or clerks in two business centers allows to conclude that:

1. VDUs are the source of e-m fields having low intensity but complex nature.
2. The incidence of spontaneous miscarriages was higher in women VDU operators performing stressing tasks than in clerk women.
3. High susceptibility of the neuroendocrine system to the influence of e-m fields forms a basis to suggest that there are contraindications to employ pregnant women at VDUs.

REFERENCES

[1] Adey, W.R., Physiol Revs (1981) 61, 435.
[2] Benoit, F.M., LeBel, G.L. and Williams, D.T., Int Arch Occup Environ Hlth (1984) 53, 261.
[3] Berquist, U.O.V., Scand J Work Environ Hlth (1984) 10, suppl. 2, 87.
[4] Chappel, S.C., Life Sci (1985) 36, 97
[5] Denning, J., New Scientist (1985) 105, 12
[6] Gaspard, U., Foidart, J.M., Lambotte, R., Reuter, A.M. and Franchimot, P., Ann d Endocrinol Paris , (1984) 45, 269.
[7] Harvey, S.M., Bioelectromagnetics (1984) 5, 1.
[8] Kameduła, T., Bezpieczeństwo Pracy (1985) 4, 13.
[9] Kruppa, K., Holmberg, P.C., Rantala, K., Nurminen, T. and Saxen, L., Scand J Work Environ Hlth (1985) 11, 353.
[10] Mikołajczyk, H., Electromagnetic fields and regulatory systems in living organizm, in Polish with English summary, in: Sedlak, W. (ed) Bioelektronika (Sci Soc KUL, Lublin, 1979) pp. 119-139.
[11] Mikołajczyk, H., Indulski, J., Kameduła, T. and Pawlaczyk, M., Effects of TV sets e-m fields on rats, this volume.
[12] Murray, W.E., Moss, C.E., Parr, W.H., Cox, C., Smith, W.J., Cohen, B.F.G., Stanmarjohn, L.W. and Happ, A., Potential Hazards of Video Display Terminals, DHHS (NIOSH) Publication No. 81-129 (U.S. Government Printing Office, Washington, 1981) .
[13] Nashel, D.J., Korman, L.Y. and Bowman, J.O., New Engl J Med (1982) 307, 891.

[14] Pulsed magnetic fields: conflicting results, Microwave News (1984) 4, 5, 1.
[15] Stuchly, M.A., Lecuyer, D.W. and Mann, R.D., Health Physics (1983) 45, 713.
[16] Stuchly, M.A., Rpacholi, M.A., Lecuyer, D.W. and Mann, R.D., Health Physics (1983) 45, 772.
[17] Taraskevich, P.S. and Douglas, W.W., Fed Proc (1984) 43, 2373.
[18] VDT - pregnancy clusters prompt NIOSH research, Microwave News (1984) 4, 4, 1.
[19] Weiss, M.M. and Petersen, R.C., Ann Industr Hyg Assoc J (1979) 40, 300.

WORK WITH DISPLAY UNITS 86
B. Knave and P.-G. Wideback (eds.)

EFFECTS OF TV SETS ELECTROMAGNETIC FIELDS ON RATS*

H. Mikołajczyk, J. Indulski, T. Kameduła, M. Pawlaczyk

Institute of Occupational Medicine, 90-950 Łódź, Poland

Exposure of female rats to e-m fields of TV sets before fecundation and during pregnancy resulted in body weight reduction of foetuses in comparison with foetuses of control females. Exposure of male rats to such fields caused weight reduction of testicles and some shifts of Na^+ and K^+ contents in brain tissue. Shifts of these ions were also found in brain tissue of rats exposed to 10 kHz e-m field of intensity 320 V/m.

1. INTRODUCTION

The present-day television sets (TV) and video display units (VDU) equipped with cathode-ray tube (CRT), flyback transformer, quartz generator, deflecting coils and other electric subsystems after being swiched on dissipate broad-band, pulse modulated electromagnetic (e-m) fields. The frequencies of these fields are of range 1 kHz to 1 GHz but most energy (about 95%) is contained within 10 - 125 kHz. Total intensity of e-m fields around these sets is of an order 0.1 - 10 V/m for E field and 80 - 200 μA/m for H field depending on the type of set and the distance from it. The screen collects static electric charges what results in static electric field of intensity 500 - 5000 V/m. Thus it is evident that TV and VDUs e-m fields are of complex physical nature. In the case of VDUs employment, the hygienic problems exist because of watching the sceen from a short distance about (40 cm). Such an exposure can create health problems especially in pregnant women being VDU operators [12]. This paper presents the results of investigations on the effects of TV e-m fields on pregnancy and on various biological parameters in female and male rats.

2. MATERIALS AND METHODS

Three series of investigations have been carried out in rats. In two series female and male rats were exposed repeatedly 4 hrs daily at 30 cm distance below the screen of black-white or colour TV sets. It means that animals were exposed from the backside. At 30 cm distance below the screen the intensity of broadband E field was found to be 1.35 - 1.73 V/m before black-white TV and 0.63 - 0.81 V/m before colour TV. The electrostatic potential at such distance was 200 - 300 V [12]. In the 1st series the female rats after 15 control and 20 prefecundation exposures were coupled with males and they were further exposed until late pregnancy when autopsy was performed. In the second series the females after 18 exposures during juvenile life and 42 prefecundation exposures

---

* This study was implemented within the project CPBR 11.1.04 coordinated by Central Institute of Labour Safety, Poland.

under the same conditions were coupled with males and they were further exposed until expected half time of pregnancy when autopsy was performed. TV sets were loaded with standard picture excluding audible sounds. In 3rd series male rats were exposed repeatedly 4 hrs daily to low frequency e-m fields obtained in the condenser of two 60x60 cm copper plates with inside distance 0.25 m. The plates were connected to: 1) RC decade generator type KZ 1115 (KABID ZOPAN, Warszawa, Poland), 2) stereo amplifier PW-7020 (FONICA, Łódź, Poland), and 3) adjusting transformer of high tension (made in the Unit of Instruments at this Institute). The intensity of the applied E field of 1 kHz or 10 kHz has been read out from the transformer scale and it was also measured inside the condenser using the e-m field meter MEH-1a with short dipole probe (Wrocław Technical University, Poland). The described set of instruments was placed in Faraday chamber 2.5x1.5x1.8 m lined inside with cardboard egg containers that had been coated with colloidal graphite. Female and male rats kept in group of 10 in plastic cages with perforated aluminium covers were housed under standard conditions (12 hrs light - 12 hrs dark cycle, temperature 22 $\pm$ 2° C, relative humidity 50 - 60 %, murigran food and degased tap water). The animals were not accustomed to experimental environment because of chronic character of the present experimental procedure. However, there was always similar handling of control and exposed rats. Every day the experimental and control animals in groups of 10 were moved to perforated plastic cages and the cages with experimental animals were placed under TV screen or between the plates of condenser. The cages with control animals were put in the shielded box placed in neighbouring room. The animals were exposed between 8.00 and 12.00 a.m. and at that period they had no access to food and water. The applied e-m fields are specified in tables containing the results. After termination of exposure the animals were moved back to the cages in vivarium. During the fecundation period two females and one male were kept in separate cages. At the beginning of the experiment and every Monday after termination of exposure the animals were weighed. After termination of the last exposure the autopsy of animals was performed. Beside macroscopic inspection and weighting of respective organs or foetuses, water content in some organs was estimated from the difference in weight of fresh and desiccted organs. Na^+ and K^+ contents in submandibular salivary gland (SSG) and in major parts of brain was measured by flame photometry (Flapho 4, Carl Zeiss, Jena) in samples of desiccated organs after their combustion in HNO_3 supplemented with H_2O_2 [7]. The numerical results in exposed and control animals were compared with "t" test for small number of data.

3. RESULTS

The autopsy of uterus content in pregnant female rats revealed higher number of involuted foetuses in females exposed to e-m field of bl-wt TV, and some reduction of foetuses weight highly significant in females exposed to e-m field of colour TV in the 2nd series. There was no macroscopic developmental defects in foetuses of control and exposed females. In general, these experiments showed no evident harmful effects of TV e-m fields on fertility and pregnancy course in female rats (Table 1).
Exposure of male rats to TV e-m fields caused significant reduction of testicles weight, reduction of glycogen content in SSG of rats exposed for 45 days, and several shifts of ions contents in SSG and in several major brain parts of rats exposed for 50 days to e-m field of colour TV (Table 2).

Growth rate of control and exposed rats to e-m fields of 1 kHz and 10 kHz was of regular course but after 6 weeks in rats exposed to 1 kHz and 200 V/m, and after 5 weeks in rats exposed to 10 kHz and 320 V/m, the reterdation of growth rate has been noted in comparison to that in control rats. However, significant reduction of body weight of rats was caused by 10 kHz e-m field. Significantly higher amounts of Na^+ have been found in hypothalamus, midbrain and brain cortex in rats exposed to 1 kHz and 10 kHz e-m fields. K^+ content was significantly augmented in these parts of brain in rats exposed to 10 kHz e-m field (Table 3).
Earlier investigations showed that microwave radiation even of very low power density influenced the gonadotropic function of anterior pituitary gland (Table 4). The gonadotropic activity was augmented in glands assayed immediately after last exposure and it was diminished in glands removed for assay several hours after termination of exposure of animals [10].

TABLE 1
Effects of TV e-m fields on pregnancy in rats

Experimental procedure	1st series cont-rols	1st series bl-wt TV	1st series col TV	2nd series* cont-rols	2nd series* col TV
number of female rats	10	9	10	10	10
body weight (g) : initial	195 ±5	202 ±6	197 ±3	78 ±5	77 ±5
before fecundation	235 ±6	242 ±8	236 ±6	175 ±13	187 ±8
periods of exposure (days) :					
1) control or juvenile	15	15	15	18	18
2) prefecundation	20	20	20	42	42
3) fecundation and pregnancy	17	17	17	15	15
nonpregnat females	0	2	1	2	0
pregnant females	10	7	9	8	10
total number of foetuses	123	84	103	83	112
(number per litter)	12.3	12.0	11.4	10.4	11.2
number of involuted foetuses	4	9	5	5	6
weight of alive foetuses	*1.90 ±.6	*1.78 ±.6	1.83 ±.75	*0.52 ±.21	*0.35 ±.2

* The autopsy of 5 control and 5 exposed females after juvenile and prefecundation periods (60 exposures) showed significantly lower weight of SSG and adrenal glands in exposed than in control animals i.e. 290 ± 40 mg and 37.9 ± 5.0 mg, and 324 ± 6.0 mg and 46.1 ± 6.0 mg, respectively.
*Statistically different at $p < 0.1$ or $p < 0.01$.

4. DISCUSSION

The rats were exposed from the back side with screen above them in order to diminish the effect of screen light on their eyes. TV sets fed with standard picture without audible sounds were the source of broad-band e-m field typical for such systems. However, ultrasounds emitted by fly back transformer have not been excluded. Both macroscopic changes i.e. higher number of involuted foetuses (deaths and resorptions) as well as lower weight of foetuses in females exposed to TV e-m fields than in control females indicate an involvement of endocrine system in these processes. Such mechanism of the effect of the applied e-m fields is also suggested by

TABLE 2
Effects of TV e-m fields on male rats

Investigated parameters in groups of 10 male rats	Exposure under TV at 30 cm from the screen, 4 hrs daily for: 35 days		45 days		50 days	
	controls	bl-wt TV	controls	col TV	controls	col TV
body weight (g) : initial	237 ±13	225 ±9	178 ±4	163 ±5	*108 ±9	*89 ±8
final	282 ±15	277 ±10	300 ±21	289 ±15	*275 ±20	*252 ±9
colonic temperature, °C	36.9 ±.7	36.9 ±.2	37.5 ±.7	37.4 ±.4	37.2 ±.5	37.3 ±.5
anterior pituitary gland, (mg)	6.7 ±1.2	7.2 ±.7	7.9 ±1.0	7.7 ±.9	7.3 ±.9	6.7 ±1.0
adrenal glands (mg)	43.5 ±3.7	45.9 ±6.2	54.2 ±6.2	47.7 ±4.9	46.8 ±4.9	44.1 ±4.0
testicles (mg/100 g body weight)	*1181 ±147	*1138 ±100	*1148 ±42	*1109 ±77	*1190 ±96	*1142 ±83
SSG (mg/100 g body weight)	76.6 ±4.5	77.5 ±7.1	87.2 ±7.8	87.9 ±7.0	92.6 ±9.4	87.9 ±5.2
left kidney (mg)	876 ±83	832 ±45	1028 ±53	943 ±106	908 ±58	863 ±65
water content (%) : SSG	74.6 ±.7	74.2 ±.8	74.2 ±1.0	74.3 ±1.0	74.8 ±.9	75.2 ±.9
kidney	76.8 ±.3	76.7 ±.4	76.4 ±.4	76.3 ±.5	76.4 ±.6	76.5 ±.4
glycogen (mg/1 g) : SSG	2.96 ±.8	3.36 ±.9	*3.5 ±.8	*2.7 ±.8	...	...
liver	34.0 ±4.2	35.3 ±3.0	28.6 ±4.5	32.5 ±5.2	...	...
SSG: Na^+ (µg/100 mg desiccated tissue)	262 ±27	235 ±20	266 ±27	258 ±23	*174 ±38	*218 ±22
K^+ " " "	743 ±56	728 ±48	*705 ±70	*635 ±29	*1028 ±111	*1142 ±77
Na^+ (µg/100 mg desic.tissue) : cerebellum	478 ±35	463 ±41	365 ±45	367 ±24	331 ±25	331 ±30
med.oblong.	404 ±18	376 ±44	285 ±15	266 ±22	212 ±24	234 ±14
hypothalamus	459 ±29	449 ±40	415 ±19	402 ±21	*322 ±22	*351 ±19
midbrain	465 ±30	454 ±31	310 ±19	291 ±17	*328 ±17	*361 ±15
brain cortex	500 ±43	477 ±44	281 ±27	286 ±32	*294 ±32	*329 ±32
K^+ (µg/100 mg desic.tissue) : cerebellum	912 ±93	910 ±65	1314 ±147	1332 ±81	1132 ±61	1162 ±82
med.oblong.	646 ±59	606 ±45	883 ±50	844 ±39	*737 ±61	*854 ±46
hypothalamus	818 ±81	826 ±59	1123 ±70	1169 ±116	*1050 ±99	*1136 ±57
midbrain	941 ±90	945 ±60	1186 ±45	1224 ±48	*1018 ±58	*979 ±29
brain cortex	1104 ±99	1066 ±118	1314 ±144	1256 ±90	892 ±61	911 ±48

*difference significant at least at $p < 0.05$

TABLE 3
Na^+ and K^+ contents in brain of rats exposed to e-m fields

Investidated parameters in groups of 10 male rats	Exposure to 1 kHz 200 V/m, 4 h/daily for 50 days: controls	exposed a	exposed b	Exposure to 10 kHz 320 V/m, 4 h/daily for 55 days: controls	exposed a	exposed b
body weight (g):						
initial	108 ±9	104 ±14	106 ±11	101 ±7	104 ±8	111 ±9
final	275 ±20	271 ±19	271 ±12	278 ±25	268 ±19	274 ±15
Na^+ (μg/100 mg)**:						
hypothalamus	322 ±22	339 ±25	361 ±30	*277 ±37	*313 ±17	*330 ±13
midbrain	*328 ±17	*365 ±13	*382 ±22	*277 ±23	*322 ±15	*360 ±22
brain cortex	*294 ±32	*327 ±17	*357 ±16	*296 ±22	*356 ±25	*358 ±24
K^+ (μg/100 mg)**:						
hypothalamus	1050 ±99	1088 ±79	1126 ±83	*1109 ±83	*1207 ±49	*1220 ±38
midbrain	1017 ±58	968 ±39	899 ±41	*1192 ±115	*1271 ±83	*1317 ±71
brain cortex	892 ±61	868 ±37	868 ±50	*1266 ±104	*1475 ±107	*1457 ±71

**desiccated tissue: * difference significant at least at $p < 0.05$

TABLE 4
FSH and LH in pituitary gland of rats exposed to microwaves

Investigated parameters in groups of 10 male rats	Controls	Exposed
body weight (g): initial	80 ± 5	83 ± 4
final	232 ± 15	239 ± 18
weight of ant.pit.gland (mg)	7.2 ± 0.8	6.0 ± 0.9
weight of adrenal glands (mg)	39.5 ± 1.5	41.5 ± 1.6
weight of testicles (mg)	3050 ± 150	2900 ± 390
ᵃFSH (μg/pituitary gland)	308 ± 8	478 ± 75
ᵇLH (μg/pituitary gland)	311 ± 180	363 ± 152

* Exposure to 3 GHz cw, 70 μW/cm^2, 4 hrs/daily for 50 days. Hormones assayed by ovaries augmentation test (a) or by prostata augmentation test (b) in hypophysectomized immature female or male rats, respectively.

the observed mass reduction of SSG and adrenal glands in female rats of small group investigated after 60 exposures (see footnote to Table 1). Weight reduction of testicles and shifts of Na^+ and K^+ content in investigated tissues, especially in hypothalamus and midbrain of male rats exposed to TV e-m fields seems to be also of endocrinological origin at the hypothalamo-hypophyseal level. The same interpretation can be applied to the observed retardation of growth rate and shifts of ions content in hypothalamus and midbrain of rats exposed to e-m fields of 10 kHz. In more detailed analysis of these results [11] the mass reduction of pituitary gland in exposed rats has been mentioned. However, there was significant shifts of Na^+ and K^+ content in major parts of brain, especially in hypothalamus and midbrain of rats exposed in e-m field of the same frequency but of intensity ten times higher i.e. 3000 V/m [11].

Experimental animals respond to incident e-m radiation by various mechanisms including anatomical, functional, biochemical or biophysical changes within the major regulatory systems and tissues, and by shifts of water and ions distribution [1, 2, 3, 4, 5, 6, 8, 9, 10, 13, 14, 15]. Some of such changes are related to field intensity and/or to definite frequency of electromagnetic spectrum [1]. The mechanism of Na^+ and K^+ shifts in hypothalamus, midbrain and brain cortex of rats exposed to low frequency e-m fields of low intensity is not clear. It has been suggested [11] that when low frequency e-m field of high intensity influences biological object like experimental animal, some kind of biological "blockade" could be activated by systematic regulation or at the cellular level.

The neuroendocrine system, especially on the hypothalamo-hypophyseal level is highly sensitive to e-m fields and responds with quantitative shifts of hormone secretion even under the effect of very low level of e-m energy [9, 10]. It is possible that e-m fields influence also secretion of placental hormones, especially chorionic gonadotropin.

The above consideration of the described in this paper results seems to support the suggestion of the endocrine background of miscarriage risk in pregnant women employed at VDUs [12].

5. CONCLUSIONS

The described results and discussion allow to draw the following conclusions: 1) Exposure of female rats before and during pregnancy to e-m field of black-white or colour TV sets caused detectable but not clear unfavourable macroscopic effects on foetuses. Exposure of male rats to such fields resulted in lowe weight of testicles and in shifts of Na^+ and K^+ content in hypothalamus and midbrain. 2) E-m field of 10 kHz and intensity of 320 V/m caused retardation of growth rate and Na^+ and K^+ shifts in hypothalamus, midbrain and brain cortex of male rats. 3) The mechanisms of the described changes could be of neuroendocrine nature.

REFERENCES

[1] Adey, W.R., Physiol Revs (1981), 61, 435.
[2] Bawin, S.M., Sheppard, A. and Adey, W.R., Bioelectrochem a Bioelectroenerg (1978), 5, 67.
[3] Bernhardt, J., Radiat a Environ Biophys (1979), 16, 309.
[4] Chou, C.K. and Guy, A.W., IEEE Trans Microwave Theory Techn (1978), MTT-26, 141.
[5] Gunn, S.A., Gould, T.C. and Anderson, V.A.D., Laboratory Invest (1961), 10, 301.
[6] Hanson, H.A., Brain Res (1981), 216, 187.
[7] Hvidberg, E., Jensen-Holm, J. and Langgard, H., Acta Pharmacol et Toxicol (1963), 20, 131.
[8] Michaelson, S.M., Amer Industr Hyg Assoc J (1971), 32, 338.

[9] Mikołajczyk, H., Microwave irradiation and endocrine function, in: Czerski, P., Ostrowski, K., Shore, M.L., Silverman, Ch., Suess, M.J. and Waldeskog, B. (eds.), Biological Effects and Health Hazards of Microwave Radiation (Polish Medical Publishers, Warszawa, 1974) pp. 46-51.

[10] Mikołajczyk, H., Electromagnetic fields and regulatory systems of living organism (in Polish with English summary) in: Sedlak, W. (ed), Bioelektronika (Sci Soc KUL, Lublin, Poland, 1979) pp. 119-139.

[11] Mikołajczyk, H., Low frequency electromagnetic fields and biological systems, in: Moroń, W., Sęga, W. and Waszkis, W. (eds), Electromagnetic Compatibility 86 (Wrocław Technical University Press, Wrocław, Poland, 1986) pp. 101-109.

[12] Mikołajczyk, H., Indulski, J., Kameduła, T., Pawlaczyk, M., Walicka, L. and Bieńkowska-Januszko, E., Task-Load at VDU and Endocrinological Risk for Pregnancy, this volume.

[13] Takashima, S., Onaral, B. and Schwan, H.P., Environ Biophys (1979) 16, 15.

[14] Tołgskaja, M.S. and Gordon, Z.V., Morphological Changes Under the Effect of Radiofrequency Radiation (in Russian), (ed. Moskwa, 1971).

[15] Schwan, H.P. and Foster, K.R., Proc IEEE (1980) 68, 104.

WORK WITH DISPLAY UNITS 86
B. Knave and P.-G. Widebäck (eds.)

EFFECTS OF PULSED MAGNETIC FIELDS ON EMBRYONIC DEVELOPMENT IN MICE

Bernhard TRIBUKAIT, Eva CEKAN and Lars-Erik PAULSSON

Department of Medical Radiobiology, Karolinska Institute, and National Institute of Radiation Protection, Box 60204, S-104 01 Stockholm, Sweden.

1. INTRODUCTION

Various possible biological effects of pulsed magnetic fields (PMF) in visual display terminal operators have been discussed (1), among them unsuccessful pregnancy outcomes and foetal congenital anomalies. To our knowledge, experimental data from animals exposed to PMF supporting the view of harmful effects of PMF on the foetal development in human beings, are lacking. In this contribution we present preliminary results from an ongoing study on pregnant mice exposed to PMF.

2. MATERIAL, METHODS AND EXPOSURE CONDITIONS

Primiparous inbred C_3H mice, 3-5 months old, were kept in macrolon cages at a constant temperature of 23^oC and relative humidity 50-55%. The light was regulated automatically from 7 a.m. to 7 p.m. The mice were given a standard diet (Astra-Ewos, Södertälje, Sweden) and tap water ad libitum. The C_3H strain has been used for about 10 years in our laboratory for various teratologic experiments and no changes in the frequency of resorption or the frequency and type of malformations have been observed. The female C_3H mice were mated overnight and examined for the presence of a vaginal plug next morning. The day on which the vaginal plug was found was denoted as day zero of pregnancy.

The pregnant mice were exposed to PMF as described below continuously from day 0 to day 14 of pregnancy. Controls were collected in the course of the exposure experiments and kept under identical conditions except for the exposures. On day 18 of gestation the animals were sacrificed by cervical dislocation and dissected. The pregnant uterus was examined for number of total implantations, resorptions, living and dead foetuses, normal and grossly malformed foetuses. The foetuses were weighed and examined after 3.5 days of fixation in ethanol. All foetuses were examined under a dissecting microscope for external malformations including various malformation of the central nervous system, malformation of the ear, eye, cleft palate, umbilical hernia and various malformations of the skeleton such as polydactyly. The foetuses were then cleared in 1% potassium hydroxide and stained with Alizarin red S for further examination of skeletal malformations, mostly of the vertebrae and ribs (2). In addition, retardation of the sternum was studied.

The animals were exposed to PMF fields with either rectangular pulses similar to those described by Ubeda et al (3), or to the sawtooth pulses typical for the fields from ordinary VDUs (4). The fields were generated by a large coil with six sections arranged in a Helmholtz-coil-like configuration. In order to create a fairly homogenous field the end section coils consisted of three turns of wire while all the four inner coils had only two turns. With this arrangement the field in the center varied less than 4% between different coils. The variation in the magnetic field strength in the plane of the coil sections was less than 1% within the exposure area. The mean diameter of all coil sections was 60 cm and the distance between them 25 cm. About 10 μT were generated by a current of 1 A. The three upper coil sections were connected in series and called the upper half coil. The lower half coil was made in the same way. Each half coil was connected in series with a noninductive power resistor of about 75Ω. The coil halves with their resistors were connected in parallel and fed directly from the 50Ω output of the pulse generator, Hewlett Packard 8112A, so that a field strength of 1 μT was generated. For the higher field strength, 15 μT, a wideband power amplifier, KrohnHite 7500, was used between the generator and the coil. In this case the coil halves with their resistors were connected in series in order to create a reasonable match to the output of the amplifier. In all cases a 200 μF nonpolar capacitor was connected in series with the coils for DC blocking. To be able to utilize the full output voltage swing of the amplifier when using nonsymmetrical pulses a DC path to earth, consisting of a 5H choke in series with two smaller chokes in the mH-μH range, was connected in parallel with the amplifier output.

Four different exposure conditions were used: I. rectangular pulses, 1 μT peak to peak; II. rectangular pulses, 15 μT peak to peak; III. sawtooth pulses, 1 μT peak to peak; IV. sawtooth pulses, 15 μT peak to peak. For pulse shapes I and II, the following timing parameters were used: repetition frequency 100 Hz, pulse width 0.5 ms, rise and fall time 2 μs. The R/L combination of the coils and their serie resistors enabled the generation of accurate 2 μs rise and fall times when fed by pulses with 1.7 μs rise and fall times from the generator. For pulse shapes III and IV, the following values were used: frequency 20 kHz, rise time 45 μs and fall time 5 μs.

The power amplifier was used at a fixed gain of 10. The output voltage from the pulse generator was adjusted in order to obtain the desired current in the coils. The current was measured with a current probe and an oscilloscope. The calculated field strength was examined by measurements using a calibrated test coil.

3. RESULTS

Pregnant mice were exposed to PMF with rectangular or sawtooth pulses continously from day 0 to day 14. There were no effects on the frequency of implantations, resorptions or dead foetuses or body weight of surviving foetuses. The frequency of occurrence of malformed foetuses was unchanged in animals exposed to rectangular magnet pulses but increased in sawtooth exposed animals. This increase did, however, not reach the level of significance. Malformations seen after Alizarin staining were unchanged. External malformations, however, increased in sawtooth exposed animals. The difference of foetuses showing external malformations between control animals and animals exposed to 15 μT sawtooth magnetic fields was significant ($p = 0.02$).

4. CONCLUSION

Based on the actual controls and taking into account the experience from a larger material of historical controls, both the frequency and the type of malformation found after exposure to PMF with sawtooth pulses during early pregnancy including the whole period of organogenesis might indicate that PMF of this specific type has teratogeneic effects. Further experiments are being carried out to clarify this question.

REFERENCES

1 Källén, B.: Dataskärmsarbete och graviditet. Svenska Läkartidningen 82, 1339, 1985 (in Swedish).

2 Wilson, J.G. et al.: Teratology, principles and techniques. Univ. Chicago Press (1965).

3 Ubeda, A. et al.: Pulse shape of magnetic fields influences chick embryogenesis. J. Anat. 137, 513, 1983.

EFFECTS OF PULSED MAGNETIC FIELDS ON IMPLANTATION, FOETAL RESORPTION, MORTALITY AND WEIGHT OF SURVIVING FOETUSES AT DAY 18 OF GESTATION

AMPLITUDE PULSE FORM	No Litters	Total Implants	Impl. /Female	Surviving foetuses	Body weight g	Resorption	Dead foetuses after day 15
CONTROLS	109	578	5.3±2.5	517 (89.4%)	0.97±0.12	53 (9.2%)	8 (1.38%)
1 µT RECTANGULAR	28	139	5.0±2.2	123 (88.5%)	0.94±0.12	15 (10.8%)	1 (0.72%)
15 µT RECTANGULAR	35	196	5.6±2.9	181 (92.3%)	0.99±0.11	13 (6.6%)	2 (1.02%)
1 µT SAWTOOTH	81	445	5.5±2.7	386 (86.7%)	0.98±0.13	53 (11.9%)	6 (1.35%)
15 µT SAWTOOTH	76	420	5.5±2.6	375 (89.3%)	0.98±0.13	43 (10.2%)	2 (0.48%)

TYPE OF MALFORMATIONS EXPOSED TO PULSED MAGNETIC FIELDS

	Malformations										
	Seen after Alizarin staining			External							
AMPLITUDE PULSE FORM	Total	Rib and vertebral malform.	Retina or iris deform.	Total	Umbilical hernia	Exen-cephaly	Hydro-cephaly	Club foot	Poly-dact-yly	Open eye	Ears mal-form.
CONTROLS	6	6	0	1	1	0	0	0	0	0	0
1 μT RECTANGULAR	0	0	0	1	0	0	0	0	0	1	0
15 μT RECTANTULAR	2	1	1	1	1	0	0	0	0	0	0
1 μT SAWTOOTH	5	5	0	5	0	1	0	0	1	3	0
15 μT SAWTOOTH	4	4	0	10	5	0	1	1	0	2	1

EFFECTS OF PULSED MAGNETIC FIELDS ON FOETAL MALFORMATIONS

AMPLITUDE PULSE FORM	Foetuses inspected	Foetuses malformed	Total no. of malfor-mations	Malformations seen after Alizarin staining		External malformations	
				Foetuses malformed	Total number of malformations	Foetuses malformed	Total number of malformations
CONTROLS	517	7 (1.35%)	7	6 (1.16%)	6	1 (0.19%)	1
1 μT RECTANGULAR	123	1 (0.81%)	1	0	0	1 (0.81%)	1
15 μT RECTANGULAR	181	3 (1.66%)	3	2 (1.10%)	2	1 (0.55%)	1
1 μT SAWTOOTH	386	9 (2.33%)	10	5 (1.30%)	5	4 (1.03%)	5
15 μT SAWTOOTH	375	11 (2.93%)	14	4 (1.07%)	4	7 (1.87%)	10

WORK WITH DISPLAY UNITS 86
B. Knave and P.-G. Wideback (eds.)

EFFECTS OF WEAK PULSED MAGNETIC FIELDS ON CHICK EMBRYOGENESIS

Monica Sandström[1], Kjell Hansson Mild[2] and Søren Løvtrup[1]

1) Department of Zoophysiology, University of Umeå, Umeå
2) National Board of Occupational Safety and Health, Umeå, Sweden

In order to investigate if magnetic fields with a asymmetrical sawtooth waveform could influence the early development of chick embryos, we have exposed fertilized hen eggs, during the first two days of development, to three different intensities of magnetic fields, 0.1, 1.5, and 16 µT with the corresponding time derivatives 0.03, 0.3, and 3.3 T/s. Neither signal produced any significant increase of abnormalities as compared to the controls.

1. INTRODUCTION

Several recent studies have shown that weak low-frequency magnetic fields may interact with biological systems. Thus, effects have been demonstrated in both cellular systems and in whole embryos. Aarholt et al.[1], using a square-wave magnetic field with intensities up to a few hundred µT, found a marked reduction of the mean generation time of the bacterium E. coli after exposure, as compared to the controls. A reduction of the generation time was found in slime mold cultures after long term exposure to 75 Hz magnetic fields [2]. Stimulatory effects of pulsed fields have also been found; the most well-known of these are the use of pulsed magnetic fields in bone repairs and in the clinical care of so-called "nonunion" fractures [3]. Stimulatory effects using much lower field strengths have been reported by Dixey and Rein [4], who found a stimulated release of noradrenaline from a nerve cell line. Liboff et al.[5] showed that human fibroblasts exhibit enhanced DNA synthesis when exposed to sinusoidally varying magnetic fields.

The effect of weak pulsed magnetic fields on chick embryogenesis have been investigated by Delgado and his associates [6, 7]. The embryos were exposed to pulses of various shapes, intensities and repetition rates. They found a significantly higher number of abnormalities in the exposed embryos than in the controls. A delay in development of the normal embryos in the exposed group was also seen, indicating that the electromagnetic fields interfere with the development of all embryos. Juutilainen et al. [8] found that weak magnetic fields - both sinusoidal, square and pulsed waveforms - may effect the development of chick embryo. Recently Siskens et al. [9], in their exposure of chick embryos to two different clinical type signals of electromagnetic fields, saw an increase in the percentage of abnormalities due to the exposure in each experiment, but the increase was not statistically significant.

The magnetic fields from VDTs have an asymmetrical, sawtooth waveform with a time derivative of the order of 100 - 500 mT/s at the position of the operator. It was therefore thought of interest to see whether such fields can influence the chick embryogenesis, and if so, give a clue to the mode of interaction, and hence be of value in the assessment of possible reproduction disturbances among VDT operators.

2. MATERIAL AND METHODS

2.1 Handling of the eggs

Freshly fertilized White Leghorn eggs were used in the experiments. The eggs were collected one day before the incubation started and stored at room temperature with the blunt end pointing west and their long axes in a horizontal direction. The last point ensures that the blastoderm gets on top of the yolk. The eggs were carefully moved to the incubator and placed in the same direction as before.

2.2 Exposure

The exposure took place in 8 identical coils, each made of 98 turns of 0.7 mm enamelled copper wire. The coils are 8.3 cm long and have a diameter of 6.0 cm, and they are fed from a signal generator and a P 2201 Yamaha power amplifier. In test 1 and 2, the coils are connected in parallel and the group of coils is connected in series with a 2.2 kΩ resistor, which is used for monitoring the current in the coils on an oscilloscope (Fig. 1A). For the highest intensity used, each coils was connected in series with a resistor (Fig. 1B).

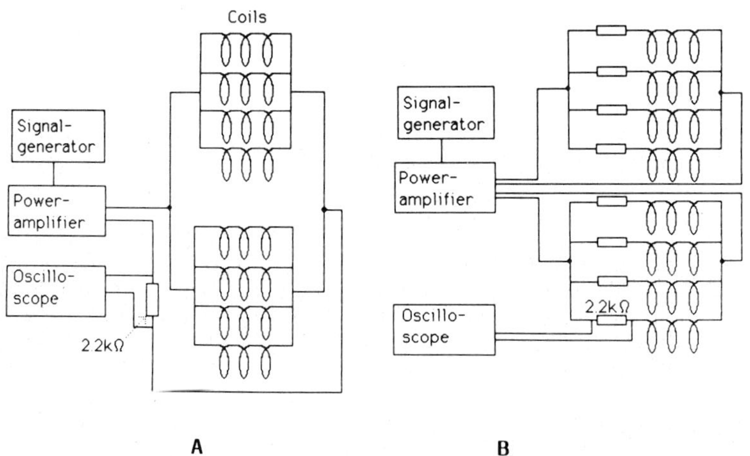

FIGURE 1 Schematic drawing of the electrical wiring. A: test 1 and 2, B: test 3.

Three different sequences of triangular pulses were used in the experiment (Fig. 2); the frequency was always 20 kHz, the rise time 45 μs and the fall time 5 μs, but the peak value of the magnetic flux density and the corresponding dB/dt were varied.

Both the controls and the exposed eggs were placed in the same incubator (TERMAX). This incubator, equipped with forced air, was rebuilt in order tc minimize the background field. The electric equipment was placed half a meter from the incubator chamber, and the fan was covered with magnetic shielding alloy in order to limit the 50 Hz background fields to a maximum of 0.1 μT. The temperature was kept at 38°C ± 0.2°C and the humidity at 75% ± 5%. These parameters were registered continously throughout the experiment.

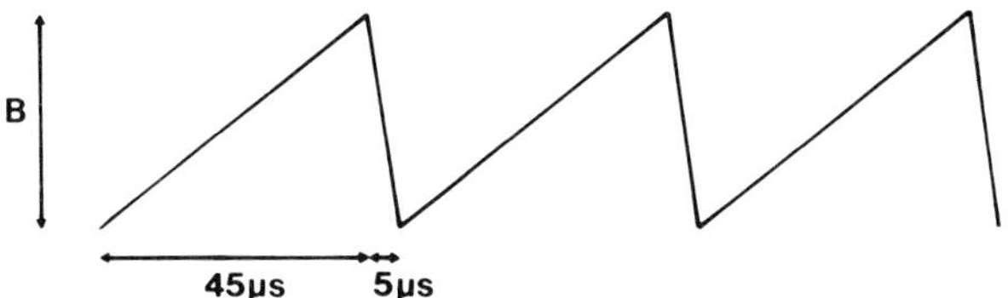

FIGURE 2 The sawtooth waveform used in the experiments. The peak value of the magnetic flux density (B) was in test 1; 0.1 µT, test 2; 1.5 µT, and in test 3; 16 µT. The corresponding time derivatives, dB/dt, were 0.03, 0.3 and 3.3 T/s, respectively.

2.3 Classification of the embryos

After a fixed incubation time the yolk with the blastoderm was immersed in warm (37^{0}C) Tyrode-solution. The blastoderm was cut out and held in a stretched position. The examination of the embryos was made with a binocular photo stereomicroscope. The development stage of each embryo was determined according to Hamburger & Hamilton [10]. The following systems were studied in detail for possible abnormalities: cephalic nervous system (CNS), trunk nervous system (TNS), heart, extra-embryonic vascularisation and somites (Fig 3).

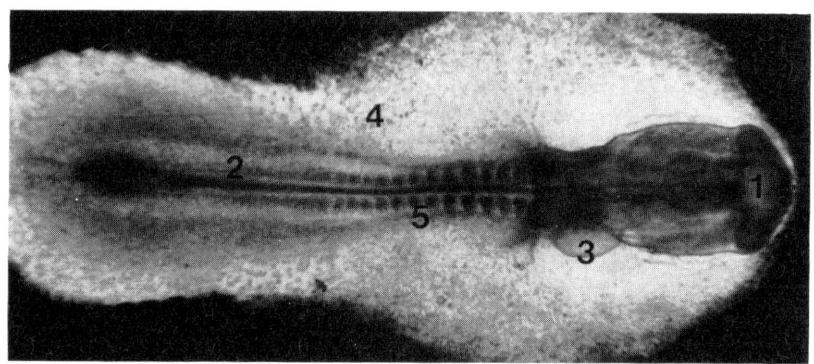

FIGURE 3 Normal embryo in stage 11 (H&H scale) with the five studied systems marked. (1) CNS; (2) TNS; (3) Heart; (4) Vasc. area; (5) somites.

Embryos which had not reached stage 4 (the definitive primitive streak stage) were classified as "nondeveloped". In test 1 and 2 the incubation time was 42 hours, and in test 3 47 hours. According to the H&H scale, normal embryos should under these circumstances reach stage 11 and 12, respectively. Embryos with a development delay of about 11 hours, i.e. having not reached stage 8 and 9^{-}, respectively, were classified as abnormal even if the morphological examination showed no abnormalities. Thus, if there is a development delay of at least 11 hours, or if there is a morphological alteration in any of the five systems, the embryo is classified as abnormal. The examinations were done blindly.

The incidence of abnormalities and non-development in the control groups is about 12%, if the eggs are treated and the embryos are studied as described above. Thus, in a studie which includes at least 30 embryos - control as well as exposed - for each test, it should be possible to detect an increase of about 30% of abnormalities due to the exposure with 95% chance (Mantel-Haenszel chi-square test).

3. RESULTS

Table 1 is a numerical survey of the experiments. No significant differences in the total number of abnormalities between the exposed embryos and the controls were found for any of the three intensities used (Table 2). In the test with the highest intensity there are nearly twice as many abnormal embryos in the exposed group as in the controls, but even that difference is far from statistically significant. There was also no difference between the normal exposed embryos and control embryos with respect to the stage reached after the incubation. There was a development delay of at least one stage for the abnormals, exposed as well as controls. The malformations were not concentrated to some particular structure, but were found in all studied systems (Table 3).

TABLE 1

Number of experiments and number of eggs in the different experimental series.

Test No.	1		2		3	
Experiments	6		8		7	
	Cont.	Exp.	Cont.	Exp.	Cont.	Exp.
No. of eggs	43	35	58	49	48	52
Invest. Embr.	39	31	52	41	37	39
Not Fertil.	1	1	1	3	5	6
Missed	3	3	5	5	6	7

TABLE 2

Total number of abnormalities and mean stage reached in the various experiments

Test No.	1		2		3	
	Cont.	Exp.	Cont.	Exp.	Cont.	Exp.
Total No of Embryos	39	31	52	41	37	39
Incubation time (h)	42		42		47	
Normal						
Number	34	27	46	39	32	32
%	87.2	87.1	88.5	95.1	86.4	82.1
Mean stage	11.2±1.0	11.0±0.9	11.3±1.0	11.1±1.1	12.4±0.9	12.5±0.9
Abnormal						
Number	4	4	4	2	3	6
%	10.3	12.9	7.7	4.9	8.1	15.4
Mean stage	10.0±0.7	10.6±2.6	10.0±0.7	7.0±0.0	10.3±0.3	10.8±2.7
Non-developed						
Number	1	0	2	0	2	1
%	2.6	-	3.8	-	5.4	2.5
Abnormal + ND						
Number	5	4	6	2	5	7
%	12.9	12.9	11.5	4.9	13.5	17.9

TABLE 3

Abnormalities in the various embryonal system studied.

Test No.	1		2		3	
	Cont.	Exp.	Cont.	Exp.	Cont.	Exp.
Total No. of Abn.Emb.	4	4	4	2	3	6
TNS	2	2	2	2	0	2
CNS	4	2	4	2	3	4
Heart	4	2	4	2	2	3
Vasc.Area	4	3	4	2	0	2
Somites	3	1	3	1	0	3

4. DISCUSSION

It is difficult to compare the various studies of chick embryogenesis under the influence of pulsed magnetic fields, since all experiments differ in one or more of the main physical parameters. For instance, in the studies of Juutilainen et al. [8] the eggs were placed standing with the blunt end up in a vertical magnetic field (Fig. 4). In the present study, and in the ones by Delgado et al. [6] and Ubeda et al. [7], the eggs were placed lying in a horizontal magnetic field. Maffeo et al. [11], in their attempt to replicate the Delgado study, placed several eggs in a long standing coil, but with the long axes of the eggs perpendicular to the magnetic field of the coil. The position of the eggs is not quite clear in the work by Siskens et al. [9].

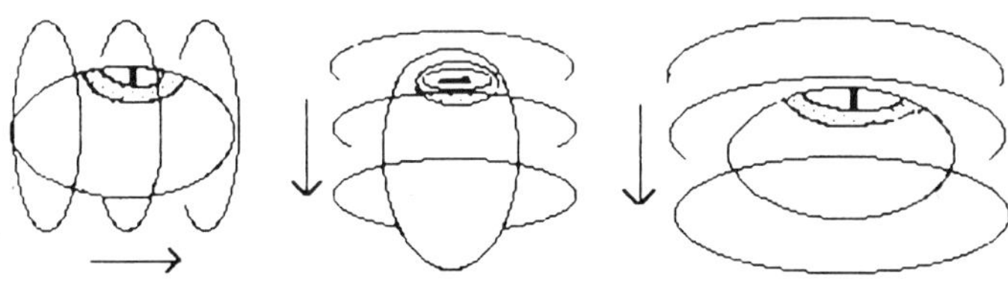

FIGURE 4 Different ways of placing the eggs in the coils. The direction of the magnetic field is pointed out. Position of the egg in the coil. (A), in the present study and the one by Ubeda et al. [6,7]; (B), the study by Juutilainen et al. [8]; (C), the study by Maffeo et al. [11].

It is known, that generally the embryo is oriented such that if one holds the egg with the blunt end to the left, the embryo in the egg will be found lying transversely to the long axes of the egg and with the head pointing away from the observer [12]. Thus, in all three exposure situations the magnitude and direction of the induced current passing the embryo is different. In the present study and in Delgado's work the induced current generally was directed along the long axis of the embryo. The exposure situation in the work of Maffeo et al. [11] and Juutilainen et al. [8] gave practically no current through the embryo. The frequency and the wave shapes used were different in the various studies.

In view of the fact that several of the reported bioeffects of weak electromagnetic fields exhibit both "intensity"- and "frequency-windows", the present result must be interpreted with caution and no far reaching conclusions should be drawn at this stage. In view of the findings of some laboratories, it is quite likely that other factors than the pulsed magnetic field are of importance for causing an effect on embryonal development. Among such factors investigators have pointed to the possible influence of a combination of the various electromagnetic fields present during exposure, i.e. the local geomagnetic field, the ambient 50/60 Hz electromagnetic field, and the pulsed magnetic field. We must await further investigations on the effects of magnetic fields on embryogenesis before these questions can be finally settled.

REFERENCES

[1] Aarholt,E., Flinn, E.A. and Smith C.W., Phys. Med. Biol. 26 (1981) 613.
[2] Greenebaum, B., Goodman, E.M. and Marron, M.T., Eur. J. Cell Biol. 27 (1982) 156.
[3] Basset, C.A., Calcif. Tissue Int. 34 (1982) 1.
[4] Dixey, R. and Rein, G., Nature 296 (1982) 253.
[5] Liboff, A.R., Williams, T., Strong, D.M. and Wistar, R., Science 223 (1984) 818.
[6] Delgado, J.M.R., Leal, J., Monteagudo, J.L. and Gracia, M., J. Anat. 134 (1982) 533.
[7] Ubeda, A., Leal, J., Trillo, M.A., Jimenez, M.A. and Delgado, J.M.R., J. Anat. 137 (1983) 513.
[8] Juutilainen, J., Harri, M., Saali, K. and Lahtinen, T., Radiat. Environ. Biophys. 25 (1986) 65.
[9] Sisken. B.F. and Fowler, J., J. Bioelectr. 5 (1986) 25.
[10] Hamburger, V., and Hamilton, H.L., J. Morphol. 88 (1951) 49.
[11] Maffeo, S., Miller, M.W., and Carstensen, E.L., J. Anat. 139 (1984) 613.
[12] Lillie, F.R., Development of the Chick, 3rd ed. (Hdt, 1952)

4. SKIN

WORK WITH DISPLAY UNITS 86
B. Knave and P.-G. Widebäck (eds.)

SOME PHYSICAL FACTORS AT VDT WORK STATIONS AND SKIN PROBLEMS

Ulf Bergqvist, Roger Wibom and Per Nylén

Occupational Neuromedicine
National Board of Occupational Safety and Health
S-171 84 Solna, Sweden.

Skin problems have been reported by some VDT operators. Investigations and the debate concerned with these skin problems have partly been centered on certain physical factors present at VDT work stations, viz. electrostatic fields and ultraviolet radiation. These factors are reviewed in this paper, largely based on an epidemiological study of office workers in Stockholm. Indications exist concerning a possible influence of the operator's potential on some skin problems, that warrant further investigations. The electrostatic fields from the VDT have not been shown to be involved, however. Ultraviolet radiation from VDTs is insignificant, and does not constitute a possible factor for skin damage.

1. INTRODUCTION

Electrostatic fields occur at many VDT work stations. Their involvement in the development of skin disorders among VDT operators have been suggested (1, 2). A few diagnosed cases of actinic elastosis among VDT operators have raised questions concerning ultraviolet radiation at VDT work stations.

Thus, a description of these phenomena and their possible relationships to skin problems is warranted.

2. GENERAL DESCRIPTION OF THE ELECTROSTATIC FIELDS

The electrostatic field component from the VDT is due to the acceleration potential applied to a metallic layer inside of the phosphorous material in the screen tube. In cases where the conductivity of the screen front is sufficiently low, this potential will be manifested outside of the VDT as an electrostatic field. The temporal appearance of this field is shown in figure 1.

Factors influencing the field strength are 1/ screen construction factors, such as acceleration voltage, inherent conductivity of surface/glass material, applied conductive layer (if any) and ground connection, and 2/ atmospheric conditions such as humidity and counter charges. We interpret the gradual decrease of the field strength to accummulation of counter charges (note also residual after switch off, figure 1), and possibly also a formation of a charge barrier against further accumulation.

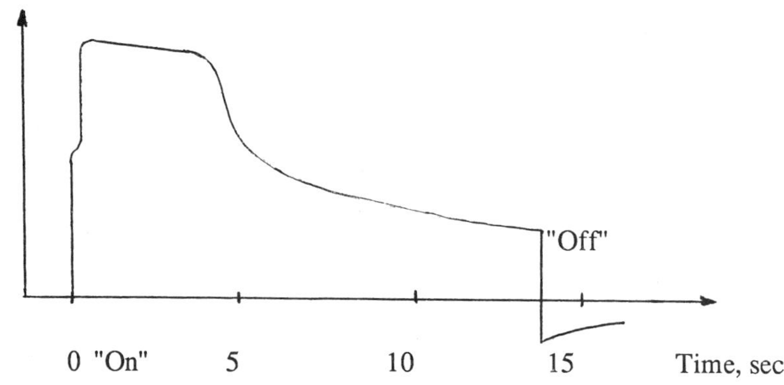

FIGURE 1
The temporal appearance of the electrostatic field from a VDT.

Humidity will also strongly affect the field strength - by changing the conductivity of the screen surface. In a series of experiments, applying distilled water to the surface effectively eliminated the electrostatic field for a short time; in moderately dry conditions, water applied by a spray bottle reduced the field by at least 90% during some 30 minutes.

The electrostatic field component due to the electrostatic charge of the operator is due to factors such as clothing, movements, air humidity, floor material etc.

3. MEASURING TECHNIQUES OF ELECTROSTATIC FIELDS

Different measuring techniques have been used to characterize electrostatic fields at VDT work stations. For the electrostatic field from the VDT, a field mill has often been used, e.g. by Cato Olsen (1) and by us (4). This field mill may be placed at varying distances from the VDT screen, and may also be placed adjacent to a larger, grounded metal plate, comparable to the technique suggested by Harvey (3). Preliminary measurements made by the authors suggest that introducing the metal plate will decrease the recorded field by about a factor two (at 10 cm measuring distance), and will also drastically reduce disturbances due to other objects in the vicinity.

Important factors are thus the measuring distances and the field distortions due to the field mill (with or without a metal plate) and other objects. Results must be expressed in relation to these data, to a calculated "unperturbed" field situation or as a corresponding potential of the screen surface. A suggested measuring technique is to place the field mill with a grounded metal plate or sheet parallell to the screen at a close distance, and then calculate the approximate average potential by treating the recorded field as a homogenuous one. (Some direct measurement of the screen potential indicate that this potential is not uniform across the screen, variations in potential of a factor two or more may appear, measured in dry conditions.)

For the electrostatic charge/potential of the operator, direct measurements by applying an electrode to e. g. the wrist appear feasible (5), although other techniques have also been used, such as measuring the field between the operator (connected to "ground" on the field mill) and a grounded metal plate (1, and our study 4). Humidity, clothing, body movements and presence of discharge possibilities (through keyboard, floor material etc) are important factors. Local variations in the field at different points of e. g. the face are also of interest, but require different measuring techniques.

4. RELATIONSHIPS BETWEEN THE DIFFERENT FIELD COMPONENTS

The "total" field between the VDT and the operator is then the sum of these (and other) field components. These fields are however not identical to those measured, since the presence of the operator will perturb the field from the VDT etc. Various methods can be used to overcome this problem, such as calculations based on the potentials of the VDT and the operator (our study, 4), simulation of the situation by a dummy operator (3) etc. For detailed examination of the field in the vicinity of e g the face, the second method appear best suited.

We have also investigated the possibility that working with a VDT having an electrostatic field could influence the electrostatic charge of the operator: In an experimental setup, 14 subjects were asked to perform identical tasks in four settings: 1/ working in front of a VDT based on CRT technique with a moderate electrostatic field, 2/ working in front of the same VDT, where the electrostatic field was eliminated, 3/ working in front of a VDT based on LCD technique (without any field) and 4/ working with only a keyboard. Activities which included increased movements were also included; 5/ writing on paper, 6/ rubbing the chair and 7/ walking. Results are shown in table 1.

No significant differences in the operators´ electrostatic potential were found due to these variations. For half, activities with paper and pen caused the highest mean potential (compared to various keyboard activities). Activities with more movements caused larger variations in body potentials. Thus, the electrostatic field from the VDT does not appear to influence body potentials. It is however possible that decreased movements (as found in VDT vs non-VDT jobs), as well as availability of grounded objects (keyboards) may influence the operators' potential.

TABLE 1. 14 operators' potential while performing various activities. All tests made the same day, room humidity 35%.

	Activity (see above for explanation)						
	CRT+ field 1/	CRT no field 2/	LCD 3/	Key- board 4/	Paper 5/	Rub- bing 6/	Wal- king 7/
Average mean potential	-12 V	-10 V	+4 V	-8 V	-6 V		
Number of subjects with highest mean in this activity	2	1	3	1	7		
Average range of potential	11 V	7 V	15 V	10 V	49 V	110 V	440 V

5. AN INVESTIGATION OF A LARGE NUMBER OF VDT WORK STATIONS

In conjunction with a large investigation of VDT work and health, 391 VDT work stations were investigated as to electrostatic fields due to VDTs and electrostatic charges on the operators (4). Both measurements used a field mill, and recorded the fields from the VDT and the operator, respectively, at a specific distance. (See discussion above.)

The electrostatic fields from the VDTs were measured by a field mill at varying distances. Recalculating the results to screen potentials, those were found to vary between 0 and 9 kV. (Comparable results have been obtained from other investigators, average values in these varied between 1.5 and 4.4 kV (1, 3, 6), for a review see (7).) Considerable differences between VDTs of different makes were also found. Humidity was recorded at the same time.

The body potentials of the operators were measured by using a field mill and a grounded metal plate. In terms of calculated body potentials, the average potential was -5 V for VDT operators, and -40 V for controls.

An estimate of the resultant field between the VDT and the operator (excluding areas close to each object) was of the order of 0 to about 15 kV/m (4).

In terms of transport velocities of aerosol size particles (0.03-1 um aerodynamic diameter), these fields do not appear to cause significant transport of such particles; a few mm/s compared to recorded air velocities in our study of about 100 mm/s. It has been suggested by Ungethüm (8), that in such circumstances, local conditions at the surface may be more important in determining charged particle deposition than the total field. (The terminal transport velocity is much higher for air ions, some m/s, and conceivably also for extremely highly unicharged heavy particles.)

6. CORRELATIONS WITH DIFFERENT SKIN DISORDERS

All participants in our study (4) reported whether they experienced skin troubles or not in a questionnaire. These responses were compared to measured VDT electrostatic fields and operators' potential, with the following results (table 2):

TABLE 2. Correlations between self-reported skin problems and some electrostatic phenomena (391 operators).

	Operator's potential	Electrostatic field from VDT
Skin problems		
- All operators	0.00	0.01
- Female operators	0.07	0.01

Thus, there was no significant correlation between measured values for electrostatic fields from the VDTs or for electrostatic charges of the operator and self-reported skin discomforts.

All participants who reported skin problems were offered a medical examination. In all, 57 cases were fully examined, and diagnoses were grouped into four groups. In none of the groups were there any correlations with electrostatic fields from VDTs. One diagnosis group - acne, rosacea and perioral dermatitis - did however have electrostatic charges that differed significantly from the other groups . The interpretation of this finding is not clear (9).

(A note on humidity is in order. The questionnaire data included questions of skin troubles at the same day as the field measurements. These responses did not differ from the more long-range questions already discussed. Thus, humidity, while important for electrostatic fields, are implicitly included in the data. The medical examinations were however performed on another day, and for these data, humidity may be a confounding factor.)

It is noticable, that the average electrostatic charges of some reported cases of skin disorders among VDT operators were quite high compared to the average levels found e.g. in our study (-600 volt in (1) compared to - 5 volt in our study). In one case (MB), the following potentials were noted: While using the keyboard 0 volt, working at the desk -300 volt and walking on the floor (wool carpet) -3000 volt.

Elimination of causes of sustained electrostatic charges of the operators have often proved effective in preventing rash outbreaks (2), but this has not been invariantly true. One such self-reported case is presented:

A 43 year old woman, who worked 17 years in the same building, the last 3-4 years with a VDT - word processing full day, varied workload.Skin troubles appeared since the outset of VDT work (self-reported): Itching, reddening and desquamation starting Tuesday or Wednesday.

Grounded mesh filter on VDT, replacement of carpeting, and air conditioning including raising humidity gave some temporary improvements only. After vacation summer 1985 problems reappeared in strength. The woman applied a grounded bracelet, which coincided with the disappearance of the skin rashes. In April 1986, skin rashes reappeared, she noted broken connection between bracelet and ground, reestablished the connection, whereupon problems again disappeared.

Measurements made in April 1986 with 40-50% humidity. VDT screen 10-15 volt, screen with grounded mesh filter 0 volt. Operator potential peaked at +200 volt during movements. No peaks when bracelet applied. In another room with wall-to-wall carpet and lower humidity, peaks were noted at -4000 volt.

7. ULTRAVIOLET RADIATION FROM VDTs AND SKIN DISORDERS

Ultraviolet (UV) radiation in the region 315-400 nm (UV_A) can frequently be detected from VDTs, but only at very low levels compared to existing occupational health limits and to those of other sources: In our study (4), we measured UV_A levels in offices with detector aimed both towards ceiling and towards VDTs. The results show that the average levels of UV_A-radiation in VDT-offices were some 0.04 W/m^2, compared to 0.13 W/m^2 in offices without VDTs. The differences are presumably caused by the darker rooms of VDT offices. Both levels are insignificant compared to (Swedish) occupational health standard of 10 W/m^2, and to levels encountered outdoors.

In addition, the levels of UV_A-radiation was not correlated with skin problems, neither self-reported nor diagnosed by the dermatologists (4, 9).

One case (MB, referred to above) has been diagnosed by one physician as having "actinic elastosis", which is 'normally caused by UV radiation'. We have measured UV_A-levels at her working place, and found some 0.009 W/m^2 (towards VDT) and 1-7 W/m^2 (towards windows, sunny day, with/without blinds).If the diagnosis and its connection with UV radiation is correct, then this disorder is clearly not connected with the VDT.

Ultraviolet radiation of shorter wavelengths (UV_{BC}, 200-315 nm) have been detected e g by us using a field instrument. Rechecking these readings with other instruments, it was apparent that these readings represent an artefact, due to the fact that the instrument, when set for UV_{BC} readings, was also sensitive to UV_A and to visible light. With more appropriate instrumentation, no UV_{BC} -radiation from VDTs was found.

8. CONCLUSIONS AND DISCUSSION

These electrostatic fields are discussed primarily in the context of skin disorders among VDT operators. It should be pointed out that a relationship between skin disorders and VDT work factors, although suggested in a few studies and by some case reports, is by no means established.

Those studies described above do indicate that the electrostatic charge of the operators may be a factor related to certain skin disorders. It should however be noted that such a relationship can only be considered as a working hypothesis, since 1/ a confounding effect of skin disorders - low humidity - high electrostatic charges is also feasible, and 2/ the observations made in our study were not the result of investigation of an a priory hypothesis. Further studies are warranted.

On the other hand, our study does not support the suggestion that electrostatic fields from VDTs are linked to skin disorders. (Likewise, we are not aware of any study that does show such a relationship.) Thus, in our opinion, there is no justification (from these points) to promote the use of grounded mesh filters to eliminate the electrostatic fields from VDTs.

Ultraviolet radiation from VDTs can not be considered a viable cause of skin disorders among VDT operators.

9. REFERENCES

1. Cato Olsen W. Electric field enhanced aerosol exposure in visual display unit environments. Chr Michelsen Institute, Bergen 1981 (CMI 803604-1).
2. Lindén V, Rolfsen S. Video computer terminals and occupational dermatitis. Scand J Work Environ Health 7 (1981) 62-63.
3. Harvey SM. Electric-field exposure of persons using video display units. Bioelectromagnetics 5 (1984) 1-12.
4. Knave BG, Wibom RI, Bergqvist UOV, Carlsson LLW, Levin MIB, Nylén PR. Work at video display terminals. An epidemiological health investigation of office employees. II. Physical exposure factors. Scand J Work Environ Health 11 (1985) 467-474.

5. Ancker K, Bjurström R, Göthe C-J, Holms S, Langworth S. Electrostatic charge in office environments. In: Proceedings of the 3rd International Conference on Indoor Air Quality and Climate, Stockholm August 20-24 1984. Volume 3. Swedish Council for Building Research, Stockholm 1984, pp 157-162.
6. Paulsson LE, Kristiansson I, Malmström I. Strålning från dataskärmar, arbetsdokument a 84-08 (Radiation from VDTs, in Swedish) Statens Strålskyddsinstitut, Stockholm 1984.
7. The use of visual display terminals. WHO 1986 (in press).
8. Ungethüm E. Elektrostatiska fält i närheten av dataskärmar och dess betydelse för transport av luftburen förorening (Electrostatic fields in the vicinity of VDTs and their importance for the transport of air contaminants, in Swedish). Resumé, 33 Nordiske yrkeshygieniske möte. Yrkeshygienisk institutt, Oslo 1984, p 17.
9. Lidén C, Wahlberg JE. Work at video display terminals. An epidemological health investigation of office employees. V. Dermatologic factors. Scand J Work Environ Health 11 (1985) 489-493.

WORK WITH DISPLAY UNITS 86
B. Knave and P.-G. Widebäck (eds.)

FACIAL PARTICLE EXPOSURE IN THE VDU ENVIRONMENT: THE ROLE OF STATIC ELECTRICITY

WALTER C. WEDBERG*

Chr. Michelsen Institute
N-5036 Fantoft/Bergen, Norway.

Electrostatic charging of the human body creates an electric field in the vicinity of the face. The existence of such fields leads to an increase in the facial deposition of charged aerosol particles. It is suggested that this phenomenon explains a certain type of skin rash that occurs among VDU operators.

1. INTRODUCTION

In an earlier study done at Chr. Michelsen Institute (CMI) it was shown that high levels of static electricity in the office environment could lead to a substantial increase in the facial deposition of airborne particles [1]. It was suggested that such particle exposure could be the cause of certain facial rashes experienced by some visual display unit (VDU) operators [2].

The original study left several important aspects of the exposure phenomenon unresolved. Therefore, a follow-up research programme was initiated at CMI in 1985, to be completed in the spring of 1987. The programme is divided into several parts, the most important of which are:

(1) A comprehensive study of the electrostatic phenomena that lead to enhanced facial depositions.

(2) A more detailed evaluation of the deposition process itself, and of the particulate species that participate in the process, under various environmental conditions.

(3) A series of provocation experiments aimed at demonstrating directly the link between electric field enhanced particle exposure and the occurrence of facial rash, if such a link does exist.

The most essential findings of the original study and some preliminary results of the present programme are reported here. Also included is a discussion on how these results relate to other, recently reported research in this field.

2. ORIGINAL RASH EPISODES

Out of a total of about 35 reports of VDU-associated rashes received by the Norwegian Labour Inspectorate in 1979/80, twelve cases in the Bergen area were selected for a closer dermatological evaluation. For six of these no cause could be identified, except that the problems appeared to be work-related. The clinical picture of these skin rashes has been de-

---

*formerly: Walter Cato Olsen

scribed elsewhere [2]. In that publication the rash episodes themselves were characterized as follows:

"There was agreement among the patients as to the time periods when the rash occurred, and as to the correlation between facial rash, low relative humidity (recorded by the employees as low as 20%) and troublesome electrostatic phenomena. All reported itching or a tingling sensation in the affected skin areas, and the rash was mainly localised to the zygomatic region. The rash was not consistent with rosacea or perioral dermatitis, and allergic contact dermatitis seems to be excluded."

A subsequent survey of environmental conditions in the rash-affected areas established that (a) the aerosol mass concentrations were normal, (b) the voltage levels of the VDU's present were similar to those found in other VDU environments, and (c) the state of charge of the operators themselves was unusually high.

On the basis of these observations it was proposed that the rashes were caused by a facial deposition of charged particles. This hypothesis was supported by the following known characteristics of aerosol particles in the size range 0.1 - 1 μm (μm = micrometers): (a) typical urban concentrations are of the order of 10^3 - 10^4 particles/cm^3, (b) most of these particles carry an electric charge, (c) such charged particles may attain velocities in the range 0.2 - 4 mm/sec under the influence of ambient electrostatic fields, and (d) particles of this size are likely to adhere if impacting on a solid surface.

By the time the original CMI study got under way, the series of rash outbreaks among the six patients referred to above had subsided. The reason for this is believed to be that various measures had already been taken to avoid the problem, the most important of which was a reduction in the time allowed for VDU work.

3. STATIC ELECTRICITY IN THE VDU ENVIRONMENT

A number of surveys have shown that VDU's commonly exhibit high positive potentials at the viewing surface. About 1/3 of the office VDU's that have been investigated by CMI over the last few years have been charged to potentials above +3000 volts. These potentials develop as a result of a positive electric voltage applied to the inner, phosphor-coated surface of the VDU screen. If not shielded, this internal voltage will create a strong electric field in front of the unit as depicted in figure 1a.

The effective potential of an activated VDU may at any given time be different from (that is, lower than) the internally applied voltage because of charge accumulation on the outer surface of the screen. Sufficient negative charge may accrue to completely counteract the applied voltage, in which case no external field will exist, as illustrated in figure 1b. Such neutralized VDU's are commonly referred to as "uncharged", even though charge actually does reside on the outer surface of the units.

The electrostatic condition of a VDU can be determined with a field meter, which is an instrument that registers the charge induced on a grounded sensor held in the proximity of the screen as shown in figure 1c.

In office environments neutralizing charge may to some extent be supplied to the VDU screen by the surrounding air. However, a transport of charge along the screen surface will normally be more important. Such charge transport may be induced by treating the surface with "antistatic"

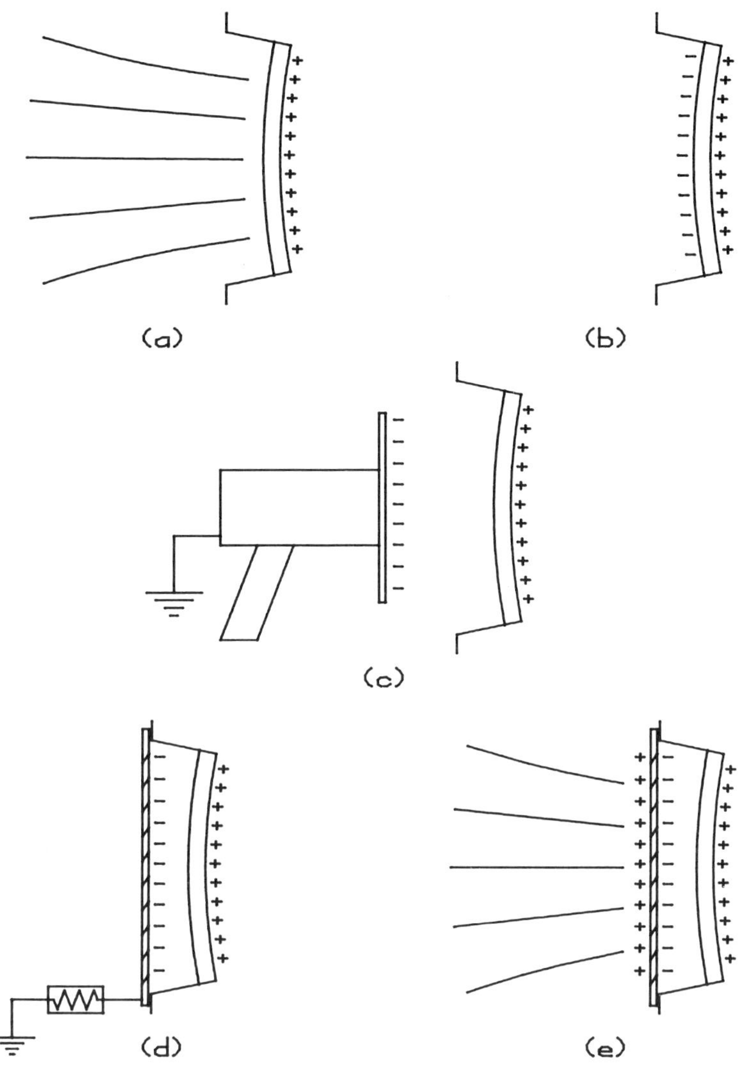

FIGURE 1
Various electrostatic conditions of a VDU: (a) external field created by the high voltage on the inside of the VDU screen ("charged" VDU), (b) external field neutralized by accumulated charge on the screen surface ("uncharged" VDU), (c) field meter measurement of effective screen potential, (d) and (e) effect of using an antistatic raster with, and without a ground connection, respectively.

agents, which are chemicals that temporarily improve the surface conductivity. An external electric field may also be neutralized by mounting a grounded, conductive screen in front of the VDU as shown in figure 1d. (A series resistance is usually incorporated in the grounding cable to protect personnel from electric shocks.) Without a ground connection such antistatic screens may not function as intended, in that there is no guarantee that the required (net) accumulation of charge will occur (figure 1e).

Over the last 25 years, electrostatic charging of the human body has been the subject of many investigations, and a number of causes have been identified. It is CMI's experience that two charge-generating activities dominate in the VDU environment, one being walking on insulating floor coverings, while the other is the rubbing of garments against the upholstery of chairs. Both these charging mechanisms may lead to body potentials of several thousand volts, especially if the ambient humidity is low. (The level below which problems may arise is often quoted to be about 30% RH, but for a given environment the actual level will depend on the electric properties of the specific clothes, upholstery and floor coverings used.)

Changes in working posture during operation of the VDU may cause these body potentials to increase further, due to corresponding changes in the electrical capacitance to ground. This situation is illustrated in figure 2, which shows the result of monitoring the voltage of a human subject during some typical office activities.

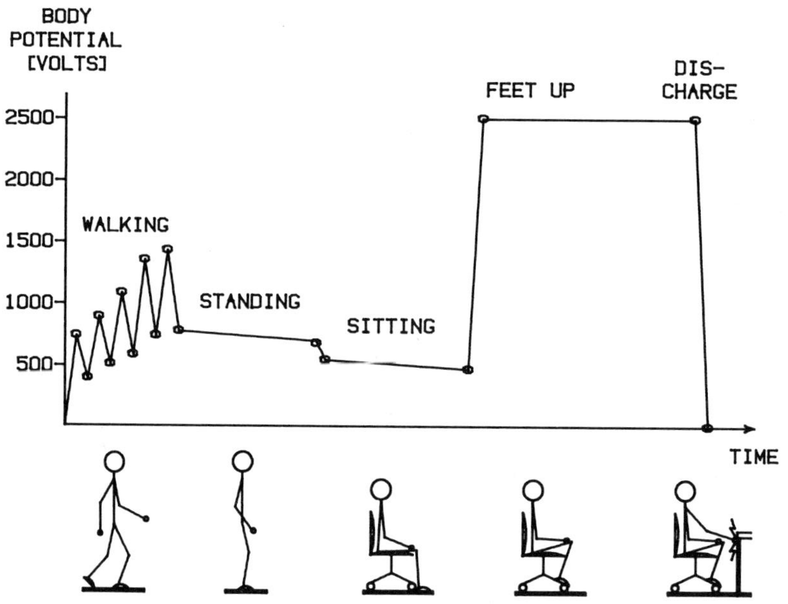

FIGURE 2
Body voltage variations of human subject in a carpeted office at an ambient relative humidity of 40%.

First, charge is being picked up by the body as the subject walks on the carpeted floor. When the subject stops, and subsequently sits down on a chair, the acquired body voltage slowly decreases because charge is dissipating through the shoe soles. At some instant the subject pulls his or her feet up under the chair, however, with the result that the body potential increases several-fold (due entirely to changes in capacitance). Since the chair in this case is equipped with insulating rollers, further dissipation of charge is prevented, and the elevated body potential is sustained until the subject at some later time touches a nearby conducting object and thereby causes a rapid discharge.

On a theoretical basis it can be estimated that body potentials in the range 5000 to 10 000 volts (which are not uncommon in areas where static electricity is a problem) may result in electric field intensities in the vicinity of the face of 500-1000 volts/cm. These values have been confirmed by laboratory measurements using the special experimental arrangement shown in figure 3. This setup differs from an ordinary field measurement in that an electric potential (equal to the body voltage of interest) is applied to the field meter, which in this case is provided with a hemispherical sensor serving as a model of the human head.

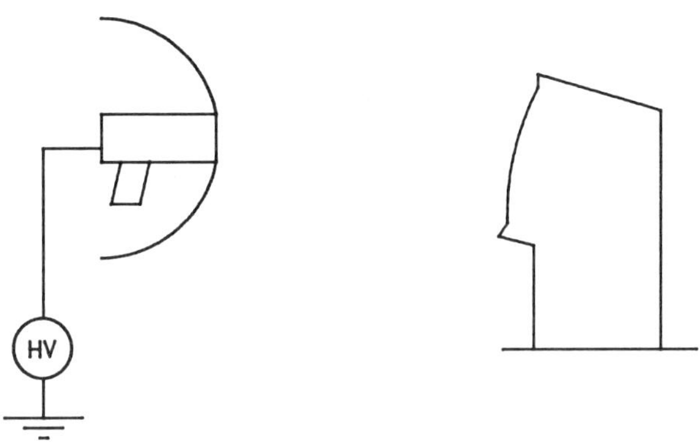

FIGURE 3
Measuring the electrostatic field at the surface of a charged hemisphere serving as a model of a VDU operator's head.

Such model measurements have also been used to determine to what extent a charged VDU influences an electric field of the noted magnitude near a charged human body. It is found that for VDU potentials up to 10 000 volts, at a distance of 60 cm (i.e. typical working distance), the induced changes are no more than 20%, the actual amount being dependent upon charge polarities and work-station lay-out. It thus appears that operator charge is much more important than VDU charge in causing increased particle exposure in office environments.

4. ELECTRIC FIELD ENHANCED PARTICLE DEPOSITION

The preliminary survey did not reveal any unusual ambient particle concentrations in the rash-affected areas. However, as stated earlier, the number of submicron particles in the air is substantial even under normal environmental conditions. Since most of these particles carry a charge, the number of particles that will be influenced by an electrostatic field will also be large.

In order to establish to what extent a field in front of a VDU operator causes particles to precipitate on the skin, deposits were collected on substrates attached directly to the face of charged human subjects. The deposition rate was determined by subsequently analyzing the precipitates in a scanning electron microscope.

By means of this procedure it was established that the facial deposition of aerosol particles indeed increases in the presence of an electric field outside the human body. Particle deposition rates of the order 1000 particles per square millimetre per hour of exposure have been registered with moderately high body charge levels. Under conditions of extreme electric fields, deposition rates in excess of 10 000 part./mm^2/hr have been measured, whereas the rates in the absence of a field appears to be of the order 100 part./mm^2/hr. (It is not known what particle deposition rates are in effect during actual rash episodes.)

The measurements show that particles deposit on the nose as well as on the cheeks. Thus, the fact that rashes are not observed on the nose cannot be explained by any lack of exposure in this region. Recent measurements have also shown that the rate of deposition in the face is similar to that on an equivalently charged metal hemisphere of radius 11 cm, serving as a model of the human head.

As far as particle counts are concerned, the increase in deposition appears to be associated primarily with the submicron aerosol fraction. Recent results have suggested, however, that although few in number, larger particles may contribute significantly to the deposited mass. Nevertheless, it is to be emphasized that the total mass collected on the cheeks is quite small, being only a few micrograms per hour of exposure.

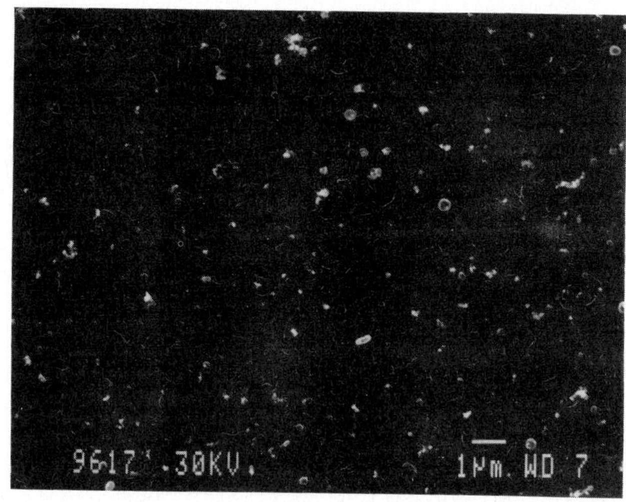

FIGURE 4
Particles collected in a VDU environment under the influence of an electric field for a period of about one month. The photograph was taken with a scanning electron microscope at a magnification of 4500X.

Figure 4 is a scanning electron micrograph showing a particle deposit collected over a period of about one month. The resulting particle density is of the order of 10^6 part./mm^2, and it can be noted that even with this extreme loading of the substrate, the deposited particles do not form a continous layer.

A limited x-ray fluorescence analysis of a long-term particle deposit in one affected area indicated that the elements sulphur and chlorine may be concentrated in the submicron fraction [1]. These elements are common constituents of the general outdoor aerosol in the coastal regions of Southern Norway.

5. RELATED RESEARCH

In some recent investigations various types of employee discomforts, including skin disorders, have been compared with specific physical exposure factors in the work environment, among these static electricity [3,4,5,6,7,8]. Although not in conflict with the CMI-findings, the results of these studies do not lend support to the particle exposure hypothesis. A number of reasons for this discrepancy may be suggested, some of which have already been noted in the reports referred to.

(1) The proportion of VDU workers (and other office employees) that report skin discomforts in response to questionnaires is usually quite large, typically in the range 30-70%. It is believed that most of these complaints are related to other factors than the electrostatic conditions of the workplace. The fraction that may be so related, if any at all, may be so small that it will not show up in the statistics of a survey unless all skin disorders for which other explanations are more likely, are treated separately.

(2) In the CMI hypothesis, a necessary condition for a significant increase in particle exposure is that a relatively high electrostatic field is present in front of the face during a significant part of the working day. If this hypothesis is to be tested therefore, the anticipated, if not proven, existence of such fields will have to become the major criterion for selecting the "exposed" group. As pointed out in section 3 before, to demonstrate the presence of such fields is a far from trivial task, in that the relevant measurement parameters (whether these be charge, voltage or field intensity) will vary throughout the day along with the movements of the operator. It may be sufficient in an epidemiological investigation, however, to ascertain that the selected operators frequently carry high body charges while the survey is being made.

(3) Although its significance cannot be excluded, the VDU itself does not appear to be of major importance in the selection of an "exposed" group. It is to be recommended that much more emphasis be put on the prevailing ambient humidity and the electrostatic properties of furniture and floor coverings in the environment in question.

(4) Little is known about the chemical composition of the ambient aerosol during rash episodes. The possibility cannot be excluded, therefore, that specific outdoor and/or indoor air pollutants may play a significant role in the development of these rashes.

As indicated by the discussion above, a number of factors may be involved in the generation of the observed facial rashes and thus may have to be taken into account if this phenomenon is to be studied in depth. A listing of factors hitherto identified by CMI, is presented in table 1.

TABLE 1
Factors that may influence the development of skin rashes associated with exposure to charged particles in office environments.

Primary factors	Related factors
body charge level	pattern of movement ambient humidity electrostatic properties of furniture, carpets, VDU keyboard, etc.
body capacitance	posture nature of shoe soles, foot rest, chair rollers, etc.
extraneous fields	charged VDU electrical equipment
aerosol concentration and composition	indoor/outdoor pollution sources air ventilation/filtration
aerosol state of charge	ion sources and sinks
operator susceptibility	skin sensitivity cleanliness/use of cosmetics

6. CONCLUDING REMARKS

In the time that has passed since the original CMI study was completed few formal reports of rash episodes have been received by the Norwegian health authorities. A possible reason for this apparent reduction in the frequency of incidences may be suggested.

The original series of rash reports came at a time when the subject of alleged radiation hazards of VDU's was a public issue, with frequent coverage in the news media. No doubt, this inspired many anxious VDU operators to report any work-related outbreak of skin rashes. However, many studies have since refuted these allegations, or as in the case of the work at CMI, have pointed to other, less alarming explanations for this phenomenon. The progress that have been made over the last few years is known to have reduced operator anxiety considerably. Thus, the incentive to formally report rash occurrences may to a large extent have been removed.

The lack of formal reports notwithstanding, the epidemiological studies quoted above show that a high percentage of office employees experiences skin-related discomforts, so there is no reason to believe the problem has been eliminated. A number of identified cases of skin disorders are being registered as part of the research programme presently in progress at CMI. These will be further evaluated, for the purpose of possibly including them in future provocation experiments.

REFERENCES

[1] Cato Olsen, W., Electric field enhanced particle exposure in visual display unit environments (Report no. 803604-1, Chr. Michelsen Institute, Bergen, Norway, 1981)

[2] Nilsen, A., Contact Dermatitis 8 (1982) 25

[3] Ancker, K., Bjurström, R., Göthe, C-J., Holm, S. and Langworth, S., Electrostatic charge in office environments, in: Proceedings of the 3rd International Conference on Indoor Air Quality and Climate, Stockholm, August 20-24 1984, Volume 3 (Swedish Council for Building Research, Stockholm, 1984) pp 157-162

[4] Nylén, P., Bergqvist, U., Wibom, R. and Knave, B, Physical and Chemical Environment at VDT Work Stations: Air Ions, Electrostatic Fields and PCBs, in: Proceedings of the 3rd International Conference on Indoor Air Quality and Climate, Stockholm, August 20-24 1984, Volume 3 (Swedish Council for Building Research, Stockholm, 1984) pp 163-167

[5] Bergqvist, U.O.V., Video Display Terminals and Health: A Technical and Medical Appraisal of the State of the Art, Scan J Work Environ Health 10, suppl 2, (1984) pp. 1-87

[6] Knave, B.G., Wibom, R.I., Voss, M., Hedström, L.D. and Bergquist, U.O.V., Scan J Work Environ Health 11 (1985) 457

[7] Knave, B.G., Wibom, R.I., Bergqvist, U.O., Carlsson, L.L.W., Levin, M.I.B. and Nylén, P.R., Scan J Work Environ Health 11 (1985) 467

[8] Lidén, C. and Wahlberg, J.E., Scan J Work Environ Health 11 (1985) 489

WORK WITH DISPLAY UNITS 86
B. Knave and P.-G. Wideback (eds.)

A ROSACEA-LIKE SKIN RASH IN VDU-OPERATORS

Berndt STENBERG

Department of Dermatology, University of Umeå,
S-901 85 Umeå, Sweden

Following the introduction of VDU-work in an office adjacent to a paper pulp mill, nine of the fourteen VDU-operators have developed facial skin complaints. Five of them suffered from skin rash with clinical and histological signs of rosacea, three had facial erythema and one sensory symptoms only. All nine workers suffered from itching, burning and swelling of the skin on cheeks, forehead and chin. Two of fourteen workers, not engaged in VDU-work, reported slight symptoms of the same kind. When terminating VDU-work it was observed that most of the visible rash diminished.

In skin biopsies the degree of elastosis was evaluated. Patch tests for delayed and immediate hypersensitivity as well as photoallergy have so far all been negative. Indoor air factors such as concentration of air ions, radon daughters, formaldehyde and terpenes have been analyzed and found to be within normal limits.

Volatile and particle bound indoor air pollutants in the office have been found to be considerably higher than what was found in a reference office in the same city. The electrostatic field from the screen used (IBM 3180) is known to be quite high and antistatic screens used were shown to have lost their function, probably because of improper handling. Still measurements undertaken to minimize the effect of electrostatic fields have not been able to stop recurrencies of the skin rash. Though not fully explained there seems to be an obvious relation between VDU-work and the skin rash. At present the deteriorating effects of indoor air particles and volatile substances are being studied.

1. INTRODUCTION

Very soon after the introduction of display units in an office building belonging to a paper pulp mill, nine of fourteen operators reported facial skin symptoms. The first case was reported in late autumn 1984. This is a report of the findings at clinical and technical investigations carried out so far.

Hitherto skin complaints related to VDU-work have rarely been reported. In 1981 some cases of facial dermatitis related to VDU-work were reported from Bergen, Norway [1]. In a recent Swedish study a relationship between rosacea and VDU-work was suggested [2]. Though sporadic cases of VDU-related dermatitis formerly had been admitted to our clinic this outbreak came as quite a surprise.

Cato Olsen has suggested an explanation to the formerly mentioned cases of facial rash reported from Norway. He suggests that electrostatic fields from the VDU screens increase the deposition of indoor air pollutants in the faces of the operators and in such a way causes skin irritation [3]. This explains why we have focused our interest on indoor air-borne factors.

2. MATERIAL AND METHODS

The workplace is a brick building adjacent to a paper pulp mill that produces mechanical and chemo-mechanical pulp.

At the time of the investigation the office had 28 employees. Fourteen of these had for a different period of time been engaged in VDU-work. They all had a positive attitude towards VDU work at the beginning and all were formerly healthy regarding relevant skin diseases.

The mill is located in Umeå in the northern part of Sweden. The climatic conditions in this region are characterized by cold dry air during wintertime. The average outdoor temperature in January is -9.7 ^{o}C and the relative humidity at 20 ^{o}C indoor is only 10%.

Though the city of Umeå is not a heavily polluted town several air pollutants are found e.g. sulphur dioxide, nitrogen oxides, hydrocarbones, chlorophenols and chlorobenzenes, phtalates, hydrochloric acid, dioxines and dibenzofurans. All of these are below existing safety limits. These air pollutants are produced by cars and oil burning but most of them are emitted by a central refuse disposal unit.

Chemical substances are added into the process of producing paper pulp. The function of the substances is mainly to break down the wood fibers (caustic soda, silicate of soda and lime), to chelate undesired metals (DTPA) and finally to bleech the pulp (hydroperoxide). It is reasonable to believe that some of these substances leave the mill through the chimneys and seek their way to the office via the ventilation system.

The office building is mechanically ventilated which includes a heat exchanger. As far as we know no recycling of air is taking place. Some of the rooms were reconditioned when the terminals were installed. Standard furniture, painting and carpeting were used and none of the chemicals emitted by these materials are known to produce this kind of skin rash.

The display units are quite common, IBM type 3180. Different kinds of radiation from the screen are known from measurements by The National Institute of Radiation Protection. The electrostatic field strength is about 19.5 kV/m at a distance of 0.3 m. The magnetic fields are of moderate strength, top value 92 mT/s. X-rays are less than 30 nG/h which is lower than background values.

About half a year after the first VDU had been taken into operation antistatic filters, Power screens, were mounted upon the terminals.

All 28 employees were investigated with a questionnaire and interviewed by a nurse. Those who reported any symptoms were investigated by the author. The diagnosis rosacea was based on the existance of erythema, papules, pustules and ectatic small blood vessels. Some of those who revealed any objective findings were tested for delayed hyposensitivity using patch test and the European standard allergens with reading at 72 hours. The standard allergens were completed with allergens from the work environment.

Samples from the work environment were tested for immediate hypersensitivity using closed patch testing for 20 minutes with readings during one hour. These tests were performed on forearm, back and face. The same substances were tested using standard photopatch technique in order to rule out photoallergic disease. Tests for sensitivity to UVA and UVB were performed on some patients.

Biopsies for histopathology were taken from facial skin.

Volatile air pollutants were analyzed by gas chromatography which estimated the total amount of organic substances. Individual substances were not identified. Particle-bound air pollutants were estimated using an optical partical counting device (Royco 225). Dust collected from ventilation filters was studied in electron microscope. These investigations were carried out by the National Defense Research Institute in Umeå.

Terpenes in indoor air adsorbed on the surface of active charcoal and formaldehyde adsorbed in XAD tubes were analyzed by The National Board of Occupational Safety and Health in Umeå.

The concentration of radon daughters was analyzed because of the debate in Swedish papers emerging from a report about suspected radiation injuries in VDU-operators [4]. In this debate it has been suggested that radon daughters might be deposited in the face of the operators and that alpha-radiation can produce radiation injury.

The radon daughters were analyzed by The National Testing Institute using passive sampling equipment.

Small air ions were calculated by The National Board of Occupational Safety and Health in Umeå using a micro processor ion counter (Type A 7803, Allen Weston).

The electrostatic field strength in front of the VDUs was measured using a field mill (Eltex Q 475/C). The field strength was estimated with and without antistatic filters at a distance of 20 cm. These measurements were carried out by the National Board of Occupational Safety and Health and IBM.

3. RESULTS

Five of the operators showed a rash with clinical signs of rosacea, three suffered from an erythema and one reported sensory symptoms only. In most patients the rash was more pronounced on the side most often turned towards the terminal. The erythema was located to the flushing area, i.e. in the center of the forehead, on both cheeks and on the chin. Some patients showed erythema on the side of the neck. Two patients had a confluent erythema, one patient a patchy erythema.

Nine operators, including those with objective findings, suffered from itching, burning sensations and swelling of the skin on cheeks, forehead and chin.

Two of the 14 workers, not engaged in VDU-work reported slight sensory symptoms of the same kind. The objective findings in these two persons were discrete and did not permit any clinical diagnosis.

The skin rash seemed to worsen during cold periods, still recurrencies were reported during the summer period. When terminating VDU-work, most of the visible rash diminished. Interestingly the sensory symptoms sometimes have recurred in the operators at work even if they have not been operating VDUs for a long time. These sensory symptoms are seldom reported during weekends and vacation.

Sunbathing and the use of UVA solarium have been reported by the operators to diminish the symptoms. Treatment with tetracyclines proved effective. Metronidazole cream 1% did not seem to have any effect, nor did protective creams.

The use of electrostatic air cleaners, air humidifiers, air ionizers, anti-static filter screens and conducting carpeting have not been able to stop recurrencies of the rash.

All tests with relevant substances have been negative.

The skin biopsies have been examined by histopathologists. A typical finding was slight elastosis and signs of rosacea. There was no finding of advanced elastosis beyond what we consider as part of normal aging.

Volatile air pollutants were found in concentrations twenty times higher than those found in a reference building in Umeå. Particle-bound air pollutants were four times higher.

Terpenes (beta-carene and alpha-pinene), formaldehyde and radon daughters were found in concentrations well below Swedish safety limits. Of course these safety limits might not be of any relevance for this kind of health effects.

The concentration of small air ions was found to be the same as in some reference buildings in Umeå.

Electrostatic field strength was 20 kV/m without filter screen. New screens reduced the field strength down to 1.5-4 kV/m. However, after eight months' use the function was checked and now only one of eight filters had any function at all. We do not know why the function of the filter screens was lost, but the reason is probably incorrect cleaning routines leading to destruction of the conducting layer by detergents.

4. DISCUSSION

The investigation of this outbreak of skin rash in VDU-operators clearly indicates a relation to work. All patients have shown improvement during vacation and they have all reported that most sensory symptoms disappeared during weekends.

Air-borne factors are suspected to be part of the cause because of the location of the symptoms and because many of the operators, after the rash had started, often have reported sensory symptoms when being at work even without VDUs. The finding of elevated concentrations of volatile and particle bound indoor air pollutants, compared with a reference building, is of interest to this respect. However, there is a need of more reference values and the identification of the air pollutants is of most interest. The importance of the general air pollutants in Umeå and local pollutants produced by the mill is so far obscure.

Is the rash related to VDU-work? Yes, probably because these skin symptoms started when VDU-terminals were taken into operation. Most of the operators had been working for many years in this office without any symptoms of this kind. As mentioned, when terminating VDU-work, it was observed that most of the visible rash diminished even when other kinds of office work was continued in the same room. When VDUs were installed nothing else was changed in the office except what has been mentioned about reconditioning of the rooms. Several trials have been made to return to VDU-work but all these trials have been followed quickly by recurrencies. The frequency of skin complaints obviously is significantly higher in the operator group compared to the non-VDU-operating group.

What exposure factor associated to VDU-work could be of importance to this rash?

The electrostatic fields might be of importance. The VDU-screen used has a considerably high electrostatic field strength and as we have seen the filter screens lost most of their function during the year they were used. Also the finding that the symptoms seemed to increase during wintertime might indicate the importance of electrostatic fields as these fields increase in a low relative air humidity. However, the explanation to this seasonal variation could also be the chapping of the skin which is normally occurring and which might increase the susceptibility of the skin to irritation.

As the counter-measures taken towards the effect of electrostatic fields seem to have been of limited value other possible explanations to this outbreak of skin rash in VDU-operators must be sought. One critical point concerning the hypothesis of deposition of air-borne particles is that it has never been shown that these particles actually can give rise to skin symptoms. At the moment we are trying to find ways to estimate the deteriorating effect of volatile and particle-bound indoor air pollutants. Another question which has no answer today is whether magnetic fields and electric fields influence the skin reactivity in VDU-operators.

REFERENCES

[1] Lindén, V. and Rolfsen, F., Scand J Work Environ Health 7 (1981) 62.
[2] Lidén, C. and Wahlberg, J., Contact Dermatitis 12 (1985) 235.
[3] Cato Olsen, W., Electric field enhanced aerosol exposure in visual display unit environments. Christian Michelsen Institute, CMI 803604-1 (Bergen, 1981)
[4] Lagerholm, B., Läkartidningen 83 (1986) 60.

WORK WITH DISPLAY UNITS 86
B. Knave and P.-G. Widebäck (eds.)

VDT WORK AND THE SKIN

Carola LIDÉN and Jan E WAHLBERG

Department of Occupational Dermatology
National Board of Occupational Safety and Health, and Karolinska Hospital
S-104 01 Stockholm, Sweden.

According to some reports, mainly from Norway, VDT work has been suspected to cause skin rashes. In three different studies we have tried to elucidate the question in Stockholm. Our studies indicate that there might be a relationship between VDT work and aggravation of some common skin diseases as rosacea, seborrhoeic dermatitis and acne. Whether this depends on physical or psychological factors is still unknown.

1. INTRODUCTION

On the basis of a few case reports it has been discussed for some years whether video display terminal (VDT) work can give rise to skin rashes [1-3]. The reports have described transitory redness and sometimes papules on the cheeks during days on VDT work and improvement on non-working days. Different physical exposure factors have been suggested being the cause, e.g. electrostatic fields and deposition of air-borne particles [4], electrostatic charge, X-ray emission and UV radiation. Psychological factors have also been proposed. No factor has yet been proved being the cause of the suggested symptoms. Since the autumn of 1985 there has been an ongoing debate in Sweden in the mass media and the salaried employees' movement press, and it has been claimed that skin disease from VDT work is common. The basis for this debate was one case with the diagnoses poikiloderma of Civatte and solar elastosis, notified as occupational diseases from VDT work. In three studies (I-III) we have tried to elucidate the question whether VDT work causes or aggravates skin disease.

2. METHODS

2.1. I. Participation in an epidemiologic study among office employees [5-7]

A questionnaire concerning subjective disorders and symptoms was answered by 536 subjects (395 VDT operators and 141 referents). One question concerning skin symptoms was included: "Have you ever had symptoms in the form of skin rashes (skin lesions, redness, eczema, dry skin, itch or the like) on the face, neck, hands or arms?" All subjects (N=96) who stated that they had current symptoms were called for a clinical examination (74 were available). Skin lesions were recorded as "objective skin lesions" (visible in the examination, based on dermatologic diagnosis) and "anamnestic skin symptoms" (not visible in the examination but experienced during the last year, probable diagnosis). The result of the dermatologic examination was compared with particulars of the subjective symptoms and physical exposure factors [5-7], e.g. VDT exposure/non-exposure, sex, electrostatic charge, electrostatic field strength and ultraviolet radiation (UV-A). For this comparison the various dermatologic diagnoses were grouped and each group was compared with the examined respectively the rest of the entire population, regarding the various mentioned factors.

2.2. II. Study among patients with rosacea [8]

A questionnaire was sent to all patients, 16-66 years old, diagnosed as rosacea or perioral dermatitis at a department of general dermatology in 1982 (N=179). The questions related to occupation, occurence of VDT work, and whether the subjects suspected that the skin disease had been aggravated, improved or unaffected by the VDT work. Those who reported aggravation by VDT work were invited to a clinical examination and interview (N=8). Telephone interviews were held with the others diagnosed as rosacea, who had reported regular VDT work (N=17) and with all office-workers who had never worked with VDT (N=12). The questions related to work-tasks, course of the disease, and effects of various factors generally regarded as aggravating rosacea.

2.3. III. Clinical examination of referred cases [9]

All cases referred to the Department of Occupational Dermatology, Karolinska Hospital under the suspicion of skin disease related to VDT work were admitted with priority within two weeks. They were clinically examined, generally at the end of the week in order to obtain optimal exposure conditions. When indicated they underwent patch testing, photo testing, punch-biopsy for histopathology or treatment.

3. RESULTS

3.1. I. Epidemiologic study among office employees

For detailed results see [7]. 61 subjects had current skin lesions or had recently had the symptoms inquired about. Altogether 15 types of skin lesions were recorded, and the most frequent diagnoses were: eczema; dry skin; redness; itch and/or dryness; papules, unclassified; seborrhoeic dermatitis; rosacea; acne; psoriasis. No case with the clinical picture described among VDT operators in Norway was found. There was a tendency towards a higher frequency of the diagnoses seborrhoeic dermatitis, acne and rosacea (one diagnosis group) among the VDT exposed subjects than among the referents ($p<0.05$). There was also a tendency towards a more positive electrostatic charge in this diagnosis group compared with the rest of the population ($p<0.01$). Otherwise no statistically significant differences were found when comparing the diagnoses and physical exposure factors.

3.2. II. Study among patients with rosacea

For detailed results see [8]. The questionnaire was answered by 166 subjects (93%). 42 had worked with VDT, 29 of them daily or once or twice a week. Eight of them suspected aggravation of rosacea due to VDT work. No difference was found between the three groups (worse by VDT; not worse by VDT; no VDT work) with respect to aggravating factors, degree of severity or treatment. The only difference found was that the mean age at onset of rosacea was higher among the persons who started VDT work before the onset of rosacea and reporting aggravation due to VDT work (46 years) compared with the entire material (37 years).

3.3. III. Clinical examination of referred cases

During the period 1979 to October 1985 seven cases were referred to our department under the suspicion of VDT related skin disease. During November 1985 to May 1986 100 cases were examined and the diagnoses are shown in Table 1 [9].The patients were treated

Table 1. Diagnoses in 100 cases (95 women and 5 men) referred under the suspicion of VDT related skin disease

Diagnosis	N
Seborrhoeic dermatitis	22
Acne	16
Rosacea, perioral dermatitis	15
Telangiectases	11
Atopic dermatitis	8
Mild, unspecific changes	9
Pustulosis, urticaria, otitis etc.	13
Normal skin	6

in accordance with the diagnoses. At reexamination it was noticed that given therapy had had a favourable effect in spite of continuous VDT exposure.

4. DISCUSSION

The single case notifed as an occupational skin disease from VDT work in Sweden was a 47 year old woman examined in 1984. She had all her life been sensitive to sunlight. The poikiloderma of Civatte was noticed as a slight red to brown pigmentation on her neck with smarting pain and pricking sensation. The diagnosis solar elastosis was based on histological examination only showing slight elastic hyperplasia, and it was by the dermato-histopathologist judged as more prominent than expected and probably caused by "radiation in the work place" [10]. However, Kligman [11] showed that elastic hyperplasia develops early in life and is found in 100% of individuals at the age of 40-49 (Table 2). Our opinion is that the natural exposure to sunlight might well explain the findings in this case. This statement is also based on the fact that measurements of her VDT equipment regarding ultraviolet radiation [12] and ionizing radiation [13] showed nothing remarkable.

Table 2. Elastic hyperplasia on the face in % of patients by decades. Adopted from Kligman [11]

Age year	No. of patients	%
5-9	16	19
10-19	26	77
20-29	31	87
30-39	40	95
40-49	31	100

Our studies indicate that there might be a relationship between VDT work and aggravation of e.g. rosacea, seborrhoeic dermatitis and acne. Stenberg [14] has also reported cases of rosacea from VDT work. These are common skin diseases, with multiple causes and variable course. At present we do not know if the reported aggravations depend on physical or psychological factors.

The electrostatic charge of the subjects was the only physical exposure factor (study I) statistically connected with skin disease [7]. We wish to point out that the electrostatic charge of the subjects is due to friction between materials and is not dependent on the electrostatic field from the VDT [15, 16]. Its relation to reported skin symptoms is still unclear.

Dermatoses on the face are common in the general population. Likewise the total number of dermatologic diagnoses in the study among the office employees was high. It is very unlikely that all the different types of skin lesions found would be caused or aggravated by one common exposure factor, originating from the VDT. This also reflects the necessity of being careful when interpreting answers on skin symptoms from questionnaires. To obtain correct diagnoses clinical examination by an experienced dermatologist is essential.

It is probable that VDT operators, at least in Sweden and Norway, are more prone to report skin symptoms than other office workers. Therefor, today it might be impossible to analyze the relationship between VDT work and skin symptoms by selecting the subjects from questionnaires.

To further elucidate the question more research is necessary, both epidemiologic and experimental studies including provocation tests. For those individuals who suspect VDT related skin disease referral to a dermatologist - if possible an occupational dermatologist - is recommended.

REFERENCES

[1] Nilsen A, Contact Dermatitis 8 (1982) 25.

[2] Rycroft R J G, Calnan C D, Facial rashes among visual display unit operators, in: Pearce B G (ed), Health hazards of VDT's? (John Wiley & Sons, Chichester, 1984) pp 13-15.

[3] Tjønn H H, Report of facial rashes among VDU operators in Norway, in: Pearce B G (ed), Health hazards of VDT's? (John Wiley & Sons, Chichester, 1984) pp 17-23.

[4] Cato Olsen W, Electric field enhanced aerosol exposure in visual display unit environments. (The Chr Michelsen Institute, Department of Science and Technology, Bergen, April 1981) .

[5] Knave B G, Wibom R I, Voss M, Hedström L D, Bergqvist U O V, Scand J Work Environ Health 11 (1985) 457.

[6] Knave B G, Wibom R I, Bergqvist U O V, Carlsson L L W, Levin M I B, Nylén P R, Scand J Work Environ Health 11 (1985) 467.

[7] Lidén C, Wahlberg J E, Scand J Work Environ Health 11 (1985) 489.

[8] Lidén C, Wahlberg J E, Contact Dermatitis 13 (1985) 235.

[9] Wahlberg J E, Läkartidningen, accepted for publication.

[10] Lagerholm B, Läkartidningen 83 (1986) 60.

[11] Kligman A M, JAMA 210 (1969) 2377.

[12] Lidén C, Bergqvist U, Wennersten G, J theor Biol, in print.

[13] Statens strålskyddsinstitut , (personal communication, 1984).

[14] Stenberg B, An outbreak of a rosacea like skin rash in VDU-operators, this volume.

[15] Cato Olsen W, Facial particle exposure in the VDU environment: The role of static electricity, this volume.

[16] Bergqvist U, Wibom R, Nylén P, Electrostatic fields at VDT work stations, this volume.

WORK WITH DISPLAY UNITS 86
B. Knave and P.-G. Widebäck (eds.)

SKIN PROBLEMS FROM VDT WORK - A SUMMARY

Gunnar SWANBECK

Department of Dermatology, Sahlgrenska sjukhuset,
S-413 45 Gothenburg, Sweden

For some years there has been complaints about skin problems from people working at VDT-stations. The greatest problems seem to have been in Norway and Sweden.

The skin problems that have been reported are either unspecific reddening of the skin or common skin diseases like rosacea, acne vulgaris or seborrhoeic dermatitis. The epidemiological studies that have been made as yet, have not shown any convincing correlation between these skin problems and VDT work. There are no reports on provokation of skin changes by VDT work experimentally.

The complaints about skin problems from VDT workers have still been taking seriously and one has looked for different possibilities of the mechanism for the induction of such skin problems. As electrons are accelerated in an electric field and hitting the VDT screen both x-rays and ultraviolet radiation is produced. Careful measurements have been made with regard to both these types of radiation. X-rays are not detected above the ordinary background level at the place of the VDT operator. Ultraviolet radiation can however be detected but in such low intensities that working for several hours corresponds to seconds of outdoor work. The contribution of ultraviolet light from the VDT is thus negligible compared to that from the sky at daytime. Therefore both x-rays and ultraviolet light can be excluded as possible etiological factors to the skin problems reported. With regard to possible skin hazards caused by electromagnetic radiation we have a solid scientific basis for our evaluation.

Another factor that has been discussed is the electric field created by a VDT. We have earlier not had reason to study possible effects on skin of electrostatic fields. Therefore we do not have the solid scientific basis that we have for electromagnetic radiation. This is thus an area that has to be looked into further experimentally. The situation is however complicated as in the countries where skin problems from VDT work has been reported the winter is cold and the humidity indoors in offices is usually very low. Therefore the friction between clothing and furniture may build up electric charges causing strong electrostatic fields. The low humidity in itself might also be causing the skin considerable problem. The barrier between our interior and the exterior with regard to evaporation of water is an extremely thin membrane in the upper part of the epidermis.

The electrostatic field may cause movement of charge particles in the air causing a deposition of some foreign material on the skin of the face. This is something that has to be looked into even if it may seem improbable that we in our working environment have such an amount of skin irritating substances in the air.

Another area that has to be looked into further with regard to skin problems form VDT work is the psychological stress that is caused by the monotonous work requiring continues concentration. What are the activities during the relaxation periods when the worker rests a few times a day. Is it smoking, coffee drinking and what could the effect of these habits be on the common skin problems that are reported?

More research has also to be done on the effect of psychological stress on skin diseases in general especially rosacea, seborrhoeic dermatitis and acne. All of these diseases seem to have some connection with sebaceous gland activity.

In conclusion it seems highly unlikely that electromagnetic radiation has anything to do with skin problems from VDT work. More research has however to be done with regard to the effect of electrostatic fields and psychological stress in connection with VDT work.

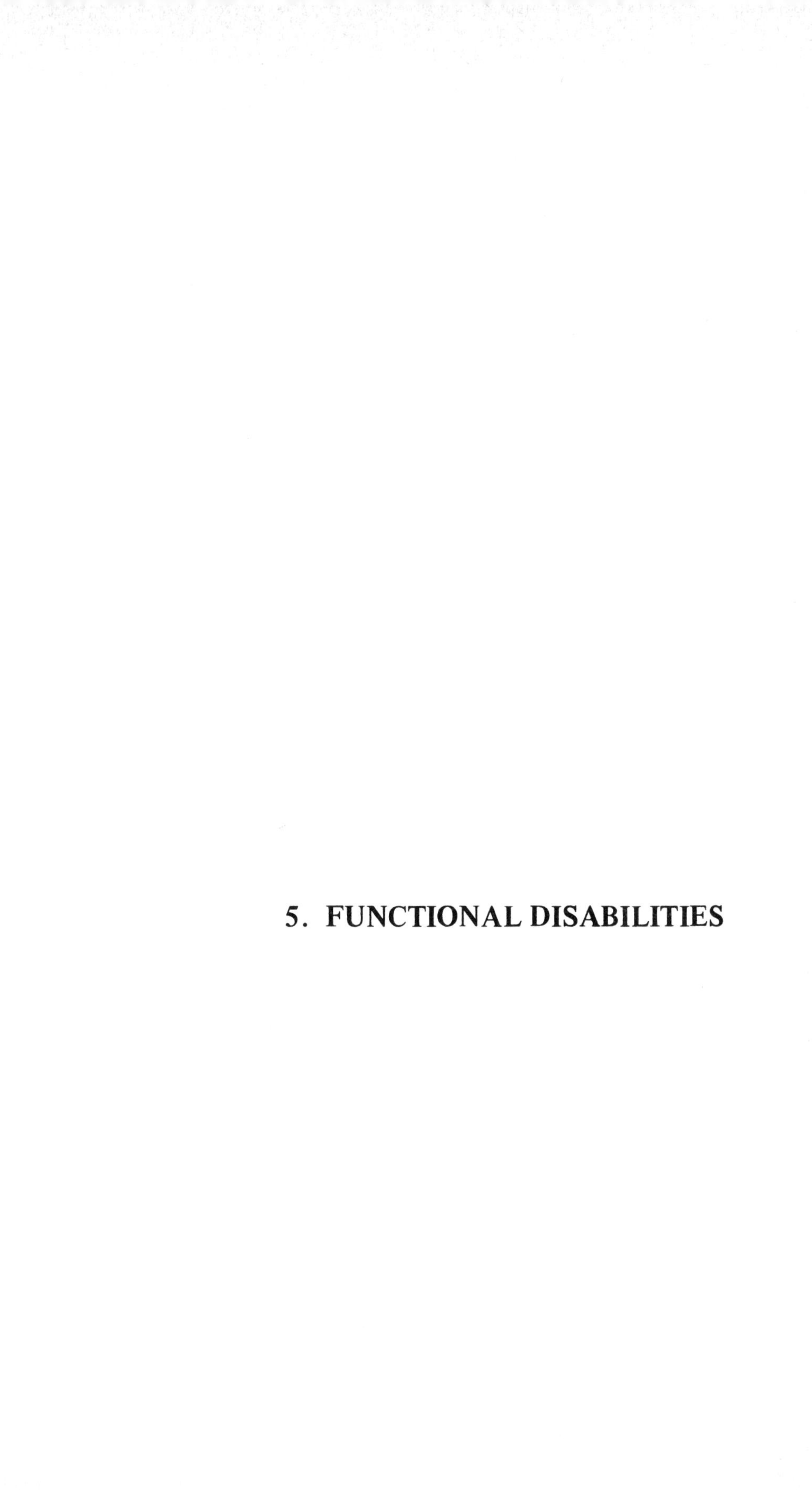

5. FUNCTIONAL DISABILITIES

WORK WITH DISPLAY UNITS 86
B. Knave and P.-G. Wideback (eds.)

HUMAN FACTORS CONSIDERATIONS IN THE DESIGN OF A VDU FOR VISUALLY IMPAIRED PERSONS

Gary W. Kelly, B.S. Psy and David A. Ross, M.Ed., M.S.E.E

Atlanta Veterans Administration Medical Center
Rehabilitation Research and Development Unit
1670 Clairmont Road
Atlanta, Georgia 30033

ABSTRACT

This paper describes research which is being conducted by the Atlanta Veterans Administration Medical Center Rehabilitation Research and Development Unit (VAMC Rehab R&D Unit) in the area of computer usage by persons with visual impairments. Specifically, the design of a device which reformats Visual Display Units (VDUs) for use by persons with limited usable vision will be discussed. The goal of the current design project, that began in January 1986, is to design, build, and test a video/video control interface which can be connected to and will reformat the video data of any general purpose computer/word processor. It is intended that the user of this device be able to choose among several possible text and presentation formats, choosing the one which best suits his particular need and application.

1. Specific Aims

The primary aim of this VDU project is to develop a universal device for persons with visual impairments which, when connected to any computer/computer terminal/word processor, will provide the person with an optimally reformated viewing screen. It is intended that persons with visual impairments interact with the computer in as "normal" a fashion as possible given the particular aspects of the disability. Since the standard output of most computers is the NTSC composite "Video Out" signal which goes to the CRT monitor, a device will be connected to the computer at this point to intercept and reformat this video signal. This video interface device is called a Video Monitor Emulator and Display (VMED) interface. The planned VMED device would be user interactive, offering each user a choice of type styles, sizes, colors (foreground and background), horizontal spacing between characters, vertical spacing between lines, and some types of line and/or screen scrolling. Various sonic and speech outputs could also be provided by this device via RS-232 interface.

All variables which are pertinent to the optimization of visually-impaired-user-to-computer interactions will be determined by an initial human factors study. This initial study of the VMED system variables began in January and will extend through December, 1986. Human factors evaluations will also be an ongoing part of the proposed work. It is the full intention of the staff to design this device with a major emphasis on ease of use and high user acceptance.

2. Significance

There are approximately two million functionally blind persons in the United States, [1] and 70% of these people have enough usable vision to read large print [2]. According to the National Eye Institute, 2.5 million eye injuries occur annually, one million of which cause permanent visual impairment, and 50,000 of which are classified as legally blind [3,4]. In addition, one out of every 500 school-age children has visual problems that are severe enough to be called a visual handicap [5]. More than ten years ago Goldish [1,6] speculated that this population could greatly benefit from the use of more sophisticated low vision aids.

Recently, the Veterans Administration [7] determined that 95% of blinded veterans have enough vision to allow the use of large print or normal print with low vision aids. It is apparent that the number of persons who can benefit from the use of large print is greater than the approximately 10% [8] of the blind population that uses braille.

Thus there is a great need for large print material or some means of access to books and other common reading materials. However, large print materials are scarce and expensive, often bulky and unmanageable, and not offered in a variety of colors, type fonts, or sizes. With the exception of the *New York* Times Large Type Weekly and the large type edition of the *Reader's Digest* which are specially type set for visually impaired persons, most large print material is simply an enlarged photocopy of the original work.

There are a number of braille reading devices for persons with severe visual impairments, along with computerized braille presses for the printing of braille books, newspapers, and other documents. The Optacon is a device for reading print in a direct tactile fashion, and, most recently, paperless braille systems and microcomputers have been developed and marketed [8,9]. However, while these devices are helpful and useful for the severely visually impaired person, they do nothing to help the overwhelming majority of visually impaired persons who are able to read large print but who do not know and are unwilling to learn braille or any other form of tactile communication.

Closed Circuit TV has been available for some time, but it is expensive, awkward to carry, difficult to use with non-flat reading materials, such as paperbacks, and even under optimum conditions cannot be used to read at anywhere near a "normal" reading speed [1,7,8,10]. More recently, large print devices that connect to popular microcomputers have become available. These devices allow the user to adjust magnification of the original screen, and then scan around the screen with the use of a joystick control. This is a very exciting innovation because it could be the start of a new type of large print reader, information source, and information recall (note taker) device. Information, books, papers, etc., could be stored on inexpensive floppy disks and read with the aid of a microcomputer. This type of innovation could also open the door to computer/word processor jobs for many visually impaired persons.

There are, however, some problems with these devices as they have been conceived and developed thus far. First, there are no standards for computer hardware design, and most computers do not provide direct access to their video screen data. Because of this, a different video interface device must be designed for each popular brand of computer on the market. Hence, the market for each large print re-formatting device will be small and the price of the device higher than necessary. Also, there will necessarily be a year or more lag from the time each "newest and greatest" computer is introduced until a large-print device interface is developed for the new computer.

Second, the manner in which the present devices plug into the I/O slots of these computers can be a problem because they depend on standard I/O protocols. Many of the newer software packages now on the market do not follow standard I/O protocols because often software can be made to run faster, be more efficient and competitive, and be more copy resistant if standard protocols are avoided. It is well known in the software industry that pirates take advantage of standard machine protocols to intercept and illegally copy expensive software. As a result, fewer and fewer of the new and more powerful word processing and financial management software packages will function properly with these video interface devices.

Lastly, the designs of these video reformatters are not based on human factors studies of the visually impaired human to computer interface. The Atlanta VAMC is the only research facility which is conducting such a study.

Based on a search of the literature concerning information criteria and time requirements for text editing, and on the perceptions of a small sample of visually impaired computer users trained at the Georgia Institute of Technology [11], clearly several points need to be addressed in the design of any large print display. First, simple magnification schemes are inadequate and difficult to use, as they provide no cues to the user regarding his position on the "page" he is scanning. The user can easily become lost in a "forest" of large letters with no direction signs pointing to where he wishes to go. With such a system, it is difficult to locate one's place or go back and re-read something important. Research using typists with normal vision has shown that most of the time spent in text editing is spent in deciding where and how to move the cursor [12]. If visual cues are not present, cursor moves take significantly longer [13]. The type and amount of feedback necessary for efficient use of a display would be dependent upon the application (i.e., programming, word processing, spreadsheeting, etc.).

The ever increasing use of computers in professional and private settings has spawned a proliferation of research in the human factors aspects of computer displays [14-20]. This research has addressed every aspect of the display from print size and style to the information requirements and control strategies. It has almost exclusively been related to persons with normal vision, so the results in many cases cannot be applied to the design of a large print display for persons with visual impairments. Given the varied and unique vision characteristics of the visually impaired population (which cannot be extrapolated from those of a population with normal vision), great care should be taken before even the general trends noted in these studies are applied to displays for persons with visual impairments. However, the results of this large body of research have been used as a starting point in the investigation of large print displays and display controls.

The present research and design work at the Atlanta VAMC will be complete when a universal electronic video reformatter has been built based upon the findings of the human factors study, and evaluated in terms of the needs and perceptions of a significant sample of visually impaired computer users. Assuming continued funding, this will be completed within the next two years. The retail price for the VMED, when manufactured in quantity, is expected to be less than $1000.

3. Preliminary Studies

An initial human factors study began in January, 1986, and will continue through December. The first part of this investigation quantified the relative significance of varying print font and format parameters, including: character height and width, thickness of character elements, style of text, horizontal and vertical space between characters, and color of text and background. The research staff has developed large print presentation software for the Apple II and the Hewlett-Packard 310. This software is a text presentation system which gives the user the ability to select a preferred font style, and then adjust each of the above listed parameters for optimal reading ease. The software is capable of presenting reading material in three formats: 1) as a series of sequential static display screens, 2) as a continuous vertical scroll, and 3) as a continous single-line horizontal scroll. The vertical and horizontal scrolling is very smooth, and the speed and direction of scrolling is determined by the user's control device.

Each visually impaired test subject will be asked to adjust text parameters until he has found two or three preferred combinations. Standardized reading material will then be presented in the chosen format, and the subject will be given a timed reading comprehension test. As a means of comparison, each subject will read a similar section of standardized text with a Closed Circuit TV system. These tests and along with the stated preferences of the subjects will then be used to determine which variables are most important. The tests will also show the range of values of each variable which must be made available to users of the VMED.

The user control device is also a variable in this study. Four different control devices will be tested for user preference: a joystick, a track ball, a mouse, and touch pad. These controls will be each operable in 3 modes: position control mode, velocity control mode, and acceleration control mode. Each subject will be asked to control text presentation and indicate the preferred control and control mode.

4. Experimental Design

4.1 Prototype Design and Development

Character manipulation and screen formatting are critical human factors issues. The system must be responsive to the user's needs, assisting and facilitating the user's tasks whenever possible. If the VMED were simply an electronic image magnifier with a magnification knob and an X-Y positioning stick, it would be very difficult for the user to get a "feel" for his current position within the text screen. The final VMED design will be somewhat dependent upon the results of the initial human factors study; however, the general design of this system has been well considered and many design decisions made, as will be described below. These decisions have been based upon previous work and considerations as described above. Basic design decisions made thus far are as follows:

[1] To be a universal device, the VMED must be connected to the Video Output of the computer, as this is the only output standard among all computers.

[2] The VMED must be a software-based device so there can be adequate user flexibility.

[3] The VMED must be built with high-speed electronics and processors to keep pace with the video signal and to decode that signal in real time.

[4] It must be built around state-of-the-art microprocessor technology to remain inexpensive and small in size.

[5] It must have a fast buffer circuit which can capture and hold specific video lines for decoding by the microprocessor.

[6] It must be able to generate high-resolution, solid video images of text and graphics.

[7] It must be capable of "zooming," smooth horizontal and vertical scrolling, and of formatting the screen in multiple "windows" or multipli-formated "split" screens.

[8] It must be capable of data recognition and parsing such that only the relevant data is formated and placed on the screen.

[9] It must be capable of immediately changing format modes as the task and user require.

[10] It must be able to dynamically track information which is being typed into the computer and keep that information in view on the reformated screen.

In reference to the first point, it should be noted that decoding and reformating a video screen via the video output is not a trivial task, nor is there off-the-shelf equipment available for this purpose; however, the only video display standard that is common to most computers is the composite video output signal. Also, most computers have a standard external video jack through which the user may readily connect the VMED system to his computer. The only way to make a truly universal and portable video reformatter for most computers is to use this composite video output.

The above points are very stringent, calling for a microprocessor system with special high-speed Input/Output capabilities. The Motorola 68000 has been chosen for this purpose, as it is one of the fastest and most sophisticated 16-bit microprocessors available today. Because it has received such wide acceptance in the industry, system development with the 68000 is well supported with high level software and hardware development systems. The price of this chip has been dropping dramatically and will soon be below $20.

The present design concept specifies that a 68000 microprocessor together with a high-speed video screen-line buffer will do the necessary real-time processing. Also, a high-resolution display chip set will be used which will provide a 512 X 340 line display. This will provide excellent quality characters in sizes of one-twenty-fourth to one-third total screen height. It is possible to increase the magnification beyond this, but this would greatly limit the amount of text which could be displayed at any one time, as the above mentioned maximum magnification would allow only four characters to reside side-by-side on the screen at any point in time. If larger character sizes are needed by the user, it would be better to achieve an increased character size by obtaining a larger video monitor screen.

The composite video signal which is sent to a video monitor contains all the information needed to reconstruct, and reformat, an alphanumeric computer-generated display. This may be done by taking advantage of the means by which a composite video signal is coded. This video signal is simply a serial string of pulses representing the dots which comprise each alphanumeric character on the video screen. This string is divided into individual lines by horizontal sync pulses, and into screens by vertical sync pulses. To decode the composite video signal, the VMED need only intercept this stream of pulses and store it in array form in the VMED memory for examination. The VMED processor would then determine the identity and placement of the original ASCII characters by comparing the dot patterns of known alphanumeric characters with the dot patterns in the video array.

Having determined the location of characters on the original screen, a scenario similar to the following may ensue. The processor would look for headings, column numbers, line numbers, etc., which had been picked by the user to remain in view. Having located these, the processor would format the user's screen such that these items are always in a known location. Text which must be left off the screen because of its larger size, may be formated into a long single-line of text to be moved horizontally across the screen via a user control; or it may be formated into multiple short lines to be moved vertically via the user's control (i.e., joystick, trackball, etc.). As text is scrolled onto the screen, the stationary headings would be automatically updated according to the position of the text on the screen. The rate at which text is moved across the viewers screen would be determined by the position of the user's control interface if he were in a "reading" mode, or by the typing speed of the user if he were in a "typing" mode. In every case, the information being reviewed or typed is always centered on the screen.

Figure 1 illustrates via block diagram the hardware structure and flow of data for video signal decoding and processing with the use of a high speed bit-mapped screen-line input buffer, and a 512 by 340 bit-mapped screen memory output to the composite video circuitry. Figure 2 shows a typical software flow diagram which manages the complete process. In order of occurrence, then, the high speed memory, under control of the 68000, "captures" the discrete pixels from each horizontal line and holds them for the processor which, when it is ready, transfers them to a temporary character matrix memory for interpretation. By sequencing through screen-line memory, the 68000 builds each character dot matrix in a line by line fashion. It then compares the resultant matrix to a table of character matrices, identifying each particular character. The processor would keep a record of each character and its original screen location in its own memory, constantly updating this memory as the original screen changed. Any graphics character or image (i.e., an icon) which was not a known character would be stored in its original dot-matrix pattern in memory to be retrieved, magnified in block form, and placed on the screen together with identified ASCII characters on the reformated screen.

The actual scrolling, graphics manipulations of characters, and control of character and text variables (i.e., size, spacing, color, etc.) will be handled by a dedicated graphics controller chip set made by NEC -- a chip set which NEC has very successfully implemented in their own APC (Advanced Personal Computer) 68000-based machine. The NEC chip set is capable of interpreting high level commands from the microprocessor and controlling zoom, split screen, foreground/background color, and vertical and horizontal scrolling of windowed sections of the monitor screen. Preliminary calculations show that the Motorola 68010 microprocessor with a 12 MHz clock, when paired with the NEC chip set, is capable of simultaneously "watching" the original screen for changes, monitoring inputs from the user, and maintaining a worst case scrolling rate on the user's screen of 206 words per minute. These calculations also show that this system could support a user typing no

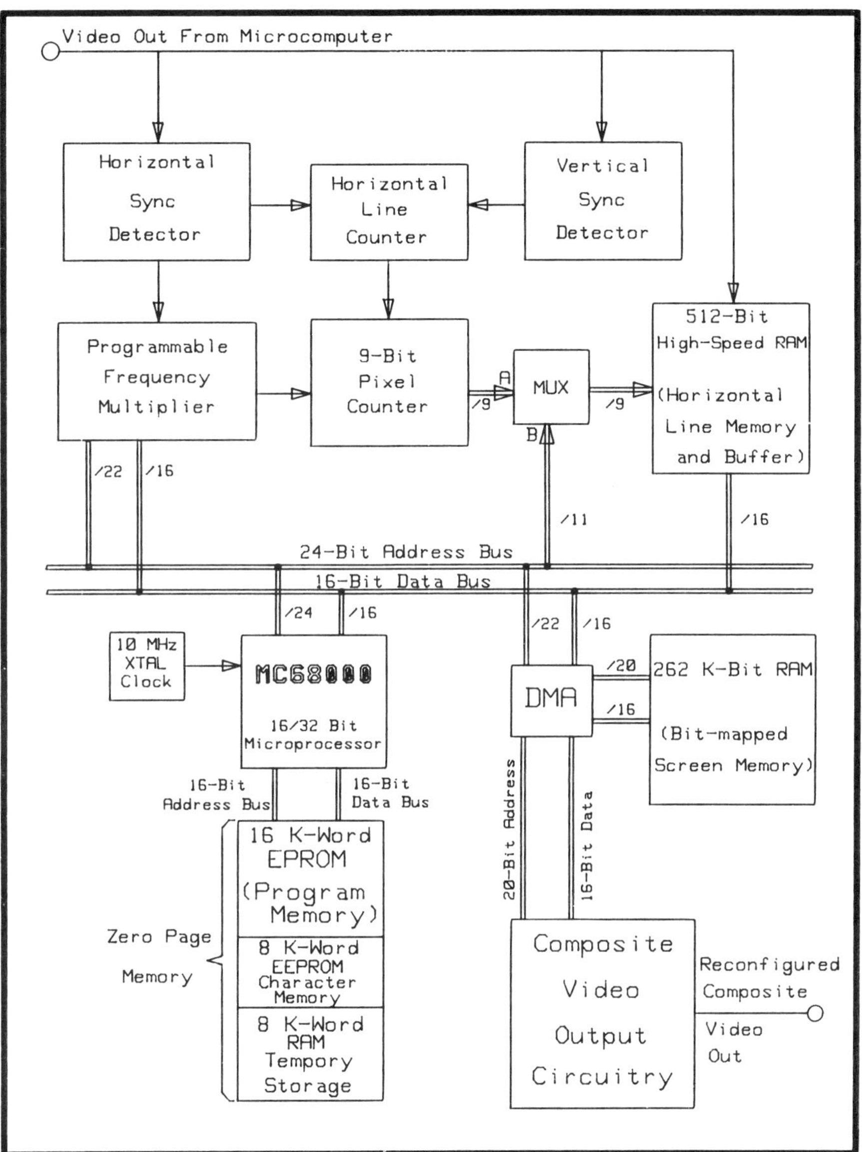

Figure 1. VMED Hardware Block Diagram

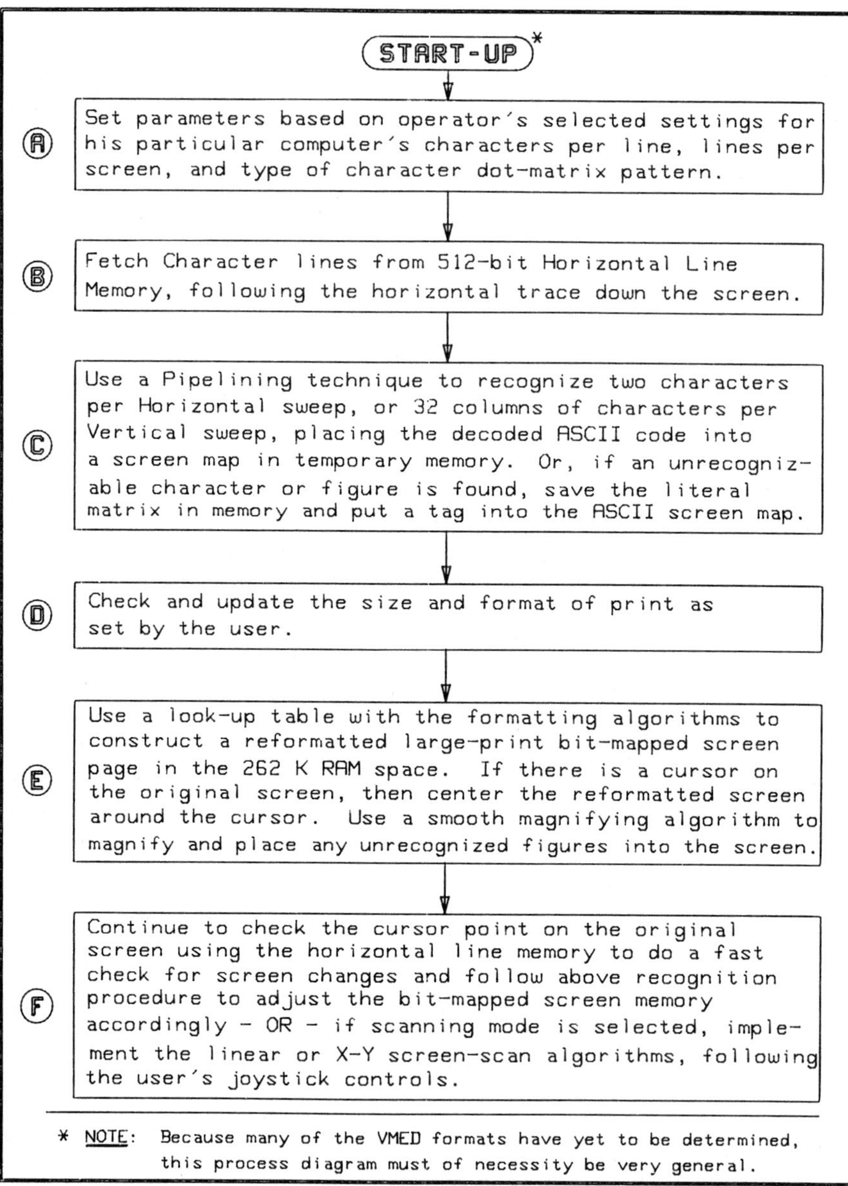

Figure 2. VMED Process Flow Diagram

more than 240 words per minute. These worst case situations show that the hardware design is more than adequate to meet the needs of most visually impaired persons using computers.

Although the type of physical instrument by which the user will control the reformated display is yet to be determined, it is assumed that the particular device used will provide numbers to the processor proportional to the speed, direction, magnification, etc., which the user wishes in each situation. Figure 1 does not show how this control is interfaced to the processor since the type of interface will be indicated by the device itself. The interface for this device will, however, be connected to the main bus of the processor and be read by the processor as a memory location at regular intervals of approximately one millisecond.

Since every computer generates a standard alphanumeric character set using slightly varied dot-matrix patterns, the VMED must be taught what each standard character "looks" like on each computer wherewith it is to be used. This will be done simply by typing each new character for each different computer in a specific order. Also, in this fashion, the VMED could be trained to recognize special non-standard characters and icons. All the VMED really does when it "learns" characters is to store each character's distinctive dot pattern in its permanent memory (EEPROM) in a specific order at a known location.

A number of large print character sets will be resident in the VMED from which the user may choose his preference. The exact nature of these sets is yet to be determined by the human factors study. Some screen display formats will also be available to the user, and again the exact nature of these will be determined by the initial human factors study. However, when this initial study is complete, the VMED will be programmed to identify certain structures and critical pieces of data (i.e., column headings, line numbers, etc.) in the original screen and to place these at known locations around the central data being viewed.

The VMED design will also provide a serial and parallel output of all reformated screen data such that this data could be used by a standard speech synthesizer, electronic brailler, or portable large single line display device (such as that developed by the Atlanta VA Medical Center for the Sony Typecorder).

Further development and testing of the VMED prototype will ensue following the completion of the human factors study, and as funding permits. Once begun, the work should be completed within approximately two years.

References

[1.] **Goldish, Louis H.**, "The Severely Visually Impaired Population as a Market for Sensory Aids and Services: Part One." *The New Outlook*, June 1972, 183-190.

[2.] **Hatfield, E.M.** "Estimates of Blindness in the United States." *The Sight-Saving Review*, 1973, 43, 69-80.

[3.] **Goldish, Louis H., and Marx, Michael H.** (1973), "The Visually Impaired Population as a Market for Sensory Aids and Services: Part Two - Aids and Services for Partly Sighted Persons." *The New Outlook*, September 1973, 289-296.

[4.] **Kirchner C., & Peterson R.** "The Latest Data on Visual Disability from NCHS." *Journal of Visual Impairment and Blindness*, April 1979, 151-153.

[5.] **Roessing L.J.** "Identifying Visually Impaired Children in a California School District." *The Journal of Visual Impairment and Blindness*, December 1980, 369.

[6.] Vision Research: A National Plan 1983-1987, *The 1983 Report of the National Advisory Eye Council*, Volume 1, 1983, p. 13.

[7.] **Mike, Edwin B.**, "Experience With CCTV in the Blind Rehabilitation Program of the Veterans Administration." *Bulletin for Prosthetics Research, Spring 1974*, 54-68.

[8.] **Pan, E.L., Backer, T.E., & Vash, C.L.**, *Annual Review of Rehabilitation*, Volume 1, 1980, pp. IX-XVI.

[9.] **Goldish, Louis H. & Taylor, H.E.** "The Optacon: A Valuable Device for Blind Persons." *The New Outlook*, February 1964, 49-55, 68.

[10.] **Kuck, J.H.** (1972), "A TV Reader With Some Novel Design Features." Applied Physics Laboratory, John Hopkins University, cp 024.

[11.] **Ross, D.A.**, "Human factors considerations in the development of a large print display for the visually impaired computer user," *Proceedings of* the 1984 ACM Southeast Regional Conference, 1984, Atlanta. New York: ACM.

[12.] **Gould, J.D., and Alfaro, L.**, "Revising documents with text editors, handwriting-recognition systems, and speech-recognition systems." *Human* Factors, 1984, 26(4), 391-406.

[13.] **Neal, A.S., and Darnell, M.J.**, "Text-editing performance with partial-line, partial-page, and full-page displays." *Human Factors*, 1984, 26(4), 431-441.

[14.] **Beldie, I.P., Pastoor, S., and Schwarz, E.**, "Fixed versus variable letter width for televised text." *Human Factors*, 1983, 25(3), 273-277.

[15.] **Bury, K.F., Boyle, J.M., Evey, R.J., and Neal, A.S.**, "Windowing vs scrolling on a visual display terminal." *Human Factors*, 1982, 24(4), 385-394.

[16.] **Curry, R.E., Kleinman, D.L., and Hoffman, W.C.**, "A design procedure for control/display systems," *Human Factors*, vol. 19, no. 4, October 1977, pp.421-436.

[17.] **Hammer, J.M., and Rouse, W.B.**, "Analysis and modeling of freeform text editing behavior," *Proceedings of the 1979 Conference on Cybernetics* and Society, Denver. New York: IEEE.

[18.] **McGillivray, R. (Ed.)**, "Large print." *Aids and Appliances Review*, 1979, no. 2.

[19.] **Pastoor, S., Schwartz, E., and Beldie, I.P.**, "The relative suitability of 4 dot matrix sizes for text presentation on color television screens." *Human Factors*, 1983, 25(3), 265-272.

[20.] **Schwarz, E., Beldie, I.P., and Pastoor, S.**, "A comparison of paging and scrolling for changing screen contents by inexperienced users." *Human* Factors, 1983, 25(3), 279-282.

WORK WITH DISPLAY UNITS 86
B. Knave and P.-G. Wideback (eds.)

VDU-WORK AND DYSLEXIA. A CASE REPORT

Knutsson A, MD

National Institute for Psychosocial Factors and Health (IPM)
Box 60210, S-10401 Stockholm, Sweden

The rapid introduction of computers in industry makes it even more essential that employees are able to read and write well. Very soon, almost all industrial jobs will involve some work at VDUs. The proportion of adult persons in Sweden who have difficulties in reading and writing is estimated at some 20 % among those with only an elementary education. Reading and writing difficulties are therefore the most common medical disability when people in industry have to learn to use a VDU. This case report describes ways in which the problem can manifest itself. Better education at elementary school and at workplaces in connection with the introduction of computers is the most important means of combating the problem. Furthermore, computer programs can be made more "user-friendly".

1. INTRODUCTION

The computerization of Swedish industry has taken place very rapidly. As the following figure shows, the installation of computers really began to take off in the seventies.

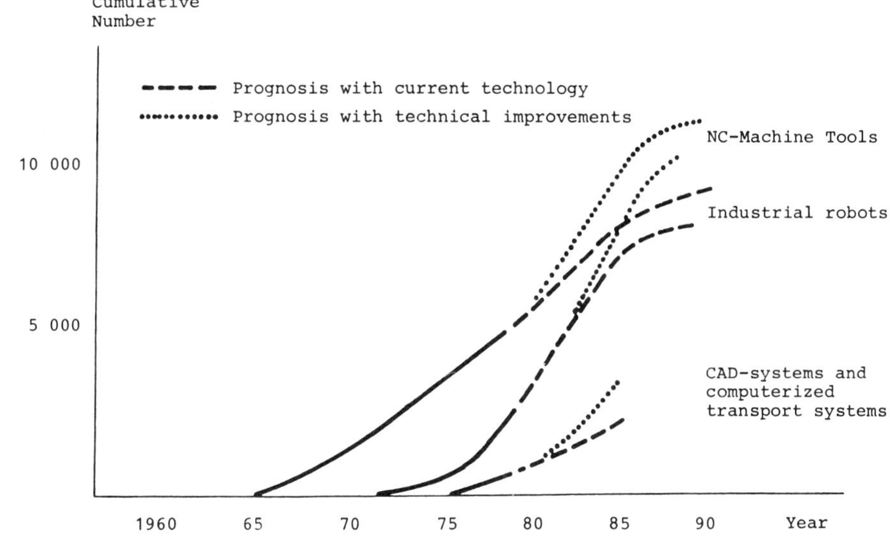

FIGURE 1. Investment in NC-machine tools, industrial robots, CAD-systems and computerized transport systems in Swedish industry. (Source: Datateknik i verkstadsindustrin. Rapport från data- och elektronikkommittén. SOU 1981:10. Liber Förlag, Stockholm, 1981)

Some increase in the rate of installation is foreseen for the second half of the eighties. Within the next decade, most industrial work will probably involve working at a VDU, at least for part of each working day. An earlier report described how three Swedish industrial workers with reading and writing difficulties experienced their problem when their workplaces were computerized [1]. This paper is a case report which deals with an immigrant.

2. CASE REPORT

The case concerns a 45-year-old man who came to Sweden from Finland in 1977 and started to work as a building labourer at a metalworking plant.In 1980, he changed job and started to work at a newsprint mill. He approached the occupational health unit in 1985 on account of pains in his feet. Later, pains were also felt in the lower lumbar region and legs. He felt that his work was far too haevy physically and he wished to be transferred to a process supervision position. However, the suprevisors maintained that he had already tried process supervision, which involved work at a VDU, and that he could not handle it. However, the patient could not describe in more detail what the problem at the VDU really involved. He spoke good Swedish with a slight Finnish accent. A writing test was arranged in which the patient had to write down a number of words which were read out to him. The following is an extract from this test:

Word read	What the patient wrote
Stolt	Stålt
Såpbubblor	Sopp
Gott	Kått
Verktyg	Värtyk
Kålsoppa	Kålsoppa
Dunsovsäck	Nydsovsek
Kökshandduk	Säkhandyk
Gamla	Kamla
Bråttom	Protlom
Rykte	Rykte
Fällt	Felt

Only two of the twelve words are correctly written. It was now possible to discuss his writing difficulties seriously for the first time with the patient. A test showed that he had reading and writing difficulties also in his native language. The outcome of this is a long period of training in order to supplement his elementary school knowledge, above all in reading and writing.

3. READING AND WRITING DIFFICULTIES

Reading and writing difficulties are common, even in highly industrialized countries. Their occurrence in Sweden varies from one survey to another between 8,5 % and 20 % [2,3]. Surveys in the USA show rates of between 10 % and 25 % [2,4].

Specific reading and writing difficulties occur more rarely. Prevalence figures for the Western world of between 1 % and 2 % are commonly mentioned.

Three types of reading and writing difficulty can be distinguished [5]:

a) Difficulties which are due to impaired development or brain damage.

b) Poor reading and writing abilities which are due to incomplete learning. This group is the largest and at the same time the area where treatment produces the best results.

c) People with specific reading and writing difficulties or dyslexia. This group is relatively small, in Sweden probably 1 % to 2 % of adult population.

People with reading and writing difficulties are often embarrassed by their lack of ability and do not even mention it to their closes friends. When visiting banks, post offices or government departments, where they are expected to fill in forms, they have hidden their lack of ability in various ways, for example, by saying that they have left their spectacles at home and asking the person behind the counter to fill in the form for them.

The feeling of shame that is associated with reading and writing difficulties makes it difficult for relations, colleagues at work, supervisors and occupational health units to discover the problem. Often a reading and writing test has to be arranged for the person in order to make the diagnosis.

4. DISCUSSION

Until the sixties, industrial work was mostly manual in character. Very few industrial jobs involved an ability to read and write. Computerization has changed this situation in a very short space of time. In order to work at a VDU it is necessary to be able to read and write well.

Firstly, the next on the screen has to be understood and secondly, the operator must be able to enter data via the keyboard. The programs are so designed that they require absolutely correct spelling. Even minor failings in the ability to read and write reduce the speed of VDU work and serve to increase stress, since it takes longer to understand and react correctly to information that some aspect of the production process is not functioning properbly, for instance. The handling of the language and the ability to understand the language therefore become important factors enabling a person to perform an industrial job.

As the people who have reading and writing difficulties are embarrased by their problem they try by a variety of means to conceal their lack of ability when computerization of their workplace means that good reading and writing skills are needed. Sometimes, they contact the occupational health unit on account of other physical complaints and ask to be transferred in order to avoid having to work at the screen [1].

People with a poor reading and writing capabilities can above all be found in groups, who are socially disadvantaged for other reasons and who have lost their foothold in the labour market to a greater degree, such as people who lived in socially miserable conditions during their childhood as well as immigrants. Computerization within industry leads to a selection of workers where those with poor reading and writing capabilities run the risk of failing and ending up in unemployment or in receipt of disability pension.

This problem can be tackled in various ways:

- Better education at elementary school, where it is made sure that the pupils learn to read and write.

- In connection with computerization in industry the employees must be offered a training that is good enough to enable them to cope with their work.

By testing reading and writing ability, it is possible to offer those who are poor at reading and writing supplementary elementary education.

- Software can be produced that is more suited for use by people with reading and writing difficulties. More research is needed in order to find out how persons with difficulties in reading and writing perform when working at a VDU.

Training of employees involves heavy costs. Deficiencies in reading and writing capabilities often require individualized training for a long period, perhaps one to two years. Who is to pay for it - the company or society?

REFERENCES

[1] Knutsson, A., Computerization in Industry Causes Problems for People with Reading and Writing Difficulties (Dyslexia). Scand J Soc Med, in print.
[2] Malmquist, E., Att förebygga och behandla läs- och skrivsvårigheter (Liber Läromedel, Lund, 1974).
[3] Grundin, H.U., Läs- och skrivfärdigheter hos vuxna (Skolöverstyrelsen och Liber Läromedel/Utbildningsförlaget, Stockholm, 1977).
[4] Robinson, H., Provisions made for Children, who have Difficulties in Reading. Proceedings of the First World Congress on Reading, held at the UNESCO House (Paris, 1967) pp. 125-133.
[5] Grogarn, M., Tråkig läsning (Liber Förlag, Malmö 1984).

WORK WITH DISPLAY UNITS 86
B. Knave and P.-G. Widebäck (eds.)

PSYCHOLOGICAL ASPECTS ON BLIND PEOPLE'S READING OF RADIO-DISTRIBUTED DAILY NEWSPAPERS

ERLAND HJELMQUIST, BENGT JANSSON, and GUNILLA TORELL

Department of Psychology, University of Göteborg, Göteborg, Sweden*

In this study, twelve blind or visually handicapped subjects participated in a reseach project where a daily newspaper was transmitted to the subjects' homes and read with braille (tactile reading) or speech synthesis. This was made possible through the use of computer and telecommunication technique. Almost the entire paper was transmitted to the subjects, signifying an important change in the blind people's information situation, since newspaper material usually is made available through summaries by sighted people, i.e. blind people have very limited possibilities to choose what they want to read themselves. Questions of interest in this study included the subjects opinions about the reading device, and their use of the different reading facilities, i.e. different commands to the computer. Comparisons in both these respects between braille and speech synthesis were made in interviews. Furthermore, the actual reading process, use of different commands and reading time were analyzed. These data were stored and available in each subject's computer. The results showed very positive attitudes and expectations of the new technique. The possibility to choose freely what to read was stressed. It made the information situation more similar to that of sighted people. Both reading modalities (braille and speech synthesis) were appreciated (all subjects were good braille readers). Braille reading was considered to give a more direct contact with the text, but more text was read at a greater speed with speech synthesis. The use of commands seemed more varied with speech synthesis as compared to braille. The subjects got acquainted rather quickly to the "voice" of the speech synthesizer, though it was considered inappropriate for certain text types, such as poetry and novels.

1. INTRODUCTION

Blind people's access to daily information is mainly dependent on radio, TV and direct communication with other people. Newspapers, which constitute a very significant source of information for sighted people, have not been available to the blind except in shortened versions, and then are often received long after sighted people get their newspapers. A technique for overcoming

* This study was supported by a grant from the Bank of Sweden Tercentenary Foundation and the Swedish State Committe on Spoken Newspapers.

some major drawbacks in this situation has recently been developed (Rubinstein, 1984). In the present study, this technique was applied to reading a daily newspaper, one of the largest in Sweden. There are a number of interesting questions to look at when introducing a new technique of this kind. One domain of questions has to do with the user's acceptance of it, another with the reliability of the technique, and a third with the reading process per se and the outcome of it, i.e., how well the content is understood and remembered. In the studies we have done so far, and in the studies underway and planned, we will investigate all three domains.

Braille reading, i.e. tactile presentation of text, as well as speech synthesis has been used. This is an interesting point of comparison, not least because it is important to study the reactions to speech synthesis and its comprehensibility, since it is likely that speech synthesis will become the reading mode if the technique is introduced on a larger scale. This, in turn, is dependent on the fact that only a minority of blind people are good braille readers. Evidently, the quality of the speech synthesis signal must be good enough so as not to create problems that affect the processing of text information dramatically. However, so far little is known about such possible effects. There are also a number of questions of a theoretical nature that can be studied. These are related to the way text is processed in different modes, i.e., writing, braille, speech synthesis and the human voice. Here we will present results pertaining mainly to the users' experience of the technique as reported in interviews and how they used the specific facilities for reading provided by the computer equipment.

2. METHOD

2.1. Subjects

Twelve blind or visually-impaired people participated in the study. There were two subgroups of five and seven subjects respectively. The two groups used the same technical equipment, which meant that they read at two different time periods. The first group consisted of two men and three women, with a mean age of 44.5 years. Two subjects had been blind almost all their life and the remaining three were severely visually impaired at birth and lost their sight as children or teenagers. Two participants had been able to read the headlines in newspapers as children. The second group consisted of four women and three men, with a mean age of 43.5 years. Four subjects had been blind since birth, two persons had been visually impaired all their life but could use a magnevision for reading single words. They had never been able to read newspapers. The seventh participant went blind at the age of 19. He had read papers as a teenager 40 years ago.

There were two married couples in the research group and two other participants had a visually-impaired spouse. Two of the 12 participants were married to persons with normal sight. The remaining four participants were single.

All the participants were familiar beforehand with the newspaper through a cassette-recorded version (human voice). During the reseach period they also used this version of the paper.

The subjects cannot be regarded as a representative group of visually-impaired people as they had been selectively chosen because of their ability to read braille. Furthermore, they were willing to spend time reading the newspaper, answering questions and participating in three memory experiments.

2.2. Technical Equipment

The technique applied in the present study utilized the fact that daily papers are being produced more and more by computerized processes. This means that the information in a newspaper is stored in a computer in the first place. In the present project, this information was transmitted from the newspaper composing computer to the FM site by a link, see Figure 1.

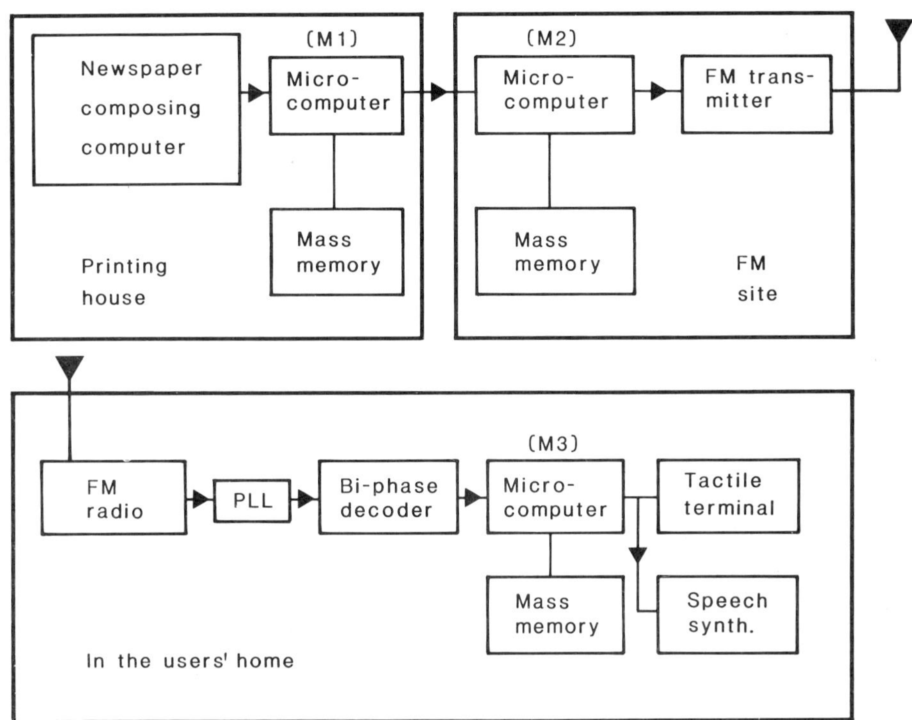

FIGURE 1
A schematic outline of the transmission of the newspaper (after Rubinstein, 1984).

Furthermore, each participant had in his or her home an FM-radio via which the newspaper was received, a mass memory (a Winchester disc), where the paper was stored, a braille terminal (for one part of the project) and a speech synthesizer (for the other part of the project). The equipment was controlled by a microcomputer which also controlled the reading procedures. The transmission of the text from the FM site started automatically after the ordinary radio programmes finished at night. The transmission took approximately 90 seconds and contained about 600 000 characters, i.e., almost the complete newspaper with the exception of photos and logotypes, etc., which were not included in the newspaper computer (Rubinstein, 1984). The tactile device used was a VersaBraille terminal, which required a specific starting-up routine, i.e., two cassettes had to be loaded before reading was possible. The display of the terminal had rather sharp dots and a reading line with 20 characters. The speech synthesis apparatus, the SA 101, was produced by INFOVOX AB, Sweden.

2.3. Search and Reading Routines

A search and reading system for the newspaper was developed and organized in a tree-like structure (Rubinstein, 1984), see Figure 2.

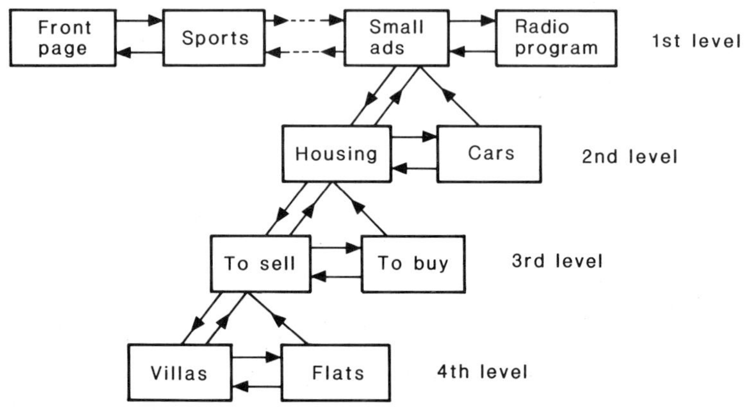

FIGURE 2
Design of the hierarchical structure of the newspaper (after Rubinstein, 1984).

At the top of the hierarchical structure, there were about 20 main classes, for example, "first page", "culture", "sports", etc. There was a maximum of four levels in the structure, but not all main classes contained sublevels. The commands available for reading a newspaper could be categorized into four functional groups; text generation, movements in text, position indications, and specific commands for speech synthesis. Each of the main groups contained two or more subgroups. The "text" commands generated text either in a stepwise or a continuous manner. When using the equipment for tactile reading, stepwise commands were the only alternative.

To facilitate movements in the text, there were several sublevels. Direct selection could be made between classes, i.e. editorials, sports, etc. Within a class, moves could be made to articles or graphical changes (i.e headings) using either of the three additional commands; "next", "previous", or "same". Furthermore, there were commands for moving to nearby located main levels or sublevels in the newspaper. These commands functioned as "forwards", "backwards", "up", and "down" in the text structure. Moreover, search in the text could be performed by using a specific combination of letters. The main classes could be reached immediately by the command "c" class, linked with the appropriate first three letters describing the requested class. For example "cspo" was used for reaching the sports main class.

Commands indicating a position in the text had two functions; to save a position in the text, and to return to the previously saved position. It should be noted that there was no possibility to save a piece of the text mass "outside" the newspaper for later reading.

When using speech synthesis, five additional commands could be given; "speak faster" or "slower", "speak in sentences", "words" or "letters".

2.4. Data Collection

Interviews were conducted three times during the investigation period, which lasted four months for each of the two groups. Both groups started with two months of braille and then switched to two months of speech synthesis reading. The participants were interviewed twice during the two months of braille reading and once during the speech synthesis reading. All the interviews were tape-recorded.

The first interview was carried out over the phone about 10 days after the reading device had been installed in the participants' homes. Points raised were demographic data, braille reading capacity, earlier contact with daily newspapers, available sources of information, expectations of the new technology in general and participation in the project in particular. The participants were also asked about their reactions to the reading device, what proceedure they adopted when reading the paper, which of the available commands they used and what they considered interesting and/or important information and which parts of the paper they were less interested in.

The second interview was conducted at the end of the braille reading period and took place in the participants' homes in connection with a memory experiment. During this interview the participants were asked almost the same questions as at the first interview and some of those questions were also asked at the third interview in order to make a comparison over time possible. One person was not available for the second interview because of work duties.

The third interview was conducted after one month of speech synthesis reading. Two participants were not available due to vacation. Six persons were interviewed over the phone and four persons in their homes. During this interview the participants were asked to compare the two reading modalities with respect to ease of handling the device, reading satisfaction and access to specific text material and information. Those two reading modalities were also compared to cassette-recorded newspapers as well as other information media.

The readers' use of the different commands was registered. Each keystroke was recorded on the Winchester disc. The recording was done in one of the following two ways. Each character was associated with a continuous time reference. If a single character or a combination of characters matched a preprogrammed command, then the location in the newspaper, i.e. on the Winchester disc, was recorded. Thus, the amount of text read during the corresponding time could be computed. However, a problem occurred at longer periods of reading when subjects took a pause without turning off the equipment. In these cases the time for pausing was included in the reading time. This problem had an acceptable solution by using mean values of reading rate over the days. Reading times was computed by dividing text with mean values of reading rates.

The recording of commands were not complete for all subjects due to technical failures. For five subjects, data was not available in any modality, and for three subjects data was available in one or the other of the two modalities. Furthermore, the registrations were based on a different number of days for different subjects. Altogether there were 188 days of braille reading and 70 days of speech synthesis reading.

3. RESULTS

3.1. Interviews

For visually impaired people in general the new technology was thought to be a revolutionary way of getting access to information. In the future, the participants expected that all kinds of computerized material would be as available to visually impaired persons as to sighted people. If these hopes come true, the handicapping effects of being blind would diminish and new sectors of the labour-market would open up for the visually impaired. As for the participants, in particular, they expected to get access to a complete newspaper, which they would be able to read independently of other people and so have freedom of choice of what to read. The project itself was expected to bring the visually-impaired people closer to sighted persons' access to a daily newspaper The participants had a positive attitude towards the project throughout the whole reading period. Actually, their attitudes seemed to grow more positive as the project went on and as they got accustomed to the equipment.

The participants' first reactions to the equipment were joy, excitement, curiosity and fascination but also irritation as the device did not function all the time and was a bit awkward to handle, and was considered too noisy. From the start of the project five of the 12 participants were already familiar with the VersaBraille terminal but they had some initial problems as the commands they were used to when working with the VersaBraille differed somewhat from the commands used when reading the newspaper. The other subjects experienced initial difficulties in getteing acquainted with the VersaBraille and acccessing the paper in the computer. The hard part was not to read the paper but to boot the computer terminal. The participants estimated the time for an ordinary person to learn how to handle the apparatus and to read the paper from a couple of hours to six months. The participants pointed out that it was very individual, partly depending on the person's braille reading skills and prior experience of computers. Older people, however, were thought to need more time to learn how to read the paper with this technique. According to the participants, the only previous knowledge necessary in order to read the newspaper, was the ability to read braille, but a positive attitude towards the new technique and motivation to read the paper would facilitate reading. After three months of reading all participants thought that they controlled the equipment satisfactorily.

On the average, the participants failed to get the newspaper, twice a week, depending either on equipment and/or transmission failure or on the participants themselves. They were disappointed and irritated about this, although some of them pointed out that they were testing the apparatus as well as the reading procedure and had to expect problems with the equipment. Most of the subjects experienced more trouble during the speech synthesis reading period compared to the braille reading period. They reported that it was harder to use the search routines and that the computer got stuck so they had to start all over again.

The signs on the tactile display were judged as very good and the quality of the "voice" of the speech synthesizer was acceptable. However, one man with a hearing impairment was unable to catch the speech synthesis sound. Six of the participants thought that the 20-sign display was too short and made it hard to read.

Some complaints of an ergonomic nature were made about the equipment. The participants got tired in their arms, hands and back when they read braille and would like some kind of support for their forearms.

The way the participants used the reading commands differed from person to person. They seemed to have tried out some of the commands and then used the ones which seemed to function the best. After two months of reading, most of the participants still used the same commands as they did in the beginning. Why change a winning team? At this time, however, three of the subjects began to try out some of the search commands. Some of the commands were never used as they had been forgotten. With the exception of "continuous reading", a command which could only be used when listening to the speech synthesizer, the participants said they used the same commands during the braille reading period as during the speech synthesis period. The most frequently used commands according to the interviews were "forwards", "backwards", "next article", "next graphic change" and "proceed to next class" or "go to a specific class" and "continuous reading". The different repetition commands were hardly ever used. When reading the advertisment columns, some of the participants made use of the "upwards" and "downwards" commands, otherwise these commands were seldom used. "Talk in letters" was only used when the participants came across a name, mostly foreign, or a word which they did not recognize, and at the beginning of the session when they did not catch what the speech synthesizer said. No one reported any use of "talk in words".

The participants estimated their mean reading time to 45 min. a day during the braille reading period and 40 min. during the speech synthesis reading. Although they spent a little less time with the newspaper during the latter part of the project, the participants thought they read a larger part of the paper as they could speed up the speech synthesizer. The subjects' estimate of how much of the newspaper they actually read varied between a few percent and half the paper.

The participants did not really change their daily routines due to the project. However, there were some small changes like rising a little earlier in the morning to get time to read, reading the paper instead of listening to the TV-news or the cassette-recorded version of the newspaper. The participants said that they did not want to change their habits for only four months. They estimated that it would take something between one month and six months before this way of reading the newspaper would be intergrated into their everyday routines.

The participants' preferences for what to read in the paper varied considerably, a fact which should be noted since blind people mostly have to accept what others select and make available to them. The participants made a strong point of their satisfaction of having access to a fresh and complete newspaper. The most attractive information seemed to be that which was not provided by radio or TV. In the future the participants hoped to make their own choice among newspapers and to be able to subscribe to more than one daily paper.

The participants did not report any difficulties in comprehending the different kinds of articles in the paper. However, articles written in straightforward and simple language were easier to comprehend than more specialized articles. Newspaper materials of personal interest were considered both easier to comprehend and recall. The abbreviation of words in the advertisements was sometimes hard to understand. As the braille display could take only 20 signs at a time, tables were difficult to read.

Concentration was considered important for the comprehension of text. The participants said that they had a more immediate understanding of what they read when reading braille compared to speech synthesis and recorded cassettes. Braille was considered an active way of reading which made it easier to stay concentrated on what was read, a finding which has been reported in previous studies (Drottz, 1986; Drottz & Hjelmquist, 1986). Listening to speech synthesis and cassettes had the advantage that the participants could combine the reading with other things, like domestic duties, but this way of reading also allowed the mind to drift. The participants thought it was much more difficult to stay concentrated or even awake when listening to the speech synthesizer.

The reading speed, on the other hand, was thought to influence the understanding of text. The 20-sign display and the manual feeding of every new line decreased the participants' normal braille reading speed, which was thought to have a negative effect on their text comprehension. The quality of the speech synthesizer "voice" was considered important, especially in the beginning, but as the participants got used to the "voice", they had very little trouble in comprehending what was read. They regarded the speech synthesizer's way of talking as any other Swedish accent. Peculiar pronunciations, however, did contribute to some comprehension disturbances as the reader became distracted from the text itself. If the reading speed was important when reading braille, it was reported even more so when listening to speech synthesis or tapes. As the participants got used to speech synthesis they preferred a high speed and thought it increased their text comprehension as they had to be more

concentrated. Actually the speech synthesizer was thought to sound more human when the speed was increased.
Most of the participants preferred to read in braille as it is a written language and they got amore immediate contact with the text, and a better feeling for the words and how they were spelt. However, five of the participants preferred to get the newspaper on speech synthesizer since they could consume more of the paper compared to reading braille. When reading poems or novels the speech synthesizer was rejected by all the participants. Except for the man with a hearing impairment, all the participants would rather have a complete newspaper in speech synthesis than only parts of the paper on cassettes.

The best way of getting a daily paper, according to the subjects, would be a combination of braille and speech synthesis with easy access to either modality. The readers would then be able to choose the modality most suitable for any given newspaper material. However, the subjects were well aware that the large majority of the visually impaired is not able to read braille and this group could only get access to the paper through a speech synthesizer.

If an article of interest was available on tape, most of the participants preferred to listen to the cassette rather than to the speech synthesizer. If it was a long article they also preferred listening to the cassette as it was considered a faster way of reading than using the VersaBraille. Regardless of whether they read braille or speech synthesis, the subjects in the present study chose to read newspaper material not provided on cassettes.

3.2. Analyses of Registered Information

The results referring to reading and search behavior were based on about 194 000 commands. The main part consisted of one-letter-commands with the function of generating text. In braille reading almost 90% of the commands were used for this purpose, while the corresponding percentage for speech synthesis was about 40% for sentence reading and about 25% for continuous reading, i.e. about 65% together. The commands used for movements in the text were primarily the next article and the forward commands. Both these ways of moving in text were about three times more frequent when using speech synthesis compared to braille reading. The other commands for search and movement in text were used more seldom, such as the commands for graphical changes, and for searching of a specific letter combination. The subjects used the class command on the average a little less than once a day, irrespective of modality. Thus, when engaged in a "typical" way of braille reading, subjects seemed to choose some class. Within the chosen class many commands were used for reading, and then moving to next article. After having read some articles, change to a higher level in the text structure was done by using the forward command. Thus, getting an overview of the newspaper required a lot of commands. Given these results one might be somewhat surprised over the infrequent use of saving positions. Direct return to a previously noted position for an interesting article ought to facilitate reading.

On the other hand, using continuous listening with speech synthesis required about one third of the commands for text generation as compared to braille reading (see Table 1 below).

Table 1

The total amount of frequencies and percentages within each reading modality. For multilevel command categories a part sum is noted

	MODALITY			
	BRAILLE		SPEECH SYNTH.	
COMMANDS	SUM	%	SUM	%
Stepwise reading:				
Next sentence	155576	85.95	3832	30.56
Same sentence	96	0.05	509	4.06
Previous sentence	2795	1.54	355	2.83
PART SUM	158467	87.55	4696	37.45
Structure moves:				
Down	1116	0.62	134	1.07
Up	556	0.31	23	0.18
Forward	4322	2.39	911	7.27
Backward	1013	0.56	221	1.76
PART SUM	7007	3.87	1289	10.28
Article search:				
Next	7980	4.41	1650	13.16
Top	12	0.01	5	0.04
Previous	440	0.24	88	0.70
PART SUM	8432	4.66	1743	13.90
Graphic changes:				
Next	20	0.01	0	0.00
Top	9	0.00	0	0.00
Previous	30	0.02	1	0.01
PART SUM	59	0.03	1	0.01
Classes	794	0.44	278	2.22
Find	712	0.39	157	1.25
Saved positions	32	0.02	2	0.02
Continous reading:				
Start	-	-	1752	13.97
Break	-	-	1619	12.70
PART SUM			3367	26.89
Speech modifications:				
Talk faster	-	-	6	0.05
Talk slower	-	-	10	0.08
Talk in sentences	-	-	11	0.09
Talk in words	-	-	14	0.11
Talk in letters	-	-	14	0.11
PART SUM			55	0.44
Combinations	5499	3.04	946	7.55
Total	181002	100.00	12538	100.00

Besides continuous reading being on the average more than four times faster than sentence reading (up to at most 20 characters a time), a larger proportion of keystrokes was more likely to be used for other commands than for text generation. The total amount of keystrokes, adjusted for the different number of days in the two modes of reading, was significantly higher for braille than for listening to speech synthesis ($F(1,9)=5.29$, $p=.02$). The reading process seemed to be more flexible when using speech synthesis, i.e. command giving was to a higher degree aimed at movements in the text. The category labelled "combinations" consists of commands not correctly written, and clusters of commands written rapidly.

Text consumption with speech synthesis was not only faster, as already mentioned, but also the total amount of consumed text was on the average almost three times larger. The mean values of consumed text in the two reading modalities were fairly equal for the different subjects, with some exceptions. Subject 2 decreased her reading time with braille over the recorded days. Furthermore, subject 8 and subject 9 had listened to about five times more speech synthesis compared to the other subjects (see Table 2). It should be noted that the amount of text in Table 2 is measured in kilobytes containing no blank characters. Transformation of 1 kilobyte text mass into an "ordinary" text would correspond to about 175 words.

Table 2

The amount of read text for each subject with braille and speech synthesis reading respectively. Stepwise and continuous reading is separated for speech synthesis

	MODALITY					
	BRAILLE		SPEECH SYNTHESIS			
	Stepwise reading		Stepwise reading		Continous reading	
Ss	N[1]	MEAN[2]	N	MEAN	N	MEAN
1	81	12.1	23	0.8	32	8.6
2	26	3.1	-	-	-	-
6	-	-	4	0.4	5	10.4
7	40	13.1	-	-	-	-
8	20[3]	10.0	9	2.7	10	55.8
9	5	12.9	4	0.5	16	63.9
10	4	15.8	7	5.2	7	6.0
ALL	176	10.9	47	1.8	70	27.9

Note 1. N=number of days.
Note 2. Text is measured in kilobytes (1024 bytes).
Note 3. Twelve days were lost due to technical errors.

Reading times were computed as a ratio between mean text mass and the mean rate of reading/listening. The mean values for the subjects using braille ranged from about 30 to 45 minutes. However, a rather extreme mean value for subject 10 was noted, two and a half hours a day. This value is based on only four recording days and the explanation seem to be that this subject did not turn off the equipment between different reading sessions. The mean value of reading in speech synthesis was about 30 minutes. In Table 3 it is interesting to note the use of the stepwise reading technique when using speech synthesis. The reading rate is about half or less of the corresponding rate when using continuous listening. Consequently, it seems that the stepwise wəy of listening is used for some texts requiring more attention.

Table 3

The daily mean reading time for each subject for braille and speech synthesis reading respectively. Stepwise and continuous reading is separated for speech synthesis

	BRAILLE		SPEECH SYNTHESIS			
	Stepwise reading		Stepwise reading		Continous reading	
Ss	Mean time	Text/ time	Mean time	Text/ time	Mean time	Text/ time
1	43.3	0.28	2.1	0.39	11.1	0.78
2	39.3	0.08	-	-	-	-
6	-	-	1.6	0.23	11.2	0.93
7	48.4	0.27	-	-	-	-
8	33.3	0.30	5.6	0.49	52.6	1.06
9	47.8	0.27	1.1	0.42	52.8	1.21
10	158.3	0.10	37.4	0.14	10.4	0.58
ALL	61.7	0.22	9.6	0.33	27.6	0.91

Note. The Time/text column is the ratio between text measured in kilobytes (1024 bytes) and time measured in minutes.

To summarize, when using speech synthesis, subjects could consume more text per time unit. A larger proportion of commands was also used for reading new articles and moving to new levels, rather than just using the "next sentence" command.

4. DISCUSSION

The present study is one in a series of investigations of blind people's reading of a computerized daily newspaper. Previous results were reported in Drottz (1986), and Drottz and Hjelmquist (1985, 1986). The results of the studies are quite similar. With respect to the interviews it was found that the subjects expressed positive or very positive attitudes towards the new reading possibility. They all strongly stressed blind people's needs for current daily news, chosen by themselves, and easily accessible whenever they want to read, without relying on sighted people. The access to a complete daily newspaper not only increases visually-impaired people's general knowledge of every-day events but also their self-esteem as they feel less different from sighted people. The information was also available at the same time, or even earlier, as the sighted people got their morning paper. Another aspect of this is that the preferences for what kind of material to read varied considerably between the 12 subjects. The more restricted the information made available to blind people, the less these differences in preferences can be satisfied. Access to a complete newspaper is a change in this situation.

An important difference between the present study and the previous ones is that in this study the subjects had access to a tape-recorded version of the newspaper throughout the whole investigation period. This fact probably explains why the reported mean reading time in this study was only half or a quarter of the value in Drottz (1986).

As the participants in this study were familiar with the newspaper through tapes it could be supposed that it was easier for them to find their way through the paper than for the previous subjects. Furthermore, the previous groups, (Drottz & Hjelmquist; 1985, 1986), seemed to be more frustrated when they did not get the paper, than the present group. One likely explanation is that the participants in this study at least had the cassette recorded version to read while the previous subjects did not get any paper at all.

The participants thought that they used the same commands for reading, and about the same reading time per day, independent of whether they read braille or speech synthesis. However, they expressed different reactions to the two reading modalities. Braille was thought to be a more active way of reading, giving a more immediate contact and understanding of the text. But the picture is more complicated than this, since they also thought that the rather slow presentation rate of text in the braille modality interfered with getting an overview of the text content. Speech synthesis allowed a more rapid text generation which was considered to facilitate understanding. The peculiarities of the speech synthesizer "voice" did not create any great problems in this respect. About half of the participants said they would prefer speech synthesis in general due to the greater speed and consequently the possibility for comsuming more text than with the VersaBraille.

The subjects did not report any clear differences between different types of text with respect to comprehension, though they pointed out that material of personal interest would be easier to understand, as well as articles written in a "simple" language.

A further interesting finding was that the participants seemed to use the new technique and the cassette-recorded version as complementary reading facilities. Material not available on the cassette was read with the new device. Articles of particular interest and long articles also seemed to be preferred in the cassette version, especially during the braille reading period.

There were clear differences in command use between the two modalities. The total amount of keystrokes was significantly higher for the braille reading. The pattern of command use also differed. When reading braille almost 90% of all commands were next sentence commands. When reading speech synthesis, the corresponding figure was only about 40% and about 25% were continuous reading commands. This difference is of course partly dependent on the fact that "continuous reading" was not available for braille reading, (the possibility for continuous reading with braille was actually pointed out as a possible improvement by the subjects). However, there are other indications that the use of commands differ in the two modalities. Thus, when reading speech synthesis, moves in the hierarchical structure were more frequent. Article search was also more common in speech synthesis. Altogether, reading with speech synthesis gives the impression of being more flexible than braille reading. The differences between reading strategies in the two modalities thus seem greater than reported by the subjects.

It could also be noted that, independent of modality, the possibility for saving positions was hardly ever used, and that when reading speech synthesis, the different repetition commands (same sentence, same article) were also very rarely used. The same was true for speech modification commands. These results fit very well with what the subjects reported.

Our study shows that the technique applied to transmission of daily newspapers to blind and severely visually-impaired persons is an efficient way of increasing the quantity and quality of information for these people. The technique was well received by the participants, who reported good comprehension of the text material independent of reading modality. The participants clearly showed different preferences for what text material to read, but at the same time a rather stereotypic way of using the reading commands, especially in the braille modality.

In the future we will study larger groups of users to see if the results of the present study will be replicated. We will also investigate the comprehension and memory for text, in different modalities, in more detail. A larger group of subjects will also make possible comparisons with sighted people's reading habits, e.g. with respect to time spent reading the paper and preferences for different text contents.

REFERENCES

Drottz, B.-M., Facilitating Reading for Blind People: A Study of Braille- and Speech Synthesis Presentation of a Computerized Daily Newspaper, Göteborg Psychological Reports, No 3 (University of Göteborg, 1986).

Drottz, B.-M., and Hjelmquist, E., Reaktioner på läsning av radioöverförd dagstidning - talsyntes och punkskrift. Synskadade i Malmö, Rapport från Psykologiska institutionen, No. 3, (University of Göteborg, 1985).

Drottz, B.-M., and Hjelmquist, E., Blind People Reading a Daily Radio Distributed Newspaper: Braille and Speech Synthesis, in: Hjelmquist, E. and Nilsson L.-G., (eds.), Communication and handicap, (North-Holland, Amsterdam, 1986) pp. 127-140.

Rubinstein, H., FM Transmission of Digitalized Daily Newspaper for Blind People, Global Telecommunication Conference, Vol 1, (Atlanta: IEEE Communication Society, 1984) pp. 532-534.

WORK WITH DISPLAY UNITS 86
B. Knave and P.-G. Wideback (eds.)

STUDY OF VISUAL PERFORMANCE ON A MULTI-COLOR VDU OF COLOR DEFECTIVE AND NORMAL TRICHROMATIC SUBJECTS

Guy VERRIEST*, Ian ANDREW** and André UVIJLS*

SUMMARY

Seventy-two normal people, males and females subdivided in 3 age groups and in 3 groups of academic achievement, and also 14 protanomals, 16 protanopes, 16 deuteranomals and 15 deuteranopes were subjected to several tests using 14 colors displayed by a multi-color VDU.

Two color naming tests showed big differences between the manufacturer's color names and those used by the normal subjects, and much poorer performances in the color defectives.

Two color discrimination tests showed (1) that, even in normal subjects, colors become confused along tritan isochromatic lines if they are presented successively instead of simultaneously, (2) that different stimuli are more often called same by the anomalous trichromats, while on the contrary, same stimuli are more often called different by the anomalous trichromats, and (3) that the colors frequently confused by the defectives can easily be predicted from the convergence centres. Response time can be considered as a measure of the difficulty of the task, but is at the interindividual level much influenced by age.

The performances in color naming and discrimination were poorer in the older normal, in the males and in the people with lower academic achievement.

A conspicuity test showed (1) that letters in more saturated colors are detected over a wider area, and (2) that such performance is worse in older subjects, but not necessarily worse in color defective individuals.

Correlation assessment showed that performance cannot be predicted precisely by standard color vision tests.

INTRODUCTION

The most usual and straightforward way of displaying colors on a shadow mask cathode ray tube with three electron guns and three phosphors is to control the output from each gun to give

*Dept. of Ophthalmology of the Univ. of Ghent, Akademisch Ziekenhuis, De Pintelaan 185, B-9000 GENT, Belgium.
**Human Factors Laboratory, IBM United Kingdom Laboratories Ltd., Hursley Park, WINCHESTER, England.

7 possibilities : the 3 primary colors (red, green, and blue), 3 secondary colors each obtained by additive mixture of 2 primary colors (yellow, cyan, and magenta) and only 1 tertiary mixture (white). The multicolor monitor that we used is somewhat more sophisticated, because it is possible to obtain on it not only 7 such "dark" or saturated colors, but also 7 similar but more intense "light" colors. We know the manufacturer's names for the colors, the spectral energy distribution curves, the chromaticity coordinates, and the photopic luminances : see Table I. For most of the tests the colors were displayed as rectangular targets of 4 sizes.

Colors Used	Chromaticity Coordinates x	y	Luminance $\log_{10}$ cd.m^{-2}
(1) Blue	0.149	0.073	1.33
(2) Green	0.302	0.566	2.33
(3) Cyan	0.237	0.333	1.80
(4) Red	0.643	0.339	1.68
(5) Magenta	0.325	0.180	1.42
(6) Brown	0.534	0.415	1.78
(7) White	0.292	0.287	2.11
(9) Light Blue	0.189	0.195	1.86
(10) Light Green	0.289	0.428	2.13
(11) Light Cyan	0.257	0.295	2.13
(12) Light Red	0.435	0.293	1.88
(13) Light Magenta	0.308	0.199	1.89
(14) Yellow	0.341	0.478	2.16
(15) High-Intensity White	0.306	0.301	2.15

On the other hand we had 72 subjects with normal color vision, selected so that this group could be subdivided for analysis into subgroups of equal numbers according to age, sex, and educational level. Protanomaly, protanopia, deuteranomaly and deuteranopia were each represented by at least 14 subjects.

The multicolor VDU was used in a blacked-out room, the walls of which had approximately 60% reflectance. The room luminance measured on a horizontal surface immediately in front of the VDU screen was 500 lx. The experimental program was stored on a diskette and presented on the VDU by a computer. For most tests the responses were made on the keyboard and recorded on diskette. The computer also recorded response times.

FREE COLOR NAMING

Targets with all 56 combinations of the 14 colors and the 4 targets sizes were presented successively on the screen in fixed pseudo-random order and for periods of 1 s. The subject was asked to name each color.

For analysis, we took account only of the hue names. Of course, we had to accept the manufactuere's terminology. However, "cyan" and "magenta" are used mainly by photographers. It soon became evident also that we have to accept "turquoise" and "blue-green" as synonyms of "cyan", "orange", "ochre" and "beige" as synonyms of "brown", "purple", "mauve", "violet", "lilac" as synonyms of "magenta". Assessing all other hue namings as errors, the scores showed that older normals make more errors than younger normals, the male more errors than the female, and the subjects with lower educational level more errors than the others. The anomalous trichromats make many more errors than the normals and the dichromats make many more errors than the corresponding anomalous trichromats. Protans make more errors than the deutans.

Magenta is often called blue by the defectives. The normals name white as blue, purple, and white in nearly equal proportions; the defective subjects use much more the color name blue.

GUIDED COLOR NAMING

For this test the subject was asked to look at color names coded by numbers namely : blue, green, turquoise, red, purple, yellow, white, pink, orange, nothing. The test consisted of the presentation of the same targets as in the first test, but the subject was asked to identify each presented color by its code number.

For analysis distinction was made between "no answer", "allowable errors", and "full errors". Allowable errors were defined from the normals' results in the first test. All kinds of errors are more frequent in the older normals, in the male and in the subjects with primary education level. Furthermore, the dichromats make fewer "allowable errors" than the corresponding anomalous trichromats and than the normals while, on the contrary, the dichromats make more "full errors" than the corresponding anomalous trichromats and many more than the normals. White is much less frequently called blue or purple than in the first test.

Our results confirm that for normal subjects under good conditions but without training, there are no more than 8-10 absolutely identifiable colors. Cyan stimuli were rarely recognized as representing an identifiable color between blue and green. For our subjects "magenta" was purple and "brown" was orange. White was too often called blue.

SPATIAL COLOR DISCRIMINATION

Pairs of equally sized targets were presented simultaneously. The 105 pairs used included all possible combinations of different colors either from the group of "dark" colors, or from the group of "light" colors. In 20% of cases, the pairs of colors were identifical. The subject had to say for each pair either "different" or "same".

A "same" error is realized when different stimuli are wrongly called same. A "different" error is realized when same stimuli are wrongly called different. University level subjects make just a quarter as many "same" errors as the people who went only to primary school. Color-defectives make much more "same" errors than the normals. When pairs of same stimuli are presented, the anomalous trichromats make more "different" errors than the normals and than the dichromats, by greater attempted compensation of the believed inferiority.

In the normals group light red and light magenta were confused in 27% of the presentations, while light cyan and high-intensity white were confused in 23% of the presentations. This confusion occurred still more in the defectives. Moreover, all defectives often confuse green and brown. Defectives also often confuse red and brown. Errors were also noted that are typical for the type of color vision defect. So protans confuse specifically light blue and light magenta and the pair blue and magenta. Deutans confuse specifically light green and light red.

As expected, the color confusions occur chiefly along the confusion lines pertaining to the defect. Our data show only a small and generally nonsignificant increase of the response time because of color-vision defectiveness.

TEMPORAL COLOR DISCRIMINATION

For this test the two colors of each pair were not displayed simultaneously, but one after the other at the same place on the screen. The first color was shown for 0.5 s; then, after a one-second interval, the second color was shown for 0.5 s.

For the normals we now find five new pairs of colors confused in more than 10% of the presentations. They all typify tritan confusions, perhaps an instance of "tachitoscopic tritanopia". Normals' confusions are found in the defective groups. We find again pairs that are confused by both protans and deutans, typically protan confusions and typically deutan confusions. The very distant colors green and red - in fact two primaries of the color system - are confused by the deuteranopes in 37% of the presentations.

COLOR CONSPICUITY

Each of the parts of this test consisted of a display of 23 contiguous rows of 80 white capital letters. After 4.5 s the color of one single letter changed for a further 2 s from white to one of the other "dark" colors. The subject was asked to name this letter, and then the color itself.

We calculated the number of times in which the presented color was not correctly matched, the number of times in which the letter was not correctly identified and the number of times in which the target was not seen at all.

The color errors are more frequent in the younger, in the male, in lower educational level and in color vision defectiveness. The letter errors are much more frequent in the older normals than in the younger ones, while the color-defectives make fewer such mistakes than the normals. The number of "not seen" errors was higher in older normals and in protanopes, but not necessarily in the other color defects.

The comparison of the results for the 6 colors used shows that the color errors occur more frequently for cyan in the normals and for all other colors in the defectives. With normals, letter errors occur most with blue and least with red. With normals "not seen" occurs frequently for cyan.

Admitting that the frequency of "not seen" is inversely correlated with conspicuity, our data confirm the view that color and brightness differences determines the conspicuousness of a color target. The color errors have to be interpreted in terms of color discrimination. The letter errors have to be considered in terms of readability. But let us first speak about another readability test.

SUBJECTIVE READABILITY

In each part of this test the same one line of text in lowercase was presented simultaneously in the 7 colors of one group of colors. The subject had to rank the 7 colors from most easy to read to least easy to read.

When we compare the results of this test with that of another test, in which the subject had to rank the different colors from brightest to dimmest, we state that for normal observers red is not only brighter than it is luminous, but moreover that it is more (subjectively) readable than it is bright.

Our subjective readability data are confirmed by objective readability data from the letter errors in the conspicuity test. Indeed, we found also best readability for red and worst readability for blue.

CORRELATIONS

We calculated the correlation coefficients between the results of quantitative color vision tests and the scores of the quantitative VDU tests. We found that the different grades of an individual's color vision test results do not enable the performance at the VDU to be predicted.

We also calculated the correlation coefficients between the results of different VDU tests and found that correlation is higher for tests implying similar tasks.

CONCLUSION

We may conclude from our experiment that, in comparison with normal users, people who suffer from sex-linked color-defective vision experience difficulties in tasks involving naming, discriminating, or matching the colors on commercial multicolor shadow-mask VDUs. To a lesser extent, among users with normal color vision, the older people can also find these functions relatively more difficult than the younger ones, while people who had only basic school education can make considerably more mistakes of certain types than users with higher education.

The occurrence of congenital color vision defectiveness in the male population and the increasing use of color VDUs make it important to take account of the described difficulties. Possible approaches involve the design of the VDU hardware and software that generate the displays, and may also include investigation into the nature of the illumination of VDU workplaces.

More data and bibliographic references can be found in the IBM Hursley Technical Report TR. 12. 241 (March 1985).

6. AGE

WORK WITH DISPLAY UNITS 86
B. Knave and P.-G. Wideback (eds.)

INFLUENCE OF AGE ON PERFORMANCE AND HEALTH OF VDU WORKERS

Choon-Nam Ong & Wai-On Phoon

Department of Social Medicine & Public Health
National University of Singapore
Kent Ridge
Singapore 0511

ABSTRACT

Many recent studies have indicated that visual fatigue and musculoskeletal problems are associated with the use of visual display units. However, little is known about the influence of age on performance and well-being of VDU operators. This study was conducted in a high speed data entry centre with intensive work load. The average keying speed of the operator was about 10,000 key strokes per hour. A survey on the subjective symptoms and feelings of fatigue of 68 experienced data entry operators revealed that there was no significant difference on physical health for the 42 young (18 – 30 years old) and 26 older operators (31 – 45 years old). However, there was a higher prevalence of visual strain and musculo-skeletal complaints among the older workers. It is believed that domestic chores may aggravate the feeling of strain among the older operators as majority of them were working mothers. A follow-up study on the performances of 22 operators for 5 years showed that there was a significant reverse correlation between age and keying speed. A lower but significant correlation was also noted for typing errors and age.

1. INTRODUCTION

Many recent studies have indicated that VDU operators have more health complaints than the conventional hard-copy office workers (Hultgren & Knave, 1974; Ong et al, 1981; Grandjean, 1984). Furthermore, working with VDUs was also found to be associated with high level of job stress (Elias, 1982). However, there are relatively few reports on the long term health effects of VDU usage and how they affect the performance and well-being of the operators. In this study, we attempted to look into the influence of age on the speed, accuracy and health of 68 experienced VDU operators in a data processing centre with intensive workload.

2. METHODS

2.1 Subjects

This study was conducted on sixty-eight female VDU data-entry operators in a data processing centre. The main task of the operators was to enter alphanumeric information through VDUs to the main computer. The source materials included airline tickets, written documents, computer print-outs, etc. All of the subjects studied were free of any ocular defects discernible under usual clinical examination and had a visual acuity corrected or uncorrected of at least 20/30.

In this study, the 68 operators were divided into two groups: 42 operators of ages 18 – 30 years old (Group I) and 26 of ages 31 – 45 years old (Group II). The average daily working hours in this centre were 8.8 hours. The work place design and VDT task were as described earlier (Ong, Hoong & Phoon, 1981).

2.2. Questionnaire survey

Each subject was required to complete a questionnaire concerning subjective symptoms, working conditions and job stress. The questionnaire on subjective symptoms was adapted from that proposed by the Committee on cervico-brochial syndrome of the Japanese Association of Industrial Health (Maeda, 1977). Relevant information on personal profile such as age, family commitments, etc were also included in the questionnaire.

2.3. Performance of the operators

The keying speed (in key stroke/hour) and key-punching errors (in percentage) were monitored daily. These results were further analysed by an IBM personal computer using a SPSS programme. The performance of 23 operators was followed up for a total period of 5 years (1980–1984) in order to minimise bias.

3. RESULTS

The profiles of the 68 subjects are as shown in Table 1. About 2/3 of the operators were younger than 30 years of age. The means of duration of service for young and older group were less than 4 years and over 10 years, respectively. Majority (88%) of the older subjects claimed that they have to do domestic work, compared to 50% of the younger workers.

Table 1. Age distribution, length of service and marital status of the VDU operators

Group	No. of persons	Age (Yrs)	Length of service (yrs)	Married: Single	No. of Children
I	42	24.17 ± 2.95 (18–30)	3.67 ± 1.67 (1–7)	24:80	1.38 ± 0.6
II	26	37.8 ± 3.96 (31–45)	11.0 ± 3.32 (6–17)	20:6	1.74 ± 0.7

The prevalence of subjective symptoms among the two groups of VDT operators is shown in Fig. 1 and Fig. 2. It is noted that "tiredness without knowing why", "visual fatigue" and "musculoskeletal aches" were general stresses reported by both group of the workers. There was no difference observed on the psychological stress in the two groups (Fig. 1).

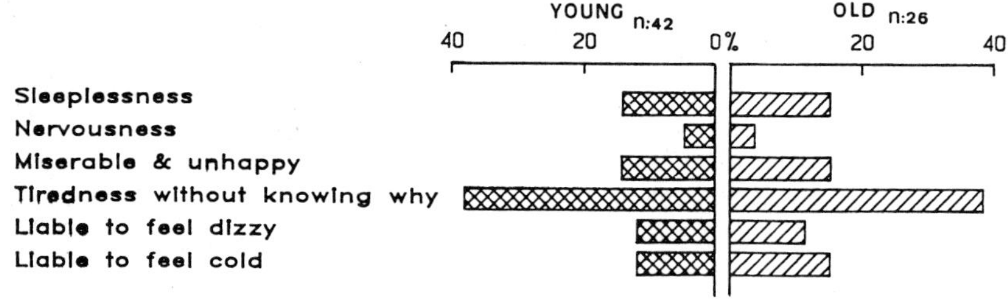

Fig. 1. Subjective symptoms of young and old VDU operators (sychological)

However, visual and musculoskeletal stresses were more pronounced in the older operators (Fig. 2). Over 78% of the operators older than 30 years claimed to have some visual problems. A similar observation was noted for musculoskeletal complaints. They were more common among the older group.

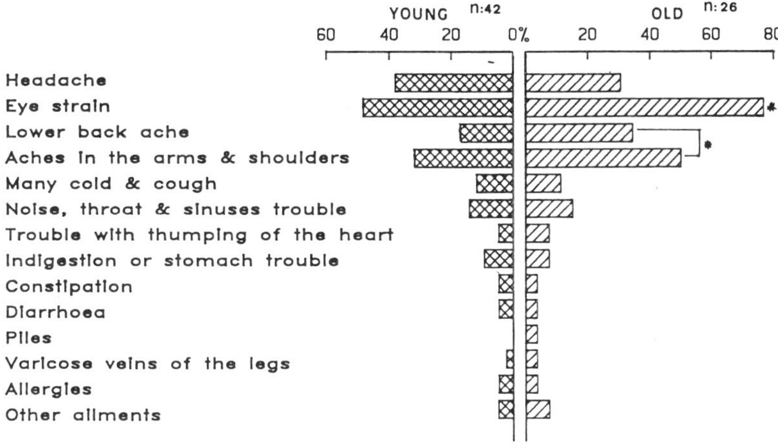

Fig. 2. Subjective symptoms of young and old VDU operators (Physiological complaints) * $p < 0.05$

Performance and errors

Fig. 3 shows the relation between keying speed and age of the 23 operators of age 23 to 42 years old. The average keying speed of these operators was about 11,600 key strokes/hour. The scattergram suggests a significant coefficient of correlation ($r = -0.74$, $p < 0.01$). There was a clear indication of the decrease of speed with age.

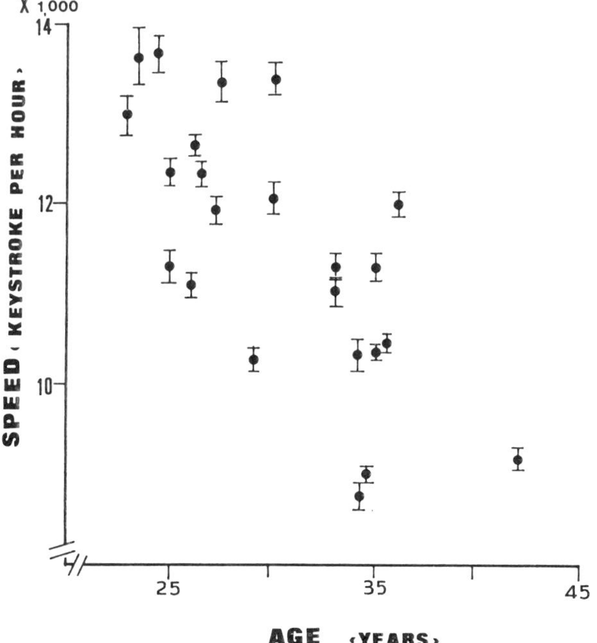

Fig. 3. The relationship between age and keying speed, $r = -0.74$ $Y = -225.883 + 14441.6$

Fig. 4 shows the means and 95% confidence intervals for keying errors of VDT categorised according to their age. A significant increase of error was found to correspond closely to the increase of age ($r=0.5$, $p<0.05$).

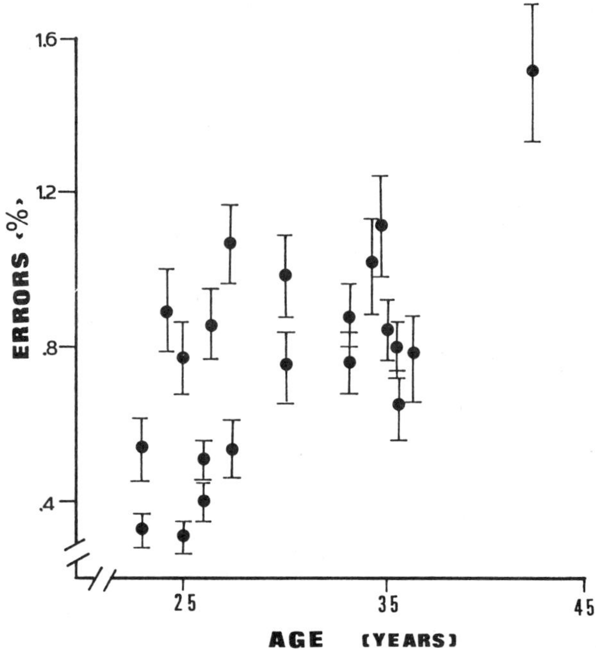

Fig. 4. The relationship between age and keying errors, $r=0.05$ $Y=0.028\,x-0.118$

4. DISCUSSION

Headache has been found to be a common symptom among office workers (Ostberg, 1979). In the present survey, about 34% of data entry operators complained of frequent headaches. This was slightly higher than the 30% of conventional office workers studied earlier in Singapore (Ong et al, 1981). However, no significant difference was observed between the young and the older group as far as the psychological stresses were concerned (Fig. 1).

Epidemiological studies have clearly indicated that musculoskeletal strain is one of the most common subjective complaints among VDU operators (Hultgreen & Knave, 1974; Grandjean, 1984; Ong et al, 1984). It is also generally agreed that this work-related symptom is the result of the peculiar VDU task, which demands a specific pattern of work design, i.e. the combination of repetitive, stereotyped exertion on upper arms, static postures, mental and visual taxing activity. Traditional office lighting and furniture are designed for workers reading papers flat on a desk and are not necessarily right when they need to read characters on reflecting, vertical glass screen. As for the present case, operators must maintain attention to the task for over 8 hours a day. The constraint on posture would no doubt cause muscular discomfort. The results here also indicated that the effects were more pronounced among the older VDU operators. However, it is necessary to point out that majority of the older operators were working mothers, who in addition to their daily work were responsible for domestic duties and maternal activities. The fatigue resulting from constraint of the work environment may be similar for both groups, but the domestic chores may aggravate the feeling 1984). It is believed that individual activities after work could also influence the above observation.

There is no evidence that working with VDUs can harm the eye sight (Lee, 1985). It was noted in the present study that, although none of the older operators was having any visual defects, they had a higher prevalence of visual complaints. In addition, there were close correlations between keying speed and age, and keying errors and age. It is believed that aging of visual mechanism and the decrease in visual ability may have contributed to the above observations. An additional important aspect could be the physiological changes of aging on information processing. According to Ostberg (1979), the main visual functions at VDT work are accommodation and adaptation. Kurimoto et at (1983) showed that VDU work might lead to inhibition on visual accommodation and this inhibition was more severe than the conventional office work. They also demonstrated that the inhibition was more evident in the elderly and middle age operators than in the young VDU operators. Older workers are known to be slower in their movement than the young and they also differ in physical and mental abilities (Yokomizo, 1985). Evaluations on manual calculation, copying of sentences, short-term memory and concentration at work of workers from age 20 – 69, Yokomizo and Sato (1985) showed that deleterioration of these abilities increases with people in their twenties to forties. In a more recent study measuring the visual evoke potential of VDU operators, Camisa & Schmidt (1984) showed that older operators required a longer visual processing time than the young operators.

The scope of the present study was limited to the influence of age on keying speed, accuracy and the general health status of VDU operators. As such, many pertinent questions related to the aging of the operators such as visual deterioration, psychomotor process of keyboarding, and visual muscular coordinations were not discussed. As there will be more and more people involving with VDUs, there is obviously a need to look into these important factors. When discussing on ergonomic approach to VDU work, we often focussed only on the physical environment, such as chair, table and work place design. This is the right time now for us to look into the matching of user and technology, task and organisation, in order to enhance the quality of working life.

REFERENCES

[1] Camisa JM & MJ Schmidt (1984). Performance, fatigue and stress for the older VDT user. In Ergonomics and Health in Modern Offices. Ed. E Grandjean, Taylor and Francis, pp. 276-279.

[2] Elias R, F Cail, M Tisserand, H Christmann (1982). Investigations in operators working with CRT display terminals: relationships between task content and psychological alterations. In Grandjean E, Vigliani E ed. Ergonomics Aspects of VDT, Taylor & Francis, London, pp. 211-217.

[3] Grandjean E (1984). Postural problems at office machine work station. In Ergonomics and Health in Modern Offices. Ed. E Grandjean, Taylor & Francis, pp. 445-455.

[4] Hultgren GV & B Knave (1974). Discomfort glare and disturbances from light reflections in an office with CRT display terminals. Appl. Ergo. 5, 2 – 8.

[5] Kurimoto S, T Iwasaki, T Nomura, K Noro, S Yamamoto (1983). Influence of VDT work on eye accommodation. J UOEH 5, 101-110.

[6] Lee, WR. (1985) working with Visual Display Units. Br. Med. J. 291, 989-991.

[7] Maeda K (1977). Occupational cervicobrachial disorder and its causative factors. J Human Ergo. 6, 193-202.

[8] Ong CN, BT Hoong & WO Phoon (1981). Visual and muscular fatigue in operators using visual display terminals. J Human Ergo. 10, 161-171.

[9] Ong CN (1984). VDT work place design and physical fatigue. In Ergonomics and Health in Modern Offices. Ed. E Grandjean, Taylor & Francis, pp. 477-483.

[10] Ostberg O (1980). Accommodation and visual fatigue in display work. Display, 7, 81-85.

[11] Sauter SL (1984). Predictors of strain in VDT users and traditional office workers. In Ergonomics and Health in Modern Offices. Ed. E Grandjean, Taylor & Francis, pp. 129-135.

[12] Tan TC & CN Ong (1983). Chronic fatigue in female keypunch operator's work related or menses related. In Proceedings of 10th Asian Conference on Occupational Health, Ed. CS Lai, HP Lee, WF LOW & CN Ong, pp. 239-246.

[13] Yokomizo, Y (1985). Measurement of ability of older workers, Ergonomises, 28, 843-854.

[14] Yokomizo, Y & Sato T, (1980). MODAPTS Assessment manual, Tokyo, Japan MODAPTS Association.

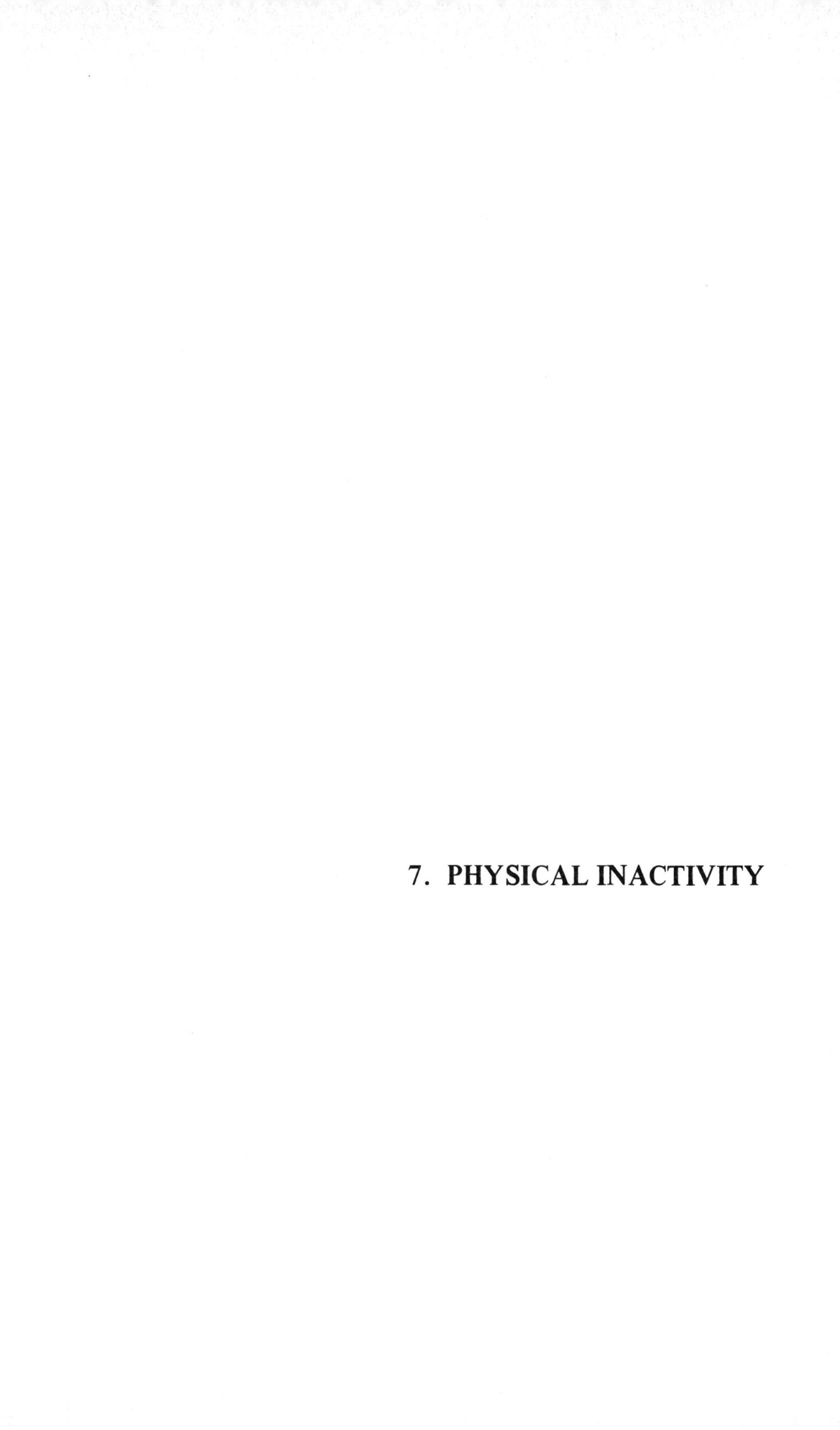

7. PHYSICAL INACTIVITY

WORK WITH DISPLAY UNITS 86
B. Knave and P.-G. Wideback (eds.)

SHORT-AND LONG-TERM EFFECTS OF EXTREME PHYSICAL INACTIVITY - A REVIEW

Åsa KILBOM

Work Physiology Unit, Research Department of the Swedish National Board of Occupational Safety and Health, S-171 84 Solna, Sweden

Apart from effects on cardiovascular disease, little is known about the adverse health effects of a sedentary life style.Marked disturbances in metabolism, cardiovascular responses, fluid-electrolyte balance, aerobic power and muscle-connective tissue strength have been observed as an effect of extreme physical inactivty during prolonged bed rest or passive sitting. Some of these changes take place within the first hours or days of passivity, and many of the underlying mechanisms are demonstrable also in less extreme physical inactivity. Adverse health effects related to physical inactivity should therefore be investigated more in studies of sedentary groups, like VDT-operators. Prevention, using gymnastics and integrating physically more active tasks in the work routines, should be initiated. The feasibility and efficiency of different preventive strategies remain to be evaluated.

1.INTRODUCTION

1.1. Health effects of physical inactivity.

In ergonomics, static and dynamic overexertion, fatigue and ensuing musculo-skeletal injuries have been the focus of interest for many years. The trend has been towards a gradual decrease in the amount of physical work performed occupationally. The benefits, in terms of available employment opportunities for physically disabled and weak individuals are obvious. However, humans are equipped with a cardiovascular system, muscles, tendons and bones which have adapted to physical activity over millions of years. As the degree of occupational physical activity decreases, less and less use is made of the capacity for exercise. In VDT work the lack of physical activity is probably more marked than in any other modern tasks, Fig. 1. The question of possible short- and longterm health effects, related to lack of physical activity in such jobs, should therefore be raised.

To date, no epidemiological studies aimed at this specific question have been performed in VDT operators. However, several previous and some recent studies indicate, that adverse health effects of sedentary occupations can be identified. The role played by physical inactivity in cardiovascular disease has been studied extensively. In some other diseases like osteoporosis, muscle-joint disease and colon cancer, a relationship has been suggested, but needs further scientific support.

Fig 1. Sedentary - prolonged sitting.
Drawing by Bo Näsström.

One aim of this review is to:

- summarize some recent epidemiological studies concerning longterm health effects of sedentary occupations.

1.2. Extreme physical inactivity

One approach that might lead to a better understanding of possible health effects in sedentary jobs, is to study the effects of prolonged extreme physical inactivity.

Already in the 1940's some basic studies were made to increase our understanding of the effects of prolonged bed rest. The incentive was the concern about the laborious reconditioning necessary for patients for whom prolonged bed rest had been prescribed. Effects like muscular weakness, muscle shortening, restriction of joint movement, orthostatic intolerance, constipation and tendency to urinary calculi were orginally ascribed to the underlying disease, not to the bed rest as such.Studies by i.a. Deitrick et al (7), Taylor et al (32) and Whedon et al (36) originally identified physiological consequences of bed rest as separate from disease, and formed the basis for most of the subsequent work. Fig. 2.

During the last two decades physiological responses during extreme physical inactivity have been studied. The reason was the extreme conditions encountered during manned space flights. Hence, a large variety of extreme conditions, like immobilization, horizontal or head down positions, variations in external pressure during water immersion and lower body negative pressure, were studied. The physiological effects - physical deconditioning, decreased orthostatic tolerance, water and electrolyte disturbances, weight loss, bone demineralization and glucose intolerance have since been reviewed by several authors (14, 15, 26, 34).

In fact, Greenleaf (15) after an extensive summary of the negative effects, concludes that "the only positive benefit to the organism from prolonged maintenance in the horizontal body position seems to be the reduction of energy consumption". According to the same author the ability of man to withstand gravity, stand upright and perform physical exercise should be looked upon as an adaptation, gained from our original state of immersion in the womb.
Other aims of this review are to:

- summarize present knowledge about the effects of extreme physical inactivity during bed rest and prolonged sitting.

- discuss to what extent such results can be used to predict responses to moderate inactivity in sedentary occupational tasks, e.g. VDT-work.

Such extrapolations may be misleading, unless the underlying physiological responses are well understood. For example, bed rest implies decreased joint movements, lack of muscular exercise and energetic demands, lack of hydrostatic pressure, and/or lack of longitudinal compression of long bones. These factors can to varying extent occur in sedentary jobs. Thus a critical appraisal of the different effects of bedrest vs. their specific causative factors is necessary.

One factor that warrants such extrapolations is that the adaptation to bed rest, physical inactivity or weightlessness is a fast process (hours and days). Thus, many of the accompanying physiological changes start within minutes or hours of the onset of bed rest and develop within a few days, or even within an eight hour working day. Moreover, studies on long-term physiological effects of sedentary or seated work are scarce.

Winkel (37) and Shvartz et al (28) have studied the shortterm effects of inactive sitting. Some of these results, especially those concerned with macro- and microcirculation will be summarized in the paper by Winkel (38). The psychological effects of prolonged physical inactivity and monotony will be described in the paper by Åkerstedt (1). The effects on the low back - demineralization and reduced disk metabolism will be described in the paper by Hansson (18).

2. SHORTTERM PHYSIOLOGICAL EFFECTS OF EXTREME PHYSICAL INACTIVITY

2.1. Physical work capacity

In a classical study by Saltin et al (27), three weeks of strict bed rest led to 26% reduction of maximum oxygen uptake (max VO_2), caused mainly by a reduced stroke volume. Heart volume was reduced, heart rate at submaximal exercise was increased, but arterio-venous O_2 difference during exercise was unchanged. In other studies reductions of max VO_2 from 5 to 15 % have been reported (cf.31). The major mechanism of these changes is the lack of physical exercise which affects myocardinal function and/or peripheral oxygen delivery. However this does not seem to give the full explanation, as inactivity during chair rest seems to cause a less marked reduction in max VO_2 (24). Thus, the maintenance of hydrostatic pressure may be another mechanism which helps to maintain working capacity.

The effects of any change in physical activity depends to a large extent on the subjects' initial physical capacity (9). Therefore prolonged chair rest can be expected to affect unfit individuals less, whereas the capacity of well trained persons will be seriously affected, unless leisure time physical training is undertaken. The problem, according to observations in different occupational categories, is that sedentary daily work tends to become a life style, and makes people less prone to undertake leisure physical training.

Fig 2. Sedentary - prolonged bedrest.
Drawing by Bo Nässtrӧm.

2.2. Orthostatic tolerance

One of the most obvious effects of prolonged bed rest is a decreased orthostatic tolerance. Some of the components of this orthostatic intolerance, like changes in plasma volume and venous compliance take place within the first 3 days of bed rest (14).

The effect of bed rest on orthostatic tolerance is usually ascribed to the lack of hydrostatic pressure in the lower part of the body, which affects the vascular tone and thereby the venous return to the heart (cf. 14). Accordingly, passive daily sitting during a period of bed rest partly maintained orthostatic tolerance in 4 subjects (26). Other effects of bed rest, like decreased plasma volume and red blood cell mass, also affect the venous return and contribute to a decreased orthostatic tolerance. These effects are caused mainly by the decrease in physical activity, and training experiments demonstrate that the orthostatic tolerance improves during a period of physical training (21).

In several studies Lamb et al have shown that orthostatic intolerance can also be caused by physical inactivity (22). Thus, for 4 to 10 days they exposed subjects to passive sitting in an upright position, with the legs supported. Signs of orthostatic intolerance were noted after 4 days already and then gradually became more pronounced. These results are at variance with the study of passive sitting cited above (26), possibly because of differences in degree of physical inactivity. In the study by Lamb et al (22) the subjects were permitted to transfer themselves to wheelchairs to visit the toilet - otherwise they were confined to sitting 16 hours per day and to recumbency for 8 hours. In this way an extreme degree of physical inactivity was obtained, but hydrostatic pressure was maintained nearly as high as in passive standing.

Although the physical inactivity in these studies was extreme, they indicate that occupations implying long-term passive sitting may affect orthostatic tolerance.

2.3. Reduced muscle and connective tissue strength

Muscle wasting and reduced strength is a well-known effect of physical inactivity. The decrease in strength is obvious after a few days and is directly related to the degree of inactivity (10,17). Studies on reduced muscle and connective tissue strength due to inactivity are important for the understanding of individual differences in susceptibility to trauma and overload. They may also help us to understand the mechanisms of occupational musculoskeletal injury. The discussions have so far mainly focused on the significance of muscle strength, but the connective tissue strength is probably just as important.

It is not until the past 10-15 years, that it has been possible to study experimentally the reduction in strength of connective tissue in entire muscle-tendon-bone sections of animals. Studies of increased as well as decreased physical activity have been performed - the decrease has usually been brought about by immobilizing a limb in plaster for some weeks (5, 6, 33). It has been demonstrated that the strength of the medial collateral ligament in animals is decreased after immobilization, i.e. a given external load gives rise to a much higher relative strain. We also know that the opposite occurs after physical training.

2.4. Ca^{++} -loss

Already within the first two days of bed rest, an increased output of Ca^{++} and phosphorus in the urine and faeces takes place (7,13). The rate of Ca^{++}-loss during prolonged bed rest seems to remain constant for a long period of time. The mechanism is incompletely known.
Daily physical exercise (isotonic or isometric) during bed rest does not seem to protect the body from Ca^{++}-loss. Thus the intermittent tension exerted by muscles on bone structure does not protect against Ca^{++}-loss during bed rest, although it may accelerate the remineralization of bone once bed rest has been abandoned.

The daily longitudinal compression of the long bones during normal daily activities has been put forward as the mechanism whereby a normal skeletal Ca^{++} balance is maintained. However longitudinal skeletal pressure applied intermittently through the legs for 3-4 hours per day was ineffective (19,26). Neither did the moderate compression of the spinal column, and the hydrostatic pressure obtained during passive sitting prevent Ca^{++}-losses (26). However, if the hydrostatic pressure was varied by oscillating subjects from horizontal to 20° head down during bed rest, urine Ca^{++}-output was normalized, possibly through an effect on renal blood flow (36). Thus the only effective remedy against Ca^{++}-losses appears to be the long-term continuous change in posture, as normally encountered in the ambulatory state.

2.5. Electrolyte and fluid balance

Already during the first day of bed rest diuresis increases (30); the fluid is mainly taken from the extracellular space. This decrease in extracellular volume predominantly affects plasma volume, with the wellknown effects on orthostatic tolerance. Thus after 4 days of bed rest plasma volume was reduced by ca 440 ml. Plasma volume remained low even in prolonged bed rest, while extracellular volume was restored (13). The increased water loss through diuresis is associated with urine losses of protein, creatinine, chloride, phosphorus and glucose, so that the plasma concentrations are maintained. The main cause of these changes has been assumed to be the changes in hydrostatic pressure. However, Lamb et al (22) in their studies of extreme physical inactivity by chair rest, obtained nearly the same plasma volume changes as during bed rest. The effects of chair rest on extracellular volumes and electrolytes remain to be studied. Thus, in order to predict effects of occupational long-term sitting on fluid and electrolyte balance more needs to be known about the relative importance of hydrostatic pressure and physical inactivity.

2.6. Glucose intolerance

During prolonged bed rest, glucose tolerance tests reveal both an exaggerated hyperglycemia and a hyperinsulinemia (8,23). These responses can be evoked after only two days of bed rest. Exogenous insulin is just as ineffective as endogenous, suggesting either release of an insulin inhibitor or changes in sensitivity to insulin at the receptor site (muscle cell membrane) in response to bed rest (cf. 14). It is clear that the effect is related to lack of physical activity, and that it can be counteracted by energy expenditure of any kind (isometric or isotonic) in sufficient amounts. Thus physical training has an effect opposite to bed rest, increasing insulin sensivity (29). The exact mechanism, however, is unknown as are the possible health effects. In addition, it is unknown if a less extreme physical inactivity, as in prolonged constrained sitting, increases the glucose intolerance.

3 LONGTERM HEALTH EFFECTS OF PHYSICAL INACTIVITY

3.1 Everyday fatigue and cardiovascular disease

A sedentary occupation is always associated with a low physical fitness, unless leisure time physical activity is undertaken. The long term effects of a low fitness level on cardiovascular disease have been discussed extensively and the reader is referred to e.g. Åstrand and Rodahl or WHO publications for further reading (3, 16). The likely mechanisms are through a lowering of blood lipid concentration, especially cholesterol levels and LDL/HDL ratio, lowering of catecholamine concentration and effects on blood pressure. Although it has not been possible to prove conclusively that mortality from degenerative cardiovascular disease is increased in unfit individuals, there is no doubt that the time necessary for rehabilitation after a myocardial infarction is increased, and so is the risk of secondary infarction. Another aspect which is often overlooked is that a low fitness level induces a large strain on the individual in his/her everyday life. Ordinary demands, like walking upstairs, performing manual materials handling etc lead to much greater fatigue in an unfit individual (2).

3.2 Osteoporosis

Urinary Ca^{++} loss due to physical inactivity has been put forward as one likely cause of osteoporosis. Others are hormonal changes (mainly in women), smoking, and reduced Ca^{++} uptake due to deficient absorption or diet. The relationship with physical activity is strengthened by studies demonstrating a higher bone mineral content in athletes than in non-athletes (25).

Over the past 5 years a series of studies have been performed in Malmö, demonstrating that so called fragility fractures (in distal radius, trochanter and ankle) have increased over the past 30 years (4, 20). The incidence has grown rapidly mainly in individuals above 50 years of age, and the medical care system is sagging under the large demands. The causes are still obscure; smoking patters and effects of urbanization (traffic) are some possible explanations. It is also a likely hypothesis that decrease in physical activity in some subgroups of the population during the past 30 years plays a role. It has not been possible to demonstrate a lowering of average fitness level in the Swedish population during this period, but it is likely that the *variation* in fitness among different categories is now larger than before. Some admittedly participate in jogging, but others are probably more inactive than 30 years ago. A further reduction in activity level may thus lead to an even larger incidence of osteoporosis.

3.3 Colon cancer

Recently several epidemiological studies have demonstrated a increased incidence of colon cancer in individuals with sedentary occupations (11, 12, 35). In two of these studies, a negative relationship between years in strenuous jobs and risk ratio was demonstrated. The mechanism is still unknown, but a slowing of bowel movements during prolonged sitting, leading to a increased exposure of the bowel mucosa to cancerogenic substances in the faeces can be suspected. In the study of Gerhardsson (12) there was also indirect evidence that food habits had not confounded the results.

4. CONCLUSIONS

A large number of short and longterm negative effects of physical inactivity have been suggested or demonstrated. Table 1. The longterm effects need further substantiation in epidemiological studies of e.g. VDT-operators.

Table 1. Summary of short- and longterm effects of reduced physical activity

Shortterm (hours, days, weeks)			**Longterm** (years)
	Bedrest	Prolonged passive sitting	
Fitness level	↘	↘	Fatigue, cardiovascular disease
Orthostatic tolerance	↘	↘?	?
Connective and muscle tissue strength	↘	↘?	Muscle/joint disease ?
Glucose intolerance	↘	?	?
Plasma volume	↘	↘	?
Ca^{++} loss	↗	?	Osteoporosis, fragility fractures ?
Bowel movements	↘	↘	Colon cancer ?

Many of the effects have been observed in conjunction with experimental and epidemiological studies of physical training. Thus a large amount of knowledge concerned with methods to improve physical fitness has been gathered. What still remains to be investigated, and what training experts have not yet considered, is how to make *occupational* work more physically active. We know that many people because of house work, children and long journeys can not spend as much leisure time as they want being physically active. Moreover, it is a common observation that extreme occupational physical inactivity is seldom compensated by an increased activity in leisure time. Therefore no efforts should be saved in order to reorganize physically inactive jobs. Some pertinent questions are the following:

- Is the traditional pause gymnastic good enough?
- How often should the activity be performed?
- What activity level is necessary to bring about a risk reduction?
- Is it possible to integrate physical activity as a normal part of the work routines?

REFERENCES

[1] Åkerstedt T, Torsvall L and Gillberg M. Inactivity, night work and fatigue,this volume.
[2] Åstrand I and Kilbom Å (1969) Aerospace Med 40, 885-890.
[3] Åstrand P O and Rodahl K (1986). Textbook of Work Physiology 3rd Ed. MacGraw-Hill, New York.
[4] Bengnér U and Johnell O (1985) Acta Orthop Scand 56. 158-160.
[5] Booth FW and Gollnick PD (1983) Med Sci Sports Exerc 15, 415.
[6] Booth FW and Gould EW (1975) Effects of training and disease on connective tissue, in: Wilmore J H and Keogh J E (eds) Exercise and sports Sciences reviews, 3, Academic Press, New York 83-101.
[7] Deitrick J E, Whedon G D, Toscani V and Davis V D (1948) Am J Med 4, 3-35.
[8] Dolkas C and Greenleaf J E (1977) J appl Physiol 43, 1033-1038.
[9] Ekblom B (1969) Acta Physiol Scand, Suppl 328.
[10] Friman G (1976) Effects of acute infectious disease on human physical fitness and skeletal muscle. Acta Universitalis Upsaliensis, No 245.
[11] Garabrant P H, Peters J M, Mack T M (1983) Am J Epidemiol 119, 1005-14.
[12] Gerhardsson M (1986) Läkartidn 83, 1581.
[13] Greenleaf J E, Bernauer E M, Young H L, Morse J T, Staley R W, Juhos I T and Van Beaumont W (1977) J appl Physiol 42, 59.66.
[14] Greenleaf J E and Kozlowski S (1982) in (ed R J Terjung) Exercise and Sports Sciences Reviews, Franklin Inst Press, Phildelphia PA.
[15] Greenleaf J E (1984) J appl Physiol 57 (3), 619-633.
[16] Habitual physiol activity and health (1978). WHO Regional Publications, European Series No 6, Copenhagen.
[17] Halkjaer Kristensen J and Ingemann Hansen T (1985) Scand J Rehab Med Suppl 13.
[18] Hansson T. Prolonged sitting and the back, this volume.
[19] Hantman D A, Vogel J M, Donaldson C L, Friedman R, Goldsmith R S and Hulley S B (1973) J Clin Endocrin Met 36, 845-858.
[20] Johnell O, Nilsson B, Obrant K and Sernbo I (1984) Acta Orthop Scand 55, 290-292.
[21] Kilbom Å (1971) Scand J Clin Lab Invest 28, 141-161.
[22] Lamb L E, Stevens P M and Johnson R L (1965) Aerospace Med 36, 755-763.
[23] Lipman R L, Roskin P, Love T, Triebwasser J, Lecocq F R and Schnure J J (1972) Diabetes 21, 101-107.
[24] Lynch T N, Jensen R L, Stevens P M, Johnson R L and Lamb L E (1967) Aerospace Med 38, 10-20.
[25] Nilsson B E, Westlin N E (1971) Clin Orthop 77, 179-82.
[26] Rodahl K, Birkhead N C, Blizzard J J, Issekutz Jr B and Pruett E D R (1967) in (ed G Blix) Nutrition and physical activity, Almqvist & Wiksell, Stockholm.

[27] Saltin B, Blomqvist G B, Mitchell J H, Johnson R L, Wildenthal K and Chapman C B. (1968) Circulation 38, Suppl 7.
[28] Schvartz E, Reibold R C, White R T, Gaume J G (1982) Aviat Space Environ Med 53, 226-231.
[29] Serman V R, Koivisto V A, Deibert D, Felig P and DeFronzo R A (1979) N Ergl J Med 301, 1200-1204.
[30] Stevens D M, Miller P B, Lynch T N, Gilbert C A, Johnson R L and Lamb L E (1966) Aerospace Med 37, 466-474.
[31] Stremel R W, Convertino V A, Bernauer E M and Greenleaf J E (1976) J appl Physiol 41, 905-909.
[32] Taylor H L, Henschel A, Brozek J and Keys A (1949) J appl Physiol 2, 223-239.
[33] Tipton CM, Matthes RD and Sandage DS (1974) J appl Physiol 37, 758-762.
[34] Vallbona C, Vogt F B, Cardus O, Spences W A and Walters M (1965) NASA Contractor Report, NASA CR-171.
[35] Vena J E, Graham S, Zielezny M, Swanson M K, Barnes R E and Nolan J (1985) 122, 357-65.
[36] Whedon G D, Deitrick J E and Shorr E (1949) Am J Med 6, 684-711.
[37] Winkel J (1985) Arbete och Hälsa nr 35. Arbetarskyddsstyrelsen, Solna, Sweden.
[38] Winkel J. On the significance of physical activity in sedentary work, this volume.

WORK WITH DISPLAY UNITS 86
B. Knave and P.-G. Widebäck (eds.)

ON THE SIGNIFICANCE OF PHYSICAL ACTIVITY IN SEDENTARY WORK

Jørgen WINKEL

National Board of Occupational Safety and Health, Research Department, Unit of Work Physiology, S-171 84 Solna, Sweden

SUMMARY: The innovation of technologies in the industrial countries during the last decades has greatly increased the number of jobs performed in the sitting position (in particular VDU-tasks). The ergonomic quality of workstation design has also been improved considerably. But the corresponding reduction in physical stress does not seem to reduce frequency of complaints from the locomotor system. Based on a number of studies carried out during recent years, a U-shaped relationship between stress and strain is suggested, i.e. strain reactions increase not only when the stress is high but also when it becomes very low. Strain-reducing effects of modest physical activity on circulation in sedentary work is given as an example. It is concluded that further research on acceptable/recommendable physical work stress should comprise studies aimed not only at upper but also at lower limit values.

1. MECHANISATION AND AUTOMATION IN WORKING LIFE REDUCE PHYSICAL STRESS* ON THE WORKER

Extensive mechanisation during the last few decades has radically changed the physical stress pattern of many occupations. Machines have partially replaced human beings, who now become operators. The new work tasks are mainly carried out in a seated position (see Grieco 1986). Work has become less heavy in the traditional sense of the word - the *total* physical stress on the body has decreased.

During this fast development we have often failed to consider man's anthropometry when designing work tasks, workstations and products. Employees are "locked" into unfavourable positions and movements, which are dictated by the shape and function of the equipment. For long periods joints and small muscle groups are burdened with keeping the body or parts of the body in uncomfortable positions. The result is high *local* stress.

Mechanisation is now developing into automation by the introduction of more and more complicated and expensive computer systems. It is estimated that in Sweden these systems will increase by 25-30% every year (Gunnarsson and Söderberg 1983). Many jobs, which were previously quite different and had a large variation in physical stress during the day, are now carried out in the same seated and "locked" working position in front of a terminal (Fig. 1). The increased capital intensity (capital which is tied up in machines, property, products etc) also means that the work periods in front of the terminal often become long, in order to use the equipment efficiently.

* Stress: External force which acts to disturb a person's physiological state and thus cause strain.

As the variation in types of work is decreasing, this creates opportunities for developing purpose-designed seated workstations. These can take into consideration special demands of the work, so that stress on muscles and joints become minimal. Such workstations have been developed for many occupational groups, e.g. lorry drivers, dentists, supermarket cashiers and machine operators in modern processes. An example is given in Fig. 2. In this and equivalent cases further constructional changes can hardly reduce the stress any further. Sometimes the workstation has become so comfortable that the operator does not wish to leave it even during the lunch-breaks (Almqvist 1977)("over-comfortable" seated work stations?).

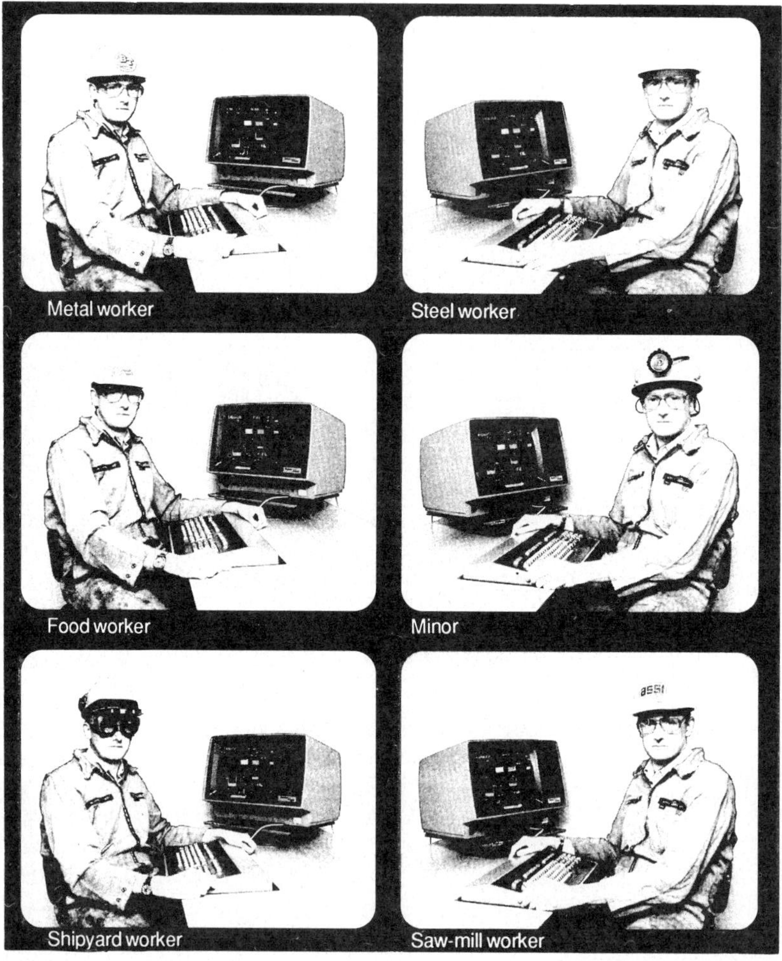

Figure 1. The number of types of workstations is decreasing; the terminal workstation is becoming more and more common (Lindström et al. 1981).

2. REDUCED STRESS LEVEL MAY INCREASE THE STRAIN

The ergonomic advantages of improved design of seated workstations may partly be eliminated by the increased time spent in the same position. Thus, a reduced load (stress) l*evel* on muscles and joints is counterbalanced by an increased exposure *time* so that the *dose* of stress (load level x time) may remain constant. Reduced *variation* in stress may also reduce nutrition of the tissues causing increased strain reactions, e.g. in the intervertebral discs (Adams and Hutton 1983, Holm and Nachemson 1983, Kraemer et al. 1985, Magora 1972). These aspects are rarely considered by ergonomists and work physiologists (e.g. Jonsson 1982).

Figure 2. A prototype workstation for microscope work (Winkel 1984).

Even if the ergonomist should succeed in reducing the stress dose to "zero", this may also be injurious to several organs, e.g. the skeleton (see Kilbom, this volume).

Thus, not only high but also low physical stress seem to increase strain (Fig. 3). Accordingly, Arndt (1983) reported that "even when guidelines are followed and workstations are adjusted to fit individuals, a variety of postural complaints may arise". The aim of ergonomic interventions should therefore be to optimize rather than reduce physical stress as far as possible. This may be obtained by organizational changes in working routines rather than constructional improvements of the workstation.

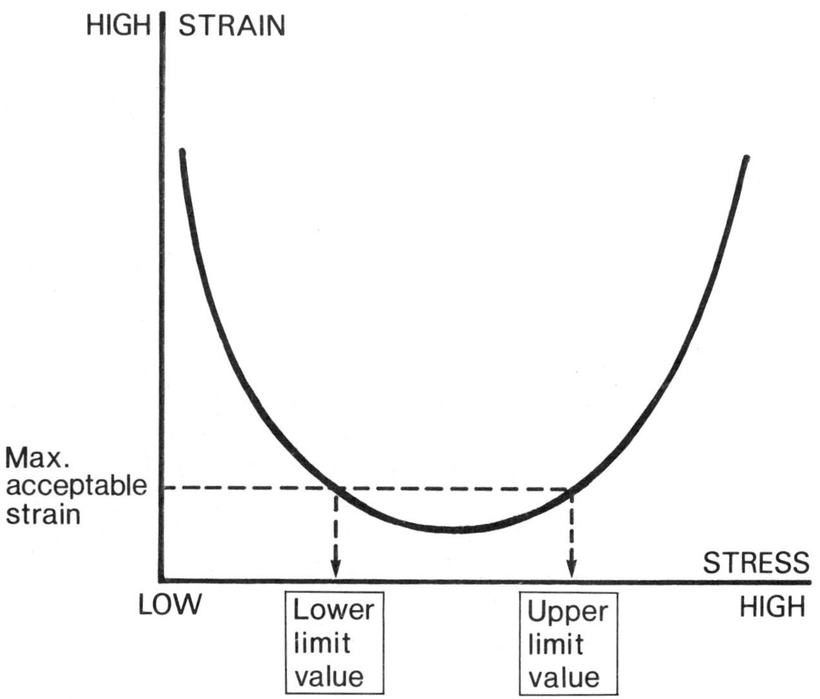

Figure 3. Presumed relationship between stress and strain suggesting introduction of the concept "lower limit value" in addition to "upper limit value".

Unfortunately, we still know very little about the physiological effects of that kind of physical inactivity which occurs in working life (e.g.8 hours of relaxed sitting in front of a terminal interrupted by a few breaks). Most experiments have either been carried out on animals or during extreme inactivity, e.g. bed rest or space flights. Therefore, it is not possible to indicate acceptable lower stress limits for the different organs in the body. However, during recent years some data have appeared on circulatory changes (strain-reactions) during prolonged sitting and the effects of modest leg activity. Below a brief survey of these findings is summarized.

3. CIRCULATORY CHANGES DURING PROLONGED SITTING

It is well-known that high leg activity causes high cardio-vascular strain. However, lack of activity may also increase the strain on circulation.

3.1. Macro-circulatory changes

Towards the end of an 8 hour working day the heart rate (HR) became significantly elevated by 4 min^{-1} during "inactive sitting" (no leg movements) compared with "active sitting" (Winkel and Jørgensen 1986a). The latter task included leg movements to role on the chair between different workstations (distance: 1.75 cm) every 5th min. This may have increased the oxygen consumption and HR. The orthostatic effect on HR during "inactive sitting" may therefore have been larger than 4 min^{-1}.

Shvartz et al. (1982a) showed that mean arterial pressure (MAP) increased by 0.9 kPa (~7 mmHg) during 5 hours of sitting, mainly due to increased diastolic pressure. Thus, prolonged quiet sitting seems to imply a gradual but modest increase in cardio-vascular strain (HR x MAP). During standing, the cardio-vascular adjustments deteriorate if this position is preceded by 5 hours of quiet sitting rather than recumbency (Shvartz et al. 1982b). An increase in cardio-vascular strain during prolonged relaxed sitting may partly be due to a gradual loss in total plasma volume (PV). During "inactive sitting" it was 6-7% (Winkel and Jørgensen 1986b) which may impair venous return from the dependent lower limbs and increase total peripheral resistance. Reduction in PV could be avoided by intermittent walking.

These macro-circulatory changes are small and may cause no major problems for healthy workers. For certain groups of subjects the responses as well as their implications may be different (e.g. pregnant females and patients with varicose veins or resting diastolic blood pressure above 90-95 mmHg).

3.2. Micro-circulatory changes

Orthostasis (e.g. quiet sitting) implies pronounced changes of micro-circulation in the lower limbs. The venous pressure increases and equals a hydrostatic pressure corresponding to the height of the column of blood to the heart (Arnoldi 1965). The resulting increase in net transfer of fluid from plasma to interstitium is counteracted by changes in "the Starling forces": hydrostatic and colloid osmotic pressures of capillary blood and interstitial fluid (Aukland 1984, Noddeland 1984). In addition, lymph flow is raised (Olszewski and Engeset 1980, Olszewski et al. 1977). However, these "oedema-preventing mechanisms" are not sufficient to prevent a gradual increase in interstitial fluid volume (IFV). Thus, 8 hours of "inactive sitting" causes a foot swelling of 4-6% among healthy female subjects.

(Noddeland et al. 1985, Winkel 1981, Winkel and Jørgensen 1986a and b).

Several investigations demonstrate that prolonged sedentary work causes increased foot/lower leg discomfort (e.g. Søndergård Kristensen 1978). It is generally assumed that this is directly or indirectly related to the swelling of the same body segments. Therefore, data on swelling and discomfort obtained in a number of different studies have been put together in Fig. 4 according to the estimated leg activity. When this approaches zero (no leg movements), a pronounced increase in swelling can be observed. Correspondingly, the perceived discomfort increased. If leg activity exceeds a certain level, the effect on swelling seems to be

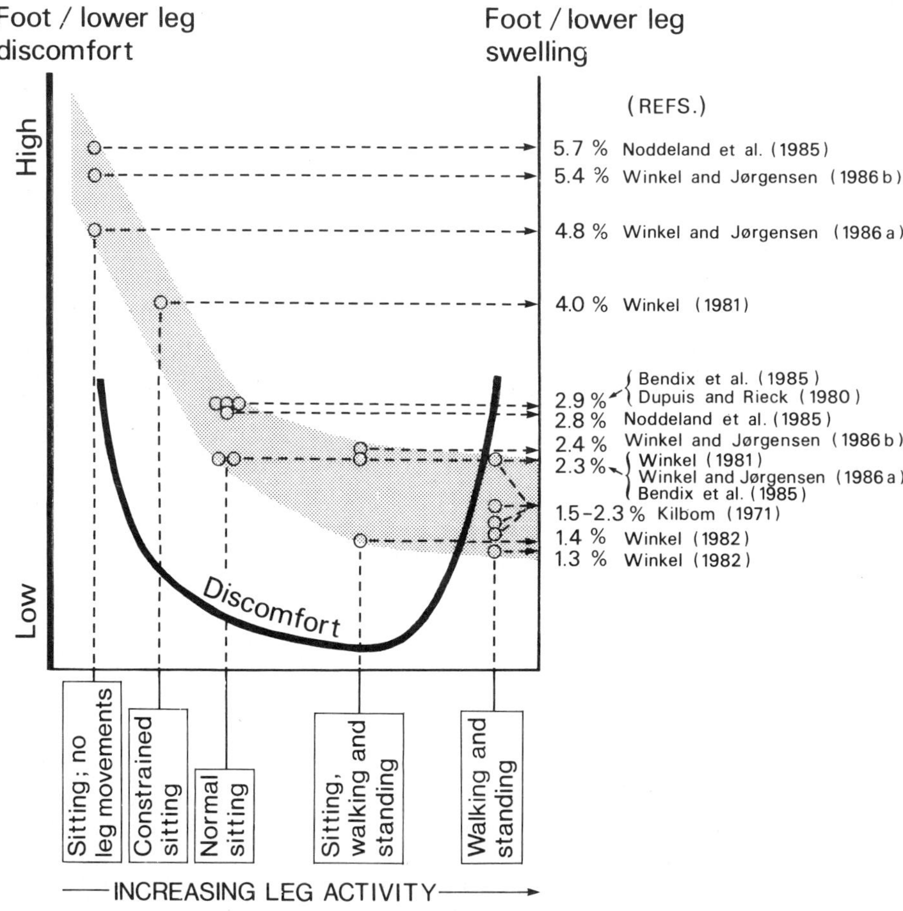

Figure 4. Foot/lower leg swelling and discomfort after an 8-hour working day in relation to estimated leg activity. As the discomfort - in contrast to the swelling - has not been measured in comparable units, the discomfort curve only illustrates principal changes (Buckle et al. 1986, Noddeland et al. 1985, Shvartz et al. 1982a, Winkel 1981, Winkel 1982, Winkel and Jørgensen 1986a). (Modified from Winkel 1985).

small. Thus, moderate ("normal sitting") as well as high leg activity ("walking and standing") apparently cause almost the same swelling ranging from 1 to 3%; i.e. a pronounced oedema-preventing effect may be obtained while seated. The highest activity level also implies an increased discomfort. This may be due to the long period spent in the upright position causing mechanical strain-reactions in the passive structures (e.g. "ligament fatigue") and/or muscles of the feet (cf. Bojsen-Møller 1982, Basmajian and Deluca 1985).

3.3. Long-term circulatory effects

Oedema formation during prolonged sitting is a short-term effect as the swelling disappears after a night's sleep (Winkel and Jørgensen 1986b). Prolonged sitting every day during several years may increase the risk of developing pathological reactions such as varicose veins, thrombosis and pulmonary embolism if one or more predisposing factors are present. Although this view is supported by several studies (for references, see Winkel 1985), we still lack clear epidemiological evidence. Accordingly, the significance of modest leg activity for the long-term effects is unknown.

4. CONCLUSION

Present data indicate that lower limb discomfort as well as cardio-vascular strain may increase during high as well as low leg activity. Such U-shaped stress/strain-curves probably exist for most organs/tissues. Further research on acceptable/recommendable physical work stress should thus comprise studies aimed not only at *upper* but also at *lower* limit values.

REFERENCES

Adams, M.A. and Hutton W.C., Spine, 8 (1983) 665-671.
Almqvist, R., Sveriges Skogsvårdsförbunds Tidskrift, 1-2 (1978) 13-19. (In Swedish).
Arndt, R., Am. Ing. Hyg. assoc. J., 44 (1983) 437-446.
Arnoldi, C.C., Acta Chir. Scand., 130 (1965) 570-583.
Aukland, K., J. Physiol. (Paris), 79 (1984) 395-400.
Basmajian, J.V. and Deluca, C.J., Muscles Alive. Their Functions Revealed by Electromyography (Williams & Wilkins, Baltimore, 1985).
Bendix, T., Winkel, J. and Jessen, F., Eur. J. Appl. Physiol., 54 (1985) 378-385.
Bojsen-Møller, F., Kan ligamenter blive trætte?, in: Bonde-Petersen, F. (Ed.), Lokal træthed (F.A.D.L' s forlag, Copenhagen, 1982) pp. 106-122. (In Danish).
Buckle, P., Stubbs, D.A. and Baty, D., Musculo-skeletal disorders (and discomfort) and associated work factors, in: Proceedings of the Ergonomics of Working Postures, Models and Methods Symposium (Taylor and Francis, London, 1986).
Dupuis, H. and Rieck, A., Z. Arb. wiss, 34 (1980) 56-60.
Grieco, A., Ergonomics, 29 (1986) 345-362.
Gunnarsson, E. and Söderberg, I., Appl. Ergonomics, 14 (1983) 61-69.
Holm, S. and Nachemson, A., Spine, 8 (1983) 866-874.
Jonsson, B., J. Human Ergol. (Tokyo), 11 (1982) 73-88.
Kilbom, Å., Scand. J. Clin. Lab. Invest., 28 (1971) 331-343.
Kraemer, J., Kolditz, D. and Gowin, R., Spine, 10 (1985) 69-71.
Lindström, S., Peterson, R. and Selg, H., Elektroniken i fabriken - hot eller hopp (Liber förlag, Stockholm, 1981). (In Swedish).
Magora, A., Ind. Med. Surg., 41 (1972) 5-9.

Noddeland, H., Transcapillary pressures in human subcutaneous tissue. (University of Bergen, Norway, 1984). (Thesis).
Noddeland, H., Winkel, J. and Andersen, H.T., Acta Physiol. Scand. (Suppl. 542), 124 (1985) 130.
Olszewski, W.L. and Engeset, A., Am. J. Physiol., 239 (1980) H775-H783.
Olszewski, W.L., Engeset, A., Jæger, P.M., Sokolowski, J. and Theodorsen, L., Acta Physiol. Scand., 99 (1977) 149-155.
Shvartz, E., Gaume, J.G., Reibold, R.C., Glassford, E.J. and White, R.T., Aviat. Space Environ. Med., 53 (1982a) 795-802.
Shvartz, E., Reibold, R.C., White, R.T. and Gaume, J.G., Aviat. Space Environ. Med., 53 (1982b) 226-231.
Søndergård Kristensen, T., Kvinders arbejdsmiljø (Fagbevægelsens forskningsråd, Fremad/LO, 1978). (In Danish).
Winkel, J., J. Human Ergol. (Tokyo), 10 (1981) 139-149.
Winkel, J., An ergonomic evaluation of foot complaints among waiters as a basis for job design, in: Noro, K. (Ed.), IEA '82, The 8th Congress of the International Ergonomics Association (Inter Group, Japan, 1982) pp. 630-631.
Winkel, J., Fysiska belastningar vid mikroskoparbete. Kartläggning och åtgärder. Technical Report 1984:60T (University of Luleå, 1984). (In Swedish).
Winkel, J., On foot swelling during prolonged sedentary work and the significance of leg activity. Arbete och Hälsa 1985:35. (Karolinska Institute, Stockholm, 1985). (Thesis).
Winkel, J. and Jørgensen, K., Ergonomics, 29 (1986a) 313-328.
Winkel, J. and Jørgensen, K., Eur. J. Appl. Physiol., 55 (1986b) 162-166.

WORK WITH DISPLAY UNITS 86
B. Knave and P.-G. Wideback (eds.)

INACTIVITY, NIGHT WORK, AND FATIGUE

Torbjörn ÅKERSTEDT, Lars TORSVALL, Katja GILLANDER, Anders KNUTSSON*

Stress Research, Karolinska Institute, 104 01 Stockholm, Sweden
Nat. Inst. for Psychosocial Factors and Health, 104 01 Stockholm, Sweden

20 subjects who were engaged in semiautomated or computerized control of process operations were monitored with respect to physical activity, EEG, EOG, ECG, urinary excretion of stress hormones, and self-ratings. The results showed that, whereas the two groups showed equal amounts of activity during leisure time the computerized group showed more inactivity during work. The amount of activity, in turn, was related to perceived sleepiness. These effects were particularly pronounced on the night shift. The results indicate that computerized process operations may be associated with reduced activity and increased sleepiness.

1. INTRODUCTION

It is a general observation that the introduction of computers in many companies leads to physical inactivity, at least in the sense that work becomes more sedentary (1). However, also on this sedentary level tasks may differ with respect to the amount of activity required - from passive VDU supervision of industrial processes to piece-wage based data entry work.

Such differences in activity on a sedentary level were observed in a study of automatization in industry by Johansson and Sandén (2). These authors compared a group of "passive" process supervisors with a group of "active" process operators. The latter continuously monitored the process, made decisions and directly influenced the output. The former mainly monitored alarm functions of another process. The questionnaires showed that the process supervisors rated work as calmer, more passive, more monotonous, less interesting and more isolated. The process operators were rushed but gained a greater satisfaction from work. An interesting aspect was that the night shift enhanced the feelings of boredom and being ill at ease in the supervisors.

One reason for the attitudes of the supervisors may be the lack of control (3) of the work situation. Another may be understimulation (4). We also know that understimulation/monotony reduces wakefulness (5). When these factors are combined with the pronounced sleepiness that occurs during night work (6) there is an increased risk for accidents (7,8,9).

The present paper constitutes a preliminary report on inactivity, sleep and sleepiness in a recently computerized group of process operators (and a control group). Particular emphasis is laid on a new "actograph" instrument to monitor activity.

---

* This work was supported by the Swedish Work Environment Fund and the Swedish Medical Research Council.

2. METHODS

Twenty male papermill workers participated (25-55 years of age). They were recruited from two departments with approximately similar amounts of automation of the production process. One of the departments was scheduled for a complete computerization of the production process (experimental group).

All subjects worked a continuous, rapidly rotating 3-shift system with shift changes at 0600h, 1400h, and 2200h. The shift cycle spanned 5 weeks. During each cycle two shifts were extended to 12 hours.

Before and after computerization the subjects went through medical check-ups and filled out questionnaires. In addition, during two 24 hour periods their EEG, EOG, and EKG were recorded on portable Medilog tape recorders (6). The two 24 hour periods contained one night and one afternoon shift. The recordings were used to obtain objective data on the sleep/wakefulness pattern of the subjects (10).

Furthermore, at 3-5 hour intervals during these days urine was sampled for analysis of catecholamines (11). At the same time intervals also ratings of sleepiness were carried out (scale 7 = sleepy, 1 = alert). The work periods were also rated with respect to the amount of physical activity and intensity of supervision of the process (active/passive).

At the occasion of post-computerization measurement we also got the opportunity to measure activity objectively by using wrist-worn activity monitors, or "actographs" (12). This monitor was worn during a 12 day period which included days with morning, evening, and night work, as well as recovery days. The monitor integrates activity over 15 min intervals and stores the data in a solid state memory (also worn on the wrist encapsulated together with the sensor). During the 12 day period the subjects also filled out a sleep diary with questions about sleep times, naps, sleep quality and recuperation.

Differences between conditions were tested using analysis of variance or t-tests for repeated or independent measures, depending on the characteristics of the data.

3. RESULTS

The measurement before the introduction of the computers showed moderate levels of rated activity (13). Rated sleepiness during night work reached 5.4 units as compared to the daytime normal of 3.0 ($p<.001$). Night shift sleepiness was, furthermore, emphasized by the fact that 20% of the subjects actually fell asleep during work. The mean length of these involuntary work time naps was 48 minutes. None fell asleep during afternoon work but 1/3 took naps during leisure time after the night shift.

The involuntary naps during work occurred in close association with maximum sleepiness, i.e. towards the end of the night shift. The leisure time nappers were characterized by curtailed recovery sleep after night work (4.6 hours), whereas those who napped involuntarily during night work had a comparatively good (5.6 hours) recovery sleep. The latter group was, instead, characterized by higher levels of rated monotony and inactivity during night work.

After introduction of computerized process control the experimental group thought their work had become more interesting and meaningful, less physically demanding, but also more mentally demanding. Their reactions to their new tasks were clearly very positive. The control group did not report any changes at all.

Figure 1 a displays an example of the activity measure in 15 min intervals across two 24 hour periods with afternoon and night work, respectively. As may be seen, the amount of activity varies greatly over the day and is virtually zero during sleep. Figure 1 b shows the mean values for the two groups. The day pattern is highly significant.

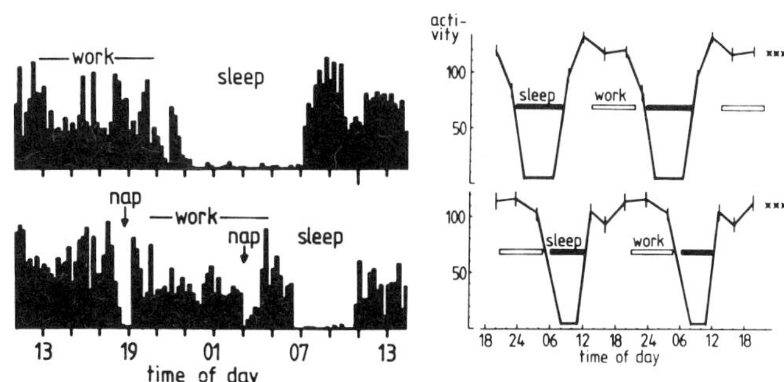

FIGURE 1
Left: Individual example of monitored activity (15 min periods) during two 24 hour periods with afternoon and night work, respectively. Right: Mean activity ($\pm$1SE) in 3-5 hour intervals during two 24 hour periods with afternoon and night work, respectively. (N=20).
*** = p<.001 for 24h analysis of variance.

In figure 2 is shown the sleep/wake pattern over twelve days of shift work for one individual. This was obtained by setting a criterion equal to mean activity during sleep plus 3 SD and having the computer identify the points in time when activity was below this level. The figure identifies several naps or rest periods after the morning shift, two naps/rest periods before the night shifts and a nap during the last night shift. The breaks during sleep represent awakenings or periods with large body movements.

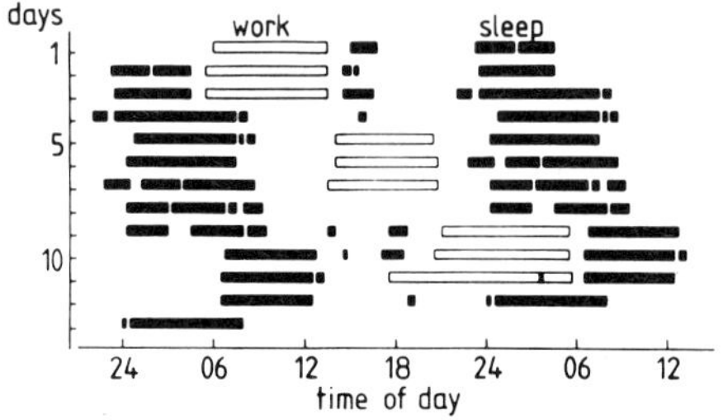

FIGURE 2
Individual example of sleep/wake pattern obtained from the actograph over a 12-day shift period with morning, afternoon, and night work, plus days off. NB sleep is plotted twice.

For further validation of the activity measure we computed intraindividual correlations with other variables across the two days (12 data points). This resulted in significant correlations with heart rate ($\bar{r}$ = 0.83, p<0.001), adrenaline excretion ($\bar{r}$ = 0.63, p<0.001), and noradrenaline excretion ($\bar{r}$ = 0,68, p<0.001).

Figure 3 displays the activity of the two groups across work, leisure, and sleep during the three shifts. During sleep and leisure time their levels of activity are virtually equal. During work, however, the control group has a significantly higher activity than the computerized group. The difference was largest during the afternoon shift. It is rather striking that for the computerized group work does not carry with it any increase in activity compared to leisure time.

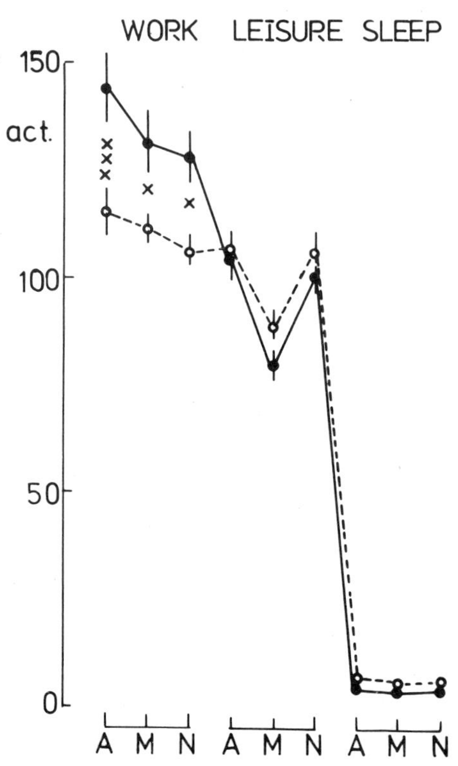

FIGURE 3
Mean activity (+1SE) for the computerized (---) and control (——) groups across work, leisure, and sleep during afternoon (A), morning (M), and night shifts (N). The data are based on 12 days of recordings from 20 subjects.
* = p<.05, ** = p<.01, *** = p<.001.

During the days when physiological parameters were measured, activity during the night shift reached 128±8 in the control group and 97±6 in the computerized group (<.01). The corresponding ratings of "active" (as opposed to "passive") process operation was 70±13% and 35±7%, respectively (p<.05), i.e. the lower level of monitored work activity in the computerized group was reflected in its rated lower "proportion of time spent in active work".

One of the hypotheses of the present study was that the amount of activity would be related to the amount of sleepiness perceived during work. The EEG data are not yet available. Instead, we compared the activity during the alert half (rating of 3.6±0.2) of the night shift with the sleepy half of the same shift (4.8±0.2) for each individual. Figure 4 shows that sleepiness was associated with significantly lower amounts of activity. (For the afternoon shift dichotomization with respect to sleepiness was not meaningful).

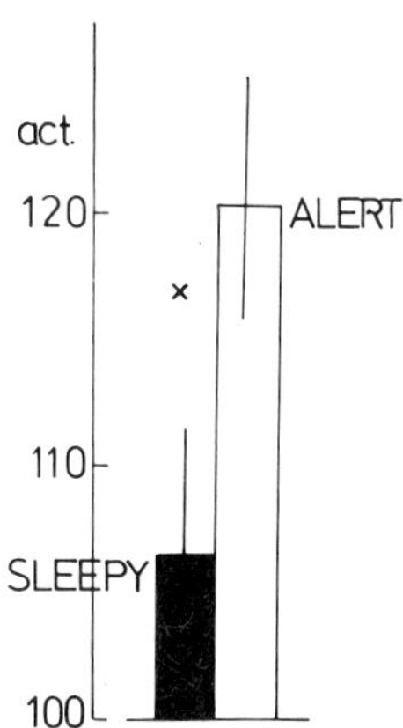

FIGURE 4
Mean activity (±1SE) for both groups during the half of the night shift in which most sleepiness was reported, compared with that with most alertness. (N=17, i.e. all who exhibited a difference between the two halves).

It may be remarked that the two most sleepy subjects actually happened to fall asleep at work (figure 1). This was associated with a strongly reduced activity.

The analysis of rated sleep quality and sleep EEG recordings did not reveal any effects of the introduction of computerized process operations.

4. DISCUSSION AND CONCLUSION

The present study has demonstrated that night work is associated with sleepiness - even to the extent that outright sleep may occur. It has also demonstrated that activity may be measured by a small wrist worn instrument and that these measures correlated closely with ratings and physiological indicators of physical activity.

Furthermore, VDU work as a part of process supervision was associated with reduced amounts of physical activity. This reduced level of activity, in turn, appears to be associated with an inability to maintain wakefulness. Even if the connection is common-sensical it will still have to be corroborated in further studies. It should be emphasized that it is not only the risk of accidents that is of importance in relation to reduced wakefulness. Other effects involve the long term health consequences of having to maintain attention, waiting for emergency action, while at the same time feeling very sleepy. One might assume that this demands a major effort and there is reason to believe that this effort may be one of the more important contributors to the negative effect of monotonous tasks (14).

ACKNOWLEDGEMENT

We would like to thank the subjects who participated in the study as well as Professor Alexander Borbély and Dr Irène Tobler who provided the actograph system.

REFERENCES

(1) See chapters by Kihlbom and others in this volume.
(2) Johansson, G. and Sandén, P.-O. Mental belastning och arbetstillfredsställelse i kontrollrumsarbete. Rapporter från Psykologiska institutionen. Stockholms Universitet (1982) 40.
(3) Johansson, G. Individual control in a monotonous task: Effects of performance, effort, and physiological arousal. Reports from the Department of Psychology, University of Stockholm, (1981) 579.
(4) Frankenhaeuser, M. and Johansson, G. On the psychophysiological consesequences of understimulation and overstimulation. In: Levi, L. (ed), Society, Stress and Disease vol 4 - Working Life (Oxford University Press, London, 1981) pp. 82-89.
(5) Davies, D.R. and Parasuraman, R. The Psychology of Vigilance (Academic Press, London, 1982).
(6) Torsvall, L. and Åkerstedt, T. Sleepiness on the job: continuously measured EEG changes in train drivers. Electroencephalography and clinical Neurophysiology (1986), in press.
(7) Harris, W. Fatigue, circadian rhythm, and truck accidents. In: Mackie, R.R. (ed), Vigilance (Plenum Press, New York, 1977) pp. 133-146.
(8) Hamelin, P. Les conditions temporelles de travail des conducteurs routiers et la sécurité routière. Travail Humain, 44 (1981) 5-21.
(9) Ehret, C.F. New approaches to chronohygiene for the shift worker in the nuclear power industry. In: Reinberg, A., Vieux, N., and Andlauer, P. (eds), Night and Shift work: Biological and Social Aspects (Pergamon Press, Oxford, 1981) pp. 263-271.
(10) Rechtschaffen, A. and Kales, A. A manual of standardized terminology, techniques, and scoring system for sleep stages of human subjects. Brain Information Service, Brain Research Institute, University of California (1968).
(11) Andersson, B., Hovmöller, S., Karlsson, C.-G., and Svensson, S. Analysis of urinary catecholamines: An improved auto-analyzer fluorescence method. Clinica Chimica Acta 51 (1974) 13-28.
(12) Borbély, A.A., Neuhaus, H.U., Mattmann, P., and Waser, P.G. Langzeitregistrierung der Bewegungsaktivität: Anwendung in Forschung und Klinik. Schweizerische medizinische Wochenschrift, 111 (1981) 730-735.
(13) Torsvall, L., Åkerstedt, T., Gillander, K., and Knutsson, A. 24h recordings of sleep/wakefulness in shift work. In: Haider, M., Koller, M., and Cervinka, R. (eds), Night and Shift work: Longterm Effects and their Prevention (Verlag Peter Lang, Frankfurt am Main, 1986) pp. 37-43.
(14) Thackray, R.I. The stress of boredom and monotony: A consideration of the evidence. Psychosomatic Medicine 43 (1981) 165-176.

WORK WITH DISPLAY UNITS 86
B. Knave and P.-G. Widebäck (eds.)

THE BACK DURING PROLONGED SITTING

Tommy Hansson, M.D., Ph,D.

Department of Orthopaedic Surgery, Sahlgren Hospital,
Gothenburg University
S-413 45 Göteborg, Sweden

The aim at a sitting working position is a basic ergonomic principle. Compared to a standing working posture sitting has several advantages. Some of these advantages are:

- a lower energy requirement

- a better stabilization of the trunk and the head when for example high motor and/or visual control is needed

- a reduction of the hydrostatic pressure in the legs

- a reduction of the load carried by the joints in the lower extremities.

Altogether these conditions make sitting to a relatively effortless working position which can be sustained for considerable time. With an increasing number of tasks requiring or being most efficiently executed when sitting, for example work with display units, it is reasonable to assume that more and more disadvantages will be disclosed due to the prolonged sitting. The predictable disadvantages for the back and especially the low back in connection with prolonged sitting will be caused by the effect of the sitting posture itself and the inactivity it will encourage. The posture and the inactivity will influence on the physiology and the biomechanics of the spine in a way which can cause both acute and chronic damages to the structures of the low back.

No studies so far have shown, however, that sitting in itself will cause for example back pain. It is on the other hand well known that people with back pain avoid sitting and also that most back pain treatment programs ban sitting at least during periods of acute pain.

In combination with vibrations, for example driving or riding different types of vehicles, several investigators, however, have found that sitting increases the risks of achieving not only back pain at large but also herniation of the nucleus pulposus (1,2,3).

In vivo intradiscal pressure measurements have shown a considerably higher disc pressure during unsupported sitting than in upright standing (4,5). It has also been found that both the intradiscal pressure and the back muscle EMG-activity are reduced when a back-rest is used and especially when the back-rest is tilted from upright (vertical) to 110° indicating that a bigger portion of a trunk load is carried by the back-rest. A further reduction of both disc pressure and EMG-activities can be obtained by adding a lumbar support and arm rests. A similar relieving effect as the one caused by the use of the arm rests was found when the arms were supported by the desk in front of the sitting subject (6,7,8).

These studies reveal how to reduce the stresses on the intervertebral discs and how to improve the comfort when sitting. Stress relieving and especially when combined with inactivity is, however, not always favourable for the human spine. Inactivity will effect both the soft and hard tissues of the spine and will cause disturbances which can develop into both known and assumed pathological changes.

It is well known that physical inactivity will cause bone mineral losses from the skeleton. Such losses predominantly occur in cancellous bone. For this reason the vertebral bodies with their uniquely high content of cancellous bone are especially susceptible. The female spine is especially exposed to these losses since it generally is equipped with a lower amount of bone mineral than the male spine. Even minor losses can thus bring the bone mineral in the female spine down to a level which is pathologically low. Since the bone mineral is directly related to the strength of the vertebrae in the spine a reduction of the bone mineral will also directly reduce the strength and increase the risks of obtaining fragility fractures for example in the distal radius, proximal humerus, neck of femur or the vertebral bodies (9).

In addition to factors like age and menopause physical activity or inactivity are among the strongest determinants for the amount of bone mineral in the spine (10,11,12). Inactivity in the form of strict bed rest for 6-8 weeks has for example in a group of young adult women been shown to cause bone mineral losses from the lumbar vertebrae of almost 30% (13). The consequences of these losses became even more serious when it was found that the majority of the young women had not regained the losses five years after the inactivity period (14). Even if the inactivity losses caused by sitting ought to be much smaller than after immobilization in bed the inability of at least some women to restitute bone losses indicate the seriousness of physical inactivity.

Experimental studies have suggested that inactivity in addition to the negative influence upon the bony tissue also seriously will disturb the nutrition of the intervertebral disc (15). It is possible that these disturbances of the transfer of metabolites in and out of the disc can accelerate degenerative changes especially in the avascular disc. An increase in the incidence of disc herniations and an acceleration of spondylotic changes are thus other changes which can be hypothesized as a consequence of inactivity of the spine.

It is quite possible that all the inactivity changes discussed here and seen both in the vertebral bodies and in the intervertebral discs will be exaggerated by smoking. Recent findings indicate that smoking is a powerful demineralizing agent which in a negative way affect both the nutrition of the intervertebral discs and the amount of bone mineral in the vertebral bodies (16).

REFERENCES

(1) Kelsey, J.L., An epidemiological study of the relationship between occupations and acute herniated lumbar intervertebral discs. Int J Epidemiol 4 (1975) pp. 197-205.
(2) Kelsey, J.L. and Hardy, R.J., Driving of motor vehicles as a risk factor for acute herniated lumbar intervertebral disc. Am J Epid 102 (1975) pp. 63-73.

(3) Frymoyer, J.W., Pope, M.H., Rosen, J., Goggin, J., Wilder, D. and Costanza, M., Epidemiological studies of low back pain. 6th Ann Mtg ISSLS, Göteborg, May-June 1979.
(4) Nachemson, A. and Morris, J.M., In vivo measurements of intradiscal pressure. Journal of Bone and Joint Surgery 46-A (1964) 1077.
(5) Andersson, G.B.J., On myoelectric back muscle activity and lumbar disc pressure in sitting postures. Doctoral dissertation, Gotab, University of Göteborg, Göteborg (1974).
(6) Andersson, G.B.J. and Örtengren, R., Myoelectric back muscle activity during sitting. Scandinavian Journal of Rehabilitation Medicine, Supplement 3 (1974) pp. 73-90.
(7) Andersson, G.B.J., Jonsson, B. and Örtengren, R., Myoelectric activity in individual lumbar erector spinae muscles in sitting. A study with surface and wire electrodes. Scandinavian Journal of Rehabilitation Medicine, Supplement 3 (1974) pp. 91-108.
(8) Andersson, G.B.J., Örtengren, R., Nachemson, A. and Elfström, G., Lumbar disc pressure and myoelectric back muscle activity during sitting. I. Studies on an experimental chair. Scandinavian Journal of Rehabilitation Medicine 3 (1974) pp. 104-114.
(9) Hansson, T., Roos, B. and Nachemson, A., The bone mineral content and ultimate compressive strength in lumbar vertebrae. Spine 1 (1980) pp. 46-55.
(10) Riggs, B.L., Wahner, H.W., Dunn, W.L., Mazess, R.B., Offord, K.P. and Melton, L.J., Differential changes in bone mineral density of the appendicular and axial skeleton with aging. J. Clin. Invest. 67 (1981) pp. 328-335.
(11) Hansson, T. and Roos, B., The changes with age in the bone mineral of the lumbar spine in normal women. Calcif Tissue Int. 38 (1986) pp. 249-251.
(12) Lindquist, O., Bengtsson, C., Hansson, T., Roos, B. and Jonson, R., Changes in bone mineral conten of the axial skeleton in relation to aging and the menopause. Results from a longitudinal population study of women in Gothenburg, Sweden. Scand J Clin Lab Invest 43 (1983) pp. 333-338.
(13) Hansson, T., Roos, B. and Nachemson, A., Development of osteopenia in the fourth lumbar vertebra during prolonged bed rest after operation for scoliosis. Acta Orthop Scand 46 (1975) pp. 621-630.
(14) Hansson, T., Roos, B. and Nachemson, A., The ability of the operated scoliosis patient to regain bone mineral lost from the axial skeleton. Scoliosis Research Society, Denver, USA, 1982.
(15) Holm, S. and Nachemson, A., Nutritional changes in the canine intervertebral disc after spinal fusion. Clinical Orthopaedics and Related Research 169 (1982) pp. 243-258.
(16) Holm, S. and Nachemson, A., Nutrition of the intervertebral disc: Acute effects of cigarette smoking. An experimental animal study. ISSLS, Sydney, Australia, 1985.

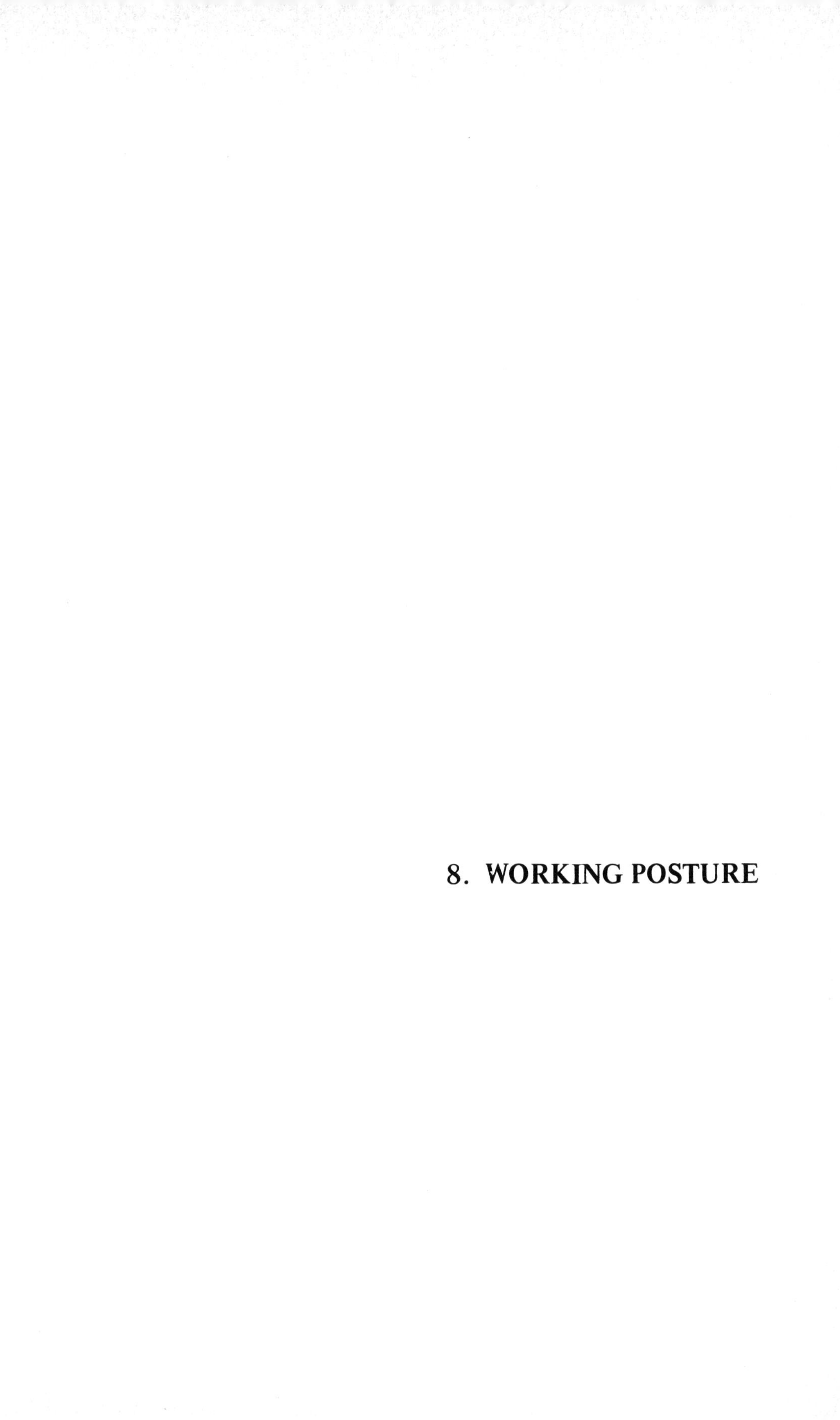

8. WORKING POSTURE

WORK WITH DISPLAY UNITS 86
B. Knave and P.-G. Wideback (eds.)

PREFERRED SETTINGS IN VDT WORK: THE ZUERICH EXPERIENCE

Thomas Laeubli

Institut fuer Hygiene und Arbeitsphysiologie,
Eidgenoessische Technische Hochschule, ETH Zentrum
CH-8092 Zuerich, Switzerland.

Six field studies and four laboratory studies are reviewed. The studies were conducted to develop guidelines for the proper design of keyboards and VDT workstations. The field studies show that musculoskeletal discomfort is increased in repetitive work on keyboards, whether or not a VDT is used. Ergonomic shortcomings precipitate constrained postures and musculoskeletal disorders. Experiments using fully adjustable workstations reveal that VDT operators prefer to recline the upper body and to rest the hands on a support. Preferred settings are presented in the paper. Preferred settings distinctly differ from textbook recommendations that rely on anthropometric measurements and an upright upper body. Based on biomechanical considerations, a "split keyboard" was developed that allows a more natural hand posture and is easily accepted by typists that are trained at the traditional keyboard.

1. INTRODUCTION

How an optimal VDT workplace should be equipped and what the most healthful sitting posture looks like is controversial. Standards and guidelines [1-7] differ considerably in their recommendations. Former conclusions how to set up an optimal workplace must be reconsidered. In a traditional office, using a mechanical typewriter, the postural demands are different from those of working at a VDT. Furthermore, the introduction of VDTs into offices is combined with many changes in working methods and other factors that also affect well-being and health. At the traditional office desk, an employee carries out a number of physical activities: he looks for documents, takes notes, uses the telephone, reads a text, exchanges information with colleagues and types. Working posture changes continuously. The situation is entirely different for an operator working on a VDT (or another business machine) for several hours without interruptions. Such an operator is tied to a man-machine system; movements are restricted, attention is directed towards the screen (or source document) and hands are fixed to the keyboard. A VDT user is much more exposed to ergonomic shortcomings because of long working periods and prolonged retention of unavoidably constrained postures.
This paper presents a survey of laboratory and field studies [8-18] that were guided by Prof. E. Grandjean in Zuerich. Researchers aimed to develop guidelines for the proper design of VDT workstations.

Present address: National Institute for Occupational Safety and Health,
4676 Columbia Parkway, MB:R10 Cincinnati, OH 45226, U.S.A.

2. FIELD STUDIES ON WORKING POSTURE AND POSTURAL DISCOMFORT

2.1 Prevalence of postural discomfort

The results of five field studies were compared to each other, because the same questionnaire was used in each [8,9,11,18,19]. The questionnaire referred to parts of the body (neck, shoulder, back, low back, arms, hands, legs and feet) that were illustrated by an anatomical drawing. Subjects were asked about the occurrence (daily, occasionally, seldom or never) of symptoms (pain, stiffness, fatigue, cramps, numbness) within the last few months.
The management informed the subjects that a study on work posture was to be conducted and invited them to participate. Questionnaires were distributed by the examiners during working hours. This procedure resulted in a response rate of about ninety-five percent. The samples were representative but not random samples of the studied occupations. The samples were determined after discussions with the respective company managements and it was assured that all questionnaire participants with similar job titles had near identical tasks. Some characteristics of the ten studied groups of employees are presented in Table 1.

Table 1 Some characteristics of the ten groups involved in five studies.
VDT + = working with VDT; (sd) = standard deviation.
100% = number of subjects in each group.

Groups	VDT	N	Age mean (sd)	Women %	≥6h/day at keyboard or terminal %
Accounting machine operating	-	119	21 (3)	100	80
Data entry tasks	+	53	30 (8)	94	81
Full-time typists	-	78	34 (13)	95	65
Space control in an airline	+	45	29 (7)	58	100
Payment transactions	+	109	34 (12)	50	73
Traditional clerical work	-	55	28 (11)	60	30
CAD operators	+	69	33 (8)	23	20
Mechanical/ wiring board design	-	52	34 (12)	31	-
Domestic directory assistance	+	58	20 (2)	100	100
International directory assistance	-	59	21 (3)	100	-

The jobs of the ten groups can be described as follows:

- Accounting machine operating. Full-time numeric data entry, taken from coupons and typed in with the right hand only. High typing speed.
- Data-entry task. Full-time numeric data entry with the right hand. 12000 to 17000 strokes/hour.
- Full-time typing. Partly copying documents, partly using dictating machine. High typing speed.
- Space control in airline. Conversational type of job. No source documents; all information is presented on the screen. Seventy percent of the machines have a fixed keyboard.

- Payment transactions into two banks. Both hands operate keyboard. Visual activity is directed fifty percent of the time on screen and fifty percent on source document. Low stroke speed.
- Traditional clerical work. Payment transactions in branch offices of a bank (without VDT), keyboards are used only occasionally. There is a great diversity of body movements.
- CAD operating. Mechanical design, printed circuit board and electrical schematics design. Tablets are used for approximately forty percent and keyboards approximately twenty percent of the working time. Great diversity of body movements.
- Mechanical and wiring board design. The same job as CAD operating, but without VDT.
- Domestic directory assistance. Operators from telephone offices of two smaller towns. Retrievals from VDT.
- International directory assistance. Operators from a telephone office of a big city working with directory listings printed in paper books. Operators must often stand up to get the various directories.

Table 2 lists the results concerning daily or occasional pains in the low back, neck, right arm and hand.

Table 2 Prevalence of daily or occasional pains in the low back, neck, right arm and hand areas, reported from five field studies. r = right, VDT + = working with VDTs. 100% = the number of subjects in each group.

Groups	VDT	Subjects with daily or occasional pains in			
		low back %	neck %	r arm %	r hand %
Accounting machine operating	-	32	19	42	46
Data entry task	+	43	23	58	38
Full-time typists	-	44	23	21	19
Space control in an airline	+	36	48	33	42
Payment transactions	+	38	16	18	26
Traditional clerical work	-	36	9	13	16
CAD operators	+	20	7	6	6
Mechanical/ wiring board design	-	21	6	21	4
Domestic directory assistance	+	56	21	11	16
International directory assistance	-	37	22	6	22

The figures reveal that localized musculoskeletal troubles were observed in each group. The highest figures were found in jobs involving repetitive work on keyboards. The lowest figures were reported by CAD operators and their control group (draughtsmen) as well as by the group engaged in traditional clerical work. More detailed analysis showed that arm pains were related to the number of daily keystrokes. The complaints must be taken seriously since thirteen to twenty-seven percent of the examined employees indicated that they had consulted a physician for this reason.

2.2 Medical examinations

To validate the questionnaire, operators were examined for the presence of painful pressure points on muscles and tendon-insertions. The reliability of this clinical examination of musculoskeletal disorders was tested in 30 young female VDT operators [20]. Two independent pairs of examiners palpated pressure points of muscles and tendon-insertions. The number and intensity of findings were summed; a corresponding index was developed. The indices of the two separate examination teams correlated with Pearson r, 0.7. A similar clinical examination was included in two other field studies [9,19]. In one [19], the index from the clinical examination was correlated with an index that was created from the questionnaire. The correlation of the two indices equaled Pearson r, 0.5. We concluded that questionnaire results about postural discomfort are a reasonable measure of physical reactions in the musculoskeletal system due to chronic overstrain. The relationship was only moderate; partly because the questionnaire asked about the previous experience of postural discomfort, while the clinical examination evaluated the present condition. Reporting bias as related to factors like job satisfaction or personality should also be considered [19].

2.3. Ergonomic shortcomings, postural adaptations and discomfort

The cross-sectional studies showed different prevalences of postural discomfort for various occupational groups. However, based on these results alone it is very difficult to identify underlying causes. Within the "payment transactions" and "space control" groups, equipment with VDTs and both fixed and movable keyboards were used. Thus it was possible to compare different exposures within a group.

The "payment transactions" group was selected from two banks. In one, a special desk with a built-in keyboard and display was used. In the other, various kinds of office desks were used that were equipped with movable visual displays and movable keyboards. In the "space control" group, thirty-two subjects used an older VDT with a built-in keyboard that was fixed on the table, and thirteen subjects used newer equipment with a separately movable keyboard and display for the very same task. Table 3 shows some measures of the workplace layout and postural elements for the four subgroups.

When allowed to move the keyboard and screen, subjects chose a distinctly longer viewing distance than avaible on fixed equipment. Variability in type of display available with the movable versus fixed furniture was not a con-

Table 3. Movable and fixed keyboards, postural adaptation and back pain in the groups "payment transactions" and "space control". Movable: keyboard and display independently movable in horizontal plane on desk surface. 100% = n of subjects within group.

	"Payment transactions"			"Space control"		
Keyboard and visual display	movable		fixed	movable		fixed
Keyboard height above floor, mean (cm)	84		78 fixed	81 fixed		81 fixed
Visual distance eye - screen, mean (cm)	62	**	43	57	**	47
Hands rested (expert rating)	95%	**	50%	91%	**	46%
Back pains	35%		47%	8%	*	41%
N of subjects	55		54	13		32

* $p \leq 0.05$, ** $p \leq 0.01$ t-test or CHI^2- test as appropriate

founding factor. Movable keyboards were often arranged in such a way that hands or forearms could be rested on the table. The more constrained postures tended to be combined with more back pain.
Another relationship that was repeatedly found was increased postural discomfort in operators disclosing a marked sidewards twisting of the hands, when operating the keyboard. This is shown in Table 4, where four studied groups are divided into two subgroups, one with an angle of sidewards twisting of the hand of 20 and fewer degrees, the other with a sidewards twisting of more than 20 degrees. The angle was defined by the axis of the forearm and the axis of the middle finger.

Table 4. Prevalence of pain caused by isometric contractions of forearm muscles in subgroups operating the keyboard with normal and increased sidewards twisting of the right hand for four occupational groups. 100% = n of subjects in each subgroup.

	Data entry		Payment transactions movable keyboard		Payment transactions fixed keyboard		Typists	
Sidewards twisting of hand (ulnar deviation)	≤20	>20	≤20	>20	≤20	>20	≤20	>20
N of subjects	46	7	46	7	43	10	54	22
Prevalence of pain (%) due to:								
- Supination	9	29	2 **	29	12	10	4 **	23
- Sidewards twisting	4	14	0 **	14	9	10	2	5
- At least one of six hand movements	26 **	72	4 *	29	19	30	20	32

* $p \leq 0.05$ ** $p \leq 0.01$ by CHI^2-test

Additional significant relationships were discovered between the design of workstations or postures and the prevalence of complaints. The following is a summary of the results. Postural discomfort was likely to increase when:
- the keyboard level above the floor was too low,
- forearms or hands were not rested on a support (surface of desk),
- space for the legs (below desk) was insufficient,
- operators showed a marked head inclination.

2.4 Postures of VDT operators

In the first studies, it was observed that VDT operators often reclined the upper body. In subsequent studies, inclination of the upper body was measured in the "space control" group and in a group of fifteen bank tellers working at VDTs. From several walk-throughs, it was concluded that their working postures were rather constant and the operators assured that they nearly always adapted the observed postures. Only the results about the degree of inclination of the upper body are reported here. This was measured by drawing a line through the middle of the shoulder (acromion) and the middle of the hip (trochanter major). The angle between that line and a horizontal line was than measured, providing the degree of inclination. Therefore, an angle of 90 degrees indicated an upright position, and an angle of more than 90 degrees a reclined upper body. The mean angle measured was 114 degrees for "bank tellers", 108 deg for "space control with movable equipment" and 112 deg for "space control with fixed equipment". Subjects tended to recline the upper body in each group. The upper arms were slightly stretched forward, and it was observed that subjects frequently rested forearms or hands on the table or on the frame of the keyboard.

A comment on ergonomic guidelines for typewriting: Many VDT manuals suggest that the trunk ought to be upright, forearms freely movable and kept horizontal. This seems adequate for the old mechanical typewriters that require key forces of several hundred grams, and can only be operated by movements of the fingers and forearms together. However, electronic keyboards permit very rapid keying with low forces of 40 to 80 g by movements of the fingers alone; assistance of the forearms is no longer needed. Hands and/or forearms may be rested on the table or on the keyboard's frame, and only the muscles which control the fingers are used to press the keys. By resting the arms, the force that is needed to hold them or stretch them out is reduced and, therefore, the shoulder muscles are relieved of some mechanical stress.

With a reclined upper body, it is possible to transfer a great part of the body weight onto the backrest. It has been shown that a reclined upper body is associated with a decreased pressure inside the lumbar intervertebral discs and a lower electromyographic activity of the back muscles compared to an upright sitting posture [23-27]. Both measures are an indication of a decreased load on the back. VDT operators seem to instinctively adopt the least stressful position when they choose to recline the upper body and ignore the recommended upright trunk position.

It was assumed that the postures which were observed in the field studies represent a compromise between preferred posture and the constraints due to the respective equipments. Based on these considerations and observations, research was directed to the following questions:

What are the preferred postures and settings at a fully adjustable VDT workstation?

What are the effects of hand/forearms supports on postural load and preferred posture?

To what extent can the traditional keyboard be modified so that postural constraints due to the inwards turning and sidewards twisting of the hands are reasonably reduced, but still be easily accepted by trained typists?

3. Preferred postures and settings at a fully adjustable VDT workstation

A fully adjustable VDT workstation was constructed. It was adjustable for the following dimensions:

- keyboard height (top of middle row), 62 to 88 cm above floor,
- screen height (centre of screen), 90 to 128 cm above floor ,
- screen distance (centre of screen), 40 to 115cm from table edge,
- screen inclination (angle between table surface and screen surface), 75 to 110 deg (90 deg = perpendicular).

The keyboard was a standard model. The top of the middle row of the keyboard was 8 cm above desk level. The chair had a high backrest with an adjustable inclination that could be fixed at a desired position. It is important to note that the experiments were done using office chairs that provided good lumbar support in an upright position, but also allowed the upper body to recline and the trunk to lean on the backrest.

The adjustable range of the equipment was shown to each subject and it was explained that the experiments were conducted to register preferred settings for VDT workplaces. A preference was not specified by the experimenter, nor was any discussion held about good or bad postures before or after the experiments.

In the laboratory [12], thirty skilled typists performed several consecutive ten-minute typing tasks at the adjustable VDT workstation. The experiment consisted of three parts. Initially, the experiments were conducted with "user preferred" settings. The preferred keyboard heights were assessed with and

without a hand/forearm support and with and without a document holder. Secondly, twelve different settings were imposed upon the subjects, one after another. Thirdly, the "user preferred" settings were again determined and tolerable ranges of adjustments were assessed.
During the typing task, the body postures were measured. At the end of each session subjects filled out questionnaires about their physical feelings in various parts of the body.
The results were as follows: The preferred settings were nearly the same with and without hand/forearm support or a document holder, and settings did not differ between the initial and final assessment. Table 5 shows the preferred settings and some measured postural elements for this laboratory experiment, together with information from two other studies.
The preferred keyboard levels were higher than those usually recommended in standards or brochures; they were only partly related to the body length (Pearson r, 0.5).
The posture at the preferred settings was characterized by a slightly reclined or upright body with the upper arms a little extended and sidewards abducted.
The preferred visual distances showed a great variance ranging from 53 to 80 cm.
Imposed settings, even if they were very similar to the mean values of the preferred ones, were combined with significantly more postural discomfort than the preferred ones. Different settings caused different postural adaptations.

Table 5 Preferred settings and postures at VDT workstations in two laboratories and a field study (all heights are reported to the floor).

Study	Laboratory [12]		Laboratory [14]		Field [13]	
N of subjects	30		20		59	
N of measurements	30		20		235	
	Mean	Range	Mean	Range	Mean	Range
Body length (cm)	166	145-176	-		168	155-181
Seat height (cm)	47	43- 51	47	43- 55	48	42- 55
Keyboard height (cm)+	77	71- 84	78	74- 84	80	73- 97
Screen height (cm)++	109	94-118	97	85-108	103	92-116
Screen inclination (deg)#	94	90-106	101	90-111	94	82-104
Screen distance to table edge (cm)++	65	47- 94	71	60- 96	65	42- 83
Visual distance (cm)++	66	54- 80	-		76	61- 93
Inclination of trunk (deg)##	91	-	99	92-106	104	91-120
Extension of upper arm (deg)	11	-	31	-	23	1- 50
Abduction of upper arm (deg)	18	-	18	-	22	11- 44
Elbow angle (deg)	86	-	99	-	99	75-125

+ top level of middle row; ++ centre of the screen; # > 90 deg means backwards inclination of upper edge; ## > 90 deg means reclined upper body.

The tolerable ranges of keyboard levels varied from 1 to 10 cm. There was no single value of a keyboard height that suited the tolerable range of each subject.

It is concluded that imposed settings are associated with constrained postures. These undesirable postures may be successfully avoided with adjustable workstations since individual operators may properly make adjustments based upon feelings of relaxed posture. There is no recommended single uniform dimension that can suit everybody.

Comparisons with results by other authors revealed some differences in the preferred settings. Miller and Suther [28] observed a much lower preferred keyboard height of 71 cm (range: 64 to 80 cm); however, their experimental conditions were different. In their study, the subjects did not need to look at the screens, and it was not reported as to whether or not subjects were allowed to rest hands or forearms against any support during typing. Brown and Schaum [29] reported similar ranges of preferred settings, but the mean distance between seat surface and keyboard was only 24 cm, compared to 30 cm in the Zuerich study. Cushman [30] reported that in an experiment using chairs with a high backrest, keying rate, error rate and comfort were best at keyboard heights of 74 to 78 cm. This corresponds to the preferred heights found by the Zuerich study. Rubin and Marshall reported a very low preferred keyboard height, of 70.5 cm, in naive users of VDTs and keyboards [31].

To overcome the artificial conditions of laboratory experiments that make it doubtful to generalize results concerning preferred settings, preferred settings were tested while subjects worked normally in their offices [13]. Experiments were conducted on 68 operators (48 females and 20 males, aged 28 years on average) in four companies. Forty-five subjects had a conversational job in an airline company, seventeen subjects performed primarily data entry activities in two banks, and six subjects were engaged in word processing operations. Each subject used an adjustable workstation that was identical to the one used in the laboratory experiment.

The keyboard height was 8 cm above desk level. A chair was provided with a high backrest and an adjustable inclination. For the first two days, a hand-forearm support was used; on the following two days the subjects operated the keyboard without support. On the last day, subjects were given the option to use or not use the forearm-hand support. Document holders were provided as an option. The preferred settings and postures were assessed daily.

The preferred settings did not differ notably over the five days, independent of the use of a support. As such, the data obtained during the week could be put together for evaluation. Table 5 shows the preferred settings as well as some measured postural elements that were observed at the preferred settings.

The results obtained in the field study revealed slightly higher keyboard levels than were found in the above discussed laboratory studies. It is assumed that in short-term experiments, subjects are less relaxed, sit more upright and try to keep the elbows low and the forearms in a horizontal position, thus giving preference to a slightly lower keyboard height. In the second laboratory experiment, to be discussed below, subjects were asked to make use of a very comfortable forearm-hand support; this procedure provoked a very similar posture as in the field study.

The preferred screen heights and screen inclinations were influenced by the attempt of operators to reduce glare which occurred in the everyday office environment. Many operators reported less annoyance by glare with the adjustable screen. As such, the preferred settings of the screen did not represent generally optimal positions, but were chosen for the lighting conditions of the experiments.

The capital letters on the screen were 3.4 mm high; this corresponds to a comfortable visual distance of 68 cm. At the adjustable VDT workstation, the operators tended to choose greater viewing distances, seventy-five percent of them had visual distances between 71 and 93 cm.

The calculation of Pearson correlation coefficients between the body length and preferred keyboard levels (r = 0.13) and between eye levels and preferred screen heights (r = 0.25) revealed only weak relationships. Therefore, it is concluded that preferred settings of VDT workstations are only little influenced by anthropometric factors.

Subjects tended to recline the upper body. Only ten percent demonstrated an upright posture; the arms were moved towards the work surface and the elbow angles slightly opened. Eighty percent of the subjects rested their forearms or hands if a support was available. If no such device was provided, about fifty percent of the subjects rested forearms and/or hands on the desk surface in front of the keyboard. The observed postures at the previous workstations were characterized by a similarly reclined upper body, so observed reclined postures in this case were deemed not due to the experimental workstation.

Ratings of postural discomfort were obtained by questionnaire. The frequency of complaints of discomfort was distinctly higher at the previous workstation than with the preferred settings. At the previous workstation, subjects sat on traditional office chairs with relatively small backrests. At the adjustable workstations, however, they were provided with particularly suitable office chairs featuring high backrests with adjustable inclinations that allowed the whole back to relax. It is therefore reasonable to assume that the decrease of physical discomfort reported at the adjustable workstation was due to both the preferred settings and the proper chairs.

In a second laboratory experiment [14], again, the preferred settings were recorded both with and without a forearm-hand support. Six experiments, involving a ten-minute typing task, were carried out. Work was performed at preferred keyboard heights as well as 5 cm above and 5 cm below; each height with and without forearm-hand support. Twenty subjects participated in the experiments. During work, electromyographic (EMG) signals were recorded from the right trapezius pars descendens (a neck muscle) and the pressure of forearms and hands on the support and the keyboard was simultaneously measured. Table 5 shows the preferred settings and respective postures for the condition with hand support.

A support was preferred by two-thirds of the subjects. The preferred settings were very similar with and without a support, but some differences in the related postures were noted. With supports, subjects tended to stretch out the arm more and open the elbow. With a support, adaptation to the three different keyboard heights was largely accomplished by the flexion of the shoulder and abduction of the arm, without support the elbow angle decreased with increasing keyboard height.

The EMG activity of the trapezius muscle was lower if it was supported. The load on the support (15 to 30 N) correlated with the amont of EMG activity (Pearson r, -0.8) in each of the three conditions. As such, one may conclude that resting arms on a support lowers the load on the neck muscles and, consequently, on the whole back. Furthermore, a support for the forearm allows shoulder flexion without creating strain in the shoulder muscles.

4. Ergonomically designed alphanumeric keyboards

As mentioned above, the modern electronic keyboard requires comparatively reduced forces to press the keys, but its layout is still the same as it is in mechanical typewriters. This design, with the parallel arrangement of rows, is more than hundred years old. It was developed to decrease the possibility of mechanical interferences of the internal mechanisms of the typewriting machine and not to attain efficiency. More efficient arrangements of keys have been recommended but have not penetrated into the market due to the subsequent need to re-educate all keyboard users; the cost would be prohibitive [32].

Klockenberg [33] and Kroemer [34,35] proposed to split the keyboard into two parts and arrange them in such a way that the hands could be kept in a more natural position. With the existing keyboards, operators seek a hand position that brings the fingers perpendicular to the rows of the keyboard. Such a hand position enforces a marked pronation (inwards turning) and lateral deviation (sidewards twisting) of the hand. In order to decrease the degree of prona-

tion, the operators often laterally elevate the elbows, which automatically increases the lateral deviation of the hands. As it is pointed out above, an increased lateral deviation results in increased muscular strain. From these considerations, it becomes evident that the keyboard should be redesigned according to the principles described by Klockenberg and Kroemer.
In a first experiment, the keyboard was split into two half-keyboards, and the preferred settings of opening angles, lateral and frontal inclinations and distances of the split keyboards were determined [15,16]. The resulting layout is shown in Figure 1.
The preferred opening angle (25 deg) and lateral inclination (10 deg) correspond to solutions with biomechanical criteria. The operators preferred a very small distance between the two halves of the keyboard, which might be explained by a disturbance of the hand-hand coordination.

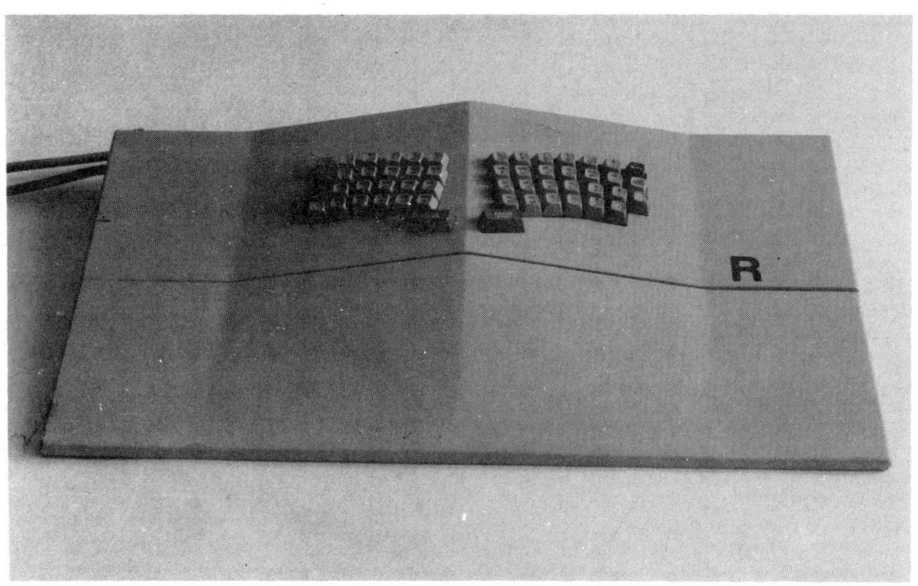

Figure 1. The experimental keyboard with a large forearm-hand support (by Huenting, 1982)

In a second experiment [17], the experimental keyboard was tested by 31 trained typists. Three keyboards were compared at random order: the experimental keyboard with a large support (see Figure 1), the experimental keyboard with a small support, a traditional keyboard with a large support. Each trial involved thirty minutes of continuous typing from a source document. Each subject selected a preferred seat height and a preferred height for the keyboard. The preferred height of the keyboard and some postural elements were recorded. The pressure of the forearms and hands on the support was continuously measured. The results of the three experimental conditions are reported in Table 6. Additionally, the subjects used a rating scale to report pain in different parts of the body.

The proposed configuration clearly decreased the sidewards twisting of hands. A large forearm support was preferred. With such a support, subjects reclined the upper body and increased the pressure onto the support, as was observed in the study by Annetta Weber [14]. The preferred keyboard heights were signifi-

Table 6. Preferred settings and related postural elements in 31 subjects working with an experimental and a traditional keyboard.

	Experimental keyboard large support mean (sd)	Experimental keyboard small support mean (sd)	Traditional keyboard large support mean (sd)
Keyboard height (cm)	80 (2)	79 (2)	78 (2)
Seat height (cm)	46 (1)	46 (1)	46 (1)
Distance shoulder key "G"	44 (4)	39 (4)**	43 (4)
Elbow angle (deg)	97 (8)	87 (6)**	94 (8)
Elbow height (cm)	76 (3)	72 (3)**	75 (3)
Lateral deviation (deg)	10 -	11 -	20 -**
Pressure on support (N)	38 -	18 -	38 -

** significantly different from the two other conditions ($p \leq 0.01$); - not reported

cantly higher at the experimental keyboard with a large support compared to the traditional keyboard. The typing task at the experimental keyboard with the large support was associated with significantly more feelings of relaxation in arms, hands and back than in the other two conditions.

Taking all the experiments together, it can be stated that out of fifty-one subjects, forty preferred the split keyboard models. A training period of less than an hour allowed full adaptation to the new keyboard.

5. Discussion

Questionnaire results as well as clinical examinations make it clear that musculoskeletal disorders are a prevalent problem in office work. Although such disorders are frequently found in VDT operators, it is concluded that they are more directly related to one-sided loads, repetitive movements and constrained postures.

The sitting posture itself induces a considerable load on the back muscles and spine, and seems to be an important cause for the high prevalence of low back pain in office employees. There are several concepts defining a healthful sitting posture that contradict each other. One proposal suggests use of an unstable seat (big ball, spring) so that the body has to be constantly balanced in equilibrium. While this proposal offers a clue to prevention of continuous and uninterrupted postures, it makes it very hard to stabilize the eyes for reading, as well as the hands for keying or writing. Another suggestion is to tilt the surface of the seat forwards, so that the angle between the upper body and the thighs is opened. Opening this angle, the muscular effort needed to hold the trunk errect is effectivly reduced [5,6]. We found that in the short run the tilted chair is comfortable [7], but after a while one gets tired from planting one's feet against slipping, or if a support for the knee is provided, the knee becomes sensitive to pressure. Finally, there is the classical office chair provided with a horizontal surface and a lumbar support. It is designed to sustain the upright posture, allow bending forward with the arms rested on the table, or to occasionally recline the upper body and relax the back. The horizontal surface of the seat with the thighs kept horizontal has the advantage of being a stable base for the trunk. The upright upper body, as recommended by many textbooks, allows to freely move arms and head. As it is pointed out above, this is needed for operating a traditional mechanical keyboard that requires movements of the forearms to press the keys. Other than this advantage, the ninety-degree angle between upper body and thighs is a constraint posture. It almost exceeds the range of the joints between the pelvis and thighs and, therefore, the lumbar lordosis of the spine is flatened. It cannot be denied that there are good arguments as to why the angle between upper body and thighs should be greater than ninety degrees. While a tilted chair seems not to be an appropriate remedy, the observed reclined upper body of many VDT operators represents a better solution to opening the angle between upper body and thighs. If the entire back is supported by a well-shaped backrest, the posture is healthful and decreases the load on the spine and back muscles. But this posture also poses some problems because the arms have to be stretched out to reach the table or keyboard. This creates an increased load on the shoulder muscles, if forearms or hands are not rested. It is exactly this posture, a reclined upper body and rested forearms, that has been preferred in all our experiments. It must again be pointed out that an office chair, provided with a high backrest that could be fixed at the preferred inclination and allowed to relax the back, was used in the experiments.

Preferred postures vary considerably from person to person. For this reason, it is important to provide adjustable equipment. It has been found that the preferred settings partly depend on the experimental settings, which makes it very difficult to define exactly the necessary range for adjustments. Nevertheless, it seems reasonable to base recommendations on the results of the field study. Pertinent results are listed in Table 5. Built-in or fixed keyboards and VDTs are to be avoided. There should be enough space between the table edge and keyboard to rest forearms or hands. A special support may sometimes be useful, especially if the keyboard is not dimensionally flat.

The split keyboard layout allows a better positioning of the hand and diminishes postural constraints. This keyboard is readily accepted by persons trained at the traditional keyboard, and we hope it will be accepted by the commercial market.

Acknowledgments

To participate in these projects was a great pleasure and I wish to thank the spiritus rector Prof. E. Grandjean and the many researchers: W. Fasser, W. Huenting, H. Krueger, K. Maeda, H. Mion, M. Nakaseko, K. Nishiyama, M. Pidermann, Elisabeth Sancin, E. Senn, C. Thomas, G. vanderHeiden, Annetta Weber, H. Zeier, as well as F. Richardson, J. Carpenter, M. London and F. Cantor who reviewed the manuscript.

Literature

[1] H.W. Juergens, K. Helbig, U. Voelch: "Arbeitsflaechenund Sitzflaechenhoehen. Anthropometrisch-ergonomische Untersuchungen zur Gestaltung des Arbeitsplatzes", Der Bundesminister fuer Arbeit und Sozialordnung, Bonn, 1974.

[2] VerwaltungsBerufsgenossenschaft: "Sicherheitsregeln fuer Bildschirm-Arbeitsplaetze im Buerobereich", Ueberseering 8, 2000 Hamburg, 1981.

[3] D.I.N. Norm 4549, June 1981: "Schreibtische, Bueromaschinentische und Bildschirmarbeitstische", Benth Verlag, Berlin, 1981.

[4] H. Schoberth: "Sitzhaltung-Sitzschaden-Sitzmoebel", Springer, Berlin, 1962.

[5] A.C. Mandal: "What is the correct height of furniture?", in E. Grandjean, ed., Ergonomics and health in modern offices, Taylor and Francis, London, 1984.

[6] C.G. Drury and M. Francher: "Evaluation of a forwardsloping chair", Applied Ergonomics 16, 41-47, 1985.

[7] H. Krueger: "Zur Ergonomie von Balans-Sitzelementen in Hinblick auf ihre Verwendbarkeit als regulaere Arbeitsstuehle", Report of the Dep. of Ergonomics, Swiss Federal Institute of Technology, 8092 Zuerich, CH, 1984.
[8] K. Maeda, W. Huenting and E. Grandjean: "Localized fatigue in accounting-machine operators", J. of Occup. Medicine 22, 810-816, 1980.
[9] W. Huenting, Th. Laeubli and E. Grandjean: "Postural and visual loads at VDT workplaces, Part 1: Constrained postures", Ergonomics 24, 917-931, 1981.
[10] Th. Laeubli: "Das arbeitsbedingte cervicobrachiale Ueberlastungssyndrom", Thesis Med. Faculty, University of Zuerich, 1981.
[11] G. vanderHeiden and H. Krueger: "Evaluation of ergonomic features of the Computer Vision Instaview Graphics Terminal", Report of the Dep. of Ergonomics, Swiss Federal Institute of Technology, 8092 Zuerich, 1984.
[12] E. Grandjean, K. Nishiyama, W. Huenting and M. Piderman: "A laboratory study on preferred and imposed settings of a VDT workstation", Behaviour and Information Technology, 1, 289-304, 1982.
[13] E. Grandjean, W, Huenting, and M. Pidermann: "VDT workstation design: preferred settings and their effects", Human Factors 25, 161-175, 1983.
[14] Annetta Weber, Elisabeth Sancin and E. Grandjean: "The effects of various keyboard heights on EMG and physical discomfort", in E. Grandjean, ed., Ergonomic and Health Aspects in Modern Offices, Taylor and Francis, London, 1984.
[15] W. Huenting, M. Nakaseko, R. Gierer and E. Grandjean: "Ergonomische Gestaltung von alphanumerischen Tastaturen", Sozialund Praeventivmedizin, 27, 251-252, 1982.
[16] E. Grandjean, M. Nakaseko, W. Huenting and Th. Laeubli: "Ergonomische Untersuchungen zur Entwicklung einer neuen Tastatur fuer Bueromaschinen", Z. Arbeitswissenschaft 35, 221-226, 1981.
[17] M. Nakaseko, E. Grandjean, W. Huenting and R. Gierer: "Studies on ergonomically designed alphanumeric keyboards", Human Factors, 27, 157-187, 1985.
[18] Th. Laeubli, H. Mion, E. Senn, C. Thomas and H. Zeier: "Rheumatische Beschwerden und Bueroarbeit", Sozialund Praeventivmedizin 30, 278-279, 1985.
[19] H. Zeier, H. Mion, Th. Laeubli, C. Thomas, W. Fasser and E. Senn: "Psychophysiological correlates between postural discomfort, personality and muscle tension", in this volume, 1986.
[20] H. Mion, Th. Laeubli, E. Senn and H. Zeier: "Beschwerden im Bewegungsapparat", Der informierte Arzt, 5, 62-71, 1986.
[21] Th. Laeubli and E. Grandjean: "The magic of control groups in VDT fieldstudies", in E. Grandjean, ed., Ergonomic and Health Aspects in Modern Offices, Taylor and Francis, London, 1984.
[22] unpublished
[23] A. Lundervolt: "Electromyographic investigations during typewriting", Ergonomics, 1, 226-233, 1958.
[24] E. Occipinti, D. Colombini, C. Frigo, A. Pedotti and A. Grieco: "Sitting posture: analysis of lumbar stresses with upper limbs supported", Ergonomics, 28, 1333-1346, 1985.
[25] A. Nachemson and G. Elfstroem: "Intravital dynamic pressure measurements in lumbar discs", Scand. J. Rehabilitation Medicine, Suppl. 1, Almquist and Wiksell, Stockholm, 1970.
[26] B.J.G. Andersson and R. Ortengreu: "Lumbar disc pressure and myoelectric back muscle activity during sitting", Scand. J. Rehabilitation Medicine, 3, 104-135, 1974.
[27] Y. Yamaguchi, F. Umezawa and Y. Ishinada: "Sitting posture: an electromyographic study on healthy and notalgic people", J. Jap. Orthopaedic Ass. 46, 51-56, 1972.
[28] I. Miller and T.W. Suther: "Preferred height and angle setting of CRT and keyboard for a display station input task", Proc. Human Factors Society, 25th annual meeting, Santa Monica, CA, Human Factors Society, 1981.

[29] C.R. Brown and D.L. Schaum: "User adjusted VDT parameters" in E. Grandjean and E. Vigliani, eds., Ergonomic aspects of visual display terminals, Taylor and Francis, London, 1980.
[30] W.H. Cushman: "Data entry performance and operator preferences for various keyboard heights", in E. Grandjean, ed. Ergonomic and Health Aspects in Modern Offices, Taylor and Francis, London, 1984.
[31] T. Rubin and C.J. Marshall: "Adjustable VDT workstations: Can naive users achieve a human factors solution?", Int. Conference on Man-Machine Systems, I.E.E. Conf. Publ. No. 121, Manchester, 1982.
[32] D.G. Alden, R.W. Daniels and A.F. Kanarick: "Keyboard design and operation: A review of the major issues", Human Factors, 14, 275-293, 1972.
[33] .A. Klockenberg: "Rationalisierung der Schreibmaschine und ihrer Bedienung", Springer, Berlin, 1926.
[34] K.H.E. Kroemer: "Ueber den Einfluss der raeumlichen Lage von Tastenfeldern auf die Leistung an Schreibmaschinen", Int. Zschr. ang. Physiologie, 20, 453-464, 1965.
[35] K.H.E. Kroemer: "Human engineering - the Keyboard", Human Factors, 14, 51-63, 1972.

WORK WITH DISPLAY UNITS 86
B. Knave and P.-G. Wideback (eds.)

SUBJECTIVE REPORTS ABOUT MUSCULOSKELETAL DISCOMFORT IN VDU WORK AS A COMPLEX PHENOMENON

Hans Zeier, Hans Mion, Thomas Läubli, Carlo Thomas, Wolfgang Fasser, and Edward Senn

Swiss Federal Institute of Technology and University Hospital Zürich,
CH-8092 Zürich, Switzerland

Subjective reports about physical discomfort usually show large interindividual differences. The subjective judgement about the severity of discomfort depends, in a differential and interactive way, on a variety of very different factors. However, such complaints are an important message, which has to be decoded with respect to individuality and situation. In order to compare different work situations it is very important to take indicators from the ergonomic, biological and psychosocial levels of the system man and work. Only by means of an integrated analysis of indicators from different levels of this system is it possible to decide if an elevated amount of subjective complaints found in a given work situation is mainly due to ergonomic, biological or psychosocial influences.

1. INTRODUCTION

Questionnaire surveys about physical discomfort in VDU work usually report a relatively high frequency of musculoskeletal complaints, often considered to be job related. However, such subjective reports depend on a wide variety of interacting ergonomic, biological, psychological and social factors. Therefore, it is not unusual to find, in a given situation, some subjects with a high amount of physical complaints, while others report none at all. The limited value of questionnaire surveys is primarily determined by the fact that subjects, asked about such an important aspect of their personal situation as their work, consciously as well as unconsciously tend to convey a message. This message has to be decoded in respect to the specific individual and situation.

Physical complaints cannot be directly considered as a disease. Although reports about pain or discomfort always contain a subjective judgement about their severity, for medical diagnostics they are not clear symptoms. However, one tries to group them, as well as is feasible, to different syndromes (see e.g. Waris [1] and Waris et al. [2]). Reliable findings can only be achieved if the critical aspects of a given situation are taken into account. Therefore, in the present study, data were collected from different levels of the system encompassed by man and work. Question-

---

This work was supported by the Swiss National Foundation for Scientific Research (Project No 4.666.0.83.15 within the National Research Program "Arbeitswelt").

naire data about physical discomfort, work situation and job satisfaction have been complemented with an ergonomic analysis of the work stations, physiological recordings and medical examinations, as well as data about the personality and behavioural habits of the investigated subjects. With this broad set of data, the present report analyses how the reports of musculoskeletal discomfort given in a questionnaire relate to a variety of different factors such as medical findings, muscle tension, personality, ergonomic properties of the workstation as well as psychosocial aspects of the work performed and how the job is experienced. Relations between data about visual discomfort, clinical eye examination and various other parameters are reported elsewhere [3].

2. MATERIAL AND METHODS

2.1 Subjects

A sample of 196 subjects, divided into five different groups, was examined. Three groups consisted of subjects working with VDUs and two control groups performed comparable jobs without VDUs. The first group contained 24 subjects from three different companies performing data entry (DE). The second group were 58 operators of the domestic Directory Assistance (DD) from the telephone offices of two smaller towns. The third group consisted of 32 subjects from three different companies performing qualified dialog work (DI) on VDUs, such as programming or clerical work in a bank or public administration. The 59 subjects of the fourth group were operators from the international Directory Assistance (ID) of a big city working with directory listings printed in paper books. The 23 subjects of the fifth group were clerks (CL) from a bank doing no VDU work. Most subjects were female, only the DI and CL group were mixed (see Table 1).

2.2 Test instruments and procedure

After a general orientation about the purpose of the investigation each subject completed a combined questionnaire (CQ) at his or her work place. This first questionnaire survey was done in small groups, office by office, under supervision of either one of two investigators. In this way the subjects could check back if they had difficulties in understanding a particular question. The combined questionnaire collected data about physical complaints, drug consumption, ergonomic aspects of the workstation, job satisfaction and behavioural habits.

The prevalance and degree of postural discomfort were evaluated with a German version of the questionnaire of the Japanese Commission on Occupational Cervicobrachial Disorder [4]. Several figures served to illustrate the different areas of the back to the tested subjects. By means of these illustrations, frequency of stiffness and pain in the back during the previous few weeks was asked for. Cramps, pain and fatigue in the upper and lower extremities were assessed analogously. The answer "almost daily" earned 2 points, "occasionally" 1 point and "seldom or never" 0 points. An index "Musculoskeletal complaints" was computed by summing up the points given on each of the 39 items (see section 2.3). Eye discomfort was assessed by asking for frequency ("almost daily", "occasionally", " seldom or never") of tired, aching, red, teary or burning eyes, as well as for associated symptoms like blurred vision (9 items). With respect to drug consumption, the CQ asked, on a threefold scale, for daily, occasional or seldom use of the following 7 categories: analgesics, sleeping pills, tranquilizers, eye-drops, gastrointestinal drugs, internal and external remedies against rheumatism. The subjective evaluation of the room climate at the work place was assessed with 5 questions about temperature-suitability during summer and winter, stale air, bad smells and bothersome draughts of air.

Satisfaction and dissatisfaction with the job was measured with two special sets of questions [5]. The first set of 19 items asks for the subjective importance of different aspects of work such as salary system, work organisation, social contacts with peers and superiors, occasions for using and improving skills. ("No importance" gives 1 point," some importance" 2," quite much importance" 3 and "very much importance" 4 points). A score "Job ideals" is achieved by summarizing the points given on each item. The second set uses the same 19 aspects of work, but asks for satisfaction with these aspects at the present job. Again, points are given for each item: 0 for "very much dissatisfied", 1 for "rather dissatisfied", 2 for "rather satisfied" and 3 for "very much satisfied". The summation of all points leads to a score called "Job satisfaction". A third score, called "Job dissatisfaction" is simply the numerical difference between the two aforementioned scores. For the present study, all three scores were numerically transformed in order to reach a theoretical range from 0 (0 points on all 19 items) to 100 (3 points on all 19 items). As the job satisfaction and dissatisfaction scores are mathematically dependent, they usually correlate very strongly with each other. However, the job dissatisfaction score is more differentiated, as it weights the 19 aspects according to their importance for the tested individual.

Following completion of the CQ, each subject underwent a brief medical examination. The pressure sensitivity of tendon-insertions and muscles of the neck-shoulder-arm area was assessed by palpation. Cervical vertebrae and wrists were tested for mobility and pain in extreme positions. These observations were quantified on a threefold scale ("none" with 1, "little" with 2, "much pain" with 3 points) and summed up to a score called "Palpation findings".

The ergonomic aspects of the workstation were examined by a particular investigator and rated with points. Taken into account were the geometry and adjustability of the office equipment and the appropriateness of the settings chosen by the individual subject, sitting posture at the workstation and distance between body and keyboard, display screen and front end of the desk. VDU quality (flicker, size and quality of the characters, image stability) and lighting situation (visual contrasts and reflexions), as well as general aspects of the job (duration and number of different elements in the principal cycle of the job, job organisation, responsibility, required qualifications, social contacts and cooperation at work) were also assessed.

The first part of the investigation with the combined questionnaire and the medical and ergonomic examinations was followed by a second part, taking physiological recordings and administering further questionnaires. Heart rate, body movements and integrated electromyograms (EMG) were continuously recorded for about four hours from each subject on two different work days. Surface EMG electrodes were placed, according to Lippold [6], on the frontalis muscles and on the pars descendens of the right trapezius muscle. From the EMG signals the activity between 100 and 600 Hz was integrated for successive 3-sec. intervals. These values were stored on a portable recording device (ZAK, Bioport) together with the output of an activity transducer, integrated for the corresponding 3-sec. intervals, and the heart rate, computed for successive 15-sec. intervals. The availability of two instruments usually made it possible to perform simultaneous recordings from two subjects on each test day. The interval between the two individual recording sessions ranged from one day to six weeks. From these physiological recordings, the present report considers only the mean baseline measured on the trapezius muscle. These baseline measurements were taken at the beginning and at the end of each recording session while the subjects had to sit quietly in a resting position for at least 30 sec. By averaging the values of these four 30-sec. periods a mean baseline was computed for each subject.

At the beginning of their individual test day, the subjects were first equipped with the portable recording instrument and the electrical electrode resistance was determined in kilo-ohms. Then, the signals to be recorded were checked and the recording session started by taking the first baseline measurement. During the first 30 min. of the recording session subjects had to complete questionnaires, assessing personality and subjectively experienced aspects of work. Then, they resumed their daily work schedule.

For personality assessment two different instruments were used: the abbreviated form of Fahrenberg's [7] Freiburg Personality Questionnaire (FPI) and an unvalidated German translation of Tellegen's [8] Multidimensional Personality Questionnaire (MPQ). The FPI distinguishes between 9 factoranalytically constructed primary factors. Factors E and N following Eysenck's concept of Extraversion and Neuroticism and an M scale, representing Masculinity, according to Terman and Miles, are affiliated. Each factor of the abbreviated FPI consists of 7 items. E, N and M are not fully independent, since several items of these scales are in common with one of the primary factors. The MPQ has 11 primary factors with 11 to 34 items each and 3 higher order traits. The latter are linear combinations of the total set of primary personality dimensions. Additional factors serve to detect constant or variable tendencies of answering. Since the results of the MPQ were similar to those of the FPI, they are only used in section 3.2 of the present report.

Subjectively experienced aspects of work were assessed with two questionnaires [9] called "Situationsbewertung" (SB) and "Emotionalitätsinventar" (EMI). Originally they were constructed for application in behavioural modification treatments. The SB quantifies self-ratings of optional situations. It comprises 55 bipolar items divided into four groups. Adapted for evaluating the work situation, the following four test questions had to be answered on 10 to 20 bipolar items with a sixfold scale: "At present, I find my work", "Doing my work, I would prefer most to", "Doing my work, I find myself just now" and "If people of my personal surroundings which I am seeing most often (e.g. family members, friends, colleagues, neighbours, etc.) could observe me doing my work, or if I told them about it, they would probably react with". The six factors of the SB-test are called: "Difficulty", "Threat", "Tendency of avoidance", "Positive expectations", "Negative expectations" and "Positive self-rating". The EMI-test evaluates tendencies for emotional reactions in a specific situation. Adapted for the work situation, the following question had to be answered with a sixfold scale on the 70 bipolar test items: "Doing my work, I feel myself mainly". The seven factors extracted by the EMI-test are called: "Anxious-constrained vs. relaxed-self-assured reaction", "Depressive-sad vs. satisfied-cheerful reaction", "Exhausted-passive vs. dynamic-active reaction", "Aggressive-hostile vs. peaceful-flexible reaction", "Optimistic-positive vs. pessimistic-resignative reaction", "Risky-openhearted vs. considerate-reserved reaction" and "Feelings of isolation vs. feelings of security".

2.3 Data analysis

All statistical analyses were performed with version 9 of the SPSS (Statistical Package for Social Sciences). From the standardized questionnaires (FPI, MPQ, EMI, SB) and the EMG baseline, the individual raw data were used. The remaining data were grouped into thematic indices by summing up the points given on the corresponding items. Following Fahrenberg [10], only those variables were used for statistical computation which did not have extreme distribution anomalies (|skewness| >3; kurtosis >10, or < -4, respectively) or missing values in more than 15% of the subjects.

Of the a priori defined indices of the combined questionnaire, the medical examination and the data observed or measured at the workstation, most fulfilled these requirements. The present report uses the following indices computed for each subject:

- "Musculoskeletal discomfort": Sum of 39, threefold rated items of the CQ (as well as subindices, correspondingly computed for particular regions of the body)
- "Eye discomfort": Sum of 9, threefold rated items of the CQ
- "Palpation findings": Sum of 48, threefold rated items of the medical examination (as well as subindices, correspondingly computed for particular regions of the body)
- "Complaints about chair": Sum of 4, threefold rated items of the CQ
- "Complaints about room climate": Sum of 5 twofold rated items of the CQ
- "Variety of work": Sum from the duration of the principal cycle (the mean time interval between repetitions of the principal activity in the daily job schedule was rated with 1 to 5 points according to the following classes: 1-14 sec., 15-179 sec., 3-15 min., 16-119 min., 2-8 h; 6 points were given if no clear principal activity or cycle time could be determined) and the number of different elements in the principal activity (5 levels: 1-2, 3-6, 7-14, 15-30 and more than 30).

The combined questionnaire asked VDU subjects also about possible dissatisfaction with ergonomic aspects of their workstation. These data were summarized into the following nine indices:

- "Computer efficiency": Sum of 5, threefold rated items
- "Character quality": Sum of 4, twofold rated items
- "Text layout": Sum of 5, twofold rated items
- "Screen quality": Sum of 9, threefold rated items
- "Annoying reflexions on the screen": Sum of 5, twofold rated items
- "Annoying contrasts in the visual field": Sum of 6, twofold rated items
- "Lighting conditions at the workstation": Sum of 12, twofold rated items
- "Screen position": Sum of 3, twofold rated items
- "Keyboard position": Sum of 3, twofold rated items.

All individual values of the above listed indices were numerically transformed onto a scale with a theoretical range from 0 to 100. An index value of 0 means that the lowest level (e.g. "No discomfort at all") was marked on all items summed up into this index. Correspondingly, a value of 100 is reached, if a subject marked the top level (e.g. discomfort intensity "almost daily") on all items of a particular index.

From the measured ergonomic data concerning VDU quality and lighting conditions at the workstation, the following eight, not further transformed indices were computed: "Contrast ratio between horizontal desk plane and VDU screen", "Contrast ratio between keyboard and VDU screen", "Contrast ratio between case and screen of the VDU", "Maximal contrast ratio to the VDU screen", "Maximal contrast ratio in the visual field", "Reflexion ratio on the VDU screen", "Reflexion ratio on the horizontal desk plane" and "Screen adjustability" (the existence of a screen adjustability with respect to height, left/right, forward/backward and rotation around the vertical and horizontal axis was each counted as one point. An additional point was given for each of these 5 features if they were set in an appropriate way for the corresponding subject).

Statistical significance of differences between the investigated groups was tested with analysis of variance and Scheffe-tests, the significance of differences between the two telephone operator groups also with t-tests and Mann-Whitney-U-tests. The sensitivity of the test instruments used for discriminating subjects reporting a high amount of musculoskeletal discomforts from subjects with a low amount was evaluated with a discriminant analysis (classification performed with the same subject sample from which discrimination function was extracted). Correlative relations were tested by computing partial correlations, corrected for age and sex, and with a principal component analysis. A correction for age and sex was applied, since the amount of physical discomforts increases with age and is usually higher in females than in males.

3. RESULTS

3.1 Differences between investigated groups

The demographic characteristics of the five groups are given in Table 1.

The five groups have to be considered as rather different samples. Most comparable are the two telephone operator groups. They not only have the same sex and are practically identical with respect to age distribution, but also have the same work schedules, employment conditions and salary system.

Mean values of various indices for the five different groups are given in Table 2. With respect to eye and musculoskeletal discomfort, within group variance was larger than between group variance. Therefore, these scores showed no significant group differences. At most, there was a tendency toward higher musculoskeletal discomfort in the data entry group, in which the amount of such complaints was positively correlated with the hours working at the VDU per day ($r = .40$, $p < .05$, partial correlation corrected for age). With respect to eye discomfort, the corresponding correlation did not reach significance ($r = .30$). In the dialog group,

Table 1: Demographic characteristics of the 5 groups (in brackets: standard deviation)

	DE	DD	DI	ID	CL	Total
No. of subjects	24	58	32	59	23	196
Age	33(12)	20(2)	35(11)	21(3)	37(13)	26(11)
No. of females	24	58	11	59	14	166
Age	33(12)	20(2)	35(13)	21(3)	36(12)	24(9)
No. of males	--	--	21	--	9	30
Age			35(10)		39(14)	37(11)
Smokers (%)	67	53	22	49	40	47
Hours at VDU per day	7.0 (1.5)	8.0 (0)	6.9 (1.2)	--	--	--
Years working at VDU	4.7 (3.1)	2.1 (1.1)	4.8 (2.3)	--	--	--

Table 2: Group means (and standard deviations) of various indices, computed by summing up individual data of related items.

	Actual Range	VDU-Groups DE	VDU-Groups DD	VDU-Groups DI	Control-Groups ID	Control-Groups CL
1) Eye discomfort	0-71	21 (19)	18 (15)	21 (21)	18 (16)	11 (16)
2) Musculoskeletal discomfort	0-58	17 (16)	10 (9)	9 (12)	9 (8)	10 (9)
3) Musculoskeletal discomfort in the right arm	0-88	20 (23)	8 (14)	8 (16)	5 (9)	8 (12)
Medical examination:						
4) Palpation findings in neck, back and arms	0-42	8 (9)	4 (7)	4 (5)	3 (4)	4 (6)
5) Palpation findings in the right arm	0-61	9 (17)	1 (5)	1 (4)	1 (3)	1 (3)
6) Job satisfaction	4-92	68 (17)	54 (13)	65 (15)	61 (13)	69 (8)
7) Sick leave (Number of days p.a.)	0-54	5.0 (6.1)	8.2 (7.4)	2.4 (4.9)	10.7 (11.0)	4.5 (8.4)

Abbreviations: DE = Data entry; DD = Domestic Directory Assistance; DI = Dialog work; ID = International Directory Assistance; CL = Clerical work.

Significant differences between groups (Scheffe tests): 1) none; 2) none; 3) DE versus DD, DI, ID, CL; 4) DE versus ID; 5) DE versus DD, DI, ID, CL; 6) DD versus DE, DI, CL; 7) DI versus ID.

---

also spending different amounts of time at the VDU per day, there were no such correlations (r = -.06 and .05, respectively). The data entry group also had a significantly higher score on the index "musculoskeletal discomfort in the right arm" and more palpation findings in the medical examination.

Among the DD telephone operators, job satisfaction was significantly lower than in the remaining VDU groups or among the clerical workers. In a direct t- and U-test comparison, their job satisfaction was also significantly lower than among the ID telephone operators ($p < .01$). Furthermore, there was a significantly positive correlation between the number of years working as a DD telephone operator and job dissatisfaction (Spearman correlation coefficient $r = .38$, $p < .01$, for job dissatisfaction and $r = -.43$, $p < .001$, for job satisfaction). With increasing number of years working as DD telephone operator, reports about eye and musculoskeletal discomfort showed an increasing tendency (Spearman correlation coefficient $r = .20$ and $r = .18$, respectively, $p < .10$), while the palpation findings of the medical examination significantly decreased ($r = -.30$, $p < .05$). Such a discrepancy between subjective reports about physical complaints and medical findings did not show up in any of the other groups.

The ID telephone operators had significantly more sick days during the 12 months previous to the investigation date than the subjects of the data entry group. A direct t- and U-test comparison between the two telephone operator groups revealed no significant difference in this respect. Furthermore, these two groups were not significantly different in their eye and musculoskeletal discomfort, palpation findings of the medical examination, drug and cigarette consumption. As the only difference among the 11 FPI factors, the ID telephone operators showed less "behavioural constraint" (t-test: $p = .062$, U-test: $p = .049$), as well as greater "social potency" (t-test: $p = .011$, U-test: $p = .013$), one of the 20 MPQ factors. In the total sample, smokers had more sickness days than non-smokers ($t = 2.12$, $p < .05$). However, if this comparison is done separately within the five groups, the differences always remain below the level of statistical significance.

In addition to the above mentioned difference in job satisfaction between the two telephone operator groups and the decrease in satisfaction with increasing experience as DD telephone operator, remarkable differences between these two groups were also found with respect to the SB and EMI questionnaires, testing how the job is emotionally experienced. Compared with the ID telephone operators, DD telephone operators had significantly higher scores on the SB-scales "threat" (t-test: $p = .007$, U-test: $p = .013$), "tendency of job avoidance" (t-test: $p = .006$, U-test: $p = .009$) and "negative job expectations (t-test: $p = .026$, U-test: $p = .045$), as well as on the EMI-scales "depressive-sad reaction" (t-test: $p = .001$, U-test: $p = .002$), "exhausted-passive reaction" (t-test: $p = .001$, U-test: $p = .002$) and "feelings of isolation" (t-test: $p = .008$, U-test: n.s.) Furthermore, they scored significantly lower on the SB-scales "positive job expectations" (t-test: $p = .027$, U-test:

n.s.) and "positive self-rating on the job" (t-test: p = .001, U-test: p = .003), as well as on the EMI-scales "optimistic-positive reaction" (t-test: p = .001, U-test: p = .001) and "risky-open-hearted reaction" (t-test: p = .020, U-test: n.s.).

3.2 Sensitivity of the test instruments

The efficiency of the test instruments used in separating between individuals with a high and low amount of musculoskeletal discomfort was evaluated with the discriminant analysis method. For this purpose, subsamples with subjects reporting a high and low amount of musculoskeletal discomfort, respectively, were extracted from the total sample, the VDU and the control groups. In each of these three cases, discriminant analyses were performed for all test instruments to be evaluated by comparing the corresponding 25% of the subjects with the highest amount of musculoskeletal discomfort with the 25% of the subjects with the lowest amount of musculoskeletal discomfort.

Table 3: Discriminant analyses between subsamples with high and low amount of postural discomfort. Indicated are the percent values of correctly classified cases.

Test instrument	No. of test parameters	VDU groups	Control groups	Total sample
Medical examination (Palpation findings)	15	77 %	74 %	74 %
Freiburg Personality Inventory (FPI)	9	71 %	86 %	73 %
Multidim. Personality Questionnaire (MPQ)	11	88 %	78 %	71 %
Subjective rating of work situation (SB)	6	73 %	64 %	62 %
Emotional experience of work situation (EMI)	7	77 %	57 %	69 %
VDU display quality and lighting	8	63 %	--	--
Ergonomic complaints about VDU station	9	76 %	--	--

The results of this analysis (Table 3) show that the test instruments used were differentially efficient in separating between individuals with a high and low amount of musculoskeletal discomfort. None of them reached a perfect separation. A substantial selectivity with more than 80% correctly classified cases was partly obtained with personality tests. The medical examination, the SB and EMI tests and the complaints about ergonomic properties of the VDU station attained a slightly lower selectivity, while the ergonomic data of the VDU station, measured by the investigator, could only correctly classify about 60% of the cases, which is not much above the 50% chance level.

3.3 Correlational analysis

Several of the variables used in this investigation were dependent on age and/or sex. Some of them are shown in Table 4. Eye discomfort, musculoskeletal discomfort, palpation findings and drug consumption increased with age. In addition, musculoskeletal discomfort, but not eye discomfort, and palpation findings were higher in females than in males. EMG baseline was slightly higher in older subjects, which could be due to an age dependent increase in mean action potential duration, reported by Buchtal et al. [11], and/or greater synchrony of individual muscle potential units in older people [12]. No significant differences in EMG baseline were found with respect to sex. Among females, there was a slight tendency for lower EMG values in subjects with higher relative body weight (Spearman correlation between EMG baseline and body weight divided by cubed body height: $r = -.11$, $p = .08$). A decrease of EMG baseline with a thicker fat layer in the skin is to be expected [12, 13]. However, this effect was minimal and it did not show up in the total sample or within males. Furthermore, older subjects had lower scores on the personality scales "Depressivity" and "Emotional lability" and females showed more "Nervousness", complaints about room climate and number of sick days. Job satisfaction was dependent on neither age nor sex.

Table 4: Partial correlations, corrected for age or sex, between sex (male = 1, female = 2) and age, respectively, and the variables given below.

Variable	Correlation with Sex	Age
Eye discomfort	.07	.16*
Musculoskeletal discomfort	.15*	.25***
Palpation findings	.19**	.31***
Drug comsumption	.08	.18**
EMG baseline (Trapezius)	-.08	.15*
Depressivity (FPI)	.00	-.29***
Emotional lability (FPI)	.10	-.31***
Nervousness (FPI)	.21***	.07
Complaints about room climate	.18**	.02
Number of sick days p.a.	.26***	.11
Job satisfaction	-.09	.13

* $p < .05$ ** $p < .01$ *** $p < .001$

The reported eye and musculoskeletal discomforts were highly correlated with each other, within the total sample as well as within the five investigated groups. The corresponding correlation coefficients, computed according to Pearson or Spearman, were all within a range of $r = .45$ to $r = .63$. Musculoskeletal discomfort was also correlated with the EMG baseline and the palpation findings of the medical examination (see Table 5). However, the palpation findings did not correlate with the EMG baseline, neither in the total sample (Pearson correlation $r = -.06$) nor within any of the investigated groups.

The variables in the total sample showing the highest correlations with musculoskeletal discomfort and, except EMG baseline, also with eye discomfort are listed in Table 5. Indicated are the coefficients of partial correlations, corrected for age, and in mixed groups also for sex. They were computed for the total sample, as well as within the five investigated groups. Several of the correlations found in the total sample could not be detected within all five groups. Most such deviations were found in the data entry group. No relationships at all were found between overall musculoskeletal discomfort and the type of work performed, the number of sick days and the ergonomic properties of the workstation.

Table 5: Partial correlations (r•100), corrected for age, and in mixed groups also for sex, between musculoskeletal discomfort and the variables given below.

Factor	Variable	Total sample	Correlations within groups VDU - Groups DE	DD	DI	Controls ID	CL
1	Depressive feelings (EMI)	23	09!	35	22!	19!	12!
1	Passivity & exhaustion(EMI)	30	14!	43	36	25	21!
1	Feelings of isolation (EMI)	21	08!	27	26	25	-07!
1	Positive self-rating (SB)	-20	-11!	-04!	-23	-28	-21
1	Anxious feelings (EMI)	26	04!	44	17!	33	23!
1	Avoidance tendencies (SB)	16	-07!	06!	32	26	-04!
1	Positive expectations (SB)	-25	-33	-29	-37	-10!	-19!
2	Depressivity (FPI)	26	-11!	30	28	45	30
2	Emotional lability (FPI)	23	-21!	29	20!	31	43
2	Masculinity (FPI)	-22	-11!	06!	-53	-35	-37
2	Nervousness (FPI)	33	09!	24	39	35	70
3	Variety of work	-24	-31	NC	-08!	NC	-63
3	Smoking	19	04!	27	11!	20	27
4	Complaints about chair	26	26	30	40	29	06!
4	Job dissatisfaction	22	-08!	34	44	32	-12!
5	Palpation findings	42	52	29	61	22	36
5	Drug comsumption	27	19!	20!	56	13!	34
6	Muscle tension (Trapezius)	19	31	20	42	01!	23
6	Compl. about room climate	28	10!	24	51	19!	55

Abbreviations: DE = Data entry; DD = Domestic Directory Assistance; DI = Dialog work; ID = International Directory Assistance, CL = Clerical work; EMI = Emotional Inventory; SB = Subjective rating of job situation; FPI = Freiburg Personality Inventory; NC = Not computable, due to no within-group variance.
Levels of significance for total sample: r 100 = 12-16 ($p < .05$); 17-20 ($p < .01$); 21-100 ($p < .001$). ! = non-significant within-group correlations below correlation coefficient of total sample.

With the variables listed in Table 5, being critical with respect to subjective reports about musculoskeletal discomfort, a factor analysis (principal components analysis) was performed. The resulting six factors explain 65% of the total variance. They are called: "Emotional experience of the work situation", "Personality", "Little variety in work and smoking", "Dissatisfaction with job and chair", "Medical findings" and "Muscle tension and complaints about room climate". For each of these factors an index was calculated. For this purpose, the individual data were normalized with a z-transformation, then multiplied by the factor loading and summed up for the corresponding factor. Table 6 shows how the index values of these six factors are correlated with the subjective reports about musculoskeletal complaints. Again, partial correlations were computed for the total sample and the five groups.

Table 6: Partial correlations (r•100), corrected for age, and in mixed groups also for sex, between musculoskeletal discomfort and the factors extracted by a principal components analysis.

Factor	Variable	Total sample	Correlations within groups VDU - Groups DE	DD	DI	Controls ID	CL
1	Emotional experience of the work situation	30	13!	37	35	34	16!
2	Personality	32	-03!	25	45	45	53
3	Little variety in work; and smoking	28	17!	36	11!	20!	64
4	Dissatisfaction with job and chair	32	14!	39	65	37	-09!
5	Medical findings	45	45	27	68	17!	45
6	Muscle tension; and complaints about room climate	29	26!	29	56	13!	39

Abbreviations: DE = Data entry; DD = Domestic Directory Assistance; DI = Dialog work; ID = International Directory Assistance; CL = Clerical work.
Levels of significance for total sample: r•100 > 21 ($p < .001$).
! = non-significant within-group correlations below correlation coefficient of total sample.

The six factors were of differing importance within the five groups. In the data entry group, for example, the factor "medical findings" played a predominant role, while most other factors, such as "personality" or "emotional experience of the work situation" were of less importance. On the other hand, in the two telephone operator groups, the psychological factors predominated.

4. DISCUSSION

The present study shows that musculoskeletal discomforts, assessed with a questionnaire, are a complex phenomenon encompassing numerous factors. These factors can partly be identified by a comparative analysis of the physical-ergonomic, biological and psychosocial level of the system man and work. In this analysis, the feature "VDU" per se did not show up as a critical factor, since the five investigated groups did not report significantly different amounts of musculoskeletal discomfort. Especially the two telephone operator groups, being very similar in age, sex and socioeconomic status, showed practically identical values with respect to all tested forms of physical discomfort and the palpation findings of the medical examination. Critical for musculoskeletal discomfort is therefore not the use of a VDU at work but the entire work environment.

Factors of the physical-ergonomic level were primarily manifested in the data entry group. Elevated discomfort in the right arm in correspondence with more palpation findings in the medical examination point to a one-sided mechanical strain of the body, connected with a constrained posture. In addition, the amount of musculoskeletal discomfort increased with the hours working at VDU per day only in the data entry group. Probably, the one-sided physical strain masked in this group the effect of certain other factors, which had a significant effect in the total sample and within other groups. These results support the recommendation that pure data entry work be limited, not only in the number of daily working hours but also in the length of a single working block. Appropriate as relaxing interruptions are not only pauses but also tasks involving physical activity such as supplying work material.

On the biological level, age played an important role. As was to be expected, eye discomfort, musculoskeletal discomfort and palpation findings increased with age. Outstanding psychosocial factors were personality, job satisfaction and how the job is experienced.

The combined view of the indices from the physical-ergonomic, biological and psychosocial levels helps to detect the specific factors critical for a particular situation. An isolated consideration of the correlation between eye and musculoskeletal discomfort, for instance, found in the total sample as well as within all investigated groups, suggests a simple causality, since intensive looking can lead to constrained posture and elevated muscle tension. A multilevel analysis, however, shows that, in the present study, additional and in part more important factors are responsible for this correlation. First, this correlation was found to be about the same in the VDU groups and in the ID telephone operators, working with printed directory listing. As the latter have relatively much physical activity, they are hardly restricted to constrained postures. It is further of imporantance that the same method was used for assessing musculoskeletal and eye discomfort, namely a questionnaire. By assessing the same phenomenon with different methods, greater differences can result than by investigating different phenomena with the same method. This is illustrated in the comparison of musculoskeletal discomfort, reported in a questionnaire, with the palpation findings of the medical examination. A correlation was to be expected, as in both cases painful sensations are involved, but with $r = .42$ for the total sample it turned out to be rather moderate, it was smaller than the correlation between eye and musculoskeletal discomfort ($r = .56$), and even surprisingly weak within the two telephone operator groups ($r = .29$ and $r = .22$, respectively). Furthermore, in the DD telephone operators palpation findings significantly decreased with increased number of years working on this job, while the reports about musculoskeletal discomfort showed an opposite tendency. This increase in reported musculoskeletal discomfort is probably due to increasing dissatisfaction with the job, for job dissatisfaction increased significantly with the number of years working on the job. The DD telephone operators also showed a possible secondary effect of VDU work. The prolonged use of a single and also very fast-working instrument makes a job more one-sided and monotonous and reduces social contacts. Compared with the telephone operators using conventional methods, the VDU telephone operators experience their work as more threatening and associated with less positive and more negative consequences. They see themselves less positively in their work and have stronger tendencies to avoid it.

VDU work has to be considered as one factor among others. It is not a uniform factor, as the forms of VDU work are so different that they can hardly be compared with each other. The different aspects of VDU work interact with numerous other factors. As a general model one could postulate that the effects of potentially critical factors depend on their magnitude and interaction with other factors. In a lower range, such factors have no effects at all. In a middle range, their effects can be compensated, masked or reinforced by others. In an upper range, they are likely to cause serious health problems.

The factors identified in the present study using factor analysis are certainly not the only possible ones, as even a broad, multilevel analysis remains incomplete and, therefore, could miss important factors. Yet, it is remarkable how the variables associated with musculoskeletal discomfort were grouped by a factor analysis and how relevant factors were specifically prominent within different groups. A first factor encompassed scales of two different questionnaires assessing emotional experience and subjective rating of the work situation, in which feelings of threat, lack of success experience, tendencies for job avoidance, and depressive-passive reactions were predominant. The personality scales "Depressivity", "Emotional lability", "Nervousness", and "Masculinity" (inversely correlated) of the FPI formed a second factor. Interestingly, the subjects reporting the highest amount of musculoskeletal discomfort showed a personality structure often found in patients with rheumatic disorders. Such a personality can be characterized as being nervous, stress sensitive, depressive, frustrated, and rather passive, thus suffering from a lack of positive reinforcement. In this situation it is to be expected that the lack of successful experiences reinforces the tendency to behavioural passivity. The remaining activity then primarily consists of nervous avoidance behaviour. Rising musculoskeletal discomfort could specifically lead to physical passivity and, in this way, advance a rheumatic disease. This finding suggests, as a means of preventive intervention in such cases, applying behavioural modification programs [15], generating active behaviour instead of avoidance behaviour and, in this way, shifting the balance from negative to positive reinforcement. The association between little variety in work and smoking in the third factor is consistent with the known fact that there are proportionally more smokers in lower than in upper socio-ecnomonic classes. However, the present study does not reveal, whether the increased amount of musculoskeletal discomfort is due to smoking, to little variety in work or to other characteristics correlating with the social class. Nevertheless, the difference in sick days found between smokers and non-smokers of the total sample, is in accordance with findings showing higher morbidity in smokers [16]. The linkage between dissatisfaction with job and chair reflects, on the one hand, the importance a chair has for physical well-being if one is working in a sitting position. On the other hand, the chair at the work place is not only an instrument for work but also a status symbol. The palpation findings and the reported drug consumption, summarized into a fifth factor, can both be regarded as medical findings in a larger sense. The connection between EMG baseline and complaints about room climate in the sixth factor suggests that people with higher muscle tension might be more sensitive to influences of the room climate, for example temperature changes or draughts of air. Remarkable is the finding that EMG baseline was positively correlated with musculoskeletal discomfort but not with the palpation findings of the medical examination. This could signify that musculoskeletal discomfort is primarily associated with increased muscle tension, whereas the pain sensations elicited by palpation remain, in everyday life, below the threshold of sensation. However, they may suddenly and very strongly manifest themselves with the onset of a rheumatic disease.

The six factors were of differing importance within the five groups. In the data entry group, subjected to the greatest physical strain, the factor "Medical findings" played a predominant role and masked the effects of most other factors, such as "Personality" or "Emotional experience of the work situation". In the two telephone operator groups, apparently experiencing more psychological than physical stress, the psychological factors predominated.

Subjective complaints are an important message. However, this message has to be decoded with respect to the individual and the situation. Only by analysing the specific circumstances is it possible to show which factors are critical for a particular case, as increased complaints about physical discomfort are not only just given by generally dissatisfied people. Critical is primarily the way the work situation is experienced. This experience is formed in an interactive way by the work in itself, the tools used, the personality of the people involved, and above all the climate and organisation of work. The way one is experiencing his or her work influences in return the behaviour at work. A bad work climate, for example, can lead to muscular tension and bad posture and, in this way, cause physical discomfort. Physiological and psychological differences in individuals might be responsible for the fact that work performed under identical external conditions can be very differently experienced. This fact can be taken into account by granting a certain individual freedom in work organisation and performance.

As the study shows, the physical and psychic well-being at the work place, and consequently also the efficiency on the job are related to ergonomic, biological, psychological and social factors in a differential and interactive way. The individual biological and psychological properties can hardly be influenced, whereas optimization of ergonomic and organizational aspects of the job are not only possible but also contribute to efficiency and convenience.

REFERENCES

[1] Waris, P., Occupational cervicobrachial syndromes, Scandinavian Journal of Work, Environment & Health 5, suppl. 3 (1979) 3-14.

[2] Waris, P., Kuorinka, I., Kurppa, K., Virolainen, M., Pesonen, K., Nummi, J., and Kukkonen, R., Epidemiologic screening of occupational neck and upper limb disorders, Scandinavian Journal of Work, Environment & Health 5, suppl. 3 (1979) 25-38.

[3] Zeier, H., Mion, H., Läubli, T., Thomas, C., and Senn, E., Augen- und Rückenbeschwerden bei Bildschirmarbeit in Abhängigkeit von ergonomischen und biopsychosozialen Faktoren, Zeitschrift für angewandte und experimentelle Psychologie (1986), in print.
[4] Maeda, K., Hünting, W., and Grandjean, E., Localized fatigue in accounting machine operators, Journal of Occupational Medicine 22 (1980) 810-816.
[5] Oegerli, K., Arbeitszufriedenheit, Versuche einer qualitativen Bestimmung, Unpublished doctoral disseration, Psychological Institute, University of Berne (1984)
[6] Lippold, O.C.J., Electromyography, in: Venables, P.H. and Martin, I., (eds.), A Manual for Psychophysiological Methods (North-Holland Publishing Company, Amsterdam, London, 1967) pp. 245-297.
[7] Fahrenberg, J., Selg, H., and Hampel, R., Das Freiburger Persönlichkeitsinventar FPI, (Hogrefe, Göttingen, 1978)
[8] Tellegen, A., The Multidimensional Personality Questionnaire, Unpublished test materials, University of Minnesota (1982)
[9] Ullrich, R. and Ullrich de Muynck, R., Testmappe SB/EMI-S (Pfeiffer, München, 1979)
[10] Fahrenberg, J., Foerster, F., Schneider, H.J., Müller, W., and Myrtek, M., Aktivierungsforschung im Labor-Feld-Vergleich (Minerva-Publikation, München 1984)
[11] Buchthal, F., Pinelle, P. and Rosenfalck, P., Action potential parameters in normal human muscle and their physiological determinants, Acta Physiologica Scandinavica 32 (1954) 219-229.
[12] Nidever, J.E., A factor analytic study of general muscular tension, Unpublished doctoral dissertation, University of California, Los Angeles (1959).
[13] Balshan, I.D., Muscle tension and personality in women, Archives of General Psychiatry 7 (1962) 436-448.
[14] Hell, D., Balmer, R., Battegay, R., Labhardt, F. and Müller, W., Weichteilrheumatismus und Persönlichkeit: eine kontrollierte Studie, Schweizerische Rundschau für Medizin (Praxis) 71 (1982) 1014-1021.
[15] Zeier, H. (ed.), Lernen und Verhalten, Vol. 2: Verhaltensmodifikation (Beltz Verlag, Weinheim, Basel, 1984)
[16] Leu, R.E. and Schaub, T., Does smoking increase medical care expenditure? Social Sciences and Medicine 17 (1983) 1907-1914.

WORK WITH DISPLAY UNITS 86
B. Knave and P.-G. Wideback (eds.)

VDUs AND MUSCULO-SKELETAL PROBLEMS AT THE AUSTRALIAN NATIONAL UNIVERSITY - A CASE STUDY

Gabriele BAMMER

Director's Section, Research School of Social Sciences, Australian National University, GPO Box 4, Canberra, ACT 2601, Australia

Preliminary results of a detailed retrospective examination of the relationship between the increased incidence of musculo-skeletal problems in the neck, shoulders, arms and hands and the introduction of VDU technology at the Australian National University (ANU) are reported here. It is suggested that changes in work practices associated with VDU technology, as well as the technology itself, contribute significantly to increased musculo-skeletal problems. The results are compared with those found in the Australian Public Service and in studies conducted in Japan, Europe and the United States of America.

1. INTRODUCTION

There are a number of health hazards associated with office work [1,2] and these seem to have increased with the introduction of VDU technology. Among the problems which seem to have become more prominent are musculo-skeletal complaints among keyboard operators, especially problems in the neck, shoulders, arms and hands. These have been recognised in most countries where VDU technology is widely used [3] and have been given a variety of names including repetition strain injuries (RSI), occupational cervico-brachial disorders (OCD) and cumulative trauma disorders (CTD). However, it is not clear how common these problems are or if the prevalence differs between countries.

Musculo-skeletal problems among keyboard operators are generally accepted to have two causes - 1) rapid repetitive movements and 2) static loading i.e. sustained isometric contraction required of the muscles of the neck, shoulders and upper arms to support and fix the arms in a position of function [4,5,6].

These causes can be influenced by a variety of factors, including the physical features of VDUs and changes in work practices associated with VDU technology. For example, physical features which may increase static loading include poor design of equipment and furniture and elimination of non-keying tasks when typing, such as changing paper, waiting for the carriage return and use of correction fluid. Physical features which can increase repetitive movements include the 'soft touch' keyboard. Changes in work practices which may be associated with the introduction of VDU technology include reduction in task diversity and reduction in keyboard staff numbers coupled with demands for increased productivity. Both of these may lead to increases in repetitive movements and static loading and thus to musculo-skeletal problems.

This study is examining whether there is an association between the introduction of VDU technology and the increased incidence of musculo-skeletal problems and if the factors outlined above could explain the increase. Preliminary results are reported here. The results are also compared with those obtained in studies of the Australian Public Service (i.e. government employees) and also with studies in Japan, Europe and the United States of America.

2. METHODS

The incidence of musculo-skeletal problems among keyboard operators at the ANU was obtained from University Health Service records and from records of claims made for workers' compensation. These records provide conservative estimates of the number of sufferers.

The other information used in this study was obtained from a survey of all areas of the ANU which was conducted at the end of 1984. Information was collected on 1) staff who were employed between January 1980 and November 1984 and who operated keyboards for more than one hour per day, and 2) the types of keyboards that such staff used. The survey covered all members of staff except academics and research assistants. The information collected was checked extensively using the university's annual reports, personnel files, equipment and wage lists and telephone calls to selected members of staff.

3. RESULTS

3.1 The incidence of musculo-skeletal problems

The incidence of musculo-skeletal problems among general staff operating keyboards at the ANU between 1980 and 1984 is shown in Figure 1. A total of 185

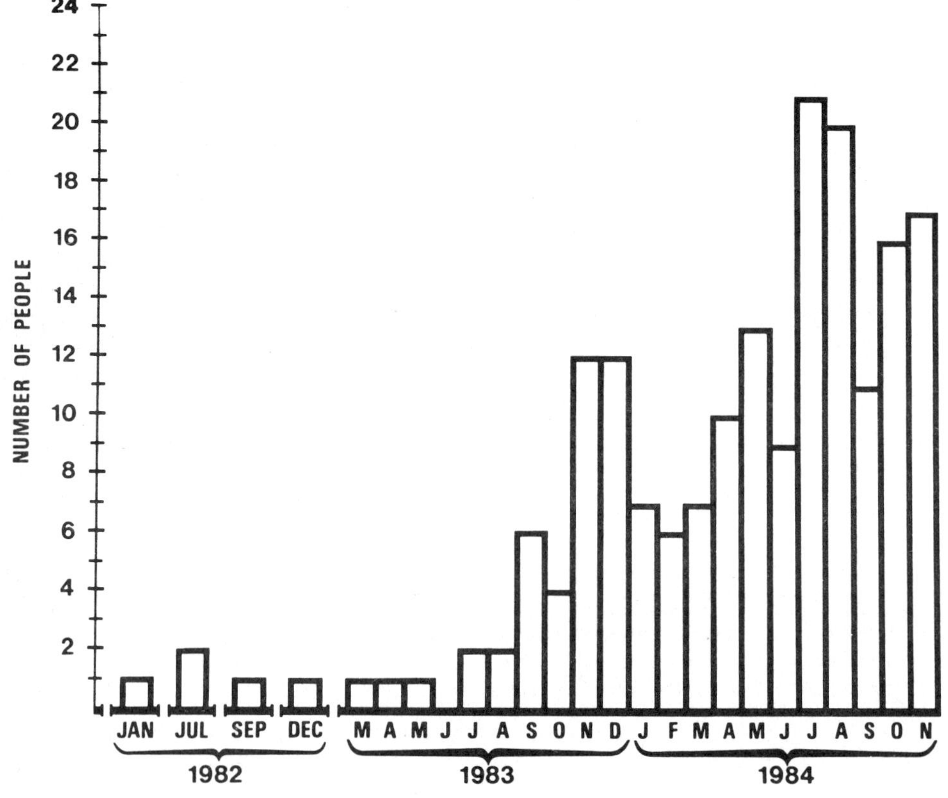

FIGURE 1
Number of people first reporting musculo-skeletal problems to a doctor in each month (since 1980).

people were affected and the month of first reporting was available for 183 of them. One of the two people where this was not known developed musculo-skeletal problems in 1981. Apart from this person, it can be seen that there were no cases until 1982, then there was a low rate of reporting until late 1983, after which the number of cases increased dramatically.

In general, people reported to a doctor between 1 and 3 months after symptoms first appeared and this latency was rather consistent across the 5 years (Figure 2). However, there was a wide range in the latencies, from 1 week to several years (with one person having had problems for 20 years).

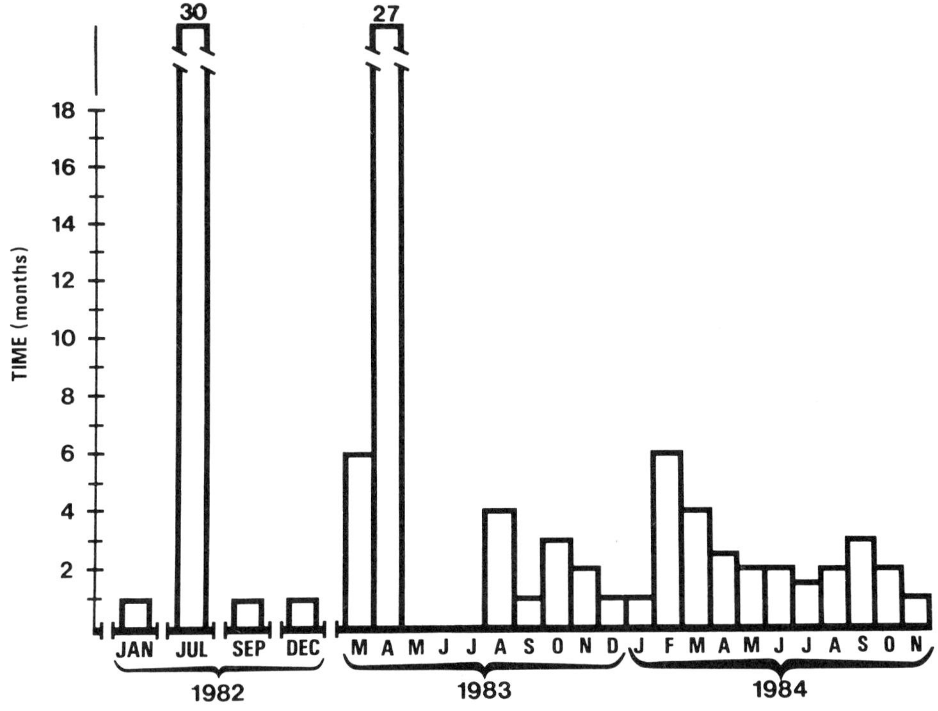

FIGURE 2
Median time (months) between noticing the problem and first reporting to a doctor.

A variety of parameters which may help to explain the increase in musculo-skeletal problems were examined for approximately one-third of the staff and are outlined below.

3.2 The equipment used

Between 1980 and 1984, the number of people working on computers or word processors (i.e. VDUs) increased dramatically, while the number using electric typewriters remained much the same (Figure 3). In general, people working on VDUs had either not worked on keyboards before or had previously worked on electric typewriters and were now working on both types of equipment.

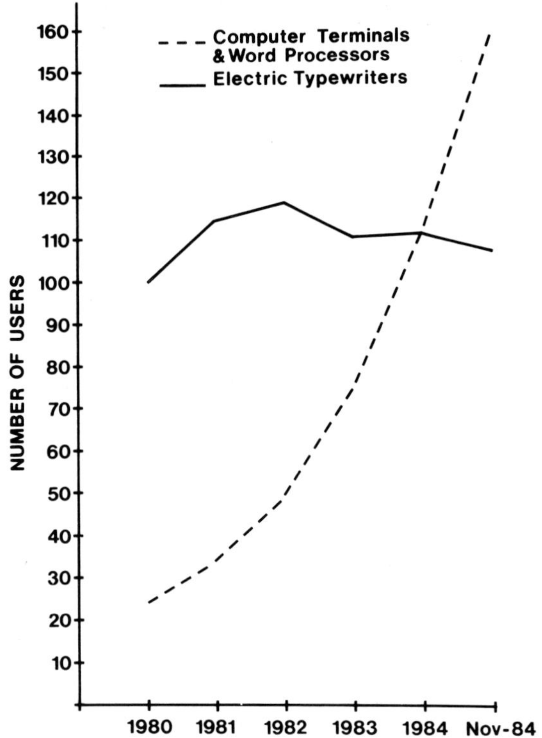

FIGURE 3
Changes in types of keyboards used between 1980 and 1984.

The relationship of musculo-skeletal problems to the type of equipment used is shown in Table 1. The whole 5 year period was examined and the analysis involved equipment used for more than 6 months (unless problems developed earlier). People who changed equipment during the 5 year period were therefore counted more than once. In addition, absolute latencies could not be calculated for people who started using equipment before 1980 and this is indicated by the use of the '>' sign.

It can be seen that people using VDUs plus electric typewriters had the highest incidence of musculo-skeletal problems, while those using only electric typewriters had the lowest incidence. In addition, it would appear that people using VDUs only had a lower incidence of musculo-skeletal problems than those using VDUs plus electric typewriters.

People using VDUs generally developed problems very quickly - the median latency being a matter of months. In contrast, people who only used electric typewriters took much longer to develop problems - the median latency being about 3 years.

A wide range of brands of VDUs is in use at the University and many staff use more than one machine. It was therefore not possible to determine if problems were more commonly associated with some brands than others. However, it is possible that such associations exist.

Table 1. The relationship of musculo-skeletal problems to the type of equipment used

	Equipment		
	electric typewriter only	VDU only	VDU plus electric typewriter
number of users	172	80	71
% with musculo-skeletal problems	5	18	35
time to develop problems (mo)			
median	37	2	10
range	1->59	1->46	1->46

3.3 Changes in staff ratios

Changes in the ratios of academic staff to keyboard staff and in ratios of total staff to keyboard staff are shown in Table 2.

Table 2. Changes in staff ratios

Year	Academic staff/keyboard staff	Total staff/keyboard staff
1980	6.34	16.82
1981	DATA NOT AVAILABLE	
1982	6.95	17.91
1983	7.16	19.42
1984	6.41	18.32

It can be seen that between 1980 and 1983 the ratios increased steadily, in other words keyboard staff worked for more people than had previously been the case. The increases were of 13% and 16% respectively. The reduction in 1984 is apparent rather than real. During this year many of those suffering from musculo-skeletal problems were absent from work (for periods ranging from a few weeks to the whole year) and were replaced by casual staff. The keyboard staff numbers include both absent and replacement staff.

3.4 Classification of the keyboard staff

The percentage of staff who suffered from musculo-skeletal problems in each year was calculated according to their job classification (Table 3).

It can be seen that the groups at highest risk were secretaries, word processor operators and data processing operators. Data processing operators and word processor operators spend most of their time operating VDUs, while secretaries generally perform a range of duties. Typists and stenographers had a much lower rate of musculo-skeletal problems and although they also spend most of their working day operating keyboards, they generally use electric typewriters rather than VDUs. Among other staff with lower rates of musculo-skeletal problems (clerks, programmers, programming assistants, librarians, administrators etc.), most only operate keyboards for part of their working day. However, as keyboard use increases among these groups, the incidence of musculo-skeletal problems may be expected to increase. This has been found in clerks; for example, in 1980 32% of clerks operated keyboards for more than one hour per day, whereas by 1984 this had increased to 48%. From Table 3 it can be seen that the incidence of musculo-skeletal problems increased, as expected.

Table 3. Prevalence of musculo-skeletal problems according to job classification

Classification	Percentage of staff with musculo-skeletal problems				
	Year				
	1980	1981	1982	1983	1984
Secretary	0%(55)*	0%(62)	3%(58)	13%(62)	38%(61)
Typist or stenographer	0%(26)	4%(27)	0%(25)	0%(19)	13%(16)
Word processor operator	0%(0)	0%(0)	0%(4)	11%(9)	36%(11)
Data processing operator	0%(5)	0%(9)	0%(8)	25%(8)	46%(11)
Clerk	0%(39)	0%(44)	0%(58)	9%(53)	13%(45)
Programmer or programming assistant	0%(17)	0%(19)	0%(21)	4%(24)	11%(19)
Other	0%(13)	0%(16)	0%(17)	0%(16)	18%(22)
Total	0%(155)	1%(177)	1%(191)	9%(191)	25%(185)

* the number in brackets is the total number of people in that classification who use keyboards for more than one hour per day.

4. DISCUSSION

4.1 The incidence and prevalence of musculo-skeletal problems

In 1984, 25% of the ANU staff studied who operated keyboards for more than one hour per day had musculo-skeletal problems, with much higher levels in particular groups (Table 3). These figures are somewhat higher than those reported in the Australian Public Service [3]. There 20% of secretaries (compared with 38% at the ANU), 32% of word processor operators (compared with 36%), 22% of data processing operators (compared with 46%) and 7% of typists (compared with 18%) reported musculo-skeletal problems. However, the pattern of reporting in the 2 institutions was similar. Of the people who reported to the end of 1984 in the Australian Public Service, 8% reported in 1982 or earlier, 14% in 1983 and 78% in 1984. The percentages for the ANU were 3%, 22% and 75%, respectively.

Table 4 illustrates some selected findings which have been obtained in other countries.

Table 4. The prevalence of musculo-skeletal problems in other countries (selected results)

Country	Occupational group	Type of problem	Prevalence	Reference
France	off-line data acquisition operators	neck pain	52%	7
		R shoulder pain	32%	
Japan	office machine operators	dullness & pain		8
		in neck	22%	
		in R arm	10%	
Sweden	VDU operators	neck & shoulder complaints	44%	9
Switzerland	data-entry terminal operators	visits to doctor for arm or hand impairments	19%	10
	typists	visits to doctor for arm or hand impairments	27%	
U.S.A.	VDT users	neck/shoulder ache	79%	11
		stiff or sore wrist	26%	
		hand/finger cramps	26%	

It is clear from these figures that musculo-skeletal problems affecting the neck, shoulders, arms and hands are of significance for office workers in a number of countries.

However it is difficult to make in depth comparisons, not only because occupational groups may differ significantly between countries, but also because different measures of musculo-skeletal problems are used in different countries. In particular, there are differences in the type of problem examined (pain, complaint, ache etc.), the method of investigation (questionnaire, medical examination, use of official statistics) and the body area investigated. In the last case, Australian studies, including this one, tend to combine neck, shoulder, arm and hand problems and refer to any and all of them as RSI. Most studies in other countries have concentrated on more specific areas of the body.

Examinations of changes in the incidence of musculo-skeletal problems only seem to have been conducted in Japan. Hosokawa [12] has reviewed Japanese studies and has shown changes in the incidence of musculo-skeletal problems in a variety of occupations. The pattern found in this study is very similar to those reviewed by Hosokawa. The most likely explanation for the pattern is as follows: A change in technology and/or work practices leads to the development of severe problems in a relatively small group of workers. Concern associated with this leads to an increase in reporting of problems (the severity of these problems has not been established, but anecdotal evidence suggests that they are generally less severe). With the introduction of prevention measures there is a gradual reduction in the number of people with problems (this stage had not been reached at the ANU in 1984, but seems to have been reached now).

4.2 Factors involved in causing musculo-skeletal problems

From the results it seems likely that both the physical features of VDU technology and changes in work and management practices associated with the introduction of the new technology are involved in increasing musculo-skeletal problems and these are discussed briefly below.

The higher incidence of musculo-skeletal problems among workers who use VDUs compared with those who only use electric typewriters (Table 1) suggests that some physical aspect(s) of VDU technology may be directly involved in causing problems.

However, other results suggest that work and management practices may have changed since the introduction of VDU technology and these may also contribute to the increase in musculo-skeletal problems. Most notably there was a reduction in the ratios of keyboard staff to both academic and total staff (Table 2) and it is therefore likely that the amount of work expected of keyboard staff increased. This study also suggests that a reduction in task diversity may be a factor involved in the increased incidence of musculo-skeletal problems. Table 3 indicates that groups with a low task diversity (word processor operators and data processing operators) have a higher incidence of musculo-skeletal problems than those with a high task diversity (clerks, programmers and others). There seem to be two anomolous findings, however. One is the relatively low incidence of musculo-skeletal problems among typists and stenographers who also have a low task diversity. However, as indicated earlier, this may be because they generally only use electric typewriters. The other interesting finding is the high incidence of musculo-skeletal problems among secretaries, who generally have a high task diversity. The reasons for this still need careful investigation. Anecdotal evidence suggests that secretaries are often most affected by increases in workloads when numbers of keyboard staff are reduced. In addition, it has been suggested that secretaries are subjected to more work stress than other categories of staff.

Two other interesting findings that need further investigation are that musculo-skeletal problems are commoner among people who use VDUs plus electric typewriters than among those who use VDUs only and that users of VDUs develop problems more rapidly than people who only use electric typewriters.

ACKNOWLEDGEMENTS

The cooperation of the staff of the Australian National University and financial assistance provided by the Secretary, Warwick Williams, is gratefully acknowledged. Valuable assistance was provided by Gail McGruddy and Shirley Taylor as well as by John Gordon, Peter Hill, Lesley Piper and Lisa Robertson. Thanks also to Robyn Savory who typed the manuscript and to Jorge Bontes and the staff of ANU Photographic Services for the figures.

REFERENCES

[1] BSSRS, 1981, Office Workers' Survival Handbook: a guide to fighting health hazards in the office. British Society for Social Responsibility in Science, London.

[2] Makower, J., 1981, Office Hazards: how your job can make you sick. Tilden, Washington D.C.

[3] Task Force Report on Repetition Strain Injury in the Australian Public Service, 1985,Australian Government Publishing Service, Canberra.

[4] Arndt, R., 1983, Working posture and musculoskeletal problems of video display terminal operators - review and reappraisal. American Industrial Hygiene Association Journal, 44, 437-446.

[5] Browne, C.D., Nolan, B.M. and Faithfull, D.K., 1984, Occupational repetition strain injuries: guidelines for diagnosis and management. Medical Journal of Australia, 140, 329-332.

[6] Stone, W.E., 1983, Repetitive strain injuries, Medical Journal of Australia, 139, 616-618.

[7] Elias, R., Cail, F., Tisserand, M., and Christmann, H., 1980, Investigations in operators working with CRT display terminals: relationships between task content and psychophysiological alterations. In Grandjean, E. and Vigliani, E., eds, Ergonomic Aspects of Visual Display Terminals. Taylor and Francis, London, 211-217.

[8] Ohara, H., Aoyama, H., and Itani, T., 1976, Health hazards among cash register operators and the effects of improved working conditions. Journal of Human Ergology, 5, 31-40.

[9] Kvarnström, S., 1983, Occurance of musculoskeletal disorders in a manufacturing industry with special attention to occupational shoulder disorders. Scandinavian Journal of Rehabilitation Medicine, Supplement 8, 1-60.

[10] Hünting, W., Läubli, Th., and Grandjean, E., 1980, Constrained postures of VDU operators. In Grandjean, E. and Vigliani, E., eds., Ergonomic Aspects of Visual Display Terminals. Taylor and Francis, London, 175-184.

[11] Sauter, S.L., Gottlieb, M.S., Rohrer, K.M. and Dodson, V.N., 1983, The well-being of video display terminal users: an exploratory study. National Institute for Occupational Safety and Health, Cincinnati, Ohio.

[12] Hosokawa, M., 1985, The study on occupational cervicobrachial disorders (OCD). Academic Reports of Kyoto Prefectural University, number 37.

WORK WITH DISPLAY UNITS 86
B. Knave and P.-G. Wideback (eds.)

GENERATION OF MUSCLE TENSION RELATED TO A DEMAND OF CONTINUING ATTENTION

M. WÆRSTED, R. BJØRKLUND and R.H. WESTGAARD

Institute of Work Physiology, Gydas vei 8, Oslo, Norway

Muscle activity (EMG) of the trapezius muscles and heart rate (EKG) were recorded in 12 VDU operators while they were performing various VDU-based psycho-physical tests. Eight of 11 subjects generated "attention- related muscle loads" of 1 % MVC or more for periods of at least 2 minutes while performing these tests. Two striking features were observed: 1) low variability in muscle tension during the tests, and 2) sudden, stepwise changes in mean tension. These features do not appear while the subjects perform a "paper and pencil" test. This result indicates that static muscle load may be generated to a much larger extent for VDU-based work tasks than for paper tasks.

1. INTRODUCTION

Muscle loads necessary to maintain posture or perform movements are relatively low when performing VDU-based work tasks, but the work situation is often perceived as strenuous. Such feelings of discomfort will almost certainly reduce the performance, and may be significant in the developement of musculo-skeletal complaints affecting a growing number of VDU operators. This effect was demonstrated in preliminary experiments by Westgaard and Bjørklund (1), and is studied in more detail in the present series of experiments by including recording of heart rate and subjective rating of discomfort and mental functions, in addition to electromyographic recordings of muscle tension.

2. METHODS

Twelve experienced female VDU operators were asked to carry out VDU-based tasks with little postural or physical demand. Postural tension was minimised by seating the subjects in a well-balanced position with the upper body erect. The lower arms were supported on the table, and the VDU tasks involved only the use of 1-4 keys operated by fingers of the dominant hand or both hands.

Electromyographic signals were recorded from the upper trapezius muscles of right and left shoulders in all subjects. (The EMG recordings failed for one subject, leaving only the heart rate recording.) The EMG signals were recorded by surface electrodes, diameter 6 mm and center distance 20 mm, giving a relatively localised recording from the the underlying muscle. After suitable amplification and filtration (bandwith 10-500Hz), the EMG signals were recorded on a FM tape recorder, and later quantified by digital full-wave rectification and integration. The recordings from the trapezius muscles were calibrated to indicate muscle force by performing a force-EMG calibration procedure (2) before and after the experimental recordings. If the calibration procedure failed the result is given as a percentage of EMG amplitude at maximal contraction. This provide a rough estimate of muscle force, but these recordings can not be used in a formal analysis of load level.

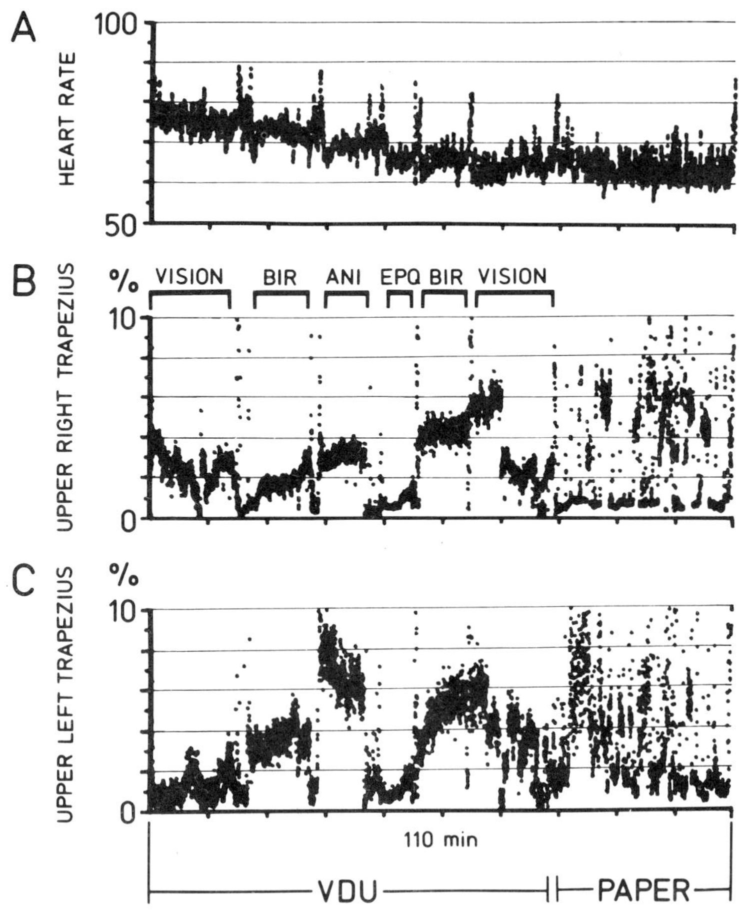

FIGURE 1
Simultaneous physiological registrations from one of the subjects. (A) Heart rate (beats pr.min.) smoothed by a five point rectangular moving window procedure. Muscle load on the upper right (B) and left (C) trapezius muscles. Muscle load is calibrated as a percentage of the EMG amplitude at maximal contraction, due to problems with the EMG - force calibration curve for this subject. Each point in panels B and C gives mean muscle load in one second period. The bars on top of panel B indicate the time periods of the different psyco-physical tests.

Perceived discomfort in different body regions was rated by using a modified Borg scale (3) at fixed intervals in the VDU task session. On the same occasion the subjects rated their mental functions with a modified Osgood technique (4).

Four different VDU-based tests were used, two more than in the first study (the "VISION" and "BIR" tests were used in both studies). After the session with VDU-based tests (lasting approximately 90 min.), the subjects also solved a paper-based psycologial test ("PAPER") not involving the VDU monitor.

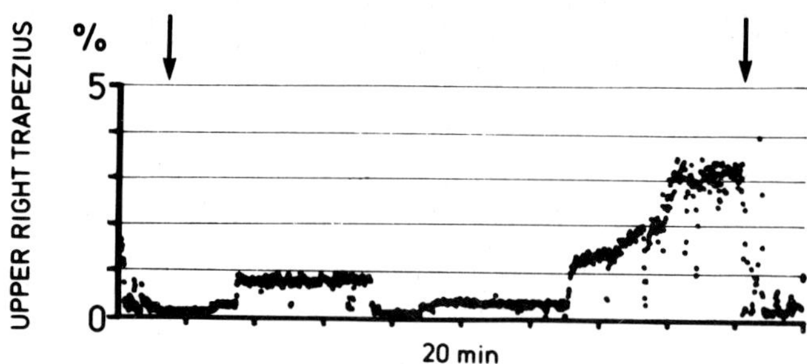

FIGURE 2
Muscle load on the upper right trapezius muscles generated by one of the subjects in the first "BIR" test (start and end of test indicated by arrows). The points give the load in one second periods calibrated as a percentage of maximal voluntary force.

"VISION": Lateral phoria eye test for continous registration of vertical phoria during 15 min. observation of a video monitor.

"BIR": Complex two choice time reaction test. This test involves problem-solving over 200 trials. Test duration 10-22 min. depending on speed of the subject.

"ANI": Four choice time reaction test. Each test consists of 200 trials. Test duration approximately 8 min.

"EPQ": The Eysenck Personality Questionnaire in a personal computer version.

"PAPER": Raven Standard Progressive Matrices. Test time limit 45 min.

(The test names in quotation-marks refer to the labels in Fig.1.)

3. RESULTS

Eight out of 11 subjects generated "attention-related muscle loads" of 1% MVC or more continuously for at least 2 minutes while performing the VDU-based tests. Fig.1B and 1C show loads generated by the two trapezius muscles of one of the subjects. The points indicate mean muscle load over one second periods, and are plotted consecutively to show variation in load throughout the test period. In Fig.2 the load on the right trapezius of another subject is plotted in the same manner as in Fig.1, except that Fig.2 only shows the result from one of the VDU-based tests. A striking feature of the load pattern in the VDU tests, as illustrated in these two figures, is a very low variability in muscle tension resulting in a narrow band of points. It is seen that the lower edge of this band is shifted away from zero load, indicating that a continuous (static) load is present during the tests. (Static load is defined according to Jonsson (2).) The subject in Fig.1 is the one generating the highest load in the test situation. However, the pattern of low variability was common to all subjects. The level of static load was with most subjects maintained at a relatively low level, rarely exceeding 2-3% MVC. The load pattern is quite different in the pauses between the different VDU tests, with the static component typically falling to zero or near zero, combined with peaks of much higher load (up to or above 10% MVC) due to postural changes and arm movements. The tendency to generate "attention-related muscle loads" differed considerably from one individual to another. The level of these loads varied from virtually non-existing up to 6% MVC, and lasting from 0.5-1 minute to whole test periods (6-22 min.).

Another feature of the load pattern while performing the VDU tests was sudden step-wise changes in the load. Fig.2 gives an example of this. Between these sudden changes, the median load level would either be very stable or slowly increase or decrease. In Fig.1 all of these patterns are seen. Other subjects seemed to predominantly generate one or the other pattern.

The tendency to generate "attention-related muscle loads" also varied between the different tests in the same session. In Fig.1 tension is low during the "EPQ" test. The same was, with few exceptions, true for all the subjects. The "VISION" and "BIR" tests did on the contrary provoke periods of relatively high loads for a majority of the subjects. The different individuals reacted similarly to the same test when it was repeated later in the session. The "ANI" test, which is a simple choice reaction time test, was with most subjects associated with low tension. (One of the exceptions is the subject in Fig.1.)

The same experimental procedure were repeated six months later by 6 of the 12 subjects. For 5 of 6 subjects the results of the second session were similar to those of the first session, i.e. individuals who showed a tendency to generate muscle tension in the first test session, had a similar tendency to generate such loads in the corresponding test session half a year later.

The low variability of median muscle load in the VDU-based tests stand in contrast to the load pattern while solving the paper-based test. Here the pattern was more dynamic, as is seen in Fig.1. Half the subjects recorded frequent one second periods with muscle load down towards 0% MVC in this test, while the rest of the subjects seemed to maintain a basic level of tension, upon which a more dynamic load pattern was superimposed. This is illustrated in the recording in Fig.1B, where the load level in the major part of the "PAPER" test do not fall below 0.5% MVC. It is not possible at this stage to exclude that this is due to a component of postural tension, but the recording may alternatively indicate the presence of "attention-related muscle loads", adding to a more dynamic pattern of muscle usage.

The heart rate in Fig.1 shows a slow decline, possibly due to the person initially being apprehensive, then slowly getting used to the test situation. The factor that heighten the heart rate early in the experiment does not seem to influence the level of muscle tension. In addition to the general downward trend the heart rate also shows minor variations reflecting similar changes in the level of muscle tension. Eight out of the 12 subjects showed a declining heart rate during the test period. (Of the 6 subjects retested, 5 had this tendency of a declining heart rate in the first session, compared to only one in the retest session.) A quantitative analysis of heart rate variability will be performed at a later stage, but is not available at present.

The VDU operators scored their perceived discomfort ratings in different body regions before, in the middle and after the VDU part of the test session. Fig.3A gives mean scores on a modified Borg scale. Fig.3B gives the corresponding results of the scoring of mental functions with a modified Osgood technique. The subjects did perceive a growing discomfort and a reduction of mental capacity in the test situation. (Only the "at ease - excited" parameter in the Osgood scoring showed a (slightly) positive trend, possibly reflecting an initial apprehension towards the test session as previously mentioned. In the retest this parameter followed the trend of the other Osgood parameters.) At present it is difficult to know to what extent there is a correlation between subjective ratings and level of muscle load generated. This will be looked further into in the follow-up studies.

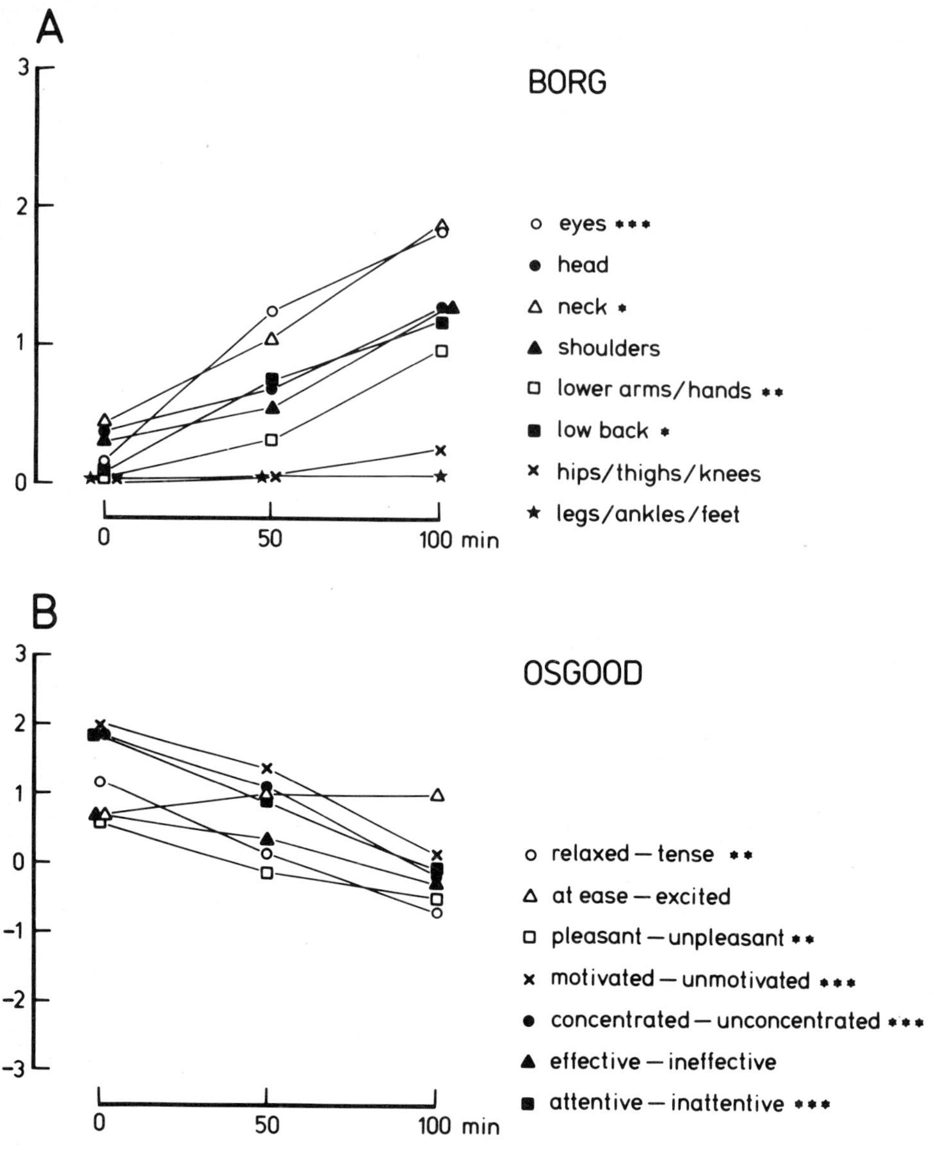

FIGURE 3
A. Mean score of the 12 VDU operators on a modified Borg scale with range 0-10, 0 indicating no discomfort, 1 light discomfort and 3 indicating moderate discomfort. B. Mean score of mental functions on a modified Osgood scale, 0 indicating the neutral position between the opposite statements and the first cited statement being the positive alternative. The scores were given on three occasions - before start ("0 min"), in the middle of the VDU part ("50 min") and after the VDU part ("100 min") of the test session. Statistical evaluation (t-test): Stars after labels indicate that the test scores at the end is significantly different from those obtained before start. (* $p<0.05$; ** $p<0.01$; *** $p<0.005$).

4. CONCLUSION

These experiments have demonstrated that muscle tension may be provoked by creating additional demands on the performance of the experimental subject. Muscle tension related to mental activities (5) and anxiety (6) has previously been demonstrated. However, attention-related muscle load has not to our knowledge previously been demonstrated in a VDU-based experimental situation. This tension appears to be unrelated to body posture or movements of body segments, a point which will be examined in studies presently in progress. Such task-related demands may easily be associated with similar demands in real-life VDU work situations. The reaction of the subjects to the different VDU-based tests gives some indication of a graded response in terms of muscle tension depending on the complexity and other characteristics of the test. The experiments also demonstrated that the fixed VDU-based test setting is characterised by low variability in tension of the shoulder muscles, compared to the more dynamic load pattern in a paper-based test. The static load generated during the VDU-based tests must be considered to be at a low level compared to most work situations with postural load components, but is probably high enough to cause considerable discomfort if maintained for long enough time. The inter-individual variation regarding both the temporal pattern and the level of these "attention-related loads" may in part explain why some persons are more susceptible to develop musculo-skeletal complaints in VDU-type work situations.

REFERENCES

(1) Westgaard, R.H. and Bjørklund, R. Generation of muscle tension independently of body posture. Sub. for publ. (1986).

(2) Jonsson, B. Kinesiology - with special reference to electromyographic kinesiology. In: Cobb, W.A. and van Dui, H. (Eds.) Contemp. Clin. Neurophysiol. suppl.no.34 (1978), 417-428; Elsevier Amsterdam.

(3) Borg, G. and Lindblad, I. A comparison between different category scales for evaluation of subjective symptoms. Reports from the Inst. of Applied Psych., no.78 (1979); Univ. of Stockholm.

(4) Osgood, C.E. et al. The measurment of meaning. Urbana, Ill.; University of Illinois Press (1957).

(5) Jacobson, E. Electrical measurements of neuromuscular states during mental activities VII. Am.J.Physiol. 97 (1931), 200-209.

(6) Sainsbury, P. and Gibson, J.G. Symptoms of anxiety and tension and the accompanying physiological changes in the muscular system. J.Neurol. Neurosurg. Psychiat. 17 (1954), 216-224.

WORK WITH DISPLAY UNITS 86
B. Knave and P.-G. Widebäck (eds.)

TASK AND THE ADJUSTMENT OF ERGONOMIC CHAIRS

Marvin J. Dainoff and Leonard S. Mark

Center for Ergonomic Research and Department of Psychology
Miami University
Oxford, Ohio 45056 USA

Studies evaluating the effectiveness of ergonomic chairs often fail to consider how the task affects workers' postural demands. In light of the different physical demands of various jobs performed at VDUs, it is highly unlikely that a single posture would suffice across tasks. Moreover, movement is essential for maintaining a stable sitting posture for prolonged periods of time, in order to avoid skeletal and muscular discomfort as well as circulatory problems resulting from diminished blood flow to areas supporting body weight. The current study investigates the influence of task requirements on the effectiveness of forward and backward tilt mechanisms on ergonomic chairs. Experienced clerical workers were provided with information concerning the postural requirements for sitting and were trained in adjusting an ergonomic chair, which could assume both forward and backward tilt positions. Subjects alternately performed data entry and verification tasks in 30-min sessions for periods of three hours each day for five days. Adjustments of the chair and body posture were continuously monitored to determine how often subjects adjusted the chair configuration and working posture. These adjustments were compared to measures of task performance and body comfort. Analyses were designed to determine: whether subjects, when given the opportunity to utilize adjustable furniture would, in fact, take advantage of these features; the temporal period from one adjustment to another; and whether certain postures were more effective for particular tasks than other postures.

1. INTRODUCTION

Studies evaluating the effectiveness of ergonomic chairs often fail to consider how the characteristics of the task affect worker's postural requirements. In light of the different physical demands of various jobs performed at VDUs, it is highly unlikely that a single posture would suffice across tasks. Moreover, when the task requires prolonged periods of sitting (static load), some degree of operator movement is essential in order to avoid skeletal and muscular discomfort associated with diminished blood flow to areas supporting body weight (Branton, 1976) as well as to maintain the viscosity of the vertebral discs (Nachemson, 1975). Many current guidelines and recommendations for ergonomic design of VDU workplaces assume an <u>upright</u> (trunk angle circa 90 deg to the horizontal) operator with upper and lower limbs of the arms and legs at right angles to each other. However, two alternative seated postures have been proposed. Grandjean et al. (1983) have argued that proper design of an ergonomic chair should allow the operator to assume a backward leaning position, with the arms supported by an adjustable keyboard with a wrist/palm rest. Anatomically, this posture provides support to the lower back by maintaining the weight of the trunk against the backrest. Moreover, operators seem to prefer this orientation to being upright. On the other hand, Mandel (1981) has argued for the effectiveness of a chair with forward tilt in the seat pan; this postural orientation allows the operator's pelvis to rotate forward, thereby causing the lumbar spine to assume a concave (lordosis) posture, which relieves pressure on lumbar discs.

Our contention is that each of the proposed alternatives has important advantages and disadvantages. Optimum postural orientation depends on the task to be performed. Any one of the three postures may be appropriate in a given set of working conditions. In our view, the choice of an appropriate posture should be determined by visual demands associated with the task as well as biomechanical factors. To what extent does the posture provide the operator with a visual display of sufficient size and clarity? We argue that, for tasks which require intensive use of paper copy, most operators will need to lean forward to see the copy more clearly. Under these conditions, the backward tilt would result in an excessively long viewing distance; thus, forward tilt would be more appropriate. However, for more screen intensive work, the viewing distance is less critical, since the size of VDU characters tends to be larger than the size of characters on paper. Therefore, in such cases, the load-bearing advantages of backward tilt might be utilized effectively.

In addition to providing for optimum static orientation, an ergonomic chair should afford the operator opportunities for movement so as to minimize the circulatory problems identified above. This is particularly important for forward tilt, since the inherent instability in this orientation can generate excessive loads on the lower limbs (Corlett and Eklund, 1984). The resulting chair criteria must, therefore, include provisions allowing the operator to adjust seatpan angle (forward and back), and backrest angle, along with the usual seat height and backrest height adjustments. In such a chair, if the operator is alternating between screen intensive and copy intensive work (as in composing and then proofreading a manuscript), the operator may simply alternate between forward and backward tilt postures, thereby obtaining what we believe is an optimum orientation for each task. If the job does not provide such variety, the operator still has the option of some degree of adjustability within the optimal range. (e.g., movement between greater and lesser degree of back angle.) In any case, such a chair would seem to provide an effective compromise between the dual but conflicting requirements of stability and movement for seated posture. (Branton, 1976).

On the other hand, a chair with four degrees of freedom of adjustability is not only expensive, but complex. Some have argued that such a chair is too complicated for an average worker to use effectively. We propose that a four degree of freedom ergonomic chair can be used effectively if the user is provided with a proper course of training--one that includes information on why adjustability is important as well as how adjustments are to be made. The following study examines this proposal.

2. METHOD

2.1. Design

Ten trained clerical workers spent 3 hours per day for five days performing copy intensive (data entry) and screen intensive (verification) work. A fully adjustable four degree of freedom ergonomic chair was provided. The first work day (Day 0) was devoted to training in use of the chair as well as performance of the task. On subsequent days (1-4), subjects alternated between data entry and verification tasks; spending 30 minutes at each. No rest breaks were employed. (The final hour of day 4 was used for a post-experimental interview and subject debriefing.) All sessions were video-taped. Video records were used subsequently for postural analysis. Discomfort complaints were assessed before and after each 30 minute work session. The intent of the investigation was to examine whether or not the subjects would, if provided with a course of instruction, actually use the chair as instructed throughout the course of a week long study.

2.2. Apparatus

The chair was a Fixtures Furniture Discovery task chair with adjustable seat pan angle (-8 deg to +7 deg), backrest angle (-8 deg to +32 deg), seat height (43.2-55.9 cm), and backrest height (7.6 cm). Adjustments were made by push-buttons located on the underside of the chair. The chair was used in combination with a Steelcase terminal table with independent adjustability for VDU keyboard and monitor. An IBM PC with a Zenith monochrome amber monitor was used for task simulation. A Panasonic video cassette recorder (Model 8950) and camera (Model 3240) system with date/time capability recorded the side view of the operator from a distance of 80.1 cm. Appropriate anatomical and structural landmarks on the subject and chair were identified with pieces of tape. Distances and angles were later digitized from video tape using an IBM PC and graphics tablet.

2.3 Training

On the initial training day, the subjects were shown a 20 minute video tape which presented a brief discussion of spinal anatomy and muscular fatigue, and then illustrated the adjustable functions of the chair. Subjects sat in the chair and operated adjustability controls while watching the tape. The subjects were then introduced to the adjustable terminal table, and the two tasks were demonstrated. The remainder of the training period was used for practicing the two tasks. Throughout the training period, subjects were instructed to use forward tilt for the data entry task (copy intensive) and backward tilt for the verification task (screen intensive). However, it was emphasized that these recommended postures were still only theoretical, and that, throughout the study itself, subjects should simply pick the posture that was most comfortable.

On Day 1, at the beginning of the first session of each task (entry/verification), the subjects were asked to take the appropriate posture (forward tilt/backward tilt.) From this point on, subjects were free to assume whatever postures they wished.

2.4 Operating Procedure

The entry task required subjects to type in 15 alphanumeric characters from a page of paper copy in response to a prompt on the display screen. There were five prompts per file. In the verification task, two files were displayed side by side and and subjects were required to make a Same/Different judgement by pressing one of two keys. In addition to subjects' hourly wages, an incentive pay system was employed in which both speed and accuracy were rewarded. A version of the Body Part Discomfort Scale (Corlett and Bishop, 1976) was administered at the conclusion of each of the 6 daily task sessions.

2.5. Postural Analysis Procedure

2.5.1. Identification of Landmarks

Measurement of key body and workstation dimensions was accomplished by marking 20 major landmarks with adhesive tape such that they would be visible on the videotape.

2.5.1.1. Workstation Landmarks

A frame of reference was established by placing horizontal tape markers on the side of the terminal table located precisely 30.48 cm apart and by placing two vertical strips on the background wall. For measurement of seatpan height, a horizontal calibration mark was placed on the base of the chair and a second horizontal mark near the seat pan itself. Two additional marks were placed on the armrest such that these marks were horizontal when seat pan angle was zero. Finally, two marks were placed on the side of the backrest such that these marks were vertical when the backrest was vertical.

2.5.1.2. Body Landmarks

Medical bandage tape squares were placed (by subjects themselves under the direction of the experimenter) on bodily locations facing the camera. These included: ankle joint, knee joint, hip joint, wrist, and elbow joint.

2.5.2. Direct Measurement of Chair

The particular physical construction and geometric configuration of ergonomic chairs often leads to considerable uncertainty as to how even simple physical measurements are to be made. For example, chair cushion materials are differentially compressible, and hydraulically adjustable surfaces add to the uncertainty. In an attempt to standardize such measurements, a draft methodology has been proposed by the Human Factors Society/ANSI Committee on VDT Workstation Standards (1985). This methodology will be employed in the current study to validate the measures of posture and chair position made off of the video records (see Section 2.5.3).

Three basic measurements were made with the HFS/ANSI method: compressed seat height, seatpan angle, and backrest angle. Each measurement utilized an articulated wooden mannequin constructed to the dimensions of a 50th percentile adult. Built into the surface of the mannequin was a protractor and spirit level.

For compressed seat height, the mannequin was placed in the chair and used to level the seatpan. Next, a 45.45 kg weight was placed in the center of the seatpan and a 2.27 kg supplemental weight was placed close to the front edge of the seatpan. Distance from floor to top of supplemental weight was measured (and thickness of the weight subtracted.) Seatpan angles and backrest angles were read directly from the mannequin protractor when the thigh regions were in contact with the seatpan surface and the lumbar region was in contact with the backrest.

2.5.3 Video Measurement Procedure

Continuous video tape records were made of all sessions. During subsequent analysis, the tape was stopped at specific designated points within the recorded work day (5 min after the beginning of each day, 5 min after each change in task, 5 min before the end of the day, and after any spontaneous chair or workstation adjustment). At this point, a piece of transparent vellum was placed over the face of the TV monitor, and the landmarks described above were recorded. The locations of the points were then digitized by means of a Micro Control Systems Advanced Space Graphics System interfaced to an IBM PC computer. The resulting coordinates formed the input data for a series of equations from which a set of workstation and body dimensions (distances and angles) were derived. A total of 6 workstation and 8 body measures were obtained. However, in this report, only four will be examined: seat height, seatpan angle, backrest angle, and seatpan-to-backrest included angle.

2.5.4. Calibration of Video Measures with ANSI Measures

In order to compare the sensitivity of the video measurement procedure against the ANSI technique, a series of simultaneous measures were carried out. The chair was set to ten different heights; five at the upper range (around 50 cm) and five at the lower range (around 43 cm). At each height, the mannequin was used to set seatpan angle and backrest angle to zero, after which the compressed seat height measures were carried out as described above. At each chair setting, video records were made, and indicated landmarks picked off the screen and transferred to the digitizer. This was done independently by each of two experimenters who were to perform this task for the regular experimental sessions. Subsequently, derived values of seat height, seatpan angle, and backrest angle were obtained from the digitized values. These values were compared with the ANSI measures obtained directly. Table 1 indicates the results of the seat height calibration for each of the two experimenters (E1 and E2). (Note that the difference scores for each experimenter were computed by subtracting the video measures from the ANSI measures. The standard deviation, SD, refers to the distribution of these differences.)

Table 1.
Comparison of ANSI and Video Measures for Seat Height (cm)

		ANSI	E1	DIFF	E2	DIFF	AVERAGE DIFF
Low	Mean	44.32	44.48	-0.15	43.64	0.69	0.25
Range	SD	0.18	0.44	0.48	0.51	0.50	0.50
(N=5)	SEM	0.09	0.22	0.24	0.25	0.25	0.25
High	Mean	55.58	56.41	-0.84	55.19	0.36	-0.23
Range	SD	0.18	0.44	0.36	0.44	0.51	0.43
(N=5)	SEM	0.09	0.22	0.18	0.22	0.25	0.22
Both	Mean			-0.51		0.53	0.03
	SD			0.41		0.25	0.46
	SEM			0.22		0.13	0.23

As expected, within each range, the variability of the ANSI measures is greater than that of the derived video measures. However, the magnitude of the discrepancy between video and ANSI measures (approximately 0.5 cm) is small enough to justify the use of our video measurements in this study. In point of fact, while each of the experimenters was remarkable consistent in their stability (SDs of 0.54 and 0.51), the direction of their respective errors seemed to cancel each other. In sum, the video values of seat height seem to be accurate within +/- 0.36 cm. (2 SEMs).

Comparable results for seatpan and backrest angles are reported in Table 2. In this case, recall that ANSI measures of these variables were always set to zero; hence, the table reflects differences from zero.

Table 2.
Video Measures for Seatpan And Backrest Angle (deg)

		E1	E2	AVERAGE
Seatpan Angle				
	Mean	2.59	1.11	1.85
(N=10)	SD	0.951	1.43	1.19
	SEM	0.317	0.475	0.396
Backrest Angle				
	Mean	0.94	0.25	0.60
(N=10)	SD	1.55	1.29	1.42
	SEM	0.52	0.43	0.48

Although the variability in taking both sets of measures was about the same, the constant error for seatpan angle was more than twice that of backrest angle (1.85 deg vs. 0.60 deg). However, here again, it appears that the size of the anticipated error, 1.85 +/- 0.8 deg for seatpan; 0.6 +/- 0.96 deg for backrest (mean +/- 2 SEM) is reasonable given the degree of accuracy required. With regard to seatpan angle, the sign of the constant error is positive. As a result, the video procedure resulted in an overestimate of seatpan angle in the backward direction. In effect, the error is in the opposite direction from our predictions in the entry task.

2.5.5. Reliability of Video Measures

Reliability of the video measures was further assessed by selecting one frame from the complete video record of each of the ten subjects. As above, landmark locations were digitized independently by two experimenters for each of the 10 frames; yielding two complete sets of body and workstation measures. Correlation coefficients between the two sets of data produced average reliability coefficients of r=0.97 among the workstation measures, and r=0.92 among the body measures. The reliability coefficients for specific measures utilized in this study were: Chair height, r=0.99; Seatpan angle, r=0.84; Backrest angle, r=0.96; Included angle. r=0.74.

3. RESULTS

3.1. Were the instructions followed?

Each time the task changed (entry to verification and vice versa) the subjects moved the three controls (seat pan angle, height, backrest angle) in the predicted direction. Thus, subjects were unanimous in wanting to change orientation in response to different task demands.

3.2. What were the resulting orientations?

From the following video measurements made during each of the six daily sessions, the postures taken during the two tasks conformed to our training instructions. Table 3 summarizes the four critical variables, averaged across day and session.

In entry, the mean seat pan angle was tilted forward -3.65 deg (SEM 0.25 deg), whereas the comparable value for verification was backward, +4.57 deg (SEM 0.16). In entry, backrest angle was virtually vertical, -0.47 deg (SEM 0.31); however, in verification, subjects assumed a backward leaning posture, 15.51 deg (SEM 0.38). Finally, mean chair height was higher for entry than for verification: 50.0 vs 47.1 cm (SEMs 0.16, 0.12 cm).

In addition, there was a significant correlation between chair height and seatpan angle for the entry task ($r=-.60$; $p<.001$), but not for the verification task ($r= -.18$; $p>.05$). It is important to realize that in assuming a forward tilt posture, the chair height must be raised. Subjects were instructed to do so in the training session. The above data suggest that they did, indeed, follow our instructions.

Table 3.
Table of Video Analyses

Task	Variable	N	Mean	SD	min	max
ENTRY						
	pan angle	295	-3.65	4.29	-12.53	8.60
	backrest angle	295	0.47	5.32	-13.16	15.26
	included angle	295	94.13	5.44	80.04	107.92
	chair height (cm)	295	49.98	2.79	43.92	57.10
VERIFICATION						
	pan angle	276	4.57	2.60	-8.80	11.06
	backrest angle	276	15.51	6.31	-1.23	29.85
	included angle	276	100.94	5.89	85.29	114.28
	chair height (cm)	276	47.12	2.08	43.36	53.90

Tables 4 and 5 indicate mean values of seat pan angle and backrest angle across Days 1-4. Although the preponderance of the variance was accounted for by task (as seen above), there was some tendency, as the week progressed, for the seatpan (forward tilt) angle to decrease in the entry condition, as the backrest angle did in the verification condition. (All analyses were significant at $p<.05$.) These findings are congruent with an explanation that holds subjects gradually adapted to the situation; finding their own optimum positions within the overall recommended postures. Comments during interviews by subjects support this argument.

Table 4.
Seatpan Angle (deg) by Day and Session
for Entry and Verification

	ENTRY				VERIFICATION			
	Day				Day			
Session	1	2	3	4	1	2	3	4
1	-4.77	-5.31	-5.18	-5.44	4.25	3.73	4.85	4.06
2	-5.81	-2.30	-1.62	-2.16	5.08	4.55	5.05	4.04
3	-5.15	-1.42	-1.12	----	5.19	4.99	4.74	----
$\bar{X}$	-5.24	-3.01	-2.64	-3.80	4.84	4.42	4.88	4.05

Table 5.
Backrest Angle by Task, Day
and Session as Measured in Degrees.

	ENTRY				VERIFICATION			
	Day				Day			
Session	1	2	3	4	1	2	3	4
1	1.17	1.67	1.01	1.08	18.35	16.07	16.10	15.01
2	1.35	2.41	0.25	-2.07	17.30	13.10	14.71	14.59
3	-0.29	1.77	-0.04	----	18.29	13.63	14.22	----
$\bar{X}$	0.74	1.95	0.41	-1.62	17.98	14.27	15.01	14.80

Table 6
Mean Severity of Discomfort Responses
By Task, Day and Session Within Day

	ENTRY				VERIFICATION			
	Day				Day			
Session	1	2	3	4	1	2	3	4
1	4.40	4.40	2.70	2.60	5.90	4.22	3.40	2.20
2	6.50	6.60	4.80	3.50	6.30	6.60	3.70	3.80
3	6.50	6.20	6.40	----	8.10	7.44	5.40	----
$\bar{X}$	6.13	5.73	4.63	2.75	6.77	6.09	4.17	3.00

The Body Part Discomfort Scale consisted of 42 body segments (21 each, front and back) which could be responded to on a scale of 0 to 5. Table 6 shows the means (across subjects) of the total non-zero scale values. There was no significant difference in discomfort between tasks. As expected, discomfort increased throughout the day ($p<.02$). However, discomfort also decreased as the week progressed ($p<.02$). This finding is consistent with subjects' comments that as they became more familiar with the chair operation, it was perceived as more comfortable.

4. DISCUSSION

The postural analyses confirm that our subjects were willing to follow our instructions and adjust the chair orientation to a position optimal for the task at hand. The seat pan was tilted forward when the task was copy intensive; the backrest was tilted backwards when the task was screen intensive. The slight decreases in these values across the week, along with a parallel decrease in discomfort scores, as well as interview comments, indicates a process of adaptation to the chair and its features. The lack of difference in discomfort between tasks indicates that potential problems with forward tilt did not materialize.

Alternately, one might argue that these findings are due to subjects' response to demand characteristics of our training program (i.e., "Hawthorne effect"). In part, this can be answered by our strong assertion that, for chairs of this complexity, instructions are integral to the successful use of the chair. It is not necessary to conduct an experiment with a "no-instruction" condition to know that instructions are crucial. Misuse of ergonomic adjustments in the field is common. The questions for further research should focus on differential effectiveness of alternative training approaches combined with alternative adjustment mechanisms.

ACKNOWLEDGMENTS

This research was supported by a grant from Fixtures Furniture, Inc., of Kansas City, Missouri, USA. We wish to acknowledge the assistance of Ray Daley, Robert Moritz, and David Vogele throughout the course of this study.

REFERENCES

Branton, P. Behavior, body mechanics, and discomfort. In E. Grandjean (Ed.), Sitting Posture. London: Taylor & Francis, 1976.

Corlett, E.N. and Bishop, R.P. A technique for assessing postural discomfort. Ergonomics. 1976, 19,175-82.

Corlett, E.N. and Eklund, J.A.E. How does a backrest work? Applied Ergonomics, 1984,15.2,111-114.

Grandjean, E., Hunting, W., and Piedermann, M. VDT workstation design: preferred settings and their effects. Human Factors, 1983,25,161-175.

Mandel, A.C. The seated man (Homo Sedans), the seated work position, theory and practice. Applied Ergonomics, 1981,12,19-26.

Nachemson, A. Towards a better understanding of low-back pain: a review of the mechanics of the lumbar disc. Rheumatology and Rehabilitation, 1975,14,129-143.

9. WORK PLACE DESIGN

WORK WITH DISPLAY UNITS 86
B. Knave and P.-G. Widebäck (eds.)

EQUIPMENT AND WORKSTATION DESIGN FOR BANKING SERVICES

Salovaara, Juhani. Ergonomiadesign Oy, Turku, Finland

In Finland banking services are in a time of major transfer in the level of technology. Real time systems were introduced by major banks in Finland over eight years ago. New multifunction systems (MFS) are presently being installed in branch offices around the country. This is manifested by the introduction of VDU:s in the workstations. Tools, system and content of every cashierś work is changing.
This case-study represents the wiewpoint of a consulting industrial designer applying ergonomics to design hardware in a highly competitive environment. The paper is based on personal involvement, interwiews and an end-user questionnare.

1. DEVELOPMENT AND DESIGN PROCESS.

1.1. BACKGROUND

The four partners referred to throughout the paper are: Producer, designer, bank A and bank B. Producer stands for Nokia, the major electronics company in the country. Designer stands for Ergonomiadesign, design consultants. Bank A stands for Postipankki, which offers services in connection with PTT. Bank B stands for Kansallisosakepankki, the major commercial bank in Finland. Characteristic of the Scandinavian social climate is the collaboration between employers and amployees. Both involved banks had mature and experienced organisations to handle ergonomic questions of their trade. These same aspects require equal competence from the producer, who relies on consultants in matters of ergonomics and industrial design for product development. Good ergonomics is a valid argument for a small (on global scale) producer. It may be added, that Nordic industrial designers have been involved in ergonomics since late sixties. Diagram 1 gives an overwiew of the process and focuses on points of contact between partners, which were dececive for the ergonomic quality of the cashierś desk at introduction of MFS, the multifunction banking system. Most contacts refer to design of different hardware and itś introduction into the market. The partners were involved in a trial and error process, **the objectives** of which **were defined, but the pragmatics and the resulting hardware-solutations unforseeable.**

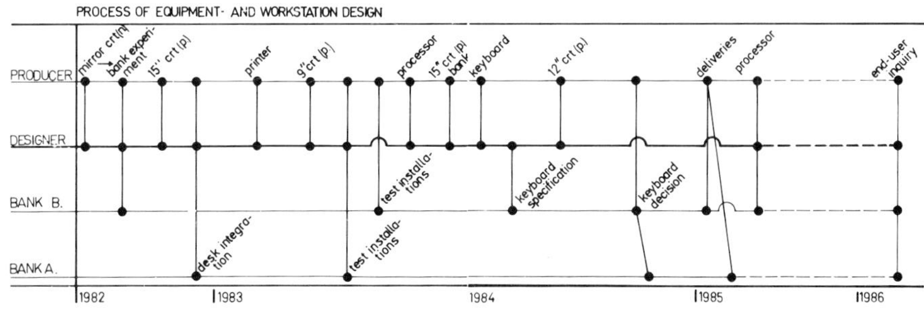

Diagram 1. Process of equipment- and workstation design.

Existing desk solutions are problematic. They are not developed with computer hardware and connected ergonomic requirements in mind. In our case the typical post office desk gave least space for incorporating all hardware, required when introducing MFS.

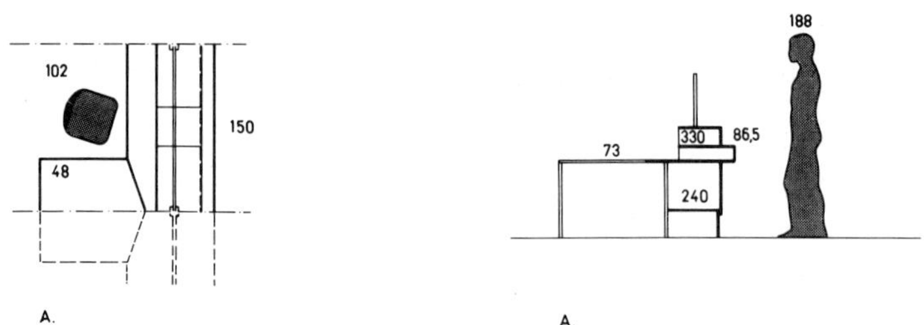

Drawing 1. Plan and section of post-office counter. Bank A.

Both banks have developed counters individually. The result, present cashierś desks are nearly identical from ergonomic point of wiew. Important dimensions differ slightly but the general lay-out is equal.Designwise bank A is using radiussed and bank B a more angled look.

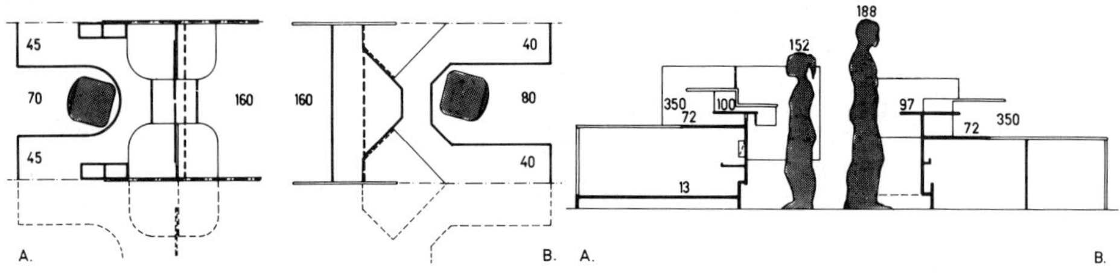

Drawing 2. Present cashier-desk types of the two banks. Plans and sections.

Designer and producer had experimented with a recessed VDU. (Negative polarity) The screen was mounted below the tilting back partition of the tabletop. A mirror was mounted on this tilting part. The display could be wiewed from proper posture by adjusting the tilt of the mirror.
Keyboard, manuscript and display can all be seen within a small visual angle. It was also believed, that problems of glare could be reduced. Although this concept was developed for normal office use, it was tested in a cashierś desk of bank B. **This experiment later gave the idea** for a vertically feeding recessed printer.

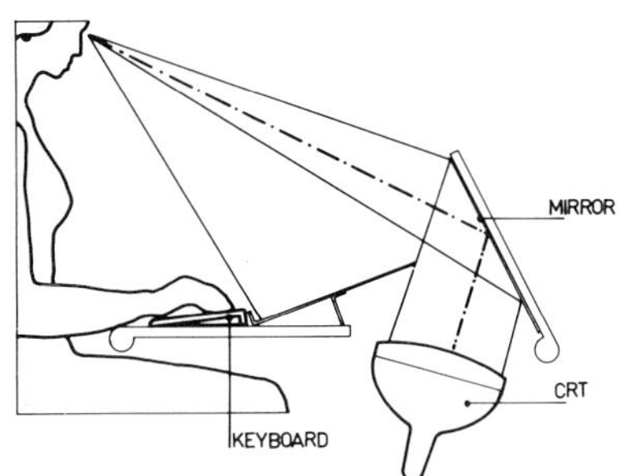

Drawing 3. Concept of the Nokia mirror-table.

1.2. Ergonomic design approach.
Different hardware lay-outs could be evaluated as "table-top" study based on standard procedures available in bank A. Such study and prototyping was performed for the post-office counter. Different sizes of VDU:s and types of printers were tested. These **experiments led towards the final workstation lay-out** and clearly identified available printers as main source of problems.

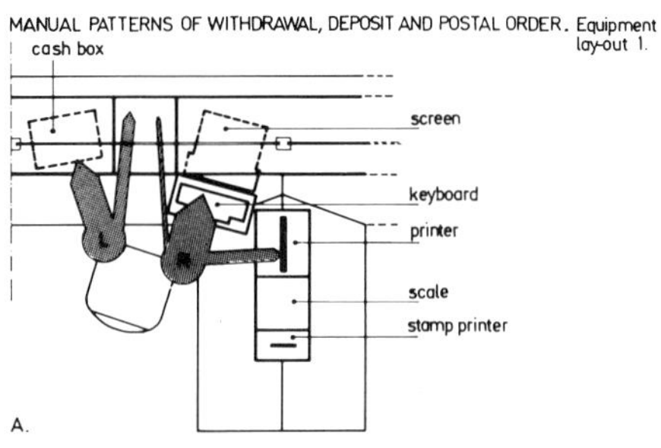

Drawing 4. Work-flow pattern for left and right arm of a proposed lay-out. Post-office, bank A.

The keyboard in the end became the hardest user-interface item in **define, design and decide of.** The designer involved a psychologist in this work. Besides consulting the producer the designer was also contracted by bank B to establish criteria for evaluating keyboards of various suppliers and to present one "ideal" solution. The required key sub-groups were classified according to **psychomotoric skill levels** of cashiers and other typical keyboard criteria from litterature was listed. Special attention was given to **keying error reduction.**
The designer suggested a solution with **two separate keyboards.** The left side keyboard for cashier was kept to minimal size, the right hand side keyboard was extended with a std. Qwerty key-set for routine office functions in the banks. In both cases a new key subgroup (skill level 5) was needed to command the MFS.

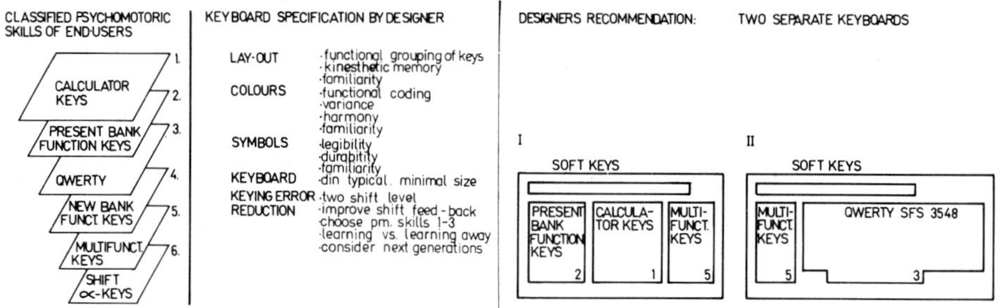

Drawing 5. Defining the keyboard.

The form of the keyboard, shown below in a side-wiew sketch, incorporates a palm support. With a credit card reader attached the support is wider. This feature was added to the keyboard keeping in mind the vertically feeding printer between the keyboard and VDU. It was known from previous systems, that printers occasionally take their time to print. Thus the **palm support and fingertip reach** to the printer.

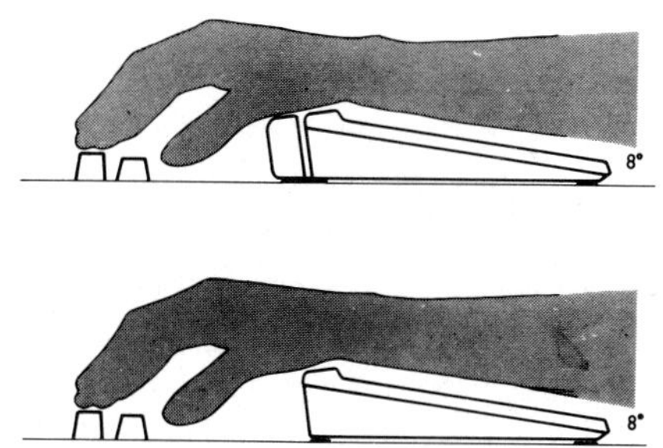

Drawing 6. Designing the keyboard.

How was the keyboard problem solved ? The illustration below gives some explanation. The producer involved in development their specialized banking-systems team. The designer involved a psychologist, bank B established a council to advice on the introduction of MFS, bank A established a MFS Project group.
In broad outlines the steps were following: Producer commissioned designer to modify existing office keyboard for banking purposes. Prototypes are presented to both banks. Prototypes were not favoured so producer asked designer to design a keyboard specially for banking applications. In the meantime bank B employed the designer to write a specification for banking keyboard and to join their advisory council. Designer produced **keyboard specification (BKB 1),** which **was approved.** Bank B sets a **small project group,** with the task to define and select among other, the keyboard.
Their choise was **one single keyboard for all tasks.** This keyboard was rapidly chosen and installed by bank A and others thereafter.

Abbreviations:
OKB = Office keyboard
BKB = Banking keyboard
BKB 1 = Banking keyboards, designers recommendation
BKB 2 = Banking keyboard, selected for realisation by User-interface group of bank B.

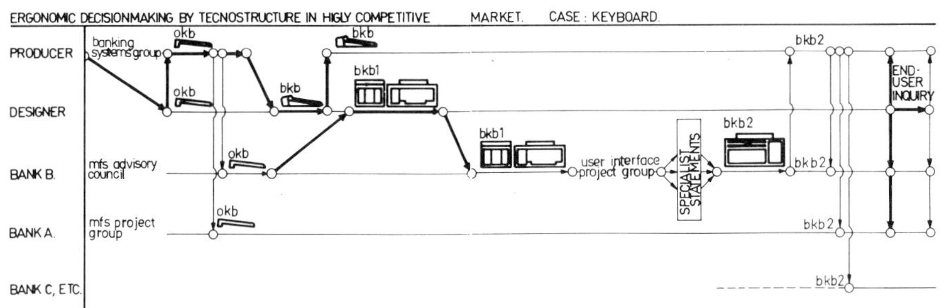

Diagram 2. The making of ergonomic decisions. Case keyboard.

2. End-user questionnary.

The questionnare was proposed by designer and approved by all partners. It was considered usefull to learn about end-user attitudes at introduction of MFS and about the fit of the selected hardware.

All subjects were using hardware delivered by the producer. Two sizes of VDU:s were used, both with positive polarity CRT. All utilized keyboards were physically identical but banking functions and their keytop lay-outs were specific of respective banks. Vertically feeding printers were installed in most workstations, but one fifth of the subjects were using horisontally fed printers of another brand.

Results:

END-USER INQUIRY

25 WOMEN FROM FOUR BRANCH OFFICES OF BANKS A AND B
WORKING EXPERIENCE: RANGE: 0,4-26y. AVERAGE 7,1y.
PREVIOUS REAL TIME SYSTEM USED BY 75%
MULTIFUNCTION SYSTEM IN USE FOR 5,4 MONTHS AVERAGE.
TRAINING AT INTRODUCTION FOR 3.7 DAYS AVERAGE.

BODY HEIGHT: RANGE 156 CM-181 CM. AVERAGE 165 CM.
MEASURED SEAT HEIGHTS. RANGE 40-56 CM. AVERAGE 50 CM.
SPECTACLES WORN BY 52% OF TOTAL.

15 INC CRT USED BY 40%
12 INC CRT USED BY 60%.

Table 1

ATTITUDES AT INTRODUCTION OF MFS.

WORK CONTENT:	POORER	5%	INTRODUCTION:	INTERESTING	96%
	ENRICHED	55%		FLUENT, EASY	27%
WORK-LOAD:	INCREASED	31%		DEMANDING	9%
	REDUCED	9%		DIFFICULT	9%

PROBLEMS AT INTRODUCTION WITH:		
	SOFTWARE INTERFACE	1.57
	SOFTWARE RELIABILITY	1.29
	CRT-DISPLAY UNIT	1.0
	UTILISATION OF SPACE IN WORK STATION	0.57
	KEYBOARD	0.33
	PRINTER	0.1
	WORKING POSTURE	0.1

(WEIGHED SCALE)

Table 2.

KEYBOARD				
LAYOUT	POOR	8%	GOOD	92%
SIZE	TOO BIG	8%	ACCEPTABLE	92%
KEY RESISTANCE	TOO LIGHT	12%	GOOD	88%
USE OF QWERTY KB	SELDOM	4%	CONTINOUSLY	96%
KEYING ERRORS	SELDOM	28%	SOME	72%
HAND SUPPORT USED	SOMETIMES	30%	OFTEN	70%
ACCIDENTAL ACTIVATION OF TOP-ROW KEYS	NO	52%	YES	48%

Table 3.

PRINTER			
TYPE: ERICSSON 20%		TYPE: NOKIA 80%	
PREFERENCE FOR HORISONTAL	20%	VERTICAL FEED	80%
OTHER PLACE OF PRINTER	16%	BETWEEN KB/CRT	84%
SETTING AND WAITING FOR PAPER AND PRINTOUT	76%	FLUENT OPERATION	24%
VDU			
CHARACTER SIZE SMALL	4%	GOOD	96%
PREFER NEGATIVE IMAGE	16%	POSITIVE IMAGE	84%
FLICKER PERCEIVED	32%	NO FLICKER	68%
GLARE ON THE SCREEN	52%	NO GLARE	48%

Table 4.

3. Conclusion.

How to make ergonomic decisions about something one does not know ? Basic ergonomic data is rarely directly transferable to design solutions.

Real-life competitive environment asks for rapid adaption and improvement of products to transforming needs.

Ergonomic data serves as a source capable of generating alternative approaches and concepts. Ergonomic effect is achieved by applying basic data to **induce** solutions, test them and decide of, within the time restriction and pressure of projected work procedures.

The "designerly mode of inquiry" is becoming a useful tool in itś own right.

The grass-root level inquiry of tasks, processes and tools through **personal involvement**; playful and undogmatic way of **generating various combinations of problem-elements;** modelling and mock-up abilities useful for rapid testing and evaluation are skills, that have proven their value. It is thus justifiable to speak of a discipline in itś own right.

End-user involvement it necessary stepwise; at problem definition and evaluation of proposed solutions.

End-users are exceptionally effective informants **in the beginning of development process** when project group is planning the operation. Their involvement is equally usefull when preliminary solutions are **evaluated** and more development ones are **tested.**

In group-decisions ergonomic quality is easily lost.

In **participating design** the dynamics of human relationship of the group become decisive. The risk exists, that ergonomic quality is traded off in order to maintain the groupś unity or by resorting, in short perspective, to something more measurable effects.

Tweiwe inch VDU, vertically feeding printer and banking keyboard by Nokia Information Systems. Installed in cashierś workstation.

WORK WITH DISPLAY UNITS 86
B. Knave and P.-G. Widebäck (eds.)

ON THE DESIGN OF DEALING DESKS

T W Trickett

Trickett Associates, The Factory, 84 Marchmont Street, London WC1N 1HE, England

The challenge facing those responsible for the effective and profitable operation of dealing and trading rooms is how to obtain and sustain a competitive edge by making the best use of the three primary resources involved: people, information technology, and the work environment.

The problems involved converge at the dealer's desk. The tools for trading (internal information systems, external information systems and telecommunications) make immense demands on the dealer and yet, in many cases, little effort is made to 'fit the task to the man'. Instead, ease of view and ease of reach take second place alongside the primary need to place more and more equipment on the dealer's desk.

In this paper, the author describes how improved levels of flexibility and adjustability can be achieved which allow the individual dealer an increased degree of comfort and control at his work place.

1.0 THE PROBLEM

1.1 A dealing or trading room is not an ordinary office. It is not even a high-performance office. Instead, it respresents an extreme working situation where the three primary resources involved - people, information technology and the internal environment - must be brought together with the minimum of conflict. The challenge facing those responsible for the effective and profitable operation of dealing/trading rooms must be how to obtain and sustain a competitive edge by focusing critical attention on every factor, however small. Nowhere is this more apparent than in the design of the dealing desk itself.

1.2 Why are dealing rooms extreme working situations? First, new technology has created a condition of information overload which forces dealers to work under severe pressure. Secondly, increasing competition between financial organisations means that success depends not just on how much equipment and information they have, but also on how effectively it is used. The third

---

* Trickett Associates is a group of architects and designers specialising in the design of working environments, particularly those with a new technology dimension. Recently, in the City of London, the consultancy has carried out projects for a number of financial organisations. 'On the Design of Dealing Desks' is based on this recent experience and an examination of equivalent situations in New York. Research has been carried out by Terry Trickett and Jeremy Bishop.

reason is the pace of dealing; the time factor has already become critical in activities like foreign exchange and Eurobonds and it is likely to become more critical in broking.

1.3 For these three reasons, the pressures on people operating dealing/trading systems is considerable. Not only do dealers have to register and instantly absorb information on display units, they must also get quick input and reactions from colleagues in order to respond, as a trading team, to specific enquiries and dealing opportunities. For many of us, such demands would generate conditions of "communication stress" but dealers thrive on it. So we must not try to eliminate the "buzz" of excitement from dealing room environments but, instead, ensure that it stimulates action rather than destroys concentration.

1.4 A glance at many existing dealing rooms reveals that conflicts occur where the increasing demands of information technology become incompatible with the needs of people. In other words, the amount of equipment at the dealer's position prevents him working effectively as a team member; often, he can see information on display units but tends to lose contact with his colleagues. In the City of London, for instance, the traditional approach is to produce a dealing desk which resembles an upright piano. The equipment is arranged vertically and is stacked in such a way that nobody can see over or round it.

1.5 This built-in approach generates other disadvantages. Groups of desks are difficult to move and the individual dealer is allowed little flexibility in the way he arranges display units, keyboards etc to suit his own working methods or physical characteristics. Further, furniture of this type usually needs to be scrapped if revised information delivery and presentation systems are introduced; items of new equipment (of a different size) cannot easily be accommodated.

1.6 But we do not have to accept such inadequate solutions. Although the conflict between the demands of information technology and needs of people in dealing rooms may be one that we can never fully resolve, there is much we can do to help. An examination of the essential criteria which a dealing desk must meet can be identified under three main headings - Planning, User Requirements and Servicing.

2.0 PLANNING

2.1 Group alterations and reconfigurations can occur more often than in the conventional office. These involve small groups (2-3) or large (12+) and need to be effected as quickly as possible.

2.2 Flexibility is needed to allow the widest possible variety of planning relationships within and between groups.

2.3 The plan-shape of the desk should be such as to increase the speed and effectiveness of re-planning/re-arranging groups, especially when this is done in-house.

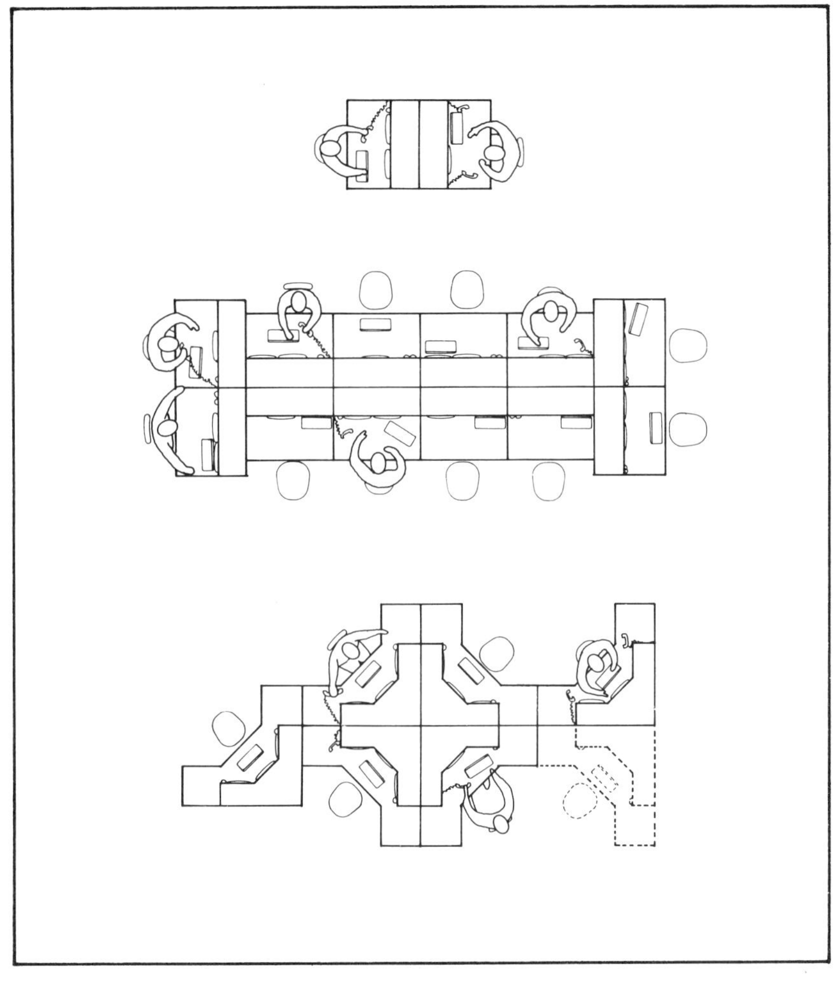

Illustration 1
Planning configurations for dealers can involve small groups (2-3) or large (12+). Flexibility is needed to allow the widest possible variety of planning relationships within and between groups.

3.0 USER REQUIREMENTS

3.1 Typical equipment in use per desk at present:

Display units (up to 6, often incompatible shapes and sizes)
Dealer board (V-Band unit or other with handsets)
Keyboard (Reuters or other)
Personal computer (IBM AT or XT)
Squawk boxes (up to 6) and microphone
Telecom handsets
Calculator
Task light
Uplighter

3.2 The amount of equipment varies widely from one dealer to another and the desk must be able to grow (in ways which are simple to understand and simple to execute) from a basic unit to one which can accommodate most of the items listed in 3.1 above. It must be possible for the dealer to move items of equipment around according to personal preference, and desk mounted accessories (eg tasklight) should be easily detachable.

3.3 Although some recent ergonomic studies have advocated radical change where there is concentrated use of display units (eg adoption of a "car-driving" posture) the assumption here is that a conventional worktop is needed to carry keyboards, paper, cups of coffee, calculators and other equipment. Display units in their current shapes and sizes have to sit clear of this zone of work, therefore a minimum worktop depth of 1000mm is required.

3.4 With the display units sited beyond the worktop, either at worktop height or a little higher, it is essential that the overall height of the desk should be low enough to give a clear field of vision over the top of all equipment (ie for the seated dealer). Any interruptions to this field of vision (eg support for uplighter - see 3.13 below) need to be minimal. A maximum height of 1100mm should be observed and any possible reduction from this is desirable.

3.5 Height adjustability of the worktop must be considered, both above and below the average (and in Germany statutory) height of 720mm. A worktop height of 680mm has been found satisfactory and where this is permitted the consequent reduction of overall height by 40mm is worthwhile. The facility to raise the worktop above 720mm would contribute to user-comfort in some instances, but the penalty of increased overall height could rule this out.

3.6 Paper storage slots in line with display units, or above, are required by most dealers.

3.7 A facility for sharing display units between adjacent desks is required.

3.8 "Squawk boxes" need to be close to the user's ear level in order for effective volume to be as low as possible.

3.9 Personal computers are at present relatively bulky items requiring infrequent user-access (ie changing discs). It is therefore desirable that these should occupy an otherwise "vacant" portion of the desk volume while being accessible when required.

3.10 A lockable storage facility is needed for discs, paper, reference material and personal effects. The need to keep the useable desk width to a minimum suggests that the "traditional office furniture" solution of a below worktop pedestal may not be satisfactory. The storage facility should in any case be easily mobile to maintain flexibility of individual arrangement.

3.11 Conditions observed in existing dealing rooms show that any dealer desk needs to be of robust construction and that workshop/industrial standards should be referred to rather than those of traditional office furniture.

3.12 Individual task-lighting must be included, as is now customary in areas with low ambient lighting.

3.13 A desk-mounted uplighter as an optional accessory should be considered. While one would not be required at every desk the opportunity of uplighting a dealing room with a suitable number per group, as part of the furniture package, could be valuable.

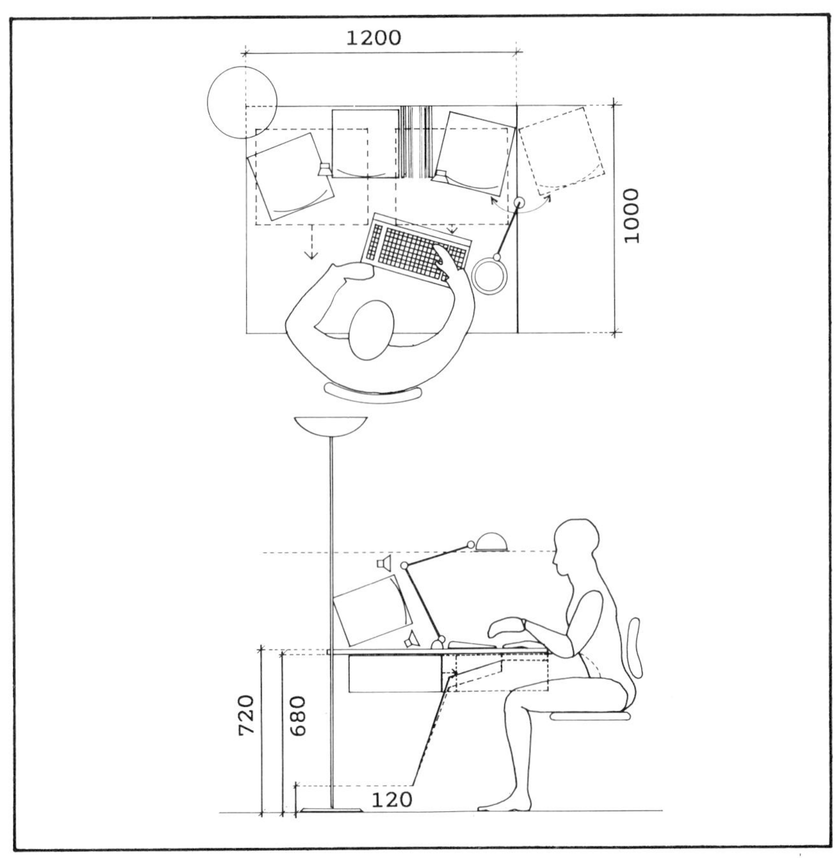

Illustration 2
What every dealer needs at the desk: a minimum worktop depth of 1000mm with space for a personal computer and storage under; task lights and optional uplighters; an unobstructed view.

4.0 SERVICING

4.1 Wired servicing to an individual dealer desk can at present be categorised as follows:

4.1.1 Power in the form of "clean" and "dirty" supplies. Typically 1 dirty and 3 or more clean supplies.

4.1.2 Signal in the form of data lines, local networks, telecom lines.

4.2 Wired servicing is taken to the desk position either underfloor (most usual) or overhead (rare but sometimes advantageous).

4.3 For underfloor servicing the modular 600 x 600mm access floor is almost universal. Generous access to the underfloor space for maintenance and repairs is particularly important in dealer rooms and the desk (and other furniture) must leave as many panels as possible free to be lifted out. An improvement on conventional office furniture should be sought in this respect.

4.4 With underfloor servicing it is usual for power supplies to terminate at a socket outlet box contained within a floor panel which may be associated with an individual desk or with a group of desks. Signal wiring usually passes without interruption through a hole or cut-out in a floor panel (often the one containing the outlet box) thence via the desk or desks to the relevant equipment. If it is not possible to guarantee the position of the floor outlet panel in relation to the desk (and this seems likely), some means of taking wiring easily and tidily up from floor level to work level must be provided. This should be to some extent movable (obviously avoiding user's feet) to help prevent final desk positioning being constrained by floor outlet location. This requirement is poorly catered for in conventional systems furniture.

4.5 If the adoption of central switching systems increases, it is possible that the practice of wiring services to dealer desks discretely with no cables running horizontally from one desk to another, will follow. This would nicely complement planning requirements that each desk should be a structural entity; nevertheless no assumptions can be made in this respect and facilities for horizontal servicing ("interlinking") must be provided. These must cause the least possible hindrance and delay when re-planning moves are carried out (2.1 above) and wiring should always be able to be "laid" in its designed routing without the need for drawing through or threading. Advanced examples of office systems furniture might be referred to although few offer the degree of "mobility" needed.

4.6 With overhead servicing, the number of "drops" would have to be kept to a minimum to avoid visual obstruction; the horizontal interlinking facility would be essential in this case.

4.7 Whichever method of taking wired servicing to the dealer desk is used, the desk itself will need the following facilities:

4.7.1 In-built socket outlets for clean and dirty power supplies. The dirty socket outlets must be easily accessible to the user. The clean socket outlets should not be inaccessible but they must be protected against improper use.

4.7.2 Easy routeing of uninterrupted signal wiring to items of equipment.

4.7.3 Generous amount of dumping space to contain excess lengths of cable resulting from the "arriving" services (it cannot be assumed that this can be kept underfloor), and also surplus wiring between desk-mounted outlets and items of equipment.

4.7.4 Horizontal interlinking facility already referred to (see 4.6 above) for power and signal wiring.

4.7.5 Means of receiving "drops" from overhead, similar to the riser facility referred to in 4.4 above.

4.7.6 Access from the user side for all servicing purposes. This is necessary because of the frequent use of face-to-face planning arrangements.

4.7.7 Segregation of signal from power wiring. The need for this is diminishing in practice but a study to ensure conformity with current UK, European and US standards must be carried out.

4.8 Apart from wired services, the need for accommodating personal air conditioning within the dealer desk should be investigated.

4.9 For dispersing the heat generated by equipment the dealer desk must allow easy paths for natural convection and the need to accommodate mechanical assistance should be investigated.

4.10 All servicing must be protected against spillage of liquids.

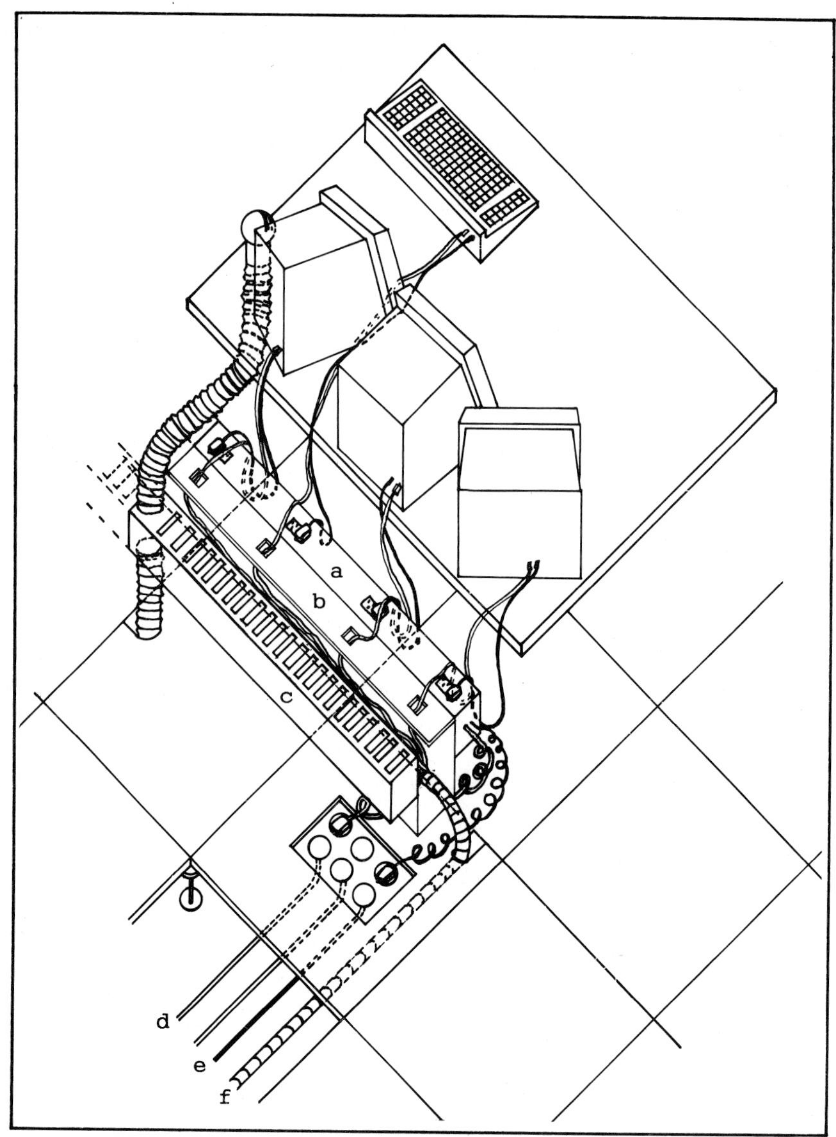

Illustration 3
Servicing to an individual dealer desk involves:
(a) The horizontal routeing of 'clean' and 'dirty' power
(b) A generous amount of 'dumping' space to contain excess lengths of wire
(c) Personal air conditioning combined with a method of dispersing heat from equipment
(d) 'Clean' supply
(e) 'Dirty' supply
(f) Coaxial cables (or fibre optics)

5.0 THE SEARCH FOR ANSWERS

5.1 It will be evident that a comprehensive design brief, which takes into consideration all elements of flexibility required, must be answered by a range of options. No single desk type can ever be expected to cope with all eventualities. Further, there is no reason to assume that the chosen desk must always be rectangular in shape; many other configurations need to be explored. Even in a single dealing room the layout needs of different trading teams are likely to vary. For this reason, plans must not become standardised; both individual and team "personalization" is required.

5.2 Future dealing requirements are likely to vary significantly from current needs. The adoption of new technology in dealing rooms tends to be sweeping and immediate rather than gradually phased as is the case in conventional offices. For this reason, an assessment of future requirements (as far as they can be foreseen) must feature in any design brief for dealing desks. Known developments include:

5.2.1 Flat screens - the present bulky shape of display units will change and the need for a "superstructure" to house them will disappear.

5.2.2 Touch screens - these may not constitute straight-forward replacements for existing keyboards. They may need to be let into worktops, or sited differently.

5.2.3 A single touch screen serving all existing dealer functions is already being assessed in pilot schemes. (Stock Exchange ORBIT system).

5.3 Considerations in 5.2 suggest that a dealer desk may need to revert from the relative complexity required to cope with present equipment to something approaching a simple work table in the near future. The ability to "grow" referred to in 3.2 above would thus equally need to work in reverse.

5.4 So far, at Trickett Associates, we have produced an interim solution by turning to the electronics industry. Here, we found a highly serviced "electronic work bench" which, with some adaptation, was capable of becoming a "loose-fit" dealing desk. This interim solution goes some way towards meeting crucial flexibility needs; it has already been used successfully in a number of dealing room installations. But the needs and expectations of dealers become ever more demanding and in situations where many competing financial organisatins are trying to attract the best possible staff, the desk becomes a subject of close scrutiny. It is for this reason that the advantages of offering a flexible "loose-fit" answer cannot be overstated. New and better answers need to be found.

WORK WITH DISPLAY UNITS 86
B. Knave and P.-G. Wideback (eds.)

THE EFFECT OF VDU ON THE INTERIOR DESIGN OF OFFICES

Edna Ishai

Senior Lecturer of Architecture, Faculty of Architecture,
Technion-Israel Institute of Technology, Haifa 32000, Israel.

1. INTRODUCTION

The work format in an office is the result of more than 150 years of development. The development of the textile industry on a large scale around 1850 and the development of the railroad in 1890 brought about the first attempts to gather people together and enable them to have office services.

The design of the office is set by the needs of the user, which in turn is connected with the activity that had to be fulfilled and the atmosphere that the designer is interested in imparting.

For the design of offices making use of the VDU, a reexamination has to be made of the changes in the nature of the machinery and equipment, the way of working, and all that these changes imply for office design: the general characteristics of an office, its furniture, and its other equipment.

2. PRINCIPAL DIFFERENCES IN EQUIPMENT BETWEEN THE COMPUTERIZED AND CONVENTIONAL OFFICE.

2.1. Information Storage

The quantity of information that is needed in an office has been increasing, and the method of storing it has been changing. In place of shelves holding books, files, and other papers, a system of diskettes and cassettes now permits the concentration of information in a very small storage volume. The information is centralized and within the immediate reach of the user, who no longer has to get up in order to search for a file or a book in the midst of a long series of shelves, nor to walk to the archives or library for material. A considerable proportion of the information is obtainable through the computer--see Figure 1.

2.2. Equipment for Information Transferral and Retrieval

There is no need for typewriters and there is no paper work. Information retrieval is accomplished through reading it off the screen, and its transferral by pressing on keys. The two activities are done simultaneously. The size of the screen and its distance from the user determine and limit the amount of information that can be obtained at the same time. The work of retrieving and processing the information does not necessarily obligate one to sit at a table in the normal manner. The two activities may be done, too, at different stations.

Fig. 1: Vast amount of books, files and paper work is replaced by...???

2.3. Communication with Other Employees

The form of information storage and its transferral do not necessitate meeting or direct contact with other employees as is the case in the conventional office. No one must go to some one else in order to receive material or to talk with that person. Most of the information is obtained through the screen. The office thus loses its importance as a place of social communication, and work becomes more and more individualized.

2.4. Basic Assumptions and Conclusions for Design

The long sitting periods without any need to stand up and the loss of direct contact with other workers create psychological and physical problems: mental fatigue, irritability, and back problems. The basic assumption behind the conclusions that will be presented here in due course is that one of the principal causes of the lack of comfort and physical tiredness in an office is the continuance of a certain physical situation, of whatever kind: "Man's physical machine has evolved to do many things well, but no single thing continuously." Thus a sitting situation, be it in the easiest of easy chairs, which lacks postural variation, accentuates the problem of maintaining reasonable body tone. A situation of repeated routine, like typing, is very fatiguing. There is need, therefore, to encourage an office design that will create variations in physical activity.

Two types of solutions are accordingly proposed: the first solution has as its purpose the encouragement of varied physical activity during office hours; the second, aimed at relaxation in the form of semi-reclining, permits relaxation during a work break or work in a different posture from that characterizing most of the hours that one stays in an office.

3. VARIATION IN PHYSICAL ACTIVITY

3.1. High Table or Stand-Up Table

The most serious health problems in offices result from the sedentary nature of the work. Office workers are compelled to conduct most office activity in a sitting position. This results in a steady decline in vitality, energy, and general body tone. Figure 2 shows Winston Churchill working at his stand-up table. Churchill was one of many such "performers" who avoided the sedentary effect by using stand-up desks. Others included Victor Hugo and Ernest Hemingway.

Figure 3 shows a schematic drawing of the proposed version of a "high table." The suggested unit includes a wall-integrated display and a high chair. The system is modular and adjustable for height and table angle. A series of tables of this sort enables information retrieval and processing simultaneously; it is possible to increase or change the table angle by means of a foot pedal.

3.2. Action Chair

Figure 4 illustrates the suggestion for an office chair with special accessories enabling a person sitting in it to carry on semi-sport activities while reclining. A number of assumptions lie at the basis of the design of this special chair:

- Physical freshness does not necessarily have to be done through putting to work tired or painful parts of the body. For example, moving only one limb, such as the legs, can lead to a certain easing of muscle tension in other places in the body (such as the back).
- Even partial physical activity (i.e., of several body parts, such as only

Fig. 2: Long sitting duration causes back troubles.

Fig. 3: High table for standing position.

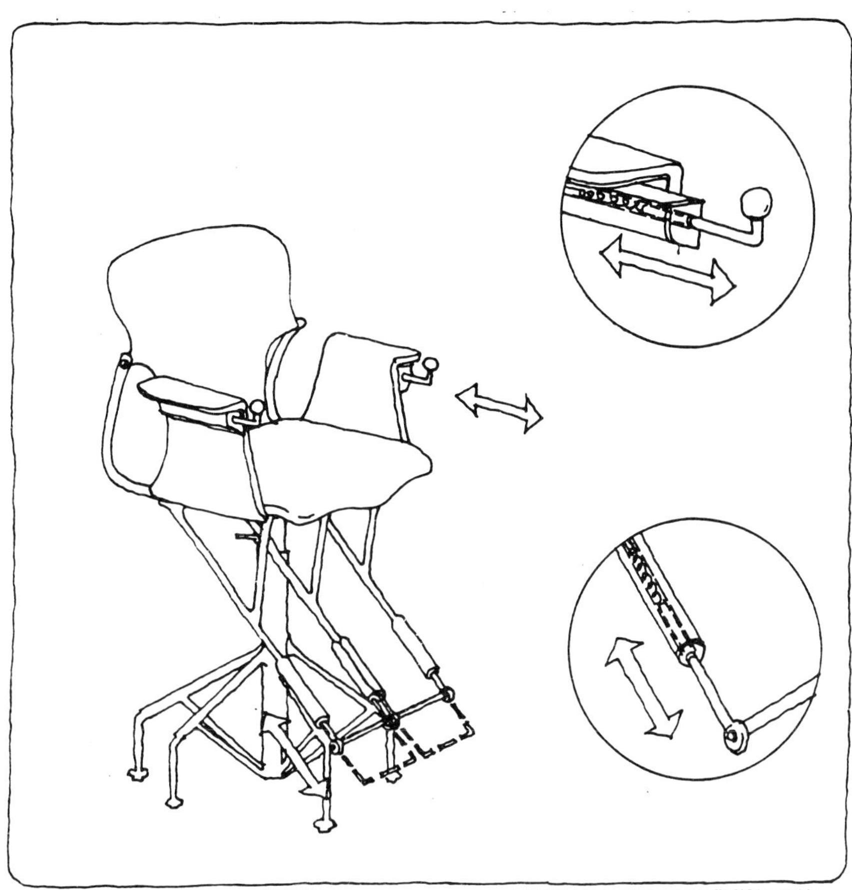

Fig. 4: Action chair for semi-sport action.

the hands or only the feet) may bring about a stimulation of blood circulation to operate the muscles of the body and to dispel general weariness.

- Simple physical activity that is done for a few seconds or minutes, but with some frequency, helps dissipate a feeling of tiredness.

The designed chair enables semi-sport activity of the hands and feet while working or during short breaks of minutes or even seconds duration. Attached to the arms of the chair are special springs that may be stretched, thereby putting to work the hand and shoulder muscles. The ball element at the edge of the arm may be turned and squeezed by operating the palm joint. Working the leg muscles is done through spring pedals that can be operated in similar fashion to a non-circular bicycle movement.

4. RELAXATION WORKING POSTURE

Relaxation in the form of semi-reclining constitutes a serious change in the condition of the body's posture. Figure 5 shows an example of a flexible armchair designed with a back "spinal construction", enabling different support postures, from sitting to lying. These reclining postures constitute a significant change in the condition of the spinal cord. Attaching to the armchair a system of computer operation devices in the form of a distant sign enables operating a computer in a semi-reclining position. The dimensions of the screen need to be designed by taking into consideration its distance from the viewer. The angle of the screen may be adjusted and changed according to the convenience of the viewers and their recumbant body posture.

5. ATMOSPHERE OF THE VDU OFFICE

High-tech technology has created a special, fashionable architectural expression, which is cold, strange, and non-personal. The materials are artificial, and usually textureless. The surfaces are smooth, unified and shining. In the existing modern office, there is not enough place for self-expression. The worker sits alone and communicates with a strange screen instead of with human beings.

As an alternative atmosphere, a different architectural treatment is suggested. The preferred materials will be natural, soft (carpets and garments), and will have some texture (textured materials are also less reflecting). Colours will be neutral and non-contrasting in order to avoid fatigue and distortion of screen colour. The sources of natural and artificial lighting will be designed to avoid reflection. Use of natural elements, such as plants, and even an aquarium, is also recommended.

The individual expression is achieved by a modular design, which enables each operator to alternate his or her own environment according to needs and moods.

6. SERIES OF MODULAR DISPLAYS

The use of the single VDU creates a new situation in which the user can do only one job at a time. The conventional working habits, using books and files, enable seeing and responding to different sources of information and input at the same time. The information the user obtains from the VDU at a certain moment is limited to the size of the screen and the symbols used. The single screen does not permit a comfortable two-to-three people conference (using the same screen at the same time).

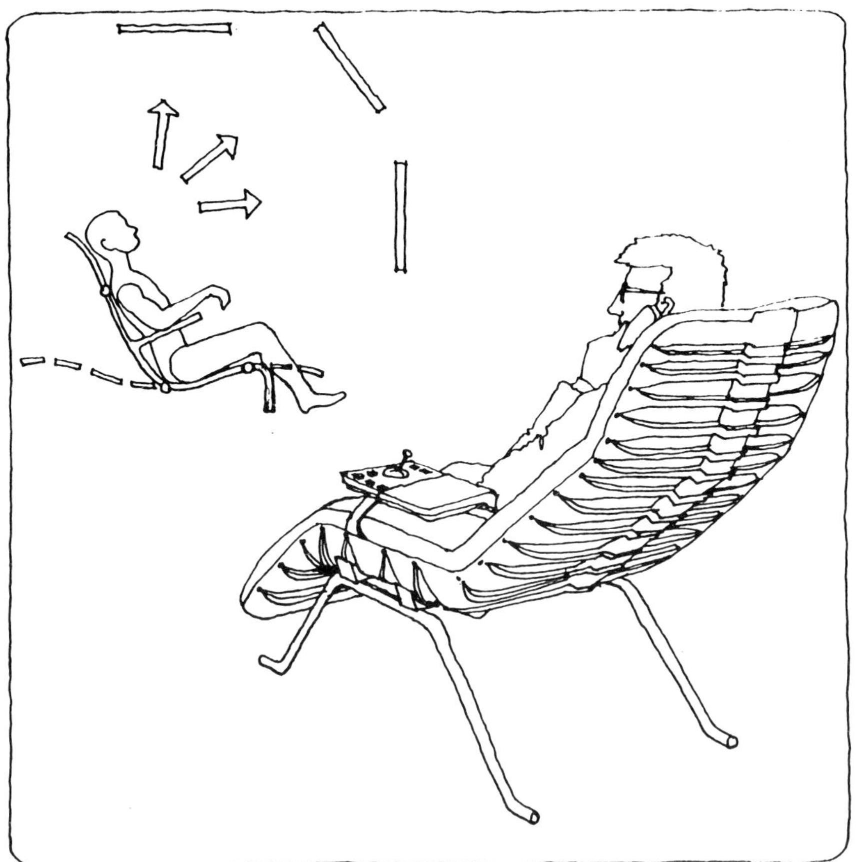

Fig. 5: Flexible arm chair for relaxation working posture.

The future VDU office will include a series of modular display units integrated in the wall and ceiling. The modular units will be flexible and adjustable. This will offer a parallel use of several displays at the same time for diverse input and response requirements (see Fig. 6).

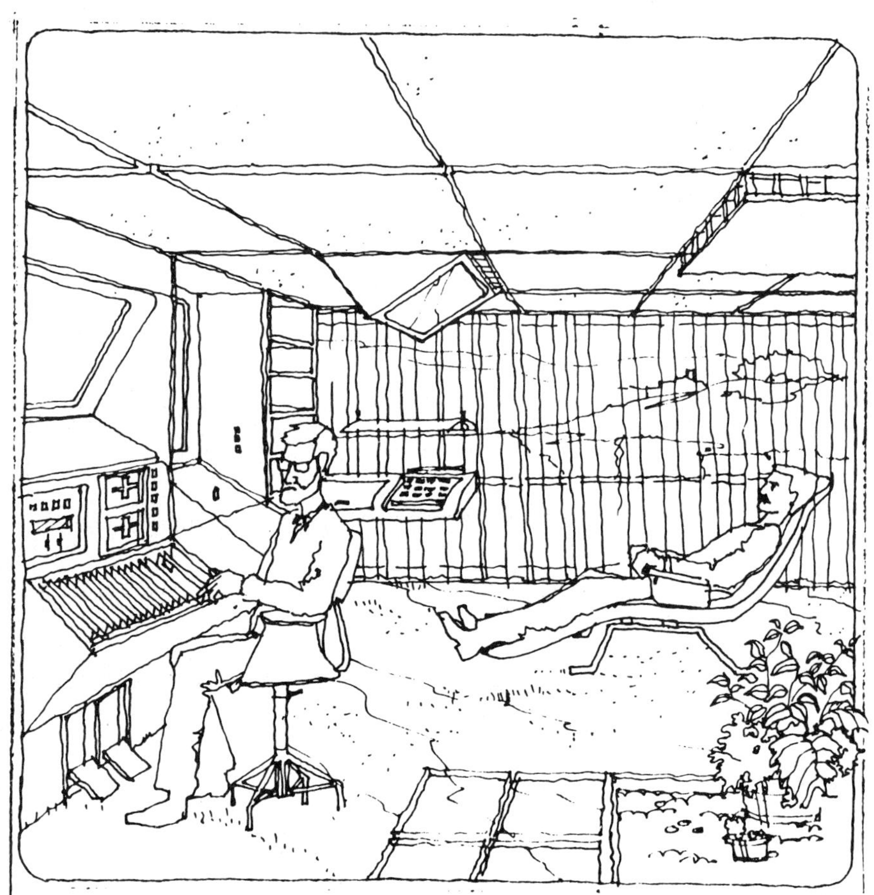

Fig. 6: Atmosphere of VDU office - high-tech with worn individual expression.

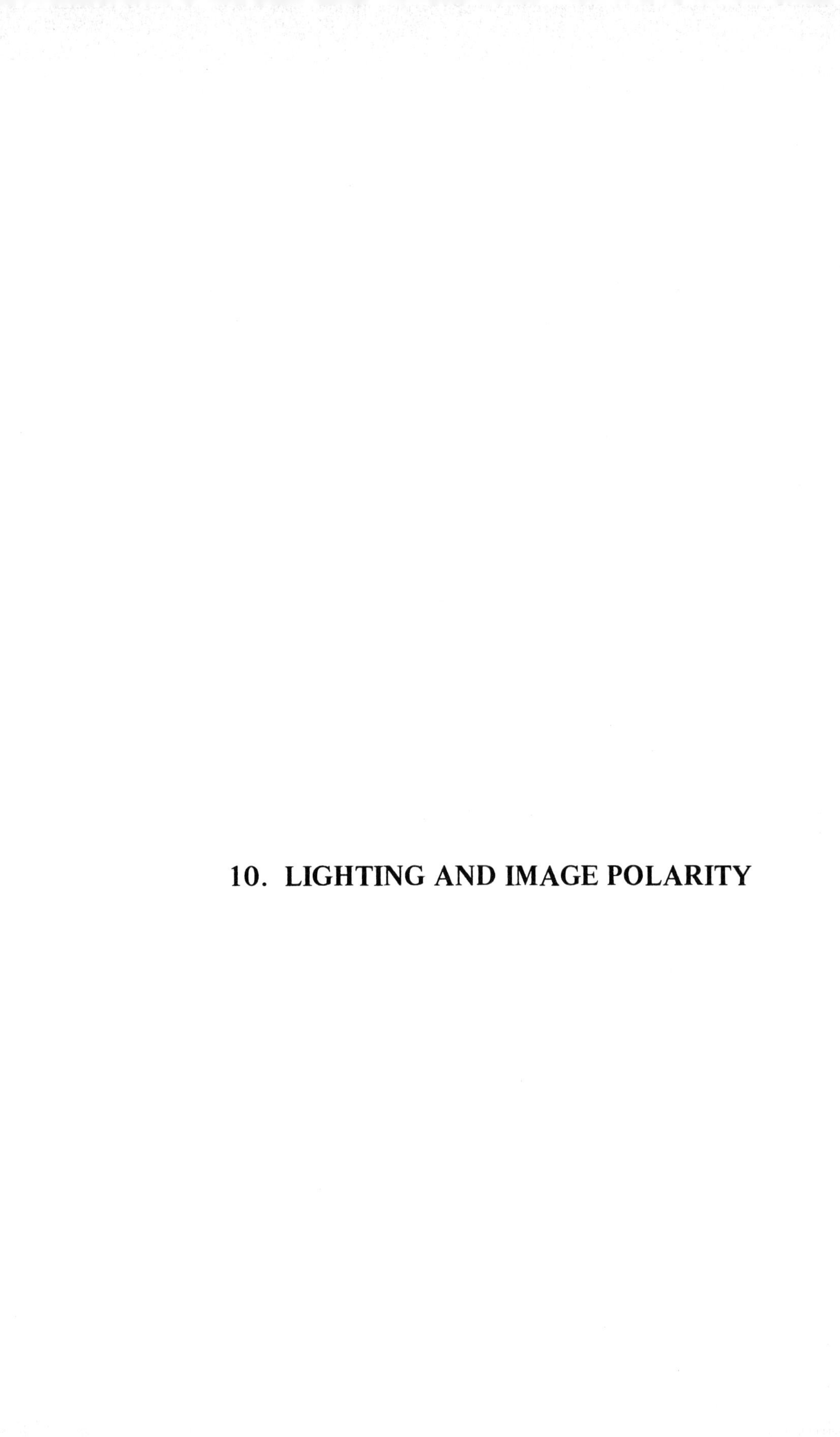

10. LIGHTING AND IMAGE POLARITY

WORK WITH DISPLAY UNITS 86
B. Knave and P.-G. Wideback (eds.)

LIGHTING FOR VISUAL DISPLAY UNIT WORKPLACES

Hans-Henrik Bjørset*

VDUs with bright, flickerfree screens and dark characters give satisfying visual conditions and greater freedom in planning good VDU workplaces. A very satisfying model lighting solution is localised lighting at each VDU workplace, consisting of two suspended luminaires, each for two 36 W fluorescent tubes, or equivalent, with about 25% of the luminous flux diffused upward to the ceiling. This solution fulfills very well the set lighting criteria and gives a good working environment.

1. INTRODUCTION

At the Lighting Engineering Laboratory, University of Trondheim, a report "Workplaces with VDUs. Ergonomics, Vision and Lighting Condition" (in Norwegian) [1] was published autumn 1985. The report covers a range of items: Ergonomics, vision and lighting criteria, model workplaces and lighting solutions, daylight and windows, criteria for spectacles, the format of the VDU screen versus the paper forms in use. Experts within the different subjects took part in the project work. At the laboratory mainly the lighting problems were studied and my paper will cover this item.

2. VISUAL CONDITIONS

Most of the serious visual problems with VDU workplaces have been due to the common dark, specular display screens with light characters, i.e. positiv contrast. To cope with some of the problems it has been recommended to have very low lighting levels, far beyond levels for conventional office work. This has, however, caused other severe visual and environmental problems. Little by little ergonomic requests have resulted in much better VDUs and display screens, so today many firms can offer screens with dark characters on a bright flickerfree background, i.e. negativ contrast.

Compared with dark screens the bright screens will give:

- increased adaptation level with increased visual acuity and contrast sensitivity
- reduced sensitivity of glare
- reduced pupil aperture with reduced optical distortions, improved depth of field and faster accomodation

* Lighting Engineering Laboratory EFI-NTH
University of Trondheim, N-7034 Trondheim-NTH.

- less problems with specular reflections in the screens and more freedom in workplace design.

Bauer and Cavonius [2] have found that by working with a bright flickerfree screen with dark characters, in comparison when doing the same operations with a screen with light characters on dark background, the performance was significantly improved:

- the mean error rate was reduced by 23% and 26%

- the timne required to perform the task was reduced with 8%.

Leibig and Roll [3] found that 95% of the observers accepted a 65% higher lightsource luminance reflected in a bright flickerfree screen compared with a dark screen.

Bauer [4] has also reported on the development of a physiologically optimized bright screen with dark characters which tolerates even very high vertical illuminances and source luminances. It is stated that for the best system performance the adaptation lumincance should be 100 cd/m^2 or more, so a screen background luminance of about 100 cd/m^2 was chosen. Such a screen, also given an antireflective coating with reflectance better than r = 0,3% will give sufficient attenuation of reflected sources up to luminances of about 2000 cd/m^2. If a suitable micromesh is also applied the maximum tolerable reflex source luminance is increased to about 6000-8000 cd/m^2.

Such display screens will give a considerable degree of freedom in the planning and the use of VDU workplaces. It may take some time before such very developed screens are on the market, however, it seems obvious that the number of VDUs with bright, flickerfree screens and dark characters, negative contrast, will increase substantially in the future.

3. LIGHTING CRITERIA

Recommendations on lighting criteria for VDU workplaces should be based on such facts as mentioned above.

By working out our proposal for lighting criteria we also took into account recommendations from other countries and the CIE.
The main points from our report are:

3.1. Illuminance

The service illuminance on the horizontal working plane (E_H) should be in the range 500-1000 lux. The upper end of this range is ment to be used when source documents are difficult to read. If the workplace is equipped with a dark, specular display screen it may be necessary to choose values within a lower range, 300-500 lux.

The vertical illuminance (E_V) should be at least 30%, preferably 50-60% of E_H.

3.2. Glare

For VDU workplaces the limitation of glare is even more important then for conventional office workplaces, so a limiting glare index = 16 is recommended (Hopkinson's formulae). Luminaires with very effective cut-off screening may, by ordinary calculation, come up with glare indexes far below 16, however, the workplaces and the luminaires must always have an optimal mutual position to avoid direct glare and glare by reflection.

3.3. Contrast

For reading and writing at the VDU workplaces the relative contrast reduction should be as low as possible and not more than 15%, respectively 30%, in the reflection standard, when the working materials are glossy, respectively matt. These figures are in accordance with the general Scandinavian recommendation [5].

We think this concept is the most logical, however, we may change over to the corresponding figures for the concept using the contrast rendering factor.

3.4. Surface reflectances, rel.illum. and lum.ratios

Our recommendations here are completely in accordance with the general requests for good environment and lighting in offices.

3.5. Cut-off angle and luminance of luminaire

Luminaire cut-off angle up to 60^0, in some cases up to 65^0, is recommended. The most suitable cut-off angle is dependent on the mounting height: Small mounting heights make it possible to have the largest cut-off angles, while bigger mounting heights lead to smaller cut-off angles. Luminaires with large cut-off angles will have a wide light distribution, which in many ways is preferable.

The luminaire luminance above the cut-off angle should be maximum 200 cd/m^2. By dark and very specular display screens it may be necessary with lower limits, 100-150 cd/m^2 or less.

These limits for the luminaire luminance should also apply for the ceiling luminance.

4. MODEL LIGHTING SOLUTION

Several lighting alternatives were tested and measured at the laboratory for a simulated workplace that easily could be changed between two model VDU workplaces, no. 1 and no. 2, see figure 1. Each of them was given a low and a high position for small and tall persons. That means that for each lighting alternative four series of measurements were taken.

The model workplaces fulfilled all relevant requests on ergonomics and covered all known practical types of VDU workplaces. Figure 2 shows the practical variation possibilities of the chosen motorised working table.

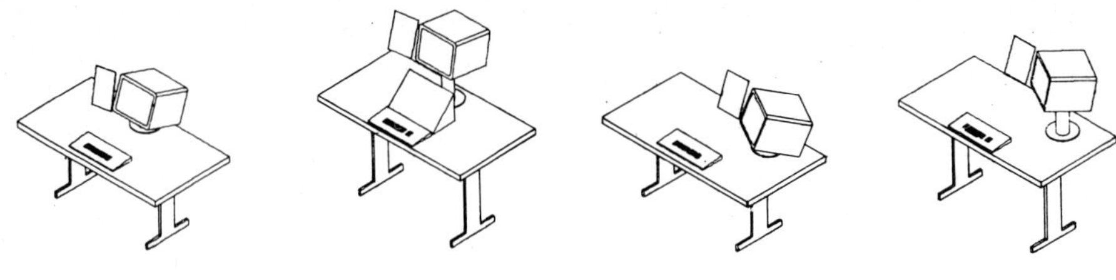

FIGURE 1
Schematic drawings of the model workplaces with low and high positions. The part of the tabletop on which the display screen is placed could be regulated in height independent of the main tabletop.

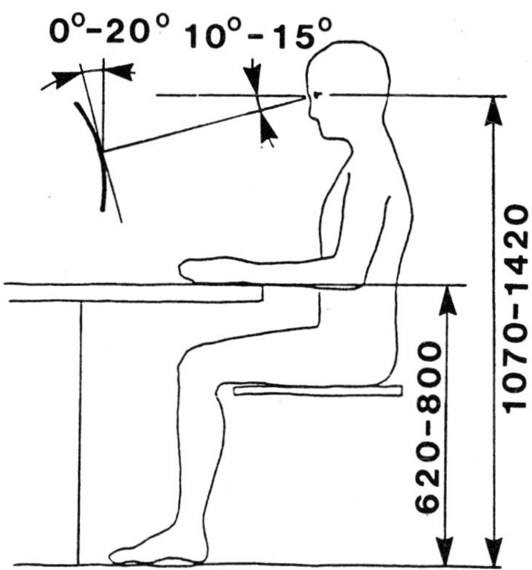

FIGURE 2
Variation possibilities of the chosen motorised working table.

The lay-out at the laboratory is shown for one of the lighting alternatives with workplace no.2, low position, in figure 3. The extensive measurements covered:

- Illuminances at the workplace.
- Contrast reduction at relevant areas.
- Luminances of the surfaces of the workplace and the room.
- Cut-off angle of the luminaires.
- Tilting angle of the display screen when no reflection of luminaires could be observed.

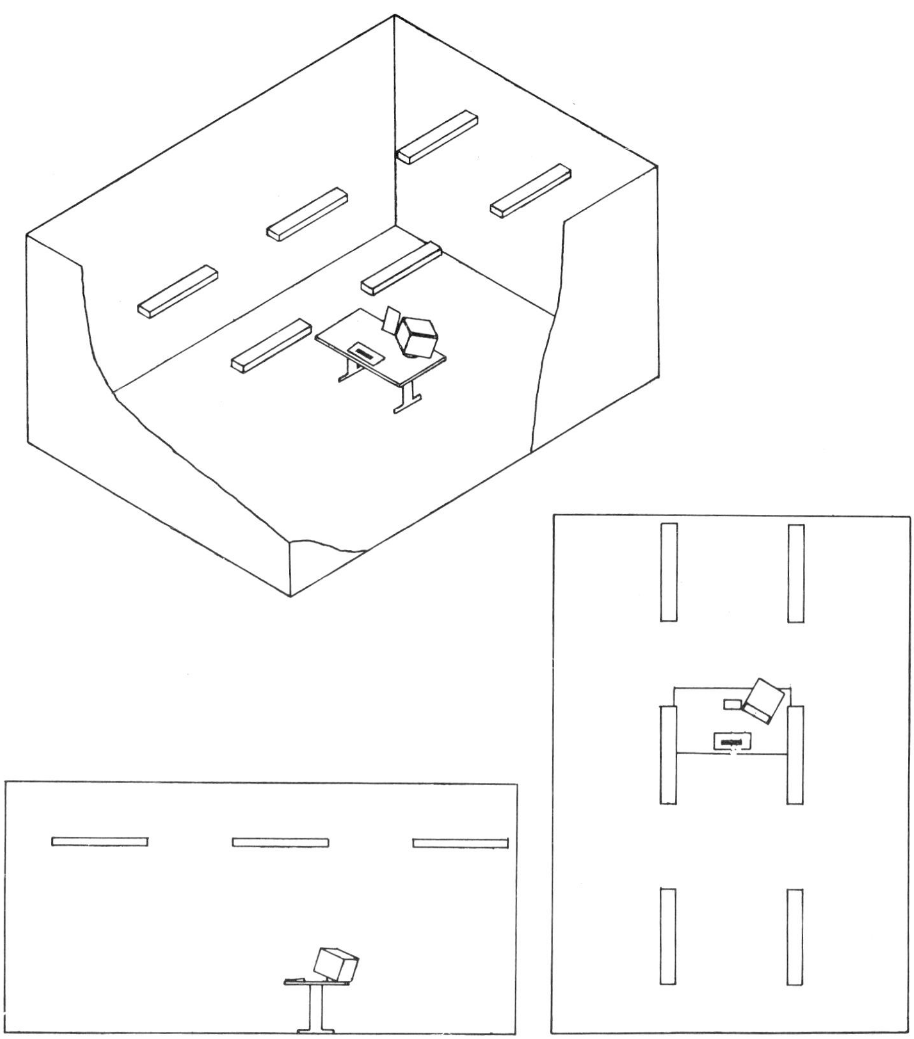

FIGURE 3

Figure 3 shows for one of the alternatives the lay-out at the laboratory with 2 suspended luminaires, each for two 36 W fluorescent tubes, for localised lighting at each VDU workplace. Altogether 6 luminaires in the room.

The results of the measurements are in the report presented in full detail. An example is just given in figure 4 showing for the lighting alternative (Figure 3) the initial illuminances at workplace no. 1, high position, and workplace no. 2, low position.

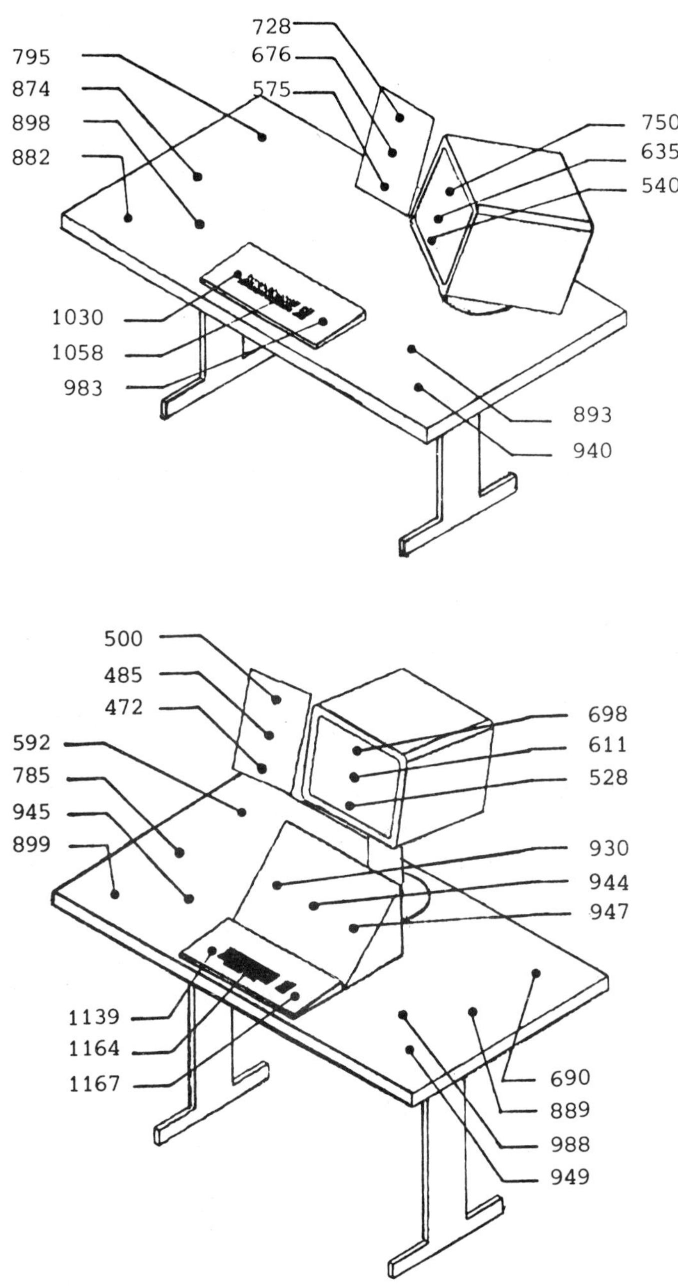

FIGURE 4
Figure 4 gives just two examples of the detailed presentation of the measured values, here initial illuminances in lux.

The contrast reduction was measured within the agreed working area shown in figure 5. The figures at the measuring points give the contrast reduction in percent of the maximum contrast in the reflection standard. The example shows good conditions with very low contrast reduction.

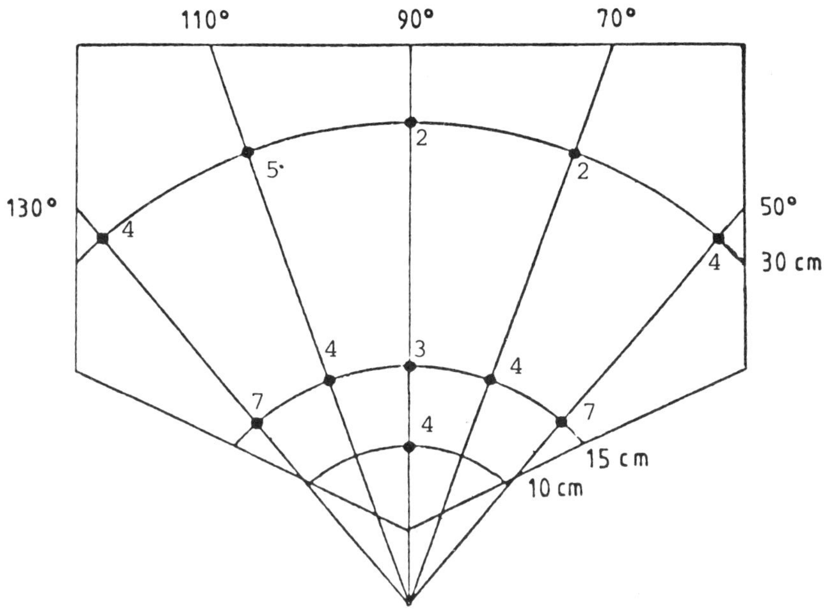

FIGURE 5
Relative contrast reduction in percent measured in front of the operator.

The detailed results were condensed and mean illuminances, initial and service values, were calculated for the relevant areas. This information was tabulated for each lighting alternative. Figur 6 gives the tabulated results for an alternative as shown in figure 3. The tables make it easy to compare the results with the criteria we have set up and to see if the requests are satisfied.

SERIES NO. X		WORKPLACE NO. 1		WORKPLACE NO. 2	
LUMINAIRE: XX 2X36W		LOW POSITION	HIGH POSITION	LOW POSITION	HIGH POSITION
ILLUMINANCE ON:					
- WORKING TABLE	[LUX]	823 (660)	824 (660)	882 (705)	927 (740)
- KEYBOARD	"	1009 (805)	1058 (845)	964 (770)	1106 (885)
- DOCUMENT HOLDER (≈70°)	"	635 (510)	771 (615)	641 (515)	804 (645)
- DOCUMENT HOLDER (≈45°)	"	-	929 (745)	-	-
- VDU SCREEN	"	670 (535)	734 (585)	630 (505)	639 (510)
- OPERATOR	"	285 (230)	283 (225)	-	-
CONTRAST REDUCTION	[%]	0 - 13	0 - 14	2 - 12	2 - 12
LUMINANCES:					
- WALLS	[CD/M²]	11 - 31	11 - 41	-	-
- CEILING	"	25 - 110	25 - 110	-	-
- DOCUMENT (≈70°)	"	110	145	110	160
- DOCUMENT (≈45°)	"	-	155	-	-
- SCREEN A:BACKGROUND	"	31	31	29	30
- SCREEN B:BACKGROUND	"	-	-	-	-
TILTING ANGLE					
- SCREEN A	[°]	18	10	15	8
- SCREEN B	"	-	-	-	-

FIGURE 6

Figure 6 gives the main results put together for the lighting alternative. The mean initial illuminances and service illuminances (within brackets, maintenance factor 0,8) are given. The luminances are initial values.

5. CONCLUSION

The general conclusion was that very satisfying lighting conditions are achieved with localised lighting consisting of two suspended luminaires, each for two 36 W fluorescent tubes, at each VDU workplace.

The luminaires should be mounted lengthwise symmetrically on each side of the operator, with a c-c distance of 1,2 m - 1,6 m (or more), and drawn a little backwards. The situation is shown in figure 3. Mounting height should be 2,0-2,3 m above the floor.

The distances to the nearest luminaires in front of and behind the operator must be sufficient and depend on the mounting height and the cut-off angle.

The luminaires should have an effective screening with cut-off angles and limited luminances above the cut-off angles in accordance with the set criteria.

About 25% of the luminous flux should be upwards, preferably diffused by opal acrylic plastic sheets to get an even lighted ceiling.

Lighting solutions within this model will give the operator:

- Very satisfying illuminance levels and luminance distribution at the workplace, as well as in the room.
- Little or no glare, direct or by reflection, from "his own" luminaires or those in front of him.
- Very limited contrast reductions.
- Very limited reflection problems in the display screen.

Even in a situation when you are planning a new lighting and have to choose a low lighting level due to dark, specular display screens, you could plan for this model solution and just put one lamp in each luminaire until the old VDU units are replaced by modern ones.

REFERENCES

[1] Bjørset, H.-H. et al., Arbeidsplasser med dataterminaler. Ergonomi, syns- og belysningsforhold. EFI TR Nr. 3219. (1985) EFI, N-7034 Trondheim-NTH

[2] Bauer, D. and Cavonius, C.R., Improving the Legibility of Visual Display Units through Contrast Reversal. E. Grandjean & E. Vigliani, Ergonomic Aspects of Visual Display Terminals. Taylor & Francis Ltd., London 1980.(137-142).

[3] Leibig, J., Roll, K.-F., Bildschirm - Arbeidsplatzbeleuchtung Licht 7/1984, 494-497.

[4] Bauer, D., Improving VDT Workplaces in Offices by Use of a Physiologically Optimized Screen with Black Symbols on a Light Background: Basic Considerations. Behaviour and Information Technology, 1984, Vol. 3, No. 4, 363-369.

[5] Bjørset, H.-H. and Frederiksen, E., A Proposal for Recommentions for the Limitation of the Contrast Reduction in Office Lighting. CIE Publication No. 50 (1980), pp. 310-314.

[6] CIE. Vision and the Visual Display Unit Work Station. CIE Publication No. 60 (1984).

WORK WITH DISPLAY UNITS 86
B. Knave and P.-G. Wideback (eds.)

LIGHTING THE DISPLAY OR DISPLAYING THE LIGHTING

Peter R. Boyce, Electricity Council Research Centre, Capenhurst, Chester, CH1 6ES, United Kingdom.

SUMMARY

Work with visual display units often produces adverse reactions. Inappropriate lighting conditions are one cause of such reactions. Three aspects of the visual environment can cause discomfort to display unit operators: high luminance reflections in the screen, static luminance imbalance in the room and dynamic luminance imbalance around the workplace. These problems can be attacked at the screen or at the lighting installation. Reducing the specular reflectivity and/or the diffuse reflectivity of the screen will reduce the significance of any reflections as will increasing the background luminance of the display. Designing the lighting to give a uniform, low luminance in the room will also reduce the problems. Uniform, low luminances can be produced either by using low luminance luminaires with a sharply downward directional lighting effect or by indirect lighting. The choice between these two approaches is largely governed by the specularity of the screen of the display and the appearance required for the room.

1. LIGHTING IN CONTEXT

There can be little doubt that work with visual display units can produce a number of adverse reactions. The causes of these reactions are many and varied but, for convenience, can be grouped into four categories: namely, the quality of the display itself, the physical environment in which the display is set, the physical characteristics of the operators themselves and the nature of the work that has to be done. This paper is concerned solely with the effects of one aspect of the physical environment: the visual environment created by the lighting installation. It is important to recognise that even if the lighting is perfect for working with display units, all the other potential causes of complaint can still occur and that it is not possible to compensate for one by eliminating another.

2. THE PROBLEMS OF THE VISUAL ENVIRONMENT

There are three aspects of the visual environment created by lighting installations which can cause discomfort to display unit operators. They are high luminance reflections from the display screen, static imbalance in the luminance distribution around the main lines of sight and dynamic luminance imbalance between the surfaces regularly looked at by the operator.

High luminance reflections can take several different forms. The simplest to consider is a reflection which is spread uniformly over the screen. The effect of this is to reduce the luminance contrast of the display. It is well established that the ability of people to perform alphanumeric tasks is related to luminance contrast [1]. Therefore, such reflections may cause a reduction in visual performance and adversely affect people's satisfaction with the display.

Another problem occurs when diffuse reflections are unevenly distributed across the display. These reduce the luminance contrast of the display differently in different parts and may make some parts of the display difficult to see. The high luminances on the screen may also cause discomfort or disability glare, since they are inevitably close to the line of sight. In addition, they may be distracting, partly because of the attention gathering power of high luminances and partly because the reflected images will move on the screen whenever the operator changes the position of his/her head.

The worst situation for reflections occurs when a sharp, well defined image of a high luminance object is produced (fig. 1). This situation has all the effects of the diffuse, uneven reflections but in addition it offers a strong cue to the accommodative mechanism of the eye. If the difference in apparent position of the screen and the reflected image is large then difficulties in focussing on the display may occur.

Fig. 1 Well-formed reflections of luminaires in a plain untreated screen.

Static luminance imbalance occurs when luminances close to a line of sight vary widely. A typical example of this phenomenon occurs when a display screen is seen against a window (fig. 2). The high luminance of the window may cause a reduction in the perceived luminance contrast of the display because of scattered light in the eye and/or it may be distracting. Whatever the mechanism there is evidence that such a situation can cause a reduction in task performance and will certainly be considered uncomfortable [2,3].

As for dynamic luminance imbalance, this occurs when there are very large differences between the luminances of objects viewed by the operator in succession (fig. 3), e.g. a source document and the display screen. If the luminances of the two objects are markedly different then the visual system will have to make a large adjustment in sensitivity to light each time the direction of regard changes. This may lead to operators not being fully adapted immediately after changing their direction of regard, which is disturbing, and may lead to adverse ocular symptoms [3].

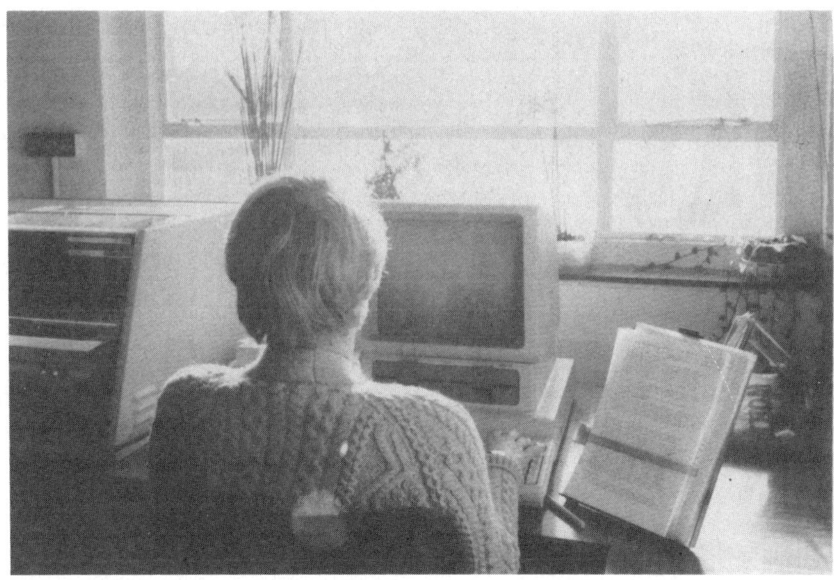

Fig. 2 A situation in which static luminance imbalance is likely to occur

Fig. 3 A situation in which dynamic luminance imbalance is likely to occur. The lighting installation produces narrow directional lighting from low luminance luminaires.

3. SOLUTIONS IN PRINCIPLE

The solutions to these difficulties can be found in two locations: the screen and the lighting installation. In principle, reflections from the display screen can be dealt with by changing the reflection properties of the screen. The relevant properties are the specular and diffuse reflectivity and the background luminance produced by the display.

The worst type of screen as far as reflections are concerned is a plain untreated surface. In essence, this is a mirror with a low percentage specular reflectivity so sharp, well defined images of any high luminance object can easily be seen in it. However, if the specularity of the screen can be reduced the probability of sharp, well defined reflections occurring will be reduced. This is what happens when etching is applied to a screen.

If the diffuse reflectance can be reduced then the likelihood of any reflections occurring is reduced. This can be done by means of a mesh filter of some sort.

If the background luminance generated by the VDU can be increased then the significance of any reflections will be diminished because their contrast with the rest of the screen will be reduced. For a positive contrast display (light characters on a dark background) the background luminance can sometimes be increased directly by using controls on the display unit, or indirectly by increasing the brightness of the characters. In a negative contrast display (dark characters on a light background) the background luminance does not usually need any increasing.

Of course, these options are not without problems of their own. The use of etched surfaces and mesh filters may degrade the quality of the display by spreading and/or reducing the character luminance. Decreasing the diffuse reflectance and hence the luminance of the screen may well make the luminance imbalance in the visual environment greater. Increasing the background luminance of a positive contrast display carries the risk of degrading the displayed characters. Using a negative contrast display increases the probability that the whole display will be seen to flicker.

An alternative approach to avoiding reflections is to eliminate the sources of luminance which are reflected in the display screen. In an extreme form this implies that the lighting should be concentrated on the working area; the general lighting in the room should be reduced to the level necessary for circulation only and low reflectances should be used for all room surfaces. This approach has been tried (fig. 3) but disturbing reflections can still occur because objects in the room tend to contrast strongly with the dark background; the most common example being when the operator wears a white blouse or shirt. In addition, most people using display units also have to use other media, such as printed material and this is difficult in a room where large areas are lit only for circulation.

Another and more realistic approach is to limit the effect of lighting on screen reflections to producing a low, uniform luminance across the whole display. Because most display units are curved in shape, the area of a room that may be reflected in the screen is large. Therefore attention needs to be given to the luminances of many of the surfaces and objects in the room, especially if there are several display screens facing different directions. In order to create a uniform, low luminance, the first step is to remove all sources of high luminance from the room. By far the highest luminances in most rooms come from the sky and sun seen through windows and electric lamps and luminaires. Blinds which provide a uniform luminance, e.g. roller blinds rather than venetian blinds, need to be fitted to windows. Luminaires should have low luminances in directions which can be reflected in a screen towards the observer. It should be noted that information on luminaire luminance cannot be gained just from a luminous intensity distribution. It is always necessary to examine the luminaire itself to ensure that it has no bright surfaces which can be seen from significant directions.

Once all the sources of high luminance have been eliminated, the remaining area requiring attention is the reflectances of the surfaces of the room. The problems associated with very low reflectances have already been mentioned. Very high reflectance surfaces run the risk of creating static luminance imbalance or of producing such a high luminance uniformly on the screen that the luminance contrast of the display is reduced beyond the range for which it can be compensated by the contrast adjustment available on most display units. Usually, reflectances of 0.7 for the ceiling, 0.5 to 0.7 for the walls, and up to 0.3 for the floor represent the best compromise. Whatever the reflectances chosen the ultimate aim is a uniform low luminance on all relevant surfaces. Sudden changes of luminance should always be avoided if disruptive reflections are to be eliminated. High uniform luminances should be avoided if the contrast of the display is to be kept at a reasonable level.

Fortunately for simplicity, this uniform, low luminance approach tends to eliminate the problem of static luminance imbalance because high luminances are removed from the room. It may also diminish the problem of dynamic luminance imbalance bcause by uniformly increasing the luminance of the display screen, the difference between the luminance of the screen and any source document will be reduced.

4. PRACTICAL SOLUTIONS

The benefits and limitations of display screen filters or treatments have already been discussed. Therefore, this discussion concentrates on the effects of different types of lighting installation. There are three types of lighting installation which are commonly used for lighting rooms containing visual display units. They are local lighting, conventional uniform lighting from a regular array of luminaires with a narrow luminous intensity distribution and indirect lighting.

Local lighting is usually done by an adjustable luminaire mounted on the workstation. This is used to light the source document or the keyboard. Provided the local lighting luminaire is located where it cannot be reflected from the display screen, this is good for reflections and for static luminance imbalance. However, unless the luminance of the source document lit by the local lighting luminaire is kept low, there is a likelihood of dynamic luminance imbalance occurring and, if the operator is lit by the scattered light from the local lighting unit, he/she will be seen by reflection in the screen against a dark background. Local lighting alone is not really suitable for lighting rooms containing display units. It may be appropriate to supplement general room lighting but even then it needs to be used carefully.

Conventional lighting from a regular array of luminaires calls for careful selection of the luminaires. Specifically, it has been shown [4] that the parts of the luminaire which may be reflected in the screen towards the observer should have a luminance less than 200 cd m^{-2}. For conventional desk mounted display units, geometry suggests that this limit applies to those surfaces seen at angles of more than 55° from the downward vertical. This recommendation has been widely adopted [5,6]. Luminaires which meet this requirement are of low luminance when seen from the usual directions and hence are unlikely to cause any static luminance imbalance or reflection problems. The main problems with this type of luminaire arise because the luminous intensity distribution produces a concentrated downward beam of light. This can have three undesirable effects. The first is that a wide variation in illuminance can occur within the room unless the luminaires are closely spaced. The second is that an operator sitting directly underneath such a luminaire can be brightly lit compared with the background against which he/she is seen which may lead to marked reflections of the operator being seen in the display screen (fig.4). The third is that this type of luminaire tends to produce high illuminances on the horizontal plane so the probability of dynamic luminance imbalance occurring may be increased (fig. 3). In spite of these problems these luminaires can be guaranteed not to produce reflections of themselves in the screens of conventionally positioned display units.

Fig. 4 An installation of low luminance luminaires. Note the reflection of the operator in the screen.

The other practical solution is indirect lighting in which all the light from the luminaires is first directed up to the ceiling and then reflected around the room. This approach effectively uses the ceiling as a large area, low luminance luminaire. The success or otherwise of indirect lighting depends on the uniformity of luminance on the ceiling and walls and hence on the light distribution from the uplighter. If a series of high luminance spots is formed on the ceiling then high luminance reflections will be seen in the screen. However, if a uniform luminance distribution can be created then a uniform reflection can be produced across the screen. Since indirect lighting depends on inter-reflections to create the uniformity of luminance it is desirable that medium to high reflectances are used on all surfaces of the room.

Several authors have tried to demonstrate the preference of VDU users for one or other of these systems [4,7]. For example, Leibig and Roll [4] asked people to read continuous text from display units with different screen reflectance properties under different sorts of lighting installation, using low luminance luminaires or indirect lighting. In addition, the subjects were asked to set the luminance of the luminaire or ceiling so that it was at the borderline between being distracting and not distracting. The results of these settings showed that using a negative contrast display (dark characters on a bright background) and using an etched screen treatment allowed higher luminances to be used before distraction occurred compared with an untreated screen and a positive contrast display (bright characters on a dark background). They also showed that indirect lighting was considered distracting at a lower ceiling luminance than was the direct lighting produced by the low luminance luminaire. This may have been because of the form of indirect lighting used, a suspended uplighter, where reflections in the display screen would show the uplighter itself silhouetted against the bright ceiling. This type of indirect lighting does not fully conform with the principle of uniformity of luminance.

Harvey et al. [7] had people perform a task involving checking lists of numbers printed on paper against a similar list displayed on a VDU screen. After doing this for about an hour the subjects were asked to give ratings to various aspects of the 'quality' of the direct and indirect lighting systems used. There was no difference in performance for the three lighting systems used but there was a clear difference in preference. The two indirect lighting systems were clearly preferred to the low luminance luminaire system using a recessed parabolic louvre luminaire. This occurred even though the indirect lighting was using suspended uplighters. This paper clearly shows the differences in reflections produced by the three types of lighting system used; the recessed parabolic luminaire providing much sharper and brighter reflections than the indirect lighting installations.

The only real conclusion that can be drawn from such studies is that either approach can be satisfactory but it all depends on how it is done. Low luminance luminaires need to have carefully controlled luminous intensity distributions in all directions and to be free of high luminance surfaces which can be seen from relevant directions. Indirect lighting needs to create uniform luminances across the ceiling and upper walls. If the luminance of the ceiling is markedly non-uniform or the luminaire can be seen in silhouette against the ceiling, complaints about reflections may still occur.

A choice between these two approaches is largely a matter of judgement. However, there are two factors which may be used to guide that judgement. The first is the specularity of the display screen. If the screen is completely untreated so that it is a mirror in all but name, then the low luminance luminaire approach is probably the better of the two. This is because a carefully designed installation of this type can guarantee that conventionally mounted display units will be free of reflections of the luminaires themselves. By comparison an indirect lighting system will inevitably produce a higher luminance on the ceiling and this may be distracting if it is seen as a well defined image on the screen. Whether this occurs or not will depend on the background luminance generated by the display and the specularity of the screen. For screens which have been treated in some way to reduce specularity, e.g. by etching, this advantage of low luminance luminaires will be much reduced, because the reflections which occur will no longer be well defined. In this situation the choice between the two lighting approaches can be made on the basis of the other important factor: the appearance of the room. Whilst both conventional narrow luminous intensity distribution lighting and indirect lighting are capable of providing satisfactory conditions for working with display units, they do produce a very different appearance in the same room. A conventional array of narrowly directional, low luminance luminaires tends to produce high illuminances on horizontal surfaces but low illuminances on vertical surfaces. Unless care is taken with the reflection of the floor, this tends to produce a gloomy appearance to an interior with strong shadows (fig. 5).

Fig. 5 A typical installation of low luminance luminaires. Note the rather dark appearance given to the upper elements in the room and the strong shadows that are apparent.

Indirect lighting tends to give high brightnesses to the ceiling and, because it depends on inter-reflected light, a very uniform illuminance on all surfaces without any shadows (figs. 6 and 7). This tends to make an interior look spacious with a high ceiling. The very diffuse nature of the lighting has been variously described as bland or relaxing. However, experience suggests that the indirect lighting approach tends to be preferred to strongly directional low luminance luminaires when the appearance of the interior is being considered.

The balance of advantage between these two approaches has led to the recent developments of hybrid systems which use low luminance luminaires to produce direct lighting but with a significant element of indirect lighting as well [8]. Installations of this type appear to be well received. It remains to be seen if such systems are satisfactory for the worst case of a high specularity, untreated, display screen.

It can be concluded that by following the principle of uniformity of luminance, lighting which is comfortable for work with display units can be created. However the need to follow this principle may only be temporary. Developments in technology, particularly the development of flicker free negative contrast displays will do much to make this restriction on lighting design unnecessary.

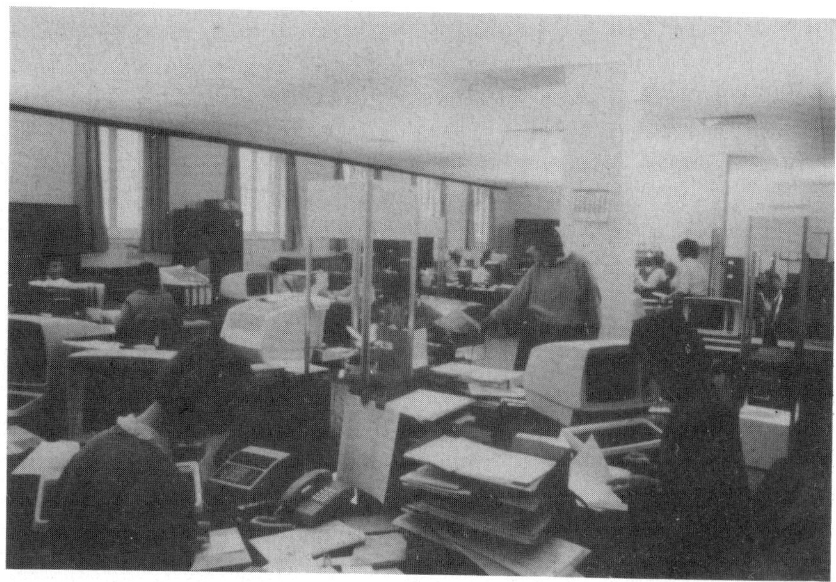

Fig. 6 A typical indirect lighting installation using free standing luminaires. Note the diffuse nature of the lighting.

Fig. 7 An indirect lighting installation using suspended uplighting

ACKNOWLEDGEMENTS

It is a pleasure to acknowledge the help of the following people in supplying some of the illustrations in this paper: Dr. M.S. Rea, National Research Council of Canada, Mr. J. Wood, Communication Complex Design, and Mr. M. Wood-Robinson, South Western Electricity Board.

REFERENCES

[1] Rea, M.S. Visual performance with realistic methods of changing contrast. Journal of the Illuminating Engineering Society, 10 (3), 164-177, 1981.

[2] Radl, G.W. Experimental investigation for optimal presentation mode and colour of symbols on the CRT screen, in Ergonomic Aspects of Visual Display Terminals. Edited by E. Grandjean and E. Vigliani. Taylor and Francis, London 1982.

[3] Laubli, T., Hunting, W. and Grandjean, E. Visual ergonomics in VDU operators related to environmental conditions, in Ergonomic Aspects of Visual Display Terminals. Edited by E. Grandjean and E. Vigliani. Taylor and Francis, London 1982.

[4] Leibig, J. and Roll, K.F. Acceptable luminance reflected on VDU screens in relation to the type of contrast and illumination. Commission Internationale de l'Eclairage, 20th Session, Vol. 2, D313/1, Amsterdam 1983.

[5] Commission Internationale de l'Eclairage. Vision and the visual display unit work station. CIE Publication 60, CIE, Paris 1984.

[6] Chartered Institution of Building Services, Technical Memorandum No. 6, Lighting for visual display units, CIBS, London 1981.

[7] Harvey, L.O., DiLaura, D.L. and Mistrick, R.J. Quantifying reactions of visual display operators to indirect lighting. Journal of the Illuminating Engineering Society 14, (1), 515-546, 1984.

[8] Bjorset, H.H. Lighting for visual display unit workplaces. Work with display units conference, Stockholm 1986, this volume.

WORK WITH DISPLAY UNITS 86
B. Knave and P.-G. Wideback (eds.)

LIGHTING THE ELECTRONIC OFFICE

M.H.F. van Ooyen
S.H.A. Begemann

Lighting Division
Lighting Design and Engineering Centre
Philips International B.V.
Eindhoven, The Netherlands

With the nowadays widely used dark VDU-screens, two problems are often encountered: reflections and adaptation. Reflections can occur in VDU-screens as a result of high wall luminances, while in larger offices these reflections can result from the wide light distributions employed. The combination of dark VDU-screens and rather bright walls can also result in transient adaptation problems. Adapting the lighting in an attempt to solve these problems will not result in a correct and complete solution. These problems will be analysed and some potential solutions will be presented in the paper.

1. INTRODUCTION

In the past decade there has been a marked shift away from traditional office work, mainly involving reading and writing dark text on white paper, toward direct communication with colleagues and office machines.

An analysis of office work (1) has revealed that the visual tasks office workers are most frequently confronted with are:
- writing, most of the time on matt paper;
- reading, from both matt and glossy paper;
- verbal communication with colleagues and others;
- working with VDUs connected to word processors, computer terminals and the like.

The introduction of VDU screens in offices has done much to bring about important changes in office-lighting practice. The first VDUs had dark screens, and problems involving disturbing reflections in these screens and the need to visually adapt between dark screen and white working documents were often encountered.

Reflections occurred in dark-screen VDUs as a result of high wall luminances, whilst in larger offices similar reflections resulted from the wide light distributions of the luminaires employed. The combination of dark-screen VDUs and bright walls also gave rise to the problem of transient adaptation.

Adapting the lighting by lowering the lighting levels or using luminaires having a narrower light distribution, or both, in an attempt to solve these problems failed to provide a correct and satisfactory solution.

2. LIGHTING REQUIREMENTS

Good lighting is necessary both for the assimilation of the visual information needed for the performance of the various visual tasks and to enhance the working environment (2). Just how well a person will perform a visual task will depend on how complete and unimpaired is the scene presented to the eye.

Two different aspects should be distinguished here:
- Visual performance: How well does the worker perform in terms of speed and accuracy?
- Visual satisfaction: Is what the worker sees experienced as being pleasant and in harmony with the environment?

In order to achieve both good visual performance and good visual satisfaction, the following lighting criteria should be considered:
- lighting level
- modelling
- luminance distribution
- direct and reflected glare
- light colour and colour rendering

These criteria should not be considered in isolation, but as forming a set of interdependent parameters that when combined in the right way will ensure good lighting.

Since the variety of fluorescent lamps currently available is wide enough to permit of the proper choice with regard to colour and colour rendering for any specific application, the question of colour will not be dealt with here.

2.1 Lighting Levels

Needless to say, there is generally more to office work than simply working with VDUs. For reading and writing tasks in most European countries, and in the USA as well, horizontal illuminances ranging from 500 lux to 1000 lux are recommended (3, 4, 5, 6). The actual level decided upon in a given situation will depend on the type of work (size, speed, accuracy), the age of the office workers, the dimensions of the office and the presence (or absence) of daylight. In practice, illuminances may vary between 500 lux and 750 lux.

For ergonomic reasons, near-vertical paper supports are now coming into use in combination with VDUs (especially with word processors). In such cases, the vertical illuminance has to be between 500 lux and 750 lux.

These illuminances can only be achieved by using luminaires having a wide light distribution, or with low-brightness luminaires in combination with additional task lighting.

2.2 Modelling

The modelling effect of the lighting, or its ability to produce acceptable shadow working, is determined by the illumination vectors; in other words, by the ratio of the horizontal to the vertical illuminance at a given point.

Good modelling will be obtained when this ratio lies between 1.5 and 2 (7). In lighting installations employing low-brightness luminaires having a narrow light distribution, a ratio of about 3 is achieved, resulting in harsh shadows. With uplighting, on the other hand, the ratio will be in the order of 1, resulting in a very diffuse and dull luminous environment.

2.3 Luminance Distribution

Because of the shift away from reading and writing tasks toward tasks of a more communicative nature, the main direction of view is no longer almost vertically downwards but horizontal. As a consequence, more emphasis has to be laid upon achieving satisfactory luminance values in the vertical plane.

Recent research (8) has produced the wall and working-plane luminances preferred in offices for reading, writing, discussion and VDU work (Fig. 1). The VDU used had bright characters on a dark screen.

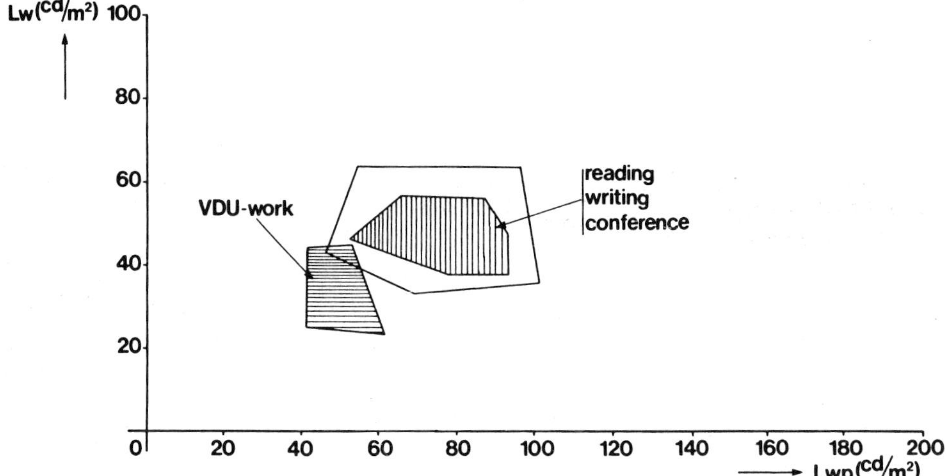

fig.1 Preferred combination area for wall and working plane luminances

It was found that reading, writing and discussion resulted in preferences that were all within the ranges:

wall luminance: 30 cd/m^2 - 60 cd/m^2
working-plane luminance: 45 cd/m^2 - 105 cd/m^2

while for VDU work the preferences were for:

wall luminance: 20 cd/m^2 - 45 cd/m^2
working-plane luminance: 40 cd/m^2 - 65 cd/m^2

This difference between the luminances preferred for VDU work and those preferred for other office tasks is attributable to the existence of adaptation problems caused by the use of the dark-screen VDU in (the preferably) bright surroundings.

2.4 Direct Glare

Various glare limitation systems are in use in different countries. The European Glare Limiting Method, which has been adopted by the CIE (9), limits the luminance of a luminaire as viewed from between 45° and 85° to the vertical, to between roughly 1000 cd/m^2 and 3000 cd/m^2 (depending on the overall lighting level). For luminous ceilings, a maximum value of 500 cd/m^2 is recommended.

Since uplighting creates a lighting situation that comes close to that produced by a luminous ceiling, it seems appropriate to limit the ceiling luminances here to 500 cd/m^2. The uplighting provided by HID lamps carries the risk of creating ceiling luminances that are too high.

2.5 Reflected Glare

The most frequent complaint among VDU workers is that of being disturbed by specular reflections in the screen (10). This acts as a convex mirror and so forms images of bright parts of the room, including the operator. These mirror images are unwanted for several reasons:

- They contain information that is irrelevant to the performance of the task but that demands involuntary attention, thus distracting the worker - sometimes to the point of irritation.

- Their apparent distance is greater than that between eye and screen and this causes involuntary changes in the accommodation of the eye when looking back and forth from text to image. This can lead to visual fatigue.

- They may conceal those parts of the text whose luminance is high, so making it more difficult to assimilate the information necessary for the performance of the task.

3. BRIGHT-SCREEN VDUs

One of the most attractive solutions to the above problems is to increase the luminance of the screen. This can be done by using VDUs in which the text is dark against a bright background - the so-called bright-screen or negative-contrast VDU. Using a bright screen will bring the preferred luminances within the range of the other office tasks, thus creating a luminous office environment in which all major tasks can be performed in comfort.

The maximum luminance levels permissible in the interior are proportional to the background luminance of the screen, which means that they can be almost ten times higher for VDUs with negative contrast than for those with positive contrast. As a consequence, good quality fluorescent luminaires (such as those employed in normal working interiors to avoid direct glare) can be used to advantage as they will not produce disturbing mirror images in the bright screen. High-luminance windows, however, will still prove troublesome in this respect.

To illustrate these effects, the contrast losses encountered in both dark-screen and bright-screen VDUs have been calculated for various disturbing luminance levels.

The background luminance (L_b) of the dark screen was 13 cd/m^2 and of the bright screen 105 cd/m^2. The bright characters had a luminance (L_{ch}) of 65 cd/m^2, against the 59 cd/m^2 of the "dark" characters. The specular reflectance of both screens was 0.04.

The contrast on the screen is defined as:

$$C = \frac{L_{ch} - L_b}{L_b}$$

In tables I and II the contrast loss $\Delta C/C$ is shown for disturbing luminances (L_r) ranging from 50 cd/m^2 to 1000 cd/m^2. (See also Fig. 2).

Table I: Contrast reduction ($\Delta C/C$) in dark-screen VDUs:

L_r	L_{ch}	L_b	C	$\Delta C/C$
cd/m^2				
0	65	13	4.00	
50	67	15	3.47	- 0.13
100	69	17	3.06	- 0.23
200	73	21	2.48	- 0.38
500	85	33	1.58	- 0.61
1000	105	53	0.98	- 0.76

background luminance: L_b = 13 cd/m^2
character luminance : L_{ch} = 65 cd/m^2

Table II: Contrast reduction ($\Delta C/C$) in bright-screen VDUs:

L_r	L_{ch}	L_b	C	$\Delta C/C$
cd/m^2				
0	59	105	0.44	
50	61	107	0.43	- 0.02
100	63	109	0.42	- 0.04
200	67	113	0.41	- 0.07
500	79	125	0.37	- 0.16
1000	99	145	0.32	- 0.28

background luminance: L_b = 105 cd/m^2
character luminance :L_{ch} = 59 cd/m^2

Measures taken to decrease the effect of disturbing reflections in dark screens - such as the use of filters or anti-reflection layers - will only serve to decrease still further the screen luminance, thereby adding to the problem of transient adaptation.

The alternative approach of reducing illuminance levels and making extensive use of low-brightness luminaires will merely result in an unacceptable luminous environment in the office. As a consequence, the office workers will feel uncomfortable and productivity will inevitably fall off.

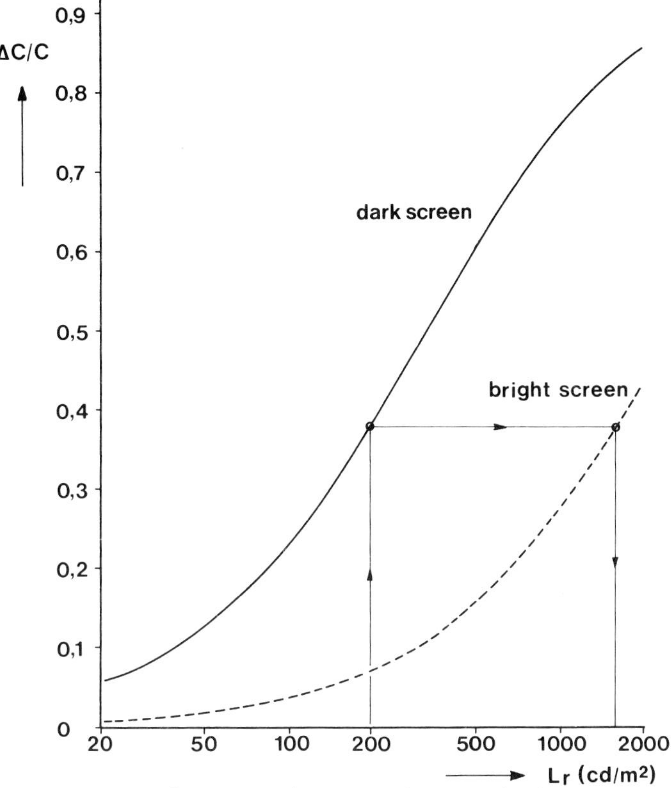

fig.2 Contrast reduction vs. disturbing luminances

4. CONCLUSIONS

The optimum luminous environment in an office can be created by:

1. Providing illuminance levels of 500-750 lux on both the horizontal and the vertical planes.

2. Providing an acceptable luminance distribution by ensuring that the wall and working plane reflectances are sufficiently high and that the light distribution of the luminaires is not too narrow.

In those offices where the above measures have been adopted and where bright-screen VDUs are in use, VDU work can be satisfactorily combined with other office tasks.

5. REFERENCES

(1) Vincent, R.L., Survey of Office Seeing Tasks, Illuminating Engineering Research Institute, Project 107.

(2) Begemann, S.H.A. and Hendriks, R.T.A., The Ups and Downs of Office Lighting, in: Proceedings of the National Lighting Conference 1984, (The Chameleon Press Limited, London, 1984) pp 7-17.

(3) IES Lighting Handbook, Application Volume, (Waverly, Press, Inc., Baltimore, U.S.A., 1981)

(4) CIBS Code For Interior Lighting, (Yale Press Ltd, London, 1984).

(5) DIN 5035, Innenraumbeleuchtung mit künstlichem Licht, (Beuth Verlag, Berlin, Germany)

(6) NSvV, Aanbevelingen voor binnenverlichting (Dutch), Arnhem, The Netherlands 1981

(7) de Boer, J.B. and Fischer, D., Interior Lighting, (Kluwer Technische Boeken B.V., Deventer, 1981).

(8) van Ooyen, M.H.F., van de Weygert, J.C.A. and Begemann, S.H.A., Luminance Distribution as a basis for Office Lighting Design, in: Proceedings of the National Lighting Conference 1986, U.K.

(9) Guide on Interior Lighting, Publication CIE no. 29/2, 1985.

(10) de Graaff, A.B., Some observations about Lighting and VDU work, Fourth World Congress of Ergophalmology, Sorrento, Italy, 1985.

WORK WITH DISPLAY UNITS 86
B. Knave and P.-G. Wideback (eds.)

WORK AT VIDEO DISPLAY TERMINALS AMONG OFFICE EMPLOYEES

Visual ergonomics and lighting

Roger I WIBOM and Lars W CARLSSON

Occupational Neuromedicine, Research Department, National Board of Occupational Safety and Health, S-171 84 Solna, Sweden

1. INTRODUCTION

In the project "Work with video display terminals among office employees" five reports have hitherto been published (Scand J Work Environ Health 11, 1985, Report 1-5). The project, which was largely carried out in 1982, investigated 400 VDT operators and 150 selected controls (i e office workers not using VDTs) in the Stockholm area.

The present report is based on report 1 and 2 , and is concerned with visual ergonomics and lighting.

Since VDTs were introduced, problems with lighting have been reported (concerning both artificial and natural light sources), and various subjective discomforts and symptoms have appeared among VDT operators, e g visual and musculoskeletal discomforts.

It is known that large luminance differences between two adjacent objects in the working visual field can cause contrast glare which may adversely affect the visual performance.

All VDT operators investigated in this project worked with VDTs displaying negative polarity, i e with light characters on dark background. The VDT and the manuscript (normally on white paper) are in many situations the two most important objects in the working visual field and, depending on the work, the visual emphasis will often shift between these objects. Every time the worker first regards the white manuscript (high luminance) and then the dark VDT (low luminance), there is a substantial risk of experiencing contrast glare.

The lighting conditions at each workplace were determined by objective measurements of illuminances, luminances and contrast reductions. Furthermore, the working visual distances were measured, and at the same time, subjective evaluations regarding reflexions at the work desk, VDT and keyboard were noted.

Subjective discomforts and symptoms concerning e g the eyes were taken from a questionnaire.

Visual statuses were also evaluated in routine ophthalmological examinations, and furthermore, special investigations were performed as to accommodation, convergence and refraction during the workday (Report 3 and 4). Report 5 describes a dermatological investigation.

2. MATERIAL

2.1 Groups investigated.

All office employees doing more than five hours VDT work at an insurance company (group A) an airline and a post office (group B) and personnel from three daily newspapers (group C) comprised the exposed group. To make up the reference group (R in the figures), persons whose work tasks were as similar as possible to those of the exposed subjects but did not include VDT work were selected from each of these enterprises. The sample was taken with the assistance of a working party comprising representatives of employers, trade unions and occupational safety and health services.
A preliminary estimate of the size of the material, following an initial contact with the enterprises, indicated some 450 exposed employees, relatively evenly distributet between the three sub-groups (A B and C).
It was therefore decided that the reference group was to include about 150 persons and that these ought preferably to be evenly distributed between the various enterprise groups and matched in terms of age and sex.
The aim of this grouping was to create about 150 "quartets", each including one representative of the three exposed groups and one representative of the three reference groups. In practice this grouping and matching was not feasible for all sub-groups, but it worked fairly well for the exposed group and reference group as a whole for age and sex (Tables I and II).
The match between the exposed and reference subjects was relatively good in group A , could be termed fair in group B, and, as regards the balance between the sexes, unsatisfactory in group C (tabell II).
The male predominance in group C is essentially due to the majority of newspaper VDT operators being printing workers who were retrained a couple of years ago to use VDT-based computer techniques instead of lead typesetting for newspaper printing.

The exposed groups were also classified according to work tasks in three groups, (1) data entry, (2) data aquisition, (3) interactive communication (i. e. a combination of data entry and aquisition). The group was also divided up according to VDT make and model. Six sub-groups could be defined in this way.

Table 1. Number of persons in the investigation.

Subjects in different phases of the investigation[a]	Examined groups[b]							
	A		B		C		Total	
	Exposed	Reference	Exposed	Reference	Exposed	Reference	Exposed	Reference
1	156	29	168	75	114	46	438	150
2	151	29	154	75	109	45	414	149
3	149	27	144	72	102	42	395	141
4	142	21	140	68	97	37	379	126

[a] 1 = those reported by the enterprises before the investigation, 2 = those examined in one or more of the substudies, 3 = those replying to the questionnaire, and 4 = those completing all substudies.
[b] A = subjects from an insurance company, B = subjects from an airline and a post office, C = subjects from three daily newspapers.

Table 2. Number of persons and the mean, median and standard deviation of the mean of the age of the examined groups by sex.

Sex	Examined groups[a]							
	A		B		C		Total	
	Exposed	Reference	Exposed	Reference	Exposed	Reference	Exposed	Reference
Male								
Number of subjects	41	6	16	16	57	8	114	30
Age (years)								
Mean	36	33	39	45	43	34	40	40
Median	34	31	35	48	43	34	39	40
Female								
Number of subjects	108	21	128	56	45	34	281	111
Age (years)								
Mean	39	37	40	43	42	45	41	42
Median	39	38	40	42	41	45	40	43
Total								
Number of subjects	149	27	144	72	102	42	395	141
Age (years)								
Mean	38	36	41	43	43	43	41	42
Median	38	35	40	44	42	44	40	42
Range	.	.	.	.	.	.	19—64	23—62
SD	.	.	.	.	.	.	11.2	10.9

[a] A = subjects from an insurance company, B = subjects from an airline and a post office, C = subjects from three daily newspapers.

3. METHODS

3.1 Subjective symtoms and discomforts.

The questionnaire, concerning subjective symtoms and discomfort, was collected on the same day as the orthoptist conducted the special eye examination.

The ophthalmological examinations, performed at specialist receptions, took place on another day.

The questionnaire included questions concerning the occurrence, frequency and intensity of ocular discomforts (smarting, itching gritty feeling, aches,sensitivity to light, redness, tearness and dryness) and headache. The frequency and intensity of pain or discomfort from muscles and the skeleton (hands, forearms, elbows, upper arms, shoulders, neck and back) were charted, as well as the occurrence of skin rashes and disorders in the face, neck, hands and arms.

On the day of the special eye examinations, the subjects were asked to state the occurrence of eye discomfort and headache and also to specify the hours at which they did VDT work, did other work or took breaks.

Special discomfort indices were constructed for eye discomfort, for headache and musculo-skeletal discomforts. Symptom scores were obtained for the eight eye symptoms and for headache, by multiplying the frequency score (occasionally = 1, weekly = 2, daily = 3) by the intensity score (negligeble = 1, slight= 2, pronounced = 3) Asymptomatic subjects scored zero. The eye discomfort index was the sum of the eight various eye symptom scores. The symptom score for musculo-skeletal complaints was based on intensity scores alone.

3.2 Duration of working hours.

Numbers of years on VDT work and numbers of hours VDT work during the past year were obtained from the questionnaire. Total working hours and time spent on VDT work were noted by the employees themselves on the day of the special eye examination. On another occasion, 132 randomly selected VDT operators were followed during a normal working day by means of a special gaze direction instrument. A small IR transmitter was fitted on one side of the frames of spectacles (persons not normally wearing spectacles were given "hollow" glasses for the day of the experiment) in such a way that the time which the wearer spent looking at the screen was recorded on a special reciever on the top of the VDT . In this way it was possible to determine total working hours and the length of time spent looking at the VDT screen.

3.3 Lighting

The lighting conditions at each workplace were determined by objective measurments of illuminances, luminances and contrast reductions. Furthermore, the working visual distances were measured, and at the same time, subjective evaluations regarding reflexions at the work desk, VDT and keyboard were noted. Illuminances and luminances were measured while work was in progress, against horizontal and vertical surfaces at the workstations (manuscript, screen, keyboard) and horizontally in the offices (general lighting) using a Hagner universal light meter (model S2). Luminance was also measured in the paracentral part (referred to as "surround" in the figures and as "close surroundings" in the text) and periphery of the visual fields for each subject in the normal work position. The luminance measurements were recorded with the normal measuring angle (1°) of the instrument and also as luminance averages for a visual field restricted by a cone having an angle of 60°. The luminance on 0,5 $cm^2$of the screen surface was measured with a measuring angle of 1° and with the instrument positioned 0,5 m away from screen. A measuring angle of 60° gave a corresponding measuring field of 0,25 m^2, wich included the whole of the VDT screen and part of the workstation. Contrast reduction on the manuscript and keyboard was measured with a Brüel & Kjaer contrast meter (type 1100). Contrast (C), which is the relative difference in luminance between surfaces (L_1 and L_2), can be defined as $C=100(L_2-L_1)/L_1$ (percent).

Contrast reduction (CR) expresses the relation between observed contrast and the best possible contrast, CR =$100(1-C/C_{max})$ (percent)

3.4. Statistical methods.

The twosample t-test, the X2-test, and the Wilcoxon rank-sum-test were used in the statistical evaluations of differences between the various groups. In the figures, statistical significance is indicated as follows: *:p<0.05, **:p<0.01, ***:p<0.001.

Other statistical methods were also attempted, e g linear regression analysis. However these methods did not lead to any further conclusions based on the present material. The character and size of the material precluded attemps of multidimensional stratification.

4 RESULTS

4.1 Subjective symtoms and discomforts.

One or more of the eight eye discomfort symptoms were reported by 64% of the exposed employees as against 46% of the reference employees (p<0.001). The exposed group had a higher level of discomfort with reference to all sub-symptoms, and the differences were significant for five of them.

When the material was separated into enterprises the differences in discomfort were found in enterprises A and B but not in C. Enterprise C also differed from the others as to sex distribution. The relative numbers of men in the exposed group was 55% in enterprise C , compared to 29% for the whole material, 26% in enterprise A and 12% in enterprise B.

The frequency of discomfort was also found to vary between men and women, and this applied to both exposed and reference subjects. This was true of all sub-symptoms, the difference being statistically significant for four of them, and for eye discomfort in general. The sex related differences in discomfort could be the reason why no differences in discomfort could be established between exposed and reference subjects in enterprise C (Figs. 1A and 1B).

Various discomfort scores, separated whith reference to VDT and reference groups and to sex , are presented in Figs. 2A-C. As mentioned above, the exposed subjects had significantly higher eye discomfort scores than the reference subjects and the women had more discomfort than men (fig. 2A) . Musculo-skeletal discomfort scores were also found to be higher among women but - with no statistic significance- more among exposed subjects than reference subjects (Fig. 2B). There was a tendency of higher discomfort scores in proximal locations (shoulder, neck and back) among the exposed group compared to the referents. Women reported more headache and a higher frequency of skin disorders. than men (Fig 2C). Significant correlation coefficients were found between scores of eye discomfort, headache and musculo-skeletal discomfort.

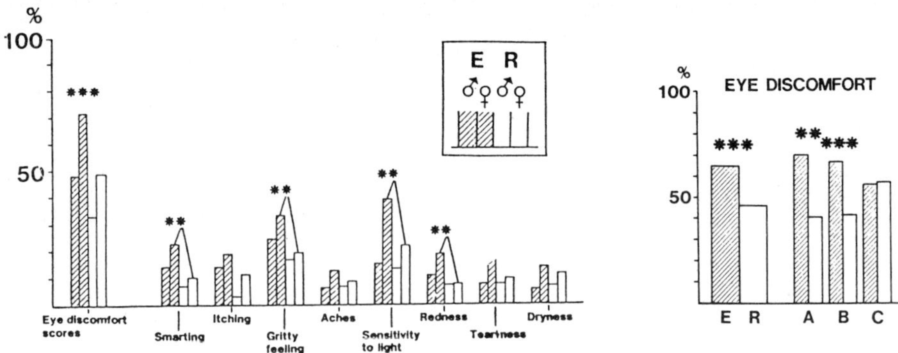

Figure 1 A. Frequency of eye discomfort (one or several eye symptoms) and the various eye symptoms in the VDT group (diagonally filled columns) and reference group, for the whole material.

Figure 1 B Frequency of eye discomfort in the material as a whole, for the VDT group (E), the reference group (R) and in the three different typs of enterprise. (A denotes the insurance company, B the airline and the post office and C the newspapers.)

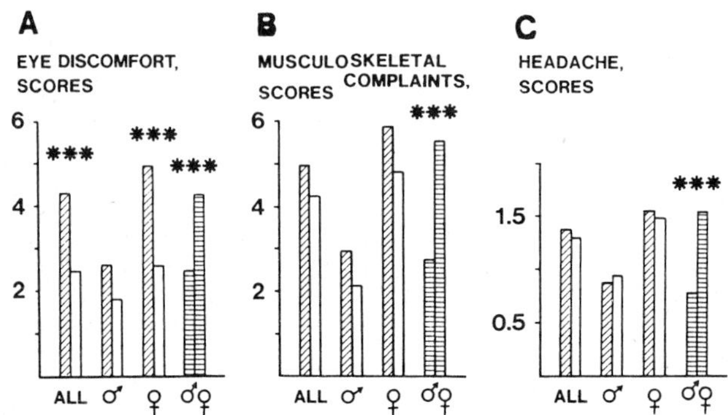

Figure 2 A-C . Discomfort scores for eye discomfort, musculo-skeletal complaints and headache for the VDT and reference groups (the whole material, men and women respectively) and for men and women.

4.2. Duration of working hours for the exposed groups.

Figs. 3A-D show the duration of working hours for all and female VDT operators related to sex and occurrence of subjective symptoms and discomforts. The subjects reporting eye discomfort were found to have worked somewhat longer than those without eye discomfort (n.s.) , but otherwise there were no observable differences worth mentioning (Fig 3A). More substantial differences were noted with regard to the number of hours per week devoted to VDT work (Fig 3B). Women worked slightly fewer hours per week than men (n.s.) and where eye discomfort and musculo-skeletal complaints were concerned, those with complaints worked longer hours at VDTs ($p<0.05$).

The measurements undertaken using the special gaze direction instrument (Figs. 3C) revealed several significant differences of interest. Subjects with eye discomfort and musculo-skeletal discomfort spent more time looking at the screen and had longer working hours on that particular day. Those reporting headache also had longer working hours than others.

4.2. Duration of hours for the exposed groups

Altogether the operators taking part in our investigation used eleven different VDTs, all with dark screens (bright characters on a dark background). Only the results obtained for the women at the insurance company and post office were used when comparing different screens. Thus the comparison included six different types of screen, marked K, L, M, N, O and P in Figs. 4 A-E. This comparison

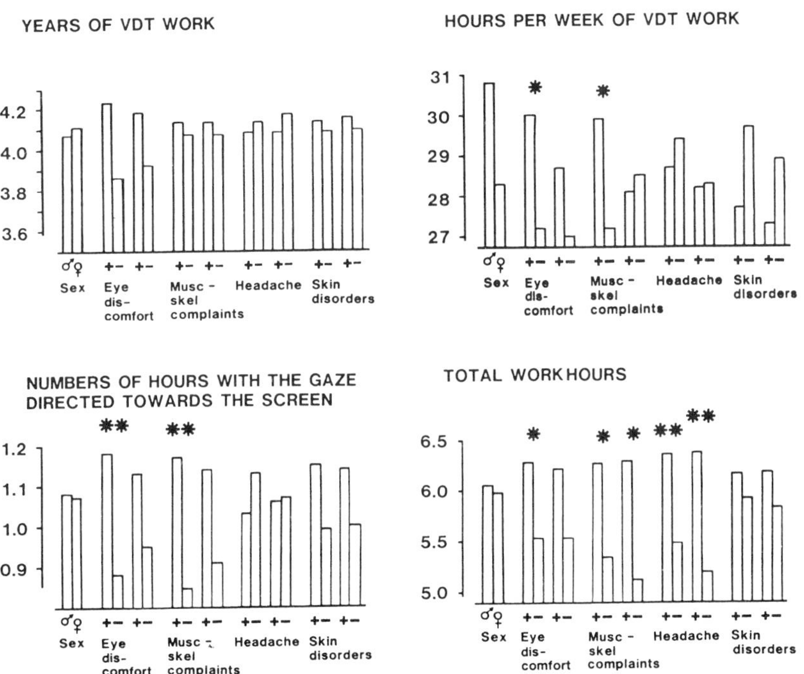

Figs. 3 A-D Duration of work with VDTs, and different measures of VDT work and total working time for exposed subjects, reporting (+) and not reporting (-) discomforts. The two left hand columns for each discomfort are for both men and women, and the two right hand columns are for women only.

revealed certain differences. Screen K, for example, is definitely more "discomfort prone" than screen P (p<0.001). but there are other differences as well (for example, screens K and L are associated with more discomforts than screens O and P.

In determining the duration of working hours (Figs 4 D,E), both shorter total working hours and shorter duration of gaze at the screen were recorded for screen P compared with the material as a whole (both p<0.001). The differences between certain screens as regards the degree of discomfort may be related to variations in the durations of working hours.

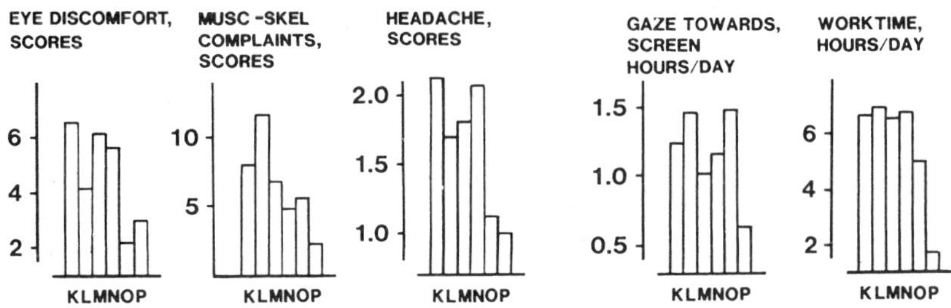

Figs. 4 A-C. Eye discomfort, musculo-skeletal complaints, and headache at the different enterprises, (denotes K,L,M,N,O and P) for the woman at the insurance company and the post office.

Figs 4 D and E. The hours per day with the gaze directed towards the screen, and the total working hours per day at the different enterprises. The figures refer to a sub-group, viz 132 randomly selected VDT operators from the same enterprises as in Figs. 4A-C.

4.3. Lighting

As regards the lighting factors investigated, there were clear differences between the exposed and reference groups. The VDT operators had both lower room illuminances and lower illuminances on the manuscript (Fig 5A and B). Luminances was lower on the manuscripts and in the close surroundings (Figs 5 C,D). The luminance ratios between the manuscript and the close surroundings and the contrast reduction on the manuscript were considerably higher among the exposed subjects than among the referents (Figs 5 E,F).

There were also differences in lighting between the men's and women's workstations, although these differences were conspicuous than those between the exposed and reference subjects. Statistically significant differences were only found regard to manuscript illuminance and luminance; lower values were recorded for the women.

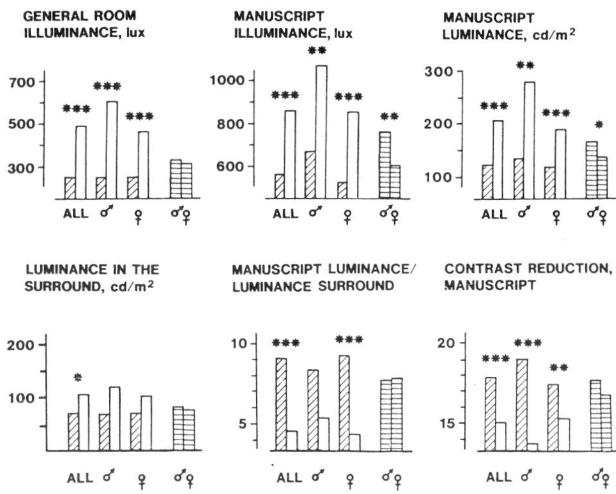

Figs 5 A-F. General room illuminance, manuscript illuminance and luminance, surround luminance, ratio between the luminance on the manuscript and the surround, and contrast reduction on the manuscript for the VDT group, the reference group and for men and women.

There were high correlation coefficients between the various lighting factors, but not such association could be established between the lighting factors and the reported subjective discomfort.

It is a well known fact that large luminance ratios between adjoining areas within the working field of vision can generate what is termed contrast glare. Luminance ratios in the region of 3:1 have been stated as a guidance for a good visual environment. The diagram in figure 6 has been made to include (for female VDT operators) eye discomfort scores versus luminance ratios for manuscript : screen(solid line), manuscript: close surroundings(broken line) and for close surroundings: periphery(dotted line). The data, as presented in the figure, suggest that the eye discomfort increases with larger luminance ratios. This findings applies particulary to the manuscript : screen luminance ratio (solid line)

The eye discomfort score for a luminance ratio of 20:1 differs from the other values in that curve ($p<0,05$). It is also worth noting that screen luminance was significantly negative correlated with the various luminance ratios. This fact indicates that the cause of the large luminance ratios may be found in the low-luminance, dark VDT screens.

It is also worth noting that the use of screenfilters (i.e. dark micromeshfilters) is unfavourable as regards the luminance and furthermore can detoriate the image quality on the screen. The subjects using screen filters in this study had slightly higher frequence of eye discomfort than the subjects not using screenfilters.

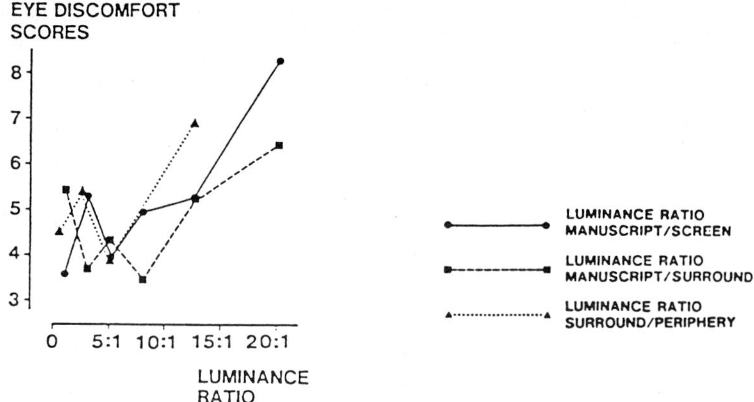

Fig 6. Relationship between the luminans ratios and eye discomfort for the women in the exposed group.

4.4. Visual distance

Measured distances between the eyes and various visual objects showed that female VDT operators worked at shorter distances than their male colleagues, in relation to both screen, keyboard and manuscript(fig 7 A,B).

Furthermore, exposed women were found to be working with the manuscript further away (about 8 cm mean) than women in the referece group. There was a clear correlation between the various visual distances, but no relation could be established with relevant subjective discomforts (eye discomfort, musculo.skeletal complaints, headache).

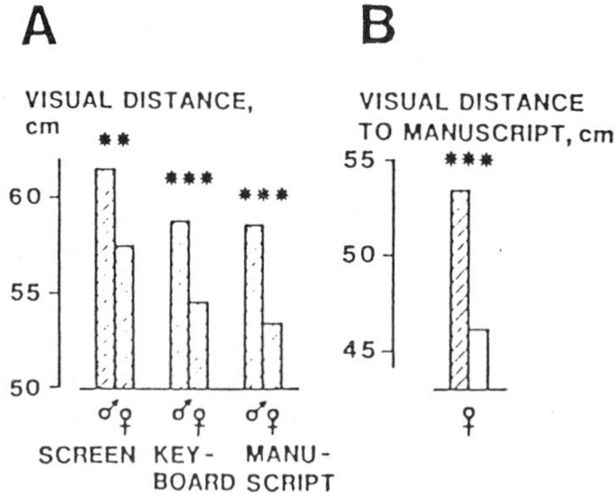

Figure 7. Visual distance to the screen,the keyboard and the manuscript for the men and women in the exposed group(A) and the visual distance to the manuscript for the women in the exposed (diagonally scriped column) and reference (unscriped column) groups(B). (** p>0,01, *** p>0,001).

5. DISCUSSION

The results in our investigation show that the VDT operators reported more eye discomforts than the controls. The VDT operators also noted a tendency of increasing discomforts in the shoulders, neck and back compared to the controls. There were no differences as to discomforts in the hands, forearms or elbows between the VDT operatoprs and the controls. Furthermore, the women reported more dicomforts than the men, regardless of VDT work or not.

The total working time per day as well as the duration of VDT work appear in our study to be related to the subjectively reported discomforts. When the investigated persons were separated into subgroups regarding workplace, type of work and VDT make, we found differences which appeared to be related to variations in work duration.

The four types of discomforts which we investigated were correlated, i e subjects reporting visual discomforts also tended to report headache and/or musculoskeletal discomforts. A number of possible explanations to these correlations are feasible, e g relations due to the work duration. It is also possible that some suboptimal reading conditions on the display, while leading to visual discomforts, may also lead to musculoskeletal discomforts when the subject attempts to compensate for the reading conditions.

There were clear differences at the lighting factors between the exposed and reference group. The VDT operators had both lower room illuminances and lower illuminances on the manuscript. The luminance ratios between the manuscript and the close surroundings and the contrast reduction on the manuscript were considerably higher among the exposed subjects than among the referents.

There were also differences in lighting between the men's and women's workstation, although these differences were less conspicuous than those between the exposed and reference subjects.

It is also worth noting that subjects using screen filters in this study had slightly higher frequence of eye discomfort than the subjects not using screenfilters.

The greater the luminance ratios in the working field of vision, the greater the eye discomfort experienced by the subjects. This finding makes it worth emphasizing once again that the large luminance ratios are partly attributable to the dark screens. The introduction of bright screens, (positive polarity) therefore, might possibly improve the situation, i.e., reduce the occurrence of eye discomfort.

WORK WITH DISPLAY UNITS 86
B. Knave and P.-G. Wideböck (eds.)

RECENT RESULTS ON THE ILLUMINATION OF VDU AND CAD WORKSTATIONS

Roll, K.-F. *

It is shown by several investigations and fieldtests, that two features of good illumination are of major importance for the work at VDU- and CAD-workstations: to avoid disturbing reflections from the environment on the screen and to design a well-ballanced luminance-distribution in the visual field. The one means shielding luminairs above an angle to the vertical of 50 degrees to a luminance limit of 200 cd/m², the other for example an illumination with an indirect component. The luminance pattern of the last on the ceiling should not show bright patches with more than 400 cd/m². For CAD-workstations, especially with storage-tubes, special requirements are neccessary.

1. INTRODUCTION

So much research has been carried out and so much published on the subject of lighting at places of work where visual display units are used (abbreviated in the following to VDU workstations) that there should by now really be a consensus of opinion among planers and users about the criteria for such lighting. But unfortunately this is not the case, at least not to the degree which might have been expected. Quite contradictory views are still frequnetly expressed in the technical press, in company brochures and in discussions with planers and other experts. Against this background, the following remarks are intended to outline the present state of knowledge and our investigations in this field, backed as it now is by wide-ranging experience, and to derive from this a basis for standardization and rules for planers.

2. LIGHTING REQUIREMENTS AT VDU WORKSTATIONS

2.1 Limiting values of the luminance of sources of disturbing light

The most frequent type of visual disturbance occurring with VDU's is the superimposition on the information on the screen of annoying reflections from surfaces with too great a luminance. These reflections, on the one hand, reduce contrast and, on the other, generate a sensation of disturbance in the person using the VDU. Figure 1 shows the result of a series of our investigations with different types of VDU [1]. It shows the relationship between the luminance of the source of disturbing light and the number of satisfied users, divided up according to type of VDU and type of lighting. In Figure 1, VDU 1 means a screen with light characters on a dark background, and untreated surface, VDU 2 a screen with

*) Siemens AG, Installation Equipment, Lighting Systems and Automotive Electronic Components Division, Technical Research Division, Postbox 1520, D-8225 Traunreut, FRG

dark characters against a light background, and untreated surface; VDU 3 the same screen as with VDU 2 except that the surface has been etched, i.e. given an anti-reflection treatment. The three types of VDU were assessed under direct and indirect lighting, with the horizontal illuminance at the workstation always 500 lx.

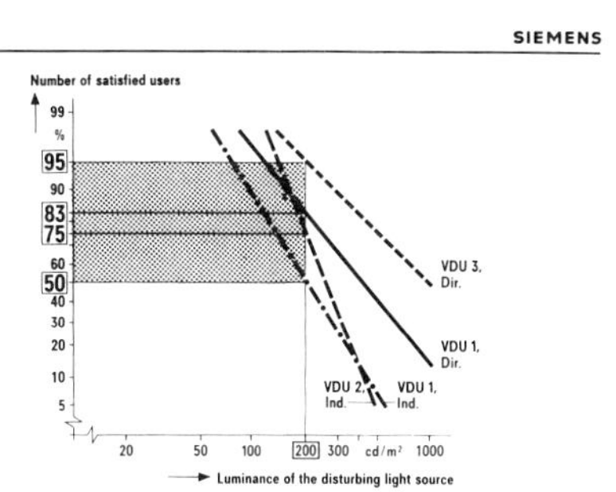

FIGURE 1
Upper luminance limit
L = 200 cd/m^2

According to a basic rule of ergonomics, achieving high-degree acceptance means, if possible, satisfying 95 % of users. Given a favourable type of lighting (direct lighting) and a screen that has undergone anti-reflection treatment, with dark characters displayed on a light background, this condition can be met with a maximum luminance of 200 cd/m^2. However, this condition **cannot** be met with the other types of lighting and types of screen investigated here. In these cases, the extraneous disturbing luminance would have to be kept to a lower level. For example, with VDU 1 and indirect lighting, the maximum permissible luminance level would be just 80 cd/m^2.

But Figure 1 also enables us to draw other conclusions as well:

- the alleged advantages of indirect lighting do not become apparent in the form of a higher permissible luminance, quite the opposite in fact!

- screens with dark characters displayed against a light background do possess advantages as regards sensitivity to reflections but they still do not provide the intended result.

- screens which have been given anti-reflection treatment (VDU 3) permit higher disturbing luminance.

From all this we may conclude that to achieve a satisfactory result the system **USER-LIGHTING-SCREEN** has to be optimized:

User: - as high a degree of acceptance as possible, i.e. at least 50 % satisfied users (i.e. L (max) between 200 cd/m^2 and 1,000 cd/m^2), but preferably 95 % (i.e. L(max) between 80 cd/m^2 and 200 cd/m^2,

Lighting - Meeting all important lighting quality criteria such as pleasant luminance distribution, balanced shadowiness, functionally appropiate level of lighting,

- Good balance between technical feasibility and economy, e.g. using high-efficiency luminaires,

- Possibility of using different lighting systems, e.g. direct lighting, direct/indirect lighting, indirect lighting.

Screen - Suitable anti-reflection treatment with discernibility loss kept as low as possible.

- Use of non-flicker screen with dark characters against a light background.

With a view to optimizing these main influencing factors, it would seem a sensible compromise to limit the luminance reflected on the screen to values of L $\leq$ 200 cd/m^2 [1, 9, 10, 11].

2.2 Assessing the indirect lighting component at VDU workstations

In a series of systematic experiments [1, 2, 11, 12], luminance patterns in the office interior were investigated, with particular reference to the indirect component and its influence on both conventional office work and work at a VDU.

Figure 2 shows how the luminance pattern in the room as a whole and at the ceiling was assessed by a group of observers under reproducible conditions. With direct lighting, it is felt that the lower part of the room is emphasized somewhat more strongly and there is a tendency to regard the ceiling as somewhat too dark, whereas in the case of direct lighting with an **indirect component** and a mean ceiling luminance of around 200 cd/m^2, luminance conditions are assessed as very well-balanced. Given purely indirect lighting with a rated illuminance of 500 lx (the same for all four installations), ceiling luminances of up to 1300 cd/m^2 occur, in the case of a uneven illumination of the ceiling. The top part of the room as a whole is regarded as over-emphasized and the ceiling is assessed as too bright.

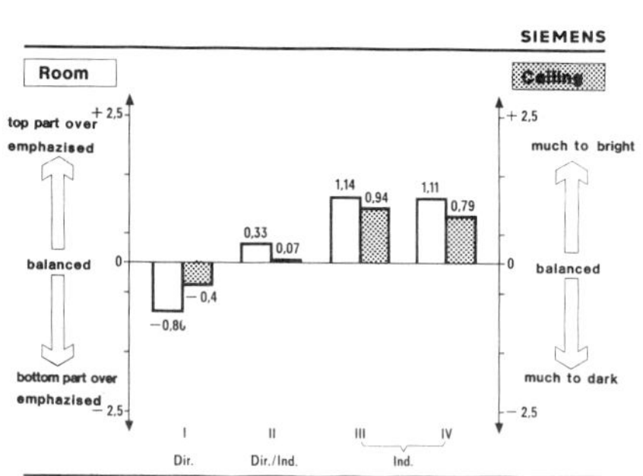

FIGURE 2

Assessmant of luminesity: Room/ceiling

If all four of these lighting installations are judged in relation to conventional office work, all are initially more or less equal in the overall assessment [11].

The picture changes, however, if we turn to work at VDU workstations. A group of observers were, for example, asked to assess the reflections on the screen (light characters on a dark background). The best assessmant was given to the direct lighting, limited to 200 cd/m^2 at $\gamma \geqq 50^{\circ}$.

With all three other types of lighting, reflections on the screen were always perceived, but it was only with purely indirect lighting that they were regarded as disturbing, as Figure 3 shows.

A repetition of this experiment with a screen displaying dark characters against a light background (cf. Figure 4) and with direct and direct/indirect lighting reveals considerably less pronounced reflections, and these are assessed accordingly.

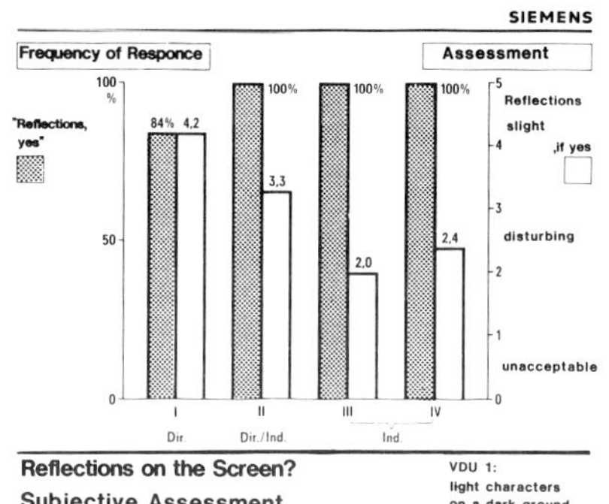

FIGURE 3

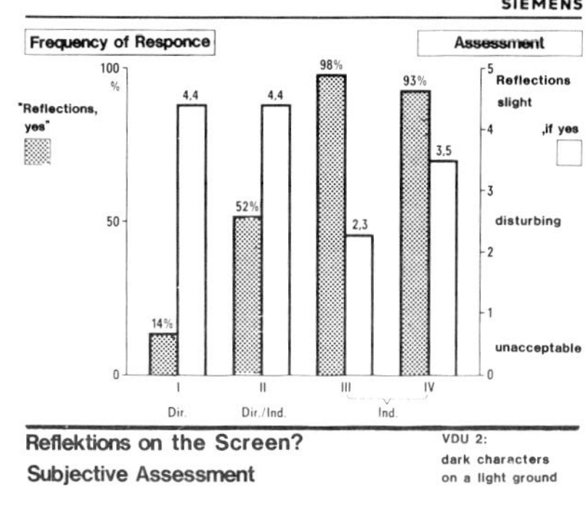

FIGURE 4

In contrast, when the room has exclusively indirect lighting, reflections make themselves strongly felt and, given the uneven workstation-oriented indirect lighting III with peak luminance values at the ceiling of over 1300 cd/m^2, are regarded as disturbing.

Finally the test persons were asked to give their overall assessment as to the suitability of these installations for work at the VDU. Figure 5 shows the findings.
By far the best results were achieved by Systems I and II (direct and direct/indirect lighting), which were limited to luminances of under 200 cd/m^2. The significantly worst assessment was given to the uneven, workstation- oriented indirect lighting III. Depending on the situation, a screen displaying dark characters against a light background can have slight advantages.

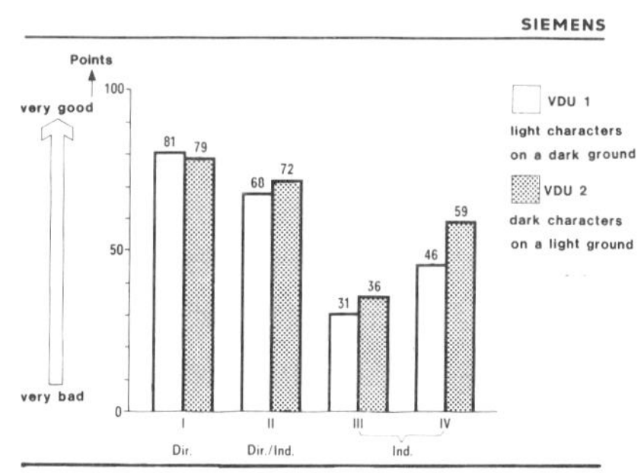

FIGURE 5

Finally overall assessment for screen activities

2.3 Critical angle of radiation

From the geometry of the screen (e.g. screen diagonal, screen height, radius of curvature of the screen) an the ergonomically most favourable position of observer and screen [3, 4] we can derive a certain critical angle γc of the light radiated from luminaires (Figure 6). From this critical angle on, the mean luminance of the luminaires or reflecting surfaces should be restricted to values under 200 cd/m^2, since reflections are then no longer regarded as disturbing, as explained above.

For most of the VDU's on the market, a critical angle of radiation $\gamma c = 50^{\circ}$ is recommended (Figure 7). Only then is an ergonomically favourable positioning of the VDU possible, with positive effects on both the employee's well-being (physiologically favourable working posture possible) and on working performance (much lower error rate [5,4]).

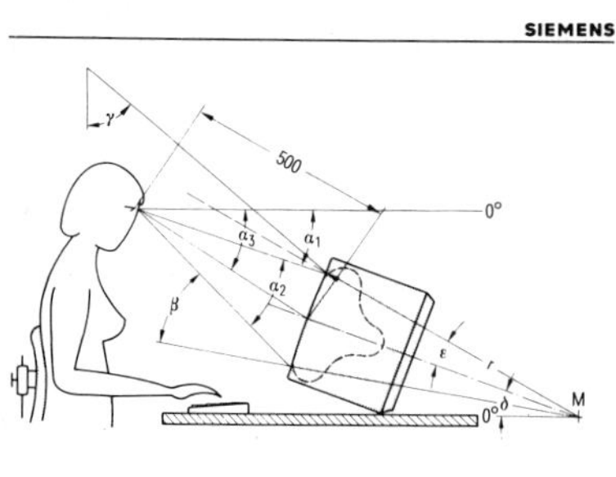

FIGURE 6

Relation of angles at VDU-workplaces

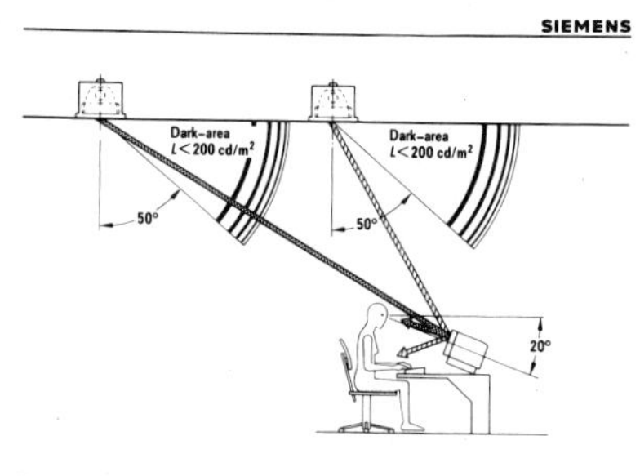

FIGURE 7

Effects of special VDU-specular reflector luminaires

3. SPECIAL REQUIREMENTS AT CAD WORKSTATIONS

The VDU's we have been dealing with so far in our investigations have been ones in which the information consists primarily of alphanumeric characters and simple graphics. In comparison, the criteria for sources of disturbing light at CAD (computer-aided design) workstations are considerably stricter.

From the lighting technology point of view is to be differentiated CAD workstations with what's called a storage tube, on which the fine lines of the construction drawing are presented with much less contrast than is the case with the screens mentioned above. Much greater contrast, though usually combined with the disadvantage of somewhat lower resolution, is offered by the so-called raster screens at CAD workstations which function with the usual refresh memory. Here, too, extremely fine lines and details have to be distinguished, so that basically the task is just as difficult as with storage tubes.

Investigations [6] recommend a minimum contrast of 3:1 for work at a VDU, but ratios between 6:1 and 10:1 are preferable. Figure 8 shows the curves indicating maximum possible character contrast on two selected screens of this kind. This reveals that, given the horizontal illuminance of 500 lx normally recommended for VDU's, the contrast achieved with a **storage tube** is just 3:1. Higher contrast values are only achieved with lower illuminance - infact optimum contrast ratios of over 6:1 only with horizontal illuminance of less than 100 lx.

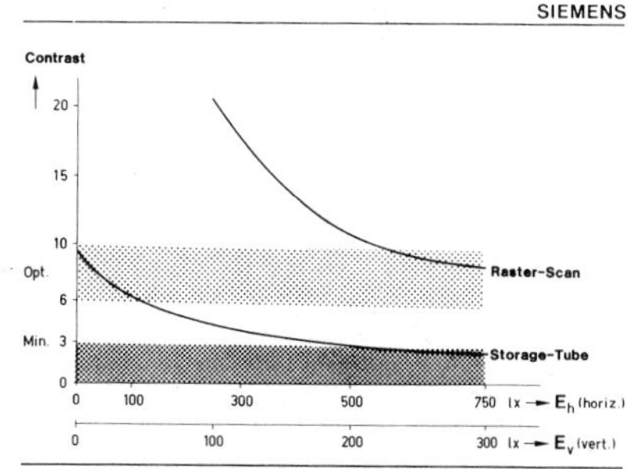

FIGURE 8

Max. character contrast at typical CAD-workstations

The conclusion to be drawn from this is that such systems can definitely not be integrated into normal office premises. Special lighting solutions are required. Experiments and measurements in the Siemens lighting laboratory have shown that a satisfactory solution can be achieved by a special positioning of luminaires in relation to the workstation and by specific switching measures.

The aim must be to limit the **vertical** illuminance E_V to values of below 40 lx in order to achieve good contrast on the screen (cf. Figure 8). On the other hand, the **horizontal** illuminance should be between 200 and 300 lx, to permit satisfactory reading of the passive indicators (e.g. menu, tablet, keyboard, original). Illuminance distribution of this kind could be effected by specular louver luminaires mounted above and to the side of the workstation, with the front edge of the luminaire being more or less aligned with the front edge of the screen in order to keep extraneous light and the vertical illuminance on the screen as low as possible [7].

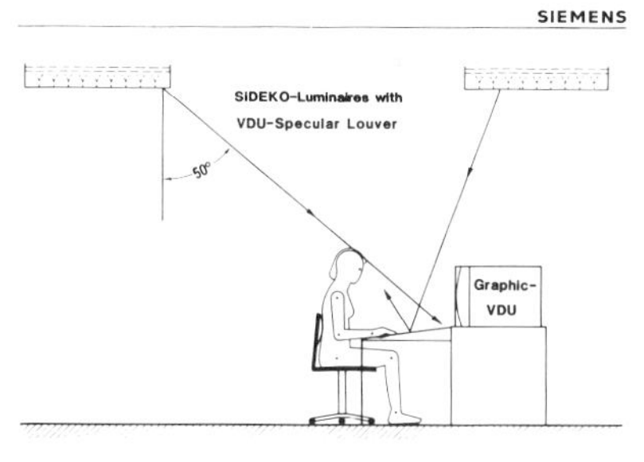

FIGURE 9 a

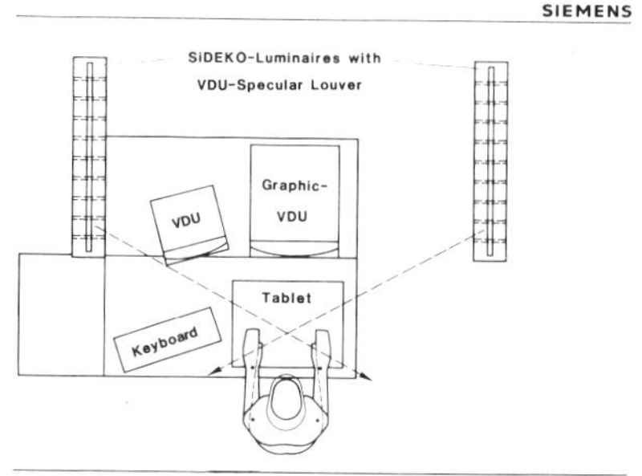

FIGURE 9 b

Arrangement of luminaires for graphic VDU-workplaces with storage-tubes

The latter consideration also applies to the positioning of the luminaires behind the workstation (cf. Figure 9a, b). Through the use of special specular louvers (for $\gamma \geq 50^{\circ}$, $L \leq 200$ cd/m²), disturbing reflections are avoided. In many cases, a facility for individual dimming of the lighting will be an advantage, and given the present state of the art, this can be achieved with relatively little technical effort [8].

From these remarks it is clear that for the lighting of CAD workstations with storage tubes, only purely direct lighting systems should be used, since the indirect component would reduce contrast far too much.

Somewhat less critical are the more modern screens with **raster scan,** which will presumably be used more frequently in future. Among other things they have a much higher character contrast (cf. Figure 8), although this can be reduced quite considerably as a result of much lower stroke width. In addition, these screens usually have relatively large diagonale making it essential to limit the angle of the light radiated by the luminaires to $\gamma_c = 50^{\circ}$.

Often, for organizational, system-related and also lighting-related reasons, several different - frequently in fact very different - types of CAD facility are brought together in CAD pools. In such pools, it is recommended that in addition to the shielding conditions mentioned above, it should be possible for the lighting to be dimmed in zones, making it easier to cater for individual requirements. As to the type of lighting here, the same sort of criteria apply as for conventional VDU's.

4. CONCLUSIONS

As mentioned at the beginning, the present state of the art in this field is documented by numerous investigations, publications and experiences. But the formulation of standards and rules is only just beginning. From the investigations mentioned you can only draw the conclusion that in standards and rules for normal situations in lighting for VDU workstations, in which bright surfaces or the luminaires themselves can cause reflections on the screen, luminance values should be restricted, with 200 cd/m^2 being a mean value, the upper limit for the luminance of surfaces of the room should be 400 cd/m^2. In addition, the mean luminance of the luminaires in the planes perpendicular and parallel to the fluorescent lamp under a critical angle of light radiation of 50° should be limited to this value of 200 cd/m^2. Since several years, on the market are various lighting systems available, which will fulfil these lighting conditions with great success.

REFERENCES

[1] Leibig, J.; Roll, K.-F., Acceptable luminances reflected on VDU - screens in relation to the typ of contrast and illumination. CIE 20th session Amsterdam 31.8.-8.9.1983, Vol. 2 Reports, P.No. 313p. 1-4, CIE-Paris 1983, France

[2] Breitfuß, W.; Hentschel, H.-J.; Leibig, J.; Pusch, R., Neue Lichtatmosphäre im Büro - Direkt-Indirektbeleuchtung und ihre Bewertung
Licht 34 (1982), Heft 6, S. 366-372, München, FRG

[3] Koch, H., Ergonomische Grenzwerte für die Anordnung von Bildschirmen. Feinwerktechnik und Meßtechnik, 89. Jahrgang, Heft 3, April 1981, S. 105-110, München, FRG

[4] Hartmann, E.; Leibig, J.; Roll, K.-F., Optimale Sehbedingungen am Bildschirmarbeitsplatz I, II, III. Licht 35 (1983), Heft 7/8, S. 442-446, Heft 9, S. 507-510, Heft 10, S.564-570, München, FRG

[5] Schmidtke, H., Lehrbuch der Ergonomie, Betriebsmittelgestaltung. Carl Hanser Verlag München, Wien 1981

[6] Kokoschka, S.; Bodmann, H.W., Kontrast und Beleuchtungsniveau am Bildschirmarbeitsplatz Publikation CIE Nr. 50 (1980), Paris, France

[7] Grob, R.; Roll, K.-F., Gestalten der Sehbedingungen an Arbeitsplatz-Beispielen aus der Elektroindustrie. Refa Nachrichten 5 (1984) Heft 5, S. 17 - 23, Darmstadt, FRG

[8] Kerscher, M.; Schwarz, M., Elektronik und Leuchtstofflampen Siemens-Elektrodienst 25 (1983) Heft 1, S. 23, Erlangen, FRG
[9] Bjoerset, H.-H., Lighting of VDU Workplaces, EFI-Trontheim (1982), Forschungsbericht-Nr.: 2866, Norway
[10] Bjoerset, H.-H., Workplaces with VDU's, ergonomics, Vision lighting conditions, EFI-Trontheim (1985), Forschungsbericht-Nr.: 3219, Norway
[11] Leibig, J.; Roll, K.-F., Leuchtdichteoptimierung und ihre Auswirkung auf Arbeitsplätze und Bildschirmgeräte, Humane Produktion, humane Arbeitsplätze 7 (1985) Heft 9, S.10-14, Dreieich-Sprendlingen, FRG
[12] Hentschel, H.-J., The indirect lighting component and comfortable luminance patterns in interiors, CIE 20th session Amsterdam 31.8.-8.9.1983, Vol. 1 Papers, P.No. D 308 p. 1-4, CIE-Paris 1983, France

WORK WITH DISPLAY UNITS 86
B. Knave and P.-G. Widebäck (eds.)

NON-VISUAL EFFECTS OF VISUAL SURROUNDINGS*

Rikard KüLLER

Environmental Psychology Unit
School of Architecture, Lund Institute of Technology
Box 118, S-221 00 Lund, Sweden

In work with display units the surrounding visual environment takes on importance in the following respects: visual performance; visual fatigue; central nervous activation; influence on diurnal bio-rhythm. The focus in the present paper is on the last two questions. One line of investigation carried out at the Environmental Psychology Laboratory, concerns the influence of colour and visual complexity on EEG, EKG and subjective mood. The second line, which consists of field studies, deals with the effect of various types of fluorescent light on melatonin, cortisol and subjective mood. It is argued that the non-visual effects, although generally neglected, may be of great importance for health and well-being in long term work with display units.

1. INTRODUCTION

The visual display unit (VDU) is often introduced into an environment which originally was not designed with this type of work in mind. Sometimes the VDU is simply placed at the existing desk, at other times a special table and chair are provided. Occasionally nearby light sources might be adjusted or exchanged, and windows supplied with special curtains. The result becomes a compromise, where the legitimate requirements of conventional work - a well lit desk and stimulating visual surroundings, including a nice view through the window - will be regarded by the VDU-personnel with suspicion.

Even newly designed VDU-environments often end up as an unsuccessful compromise between opposing requirements, which points to the insecurity that exists today amongst those who design for VDU. This is not astonishing, because there is so much going on not only in product development but also in basic ergonomic and environmental health research.

Recently, there has been a growing awareness of the adverse health effects that might result from the intense use of VDU. Problems like visual fatigue, eye strain, muscular discomfort, and skin disorders, seem to be fairly well established (1), while damage of a more serious kind, presumably caused by low frequency electrostatic and electromagnetic fields is only suspected. This has led to requirements to diminish the use of VDU wherever possible. In Sweden, pregnant women are advised not to work with VDU, and recent work and health legislation also gives them a right to refuse this kind of work. There are also demands for a general hour-per-day limit for VDU-work.

There are still other aspects of the VDU-environment which have until now received very little attention. I am referring to so called non-visual effects of two kinds, the influence of indoor light on the diurnal rhythm, and

* The research presented in this paper was supported by the Swedish Council for Building Research and the Swedish Work Environment Fund.

reticular activation caused by the visual surroundings. Symptoms such as headaches, tiredness, and general stress have been shown to be attributed to work in inappropriate lighting or windowless environments. This can in turn result in increased absenteeism, and worse work performance and might, in the longer run, even affect the general health status of specially exposed groups in environments where the conditions are unfavourable.

2. INFLUENCE OF LIGHT ON THE DIURNAL RHYTHM

When light penetrates the eye, impulses are transmitted not only to the various visual areas of the brain, but also to other parts of the central nervous system. The most conspicuous outcome is the complex variations of wakefulness and sleep usually called the diurnal rhythm. It seems the synthesis of melatonin in the pineal gland holds a central position in mediating the effects of ocular light.

Melatonin, which is popularly known as a sleep hormone, is mostly produced during night, while daylight will suppress its production more or less completely. Melatonin in its turn will affect both the hypothalamus and the pituitary gland. This means daylight entering the eye will control many of the highly complex endocrine and autonomic processes taking place in the human body. The pineal gland will also produce more melatonin during the winter than the summer. This is one of the reasons why people from the northern latitudes are more active during the summer when there is more daylight.

Numerous studies show that the amount and quality of light will influence body metabolism and temperature, hormone secretion, ovulation and a variety of other basic functions of the human organism (2, 3, for a review see 4). There is also some evidence relating melatonin to psychiatric disorders, e.g. certain types of depression (5). Results from amongst others Hollwich et al (6), Stone et al (7), and Sugimoto and Ikeda (8), indicate that artificial light might be more stressful to the human organism than natural daylight.

In an experiment carried out by Erikson and Küller (9, see also 10), two offices at a large factory in central Sweden were supplied with different types of fluorescent lighting (white and daylight type) and the health conditions of the personnel studied from November until June. Measurements included subjective reports of emotions and wellbeing as well as the analysis of the hormones melatonin and cortisol.

The results clearly showed that the personnel working in fluorescent light of the daylight type, complained less of visual fatigue (figure 1). By using daylight tubes, it was also possible to suppress the production of melatonin during the winter. These persons also felt slightly more stimulated. However, this improvement was temporary, and it is therefore difficult to draw any definite conclusions about which light should be preferred. While the persons working under the conventional light tubes showed very little variation in mood between summer and winter there was a clear shift for the other group, from more positive moods in December to more negative moods in June.

Another salient finding was that independent of the type of artificial illumination, people working close to a window produced more of the stress hormone cortisol in summer than in winter. The reverse was true for persons sitting far away from the window.

In another recently completed study, Lindsten and Küller (11) investigated the reactions of four groups of school children, who were working in different classroom environments. Two of the classrooms had no windows, while one had windows on the longer wall and another carried a lantern situated centrally, in the ceiling.

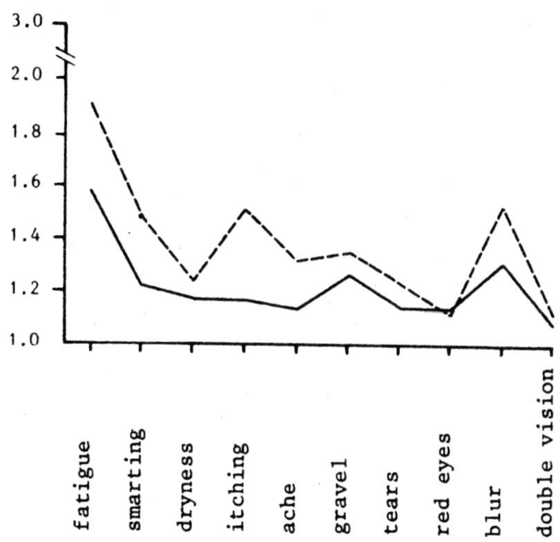

FIGURE 1
Prevalence of various kinds of visual deficiencies in December in two offices, one with daylight tubes (——) and the other with conventional fluorescent tubes (---) (after Küller; 10).

The cildren were studied for one year by means of behaviour observations. In addition, samples of urine cortisol were taken on four occasions during the fall, winter and spring.

The preliminary results revealed the existence of an annual rhythm in behaviour as well as in the secretion of cortisol. However, also the different lighting conditions seem to have an impact on these parameters. Those children in classrooms lacking natural daylight displayed a marked deviation from the normal annual patterns.

The results from the two studies mentioned above support the conclusion that in localities without windows hormone production becomes dependent on artificial lighting. This can eventually produce a disturbance or even a partial reversal in the annual biological rhythm.

3. RETICULAR ACTIVATION FROM VISUAL SURROUNDINGS

Light and colour might also affect the central nervous system through reticular activation. The reticular formation situated in the brain stem is reached by signals from all senses, i.e. not only vision, but hearing, smell, taste, touch, etc. The stronger the signal the higher the activation will be (12, 13). This might be recorded in terms of the electrical activity of the brain (EEG), heart beat (EKG) or subjective emotional mood. Glaring or flickering light especially in the long wave range causes severe activation and stress (4, 7, 14, 15, 16).

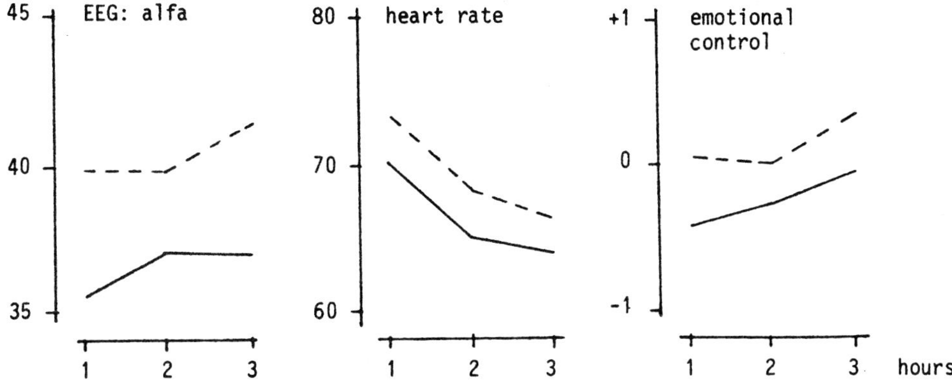

FIGURE 2
Average values in grey (---) and colourful (——) room after one, two and three hours (after Küller; 17, 18).

In a study by the present author, the subjects, one at a time, were placed in one of two rooms for a period of three hours. The one room was grey and sterile, the other extremely colourful and diversified. The two rooms differed in visual complexity and unity but not in pleasantness (17). Measurements taken during the first, second and third hour showed that the subjects generally experienced a lack of emotional control in the colourful room. The chaotic visual impact made them feel silent and subdued (figure 2).

Also, the alpha-component of the EEG was considerably lower in the colourful room than in the grey one as long as the subjects' eyes were open. This difference disappeared more or less when the subjects closed their eyes. The difference in alpha level between the subjects in the two rooms can be explained in terms of cortical arousal. In addition, stress reactions were more noticeable in men whan in women. Subjects' EKG were lower in the colourful room than in the grey one, which is in agreement with a hypothesis of Lacey et al (19), i.e. intense attention might be accompanied by cardiac deceleration. For introverts this effect was much more pronounced than for extroverts.

Thus, it was demonstrated that the colours and visual patterns of a room might have a profound physiological and psychological effect and this effect might vary between different groups of subjects. Our data also suggested that a room lacking in visual complexity might have a pronounced negative influence on performance and wellbeing.

4. CONCLUSION

In addition to affecting visual comfort and performance it has become clear that light and colour will influence man in a number of other ways. However, up to now few attempts have been made to relate these non-visual effects to the design process. Results from studies like those cited above are seldom considered by architects, interior decoraters or lighting consultants. Yet, there are some obvious consequences that might be drawn from these results in regard to the design of VDU-environments.

By using artificial light the delicate balance between sleep hormones on one side and stress hormones on the other, may become disturbed. In this respect some artificial light sources might be more damaging than others. This seems to be a question about intensity and spectral quality, amongst others. There is an obvious risk that in designing for VDU there will be less light and especially less daylight, left in the work environment.

The more advanced VDU environments also tend to become visually purified. Bright colours and patterns are generally avoided for performance reasons not only on the equipment as such, but also on desks and adjoining walls. When the visual complexity is thus reduced the work environment might become too monotonous and tend towards understimulation of the reticular activation system.

On these grounds the slogan 'One VDU on each desk!' may be seriously questioned. It is time to consider in detail where and when the VDU is really important or necessary, and how it should be brought into environmental design without causing unnecessary strain or hazard. We are at present trying to get some answers to these questions in a combined series of laboratory and field studies at the Environmental Psychology Unit in Lund.

REFERENCES

(1) Knave, B. et al. 1985. Bildskärmsarbete och hälsa. Läkartidningen, 82, 9, 689-712
(2) Hollwich, F. 1979. The influence of ocular light perception on metabolism in man and in animal. Springer-Verlag, New York, Heidelberg, Berlin
(3) Wurtman, R.J. 1975. The effect of light on the human body. Scientific American. 233, 1, 68-77
(4) Küller, R. 1981. Non-visual effects of light and colour. Annotated bibliography. Swedish Council for Building Research, Stockholm, Document D15
(5) Wetterberg, L. 1978. Melatonin in humans. Physiological and clinical studies. Journal of Neural Transmission. Suppl. 13, 289-310
(6) Hollwich, F., Dieckhues, B. & Schrameyer, B. 1977. Die Wirkung des natürlichen und künstlichen Lichtes über das Auge auf den Hormon- und Stoffwechselhaushalt des Menschen. Klin. Mbl. Augenheilk. 171, 98-104
(7) Stone, P.T. et al. 1974. Light, endocrine mechanisms and stress. Department of Human Sciences, Loughborough. LUTERG Report No. 156
(8) Sugimoto, S. & Ikeda, I. 1983. Illuminance and physiological load. Proc. CIE 20th Session, Vol. 1, D310, 1-4
(9) Erikson, C. & Küller, R. 1983. Non-visual effects of office lighting. Proc. CIE 20th Session, Vol. 2, D602, 1-4
(10) Küller, R. 1986. Hur inverkar belysningen på människan? Miljöpsykologisk forskning vid Sektion A. Ordo 2, 23-28
(11) Lindsten, C. & Küller, R. Health impact on school children from lack of natural daylight. Research project in progress. Lund Institute of Technology, Environmental Psychology Unit, Lund
(12) Lindsley, D.B. 1951. Emotion. In: S.S. Stevens (Ed). Handbook of experimental psychology. John Wiley & Sons, New York
(13) Moruzzi, G. & Magoun, H.W. 1949. Brain stem reticular formation and activation of the EEG. Eletroenceph. Clin. Neurophysiol. 1, 455-473
(14) Ali, M.R. 1972. Pattern of EEG recovery under photic stimulation by light of different colors. Electroenceph. Clin. Neurophysiol. 33, 332-335
(15) Brundrett, G.W. 1974. Human sensitivity to flicker. Lighting Research and Technology. 6, 3, 127-143
(16) Gerard, R.M. 1958. Differential effects of colored lights on psychophysiological functions. Doctoral dissertation. University of California, Los Angeles

(17) Küller. R. 1976. The use of space. Some physiological and philosophical aspects. In: P. Korosec-Serfaty (Ed). Appropriation of space. Proceedings of the Strasbourg Conference. CIACO, Louvain-la-Neuve, 154-163
(18) Küller, R. 1983. Ljus och färg påverkar hur vi mår. Forskning och Framsteg. 1, 35-39
(19) Lacey, J.I. et. al. 1963. The viceral level: Situational determinant and behavioral correlates of autonomic response patterns. In: P.H. Knapp (Ed). Expression of the emotions in man. International Universities Press, New York

WORK WITH DISPLAY UNITS 86
B. Knave and P.-G. Widebäck (eds.)

IMPROVING THE VDU WORKPLACE BY INTRODUCING A PHYSIOLOGICALLY OPTIMIZED BRIGHT-BACKGROUND SCREEN WITH DARK CHARACTERS: ADVANTAGES AND REQUIREMENTS

DIETER BAUER

Institut für Arbeitsphysiologie an der Universität Dortmund, Ardeystrasse 67, D-4600 Dortmund 1, FRG

It is possible to construct a light-background screen in such a way that any visual interferences are reduced below the psychophysical perception threshold. A list of critical parameters is developed, which guarantees a physiologically-matched screen design. If these recommendations areimplemented, a character quality is obtained which is superior to that of dark background screens: indeed, it is comparable to the quality of printed text. Reflexions of external light can bereduced to non-interfering levels at the real workplace only by using light-background screens, but not with dark background screens.

1. INTRODUCTION

Despite some technical improvements in recent years, many VDU workplaces still present visual problems to many users. Our goal has been to find out whether it is possible to develop a VDU which, with regard to vision, has the properties of a printed document. Thus, the starting point has been a critique of the conventional display which - when we began our work- was almost exclusively the 50 or 60 Hz-dark-background-display derived from TV-technology. The problems which are inherent in the dark background VDU still remain today; they may be classified into two categories :

A. Acuity problems and problems caused by transient adaptational states, resulting from the low luminance of the screen and
B. Inadequate suppression of external light reflexions (from clothes, lamps and windows), which may cause considerable masking of the screen text.

These inherent problems of the dark screen are being recognized by a growing number of manufacturers: the proportion of light-background screens on the market is growing; but not all of the constructions offered are satisfactory. The choice of a light background *per se* does not guarantee that the equipment will be visually adequate. Indeed, bright-background screens may be as poorly matched to the visual system as dark-background screens. A poor light-background construction may introduce additional visual problems that exceed the potential benefits. The question then is: what kind of light background screen should be introduced in order to materially improve the VDU situation? To identify the pitfalls and the benefits, let us consider the results of different experimental dark/light screen comparisons:

2. DEVELOPMENT OF THE PHYSIOLOGICALLY-OPTIMIZED BRIGHT-BACKGROUND SCREEN

2. 1. First experiment: advantage of the light background screen with dark characters measured with a conventional screen, when reflexions of external light are experimentally avoided.

In 1980 (Bauer et al.) a light/dark screen comparison was carried out in which observers had to recognize nonsense words while performing a dynamic oculomotor task.

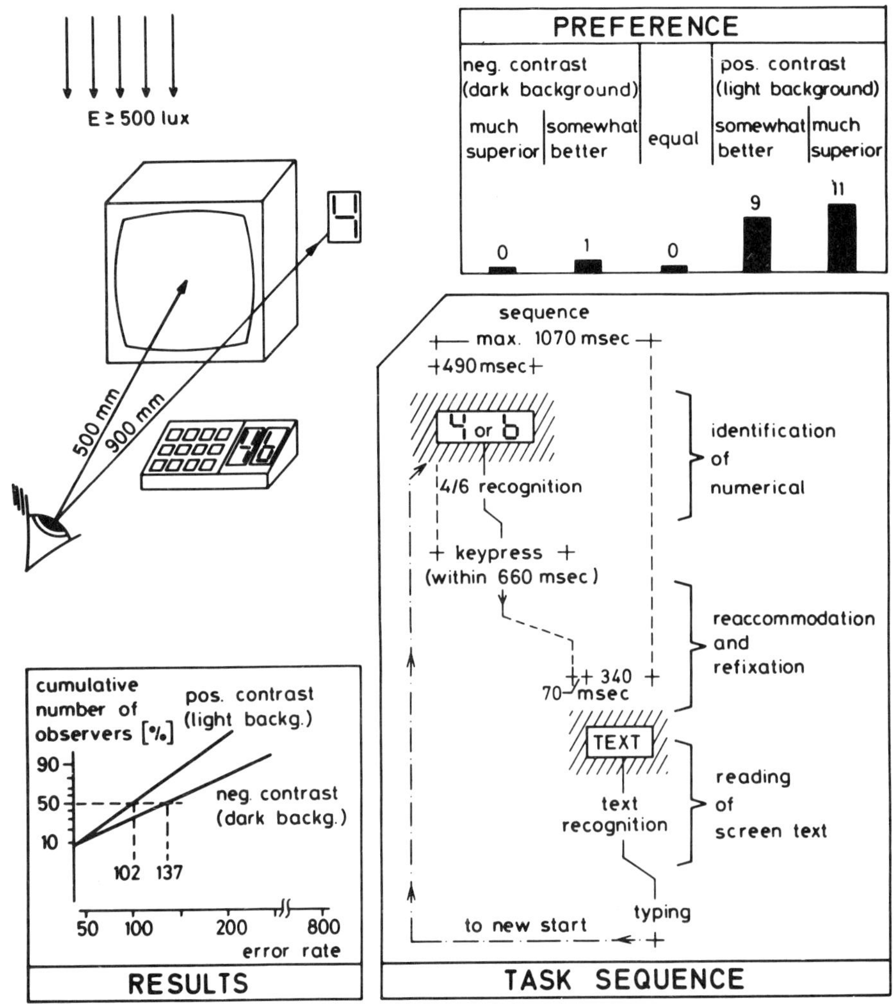

Fig. 1 Comparison of dark background (10 cd/m^2) and light background (80 cd/m^2) screens. The stroke width of dark and light strokes is visually equated. The text recognition task requires a change of fixation and accommodation within a fixed time interval.

First, the observer had to detect a number, which was either a 4 or 6, randomly selected. These were presented on a 7-segment display at a distance of 90 cm, placed about 30 degrees to the side of the center of the screen. After the observer responded by pressing the appropriate character (4 or 6) on the keyboard of the display, a four-letter nonsense word was presented at a random position near the center of the screen, and the observer responded by typing this word on the keyboard. The number of errors that the observer made was recorded. The results show that under conditions of high visual workload (low S/N ratio) the advantage of the light screen is measurable both in terms of improved performance: fewer errors (Fig 1), and more rapid completion of the task, and in terms of preference. It should be emphasized that only under the specific timing conditions - as outlined in Fig.1 - could a performance difference be measured. The differences in the error rate between the light- and the dark-background screen are shown at the bottom left for a presentation time of 340 msec.
When the workload was reduced - for instance by increasing the presentation time - no performance difference was found. However, the preference differences (see Fig.1, top) remained.
An analysis of the visual situation suggested that the observers' preference for the light screen may be caused by the increased visual resolution that is made possible by the light screen and by the reduction of transient adaptation: both will reduce the workload of the sensory system as a whole.

2. 2. Second experiment: advantage of the light screen with dark characters measured with high resolution equipment, when external reflexions are avoided experimentally

In 1983, an extension of the first experiment was carried out to answer the question of whether the preference results of the first experiment could be replicated with much improved screens: 1.) the resolution of the screen was increased by using a high resolution tube; thus, the sharpness of the characters was increased considerably, 2.) an enlarged character matrix of 14x12 pixels was used, thus it was ensured that the character strokes consisted visually of closed lines and not of single dots, 3.) care was taken to suppress visible spatio-temporal instabilities caused by technical instabilities (in particular by jitter); 4). high contrast (better than 10:1) between characters and background was maintained under the illumination conditions used.
In addition, we reduced the workload by using a visual screen-document-comparison task without the time pressure of the previous experiment; large changes of accommodation were avoided by keeping the screen and document at similar viewing distances.

From the results of the first experiment it was clear that performance differences could not be expected under the conditions of a reduced workload. Instead, visual comfort was evaluated according to four criteria, these were: readability, sharpness, flicker and contrast. The observers made ratings on a scale from 1 (for excellent) to 4 (for satisfactory). The mean ratings are given in Fig. 2. We see that the differences between the values for dark and light backgrounds are not very large. This may be explained partly by the use of totally inexperienced observers who had problems of maintaining stable criteria. Nevertheless, the comfort estimations for "sharpness" and "readability" were significantly higher for light backgrounds than for dark backgrounds. Judgements of flicker were significantly higher for bright backgrounds than for dark backgrounds. This was unexpected, since the frame repetition rate was as high as 85 Hz, which is substantially above most published values for flicker fusion frequency. When we analyzed the data of this experiment in more detail, we found that the quality of the bright screen was not strictly comparable with that of the dark screen: We found 3 unfavourably chosen parameters, which, in subsequent experiments, were shown to have negatively influenced the

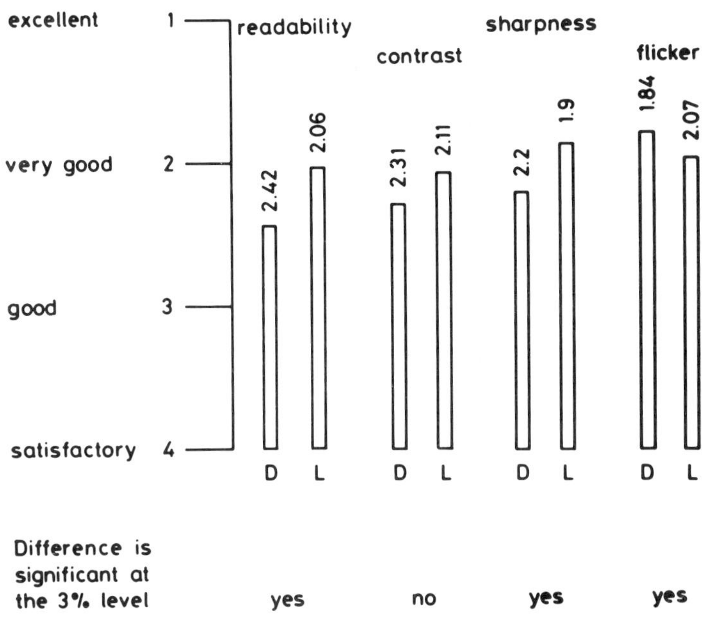

Fig. 2 Comfort/discomfort judgments with respect to readability, subjective character contast, character sharpness, suppression of screen flicker
D := Dark background screen
L := Light background screen

preference level for the light screen. Unfavourable viewing conditions were established 1.) by boundary flicker 2.) by a too bluish background colour and 3.) by the fact that the screen was seen as a light source (that is, in aperture mode).

Boundary flicker (cf. Bauer, 1984a) is a subjective movement of the border between the light screen and the light surround. It is perceived when the contrast between screen and surround is rather low. It may be a kind of sampling-interference between image repetition and oscillatory eye movements. The perception of boundary flicker may be enhanced by inducing stronger eye movements or eye movements with longer oscillatory phases. Natural eye movements with oscillatory phases occur if fixation changes in a text-document comparison task are being performed. We therefore suggest that boundary flicker had indeed increased the flicker ratings for the light screen in the second experiment.

Various methods to eliminate boundary flicker for "fast" and for "slow" phosphors are indicated on the right side of Fig.3 .

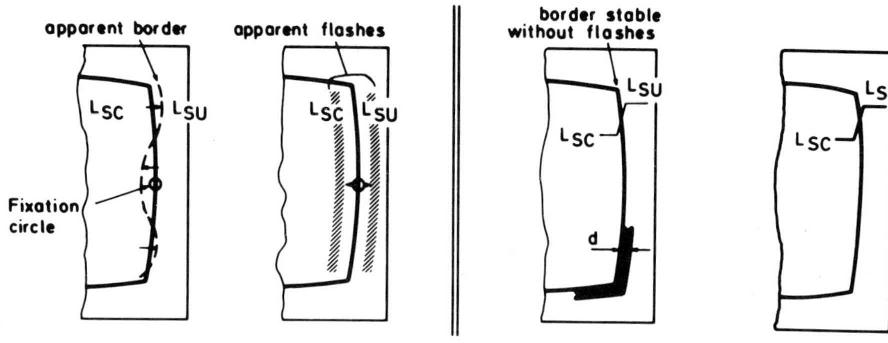

L_{SC}: Screen Luminance = L_{SU}: Surround Luminance

a)
Steady fixation causes irregular shifting or jumping of the border

b)
Saccadic jumps of the eye cause bright and /or dark flashes on or near the border

c)
"Fast" phosphor: ($\tau_{1\%}$ = 0.38 msec) Suppression of border effects by a border-contrast $L_{SU}:L_{SC} \geq 2:1$ or/ and a dark separation line (width d~5mm)

d)
"Slow" phosphor: Border flicker may be suppressed by the use of a "slow" phosphor with a persistence of $\tau_{1\%}$ = 30 msec (frame repetition = 72 Hz)

Fig. 3a Border flicker and its suppression
b Generally, the solution c. -the use of a small black
c separation- should be chosen to suppress border flicker
d since solution d.-the use of "slow" phosphors- creates new problems in situations where the screen content is being scrolled.

The second unfavourable condition was the use of screen colours that were too bluish compared to the room illumination. In the course of some experiments, many observers spontaneously complained about the blue screen colour. That gave us grounds to check the preference of our observers for some pre-selected near-white colours. In Fig.4, the colour loci of all background colours further used are plotted as full circles on a chromaticity diagram. Theobservers judged the ease of reading continuous text written with black characters on each of the indicated coloured backgrounds which were equated for brightness. The numbers following the colon are the mean ratings which were given on a scale from 1 (excellent) to 4 (satisfactory). In brackets are given the number of observers who would choose that colour for continuous VDU work.
We may see that the colours which are close to the illuminant

colour are mostly preferred. That means that screen colour and illumination colour should be closely matched. (Thus, "warm white"

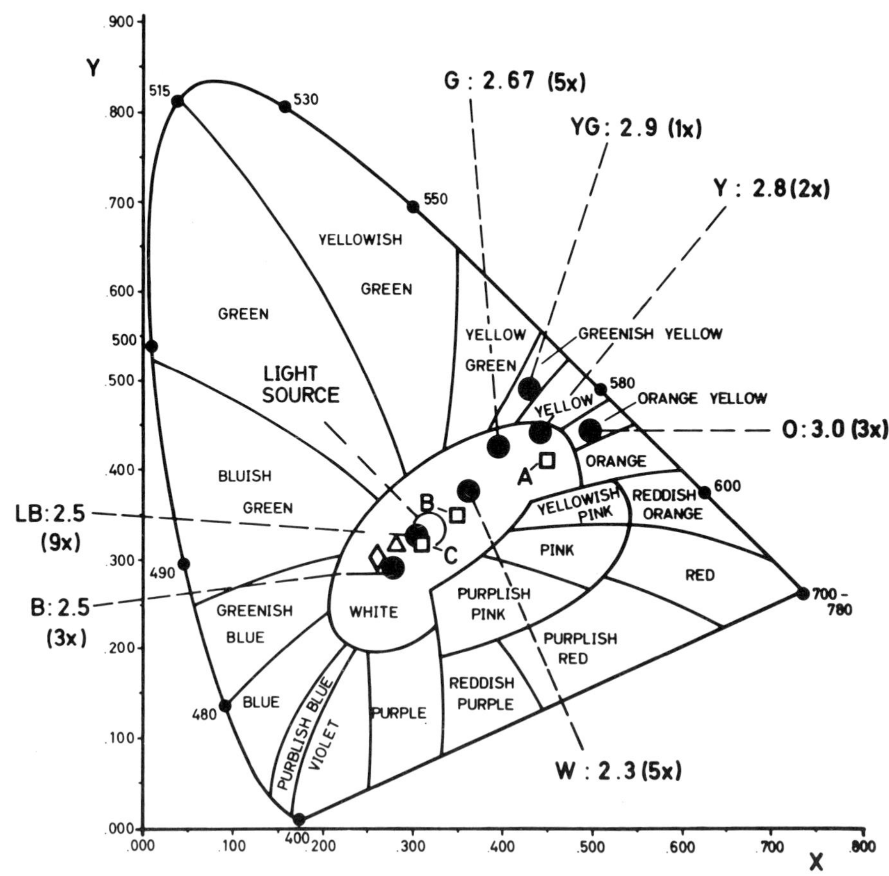

Fig. 4 Colour preference for the light background screen with dark characters
Judgments are given on a scale from 1 (excellent) to 4 (satisfactory); number of observers: 21, mean judgements are given behind the colon. Numbers in brackets show how many observers would choose that colour for continuous work.
Colour coordinates of the light source: x=0.316 ,y=0.334 .

fluorescent tubes -unlike ours- require phosphor coordinates which are shifted towards lower colour temperature coordinates.)

The third unfavourable condition was the choice of a fixed screen luminance, which was too high in relation to the surround: the perceptual effect is that the screen is perceived as a light-source and rather than an object which is being illuminated. Thus a perceptual difference between screen and document is created. To

find out the preferred screen background luminance, we asked our observers to adjust the screen luminance to their preferred level. In subsequent experiments, we used two illumination conditions. The result of the medium-to-low-level-illumination is shown in Fig.5 that of the high-level-illumination is shown in Fig.6 (The latter situation was established by spotlights, beams of which were used to brighten several colour photographs).
We see from the distribution of preferred background luminances

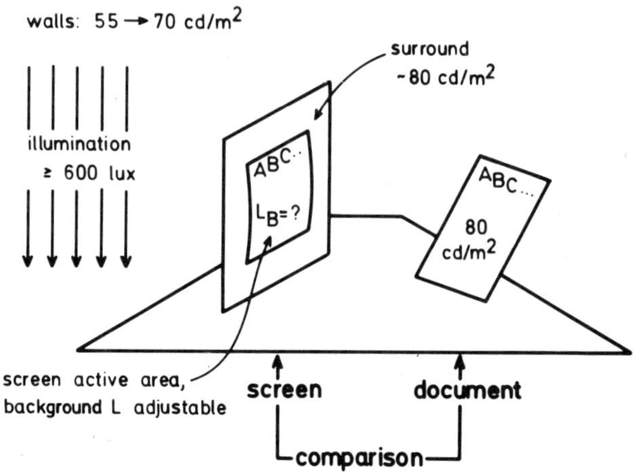

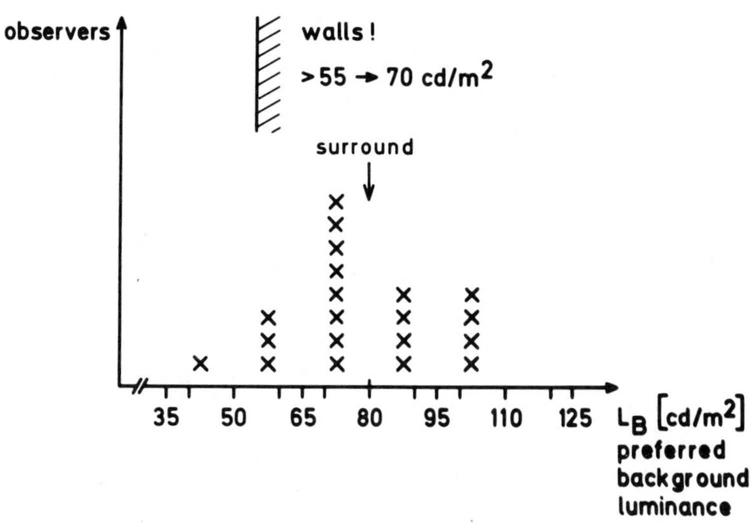

Fig. 5 Evaluation of the preferred background luminance of a light screen with dark characters under office conditions
- low level wall luminance -
One cross is the mean of 5 luminance adjustments made by one observer.

that most observers chose values which were slightly below the screen surround luminance and much below the luminance of the walls

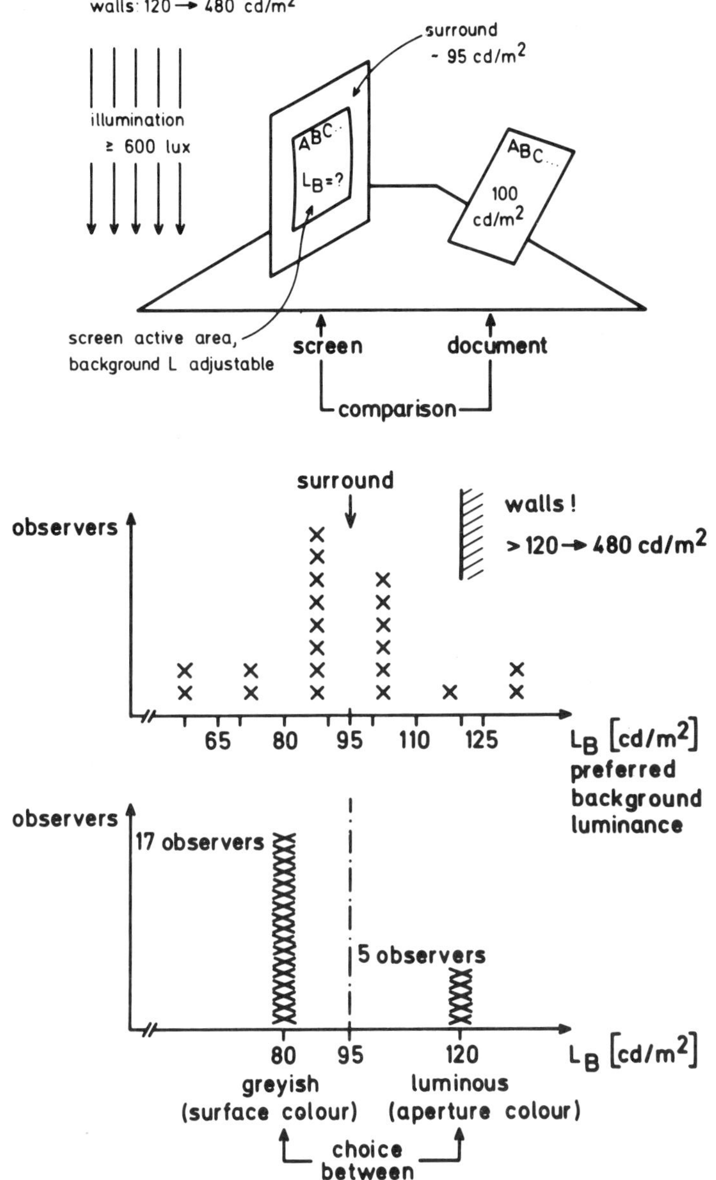

Fig. 6 Evaluation of the preferred background luminance of a light screen with dark characters under office conditions (as in Fig. 5 but with high-level wall luminance). In addition, the lower part of the graph shows the choices of 22 observers in a forced choice situation.

in the high level situation (Fig.6): In both cases this choice made the screen colour slightly greyish.
This preferred adjustment is seen even clearer if the observers are asked to make their decision in a forced choice situation. If they have to choose either the definitely greyish VDU-screen of 80 cd/m^2 or the definitely luminous screen of 120 cd/m^2 , 17 out of 22 observers preferred the greyish screen for continuous vdu work (see the lower part of Fig.6). These results suggest that in a text comparison task the object mode of the screen is generally preferred to the aperture mode.

The variables considered so far may be called internal variables, since they are fixed by the intrinsic construction of the monitor screen plus electronics. We still have to consider the effect of external conditions, especially problems caused by the ambient illumination. The corresponding variables will be called external variables:

3. ATTENUATING EXTERNAL REFLEXIONS

To make a complete comparison between light and dark screens, we still have to consider the merits of both designs in terms of their ability to suppress the adverse effects of external illumination -

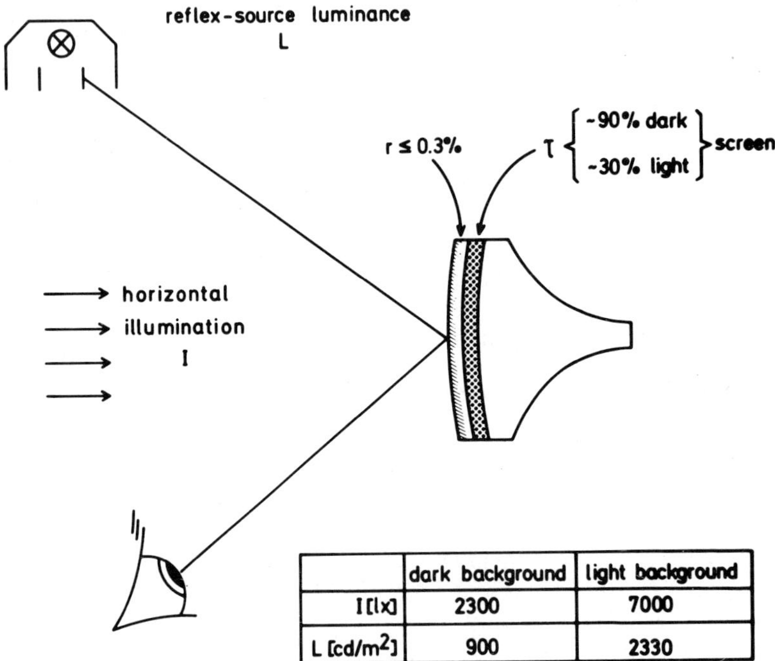

	dark background	light background
I [lx]	2300	7000
L [cd/m^2]	900	2330

Fig. 7 Rejection of diffuse and specular reflexions from light and dark background screens - a comparison of the best possible configuration for each kind.

the second source of trouble that the VDU brings into the office. To quantify the effects, we have to consider two aspects: diffuse reflexions and specular reflexions.
Light that is diffusely reflected by the matte surface of the screen may dilute the contrast of the displayed characters. For a given VDU there is an upper limit of (horizontal) illuminance: If this is exceeded, the contrast between characters and background becomes loo low. We recommend a minimum contrast of 1:5 to avoid any loss of optical information -even in depth space- which is particular important in viewing tasks which are not confined to a single depth-of-focus region. To make a fair comparison, we tried to set up a best possible dark-background VDU and a best - possible light-background VDU. Among the many configurations tested those of Fig.7 turned out to be the local quality maxima. (The light transmission in the case of the dark-background screen had to be made higher (=90% instead of 30%) to prevent the screen appearing black to the observer under real-office conditions (a situation which was complained about by the majority of our observers). Under these conditions the best dark-background screen may be illuminated by about 2000 lux whereas the best light-background screen tolerates about 7000 lux. A limit of 7000 lux is sufficient to admit natural daylight through windows.

Specular reflexions tend to mask the screen characters. In Fig.7, maximum permissible luminance values are given which correspond to an equivalent comfort level. The comfort level used here may be characterized by "no essential disturbance is experienced by the observers". Then, the light screen rejects more than 2000 cd/m^2, the dark screen only 900 cd/m^2. Therefore, the light screen rejects reflexions from normal artificial office lighting at a high comfort level; the dark screen does not.

4. REQUIREMENTS FOR A LIGHT SCREEN WHICH IS PHYSIOLOGICALLY MATCHED TO THE VISUAL SYSTEM

If we compare the above results to the previously evaluated requirements, we may define the physiologically optimized light-background screen by a list of all psychophysical variables that should be considered and their physical limits so as to guarantee a VDU that has no visual interference for 95% of the population.
Table I lists the main perceptual variables for the light screen, which are

1. large-field flicker (see Bauer et al., 1983)
4. stroke blur(width) (see Bauer, 1984b)
6. background grating adaptation (unpublished results)
7. induced movement (jitter see Bauer, 1984a)
8. maximum contrast of unblurred characters (unpublished results)

In addition, the following internal parameters must be considered:

2. border flicker (see Bauer, 1984a)
3. perceptual screen mode (object mode vs. aperture mode)
5. background colour

and the external variables

9. max. illuminance permissible for stroke contrasts 1:5
10. max. reflex source peak luminance (see Bauer, 1986).

Points 11. and 12. of Table I must be considered if contrast reversal is required: for exemple, when the VDU is used in dark rooms.

requirements with regard to psychophysical variables	technical parameters	specification
1. suppress large-field-flicker	1. frame repetition rate ω	about 90 Hz at 80 cd/m^2
2. suppress border flicker	2. border contrast, separation, ω	120 Hz or k ≥ 2:1 or 5mm separating dark line
3. avoid aperture mode	3. auto-range of background luminances	40 to 100 cd/m^2
4. avoid stroke blur	4. stroke flank-gradient	about 30 sec arc (preliminary)
5. use preferred background colours	5. colour locus	near white, i.e. between source E and A
6. avoid background grating adaptation	6. line density	>0.5 l/min arc
7. avoid induced movement	7. jitter amplitude/frequency	<10 sec arc at 10 Hz (preliminary)
8. provide for maximum (internal) screen contrast without blur	8. max. phosphor screen contrast	>10:1
9. make provision against contrast dilution by external light	9. max. illuminance admittable for stroke contrasts ≥1:5	about 3000 lux (natural lighting)
10. make provision against disturbing reflex pattern strength	10. max. reflex peak luminance (for admittable reflex increment ≤ 7 %)	about 2000 cd/m^2
(11.) provide for a corrected stroke width if switched to the reversed contrast	11. 50 % stroke width	about ≥ 2 min arc for pos. contrast
(12.) avoid screen blackness if switched to the reversed contrast	12. mean background luminance of empty screen	adjustable up to ≈ 25 cd/m^2

Table I Recommendations for the construction of a light background vdu which is physiologically matched to the visual system of the vdu worker -on a 95 percentile level.

5. CONCLUSIONS

If the artificial (laboratory) condition of "no external reflexions" is abandoned, and the comparison of light and dark displays is made under the constraint of "reflexions from artificial office lighting present", the main benefit of the light-background screen becomes obvious: The screen may be designed in such a way that even under conditions of high lighting levels (which are necessary to optimize the information-handling ability of the visual system, and thus to minimize the visual workload), reflexions are suppressed to such a degree that the text on the screen closely resembles the text of a well printed document.
Further, this can be achieved with normal office lighting (including daylight), without resorting to special "anti-reflexion" lighting systems.

ACKNOWLEDGEMENT

This reseach was sponsored by the Bundesanstalt für Arbeitsschutz, (BAU), Dortmund, FRG.

KEYWORDS

light background VDUs, positive contrast, high resolution screen, flicker, sharpness, readability, contrast, lighting of VDUs, reflexions on VDUs

REFERENCES

Bauer ,D. and Cavonius ,C.R.,1980, Improving the legibility of visual display units through contrast reversal, in: Ergonomic Aspects of Visual Display Terminals, E. Grandjean and E. Vigliani,(London: Taylor & Francis Ltd.), 137-142

Bauer ,D.,Bonacker ,M.,Cavonius ,C.,1983, Frame repetition rate for flicker-free viewing of bright VDU screens, Displays, 4, 31-33

Bauer ,D.,1984a, Causes of flicker at VDUs with bright background and ways of eliminating interference, in: Ergonomics and Health in Modern Offices, E. Grandjean (London and Philadelphia: Taylor &Francis), 364-370

Bauer ,D.,1984b, Improving VDT workplaces in offices by use of a physiologically optimized screen with black symbols on a light background : basic considerations, Behaviour and Information Technology, 3, 363 -369

Bauer ,D.,1986, Reducing reflexions of external light on vdu screens -comparison of bright and dark background screens; considerations and a case study, in: Proceedings of the International Scientific Conference: Work with display units, Stockholm May 1986, Swedish National Board of Occupational Safety and Health

WORK WITH DISPLAY UNITS 86
B. Knave and P.-G. Wideback (eds.)

DISPLAY IMAGE CHARACTERISTICS AND VISUAL RESPONSE

Stanley E. TAYLOR and Bruce A. RUPP

Human Factors Center, International Business Machines Corporation, San Jose, California, United States of America

Several studies concerning display image characteristics and visual response are summarized. In large part these studies have addressed issues raised by developing video display terminal (VDT) standards and guidelines. The studies show that adaptation to an irregular field, such as the characters against a background on a VDT, is biased significantly in the direction of the peak luminance rather than the average luminance, thereby obviating a recommendation for highly reflective backgrounds or positive image polarity based on misconceptions about "maladaptation"; that consistent with extant literature and in contradiction to conclusions based only on CIE relative contrast sensitivity data, negative image polarity actually provides slightly better acuity; that operators do not set limits on preferred contrast, but rather seek contrast levels which are comfortable and which allow a minimum character luminance of about 30 cd/m²; that the pupillary system is not stressed when fixating between a white paper source document and a negative image polarity VDT display, even with a fairly low background luminance; and that the accommodative mechanisms of the eye are not stressed by CRT viewing to any degree greater than would be found with printed material, regardless of image polarity, nor do multimodal phosphors present difficulty for the accommodative mechanisms.

1. INTRODUCTION

For some years now video display terminal ergonomics, particularly concerning vision, have been a source of much activity. It has led to an explosion of standards and guidelines ([8] [17]), and to many research symposia. There have been excellent reviews of the research conducted to determine what are the effects on vision of working with video display terminals (for example, [7] and [16]).

This paper will summarize some research conducted to examine certain issues raised by the developing standards and guidelines, such as the issue of image polarity, possible stress on the focal mechanism of the eye related to the edge characteristics of CRT presentations, potential difficulties related to luminance balances and brightnesses, and possible stress associated with the spectral characteristics of phosphors ([18], [19], [20], [21], [22], [25]). In attempting to understand these issues, we have looked at dynamic accommodative responses, pupillary responses, various psychological measures (adaptation responses, reaction times, preferences), and task performance.

2. ADAPTATION STUDY

2.1. Rationale

One of the often heard rationales for preferring positive image polarity or standardizing very restrictive luminance balances near CRT workstations is the belief that visual re-adaptation must be prevented and that visual adaptation depends on background luminances or average luminances (German Standards Institute, DIN). However, other evidence suggests that peak luminances in the information to be accessed are more important in determining adaptation. The following study attempted to determine whether or not peak luminance or average luminance played a greater role in determining adaptation.

2.2. Method

After 10 min of dark adaptation, four subjects adapted for 2 min on each trial to one of four uniform adapting fields (2200, 875, 345, or 140 cd/m^2) or to one of two patterns, a 50 % duty cycle square wave grating with a bar thickness of 15′ arc, with a light bar luminance of 2200 cd/m^2 and a dark bar luminance of less than 1 cd/m^2. The other pattern was a set of dots each of which subtended 5′ arc with centers separated by 20′ arc from all adjacent dots. The dots were at 2200 cd/m^2 with the inter-dot spaces at less than 1 cd/m^2. The average luminance of the bar pattern was 1100 cd/m^2; of the dots pattern, 132 cd/m^2. Each pattern was viewed through a 3° aperture. After adaptation, subjects fixated an illuminated opal glass plate subtending 1° by 0.8° on which one of two lights would appear, one to the left and one to the right of a middle vertical black line. The lights were 5.5 cd/m^2 against a 5 cd/m^2 background. The subject's task was to detect which of the two lights had appeared. Time to accurately detect which of the two lights had appeared was the measure of amount of adaptation. Subjects completed a total of 10 trials, 5 with each of the 6 patterns in each of two sessions.

2.3. Results

Mean response times for each pattern were computed and are shown in Figure 1. Response times increase linearly with increasing average luminance of the uniform fields. To index the adaptation effects of the DOTS and BARS patterns, the equivalent average adapting luminance was found by regression. That is, a line was fit to the response times to the uniform adapting fields. Then the uniform adapting luminance was found which corresponded to the response time actually observed for the DOTS pattern and for the BARS pattern. For the DOTS pattern, it was 1197 cd/m^2, even though the average luminance of this pattern was only 132 cd/m^2. For the BARS pattern, it was 1486 cd/m^2, even though its average luminance was only 1100 cd/m^2. Statistically, planned comparisons showed that BARS and DOTS patterns had reaction times which were significantly different from the reaction times that would be predicted from their respective average luminances, but also significantly different from that of the 2200 cd/m^2 adapting field, equivalent to their peak luminances ($p < 0.05$).

2.4. Discussion

These data suggest that the adaptation to an irregular field is biased significantly in the direction of the peak luminance. This suggests that adaptation to source documents and displays has to do more with the peak luminance than with the average luminance. Such a difference is very small, and thus one would not expect maladaptation. For that reason, adaptation does not appear to be a concern at VDT workstations and does not justify recommendations for one image polarity over the other.

3. IMAGE POLARITY AND ACUITY

3.1. RCS Analysis

Visual acuity is one of the issues in the display image polarity debate. It has been assumed by some ([2],[4], [12],[26], etc.) that a positive image display, that is, a display of dark characters on a light background, will provide for higher visual acuity than an otherwise equal negative image presentation. The main reason for making that assumption is that Relative Contrast Sensitivity (RCS) does increase as luminance is increased ([5], p. 60). However, neither experimental data, the classic Berger study for example [3], or the data contained in CIE Publication 19 [5] would support the position that a positive polarity display would provide for higher visual performance.

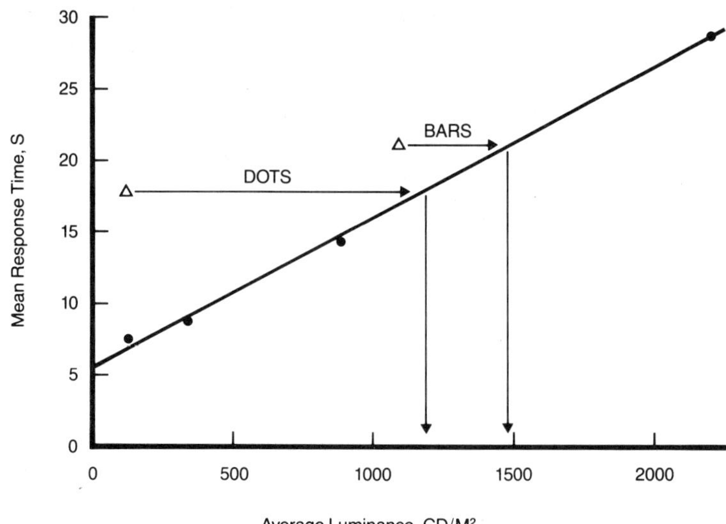

Figure 1. Mean response time for uniform adapting fields. The arrows indicate the derivation of the equivalent adapting luminance based on the observed response times for the DOTS and BARS patterns.

The Berger study investigated the effects of both strokewidth and polarity on the threshold legibility of numeric symbols. Maximum visual performance was found to be with light symbols on a dark background and with a strokewidth of about 1/15 of the character height. Performance on the positive polarity presentation was superior only when strokewidths were larger than 1/6 of the character height.

CIE Publication Number 19 [5] describes a standardized method for collecting contrast sensitivity data and contains a table of Relative Contrast Sensitivity (RCS) values for adapting luminances from 1 to 10,000 cd/m². The RCS values use the contrast sensitivity of the 10,000 cd/m² adapting luminance condition as the reference value, 100%. The RCS values for other adapting luminances are stated in terms of relative efficiency compared to the reference value. The RCS table does show that as luminance is increased relative contrast sensitivity is increased. However, as the adapting luminance is increased the absolute luminance difference required for the target to be just perceptible also increases.

The CIE publication also describes a method to determine the Effective Visibility Level (VL_{eff}) of a specific target presented on a given background. The VL_{eff} is essentially the number of threshold steps separating the target from the background: the larger the separation, the more visible the target. The VL_{eff} value may be used with Table II (page 80) of the CIE publication to predict the percentage of maximum visual performance capability that would be provided by that VL_{eff} value. It is clear from these data that for a given absolute luminance difference between the target and its background, maximum visibility is achieved with the lowest possible background luminance. This would indicate that a negative polarity presentation would provide for higher visual acuity, and it would also question the validity of requiring a minimum background luminance for negative polarity displays as specified in one set of safety regulations [26].

Table 1 is provided to illustrate the conflict in the use of the CIE RCS data to support a recommendation for negative image polarity. Note that for a phosphor brightness of 100 cd/m², the RCS value is greater for positive polarity. However, the VL_{eff} is much greater for negative image polarity, as is the percentage of maximum visual performance capability.

Table 1
Example of RCS Analysis from CIE Tables

Adapting (Background) Luminance	Target Luminance	Luminance Difference	RCS Value	Threshold Units	VL_{eff}	% Maximum Visual Performance Capability
Positive Polarity:						
100.0	10.0	90.0	62.2	9.23	9.75	87.7
Negative Polarity:						
10.0	100.0	90.0	36.2	1.59	56.60	>99.9

3.2. Snellen Study Rationale

The CIE contrast sensitivity material has been used to claim that positive image displays will provide for higher acuity. However, as shown, if correctly applied, that same material may be used to come to the opposite conclusion, that a negative polarity presentation would provide for higher visual acuity.

The object of this study was to test visual acuity by the use of both positive and negative polarity acuity charts under otherwise equal viewing conditions. If the RCS value is in fact an appropriate predictor of visual performance, then performance with the positive polarity chart, dark letters on a light background, would be expected to be superior. On the other hand, if the VL_{eff} value is a more appropriate predictor, then performance on the negative polarity acuity chart should be superior.

3.3. Method

Two acuity charts using a modified "Tumbling E" pattern were constructed: one with black characters on a white background (positive polarity) and one with white characters on a black background (negative polarity). The symbols had a strokewidth of 1/7 of character height. The separations between the bars of the E were two strokewidths wide and the width of the characters was the same as the height. Each chart was composed of seven lines of five randomly oriented characters. The character height of the top line was 9.09 mm with a between bar separation of 2.6 mm. The character heights of each succeeding line of characters were reduced by 0.91 mm. The bottom line, the line with the smallest characters, had a character height of 3.64 mm. The viewing distance was set at 6 m. The separation between the bars was used as the index of resolution. The seven lines of the acuity chart thus represented levels of acuity of 0.67, 0.79, 0.84, 0.95, 1.12, 1.34, and 1.71.

The dark areas of the charts measured 3.11 cd/m^2 and the light areas were 33.6 cd/m^2. This produced a Cm of 0.83, or a contrast ratio of 10.8:1, between the characters and the background. The acuity charts were mounted on a neutral colored wall that had a luminance of 32 cd/m^2 in the area where the charts were positioned.

The subject's task was to report the orientation of each of the symbols of each line starting with the top line, the line with the largest symbols. The experimenter recorded the responses. Performance was determined by prorating the number of correct responses on the line of the smallest characters that the subject could resolve. Twenty subjects were run in a counter balanced order and only one chart was present at a time.

3.4. Results

The mean visual acuity for performance on the negative polarity (white symbols on a black background) acuity chart was 1.18 (6/5.1), and on the positive polarity acuity chart, 1.12 (6/5.4). The difference was significant at the $p < 0.05$ level, $F(1,19) = 5.295$.

3.5. Discussion

The assumption that a positive polarity presentation, dark characters on a light background, will provide for higher acuity than a negative polarity presentation may be rejected. If visual performance, acuity, was simply a function of the RCS value of the background luminance, then performance with the positive polarity acuity chart, the chart with black characters on a white background, should have been about twice that of the negative polarity condition. The RCS value for 33.6 cd/m² is 51.2% and the value for 3.11 cd/m² is 22.8%. However, the use of the VL_{eff} to predict visual performance under the two conditions would have resulted in an overestimation of the superiority of the negative polarity condition.

The threshold difference, in percent, may be estimated by dividing 5.74 by the RCS value for the adapting luminance. A threshold unit for the 33.6 cd/m² adapting luminance would be 3.77 cd/m² and 0.78 cd/m² for the 3.11 cd/m² adapting luminance. The luminance difference between the symbols and the background was 30.5 cd/m² for both conditions. The number of threshold units, or steps, between the background and the symbol would be 39 for the negative polarity presentation and only 8 for the positive polarity presentation. Table II of the CIE publication would predict that the negative polarity acuity chart would provide for about 99% of visual capability while the positive polarity presentation would provide for only 85%. Only a 5% difference was found in the average performance for the two acuity charts, about 1/3 of that which would be predicted by the CIE material. That difference was not unexpected as the CIE contrast sensitivity material was collected under significantly different conditions.

The results of this study are also consistent with those of Berger. That study found a superiority for the negative polarity mode of presentation when the strokewidth was less than 1/6 of character height. Visual display terminals will generally have strokewidths of from about 1/7 to 1/10 of character height. The relationship between acuity, strokewidth, and polarity should also consider retinal modulation. The optics of the eye are not perfect; even at best focus there is some blurring of the image. That blurring will reduce the retinal illuminance modulation of small patterns. This effect is most noticeable when the strokewidth of a bright character display is thicker than the separation between the strokes.

It is also interesting to note that in the positive polarity condition, the luminance of the background of the acuity chart and the luminance of the immediate surrounds were about equal, while for the negative polarity condition there was close to a 10:1 difference. There are frequent recommendations that there should not be more than a 3:1 luminance difference between the task area and its immediate surround. However, that does not seem to be particularly important or to have any influence on visual performance, as has been noted previously [10] [14].

4. PREFERENCE FOR CONTRAST

4.1. Rationale

The German Trade Cooperative Association safety regulations for visual display terminals [26] require that the contrast ratio between the symbol and the background of a bright character display range between 3:1 and 15:1. Those regulations also require that the display have a background luminance of at least 10 cd/m². German DIN Standard 66234, Part 2 [6] recommends a contrast ratio of from 6:1 to 10:1 and advises against contrast ratios of less than 3:1 or more than 15:1. The reason for the caution for higher contrast ratios is that they assume that they would be "experienced as unpleasant." Neither MIL-STD 1472c [15] or the draft ANSI

[1] or ISO [11] standards recommend any upper limit for contrast. Previous work in the area has indicated that higher contrast was associated with higher levels of visual performance ([5],[9],[23]) and levels of contrast above 15:1 have been recommended. For example, Shurtleff [23] and Snyder [24] have recommended that displays be able to achieve a minimum contrast ratio of at least 18:1, and Snyder has recommended a minimum contrast ratio of 18:1 (a modulation of 90%) for noncontextual material. Howell and Kraft [9] recommended even a higher modulation, 94% (about 30:1).

A separate concern has been expressed by Kokoschka [13]. The concern is that as large area contrast is increased, the contrast of the details of the characters may decrease. There are various methods used to characterize display contrast. Large area photometric techniques measure the integrated luminance of an area of a screen with all pixels on and compare that with a similar measure of an area of the screen where all the pixels are in the off state. The large area contrast measure may over- or under- estimate the actual contrast of the details to be resolved depending on different factors. Large area photometric techniques may integrate luminances that the eye does not integrate. That would underestimate effective contrast. However, large area measures are relatively insensitive to blur. If there is significant blurring at a particular display luminance level, then the contrast of the details to be resolved may be reduced; that would not be detected by large area photometric techniques.

4.2. Method

A modified IBM 3101 display unit was used to present sets of random characters. The display was modified to produce three different display background luminances while maintaining a constant ambient illumination of 500 lux measured on a horizontal surface in front of the display. The three background luminances were 11.5, 1.6, and 0.67 cd/m². The 11.5 cd/m² background luminance was obtained by removing the contrast enhancing filter that was supplied with the display (this was a bare tube condition). The 1.6 and 0.67 cd/m² background luminances were achieved by placing supplementary neutral density filters over the screen of the display, having transmissions of 0.37 and 0.21 respectively. Both of the supplementary neutral density filters also had thin film anti-reflection coatings on their first surfaces.

The screen of the display was filled with a pattern of random character blocks. The characters presented on the display had a vertical height of 3 mm and the brightness control operated by the subject was located on the front surface of the display frame. The typical viewing distance, while the subject was operating the symbol brightness control, was about 400 mm. That would result in an angular character height of approximately 25 minutes of arc.

Each of the 21 subjects was instructed in the use of the brightness control of the display and asked to make three character luminance settings for each of the three display background luminance conditions. They were:

1. The preferred character contrast.
2. The lowest character contrast that would be considered useable and acceptably comfortable.
3. The highest character contrast that would be considered useable and acceptably comfortable.

4.3. Results

Table 2 shows the results of the study in terms of contrast ratios. The subjects, in every case, selected higher contrast ratios for lower background luminances. For each one of the given instructions, the Preferred, the Lowest, or the Highest Comfortable contrast setting, the contrast setting selected by the subject was the highest for the 0.67 cd/m² background condition, the second highest for the 1.6 cd/m² background, and the lowest for the 11.5 cd/m² background condition. Any appropriate nonparametric test would show the differences to be highly significant. However, the use of contrast ratios may be misleading.

Table 2.
Preferred and Lowest and Highest Acceptable Contrast Ratios

Display Background Luminance		Contrast Ratio Mean	S.D.	Range Low	Range High
11.5 cd/m²					
	Preferred Setting	6.08:1	3.84:1	1.87:1	15.78:1
	Lowest Acceptable	2.10:1	1.13:1	1.09:1	6.04:1
	Highest Acceptable	12.57:1	5.85:1	3.26:1	19.00:1 (5)*
1.6 cd/m²					
	Preferred Setting	19.78:1	11.56:1	4.73:1	49.26:1 (1)
	Lowest Acceptable	5.17:1	3.42:1	1.23:1	13.36:1
	Highest Acceptable	38.25:1	14.39:1	9.63:1	49.26:1 (11)
0.67 cd/m²					
	Preferred Setting	43.10:1	23.76:1	10.35:1	75.46:1 (3)
	Lowest Acceptable	12.53:1	7.75:1	3.16:1	27.62:1
	Highest Acceptable	66.00:1	17.44:1	25.46:1	75.46:1 (14)

* The numbers within the parentheses indicate the frequency of trials where contrast was adjusted to the maximum obtainable.

Table 3 shows the same data as Table 2 but in terms of symbol luminance rather than contrast ratios. The Highest Comfortable data were deleted because of the frequency with which the settings were limited by the range of the control. When symbol luminance is considered, the differences in the settings for the 1.6 and 0.67 cd/m² backgrounds disappear.

Table 3
Preferred Character Luminances

Background Luminance (cd/m²)	Preferred Character Luminance Mean	S.D.	Minimum Comfortable Character Luminance Mean	S.D.
11.5	69.92	44.16	24.15	13.00
1.6	31.65	18.50	8.27	5.47
0.67	28.88	15.92	8.40	5.19

The responses for the 11.5 cd/m² were significantly different ($p < .01$, Wilcoxin Matched-pairs Signed-ranks Test) from those for the 1.6 or 0.67 backgrounds. However, the responses for the 1.6 and 0.67 cd/m² background conditions were not significantly different from each other.

4.4. Discussion

There is an inverse relationship between comfortable contrast ranges and the background luminance of a bright character display. However, in this study as well as most others, contrast was confounded with symbol luminance and, to some extent, display resolution. This study used three display background reflectivities in a constant ambient illumination to set the display background luminance. For each background luminance, contrast was adjusted by adjusting the luminance of the displayed symbol. When the results of the study were stated in terms of contrast, each subject always selected a higher contrast ratio for a lower background luminance. Statistically, and considering the number of subjects, 21, that is highly significant. However, it is interesting to note that when symbol luminance, rather than contrast, was considered, there is no significant difference between the responses for the 0.67 and 1.6 cd/m² background conditions. Regardless of the instructions, the subjects may well have been basing their judgements on symbol luminance rather than contrast, at least for those two background conditions.

The degree of between subject variability is high, the standard deviation being about one half of the mean. That would indicate, at least for operator preference, that it would be inappropriate to recommend a relatively limited contrast ratio range. On the other hand, recommendations for a minimum obtainable symbol luminance do appear reasonable if, in fact, the subjects were adjusting for symbol luminance rather than contrast during the trials with the two lower background luminances. It would be interesting to extend the study to include background luminances of 5 and 20 cd/m² to determine if the basis for preference does transition from symbol luminance to contrast as the background luminance is increased.

5. PUPILLARY STRESS STUDY

5.1 Rationale

A study reported by Cakir, Reuter, von Schmude, and Armbruster [4] claimed that when changing the point of fixation between a negative image display (e.g., a CRT with light characters on a dark background) and a positive image display (a typical print source document), the initial pupillary response is excessive, often resulting in complete dilation or constriction, respectively. This finding was offered as evidence that the pupil was stressed by such a situation, often found in CRT work. It has contributed to a belief that positive image polarity should be preferred over negative image polarity to avoid the luminance differences which lead to the pupillary response.

5.2 Method

In the present study, this hypothesis was examined carefully. Four subjects fixated back and forth on command between a CRT display with a single bright "X" against a background of either 2.5 cd/m² or 15.1 cd/m², with a contrast in either case of at least 10:1, and a single black "X" on paper with a background luminance of 84.3 cd/m². These conditions are typical of VDT working conditions and would tend to show the greatest pupil activity, since only a single character interrupted the background luminances thought to be contributing to pupil diameter. Pupil diameter was tracked with a Gulf & Western Series 1000 Pupillometer.

5.3 Results and Discussion

Pupil diameter shifts were the same for the two display backgrounds, and in both cases averaged less than about 0.3 mm. The changes associated with fixation changes were typically no larger than the magnitude of the natural oscillations of the pupil when fixating a target of steady luminance (called hippus or pupillary unrest).

These results, together with those of Zwahlen [27] for average pupil size over extended time periods while working with VDTs, suggest that the luminance balances typically found with VDT work are not a source of stress to the pupillary control system.

6. OTHER RELATED RESEARCH

The studies cited join other research of our own and others that, as a body of literature, show that there is no unusual stress or demand placed on the visual system when working at a video display terminal. As has been pointed out, all too often restrictive, ill-founded recommendations for standards or guidelines have been proposed which do not survive the test of scientific inquiry.

In addition to those studies just summarized, a few other studies merit a brief discussion which concern accommodation and VDT viewing ([21] [25]).

In the first, we examined the frequent speculation that the edge characteristics of CRT characters would create difficulty in accommodation and might result in instability (perhaps a searching behavior). We compared accommodation to printed material, to a normal CRT, and to a CRT that was defocused. Accommodation was continuously monitored by an SRI International Infrared Optometer incorporated in a Fifth Generation Dual Purkinje Image Eyetracker.

Steady state accommodation showed only a small difference between CRT and hardcopy due to chromatic aberration associated with using a green phosphor (at a distance of 2 diopters, 1.82 diopters for the print material, 1.61 for the CRT focused and defocused). For all 3 conditions there was a slight accommodative lag. The accommodative stability was the same for all conditions, about 0.1 diopters rms. Thus the accommodative response did not differ as a function of the edge characteristics in these conditions. Clearly the many other cues to distance enabled the accommodative system to focus to the proper distance. In another study, which compared positive image polarity and negative image polarity, both steady-state accommodation and accommodative stability were the same.

Finally, accommodation to bimodal phosphors had been hypothesized to result in accommodative instability. We simulated the condition by rear illuminating a glass slide with two Wratten filters (No. 55 and 22). The green filter resulted in 1.6 diopters of accommodation; the orange, in 1.87; and the two together, in 1.74. In all three cases, accommodative stability was the same (0.08, 0.09, and 0.08 diopters respectively). Thus accommodative stability is not affected by using phosphors with bimodal spectral distributions.

ACKNOWLEDGEMENTS

The following other individuals have contributed to the Visual Performance Laboratory's research: Maryellen Ciak, Calvin K. Clauer, William H. Emmons, R. James Evey, Timothy M. Floyd, Timothy Hogan, David Marcarian, Bernard W. McVey, Victor M. Ramos, and Ann Sorknes.

REFERENCES

[1] ANSI/HFS100. 1986. *American National Standard for Human Factors Engineering of Visual Display Workstations.* Santa Monica, CA: The Human Factors Society.

[2] Bauer, D., & Cavonius, C.R.. 1980. Improving the legibility of visual display units through contrast reversal. In E. Grandjean and E. Vigliani (Eds.), *Ergonomic Aspects of Visual Display Terminals* London: Taylor & Francis. Pp. 137-142.

[3] Berger, C. 1944. Stroke-width, form and horizontal spacing of numerals as determinants of the threshold of recognition. *Journal of Applied Psychology, 28,* 208-231

[4] Cakir, A., Reuter, H., von Schmude, L., & Armbruster, A. 1978. *Untersuchungen zur Anpassung von Bildschirmarbeitsplatzen an die physische und psychische Funktionsweise des Menschen.* Bonn: Der Bundesminister fuer Arbeit und Sozialordnung.

[5] Commission Internationale de L'Eclairage. 1972. *A Unified Framework of Methods for Evaluating Visual Performance Aspects of Lighting.* Paris: Publication CIE No. 19 (tc 3.1).

[6] DIN 66234, Part 2. 1983. *Display Workstations, Perceptibility of Characters.*

[7] Helander, M.G., Billingsley, P.A., Schurick, J.M. 1984. An evaluation of human factors research on visual display terminals in the workplace. In F.A. Muckler (Ed.), *Human Factors Review: 1984.* Santa Monica, CA: The Human Factors Society, Inc.. Pp. 55-129.

[8] Helander, M.G., & Rupp, B.A. 1984. An overview of standards and guidelines for visual display terminals. *Applied Ergonomics, 15,* 185-195.

[9] Howell, W.C., & Kraft, C.L. 1959. *Blur and Contrast as Variables Affecting the Legibility of Alpha-Numeric Symbols on Radar Type Displays.* WADC Technical Report 59-36.

[10] Ireland, F.H., Kinslow, W., Levin, E., & Page, D. 1967. *Experimental Study of the Effects of Surround Brightness and Size on Visual Performance* (AMRL-TR67-102). Wright-Patterson Air Force Base. OH: Aerospace Medical Research Lab.
[11] ISO. 1986. *Ergonomics of Office Visual Display Units: Visual Requirements* (Draft). International Standards Organization Document ISO/TC 159/SC4 N102.
[12] Klittervall, T. 1979. Synarbetet vid Bildskarm. *Optik och Optometric,579*, 14-18.
[13] Kokoschka, S. 1986. Visibility aspects of VDUs in terms of contrast and luminance. *Behaviour and Information Technology*, In press.
[14] Kokoschka, S., & Haubner, P. 1985. Luminance ratios at visual display workstations and visual performance. *Lighting Research and Technology (London), 17(3)*, 138-144.
[15] MIL-STD 1472C. 1981. *Human Engineering Design Criteria for Military Systems, Equipment, and Facilities.* Washington, DC: Department of Defense.
[16] National Research Council. 1983. *Video Displays, Work, and Vision.* Washington, DC: National Academy Press.
[17] Rupp, B.A. 1981. Visual display standards: A review of issues. *Proceedings of the SID, 22*, 63-72.
[18] Rupp, B.A., & Clauer, C.K. 1986. *Pupillary Responses as a Source of Stress During Display Viewing.* San Jose, CA: IBM Human Factors Center, HFC-59.
[19] Rupp, B.A., & Floyd, T. 1986. *Image Polarity and Visual Acuity.* San Jose, CA: IBM Human Factors Center, HFC-58.
[20] Rupp, B.A., & McVey, C.K. 1986. *Preferred and Ranges of Acceptable Contrast for Three Levels of Display Background Luminance.* San Jose, CA: IBM Human Factors Center, HFC-60.
[21] Rupp, B.A., McVey, B.W., & Taylor, S.E. 1984. Image quality and the accommodation response. In E. Grandjean (Ed.), *Ergonomics and Health in Modern Offices.* London: Taylor & Francis. Pp. 254-259.
[22] Rupp, B.A., & Taylor, S.E. 1986. Retinal adaptation to video display terminals: Average luminance or symbol luminance? *Behaviour & Information Technology.* In press.
[23] Shurtleff, D.A. 1980. *How to Make Displays Legible.* La Mirada, CA: Human Interface Design.
[24] Snyder, H.L., & Maddox, M.E. 1978. *Information Transfer from Computer Generated Dot-Matrix Displays* (HFL-78-3/ARO-78-1). Blacksburg, VA: Department of Industrial Engineering and Operations Research, Virginia Polytechnic Institute and State University.
[25] Taylor, S.E., & McVey, B.W. 1984. The dynamics of dark focus and accommodation to dark and light character CRT displays. In E. Grandjean (Ed.), *Ergonomics and Health in Modern Offices.* London: Taylor & Francis. Pp. 248-253.
[26] Trade Cooperative Association (TCA). 1980. *Safety Regulations for Display Workplaces in the Office Sector, No. ZH 1/618.* Hamburg: 10/80 edn TCA.
[27] Zwahlen, H.T. 1984. Pupillary responses when viewing designated locations in a VDT workstation. In E. Grandjean (Ed.), *Ergonomics and Health in Modern Offices.* London: Taylor & Francis. Pp. 339-345.

11. IMAGE QUALITY

WORK WITH DISPLAY UNITS 86
B. Knave and P.-G. Wideback (eds.)

MATCHING DISPLAY CHARACTERISTICS TO HUMAN VISUAL CAPACITY

Gerald M. Murch and Robert J. Beaton

Human Factors Department, Tektronix Laboratories, Tektronix, Inc., P.O. Box 500, MS 50/320, Beaverton, Oregon 97077 USA

ABSTRACT

The perceived image quality of a digital display is affected by two independent system characteristics, namely resolution and addressability. This paper discusses a quantitative procedure for selecting optimal levels of resolution and addressability based upon the performance constraints of human vision.

INTRODUCTION

For a visual display unit to be used comfortably and efficiently, the image must be constituted in light of the imaging requirements of the human visual system. In digital-display systems employing a Cathode-Ray Tube (CRT), the critical attributes are *resolution* and *addressability*. By matching these two characteristics of the display to the imaging limits of vision, an optimized system may be obtained.

In essence, resolution is a property of the design of the display device. It is derived from the width of a line or spot imaged on the screen: The narrower the line or the smaller the spot, the higher the resolution. From the measured line width, resolution can be specified in a number of ways, such as lines per unit distance, Modulation Transfer Function (MTF), spot size, etc. We will consider the line width at 50% of the maximum luminance intensity, since simple conversions exist to translate the various metrics of resolution [1],[2].

Addressability is a characteristic of the display controller and represents the ability to select and activate a specific point or *x,y* coordinate on the screen. On rastered displays, this is usually stated in terms of the number of lines scanned from the top to the bottom of the display screen as well as the number of points along each raster line.

Since addressability is controlled by the hardware driving the CRT, and since resolution is determined by the design of the CRT, these two display characteristics are independent of one another. However, to obtain high levels of image quality, certain relations need to be maintained between resolution and addressability. For example, if resolution is too low (large spot sizes), successive lines will over-write preceding lines. Under some conditions, this may produce image artifacts such as false contours. Conversely, if addressability is too low (large spot separations), then adjacent raster lines will not merge and they will appear as visible stripes.

RELATING RESOLUTION AND ADDRESSABILITY

We assert that a primary goal in engineering a visual display system is to attain sufficient image quality to maximize the transfer of "information" from the display screen to the human operator. Although numerous factors contribute to overall image quality (e.g., ambient illumination, screen format, etc.), resolution and addressability directly impact two fundamental criteria underlying this design goal.

The first criterion, which we have termed the *adjacent* raster line (pixel) requirement, states that the raster structure of a display must be imperceptible to an operator located at a typical (46 cm) viewing distance. This requirement is intended to eliminate visible "noise," which arises from the discrete picture elements of digital display systems, and which bears no relevant information for the operator. Display systems that meet the adjacent raster line (pixel) criterion present uniformly bright solid-filled areas and alphanumeric characters, which appear continuously constructed and highly legible.

The second image-quality criterion, termed the *alternate* raster line (pixel) requirement, states that individual lines (pixels) within an alternating on-off-on-off pattern must be visible to an operator from a typical viewing distance. This requirement optimizes the visibility of high spatial frequency components, such as narrow lines and fine details within an image. For a CRT system with a smoothly decreasing MTF, optimizing the alternate raster line (pixel) criterion also optimizes the information transfer of low spatial frequency components as well [3].

The two above-mentioned image-quality criteria place opposing demands upon the optimal specification of display resolution and addressability. For example, increases in display addressability favor the adjacent raster line (pixel) criterion since the modulation (luminance contrast) between adjoining raster lines is reduced; however, this same reduction in modulation also reduces the detectability of individual lines within an on-off-on-off pattern, thereby disfavoring the alternate raster line (pixel) criterion. A similar trade-off occurs with changes in display resolution.

RESOLUTION/ADDRESSABILITY RATIO

In order to assess whether or not a display system satisfies the two image-quality criteria mentioned above, the system designer must determine the modulation between adjacent and alternate raster lines (pixels). Then, these modulation values must be evaluated in terms of human visual sensitivities to modulation at specific spatial frequencies. It is desired that the modulation between adjacent raster lines (pixels) be below a minimum level required for visual stimulation, while the modulation between alternate raster lines (pixels) should exceed this minimum visual stimulation level.

To evaluate display systems over a wide range of resolution and addressability, we employ a simple metric, termed the Resolution/Addressability Ratio (*RAR*), given as

$$RAR = \frac{W}{S} \tag{1}$$

in which W denotes the full-width of a raster line (pixel) profile at one-half its maximum luminance intensity and S denotes the peak-to-peak separation between adjacent raster lines (pixels). For example, a 48-cm diagonal display with a height of 27.5 cm and an addressability of 1024 lines has a peak-to-peak separation of 27.5/1024=0.27 mm/line. Assuming a 0.38-mm wide spot profile, the resulting *RAR* value is 1.41.

By using a numerical simulation program, modulation values for adjacent and alternate raster lines (pixels) were determined under various combinations of resolution and addressability and, hence, *RAR* values. For each *RAR* value, the simulation program constructed a waveform that represented the luminance pattern across several raster lines (pixels). These calculations were performed by convolving a Gaussian spot profile having a specific width (W) with a series of unit delta functions spaced at a specific separation (S). The modulation values, determined by Fourier analysis of the resulting periodic raster (pixel) structure, are shown in Figure 1 by the curve labeled "Adjacent Pixel." The observed trend in modulation, over a range of *RAR* values from 0.35 to 2.4, can be described by

$$M = \frac{2}{\pi} \exp \left[3.6(RAR) - 7.0(RAR)^2 + (RAR)^3\right] , \qquad (2)$$

in which M denotes modulation and RAR is defined by Eq. 1. As an example, for a display with a resolution of 0.38 mm and an addressability of 480 lines within a 27.5-cm vertical display area, the modulation between adjacent raster lines (pixels) is 0.43.

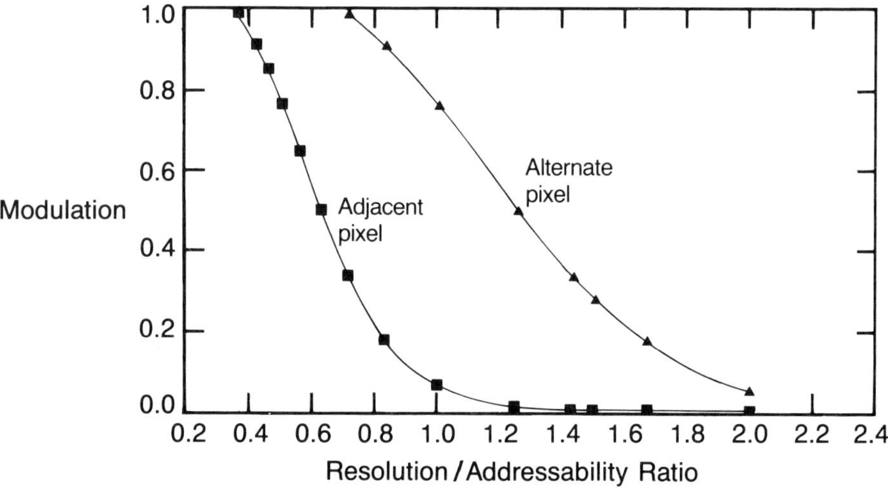

Figure 1. Adjacent and alternate raster line (pixel) modulation as a function of *RAR*.

With Eqs. 1 and 2, the alternate raster line (pixel) modulation can be computed easily by doubling the separation value used in the corresponding adjacent raster line (pixel) calculation; that is, the *RAR* value for the alternate criterion is equal to one-half of the *RAR* value for the adjacent criterion. Example calculations are shown in Figure 1 by the curve labeled "Alternate Pixel."

SELECTING AN OPTIMAL RESOLUTION AND ADDRESSABILITY

The final step in the evaluation procedure is to assess the detectability of adjacent and alternate raster line (pixel) modulation by a human operator. For this purpose, a classic finding from the field of visual science known as the Contrast Sensitivity Function (CSF) is used, which describes the minimum modulation needed by the visual system to detect a sine-wave pattern of a given spatial frequency. Figure 2 presents the 90% population CSF for sine-wave patterns subtending at least 5 degrees of visual angle and having an average luminance of 10 cd/m^2 [4]. This CSF curve is described by the following least-squares regression equation:

$$M = b_0 \exp \left[b_1(\omega) + b_2(\omega^2) + b_3(\omega^4)\right] , \qquad (3)$$

in which M denotes the modulation required for detection at spatial frequency ω, expressed in cycles per degree of visual angle. Values for the regression coefficients b_0, b_1, b_2, and b_3 are 1.7062×10^{-3}, 201.6188×10^{-3}, -2.3161×10^{-3}, and 0.2000×10^{-6}, respectively.

Equation 3 can be used in conjunction with Eq. 2 to determine the visibility of adjacent and alternate raster line modulation. Before proceeding, however, it is necessary to determine the spatial frequency, in cycles per degree of visual angle, corresponding to the adjacent and alternate raster lines (pixels) and to rewrite Eq. 3 in a form that can be used directly with Eq. 2.

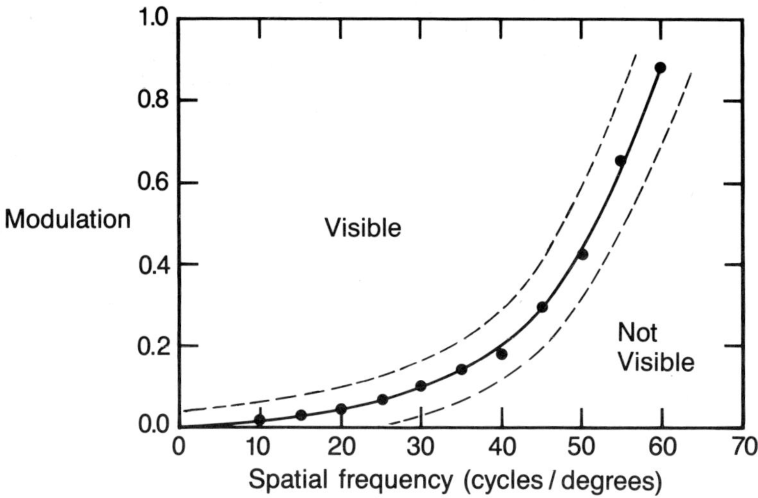

Figure 2. Human contrast sensitivity function with 90% population limits (broken lines).

For each image-quality criterion, spatial frequency is related to the separation between the raster lines (pixels) under consideration, since peak-to-peak separation equals one period of the waveform cycle. Therefore, using the fact that $S = W \div RAR$ (see Eq. 1), a separation value can be converted into cycles per degree of visual angle by

$$\omega = \frac{\pi}{180}\left[\frac{D}{S}\right] = \frac{\pi}{180}\left[\frac{D(RAR)}{W}\right], \tag{4}$$

in which D denotes the viewing distance of the operator from the display screen and S, W, and RAR are defined by Eq. 1. The right-hand side of Eq. 4 can be substituted into Eq. 3 to express the CSF as a function of RAR for various levels of display resolution.

Figure 3 presents an example of the display evaluation procedure, where a resolution level was chosen and an optimal display addressability was desired. By the use of Eq. 2, the adjacent and alternate raster line (pixel) modulations were computed for various addressabilities and, therefore, various RAR values, as shown by the two decelerating curves. Next, Eqs. 3 and 4 were used to determine the CSF values for the adjacent and alternate raster line (pixel) criteria, as shown by the two accelerating curves. One bound on the optimal addressability is provided by the intersection of the adjacent raster line (pixel) modulation curve with the corresponding CSF curve, while another bound is provided by the intersection between the two curves for the alternate raster line (pixel) criterion.

For a selected resolution level, a range of addressabilities will satisfy the adjacent and alternate raster line (pixel) criteria. In these situations, it will be convenient to choose the adjacent RAR limit since the resulting addressability maximizes the visibility of high spatial frequency components while maintaining the raster modulation at a "just detectable" level. Table 1 lists the RAR limits for a variety of frequently used resolution levels. Note that the alternate raster line (pixel) limit is twice as large as the corresponding adjacent raster line (pixel) limit.

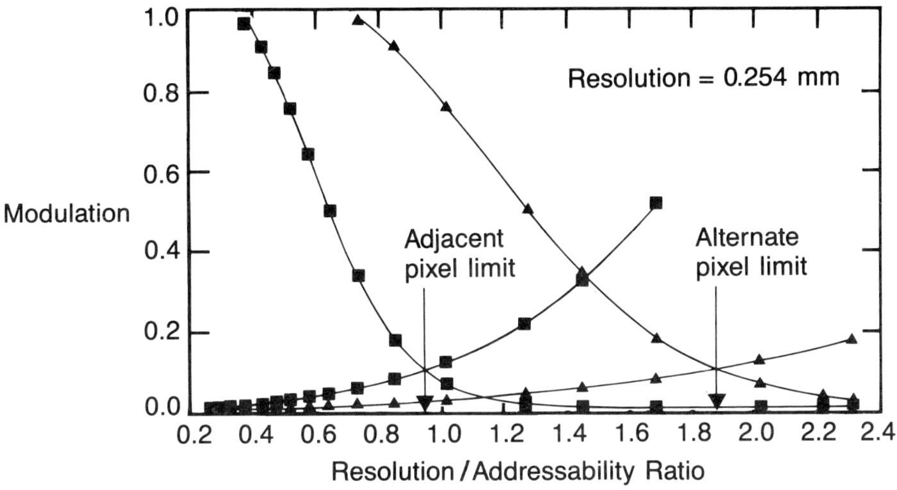

Figure 3. Modulation and visual contrast sensitivity values for the adjacent (squares) and alternate (triangles) raster line (pixels) criteria.

Table 1. Adjacent and Alternate Raster Line (Pixel) Limits.

RESOLUTION – mm	ADJACENT PIXEL LIMIT	ALTERNATE PIXEL LIMIT
0.127	0.71	1.42
0.254	0.92	1.84
0.381	1.02	2.04
0.508	1.09	2.18
0.635	1.12	2.24
0.762	1.18	2.36

CONCLUSIONS

Resolution and addressability play key roles in determining the image quality of digital-display systems. In this paper, we have discussed a straightforward procedure to match these display characteristics to human visual capacity.

REFERENCES

[1] Sherr, S., *Electronic Displays* (John Wiley & Sons, Inc., New York, 1980).

[2] Keller, P.A., "A Survey of Data-Display CRT Resolution Measurement Techniques," in *Society for Information Display, Seminar Lecture Notes*, (Los Angeles, California: Society for Information Display 1984) pp. 2.2a-1–2.2a-28.

[3] Beaton, R.J., *A Human-Performance Based Evaluation of Quality Metrics for Hard-Copy and Soft-Copy Digital Imaging Systems*, (Unpublished doctoral dissertation, Virginia Polytechnic Institute and State University, Blacksburg, Virginia, 1984).

[4] Snyder, H.L., "Human Visual Performance and Flat Panel Display Image Quality," *Technical Report No. HFL-80-1/ONR-80-1*, (Blacksburg, Virginia: Virginia Polytechnic Institute and State University, Human Factors Laboratory, 1980).

WORK WITH DISPLAY UNITS 86
B. Knave and P.-G. Wideback (eds.)

CRITERIA FOR THE SUBJECTIVE QUALITY OF VISUAL DISPLAY UNITS*

Jacques A.J. Roufs, Martinus A.M. Leermakers, Martin C. Boschman**

1. INTRODUCTION OF THE PROBLEM

Opto-electronic display techniques have undergone a rapid development during the past decade. In the case of display units, especially when used for alphanumeric information during long sessions, visual fatigue was found to be an unwanted effect of bad design. It became apparent that it is important to match physical screen parameters to the demands of the visual system. It is well known, however, that visual fatigue is difficult to measure and consequently not quite suitable as a design criterion. Therefore we took a different approach, starting from the assumption that if the text is easily legible, visual comfort is high and visual fatigue correspondingly low. This report concerns the relation between visual comfort, visual performance and characteristics of eye movements, reflecting the ease of information intake while varying the physical screen parameters. It is a part of the results of an 8 manyear research project, financially supported by the Netherlands Technology Foundation.

2. APPARATUS AND METHODS***

An image processing system was used to generate characters. The actual data apply to letterfont BEEHIVE, the x-height being 14 min of arc. Bright characters on a relatively dark background and dark characters on a bright background were the independent variables, where luminance ratio and mean luminance were varied. The images were obtained from a 512x512 points memory and displayed on a high quality monitor. For the reported case the interlace mode was used, the frame frequency being 50 Hz. In reading a normal text, the eye does not move continuously over the text but jumps from one fixation point to the other. These so-called saccades and the fixation pauses between them are, among other things, related to the legibility and to the difficulty of the text (Bouma, 1978; Roufs, Bouma, 1980). During fixations information is taken in. The more difficult the text is, the longer are the fixation pauses and the smaller the saccades (Tinker, 1965). This suggests that fixation duration and saccadic length might be a measure of the ease of information intake. Fixation duration and saccade length are stochastic variables. In order to avoid effects of text redundancy or semantic aspects, pseudo text of meaningless character strings of different length were used. For an example see Fig. 1.
The subjects, observing the screen from a distance of 1.0m, were asked to read the text, to look for a certain character and push a button every time they spotted it. Their eye movements during this search task were registered with a dual Purkinje image eye tracker of SRI and analysed by a computer. Forward saccade length, duration of fixation and search velocity were used as global dependent variables. After completing the search on a page of text which took about 1 min., the subject was asked to judge reading comfort on a ten-point

---

* This research project is supported by the Netherlands Technology Foundation granted to the first author, project number EIPOO.0024.

** Institute for Perception Research/IPO, P.O. Box 513, 5600 MB Eindhoven, The Netherlands.

*** More specific details will be published elsewhere.

```
6M 4KVGWY09L9VHVI3F TNJY0 7AFS
XDY M8HINOM4EZB6I T08 XAMP 9NF
N7ST6IG4GY YOE6 YA10SQFT BGZIH
LIT CHIL 9LA7ENQ W9HB J1RVHOWG
CSUY1X44C8G EEGITU52L44WJ215N6
I8G ZYH 1SJOQ2 ANQ 8I8X3Y 0LX7
M4 B7HH4FR1H HTU 21EP CC VUOXK
PZRB TS0Q WIWO7 VY4TMH833QI TD
F8H AI4PFYCN7I NH GTY4Q6LV0UHS
W24XD2O TVY 1J AMN2DH9FQE0WGGF
QWGRBA34QL 1R 3789 NNVFX9T5 ZU
1Q5L IY0OV P19V 3R5 IC CF0VR01
MUL VEXS 2XOA4SQL9 NT8G7T 59WI
6T EAX 4MGEZR 5JJHBH DCKY LP3V
```

Fig.1. An example of the pseudo text used (font: BEEHIVE)

scale. This kind of category scaling (e.g. Torgerson, 1958) has proven to work quite satisfactory for the evaluation of appreciation of perceived quality (e.g. Allnatt, et al., 1983). Then, a new page with different screen parameters was displayed. The different parameter combinations were ordered in randomized blocks. In one session which took some 1.5 hours, 42 pages were displayed. At the beginning of each session, during the training trials four pages covering the whole range of physical parameters were shown to the subjects. Each experiment took two sessions per subject.

3. RESULTS

Fig.2 shows the means of comfort judgement of three trained subjects as a function of the luminance contrast ratio of the characters. Their individual assessments are pretty close. Fig. 3 gives the means of 20 mostly naīve subjects. The subjects' judgement figures were found to have equal sensory intervals, which has been tested by calculating the psychological scale-values for the subjects' judgements on the basis of the well known Thurstonian type of model (Edwards, 1957). This is illustrated in Fig.7. The general trend of the results is clear. After an initial fast increase with contrast, judgement levels off. For light characters on a dark background an optimum is found at contrast ratios of about 5. For dark characters on a light background the result is at least not worse, probably better. For the present set of characters the letter-font did not allow larger contrast values, the thin parts of the characters being filled with light due to scatter. The optimal contrast is roughly 1/5. It must be emphasized, however, that details in behaviour of this judgement function depend on the letterfont used and the general viewing conditions. In Fig.5 the mean fixation durations are plotted as a function of contrast. The fixation duration is plotted downward in order to facilitate the visualization of the correlation with judgement since faster, and correspondingly easier information intake would mean shorter fixation duration. In Fig.5 the average length of the forward saccades is shown. From reading experiments we know that as stated above if text becomes more difficult the fixation duration increases and the length of the forward saccades decreases. The same thing appears to happen if the legibility is degraded. In this case there is an obvious increase in fixation duration and decrease in saccade length when contrast is lowered. Finally in Fig. 6 search velocity, expressed as the total number of inspected characters per second, is shown. Search velocity is used in literature as a measure of visual performance. It is of course closely connected with the two preceding variables and is very easy to measure.

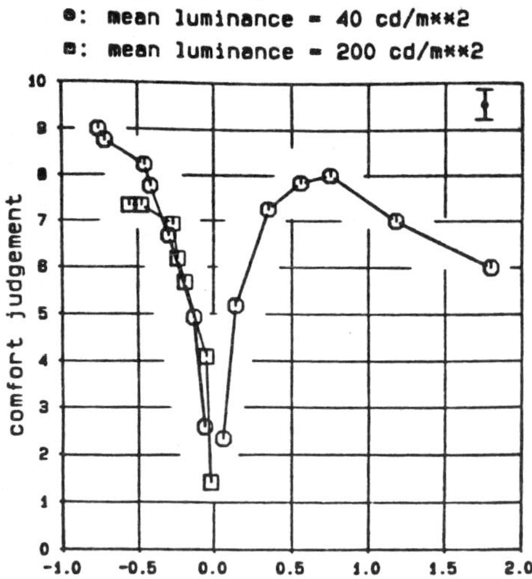

Fig. 2. The means of comfort judgements of 3 trained subjects as a function of log contrast ratio L_c = character luminance, L_b = background lumimance.

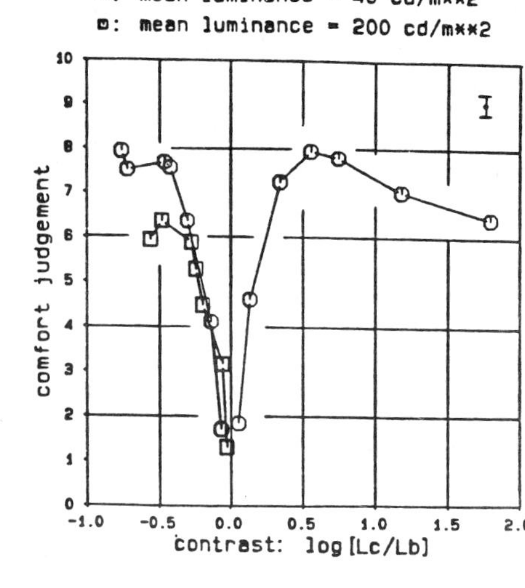

Fig. 3. The means of comfort judgements of 20 subjects (including 17 naïves) as a function of log contrast ratio.

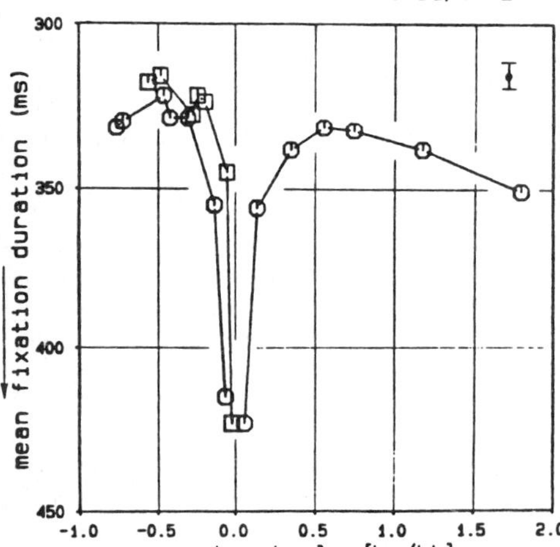

Fig. 4. Mean fixation duration (plotted downwards) for the same subjects as Fig. 2, plotted against log contrast ratio.

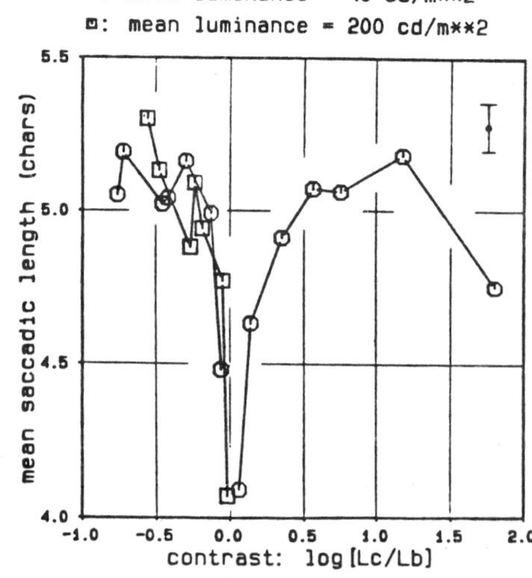

Fig. 5. Mean saccadic length (in number of characters) as a function of log contrast ratio. Same subjects as Fig. 2.

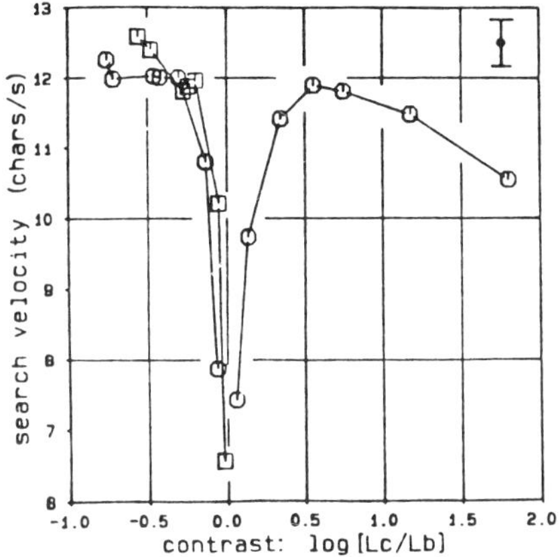

Fig. 6. Search velocity (in number of inspected characters per second) as a function of log contrast ratio. Same subjects as Fig.2.

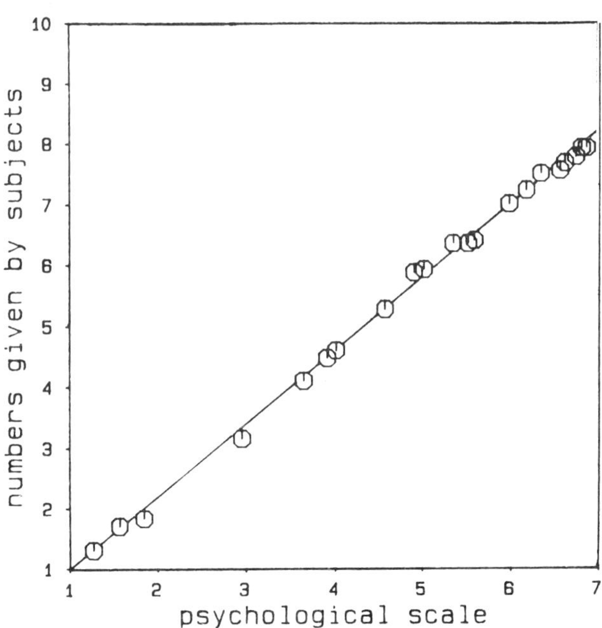

Fig. 7. Demonstration of the linearity of the 10 point-interval scale with the psychological scale, based on Thurstone's model and reconstructed using Edwards' method (1957). Every point in the plot corresponds to the averaged (scale used) or reconstructed (psychological scale) data, concerning one stimulus condition in the scaling experiment with 20 inexperienced subjects.

4. DISCUSSION AND CONCLUSIONS

The four contrast-dependent variables are obviously sufficiently sensitive to be used as criteria for an optimal design. Comparison of Figs. 2, 4, 5 and 6 shows in one glance that these curves are highly correlated. The correlation coefficient between each of the variables is given in Table 1. The overall-correlation coefficient is about 0.9. However, there is a small but significant difference between comfort judgement and the three objective variables. For small negative contrasts the latter increase faster than for positive contrast. This was confirmed in several other experiments not reported here. The reason for this discrepancy is not yet clear. Nevertheless, the results support the validity of the category scaling of reading comfort. Search velocity, using the right experimental setup, seems to be a convenient measure of performance in reading information. However, small but significant deviations from judgement do occur.* Therefore, although both output variables seem to have a common input, they do not reflect the same process. Bright characters on a relatively dark background look to be optimal for a luminance ratio of about 5. For the other polarity no clear optimum was found with this letterfont; however, the data suggest that it could also be 1/5 with a somewhat better judgement. These data are only valid for the letterfont and conditions mentioned. Although the general behaviour of judgement and performance is roughly the same for other letterfonts and conditions it is still too early to make any conclusions about the best polarity or optimal luminance contrast ratios. These variables appear to depend on quite a few physical parameters and need, therefore, considerable more study.

	comfort judgement	search speed	fixation duration
search speed	0.92	***	***
fixation duration	- 0.86	- 0.98	***
saccade length	0.85	0.93	- 0.89

Table 1 Matrix of correlation coefficient for the different dependent variables. In all cases is $p < 0.001$ (two-tailed)

5. REFERENCES

[1] Allnatt J.W.; Gleiss, N.; Kretz, F.; Sciarappa, A.; VanderZee, E. (1983) Definition and validation of methods for the subjective assessment of visual telephone picture quality. CSE 25, Rapporti technici Vol. XI pp. 59-65.

[2] Bouma, H. (1978) Visual search and reading: Eye movement and functional visual field. A tutorial review. Proc. Attention and Performance VII, Sénanque, 1976; ed. J.R. Requin, Hillsdale, Erlbaum, 1978 N.J. pp.115-147.

[3] Edwards, A.L. (1957) Techniques of attitude scale construction. NY Appleton-Century-Crofts.

[4] Roufs, J.A.J.; Bouma, H. (1980) Toward linking perception research and image quality. Proc. SID Vol. 21 pp. 247-270.

* Experiments with variable bandwidth, not reported here, show that these differences may become quite large.

[5] Tinker, M.A. (1965) Bases for effective reading. University of Minnesota Press, Minneapolis.
[6] Torgerson, W.S. (1958) Theory and methods of scaling. NY Wiley and Sons.

WORK WITH DISPLAY UNITS 86
B. Knave and P.-G. Wideback (eds.)

COLOURS IN VIDEO DISPLAYS

Gunnar TONNQUIST

Department of Photography, Royal Institute of Technology,
S-100 44 Stockholm, Sweden

Colours in a video display may be described physically by the excitation levels of the electron guns, psychophysically in the CIE colorimetric system, or psychometrically in a colour appearance system. The Natural Colour System (NCS), today widely used in architecture, design, and industrial production, is described and suggested for use in the description of video display colours.

1. WHAT IS COLOUR?

1.1. What does the word colour mean?

Colour is a perception, normally caused by electromagnetic radiation acting as a stimulus on the sense of vision. But the same word colour is also used for the stimulus causing the perception. Many languages even have the same word for the material, which by selective absorption influences the spectral quality of the colour stimulus and thereby the perceived colour.

Colour percepts may be either achromatic (white, grey, black) or chromatic (e.g. yellow, red, blue, green) but very often 'colour' is used in a more restricted sense. A colour picture e.g. is one where we see not only grey or greyish colours but also colours that are more or less chromatic. Correspondingly, a black and white picture (b&w) is regarded as one showing no colours, i.e. black, white, and the greys are deprived of their right of being colours.

1.2. Video colours

In modern video technique, the term b&w is replaced by monochrome, disregarding the colour of the background. A monochrome monitor may show 'black' characters on a white or uniformly chromatic background: Such a display is described as positive. Or the background may be 'black', contrasting against characters which are white or of one single chromatic colour, a negative display.

In these contexts, 'black' is a purely perceptive concept, as the psychophysical luminance of those areas on the screen never can be lower than that of the disconnected screen, which we usually would not describe as black. As soon as a part of the screen becomes luminous, the adjacent non-luminous parts seem to darken, due to the effect known as simultaneous contrast. In the negative mode all colours are luminous; in the positive mode they may simulate non-luminous surface colours, if the white background determines the adaptation, but they may as well be perceived as luminous colours.

A multi-colour display of the usual shadow-mask type requires three sets of phosphor dots or stripes in the screen. When hit by electrons, each phosphor emits a radiation acting as a stimulus for blue, green or red. The 'red' phosphor usually emits a line spectrum, whereas the others emit broad-band spectra (Figure 1). When radiations from different dots fuse and act on the same part of the retina, we perceive new colours by so called additive colour synthesis. Red and blue combine to a bluish red, by colour reproduction technicians called magenta. Blue and green combine to a greenish blue called

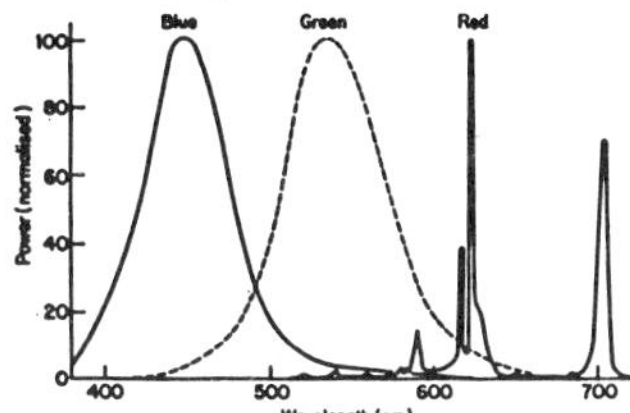

Figure 1. The emission spectra of three typical video screen phosphors. When spectrum lines are seen isolated, yellow is usually perceived around 580 nm; on the screen, yellow is generated by superposition of green red, with only a small part of the total energy in the 580 nm region. (From Sproson)

cyan. Red and green together induce the perception of yellow. Finally, all three together give us an achromatic perception of white.

In the simplest type of colour displays, each electron gun can only be trigged on or off, giving us the six already mentioned chromatic colours plus white and black. If the electron beam intensities can be regulated stepwise, e.g. from the computer, the numbers of possible combinations increases rapidly. With eight excitation levels there are 512, with sixteen levels 4096 and with 256 levels 16777216 possible stimulus combinations. The last figure exceeds the number of colours that the eye can distinguish, but the non-linearity between excitation levels and perceived colours will result in a perceptively uneven distribution om stimuli. In one part of colour space many stimuli may be undistinguishable from each other, whereas in other parts each increase inexcitation produces a clearly visible change in perceived colour. In order to produce stimuli for every conceivable colour, it is therefore necessary to use 1024 levels. Today only few monitors have this capability, and usually only a selection of all possible stimuli are available for the operator at a given moment.

2. COLOUR VISION

As already stated, the stimulus for a colour perception normally is an electromagnetic radiation of a certain spectral composition. Variations in its intensity initiate electric spikes in the nerve cells in the retina, radiations from different wavelength regions affecting different cells (Figure 2). These signals are analyzed by various kinds of transformation and differentiation before leaving the eye - in fact a part of the brain - through the optic nerve for the main part of the brain.

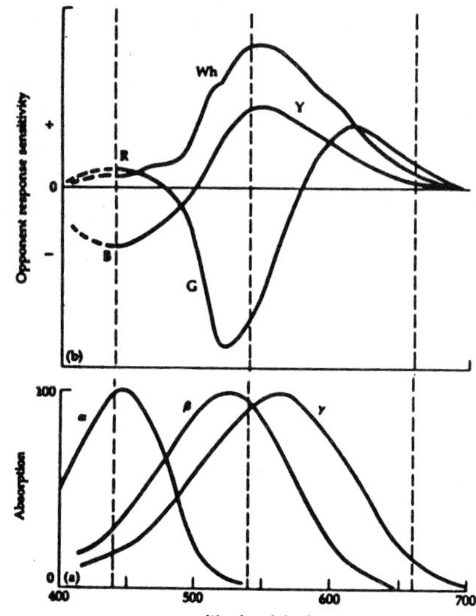

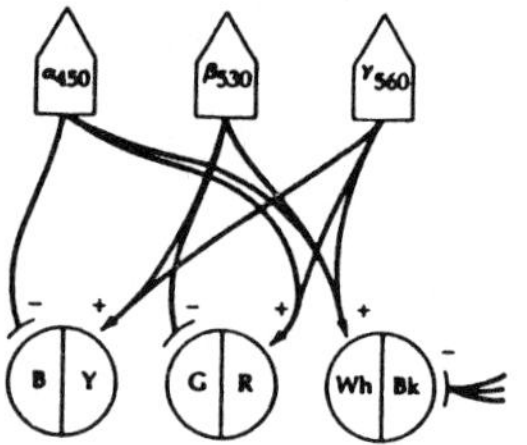

Figure 2. Spectral distributions of photopigment absorptions with maxima at 440, 540, and 660 nm (left), how they are linked to the opponent neural system (above), and the resulting achromatic and opponent chromatic responses (upper left). (From Hurvich)

Our final perception is strongly influenced by spacial and temporal induction, by chromatic adaptation and by the psychological evaluation of the nerve signals arriving at the visual centre in the brain. This evaluation includes some sort of memory retrieval - if the information through the visual nerve is insufficient we are simply apt to see what we are used to see in similar situations, or what the stimulation from other parts of the visual field makes probable. We are e.g. not aware of the blind spot in the retina except in carefully arranged experiments; our sense of vision 'fills in' the lacking information from the surround. We also 'see' colours when the visual system is affected mechanically or chemically, and even in the absence of any stimulation from the outside, as in a completely dark room.

3. PRINCIPLES FOR THE DESCRIPTION OF COLOURS

3.1. Colour names

In any language, the number of real colour names - i.e. words exclusively used for colour description - is very small. Looking up in an ethymological dictionary, we will find that even the 'real' colour names in the indo-european languages have originated from the words of objects exhibiting those particular colours. So e.g. is <u>yellow</u> (Swed. 'gul') most probably derived from <u>gold</u> (Swed. 'guld'). To the Swedish word for <u>green</u> ('grön') we have the verb 'gro' (<u>grow</u>). But the immediate connection between object and colour name has got lost in everyday speech for a few colour names: white, black, yellow, red, blue, green, and brown.

In other cases we still may be conscious of the relation between object and colour: orange, violet, turqoise etc., whereas many other colour names do not describe the colour appearance at all, leaving us with a more or less pronounced uncertainty: ultramarin, sand, sky blue, sea blue, sea green (!), lavender, mist (!) etc.

The first eight colours of a typical video display are easy to describe by their technical names, once the terms 'cyan' (from a dark blue mineral) and 'magenta' (a town where Napoleon won a battle when the French chemist first produced the pigment) have been memorized. Whith more colours on the screen we need a logical notation system to describe them.

3.2. Methods for colour specification

For many technical purposes, as in the construction and servicing of monitors, a physical method specifying the electronic signal levels in the red, green and blue channels will do. Due to nonlinear relations between signal level and the number of emitted photons, as well as between photon current and perceived luminosity, this RGB-system for the specification of video colours - although useful and necessary for the technician - gives a poor idea of what the colours really look like.

3.3. Psychophysical colour specification

Colour stimuli can be measured with physical instruments, givning the spectral partition of the radiant energy evoking the colour perception. Clearly this is not a measurement of colour itself, but using our previous experience of the relations between stimulus and perception, we can evaluate the physical measurements according to a psychophysical method.

Thus, the colorimetric system recommended 1931 by the CIE (International Commission of Illumination), was developed from matches between a series of monochromatic stimuli and suitable combinations of three reference stimuli manipulated by the observers, whose eyes only acted as null instruments. The mean values were recommended as the CIE standard observer, and different sets of reference stimuli may be substituted for each other by linear transformation. CIE also recommended a series of standard illuminants (CIE 1971). We will later discuss in more detail the validity and limitations of such a system for the specification of perceptions.

The CIE system of colorimetry was originally developed to supplement the CIE photometric function as a tool for the illumination engineer, but it was soon found useful also for the measurement of all sorts of coloured products. New instruments and evaluation routines were developed. Modern video displays have again made the measurement of luminous colours important (Sproson 1983).

The CIE system is excellent for many purposes and used world-wide as the most precise system for comparing colour stimuli, but it was never intended to describe the appearance of colours. The matching experiments were made in experimental situations (a split field with a black surround) very different from how colours are seen in everyday life. CIE data are always related to a specified standard illuminant and a specified standard observer, from which individual observers may deviate noticeably, something which is very often forgotten.

For calculation of differences between luminous colours the CIELUV system is currently recommended, as is the CIELAB transform for surface colours, but the efforts are continued to find better transformations of CIE coordinates to better conformance with the perceptive colour world.

3.4. Psychometric colour specification

Belonging to the domain of perception psychology, perceived colours should be measured and specified by psychometric analysis. Can this be done? It is still widely believed - especially among scientists and technicians - that all measurements need physical instruments. Therefore true psychometry has been substituted by physical measurements in combination with some empirical evidence of the relations between stimulus and perception. But if this evidence is obtained under conditions quite different from those where we want our psychometric specification, then it doesn't help how carefully the experiments were made. The CIE system described in the preceeding section even contains a number of terms, which are falsely designated as "psychometric".

The requirement to measure colour psychometrically was first formulated by the German physiologist Ewald Hering (1874, 1878, 1920, 1960):

> "For a systematic grouping of colours the only thing that matters is colour itself. Neither the qualitative (frequency) nor quantitative (amplitude) physical properties of the radiation are relevant."

How can this be done? Many years ago, this author had the privilege of being the subject in a private demonstration of psychometric measurement, led by no less an authority than professor S.S. Stevens at Harvard University. He taught me how to use my own senses as meter-stick and balance to measure my perceptions on an arbitrary scale invented by myself on the spot, and without any comparison with outer references.

The only modern colour system implementing this method of 'absolute scaling' of colour perceptions, is the Swedish development of what Hering called the "Natural System of Colour Perceptions" (see Section 5). All other systems are built upon the selection of a set of colour stimuli which compared with each other yield colour perceptions with equaly large differences. In the next section we will study the properties of some such systems, before the Natural Colour System and its relations to other systems will be described.

4. COLOUR DIFFERENTIATING SYSTEMS

Many efforts have been made to construct perceptive colour systems. The usual choice of variables is hue, lightness, and saturation or corresponding terms, and the usual criterion for the scaling of variables is that of a perceptively equal spacing, i.e. the distances between adjacent lattice points should represent equal differences in colour perception.

Usually, the first step in colour ordering is to separate achromatic colours from the chromatic ones. When the achromatic colours are non-luminous surface colours, they are also designated as grey and are ordered in a continuous scale from black to white according to increasing lightness.

Dealing with luminous achromatic colours, the grey scale is replaced by a series of neutral colours of increasing brightness, without any definite upper limit that could be called white.

In the first colour systems the Weber-Fechner function was used for the relation between stimulus intensity and perceived lightness/brightness, but it was soon found that more sophisticated direct experiments were necessary, leading to various forms of power or logarithmic functions.

Contrary to the achromatic colours, the chromatic colours all possess some kind of hue. All different hues can be arranged in a continuous and closed circuit, called the hue circle, running from red over organge, yellow, green, turqoise, blue, violet and purple back to red. Even if most systems claim to have equally spaced hue circles, the results are widely different. When reference points are indicated on the hue circle, they ar mostly vaguely defined and sometimes in contradiction to direct visual observation.

As the achromatic colours show different degrees of lightness/brightness, so do the chromatic colours. Equal lightness is then either defined as equal photometric luminance or reflection factor, or it is determined by separate experiments, where one often finds that chromatic colours need less luminance to appear equally bright. Such results are dependent on the situation of observation. It is therefore still uncertain, if this is really true, or if the effect is due to the inability of the observer to fully separate the concept om 'brightness' ('lightness') from other characteristics of the colour.

The chromatic colour may be more or less chromatic. If this is expressed as the degree of departure from a grey or neutral colour of the same lightness/ brightness, the attribute is usually called chroma. If the attribute is being judged in proportion to the lightness/brightness, it is called saturation.

Not only the choice of variables, but also their scaling, varies considerably between various perceptive colour systems of this type. In the absence of natural reference points, the systems are defined, not by any psychometric measurements, but by the CIE coordinates of selected stimuli. The notations do therefore not give an unambiguous description of the appearance of a colour, unless one has an illustrating colour atlas at hand for reference.

So were the Munsell system (Munsell 1905) and the German DIN system (Richter 1952) and their corresponding colour atlases developed. For video screen colours a similar system has been proposed, HCV Colour Space, using the variables hue, saturation, and value.

The principle of equal spacing can obviously not be upheld throughout a cylindrical colour space of the lightness/hue/saturation type, as e.g. hue steps necessarily become smaller with decreasing saturation. To overcome this difficulty, the UCS system of the Optical Society of America (MacAdam 1978) has replaced hue and saturation by rectangular j,g-coordinates, intended to simulate the opponent hues (see Section 5), but the efforts to obtain equal colour steps in as many directions as possible induces fairly large discrepancies.

5. THE NATURAL COLOUR SYSTEM

In another group of colour order systems, less emphasis is laid on the differentiating and equal spacing aspects. Instead the unambiguous characterizing of the appearance of colours is stressed. If colours are measured psychometrically, the description of colours can be made irrespective of by which stimuli the colour perceptions are evoked, in accordance with Hering´s requirements.

In Sweden, Hård (1969) and others further analyzed Hering´s ideas and developed them into the modern Natural Colour System (NCS). Comparisons between the basic concepts of different systems have been made by Tonnquist (1970, 1986). Even if Hård´s work was restricted to non-luminous surface colours, the basic concepts of the NCS are so general that they without much difficulty should be applicable also the colours seen in a video display.

5.1. Elementary colours

Hering had demonstrated 1) the existence of six "einfache" (elementary) colours - black, white, yellow, red, blue, and green - each of them showing no resemblance to any of the other five, and 2) that all other colours can be described by their resemblances to these elementary colours.

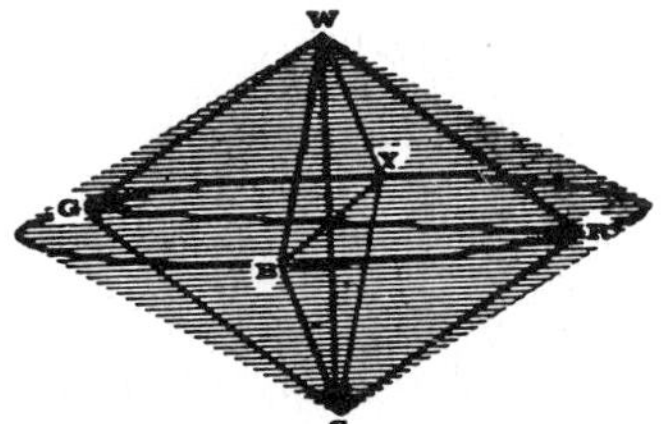

Figure 3. The NCS colour solid with the six elementary colours as the natural references. All other colours can be described by their resemblances to the elementary colours. These resemblances are called elementary attributes.

We can easily imagine a pure white and a pure black. There is also a consensus about the concepts pure yellow, pure red, pure blue, and pure green, all without any resemblance to white or black. It seems as if these six pure colours (in English usually called 'unique') are innate in all humans with normal colour vision, as there is a fairly unanimous opinion both of the meaning of the words and of the appearance of the colours.

All other colours can be described by their resemblances to the six elementary colours:

1. An (arbitrary) achromatic colour resembles white and black only.

2. An (arbitrary) chromatic colour resembles white and black and one or two of the four chromatic elementary colours.

3. If a chromatic colour has no resemblance to white or black, it is a pure chromatic colour and resembles one or two of the four chromatic elementary colours only.

The elementary colours are cornerstones in a perceptual colour system. White and black are the ends of the grey scale. Red, blue, green, and yellow divide the hue circle into four quadrants. In a series of hues, the qualitative character changes markedly when an elementary hue is passed (e.g. from a greenish yellow to a reddish yellow). A similar but less drastical change is experienced when the mid-point of each quadrant is passed (e.g. where a yellow dominance in an orange colour is changed to a reddish dominance).

5.2. Elementary attributes

For an arbitrary colour, its degree of resemblance to each of the elementary colours is described by a corresponding elementary attribute (whiteness, blackness, yellowness, redness, blueness, and greenness). These are the colour attributes primarily observed, when the appearance of a single colour has to be described without any conscious comparison with other colours.

But how do we get from the elementary attributes to the attributes used in other perceptive colour systems?

When we are comparing a colour with other colours, such as the colour samples in a colour atlas, and e.g. see more redness in one colour than in the other, there consequently is less yellowness, i.e. the ratio between its two chromatic attributes is different. This is in fact how hue ϕ is defined in the Natural Colour System. With this definition we obtain a hue scale with four easily recognizable reference points, dividing the hue circle in four quadrants. The position of each hue within the quadrant, reflected in the notation of the colour, is defined by its distances to two elementary hues. When each quadrant is divided in 100 steps, it may be so that numerically equal hue steps may appear larger in e.g. the green-yellow quadrant than in the red-blue one, but in the practical use of the system this has never proved to be of any disadvantage,

The total amount of chromaticness c in the colour is obtained be adding the amounts of chromatic elementary attributes. In the example of an orange colour the chromaticness is the sum of the yellowness and the redness.

We thus find that the elementary attributes may be combined to other derived attributes:

hue as the ratio of two chromatic attributes,
chromaticness as the sum of its chromatic attributes.

The relation between the chromaticness and the whiteness of a colour defines its saturation. Thus, while neither hue nor chromaticness/saturation are regarded as basic attributes for characterizing the appearance of a single perceived colour, they are useful to describe colour differences in complex patterns, and hence of major importance in practical work with the NCS.

5.3. Bipolar scales

Between any two adjacent elementary colours Hering established a 'bipolar' scale of colours showing a visual resemblance to both end colours. Along such a bipolar scale the resemblance to one elementary colour (e.g. white) is continuously increasing and the resemblance to the other one (in this case black) is decreasing (Figure 4). Therefore the amounts of the two attributes always sum up to unity (or 100 percent). Similar bipolar scales of particular interest may also be drawn along each quadrant of the hue circle, e.g. from yellow to red with increasing redness and decreasing yellowness. Bipolar scales do also run form white and black to each of the four chromatic elementary colours.

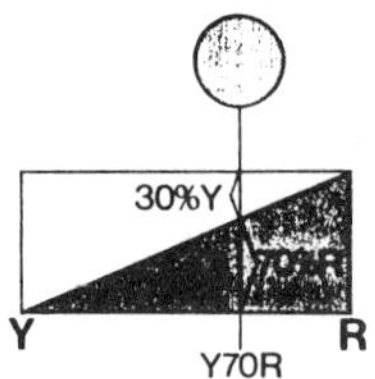

Figure 4. Example of a bipolar scale, here between yellow and red, illustrating the elementary attributes of an reddish orange colour.

But bipolar scales cannot be drawn between opposite chromatic elementary colours on the hue circle. There is no bipolar scale between yellow and blue, as there are no colours which show both yellowness and blueness. Likevise, there is no bipolar scale between red and green, as redness and greenness never appear in the same colour perception. Therefore those two pairs of elementary colours are called opponent, and in English literature the Natural Colour System is mostly known as the 'opponent-colour system'.

The opponent hues are significant for the NCS. When hue circles are constructed on the criterion of equal spacing, the opponent hues will not be oriented opposite each other or at right angles. Particularly the red-blue sector is largely expanded at the cost of the blue-green and green-yellow sectors, and Munsell used purple as a fifth principal hue. However, the real 'expansion' in red-blue is not twofold, and consequently other hues are shifted noticeably from their perceptive positions. So does the Munsell system notate an elementary blue as a purplish blue!

Obviously with the opponent-colour theory in mind, a famous American colour scientist, Dr. Deane B. Judd stated:

> Analysis of the chromatic aspect of colour perception in terms of blue, yellow, red, and green, alternative to the use of the terms, hue and saturation, is preferred by many. Anyone who practices this kind of analysis soon learns to think of colours as combinations of various amounts of these primaries and even to experience colour directly in these terms. With sufficient practice fairly reproducible estimates may be made. .... This basis for the analysis of chromatic experiences is so universal that blue, yellow, red, and green have become known as the psychological colour primaries (Judd 1965).

Hering combined his Natural Colour System with a theory for colour vision, but neither was accepted by colour scientists, who long preferred the Young-Helmholtz trichromatic theory, so readily applicable to colour stimulus specification. Much later it was suggested (von Kries 1905, Müller 1930) and confirmed (Svaetichin 1953) that colour vision really is a combination of trichromatic responses and opponent-colour transforms, and that the opponent colours are fundamental in colour perception (Hurvich 1981).

5.4. Hue circle and colour triangle

The hue circle with the chromatic elementary colours as rectangular axes may be used as a graphical representation of hue. In the same way, all colours of the same hue may be represented by a colour triangle with white, black and the pure chromatic colour of that hue as corners (Figure 5). The position of a colour within the triangle is given by its chromaticness, its blackness and its whiteness. But as the sum of all attribues is defined as 100, and because the hue is expressed by a dimensionless ratio, one of the three attributes can be left out. Thus it has been found suitable to have a standard NCS notation consisting of blackness s, chromaticness c and hue ϕ (Figure 6).

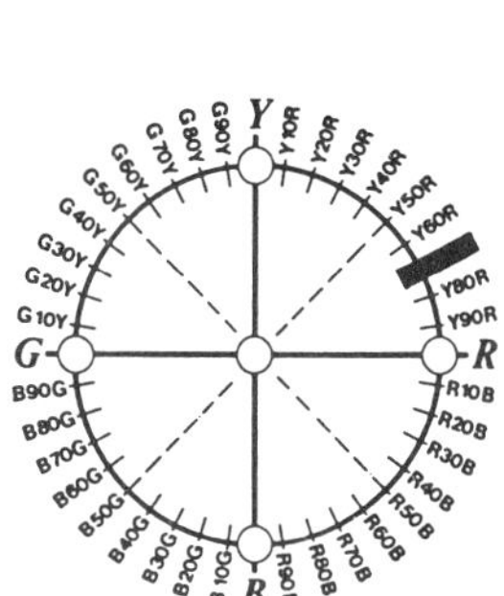

Around the perifery of the colour circle you will find the four chromatic elementary colours (yellow - red - blue - green). These form a quadrant — similar to the points of a compass.

The angle C of the triangle represents the pure chromatic colour of the hue concerned, lacking resemblance to both white and black. The angle W represents pure white and the angle S pure black.

Figure 5. The NCS notation is illustrated by the hue circle and the colour triangle.

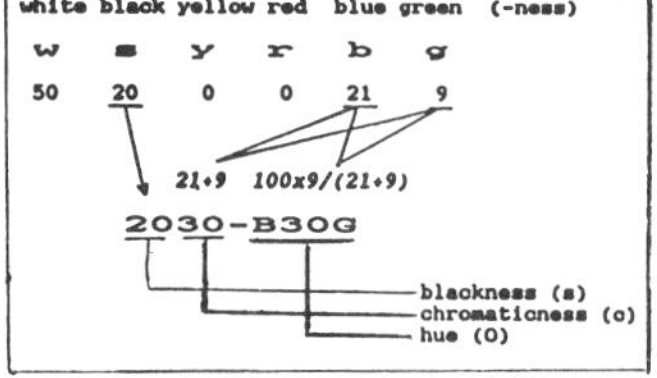

Figure 6. The NCS notation is derived from the elementary attributes and describes the appearance of the colour.

6. COLOUR ATLASES

The Munsell and DIN systems are defined by the CIE specifications of a set of colour stimuli. Where corresponding colour samples can be produced by stable pigments, they are represented in a colour atlas to be used as the reference for the appearance of the colour notations in the system. The system is therefore tightly tied to the atlas and does, strictly speaking, only exist for the illumination and the observer specified with the CIE values.

Hård (Steen 1969) found that the method of psychometric scaling was applicable to the elementary attributes, so that their values could be determined for an arbitrary colour sample without reference to any other material colours in the visual field. The colour samples used in the psychometric experiments were all measured psychophysically in the CIE system. From the CIE data relations between CIE and NCS spaces were established. The CIE data were also the basis for the production of the NCS atlas, with the same restrictions regarding illuminant and observer as all other atlases.

The NCS atlas is a helpful illustration of the system, but it does not define the colour system. The same applies for the CIE values that are published for the 1530 atlas samples. It is very important always to remember this fundamental difference between the NCS and other colour systems.

To work with the atlas and the corresponding samples (available in sizes up to ISO A2) is today the most common application of the NCS. The NCS samples have nominal notations, valid for specified illumination and observing conditions. When viewed in other surroundings, they look differently and can be assigned new NCS notations according to the general rules of the system. This can be used for a direct description of induced colurs in exceptional situation for the study of after-images etc., even if experience has indicated that the NCS samples may be used with acceptable tolerances in all ordinary daylights.

7. COLOURS IN VIDEO DISPLAYS

The general character of the NCS enables it to be used also for special applications, where other systems fall short, e.g. to describe the colours in a video display. Derefeldt (1986) has demonstrated a computer generated simulation of NCS samples in a video display. When colours are seen against a light background and the eye is adapted to the surrounding room, they may still be perceived as non-luminous object colours and the basic principles of the NCS should be applicable, even if a direct comparison with the atlas samples may be difficult or meaningless.

If the colours on the screen are seen as luminous, the main structure of the NCS still applies, even if an attribute like blackness will be of no significance. The new mode of vision opens new possibilities for colour research, but it is not the intention of this paper to report confirmed results, only to indicate ways for future development. In a following paper one such application of the NCS on video display colours will be described.

8. SUMMARY

The specification of the colours in a video display may require three different systems: one purely technical to specify the voltages applied to the image tube, one stimulus system to specify the colour-forming stimuli emitted from the screen, and one perceptive system, preferrably the Natural Colour System to describe the resulting colour perceptions.

References:

CIE Publication No 15, Colorimetry, Paris 1971. (Out of print, new edition in preparation)

Gunilla Derefeldt and Carl-Eric Hedin, A colour atlas for graphical displays, WWDU Stockholm 1986

Ewald Hering: Zur Lehre vom Lichtsinne, Gerold & Sohn, Vienna 1878, first published in S.-B. Kais. Akad. Wiss. 70 (1874), 169-204

Ewald Hering: Grundzüge der Lehre vom Lichtsinne, Springer, Berlin 1920. (Transl. by Hurvich and Jameson: Outlines of a Theory of the Light Sense, Harvard Univ. Press, Cambridge Mass. 1964)

Leo M Hurvich: Color Vision, Sinauer, Sunderland Mass. 1981

Anders Hård: Qualitative Attributes of Colour Perception, Proc. "Color 69", Stockholm 1969, pp 351-356

Deane B Judd: Handbook of Experimental Psychology, ed. Stevens, 1965, p.839

J. v.Kries: Die Gesichtsempfindungen, Nagels Handbuch der Physiologie des Menschen, Vol.3 Vieweg, Braunschweig (1905)

D.L. MacAdam: Uniform color scales, J. Opt. Soc. Am. 64 (1974), 1691-1702

A H Munsell: A Color Notation, Munsell Color Co., Baltimore 1946; 1st edition Boston 1905

G.E. Müller, Z. Psychol. 17/18, 1-430, 435-647 (1930)

Manfred Richter: Das System der DIN-Farbenkarte, Die Farbe 1, 85-98 (1952)

W N Sproson: Colour Science in Television and Display Systems. Hilger, Bristol 1983

Peter Steen, Experiments with estimations of perceptive qualitative colour attributes, Proc. Intern. Colour Meeting COLOR 69, 717-726, Stockholm 1969

Gunnar Svaetichin: The cone action potential, Acta Physiol. Scand. 29 Suppl. 106:565, 1953

Gunnar Tonnquist: The principles of colour systems, Die Farbe 19, 31-37 (1970)

Gunnar Tonnquist: Philosophy of perceptive color order systems, Color R&A 11, 51-55, (1986)

Swedish Standards Institution: SS 01 91 00 Colour notation system and SS 01 91 01 Colour Atlas, Stockholm 1979

WORK WITH DISPLAY UNITS 86
B. Knave and P.-G. Wideback (eds.)

A COLOUR ATLAS FOR GRAPHICAL DISPLAYS

Gunilla Derefeldt and Carl-Eric Hedin

National Defence Research Institute
Man and information Systems (FOA 53)
P.O. Box 1165
S-581 11 Linköping, Sweden

Colour displays are increasingly used in various applications such as computer graphics, colour VDUs etc. In colour graphics the specification, selection and presentation of colours are important. Traditionally the RGB (Red Green Blue) space has been used for these purposes. Though it is computationally easy, the RGB space is not a perceptive colour system, i.e. colours and colour differences defined in terms of RGB values are not closely related to what will be perceived by the user. To meet user demands on colour appearance and uniform colour spacing, we have developed a computerized colour atlas (CCA) based on the NCS, CIELAB and CIELUV colour order systems. When using the CCA, a colour can be selected from any of these three colour spaces and the CCA translates it to the appropriate RGB values for the system used. There are several tools in the CCA for choosing colours. For example, the CCA can display the set of colours that the graphical system can generate in different sections of the colour spaces, colours can be interactively as well as automatically selected. Ongoing research concerns the development of perceptually based algorithms for automatic selection of colours for different applications such as pseudo colour coding, colour coding of symbols, choice of background colours etc.

1. INTRODUCTION

During the last decade, perceptually based colour spaces have come into use for colour selection and presentation in computer graphics and digital image processing applications. Traditionally, the RGB (Red Green Blue) space has been used for digitally controlled colour television monitors. Though it is computationally easy, colours and colour differences defined in terms of RGB values are not closely related to the appearance of colours. Colours defined in numerical RGB values are not related to the perceptually relevant dimensions hue, chroma (chromaticness, saturation), lightness, and brightness. For instance, how does the colour defined by the RGB numerical value 15,10,1 appear? And how does this colour differ from that with the value 12,8,4 ? As the impression of colours on a display is a major function of variations in perceptual dimensions, knowledge about these is of extreme importance for a successful and effective use of colour in VDUs.

Considering the fundamentals of colour perception, there is thus a need to translate RGB values into a colour space where colours are defined in terms of hue, chroma (saturation), and lightness (brightness) and where colours expressed in terms of these attributes are uniformly spaced. Colour order systems that have been applied to computer graphics and image processing are the Munsell System and the OSA Uniform Color Scales (1) and the CIE 1976 (L* u* v*) system (2-4). The perceptually based, although not perceptually uniformly spaced, HLS system (5), which is a direct transformation from RGB to hue, lightness and saturation has also been used (6-7). Comparing the RGB, the HLS and a Colour Naming System (CNS) based on the Munsell Book of Color and natural language categories in English, Berk, Brownston and Kaufman (8-9) found the HLS system to be superior to the RGB system and the CNS system to be better than the HLS system with respect to colour selection. Thus, for interactive colour selection, the best colour space would be a space where colours are defined according to fundamental attributes perceptually as well as linguistically.

2. THE COMPUTERIZED COLOUR ATLAS

2.1 Colour Spaces

Our computerized colour atlas is based on the CIE 1976 (L* u* v*) and CIE 1976 (L* a* b*) spaces, abbreviated CIELUV and CIELAB respectively (10), and on the Swedish Natural Colour System, NCS for short (11 - 17). The CIELUV and CIELAB spaces might be considered as highly appropriate for computer graphics as they have an approximately uniform colour spacing and can be transformed from the CIE 1931 XYZ system. Neither of these two colour spaces has been found to be superior (18-19). However, CIELUV has predominantly been used among those engaged in colour television and CIELAB among those working with colour samples. The NCS is a purely perceptive colour system and its colour notation is simple and comprehensive. Colours are easily described by graphical illustrations as well as by letter-digit notations. Although the NCS Colour Atlas (14) is based on visual judgements of surface colours, we think the concept might equally well be used for colours displayed electronically. The three basic variables of the NCS are hue (ø), blackness (s), and chromaticness (c). In the NCS colour space, the six elementary colours yellow (Y), red (R), blue (B), green (G), white (W), and black (S) constitute cognitive, natural reference points. Any colour perception has a resemblance to two, three, or four of these elementary colours and the degree and composition of these relationships represent the colour we thereby identify. The degree of resemblance to black defines the blackness (s) of the perceived colour. The sum of the chromatic elementary attributes defines the chromaticness (c) and their ratio defines the hue (ø) of the colour. In the NCS hue circle, the unique hues, yellow, blue, red, and green are arranged at 90 degree intervals. The hues are notated in relation to the two related unique hues.

The CIELAB and CIELUV correlates of lightness (L*) and chroma (C^*_{ab}, C^*_{uv}) are close to natural variables of perceived colour. Hue angle (h_{ab}, h_{uv}) however, is not as close to natural language colour characterization as the NCS hue and therefore for many applications we think the NCS hue notation is superior to either CIELAB or CIELUV hue angle. The relationship between the NCS and the CIELAB and CIELUV colour spaces is illustrated in Figures 1-3. (16-17, 20-21).

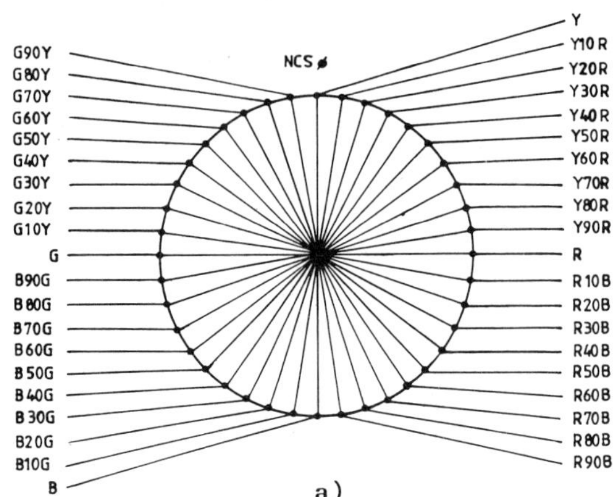

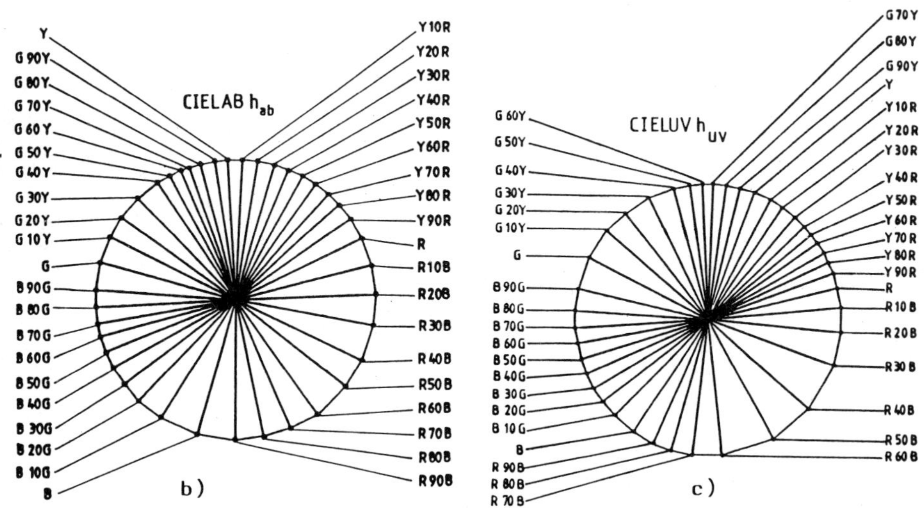

Figure 1. a) Transformation of NCS hue (ø)
b) to CIELAB hue angle (h_{ab})
c) and CIELUV hue angle (h_{uv}).

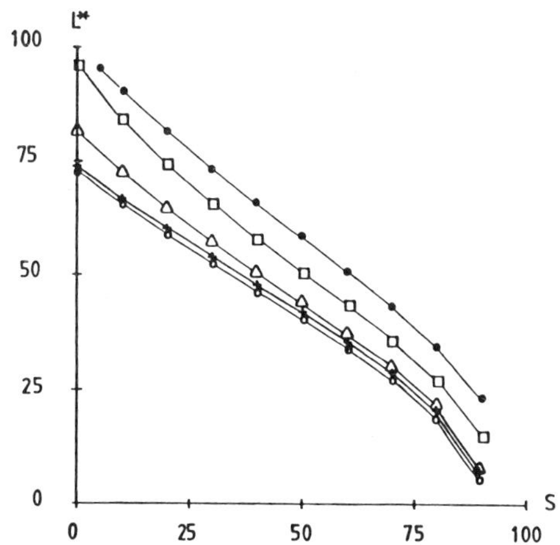

Figure 2. CIELAB and CIELUV lightness (L*) plotted against NCS blackness (s) for the purely grey colours (●—●—●) and for the NCS hues Y (□—□—□), R (○—○—○), B (×—×—×) and G (△—△—△).

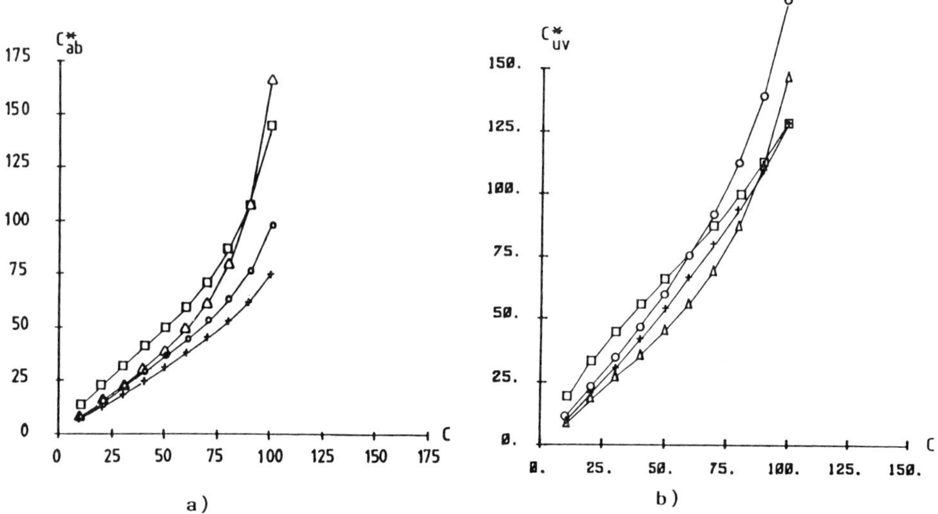

Figure 3. a) CIELAB chroma (C^*_{ab}) and b) CIELUV chroma (C^*_{uv}) plotted against NCS chromaticness (c) for the NCS hues Y (□—□—□), R (○—○—○), B (×—×—×), and G (△—△—△).

The NCS has been used and considered advantageous as a colour order system for environmental design (22). Colours that are equal in NCS blackness/chromaticness are said to be more similar than colours of the same lightness/chroma. This characteristic of the NCS, we think, is essential for certain applications.

2.2 The Colour Video Display System

The computer system on which the CCA has been implemented is a VAX 11/750 with a picture memory VS11 (Digital Equipment). With the VS11 it is possible to display simultaneously 256 out of 4096 colours. The resolution of the picture memory is 512 x 512 pixels. The colour VDU (CRT) used is a Mitsubishi C - 3910 EBM. It is driven by separate signals for RGB and separate sync, 629 lines/25 Hz 2:1 interlace. The "white " of the VDU was adjusted to the colour of the CIE standard illuminant C. The CIE 1931 X Y Z tristimulus values were measured for each electronic gun R (red), G (green) and B (blue) at each digital level. As 4 bits were used to drive each gun, the digital levels controlling each of the red, green, and blue signals could be varied in 16 steps from 0 to 15. The measurements were made with a Spectra Pritchard Photometer 1980-A. The tristimulus values X Y Z of any colour or any digital RGB combination displayed on the screen are given by :

$$X = table(Rd,Xr) + table(Gd,Xg) + table(Bd,Xb)$$
$$Y = table(Rd,Yr) + table(Gd,Yg) + table(Bd,Yb)$$
$$Z = table(Rd,Zr) + table(Gd,Zg) + table(Bd,Zb)$$

where, for example, table (Rd,Xr) indicates the X tristimulus value at the given digital level of the red gun, table (Bd,Yb) the Y tristimulus value at the given digital level of the blue gun as given by the values in a table containing the XYZ tristimulus values for each of the three guns at each of the 16 digital levels, in all 3 x 3 x 16 values.

The transformation of the RGB values into CIELAB L*, a*, b* and CIELUV L*, u*, v* coordinates was made using monitor "white" (e.g. RGB = 15,15,15) with Y_n set to 100. The tristimulus values for all the other RGB combinations were normalized accordingly. For low values of X/X_n, Y/Y_n, and Z/Z_n the modified formulae for calculating L*, a*, and b* were used (10). For each RGB combination the CIELAB and CIELUV metric correlates of the concepts lightness (L*), perceived chroma (C^*_{ab}, C^*_{uv}), and hue (h_{ab}, h_{uv}) were calculated according to the definitions (10).

Lightness: $L^* = 116\,(Y/Y_n)^{1/3} - 16$

CIE 1976 a,b chroma

$$C^*_{ab} = (a^{*2} + b^{*2})^{1/2}$$

CIE 1976 u,v chroma

$$C^*_{uv} = (u^{*2} + v^{*2})^{1/2}$$

CIE 1976 a,b hue angle

h_{ab} = arctan (b*/a*)

CIE 1976 u,v hue angle

h_{uv} = arctan (v*/u*)

where h_{ab} lies between 0 and 90 degrees if a* and b* are both positive, between 90 and 180 degrees if b* is positive and a* is negative, between 180 and 270 degrees if b* and a* are both negative, and between 270 and 360 degrees if b* is negative and a* is positive (and similarly for v* and u*)

The transformation of RGB into NCS was based on the transformation from digital RGB values into L*, a*, b* coordinates, on transforming the tristimulus values of each of the nominal NCS notations (13) into the same coordinates and on calculating the CIELAB colour differences,ΔE^*_{ab} (10), between the digital RGB combinations and the NCS notations. To find the most representative RGB - NCS combination, the pair with the very smallest colour difference was chosen to represent the translation of digital RGB into NCS hue, chromaticness and blackness.

3. APPLICATIONS OF THE CCA

When using the CCA, colours can be selected in different ways. Colours can be interactively as well as automatically selected.

- From any of the three colour spaces, the system can present different cross-sections shown against any background colour. From NCS, the system can present colours from the different NCS colour triangles. The user may also choose colours from different hue circles and blackness or chromaticness diagrams. From the CIELUV and CIELAB spaces, the system can present colours with concurrent variation of hue angle, chroma, and lightness as defined by the user. The colours can be displayed on either a u*/v* (a*/b*) or a chroma/lightness diagram. From the different plots, colours may be selected and saved for colouring.

- The system can automatically select colours that show high contrast against a particular background colour and at the same time high contrast between themselves. The algorithm for this is based on the NCS hue scale and on the CIELUV colour difference formula (10).

- Different objects of a picture presented on the screen can interactively be "painted" in different colours. A "palette" consisting of an NCS hue scale with colours of chromaticness and blackness as defined by the user may be ordered from the system. If any of the colours in the palette is unsatisfactory, different values of blackness and/or chromaticness can be ordered. Alternatively, the colour can be adjusted with small changes in hue, chromaticness or blackness.

REFERENCES

[1] Meyer, G.W., and Greenberg, P.P.: "Perceptual color spaces for computer graphics." Computer Graphics, vol. 14, 1980, pp.254-261.

[2] Santisteban, A.: "The perceptual color space of digital image display terminals." IBM Journal of Research and Development, vol. 27, 1983, PP 127-132.

[3] Tajima, J.: "Uniform color scale applications to computer graphics." Computer Vision, Graphics, and Image Processing, vol. 27, 1983, pp. 305-325.

[4] Tajima, J.: "Optimal color display using uniform color scale." NEC (Nippon Electr. Co) Research & Development, No.70, July, 1983, pp. 58-63.

[5] "Status Report of the Graphics Standards Planning Committee, Part III: Raster Extensions to the Core System." Computer Graphics, vol. 13, No.3, August, 1979.

[6] Smith, A.R. : "Color gamut transform pairs." Computer Graphics, vol.12, no.3, 1978, pp. 12-19.

[7] Ballard, D.H. and Brown, C.M.: Computer Vision. Eaglewood Cliffs,NY.: Prentice-Hall, 1982, pp. 32-33.

[8] Berk, T., Brownston, L., and Kaufman, A.: "A human factors study of color notation systems for computer graphics." Communications of the ACM, vol. 25, 1982, pp. 547- 550.

[9] Berk, T., Brownston,L., and Kaufman, A.: "A new color-naming system for graphics languages." IEEE Computer Graphics and Applications, vol. 2, 1982, pp. 37-44.

[10] Commission Internationale de l'Eclairage, Recommendations on Uniform Color Spaces, Color-Difference Equations, Psychometric Color Terms, Supplement No.2 to CIE Publication No.15 (E-1.3.1.) 1971/(TC-1.3), Paris: Bureau Central de la CIE, 1978.

[11] Hård, A. and Sivik, L.: "NCS - Natural Color System: A Swedish standard for color notation." Color Research and Application, vol. 6, 1981, pp. 129-138.

[12] Swedish Standards Institution, Swedish Standard SS 01 91 00, Colour Notation System, Stockholm: SIS, 1979.

[13] Swedish Standards Institution, Swedish Standard SS 01 91 01, CIE tristimulus values and chromaticity coordinates for some 16,000 colour notations according to SS 01 91 00, Stockholm: SIS, 1983.

[14] Swedish Standards Institution, Swedish Standard SS 01 91 02, Colour Atlas, Stockholm: SIS, 1979.

[15] Swedish Standards Institution, Swedish Standard SS 01 91 03, CIE tristimulus values and chromaticity coordinates for the colour samples in SS 01 91 02, Stockholm: SIS, 1982.

[16] Tonnquist, G.: "Comparison between CIE and NCS colour spaces." FOA Report C 30032-E1, Stockholm: Försvarets Forskningsanstalt, 1975.

[17] Tonnquist, G.: "Properties of the NCS colour space" in Proceedings of AIC Symposium Colour Dynamics, Budapest: Hungarian Electrotechnical Society, 1976, pp. 305-323.

[18] Robertson, A.R.: "The CIE 1976 color-difference formulae." Color Research and Application, vol. 2, 1977, pp. 7-11.

[19] Pointer, M.R.: "A comparison of the CIE 1976 colour spaces." Color Research and Application, vol. 6, 1981, pp.108-118.

[20] Derefeldt, G. and Sahlin, C.: "Transformation of NCS data into CIELAB colour space". Colour Research and Application, vol. 11, 1986, pp. 146-152.

[21] Derefeldt, G.: "Transformation of NCS data into CIELUV colour space." To be published.

[22] Spillman, W.: "A color order system for environmental design." In A. Hård, L. Sivik, Å. Stenius, and G.Tonnquist (eds.) Colour Report F26.The Forsius Symposium on Colour Order Systems, Stockholm: Scandinavian Colour Institute, 1983.

WORK WITH DISPLAY UNITS 86
B. Knave and P.-G. Wideback (eds.)

COLOUR ON DISPLAYS - BOON OR CURSE?

Floris L. van Nes

Institute for Perception Research/IPO
P.O. Box 513
5600 MB Eindhoven, The Netherlands

1. INTRODUCTION

The number of multicolour visual display terminals, in all sorts of applications, is rapidly increasing. However, in quite a few cases it is doubtful whether the advent of colour should be regarded as a boon; sometimes, when colour is applied injudiciously by the screen editor, it might rather be called a curse to the user.

Practice has shown that it is very difficult for screen text editors without a background in visual ergonomics to realize what effects on reading their use of colour will have. For instance, colour is often wrongly used to accentuate what is in fact secondary information in a particular screen layout. And already the alternation of two colours in a text can create unrest. Therefore, it is of paramount importance to exercise the greatest economy in choosing text colours. This paper is intended to provide some background and guidelines on colour use, which will be illustrated with display examples in the oral presentation.

Colour and spatial effects cannot really be treated in separation since particular colours of course appear at a particular position. The reader is referred to a forthcoming publication dealing with colour as well as with spatial, and typographical effects (Van Nes, 1986) to provide a more complete view of all these effects on display legibility.

2. SOME BASIC ELEMENTS OF THE VISUAL READING PROCESS

It is important to realize the distinction between the two basic processes that can be generally distinguished in reading (Bouma, 1980). When a page, on paper or an electronic display, is considered for being read, it is first necessary to search for the desired information, and secondly this information has to be taken in. To obtain optimal legibility, the page structure should be such that visual search can proceed rapidly, but without disturbance to subsequent reading of the passage of interest.

Legibility is defined here, in accordance with Tinker (1964) and Klare (1969), as the effect on the *visual* processes involved in reading, of all relevant properties of the text, such as type face, contrast, spacing and colour. In contradistinction to legibility, the readability of a text is then defined as the effect of such factors as vocabulary, density of ideas, connectedness and style on the *cognitive* processes involved in understanding the text.

When searching, the eyes skim over the page, guided by text attributes such as specific first letters or word lengths and attracted by text elements of a conspicuous nature. In print, adequate attraction to subheadings etc. may be provided by bold type, or italics. Such subtle means are not available on most displays; there the text editor has to resort to means like displaying the text parts concerned in a different colour. However, then their conspicuity in the rest of the text is often too pronounced, and attention is therefore involuntarily attracted. Consequently, reading itself may be disturbed.

3. COLOUR EFFECTS

3.1. Recognition

The recognition of a coloured text, be it on a coloured or on a 'black' background, depends mainly on the luminance contrast between letters and background; colour contrast plays a subordinate part. Therefore, on a dark or 'black' background, bright colours such as white, yellow, cyan or green are best suited for rendering text, whereas red and blue are inappropriate. But on a bright background i.e. white, yellow or cyan, the letter colour should be dark, e.g. blue, red or magenta, in order to have sufficient luminance contrast. Providing enough luminance contrast is also important when colour combinations such as red on green are used, i.e. colours which people with defective colour vision find it hard to distinguish: they might not see the colours as different, but still would be able to read because of the luminance difference between text and background.
It should be realized that high-luminance backgrounds on displays with a 50 Hz refresh rate show annoying flicker effects, especially in large areas.

3.2. Association

Identically coloured parts of a text and/or a figure are generally interpreted as belonging together. This association mechanism causing grouping of texts and/or figures only operates well, however, when not more than three of four colours are present (Reynolds, 1979). In such cases text editors should be aware of unintentional colour grouping effects.

3.3. Accentuation

If a part of a text or figure, or its background, has a colour which is different from the surround, this part will have an objectively measurable conspicuity (Engel, 1980). This means that the differently coloured part will involuntarily attract fixation of the eye when it scans the page. Colour differences therefore can be consciously used as efficient search aids, provided the reader knows which colour to look for.

3.4. Categorization

The colour of a text may be used to code it, i.e. to attach a specific meaning to it. This coding should be used consistently in a system. One example of coding, which in principle does not have to be learned, is that caused by the transfer of a colour's subjective importance to the words with this colour; words *printed* in red therefore are assumed to be important. However, this generally does not apply to words *displayed* in red on a dark background, because usually the luminance of such words is too low in comparison to that of words in other colours.

3.5. Chaos

If a display shows a structured text or graphics in not too many different colours, visual search processes are aided and subsequent reading is not impaired by distracting parts of the display. If, on the contrary, a multitude of colours is scattered over the whole display area so that structure is lacking, the reader is bewildered by this colour chaos even before he starts reading and is disturbed while he is doing so.

3.6. Esthetics

Objective, measurable effects of colour combinations on legibility, i.e. on the reader's performance, were described in the previous sections. The subjective effects of display colours on the viewer, i.e. whether he considers them to be esthetically pleasing or not, probably do not influence his reading performance directly, yet may affect his appreciation of the displayed text as a whole, and therefore the task he has to read it for.

4. PRACTICAL GUIDELINES ON COLOUR USAGE

1. Dark text on a bright background is more legible than the reverse, but only if the display refresh rate is high enough, i.e. 70 Hz or more. For television-type VDTs, having a lower refresh rate, this means that sizable quantities of text have to be displayed on a dark background, in white, yellow, cyan or green - or a comparable colour range if other colours than those provided in videotex systems are used. Text colours such as red and blue are not luminous enough for a dark background and therefore may only be applied on a bright one - which will not flicker intolerably at a low refresh rate if the area it occupies is relatively small.
2. On one display screen not more than three colours should be used for sizable quantities of text. Text parts with the same colour will be regarded as belonging together; this effect can be utilized, but may also cause confusion if there is no semantic relation among identically coloured texts.
3. A page completely filled with text is hard to read. This can only be improved substantially by the insertion of empty lines, *not* by the use of different text colours. Division of a text into paragraphs of three to five lines, with empty lines separating the paragraphs, improves legibility without too great a loss in text capacity.
4. A part of a text or figure with a colour different from its surround is conspicuous, i.e. attracts attention. This effect may be helpful when searching for certain information, provided the reader knows which colour to look for.
5. If colour coding is applied in an information system, it should be used consistently, i.e. the coupling agreed upon between colour and meaning should be the same throughout the system.

REFERENCES

Bouma, H. (1980) Visual reading processes and the quality of text displays. In: E. Grandjean and E. Vigliani (Eds): Ergonomic Aspects of Visual Display Terminals. London: Taylor & Francis Ltd, 101-114.

Engel, F.L. (1980) Information selection from visual display units. In: E. Grandjean and E. Vigliani (Eds): Ergonomic Aspects of Visual Display Terminals. London: Taylor & Francis Ltd, 121-125.

Klare, G.R. (1969) The Measurement of Readability. The Iowa State University Press, Ames, Iowa, USA, 1-2.

Nes, F.L. van (1986) Space, colour and typography on visual display terminals. Behaviour & Information Technology, 5, No. 2, 99-118.

Reynolds, L. (1979) Teletext and viewdata - a new challenge for the designer. Information Design Journal, 1, 2-14.

Tinker, M.A. (1964) Legibility of Print. The Iowa State University Press, Ames, Iowa, USA, 120-121.

WORK WITH DISPLAY UNITS 86
B. Knave and P.-G. Wideböck (eds.)

THE EFFECT OF VDT SYMBOL CHARACTERISTICS ON OPERATOR PERFORMANCE AND VISUAL COMFORT

Verna BLEWETT

Industrial Rehabilitation Service, 9th Floor, Da Costa Building, 68 Grenfell Street, Adelaide S.A. 5000 Australia

1. INTRODUCTION

Much research has been conducted since the introduction of cathode ray tube (CRT) based visual display terminals (VDT) about the needs of people using them. The mechanical and physiological aspects of VDT workstations have been addressed in many documents and the important contribution of adjustable workstations to the reduction of postural fatigue and musculo-skeletal complaints is well recognised.

Standards or guidelines covering the design and use of VDT's and workstations exist in the United Kingdom, Canada, USA, Sweden, Germany and Australia and the ISO Standard is apparently nearing completion. However, until recently, less emphasis has been placed on the interface of the information exchange and the user, i.e. the screen. The burgeoning fields of cognitive and software ergonomics are having their influence on the design of information technology software but less emphasis has been placed on the design of display characteristics.

There is a disparity between existing guidelines and specifications. Some are directed towards improving operator comfort and others to performance but none to both. That there is a relationship between operator performance and comfort is intuitively true but the nature of that relationship is not well understood. The relationship is likely to be complex and may not necessarily be a positive correlation. The report by the NIOSH Panel on the impact of Video Viewing on Vision Workers stated that, "research should be directed at unresolved questions about the effects of display workstation parameters on worker comfort and performance" [1].

Amongst the many factors which probably contribute to visual comfort the characteristics of the displayed image are under manufacturer's control as they are generally inherent in the manufacturer's hardware or firmware. It is not surprising therefore that the computer industry has conducted or assisted with research in this area in the past, particularly in Europe and the U.S.A. There is an economic incentive in this. The characteristics of the displayed image affect readability and legibility and must therefore, impinge on operator performance and visual comfort.

In these days of ever dwindling staff numbers when management is keen to extract the maximum efficiency from each individual it is presumably true that it is desirable for user industries to purchase equipment that can be shown to improve operator performance.

In Australia the research dollar is perhaps an even rarer commodity that it appears to be in other countries. Of course, money is directed at areas which are perceived as being trouble spots by the voting community as much as by those who hold the purse strings.

Visual discomfort associated with VDT work is not considered a problem in Australia. Despite the grumblings from operators about visual fatigue, poor readability and legibility or problems associated with glare, these complaints have not received the same attention that has been accorded musculo-skeletal problems in the same workplaces. There appears to be a certain resignation amongst operators that nothing can be done to improve things but it is also true that visual problems rarely result in lost time from work. As lost time is the basis for measuring the incidence of complaint in most organisations, visual problems tend to be hidden and therefore ignored.

Furthermore there is a prevailing attitude amongst managers and the computer industry that as vision is not perceived as a problem in Australia research in the area is not appropriate. There is certainly industry resistance to workplace research. This is neither resistance to the concept of research nor an unwillingness to incorporate new ideas into designs but is based on a record, in Australia, of instability in industrial relations and the difficulties of presenting change to consumers. It appears that the computer industry sees its role as meeting an existing market rather than creating a market and there have been examples which support this view. It appears then, that improvements in the design of equipment based on the results of research may best be introduced by influencing the market place to demand those changes.

This paper outlines a proposal for a research project in an area which is not considered completely acceptable in Australia and for which funding and industry assistance are difficult to find.

2. RATIONALE

This proposed research project is aimed at elucidating the relationship between visual comfort and operator performance in the working environment. That visual performance and comfort are affected by display parameters has been shown by a number of researchers. For instance Vartabedian [2] confirmed earlier work by Kinney and Showman [3] that the legibility and readability of uppercase versus lowercase letters, as perceived by operators, depends on the type of work being performed. Uppercase is preferable for isolated words while lowercase is preferable for text. In comparing methods of symbol generation, Vartebedian [2] showed that the 7 x 9 dot matrix is superior to the 5 x 7 although search time was not significantly affected by character size. More recently Roufs [4] showed in an elegant series of laboratory procedures examining the effects of luminance levels of visual comfort and performance, that there is probably a positive correlation between comfort and performance. He further suggests that the validity of self reporting on a "scale of comfort" that was used is supported by the results.

Results are not always compatible; a series of complex laboratory procedures involving the measurements of eye movements of subjects whilst reading a CRT screen suggests that smaller, rather than larger letters may require less ocular and cognitive work in their comprehension [5]. Cakir, et al [6] recommended 100% of character height between lines and inter-character spacing 20% - 50% of character height. Shurtleff [7] found that inter-character spacing can be reduced to 10% of character height if other display characteristics are optimum. Accuracy is reduced, however, if symbol width is narrow and inter-character spacing is less than 25% of character height.
Knave [8] summarises that font design depends not only on the number of dots in the matrix but the spacing between the dots - individual dots should not be distinguishable. He concludes that each character set should be closely inspected in order to maintain a high degree of legibility. In summary, although everyone agrees that fonts should be readable and legible, the method of achieving this is still not entirely known. This is further confounded because much of the research has been conducted in laboratories or using hard copy - both difficult to extrapolate to the real-time, working environment.

3. ORGANISATION

It is intended that this research will be conducted using operators of a recently introduced, on-line computer system in a large, decentralised organisation during 1987. The research will be conducted using, as subjects, intensive VDT operators performing their usual data entry or word processing tasks in the normal work environment. Negotiations are underway to obtain the active endorsement of those who will be affected by the project - the management and staff, the unions and the manufacturers of the equipment. The sensitivity of the industrial relations in the VDT workplace is such that it is expected that these negotiations will be protracted. A necessary part of the research will be to examine individual error rates and a commitment that this information will be confidential and not used for any other purpose must be made and adhered to. Individual staff will not be identifiable in or by reports. Minimal time away from normal duties will be required - time to complete questionnaires or attend interviews being the only commitment.

4. METHODOLOGY

It is intended to examine the relationship between various symbol characteristics and operator comfort and performance by varying the existing font offered to operators over a given period and comparing their performance (error rates) before and after the introduction of the change. Visual comfort will be determined subjectively at the end of each test period using a combination of questionnaire and structured interview.

Criteria selected for testing will depend on the physical constraints of the equipment but will most probably be character height; inter-character spacing; stroke width; height-to-width ratio and line spacing. Each variable will be introduced for a one week period to all terminals in the offices selected for study. As all screens in the office will look alike this may reduce the "Hawthorne effect". Variables will be introduced into each office in a randomised sequence. 'Test' weeks will alternate with 'control' weeks and both the first and last weeks will be control weeks.

In both 'control' and 'test' weeks a consistent collection period will be set to reduce confounders from daily variations in workload. Data from 'control' weeks will be compared to improve the baseline data and 'test' will be compared with 'control' weeks.

Data obtained during this part of the project will be investigated in an attempt to relate well-being with performance and with the physical parameters of the equipment. It seems logical that improvements in visual comfort will lead to improvements in operator performance. A study by Mourant et al [9] suggests that visual fatigue is achieved more readily by VDT viewing than hard-copy viewing and numerous subjective surveys support this but no attempt has been made to relate visual comfort with performance although this will not necessarily be a simple relationship.

Subjects will be volunteer, intensive keyboard operators (work processing or data entry) with normal sight. Each subject will act as their own control to reduce bias. At this stage the size of the sample is uncertain but is expected to be between 100-200 subjects.

Possible confounders which will need to be considered are variations in weekly workloads; variations in contrast/luminance settings and ambient lighting; mobility of operators during the testing period; self-selection of subjects and the low error rates amongst experienced operators, typically less than 5%.

5. CONCLUSION

There is particular worth in conducting this research project in the manner described above:-

. costs will be minimal;
. there will be little disruption of subjects at work;
. there will be no need to extrapolate the research to the workplace as subjects will be experienced operators working in a real environment on 'live' work.

"The main advantage of field research is the realism of the phenomena it studies". (Rinalducci & Fender, 1983)

REFERENCES

[1] Rinalducci, E.J. and Fender, D.H. (chairs), Video Displays, Work and Vision (National Academy Press, Washington D.C., 1983).
[2] Vartabedian, A.G., The Effects of Letter Size, Case and Generation Method on CRT Display Search Time, Human Factors (1974) 13(4):363-368.
[3] Kinney, G.C. and Showman, D.J., The Relative Legibility of Uppercase and Lowercase Typewritten Displays, Information Displays (1967) 4:34-39.
[4] Roufs, J.A.J., Leermakers, M.A.M. and Boschman, M.C., Criteria for the Subjective Quality of Visual Display Units, this volume.
[5] Kolers, P.A., Duchnicky R.L. and Fergus D.C., Eye Movement Measurement of Readability of CRT Displays, Human Factors (1981) 23(5):517-527.
[6] Cakir, A., Hart, D.J. and Stewart, T.F.M., The VDT Manual (John Wiley and Sons, Chichester, 1980).
[7] Shurtleff, D.A., How to Make Displays Legible (Human Interface Design, California, 1980).
[8] Knave, B.G., Snyder, H.L., Shackel, B., Stewart, T., Peters, T. and Kirk, N.S., Ergonomic Principles in Office Automation (Ericsson Information Systems AB, Stockholm, Sweden, 1983).
[9] Mourant, R.R., Lakshmanan, R. and Chatadisai, R., Visual Fatigue and Cathode Ray Tube Display Terminals, Human Factors (1981) 23(5):529-540.

WORK WITH DISPLAY UNITS 86
B. Knave and P.-G. Widebäck (eds.)

VISUAL PHENOMENA AND THEIR RELATION TO TOP LUMINANCE, PHOSPHOR PERSISTENCE TIME AND CONTRAST POLARITY

Per Nylén and Ulf Bergqvist*

The concepts top luminance, phosphor persistence time and contrast polarity are briefly described, and their roles in the generation of different types of flicker are discussed.

Top luminance: top luminance is defined as the peak amplitude of the luminance intensity function, see fig 1. The measurement requires a photometer with rapid time response since the peak is reached in less than 200 nS. Our group has made some preliminary measurements using an indirect method for determining the top luminance. A photometer with a rise time of less than 2 nS was used for studying time variations of the luminance intensity. No exact amplitude calibration could be done since a stable source of the same light spectra as the screen phosphore was not available. Instead, the mean luminance was measured with a Hagner S2 photometer and a photographic tecnique. By integrating the area of the luminance intensity function it was found that the P31 phosphor had a top luminance of approx. 65 000 cd m-2 and that P22 phosphor (amber) had a top luminance of approx 200-300 cd m-2. Very few data on top luminance exists in the litterature. Published data does not indicate whether a fast enough photometer has been used for the registrations.

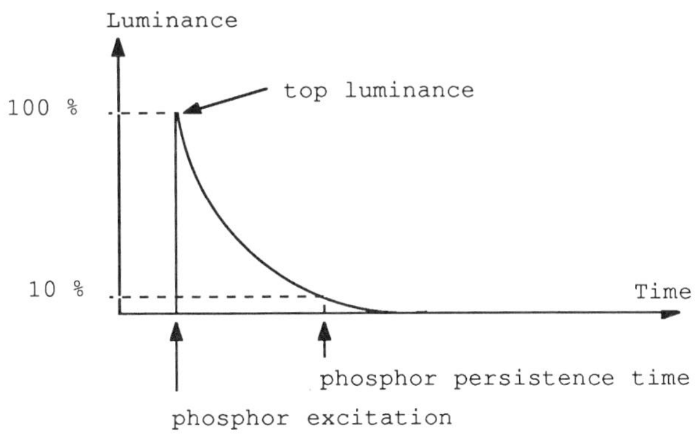

Figure 1

Phosphor persistence time: the persistence time definition used here is the time taken from excitation to the moment when the luminance is 10 % of top luminance intensity, see fig 1. The persistence time variation between different phosphors commonly used in VDUs differs by a factor of more than 1 000, from less than 20 uS to longer than 20 mS. The sweep velocity of the electron beam is roughly 4 000 m/s horisontally and 10 m/s vertically. This means that if the persistence is 20 uS only 8 cm of one single line on the screen has a luminance of 10 % or

*Ntl Board Occup Safety & Health, S-171 84 Solna, Sweden

more at every single moment. The rest of that line is darker and most of the other lines are completly dark. Persistence values found in the litterature differs a lot, probably because of improper measurements according to slow photometers used.

Screen polarity: Negative polarity means light letters on a dark background, positive polarity means dark letters on a light background. There are screens available that have a rather light background with considerably lighter letters. These screens should, according to our opinion, be defined as negative polarity screens but they have higher luminance values than the conventional negative screen (that have an almost black background).

The main disadvantage of negative polarity screens are the low luminance that demands a low overall luminance at the work area. Another serious limitation is the need of shielding from all light sources that can give rise to reflexes. Thirdly, a negative polarity screen has a considerably lower luminance than the manuscript (positive polarity) used. Positive polarity screens allows normal light levels, even day light, in the office. Reflexes can be seen but are often of the same luminance as the screen background itself. The luminance between screen and manuscript can often easily be balanced. There are however distinct differences in visual ergonomics between positive screens eg. colour and flicker tendency. The difference mainly comes from the different phosphors used. These differences will be discussed below.

Screen attention flicker: when the operator is looking directly onto a positive screen he might perceive flicker. The probabillity of doing this depends on the type of screen. The regeneration rate has earlier been considered as the only important factor but it has later been shown that the phosphor persistence time is quite important too. Phosphors with short persistence gives rise to more flicker than long persistence phosphor screens. Line jitter increases perceived flicker as a third factor to be considered. The perceived flicker is also depends on how long the operator has been watching the screen. It has been shown that the ability to perceive flicker diminishes if the operator has been watching an oscillating light source (in this case the screen) for a while. The ability to perceive flicker is therefore highest when the operator starts to look at the screen.

Pheripheral flicker: The ability of the human eye to detect flicker increases when the oscillating source is placed pheripherally. This means that a screen that is perceived as free of flicker, when looking at it directly, can be perceived as flickering when it is seen peripherally eg when performing tasks beside the screen as reading a manuscript or serving a customer. The peripheral flicker depends in the same way upon the same factors as screen attention flicker does.

Downward directed eye movement momentary flicker: As the operator moves his gaze downwards onto the screen he sometimes perceives a brightly shining horisontal band on the screen for a very short moment. The phenomenon can give rise to a slight glare effect and is a cause of discomfort if frequent vertical eye movements is performed. The phenomenon is probably caused by the downward directed vertical line displacement (as suggested by Nylén (1)). As the eye bulb is rotated downwards the same light receptors are exposed to the freshly exited lines for a prolonged time thereby giving an impression of a lighter area, the brightly shining line. The phenomenon is only perceived on screeens with short persistence.

Talk generated flicker: positive polarity screens with short persistence does sometimes appear to flicker more to the operator when he is talking. The perceptance threshold of this flicker is lowered when the operators distance from the screen is increased. It can therefore sometimes be perceived on a screen on a neighboring colleges desk but not on the operators own identical screen.

The phenomenon has not been described earlier and we here offer a possible explanation: The different frequencies produced by the vocal cords that builds up the different word is mechanically transmitted to the eye bulb. As at least parts of the eye bulb is subject to tiny vibrations in the vertical plane, see fig 2, causing the image on the retina to oscillate

Figure 2

with the same orientation. This gives rise to a different photon inflow to the retinal light receptor which builds up the flicker perceptance. The mechanism is basicly the same as described for the previously described eye movement flicker although the intensity is much lower since the velocity of the image fluctuations on the retina are much slower and has shorter time persistence. The mechanism can be further clearified by an experiment performed at our lab. If the operator is placed on a few meters distance from the screen and is asked to sing a tone, he will after some adjustment of the tone frequency perceive light and dark horisontal bands on the screen. By further adjustment of the tone frequency he can make the bands stand still. By singing a tone of higher frequency he increases the number of bands perceived. If the screen is rotated 90 degrees so that the screen is laying on its side the intensity of the perceived bands diminishes, if they are perceived at all. The bands are perceived at frequencies that are multiples of the regeneration rate. The vertical vibration of the retinal image will get time locked to fixed areas of the screen so that the image is moving upwards every time the electron beam is passing the same areas on the screen. This means that the same light receptors will be illuminated with the top luminance for a prolonged time thereby giving the operator the impression of lighter areas. When the image is moving downwards the opposite situation occurs and the operator will perceive darker areas. This phenomenon is not seen on screens with long persistence either.

References

(1) Nylén, P.R., A light phenomenon perceived when viewing CRT-based VDT screens with positive image. Appl. Ergonomics 16 (1985) 82-84.

WORK WITH DISPLAY UNITS 86
B. Knave and P.-G. Wideback (eds.)

OBJECTIVE METHODS FOR EVALUATING SCREEN FLICKER

Joyce E. Farrell

Hewlett-Packard Corporate Engineering Human Factors
3500 Deer Creek Road, Palo Alto, CA 94304

Abstract

Based on research on human temporal sensitivity, one can predict whether a visual display terminal will appear to flicker to a *theoretical standard observer*. These predictions are tested across a range of refresh frequencies, screen luminance, screen phosphors and individual users.

Introduction

Several VDT standards require visual displays to be "flicker-free" but do not specify how to determine whether a display is flicker-free. This poses a problem for display engineers who wish to design their displays so that they meet the VDT standards. It would, therefore, be of great value to have a method for determining whether a particular display appears to flicker.

Various methods have been proposed for empirically determining whether a particular VDT will appear to flicker in an experimental situation. These methods have the disadvantage that they require display engineers to conduct experiments that are both difficult to perform and difficult to verify. Ideally, one would like a single formula that display engineers could use to predict whether a screen would appear to flicker.

This paper describes an analytical method for *predicting* whether a VDT will appear to flicker given the screen phosphor persistence, refresh frequencies and other environmental factors such as the distance between the user and the VDT. Based on research on human flicker sensitivity (Kelly, 1969, 1979), one can predict the maximum screen luminance and the minimum refresh frequency that will generate a flicker-free display for a *theoretical standard observer*. These predictions are tested across a range of refresh frequencies, screen luminances, screen phosphors and individual users.

A Standard Observer for Flicker

The first step in developing a method for predicting whether a VDT will appear to flicker to a typical user is to develop a model of a standard observer for flicker. Research on human flicker sensitivity (DeLange, 1961; Kelly, 1961, 1969, 1971) indicates that when a temporally-varying light is decomposed into component temporal sine waves then flicker sensitivity can be predicted simply by the amount of stimulus energy in the lowest or fundamental temporal frequency. A standard observer, based on this previous research, detects "flicker" if the amount of energy in the fundamental frequency in any time-varying light is above a pre-determined and fixed threshold. Moreoever, Kelly (1961, 1969, 1971) found that there is a single formula that predicts the amplitude of the fundamental temporal frequency that is detected by a "normal" or "standard observer" viewing a flickering light at a standard viewing distance under a wide range of room illuminations. Kelly's analytical description of a standard observer for flicker forms the basis of the method for predicting screen flicker.

The method is based on a Fourier decomposition of the time-varying screen luminance. The Fourier analysis of the time-varying screen luminance is simplified by the fact that the fundamental temporal frequency of a VDT is equal to the refresh frequency. If one knows the amplitude of the fundamental frequency in the Fourier series describing the temporally modulated screen luminance, then one can predict whether the screen will appear to flicker.

From Kelly (1969, 1971), it is predicted that if the absolute amplitude of the fundamental temporal frequency of the VDT luminance modulation, E_{obs}, is greater than E_{pred}, then observers will perceive flicker.

$$E_{pred} = \frac{1}{a} e^{\sqrt{b 2\pi f}} \qquad [1]$$

where f is the refresh frequency and a and b are constants that depend on the size of the display.

Knowing the amount of energy in the fundamental temporal frequency of the VDT, E_{obs}, one can carry out the following tests:

If $E_{pred} > E_{obs}$, then the prediction is that people will not see flicker.

If $E_{pred} < E_{obs}$, then the prediction is that people will see flicker.

Conversely, one can predict the lowest refresh frequency that will render a VDT "flicker-free" by:

$$CFF = [\ln(aE_{obs})]^2 / [b 2\pi]$$

The method for predicting screen flicker is, then, reduced to the problem of calculating the amount of energy or the absolute amplitude of the fundamental frequency of the temporally varying screen luminance. The procedure for this calculation is outlined in Appendix A.

Evaluation of the method

Two experiments were conducted in order to evaluate the analytical method for predicting screen flicker.

Experiment One: The effect of phosphor persistence

This experiment was conducted in order to test the assumption that one can predict flicker thresholds simply by knowing the amount of energy in the fundamental temporal frequency of the display. People viewed two different phosphor displays with different refresh frequencies and luminances and indicated whether the displays appeared to flicker. One display had a very short phosphor persistence (P4) and the other display had a relatively long phosphor persistence (P39).

Appendix A describes how the time constant of the phosphor influences the amount of energy in the fundamental temporal frequency. For a fixed refresh rate, subjects will need to make the P39 displays brighter than the P4 displays in order to obtain the same amount of energy in the fundamental temporal frequency. But, having taken the phosphor time constant into account, the flicker thresholds for the P4 and P39 displays should be the same. In other words, for both the P4 and P39 displays, the probability of seeing flicker should depend only on the amount of energy in the fundamental temporal frequency.

Two Hewlett-Packard displays (with P4 and P39 phosphors) were modified to allow for variable refresh rates in a non-interlaced mode. The displays were viewed in a room illuminated with approximately 500 lux. Observers sat 12 inches away from the display. The active region of the display subtended a visual angle of 30 degrees.

Flicker thresholds for refresh rates between 40 and 100 Hz. were estimated by asking subjects to increase the luminance of the display until they first saw flicker (ascending flicker thresholds) and then to decrease the luminance of the display until they no longer could perceive flicker (descending flicker thresholds). For each of 6 observers, the average of these two thresholds was used, together with the refresh rate and phosphor time constant, to determine the amount of energy (i.e absolute amplitude) in the fundamental temporal frequency of the display. These amplitude thresholds can then be compared with the amplitude thresholds predicted from Kelly's findings for the 68 degree stimulus.

In Figure 1, the flicker thresholds are plotted as a function of the screen refresh rate for each of the 6 observers. The closed circles are the data collected when observers viewed a display with a P4 phosphor, and the open circles are the data collected when observers viewed a display with a P39 phosphor.

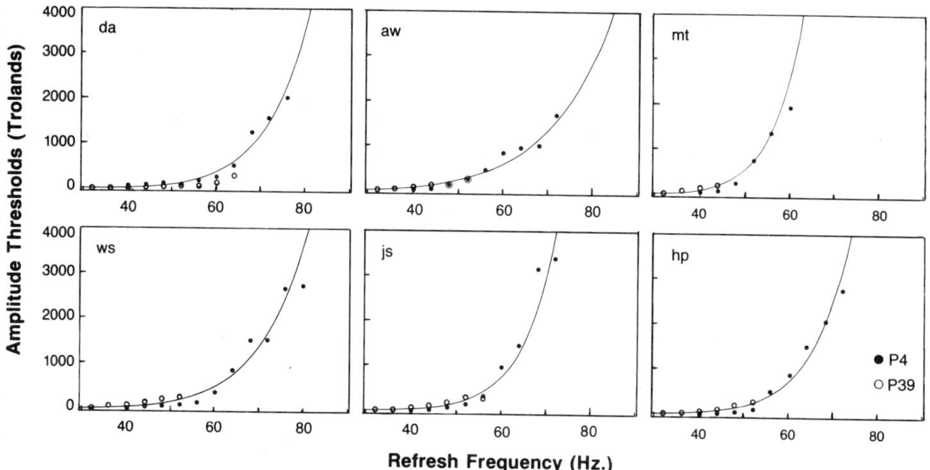

Figure1. Thresholds for perceived flicker are plotted as a function of refresh frequency for 6 observers. Solid circles represent thresholds for P4 phoshor displays and open circles represent threholds for P39 phosphor displays. Curves passing through the data are best-fitting parameter estimates of Kelly's general flicker threshold equation (Kelly, 1969).

Curves passing through data represent the best fitting parameters for Kelly's general equation:

$$E_{pred} = \frac{1}{a} e^{\sqrt{b 2\pi f}} \qquad [1]$$

where f is the refresh frequency and a and b are constants that depend on the size of the display.

The parameter values, $1/a$ and b, were derived from the intercept and slope (respectively) of a linear regression of $ln(E_{obs})$ on $\sqrt{2\pi f}$ for the P4 flicker thresholds only. The linear regression equations account for more than 95% of the variance for all observers. Although the linear equations were fit to the flicker thresholds for the P4 display, the flicker thresholds for the P39 display fall remarkably close to the curves. This is what we would expect if flicker thresholds were determined solely by the amount of energy in the fundamental frequency of the temporally modulated screen luminance (see *Appendix A: Effect of screen phosphor).*

Experiment Two : Variability of the standard observer for flicker

Having established that a single curve predicts data for different phosphors (fast and slow), a second experiment was conducted to assess the variability of flicker curves across a larger population of subjects. As in the previous experiment, subjects viewed a display with P4 phosphor at different screen luminances and refresh frequencies and indicated whether the display appeared to flicker.

The method of estimating flicker thresholds differed from the method used in the previous experiment in a number of ways (see Farrell, note1, for a complete description of the random staircase procedure for estimating flicker thresholds). The most significant difference was that at high screen luminance, flicker thresholds were estimated by varying refresh frequency, holding screen luminance constant. This difference is important because of the exponential nature of the flicker threshold curve. The luminance required to detect flicker increases rapidly at refresh frequencies beyond 60 Hz. The variability in flicker thresholds will therefore be greater if one varies screen luminance rather than refresh frequency. On the other hand, at low screen luminances the variability is greater if one varies refresh frequencies. Therefore, at low screen luminances, flicker thresholds were obtained by varying luminance, holding refresh frequency constant.

Figure 2 shows the flicker thresholds averaged across 10 observers. The horizontal and vertical lines passing through the flicker thresholds represent plus and minus one standard deviation. The solid line curve represents the best-fitting flicker threshold curve (see equation [1] above). Again, the parameter values of the flicker threshold curve [1] were derived from the intercept and slope of a linear regression of $ln(E_{obs})$ on $\sqrt{2\pi f}$. For comparison, the dashed curve represents the best-fitting flicker threshold curve derived from flicker thresholds averaged across the data obtained from the six observers in the previous experiment. The average flicker threshold curve from Experiment One falls within the standard deviation of the average flicker threshold values obtained in Experiment Two.

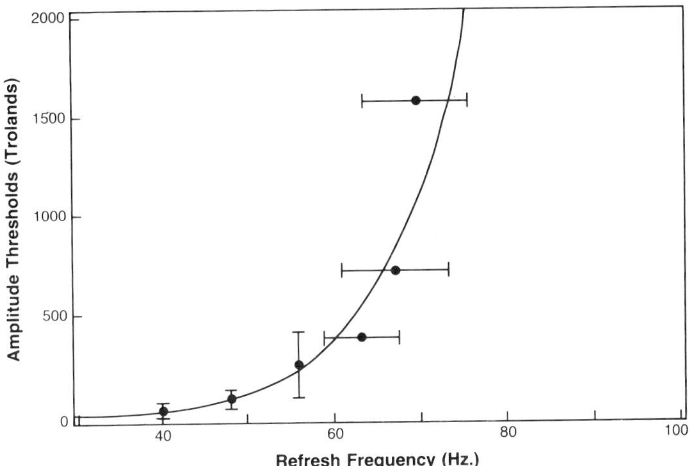

Figure 2. Flicker thresholds averaged across 10 observers and plotted as a function of refresh frequency. The horizontal and vertical lines passing through the data represent plus and minus one standard deviation of the mean flicker thresholds. The solid line passing through the data represents the best-fitting flicker threshold curve (as described in the text).

The standard deviation of average flicker thresholds can be used to estimate flicker thresholds for 10 and 90 percent of the population of observers. Figure 3 shows best-fitting flicker curves for the estimated 10 , 50 and 90 percent of the population. These estimated flicker threshold curves are then compared to flicker thresholds reported by Bauer, Bonacker and Cavonius (1983) for comparable conditions. Solid circles represent the flicker thresholds for 50% of Bauer et al subjects and vertical bars to the left and right of the circles represent flicker thresholds for 10 and 90% of Bauer et al subjects, respectively.

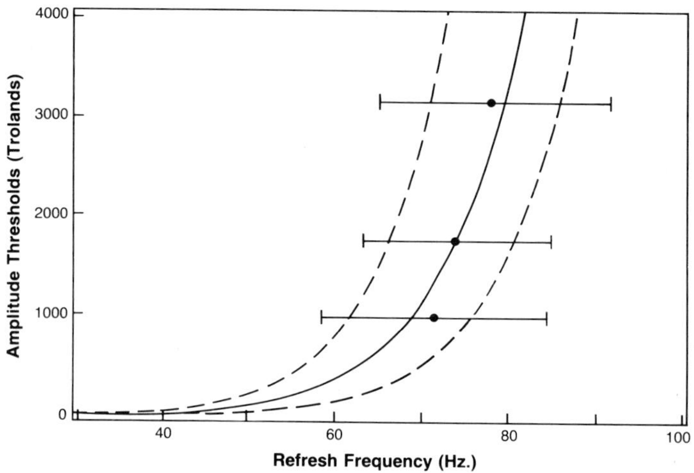

Figure 3. A comparison of flicker thresholds obtained in two independent experiments. Data points represent flicker thresholds calculated from data published by Bauer, Bonacker and Cavonius (1983). The vertical bars to the left and right of each data point represents flicker thresholds for 10 and 90 percent of the subjects in the Bauer et al study, respectively. The solid line is the flicker threshold curve estimated for 50% of the subjects in Experiment Two and the dashed lines to the left and right of the 50% curve are flicker threshold curves estimated for 10 and 90% of the subjects, respectively.

Figure 3 shows that the flicker thresholds obtained by Bauer et al for 50 percent of the subject population is comparable to the flicker thresholds obtained for 50 percent of the subjects in this experiment. The variability in flicker thresholds across observers was greater in the Bauer et al study, as evidenced by the fact that the 10 and 90 percent flicker curves estimated from the data of Experiment Two fall short of the 10 and 90 percent flicker threshold values obtained from the Bauer et al data. This result suggests that flicker thresholds should be obtained for a relatively large sample of subjects in order to accurately predict the display conditions that will appear to be flicker-free for 90 percent of the population.

Finally, Figure 4 shows that flicker threshold curves must also be defined for a standard display size: Figure 4 shows the flicker threshold curves obtained by Kelly (1969, 1971) for displays that subtend a visual angle of 7 and 68 degrees, along with the flicker threshold curve for a display that subtends a visual angle of 30 degrees (Farrell, note 1). The horizontal line indicates flicker thresholds for subjects with ages ranging between 20 and 70 who viewed a 2 degree flickering light (Rogowitz, 1984). This figure shows that the smaller a flicker display is, the lower the critical flicker frequency. This result confirms the well-documented finding that the smaller the display the less likely it is to appear to flicker (Kelly, 1974).

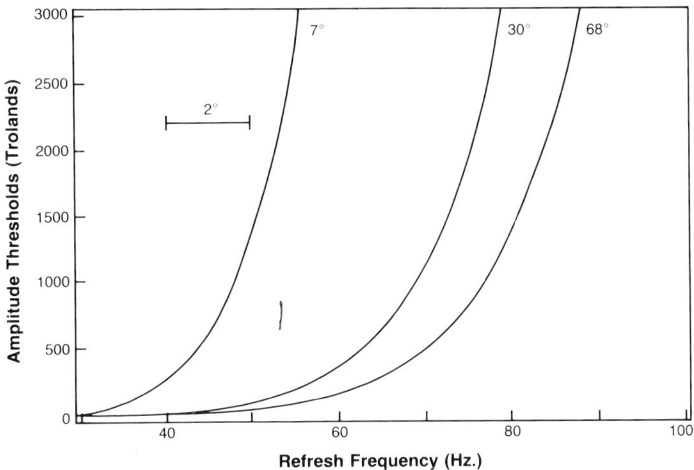

Figure 4. Flicker threshold curves estimated for displays varying in size. From left to right in the figure, the curves represent flicker threshold curves estimated for displays subtending a visual angle of 7 (Kelly, 1971), 30 (Farrell, note 1) and 68 degrees (Kelly, 1969), respectively. The horizontal bar represents the range of flicker thresholds obtained by Rogowitz (1983) for a stroboscopic light subtending a visual angle of 2 degrees.

Conclusions

In summary, this study provides independent evidence that there is a single and general equation relating the critical flicker frequency (CFF) and the screen luminance modulation (expressed as E_{obs}).

$$CFF = [\ln(aE_{obs})]^2 / [b2\pi]$$

where f is the refresh frequency and a and b are constants that depend on the size of the display.

There are two important caveats to the conclusions that can be drawn from this research. First, it is important to collect flicker threshold data for a larger sample of subjects to be confident about the parameter estimates of flicker threshold curves. We are now in the process of collecting this data.

Second, the configuration of a display that is "worst" with respect to flicker is the case in which every scan line or pixel is illuminated. This "worst case" is equivalent to a homogeneous uniform display with time-varying screen luminance. The method for predicting screen flicker outlined in this paper is, therefore, a *conservative flicker test*. If a VDT is flicker-free when every pixel or scan line is illuminated, then it will be flicker-free when approximately 85% of the pixels are illuminated, as in a character display. It is *not* the case, however, that if a VDT appears to flicker in the extreme or worst configuration it will necessarily appear to flicker in the character configuration.

Within the bounds of these two important caveats, the present findings have been useful in establishing limits on display parameters such as screen phosphor, refresh rate, screen size and luminance, that will generate a flicker-free display. From the equation above and from equation [2] in the appendix, one can deduce how variations in the display parameters will increase or decrease the probability of seeing flicker. The probability of seeing flicker decreases with refresh frequency and phosphor persistence and increases with screen luminance and display size. The probabilty of seeing flicker also increases with the number of VDT scan lines or pixels that are illuminated.

Finally, the analytical method of flicker assessment can be applied to any type of visual display, whether it be a liquid crystal display, an electroluminescent display or a cathode ray tube display. This *generality* is a consequence of two important facts. First, the temporal variation of *any* stimulus can be described as a sum of temporal sine waves. Second, one can predict human flicker sensitivity simply by knowing the amplitude of the fundamental temporal frequency of any time-varying visual stimulus.

A Standard Observer for Flicker

In this paper, I have shown that Kelly's earlier findings on human temporal sensitivity provide a firm foundation for developing a *model of the standard observer* for flicker that will allow us to predict whether any temporally varying luminance will appear to flicker. The standard observer for flicker corresponds to a *single* response curve that represents average flicker thresholds for human observers in general.

The concept of a standard observer has been useful in solving many industrial problems. For example, photometric measurements are based on standard photopic and scotopic observers and the CIE colormetric measurements are based on a standard trichromatic observer.

There are many similarities between the practical applications of a standard observer for flicker and a standard observer for color. In the early 1900's, the CIE was formed to to address the problem of how to measure and describe colors. At that time, manufacturers were faced with the practical problem of insuring that the color of a product (eg. paint) was the color that the customer ordered. Before the CIE was formed, contracts were formed between manufacturers and customers that included elaborate test methods for insuring that the color appearance of a product was the same as or close enough to the color that the customer specified. In the early 1900's, the CIE set about to define a standard observer for color and thereby eliminate the necessity of such elaborate contracts (Judd & Wyszecki, 1975).

The empirical methods of screen assessment are elaborate contracts between standards organizations and manufacturers of VDTs. These contracts are difficult to verify because we cannot be certain that empirical methods (i.e. psychophysical measurements) are performed correctly each time. A standard observer for flicker would eliminate the necessity of these contracts.

The CIE color metrics describe the psychophysical spectral properties of a two degree patch of light in terms of three chromaticity coordinates. The method proposed in this paper describes the psychophysical temporal variation of a 30 degree display surface in terms of a single coordinate defined by the fundamental temporal frequency and corresponding amplitude of the temporally modulated display. This flicker coordinate is used to predict the detectability of flicker, following Kelly (1969).

Just as there is some variability in flicker thresholds across observers (see, for example, Kelly (1962), Bauer, Bonacker & Cavonius (1983), Rogowitz (1984) and Farrell (note 1) there is variability in color matching across observers. The color matching functions of the CIE 1931 standard colorimetric observer were derived from measurements with a 2-deg stimulus by Guild (1931) who collected color matching data from 7 observers and by Wright(1928-1929) who collected data from 35 observers. Despite the variability in color matches both within and across observers (due to varying degrees of ocular pigmentation and different matching strategies), the CIE made the best approximation to a standard observer. This allowed the CIE to derive the color metrics that are in use today.

> "The CIE 1931 standard colorimetric observer and coordinate system was recommended, not because it had been proven to be a statistically reliable average of normal color vision, which it had not, but because it was believed to be intermediate to actual observers with normai color vision." Judd & Wyszecki. *Color in Business, Science and Industry, 1975.*

Similarly, it is possible to treat the variability in flicker thresholds across observers as the variability of a normal or standard observer. The ultimate goal of the research described in this paper is to develop a standard observer for flicker that can be used to solve problems in display evaluation.

Acknowledgements

The data presented in this paper were previously described in an oral presentation to the members of the DIN-SC-AAD/WD and WG 9, November 5, 1985. Parts of this paper are reproduced in Farrell, J. E. An Analytical method for predicting perceived flicker, *Behavior and Information Technology, in press.* I thank Donald H. Kelly and Brian A. Wandell for many helpful discussions of this work. I also thank Carl Haney and Michael Moran for invaluable technical assistance.

Reference Note

Farrell, J. E. A Standard observer for flicker, manuscript in preparation, 1986.

References

Bauer, D., Bonacker, M. & Cavonius, C. R. 1983, Frame repetition rate for flicker-free viewing of bright VDU screens. *Displays*, January, 31 - 33.

Crawford, B. H. 1936, The dependence of pupil size upon external light stimuli under static and variable conditions. *Proceedings of the Royal Society* (London), *B121*, 373.

DeLange, H. Dzn. 1961, Eye's response at flicker fusion to square-wave modulation of a test field surrounded by a large steady field of equal mean luminance. *Journal of the Optical Society of America, 51*, No. 4, 415-421.

Kelly, D. H. 1961, Visual responses to time-dependent stimuli, I. Amplitude sensitivity measurements. *Journal of the Optical Society of America, 59*, No. 4, 422-429.

Kelly, D. H. 1962, Visual responses to time-dependent stimuli. III. Individual Variations, *Journal of the Optical Society of America, 52*, No. 1, 89-95.

Kelly, D. H. 1964, Sine waves and flicker fusion. In H. E. Henkes and L. H. van der Tweel (Eds). *Flicker*. The Hague: Junk, 16-35.

Kelly, D. H. 1969, Diffusion model of linear flicker responses. *Journal of the Optical Society of America, 59*, No. 12, 1665-1670.

Kelly, D. H. 1971, Theory of flicker and transient responses, I. Uniform fields. *Journal of the Optical Society of America, 61*, No. 4, 537-546.

Kelly, D. H. 1974, Spatio-temporal frequency characteristics of color-vision mechanisms. *Journal of the Optical Society of America, 64*, pp. 983-990.

Oppenheim, A. V. & Willsky, A. S. 1983, *Signals and Systems*, Englewood Cliffs, New Jersey: Prentice-Hall, Inc.

Rogowitz, B. E. 1984, Measuring Perceived Flicker on Visual Displays. *Ergonomics and Health in Modern Offices*, London: Taylor & Francis, 285-293.

Appendix A

Calculating the absolute amplitude of the fundamental temporal frequency of a VDT

A. Convert the screen luminance into trolands.

1) Measure the mean screen luminance over time, L_t, in units of candelas per squared meter (cd/m^2) using a time-integrated photometer. L_t is the total amount of light generated from the screen and it includes the amount of light reflected from the screen as well as the amount of light emitted by the display phosphors.

2) Now turn the display off and simply measure the amount of light reflected from the screen, L_r, again in units of cd/m^2.

3) Estimate the area of the observer's pupil. Pupil area, A, is a function of the amount of light entering the eye. Use the formula below (taken from Crawford, 1936) to estimate the diameter of the pupil.

$$d = 5 - 3\ tanh(0.4\ \ log(L_t\ \ 3.183\ ))$$

Then, pupil area, A, is easily calculated:

$$A = \pi(d/2)^2$$

4) The DC component of the temporally varying screen luminance (specified in trolands) is:

$$DC = (L_t - L_r)\ A$$

B. The screen luminance is a series of pulses with exponentially decaying persistence, $e^{1/\alpha}$. We can compute the amplitude coefficient of the fundamental frequency of the time-varying screen luminance using a well-known formula (eg. Oppenheimer & Willsky, 1983):

$$Amp\,(f\,) = \frac{2}{\left[1 + (\alpha f\,)^2\right]^{1/2}} \qquad [2]$$

where α is the time constant of the exponential describing the phosphor persistence, $e^{\frac{1}{\alpha}}$, and f is the refresh frequency of the display.

C. Finally, the luminance modulation of the fundamental frequency, E_{obs}, is obtained by multiplying the DC component of the temporal screen variation by the amplitude coefficient of the fundamental frequency, $Amp(f)$.

$$E_{obs} = (\ DC\ )(\ Amp(f)\ )$$

The effect of screen phosphor

The absolute amplitude of the fundamental temporal frequency of the display, E_{obs}, is the product of the amplitude coefficient of the fundamental temporal frequency, *Amp* (equation [2] above), and the DC component of the temporally varying screen luminance (specified in trolands).

Fast phosphors have small decay constants. Notice that as the decay constant, α, decreases, the amplitude coefficient approaches 2. Therefore, the amplitude of the fundamental temporal frequency of a a fast phosphor display will simply be twice the time-integrating screen luminance (specified in trolands). (One can consider this fact a check on the formula for the amplitude coefficient derived from Oppenheim & Willsky (1983), since it is well-known that a periodic train of pulses (generated by a very fast phosphor display) has a fundamental sine wave at a flash (refresh) frequency that is 200% modulated.)

A display with a very fast phosphor will, therefore, have a large amplitude coefficient and require less energy or screen luminance to be seen. This is in fact what we observe. Displays with fast phosphors (and, consequently, short decay constants) appear to flicker at low luminances. The screen luminance for perceived flicker is proportional to the decay constant of the phosphor. Since this trade-off is incorporated in the calculation of the amplitude (see equation [2] above), displays with different phosphors should have the same amplitude thresholds. This prediction is true only if flicker thresholds are determined solely by the amount of energy in the fundamental frequency of the temporally modulated screen luminance, as Kelly predicts.

WORK WITH DISPLAY UNITS 86
B. Knave and P.-G. Widebäck (eds.)

TEMPORAL AND SPATIAL STABILITY IN VISUAL DISPLAYS

Sture Eriksson and Lars Bäckström

Department of Psychology, Uppsala University
Box 227, S-751 04 Uppsala, Sweden.

1. INTRODUCTION

The use of visual display units (VDU:s), especially those with a bright background, has introduced the problem of flicker perception into the workplaces of today.
The international endeavour to formulate a standard in this context implies that VDU:s should be flicker-free. However, it is not clear how a strict requirement should be formulated and under which conditions the critical flicker frequency (CFF) should be measured.
The reason for this state of uncertainty mainly is that previous research has demonstrated that CFF is multiply determined and varies between 5Hz - 60Hz depending on the specific combinations of effective stimulus variables (e.g. luminance, retinal position, size of stimulus) and observer variables (e.g. age, adapation state, pupil size). For reviews of these studies see Landis (1953), Brown (1965), and Kelly (1972).
In the present context two of these stimulus variables appear to be of first order importance, namely stimulus intensity and spatial interaction.

1.1. Stimulus intensity

The most important of of the variables which determine flicker is the luminance of the stimulus field. At low luminances (about 1 Troland or 0.03 cd/m^2) the CFF is as low as 5 Hz then it reaches a maximum (60 Hz) at about 10.000 Troland (about 1.000 cd/m^2) and finally declines somewhat at higher intensities (Hecht & Smith, 1936). The general relation between CFF and luminance is sigmoid but for intermediate luminances (10 - 300 cd/m^2), which is the interval of interest in the VDU-context, there is a linear relation between CFF and the logarithm of stimulus luminance (the Ferry-Porter law).

1.2. Spatial interaction

The term spatial interaction here is used to denote three different aspects of spatial interaction in VDU:s.

a) Stimulus size. Several investigators (Granit & Harper, 1930; Berger, 1953; Roehrig, 1959) have demonstrated that there is a linear relation between CFF and the logarithm of stimulus area (the Granit-Harper law). The increase of CFF with area is, in part, due to spatial summation (Woodworth & Schlosberg, 1958). However, a peculiar finding (Roehrig, 1959) is that the CFF for a large area remains the same even if a large central portion of the field is covered. Thus CFF appears to be determined by the edge region of the stimulus field, not the inside of the field. Consequently there is no strict spatial summation. This finding has implications for VDU design since a bright border area will produce flicker even if the central part of the screen is dark or filled with dark symbols.

b) Retinal eccentricity. Even if retinal area is kept constant it is found that flicker sensitivity varies from the periphery to the central visual field. If the stimulus area is large, then the CFF increases toward the periphery but if the test area is very small (12-minute diameter) then CFF decreases toward the periphery. At some intermediate levels of luminances the CFF may be found to be relatively independent of retinal position (Brown, 1965). The complexity of these results still is open to interpretation but for the present purposes it may be stressed that we are concerned with large areas and therefore the problem mainly can be subsumed under the problem of stimulus area, see below.

c) VDU surround. It has been demonstrated (Hecht & Smith, 1936) that use of a large surround which matches the test field luminance will reduce glare discomfort and headaches. These results obviously have implications for the design of work-stations and the environment of the VDU-worker, see also Dainoff et al., (1981).

However, since earlier investigations usually have utilized a rotating sector shutter, a so called episcotister (or equivalent stimulation) the generated stimulus deviates from that offered by a CRT where a moving electron beam generates the image in a phosphor layer. In a study by Bauer et al., (1983) a refresh rate of about 90 Hz was found to be necessary in order to avoid perceived flicker on the computer screen. This outcome is interesting in that it indicates a crucial difference between the two kinds of stimulus generation. According to previous data the visual system cannot detect flicker above 60 Hz (Barlow & Mollon, 1982, p.154). Consequently the findings based on episcotister stimulation need to be controlled in new experiments in the VDU context.

2. STIMULUS ANALYSIS

What is the effective stimulus for flicker in a VDU? In a raster-scan display there are two potential stimulus variables for flicker perception, namely the high-frequency motion of the luminous spot within a scan line (including rise time, dwell time and fall time or persistence) and the low-frequency line sweep motion.

The first potential stimulus variable can be ruled out as an effective stimulus because the writing speed definitely exceeds all conceivable perceptual thresholds (one line on the screen is generated in about 40 microseconds). Furthermore the data concerning the so called critical duration confirms this conclusion (Woodworth & Schlosberg, 1958). Thus the motion of the spot within one single line can be replaced with an equivalent single stationary line or a line generated by optional high-frequency motion of the luminous spot according to Riccoś law (op. cit.)

The second potential stimulus variable for flicker perception in a VDU consists of a line moving downwards (in a raster with horizontally lines). Since this line motion is rather slow (it is usually completed within 20 ms) it is an effective stimulus for the visual system. The main criterion for this conclusion is that a variation of the line motion speed is accompanied by definite perceptual changes. When the speed is low (below 5 Hz refresh rate) a clear motion of the line is perceived. An increase in line motion speed produces a strong flicker. Further increase in speed is followed by a decrease in flicker strength and at 50 - 80Hz, depending on luminance and display size, flicker is replaced by fusion. When the corresponding perceptual criterion was applied to the spot movement within a single line no perceptual changes whatsoever could be found when the motion was varied from 100 Hz up to 100kHz. Other tests with different curveforms confirmed the conclusion that high-frequency modulation (more than about 100 Hz) within a single line is without any perceptual effects. Hence the effective stimulus for flicker perception in a CRT VDU is the sweep line motion. Since this motion is rather close to the phi-movement treshold (Woodworth & Schlosberg, 1958) it is expected that eye-movements executed in correlation with the sweep line motion (i.e. downwards in an ordinary raster-scan display) will allow a single line to be perceived (or a few lines if the phosphor has a long persistence). Such expected effects are exemplified in the well-known 'Blitz-phenomenon' found in VDU:s.

A further implication of this stimulus analysis is that phosphor decay will have rather small effects in displays with fast phosphors. If the effective stimulus were the spot motion within a line then persistence would greatly affect the stimulus waveform. But in the case of a line motion, the velocity of which is much smaller, the effect of the decay time becomes less important. Thus a fast phosphor (like P31 and P11) would give a response- when measured over a larger area- which has much longer rise and fall times than when the response is measured in a small spot within the line. An exact stimulus definition optimally correlated with the widths of the receptive fields is not yet available and more research is needed to arrive at such a definition. Figure 1 illustrates the above discussed properties of the stimulus.

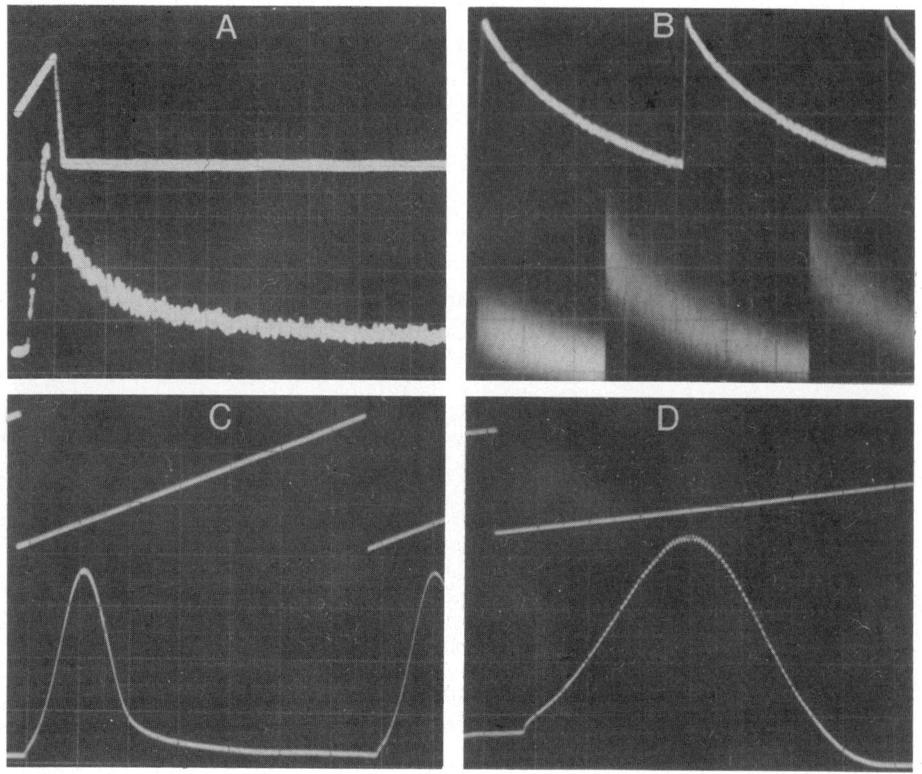

FIGURE 1

Luminance modulations for different phosphors and measurement conditions. Inset A shows a fast phosphor (P 31) and inset B shows a slow phosphor (amber) used in the Commodore DM-14. The time course of luminance was measured in one single line with a writing time of 40 microseconds. Inset C demonstrates the stimulus for flicker measured with a fast photocell (BPX 79) over a surface of 5 x 5 mm on the screen (P31 phosphor). Inset D illustrates the similar curve for a P11 phosphor. Time scales: Each horizontal division in A is 20 microsec., in B 5 ms, in C 5 ms, and in D 2ms.

3. EXPERIMENTS

3.1. Experiment 1

As explained above the effective stimulus for flicker in a VDU is a luminous line moving over the display. In the experiment we utilized such a stimulus in order to try out a simple method for studying flicker in VDU:s. A further advantage with this method is that it constitutes a way of investigating flicker per se, without any interference with the raster which is present in VDU:s and which may complicate the interpretation of the perceptual responses due to raster properties and jitter, see below.
The main purpose of the experiment was to determine CFF:s for different luminances and display sizes covering most displays in use.

Stimulus generation. The optical stimulus was generated on a Tektronix mod. 608 high intensity monitor with a 22.5 kV acceleration voltage. The phosphor was P 31 (green) and a flickering square (70 x 70 mm) was generated by function generators. The x-input of the oscilloscope was fed by a sawtooth waveform (see Fig. 1C). The frequency of the x-input could be varied by the subject or experimenter via a turning knob. The y-input of the oscilloscope was fed by a triangular waveform with a frequency of 2MHz. The z-input was a square wave synchronized with the x-voltage in such a way that the electron beam was lit during the line sweeping over the display and unlit during return motion. Thus with a low x-frequency (a few Hz) a vertical luminous line was seen moving horizontally to the left. During return motion the beam was unlit. At about 20 Hz the perceived motion was replaced by a stationary flickering square surface and over 100 Hz the observer perceived a temporally stable, homogeneous square. Viewing was monocular and a head rest was used. The viewing distance was 5 cm. To ensure that no interference between display modulation and room illumination took place a small hood was attached to the oscilloscope. The surround luminance of the interior of the display was about 1.5 cd/m^2.

Design. The experiment was designed as a 4 x 5 factorial design with four display sizes (10, 30, 50, and 70 degrees of visual angle), and five mean luminance levels (25, 50, 100, 200, and 400 cd/m^2). The luminances of the moving line were 120, 240, 490, 900, and 1900 cd/m^2 respectively with contrast modulations between 0.98 and near unity.

Procedure. The task of the subjects was to start responding in a descending (or ascending) trial, overshooting the CFF a little until clear flicker (fusion) was perceived and then moving the knob back and forth until flicker was just replaced by fusion. Every subject made four productions on each of the 20 stimulus conditions, i.e. 80 productions totally. Each CFF threshold estimate consisted of the mean of one ascending and one descending production. After each of the 20 conditions the subject looked out into the room in order to maintain the adaptation to room illumination. The luminance of the walls was 30 cd/m^2. Twelve payed subjects participated in the experiment. Mean age was 23 years, standard deviation 3 years.

Results The results demonstrate the expected increase in CFF concerning both luminance (Figure 1) and display size (Figure 2). It is evident, however, that the CFF:s are much higher than the values expected from experiments using episcotister stimulation and the combination of a high luminance and a large display gives a mean CFF which is more than 20 Hz above the curve obtained by Hecht & Smith, (1936).

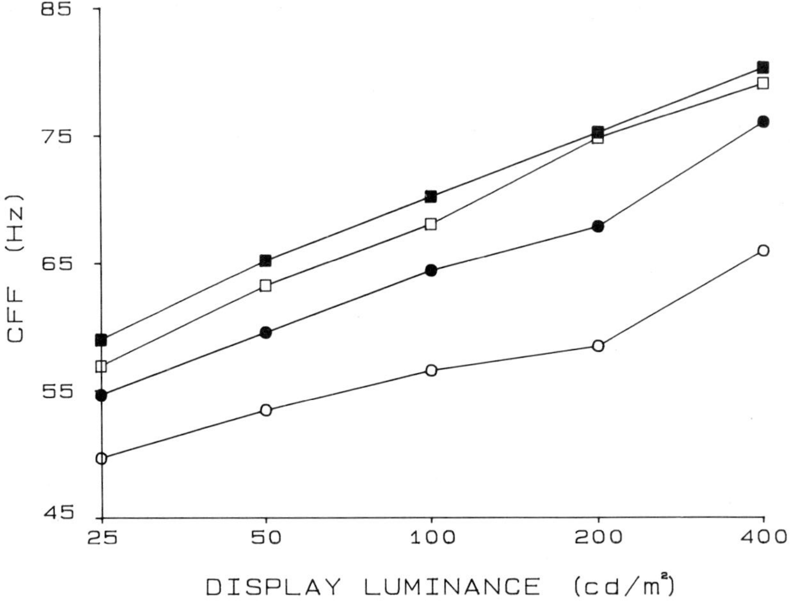

FIGURE 2

Critical flicker frequency as a function of display mean luminance and display size. Open circles represent the 10 degree display, filled circles the 30 degree display, open squares the 50 degree display, and filled squares the 70 degree display.

In order to describe the obtained results we have fitted logarithmic functions to the data using a least square criterion. The following equations describe the results showing CFF as a function of display mean luminance (I).

$$CFF = 31.82 + 12.51 \times \log I \quad (1)$$
$$CFF = 30.43 + 17.04 \times \log I \quad (2)$$
$$CFF = 31.15 + 18.63 \times \log I \quad (3)$$
$$CFF = 34.85 + 17.57 \times \log I \quad (4)$$

where formula 1 is valid for the smallest display size (10 degrees), formula 2 is valid for the 30 degree display, formula 3 for the 50 degree display and formula 4 is valid for the largest display (70 degrees of visual angle).

In Figure 3 is depicted the results when CFF is plotted against display size.

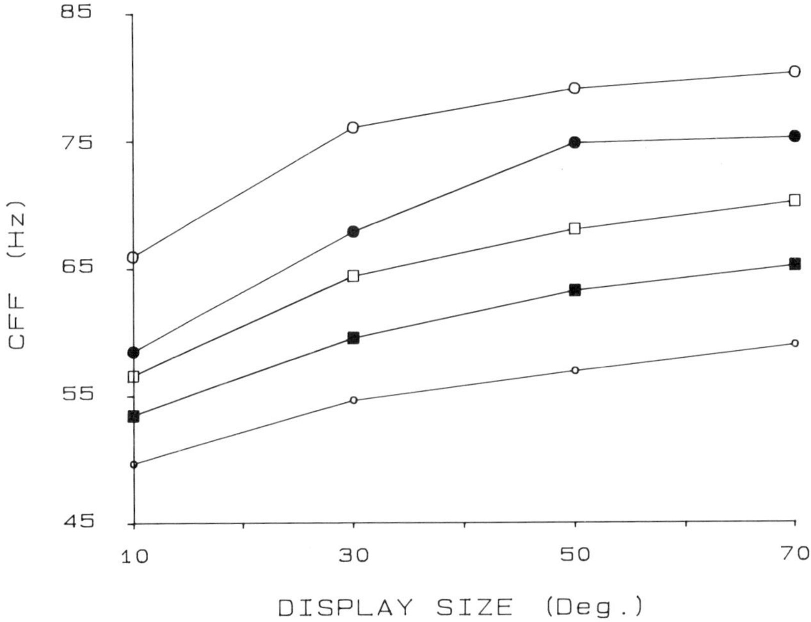

FIGURE 3

CFF as a function of display size measured in terms of degrees of visual angle. Small open circles (lowest curve) is the 25 cd/m^2 condition, filled squares denote 50 cd/m^2, open squares 100 cd/m^2, filled circles 200 cd/m^2, and open large circles 400 cd/m^2.

The following equations describe the results showing CFF as a function of display area.

$$\text{CFF} = 38.81 + 5.40 \times \log \text{Area} \quad (5)$$
$$\text{CFF} = 39.37 + 6.97 \times \log \text{Area} \quad (6)$$
$$\text{CFF} = 40.42 + 8.10 \times \log \text{Area} \quad (7)$$
$$\text{CFF} = 37.50 + 10.50 \times \log \text{Area} \quad (8)$$
$$\text{CFF} = 49.09 + 8.72 \times \log \text{Area} \quad (9)$$

Formulae 5 - 9 are valid for the luminances 25, 50, 100, 200, and 400 cd/m^2 respectively.
The above formulae can be used to predict the mean CFF for various displays. Since a wide range of luminances and display sizes have been covered in the experiment it should be possible to encompass practically all displays in use. The formulae also may be used as a first formulation of a standard for flicker-free displays, see the concluding discussion.

In Figure 4 is shown the interindividual variation (standard deviations based on the means of the subjects). The data were averaged over display sizes since the SD:s are rather similar for different sizes.

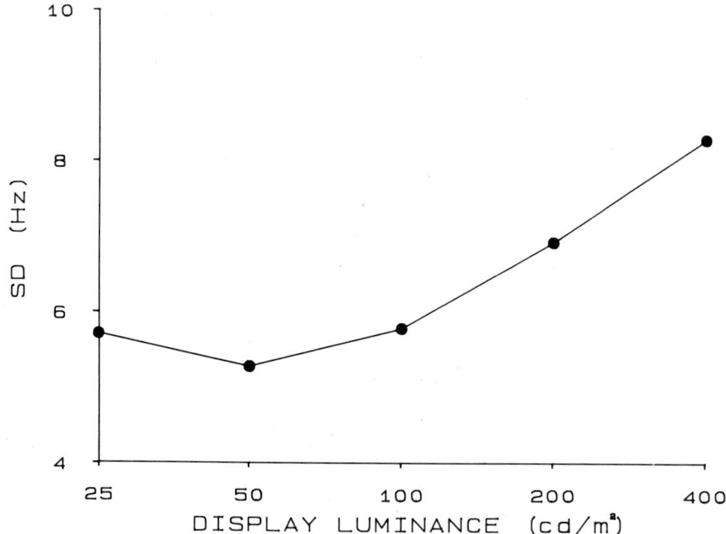

FIGURE 4
Interindividual variation (standard deviation) as a function of display luminance.

3.2. Experiment 2

The purposes of this experiment were to find out how many subjects which are necessary to provide stable data in this kind of experiments and to estimate the intraindividual and interindividual variations of the subjects. This last point is especially important in the formulation of a standard and therefore part of Experiment 1 was replicated on a large group of subjects (N=27).

Method. The same setup as in Experiment 1 was used but the subjects were presented only four display sizes (10, 30, 50, and 70 degrees of visual angle) in random order while mean screen luminance was held constant at 100 cd/m^2. Each subject participated in two sessions. In one session four productions were recorded (two ascending and two descending). In the second session 10 productions were recorded. Thus the first procedure allowed two threshold estimates (each one consisting of the mean of one ascending and one descending production) while the second procedure resulted in five threshold estimates per condition.

Results. The result of the experiment is shown in Figure 5.

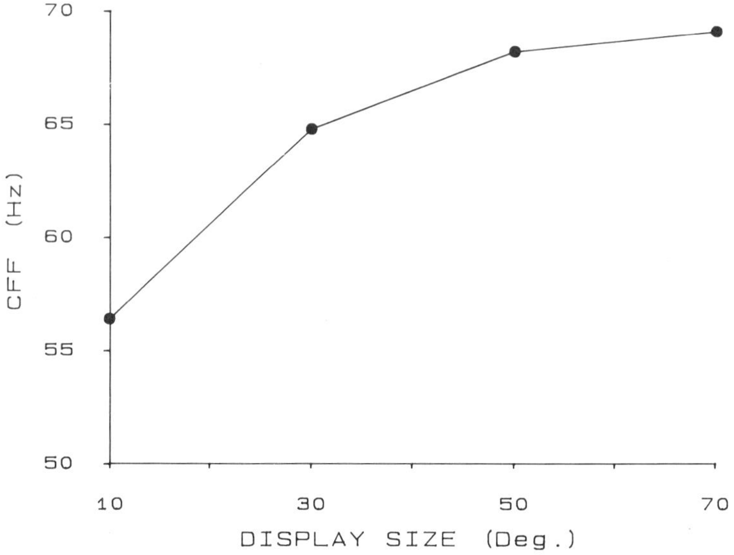

FIGURE 5

CFF as a function of display size. N=27. Mean screen luminance = 100 cd/m^2.

The results demonstrate the same relation between CFF and display size as in Experiment 1 and a least square fit gave the following equation

$$CFF = 41.21 + 7.79 \log Area \qquad (10)$$

As seen from this outcome there is a close correspondence between formula 10 and formula 7 above.

A second question to answer was how many subjects that are required in order to obtain a stable response level. Figure 6 depicts the results when CFF:s and standard deviations are plotted against the number of subjects.

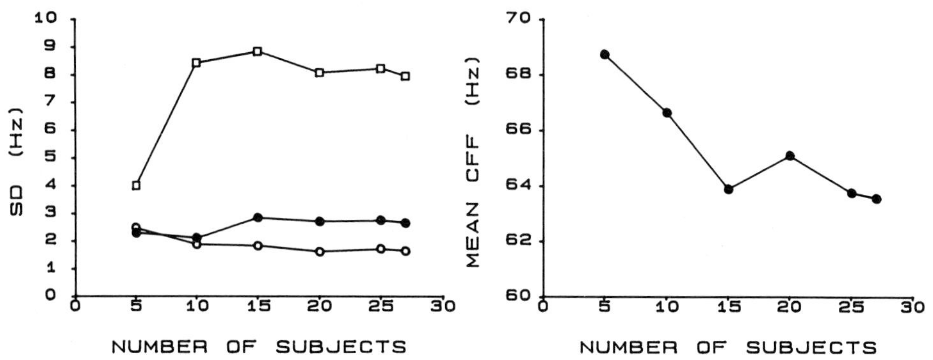

FIGURE 6

The left part of the figure shows interindividual variations (open squares), and intraindividual variations (open circles indicate two threshold estimates, filled circles five threshold estimates). The right part of the figure shows the relation between CFF and the number of subjects.

Obviously not much is gained in accuracy by including more than about 15 subjects in the experiment.

3.3. Experiment 3

The purpose of this experiment was to study the interaction between flicker and jitter in VDU:s.

Stimulus generation. The optical stimulus was generated on a Tektronix mod. 608 monitor with P31 phosphor. A specially built microprocessor made it possible to generate a raster-scan image based on 256 lines. Different patterns including a blank surface could be generated and the number of lines , their separation and luminances could be controlled. Furthermore refresh rate was variable from 45 to 100 Hz and finally a sinusoidal jitter with preselected amplitude and frequency could be superimposed on the stationary pattern. The mean screen luminance in the experiment was 44 cd/m^2. Viewing distance was 25 cm. Binocular vision was used and a hood mounted to the oscilloscope constituted the head rest and also screened of external illumination.

Design. The experiment was conducted according to a 3 x 5 factorial design with three levels of jitter and five levels of refresh rate. Each of the 15 conditions was presented during 1.5 seconds with a pause between conditions of 5 seconds. Ten replications were used. Thus each subject made 150 estimates of flicker strength in the experiment. No perceived flicker was denoted by 0, just perceptible flicker denoted by 1, clear flicker by 2 and strong flicker by 3. The subjects were instructed to disregard jitter and only judge flicker.

Results. Figure 7 shows the results of the experiment on flicker-jitter interaction. Jitter frequency was 5 Hz. 25 subjects were used.

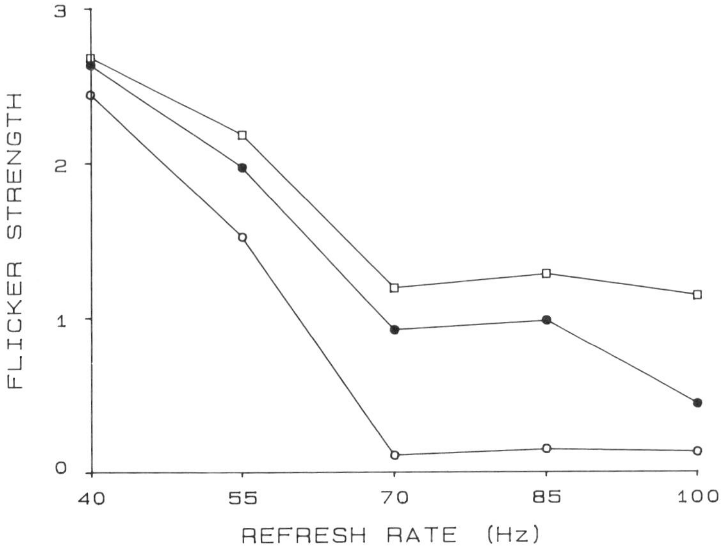

FIGURE 7

Perception of flicker strength as a function of refresh rate and jitter. The upper curve (squares) demonstrates the effect of strong jitter (0.4 mm amplitude), the middle curve (filled circles) weaker jitter (0.2 mm amplitude), and the lowest curve (open circles) shows the effect when no jitter is present.

It is evident from the data that there is a strong effect of jitter on the perception of flicker. Even though the subjects were carefully instructed to disregard jitter and only judge flicker it turned out that all subjects confused flicker and jitter.

This finding has important implications for flicker testing in VDU:s since jitter may inflate the flicker judgments. Therefore the 'pure flicker method' presented in Experiment 1 may constitute a way of providing jitter-free data in the study of flicker perception.

4. DISCUSSION

The main results of the present study are a demonstration of flicker-jitter interaction and a set of empirically derived logarithmic functions which describe CFF:s for various combinations of display luminances and display sizes. The functions are based on experiments using a stimulus which is similar to the stimulus generated by ordinary CRT-based displays. The main difference is viewing distance, the effect of which mainly is a defocusing of the sweep line for short viewing distances. In control experiments we have established that defocusing the beam has no relevant effect, neither on the photometer recording, nor on the perceptual effects in determining CFF. Consequently we regard our data as representative for most displays with phosphors similar to P31.

A comparison of the data obtained in Experiment 1 with those obtained by Bauer et al., (1983) can be used to test the generality of our formulae. Since Bauer et al. used a maximum sensitivity with regard to retinal position their data should be compared with our maximum condition (70 deg.). According to formula 1 we predict mean CFF:s of 69, 73 and 78 Hz for their displays with 80, 160, and 320 cd/m^2 mean luminances. Their data are 72, 74, and 78 Hz respectively. Thus the agreement between the two sets of data is very good.

A second prediction is made possible due to the data reported by Rogowitz (1984). She found that a group of 100 subjects had a mean CFF of 45.3 Hz for a 2 degree stimulus. Using formula 10 we predict a mean CFF of 43.6 Hz, which is in good agreement with Rogowitz data. Since she used a square wave modulation, which initially is equivalent to a slow phosphor decay, the data agreement gives support to our stimulus analysis above. Consequently our formulae may be used as a first formulation of a standard for flicker-free displays provided the standard is set to the mean CFF plus three standard deviations implying that practically no user should perceive flicker.

However, a more general method for predicting flicker in VDU:s is both desirable and possible (Eriksson & Bäckström, 1986). By using a physiologically derived impulse response which is convolved with the proper optical stimulus it is possible to derive a temporal MTF capable of predicting the "temporal Mach bands" which are indicated in empirical data (Kelly, 1962).

ACKNOWLEDGEMENT

This project has been supported by grants from the Swedish Work Environment Fund.

REFERENCES

Barlow,H.H. and Mollon,J.D. (1982). The senses. Cambridge: Cambridge Univ. Press.

Bauer,D. Bonacker,M. and Cavonius,C.R. (1983) Frame repetiotion rate for flicker-free viewing of bright VDU screens. Displays, January, 31 - 33.

Berger,C. (1953). Area of retinal image and flicker fusion frequency. Acta Physiol.Scand., 28, 224 - 233.

Brown,J.L. (1965). Flicker and intermittent stimulation. In Graham,C.H.(Ed.) Vision and visual perception. New York: J.Wiley & Sons,Inc.

Dainoff,M.J., Happ,A. and Crane,P. (1981). Visual fatigue and occupational stress in VDT operators. Human Factors,23, 421 - 438.

Eriksson,E.S. and Bäckström,L. (1986) An impulse response model of flicker perception. Departm. of Psychology, Uppsala University, in preparation.

Granit,R and Harper,P. (1930). Comparative studies on the peripheral and central retina: II. Synaptic reactions of the eye. Amer.J.Physiol., 95, 211 - 227.

Hecht,S. and Smith,E.L. (1936). Intermittent stimulation by light. VI. Area and the relation between critical frequency and intensity. J.gen.Physiol., 19, 979 - 991.

Kelly,D.H. (1962). Visual responses to time-dependent stimuli. III. Individual variations. J.Opt.Soc. Amer., 52, 89 - 95.

Kelly,D.H. (1972). Flicker. In Jameson,D. and Hurvich,L.M. (Eds.) Handbook of sensory physiology. Vol VII/4. Berlin: Springer Verlag.

Landis,C. (1953). An annotated bibliography of flicker fusion phenomena, 1740 - 1952. Univ.Michigan, Ann Arbor.

Roehrig,W.C.(1959). The influence of the portion of the retina stimulated on the critical flicker fusion threshold. J.Psychol., 48, 57 - 63.

Rogowitz.B.E.(1984). Measuring perceived flicker on visual displays. In Grandjean,E.(Ed.) Ergonomic and health in modern offices. London and Philadelphia: Taylor & Francis.

Woodworth,R.S. and Schlosberg,H. (1958). Experimental psychology. London: Methuen and Co, Ltd.

WORK WITH DISPLAY UNITS 86
B. Knave and P.-G. Widebäck (eds.)

INFLUENCE OF CRT REFRESH RATES ON ACCOMMODATION AFTEREFFECTS

Tsunehiro Takeda, Yukio Fukui, and Takeo Iida
Industrial Products Research Institute, M.I.T.I.
1-1-4 Yatabe Higashi, Tsukuba Science City, Ibaraki, JAPAN

The paper describes the basic characteristics of dynamic accommodation and demonstrates the effects of the CRT refresh rate on accommodation for both negative and positive display modes. The accommodation area (AA) is defined as a measure of visual fatigue. The experiment confirms that the AA can be satisfactorily used to access visual fatigue. The data indicate that the positive display mode is better for the eye than the negative display mode, provided that its refresh rate is sufficiently above the critical fusion frequency (CFF).

1. INTRODUCTION

An objective and reliable measurement method has long been needed to deal with still highly controversial visual display terminal (VDT) issues (Ostberg, 1980). To meet this needs, the authors have proposed the dynamic refractometer as an objective measurement device and the accommodation area (AA) of the measured accommodative response to the stepwise stimulus of a target as a measure of visual fatigue (Takeda et al., 1984, 1985a, b).

This paper reports some small changes in the measurement system and the preparatory examination on the effect of the cathode ray tube (CRT) refresh rate for both negative and positive display modes with regard to accommodation aftereffects. The study also reveals (1) that the decrease in accommodation area (DAA) of the positive display mode is greater than that of the negative display mode with a lower refresh rate, and (2) that the DAA becomes smaller with a refresh rate that is slightly higher than the critical fusion frequency (CFF) of the positive display mode. Thus the positive display mode appears to produce less visual fatigue than the negative display mode, provided that the refresh rate is higher enough than its CFF.

2. METHOD

2.1. Apparatus

The dynamic refractometer, which is described in detail by Takeda et al. (1984), is used for objective measurement of visual fatigue. A specially designed hood is attached to the device to eliminate the problem of vague reflection. With the aid of the hood, the acquired data became more stable than before. The light-emitting diodes (LEDs), which produce the measurement light, were changed from the one with a central frequency of 870 nm to the ones with 950 nm. As a result, subjects could not sense any measurement light, even in total darkness. This change permitted the dynamic and precise measurement of dark focus that is reported by Iida et al. (1986).

2.2. Basic Characteristics of Responses

Figure 1 shows the pupil-diameter and accommodative responses for a gradually approaching target. Note the unstable response for the extreme end of the subject's near point. The span of step response (SS) is determined to about 80%

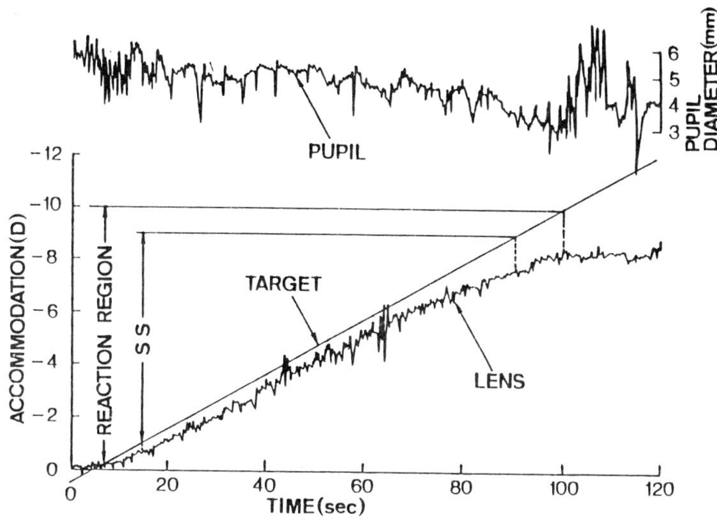

Figure 1: Accommodation and pupil-diameter responses for a gradually approaching target.

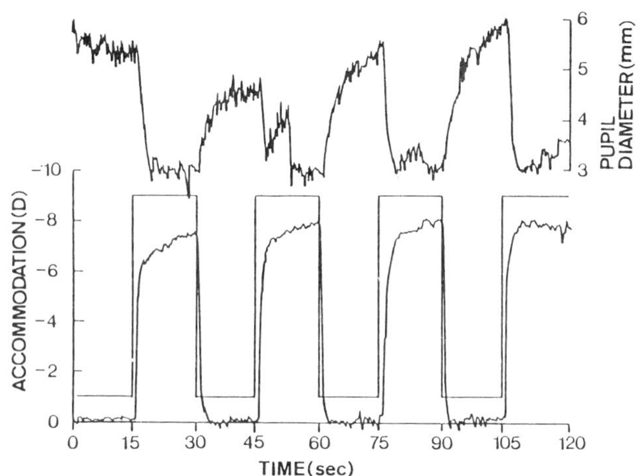

Figure 2: Accommodation and pupil-diameter responses for a suddenly changed target.

of the target span to induce as much accommodation power as possible without excessive difficulty for each subject (Figure 1). Figure 2 shows examples of pupil-diameter responses and accommodation for the stepwise stimulus of the target. The responses show a hunting behavior during the second near stimulus is presented. As shown in the figure, the accommodative response is generally faster and more stable than the pupil-diameter response. The fact that the measurement is performed monocularly may have some influence on the result, since the eye is out of the optimal vergence condition.

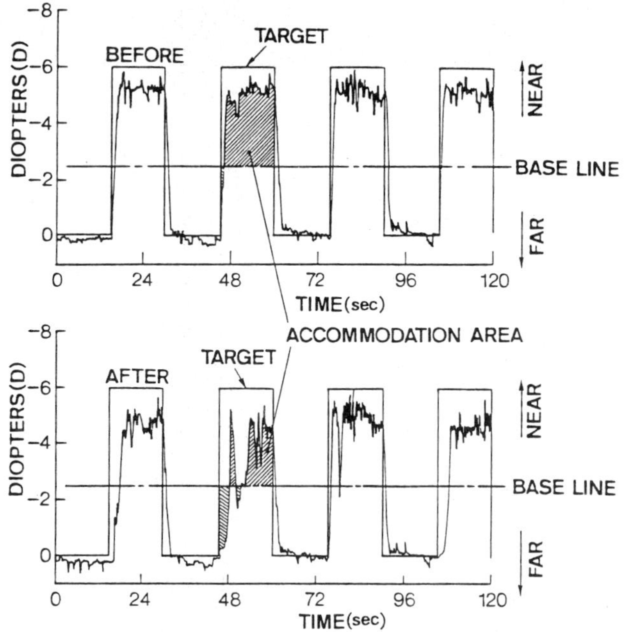

Figure 3: Examples of accommodation step responses before and after search work.

2.3. Definition of the AA

After several hours of VDT work, most cases show an accommodative response that is clearly different from the response before work (Figure 3). These differences are summarized as increased dead time, decreased response speed, increased occurrence time of defocusing from near stimulus, and decreased accommodative power. As Figure 3 shows, the AA is defined as the integrated area of the accommodative response from the base line of the averaged value of the whole response before work. The area is normalized as the perfect response to be an unity. Hence, greater AA values means better accommodative ability.

3. EXPERIMENTAL PROCEDURES

3.1. Equipment Used

The study used standard commercial CRT (Cannon CanoWord 35) with a 57.3 Hz refresh rate and non-interlace scanning. The phosphor (P4, Paper White) had a rather wide energy distribution spectrum and had yielded good results with visual fatigue in a previous experiment (Takeda, 1985). The CRTs were modified so that the refresh rate could be changed from 43 to 75 Hz by restricting the display region to 15 lines (Figure 4).

The CFFs for both display modes were measured for 11 subjects aged 19 to 45 years. Results showed averages of 48.1 and 60.1 Hz for the negative and the positive display modes respectively. Five CRTs were used, and the refresh rates were determined to be 43, 48, 56, 65, and 75 Hz for the negative display mode. The frequencies were to be equally located on a logarithmic scale for the negative display mode, taking into consideration the logarithmic nature of sensation. Because the flicker of the 43 Hz positive display mode CRT was very

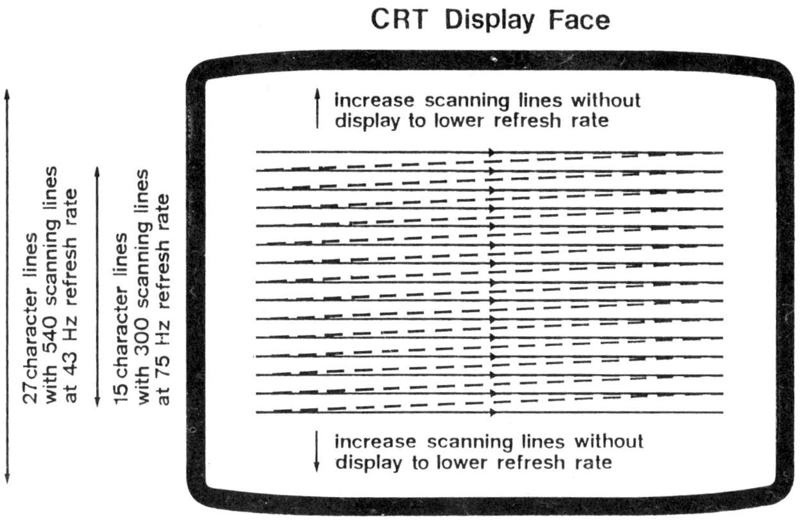

Figure 4: Method for altering the refresh rate.

strong, it was altered to 60 Hz; but the rest of the frequencies were kept the same for the positive display mode to facilitate comparison.

The luminance of the CRTs were all fixed at 56 cd/m , which was agreed to be optimal by most subjects. The illumination was 300 lux on the face of the CRTs and 540 lux on the desk.

3.2. Task

The task was to count the number of randomly specified two digit numbers out of 266 (19x14) randomly arranged numbers. The task was performed alternately on a CRT and then on white paper printed in advance in black ink. Subjects were required to solve the problem as quickly as possible. After 40 seconds, the next problem was automatically presented. Subjects worked for 2 hours in the morning and 3 hours in the afternoon without a break.

3.3. Subjects

Five emmetropic subjects were selected from some 250 new Canon, Inc., employees who have a visual acuity of 1.0 or better. Their ages ranged from 19 to 22 years, and they were all highly motivated. Two of them were males.

3.4. Procedure

Each subject used randomly selected VDTs and took part in the experiment every other day to avoid accumulated influence. Both at the beginning and at the end of the experiment involving negative and positive display modes, subjective evaluation was conducted with one by one comparison. Before and after each working day, the subjects answered 25 questions on visual fatigue and discomfort. The performance was automatically recorded and analyzed every hour. About 15 minutes were needed to gather the step responses of all five subjects. The measurements were carried out every hour for 5 hours. The negative display mode experiment was conducted in the first session, and the positive display mode experiment was performed a month later.

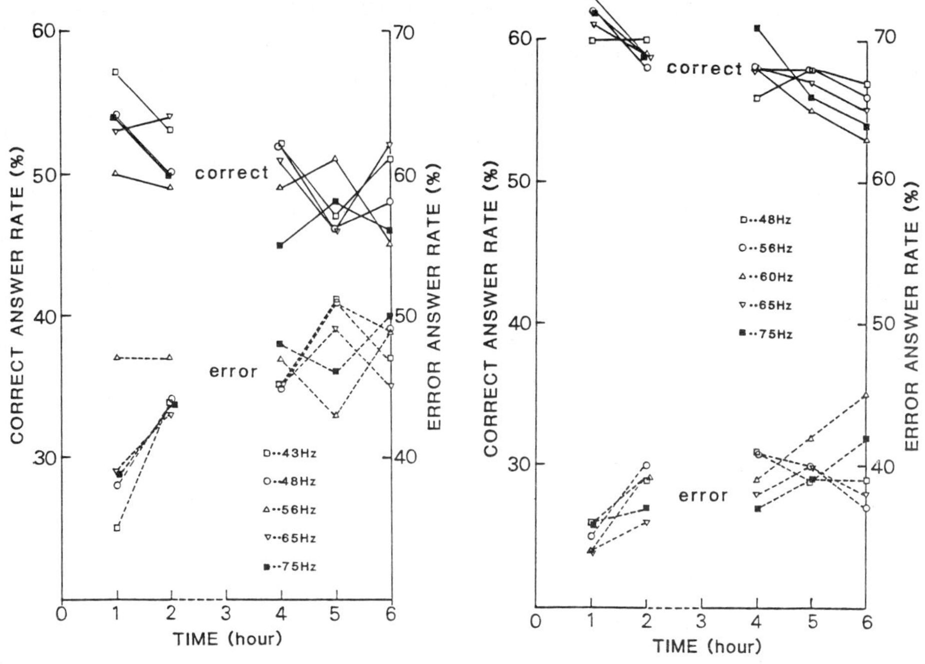

Figure 5: Averaged performance results for the negative display mode.

Figure 6: Averaged performance results for the positive display mode.

4. RESULTS AND DISCUSSION

4.1. Subjective Tests

The subjective preference for the CRTs was in accordance with the CRT refresh rate for both display modes. Subjective reports of eye fatigue and discomfort increased slightly on the 25-item questionnaire after the work on each CRT for both display modes, but no statistically meaningful differences were found between display modes with identical refresh rates.

4.2. Performance

Averaged performance results showed a decrease in the correct answer rate and an increase in the error rate as a whole (Figures 5 and 6) for the negative and positive display modes respectively. The number that each subject could not answer within 40 seconds time were only several times each hour.

Highly significant differences occurred over time. The correct answer rate was higher by several percentage points than that of the negative display mode. The inter-individual differences were so great that no clear differences could be found between the refresh rates used or between the positive and negative display modes.

4.3. Changes in AA

Figures 7 and 8 show the average change in AA for each refresh rate with the

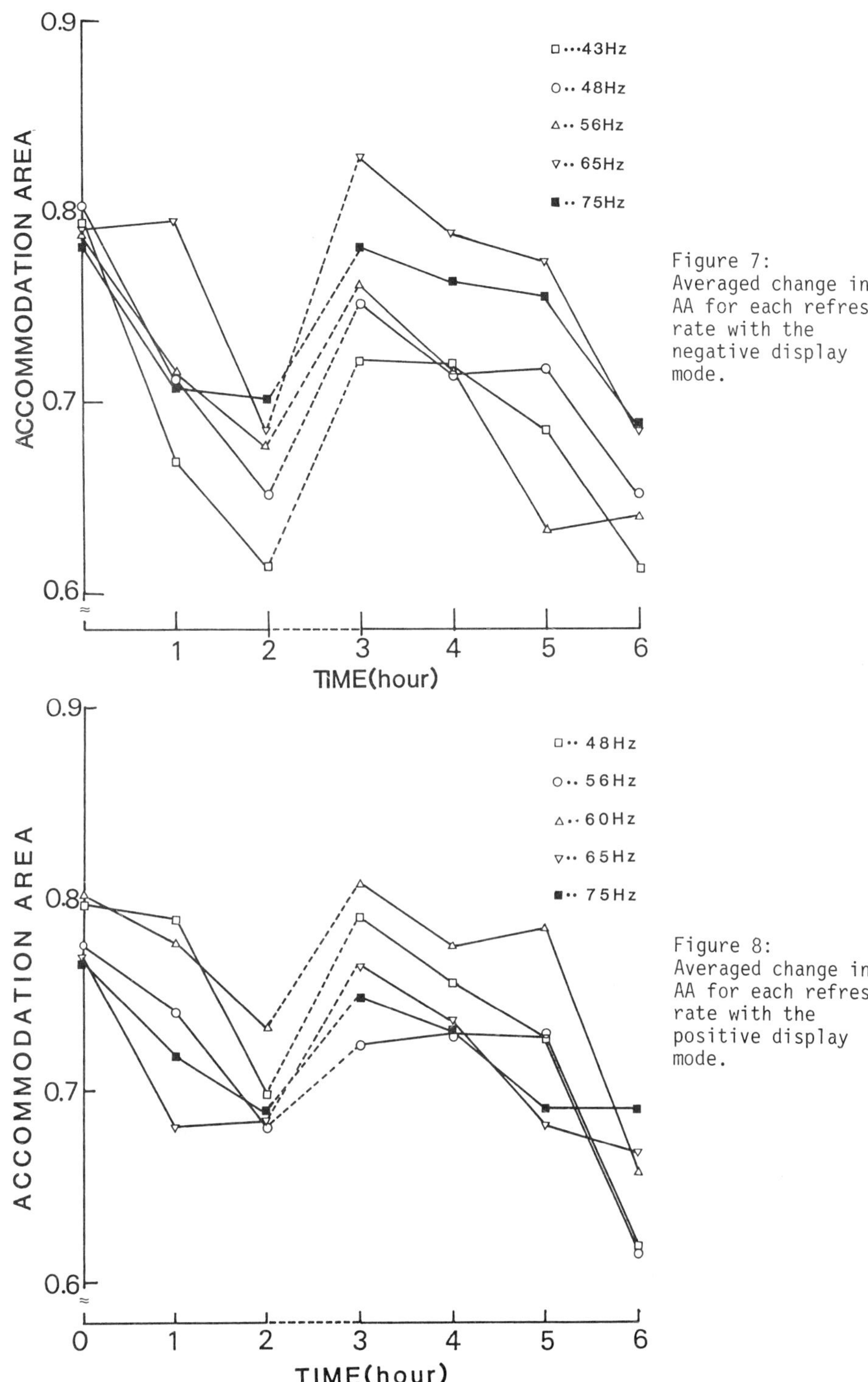

Figure 7: Averaged change in AA for each refresh rate with the negative display mode.

Figure 8: Averaged change in AA for each refresh rate with the positive display mode.

negative and positive display modes, respectively. Both figures show a clear decrease of the AA over time and an increase after a 1-hour noon recess. The dips in the morning for the negative display mode are considerably greater than those for the positive display mode.

Tables 1 and 2 shows the results of three-dimensional analysis of variance for both display modes. If the fixed-effect model were adopted, the data would indicate a highly significant difference with respect to the refresh rates in both the positive and negative display modes. However, since the inter-individual differences in the AA are so great, no statistically meaningful difference exists between the refresh rates for the two display modes, when the mixed-effect model is applied. This result indicates that it is premature to generalize the following findings. More data are needed to reach firm conclusions.

4.4. Difference of Display Modes

DAA is defined to be the difference of AA before and after work. Figure 9 shows the averaged DAA of five subjects' DAA for the respective refresh rate. The DAA is greater in the lower refresh rates because most subjects feel flicker below 48.1 Hz for the negative display mode and below 60.1 Hz for the positive display mode. The DAA of positive display mode is greater than that of negative display mode in the lower refresh rates region. Then the figure shows the intersection

Factor	Mixed-effect Model		Fixed-effect Model	
	F_0	F	F_0	F
A	0.51	3.01 (5%)	35.3 **	3.32 (1%)
B	151. **	3.32 (1%)	151. **	3.32 (1%)
C	20.0 **	3.67 (1%)	69.4 **	2.80 (1%)
A×B	68.6 **	2.01 (1%)	68.6 **	2.01 (1%)
A×C	0.79	1.65 (5%)	3.78**	1.79 (1%)
B×C	3.48**	1.79 (1%)	3.48**	1.79 (1%)
A×B×C	4.78**	1.39 (1%)	4.78**	1.39 (1%)

** p <0.01; A -- the difference of colors;
B -- the difference of subject; C -- the effect of time

Table 1: Analysis of Variance for the Accommodation Area for the Negative Display Mode.

Factor	Mixed-effect Model		Fixed-effect Model	
	F_0	F	F_0	F
A	1.54	3.01 (5%)	19.7 **	3.32 (1%)
B	46.3 **	3.32 (1%)	46.3 **	4.61 (1%)
C	8.84**	3.67 (1%)	62.6 **	2.80 (1%)
A×B	12.8 **	2.01 (1%)	12.8 **	2.51 (1%)
A×C	0.98	1.65 (5%)	3.79**	1.52 (5%)
B×C	7.08**	1.79 (1%)	7.08**	2.18 (1%)
A×B×C	3.86**	1.39 (1%)	3.86**	1.59 (1%)

** p <0.01; A -- the difference of colors;
B -- the difference of subject; C -- the effect of time

Table 2: Analysis of Variance for the Accommodation Area for the Positive Display Mode.

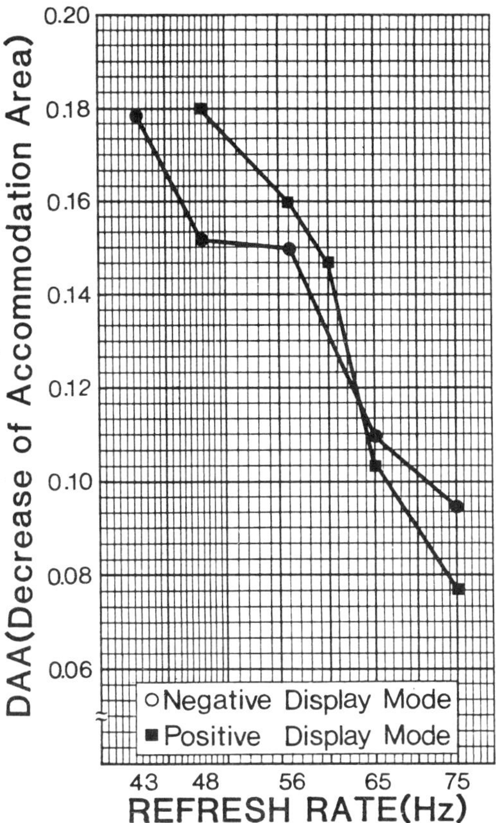

Figure 9: Relationship of the DAA to the refresh rate.

of the DAA of both display modes at about 64 Hz. This result indicates that the positive display mode is better for the eye provided that the refresh rate is a little higher than its CFF.

5. CONCLUSIONS

The decrease in AA was again confirmed as a promising objective measurement of visual fatigue and discomfort. The study shows that the positive display mode is better for the eye if the refresh rate is a little higher than the CFF. At the same time, the DAA trend seems to indicate a preference for a refresh rate that is above enough the CFF, since such a rate reduces visual fatigue with VDT work. However, the inter-individual differences are so great that more data are needed to reach a firm conclusion.

Though the dynamic refractometer is very effective for objectively measuring visual fatigue, it has the disadvantage of requiring subjects to stop working for examination. This interruption may actually veil real visual fatigue because sensitive subjects tend to try hard during the short examination, even though they are extremely tired. The authors are now developing a new measuring system to overcome this problem (Fukui et al.,1986). The system allows the eye to move freely while accommodation is being measured and will thus permit investigators to measure the effects of VDT work on accommodation in actual work situation.

ACKNOWLEDGMENTS

The authors wish to express their sincere thanks to K. Karasuyama and E. Maeda of Canon Inc., and to their assistances, M. Kouchi, and A. Numano, for handling the data.

REFERENCES

Fukui, Y., Takeda, T., and Iida, T. (1986). Development of Free Eye Movement Dynamic Refractometer (FEMDAR), Proceedings of WWDU, 1018-1021.

Iida, T., Takeda, T., and Fukui, Y. (1986). Visual Fatigue and Dark Focus of Accommodation, Proceedings of WWDU, 871-874.

Ostberg, O. (1980). Accommodation and Visual Fatigue in Display Work. In E. Grandjean and E. Vigliani (Eds.), Ergonomic Aspects of Visual Display Terminals (pp. 41-52). London: Taylor and Francis.

Takeda, T., Fukui, Y., Iida, T., Karasuyama, K., and Kigoshi, T. (1984). A New Objective Measurement Method of Visual Fatigue in VDT Work. In H.W. Hendrik and O. Brown (Eds.), Human Factors in Organizational Design and Management (pp. 193-197). Amsterdam: Elsevier Science.

Takeda, T., Fukui, Y., Iida, T., and Karasuyama, K. (1985 a). An Objective Measurement Apparatus for Accommodation Ability Change Caused by VDT Work. Journal of the Optical Society of Japan, 6, 59-66.

Takeda, T., Fukui, F., Iida, T., and Karasuyama, K. (1985 b). An Objective Measurement of Accommodation Aftereffect in terms of Display Color of VDT. In I.D. Brown, R. Goldsmith, K. Coombs, and M.A. Sinclair (Eds.), Ergonomics International 85 (pp.586-588). London: Taylor and Francis.

12. VISION

WORK WITH DISPLAY UNITS 86
B. Knave and P.-G. Widebäck (eds.)

SENSITIVITY TO LIGHT AND VISUAL STRAIN IN VDT OPERATORS : BASIC DATA FOR THE DESIGN OF WORK STATIONS

Jean-Jacques Meyer, Paule Rey, Jean-Claude Schira and Arnaud Bousquet

Institut de médecine sociale et préventive, Unité de médecine du travail et d'ergonomie, Université de Genève*

INTRODUCTION

According to our results obtained both in field studies and in laboratory experiments, the design of VDT work stations should take into account the huge variability towards light displayed by VDT users. For this purpose, we like to propose an area of possible luminances which could fit the requirements of older operators, as a function of sweep frequencies. This area is limited by the flicker sensitivity of younger subjects. It also covers the needs of operators with commonly found visual defects.

POPULATION UNDER STUDY

Variability will be demonstrated in 112 clerks of our state department who work at least 3 hours a day facing a screen. Their age distribution goes from 15 to 65 years. They were submitted to a questionnaire on subjective feelings of fatigue, signs and symptoms of asthenopia, adverse reactions to the lighting environment of their work place and to an extensive eye examination. Their work places were fully investigated.

RESULTS AND DISCUSSION

Complaints of asthenopia, in this group like in other groups, were shown to grow with age and to be more important in operators with dioptric defects (**table 1**). In other words, young people with myopic eyes or astigmatism displayed more complaints of of asthenopia than did young or older operators. Let us underline that the difficulty in assessing the influence of dioptric defects on asthenopia is due to the fact that several defects may be present in the same individual.

Age groups :	18-34	=	57 %
	35-45	=	71 %
	over 45	=	89 %
Without defects		=	59 %
With defects		=	72 %
Myopic eyes		=	65 %
Presbyopic eyes		=	77 %

Table 1 - Proportion of asthenopia in different sub-groups

* 10, avenue Jules-Crosnier, 1206 Geneva, Switzerland

From results in **table 1**, it could be concluded that with a routine visual examination and taking into account the aging process, it would be possible to eradicate all visual problems at VDTs. Unfortunately, that is not true. At first, there are still a fair number of young operators, without visual defects, who complain of visual overstrain at their work place; moreover, operators with spectacles tend to complain even more than operators with uncorrected slight defects [1].

Our hypothesis is that a large part of visual difficulties in VDT operators are better understood, using other test procedures than routine eye examination. With our prototype C45 [2], our operators were required to adjust the luminance of a Landolt ring to distinguish precisely the gap, against a background of 1 cd/m2 of 3° and a surrounding area of 30° at 10 cd/m2, for decreasing sizes of the target. We then distributed them among 6 classes of increasing requested luminances as shown in **table 2** where the size of the target is either equivalent to a visual acuity of .7 or of .3 respectively. It is obvious that our operators vary very much in sensitivity, the luminous requirements of the worst performers being from 50 to 100 times as much as the ones of the best performers. This variability increases with the decreasing size of the target.

Conditions		Classes					
		1	2	3	4	5	6
Visual accuity	= .3	up to					
Minimal Lvalue	= .1 cd/m^2	2	3	5	7	27	50
Visual acuity	= .7						
Minimal Lvalue	= .5 cd/m^2	"	"	"	10	20	200

Table 2 - C45 classes of threshold luminances expresses as a number of times the minimal value of the best performers

One of the most important parameters to explain such a wide variety of answers is age (**figure 1**), the second being visual deficiencies (**figure 2**).

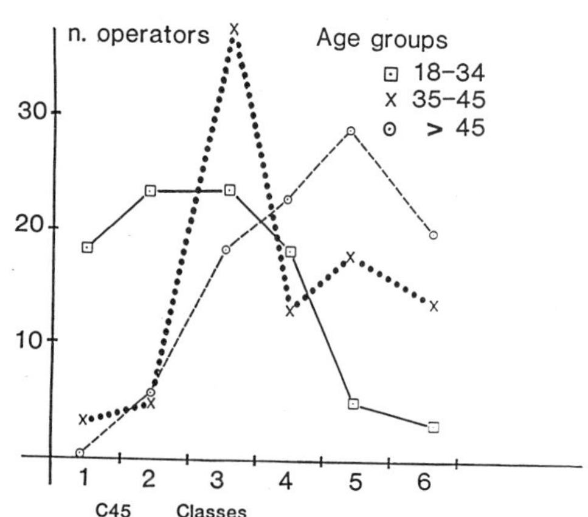

Figure 1 -

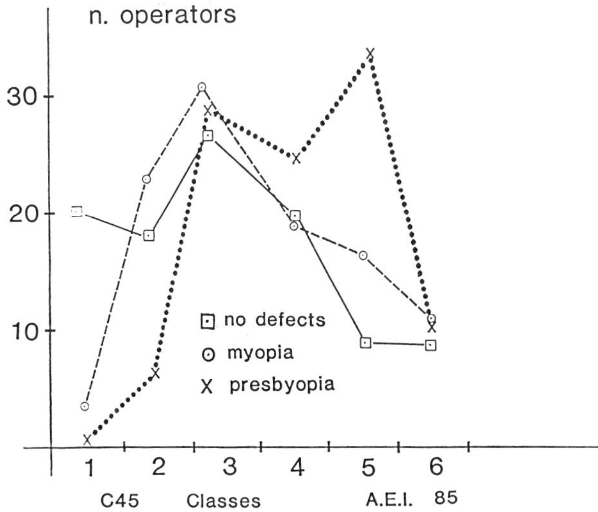

Figure 2 -

Complaints of asthenopia, however, did not change significantly from one class to the next. As shown by **table 3**, if a fair proportion of older operators with visual defects are found among the worst performers, it still remains that a high percentage of normal and young subjects are present among those subjects who need 10 to 100 times more light than the best performers for an equal performance.

Without defects	=	13.6 %
Myopic eyes	=	25.7 %
Presbyopic eyes	=	33.0 %
Astigmates	=	40.0 %
Age : 18-34	=	7.0 %
35-45	=	36.0 %
over 45	=	55.0 %

Table 3 - Who is to be found among the worst performers at C45 (V.A. = .7)

Moreover, considering only the best performers, we noticed that : one third of them complained of visual discomfort due to the illuminating conditions at their work place and another third complained of visual discomfort due to bad illuminating conditions of their office.

Thus, according to our results, it would not be reasonable for the designer to say : let us take as a reference the worst performers and provide to all operators as much light as possible. Two of our observations are against such a point of view. At first, we noticed that some operators, young or older, with or without visual defects, prefer low illumination levels at their work place while others prefer higher illuminatin levels. Secondly, as shown by **table 4**, recovery time after glare is growing from class 1 to class 6 in young like in older operators, in operators without visual defects as well as in operators with visual defects. Thus, the same persons may be expected at the same time to show a low discriminatory power at low contrast and low luminance levels and to suffer easily of glare.

Sub-groups	C45 L classes					
	1	2	3	4	5	6
Without visual defects	3.0*	3.6*	5.2*	5.4*	10.0*	?
Young operators	2.7**	4.5**	5.0**	5.2**	10.4**	10.0**
Myopic eyes	-	4.4	4.5	5.5	9.8	11.3

difference to the mean recovery time of the whole population
* p = .05 ** p = .01

Table 4 - Average recovery time after glare, in sec. (4'000 cd/m^2; 3°; exposure time : 10 sec.)

A third parameter should be taken into account : it is the wide variety in flicker sensitivity which can be noticed with our testing procedures [3] in which the subject is allowed to settle his flicker-free thresholds for different luminance levels and different sizes of the flickering field.

Combining, then all relevant data provided by our populations of VDT users, we like to suggest, for the ergonomical design of VDTs, the two following graphs : **figure 3** represents the percentage of expected annoyed operators between 15 and 65 years of age, as a function of sweep frequencies for two types of phosphors and a screen of 30° at 50 cd/m2. It has to be stressed that a sweep frequency of less than 70 Hz can be expected to disturb about one half of an ordinary population of operators.

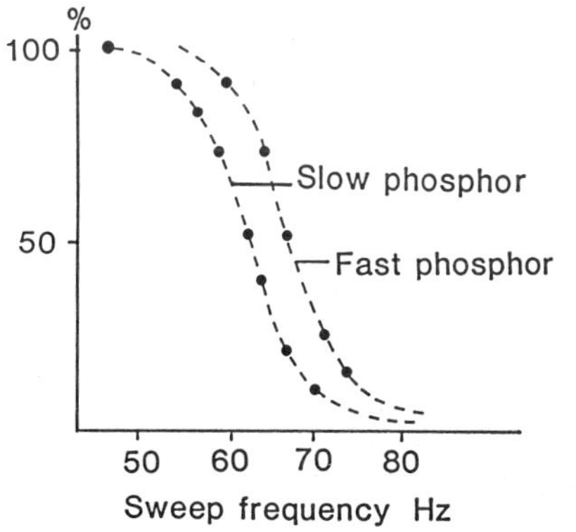

Figure 3

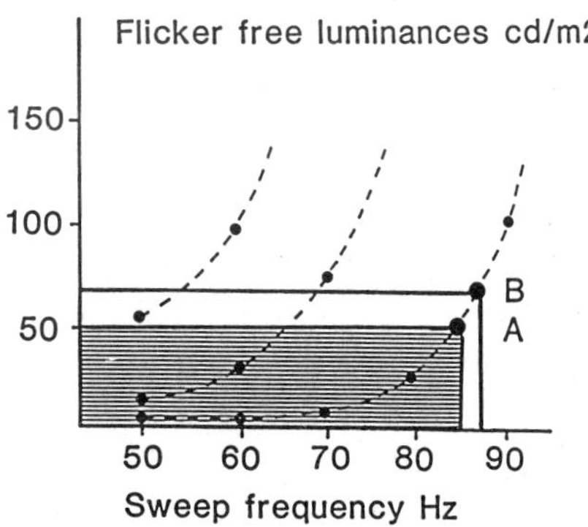

Figure 4

Figure 4 represents the relationship between luminance levels and sweep frequencies for the least (left curve), the inbetween (middle curve) and most sensitive subjects (right curve). As deduced from our results, it would be necessary, to satisfy 100 % of operators between 15 and 65 years of age, to increase the sweep frequency up to around 85 Hz, for threshold discrimination (A) and even, up to 88 to 90 Hz, for comfortable reading (B).

However, if the opportunity could be given to the operator to adjust the luminance level of the screen and also of the surrounding, this requirement of very high sweep frequencies would be less stringent.

REFERENCES

[1] Wildberger, H., Zur Arbeit an Datensichtgeräten : Untersuchung in einer Grossdruckerei. Klin. Mbl. Augenheilk., 180 (1982), pp. 367-369.

[2] Rey P. and Meyer J.J., Visual impairments and their objective correlates. Ergonomic Aspects of Visual Display Terminals, edited by E. Grandjean and E. Vigliani (Taylor and Francis, London, 1980) pp. 77-83.

[3] Meyer J.J., Bousquet A., Rey P. and Pittard J., Two New Visual Tests to define the Visual Requirements of VDU Operators. Ergonomics and Health in Modern Offices, edited by E. Granjean (Taylor and Francis, London, 1984) pp. 423-430.

WORK WITH DISPLAY UNITS 86
B. Knave and P.-G. Wideback (eds.)

ARE THERE SUBTLE CHANGES IN VISION AFTER USE OF VDTs?

George C. WOO, Graham STRONG, Elizabeth IRVING, Brian ING

Centre for Sight Enhancement
School of Optometry, University of Waterloo
Waterloo, Canada N2L 3G1

Visual function of two groups of workers is monitored in this study by means of a number of laboratory and clinical techniques. These include visual acuity, contrast sensitivity function, refraction, accommodation and phoria measurements. Our results indicate there are subtle changes in selected aspects of vision for both VDT and nonVDT subjects.

1. INTRODUCTION

Reports of visual complaints by VDT users are well publicized. Some believe them to be serious occupational problems whereas others view them as adaptation problems associated with a new technology. The purpose of the present study is to evaluate selected visual characteristics of both VDT and nonVDT users.

Östberg (1) has shown that the accommodative mechanism of the eye exhibits signs of fatigue after use of VDTs. Such findings appear to substantiate symptoms of transient blurred vision reported by VDT users. Mandatory vision testing for VDT operators at regular intervals has been implemented in Europe for quite some time (2). One of the tests recommended is the measurement of visual acuity. The fact that there is no study on transient alterations of vision due to use of VDTs could be attributed in part to the limitation of the conventional Snellen visual acuity test. Clinical visual acuity measurements are based upon the limit of resolution of high contrast small targets. An assumption has to be made about the relative visibility and object size within the resolution limit. Such an assumption is only valid when the visual abnormality can be equated with dioptric defocus. In order to measure subtle changes in vision prior to reduction in visual acuity, a laboratory technique designed to obtain the contrast sensitivity function is required (3,4). Ophthalmic practitioners have long recognized the need for such a tool. Based upon clinical observation, eye care practitioners realize that there may be a distinct difference in visual function between two patients who have identical Snellen visual acuities. One simply cannot predict a person's overall performance from his Snellen visual acuity alone.

Campbell and Green (3) first measured the sensitivity of the human eye to subtle differences in contrast. They varied the contrast of sinusoidal gratings generated on the screen of an oscilloscope. Threshold contrast measurements are made across the full range of spatial frequencies to which the human visual system is able to respond. When these findings are plotted, a contrast sensitivity function is derived. The new approach of measuring contrast sensitivity for object sizes within the resolution limit offers not only a more complete description of different types of visual loss but also a more sensitive method and possibly a more realistically correlated perceptual method of assessing the visual advantage of different optical aids. Assessment and specification of the intra-resolution abnormality, combined with an understanding of its suprathreshold consequences should allow a much more adequate description of visual loss. Using this method, it has been discovered that subtle changes of visual function can actually be measured (5).

Jaschinski-Kruza (6) found after three hours of editing text at a VDT, a significant decrease in sensitivity was found in five subjects out of seven. He used a single spatial frequency of 10 c/deg for his study.

A number of studies carried out with a variety of psychophysical and objective methods (8-10) have shown that the human eye's longitudinal chromatic aberration amounts to 1.00 - 1.50 dioptres between and C and F Fraunhofer Lines (486-656 NM). It is commonly assumed that a specific wavelength within the chromatic aberration interval is in focus on the retina. It has also been shown that the wavelength in focus varies selectively with the state of accommodation (8). When the eye is viewing a distant target or is with relaxed accommodation, it is conjugate with the wavelength of 650 NM. As the eye accommodates the wavelength which is in focus at the retinal plane becomes progressively shorter as the target is brought closer. At a distance of .5m, the wavelength in focus is about 520 NM. This hue shift has been used to explain the lag in accommodation and suggests that selective focussing within the longitudinal chromatic aberration interval is responsible for the sparing of accommodation. Bobier and Sivak (11) have reported an accurate objective procedure for assessing chromatic aberration. Chromoretinoscopy has proven useful to identify the selective focussing of the eye within the chromatic interval when viewing near and distant targets. This technique is employed to monitor accommodative changes with VDT use, and the occurrence of any shift in the wavelength which is in focus at the retinal plane as a result of prolonged viewing of a VDT screen.

As accommodation increases, the eyes converge and exhibit increased esophoria. With decreased accommodation they diverge and exhibit more exophoria. As a result of chromatic aberration, the accommodative and therefore vergence demands should be different for different coloured targets at the same distance. Since VDTs are essentially chromatic, it is important to evaluate the accommodative and convergence requirements of the eye to visualize coloured targets. In addition to chromoretinoscopy, chromophoria findings are elicited as well. In this study, we investigate possible changes of various parameters in vision. These include visual acuity, contrast sensitivity function, refraction, accommodation and convergence.

2. METHODS

Two groups of subjects participated in this study. Group I are VDT users at the University of Waterloo and Group II are nonVDT workers at the same institution. The experimental design of this study is of the observational fixed period approach. The fixed period is 6-8 hours. All the above described procedures are performed on the two groups of subjects before they commenced work and again at the end of their normal working day.

Contrast sensitivity function measurements in this study employ electronic generation of spatial gratings with a sinusoidal luminance profile on an oscilloscope. Contrast and spatial frequency can be varied in a systematic manner by a microprocessor. Two groups of subjects are carefully refracted objectively and subjectively for ametropia at specific viewing distances. Natural pupils are used. Contrast thresholds are elicited by the method of adjustment. For each of the several predetermined spatial frequencies, five readings are taken. The mean luminance of the screen was found to be 18 cd m^{-2} and contrast was modulated about this luminance and adjusted by the subject using a decibel contrast attenuator connected to the apparatus. Its colour was white (P4 phosphor). The viewing distance was varied from 114 cm. for spatial frequencies up to 5 c/deg to 570 cm for spatial frequencies higher than 5 c/deg. The angular subtense of the target was 5 deg at 115 cm and 1 deg at 570 cm. Each subject was asked to fixate the centre of the screen while the contrast was varied at .5, 1, 2, 3, 5, 10, 15 and 20, 30 and 40 c/deg. Distance Snellen visual acuities are recorded using a

University of Waterloo logarithmic chart (13). The subject was asked to read across the chart horizontally to find the smallest letter seen before reading vertically down a column of letters at a distance of 4m. Near reading acuity is obtained with a conventional reading card. The mean luminance of these charts match those of the contrast measurements so that comparisons can be made between these functions. The associated phoria was measured using vectographs and loose prisms.

With the subject viewing a distant target, static retinoscopy is performed allowing an objective measure of the subject's refraction. Following this procedure, chromoretinoscopy was performed first with a red filter (615 NM dominant wavelength) and then with a green filter (530 NM dominant wavelength) placed over the viewing aperture of the retinoscope. These same procedures are repeated in dynamic retinoscopy when the subject is asked to view a near target. In this manner, the difference in the subject's refraction for red and green is obtained respectively. The subjective refraction is then obtained with the use of a phoropter. Measures of the distance phoria, near phoria and phorias using chromatic targets are obtained using Van Graefe technique with flash exposure of the variable target. Phoria findings are used as indicators of the binocular function under specific viewing conditions. The fusional vergence limits are measured for both distance and near targets followed by push-up amplitude of accommodation with the subject wearing his/her habitual correction.

A questionnaire was sent to each of the subjects after he/she served as a subject. Appendix A is the questionnaire.

3. RESULTS

Preliminary analysis of our data of 20 VDT and 20 nonVDT users indicate there is no change in both distance and near Snellen acuities before and after work for all the subjects (change is defined as 0.04 log unit or 2 letters on the logMAR chart). Legge et al. (14) reported that if the task is to read 6/30 Snellen letters, up to 2D of defocus can be tolerated. For an acuity of 6/3 the total depth of focus is 0.4D, that is +/- 0.2D. Since the change in refraction observed in this study is never greater than 0.5D and the best corrected distance acuity of all subjects is 6/6, little or no change in visual acuity is therefore anticipated as shown in Figure 1.

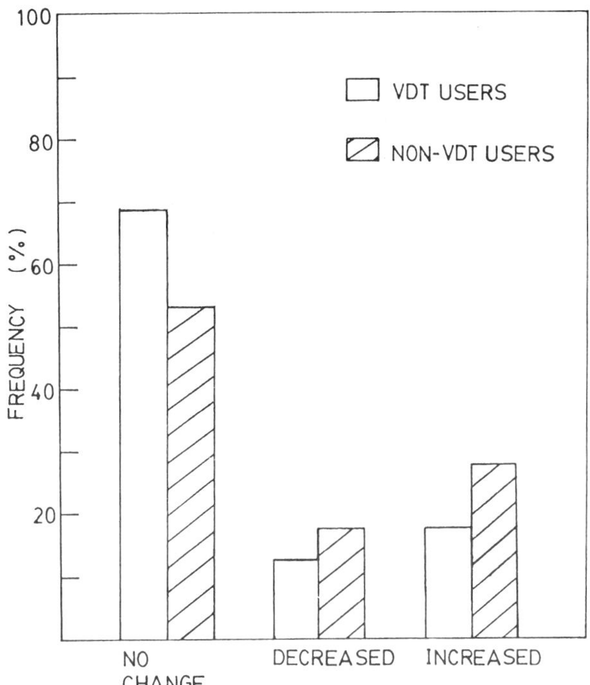

Figure 1. Frequency histogram of changes in distance visual acuity of 20 VDT users and 20 nonVDT users that demonstrate a change of 2 or more letters on the UW logMAR chart after one work day.

Although there are individual fluctuations in contrast thresholds obtained at low, medium and high spatial frequencies before and after work, the fluctuations are not systematic and cannot be attributed to any real change. Furthermore, such fluctuations are evident in both Group I and Group II subjects (see Figures 2 and 3). At 10 c/deg, our findings do not coincide with those reported by Jaschinski-Kruza. Since defocus is a purely optical effect, any threshold loss should have similar consequences for suprathreshold contrast targets. In this case, we do not have any loss in either the suprathreshold domain (letter acuity) or the threshold region (contrast sensitivity for a wide range of spatial frequencies).

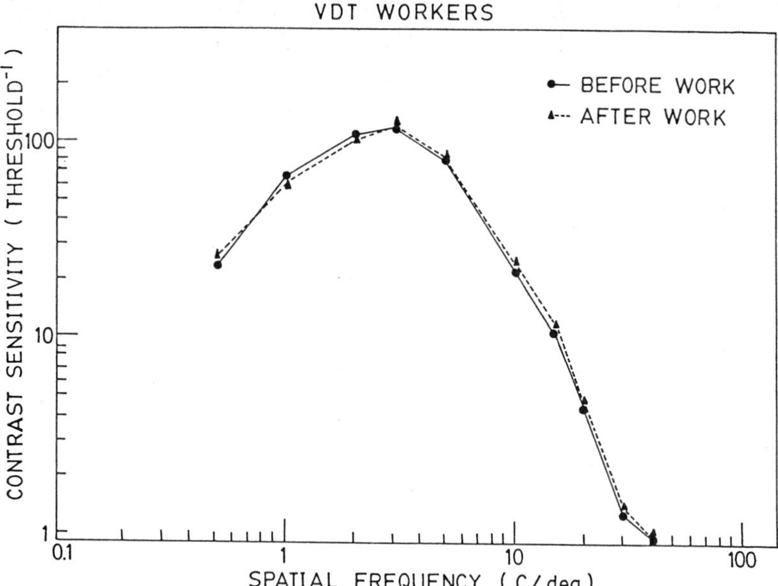

Figure 2. Contrast sensitivity function determined for users. Measurements were taken before the beginning and at the end of a single work day. Standard error of the mean is smaller than the symbol size.

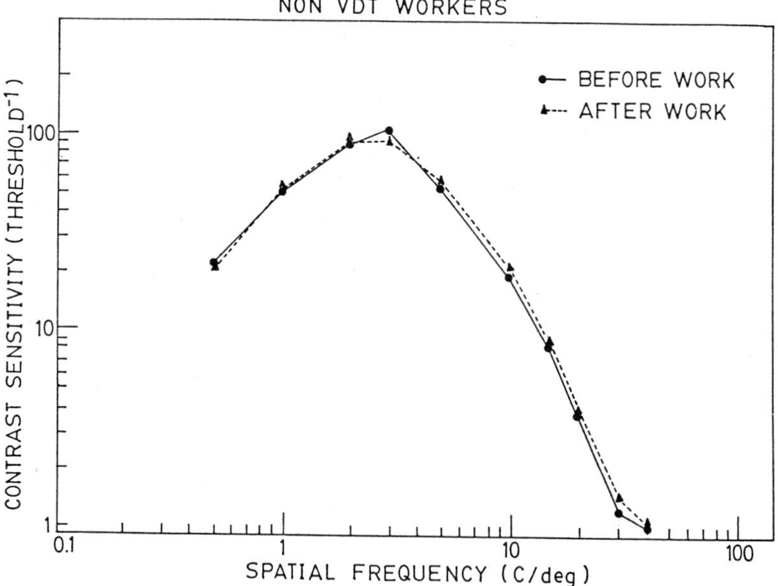

Figure 3. Contrast sensitivity function determined for nonVDT users. Measurements were taken before the beginning and at the end of a single work day. Standard error of the mean is smaller than the symbol size.

It appears that there are no changes in associated phoria measurements for either group. Figures 4 and 5 are results on objective and subjective refraction findings. It can be seen by inspection of the results that there is a distinct difference between the refraction findings. Increase in myopia as determined by objective refraction techniques is observed in many VDT users and nonusers. A smaller number of subjects in both groups exhibited decrease in myopia. However, identical changes do not necessarily occur in subjective refraction findings. Figures 6 and 7 illustrate the chromatic shift after a prolonged period of near work for both VDT and nonVDT users. What is certain is that there does appear to be a shift in the best focus position within the chromatic interval as revealed by chromoretinoscopy (see Figures 6 and 7). Essentially this shift results in relatively longer wavelengths being selectively better focussed than shorter wavelengths within the chromatic interval as a result of near work.

CHANGE IN REFRACTION

OBJECTIVE TECHNIQUE CHROMORETINOSCOPY

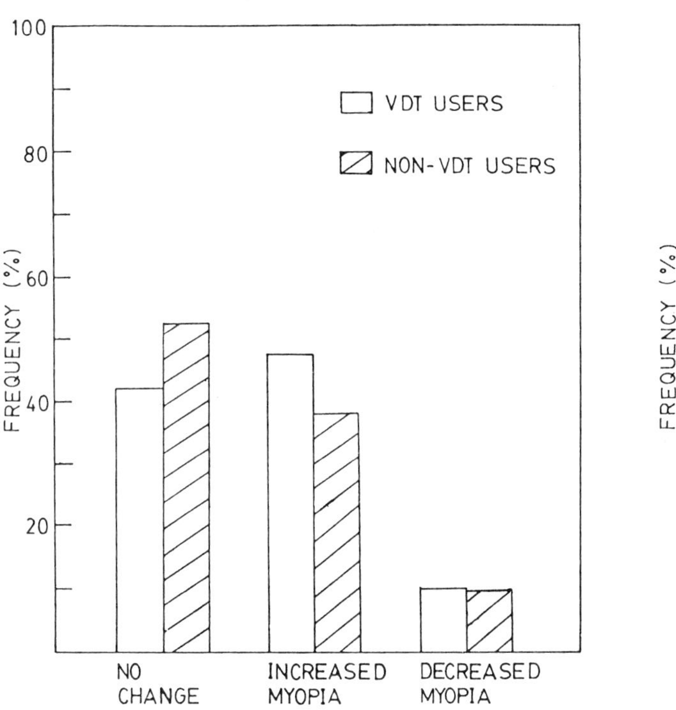

Figure 4. Frequency histogram of changes in chromoretinoscopic measurements after one work day of 20 VDT users and 20 nonVDT users. Static retinoscopic measurements of both red and green wavelengths must change by 0.25D or greater in the same direction in order to constitute a change.

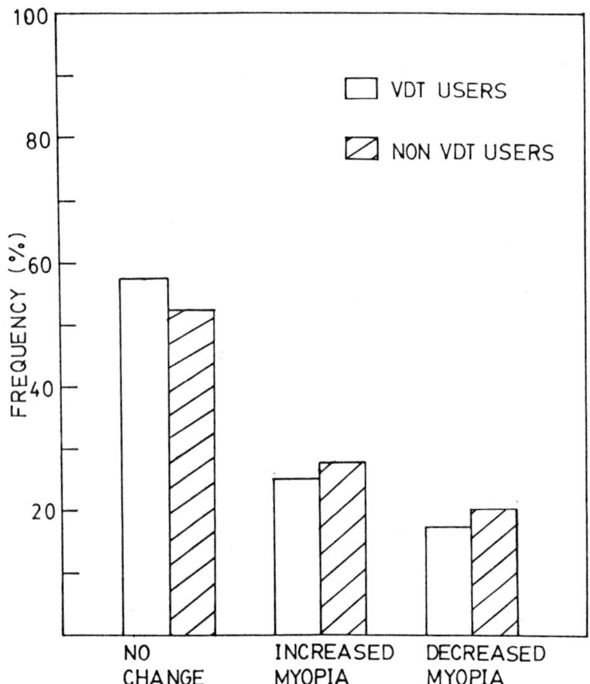

Figure 5. Frequency histogram changes of subjective refraction after one work day. Increases in myopia consisted of 0.25D or more of negative spherical power. Decreases in myopia (increased hyperopia) were noted if the lens correction increased in positive spherical power of 0.25D.

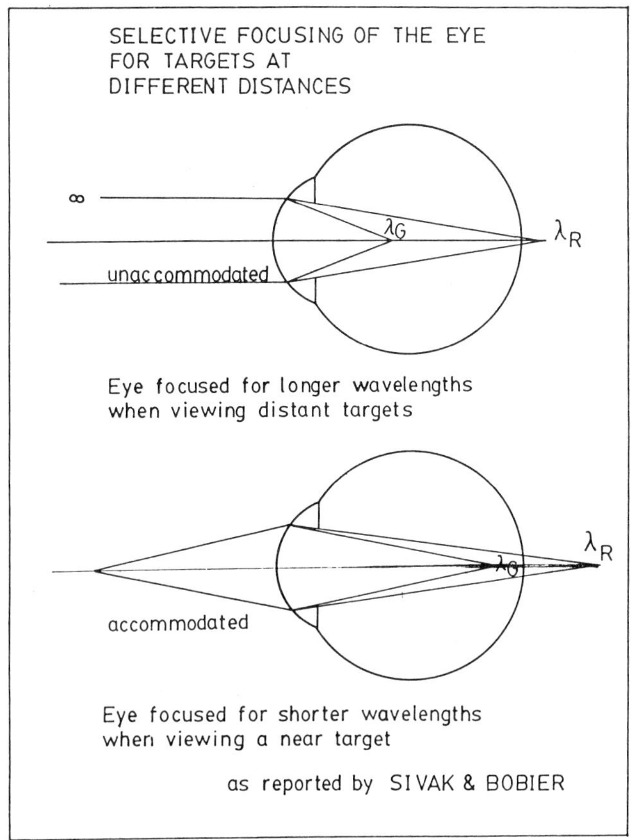

Figure 6. Selective focussing of the eye for different accommodative stimuli as indicated by chromoretinoscopy. Distance targets are focussed on the retina closer to the focus for red wavelengths (λ R) than the focus for green wavelengths (λ G). With accommodation, light of shorter wavelengths are focussed on the retina instead due to lag of accommodation.

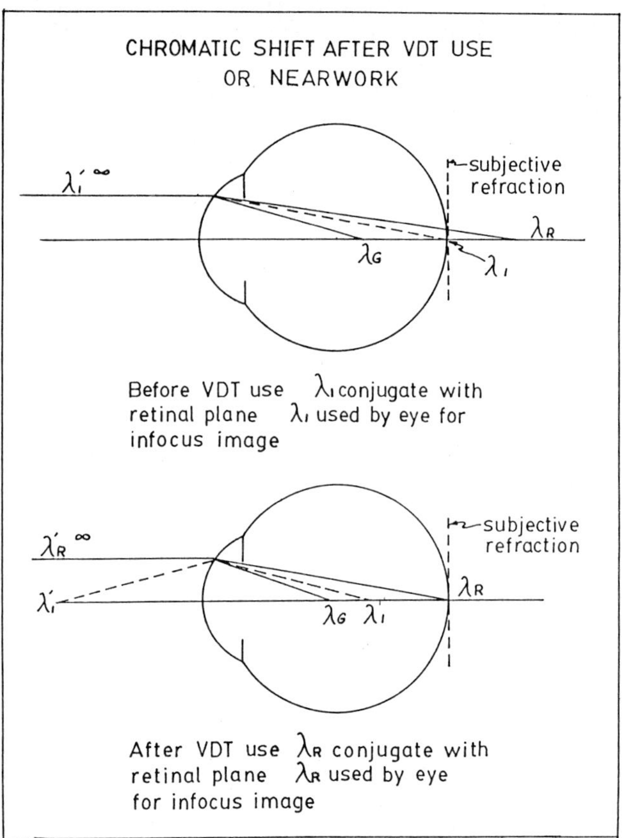

Figure 7. Diagramatic representation of the forward shift of the whole chromatic interval relative to the retina that occurs after a full work day of VDT usage or near work.

Results in dynamic retinoscopy, associated phoria and positive and negative fusional reserves are yet to be subjected to further analysis. Inspection of our raw data revealed an apparent reduction in exophoria or increase in esophoria at near for a number of subjects in both groups (see Figure 8). There are fewer subjects demonstrating less esophoria or more exophoria.

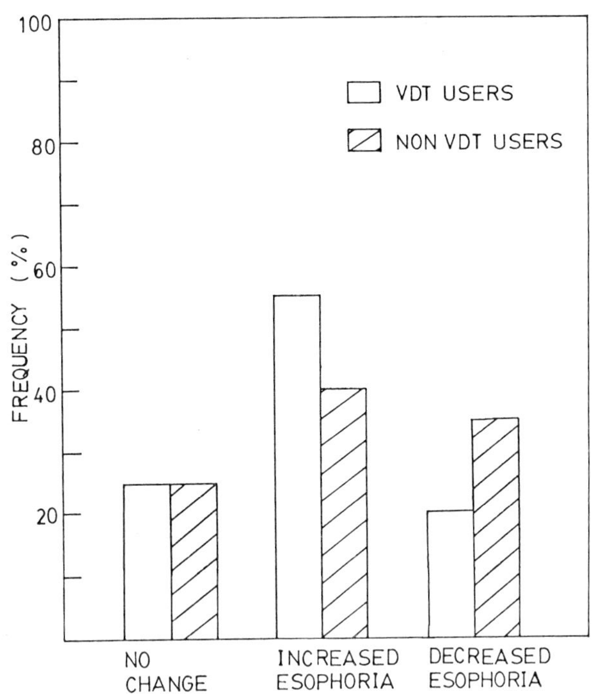

Figure 8. Frequency of changes in near phorias after one work day of 20 VDT users and 20 nonVDT users. Changes in phorias were at least 1 prism dioptre.

4. CONCLUSIONS

Our results suggest that the accommodative system of the eye does show signs of fatigue for VDT and nonVDT users. These results support Östberg's earlier findings on VDT workers (1). The trend towards myopia and esophoria in both groups was confirmed. There is no change in visual acuity or contrast sensitivity function after near work. Small changes in refraction and convergence can probably be attributed to the demand for accommodation. Further research on the relationship between accommodation and convergence of the visual system due to close work is indicated. It is concluded that there are subtle changes in selected aspects of vision after a work day. These changes occur in both VDT and non-VDT users.

ACKNOWLEDGEMENTS

This work was supported by a grant from the Ministry of Labour, Government of Ontario.

REFERENCES

(1) Östberg, O., Accommodation and Visual Fatigue in Display Work, in: Grandjean, E. (ed.), Ergonomic Aspects of Visual Display Terminals (Taylor and Francis Ltd., London, 1980) pp. 41-52.
(2) Cakir, A., Hart, D.J., and Stewart, T.F.M., Visual Display Terminals (John Wiley and Sons, Chicester, 1979)
(3) Campbell, F.W. and Green, D.G., Journal of Physiology 181 (1965) 576.
(4) Hess, G. and Woo, G., Investigate Ophthalmology and Visual Science 17 (1978) 428.
(5) Bodis-Wollner, I., Science 178 (1972) 769.
(6) Jaschinski-Kruza, W., Ergonomics 27 (1984) 1181.
(7) Wald, G. and Griffin, D.R., Journal of Optical Society of America 37 (1947) 321.
(8) Bedford, R.E. and Wyszecki, G., Journal of Optical Society of America 47 (1959) 564.
(9) Millodot, M. and Sivak, J., British Journal of Physiological Optics 28 (1973) 169.
(10) Woo, G., Optometric Monthly 69 (1978) 992.
(11) Bobier, C.W. and Sivak, J.G., Vision Research 18 (1978) 247.
(12) Strong, G. and Pace, R., American Journal of Optometry and Physiological Optics 59 (1982) 532.
(13) Strong, G. and Woo, G., Archives of Ophthalmology 103 (1985) 44.
(14) Legge, G.E., Mullen, K.T., Woo, G.C. and Campbell, F.W., Journal of Optical Society of America (1986) in print.

APPENDIX A: The Questionnaire

Thank you for participating in this study. We are interested to learn whether subtle changes in vision occur after prolonged reading or close work activities. The following questionnaire will help us to accurately profile your seeing activities for comparison with our test data. All subjects are asked to complete sections A and B. Video display terminal (VDT) users are also requested to complete section C.

Section A

Name ______________________ University extension ____________

Age ___ 20-25 years ___25-30 years ___35-40 years ___over 40 years

1. Estimate how many hours you spent today doing close work?

___ 2-4 hours ___ 4-6 hours ___ 6-8 hours ___more

2. If this was not a "normal" work day, how many hours do you usually spend doing close work?

___ 2-4 hours ___ 4-6 hours ___ 6-8 hours ___ more

3. Description of visual work environment. (Please indicate the most descriptive task from the following, and record your usual working distance as outlined.)

a. ___ Display screen and keyboard only

b. ___ Display screen, keyboard and script

c. ___ Microfiche

d. ___ Typing. Visual distance to script

e. ___ General desk work. Visual distance to "peripheral" papers.

Measure the distance from the root of the nose to the various objects you have at your work place. Make sure that you sit correctly, preferably have someone else do the measuring.

Section B

1. Circle any visual aids used
   none, contact lenses, single vision spectacles, bifocal spectacles
   other ____________

2. Indicate the reason for visual aids (if appropriate)
   reading only, distance only, constant use, VDT use only
   other ____________

3. Length of time since last vision check-up
   ___ less than 6 months ___ 6-12 months ___ 12-24 months ___ longer

4. Circle the following that describe your physical condition at the beginning of your working day.

	Not at all	Somewhat	Yes	Very
1. Are your eyes tired?	___	___	___	___
2. Feeling pain behind your eyes?	___	___	___	___
3. Feeling pain around your eyes?	___	___	___	___
4. Feeling a dullness around your eyes?	___	___	___	___
5. Feeling pressure around your eyes?	___	___	___	___

	Not at all	Somewhat	Yes	Very
6. Feeling dryness of your eyes?	____	____	____	____
7. Feeling dim?	____	____	____	____
8. Eyes irritated?	____	____	____	____
9. Tearing sensation?	____	____	____	____
10. Blinking more frequently?	____	____	____	____

5. Circle the following that describe your physical condition at the end of your working day.

	Not at all	Somewhat	Yes	Very
1. Are your eyes tired?	____	____	____	____
2. Feeling pain behind your eyes?	____	____	____	____
3. Feeling pain around your eyes?	____	____	____	____
4. Feeling a dullness around your eyes?	____	____	____	____
5. Feeling pressure around your eyes?	____	____	____	____
6. Feeling dryness of your eyes?	____	____	____	____
7. Feeling dim?	____	____	____	____
8. Eyes irritated?	____	____	____	____
9. Tearing sensation?	____	____	____	____
10. Blinking more frequently?	____	____	____	____

Section C (To be completed only by VDT users)

1. Which of the following categories do you feel best describes the nature of your VDT work?

____ Data entry - non contextual information (numbers, letters, or symbols) is entered often in a repetitive manner using a set format.
- the input rate is often high and the operator usually reads from printed material.
- in many cases the use does not involve much looking at the video terminal.

____ Data acquisition - this task involves calling up information from the computer and reading it from the screen.
- the input rate is reduced.
- this is a more screen intensive task with the operator's attention directed primarily towards the screen.

____ Interactive communication or conversational
- this involves both data entry and data acquisition.
- the input rate is medium and sometimes intermittent.
- the operator sustains a dialogue with the computer and the visual emphasis is on the video screen (some keyboard).

____ Word Processing - this task involves text entry, text recall, searching text for errors, making corrections, and organizing format.
- the input rate is usually high and often intermittent.
- the visual emphasis may either be source document-intensive or screen intensive.

____ Programming - this task involves considerable variations in the amount of time spent at a terminal
- the input rate is often low and intermittent
- the visual emphasis may either be copy intensive or screen intensive.

2. When did you first start using video display terminals? ________________

3. What type (brand) of monitor are you now using? ______________________

4. The display colour is (circle one) red/green/amber/white/other __________

5. Do you have any preference for another display colour other than the one you are now using? (circle one) no preference/red/green/amber/white/other _____

6. Estimate your daily use of the video display terminal
   ___ 2-4 hours ___ 4-6 hours ___ 6-8 hours ___ more

WORK WITH DISPLAY UNITS 86
B. Knave and P.-G. Widebäck (eds.)

VISUAL IMPAIRMENT AND SUBJECTIVE OCULAR SYMPTOMATOLOGY IN VDT OPERATORS

G.F. RUBINO*, G. MAINA* , A. SONNINO*
F.M. GRIGNOLO+, F. PESCE+, A. DIBARI+
F. MORUZZI§

ABSTRACT

Health conditions, ocular symptoms, visual function and working ergonomic conditions of two different groups of workers at VDT were examined.
The results show that there is no permanent modifications of visual function, but subjective ocular discomforts is due to work type and hours worked at VDT.

1. INTRODUCTION

The present epidemiological investigation was carried out to assess the relationship between subjective ocular symptoms reported by VDT operators and working ergonomic conditions.
VDT'S installed in offices increase in number every year. Thus, problems linked to this fact (1,2,3) are growing and do interact with occupational medicine, ergonomics, ophtalmology, psychology techniques and theories.
A body of scientific evidence supports the conclusion that VDT usage "per se" is not a health hazard (4,5,6,7) but it is clear that many VDT operator troubles are related to visual function and ergonomic workplace conditions.

2. SUBJECTS AND METHODS

2.1 Subjects

3835 subjects were examined, 90% of whom were telephone operators using VDT at the information service and 10% data entry operators; subjects who worked less then two hours per day and less then six months at the VDT were taken as the reference group.
The first table shows biodemographic items and working conditions of the groups examined.

----

* Inst. Occup. Health, University, V. Zuretti 29, Turin, Italy
+ Dpt. of Ophtalmology, University, V. Juvarra 19, Turin, Italy
§ Sip, Rome, Italy

TABLE 1
BIODEMOGRAPHIC ITEMS AND WORKING CONDITIONS

	Telephone operators				Data entry operators			
	males		females		males		females	
	E.	R.	E.	R.	E.	R.	E.	R.
NUMBER OF SUBJECTS	546	37	2816	65	63	59	158	91
AGE (YEARS)								
- mean	33.3	41.9	40.3	43.8	34.2	36.1	33.9	32.4
- s.d.	9.1	9.3	9	8.4	8.1	7.5	8.3	7.3
MONTHS AT VDT								
- mean	33.1	29.8	57	19.1	42.1	22.1	32	12.7
- s.d.	27.3	28.1	44.5	30.4	32.3	23.2	23	19.1
HOURS AT VDT								
- mean	5.8	1.3	5.9	0.5	4.9	0.9	5.9	0.7
- s.d.	1.3	0.9	1.3	0.8	1.7	0.8	1.7	0.8

E.=Exposed group R.=Reference group s.d.=Standard deviation

2.2 Methods

The investigation was subdivided into the following stages:
- 1) extensive specialized medical check-up (clinical and working history, general medical inspection) carried out by an occupational medicine specialist;
- 2) administration of a questionnaire concerning subjective general and ocular symptoms and discomfort, and workplace ergonomic condition evaluation;
- 3) assessment of the ophtalmologic status by means of routine visual test (visual acuity, colour blindness, ametropia and phorias). Subjects complaining of ophtalmologic disorders were examined by an ophtalmologist.

2.3 Questionnaire

The questionnaire included questions about eyes fatigue, smarting, teariness, redness, blinking, double vision, blurred vision, ocular aches and headache; the occurrence and frequency of discomfort of the muscoskeletal system (neck, arms, legs and back pain) were recorded.
Previous and present occupations, number of months and hours per day of VDT work and subjective evaluation of the environmental and ergonomic conditions (lighting, desk, chair, working distance from VDT) were recorded.
For each subject the mean number of the nine symptoms explored by the questionnaire was calculated and used as a measure of the discomfort for the groups in relation to the aforementioned conditions.
Lighting and chair evaluation was ranked as follows: good, satisfactory, sufficient, not sufficient, bad.

3. RESULTS

3.1 Eye discomforts

No complaints were recordedd in 25% of males and 14% of females; males always complained of less symptoms.
The frequency of each ocular symptom is reported in figure 1. Telephone operators have more symptoms than data entry operators; ocular discomfort increases for both sexes with increasing time spent at the VDT (figure 2). On the contrary there is no relationship between the length of exposure and mean number of symptoms (figure 4 and 5). Complaints start on the average about four hours after starting work in 30% of the telephone operators. Within three hours and half after stopping work symptoms disappear in 87% out of those complaining of troubles (table 2).

FIGURE 1
OCULAR SYMPTOMATOLOGY DISTRIBUTION

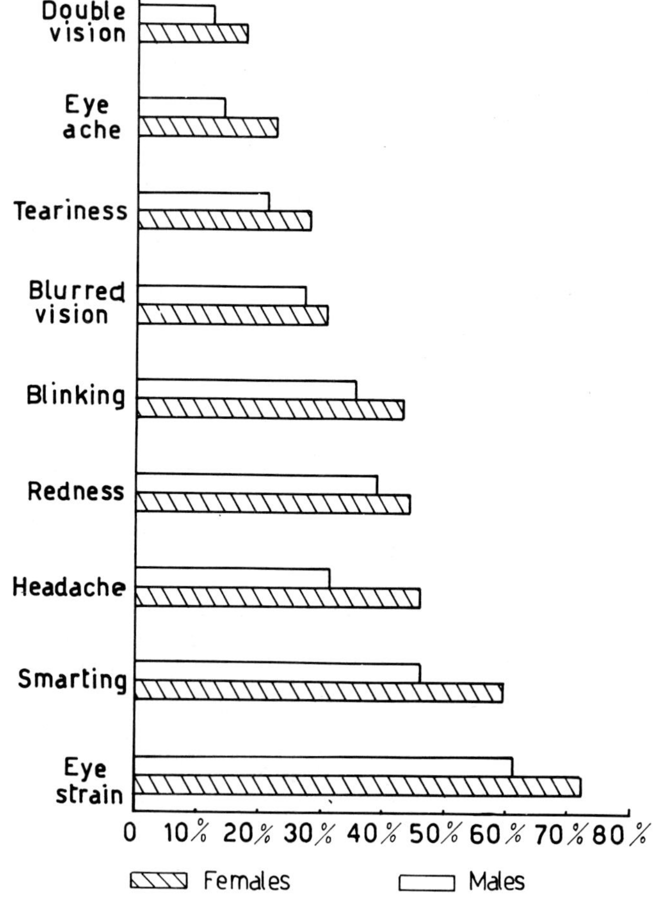

FIGURE 2
WORKING HOURS AND EYE IMPAIRMENT

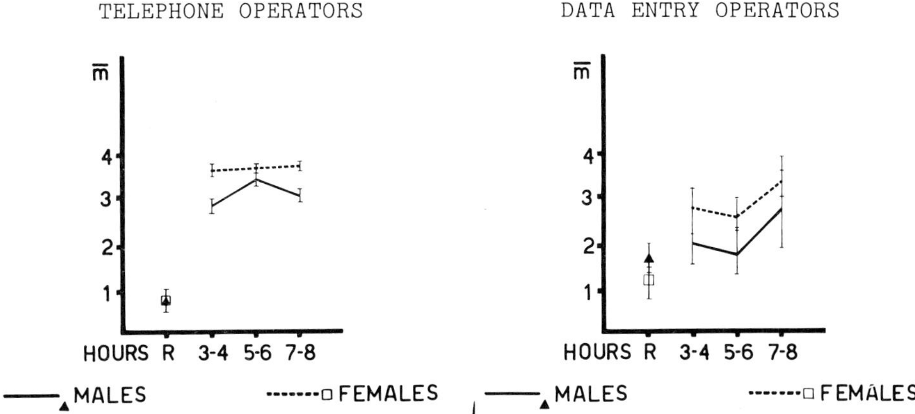

m = mean number of symptoms and standard error of the mean
R = reference group.

FIGURE 3
EXPOSURE DURATION AND EYE IMPAIRMENT: TELEPHONE OPERATORS

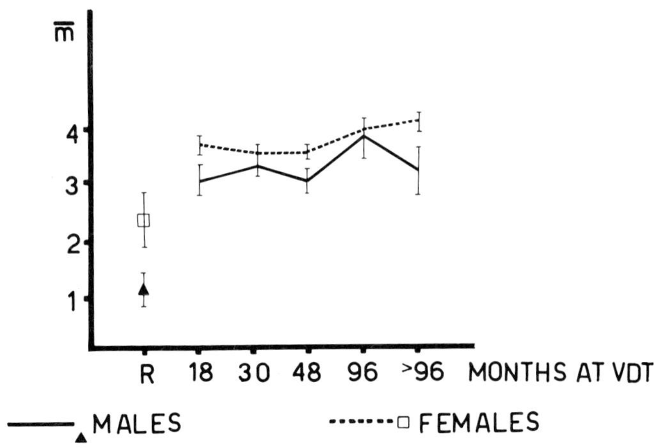

m = mean number of symptoms and standard error of the mean
R = reference group

FIGURE 4
EXPOSURE DURATION AND EYE IMPAIRMENT - DATA ENTRY OPERATORS

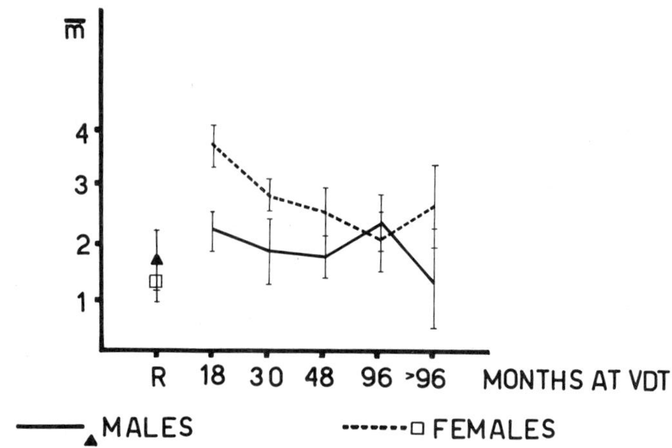

m = mean number of symptoms and standard error of the mean
R = reference group

TABLE 2
ONSET AND DISAPPEARANCE OF SYMPTOMS IN VDT OPERATORS

Telephone operators

	MALES H	MALES s.d.	MALES %*	FEMALES H	FEMALES s.d.	FEMALES %*
ONSET	3.32	1.39	29.9	3.23	1.33	29.7
DISAPPEARANCE	2.08	2.2	87.2	2.26	3.43	87.3

Data entry operators

	MALES H	MALES s.d.	MALES %*	FEMALES H	FEMALES s.d.	FEMALES %*
ONSET	3.55	1.47	20.5	4.22	1.26	12.
DISAPPEARANCE	1.24	0.36	100.	2.02	1.17	84.9

H = Mean time (hours) after starting work at which symptoms appear or time after stopping work at which they disappear

s.d. = Standard deviation

%* = Per cent of workers who complain of symptoms within two hours from beginning work or who report disappearance of symptoms within two hours since the end of work

3.2 Use of corrective lenses

The number of people using glasses increases with age, noticeably after 40. This may be explained by the presence of presbiopia and latent hyperopia and is more evident from 50 onwards. The use of

near vision lenses increases from 40 onwards.
Operators wearing glasses, particularly contact lens wearers, report more visual troubles than the others; contact lenses are usually preferred by women.
Whereas there was a small increase in symptoms in people using lenses for long sightedness, there was no difference in short sighted subjects.
However, there was a significant increase in symptoms among astigmatic people. Contact lens wearers had the highest mean number of symptoms. Spectacle wearers prevail among those who work at less than 40 cm from VDT and decrease in number among those who work at a distance between 40 and 60 cm.

3.3 Relationship between ocular impairment and visio-test

There was no difference between the mean number of symptoms for both far and near mono and binocular vision (table 3).
Symptoms do, in fact, increase rapidly when vision is below five tenths. There is no evidence of change in phorias when examined in relation to working hours or exposure duration (figure 6).
Neither stereopsis nor colour blindness are influenced by the number of hours worked at VDT or the lenght of exposure.

TABLE 3

FAR VISION

	MALES						FEMALES					
	RE		LE		EE		RE		LE		EE	
VISUS	n	mean	n	mean	n	mean	n	mean	n	mean	n	mean
<2/10	5	4.4	11	4.0	2	3.5	32	3.7	30	3.4	19	3.9
2/10	28	3.5	22	3.9	5	4.4	77	4.4	79	3.8	21	3.8
4/10	26	2.8	24	3.4	13	3.2	139	3.9	109	3.8	56	3.8
6/10	41	3.5	36	3.2	18	4.0	251	3.8	252	3.8	105	3.7
8/10	102	3.0	86	2.8	59	2.8	600	3.8	573	3.7	352	3.9
10/10	156	2.8	177	2.8	132	3.1	917	3.7	1045	3.7	902	3.7
12/10	232	2.8	234	2.8	360	2.7	913	3.4	843	3.5	1475	3.5

NEAR VISION

	MALES						FEMALES					
	RE		LE		EE		RE		LE		EE	
VISUS	n	mean	n	mean	n	mean	n	mean	n	mean	n	mean
<2/10	9	4.4	16	4.1	9	4.2	40	4.2	44	4.1	27	4.4
2/10	36	2.5	25	2.6	11	3.5	194	3.9	203	3.7	58	3.7
4/10	38	2.8	28	3.1	26	3.0	302	3.5	218	3.6	212	3.5
6/10	36	2.6	46	2.8	27	2.3	412	3.8	409	3.8	243	3.9
8/10	96	3.0	94	2.6	57	2.3	645	3.5	610	3.5	528	3.6
10/10	137	3.1	144	3.0	121	3.0	712	3.8	799	3.8	780	3.8
12/10	238	2.8	237	2.9	339	2.9	626	3.5	647	3.5	1083	3.6

RE = right eye LE = left eye EE = both eyes
n = number of subjects mean = mean number of symptoms

FIGURE 5
WORKING HOURS AND HETEROPHORIAS

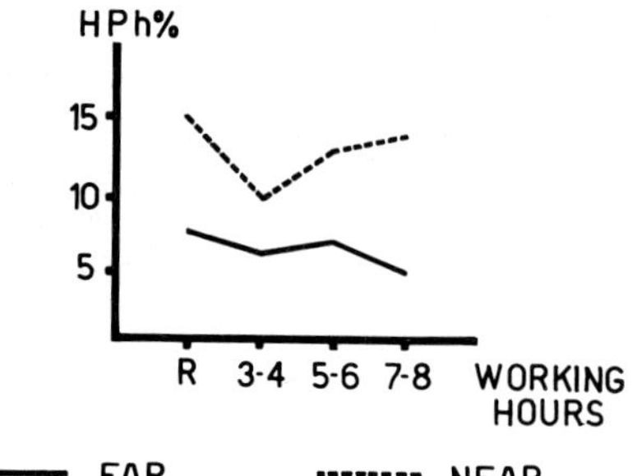

FIGURE 6
EXPOSURE DURATION AND HETEROPHORIAS

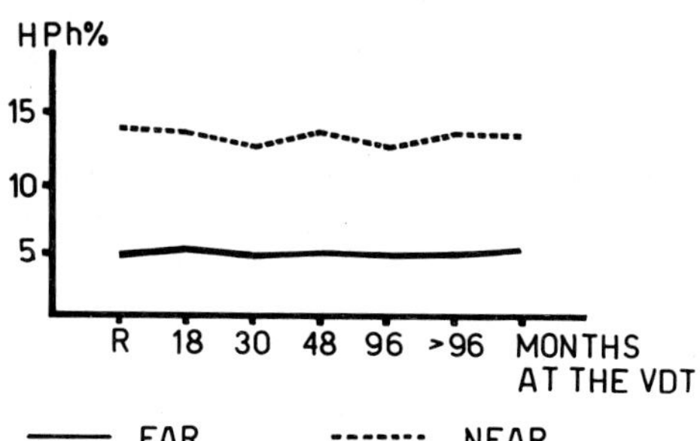

HPh% = per cent heterophorias R = reference group

4. CONCLUSIONS

Working at VDT contributes to the spreading of muscoskeletal complaints, psychosomatic and astenopia symptoms.
The number of the symptoms suffered is related to the hours daily worked at VDT'S but not to the exposure duration (years worked).
There is no indication that VDT exposure leads to permanent modifications (visual acuity, ametropia, stereopsis, phorias, colour blindness) during work or in relation to the number of years worked at VDT'S. Woman always report more symptoms then men.
There are significant differences between the two work tasks examined, but the highest number of symptoms found in telephone operators seems to be linked to psychophysiological variables related to the work organization, rather than to the visual charge at VDT.
A telephone operators job is dictated and cannot be self regulated. Moreover, in many instances conversation with users may be provocative and frustating.
In this situation the work structure itself may well be the main cause of their symptomatology.

ACKNOWLEDGEMENTS

The authors wish to tank Mr Rodolfo Orazietti for his precious technical assistance.

REFERENCES

(1) Bergquist, V.O., Scand. J. Work Environ. Health 10 (1984) suppl 2, p 87.
(2) Anfossi, D.G., Grignolo, F.M., Maina, G., Romano, C., Giornale Italiano di Oftalmologia Occupazionale 1,1 (1983)
(3) Boles Carenini, B., Rubino, G.F., Grignolo, F.M., Maina, G., Visual Fitnees for VDU Operators, in: Taylor and Francis (eds.), Ergonomics and Health Aspects in Modern Offices (London, 1984) pp. 442-444.
(4) Knave, B.G., Scand. J. Work Environ. Health 11 (1985) 457-466.
(5) Boos, S.R., Scand. J. Work Environ. Health 11 (1985) 475-481.
(6) Nyman, K.G., Scand. J. Work. Environ. Health 11 (1985) 483-487.
(7) Grandjean, E., Vigliani, E., Ergonomic Aspects of Visual Display Terminals. Taylor e Francis, London 1982.

WORK WITH DISPLAY UNITS 86
B. Knave and P.-G. Widebäck (eds.)

EFFECTS ON VISUAL ACCOMMODATION AND SUBJECTIVE VISUAL DISCOMFORT FROM VDT WORK INTENSIFIED THROUGH SPLIT SCREEN TECHNIQUE

Olov Ostberg and Michael J. Smith

Department of Industrial Engineering
University of Wisconsin-Madison
1513 University Avenue
Madison, Wisconsin 53706, U.S.A.

Many studies have tried to determine the effects of visual display terminal (VDT) viewing on the visual system by comparing VDT and non-VDT tasks. Such an approach fails to consider that VDT tasks themselves vary significantly in the amount of load they impose on the visual system. This laboratory study examined an intensified viewing VDT task versus a normal VDT task to determine if the extent of VDT viewing time influenced visual accommodation and subjective visual discomfort. Six VDT operators performed mixed tasks of data entry and file updating in normal and intensified conditions for two times three hours per day for two days. Eye movement patterns and pupil diameter were recorded continuously, while accommodation and subjective discomfort were examined before and after each three hour VDT session. The results showed that the type of VDT task influenced the eye movement patterns and that the longer the viewing time the greater the influence on accommodation and subjective complaints of discomfort.

1. INTRODUCTION

A wide range of field studies have found that VDT users report burning and itching eyes, eye strain, visual fatigue and blurred vision [1,2,3,4,5,6]. Of all the demands imposed by VDT use, that placed on the visual system appears to have an adverse effect on the greatest number of users than any other demand [7,8,9]. A few studies have questioned whether VDTs are more demanding than intense hard copy reading [10,11], yet even these studies have demonstrated a high percentage of VDT users with visual complaints.

Many studies of VDT users have found high percentages reporting subjective visual complaints, and some have even reported objective changes in visual functions. Early Austrian and Swedish work reported covariations between degree of VDT viewing, visual discomfort and changes in visual functions in the course of the working day [2,12,13,14,15]. In these studies the changes in visual functions were interpreted to support the VDT operators' claims of being subjected to taxing work demands.

However, while these early studies found changes in visual functions indicating VDT aftereffects, the changes were so small (e.g., myopization of 0.5 diopter) as to be questioned as to the practical significance for visual functioning. Of the more recent studies, some are in agreement with the early findings [e.g., 16,17,18], and some are in disagreement [e.g. 11,19,20]. The following quotation from Stark and Johnston [21] seems to be a representative summary of the over-all picture:

"[Pupil oscillation, accommodation, vergence, saccadic eye movements at several levels of integration, and blinking]--all seem to reflect and confirm subjects' verbal reports of eye fatigue. It is important to note that an objective measure, i.e., recession of accommodative near point, may be seen as an objective finding of fatigue or may equally be interpreted as a sign of helpful adaptation to the task, whereby skill and practice allow effort to be minimized while still permitting adequate (perhaps even error-free) task performance to be maintained."

2. THE NEED TO DEFINE VISUAL DEMANDS

Research has demonstrated that working at VDTs can have an adverse impact on vision. According to the U.S. National Academy of Sciences the extent of this impact is open to question [22], but none the less of concern to the U.S. Congress' Office of Technology Assessment [23]. Based on its research and the growing general problem awareness, the U.S. National Institute for Occupational Safety and Health (NIOSH) in 1981 issued the following nonbinding recommendations [24]:

"Based on our concern about potential chronic effects on the visual system and musculature and prolonged physiological distress, we recommend the following work-rest breaks for VDT operators:

(1) A 15-minute work-rest break should be taken after two hours of continuous VDT work for operators under moderate visual demands and/or workload.

(2) A 15-minute work-rest break should be taken after one hour of continuous VDT work for operators under high visual demands, high work load and/or those engaged in repetitive work tasks."

Since these 1981 recommendations, public concern about VDTs has grown in the U.S. Today it is estimated that between 10 and 14 million persons use VDTs and over 2 dozen "VDT bills" have been introduced in state legislatures to deal with health concerns, many including the NIOSH recommendations. Due to societal concern and the rapid introduction of VDTs into the workplace, a U.S. Congressional Subcommittee on Health and Safety in 1984 conducted extensive VDT hearings. A report from the hearings [25] concluded that:

"There is a real question when it comes to determining the physical stress of using a VDT for a long period of time. This stress often manifests itself in the form of headaches, eye strain and other ailments."

Fundamental questions in the debate about VDT visual effects are the definitions of high versus low visual demands and long period of VDT work, respectively. Research at NIOSH has examined the visual, musculoskeletal and performance benefits from "good" versus "poor" VDT experimental workstation configurations. The draft report [19] indicated less visual strain with the "good" conditions. However, these studies were unable to detect any clear-cut differences for the two VDT tasks examined (data entry versus file maintenance). These tasks had been designed to give the operators low and high VDT viewing time respectively, but it was later determined that the actual screen viewing times were relatively low for both; 15% for data entry and 35% for file maintenance.

The purpose of the present study was to look further into the visual aspects of the same tasks by increasing the VDT viewing time by means of a split screen technique allowing the "hard copy document" to be presented on the VDT screen. The study was carried out at the Department of Industrial and Systems Engineering, Ohio University, Athens, OH, using the same task generating software developed by Dainoff et al. [19]. More detailed research data from various aspects of this study are available in an Ohio University report [26].

3. EXPERIMENTAL DESIGN

Six subjects aged 25-40 years took part in the experiment. They were recruited from the Ohio University campus area, had experience at VDT work and a minimum typing speed of 60 words per minute, did not wear eye glasses and had a 20/20 vision or better. They were paid for their participation according to the incentive scheme used in the previous NIOSH studies [19]. The VDT work tasks and the VDT workplace configuration were also a replica of those of the NIOSH studies.

The subjects were tested individually during two VDT working days, during which they switched between data entry and file maintenance approximately every 20 minutes. The work started at 0900 hours and ended at 1600 hours. Lunch break occurred between 1200-1300, and 15-minute breaks were given in the mid-morning and mid-afternoon workperiods respectively. One AM and one PM session were each devoted to the traditional mixed task mode consisting of a VDT screen plus keyboard and paper source documents (S/P; screen/paper work mode), and one AM and one PM session each were spent with 'source documents' appearing on the left side of the split screen VDT (S/S; screen/screen work mode) rather than as paper documents. The subjects were randomly assigned to a work schedule in a counter-balanced experimental design to account for the possible learning effects of the two tasks and the two work modes.

The objective of the experiment was to explore the effects of relatively low VDT viewing time (the S/P mode) and relatively high VDT viewing time (the S/S mode) on eye strain and accommodation. The visual work was continuously monitored by means of an Applied Science Laboratory 1998 computer controlled vision evaluation system that collected eye scanning and pupil diameter data in a nonobtrusive way. Eye strain information was collected through a questionnaire appearing on the VDT screen a couple of minutes before and after each session and before and after the 15-minute breaks. The subject's accommodation when viewing a 6m distant target was measured a few minutes before and after each session by means of the laser optometer method described by Ostberg [15].

The questionnaire contained 9 items on eye strain and eye symptoms, and the subject responded by pressing the keyboard's minus-key so as to produce a line, the length of which represented the subject's felt level of discomfort on the scale from "no, not at all" (score 00) to "yes, very much so" (score 72). The questionnaire also contained items on musculoskeletal discomfort. Unfortunately the postural requirements of the system for eye scanning and pupil diameter monitoring prohibited drawing meaningful conclusions from the musculoskeletal questionnaire responses. In order to secure good data on eye scanning and pupil diameter, the subject's work posture had to be optimized imposing the constraint that the eyes always had to be 119cm above the floor, and, furthermore, the subject was required to move her head as little as possible. It was hoped that these severe postural constraints would not interact too much with the visual work. The final, experimental workplace configuration (for the S/P mode) is shown in Figure 1.

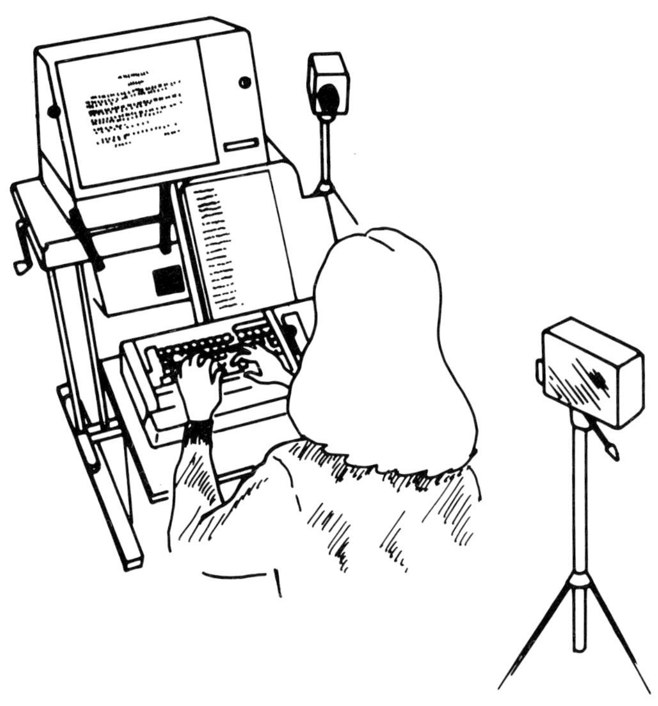

FIGURE 1
Experimental workplace configuration for the S/P mode. During the S/S mode the source document was displayed at the left half of the VDT screen. Eye movements and pupil diameter were monitored through the little window to the left of the source document.

4. RESULTS

A description of some of the viewing parameters is given in Table 1. Every 1/60 of a second eye movement and pupil diameter data were collected. As expected, the total VDT screen viewing time was considerably lower in the S/P work mode (35.9%) than in the S/S mode (85.8%). During the S/P mode the VDT viewing time was considerably lower for the data entry task (24.6%) than for the file maintenance task (47.2%). From Table 1, it can also be seen that throughout sessions the eyes were scanning back and forth approximately 100 times per minute. There were also differences in pupil diameter which were postulated to be due to differences in the luminances of the visual targets.

Table 1

Descriptive viewing parameters averaged over two days of VDT work of six subjects. Eye scanning and pupil diameter data were sampled every 1/60 of a second.

Work Modes and Tasks	Viewing Time (%)				Number of Looks per Minute				Pupil Diameter (mm)			
	Screen	Source	Keyboard	Other	Screen	Source	Keyboard	Other	Screen	Source	Keyboard	Other
Screen/Paper												
Data Entry	24.6	53.5	18.5	3.5	20.5	44.0	25.2	8.0	3.44	3.19	3.30	3.34
File Mainten.	47.2	35.0	14.5	3.3	27.4	35.5	22.6	7.7	3.50	3.27	3.41	3.41
Mean (VDT)	35.9	44.3	16.5	3.4	23.9	39.7	23.9	7.9	3.47	3.23	3.36	3.37
Screen/Screen												
Data Entry	34.5	49.0	11.7	2.8	34.4	41.4	13.9	6.6	3.66	3.64	3.54	3.48
File Mainten.	54.6	31.7	10.7	3.0	46.1	40.1	14.0	6.9	3.68	3.64	3.61	3.54
Mean (VDT)	45.5 +	40.3	11.2	2.9	40.3 +	41.0	13.5	6.8	3.66		3.58	3.51

Means of viewing distance (cm): VDT Screen 79; Paper Document 76; Keyboard 55

Luminances (cd/m^2): VDT Characters 20; VDT Character Background 2.4; Paper Document 140

As shown by the mean scores in Table 2, after the 3-hour work sessions the subjects reported increased feelings of eye strain and at the same time exhibited increased accommodation (myopic) when focusing a 6m distant target. For both these measures, the increases were larger for the more screen intensive work mode (S/S).

These results are in accordance with the hypothesis that increased VDT viewing time would be experienced as more strenous (eye strain) and result in greater accommodation aftereffects (myopization). However, due to the small number of subjects and the incomplete experimental design, the findings are plagued by a large data variability.

Table 2

Increases per session in six subjects' dioptric accommodation (laser optometer; 6m eye chart distance) and ratings of eye strain (mean of 9 questionnaire items). Data from two days of VDT work.

Subject	Session	Screen/Paper		Screen/Screen	
		Ratings	Accomm.	Ratings	Accomm.
SM	AM	3.7	0.34	---	----
	PM	---	----	1.8	0.52
	AM	---	----	0.9	-0.05
	PM	1.1	0.04	---	----
KK	AM	---	----	-2.3	-0.20
	PM	7.6	0.20	---	----
	AM	---	----	1.4	0.18
	PM	5.2	0.07	---	----
MR	AM	3.4	0.34	---	----
	PM	-0.2	0.17	---	----
	AM	---	----	18.1	0.14
	PM	---	----	13.3	0.27
TG	AM	---	----	10.2	0.81
	PM	---	----	-20.0	0.11
	AM	-19.9	0.16	----	----
	PM	5.6	0.03	----	----
CS	AM	---	----	17.9	0.09
	PM	11.2	0.34	----	____
	AM	12.6	0.10	----	----
	PM	----	----	25.6	2.24
MT	AM	10.0	-0.22	----	----
	PM	----	----	23.2	-0.40
	AM	9.0	-0.25	----	----
	PM	---	----	10.9	-0.09
Means		4.1	0.09	8.4	0.30

A time-of-day variability was observed and can be explained by the accumulative effects of the two sessions each day, or, alternatively, by circadian rhythm effects [27]. By setting each day's morning score to zero (i.e., the score before the start of the AM-session), the data from Table 2 may be recast into the time-of-day graphs of Figure 2.

Using a t-test on the accommodation scores, the end-of-day increase exhibited in Figure 2 is significantly higher for the S/S mode than for the S/P mode. There is also a restoration effect of the lunch break. For the present data the t-test analysis unfortunately can only be used to gain insight. The end-of-day scores are not independent since a balanced experimental design was not achieved. Of the 6 PM sessions spent with S/S work, 2 had an AM history of S/S and 4 of S/P. For the same reason it is not possible to draw any firm conclusion on the restoration effects of the lunch break.

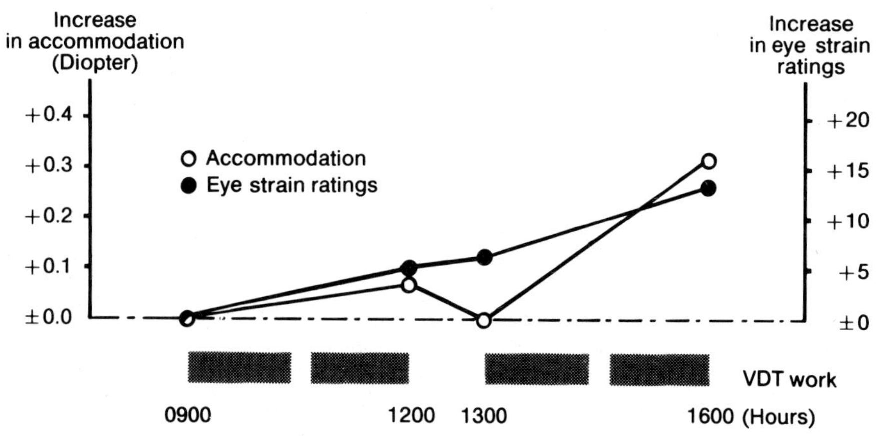

FIGURE 2
Mean increases in accommodation and ratings of eye strain of six subjects' VDT work for two days. For both days, the accommodation baseline was 0.46 diopeter (myopic). The eye strain ratings are expressed in arbitrary units and consist of the mean score of a 9 item questionnaire.

5. DISCUSSION AND CONCLUSION

The main objective of the experiment was to explore the effects of relatively low VDT viewing time (S/P) and relatively high VDT viewing time (S/S) on eye strain and accommodation. It is acknowledged that the securing of reliable eye movement data resulted in unduely constrained work posture for the subjects, which may have influenced the visual effects. It must also be stressed that accommodation is not the one and only visual fatigue load factor in VDT work. Throughout the experiment it was found, for example, that the subjects' eyes were scanning back and forth approximately 100 times per minute between source document, screen and key board. This may result in eye strain or visual fatigue without the accommodation system having been taxed [28], and for such visual system load factors other measures of visual strain than those examined here must also be explored.

The importance of delineating the visual task and environmental parameters in assessing visual effects of VDT viewing is underscored by the differences in viewing pattern between the experimental conditions. Those conditions with more extensive viewing requirements differ in eye movement pattern, operator reported eye strain and accommodation from those with less time actually watching the VDT, even though both conditions had subjects working with a VDT the same number of hours. Thus, it is not helpful in understanding VDT operator visual discomfort and disfunction to simply refer to their activities as "VDT work". For it is the nature and extent of actual VDT viewing that influences subject responses. As this study demonstrated, the extent of viewing can vary substantially from 20% on-screen viewing to 90% on-screen viewing for different tasks even though the hours of work at the VDT are equivalent.

In a real working situation the VDT viewing time is determined by the combination of the number of consecutive hours worked (work organization) and the task dependent viewing pattern (job design). The visual demands are furthermore dependent on the VDT operator's visual capacity and such workstation factors as light gradients, viewing distances and VDT screen quality. The NIOSH report [24] from which the rest-break recommendations earlier were quoted acknowledged all these aspects. In a practical situation the recommendations are difficult to implement without having access to a measure of visual load such as time actually viewing the screen.

The experimental results indicated that both subjectively reported eye strain and objectively measured accommodation are indicators of exposure to visual load. As with previous studies of visual accommodation, individual differences in accommodation make statistical analysis difficult and therefore the results are only indicators of potential visual effects. Their current reliability do not warrant their employment on an individual or clinical basis, or as routine job analysis tools. Furthermore, in comparing the results from different investigations it is important to keep in mind that "accommodation effect" is not a sufficiently well defined concept. The accommodation effects will be different for far and near test distances [15], for young and old subjects [14], and for immediate and delayed measurements [18]. It has also been pointed out that accommodation values cannot be interpreted in isolation because of the interrelatedness between accommodation, convergence and pupillary aperture [21].

Using only six subjects for two days' VDT work each, several ergophthalmological conditions and measures were explored in this experiment. The results of the visual load measurements point to their use as discriminatory tools which need further development and refinement. An ideal instrument for visual load assessment would be to add an accommodation measurement function to the infrared measurement system used to collect eye scanning and pupil diameter data 60 times per second (Table 1). Such an instrument is presently being developed by Takeda et al. [29] at the Industrial Products Research Laboratory in Japan and hopefully will provide the capability for more reliable data on visual accommodation.

ACKNOWLEDGMENT

The authors wish to acknowledge the participation of Dr. Helmut T. Zwahlen and Mr. Sudhakar L. Rangarajulu, Ohio University in this study, and the financial support of the U.S. National Institute for Occupational Safety and Health.

REFERENCES

[1] Ostberg, O., CRTs Pose Health Problems for Operators. International Journal of Occupational Health and Safety (Nov./Dec. 1975) 24-52.

[2] Gunnarsson, E. and Ostberg, O., Physical and Psychosocial Working Environment in a Terminal-Based Computer System. (AMMF 1977:35). (National Board of Occupational Safety and Health, Stockholm, 1977).

[3] Smith, M.J., Cohen, B.F.G., Stammerjoh, L.W. and Happ, A., An Investigation of Health Complaints and Job Stress in Video Display Operations. Human Factors 23 (1981) 389-400.

[4] Laubli, Th., Hunting, W. and Grandjean, E., Postural and Visual Loads at VDT Workplaces: II. Lighting Conditions and Visual Impairments. Ergonomics 24 (1981) 933-944.

[5] Smith, A.B., Tanaka, S. and Halperin, W., Correlates of Ocular and Somatic Symptoms among Video Display Terminal Users. Human Factors 26 (1984) 143-156.

[6] Sauter, S.L., Gottlieb, M.S., Jones, K.C., Dodson, V.N. and Rohrer, K.M., Job and Health Implications of VDT Use: Initial Results of the Wisconsin-NIOSH Study. Communications of the Association for Computing Machinery 26 (1983) 284-294.

[7] Dainoff, M.J., Occupational Stress Factors in Visual Display Terminal Operation: A Review of Empirical Research. Behaviour and Information Technology 1 (1982) 141-176.

[8] Smith M.J., Health Issues in VDT Work, in Sandelin, J., Bennett, J. and Smith, M.J. (Eds.), Video Display Terminals: Visibility Issues and Health Concerns. (Prentice-Hall, Englewood Cliffs, NJ, 1984) 193-228.

[9] Smith, M.J., Mental and Physical Strain at VDT Workstations. Behaviour and Information Technology, (in press).

[10] Starr, S.J., Thompson, C.R. and Shute, S.J., Effects of Video Display Terminals on Telephone Operators. Human Factors 24 (1982) 699-711.

[11] Starr, S.J., Effects of Video Display Terminals in a Business Office. Human Factors 26 (1984) 347-356.

[12] Holler, H., Kundi, M., Schmid, H., Stidl, H.G., Thaler, A. and Winter, N., Work Demands and Visual Strain from VDT Use. (In German). (Austrian Trade Union Association, OGB, Vienna, 1975).

[13] Haider, M., Kundi, M. and Weissebock, M., Worker Strain Related to VDUs with Differently Colored Characters, in Grandjean, E. and Vigliani, E. (Eds.), Ergonomic Aspects of Visual Display Terminals. (Taylor & Francis, London, 1980) 53-64.

[14] Gunnarsson, E. and Soderberg, I., Work at a VDT Presenting Textual Information at a Publishing Company: An Inventory of Visual Ergonomics Problems. (AMMF 1979:21). (National Board of Occupational Safety and Health, Stockholm, 1979).

[15] Ostberg, O., Accommodation and Visual Fatigue in Display Work. Displays (July 1980) 81-85.

[16] Wattenbarger, B.L., A Look at the VDT Issue. Proceedings of the 10th International Symposium on Human Factors in Telecommunications (1983) 173-180.

[17] Kurimoto, S., Iwasaki, T., Nomura, T., Noro, K. and Yamamoto, S., Influence of VDT Work on Eye Accommodation. Journal of University of Occupational and Environmental Health, Japan 5 (1983) 101-110.

[18] Jaschinski-Kruza, W., Transient Myopia After Visual Work. Ergonomics 27 (1984) 1181-1189.

[19] Dainoff, M.J., Frazier, L. and Taylor, B., Workstation and Enviornmental Design Factors in Best and Worst Case Conditions and Their Effects on VDT Operator Health and Performance. (National Institute for Occupational Safety and Health, Cincinnati, OH, 1984).

[20] Nyman, K.G., Knave, B.G. and Voss, M., Work with Video Display Terminals among Office Employees: IV. Refraction, Accommodation, Convergence and Binocular Vision. Scandinavian Journal of Work, Environment, Health 11 (1985) 483-487.

[21] Stark, L. and Johnston, P.G., Visual Fatigue and the VDT Workplace, in Sandelin, J., Bennett, J. and Smith, M.J. (Eds.), Video Display Terminals: Visibility Issues and Health Concerns. (Prentice-Hall, Englewood Cliffs, NJ, 1984) 229-269.

[22] Video Displays, Work and Vision. (NRC/NAS). (National Academy Press, Washington, DC, 1983).

[23] Automation of America's Offices. (OTA). (U.S. Government Printing Office, Washington, DC, 1985).

[24] Potential Health Hazards of Video Display Terminals. (National Institute for Occupational Safety and Health, Cincinnati, OH, 1981).

[25] Oversight of OSHA with Respect to Video Display Terminals in the Workplace. (Staff Report, 99th Congress, Committee Print). (U.S. Government Printing Office, Washington, DC, 1985).

[26] Zwahlen, H.T., Hartmann, A.L. and Rangarajulu, S.L., Video Display Terminal Work with Hard Copy Screen and a Split Screen Data Presentation. (Ohio University Department of Industrial and Systems Engineering, Athens, OH, 1984). (NIOSH Order No. 83-1775).

[27] Ostberg, O. and Takeda, T., Accommodation Performance as a Function of Time of Day and Line of View. Proceedings of the International Scientific Conference on Work With Display Units, Stockholm (1986) 1013-1016.

[28] Elias, R. and Cail, F., Stress and Strain Associated with CRT Screens. (In French). (Institute National de Recherche et de Securite, Paris, 1982).

[29] Fukui, Y., Takeda, T. and Iida, T., Development of Free Eye Movement Dynamic Refractometer. Proceedings of the International Scientific Conference on Work With Display Units, Stockholm (1986) 1018-1021.

WORK WITH DISPLAY UNITS 86
B. Knave and P.-G. Widebäck (eds.)

WORK DISTANCE AND OPTICAL CORRECTION

Bengt Palm

Vision Information Council,
Årstaängsvägen 1 C, S-117 43 STOCKHOLM, Sweden

INTRODUCTION

At the age of 45 difficulties in seeing at a near distance occur. That is due to the fact that the lens has lost its capacity to focus at a near distance. This condition is called presbyopia. The presbyopes need spectacles for a near distance, known as reading-glasses. Reading-glasses are always made for a fixed visual distance which results in a limited depth of vision.

In order to compensate an incorrect visual distance, a person might stress himself into a wrong posture that can lead to ergonomic problems.

This study will present the possible connection that might appear between eyestrain and muscle pains, between ergonomic problems and wearing spectacles and the need of special spectacles while working at VDUs.

The study was made at Oxen's Occupational Health Center, the project group being consisted of Inga Moberg, MD; Hans Klasén, safety engineer; Margareta Mellner, physiotherapist; Bengt Palm, optometrist.

MATERIALS AND METHODS

The study included all the employees, at enterprises (15/45) connected with the Health Center, using VDU in their daily work.

After studies of specialist literature and visits to the various enterprises included in this study, a questionnaire was worked out. This was then used in testing 17 persons, after which some changes were made. The questionnaire contained information on the persons and questions about the type of work at the VDU, the period of VDU work and possible ergonomic problems and eyestrain. The questionnaires were distributed by the local working environment committees. The staff received both oral and written information about the purpose and aim of the study. The questionnaire was distributed to 550 persons and was answered by 467, 315 women and 152 men. 15% did not answer. The middle age of the answering group was 38.

228 were called at random to visual screening.
The test was carried out by the Essilor Vision Test and included:

- The person's subjective judgment of his vision
- Test of distance vision
- Test of near vision

Persons with visual acuity under 1,0 (20/20; 6/6) or subjective problems were called to an eye examination included:

- Case history
- Unaided acuity
- Inspection
- Refraction, long distance
- Refraction, near distance
- Refraction of present working distance

RESULTS

47% of the persons stated that they had pains in parts of their body, spread into 25% of shoulders, 15% of head/neck, 15% of loin/back and 13% of chest (n=467).
Figure 1.

The study of problems in relation to the type of work shows that 54% of those who worked with registering, 44% of the persons who worked with WP (word processing) and 44% of the persons with temporary VDU routine had troubles.
Figure 2.

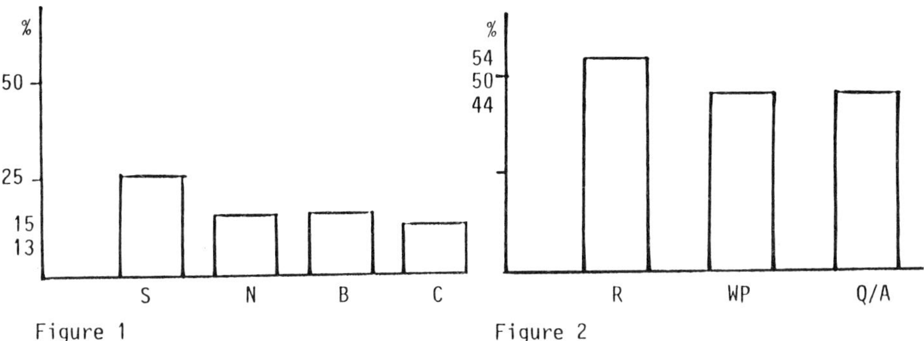

Figure 1

Figure 2

60% stated eyestrain. The problems are distributed more or less identical in the different groups of age, the younger persons having as much trouble as the older ones.
Figure 3.

Among the persons with eyestrain 57% stated ergonomic problems. That should be compared with the frequency of ergonomic problems of the total number that was 47%. There is a significant correlation between ergonomic problems and eyestrain ($p<0,001$)
Figure 4.

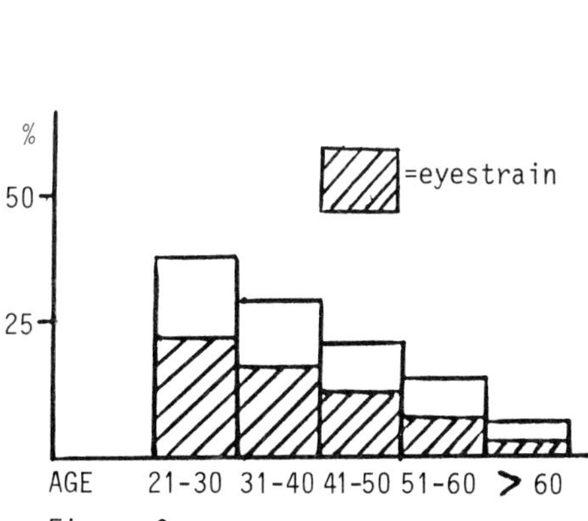

Figure 3

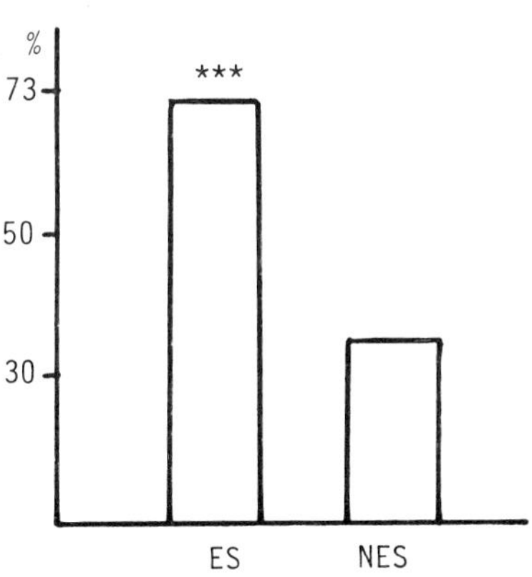

Figure 4
Correlation between ergonomic problems and eyestrain
ES=eyestrain NES=no eyestrain

50% of the group (n=467) used spectacles, 68% of those stated eyestrain while working at VDU.
51% of those who did not use spectacles had problems.

Visual screening

228 were called to visual screening.
129 persons, i.d. 57%, needed no treatment after the screening.
99 persons were called to eye examination because they had visual acuity under 1,0 (6/6; 20/20) or subjective problems.
71% of the group who had been called to the eye examination used spectacles.

The result of the eye examination

In the examined group 21% needed no treatment.
61% got prescription for normal private spectacles.
36% got prescription for spectacles for working distance.
5% of the persons who got prescriptions of spectacles for working distance, got specially made bifocal lenses.
2% were sent to an ophthalmologist, due to pathological reason.

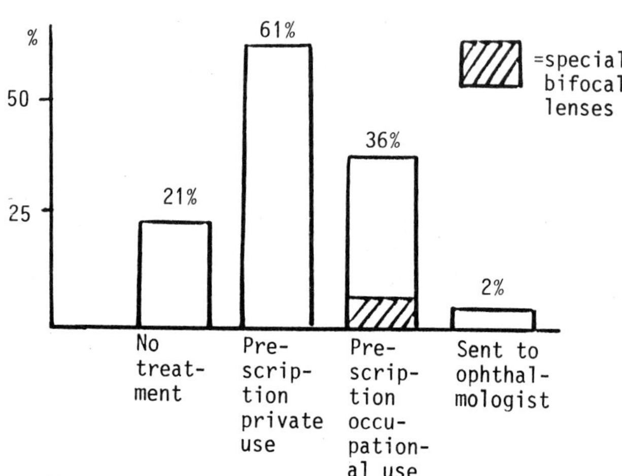

Figure 5

Among the persons who got prescriptions of spectacles for working distance, 86% were over 41 years of age.

CONCLUSIONS

Discussion

The visual distance at VDU work is about 60-70 cm which leads to the fact that reading-glasses generally do not function satisfactorily together with a proper posture. There is therefore a need of special spectacles for working distance. This study shows a significant correlation between ergonomical problems and eyestrain for people working at VDU and a correlation between people wearing spectacles and eyestrain.

36% of the examined needed special spectacles for working distance, i.e. 15% of the total number (n=228). Among these examined more than 86% were over 41 years of age.

Singel vision spectacles are generally functioning properly as special spectacles for working distance at tasks, limited to VDU distance, on condition that the employee is informed that the vision on all other distances gives a blurred image.

At places of work with several different visual distances bifocal lenses are an excellent solution.

A normal segment disposal of bifocal lenses might cause trouble in the neck. When bifocal lenses are suitable, the segment height is to be placed so that no troubles will occur.

Adjustment of bifocal lenses for working distance ought to be preceded by visiting the place of work by a person with knowledge of visual ergonomics and optometry in order to get the height of the segment and the prescriptions properly fitted to the task.

REFERENCES

Bildskärmsarbete och hälsa - en epidemiologisk studie av kontorsarbete.
Rapport 1 Subjektiva besvär och symtom.
Rapport 3 Oftalmologisk undersökning.
Bengt Knave, Ulf Bergqvist, Svante Böös, Berit Calissendorff, Lars Carlsson, Lars Hedström, Mats Levin, Per Nylén, Karl Gösta Nyman, Margareta Voss, Roger Wibom.

Arbetarskyddsstyrelsens författningssamling AFS 1983:6, Arbetsställningar och arbetsrörelser.

Arbetarskyddsstyrelsens författningssamling AFS 1985:12, Arbete vid bildskärm.

Rapport Stadshälsan 603-83-06, Rapport över Hälso- och arbetsmiljöundersökning, bildskärmsarbete vid Försvarets Forskningsanstalt.
Jan Brännström, Anita Nedstam, Lena Waldenström, Bengt Palm, Ingrid Björkegren.

Synstatus hos slumpmässigt vald grupp, 1983.
Bengt Palm, Stefan Sörensen.

Klinisk optometri, analys och korrektion.
Bengt Burman, 1983.

Ljus och belysningskrav vid arbete med textskärmar på tidningsföretag.
Tidningarnas arbetsmiljökommitté/Arbetarskyddsstyrelsen, AMMF, Lars Carlsson.

ADB Handbok för Statsförvaltningen, terminalarbete.
Statskontoret.

Bifokalglasögon som orsak till nacksyndrom.
Joakko Laitinen.

WORK WITH DISPLAY UNITS 86
B. Knave and P.-G. Widebäck (eds.)

IS THE RESTING STATE OF OUR EYES A FAVORABLE VIEWING DISTANCE FOR VDU-WORK ?

Wolfgang JASCHINSKI - KRUZA

Institut für Arbeitsphysiologie, Ardeystr. 67
D 4600 Dortmund, Fed. Rep. Germany

The generally recommended viewing distance for VDU-work is about 50 cm. However, in darkness, for most observers accommodation and convergence of the eyes are adjusted to a distance that is greater than 50 cm. We investigated whether the state in darkness constitutes a resting state in the sense that it is a favorable viewing distance, which causes less visual fatigue. The results suggest that a viewing distance greater than 50 cm is preferable for most subjects.

1. INTRODUCTION

Standards for VDU-workplaces commonly recommend viewing distances in the range of 35 - 70 cm, preferably about 50 cm [1]. However it is questionable whether this distance is physiologically reasonable for all subjects, since in the absence of any visual stimulus - e.g., in darkness - the eyes of most subjects accommodate and converge to a distance that is greater than the recommended monitor distance of about 50 cm. An extended review of the state of the eyes in darkness is given by Owens [2]. One might assume that this state in darkness is a resting state in the sense that eyestrain during VDU-work would be reduced if the monitor were positioned at or near this distance. In the oculomotor system, we have to consider the dark state of accommodation and the dark state of convergence. As it is unclear whether the load on the accomodation system or the load on the convergence system is more relevant to cause eyestrain during VDU-work, we have to take into account both factors.

The accommodative state in complete darkness, the dark focus (also called resting state of accommodation or tonic accommodation) varies widely among subjects in the range 25 cm to infinity; i.e., 4 - 0 diopter (D). Table 1 shows the distribution of the dark focus in larger groups of subjects as measured in three studies [3,4]. The mean is about 65 - 90 cm (1.1 - 1.5 D). This holds for college-age subjects; with increasing age the dark focus shifts outwards [5]. This means that more than half of the population has a dark focus that is more distant than the recommended viewing distance of about 50 cm. These subjects have to accommodate during VDU-work from their dark focus to the closer monitor distance. This prolonged static near-accommodation may contribute to eyestrain, which might be reduced if subjects put the monitor further away, at or near the dark focus. On the other hand, a smaller proportion of subjects has a dark focus near 50 cm; for these subjects the recommended viewing distance of about 50 cm might be appropriate. Thus, if the difference between dark focus and the viewing distance is a factor that contributes to eyestrain, the recommended viewing distance should be based on the individuals´ dark focus. The hypothesis that the dark focus might be a favorable viewing distance for VDU-work has been suggested before by Kintz and Bowker [6] and Krueger et al. [7]; Östberg [8] has also raised this question.

The convergence of the eyes in darkness (resting state of convergence or tonic convergence) can be expressed as the distance (in meters) at which the axes of both eyes intersect, or as the reciprocal of this distance, with the unit meter angle (ma). A study by Owens and Leibowitz [9] shows that dark convergence ranges from 0.55 m to infinity, (1.8 to 0 ma), with a mean at 1.16 m (0.86 ma). Wolf-Kelly et al. [10] found a distribution of the dark convergence with a mean at about 4 m (0.25 ma) and a standard deviation of about 0.5 ma. Thus, most subjects have a dark convergence that is more distant than the recommended viewing distance of about 50 cm; relative to the dark convergence, they have to converge the eyes stronger to fixate the 50 cm viewing distance. Supposing that the load on the convergence system is the relevant factor for eyestrain, one should generally recommend a larger viewing distance, except the very few people with a dark convergence near 50 cm.

The aim of the present study is to test these both hypothesis in laboratory VDU-work experiments and to find a physiological basis for recommending a favorable viewing distance. We had subjects work at a VDU that was placed on one day at 50 cm and on another at 100 cm viewing distance. In the 100 cm condition the characters on the monitor were doubled in height and in width. We had two groups of subjects:
(1) subjects with a dark focus of about 100 cm or more distant;
(2) subjects with a dark focus of about 50 cm.
With this design we can test whether subjects prefer the viewing distance that corresponds to their individual dark focus. This would be evidence for the bearing of the accommodative load during VDU-work. On the other hand, if both groups prefer the greater distance (irrespective of the different dark focus values), the convergence load might be more important, since the dark convergence generally agrees better with the 100 cm viewing distance.

To judge which viewing distance might be favorable, we applied the following measures:
- Performance in the VDU-task was recorded, since poorer performance might be expected under adverse visual conditions.
- A questionnaire for a subjective estimation of eyestrain was used.
- Accommodation was measured when subjects looked at the monitor. It is known that the accuracy of accommodation depends on the dark focus and the viewing distance, and it may be that the accuracy of accommodation has an effect on the performance.

Additionally to these three primary measures to judge the comfort of VDU-workstation conditions we measured the dark focus and the dark convergence, because inward shifts of these measures have been observed during prolonged near vision and it has been suggested that inward shifts of dark focus [8] or inward shifts of dark convergence [11,12] are objective correlates of visual fatigue. However, we think that shifts in dark focus or dark convergence can only be useful in judging the comfort of a VDU-workstation if it can be shown that they coincide with the results of the primary measures (performance, subjective estimation of eyestrain, accuracy of accommodation), or, if it could be shown that temporary changes in e.g. dark focus cumulate to a functional myopia, but at present this is speculation (Ebenholtz [13]).

2. METHODS

2.1. Dark focus and accommodation

In experiment 1, accommodation and dark focus were measured with a polarized vernier optometer [14]; and in experiment 2, with a laser optometer [15]. Both are subjective methods. Table 1 shows the mean dark focus values for larger groups measured with the polarized vernier optometer and the laser optometer [3] compared with an objective infrared technique [4].

Study	Leibowitz, Owens	Johnson, Post, Tsuetaki	Present study
Method	Laser optometer	Infrared optometer	Pol. vernier optom.
Dark focus	1.57 ± 0.77 D	1.10 ± 1.06 D	1.23 ± 0.56 D
Sample size	260	50	67
Subjects	emmetr. or corrected	emmetropic	emmetropic

TABLE 1. Mean dark focus in studies using different measurement techniques.

The laser optometry shows a significant ($p<0.01$) nearer mean dark focus than the objective infrared optometry [4], which might be explained in part by the observation that the mental task of judging the movement of the laser speckle produces a nearer dark focus value in some subjects [16]. The population mean measured with the polarized vernier optometer agrees well with the mean of the infrared technique. When we selected our subjects, we observed in some of them nearer dark focus values with the laser optometer compared to the polarized vernier optometer and in these cases we used the polarized vernier optometry to group the subjects according to their dark focus.

An adaptive psychmetric procedure (Best PEST [17]) and a probit analysis [18] was used to determine the accommodation and the dark focus with maximal efficiency. One measurement took about 30 s and comprised 10 presentations of the laser light or the vernier bars.

2.2. Dark convergence

In dark surround, a vernier alignment task was given with two vertical light bars (made by yellow light emitting diodes) that subtended 0.2 x 0.02 deg and were presented 10 times dichoptically for 125 ms at a distance of 2.85 m. One bar was shifted relative to the other until both appeared to the subjects to be in line. The objective displacement (despite subjective alignment) of the bars is used to calculate the intercept of the visual axes.

2.3. Subjective evaluation with questionnaires

40 questions concerning eyestrain and the VDU-workstation conditions were displayed on the VDU. Subjects answered with the keyboard on a 6 point scale. The following 5 questions had the strongest ratings during work:

Did you have tired eyes?
Did you have to exert an effort to see?
Did you have difficulties in seeing?
Did you have strained eyes?
Did you have burning eyes?

The answers to these 5 questions were added and the sum was taken as an estimation of eyestrain.
The questionnaire included the questions:

Is the screen too near?
Is the screen too far?

The difference between these ratings was used as a judgement of the comfort of the actual viewing distance.

Additionally, subjects were asked after the experiment which distance they preferred.

2.4. Statistical analysis

The interval-level measurements were tested with analysis of variance and the ordinal-level questionnaire results with the Wilcoxon test or with the Kolmogorow-Smirnov test [19].

2.5. Subjects

The subjects were tested with a visual screening test (OCULUS-Binoptometer) to have normal visual functions: near and far visual acuity (monocular and binocular), stereo vision and phoria. They were naive as to the aim of the experiment. The mean age was 23 and none had experience in VDU-work.

2.6. Visual display unit

The monitor was 14". The white characters (on dark background) were either 5 mm or 10 mm in size and subtended 0.57 deg at the viewing distances of 50 cm or 100 cm, respectively. The background luminance was 2 cd/m^2 and the luminance of the characters was 65 cd/m^2.

EXPERIMENT 1			**EXPERIMENT 2**		
t(min)			t(min)		
0			0		
	5	**visual tests**		2	**eyestrain questionnaire**
	15	**questionnaires**		3	**visual tests**
	10	number comparison task		26	search-comparison task
	10	audio visual task		3	**eyestrain questionnaire**
60	20	mental arithmetic	60	26	search-comparion task
	5	**visual tests**		3	**visual tests**
	10	number comparison task		4	pause
	15	**questionnaires**		26	search-comparison task
	10	audio visual task		3	**eyestrain questionnaire**
120	20	mental arithmetic	122	26	search-comparison task
	5	**visual tests**		4	**visual tests**
	10	number comparison task		2	**eyestrain questionnaire**
	20	mental arithmetic			
	10	audio visual task		30	pause
180	15	**questionnaires**			
	5	**visual tests**		4	**visual tests**
	30	pause			
	5	**visual tests**			

Experiment 1	Experiment 2
visual tests:- accommodation to VDU - dark focus	visual tests:- accommodation to VDU - dark focus - dark convergence
sample: 6 far-dark-focus subjects 2 near-dark-focus subjects	sample: 10 far-dark-focus subjects 6 near-dark-focus subjects

TABLE 2. Summary of both experiments.

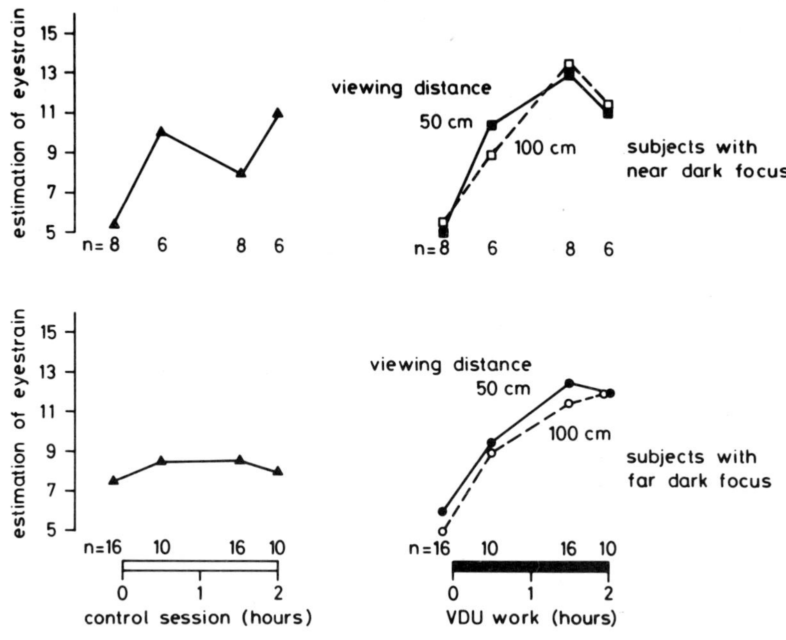

FIGURE 2a
Subjective evaluation: (a) Estimation of eyestrain (Median values).

3.2. Subjective evaluation

Figure 2a shows median values of the estimation of eyestrain as indicated by the subjects in 5 questions concerning visual fatigue (see 2.3.). Eyestrain increased with time in the VDU-work sessions. Subjects with a far dark focus estimated the eyestrain higher at the 50 cm viewing distance. This difference reaches a significance of p=0.08. Near-dark-focus subjects showed no tendency to judge eyestrain as more severe in one of viewing distances. In both groups we observed that the eyestrain estimation did not further increase after 1.5 hours of work; this might be explained by the fact that the last questionnaire (after 2 hours) was answered after the work was over and thus subjects might have felt relieved.

Figure 2b gives the median values of the ratings of the viewing distance. Positive and negative values indicate the judgement "too near" and "too far", respectively. The zero-level means that the viewing distance was judged neiter too near nor too far, thus the distance was accepted. The far-dark-focus subjects judged the VDU at 50 cm to be positioned too near; the difference to the zero-level was significant (p<0.01, Kolmogorov-Smirnov test). However, the 100 cm distance was accepted and not judged as too far. If these far-dark-focus subjects were asked after the experiment which viewing distance they preferred, 12 out of the 16 prefered 100 cm and 4 had no preference.

The group with a near dark focus showed the same pattern of result: they also judged the 50 cm as too near (p<0.01) and again 100 cm was accepted and not judged as too far. After the experiment, 5 subjects out of the 8 with a near dark focus also preferred the larger distance of 100 cm, 1 subject preferred the 50 cm and 2 subjects had no preference.

2.7. Time scheme

Table 2 shows the time schemes of the two experiments. The visual tests were made in a fixed temporal order as indicated. The first experimental day was a control session without VDU-work, during which the visual tests were made twice at the times shown, first with the VDU at 100 cm and then at 50 cm. On the second and the third day, the sessions included VDU-work; the viewing distances 50 cm and 100 cm were presented in balanced order.

The following is a preliminary report of some main results. In order to combine the results of both experiments in this report, only the data of the first two hours in experiment 1 are shown.

3. RESULTS

3.1. Performance in VDU-work

Subjects had to search for names in a list displayed on the VDU-screen and to compare 5 or 6 digit numbers and to indicated by means of a keyboard, whether these numbers were identical or not. Figure 1 shows the mean search time that subjects needed for this task in 8 periods of 12 minutes. Subjects with a far dark focus needed a longer time if the viewing distance was 50 cm (p=0.085). Near-dark-focus subjects also tended to have longer search times when working at 50 cm, but this difference is not significant.

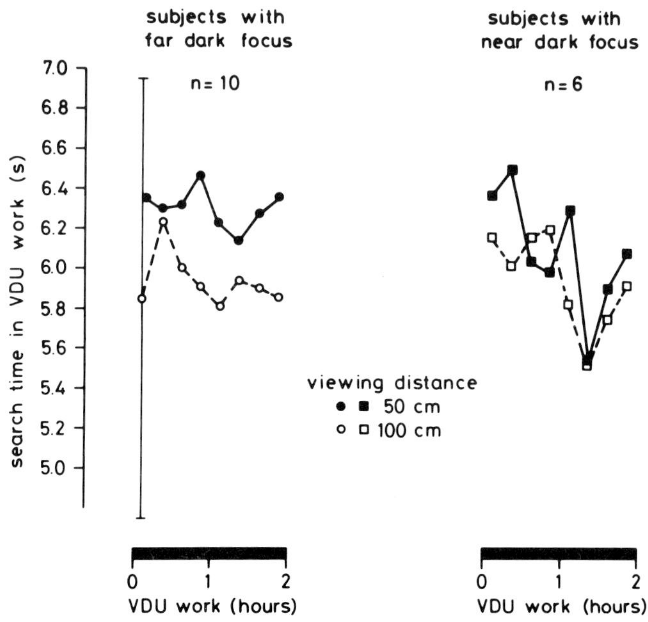

FIGURE 1
Effect of viewing distance on search time (Error bar gives a typical S.D.).

In both groups we observed that the objection to the near monitor was weaker after 2 hours of work than before; but as in the estimation of eyestrain, this might be influence by the subjects' knowing that they finished with working at the VDU after 2 hours.

These results of the subjective evaluation show that (with very few exceptions) most subjects of both groups reject the 50 cm viewing distance, irrespective of their individual dark focus.

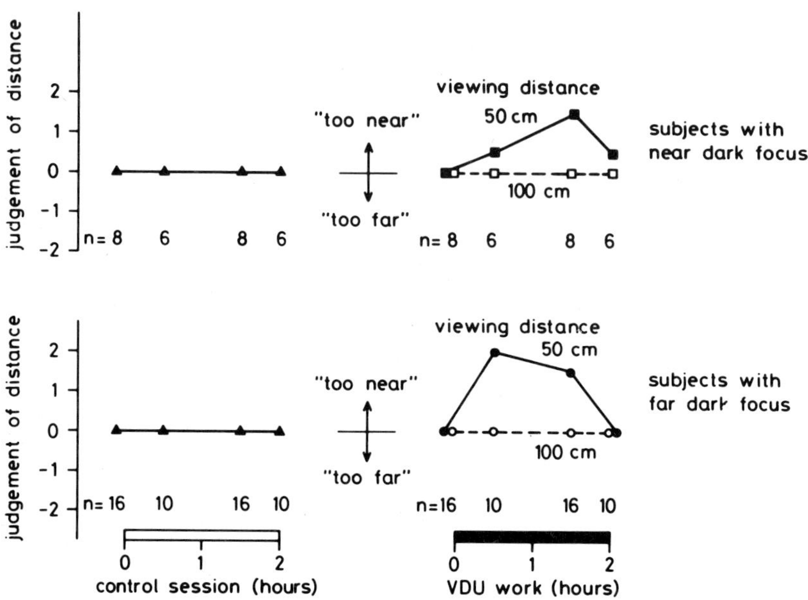

FIGURE 2b
Subjective evaluation: (b) Judgement of viewing distance (Median values)

3.3. Accuracy of accommodation

Figure 3 shows accommodation when subjects looked at the monitor. Measurements were made in the control session and in the VDU-work session, before the session, after one hour, after two hours, and after a rest pause of half an hour. In the control session, accommodation was measured twice at each time, once with the VDU at 100 cm and at 50 cm. The data points show the state of accommodation, and horizontal lines the viewing distances of 50 cm (2 D) and 100 cm (1 D). Thus the vertical lines give the accommodation errors, which are the discrepancies between viewing distances and accommodative states.

In far-dark-focus subjects (those with a mean dark focus of about 0.9 D) we observed significantly smaller accommodative errors at 100 cm than at 50 cm ($p<0.0001$), as 100 cm is closer to their dark focus. However, these errors in accommodation were not affected by VDU-work or by time. In near-dark-focus subjects, significantly smaller accommodative errors appeared at the closer viewing distance of 50 cm ($p<0.0025$), which agreed well with their mean dark

focus. The near-dark-focus subjects showed a slight over-accommodation even at the 50 cm viewing distance, as their mean dark focus was about 2.3 D (as measured by laser optometry).
These results in both groups are explained by the well-known fact that the accommodative state usually is a compromise between the physical viewing distance and the individual dark focus [2]. Thus, accommodative errors are smaller when subjects accommodate to objects near the dark focus.

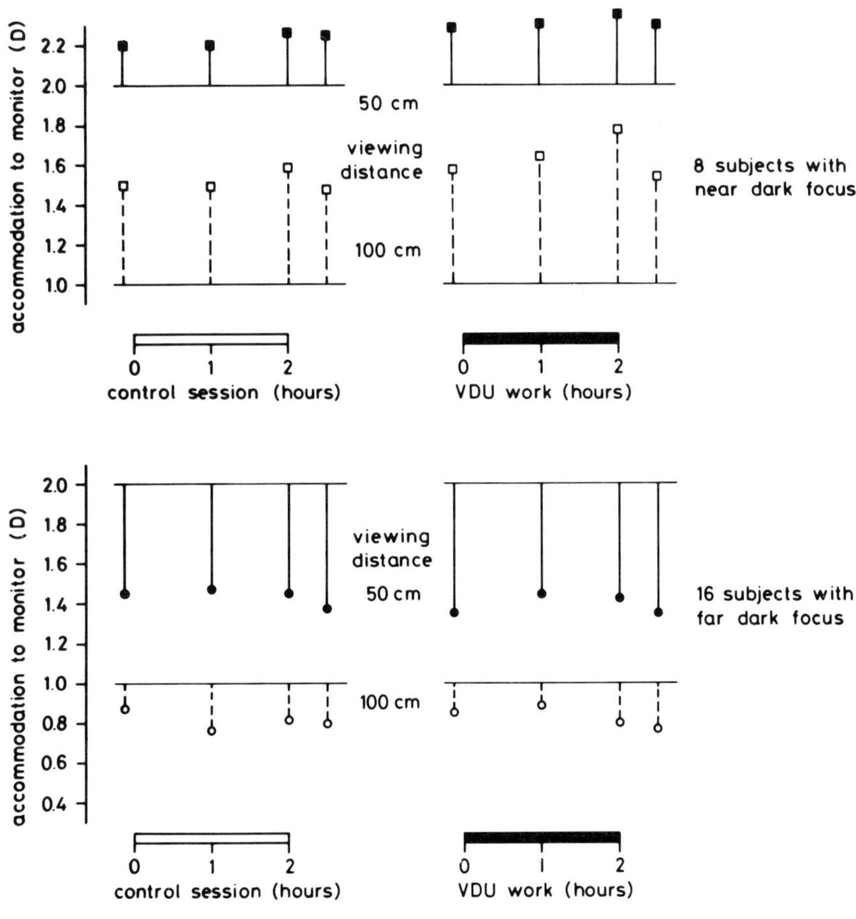

FIGURE 3
Results in accuracy of accommodation (Mean S.D. = 0.4 D)

3.4. Dark focus

The subjects' dark focus was measured immediately after every measurement of accommodation; hence, in the control session at each time two values of dark focus are given. Figure 4 shows that the mean dark focus is in every case higher at 50 cm. Thus, the dark focus tends to shift in a direction appropriate to the previous viewing distance. This phenomenon, the so-called accommodative hysteresis, has been investigated by Ebenholtz [13]. In the control session (independent of any VDU-work) this effect was significant in far-dark-focus subjects (p<0.0005) and in near-dark-focus subjects (p<0.025). In near dark-focus subjects, the strength of accommodation appears to increase during the control session, but this was not significant. Other than this, in the control session the dark focus had a rather constant time-course.

When far-dark-focus subjects worked at 100 cm (which corresponded to their dark-focus) the dark focus remained constant over the session. If they worked at 50 cm (about 1.2 D closer than their dark focus) a small but significant inward shift of 0.2 D occurred (p<0.02) after one hour of work relative to the initial level. However, the changes in dark focus during VDU-work are small and do not differ significantly from those in the control session. The small shift in the 50 cm working condition can be explained by a stronger accommodative hysteresis following the prolonged near-accommodation. In the 100 cm condition no dark focus shift appears as the viewing distance agrees well with the far dark focus of these subjects.

However, when near-dark-focus subjects worked at 50 cm, which corresponded to their dark focus, they developed an inward shift of about 0.3 D; and even if they worked at 100 cm, which is more distant than their dark focus by about 1 D, they showed an inward shift of about 0.3 D. This time effect during VDU-work was significant (p<0.05), but not different at both viewing distances.

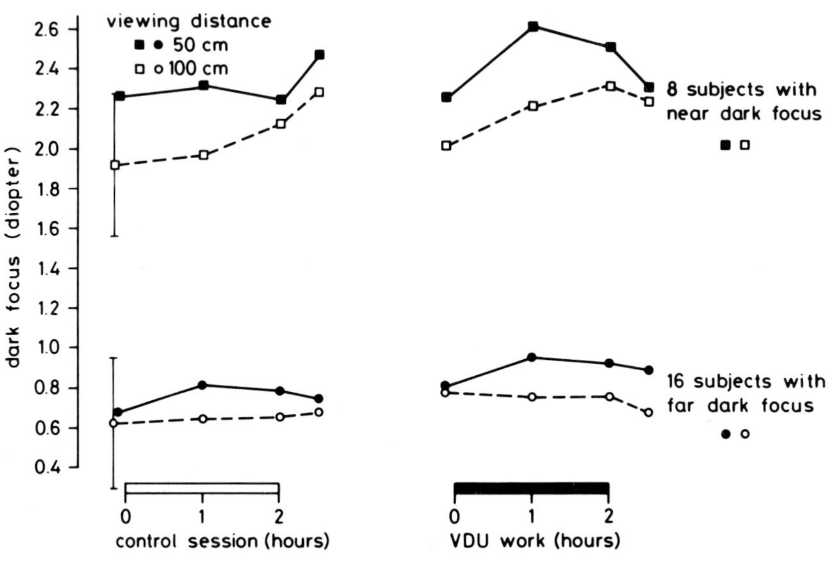

FIGURE 4
Results in dark focus (Error bars is a typical S.D.).

Thus, we observed a different characteristic of the dark focus in the two groups: if the same visual task (with the same mental demand) is given close to the individual dark focus, the dark focus shifts inwards in near-dark-focus subjects, but remains constant in far-dark-focus subjects. This surprising inward dark focus shift in near-dark-focus subjects cannot be explained by accommodative hysteresis; and, since it is inappropriate to the 50 cm viewing distance, it appears that factors other than the viewing distance must have contributed. From studies of Kruger [20,21], Malmstrom and Randle [22] or Post et al. [23] we know that the dark focus can shift inwards under mental or cognitive demand or under stress (see Westheimer [24], Leibowitz [25]). Further, Miller [26] found that in subjects with a high dark focus variability the dark focus more often tended to shift inwards as anxiety or depression increased. The VDU-work constitues a cognitive demand and perhaps a certain emotional demand in some subjects, which could produce an inward dark focus shift even when the viewing distance agrees with the dark focus, or when the viewing distance is even larger than the dark focus distance. This mental demand apparently does not affect the dark focus in subjects with a far dark focus. This agrees with the observations that in near-dark-focus subjects the dark focus varies stronger from day to day and has larger short-term fluctuations [4]; further, the dark focus shift in women at the ovulation is larger in subjects with a near-dark-focus [27].

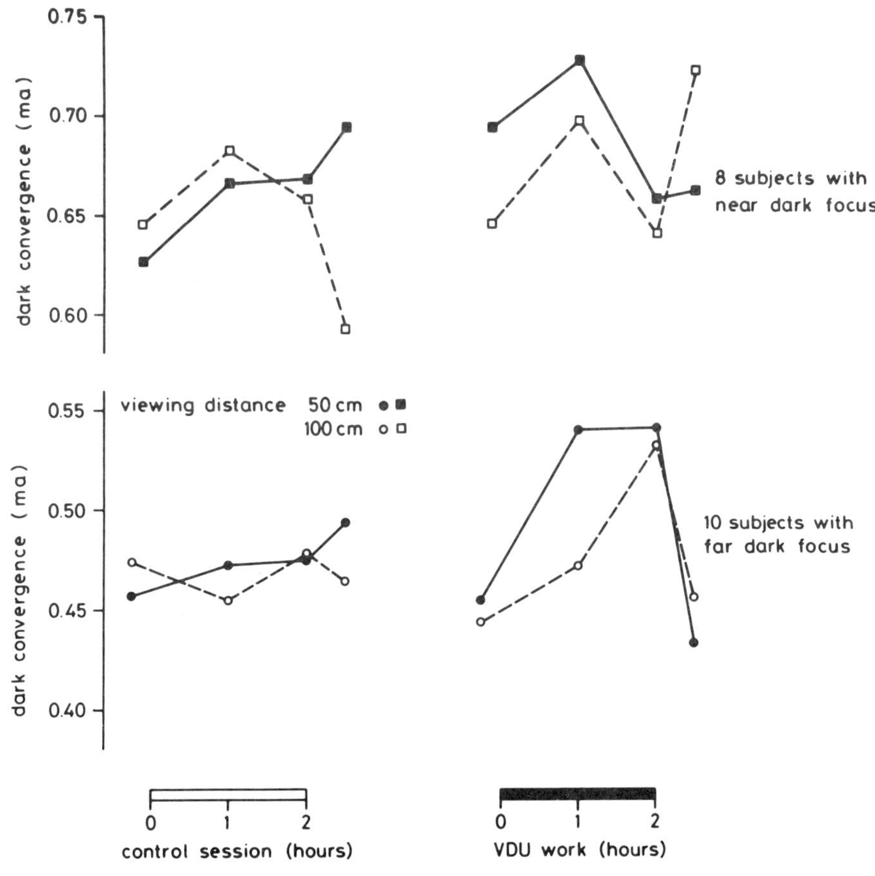

FIGURE 5
Results in dark convergence (Mean S.D. is about 0.4 ma).

These results suggest that dark focus shifts after close work are not simply an effect of the visual condition of the workstation; they also seem to depend on the mental demand and the disposition of the subject to exhibit dark focus shifts. Because of these findings, it seems questionable to regard dark focus shifts as objective correlates of visual fatigue, if visual fatigue means eyestrain due to visual conditions of a workstation.

3.5. Dark convergence

Figure 5 shows the dark convergence of the same subjects. In far-dark-focus subjects, the dark convergence remained constant in the control session. In the VDU-work sessions, their dark convergence increased during work and recovered during the pause. This time effect was significant ($p<0.01$). The increase was stronger at the 50 cm viewing distance. However the difference between both viewing distances was not significant. This inward dark convergence shift agrees with the results in other studies [10,11,12]. In near-dark-focus subjects we found no significant effects in dark convergence.

4. CONCLUSIONS

In subjects with a far dark focus, we found that in the 50 cm viewing distance the accuracy of accommodation was worse ($p<0.0001$), the search time in the VDU-task was longer ($p=0.085$) and eyestrain was higher ($p=0.08$) as compared to the 100 cm condition. Further, the 50 cm viewing distance was judged as too near ($p<0.01$) and after the experiment, 12 out of 16 subjects preferred the 100 cm viewing distance. These results provide evidence that the generally recommended viewing distance of about 50 cm is not optimal for far-dark-focus subjects. However, we cannot decide whether these subjects prefer the 100 cm because of their far dark focus of about 0.9 D, or because of their far dark convergence of about 0.5 ma (or because of any other reason).

In near-dark-focus subjects, the estimation of eyestrain and the performance in the VDU-task was not significantly different at the two viewing distances. The accuracy of accommodation was better ($p<0.0025$) in the 50 cm viewing distance, as it was expected from the near dark focus of this group. On the other hand, near-dark-focus subjects judged the 50 cm viewing distance as too near ($p<0.01$) and after the experiment 5 out of the 8 subjects preferred 100 cm, 1 subject preferred 50 cm and 2 subjects had no preference. The larger accommodation errors in the 100 cm viewing distance seem to have no adverse effect, as neither the performance nor the subjective estimation of eyestrain deteriorated in the 100 cm condition. Therefore we conclude on the basis of the subjective judgement of the viewing distances that also for most subjects with a near dark focus the recommended viewing distance of about 50 cm is too near. These results in near-dark-focus subjects are evidence against the hypothesis that the dark focus is the optimal viewing distance, as has been suggested [6,7]. The preference for the longer viewing distance in most near-dark-focus subjects indicates that visual fatigue during VDU-work is not due to the load on the accommodation system but rather due to the load on the convergence system. The dark convergence was about 0.65 ma in the near-dark-focus group and about 0.5 ma in the far-dark-focus group. In both groups, these values agree better with the 100 cm viewing distance that most subjects in both groups prefer.

It is useful to compare these results with studies of the preferred settings at VDU-workstations. In a laboratory experiment (Grandjean et al. [28]) subjects were free to adjust (among other parameters) the viewing distance of a VDU with constant letter size of 3.4 mm. The mean preferred viewing distance was 66 cm with a 95% range of 54 - 87 cm. In a field study, Grandjean et al. [29] found a mean preferred viewing distance of 76 cm with a range of 61 - 93 cm. In another field study by Hünting et al [30], mean viewing distances of 58 cm and 62 cm were found with 90% ranges of 42 - 81 cm and 44 - 82 cm, respectively. Despite the fact that in these studies the fixed conventional letter size and the limited space on the table in the field studies may have prevented the use of longer viewing distances, these studies make clear that most subjects place the screen at viewing distances greater than recommended in standards. It can be assumed that VDU-users, because of their daily experience, take a viewing distance that is most comfortable for them. Thus, the viewing distances found in practice are further evidence that the recommended viewing distance of about 50 cm is not optimal.

However, what the optimal viewing distance is still remains an open question. It cannot be deduced from the studies where the letter size or the table space is limited; thus the viewing distances found in studies of the preferred settings are rather a lower limit of the optimal viewing distance. The present study can neither propose an optimal viewing distance as just two viewing distances of 50 cm and 100 cm were compared to find out whether the dark focus might be the optimal viewing distances. The rejection of the 50 cm viewing distance does not mean that 100 cm is optimal. Further research is required to establish the optimal viewing distance.

At present we conclude from this study that VDU-users should try whether a greater viewing distance is more comfortable for them, despite recommendations of a closer viewing distance in the standards and despite the intuition that seeing is easier if the object is near. When VDU-users purchase a new VDU they should consider getting a large display with large characters, so as to be able to adjust a large viewing distance.

ACKNOWLEDGEMENTS

The auther wishes to thank Prof. C.R. Cavonius, Prof. W. Rohmert, Dipl.-Psych. G. Jordan, Dipl.-Inf. E. Schubert-Alshuth and Dipl.-Inf. H. van Truong.

REFERENCES

[1] Helander, M.G. and Rupp, B.A., An Overview of Standards and Guidelines for Visual Displays, Applied Ergonomics, **15**.3 (1984) 185-195.

[2] Owens D.A., The Resting State of the Eyes, American Scientist, **72** (1984) 378-387.

[3] Leibowitz, H.W. and Owens, D.A., New Evidence for the Intermediate Position of Relaxted Accommodation, Documenta Ophthal., **46** (1978) 133-147.

[4] Johnson, C.A., Post, R.B. and Tsuetaki, T.K., Short-term Variability of the Resting Focus of Accommodation, Ophthalmic & Physiological Optics, **4**.4 (1984) 319-325.

[5] Krueger, H., Die Funktion der Akkommodation des menschlichen Auges, in: Syrbe, M. and Thoma, M., (eds.), Aspekte der Informationsverarbeitung (Springer Verlag, Berlin, Heidelberg, New York, Tokio, 1985) pp 66-92.

[6] Kintz, R.T. and Bowker, D.O., Accommodation Response during a Prolonged Visual Serch Task, Applied Ergonomics, **13**.1 (1982) 55-59.

[7] Krueger, H., Hessen, J. and Zülch, J., Bedeutung der Akkommodation fur das Sehen am Arbeitsplatz, Z. Arb.wiss., **36** (1982) 159-163.

[8] Östberg, O., Accommodation and visual fatigue in display work, in: Grandjean, E., and Vigliani, E. (eds.), Ergonomic Aspects of Visual Display Terminals (Taylor & Francis, London, 1980) pp. 41-51.

[9] Owens, D.A. and Leibowitz, H.W., Accommodation, Convergence, and Distance Perception in Low Illumination, Am. J. Optom. and Phys. Opt., **57** (1980) 540-550.

[10] Wolf-Kelly, K., Ciuffreda, K.J. and Jacobs, S.N., Time Course and Decay of Effects of Near Work on Tonic Oculomotor Level, Proceedings of Conference "Work with Display Units" Stockholm, 1986.

[11] Owens, D.A. and Wolf, K.S., Accommodation, Binocular Vergence, and Visual Fatigue, Invest. Ophthalmol. Vis. Sci. (Suppl.), **24** (1983) 23.
[12] Owens D.A., Resting Distance of the Eyes and Problems of Near Work, Invest. Ophthalmol. Vis. Sci. (suppl.), **26** (1985) 78.
[13] Ebenholtz, S.M., Accommodative Hysteresis: A Precursor for Induced Myopia?, Invest. Ophthalmol. Vis. Sci., **24** (1983) 513-515.
[14] Simonelli, N.M., Polarized Vernier Optometer, Behavior Research Methods and Instrumentation **12.**3 (1980) 293-296.
[15] Hennesey, R.T. and Leibowitz, H.W., Laser optometer incorporating the Badal principle, Behavior Research Methods and Instrumentation, **4** (1972) 237-239.
[16] Post, R.B., Johnson, C.A. and Tsuetaki, T.K., Comparison of Laser and Infrared Techniques for Measurement of the Resting Focus of Accommodation: Mean Differences and Long-term Variability, Ophthalmic & Physiological Optics, **4.**4 (1984) 327-332.
[17] Liebermann, H.R. and Pentland, A.P., Microcomputer-based Estimation of Psychophysical Thresholds: The Best PEST, Behaviour Research Methods and Instrumentation **14.**1 (1982) 21-25.
[18] Finney, D.J., Probit Analysis, 3rd ed. (Cambridge University Press).
[19] Siegel, S, Nonparametric statistics for the behavior sciences (McGraw-Hill, New York, 1956).
[20] Kruger, P.B., The Role of Accommodation in Increasing the Luminance of the Fundus Reflex during Cognitive Processing, J. Am. Optom. Assoc., **48** (1977) 1493-1496.
[21] Kruger, P.B., The Effect of Cognitive Demand on Accommodation, Am. J. Optom. Physiol. Opt. **57** (1980) 440-445.
[22] Malstrom, F.V., Randle, R.J., The Effect of a Concurrent Counting Task on Dynamic Visual Accommodation, Am. J. Optom. Physiol. Opt. **61** (1984) 590-594.
[23] Post, R.P., Johnson, C.A. and Owens, D.A., Does Performance of Tasks Affect the Resting Focus of Accommodation?, Am. J. Optom. Physiol. Opt., **62** (1985) 533-537.
[24] Westheimer, G., Accommodation Measurements in Empty Visual Fields, J. Opt. Soc. Am., **47.**8 (1957) 714-718.
[25] Leibowitz, H.W., Visual perception and stress, in: Borg, G. (ed), Physical work and effort (Pergamon, 1976).
[26] Miller, R.J., Mood Changes and the Dark Focus of Accommodation, Perception and Psychophysics, **24.**5 (1978) 437-443.
[27] Jordan, G. and Jaschinski-Kruza, W., Dark Focus and Visual Acuity in Relation to the Menstrual Cycle, Perception, **15.**1 (1986) A20.
[28] Grandjean, E., Nishiyama, K., Hünting, W. and Piderman, M., A Laboratory Study on Preferred and Imposed Settings of a VDU workstation, Behaviour and Information Technology, **1.**3 (1982) 289-304.
[29] Grandjean, E., Hünting, W. and Piderman, M., VDT Workstation Design: Preferred Settings and Their Effects, Human Factors, **25.**2 (1983) 161-175.
[30] Hünting, W., Läubli, Th. and Grandjean, E., Postural and Visual Loads at VDU workplaces I. Constrained Postures, Ergonomics, **24,**12 (1981) 917-931.

WORK WITH DISPLAY UNITS 86
B. Knave and P.-G. Widebäck (eds.)

VISION MONITORING OF VDU OPERATORS AND RELAXATION OF VISUAL STRESS BY MEANS OF A LASER SPECKLE SYSTEM

Ove Franzén and Hans Richter. Department of Psychology, University of Uppsala, Sweden. *
Robert von Sandor. College of Applied Visual Sciences, Sweden.

Abstract Several experimental findings depict a view of the refractional system as being characterized by a complex functional relationship to external and internal factors. In the present study thirty-four subjects were exposed to the granular pattern of a bio-feedback laser system. Participants were instructed to judge the apparent motion and direction of laser speckles when eleven increasingly stronger spherical plus lenses were held in front of the right eye while the left eye was occluded. In the last session the subjects were required to stop or slow down any experienced motion of the speckles by means of accommodation through mental effort, thus reducing the tension in the ciliary muscle. Two general functions were established. Apparent speckle motion was a monotonic function of the optical lenses administered. This relationship was significantly altered under the instruction of mental effort towards relaxation of accommodation. A pattern demonstrating group-related differences revealed itself. It was inferred from these observations that remedial benefits may be obtained when employing these strategies on VDU-operators and others suffering from acquired transient or sustained myopia and/or asthenopia and eye strain.

1. INTRODUCTION

Today poor vision is, from an epidemiologic point of view, one of our most common afflictions. Most people know a few individuals in their nearest surrounding who are alleviating this disorder through prescriptions of spectacles or lenses. The present restructuring of our society and the emergence of the information society is transforming many people's lives. The demands on these people's visual system is also changing. The most striking example of this is illustrated by the considerable spread of Visual Display Units (VDUs), which is still on the increase. Unfortunately, the near work VDU operators are engaged in, has frequently been linked to various ill-effects (Bergqvist, 1984). This circumstance is evidenced in a new law issued by the Swedish National Board of Occupational Saftey and Health (Arbetarskydds-styrelsen) which states that employers are required to issue tests

*Department of Psychology, University of Uppsala, Box 227, S-751 04, Sweden

for all VDU operators and furnish glasses, when needed (Arbetarskyddsstyrelsen, 1985:12). It is thought that VDU operators may develop eye strain due to the heavy load placed on the visual system. Ciliary spasm of a medium degree may occur with or without any sensation of pain or discomfort (e. g. Cameron, 1986; Ehrlich, 1986; Koicheva et al., 1986; Koicheva and Zlateva, 1986; Viikari, 1978; Wolf-Kelly, 1986).

It is essential to understand the neurophysiological processes pertaining to accommodation. This is especially critical in attempting to understand how these processes can be and are altered through the development of a refractional error such as myopia and through therapeutic approaches. The duplex innervation of the ciliary muscle, which is at the center of the accommodative process, is an important and often investigated topic. Accommodation of the lens is a product of the requirement that the image be brought into focus at the retina, despite changes between the target and the eye (Fig. 1).

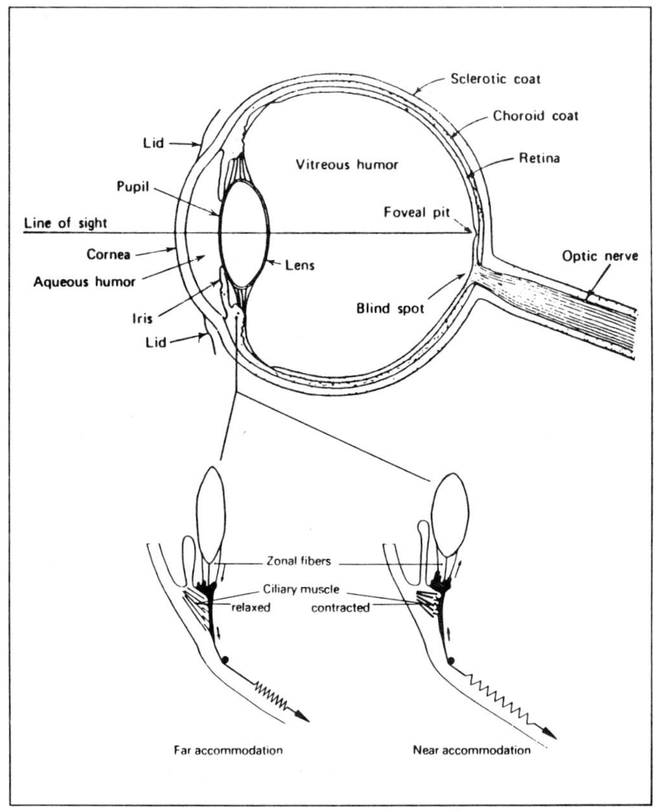

Figure 1
Diagrams of the gross structure of the eye and the operation of the ciliary muscle. In the right diagram the ciliary muscle is contracted resulting in an increased curvature of the lens and in the left diagram it is relaxed which results in a flattening of the lens (from Grüsser and Grüsser-Cornehls, 1981).

The possibility of a dual innervation of the ciliary muscle was proposed already in 1855 by von Graefe, who thought that since the iris had a double innervation why should the ciliary muscle be an exception (Toates,1972). Similarly, Pitts (1968) was able to demonstrate both positive and negative dioptrical adjustments by brain stem stimulation thereby further supporting the notion of active accommodation under central control. In an extensive review covering over two-hundred articles on accommodation Toates (1972) concluded that a dual neural innervation of the ciliary muscle exists and proposed a simple mechanical model of the network for this duplex reciprocal innervation (Fig. 2).

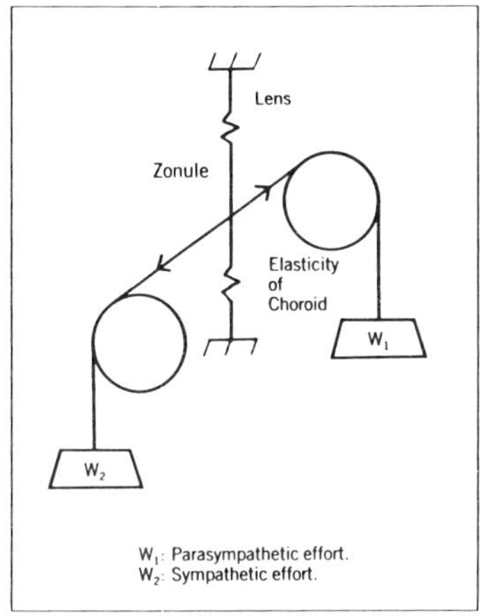

Figure 2

Mechanical model of accommodation assuming a dual innervation of the ciliary muscle (from Toates, 1972).

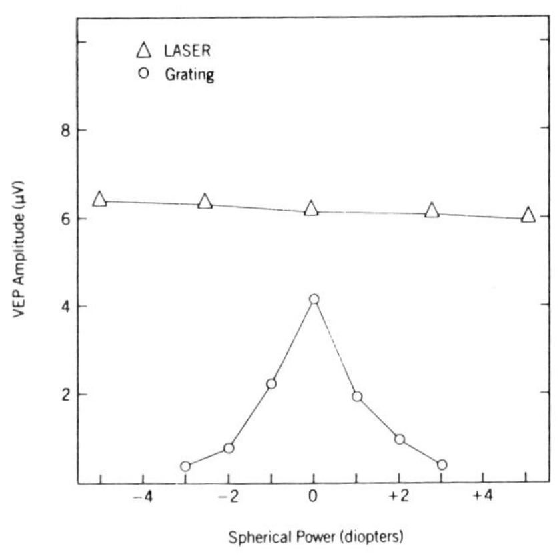

Figure 3.

Visual cortical responses evoked by a laser speckle pattern (open triangles) or by a moving grating (open circles) (from Franzén, 1982).

Already in 1914, Lancaster and Williams reported that prolonged accommodation in near viewing induced transient after-effects that were myopic in nature (Weinstein, 1969). Sato (1964) concluded, after twenty-five years of research, that adaptive changes in the refractive power of the crystaline lens and related systems, were caused by near work resulting in myopia (Lanyon and Giddings, 1974). In 1981 Birnbaum stated, "there is general agreement today among authorities that environmental factors play a significant role, and that near work is probably the most important environmental factor"(p. 554). This view is further reflected in Hedman and Briem's study (1984).

In VDU-work, the operator is located at a close distance to the keyboard and display unit, and thereby engaged in a prolonged state of positive accommodation as part of the work requirement. The near work hypothesis and the significance of accommodation in myopia etiology has gained support through various assessments on the dioptrical state in VDU-work. It has been reported that four hour work with multicolor VDU produced a clear and long lasting transient myopia (Koicheva and Zlateva, 1986). Similar reports by Wolf-Kelly (1986), and Ehrlich (1986) are consistent with this view. It should be pointed out, however, that their subjects were working at an unnatural viewing distance of twenty centimeters.

Several experimental findings depict a view of the dioptrical system as characterized by a complex functional relationship to external and internal factors. Arion (1967) argued, for instance, that the ciliary muscle responds to volition. Westheimer (1957) observed further that subjects could make a small change in their accommodation simply by thinking about far and near. Additionally, anger was found to result in momentary hypermetropia. It was argued that the importance of voluntary factors had been underestimated in clinical testing of accommodation (Weinstein, 1969). Although under many conditions accommodation behaves as a reflex, the importance of so-called higher functions should not be overlooked.

It has been suggested explicitly and implicitly, that the adaptability of the accommodative response be put to a test. The eligibility of such a view was, in the present study, acted upon. Here, an updated modernized version of a bio-feedback laser was employed. The laser optometer has been described in terms of being a promising technique that is appropriate when measuring slowly changing levels of accommodation (Leibowitz and Hennessy, 1975). In a laboratory setting assessments of the proposition that intentional control towards relaxation of the ciliary muscle could be obtained, were carried out by means of a bio-feedback laser system. This study was therefore concerned with modulation of accommodation, rather than measuring accommodation and refractive power per se.

2. METHOD

2. 1. Subjects

Thirty-four undergraduate students, twenty-two females and twelve males, participated in the study. Subjects had a median age of twenty-five and half. Students were selected according to the criteria of age and refractional stability of dioptrical apparatus of the eye as to represent a homogenous age group with varying degrees of prescription stability or need of prescription.

On the basis of whether subjects had been prescribed corrections for myopia or not they were categorized into four different groups depending upon how many times they had updated this prescription for a stronger one during the past three years. Seven (7) non-prescription receivers, seven (7) myopes, seven (7) progressive myopes, and seven (7) pronounced progressive myopes formed the different groups. The first group (emmetropes defined by self-report) were non-correction users, or non-prescription receivers. The second group (myopes) were subjects who had received a prescription for myopia, which they had not updated during the last three years. The third group (progressive myopes) had updated their prescriptions once during the classification period, and the fourth group (pronounced progressive myopes) had changed their prescriptions more than once during the same time span.

A total of six subjects were excluded from the study for the following reasons: Two persons were eliminated due to classification uncertainty, one because of a cold with concomitant swelling of the eye. One person did not show up at the proper time. Finally two participants were randomized away in order to create homogenous size groups for statistical purposes.

2. 2. Equipment

The experiment was carried out in a room illuminated by neon-light where a portable bio-feedback apparatus (390x240x 210mm), Scientific Cook LTD No. 52 model 52 (See fig. 4), was put on a table, approximately 2.5 meters away from a chair. The bio-feedback equipment was located on the table at a height which would guarantee viewing, when seated in the chair. Behind the bio-feedback apparatus and table was a large white cardboard screen (2x2 meters) in order to effectively eliminate any interfering background material.

The bio-feedback device may monitor vision and accommodation in a reliable and valid way. The technique of assessing vision and accommodation has been described by a number of investigators. (For additional information regarding usability, construction and function see; Hedman and Briem,1984; Epstein et al., 1981; Leibowitz and Hennessy, 1975; Ingelstam and Ragnarsson, 1971). A granular stimulus pattern is produced and presented from a slowly rotating drum, onto which laser light is reflected (Fig. 4a). A granular stimulus pattern produced

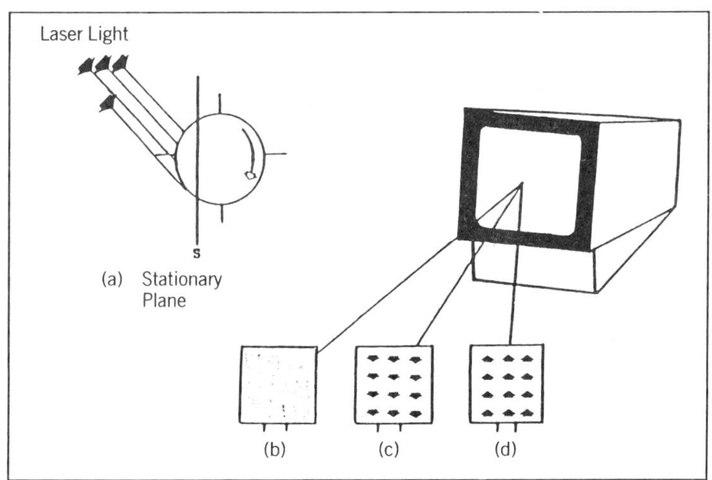

Figure 4

Bio-feedback laser system. The laser speckles are presented to the viewer through a VDU-like device. A granular pattern is produced and presented from a slowly rotating drum onto which laser light is reflected (a). The observer reports the direction of movement of the pattern. An emmetrope experiences the granular pattern as stationary or boiling (b). An uncorrected myope experiences the speckle pattern as moving downwards (c). Apparent speckle motion is perceived by an uncorrected hypermetrope as moving upwards (d).

by interference of reflected helium-neon laser light has no definite plane and its spatial frequency is approximated by a normal distribution curve. Since the speckle pattern is produced by interferences at the retina, its subjective sharpness remains unchanged over a wide range of added lens powers. A visual brain response elicited by a moving grating was systematically altered when various spherical lenses were held in front of the eye (Franzén, 1974, 1982). A cortical visual response evoked by laser-speckles, however, was almost invariant using the same procedure (Dawson and Barris, 1978. See fig. 3). Thus, the advantage of this procedure is that the subject's refractional status, inherent or provocated, does not change the contrast of the stimuli.

2. 3. Procedure

In order to determine to what degree observers could relax the ciliary muscle voluntarily, two test sessions around ten minutes each were carried out. The subjects were given introductional information and instructions. After receiving this information subjects were asked some questions regarding their visual status, and then given a standard instruction, and a short familiarization trial in order to ensure that they understood what was expected of them. These initial preparations took approximately five minutes. When the participant was ready, the laser speckles were presented through the VDU-like device. The speckles are seen as stationary or boiling for an emmetropic viewer with eyes focused in the center of the drum on the stationary plane (Fig. 4b). For myopes and hypermetropes the speckles are seen as moving downwards respectively upwards, with the eyes focused in front of the stationary plane for myopes, respectively behind it for hypermetropes. The apparent speed of the speckles is directly dependent on the magnitude of deviation from the stationary plane. The more myopic a viewer is, the faster the speckles are experienced as moving downwards, and vice versa. Subjects were asked to report the direction of movement of the pattern and its apparent speed (Fig. 4b, 4c, 4d), while lenses were added to produce errors from .5 to 5.0 Diopters. Because of the relative sluggishness of the accommodative response the speckles do not significantly influence the accommodation process, and therefore the subject's perception of the stimulus motion will not be disturbed during this observation time.

Eleven optical spherical plus (+) lenses and two minus (-) lenses were fixated in front of the right eye one at a time for approximately three seconds each. Left eye was occluded. The order of presentation was determined by means of total randomization for each person and test series. Each observer communicated his or her responses to the experimenter verbally during the sessions through his or her choice of a number or a verbal expression from a preprinted scale, which was presented to the viewer throughout the sessions. The sensory verbal descriptors were as follows: Very very slow, very slow, slow, neither slow nor fast, slightly fast, fast, very fast, and very very fast. Subjects wearing glasses or lenses were instructed to keep them on. The stimuli were then administered from the subject's non-correction (self-reported emmetropes) or correction stage. Two series of this type were carried out with approximately one minute break in between.

In the concluding experimental phase subjects were again exposed to the bio-feedback apparatus and optical lenses as previously, however now, the two minus lenses were excluded. At this point subjects were given the following instructions:

> As you now have seen, this pattern can move with different speeds or stand still. Preliminary tests have shown that one may be able to affect this motion voluntarily. We are now going to test to what degree you can affect this pattern's movement. After each lens change I want you, as before, to reply with a number or a verbal expression and to tell the direction of movement, after which I want you to attempt to bring the pattern's movement to a complete stand still or to slow down its movement as much as possible. After approximately twenty seconds I want you to report what speed the pattern now has. We will train some before starting. If you cannot affect the pattern's motion, just report the pattern's movement as you see it. Any questions?

The same procedure was followed as previously. In addition, subjects were observed to make sure that no behavior was performed that could threaten the validity of the responses, such as head movements, squinting the eye and so forth.

3. RESULTS

On a continuum of visual stability and onset of refractional disturbances, seven emmetropes occupied one end, while pronounced progressive myopes represented the extreme other end. In between these two extremes, following the emmetropes, were seven myopes and the same number of progressive myopes. Pronounced progressive myopes, closely followed by progressive myopes demonstrated a more unstable status of their visual system. These groups updated their prescriptions for corrections more often than myopes (Fig. 5). Moreover, they received prescriptions earlier in life and used them more often than myopes.
Two general functions were established (Fig. 6). First, apparent speckle motion was dependent on the magnitude of the optical lens administered. Second, apparent motion of the granular pattern was similarly a function of magnitude of lens administered even under the condition of mental effort towards intentional accommodation. Pronounced progressive myopes made evident a different response pattern in a between-group comparison. The intentional accommodative responses (dotted curve) differed less from the responses under the first two conditions.

The ability to voluntarily relax the ciliary muscle when provoked into a state of greater tension differed between individuals (Fig. 7). Response curves, (a) and (b), show a 32 year old male progressive myope, respectively a 27 year old male emmetrope. These two participants demonstrated an extraordinarily good intentional accommodative ability in comparison with the rest. A moderate similar ability is exhibited in Fig. 7 (c) and (d). The former was a 23 year old female myope (7c), and the latter (7d) a 20 year old female emmetrope. In Fig. 7 (e) and (f) a poor or nearly non-existing capability is demonstrated. Both subjects, a 23 year old male and a 24 year old female, were from the group of pronounced progressive myops. These response patterns shown in Fig. 7 represented the two extremes as well as the average.

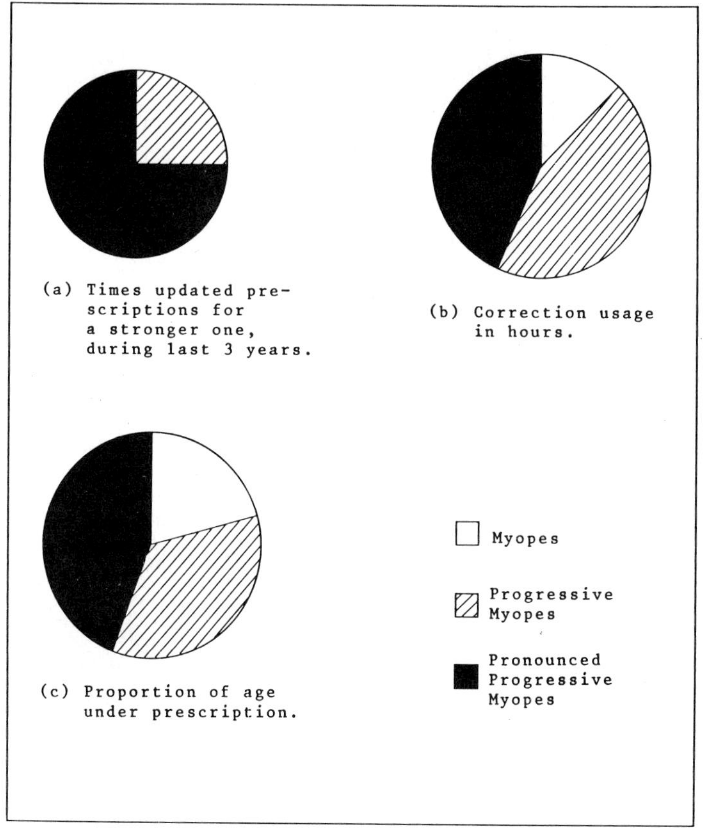

Figure 5.

Visual status among groups. The group of pronounced progressive myopes constituted seventy-five percent of those subjects who updated their prescriptions during the last three years (a). Pronounced progressive myopes and progressive myopes used their prescriptions for glasses or lenses more often than myopes (b). Pronounced progressive myopes and progressive myopes received prescriptions earlier in life than myopes (c).

Subjects were tested for their attention and alertness during the test sessions. Two minus lenses were administered in a random way in the first two test conditions. These lenses caused the granular speckle pattern to appear to go in

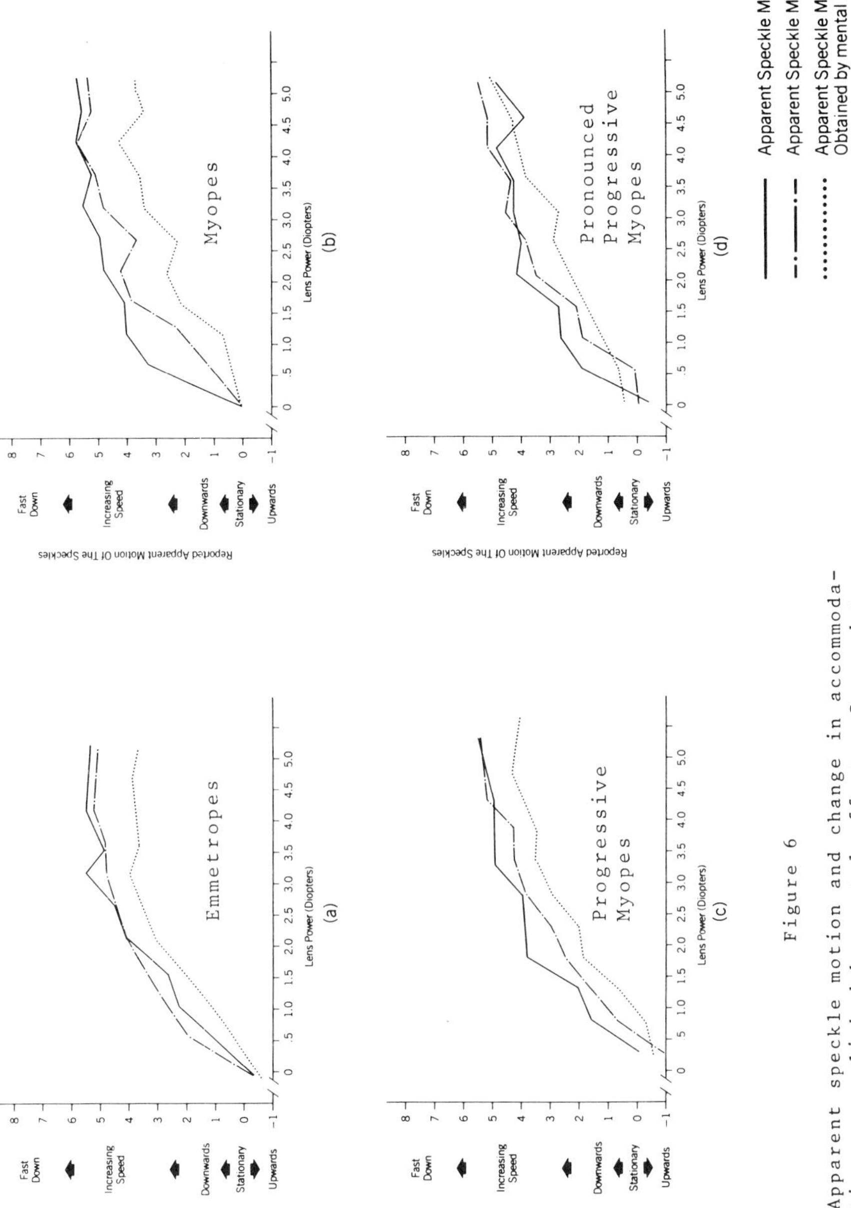

Figure 6

Apparent speckle motion and change in accommodation accomplished by mental effort. Group data.

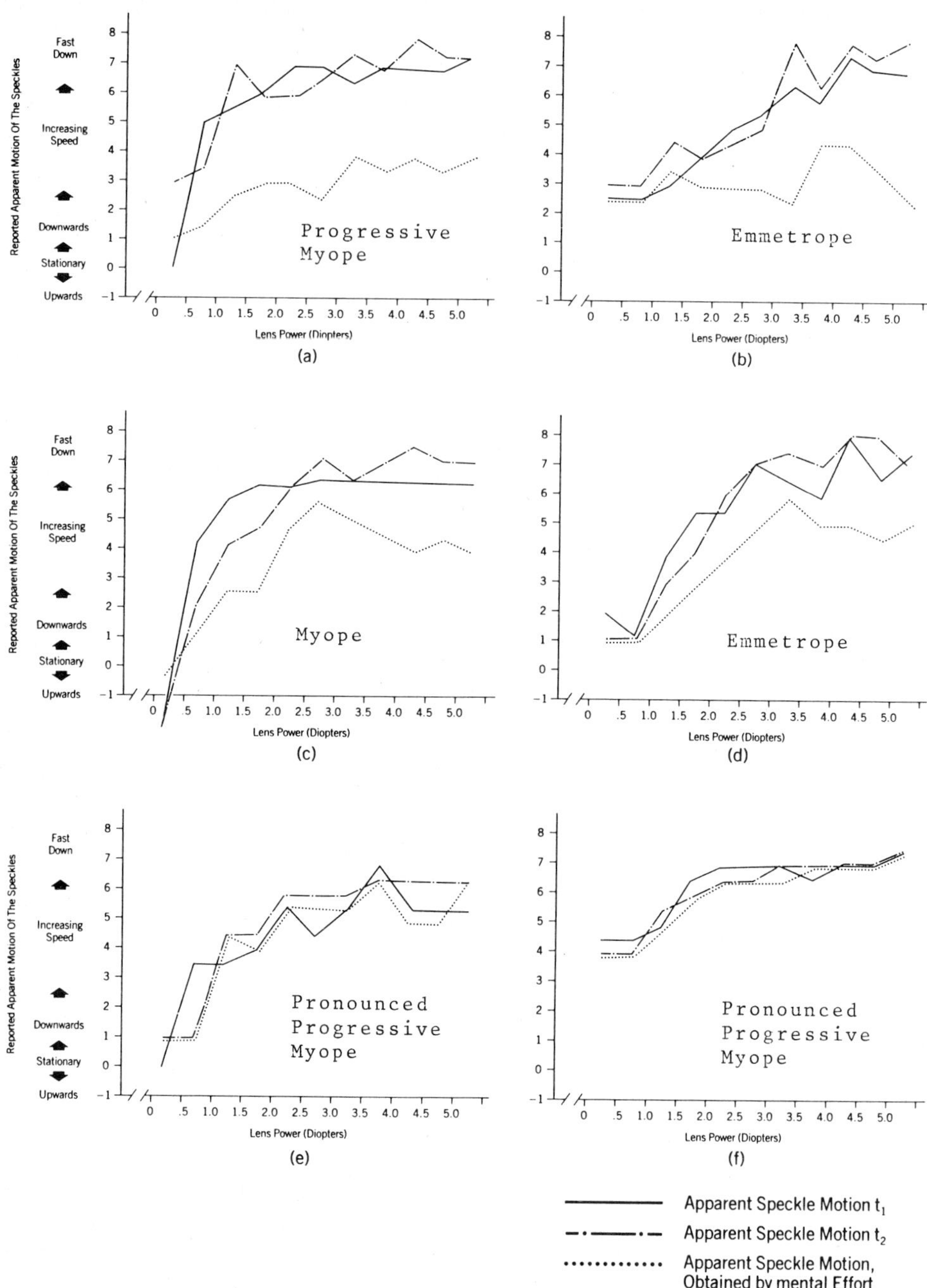

Figure 7

Apparent speckle motion and change in accommodation accomplished by mental effort.

the opposite direction (upwards) contrary to the rest of the lenses administered. Participants' responses indicated that they were alert to these test stimuli. The present data revealed furthermore a high test-retest reliability with respect to the subject's scaling of the sensory magnitude of speckle motion (r_{xy}=0.90). This observation suggested that the request to modify accommodation did not in any significant way bias their judgements of speckle motion under the conditions requiring no mental effort. The two response curves for session t_1 and t_2 were monotonically increasing and they were intertwined with one another along the sensory continuum. If any progressive effects were operative, the two response curves would systematically deviate from one another. One might also have expected that as the visual as well as the attentional system got increasingly fatigued, the subjective responses would be generated in a random fashion. Lastly, an informal observation was made that responses were generally reported in a way that indicated little hesitation or uncertainty.

4. DISCUSSION

In the present study it was concluded that the participants demonstrated an intentional accommodative ability. The results are consistent with previous views and experimental data indicating that the accommodative system is impressionable. This investigation attempted to carry these previous notions in a new direction. Hence, the accommodative response was intentionally modified by our procedure involving a bio-feedback technique.

The difference in intentional accommodative capacity between groups of subjects is interpreted in light of a hypothesis about the relative development of a tension in the ciliary muscle. Lack of changes in the subjects' response pattern under the condition of mental effort is an indication of absence of flexibility and adaptability in the accommodative system. The procedure advocated here to approach the problem of modulation of the accommodation process has the advantage of providing a new perspective on the essential role played by cognitive factors in the dynamic interaction between lower and higher levels of the nervous system.

This prelude to a bio-feedback system capitalizes, among other things, upon the visual system's exquisite sensitivity to movement (McKee, 1981). The cortical neurons of the geniculo-cortical system of mammals are uniquely sensitive to contours, motion and orientation of the contour in the visual field (Hubel and Wiesel, 1962; 1965). Orban (1985) has also advanced the hypothesis concerning the existence of specific velocity tuned cells located in the visual cortex. In this connection it is worthwhile noticing that powerful mechanisms seem to exist in the posterior parietal lobe of the cerebral cortex for directing visual attention and thus for selecting targets of importance in the external world (Mountcastle, 1978; Wurtz, Goldberg, and Robinson, 1982), and possibly these mechanisms are critically involved in the voluntary modulation of accommodation.

The inherent uniqueness of the present technique lies in the fact that the observer is furnished with useful information as to the state of accommodation of the eye which is supplied in a precise way by means of motion and which is easy to interpret and to understand.

If a person is able to control the apparent motion of the granular laser speckle pattern, he/she may also learn to relax his ciliary muscle. It is inferred from the present findings that remedial benefits may be obtained when applying these techniques to VDU-operators and other employees suffering from acquired transient/chronic myopia and/or eye strain, probably as a consequence of prolonged, intense and monotonous near work carried out under time pressure and emotional stress.

ACKNOWLEDGEMENTS

Thanks are due to all subjects who gave their time, and to Hoya Optic for providing the instrument (Bio-feedback laser optometer). Thanks also to Hemlins Glasögon, Uppsala and Tierp, for providing optical lenses.

REFERENCES

Arion, A.F. De l'intérêt des images de Purkinje dans l'étude de la dioptrique dynamique de l'oeil. Archives d' Ophtalmologie. (Paris) 1967, 27, 221-250.

Arbetarskyddsstyrelsens Författningssamling. Swedish National Board of Occupational Safety and Health. Arbete Vid Bildskärm. (1985). AFS 1985:12

Bergqvist, U. Video Display Terminals and Health. Scandinavian Journal of Work, Environment and Health. 1984, 10(2), 44-49.

Birnbaum, M.H. Clinical Management of Myopia. American Journal of Optometry and Physiological Optics. 1981, 58(7), 554-559.

Cameron, R. Space Invaders. Learning to Live with the C.R.T. Proceedings: Work With Display Units. 1986, Part 2, 1046-1049. Stockholm, Sweden.

Dawson, W. and Barris, M. Cortical Responses Evoked By Laser Speckle. Investigative Ophthalmology and Visual Science. 1978, 17(12), 1209-1212.

Ehrlich, D. Transient Myopia Following Sustained Near Work. Proceedings: Work With Display Units. 1986, Part 2, 956-959. Stockholm, Sweden.

Epstein, D., Ingelstam, E., Jansson, K. and Tengroth, B. Low Luminance Myopia as Measured with a Laser Optometer. Acta Ophtalmologica. 1981, 59, 928-943.

Franzén, O. Spatial Analysis in the Visual System. Theoretical and Clinical Considerations. Electroencephalgraphy and Clinical Neurophysiology. 1974, 37, 215-216.

Franzén, O. On Binocular Vision. Motion Perception and Cortical Responses Evoked by Moving Gratings of Fixed Spatial Frequency. Scandinavian Journal of Psychology. 1978, 19, 223-229.

Franzén, O. Den Spatiala Kontrastfunktionen Vid Normalt Seende, Närsynthet och Hjärnskada. Aktuell Optik och Optometri. 1982, 4, 11-21.

Grüsser, O.J., and Grüsser-Cornehls, U. Physiology of Vision, in: Schmidt, R., (ed.), Fundamentals of Sensory Physiology. (Springer-Verlag, New York, 1981) pp. 126-171.

Hedman, L. and Briem, V. Short Term Changes in Eyestrain of VDU Users as a Function of Age. Human Factors. 1984, 26(3), 357-370.

Hubel, D. and Wiesel, T. Receptive Fields, Binocular Interaction and Functional Architecture in the Cat's Visual Cortex. Journal of Physiology. 1962, 160, 106-154.

Hubel, D. and Wiesel, T. Receptive Fields and Functional Architecture In Two Nonstriate Visual Areas (18 and 19) of the Cat. Journal of Neurophysiology. 1965, 28, 229-289.

Ingelstam, E. and Ragnarson, S. Eye Refraction Examined by Aid of Speckle Pattern Produced by Coherent Light. Vision Research. 1972, 12(3), 411-420.

Koicheva, V. and Zlateva, V. Visual Impairments In VDU Operators. Proceedings: Work With Display Units. 1986, Part 2, 622-624. Stockholm, Sweden.

Koicheva, V., Draganova, N., Gantcheva, P., Tsenova, B., Dobrovolski, I., and Dacov, E. Psychophysiological Aspects of Work With Data Entry VDU. Proceedings: Work With Display Units. 1986, Part 1, 252-254. Stockholm, Sweden.

Lanyon, R. and Giddings, J. Psychological Approaches to Myopia: A Review. American Journal of Optometry and Physiological Optics. 1974, 51(4), 271-281.

Leibowitz, H. and Hennessy, R. The Laser Optometer and Some Implications for Behavioral Research. Journal of American Psychological Association. 1975, 349-352.

McKee, S. A Local Mechanism for Differential Velocity Detection. Vision Research. 1981, 21, 491-500.

Mountcastle, V.B. Brain Mechanisms for Directed Attention. Journal of the Royal Society of Medecine. 1978, 71, 14-28.

Orban, G. Velocity Tuned Cortical Cells and Human Velocity Discrimination, in: Ingle, D., Jeannerod, M., and Lee, D., (ed.), Brain Mechanisms and Spatial Vision (Martinus Nijhoff Publishers, Boston, 1985) pp. 371-388.

Pitts, D. Electrical Stimulation of the Occulomotor Nucleus: A Theory of the Central Control of Accommodation. American Journal of Optometry and Archives of American Academy of Optometry. 1968, 45(11), 709-718.

Toates, F. Accommodation Function of the Human Eye. Physiological Reviews. 1972, 52(4), 828-863.

Viikari, K. Panacea. The Clinical Significance of Occular Accommodation. Turku: Turun Sanomat. 1978.

Weinstein, M. Accommodation Reconsidered. American Journal of Optometry and Archives of American Academy of Optometry. 1969, 46, 250-260.

Westheimer, G. Accommodation Measurements in Empty Visual Fields. Journal of the Optical Society of America. 1957, 47(8), 714-718.

Wolf-Kelly, K., Ciuffreda, K., and Jacobs, S. Time Course and Decay of Effects of Near Work on Tonic Occulomotor levels. Proceedings: Work With Display Units. 1986, Part 2, 944-947. Stockholm, Sweden.

Wurtz, R.H., Goldberg, M.E., and Robinson, D.L. Brain Mechanisms of Visual Attention. Scientific American. 1982, 246, 124-135.

Östberg, O. Accommodation and Visual Fatigue in Display Work. Displays. 1980, 81-85.

WORK WITH DISPLAY UNITS 86
B. Knave and P.-G. Wideback (eds.)

VDU WORK, REFRACTIVE ERRORS AND BINOCULAR VISION

E. JÄRVINEN, J. MÄKITIE

Institute of Occupational Health, Helsinki, Finland

INTRODUCTION

In this study we investigated eye strain in VDU work and its possible relationship with objective ocular parameters such as refractive errors, binocular vision, range of fusion and daily accommodation.

SUBJECTS AND METHODS

The material consisted of 142 female VDU users from the age groups 25-30 (n = 61), 40-45 (n = 47) and 50-55 (n = 34) years and 78 age matched female controls (C) of various professions. The character and duration of VDU work were determined with special attention to working distance. Ophthalmological and strabismological status were examined in detail. The results were correlated to eye strain. The accommodative capasity, total and relative daily accommodation were calculated from refraction, nearpoint of accommodation, working distance, glasses worn and time with VDU per day. With total daily accommodation in this connection we mean the accommodation needed to screen multiplied with effective working hours per day. The relative daily accommodation is total accomodation divided with maximal accommodative capasity, and tells the relative accommodative stress per day.

Range of fusion was measured to convergent and divergent direction with a synophtophore.

RESULTS

Fiftyone percent of the VDU users and fortyfive percent of the controls suffered from eye strain at work. They were divided into the following subgroups: VD+ (n = 72) with eye strain, VD- (n = 70), C+ (n = 35) and C- (n = 43). VD+ had been working with VDU for 5.5 yrs (mean) and VD- for 4.8 yrs (mean), effective working time daily with VDU was 4.3 hrs (mean) in VD+ and 4.1 hrs in VD- and the mean working distance 53 cm in both groups.
Nineteen percent of VDU users and twentytwo percent of controls had glasses only for their work. Of all VDU users half of the case with bifocals or progressive lenses had eye strain, but in cases with normal near glasses 2/3 had eye strain and only 1/3 did not. The finding was not statistically significant.

Most myopic were the youngest VDs and the oldest VDs were most hyperopic. Differencves between the VDs and the controls were not statistically significant.

Table 1. Refraction, diopters (D)

	REFRACTION (Mean spheric equivalent)	
	VD	C
25-30 yrs	-1.85	-0,97
40-45 yrs	-0.15	-0.68
50-55 yrs	+0.40	-0.18

Maximal accommodative capasity was lower in the two older VDU groups than in their controls. The result is statistically significant at the level of $p < 0.01$ in both groups. No difference in accommodative capasity could be observed between VDU users with and without eyestrain.

Table 2. Mean accommodative capasity (D)

	25-30 yrs	40-45 yrs	50-55 yrs
VD	8.4	3.8	2.1
C	8.4	5.0	3.0

Table 3 summarized the

- mean accommodation needed for work with VDU in different groups
- total daily accommodation, mean (accommodation at work multiplied with effective individual working hours)
- relative daily accommodation effort, mean (total daily accommodation divided with maximal accommodative capasity)

None of these differences between VD+ and VD- groups are statistically significant.

Table 3. Accommodation at work, mean (D)

	25-30		40-45		50-55	
	VD+	VD-	VD+	VD-	VD+	VD-
Accom. to screen	2.1	2.0	1.9	1.6	0.3	0.6
Total daily accom.	8.6	8.3	8.5	7.1	0.5	1.7
Relat. daily accom.	1.1	1.1	2.5	2.0	0.4	0.8

No difference in stereoscopic vision, convergence or near and far binocularity was found between any of the examined groups. VDU users had 10-15 % more mild or moderate exophoria than the controls, but no difference between VD+ and VD- groups could be observed in exophoria or -tropia.

Esodeviations were more common among VDU users with eye strain than without it.
Two or more degrees of esotropia/phoria examined with a synophtophore was found in 16.8 % in VD+ and in 3.2 % in VD- groups. The finding is statistically significant at the level of $p = 0.01$.

Table 4. Esodeviations examined with a synophtophore

	VD+	VD-
0-1 degrees	83.2 %	96.8 %
≥ 2 degrees	16.8 %	3.2 %

Range of fusion in divergent direction was smaller in VDU users with eye strain than without it.
Four or more degrees of divergent fusion was found in 57.1 % in the VD- group and in 38.5 % in the VD+ plus group. This result is significant at the level of $p < 0.05$.

Table 5. Range of fusion to abduction

	VD+	VD-
0-3 degrees	61.5 %	42.9 %
≥ 4 degrees	38.5 %	57.1 %

No significant differences in convergent fusion could be observed betweeen the VD+ and VD- groups.

DISCUSSION

No objective signs of ocular diseases or pathological changes could be found, in the present material, related to work with VDU.

VDU users had more eye strain in their work than their age matcherd controls, allthough the difference was not statistically significant.

Lower accommodative capasity, found in VDU users, hardly explains the eye strain, for there were no difference in accommodation between groups with and without eye strain. Lower accommodative capasity, found in the VDU users, may be a result of disturbance in accommodation on the basis of more stirring nature of VDU work, compared with controls. Horisontal deviations and narrow range of fusion may cause that fixation on a flickering screen is more difficult and tiresome than on a paper. This may partly explain the more frequent eye strain observed with VDU use.

It seems, that the cause or causes of subjective ocular symptoms related to VDU use, are not directly connected to measureable objective ocular parameters.

REFERENCES

(1) Östberg,O. Accommodation and visual fatigue in display work. Displays July (1980) 81-85.

(2) Binaschi S, Albonico G, Gelli E, Morelli Di Popolo MR. Study on subjective symptomatology of fatigue in VDU operators. In: Grandjean E, Vigliani E, ed. Ergonomic aspects of visual display terminals. Taylor & Francis, London 1982, pp. 219-225.

(3) Dainoff MJ, Happ A, Crane P. Visual fatigue and occupational stress in VDT operators. Hum Factors 23 (1981) 421-438.

(4) Cunnarsson E, Söderberg I. Eye strain resulting from VDT work at the Swedish Telecommunications Administration. Appl Ergon 13 (1983) 61-69.

WORK WITH DISPLAY UNITS 86
B. Knave and P.-G. Wideback (eds.)

REFRACTION IN VDU OPERATORS - A COMPARISON WITH OTHER PROFESSIONS

Karl Gösta NYMAN

Occupational Neuomedicine, Research Department, National Board of Occupational Safety and Health, S-171 84 Solna, Sweden.
The Swedish Foundation for Occupational Health and Safety for State Employees.

In several previous studies, work with video display terminals has been related to asthenopia [1, 2, 3, 4], discomfort, cataracts [5], myopia [6, 7] as well as changes in accomodation and convergence capacity [8, 9, 10]. Some other studies did not reveal any changes in refraction or accommodation [3]. In this study we are comparing the refractional state of VDU operators with other professions with near work.

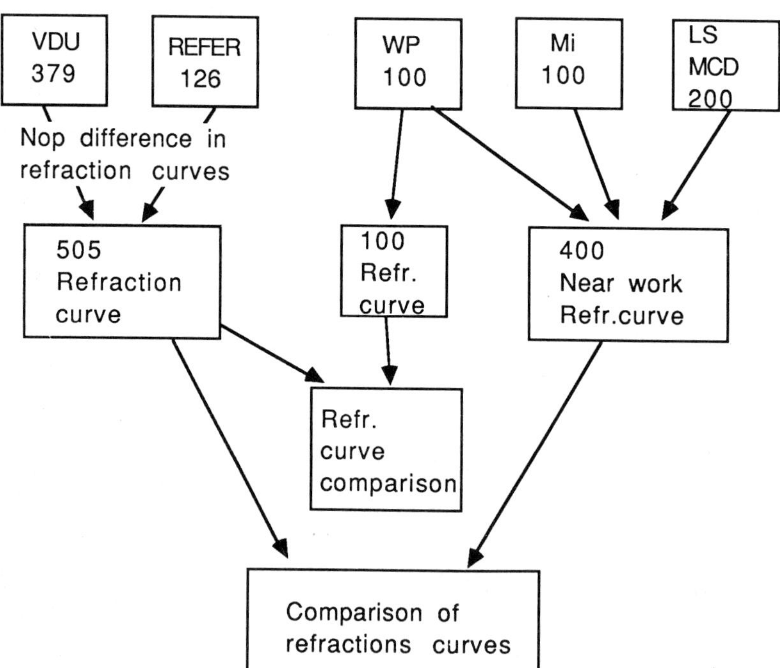

The material consists of two major groups, VDU operators with referents and a second group of map and chart drawers, operators of word processors, microscope operators and land surveyors. Microscope work is not really near work but transient accommodative pseudomyopia has been reported after working sessions.

The VDU group counted 379 exposed and the referents were 126. The VDU workers were exposed at 5 hours or more a day whereas referents were typists and worked during similar time periods. Both these groups were randomly selected, however matched with regard to age [11]. The second professional group was randomly choosen within the professions and divided into age groups. None was exposed to a VDU except the operators of word processors.

All were given a complete ophthalmological examination and an additional refractioning with a refractometer (Dioptron II) before beginning of the work and immediately before the end of work. They also had an orthoptic assessment on these two occations.

Refraction in the ophthalmologic status was measured with Donders fogging method. A test chart allowing assessment if vision accuity up to 2.0 was used at 5 meters distance. When investigated at work was assessed with the refractometer mentioned and without cycloplegia. Refraction was expressed in spherical equivalents. It was ment to discard persons with great astigmatic errors, but no such were found. Age distribution for refraction assessed with Donders method and with refractometer showed that the refractometer closely followed the values of Donders but differed in mean values 0.2 Dioptres to the myopic side.

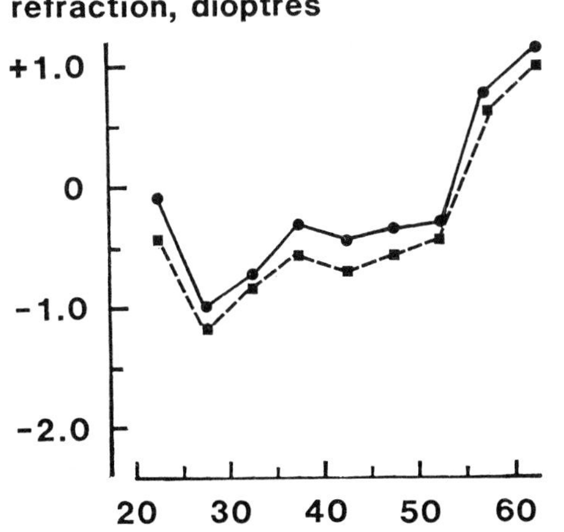

Circles. Donders method.
Squares: Dioptron.

Thus it was possible to plot an age - refraction curve which showed no difference between referents and VDU workers. The refraction difference before and after work session was very small and did not differ between exposed and referent either. There was no difference between men and women.

Thus it can be concluded that VDU work does not cause myopic shift in the refraction nor any transcient accommodative pseudomyopia compared with referents, the age refraction curve was almost identical.

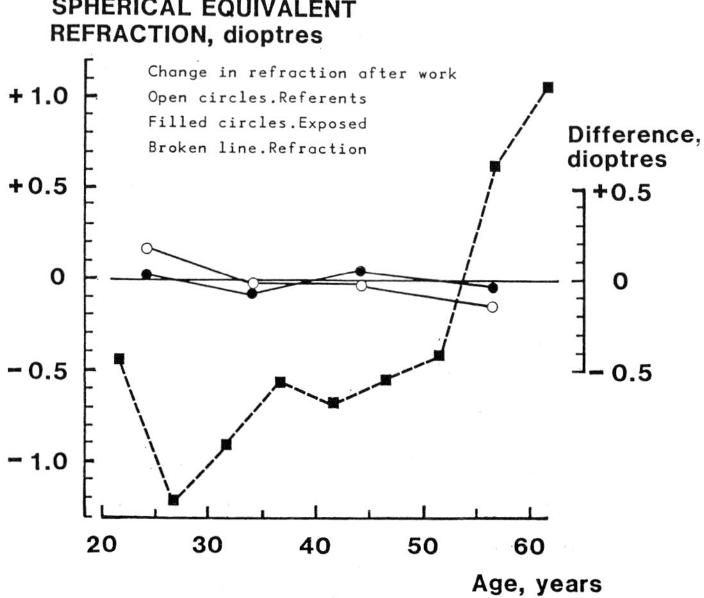

The second group of persons with near work consisted of map and chart drawers, land surveyors, microscope workers, (with earlier mentioned assumptions) and operators of word processors.

These professions are compatible with respect to near work. The mean refractions for the subgroups did not differ and therefore the main group is homogenous.

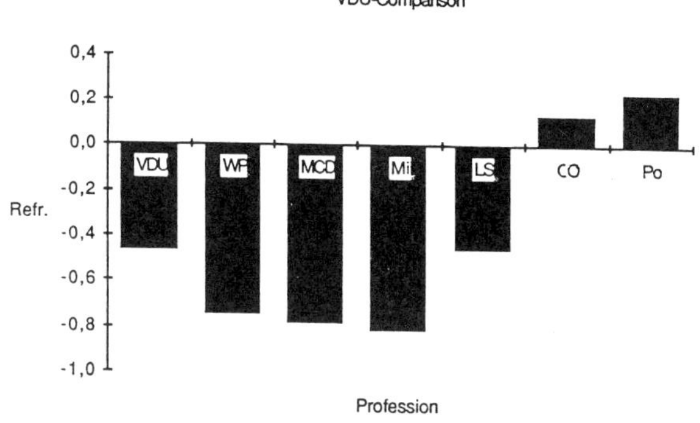

VDU
WP Word processors
MCD Map and chart drawers
MI Microscope workers
LS Land surveyors
CO Custom officers
PO Policemen

When comparing refractions in the age groups for VDU workers and the second group the VDU refraction curve has a low myopic start at the lowest age, followed by a myopic depression lasting to the age of 35-40 where it stabilizes to a slightly myopic level. Above the age of 50 it shows a hyperopic deviation.

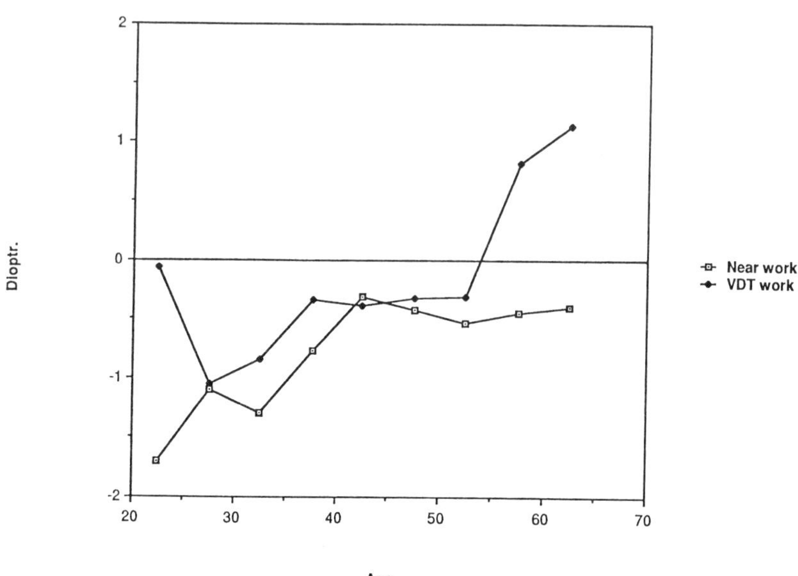

For the second group there is a deep myopic beginning and then the curve neatly follows the VDU curve and has its plateau a little more on the myopic side. However it does not show any hyperopic shift at the higher ages. These people stay myopic. The explanation of this phenomenon is not fully understood since there is a multifactoral origin to ametropia. As for the refraction of those who have a more intense near work during prolonged time this might parallel the outcome of monkey refraction when these animals are kept in a near sight situation for a prolonged time (12.13). The animals turn about 0,5 Dioptris more myopic and stay there even when let free.

These circumstances needs further research in a longitudinal study which includes assessment of refraction and simultaneous ultrasonography for lens thickness and axial length. This has already been started simultaneously with ophthalmological examination and we have got a regression line for axial length and refraction as a pilot study with 60 VDU operators showed close correlation between axial length and refraction but not lens thickness.

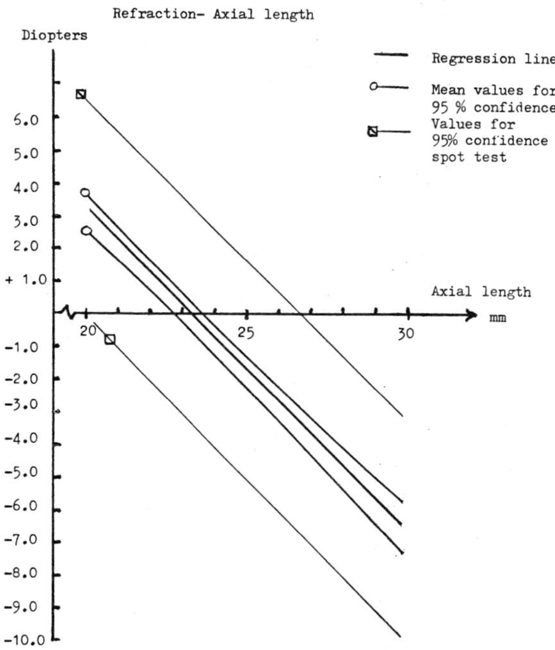

VDU operators have for every age the same refraction as general clerks(-typists) not exposed to CRT:s. There is no evidence of myopisation amongst VDU operators. Other professional groups with more intense near work might be selected or have for other reasons slightly more myopia.

REFERENCES

[1] Ong CN, Hoong BT, Phoon WO. Visual and muscular fatigue in operators using visual display terminals. J Hum Ergol 10 (1981) pp. 161-177.

[2] Rey P, Meyer JJ. Visual impairments and their objective correlates. In: Grandjean E, Vigliani E, ed. Ergonomic aspects of visual display terminals. Taylor & Francis, London 1982, pp 77-83.

[3] Smith AB, Tanaka S, Halperin W, Rickards RD. Report of a cross-sectional survey of video display terminal (VDT) users at the Baltimore Sun. National Institute for Occupational Safety and Health, Center for Disease Control, Cincinnati, OH 1982.

[4] Wallin L, Winkvist E, Svensson G. Terminalanvändares Arbetsmiljö - en enkätstudie vid Volvo i Göteborg, AB Volvo Göteborg 1983.

[5] Zaret MM. Cataracts and visual display units. In: Pearce BG ed. Health hazards of VDTs? John Wiley & Sons, Chichester 1984, pp. 47-59.

[6] Haider M, Kundi M, Weissenböck M. Worker strain related to VDUs with differently coloured characters. In: Grandjean E, Vigliani E, ed. Ergonomic aspects of visual display terminals. Taylor & Francis, London, 1982 pp. 53-64.

[7] Kajiwara S. Work and health in VDT workplaces (in Japanese). In-Service Training Institute for Safety and Health of Labour, Osaka pp. 5-82.

[8] Gunnarsson E, Söderberg I. Eye strain resulting from VDT work at the Swedish Telecommunications Administration. Appl Ergon 14 (1983) pp. 61-69.

[9] Mourant RR, Lakshmanan R, Chantadisai R. Visual fatigue and cathode ray tube display terminals. Hum Factors 23 (1981) pp. 529-540.

[10] Östberg O. Accommodation and visual figue in display work. Displays July (1980) pp. 81-85.

[11] Nyman K G, Knave B G, Voss M. Work with display terminals among office employees. Scan J Work Environ Health 11 (1985) pp. 483-487.

[12] Young FA. (1961) The effect of restricted visual space on the primate eye. Am J Ophthalm.52. pp. 799-806.

[13] Young FA. (1963) The effect of restricted visual space on the refractive young monkey eye. Invest Ophthal.2. pp. 571-577.

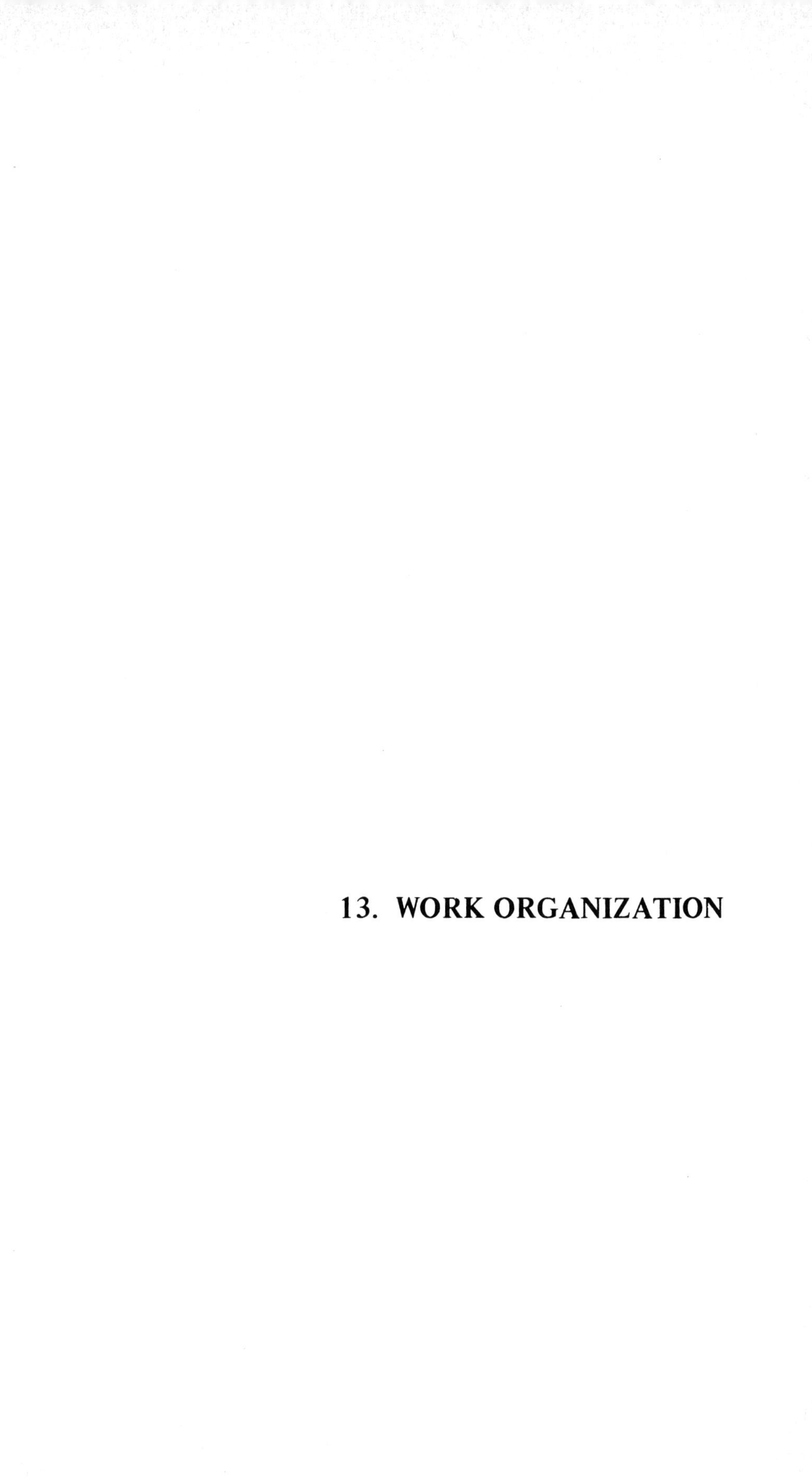

13. WORK ORGANIZATION

WORK WITH DISPLAY UNITS 86
B. Knave and P.-G. Wideback (eds.)

HOW IDENTIFY ORGANIZATIONAL FACTORS CRUCIAL OF VDU-HEALTH?
A context-oriented method approach

Gunnela Westlander

National Board of Occupational Safety and Health, Research department
S-171 84 Solna, Sweden

As in many other countries the majority of VDU-operators in Sweden are white collar workers with less than three years of occupational education. That is why extensive VDU-work mostly means office work. Office work implies a workplace with its characteristic features, easily distinguised by ergonomists, but office work also signifies a special function in relation to the main activity production of the company or public authority. Essentially office work is to provide decision-makers of the organization with basic data, systematized information, administrative service. In the scientific efforts to identify job conditions and organizational factors relevant to "VDU-health" this must not be forgotten.

When studying VDU-health and its causal patterns, what kind of organizational factors shall be made attention to and how can they be identified? At present we do not go groping about in empty nothingness. Instead the answer can be based on a considerable amount of research. It may for the issue of this paper be useful to propose two main categories of organizational factors:

1. Those which represent features of the work organization on the individual group or department level. For instance working pace, working hours, breaks, postural demands, cycle and content of the tasks, division of labour and structure. We may regard them as the very outcome of a planning process when technology (in a wider sense) is decided.

2. Those which represent the acts of organizing in order to find a suitable work pattern. For instance training, planning, pilot studies, implementation, designing the work and co-operation.

Many of the first kind of factors have been identified in the search for causes of physical illhealth in work places. The second kind of factors are looked for in a more systematic way when there is a genuine curiosity about the preparations made to design or combine jobs.

We suggest these two categories on the plea that what is most important to emphasize when talking about organizational aspects is that there is a reaction - and an action side of every work situation. Another - wellknown - way of structuring research of work and health is to think in terms of levels of analyses. Regarding the VDU it could be work station level, VDU-level, job design level, organization level. This fourfold classification (Smith [1]) invites the researcher to analyse organizational factors of the second kind (actions, interactions, interventions) separately. This could be an adequate research strategy only when experts and management level-people alone are allowed to act and plan. If on the contrary there is a democratic policy meaning that all employees should be involved and responsible for a healthy division of work, job conditions should always be looked at and studied from both points of view: how do people act and interact to create, keep or change the work organization and how do people react to the work organization created?

The health concept in VDU-research

The health concept may be operationalized into an infinite number of ways for reasons as subcultural values, changes in health - and quality of life ideals. Therefore every attempt to handle this problem of manifoldness is welcomed. To point out the great importance attached in Sweden to organizational factors we mention here a late research program concerning the psychosocial field (the Swedish Work Environment Fund, [1]). The program was based on a health concept consisting of three classes of criteria (Lennerlöf [1]) 1.ill-health, 2. well-being, 3. resources (personal or situational). Most of the dimensions of the third group refer to organizational factors.

Which health criteria are chosen by scientists seem to a certain degree depend on their definition of VDU-work. An attempt to illustrate this relationship concisely is made in table 1. When studies based on more or less complex criteria of VDU-work are compared differences in the choice of health-variables appear. In studies of type 1 and 2 (see table 1, left column) physical components of the VDU or the VDU-terminal on the whole is in focus. In type 3 and 4 it is VDU-work, usually typologized (data entry tasks, data acquisition tasks, interactive tasks, wordprocessing, see Smith [3], Sydow [2], [1] and studied on full-time workers. In type 5, 6, 7 VDU-work is embedded in a more complex unit of analysis. In other words, the variation of the core phenomenon of the studies can be described along a continuum of specificity - complexity. (Westlander [1a])

Table 1. VDU-work and health. Definitions of work and health-dimensions in applied research. (based on a review, Westlander [1a])

Health-criteria, categories of dimensions

Work situation	**1.Ill-health**			**2.Wellbeing**		**3. Resources**	
	Somatic & psychosomatic	Impaired cognitive functions	Stress and strain	Dissatisf.	Satisf.	Work.org conditions	Actions to influence org.factors
1.Physical components of VDU	x	x					
2.VDU-terminal	x		x			x	
3.VDU-terminals combined with job content	x	x	x	x		x	
4.Transition to VDT-use			x			x	
5.Computer system and work organization model					x	x	x
6.Transition to use of comp. system and related work organization	x		x		x	x	x
7.Process of initiation and implementation					x	x	x

A tendency which seems to follow this continuum is the choice of health dimensions:. from a preference of ill-health reactions and organizational conditions, to a stronger interest of well-being and behavior to influence the organizational pattern. What is more, as far as the studies referred to in table 1, these various research approaches intended to shed light upon VDU-health yield different kinds of scientific knowledge. The empirical methods of studies type 1, 2 and 3 are chosen with the researcher's ambition to obtain results on a "workplace independent level"; studies of type 4-7 on the other hand are difficult to carry through but via more or less structured case studies. Consequently the findings are mostly "workplace unique".

Workplace-independent and workplace-unique data

This distinction between workplace independent and work-place unique data takes us to the issue of the target groups of research findings. Decision makers - on more or less central levels - take what we may call workplace general decisions. Accordingly they show more interest in obtaining workplace independent results. Practicians mostly prefer workplace unique findings. These may function as models or frames of references to their own development work in situ. But, it must be added that central decision makers need abstract knowledge which can be easily interpreted on a concrete level, and many practicians benefit from findings on a concrete /local/ level only if these are applicable to other more or less similar fields so that a certain amount of external validity is possible. In other words, the question is about which kind of knowledge - abstract or concrete - should be in the suborder of the other!

These endeavours to describe research on VDU-work and health by the characteristics which signify some important differences between studies are outlined below:

Core phenomenon of the study	Specific separate qualities of the VDU or VDU-work work isolated)	Complex (VDU-work as a part of total work/main activity or computersystem-affected activity)
Human behavior-dimension chosen	Health-relevant reactions	Health-relevant actions and interactions
Research strategy	Descriptive or quasi-experimental studies	Case study approach
Empirical data	Workplace-independent	Workplace-unique
Evaluation of results	Concerning generalizability	Concerning external validity

The cluster of features indicated in the right column above is significative of the method shortly presented on the following pages.

Judging from the great number of case studies published, many social scientists seem to be aware of the necessity to investigate the processes which precede a final job design and division of work. It is indeed necessary to gain a better insight into the dynamics of initiation processes and into the circumstances where users implement office systems.

But however interesting the analysis may be of technological change in a natural setting, case studies made on the topic run the risk of being conceived as disparate and difficult to make use of. This problem of usefulness has not been passed unnoticed. An increasing number of late publications on theory and practice of case study research is a sign of this awareness.

A context-oriented method approach

The method described in this paper has been worked out with the purpose of extracting a more generalized knowledge from experiences and findings in natural settings. The method amounts to systematic comparisons of several cases. (Westlander [1])

The starting point was an ambition to investigate office work in a transition to computer use. Special attention was made to changes in job conditions of the employees so that the processes of initiation as well as implementation could be better understood. The issue required elaboration of 1. a descriptive model of computerized work as a part of total work, 2. a method apt to identify forces contributing to the job conditions and work environment of the users, 3. an evaluation in terms of health. In other words the project dealt with computerized office work and its practisers in a contextual perspective.

We shall shortly comment on research design, empirical approach and theory. As mentioned, the research design was a prospective multiple case study. This implies a focus on core phenomena explored in their natural setting, abundantly described over time to give a clearer picture of their relation to the context. (Cooley [1], Selltiz et al [1], Yin [1]). As several cases were included for comparison a rather uniform empirical investigation was given priority, but still with a certain attention to unique features of the cases. (Yin [1], Miles and Huberman [1]).

Empirical approach was so-called context-oriented, (Westlander [1b]) which allowed for organizational factors on more or less distance to the computerized work in focus. From a previous explorative study (Westlander 1986 [1]) that covered a process of decisions-making it was realized that initiators, participants and key persons were to be found in various organizational positions. Thus it seemed important to be open for hypothetical influences from the macrocontext.

A theory was developed to conceptualize work in a way that a more generalized knowledge could be extracted from detailed findings in natural setting. Three aspects of work: outcome, design (structure and content), context-relation, made up the basic dimensions which were used to describe the computerized activity (core phenomenon) as well as organizational context. The theoretical point of departure may offer a general frame of reference to case studies concerning organizational and human effects of technology. As our research findings derive from word processing technology we demonstrate the assessment model in that special application (see fig 1).

Data collection

Three workplaces were studied. The workplaces are organizational units of 1. a local government authority, 2. a private industry security service company and 3. a state-owned industry of energy supply. The first is an OD-department with 13 employees, the second handles personnel information and training and has 13 employees, the third is a public relations department with a staff of 19 persons. There are purchasing-, administrative rationalization- and EDPstaffs in all three organizations.

Fig 1. Organizational assessment according to context-oriented approach for studies of office automation and working conditions. Special application to word processing.

META-LEVEL	ORGANIZATION THEORY-LEVEL		OFFICE TECHNOLOGY LEVEL WITH SPECIAL REFERENCE TO WORD PROCESSING
		Main aspects	Main dimensions investigated in the prospective multiple-site-study
Distal context	Macro-organization	context-relation	demand-supply-situation; uncertainity-control of external environment
		design	structure; personnel composition; staffs of administrative rationalization, EDP, purchasing
		outcome	services/products
Proximal context	Organizational unit	context-relation	functional contrib. to macro-org; external demands for flexibility; external social network; dependencies outside unit
		design	task structure; division of work; number of personnel; leadership, internal social network
		outcome	services/products
Core phenomenon	Activities being computerized + computer system	context-relation	proportion writing of total work; instrumental function of documents; demands for external cooperation in composing texts; economic aim of investment in WP-system
		design	proportion of VDU-work per day; division of writing work (composing texts, typing, document storage, retrieval, communication and administration); office machines and utensils; everyday routine rationalizat.
		outcome	documents (different types); translated versions

None of the three organizational units is directly involved in the main activity/production. They have all some sort of service, support- or development-functions in the organization which means high demands for flexibility in the work. From a psychological - and mental health - point of view, the outcome of the work can be characterized as immaterial which implies difficulties for the workers to obtain a clear feedback of their achievements. One has to resort to intuitive assessments.

Data collection started at the point of time when the installation of the WP-system was approaching. The initiation phase was studied retrospectively and the implementation prospectively. The final point of time of data collection was about 15 months later. (The initiation phase was prolonged in the Public

Relations department owing to the employees' will to put off the choice of equipment). Data collection methods:

I structured and semistructured interviews recorded in questionnaires and schedules; qualitative as well as quantitative data-analyses were made. The whole staff of the three workplaces were interviewed, also one representative of the EDP-, administration- and purchasing staffs each. An indepth-interview was made with the vendor. 11 inventories were used (see table 2). The number of interviewees were 58, the vendors included.

II Detailed survey of office equipment (machines, requisites).

III Analysis of a representative sample of writings produced within the organizational unit

IV Organizational assessment of structure, main activities and policies of the company/authority.

Some findings

The method invites to an abundant empirical analysis which makes it especially suited for questions like: "in which respects does office work change after word processing systems are implemented?", "if changes have occurred, are the causes to find in the use of a new word processing equipment?", "concerning the organization of the word processing work, is it possible to get an understanding and explanation of the solution taken?"

Office work and the role of of WP-equipment

In table 3 is an outline (on a synthesis level) of empirical findings relating conditins of distal and proximal context to the core phenomenon: word processing equipment and tasks. It is seen from table 3 that writing work, - that part of office work which is directly affected of the WP equipment, had more or less changed after the implementation in all three workplaces.

In the OD-department the writing documents were the same, there were minor changes of division of the work and of how much it occupies the time of the employees. The Public Relations department showed minor changes: only in division of work, whereas the department of Personnel Information and Training had changed a great deal regarding amount of writing, their functions in the organization and regarding division of the work.

This cross-site analysis of writing work after an implementation period tells us something about changed patterns in the computerized work. Before drawing a rapid conclusion about the WP-epuipment as a causal factor, we can use within-site analyses to explore the role of the organization-context. Table 3 presents the situation of our three sites regarding more or less distal organizational events.

In the cases of OD-department and the PR-department, their organizational context has stayed rather the same during the passed 15 months, the minor changes in writing work was caused by internal personnel adjustments. What has happened in terms of psychosocial consequences and stress has its origin mainly in the internal situation, the way of coping with the WP-system, its technical fitness to the work demands of the employees. (see also Westlander [1]).
Department of Personnel Information and Training on the other hand illustrates a case where macro-organizational factors intervened during the implementation period and became the dominating sources of stress and anxiety. The troubles with the WP-system became a contributing but secondary cause to an increasing uneasiness of the VDU-operators as well as of other employees.

Table 2. Inventories of the study

Notation of	**Method**	**No of items**	Categories of people inquired: Organizational unit – Head	Organizational unit – All empl	Organizational unit – Sample of empl	Pur-chas repr	Adm-rat. repr	EDP funct repr	Vendor of suppl comp
-Office tools (machines and utensils)	Checklist	199							
	Interview schedule	45							
-Organizational assessment	Interview schedule	17	x						
-Job conditions	Interview schedule	45		x					
" "	Question-naire	42		x					
-Initiation-acqu-isition process	Interview schedule	41		x					
-The Transition stage	Question-naire	72		x					
" "	Interview schedule	77			x				
-End-user influence	Interview schedule	87		x					
-Task analysis of purch.AR,EDP functions	Question-naire	98				x	x	x	
-Attitudes of purchas.AR,EDP	Interview schedule	48				x	x	x	
-The role of the vendor	Interview schedule	117							x
-Office environm. ergonomics	Question-naire	75		x					

Table 3. Organizational conditions and the computerized office work of three workplaces (sites). At the time of about 15 months after installment of WP-equipment. Outline on an integrated prospective data level for cross-site and within-site analyses.

U =unchanged Uc=in the main unchanged
C =changed Cu=in the main changed

	Site:	Main aspects		
	OD-DEPARTMENT	**Context**	**Design**	**Outcome**
Distal context	Macro-organization (local government authority)	Unchanged constant adjustment to local recession (U)	Unchanged structure and staff resources (EDP, Adm.rationaliz. purchasing) (U)	Unchanged municipal services-supply (U)
Proximal context	Organizational unit (the OD-department)	Unchanged functions contrib. to macro-org. Intens. contacts with purchasing department (Uc)	Unchanged task structure and division of work but reduced personnel resources (Uc)	Unchanged supply of OD-projects (U)
Core phenom	Writing and wordprocessing as part of the org. unit	Unchanged instrumental functions More time-consuming (Uc)	Unchanged formal organization of writing work. Minor changes in div. of the work More VDU-work (Uc)	Unchanged scope and kind of documents (U)
	Site: **PERSONNEL INFORM. AND TRAINING DEP.**			
Distal context	Macro-organization (industrial security service comp.	Unchanged market position (successful) (U)	Changed ownership and direction.Whole business in restructuring phase (C)	Changed profile of security-services considered (Uc)
Proximal context	Organizational unit (the pers. inf. and train. dep.)	Changed functional contrib. to macro-org; departm reconsidered (C)	Changed, unstable situation; reduced personnel resources turnovers, reorganiz, transfer of employees (C)	Reduced output of personnel information and courses (C)
Core phenomenon	Writing and wordprocessing as part of the work of the org. unit	Changed functional contrib. to macro-org. regarding pers information Less time-consuming than previously (Cu)	Unchanged formal organization Minor changes in division of work Transition to VDU-work (Uc)	Reduced output of documents (C)
	Site: **PR-DEPARTMENT**			
Distal context	Macro-organization (industry of energy production)	Unchanged stable market position (U)	Unchanged structure and staff resources (EDP,admin. ration, purchasing) (U)	Unchanged production (U)
Proximal context	Organizational unit (the PR-department)	Unchanged functional contrib to macro-organis. Minor change in interaction with specialists staffs (increased) (Uc)	Unchanged task structure and division of work.Intensified social contacts. Reduced personnel resourc. (minor) (Uc)	Unchanged output of PR-services in - and outside the company (U)
Core phenomenon	Writing and wordprocessing as part of the work of organiz. unit	Unchanged instrumental functions and in oth.respects (U)	Unchanged formal organiz.Minor changes in div. of work.Transition to VDU-work (Uc)	Unchanged scope and kinds of documents (U)

An understanding and explanation of the organizational choice.

The three cases (studied for about one year) illustrate (a) leadership styles, (b) diverse ideas of optimal organizational solutions, (c) different strategies to realize these ideals and different ways of coping with emerging problems. Among these kinds of acts of organizing this paper will focus on leadership behaviour and ways of dividing the WP-work.

Leadership behaviour

Head of the OD department
The idea of sociotechnical change was in the mind of the head. All employees should be operators, which would relieve the secretaries from to much writing and give them a chance to assist in the more qualified consultant tasks. In other words: job enlargement and skill-development for the secretaries and more independence of secretarial support for the consultants of the department. The last mentioned appreciated the proposal whereas the secretaries felt hurt in their feelings and refused to accept. The social climate became hostile. The head of the department responded to this mixed refutation by taking a totally passive role. He avoided all further discussions about the organization of work and left it to the secretaries. The traditional task structure remained.

The kind of humanization of work that the head wished to encourage was not met with sympathy. In a cold atmosphere the implementation proceeded, the secretaries becoming more and more skilled in handling the word processing system. No social support was given them by their boss. He left all problems, even the technical ones, to be solved by the secretaries.

Head of the Personnel Information and Training department
This person wanted the WP-system to be to the secretaries full disposal. Their monotonous, isolated and sedentary job should be compensated by office machines of top quality. The rest of the personnel had better to keep out of it as they already were provided with qualified work.

By furnishing the secretaries with good office machines the head expected their self-esteem and occupational prestige would increase. He concentrated his social support on them, which made the others feel slight indignation. Imperfect application programs made the head take up negotiations with the supplier company. But when these negotiations did not ended in a totally satisfying way he lost the interest of the WP-system and retired, downhearted. A few months after, he was replaced by one of his subordinates. The new head was very vague and diffuse about the benefits of the new WP-system.

Head of the Public Relations department
On purpose the head of this department pursued a wait-and-see policy. The need of an automated office system should grow slowly "from inside", that is to say, the employees should not be forced into a rapid choice. This was a very deliberate delegation intended to increase interaction and willingness to take responsibility among his subordinates. He succeeded to develop these attitudes but here was no decision taken.

The head found it best to withdraw the delegation, he turned about, made the choice himself very rapidly without discussions with his subordinates, and bought two systems of different marks. He continued to be as active as the rest of the personnel during the implementation that followed.

These examples of leadership show no initial indefiniteness of the heads concerning the word processing work. On the contrary all the heads knew how they wanted it organized and which personnel categories should be given the primary advantages of the system. Their models differed from each other and so did their strategies to achieve them. They had all ideas about the most important criterias of wellbeing and how to attain them. They also tried a rather consequent leadership style, two of them had to give it up, whereas the third was successful.

The models of VDU-use chosen and its consequences.

At the time of installation the organizational preferences within these three departments looked very different: to sum up there was a full consensus in the PR department of how to find the most suitable model of using the system, a partial consensus in the Personnel Information and Training department (head and secretaries agreed) and a non-consensus in the OD department.

From these three social psychological conditions evolved various models of VDU-use. The findings from a longitudinal, prospective study of the implementation phase lead to the conclusion that the cooperative patterns within the personnel were closely connected to the VDU-use model realized and so were the psychosocial consequences. Different kinds of work environment-problems remained in the three departments. (See table 5)

Table 5. Patterns of cooperation and remaining problems related to model of VDU-use. Three workplaces.

Site	VDU-use model	Target groups supported by service from the WP-system	Internal cooperative dependencies in WP- betw. employees	Psychological relations, secretaries-other employees	Remaining problems (a year after installation)
OD-dep.ment	Only secret.; fulltime work at the VDU	High level of service from secretaries to professionals also within the dep.ment	strong	antagonistic	productivity overload and exaggerated demands of service on secretaties latent conflict; high work load (ergonomic) systems deficenies
Personnel inf. and train dep.	Only secr; parttime work (4 h /day) at the VDU	Low level of service from secretaries to profess. within the dep. High level of service fr secr to macroorganiz.	week	parallell	
PR-dep-ment	All empl. parttime work at the VDU	High level of service from all employees to macroorganiz. and external environment	miscellanous	cooperative	Lack of technical knowledge and skills

The first case - the OD department - is an excellent example of a polarization effect. The skills of the various occupational categories tend to develop into separate directions. The outcome was a paradox: increase in efficiency and effectiveness and decrease in job satisfaction.

In the case of the department of Personnel Information and Training on the other hand, the professionals are un-touched by the computerization, whereas the secretarial staff become higly involved. However, efficiency is never reached because a combination of macroorganizational changes (see table 3) and supplier neglects.

The third case - the PR department shows up a more intentional approach to the whole procurement. One of the intentions was to avoid a polarized work division, another was to be selective and fastidious about the choice of equipment. Skill development, efficiency and job satisfaction were goals strived for, which postponed an early installation.

The three cases are instances of transitions from one office technology to another. The initial strains are common but when the main difficulties in handling the equipment technically are overcome, workplaces show up and meet different problems depending, on to a high degree, how work is organized. The methodological approach described shortly in this paper leads to a differentiated knowledge of VDU and its job consequences. Crucial factors to VDU-health, ways of coping and preparations are features which distinguish workplaces where the same kind of office system is introduced - a fact that becomes salient from research based on this context-oriented method.

Characteristics of the method - concluding comments

- A context-oriented perspective implies search for crucial factors inside and outside the organizational unit to consequences of the office technology introduced. It is a way of investigating the interaction between distal and proximal forces on one hand and the activities under computerization on the other.

- The method shortly demonstrated in this paper indicates a way of coping with the linkage problem: do effects in form of job conditions and health arise from implementation of the office system or from other events occuring simultaneously in the organization?

- In its longitudinal design the method is a way of catching phase-specific stressors (or their positive correspondences!) arising during initiation-, installation-, implementation-periods - and, if the study is allowed to be prolonged, permanent ones.

- It is a dynamic approach which means among other things that presumptive and present VDU-operators can be studied not only as usually in terms of their reactions but also in terms of coping, search for control and mastering the technology. Such findings would be very useful in order to understand if and how bad job conditions could be eliminated.

- Basic and in-depth knowledge can be obtained from this context-oriented approach to clarify the causal patterns of VDU-health.

Table 4. Roles in chief positions in a context-oriented perspective. The initiation phase of an office automation. Three workplaces.

Office department	Source of initiative and support in the organization.	Kind of change from the point of view of the office department	Role taken by the head	Employee-participation during initiation (♂ = man, ♀ = woman)	Initiator	Early involved	Late involved
Org devel. EDP, ration	Initiative from the office unit itself (head and secretaries). Generally recognized by purch function and board as well as unions. Adm and EDP specialists identical with the head of the office unit	Immanent change with full support from outside	Active	Head	♂		
				Secr N=3			♀ ♀
				Others N=9	♂	♂ ♀	
Personnel information and training	Initiative from outside the office unit itself. The idea came from adm specialist function and was accepted by the personnel of the office unit. Support from the purchase departm and resistance from the direction board	Externally imposed change with full support from inside and mixed acceptance in the macroorganization	Active	Head		♂	
				Secr N=4			♀
				Others N=8			♂ ♂
Public relations and pers. information	Initiative from outside the office unit. Adm staff planned a pilot study of office automation of change unclear to all involved. Support from management level and spec. functions	Externally imposed change with a vague support from inside and vague purposes expressed from outside	Passive	Head			
				Secr N=5			♀ ♀ ♀
				Others N=13		♂♂ ♂♂	♀

References

[1] Arbetarskyddsfonden. (The Swedish Work Environment Fund) Mänsklig arbetsmiljö. Angelägen beteendevetenskaplig arbetsmiljöforskning. Rapport 1984:4. Stockholm.

[1] Cooley, C.H. Sociological Theory and Social Research. Holt and Comp. NY 1930 Chapt X and XII.

[1] Lennerlöf, L. Arbetsmiljön ur psykologisk och sociologisk synvinkel. Liber Förlag, Publica-serien. Stockholm 1981.

[1] Miles M B, Huberman A M. Qualitative Data Analysis. A Soursebook of New Methods Sage Publication Berverly Hills, London, New Delhi, 1984.

[1] Selltiz, C., Wrightman L., Cook, S. Research Methods in Social Relations 3rd ed. Holt, Rinehart and Winston, 1976.

[3] Smith, M. Health Effects of VDT: Ergonomic Aspects of Health Problems in VDT operations. In: Office Hazards: Awareness and Control. North West Center for Occupational Health and Safety. University of Washington, Seattle. 1984.

[2] Sydow, J. Sociotechnical Change and perceived Work Situations: Some Conceptual Proportions and empirical Investigations in different Office settings. Office: technology and people 1984. vol 2 no 2 .

[1] Sydow, J. Organisationsspielraum und Büroautomation. Zur Bedeutung von Spielräumen bei der Organisation automatisierter Büroarbeit. Walter de Gruyter. Berlin 1985.

[2] Westlander, G. Office Automation, Organizational Factors and Psycho-social Aspects of Health with special reference to Word Processing. Reports from the Department of Psychology, the University of Stockholm. Supplement 61, Nov 1984.

[1a] Westlander G. Kontorsarbete som objekt för arbetsmiljöforskning. En översikt i perspektivet av kontorsautomation. Undersökningsrapport 1985:6. Arbetarskyddsstyrelsen, Stockholm. (Office work and work environment. A research review.) 1985a.

[1b] Westlander,G. Om contextorienterad ansats. En metoddiskussion med anknytning till organisationspsykologisk tillämpning. Undersökningsrapport 1958:8 Arbetarskyddsstyrelsen, Stockholm. (Contextoriented approach. A methodological discussion related to organizational psychology.) 1985b.

[4] Westlander,G. Leadership styles in the implementation Phase. Paper presented at the International Conference of Work with Display units. Stockholm, 12th 16th May 1986.

[1] Westlander,G. Kontorsautomation som drivkraft - hur människor handlar och arbete förändras. Tvärfallsanalys av kontorsarbetsplatser. Studentlitteratur, Lund 1986 (Office automation as a motive power. How people act and work is changed)

[1] Yin, R.K, Case Study Research. Design and Methods. Applied Social Research and methods. Series, vol.5. Sage Publications Ltd. Beverly Hills, Calif.

WORK WITH DISPLAY UNITS 86
B. Knave and P.-G. Widebäck (eds.)

PSYCHOSOCIAL WORK ENVIRONMENT AND USE OF VISUAL DISPLAY TERMINALS - FROM THEORETICAL MODEL TO ACTION

Gunilla Bradley
Department of Sociology, University of Stockholm,
S-106 91 Stockholm, Sweden

ABSTRACT

This article is based on research performed at Stockholm University. The research group consisted of people from different disciplines (e.g. psychology, sociology, computer science, and economy). We have cooperated with reference groups both from trade unions and management. The research which is called the RAM project began in 1974. We have studied the effects of computerization at three companies. Each uses a different system of processing data. The systems correspond to three phases in the history of computer technology:

1. System of so-called batch type (a government-owned company, the Postal Giro Service)
2. On-line system with display terminals (an insurance company, Trygg-Hansa)
3. Microcomputer system (an electronic company, Philips Electronic Industries).

The results in this article are mainly from the insurance company. A theoretical model was set up for analyzing the effect of computerization on the psychosocial work environment and family life, leisure, and health.

Before and during computerization various actions to create a better work environment were taken. They are summed up in section 3.5.

1. INTRODUCTION

1.1 Theoretical Model, Purpose, and Problems

Research on computerization and psychosocial work environment (RAM project)* has been performed over the past twelve years at the Department of Sociology, the University of Stockholm. The constellation of the research group is interdisciplinary with researchers from the following disciplines: psychology, sociology, educational psychology, and computer science. The research is financed by the Swedish Work Environment Fund.

Work environment has mainly been studied from a psychosocial perspective and the concept has been given a broad meaning. It is linked to the idea that environment influences the individual at different levels: the level of society, the level of organization and the level of the individual. The factors on the different levels are regarded as interacting. Problems studied in the project include objective, structural working conditions (especially at the organiza-

* RAM is an abbreviation of the corresponding key words in Swedish: Rationalization (R) Work Environment (AM).

tional level) as well as experiences and attitudes related to work. The action strategies discussed during the successive findings are connected with this view.

A theoretical model for the analyses of the interplay between computerized information systems, psychosocial factors in the work environment and living conditions outside work (family/leisure) has been presented in earlier publications from the project, e.g. /1/.

The theoretical model can also be used as a thought model for the structuring of desired conditions in a computerized society:

* What objective conditions outside work, the definition of work as it is used today - leisure time, family, social life - do we want for the future?

* What are the ideal properties of a good work environment from a broad psychosocial point of view?

* What technology and combination of technologies can be used to bring about the prerequisites and objectives stated in the points above?

* What properties in the structure of society, the societal frameworks and norms and value systems, promote and create positive opportunities for the future growth of such a technology?

The first RAM project is called RAM:1 below. The problem areas which were explored concerning computerization in working life are represented below, using essential concepts from the model:

* General questions on work environment and work satisfaction
* Information and participation in decision-making
* Organizational design
* Work content and work load
* Promotional and development patterns
* Contact patterns and communication
* Salary conditions and working hours
* Education and training
* Evaluation of work/role at work
* Physio-ergonomic conditions
* Leisure time
* Health

1.2 Introduction to the Field Studies

Data processing systems offer various conditions for structuring work and work environments. Three main data processing systems were studied, related to three phases of the "history of computer technology":

* A *batch system* (a government-owned company, the Postal Giro Service) - company 1

* An *on-line system* with video display terminals (an insurance company, Trygg-Hansa) - company 2

* A *microcomputer-based system* (an electronic industry, Philips Electronic Industries) - company 3.

RAM:1 Project
The project's second field investigation took place at an insurance company. Approximately 1,000 persons employed at the company's main office, situated in

the Stockholm area, constituted the population. The results were based on a randomized sample of 300 persons. The methods used for collection of data were interviews, direct observation, internal documentation and questionnaires. The "terminalization process" was observed over a two year period.

About 50 indexes (or Likert-type scales) were constructed from the 400 items contained in the questionnaires. The indexes measure psychosocial aspects of the work environment, degree of co-determination in the job, health complaints, values concerning work and leisure time, effects on the work environment caused by the display terminal system and likewise by the data processing system in general (this refers to all computer operations in use before the introduction of terminals). Analyses have been performed on substructured data. Some further analyses have been undertaken with the purpose of exploring which psychosocial factors of the work environment, factors measuring democracy at the work place, and physio-ergonomic conditions, dominate in explaining

* nervousness
* health complaints
* influence of work on family and leisure time.

Various phases of the field work give various types of knowledge with regard to computerization. This article presents *selected analyses and results*.

Participators in the project's reference group in the company were involved in various action strategies. The aim was to create a better work environment. These activities were undertaken at the insurance company before and during the computer implementation process. These strategies are briefly presented in a "follow-up perspective".

Requirements for work and work environment in the context of computerization - derived from our research - are presented. *Strategies* for the (re)organization of work are proposed.

The research project has issued a report series (RAM reports), which began in 1976 and now numbers 12 (ISSN 0349-2915) (Nos. 9 and 11 in English). Results have also been published in books and articles (see list of documentation).

RAM:2 Project
The RAM:2 project began in 1982 and was completed in 1986. It constituted an expansion as well as a further penetration of the research carried out within the RAM:1 project. Primarily, the working environment was studied for a new technique variable, the microcomputer system. The program was divided into three problem areas, which are partly interwoven. In studying these, we also analyzed the work and its characteristics and the organizational structure.

* Data Processing and Communication Structure at Work Sites
* Data Processing and Leadership/Collaboration
* Analyses of the Interaction between:
    - Data Processing - Working Conditions - Health
    - Data Processing - Working Conditions - Life Styles outside "Work".

The research was structured into sub-projects, which encompassed two professional groups using microcomputer-based equipment in their work:

* Secretaries and Word Processing System
* Engineers and CAD/CAM-systems.

Empirical results have been published in books, articles, and reports. In 1986 the book "Psychosocial Work Environment and Computers" was published (in Swedish). /2/ An English version has not yet been published but negotiations are proceeding.

2. SOME EMPIRICAL FINDINGS - USE OF DISPLAY TERMINALS

Comparisons were made between *terminal users and non-users*. In 1986, most of the staff use terminals, but at the time of our investigation there were many non-users. Only statistically established differences are presented below - relevant background factors were held under control. In general, terminal users were more dissatisfied with some aspects of the psychosocial work environment, including questions of democracy at the work place. They experienced more frustration on the job. They viewed their work pace as too irregular, too dependent on other people, and too high during certain periods. Terminal users to a lesser degree saw the positive sides of promotions at work.

Work environment aspects regarding work pace, staffing, the demands for efficiency, etc. are the most dominant areas in which terminal users expressed a higher level of dissatisfaction than non-users. But the picture crumbles when sex is taken into account. For both sexes, "terminal-sensitive" areas of the work revolve around its content, with particular emphasis on the degree of independence and degree of meaningfulness in the content. Among women, however, terminal users are more positive to their work content than are non-users. The opposite is true for men. Moreover, calls for an end to discrimination between the sexes and the process of computerization have often collided up to this point. This was the case at Company 1 in the project (the Postal Giro Service) where the content of women's work was "hollowed out". /3/ The relation between sexual equality and computerization is discussed in Bradley 1983 and 1985 /4, 5/ and is seen as one of the crucial questions for the future.

Terminal users point to a number of changes in their work environment resulting from computerization - increased demands put on them (the buffer role intensified), more irregular work pace, increased demands for attentiveness, accuracy, and responsibility at the job.

With the new technology, it became possible to accelerate the rate at which work was being performed and material processed. At the same time, the number of contacts, such as with customers, was also increasing. However, it appears to be highly difficult, if not impossible, to translate this increased speed in the disposal of the matters at hand into an enhanced quality of personal contacts or into more time available to be spent with customers. As the work pace at the terminal speeds up, it tends to set the pace for other functions. In addition, as demands from a person's surroundings rise, these demands may be successively integrated by the individual and finally internalized.

Health considerations were also included. The terminal users had more difficulties with general bodily pains and headaches than did the non-users. Among the younger group, terminal users claimed to suffer periodic eye troubles, and even nervous complications during their leisure time. Other workers were less often afflicted with these conditions.

If groups with *different lengths of experience* of work at the terminal are compared, it is the terminal users who have spent less time in front of the display terminal that are the most positive. However, from these findings, it is difficult to reach any conclusions about long-term use. Among women, it is those with longer experience that are more positive to the work content itself.

Groups that sit for *differing lengths of daily terminal use* have also been compared. One risk of long daily use is the negative effect on the user's ability to receive both formal and informal information at the job. But those who work longer hours worry less about making mistakes, in the light of their increased opportunity to correct any that might arise. They feel that the new computer system has reduced the risk of error in their work. Nevertheless, more demands pour in from all over the company. This situation we define as the increased "buffer role".

The findings listed above are based on direct comparisons between mean values. We analysed a number of *stress factors*. Employees with longer hours of daily terminal use more often feel that they receive too little information, that the possibilities for promotion and individual development and growth in the work are too small as are the demands for training/continuing training. They also more often feel imprisoned by their work situation, isolated from other people during working hours, and oppressed by the physical demands - on their back, muscles, and eyes. On the other hand, those with longer hours of daily terminal use feel more secure at work (greater job security).

Comparisons were also made between employees with various degrees of *contact with the general public*. In general, employees with regular or occasional contact with the public showed higher degrees of satisfaction with their work tasks, but were also more discontent with their wage levels and with the effects of the buffer role. In the comparisons between the various groups of terminal users, the more positive aspects of their work situation vanished leaving their less positive attitudes to the buffer role, and to the work pace/work load.

If the employees were asked directly about the effects on the work environment of the terminal system and the computer system in general, along with questions on democracy etc., the group of employees with public contacts felt that the buffer role was being strengthened and that their salary conditions were somewhat worsened. Terminal users with more public contact also felt that computers had reduced their influence over their own work and in the company as a whole.

These analyses showed that from a psychosocial perspective of the work environment and working life, it is of vital importance to avoid intense and continuous work at the display terminal.

Other similar analyses have been performed. Comparisons have been made between various occupational groups, e.g. between secretaries and other female employees. Various types of systems which involve use of display terminals have been studied, e.g. query systems and dialogue systems. A special analysis has focused on differences between men and women when relevant variables are taken into account, e.g. variables related to job, family, and private life. All these analyses are presented and discussed in a separate chapter in my book. /2/ Also discussed are the successive action strategies adopted at the company together with our follow-up of them.

3. ACTIONS - INFORMATION TECHNOLOGY AND LIFE AT WORK

3.1 Desires and Requirements - from Theory to Implementation

When the RAM project started in 1974, I designed a theoretical model of the relationship between computer technology and work environment (Figure 1). For a more detailed version of this model I refer to earlier publications in the selected list of documentation, e.g. /6, 1/.

Work environment is primarily studied from a psychosocial perspective and the concept has been given a broad meaning. It is linked to the idea that environment has an influence upon the individual at three main levels: the level of society, the level of organization, and the level of the individual. The factors on the different levels are regarded as interacting. Problems studied

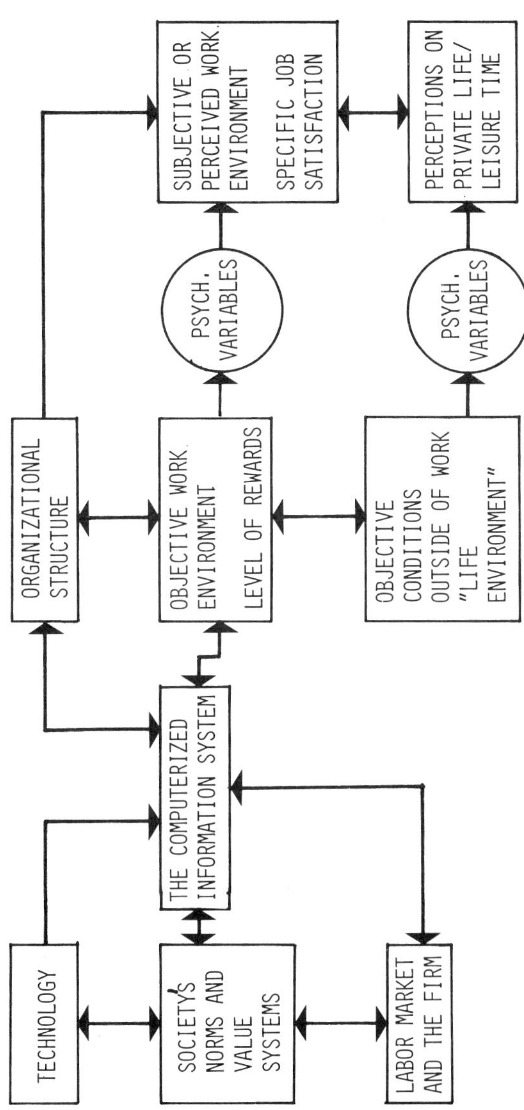

FIGURE 1
Theoretical model of the relationship between computer technology and work environment. Source: Bradley 1977, 1981 /6, 9/.

in the project include objective, structural working conditions (especially at the organizational level), as well as experiences and attitudes related to work.

Some concepts of the model can be briefly commented on, relating to stress, work load, and job satisfaction.

* Goals of labor market and of company	Efficiency
* Norms and values of society	"The rational society"
* Computerized information system	Aids to rationalization
* Technology	Power of mind and muscle become replaced by machines, during the pursuit of efficiency

For the theoretical modelling (process between Fig. 1 and Fig. 2) and for definitions of theoretical concepts and empirical indexes I refer to /2/. Figure 2 is a crude *causal model*. The variables are items (background data) and indexes related to health effects. Variables are evaluated by regression analysis to reveal, how they influence health complaints (see the special symbols, x, *, +, =). Such analyses, together with many other analyses as in section 2, help to formulate general desires and demands (section 3.2). These vary and must be revised as technology develops.

Different causal models apply for women and men. RAM report No. 12 includes the path analyses. /7/ Analyses of differences between men and women prove the need of reform activities and new technology especially designed for women. /5/

The general demands on work environment that we derived from our research include these factors (see section 3.2).

3.2 Desires and Requirements as to the Psychosocial Work Environment

There are many ways in which to present wishes and demands for the working environment in the context of computerization:

- *General demands and wishes* for an acceptable working environment, along with group-oriented demands for e.g. specific branches.

- *Check lists* for support and new suggestions for work environment issues to be considered during computerization.

- *Questionnaires* or interviews to evaluate planned computer systems or systems already in operation.

General Demands on the Psychosocial Work Environment

* Working pace
* Influence
* Education/Training
* Human contact and communication
* Information
* Intermediate position/buffer role
* Physical strain
* Replaceability
* Extrinsic equality
* Intrinsic equality.

OBJECTIVE WORK ENVIRONMENT ---->

Work-related background variables

- Time per day at the display terminal x *
- Contact with customers etc. x *
- Dependency on the DP-system x +
- Supervision
- Income = +
- Time of employment within the occupation +

Individual-related background variables

- Sex
- Age x =
- School background x
- Pre-school children

SUBJECTIVE WORK ENVIRONMENT (INDEXES) ---->

Psychosocial work environment

- Interesting work - meaningfulness (SIME) x
- Interesting work - human resources (SIMR) x
- Opportunities of contact with co-workers (SKONT)
- Cooperation with co-workers (SSAM) +
- Status of work (SAANS) =
- Attentiveness/responsibility (SUPPA) +

- Work pace/work load (SARBT) x = + *
- Irregular work pace/work load (SOJA)
- Intermediate position - buffer role (SBUFF)
- Wage conditions (SLÖN) *
- Opportunities for promotion (SBEFM) *

- System of promotion and reward (SBEFN) = +
- Information (SINFO) x
- Effectiveness (SEFF)

Democracy at work

- Influence and independence at work (SSJA) x +
- Work-leisure democracy (DEMAL) +
- Interest in promotion (VB)

EFFECTS

Health problems during working-hours

- Pain - general (HAV) x
- Headache (HAH) *
- Stomach trouble (HAM) +

Health problems during leisure

- Nervousness (HFN) =
- Pain - general (HFV) x
- Headache (HFA) *

FIGURE 2
Crude causal model

Psychosocial Aims during Computerization

* A *working pace* adjustable to the individual (work load per time unit).

* Fairly *even working pace*; not too dependent on the *pace of workmates and/or equipment*.

* Possibility of *influencing* structure and planning of work, and working hours such as the scheduling of breaks and hours of terminal use.

* Ensure good flow of *information* among staff, both vertically and horizontally, e.g. instructions, company policy etc.

* Special support to staff who have a "*buffer role*". Negative effects of this position in the middle of contradictory demands should be avoided or prevented.

* *Training* during paid working hours.

* *Development* on the job.

* Possibility of conferring with colleagues in order to fulfil need of *human contact* and *communication* during daily tasks.

* Reduce *physical strain* on eyes, neck, back, muscles etc.

* Opportunities of *replacement* on the job. Too easy and too difficult replaceability should be avoided. (Positions entailing too much specialization may need to be avoided.)

* Even distribution between the sexes of duties and positions, so-called *extrinsic equality*.

* New duties and functions should make use of both traditional female and male experiences, interests and values. This ensures so-called *intrinsic equality*.

* *Reward and promotion systems*, so that executives as well as colleagues find themselves in work situations that meet their own basic human needs and requirements.

3.3 Desires and Requirements - Stress Criteria

Computerization should also help to create working situations where as few individuals as possible are overstimulated or understimulated. It is the individual who ought to make this evaluation. There are both quantitative and qualitative aspects of overstimulation or understimulation. The number of tasks to be done per unit of time concerns quantity. The degree of complexity is a qualitative aspect.

A special chapter in my latest book /2/ summarizes our empirical results on stress and stress-related phenomena from all three companies. A broad theoretical model on stress and factors influencing stress is presented in this chapter.

Urgent reasons for avoiding under- and overstimulation:

* Health problems and stress

* Labour force becomes divided

* Exclusion from the mainstream of society.

Figure 3 - taken from Bradley 1979b /8/ - is meant to illustrate the reasoning above. The "model" was considered in the questionnaires used in the field studies. Both poles should be avoided according to experiences from "stress at work"-research /10, 11/.

Demands and wishes for the computerized work environment also affect the leisure - its content as well as form. The current definitions of the quality of life are changing. Principles for what should be paid work are already being analyzed by various pressure groups in Sweden. The aim is to provide a basis for political decisions.

Overstimulation		Understimulation
Too much <-----		-----> Too little

* Work load
  Information
  Personal contacts

* Demands for training
  Demands for development/promotion
  Conflicting demands
  Demands for physical capacity

* Variety in work
  Complexity
  Influence on work tasks
  Spatial variation
  Responsibility
  Concentration/attention

* Authority and power
  Consultation, team work
  Replaceability

FIGURE 3
Desires and Requirements - Stress Criteria

3.4 Designing and Redesigning of Roles at Work

Our results from different phases of the research process give support that during the computerization process, it is important to focus on two things: horizontal and vertical differentiation of tasks. Work can be reorganized in various ways:

* Design/redesign of organizational *structure*.
* Introduce into the chain of production other work tasks which are on the *same* level.
* Introduce planning and control tasks that are now on *another* (higher) level.
* Analyze *whether* any tasks should be done by machine.

* Analyze *which* tasks should be done by machines and which by people.
* Make clear the *goal*/goals of the work organization.

These six strategies are supported by theories on overstimulation and understimulation, by empirical research on alienation processes at the lower levels in the company, and by critical analyses of the managerial role.

3.5 Action Strategies - an Overview

Figure 4 is a picture of action strategies. It is based on research by many people in Sweden during the last twelve years /6, 12, 13, 14, 15/. It shows actions at the various levels: national level, which is the trunk, company level, which is one branch, and individual level, which is another branch. Technology is still another branch. All these factors are interacting or ought to interact (according to our theoretical model on work environment).

This picture (originally in colour) was shown for the first time at the conference Work With Display Units held in Stockholm in May 1986. It was also shown at a conference in Vancouver in August the same year (Second International Symposium on Human Factors in Organizational Design and Management). On both occasions the audience responded with interested comments - maybe because it was simple, but yet described a complex phenomenon. I invite all readers of this article to forward comments and questions on this tree, its branches, and sub-branches (address: The University of Stockholm).

What are the experiences in other countries?
What activities in the branches of this tree are going on in various countries?
What knowledge do we have now of how these factors interact?
Main interplay and interactions?
Main controversies and contradictions?
Are there any branches or sub-branches that we have not yet identified?
Where do we need more research?
Which is the most urgent matter for international collaboration?
At what level and/or branch must we collaborate?

Can we work together and supplement our national trees by an international tree of action? Such a tree would show what is going on in many countries. We can then identify the strategies of international actions. Our aim should be to strive for an information society that could be depicted as a tree of fruits for us all to share.

4. THE ALLOCATION PROBLEM

Computerization of work leads to the general *question of allocation*. It all depends upon *what we have to allocate* and *how we value it*. International competition compels rationalization, and computerization is one of the most important tools today. Whether seen in a national or an international perspective, computerization poses these questions:

- Allocation/distribution of profit
  * among sectors within a country
  * among industrial countries
  * among industrial and third-world countries
- Allocation of work (shortening of working hours, division of labour, etc.)
- Allocation of leisure
- Allocation of compulsory citizen services (paid or unpaid)
- Allocation of production and reproduction.

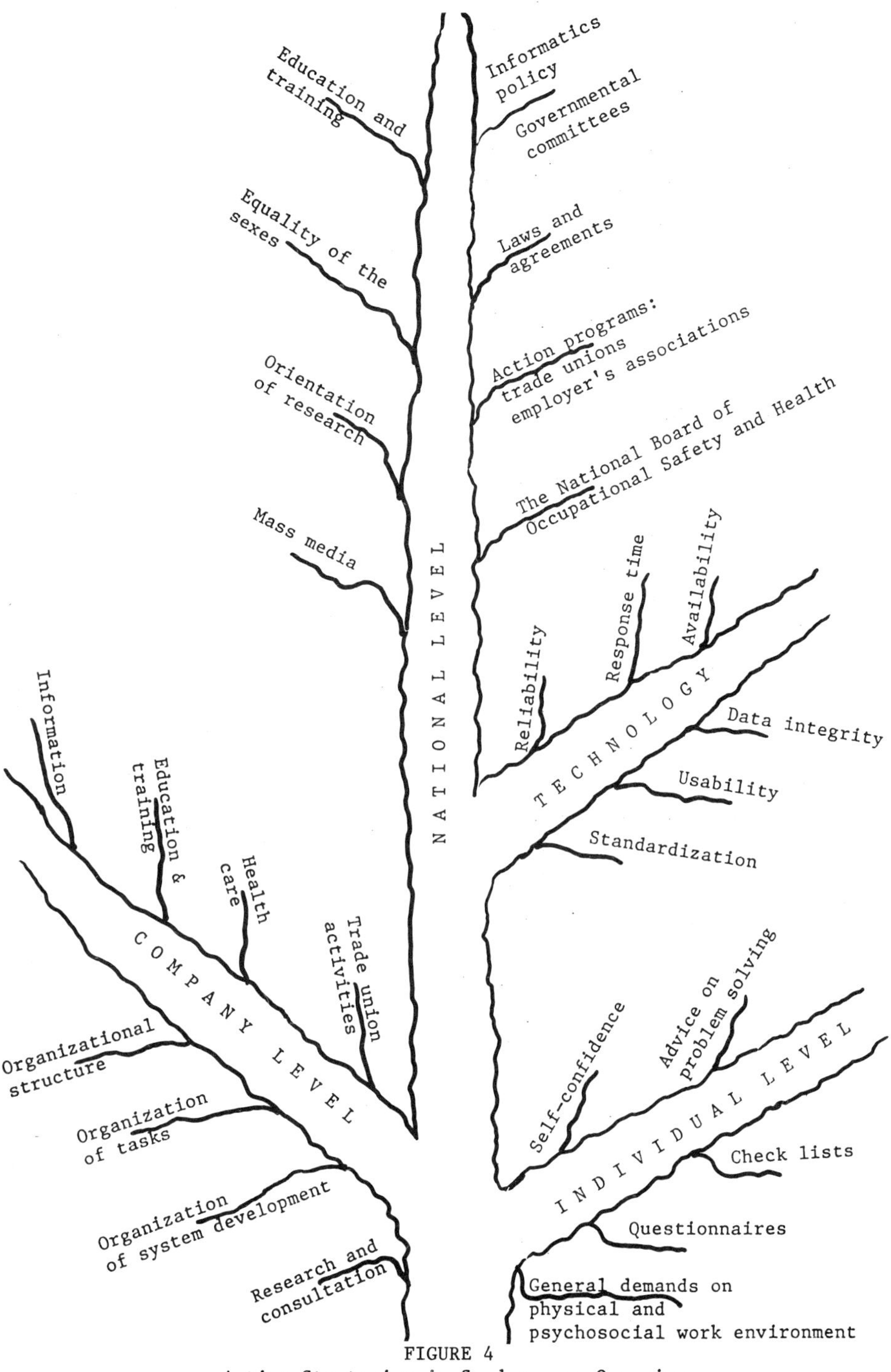

FIGURE 4
Action Strategies in Sweden - an Overview
(© Gunilla Bradley 1986)

SELECTED LIST OF DOCUMENTATION (Works marked with * are in Swedish)

/1/ Bradley, G. (1979a). Computerization and Some Psychosocial Factors in the Work Environment. Proceedings of the Conference on Reducing Occupational Stress. New York, 1977. NIOSH Publication No. 78-140, pp. 30-40. U.S. Department of Health, Education, and Welfare.

/2/ Bradley, G. (1986)*. Psykosocial arbetsmiljö och datorer (Psychosocial Work Environment and Computers). Stockholm: Akademilitteratur. ISBN 91-7410-314-8.

/3/ Bradley, G. & Nilsson, I. (1977)*. Arbetsmiljö och datorisering. (Work Environment and Computerization). A summary of Reports 1 and 2. University of Stockholm. RAM report No. 4 (ISSN 0349-2915).

/4/ Bradley, G. (1983). Effects of Computerization on Work Environment and Health: From a Perspective of Equality Between Sexes. Occupational Health Nursing Journal, November 1985, pp. 35-39.

/5/ Bradley, G. (1985). Computers and Work Content, Work Load and Stress - Analyses and Women's Participation Strategies. In: A Olerup, L Schneider & E Monod (Eds.) Women, Work and Computerization: Opportunities and Disadvantages, pp. 249-263, Proceedings of an IFIP-conference 1984. Amsterdam: Elsevier Science Publishers B.V.

/6/ Bradley, G. (1977)*. Datateknik, Arbetsliv och Kommunikation (Computer Technology, Working Life and Communication). The Swedish Committee for Future Oriented Research. Stockholm: Liber förlag/Forskningsrådsnämnden.

/7/ RAM report No. 1-12 (No. 9 and 11 in English), ISSN 0349-2915

/8/ Bradley, G. (1979b)*. Yrkesroller och livsmiljö. (Working Roles and Quality of Life). Stockholm: Wahlström & Widstrand. ISBN 91-46-13409-3.

/9/ Bradley, G. (1981)*. Arbetsmiljö och Terminaler (Work Environment and Display Terminals. Analyses of terminal systems - psychosocial aspects of the work environment). Stockholm: The Swedish Work Environment Fund/ Liber/Allmänna förlaget. ISBN 91-38-06353-0.

/10/ Frankenhaeuser, M. (1974)*. Stress, toleransgränser och livskvalitet. Stockholm: Psykologiska institutionen. Rapport nr 1.

/11/ Levi, L. (1972). Stress and Distress in Response to Psychosocial Stimuli, Acta Medica Scandinavica, suppl. 528. Stockholm: Almqvist & Wiksell.

/12/ Dockerty, P. et al (1977)*. Hur man lyckas med systemutveckling. Stockholm: EFI.

/13/ Ehn, P. & Sandberg, Å. (1979)*. Företagsstyrning och löntagarmakt. Stockholm: Prisma i samarbete med Arbetslivscentrum.

/14/ Göransson, B. (ed.) (1978)*. Ideologi och systemutveckling. Lund: Studentlitteratur.

/15/ Hedberg, B. (1978). Using computerized information system to design better organizations and jobs. Stockholm: Arbetslivscentrum, Working paper no. 04.

WORK WITH DISPLAY UNITS 86
B. Knave and P.-G. Widebäck (eds.)

ON THE USER'S OPINION ABOUT SYSTEMS DESIGN

Vincent ROGARD

Laboratoire Communication et Travail, Université PARIS-NORD, Avenue J.B. Clément - 93430 VILLETANEUSE, France

Historical analysis of design methods for business computer systems show an increasingly active role of future users. Today, the design of the software, the choice of the terminal and the content of training sessions may partially depend on the user's point of view. According to this fact project manager's needs to precise what they call a "user" because they have to choose participants for project committee.

This paper deal with a research which is a little part of a long-term project conducted in one of the major french bank company. The main purpose of this project is to promote better understanding and ccoperation between designers and users of computer systems by increasing mutual comprehension.

This research aims to show that the hierarchical position and organizational role of the user affects the judgments which are making concerning the same computer-aided work station.

1. METHOD

1.1. Subjects

Study is based on bank employees using daily the same teleprocessing terminal. They had one of the following three organizational role :

- management
- customer relations
- counter/book-keeping.

They were also classified as higher or lower level employees.

Since nineteen seventy eight, all the subjects used a financial teleprocessing terminal comprising a keyboard, screen and printer.

The <u>keyboard</u> is used for capturing data, selecting functions and for presenting system feed back.

The plasma <u>screen</u> displays the information currently being processed, in addition to system messages. Having a limiting capacity of six lines of forty characters each.

The top loading <u>printer</u> prints three types of document : standard book-keeping and administrative forms, details of the financial transactions and the daily account total.

1.2. Choice of the banks branches

The study was undertaken for a bank having 110 branches in Paris and its suburbs. Twelve of them were choosen as representative according to the following criteria :

- the number of terminals
- the number of employees
- the number of customers.

In each of these twelve branches we had choose three subjects. The first was a manager or assistant manager, the second was an employee in charge of relation with customers (private or company) and the third was a counter/book-keeping clerk. Finally, thirty six subjects were interviewed (12 per role), amongst which were sixteen higher level employees.

1.3. Recording of the judgments

A standardized interview including forty five items and lasting approximatively forty minutes was undertaken in the work place in order to know the opinion of subjects on five main themes :

- Computerization of the bank : on this point we would like to know how the subject react to the progressive computerization of his profession and more precisely of his daily work

- The ergonomic design of the hardware

- The ergonomic design of the software : we ask subjects to make judgments about easibility of use of software, screen/page organization, response time...

- The reliability of the teleprocessing network : this theme is relate to the perceived frequency of the incidents, the lenght of the breakdown but also the reactions of people in such cases.

- The training about the learning of terminal and software.

2. RESULTS

The interview transcriptions were analysed by two independant judges. The principal tendancies observed for each of the themes are presented below :

2.1. Computerization in the bank

Perceived by everybody as unavoidable, the phenomena was judged favourably. However the book-keeping/counter clerks placed greater emphasis than the others on the constraints associated with computer. They similarly stressed that teleprocessing had abolished certain tedious tasks such as the daily totting-up, but it had also resulted in a very strong dependance on the system (returning to the old procedures during a breakdown appeared impossible). In many cases, book-keeping/counter clerks were stopped during an operation because of a failure in the teleprocessing network and they were obliged to phone to a technician.

2.2. The ergonomic design of the hardware

Large differences were observed depending upon organizational role of the user :

Management : All the interviewees mentionned that the terminal was either satisfactory or that they had no particular opinion. Managers or assistant managers seems to be not concerned by the ergonomic design of the terminal.

Customer relations : A small number of these employees made three criticisms : legibility of the screen characters, the space occupied by the terminal, the slowness of the printer.

Counter/book-keeping : All these employees indicated one or more of the following difficulties : legibility, space occupied by the terminal, slowness of the printer, visual fatigue, auditory fatique, heat from the screen, heat from the control unit placed near to the clerk's legs, paper jamming in the printer.

2.3. The ergonomic design of the software

The programs were generally judged to be easy to use. The criticims concerning the programs were only made by the customer relations employees and more particularly by the counter/book-keeping clerks. They essentially included : overloading of some pages with unnecessary information, unclear coding of certain information, various operational ambigutïes (e.g. searching for a customer with a composed name).

2.4. The reliability of the teleprocessing network

Although the lack of reliability of resulting in frequent breakdown was unanimously deplored, the attitudes varied as to what information would be desirable. While the counter/book-keeping clerks wished to know the origin and foreseable duration of the failure, the other employees expressed desinterest.

2.5. Training

The training requirements were :

- mastering of the operating modes, procedures and incidents by the user

- knowledge of the bank computer system, thus permitting a global understanding of the concepts employed : description of the data bases, relational plan of the data, etc...

The latter requirement was only put forward by the higher level employees. The training requirements of the other employees concerned exclusively the mastering of the terminal and knowledge of the available transactions.

3. DISCUSSION

Results show that differences between the judgments of employees concern mainly :

- ergonomic design of the hardware

- information desirable in case of network breakdown

- training requirements.

For a part, differences on the ergonomic design of the hardware can be explain by the V.D.U. time of the three kinds of employees. In fact, V.D.U. is the principal means of work for the counter/book-keeping clerk, less so for the customer relation person, whereas the manager spent very little time (ten minutes per day). Consequently counter/book-keeping clerks are more able to feel the effects of fatigue or heat.

Our results collected with bank employees working in similar places and using the same financial terminal show that we need a more precise knowledge of user's characteristics. In our study, classification of users was only based on organizational role and hierarchical position of employees. In fact, these two informations about employees embrace a great diversity of factors which are probably playing on the user opinion. A better understanding of these factors seems to be need if we want to be able to list the informations about future users likely to be relevant for a project manager. Such work is going on in the bank company where the study was realised. The final purpose of such research could be to construct a tool-easy to use by computer project manager- for understanding and knowledge of user constraints.

WORK WITH DISPLAY UNITS 86
B. Knave and P.-G. Wideback (eds.)

IDENTIFICATION AND PREVENTION OF WORK-RELATED MENTAL AND PSYCHO-SOMATIC DISORDERS AMONG TWO CATEGORIES OF VDU USERS

Irma Wright, M.D.

BACKGROUND

Since 8 years one of the health care teams at Volvo Gothenburg has made a systematic analysis of work environment and health among our employees.
The employees in our investigations represent a variety of trades and occupations, but they are mostly white-collar workers because of the specific conditions where we work. Around 900 white-collar workers and 150 blue-collar workers are included in the present study. 293 of the employees work with VDU:s. The employees investigated make up 140 work-groups of 2-35 persons in each, the majority being 5-15. Several work-groups together form whole departments of 50-70 employees under a department manager with a number of group managers under him. Around 2/3 are men, 1/6 are managers, 1/5 work part-time. The average age is around 40. The majority have gone to high-school.

MAIN OBJECTIVES

The investigation has four main objectives:

1. To examine and assess the health, general well-being and adjustment to work of individual employees and to adopt corrective measures where necessary. The measures may either be medical or consist of modification of physical and/or psychosocial aspects of the work environment.

2. To map out and analyze the work environment of work-groups and departments by combining medical, social and technical analysis.

3. To construct a program aimed at eliminating unsatisfactory aspects of the work environment. The program should make it possible for the group itself to take remedial action.

4. To carry out research on the effects of the work environment on individuals and groups and thereby to identify risk factors.

METHODS OF WORK

Our investigation focuses on individual work-groups. It is based on voluntary participation. So far 80-100% of the employees invited to participate have done so. The method of work is divided into 8 steps:

Irma Wright, M.D.
AB Volvo, S-405 08 Göteborg

1. Information to the group about the investigation.

2. Questionnaire consisting of general information (sex, age, education, length of employment, etc.) and the employee's attitude to four main areas: The physical work environment, his/her own health, psychological stress and job satisfaction. When relevant, questions concerning the introduction of computer aids are added.

3. Personal interview by occupational nurse, physician, or social worker. The interview lasts 30-45 minutes and is strictly confidential.

4. Medical check-up, offered to all above the age of 40 and to others where illness is suspected or who for other reasons request it.

5. Assessment of the physical work environment when questionnaire and interviews indicate problems in this area.

6. Reporting back to manager and work-group of the group-results. These are based partly on the profiles revealed in the questionnaire, and partly on the personal interviews. Individuals are never exposed personally. The whole process is built on confidence between the employee and the health department.

7. Remedial program if problems are found. Measures can be taken at three levels:

    a. the individual level

    b. the group level

    c. the overall organizational level

8. Follow up, a few years later.

FACTOR DIVISION

A statistical factor analysis has been carried out the aim of which is to discover connections between the various questions in the questionnaire and group them accordingly into 25 factors. In this way, increased reliability is gained. It also makes for an easier presentation of the results. In figure 1 you can see the individual factors ranked according to their absolute weight, where 4 is "good" and 1 is "bad". As can be seen, freedom from regulations ranks the highest and tiredness/listlessness plus smoking the lowest among our employees.

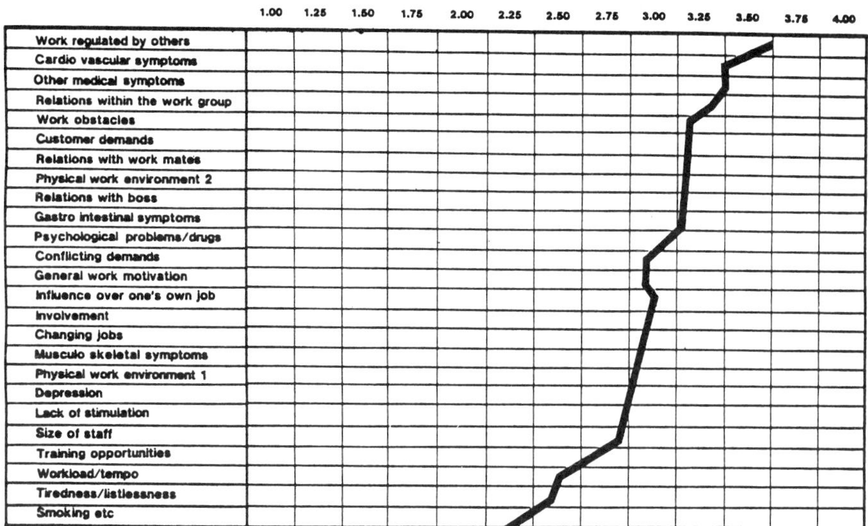

FIGURE 1: RANKING ORDER OF FACTORS N=900

Further analysis shows that the questions we ask cover four main areas (factor groups): Physical work environment, medical symptoms, psychological stress and job satisfaction. Within each of these, sub-factors can be recognized (Figure 2).

PHYSICAL ENVIRONMENT	A1 Physical work environment 1
	A2 Physical work environment 2
MEDICAL SYMPTOMS	B1 Gastro-intestinal symptoms
	B2 Musculo-skeletal symptoms
	B3 Psychological problems/drugs
	B4 Depression
	B5 Cardio-vascular symptoms
	B6 Other medical symptoms
	B7 Smoking etc
PSYCHOLOGICAL STRESS	C1 Work obstacles
	C2 Conflicting demands
	C3 Workload/tempo
	C4 Work regulated by others
	C5 Involvement
	C6 Lack of stimulation
	C7 Customer demands
JOB SATISFACTION	D1 General work-motivation
	D2 Relations with boss
	D3 Relations with work-mates
	D4 Relations within the work-group
	D5 Influence over one's own job
	D6 Tiredness/listlessness
	D7 Changing jobs
	D8 Training opportunities
	D9 Size of staff

FIGURE 2

In order to simplify the presentation of the results to the individual work-group, we refer to the means of the total number of 900 employees examined as the norm, and call each mean 100%. The work-groups are then described in percentage deviation from this norm (Figure 3). Each country and each company has its own social climate and culture: What we refer to is the norm for the areas of Volvo Gothenburg in which we work.

					NEGATIVE							POSITIVE			
		65	70	75	80	85	90	95	100	105	110	115	120	125	130
PHYSICAL ENVIRONMENT	A1 Physical work environment 1														
	A2 Physical work environment 2														
MEDICAL SYMPTOMS	B1 Gastro-intestinal symptoms														
	B2 Musculo-skeletal symptoms														
	B3 Psychological problems/drugs														
	B4 Depression														
	B5 Cardio-vascular symptoms														
	B6 Other medical symptoms														
	B7 Smoking etc														
PSYCHOLOGICAL STRESS	C1 Work obstacles														
	C2 Conflicting demands														
	C3 Workload/tempo														
	C4 Work regulated by others														
	C5 Involvement														
	C6 Lack of stimulation														
	C7 Customer demands														
JOB SATISFACTION	D1 General work-motivation														
	D2 Relations with boss														
	D3 Relations with work-mates														
	D4 Relations within the work-group														
	D5 Influence over one's own job														
	D6 Tiredness/listlessness														
	D7 Changing jobs														
	D8 Training opportunities														
	D9 Size of staff														

Figure 3: REACTION ON WORK ENVIRONMENT

THE WORK GROUPS STUDIED

In this way a thorough analysis was made of four selected work-groups in an Insurance Department a year before and a year after the introduction of VDUs (in 1978 and 1980 respectively).
A further follow-up study was carried out three years later (1983-1984). The four work-groups can be divided into two categories according to time spent at the VDU.

The extensive users (N=21, women only, average age 35) deal with administration, economic planning and customer service. 85% spend more than 3 hours a day at the screen, a third of them as much as 7 to 8 hours a day.

The limited users (N=18, a mixture of men and women, average age 37) adjust accident claims, exchange damaged cars and carry out technical follow-up. 85% of these spend less than 2 hours a day at the screen.

Within each of these categories, it was found that, in addition to spending similar amounts of time at the VDU, problems were similar, working conditions and job content were similar, and similar skills were required.

RESULTS

The 1978 study showed that the category who were to become limited VDU users suffered from a high degree of stress.
This was due to overwhelming customer demands, incompatible demands, a heavy work load and high tempo. The result was depressive disorders, feelings of psychological insufficiency and gastrointestinal troubles.
Other typical symptoms were tiredness, listlessness and slow unwinding (Figure 4).

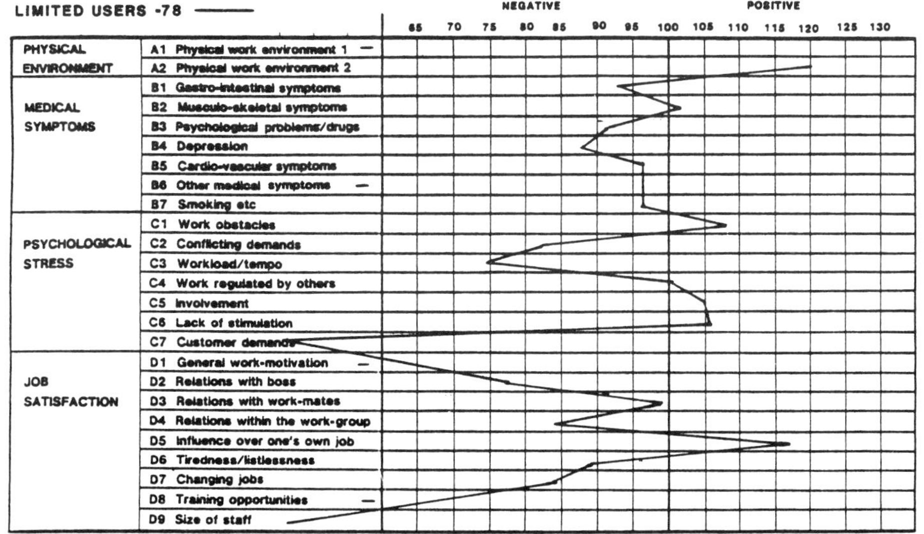

FIGURE 4: REACTION ON WORK ENVIRONMENT- LIMITED USERS -78

The health care team and the personnel together sought ways of combating these problems at the time of the introduction of the VDUs - and even through their introduction.

The result was not merely improved work organisation and increased output. The 1980 study also showed significantly reduced stress levels, reduced work load and lower tempo. Demands on the groups by customers and orhers had reached tolerable levels and relations had improved dramatically (Figure 5).

Our last analysis in 1983-84 showed extraordinarily high job satisfaction, with a further increase since 1980. The medical records showed a significant drop in depression, psychological insufficiency and fewer gastrointestinal complaints in 1980 than in 1978, an improvement that was sustained in -84, -85. Motivation has increased, work has become more varied and more interesting but calls for concentration and a sense of responsibility (Figure 6).

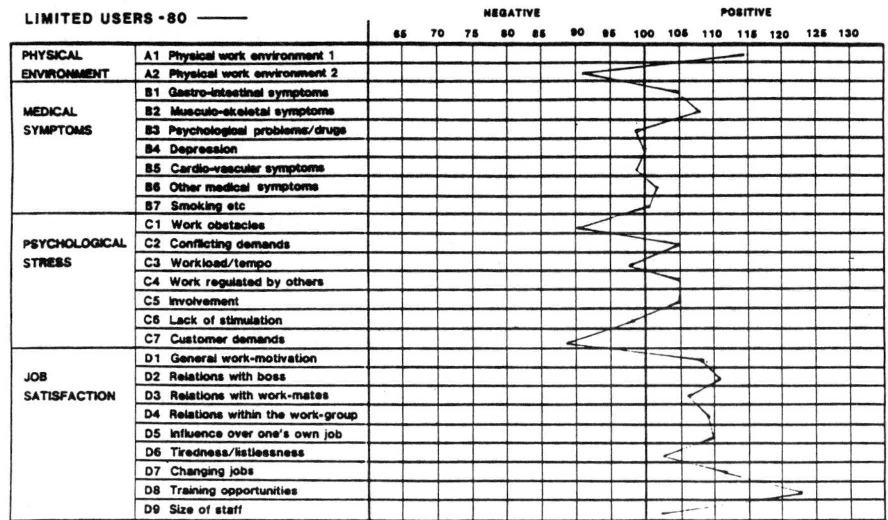

FIGURE 5: REACTION ON WORK ENVIRONMENT - LIMITED USERS -80

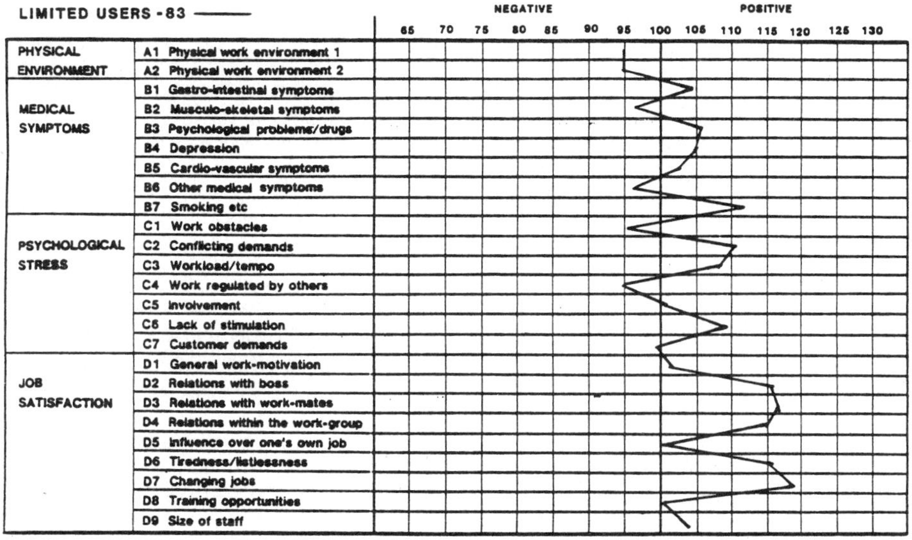

LIMITED USERS -83
NEGATIVE
POSITIVE
65 70 75 80 85 90 95 100 105 110 115 120 125 130
PHYSICAL ENVIRONMENT
A1 Physical work environment 1
A2 Physical work environment 2
MEDICAL SYMPTOMS
B1 Gastro-intestinal symptoms
B2 Musculo-skeletal symptoms
B3 Psychological problems/drugs
B4 Depression
B5 Cardio-vascular symptoms
B6 Other medical symptoms
B7 Smoking etc
PSYCHOLOGICAL STRESS
C1 Work obstacles
C2 Conflicting demands
C3 Workload/tempo
C4 Work regulated by others
C5 Involvement
C6 Lack of stimulation
C7 Customer demands
JOB SATISFACTION
D1 General work-motivation
D2 Relations with boss
D3 Relations with work-mates
D4 Relations within the work-group
D5 Influence over one's own job
D6 Tiredness/listlessness
D7 Changing jobs
D8 Training opportunities
D9 Size of staff

FIGURE 6: REACTION ON WORK ENVIRONMENT - LIMITED USERS -83

In the 1978 study, the extensive VDU users were shown to be suffering from low job involvement, lack of stimulation and lack of influence over the job (Figure 7).

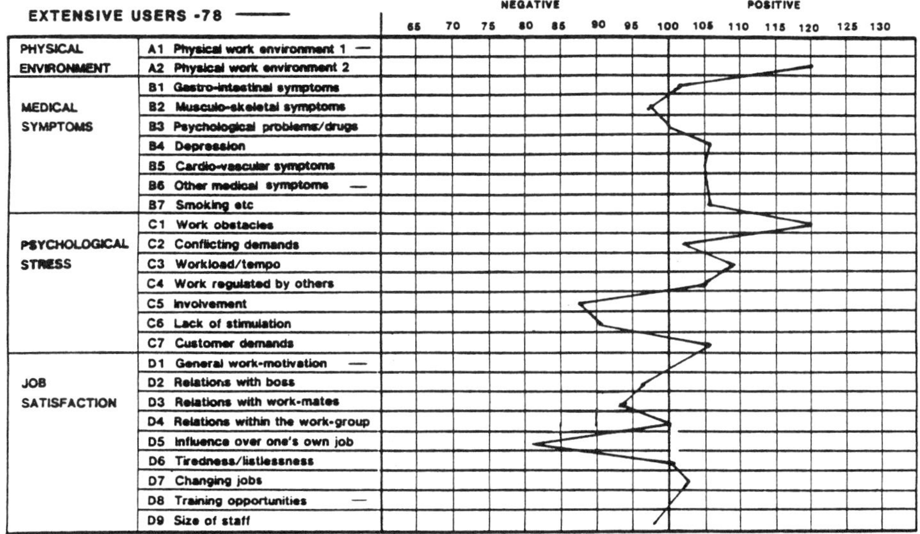

FIGURE 7: REACTION ON WORK ENVIRONMENT - EXTENSIVE USERS -78

Many worked part-time with home as their primary interest. However, some young women wanted to advance and were given the opportunity when the VDUs were introduced a year later. The whole organisational change was carried out in consultation with the staff. Job rotation and futher education were suggested by the health care team and were partly implemented. The follow-up studies show that this category have a positive attitude to the VDUs as improving the quality and quantity of their jobs and reducing the work load for the individual. But stimulation and involvement are still low and influence over the job has not increased (Figure 8 and Figure 9).

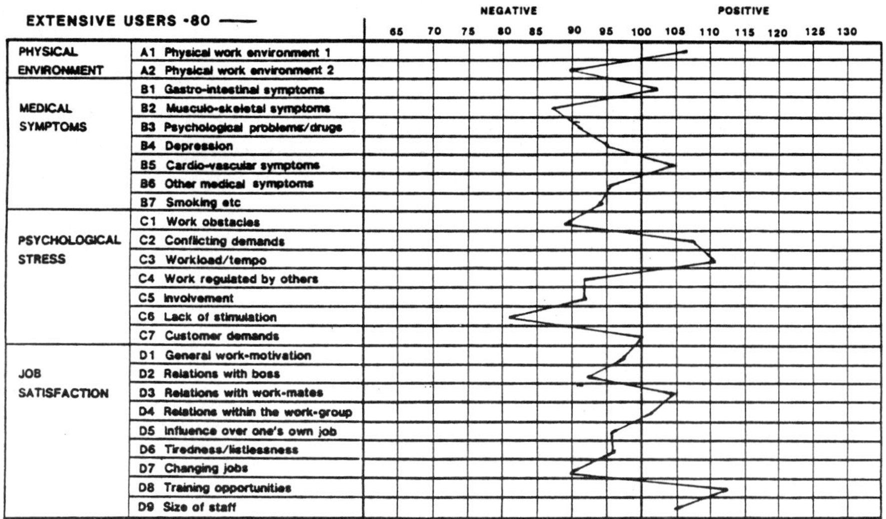

FIGURE 8: REACTION ON WORK ENVIRONMENT - EXTENSIVE USERS -80

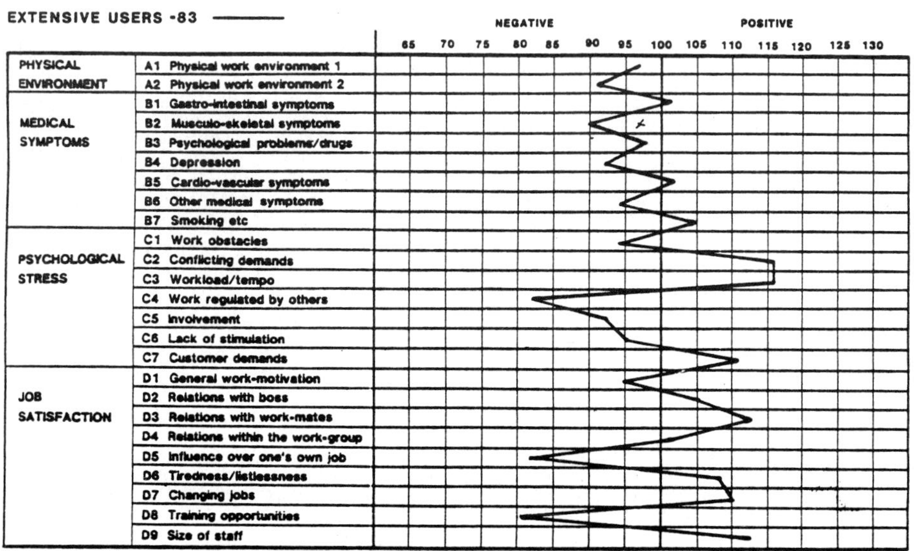

FIGURE 9: REACTION ON WORK ENVIRONMENT - EXTENSIVE USERS -83

Some find their jobs too simple and monotonous and restricted by the computers. The jobs are demanding and responsible, however, and the groups enjoy going to work. Depression has increased somewhat. Psychological insufficiency and psychosomatic symptoms remained largely unchanged over the period studied but tend to increase.

Worry over health hazards has increased for the extensive VDU users, whereas it has decreased over time for the limited users. These worries are connected especially with 'radiation' and ergonomic problems (mostly eye-strain).
Eye-strain and headaches are now twice as common here as among the limited users. This reflects findings in our larger studies where a consistent correlation is seen between time spent in front of the VDU and eye-strain and headaches, as well as neck and muscular pain. The physiotherapist and safety engineer have over the years taken a number of corrective measures in the physical work environment and in ergonomics.
For the extensive VDU users, musculoskeletal symptoms have increased slightly over the period studies, whereas they have remained constant for the limited users. Absenteeism, which is low in both groups, is, however, higher among the extensive VDU users than among the limited users.

A conscious effort has been made to keep the more interesting work tasks for man and transfer the simple ones to the computer. Thus, for the unit as a whole, there has been a reduction in the number of simple work tasks. The introduction of the VDU has not hampered the employees´ use of their work skills.
Compared with the average office unit in our larger studies, the pecture for the groups reported on here is one of better social relations, better job satisfaction and less psychological stress. There is no difference, however, in general health.

OTHER FINDINGS

1. Tiredness and listlessness decreased significantly for the limited users as did the tendency to change jobs. Small changes occurred in positive direction for the extensive users.

2. Social relations improved particularly for the limited users through better work organisation and leadership.

3. Influence over one´s own job decreased somewhat for both categories.

4. Improved quality of work especially for the extensive users.

5. Increased amount of work possible for both groups.

6. Customer and other demands now at reasonable level for both groups.

7. Risk for monotony for the extensive users who also have fairly high rates of headache and eye-strain.

8. Almost all enjoyed going to work.

CONCLUSIONS

Introducing computers, or changing the systems of already existing ones, gives us a unique chance to improve the total work environment, provided that an adequate analysis is made beforehand of individual needs, work requirements, work content and work load. A crucial role is also played by user participation in systems design, the way leadership is exercised, social relations, and opportunities for futher education and personal development. Time spent at the VDU should ideally not exceed four hours.
If all these factors are taken into account, it seems that one can successfully prevent mental and psychosomatic disorders.
The Company health care units can play an important part in influencing the organisation and its work design.

REFERENCES

[1] Wright, I, Wallin, L, Psychosocial Aspects of Work Environment Among White- and Blue Collar Workers, 1983
[2] Wallin, L, Wright, I, Psychosocial Aspects of the Work Environment - A Group Approach, American Journal of Occ. Medicine, 1986

WORK WITH DISPLAY UNITS 86
B. Knave and P.-G. Wideback (eds.)

COMPARISON OF WELL-BEING AMONG NON-MACHINE INTERACTIVE CLERICAL WORKERS AND FULL-TIME AND PART-TIME VDT USERS AND TYPISTS [a,b]

Jeanne M. Stellman,PhD*, Susan Klitzman, DrPH#, Gloria Gordon, PhD+ and Barry R. Snow, PhD**

School of Public Health, Columbia University, New York, N.Y., U.S.A.

INTRODUCTION

The implications of office automation for worker health and well-being are receiving increasing attention by the public and the professional community. Two growing concerns are the impact of office automation on the content and design of office jobs and the potential effects of video display terminals on user health. The currently available data is not conclusive and in some cases may even be contradictory. There is some evidence to suggest that there has been a positive effect in situations where office workers have been given control over the computer tasks, leading to an expansion of skills and increased productivity. [1] Other reports suggest that office automation has had negative effects on office jobs by leading to a narrowing of tasks, repetitive work and electronic surveillance of speed and productivity. A 1981 American study by the National Institute for Occupational Safety and Health found that clerical VDT workers reported much higher levels of stressful working conditions than did clerical workers who did not use automated equipment, for example. [2]

Similarly, conflicting findings on the link between office automation and health complaints have been reported. [See for example, 3-9.] Such conflicting reports may be partially explained by methodological difficulties, such as the fact that similar associations to those observed for VDTS may also be found with other clerical tasks.[10] Also, the health complaints of clerical workers tend to be non-specific and to be less severe than those of workers in heavier industries, making their definitive diagnosis, consistent reporting, and confirmation, difficult. The majority of the workforce at risk are relatively young women, where a considerable "healthy worker effect" can be expected. [11] Finally, much of the existing research on office work is observational and hence generally encumbered with serious methodological challenges which have been reviewed elsewhere [12,13].

The aim of this presentation is to examine health and well-being and the working environment of clerical workers with and without VDT based jobs.

[a]This research was supported by U.S. Department of Health and Human Service Grant NIMH MH34934.

[b] Parts of this article are adapted from an article of the same name currently in press in the _Journal of Occupational Behaviour_, John Wiley & Sons, Ltd., with permission of the publishers.

[*]To whom correspondence should be addressed at 117 St Johns Place, Brooklyn NY 11217; [#] Institute for Social Research, University of Michigan, Ann Arbor, Michigan, 48016;[+] Dept. of Psychology, St. Louis University, St. Louis, Missouri, 63103; [**] Dept. Behavioral Medicine, Hospital for Joint Diseases, New York, N.Y.,10003.

The data are drawn from a larger, more general study of office workers, carried out in six sites in the United States and Canada, originally designed to gather further information on the effects of physical environmental health factors on worker health and well-being. [14]

METHODS

A cross-sectional survey of 2412 non-managerial public service office workers employed at four different establishments, located in six different buildings, was carried out. Initial contact with the study populations was made through the Unions representing the employees and management cooperation was then obtained. The survey questionnaire was completed by participants, at their desks, during working hours. In one site, where the workforce was greater than 6,000 people, a representative sub-sample of 15% of the employees was identified. The overall participation rate was 86%.

The questionnaire consisted of groups of items on :

1. physical characteristics of the office
2. job characteristics
3. psychological and physical health and job satisfaction
4. demographic data

To the extent feasible, items were obtained from previous studies with measures known to be reliable. Survey research team interviews with workers, union representatives and management were also the source of items. More details on questionnaire construction and validation are available elsewhere. [14,15,16]

In this paper we report the results of analyses using single-item measures and of scales constructed to measure ergonomic stressors, visual and musculoskeletal symptoms, job demands, job satisfaction, office satisfaction, and decision-making latitude. Reliability estimates of scales were calculated for the entire sample using Cronbach's alpha as a measure of average inter-item correlation. Only those scales achieving moderate to high internal consistency (alpha > .67) and consisting of logically related items were used in the analysis. The individual items contained in the scales are described in the other publications cited above.

Full-time female clerical workers with at least six months of tenure were categorized on the basis of their reported job title and use of various office machinery, resulting in a sub-population of 1032 clerical workers. These workers could be further classified into 5 separate populations based on the extent to which they used either a VDT, a typewriter or neither office machine. These groups were: I - 'part day typists' (n=186); II - 'all day typists' (n=50); III - 'clerks' (n=363); IV - 'part-day' VDT users (n=241); V - 'all day' VDT users (n=192). 'Part day' was defined as 4 hours or less.

Results of univariate methods of analyses (frequencies, crosstabulations, correlations and ANOVA) and of regression analysis, using SPSS-X statistical analysis software, are given here. The regression method forced entry of the independent variables as two blocks comprised of the job characteristics and the physical environment variables given in figures 1 and 2. Variables were removed on the basis of their probability of F, until no further variables either meet the required significance level for entry or until no variables in the equation need to be removed, according to standard SPSS-X procedures. P values were based on the significance of F in the analyses of variance.

RESULTS

Relevant outcome variables representing physical and psychological symptoms were considered in the larger investigation. Of the various organ systems and physical problems surveyed, only eye and musculo-skeletal skeletal symptoms showed any meaningful variation within the population. They are further explored here. Job satisfaction and satisfaction with the office environment, as measured with a scale which we call "office satisfaction", are two psychosocial also considered. The results of the one-way analyses of variance on these outcomes based on occupational clasification are given in Figure 3.

'All day' VDT users exhibited significantly higher levels of visual symptoms and of musculo-skeletal complaints than did other clerical workers ($p < 0.05$), while the means for clerical workers who used a VDT for four hours or less per day fell within the ranges of other clerical workers. There was a significant difference in job satisfaction between 'all day' VDT users and typists, as well. 'Part day' VDT users were not significantly different from any other clerical group. The mean level of reported satisfaction with the office environment, as measured by the office satisfaction scale, was significantly different for 'all day' VDT operators. Again, this group exhibited significantly higher levels of complaints than each of the other groups, the differences with all but the 'all day' typists achieving statistical significance at the 0.05% level.

Mean levels of selected job characteristics and characteristics of the physical environment and the significance of inter-group differences were calculated. The data are presented in Figures 1 and 2, where the characteristics have been divided into two groups representing intrinsic job characteristics and characteristics of the physical environment as reported by the participants. The same direction of results was obtained for each of the job characteristics given in Figure 1: 'all day' VDT users report the highest mean levels of negative workplace characteristics, such as repetitious work, and the lowest mean levels of workplace resources, such as the opportunity to learn new things or of having decision-making latitude. The means for 'part day' VDT users were closer to the other groups with far fewer significant differences.

Interestingly, the 'all day' VDT users showed a different trend in the physical environment characteristics given in Figure 2. Here they reported the highest mean levels of adustability of lighting, of chair height and chair back (n.b. In general, they were provided with the newest, most adjustable furniture.) but also, however, reported the highest levels of ergonomic stressors, significantly different from all other groups except that the 'part day' VDT users. They also reported that the lighting was too bright. It is important to note that they worked under the same physical lighting conditions as the other workers in the study. Highly significant differences were observed in the responses to the question "Does your job require you to leave your workstation and move around the office?", with 'all day' VDT users averaging about one-tenth of the mean response level of the other occupational categories.

In addition to noting these univariate trends by occupation in both the independent and dependent variables, the results of the regression analysis, given in Table 1, also show that both the job characteristics and the physical environmental characteristics are predictive of the health and well-being outcomes. The physical factors, in fact, make a substantial contribution to the outcome measures of psycho-social well-being and the job characteristics, likewise, significantly predict the health outcomes. In all about 29% and 23% of satisfaction with the job and with the office could be explained by combinations of psycho-social and physical factors, and 15% of both visual and musculo-skeletal symptomatology could be explained.

Figure 1. Job Characteristics by Clerical Subgroup

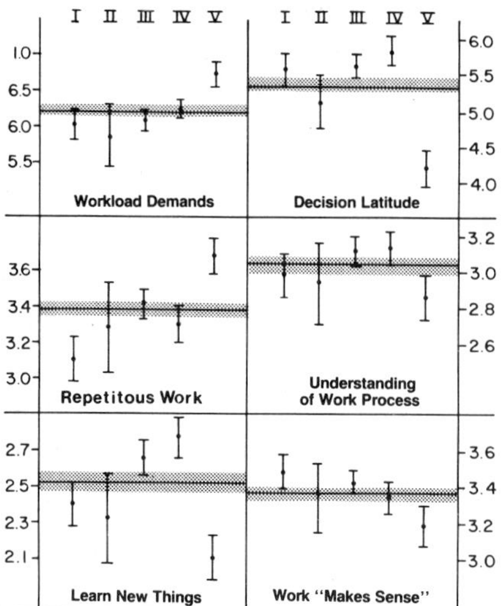

I Part Day Typist (n = 186)
II All Day Typist (n = 50)
III Clerk (n = 363)
IV Part Day VDT User (n = 241)
V All Day VDT User (n = 192)

Group Mean with 95% Confidence Interval

Note: Intergroup Differences are indicated by non-overlap of error bars (p <.05) using one way anova

Figure 2. Physical Environment Characteristics by Clerical Subgroup

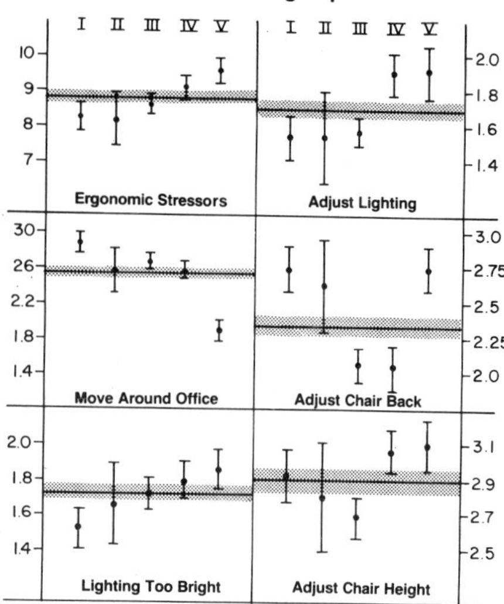

I Part Day Typist (n = 186)
II All Day Typist (n = 50)
III Clerk (n = 363)
IV Part Day VDT User (n = 241)
V All Day VDT User (n = 192)

Group mean with 95% confidence interval

Note: Intergroup Differences are Indicated by non-overlap of Error Bars
(p > .05 using one-way anova)

Figure 3. Health and Well Being Outcomes by Clerical Subgroup

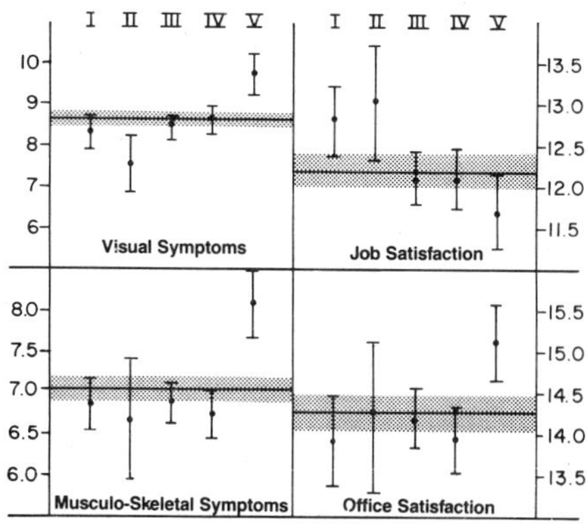

I Part Day Typist (n = 186)
II All Day Typist (n = 50)
III Clerk (n = 363)
IV Part Day VDT User (n = 241)
V All Day VDT User (n = 192)

Group mean with 95% confidence interval

Note: Intergroup Differences are indicated by non-overlap of error bars
(p < .05 using one-way anova)

TABLE 1. Effects of Physical Environment and Job Characteristics on Clerical Worker Health and Well- Being: Regression Results

<u>Dependent Variable: Job Satisfaction</u>

Multiple R .537
R Square .289

	B	Beta	Significance
Job Characteristics:			
Repetitious Work	- .593	- .159	<.0001
Work 'Makes Sense'	.628	.147	<.0001
Learn New Things	.446	.140	<.0001
Understanding of Work	.356	.096	.003
Decision Latitude	.161	.090	.006
Physical Environment:			
Ergonomic Stressors	.218	.226	<.0001
Lighting Too Bright	- .575	- .157	<.0001

<u>Dependent Variable: Office Satisfaction</u>

Multiple R .478
R Square .228

	B	Beta	Significance
Job Characteristics:			
Work 'Makes Sense'	.614	.129	<.0001
Understanding of Work	.376	.0900	.007
Decision Latitude	- .178	- .088	.007
Physical Environment:			
Ergonomic Stressors	.359	.330	<.0001
Lighting Too Bright	- .626	- .152	<.0001
Move Around Office	- .254	- .068	.03
Adjust Chair Back	.166	.059	<.0001

<u>Dependent Variable: Visual Symptoms</u>

Multiple R .380
R Square .145

	B	Beta	Significance
Job Characteristics:			
Repetitious Work	.417	.114	.0003
Workload Demands	.248	.109	.0006
Physical Environment:			
Ergonomic Stressors	- .200	- .211	<.0001
Lighting Too Bright	.658	.183	<.0001

<u>Dependent Variable: Musculo-Skeletal Symptoms</u>

Multiple R .389
R Square .151

	B	Beta	Significance
Job Characteristics:			
Repetitious Work	.317	.103	.02
Workload Demands	.126	.066	.04
Decision Latitude	- .090	- .061	.05
Physical Environment:			
Ergonomic Stressors	- .219	- .274	<.0001
Lighting Too Bright	.286	.095	.004
Adjust Lighting	.189	.067	.03

Ergonomic stressors, in fact, made the largest contribution to each of the outcomes under study. Several job characteristics, including repetitious work, the extent of decision-making latitude and the understanding of one's work also made significant and comparatively substantial contributions. The reported brightness of the light was another variable that could significantly predict each of the outcomes, an interesting finding the implications of which are discussed further below.

DISCUSSION

The data presented here shed light on a number of important and timely issues relevant to clerical work, and also more generally to occupational stress. A major purpose of this evaluation was to characterize the physical and psychosocial characteristics and health effects of computer-mediated clerical work and to compare it with more tradition forms of clerical work (i.e. typing and non-machine interactive jobs). Our findings suggest that VDT-based technology is related to a variety of job factors and health. 'All day' VDT use is characterized by different physical and psychosocial job characteristics than are other forms of clerical work. In this population, 'all day' VDT operators reported significantly higher workload demands, repetitious work, ergonomic stressors and overly bright lighting. Participants also reported that their work had less cognitive meaning for them and that they were less able to use their skills and to make decisions in carrying out their work. With respect to health, 'all day' VDT operators reported significantly higher levels of musculo-skeletal and visual strains than did the other clerical workers and lower job satisfaction than did 'all day' and 'part day' typists.

It is also noteworthy that 'part day' VDT users characterize their working conditions as less stressful than do 'all day' users. Their reports of physical and psychosocial working conditions and health appear to be more similar to typists and non-machine interactive clerical workers than to 'all day' VDT users. On the basis of these data it appears that clerical workers whose jobs require them to use a VDT for only part of the work day, while engaging in non-VDT-mediated tasks for the remaining part of the day are at lower risk for stress-related symptoms and illness than 'all day' VDT operators. Such findings suggest that integrating computer and non-computer related tasks (task rotation) may be a useful strategy for reducing the potentially stressful aspects of these jobs.

The present findings on increased musculo-skeletal and visual symptoms and extensive VDT work are supported by data from a number of investigations described in other parts of this volume, as are the findings on 'part day' versus 'all day' usage.

The results of the regression analysis are consistent with the several accepted models for occupational stress, such as that of House [17], wherein characteristics of the physical and psychological environment (as well as personal characteristics of the individual) contribute to occupational stress. These findings are also consistent with biological models of the occupational stress response, as first posited by Selye [18]. In these models the stress response is a non-specific response to physical and psychological demands. It may be multi-systemic and may manifest itself in one or in many physical and psychological symptoms or symptom-complexes. Thus the presence of ergonomic stressors, which logical should relate to the musculo-skeletal system, may also manifest themselves in visual symptomatology. This is analogous to the fact that headaches and neck pains are common responses in the general population to stressful conditions not at all placing direct demands on the neck muscles.

When considered in this light the findings in Table 1 have implications for programs designed for the improvement of working conditions and for prevention of adverse effects. Both the models and these data would imply that workplace modifications, such as reducing the numbers of hours of continuous VDT work, alternation with other tasks and a better designed physical workplace environment should be accompanied by changes in the design of work and the extent to which workers have input and control over their work and work environments. Conversely, attempts at restructuring and redesigning job content should also take into account the physical characteristics of the workplace.

The relationships observed with respect to the mean levels of "lighting too bright' would appear to bear these statements out. 'All day' VDT operators simultaneously reported the greatest ability to adjust the lighting while also reporting the lighting to be too bright and the greatest amount of eyestrain. Although the ambient lighting levels and visual characteristics of the terminal were not measured in this survey, the investigators observed that the lighting were uniform throughout the floors and was supplied by standard overhead fluorescent fixtures. It is therefore reasonable to propose that the tendency for 'all day' VDT users to report the lighting as brighter may be a reflection of differential perception of lighting rather than actual differences and can also be associated with visual fatigue arising from 'all day' VDT use. The differential perception could well be the result of the differences in the psycho-social aspects and job characteristics of 'all day' VDT work.

These data show that there is thus a strong need for further investigation into the very nature of clerical work, both physical and psychosocial, in order to more fully understand its implications for worker health and well-being. We have presented elsewhere [14-16] which shows that there is a widespread prevalence of dissatisfaction and visual and musculo-skeletal symptomatology among the group of clerical workers as a whole. Over one-third of the respondents reported eyestrain, neck and shoulder pain and over one-fourth reported back pain, either "often" or "almost all the time." Less than 20%, overall, said that they were "very satisfied" with their jobs or occupations, while only slightly more than one third said that they would "strongly recommend" their job to a friend.

There are, of course, methodological difficulties associated with a cross-sectional study of this kind, some of which have been discussed by us elsewhere.[16] However, the large size of the population and the comparability of the groups, as well as the consistency of the findings with other reports and with popularly accepted models of stress, tend to strengthen the findings. It is clear, however, that predictions about long-term health and well-being from cross-sectional data are, at best, tentative. Prospective studies, such as those reported from researchers at Volvo in Sweden, are needed.

CONCLUSION

The widely held assumption that office automation will upgrade clerical work is not supported by these findings. The data presented here suggest, in fact, that the exact opposite may be true. The introduction of office automation appears to have resulted in profound changes in the task characteristics of clerical jobs: 'all day' VDT operators have significantly less decision latitude, lower skill utilization, less overall understanding of the work process and greater task repetition and ability to physically move around the office than do other clerical workers. They also reported the highest levels of eyestrain, musculo-skeletal strain and job dissatisfaction. This is in contrast to the relatively similar job characteristics which were reported between typists and clerks. The findings strongly suggest that 'computerization' has had a substantially greater impact on the nature of clerical work than have previous forms of technological change -- such as the introduction of typewriters. Of relevance to worker well-being are the findings that increased use of VDTs in office automation is associated with changes that are all in the direction of increased stresses and decreased resources.

The contrast between reported levels of satisfaction and job characteristics between 'all day' VDT operators and 'part day' suggests that it may be possible to introduce computerization in ways which minimize stressors and maximize resources. However, the observed negative aspects of clerical work itself, the impact of physical factors on psychosocial well-being and job characteristics on physical well-being, also strongly suggest that there is a limit to positive effects of modifications of the work environment and of job design when done "piecemeal." A more holistic approach appears to be required. Indeed, the division of tasks into clerical and non-clerical may themselves be constructs in need of modification. Further and more intensive work is urgently needed in this area.

ACKNOWLEDGEMENTS

We wish to acknowledge the following organizations for their collaborative efforts: The Communications Workers of America, AFL-CIO; Canadian Union of Public Employees; British Columbia Government Employees Union; and Public Service Alliance of Canada. Cooperative managements are not identified here because of commitments to anonymity. However, we are grateful for their assistance. We also wish to thank Maury Lieberman at the National Institute of Mental Health for his continuing interest and support.

REFERENCES

1. Bradley G (1977). 'Computerization and some psychological factors in the work environment in Reducing Occupational Stress', U.S. Department of Health, Education and Welfare, Washington: NIOSH.

2. Coe JB, Cuttle K, McClellon WC, Warden NJ, and Turner PJ (1980). Visual display units report W/1/80. New Zealand Department of Health, Wellington, N.Z.

3. Cohen BFG, Smith MJ and Stammerjohn LW (1981). 'Psychosocial factors contributing to job stress of clerical VDT operators' in Salvendy G and Smith MJ eds., Machine Pacing and Occuaitonal Stress, (London: Taylor and Francis).

4. Hunting W, Laubli T, and Grandjean E (1981): Postural and visual loads at VDT workplaces: Constrained postures. Ergonomics, 24(12): 917-931.

5. Laubli T, Hunting W, and Grandjean E (1981). 'Postural and visual loads at VDT workplace: Lighting conditions and visual impairments', Ergonomics, 24(12): 933-944.

6. Mourant R, Lakshamanan R, and Chantadisai R (1981). 'Visual fatigue and cathode ray tube display terminals', Human Factors, 23(5): 529-540.

7. Sauter S, Gottlieb MS, Jones KC, Dodson VN, and Rohrer KM (1983). 'Job and health implication of VDT use: initial results of the Wisconsin-NIOSH study', Communications of the ACM, 26(4): 284-294.

8. Starr S, Thompson C, and Shute S (1982): Effects of video display terminals on telephone operators. Human Factors, 1982.

9. U.S. Department of Health and Human Services, Public Health Service, center for Disease Control, National Institue for Occupational Safety and Health, Division of Biomedical and Behavioral Science, Division of Surveillance, Hazard Evaluations and Field Studies (1981). Potential Health Hazards of video display Terminals.

10. Arndt RA (1983). 'Working posture and musculoskeletal problems of video display terminal operators - review and reappraisal,' American Industrial Hygiene Association Journal, 44(6): 437-446.

11. Shindell S, Weisberg RF, and Geifer EE (1978). 'The healthy worker effect - fact or artifact?' Journal of Occupational Medicine, 20: 807-811.

12. U.S. Office of Technology Assessment (1985): 'Automation of America's Offices', Washington D.C.

13. Schurick JM, Helander MG, and Billingsley PA (1982). 'Critique of methods employed in humans factors reserach on VDTs', Paper presented at annual meeting of The Human Factors Society. Seattle, Washington 1982.

14. Stellman JM, Gordon GC, Snow BR and Klitzman S (1984). 'Office Workers: Health and Well-Being Survey", Final Report to NIMH.

15.Stellman, J.M., S. Klitzman, G.C. Gordon and B.R. Snow (1985): 'Air Quality and Ergonomics in the Office: Survey Results and Methodologic Issues,' AIHA J. (46): 286-293.

16.Stellman, J.M., S. Klitzman, G.C. Gordon and B.R. Snow (in press): 'Work Environment and the Well-Being of VDT and Clerical Workers', J. Occ. Behav.

17. House J (1980): Occupational Stress and the Mental and Physical Health of Factory Workers. University of Michigan, Ann Arbor.

18. Levi, L (1983): 'Preventing Work Stress', Addison-Wesley, New York.

WORK WITH DISPLAY UNITS 86
B. Knave and P.-G. Wideback (eds.)

OFFICE AUTOMATION AND WORK ORGANIZATION: MAKING USE OF THE SCOPE OF CHOICE

Jörg Sydow

Institute of Management, Freie Universität Berlin, Garystr. 21, D-1000 Berlin 33.

It is widely accepted among people who are concerned with the design of office work that there is a scope for organizational choice. However, there is some controversy as to how the size of this scope is affected by modern micro-electronic based office technology. There is also a discussion as to why this scope is hardly used by systems designers for reconciling the interests of management in a more efficient work organization and the interests of office workers in a better quality of working life.
This papers presents an instrument which enables the designers of work organizations to make use of this scope of choice in order to design 'better' organizations. This instrument accepts the fact that managers, designers and those who have to work in automated office settings have different values and interests. Hence, it favours a dual analysis and evaluation of work situations, i.e. the investigation of the work situation as it has been created by the designers and the work situation as it is subjectively perceived by the office workers.

1. INTRODUCTION: THE THEME OF ORGANIZATIONAL CHOICE

All practitioners of work and organizational design and most researchers agree that there is a scope of organizational choice. If it were not so, there would be no need for organizational design but neither would there be any chance of social control. The size of this scope, at least to some extent, is said to depend upon the technology in use. While there is little controversy that the scope of organizational choice is fairly small with the assembly line-type of production and traditional centralized data processing systems, it is widely hoped that in the face of new micro-electronic production and office technologies systems designers will regain the scope they had at their disposal in times of manual-type work. For instance, van Beinum (1981) claims: "Microelectronics offers us opportunities to design jobs and organise work in accordance with the values of the quality of working life in a way that no other technology in industrialized society has done in the past" (p. 6), and Walton (1982) observes: "Information technology is less deterministic than other basic technologies that historically have affected the nature of work and people at work" (p. 1076). The less deterministic character of these new technologies, to be used for automating production as well as office work, is said to result from the fact that (programmable) software makes up the core of these technologies and that, among other things, their economics are difficult to establish.

Somewhat sceptical about these arguments this paper, on the one hand, warns of overestimating this scope of organizational choice in automated office settings; on the other hand, it demonstrates ways of how to discover the available scope and even how to enlarge it.

2. APPROACHES TO DISCOVER AND ENLARGE THE SCOPE OF ORGANIZATIONAL CHOICE

Basically, there is a theoretical and an empirical approach to discover the scope of organizational choice. The empirical approach comprises the accomplishment of impact studies and organizational experimentation. The theoretical approach adds arguments to those already presented and arranges them within a comprehensive theoretical framework such as the framework of strategic choice developed by Child (1972) or as sociotechnical systems theory (Trist 1981).

Empirical studies of the impact of modern office technology (i.e. decentralized computer systems, personal computers, word processing, electronic mailing) on the work situation of secretaries, typists and clerks have produced very diverse evidence. This seems to substantiate the existence of a scope of organizational choice.

A review of empirical studies of the change of clerical work due to the introduction of computer systems shows that the results are particularly diverse as such dimensions of work organization as work content, time structure and human interaction are concerned (Sydow 1985). However, this review also makes clear that the empirical evidence is less contradictary with regard to an intensification of work, a change of control structure, an increase of standardization and formalization, and a further abstractification of office work. The argument of abstractification is of particular relevance where office work is automated by the use of VDU. The VDU worker can no longer monitor the work process, its material inputs and outputs, but only its symbolic representation on the screen. Symbolic representation is not necessarily bound to the use of VDU (take traditional office work with paper and pencil as an example); but the use of modern micro-electronic based office technology abstractifies work once more, no matter what the organization of work may be. Pava (1983) argues similarly when he states: "Equipment that is both highly self-regulating and highly interconnected can easily make office work too abstract and intangible. Information manipulated by people running advanced processing devices can become many steps removed from the events they ostensibly control. Under these conditions equipment used for advanced information technology seals off its users from tangible reality, and encourages them to become passive, docile, and complacent" (p. 138). Zuboff (1982) expresses this tendency towards abstractification by his term of "computer-mediated work" and hypothesizes: "When work is abstracted its meaning tends to become thin" (p. 70). While the empirical evidence quoted above may not be generalized to the work situations of other office personnel, the change in the work of clerks is of outstanding importance. For they constitute the largest proportion of office workers, move more and more into the limelight of office rationalization activities, and in contrast to most data typists and text processing people will probably survive the ongoing process of work integration, which has been stipulated by the introduction of modern office technologies.

Organizational experimentation with new forms of work organization in offices clearly demonstrates that there is an opportunity of a more humane form of office work under specific cirumstances. Modern office technology seems to be only a necessary but not sufficient condition among these circumstances. In addition, most of this evidence is questionable from a methodological point of view and has been derived from studies of data-entry and text-processing jobs, which are becoming of more peripheral importance to office automation. Still, organizational experimentation enables us to explore the limits of organizational choice with reference to a specific technology and other situational factors. Or, as Kubicek (1980) puts it: "Concrete limits become visible only if you touch them in practical experiments and if you are trying in vain to defer them" (p. 57).

Systems designers and decision makers may become aware of the possibility of choice and its limitation if their learning of the functioning of an organization and their experimentation with new forms of work organization is supported by an instrument, which helps them in the process of evaluation and redesign of work. Such an instrument can make systems designers give up traditional models of men and organizations (Hedberg & Mumford 1975). So far, neither the diffusion of new technologies nor the broad discussion of the quality of working life in western countries seems to have affected the values of systems designers: "They still prefer to maximize the immediate costs of production rather than to optimize a longer-term approach to job design which recognizes the economic costs of worker frustration and emphasizes employee satisfaction and motivation" (Taylor 1977, p. 16). It may be concluded from this evidence that systems designers still need assistance so that they conceive their role in the process of office automation as that of an organization designer.

There are some theoretical arguments, which favour the existence of a non-negligible scope of organizational choice. They concern in addition to the software-character of modern office technology the alleged minor impact of work and organizational structures on organizational efficiency and the difficulty in assessing this impact (Child 1972); the existence of market structures which do not coincide with the economist's model of perfect competition (Schreyögg 1980); the contradictary demands which result from market economies on the one hand and production economies on the other (Brandt et al. 1978)*. These theoretical arguments which cannot be discussed in this paper have to be considered if practical experimentation with new forms of work organization, the purpose of which is to defer the limits of organizational choice, are to produce general empirical evidence.

3. THEORETICAL BACKGROUND OF THE DUAL ANALYSIS OF WORK SITUATIONS

An instrument, which combines these empirical and theoretical insights has been developed by Staehle and his colleagues at the Institute of Management of the Freie Universität Berlin (c.f. Elias et al. 1985). It has been named the Dual Analysis of Work Situations (Duale Arbeitssituationsanalyse) and applied to the redesign of assembly work in a medium-sized company. Its development, application and its current popularization by the German productivity center (RKW)** has been supported financially within the German Humanization of Work Programme (see Kißler & Sattler 1982 for information on this programme).

The theoretical foundation of this instrument is the sociotechnical systems theory (Trist 1981). With this theory it shares the following basic assumptions:

(1) Technology is a most significant aspect of work situations. The work situation, however, does not directly result from the technical system installed, but is formed by organizational design.
(2) The individual work situation can only be analyzed when the wider context (organizational structure and culture, industrial relations system) is taken into account.
(3) The analysis and design of work situations must be dynamic; it has to deal with the design process itself as well as with its results.
(4) The design process is participative, i.e. involves all those individuals whose work is being redesigned. Participation does not merely "mean user-cooperation in installing something that has already been designed with purposes in mind that undermine the user's position" (Shaiken 1983, p. 13). Genuine participation allows workers to change the work situation in a way which meets their interest to the exclusion of other interests.

These arguments are complemented by the insight that organizational reality has a dual character in at least two respects. Firstly, the perceived organizational world may be different from the 'real' one. Individual perception is subjective, influenced by interests, values and experiences. Secondly, perception as well as action in work organizations can be best understood if the basic conflict of interest between those who decide about the design of work situations and those who have to live in them is accepted. In these respects the Dual Analysis of Work Situations differs significantly from sociotechnical systems theory in order to insure a balanced analysis of work and a successful realistic search for the scope of organizational choice. It is for this reason that the instrument concentrates on work situations and their redesign, and does not focus on the work process (i.e. the interlinkage of singular tasks or work situations). The latter view, considered separately, favours a rationalization perspective while largely neglecting the humanization aspect.

Built upon these assumptions the dual analysis has been successfully applied in the redesign of factory work. It is just being adapted to automated office environments.

4. THE DUAL ANALYSIS OF WORK SITUATIONS IN THE FIELD OF OFFICE AUTOMATION

4.1. Office automation defined

In the past, technology has only been of overwhelming importance for the layout of work situations in factories. The introduction of electronic data processing and its spreading to about every tenth workplace via the use of VDU has changed the nature of office work dramatically. Hence, it was at hand to adopt the Dual Analysis of Work Situations to automated office work settings. Office work is said to be (partially) automated if a substantial part of the task, i.e. the production of information, is handled independently of human interaction by information and communication technology (Sydow 1985, p. 47). Or, as it has been put by Uhlig et al. (1979): "An 'automated' office is an office in which interactive computer tools are put into the hands of individual knowledge workers, at their desks, in the areas in which they are physically working" (p. 20). And it is this aspect of physical proximity of technology which makes it more and more advisable to investigate office work situations before redesigning them, to investigate the physical and psychological working conditions in automated office settings.

Office automation is considered to be an organizational strategy to enhance productivity but even more to overcome the contradictary demands of production economies (mass production of information at low cost) and market economies (individual production of strategically important information). Although maximum automation of office work may be counterproductive to the latter demands, management tends to strive for this goal instead of striving for optimum office automation. The resulting effects upon the work situation and upon office workers using VDU have been impressively demonstrated throughout this conference.

Office automation may be characterized by two interrelated dimensions, both independently and jointly even more so influencing the work situation: the technological dimension and the organizational dimension. The technological dimension, at an abstract level, may currently be best described by three kinds of tendencies towards integration:

(1) Integration of information and communication technologies, due to the digitalization of telephone terminals and networks
(2) Integration via the use of networks between computer systems (e.g. LAN)
(3) Integration at the terminal level (e.g. personal computer, multi-purpose terminals).

All three tendencies strengthen the view of the VDU as the visible peak of office automation, dominating the work situation. The organizational dimension can be best characterized by three kinds of tendencies towards integration, too:

(1) Integration of office work processes (e.g. the work of clerks and typists)
(2) Integration of office and factory work (e.g. CIM)
(3) Integration of software and organizational design (i.e. to a very significant extent work design in automated offices is and will be even more a matter of software design).

Looking at theses organizational tendencies from a sociotechnical point of view it has to be emphazised that they are likely to arise when modern micro-electronic equipment is installed in offices; however, these tendencies are not deterministic. There is at least some scope for organizational choice. Beyond that, technology itself is an outcome of design decisions and, hence, can at least to some extent be considered as a design variable. Consequently, there are at least two groups of design parameters, which have to be taken into account when analysing work situations. The Dual Analysis of Work Situations tries to meet both challenges.

4.2. Basic features of the instrument

The overwhelming feature of the Dual Analysis of Work Situations is its two-sided duality mentioned already. Accepting the basic conflict of interest between those who decide about the design of work situations and those who have to live in them it is consistent to differentiate the work situation as defined by management and as subjectively perceived by office workers.

A second feature of the instrument is that it does not concentrate on the technical and physical aspects of the work situation while neglecting organizational and psychological aspects, which are more difficult to assess. It looks rather at both, technological and organizational dimensions of automated office work. These dimensions constitute what is labeled the basic structure of the work situation (see fig. 1). These dimensions of the basic structure are related to physical, psychological and skill-related requirements (requirement structure). The Dual Analysis of Work Situations makes use of a questionnaire which combines the different dimensions of the basic structure of the work situation and of the requirement structure to a matrix, the work situation matrix. The questionnaire is given to the management in charge of the design of office work in order to survey their view of the work situation, and to the representatives of office workers, whose task is to complete the questionnaire after having interviewed those persons whose work is affected by automation. Alternatively, each office worker concerned may her-/himself fill in a separate questionnaire. Then, the questionnaires of both groups are compared. Dimensions strongly present in affecting the requirement structure, no matter if marked so by a manager or a office worker, and significant differences in the assessment of the work situation give a first hint of technical and/or organizational oddities or even deficiencies in the work situation under consideration.

The present work situation matrix shown by fig. 1 is only a conceptual framework from which the actual matrix for the evaluation of office work has to be derived. For instance, the actual matrix has to be more precise in the software aspects of modern office technology and to differentiate the relevant organizational sub-dimensions such as space, time, task and interaction. For instance, the task as an important organizational dimension of the basic structure of the work situation, influencing physical, psychological as well as skill-related requirments, has a quantitative aspect (e.g. speed of work) and a qualitative aspect (content of work). The latter embraces at least three phases of information processing/communication: receiving information, processing information, and sending information (including storing). The processing of information, the heart of the production process in offices, can be schematic, creative, and also includes manual handling (e.g. typing). And so forth.

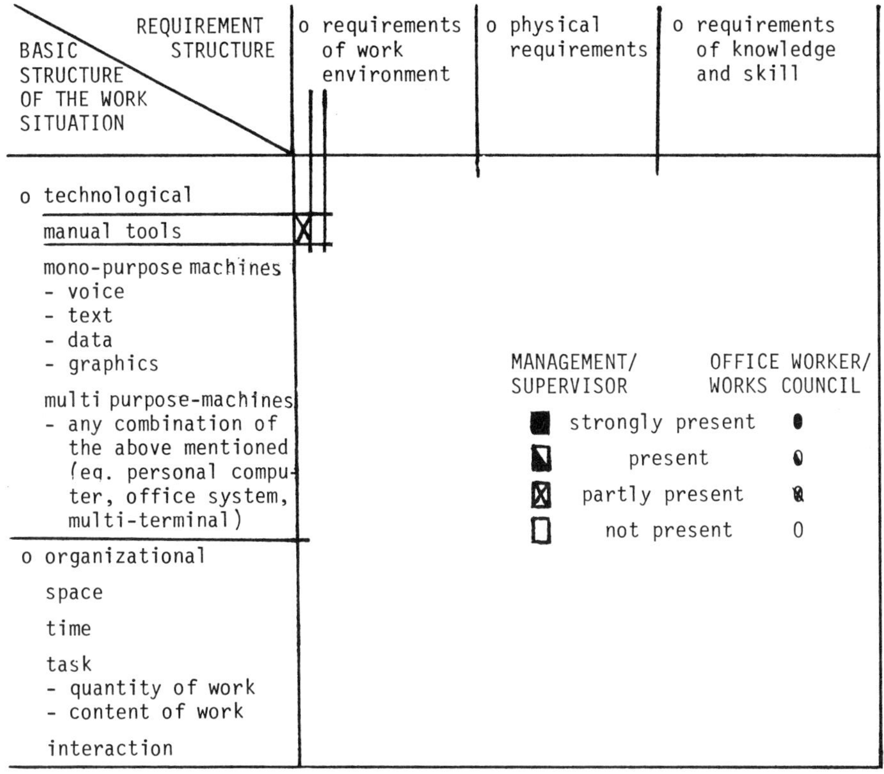

REQUIREMENT STRUCTURE
BASIC STRUCTURE OF THE WORK SITUATION
o requirements of work environment
o physical requirements
o requirements of knowledge and skill
o technological
manual tools
mono-purpose machines
- voice
- text
- data
- graphics
multi purpose-machines
- any combination of the above mentioned (eg. personal computer, office system, multi-terminal)
o organizational
space
time
task
- quantity of work
- content of work
interaction
MANAGEMENT/ SUPERVISOR
OFFICE WORKER/ WORKS COUNCIL
strongly present
present
partly present
not present
0

Fig. 1: Work situation matrix (conceptual framework)

The analysis of work situations is a necessary but not sufficient step towards a technological and organizational design incorporating the goals of management and those of office workers. The dual analysis has to be followed by a joint development of design alternatives. Consequently, and as the Dual Analysis of Work Situations aims at self-reliance, the instrument contains a detailed procedure on how to start such an evaluation process, how to classify those work situations, which need to be included in such an analysis, how to conduct the interviews, how to analyse the data collected from managers and office workers, and how to develop alternative forms of work organizations. This procedural aspect is a third important feature of the Dual Analysis of Work Situations.

4.3. The conduct of the analysis, evaluation and design

The procedure starts with an explicit formulation of goals for specific work systems. A work system usually contains several work situations of a similar shape. The goals have to be made explicit by the management/systems designers as well as by the office workers and their representatives. Following fig. 2 these goals related to the technological and/or organizational design of the work situation are compared to each other and the deviation of the actual work situation from these objectives is recorded. When a need for an analysis or even redesign of a work situation is articulated, a rough analysis of weak points is conducted, using a check list containing personnel, organizational, technological and economic aspects. This first analysis is helpful for the adjacent classification of the work systems. At least those which have to be analyzed in more depth are separated from those which deviated from the stated objectives only marginally or show no weak points. This phase may also contain a ranking of the work systems according to priority.

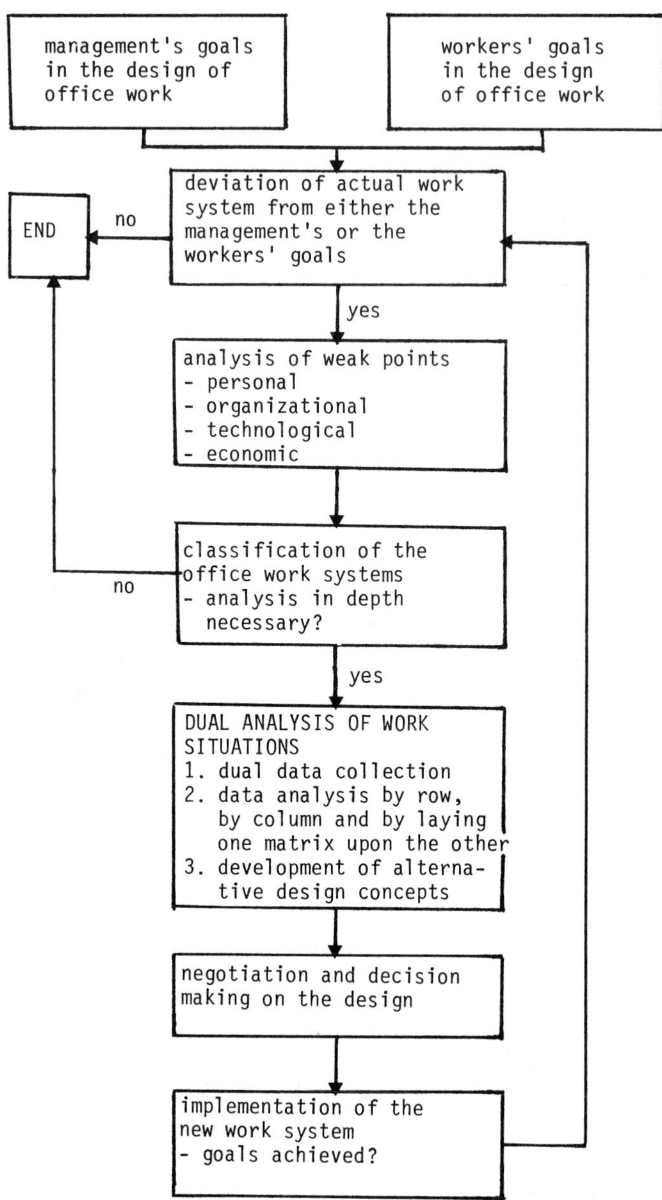

Fig. 2: The procedure of analysis and design

The phase of classification is followed by the core of the Dual Analysis of Work Situations: (1) the dual collection of data using the work situation matrix, (2) the combined data analysis, and (3) the development of alternative design concepts. Since something has been said concerning the dual collection of data depicting the work situation as defined by management and as perceived by the office workers, the following focuses on the analysis of these data and the development of design concepts.

In contrast to the separate collection of data the analysis of those data is a task which has to be carried out jointly by the managers, office workers and their representatives. For this phase of the process is narrowly related to the development of design alternatives, which has also to be done jointly. There are two basic approaches to the data analysis. Firstly, the work situation matrices are analyzed by row. This approach indicates all requirements caused by a specific element of the basic structure of the work situation. The second approach, the analysis by column, pointsto those elements of the basic structure of the work situation which cause a specific type of requirement. Nevertheless, the most important method of analysis consists of laying the matrices filled in by management upon those representing the views of the office workers. This method indicates clearly the differences in assessing the work situation in terms of basic structure and physical, psychological, and skill-related requirements.

The development of design alternatives, which is based upon the outcome of such an analysis, is also carried out by a team composed of management and office workers and their representatives. Each party makes recommendations of how to overcome the deficiencies determined. The development of design alternatives is very much complicated by the fact that an improvement in terms of one type of requirement may well be accompagnied by the worsening of another aspect. Hence, the comprehensive impact of a specific redesign upon the work situation as defined by management as well as perceived by office workers has to be assessed. Those design alternatives which do not correspond to the minimum required by a law have to be excluded immediately. If single measures are not sufficient to modify specific requirements of the office work the basic sociotechnical structure of the work situation has to be changed. Again the work situation matrix may be used to generate feasible design alternatives. For this it is necessary to combine the elements of the basic structure of the work situation (rows) in an innovative way. Combining these elements in a new way usually results in new forms of sociotechnical systems which are also an outcome of job enlargement, job enrichment, and job rotation strategies. Moreover, semi-autonomous working groups are often the recommendations of the team in charge of the analysis and redesign.

The collection and analysis of data and the development of design alternatives, the true core of the Dual Analysis of Work Situations, is to be followed by a negotiation and decision making process. In the end, management will make the decision, and it is a matter of the power structure within the organization and even more so within the industrial relations system as to which extent the interests of the office workers will be incorporated in the sociotechnical design. In any case, the usage of the Dual Analysis of Work Situations will sensitize the management towards the views of the office workers on their work and motivate the office workers themselves to get their recommendations accepted. The whole process of analysis and redesign of office work is stopped when the new features or work systems implemented correspond to the initial goals of both parties and to their interpretation of the data collected. Otherwise, single phases of the process have to be gone through again.

The Dual Analysis of Work Situations whose adaptation to automated office work settings is still in progress aims at self-reliance and, hence, will contain a detailed procedure on how to start and conduct such an analysis and redesign process (for details on factory assembly work see Elias et al. 1985). A test of the instrument in a suitable office environment is to be carried out.

5. SOME CONCLUSIONS

Office automation has been defined as an organizational strategy comprising technological as well as organizational aspects of work system design. Both technological and organizational aspects of automated office settings are met by the instrument presented, which favours a very early involvement of office workers and their representatives in the analysis and design process. This ensures that participation means more to them than user cooperation. Being aware of the fact that the proposed procedure of dual analysis and joint redesign of automated office work may produce conflict, this conflict is considered as a useful and necessary step towards real consensus.

The scope of organizational choice in automated office settings can best be discovered or even enlarged when both management and office workers are assisted in finding common interests in this process of evaluation and design. These common interests may result from the fact that new office technologies enable a spatial and a temporal decoupling and a re-integration of office work. They may also arise from the difficulty to establish the most efficient design and from the wish to avoid psychological stress and physiological strain which result from intensive VDU work. In those cases, the application of the Dual Analysis of Work Situations facilitates the utilization of the scope of organizational choice and eases the implementation of new sociotechnical systems without dehumanizing work.

NOTES

* For a discussion of these and further arguments c.f. Sydow (1985, 1986).
** The manual supporting the use of the Dual Analysis of Work Situations in factory settings (especially assembly work) may be obtained from the RKW, PO Box 5867, D-6236 Eschborn, Federal Republic of Germany.

REFERENCES

Beinum, H. van (1981): Organizational choice and micro electronics. In: QWL Focus, 1 (3), p. 1-6.

Brandt, G., Kündig, B., Papadimitriou, Z., & Thomae, J. (1978): Computer und Arbeitsprozeß. Campus. Frankfurt and New York.

Child, J. (1972): Organizational structure, environment, and performance: the role of strategic choice. In: Sociology, 6, p. 1-22.

Elias, H.J., Gottschalk, B., & Staehle, W.H. (1985): Gestaltung und Bewertung von Arbeitssystemen. Campus. Frankfurt and New York.

Hedberg, B., & Mumford, E. (1975): The design of computer systems. In: Mumford, E., & Sackman, H. (eds.): Human choice and computers. North-Holland. Amsterdam, p. 31-59.

Kißler, L., & Sattel, U. (1982): Humanization of work and social interests: Description and critical assessment of the state-sponsored program of humanization in the Federal Republic of Germany. In: Economic and Industrial Democracy, 3, p. 221-261.

Kubicek, H. (1980): Perspektiven und Fragen zur Überwindung einiger Mängel des Situativen Ansatzes. In: Potthoff, E. (Hrsg.): RKW-Handbuch Führungstechnik und Organisation. 6th part. August 1980. Berlin.

Pava, C.H.P. (1983): Managing new office technology. Free Press. New York and London.

Schreyögg, G. (1980): Contingency and choice in organization theory. In: Organization Studies, 1 (4), p. 305-326.

Shaiken, H. (1983): Choices in the development of office automation. In: Marshall, D., & Gregory, J. (eds.): Office automation: Jekyll or Hyde? Working Women Education Fund. Cleveland, Ohio, p. 5-14.
Sydow, J. (1984): Sociotechnical change and perceived work situations: Some conceptual propositions and an empirical investigation in different office settings. In: Office: Technology & People, 2, p. 121-132.
Sydow, J. (1985): Organisationsspielraum und Büroautomation. DeGruyter. Berlin and New York.
Sydow, J. (1986): Information technology and organizational choice. In: Child, J., & Bate, P. (eds.): Organizations in transition. DeGruyter. Berlin and New York (in press).
Taylor, J.C. (1977): Job design criteria twenty years later. Center for Quality of Working Life, University of California. Los Angeles; also published (1979) in: Davies, L.E., & Taylor, J.C. (eds.): Design of jobs. 2nd edition. Goodyear. Santa Monica, Calif., p. 54-63.
Trist, E.L. (1981): The evolution of sociotechnical systems. In: Van de Ven, A.H., & Joyce, W.F. (eds.): Perspectives on organization design and behavior. Wiley. New York, p. 19-75.
Uhlig, R., Faber, D.I., & Blair, J.H. (1979): The office of the future. North-Holland. Amsterdam.
Walton, R.E. (1982): Social choice in the development of advanced information technology. In: Human Relations, 35 (12), p. 1073-1084.
Zuboff, S. (1982): Statement of concern. In: Office: Technology & People, 1 (1), p. 66-70.

WORK WITH DISPLAY UNITS 86
B. Knave and P.-G. Wideback (eds.)

THE ROLE OF USER PROTOTYPING IN THE SYSTEM DESIGN PROCESS

S.D.P. HARKER
Department of Human Sciences, HUSAT Research Centre
University of Technology, Loughborough, Leics. LE11 3TU

Users find it difficult to comment on proposals for the design and implementation of new VDU systems unless they can be given some 'concrete' experience of what is being offered to them. The range of issues which must be explored covers all these aspects of interaction which will affect user acceptance, from screen and keyboard characteristics, through dialogue design and navigation, to the process of implementation. The reliability of the information gathered from the users is contingent on the extent to which the prototype under test is a realistic version of the actual system. Thus the process of testing prototypes with users goes through a series of increasingly accurate approximations, which take account of all the other features which will constrain the design as it evolves, and should be planned in such a way as to yield relevant information prior to key decision points. There will be corresponding changes in the form of evaluation which is appropriate to each stage and the methods to e used should also be planned as an integral part of the process.

The implications of these issues for the utilisation of human factors knowledge will be discussed in relation to material derived from case studies carried out in organisations developing systems for their own use and in organisations developing products for a mass market.

1. INTRODUCTION

The need to create computerised systems which are better matched to user requirements is a pervasive theme in the systems design community. It stems from the increasing recognition that good human-computer interfaces are crucial to the effective use of information technology and a concomitant acknowledgement that the design of human-computer interfaces is not yet good enough. There are, of course, many factors which will contribute to improved quality, including the development of the human factors knowledge base, the dissemination of the knowledge thus generated and the creation of tools and techniques which will enable designers to apply the knowledge. This paper is directed at one particular issue, that is the role of user prototyping as a technique for use in the design of human-computer systems.

2. WHY PROTOTYPE?

In some situations it is possible to meet user needs by reference to some universally applicable body of knowledge. This is an extremely attractive option for the technically oriented designer who is used to the application of prescriptive data formed from a standard base. However, there are many situations in the design of information technology systems which require the designer to cope with complex relationships between task and user characteristics which are unique and for which no generalised solution can be used, Harker & Eason 1984. In those circumstances there is the need to generate a specific solution. Of course there are a variety of ways in which this unique solution may be sought. It is possible to infer the particular requirements of the task and the user and draw conclusions on the basis of insightful human factors, although this will require a considerable degree of human factors expertise and experience. Even when a human factors expert is involved, users themselves should play an important role in generating information which will guide the development of a design which is satisfactory to their needs and tasks.

User involvement may take a variety of forms; these include the use of detailed checklists in order to establish user requirements, the creation of scenarios for evaluation by users, and representation on various forms of planning and steering committees. However perhaps the most obvious way in which users may be involved is to ask them to give the designers direct feedback on the design proposals as they develop.

Design is an iterative process and moves from the general to the particular. Therefore in order to provide feedback one may find that users are asked in the first instance to comment on the outline proposals and then, as the formal solutions are generated, they are asked to respond to these. Unfortunately most users have great difficulty in understanding the way in which designers present their proposed solutions at each stage and therefore are not well placed to give meaningful feedback. For example, they are unlikely to respond in any very informed way to analyses of the current or proposed tasks which are represented by paper and pencil versions of data flows and entity life histories. Even screen by screen paper presentations of dialogues give little sense of what the real system will be like. Evidence of this problem emerged from a study of designers using a Structured Design Methodology which assigns a formal role to users in approving the design as it proceeds. In theory this approach provides an effective and powerful say in how the design actually emerges. In practice although the users could make comments on the designs they found that they understood very little of what was actually intended and what its impact might be upon the tasks at which it was directed and as a consequence they provided little substantive guidance on where changes might be needed.

A way of overcoming this problem is to create prototype versions of interfaces which will provide something concrete to which users will be able to respond in a realistic manner. The creation of a prototype which presents the system in the way that it might eventually emerge to the user allows the designer to offer the opportunity to explore iterative versions of the solution which may be offered. These solutions should express requirements that the user has identified and also features which the designer feels will be of benefit to the user. One would expect people to find the concrete much easier to assimilate than the abstract, simply on the basis of our understanding of concept attainment, Bruner, Goodnow & Austin, 1956. The natural consequence is that the information which they generate will be of better quality and far more informative to the designers. In the example which I quoted above there was clear evidence that users who had a formally identified role in the design process and had actually been exposed to the paper and pencil versions of the interface dialogues as they developed, were far more informative in their comments on the utility and acceptability of what was being proposed, once it was available in prototype form. This response emerged even from a user who was a graduate computer scientist familiar with the principles of the design methodology and the way in which the solutions were represented within that methodology.

Prototyping may be used to examine the whole range of issues which impact upon user acceptance thus prototypes may simulate hardware characteristics of the system, workstation and environmental factors as well as dialogues and navigation. Prototypes may also be used if they are developed in a sufficiently elaborate fashion to allow groups of users to respond to planned implementation including training strategies. Figure 1 illustrates some of the more specific items which might be considered.

Figure 1 Prototyping can be used for:

- screens
- keyboards
- workstations

- workplace layout
- visual, thermal and acoustic factors

- task dialogue match
- navigation
- help
- error messages
- system information

- documentation

- implementation
- organisational impact
- training

Thus the scope of prototyping is potentially as great as the overall scope of the design process and gives users the opportunity to provide an input which will directly affect all aspects of the systems which they will work with in the future. However, we must recognise that it may not be possible to achieve all these goals in each case; prototyping is inevitably a fairly expensive process because of the requirement to produce a simulation of the users' interface with the system, while the simulation may not directly contribute to the technical solution which will underpin the final version of the interface. It may also prove extremely difficult to create the right kinds of user involvement and representation to test some of the more complex issues arising from the organisational ramifications of the proposed design. Nevertheless in large scale systems development this can be an extremely valuable and important part of the development process since in no other way may it be possible to understand exactly what the impact of the system will be, before many irrevocable decisions have been taken. At this point we overlap with the realm of pilot systems and what is an alternative to the development of a user interface prototype, that is the evolutionary design of the technical system in which the users' involvement is with a live working system as it is developed. These approaches are not entirely dichotomous, they may indeed be used in combination, but the choice of which provides the better route will depend upon the particular nature and circumstances of the design of the system being developed.

3. THE CONDUCT OF PROTOTYPING EXERCISES

Much attention has recently been focused upon the advent of rapid prototyping tools and application generators which are often cited as a ready made solution to the problem of designing highly usable interfaces, Tagg 1985. However, there is often little reference to the circumstances that would make the use of such application generators and tools fully effective in the design of systems. It is timely to remind ourselves that simply stating that user system problems can be resolved by the use of prototypes is a gross over-simplification of the situation and may be misconstrued by those designers who are seeking to take account of human factors issues without having any specialised knowledge of the area. While prototyping is a familiar concept to most technical designers they usually use it in relation to the performance testing of the technical functions of the products which they have designed. The methods, that are appropriate to judging whether the system works well from the users point of view are rather different from those that apply to the assessment of technical performance. It is these methods that draw upon the established discipline of ergonomics and psychology. Thus it brings in a whole range of techniques which will be unfamiliar to the systems designer but which will demand a considerable degree of experience to make effective. If we are to make effective use of prototypes in the design process we must develop ways of formalising the procedures and integrating them into the design process so that the information which can be gathered is fed back and used.

Different forms and stages of design have different requirements from prototypes in terms of the way in which exercises are conducted, the use which will be made of the information which is generated, the users who will be involved and the forms in which data is gathered. There are however a number of general principles which apply and they all fall under the broad heading of the realistic representation of the circumstances in which the system under design is expected to be used and thus the extent to which one can simulate realistic conditions for end use in the prototype.

3.1 Adherence to Design Assumptions

It is important that the prototype version incorporates the same assumptions and constraints that will govern the interface which emerges from the final design, although the prototype of the interface which the user sees does not necessarily have to be based on the anticipated form of technical solution. The designer may be able to think of a number of alternative technical routes which will achieve the required interface characteristics. In some circumstances the data collected from the prototype may be used to determine aspects of its technical solution. In either case the solution or solutions offered must be judged to be capable of being implemented.

I would like to use the issue of system response times as an example of these issues. We have sufficient information available to enable us to specify recommended values for system response times relative to broad categories of task and user. Usually these recommended values will specify maxima and the shorter the time specified the greater the resource implications for the system. Thus when any uncertainty exists about the chosen values or there is a need to trade-off the recommended values against the cost of the system, it is critical that the users are given the opportunity to provide direct feedback on a prototype version of the system, which mimics the outcome anticipated for the current design solution. Yet it is all too easy for a prototype based on a micro to produce relatively fast response times which can in no way be replicated when the final system is implemented on a central mainframe computer. It requires positive action, however, to institute features such as the predicted values for system response time in a prototype, particularly when they are known to be likely to reduce the general acceptability of the version presented to the users. A further consideration to be borne in mind is the requirement that features such as these, which are common to the whole system, may give rise to interaction effects which would not be predicted from the evaluation of the effects of single variables. Thus one must strive not only to look at the effects of individual elements in the proposed design but also to embed general features within all stages of the prototype so that the effects of their interaction with other variables may be kept under review.

In some situations it is possible to imagine that there is insufficient information to allow the full simulation of the system or it is impossible to produce the full scale of the system. This is particularly critical in relation to the accurate representation of the task attributes. For example it may be very difficult to create a realistic task scenario where a large database will normally be created in the final system. Alternatively, it may be that the task which is to be created represents some quite considerable deviation from current practice and it is not yet possible to say what form it will take, for example if it must follow some proposed change in legislation. These things do not represent a reason for not undertaking prototyping, indeed uncertainty about what is to come may well be the most powerful lever for the creation of some advance version of the system which allows outcomes to be explored. However the conduct of the prototyping exercises must take into account such limitations. Here we have an example of the need for careful and systematic planning of the use of prototypes. It is not sufficient to say 'I have created a part of this system and I have tried it out and the users like it' when one knows that it bears little resemblance to that which will ultimately emerge, either because it is different in significant respects or because it represents but a small part of the whole.

3.2 The Importance of Hands on Use

In addition to presenting users with an accurate representation of the anticipated design the users should be able to use the prototype in a realistic way if data which is directly relevant to the design is to be gathered.

Unfortunately it is not uncommon for those people who are creating prototypes to feel that they have satisfied the requirement to prototype the user interface of a system when they have created a technically viable version of the interface which senior management have approved. Passive inspection of prototype versions of computerised systems particularly when this is not done by genuine end users is not an adequate basis for informed judgement. Yet I can cite two recent examples in which this appears to be the basis upon which user involvement with the prototype was expected to operate.

In one case the primary use of the prototype was said to be concerned with its role in satisfying the steering committee, responsible for the overall implementation of the project, that it was possible to produce what they were expecting. However, it is not entirely clear that this steering committee had any firm notion of what they did expect from the computer system, and they had no opportunity to try the system out. In the other case a small team of designers, who had a long history of commitment to user involvement, became so absorbed in the technical developments which they had in hand that they managed to forget that the primary purpose of the development of their prototype was to try it out with prospective users. These people happily congratulated themselves on the fact that their steering committee had approved the design and that they could go into formal development. When it was pointed out to them that they now had a prototype available which they could use with their intended population they were quite astonished and extremely contrite because, as they said themselves, they had fallen into the trap which they so often criticised others for falling into.

It is perhaps worthwhile to speculate about some of the reasons why such problems may arise. They largely seem to be associated with the power base which authorises the design process itself. The prototype becomes a significant source of proof that the designers can deliver to those who pay the ultimate bills and this tends to dominate the thinking as difficulties become more critical and more intense. It is necessary to remind people that there are important economic and social benefits which derive from getting the users' view of the system to feed into the design process and prototyping with end users makes a critical contribution to this.

Having achieved the commitment to involve end users in the evaluation of prototypes it is still necessary to ensure that this evaluation is based on active 'hands-on' use of the system. This directly interacts with the earlier point about the need to experience concrete versions of proposals rather than abstract ones. The most effective way of making the experience more concrete, is for the users to work with the system, inputting information, using the keyboard if that is the intended device, and acting in accordance with the information which is output through the screen. This implies that the prototype of an interactive system must be capable of behaving interactively and that a degree of formality must be introduced when users are exposed to it, so that they can be directed to engage in certain activities which will use the interactive capacity. Self directed passive inspection tends to focus on static elements such as screen layout or the use of colour, which may be important, but which are less critical than the dynamic relationship between the operation of the system and the person's task. The features required in a prototype for hands-on use are summarised in figure 2.

Figure 2: Features required in a prototyping exercise involving 'hands-on' use.

- creation of a relevant task context
- availability of relevant source information (documents, telephone calls, knowledge held by task performer)
- data input
- presentation of output
- conduct of appropriate input/output transformations, or their simulation
- specified tasks or sub-tasks which the user can be directed to engage in

It is worth making the additional point that it is not simply a question of the use of the prototype in an interactive way which is at issue here. It is also necessary that the time for which the system is used is sufficient to allow users to become familiar with the way it works. The amount of experience which is required to give meaningful data depends upon the nature of the issue being studied. When one is testing the match between individual dialogues and the tasks which they are to support it may sufficient to run relatively short term tests but if one is concerned with the impact of a large scale system on job design, and work organisation, then the prototype evaluation must continue not simply over hours or even days but over weeks and possibly months. Inevitably this relates to the sampling issue and decisions about the viability of the exercises which are to be conducted. It will be usual to find that in order to provide valid and reliable data one needs large numbers of subjects. This will be precluded in long term testing and the results, consequently, may be of a more tentative nature.

In all these cases the problem of creating appropriate conditions for hands on use are rendered more complex when new tasks are to be created. One has to consider the ways in which the task will actually be performed even if one is not going to create a full simulation of a working group and some scenario must guide the terms upon which individuals are to use the system. In some circumstances this may mean that one is not only faced with the question of training the user to work the system but also to perform the task itself.

3.3 Sampling the User Population

The pursuit of realism extends to the requirement to recruit a representative sample of the projected user population, which will take part in the prototyping exercises. A major dimension affecting the creation of this sample reflects the ease with which one can gain access to the proposed user population. The ends of this dimension correspond to design processes which will result in "off-the-shelf" products at one end, and a design which has been tailored to a specific organisation's application at the other end. The suppliers of "off-the-shelf" systems are confronted with the problem that their users are at a much greater distance from them than is the case with users for whom bespoke systems are being designed. Even if their initial specification for the proposed product and its user population is well developed, they may find it impossible to recruit a representative sample of users. For example it may be intended that the product is marketed on an international basis; it becomes impractical to consider running evaluations of prototypes with the many different nationalities who may ultimately take delivery, yet they might in fact be expected to respond differently and to yield different kind of feedback to the design process.

Another problem when developing an off-the-shelf product may be that it raises issues of commercial confidentiality and that there is a reluctance to obtain a truly representative reaction lest this should also lead to premature disclosure of sensitive product information. Another factor having somewhat similarly constraining effects is the fear that if the prototype version of the system is unsatisfactory in some respects it may lead to adverse impressions in the potential customer base. These considerations operate in direct opposition to the effective early use of prototypes. The usual solution is to try and recruit a sample of users, who will test early versions of the system, from within the organisation's own employees. However this limits the use which can be made of prototypes of more specialised products because of the limited availability or complete absence of any relevant personnel. It is no accident that the products which have been most extensively evaluated in pre-production phases are secretarial workstations. Prototype testing of products at a more advanced stage of development is usually carried out within selected customer sites, having good relationships with the supplier organisations. Inevitably these users do expect that the prototype system they are testing will be more complete and in a form very close to the anticipated final versions and as has already been said, this rules out the possibility of getting early feedback before the design has become relatively fixed.

In design environments where the organisation is developing systems for its own use, or there is a close collaboration with the client, the problem of recruiting representative users is relatively simpler. In these cases there can be more systematic attention to sampling issues, such as the representation of all grades of staff who will be expected to use the system and the gathering of data from users in a representative sample of locations. These factors are important if the variance which exists within user and task requirements is to be adequately explored in relation to the development of a system which is tailored to the organisation's needs. An additional advantage which is often cited in relation to prototyping in this type of design environment is that the users who are involved in evaluation will develop a more direct stake in the outcome and become more committed to the eventual implementation. While this is undoubtedly true, it is important to consider whether it should be welcomed as a primary goal for prototyping exercises, since it can have inhibiting effects on the willingness of designers to expose somewhat imperfect designs for evaluation. The reason for this reluctance are similar to those cited in relation to the development of off-the-shelf products. It is usually more important that users understand that as the system develops, and the results of prototyping are evaluated, it may be necessary to reach compromise solutions because of the needs of different user groups. For this reason it is critical that representation does reflect all main categories of users. In a recent example I was most concerned to find that only one of three main user groups would actually be asked to evaluate the prototype. The reason for restricting the sample stemmed from certain political and organisational difficulties in involving all three. However, it was evident that when the results of the prototype evaluations were fed back, the absence of comparable data from the other two user groups would undermine their validity and could be used to argue against the acceptance of any design changes. This is clearly an unsatisfactory situation.

Up to this point discussion of the issues surrounding the sampling of users has been focussed upon the importance of having experienced task performers because they represent the current situation. In some circumstances the important consideration is the issue of creating a sample of naive users. For example if the intention is to develop a greenfield site with personnel who have not taken any part in the performance of similar tasks previously or if one wishes to assess training routines, one would need to be in a position to obtain samples which represent the potential pool of new recruits.

3.4 Ensuring the timeliness of user prototyping

The benefits of carrying out prototyping with users can only be realised if the data is generated early enough in the design cycle to affect the design decisions as they are made. This point has been referred to in relation to the need to have access to the relevant user population, in the previous section. One consequence of relatively late prototyping in supplier organisations delivering off-the-shelf products is that the alpha test prototyping is often used to inform the next enhancement of a product rather than being acted upon within the current design cycle. Nevertheless the economic benefits of early user prototyping will be much greater if testing can be carried out at a time which will allow the incorporation of the resulting data into the current round of decision making. For example I have recently had experience of a system which had undergone six months of development work before it was subjected to evaluation in prototype form. The intention had been that the prototype testing would be mainly concerned with refinements in the details of the software interface. In practice, what was a revealed was a basic defect in the ergonomics of the design of a software module, which had been incorporated into the product from its inception. This module was virtually self-contained and could in fact have been evaluated independently of the overall product. Early evaluation would have avoided an expensive period of unproductive development which resulted in the product being dropped.

In large scale design processes, and particularly in those based on 'bespoke' requirements, the role of prototyping will be incremental. Figure 3 illustrates some of the ways in which the sequencing of design decisions may structure the order in which different aspects of user needs could be studied in a prototype. This reflects progression from more generalised design decisions, which provide the infrastructure for the development, through to more detailed decisions which are made later in the process. However, it may be noted that issues such as job design or work organisation choices cannot be prototyped until the later stages of design, because they are dependent for proper evaluation upon the creation of a fully operational system. Other ways of handling the process of determining user requirements in relation to ergonomic issues such as these will be needed for use in the early stages of design.

Figure 3: Prototyping Activities in Relation to the Design Cycle

	DESIGN	USER NEEDS
Earlier	Decisions about the fundamental characteristics of the system; sizing; centralised vs. distributed applications.	HF issues relating to system response times, volume of information per screen, organisation of information flow through transactions.
	Decisions about the interface, dialogue and screen design which may be varied within limits.	HF issues relating to task fit; user knowledge; the system-paper interface; feedback.
Later	Decisions about organisation within the individual office units.	Job design options; implementation strategies; allocations of VDUs between and within offices; effect of customer access to screens.

4. DATA COLLECTION IN PROTOTYPING EXERCISES

The techniques of data collection which are relevant to prototyping are those which are fundamental to the disciplines of ergonomics and applied psychology. The major influence on the way in which those techniques are used will be the fact that the data which is to be gathered needs to be applied to decisions about current, real world problems. Therefore the most important criteria for selecting methods and techniques will derive from the design environment itself and the opportunities and constraints which it offers. From my experience with prototyping activities, I would suggest that this means that the need for a systematic approach and advance planning is critical and that it is preferable to choose simple methods and measures rather than complex ones. The reasons for this are the limitations on time and resources which are common to all design processes and the fact that it is necessary to provide designers with clear information.

Direct observation of sources of difficulty and errors and subjective measures of user response will reveal the most important issues. If necessary, these can be followed up by more detailed monitoring of interactions which are seen to be sources of special difficulty without obvious explanation or resolution. Thus the approach in selecting the methods should be to commence with the general and move to the specific when it seems necessary. Global monitoring of elementary units of behaviour, such as keystrokes, is unlikely to be an effective way of using prototyping resources. It would, of course, be extremely convenient to have access to such detailed information on demand, but such options depend upon the availability of sophisticated test environments such as that proposed in the Alvey MMI Laboratory, Alvey 1986, and this has yet to become fully operational. In the longer term one can see that such developments would be valuable to supplier organisations who will have a continuous flow of products to subject to prototype testing. It is more doubtful whether it would be worthwhile for an organisation developing its own application systems, to invest in highly sophisticated data capture devices in anticipation of the possibility that they may have problems which require detailed analysis.

It is also the case that the practice of using prototyping to improve the design of systems from the user's point of view is still so limited that current efforts should focus on getting the basic principles in place. In many design situations much of the effort relating to prototyping and the collection of data will have to come from existing members of design teams and it will be essential to focus attention on the critical human issues. This goal is likely to be better served by the gathering of simple data direct from the users.

5. INSTITUTIONALISING PROTOTYPING WITHIN THE DESIGN PROCESS

Prototyping is one way of representing the user's needs within the design process and should form part of a wider strategy which establishes the formal requirements for user involvement. Design processes are themselves increasingly subject to formalisation which can take a variety of different forms depending upon the nature of the application area and the type of organisation responsible for the development. It must be expected therefore that different approaches will be required in different circumstances and that the details of the formal approach to user involvement will reflect this variation. However, the generality of some of the issues relevant to prototyping has been discussed in this paper and sets the scene for reviewing the design process and identifying specific stages at which prototyping exercises should be conducted. The principles to be followed and the criteria for a successful activity can be established so that data becomes available in a relevant and timely manner.

However, the introduction of effective prototyping will impact on the design process and on the designers themselves. They should be getting substantive feedback from users much earlier than they are accustomed to and thus will be faced with the need to make changes to their designs. This will mean that the planning of the timescales for each stage must make allowance for this, with the longer development time in the early stages being justified by the reduction in the need to correct things at the end of the process.

Equally important is the training required both in relation to the general principles and in relation to specific skills. If prototyping is to be used successfully it should not be regarded as a threat or challenge to the designer's skills and expertise, and designers need to be made aware of the benefits which it will bring. There will also be the requirement to create design teams with the requisite range of skill and experience to conduct prototyping exercises with users. This implies the need to enlarge design teams by bringing in new expertise or by providing specialist training for existing members.

Prototyping can only make a meaningful contribution to the quality of the design if it is an integral part of the design process. This means that it is not simply a question of doing the right things but doing them in the right place at the right time where they will actually have an effect.

6. CONCLUSION

This paper has attempted to outline the potential of user prototyping as a tool for promoting good human factors design and has also attempted to identify some of the constraints which will operate on the use of the tool. The conclusions which are arrived at are based on experience of design teams who are just beginning to prototype in this way. As an ergonomist one learns much from their experience and from one's own efforts to help them and there is no doubt that there is much more to be learned from future studies in this area.

REFERENCES

Alvey, 1986, The MMI Laboratory: an Infrastructure Project, Alvey Programme Project MMI/091; poster paper at the Alvey Conference, 30 June - 4 July.

Bruner J S, Goodnow J J and Austin G A, 1956, A Study of Thinking, Wiley

Harker S D P and Eason K D, 1984, Repressing the User in the Design Process, Design Studies, Vol 5, No 2, 78-85

Tagg R M, 1985, Fourth and Fifth Generation Languages for Information Management in 'State of the Art Review: the information initiative'. Pergamon Infotech, Maidenhead.

WORK WITH DISPLAY UNITS 86
B. Knave and P.-G. Widebäck (eds.)

USE OF AN ENTIRE WORKFORCE AS COMPUTER

By Richard Tabor Greene
University of Michigan Japanese Studies Center
Inst. of Labor and Industrial Relations
Manager, Knowledge Automation, EDS/General Motors

2000 people in one organization between 1968 and 1974 participatorily managed their own psychological protocols at work; redesigned the structure and function of their entire organization in annual July 30 day workshop conferences; and in general designed and managed their organization as if it were an array of 2000 computer processors each processor of which happened to be a human being. This imaging of societal structures upon computer technology represents one instance of a growing dialog the other part of which is a growing imaging of computer systems using societal metaphors like Hewitt's Society of Experts AI.

There are three sizes of computer relation to society: micro--things like how particular kinds of work are transformed by particular features of computation; macro--things like how social properties are modified by the spread and characteristics of computerization; and macro--things like how all parts and self consciousnesses of society are subtly transformed by the impact of computerization. Studies involving computer equipment and parts of society interacting directly with that equipment are literal studies. Studies of society reacting to computer equipment trends are also literal studies. Studies of society interacting with non-computer issues and concerns but in ways spawned by the computer indirectly are non-literal or metaphoric studies. This paper concerns the latter category, in particular, how the computer has become a metaphor helping society both understand and reorganize itself in general in areas having nothing directly to do with computation. This paper tells the story of one organization that managed its people, 2000 of them, as if they were each processors in a parallel array.

Typical paranoid responders to computation envision this as the height of inhumanity; in fact, imagining and treating people as processors in a parallel array turned out, to be a pioneering form of management and design decentralization, and led to radical increases in participation by the employees of the organization in the organization.

The IEEE Journal of Man, Systems, and Cybernetics a few years ago devoted a special issue to researchers at Carnegie Mellon University who were taking various algorithms of parallel "society of experts" computation, and matching them with various extant human organizations to see whether human corporations, governments, etc. might have "algorithms", might be determined by certain axioms of information flow, and the like. Herbert Simon decades earlier had promoted "bound rationality" as a principle underlying why organizations took on the structural forms they did and why managers took on the choice behaviors they did. Recently, Thinking Machines Inc., under Mr. Hillis' leadership, developed "The Connection Machine", as an extension of previous work by Minsky and Carl Hewitt, on modelling computation itself on human social organization. Hewitt took the scientific community and its agendas, conferences, faculties, and other events and institutions and tried to build a model of "computational community" out of computer software and hardware elements that embodied this aspect of society as an algorithm of computation. It is the inverse of this pioneering Hewitt "metaphor" (taking a part of society and making computation like it) that this paper describes the accomplishment of (how one institution took a part of computation and made society like it).

I was director of Protocol for the Network Relations post of the Ecumenical Institute during the years that this experiment in "computerfying society" took place. That organization's embodiment of this "computerfying society" can be scanned by the following:

a. an organization whose workday was divided into a knowing, doing, and being section

b. an organization all of whose employees (1500 to 2000 during the years of experimentation) gathered each July for a full month of workshops during which they redesigned all parts of the organization every year

c. an organization which studied materials every week on Thursday nights which materials were exercises in specific mental protocols devised to cure problems in the organization diagnosed cognitively

d. an organization which invented the "9 Week Week" such that ordinary society activity would be enveloped in a social structure that futuricly compensated for faults in society at large (based on an analysis done in those July's mentioned above) and such that each person in the organization worked in 9 different "jobs" in 9 different rooms, with 9 different sets of colleagues, using 9 different cognitive skill sets every week.

The particular function that most clearly demonstrated the power of shaping societies of people to more closely resemble processors in parallel array computers and that most clearly demonstrated that metaphor itself was research and development in the Ecumenical Institute. One example is described below.

These "management of cognition" components were predicated on a finding that modern social structures were cognitively underpowered relative to the flood of information and interrelatedness of all social entities characterizing these latter half of the 20th century days. By cognitively refiguring common mundane social functions like eating breakfast in families versus eating breakfast in neighborhoods, taking political happenings in nations as "news" versus taking world-wide research happenings as "news" and the like, cognition as robust as societal problems might emerge.

Some 2000 employees of the Institute were assigned to abstract a different book every week for 12 weeks, which books were in certain categories assigned each of 104 regional training centers of the Institute and which abstracts were collected and published in volumes sent back to all 2000 employees. 24,000 books were thus abstracted in 3 months and those abstracts were themselves melded into a "metabuilt" model of the domain being studied. Not only this but the mental procedures used to develop the abstract were specified iteratively in each week's Thursday night procedures based on central analysis of last week's procedures and how good the results attained last week were. Not only that but a format evolved during the 12 weeks which format gave room for the different protocols employed in the abstracting while commonizing somewhat the final results achieved.

Saying all this in words obscures the immense difficulty of actually achieving processor-like human study behavior. Key to seeing the suffering society as a whole endures unnecessarily now everywhere for lack of processor-like treatment of research, study, design, and management, is investigating the problems this actual institution, the Ecumenical Institute, had in its pioneering implementations of processor-like business functions.

First, the human propensity for opinion had to be handled by the protocols of the abstract building such that it was "subtractable out" in the meshing phase of deriving a global model from the many abstracts on any one subtopic. People hated not being asked to give their opinion in the context of persuading others with verbal skill but rather being asked to mark down their opinion as a clue to overall bias to be subtracted out of their abstracts.

Second, a momentum for logical argumentation had to give way to the enormous collection of facts involved in abstracting 24,000 articles on one topic. People wanted to fight with each other over how their particular 1/24,000th of the job was righter than the other 23,999ths of the data. That the numbers made such attempts not only patently arrogant and foolish but conceptually untenable as the number of models superior to any one individual's model rapidly became large, did not stop the sheer momentum in those doing the abstracting toward "being right" in spite of all data.

Third, the suppression of individual skill and talent advantage involved in following detailed protocols frustrated just those employees who either intended to rise above all other employees thru college degrees of other talent sources not available to others or the like. That is professors and business executives, to take two examples from many, found it exceedingly frustrating to be asked not to lead others but to contribute like others their bit to the overall corporate abstracting procedures each week in a way just like everyone else contributed. Many professors involved rejected results of the abstracting along the way, not based on a better data base or model of the data but based on frustration at not being able to use special personal talent to sway the overall group of 2000 save the small room for talent afforded all alike equally in the weekly Thursday night abstracting procedures.

Some implications of the above difficulties are that the same routine "Taylorization" of work that clerks using VDTs experience, if applied to R&D, company policy design, and like functions handled today by elites, both enriches the working environment of all employees and immensely frustrates just those employees whose work satisfaction is most based on special talents or abilities not to be shared with other employees.

Also, a leap into greater cognitive intensity is fostered when work is assigned by cognitive protocol not by goal or task name. If the designing and designating of what protocols the whole body is to try out any given week, is done participatorily by the whole group itself in an annual workshop meeting (itself a protocol controlled event not a bunch of discussions) then the organization itself manages its own mental protocols to ever higher levels of performance.

Sidebenefits of this work now being applied to industry. First, the concept of the Meta-cognitive Organization, the organization that invites all its members to design their own mental protocols at work on a daily basis, is being tried out in parts of several leading US firms.

Second, a side-effect being explored in several Japanese companies is the so-called Cognitive Furniture movement wherein walls, doors, tabletops, blackboards, etc. are being transformed from partitions from other people and the elements into modes of heightening thought. The Panasonic blackboard that remembers what is written on it and prints out a copy is one commercial product derived from author's training in Cognitive Furniture principles.

Third, a form of reading based on grasping the cognitive protocol producing the text by typing "macrostructures" in the text has been invented and found by the author to be a prime discriminant of top executives from top managers. This form of reading, done by groups at first and only later by individuals, uses the mind as a processor in an unusually literal way.

Space does not permit references; key researcher names have been included in the body of the text.

WORK WITH DISPLAY UNITS 86
B. Knave and P.-G. Widebäck (eds.)

OFFICE AUTOMATION AS AN OPPORTUNITY FOR AN ORGANIZATIONAL CHECK-UP

Michele VISCIOLA, Antonio RIZZO
CNR/Istituto di Psicologia/Roma

and

Sebastiano BAGNARA
Università di Siena and
CNR/IStituto di Psicologia/Roma

The introduction of computer-based technologies in the office is often accompanied by negative effects', which are assumed to be determined by the lack of compatibility between the strategy of OA adopted and the work organization in which automation is put into action. This view, though not always inadequate, can be misleading, since a negative organizational impact may be due also to inconsistencies in the previous work organization. Since OA takes usually place step by step the inconsistencies appear mainly at the 'interfaces' between the automated and the 'manual' part of an office, where any incompatibility makes rise problems and conflicts, which, in turn, can have a negative feedback on the efficiency of the OA. This view will be illustrated through a case study where it will be shown 'negative' effects have to be attributed to inefficiency in the work procedures followed in the 'manual' part of office, whose outputs have to be handled by the automated office. It is concluded that an OA process can be seen as an opportunity to disclose previous organizational inconsistencies.

1. INTRODUCTION

The introduction of computer-based technology in the offices is often accompanied by "negative effects" or "unexpected consequences" (Diani and Bagnara, 1984). These effects are commonly attributed to the strategy of office automation (OA) adopted. When users do not play a significant role in the design of OA and the strategy of introduction of the new technologies prevents their participation, workers usually complain of many psychophysical disorders and, besides, conflicts and organizational breakdowns are very frequently observed (Wainwright and Francis, 1984; Diani, Misiti and Bagnara, 1985).

Moreover, since automation develops step by step and long-term consequences can not be anticipated in detail, it can be conceived as an adaptive process by which the technical system is fitted in with the organizational aims and constraints. This adaptive process can make appear unforeseen problems which require **ad hoc** technical, professional and organizational solutions (Rockart and

Flannery, 1984).

So, "negative effects" and/or "unexpected consequences" of OA can be due to the strategy of participation adopted and/or to the lack of compatibility between the OA system and the work organization in which the automation has to be put into action.

As for this last point, it has to be underlined that, when OA is introduced into complex systems, the process itself does not involve the whole system from the very beginning. As a matter of fact, even though a comprehensive strategy has been adopted, office automation is put into action in small-scale working units and does not involve all the functionally-linked areas.

Moreover, even within the "automatized" working unit, office automation does not affect at the same level all the work activities carried out. OA primarily affects (to a point that they are no more executed by human operators) well-structured activities, whereas the less-structured ones are only marginally modified.

Furthermore, those areas of the organization which are not within the "automatized" unit, even though related to it, are indirectly affected by OA. For example, they can receive information from and/or trasmit information to the "automatized" unit. However, information can have different level of reliability and of transparency and the control over it can very much vary and require different knowlodge and skills by the operators, and organizational procedures as a function of whether the information processing has been carried out by a human or by a computer-based tool. This is true not only for the areas related to an "automazited" unit, but also for the "automatized" unit itself. The effectiveness of the automatized office will suffer from the effects of the working modalities of other sectors functionally interdependent with it, as long as these sectors cannot rely on information processing procedures automatized or, at least, compatible with the automation. In other words, the underutilization of the automation potentialities and the distrust in initiatives of working transformation may be due to the incompatibilities between automatized and not-automatized sectors of the organization.

It follows that the design of an automatized system has to take into account the whole organization which it belongs to. From this point of view, the OA needs and offers an opportunity for an organizational check-up.

2. THE CASE STUDY

2.1. The context

The study was jointly requested by the trade unions and the management of the company and carried out by the authors as an independent research team. Since it was aimed at evaluating working conditions and operators' wellbeing after the introduction of VDTs in a office of the company, the study actually consisted of two parts: a bio-medical evaluation and psychological survey. The two parts have been carried out in parallel. The planning of the studies was the result of joint decisions and the studies themselves have been carried out having a high level of collaboration both between the two research teams and the workers' and management' representatives. Given this continuous exchange of information and the degree of collaboration, joint conclusions and recommendations had been drawn.

However, this paper will report on the psychological survey only. For sake of completeness, it has to be underlined that the bio-medical evaluation agreed with the conclusions of the psychological evaluation which will be reported later in this paper.

The study was undertaken under the umbrella of Statute of the Workers' Rights (approved in 1970) (for an extensive evaluation of the occupational health policy in Italy, see Bagnara, Biocca and Mazzonis, 1981; Misiti and Bagnara, 1986) which allows workers' control over working conditions by means of company-independent technical assistance. However, the management wellcomed the study proposed by the trade-unions since the introduction of VDT in an office area had given rise to conflitcts and worker complanints and alarm about health consequences. Since the company was up to introduce OA in a large scale, the management recognized that the study could offer the opportunity to single out possible errors made and to identify a better strategy for putting OA into action with no or very few conflicts and micro-conflicts. As a matter of fact, the first experience of OA had been accompanied by long-lasting strikes and by many individual requests not to work with VDTs and to be moved to "traditional" workplaces.

Both trade unions and management were well aware that conflicts, complaints and individual "flights" from the automatized office were to be attributed to a general perception of stressful working conditions.

As above noticed, this paper will report about possible relations between transformations in organizational procedures (automatized vs. "manual") and workers psychological wellbeing. The bio-medical health evaluation will not be discussed.

2.2. The office

The office under study belongs to an Electric Power Supply Company. It provides face-to-face and via phone assistance to customers requiring information about received, and supposed wrong, invoices, or on how to negotiate, sign, modify or cancel a contract. So, this office is an "interface" between the company and the customers and its performance is crucial in establishing the "public image" of the company itself. This is the reason why the OA was first introduced in this office: the company wanted to improve its image through a more efficient interaction with the customers.

The work done by an operator in the office can be exemplfied as follows. When a customer receives an invoice which s/he believes overcharged (it is quite unusual the opposite case), s/he can contact through the phone or directly the office and an operator will answer about the requests, by checking whether an error has been made. Before the OA, the operator, after checking the invoice for trivial errors, had to look through the files, find the data from which the amount to be payed has been calculated and detect possible errors. All the se operations were done "manually" and operators had to rely on their own knowledge and mental representation on how data were organized, where to find them, on the typical errors, and so on. After the OA, the operator has not to move from the VDT through which data can be fetched, displayed and controlled because an automatized data base can be easily reached and used.

However, an operator in this office is not in charge of the reliability of the data about a costumer, since the data bank is fed by other offices which follow "manual" procedures. Errors in the data bank can affect the VDT operators quality of work at least in three ways: a) the more errors in the data bank, the more errors in the invoices delivered and, consequently, the more customers requiring information. Of course, the degree of politeness of the customers varies as function of the number and the seriousness of the errors. So, more errors mean higher workload and stressful interactions. b) When an error can not be detected through the automatized system, a painful search has to be done to sastisfy the customer. It means that the operator has to go first through all the available automatized procedures and then to try to identify which "old and manual" procedure can be of help. The operator has to rely on at least two different mental representations of his/her work, so rendering it unnecessarily complex. What is worse is that c) the operator is less likely to find and adopt satisfactory strategy to adapt to the new conditions of work. That is, stress coping strategies are made difficult to become part of the operator behavior.

However, these consequences of errors made by "non automatized" areas were only highlighted by the introduction of OA. They were part of the everyday work experience before OA. And they were due to organizational failure present both in the areas which still produce them and of the interfaces between those areas and the office under study. The consequence was that the positive expectations toward the automation, based on the hope that it would have improved the quality of work, were not fulfilled. So, a radical change in the attitudes toward the automation was observed.

3. METHODOLOGY

When a study is aimed at analyzing the transformations in the work content, measurements and observations should be carried out both before and after modifications such as, for example, the replacement of the traditional technologies with more advanced ones.

When this methodological procedure is not applicable, as in the case of the present study, other methods have to be used. The procedure adopted in this study consists of two methods: a) Subjective evaluation of organizational stress ("Perceived Job Characteristics" Questionnaire, by Caplan et alii, 1974), and b) Analysis of work organization and individual task carried out by utilizing the "Office Analysis Methodology (Sirbu et alii, 1984). The analysis of work organization, based on OAM (which is particularly suitable for describing unstructured and/or semistructured activities which are of crucial importance in an office system) allows to identify the objective conditions to which subjective evaluations of perceived stressors can be related. In other words, this method allows to identify which component of work activity should be modified in order to reduce stress. The subjective evaluation of organizational stress should provide a measure of how much an organization fits with the needs of the humans performing their tasks within it. The assumption is that when work content prescribed and/or allowed by a work organization fulfills workers'expectations and capabilities no stress should be perceived. In other words, subjective evaluation of stress should provide a measure on how good is an organization with reference to the criterion of the psychophysical wellbeing of the people in it.

When these two methods are used in such a design that an experimental and a control group are compared, a measure of the modifications determined by an innovation (either technological or organizational or both) can be obtained. The analysis of work provides the basis for establishing whether the two groups can be safely compared, and so avoiding the well known criticism to most of the VDT studies (Laübli and Grandjean, 1984). Since, it is unlikely to find out two groups which differ only for the factor under study, it is much safer to compare them having a clear-cut knowledge of how much they differ especially for factors which can affect the variable under study. This is more true when the factor under study is complex.

By keeping in mind that the evaluation of OA is based on the criterion of psychophysical wellbeing, the comparison between a group affected and one unaffected by OA should show how much OA improved or deteriorated working conditions. As a consequence, when the comparison between groups show a difference, it can be safely attributed to OA only when a modification in work content can be identified between the two working conditions.

4. RESULTS AND DISCUSSION

The comparison between the OA and the control group on the data obtained through the subjective evaluations of the organizational stressors showed a striking similarity. The two groups significantly differed only on a few items. This similarity was confirmed by the results of the work analysis conducted by using the OAM. The work analysis showed that the OA modified the "structured activities". Almost all the routinary procedures were executed via automation, whereas the variances and most of the error correction activities were still carried out through "manual" procedures. So, the introduction of automation changed how many operations were executed, whereas no change could be observed on why the operations were performed. As a consequence, since the goals of the office organization and many relevant activities in it did not change with OA, the overall similarity between the two groups should be expected.

However, the OA did introduce modifications. The change in how an operation was performed, and the availability of a great amount of the needed information via VDT (that means less movements, high postural costrictiveness and less time to get the required information determined transformations in the work content. The procedures for searching information become standard and rigid and the degree of freedom in the choice of strategies was considerably reduced. These observations collected through the work analysis were corroborated by the subjective evaluations on organizational stressors. The decrease in uncertainty in the strategy choice was confirmed by the fact that the OA group perceived a lower level of "role ambiguity" as compared to the control group (2.32 vs. 3.38; p .01). The OA produced a beneficial effect as far as what people expected and were expected to do in their work. However, a more precise role definition did not contribute to reduce the perceived "work load variance", which depended on how many customers were waiting for assistance in a given moment during the work hours. The evaluation was actually the same for both OA and control group (3.80 vs. 3.79).

This result is of crucial importance for evaluating the impact of OA in the office organization. As anticipated before, workload did not depend on the characteristics of the office where the OA was introduced but from the related areas were the errors were made. Moreover, both the OA and the "manual" office units could not plan their workload which depended also upon the behavior of the customers. A customer could find more convenient to phone or to come to the office during only some of the working hours. However, the core problem was that the workload could be reduced not by trying to modify customers' behavior, but by rendering the whole office system more reliable, so reducing the number of customers complaining for errors. OA could reduce the average time needed to detect and to correct errors only after they had been made. It did not make them less likely. This failure could be attributed to how the office system was organized before a part of it was automatized.

This could be indirectly confirmed by the fact that both the OA (2.32) and the control group (3.38) gave subjective evaluations of the "role ambiguity" stressor very much higher than those reported in other studies, such as that of Caplan et alli, (1975))(2.06) and that of Sauter et alli (1983)(1.96). Independently from OA, the work organization in the whole office system was such that people did not exactly know who were responsible of many activities. OA did reduce such an uncertainty. So, a hint that the whole organisation could be ameliorated was provided.

This conclusion does not mean that OA such as that under study is a way to solve organisational inefficiencies. OA itself should not be considered as a criterion of evaluation. However, OA should be utilized as an opportunity to check the efficiency of the whole organization. So, the possibility that the OA might enlarge preexisting organizational discrepancies should be minimized.

When this opportunity is not caught, as was the case of the office under study, some negative consequences should be expected.

Instead of allowing operators to allocate their own attention, higher level mental resources to the objectives of the work done, as should be the case when low level, routinary actions are eliminated, people tend to concentrate themselves on <u>how</u> to execute actions. In the present study, OA operators perceived the objectives of their own work as less defined than the members of the control group (3.10 vs. 3.85; p .01). It has to be underlined that this outcome was obtained after an average of five year familiarity with VDT work. Since the OA system was relatively simple, this result could not be attributed to a poor trasparency of the system itself. After such a long practice, people had a clear cut mental representation of the automatized system and of its potentialities. What was instrumental in determining such an outcome was very likely due to the unpredictable use of two not overlapping mental representations of work activities and procedures: A computer based and a "manual based" representation of the office work. It can be suggested that OA operators tended to reduce the complex handling of the two different mental representations by unifying them at the lower level and so considering them as a single aggregate of mere sequence of actions. As a consequence, whichever the technology used, an action was mentally handeled as such, independently of the higher level objectives they were supposed to be integrated in.

This suggestion was confirmed both by the data obtained through the operators' evaluations on objectives' definition and by observational data. The observational data showed that OA operators were very likely to avoid complex problems raised by the customers by means of social skills. Alternatively, when social skills were not successful the problems were solved by employing the "old" and "manual" procedures.

Such a situation entails two negative consequences. 1) As soon as no operator anymore possesses the mental representation of the "manual" office many problems are simply not solved. This can happen sooner or later as a function of the personnel policy of a company. When OA is accompanied (as is often the case) by a policy which gives the priority to young, newly hired operators at the expense of "old ones", manually well trained employers, complex problems are very soon left apart, even though the still existing organizational failures continue to produce them. The consequence is that the office as a whole is less capable to handle variances and unpredictable events. The office becomes rigid, less adaptive because the skills and knowledge needed to handle it as a system are lost.

2) The reduction of the mental work to the execution of sequences of actions with scarse reference to the objectives prevents and/or delays the adaptation to the new working conditions. Coping strategies to new sources of stress are very unlikely to be discovered and adopted because of the use of an impoverished representation of the reality to face with. In such conditions, people keep on to make use of out-of-date mental representation of fatigue symptoms and to adopt inadequate strategies to detect and counter them (Bagnara, in press).

These effects are negative both for the office effectiveness and productivity and for operators' well being. As it has been shown throughout this paper, they cannot be considered as direct consequences of the introduction of OA, even though OA often highly increases them. They are due to previous failures in work organisation which, if not detected and corrected in time, can undermine OA itself and its expected benefits. So, it can be concluded that when OA is going to be introduced an organizational check-up is highly recommended. It has also to be underlined that the negative effects observed in the present study were quite evident because OA covered only a part of the office system. When large scale OA is introduced thses effects become less clear and can be wrongly attributed to other factors and their elimination or reduction can turn out to be very hard.

Bibliography

Bagnara S. (in press) La fatica come sistema di segnali - Sociologia del lavoro. Bologna (1986).

Bagnara S., Biocca M. and Gattegno Mazzonis D. (1981) Trends in occupational health and safety policy in Italy. International Journal of Health Services. V. 11, 431-451.

Caplan R.D., Cobb S., French J.R.P., Van Harrison R. and Pinneau S.R. Jr. (1975) Job Demands and Work Health. National Institute for Occupational Safety and Health. Pubblication No. 75-160. Cincinnati, Ohio.

Diani M. and Bagnara S. (1984) Unexpected consequences of participative methods in the development of information systems. In E. Grandjean (Ed.) Ergonomics and Health in Modern Offices. London. Taylor & Francis.

Diani M., Bagnara S. and Misiti R. (1984) Participation in technological change: Are there only unexpected consequences? In H.W. Hendrick and O. Brown, Jr. (Eds.) Human Factors in Organizational Design and Management. Amsterdam. North-Holland.

Laübli T. and Grandjean E. (1984) The magic of control groups in VDT field studies. In E. Grandjean (Ed.) Ergonomics and Health in Modern Offices. London. Taylor & Francis.

Misiti R. and Bagnara S. (1986) Participation in health control at the workplace: The Italian experience. In Bagnara S., Misiti R. and Wintersberger H. (Eds.) Work and Health in the 1980s. Berlin. Edition Sigma.

Rockart J.F. and Flannery L.S. (1983) The management of end user computers. Communication of the ACM. 26, 10-18.

Sauter S.L., Gottlieb M.S., Rohrer R.M. and Dodson V.N. (1983) The Well-being of VDT-Users. An Exploratory Study. National Institute for Occupational Safety and Health Pubblication No. 210-79-0034. Cincinnati, Ohio.

Sirbu M. et al. (1984) OAM: An office analysis methodology. Behavior and Information Technology. V. 3, 25-39.

Wainwright J. and Francis A. (1984) Office Automation. Its Design, Implementation and Impact. PR. 13, 1-9.

WORK WITH DISPLAY UNITS 86
B. Knave and P.-G. Widebäck (eds.)

AUTOMATION AND WORK CULTURE

Frigga Haug

Hochschule für Wirtschaft und Politik
Von-Melle-Park 9
D-2000 Hamburg 13
FRG

Ergonomic research in different societies on the compatibility of visual display units (VDU's) with users is certainly an advance in the treatment of working people; this must bei welcomed. Never before have there been so many joint research energies on a world scale attempting to solve a problem for working people. It has always been the case that any onesided use of men as a mere instument must have bad conseqeuences in the long run. Why is it only now, then, that in work with display units, so much attention is concentrated on it?

In my opinion the answer to this question is obscured by the concentration on one visible aspect of a new instrument of work. It is rather like doing research on the consquences of the spade on the spine and the hands - which both doubtlessly suffer, when you dig for too long a time. What we must deal with is the break from one mode of production to the next - say the urban industrial way to the agricultural one. What escapes our attention if we only look at the display unit as such are not only questions of culture and a way of life, which are radically transformed by the change in work.

On the one hand common ergonomic questions concerning work with display units tend to neglect the social nature of human beings and instead pose questions regarding the adequacy of the workers for certain machines or vice versa, thus implicitly reducing people to stimulus-response patterns; on the other hand it is a series of such ergonomic studies which allow us to learn a great deal deal about the natur of humanity.

I will give some examples for illustration:

In Australia, researchers are stirred up by a kind of public disease, which captures workers at display units like a medieval plague especially when they are women. At first they called it "Tendosinovitis", now more generally RSI (repetitive stress injury); thus they name a symptom or a set of symptoms experienced as a paralysis of arms and hands which lasts over months, sometimes more than a year. As far as I know there is no other coutnry, where we can observe the same symptoms arising with the same intensity and suddenness. Instead there is a discussion of sudden abortions and pregnancy problems as a symptom related to work with display units in Sweden; skin allergies are reported from other countries; in Finland the eyes seem mostly affected; also the neck and shoulders are favoured sites where incompatibilities are played out. The cultural differences in how people endure the same change in the arrangement of work makes obvious to us the need to look at work with display units as a societal question. However we do not doubt at all, that any onesided strain or stress of the human body causes long term injuries and should therefore be avoided. Even here though there are specific human differences. It was Lewin who proved empirically that physical stress caused by typing is more obvious, if somebody types something for someone else compared with the process where you subordinate typing to the formulation of your own ideas.

Let us look at the display unit as both a symbol and a part of a revolution in the arrangement of work in society, as a dimension of the microelectronic mode of production. The computer changes the position of the worker in the working process radically. We do not define work with computers adequately, when we say that it is merely work with information. The elements of work are presented to the individual worker not only as information, but also embody a form of a theory of the working process. Thus, there is an element of distance which develops between the worker and the material activities of the work. Rather, the relationship to his or her own work becomes necessarily more reflective. This is even valid for simple data-entry work, and of course for dialogue systems and systems analysis. The logic of a computer is a certain intervention in language an information. One could subject oneself to this logic and try to learn the commands by heart - accompanied by the constant fear and helplessness that one might be thrown out of the system. On the other hand one can appropriate the computer, which means to test its possibilities and enlarge and develop the system - according to its limits. This needs a relation to work comparable to the one usual for experimentors. Work seizes hold of you: a fascination with computers is a well konwn phenomenon:

Computers change work on the following levels:

- The position of the individual worker in the working process is changed: in a certain way he/she is more distant - standing outside the process and above it - nevertheless the relationship to work becomes more intensive and concentrated; often with the growing distance the individual workers become more engaged in work.

- Cooperation becomes at the same time more intensive and less social; the forms of the division of labour become less directly hierarchical; authorities become less competent in the work of their subordinates.

- Work itself changes its character up to the point of a growing uncertainty as to what is work and what not: Are learning times working times? Is the looking for solutions and the effort to solve a problem work or the hindrance of real work? Is looking for mistakes and failures work? Is work with computers men's work or women's work? Is it work mainly consisting of typing and writing or is it more machine work? Is it routine unqualified female work or skilled technical male work?

- Computer work changes the relation of learning and work, of theory and experience. If work has a strong part of development, how is it possible ever to be finished with learning? What sort of education do you need, to be really able to master a computer? Is it necessary to arrange work as a form of learning and how is that different from learning by doing?

- With the change in the relation to work and the change in the content of work, work culture and workers identity have to be constructed anew.

- Finally the breaks in the working process necessitate a new order of politics at work.

In my paper I want to concentrate on some of the above mentioned dimensions, the meaning of which for the working process I think to be very important. They should be included in the question of how people handle the new technology and how they are enabled to use it; what work is doing to them and they to it.

I refer to three empirical researches - on which has already been conducted in the late seventies, which has the advantage of being a very intensive piece of research on a large number of workingplaces (1); the next one was conducted in 1982. This was a qualitative analysis using biographical methods with the advantage that workers themselves were involved in the research on their work (2); and finally one which was conducted in 1985 and focused on office jobs with display units - the data coming from 200 workers (including both men and women) and the method being both quantitative and qualitative, the latter following a form of narrative method (3).

I will give some findings of the last-named empirical study. We included three different types of work:
work in the data entry
work with a dialogue system
work in systems analysis.

All three job positions certainly involved display units. We concentrated on both the actual changes and their perception of the workers themselves. Our questions concerned the fields of qualification, the variety of work, division of labour and hierarchies, forms of cooperation and solidarity, and structures of learning and education.

The first pecularity we met was a contradictory security: our informants reproduced the common opinion that automation would be followed by deskilling, monotony and a tayloristic division of labour - but they also juxtaposed this to another view: that their o w n work had become more qualified, varied, less divided, more cooperative etc. In this way they showed us their own method of coming to terms with the dominating ideas and individual self consciousness: it is done by dividing oneself from society at large and abstracting from individual experience when asked in general. This is at the same time a warning against misunderstandig opinion research as research about facts and provides first-hand information on how workers live contradictions. This idea that all other workingplaces would be bad ones also helps to construct oneself as an elite se apart from the masses. This includes the problem of a supposes solidarity among the assumed unqualified others, who have nothing to loose and a loneliness ans isolation of the qualified self.

Within this context there was a second peculiarity: whereas all these workers expressed loneliness they also reported a growing intensity of cooperation. We call this cooperation as isolation. We had earlier assumed that cooperation in the labour process would always be a positive factor. It is obvious that cooperation is useful if we take the standpoint of effectiveness and productivitiy; but cooperation as an experience of individual workers is generally assumed as being a very positive and human event, a starting point of solidarity, a testimony to the liveliness of social beings. Therefore our questions about cooperation at display units were of strategic importance. In our quantitative analysis we got the strange result that there was a growing variety of and less hierarchical structures, a dissolution of the boundaries of the former divisions of labour and that all of these factors would make working together very dense; but our informants experienced this as a decline in cooperation. We discussed this strange result with groups of office workers: they agreed that there was an increase in the way they were working together, but they did not experience this a strength, but as a kind of threat, in any case an increase in stress and compulsion, an increase in alienation. The new cooperation was understood as an objective and subjective substitution of the former so-called personal relationships. That is: birthday parties in the office, talking about weddings, births,sickness, bringing flowers and making coffee etc. They characterized these personal relationships as a fundamental basis for solidarity. In short they missed a form of relationship which we usually characterize as being a deformation of real work relations within our competitive society: a relationship which does not refer to work itself but only to the fact of being together under the same roof. On the other hand they were not even able to live those new relationships which were related to their work as a sort of developped relations between human beings. To be dependant upon each other in work was experienced as a double threat: a threat to personal relations and a threat to the private person by compulsory work relations, which leaves the individual unprotected. We formulate as a thesis: under social relations of competition and concurrence, compulsory relations within work are a paradox, which is experienced as a threat. The subjection to alienation is not weakened but strengthened. What could be a selfdetermined coordination of individual labour appears in the form of its opposite: as collective work experienced as competition and alienation. We can learn that cooperation is linked to the selfdetermined decisions of individual subjects and if determined from above, contributes to the loss of self-consciousness.

I summarize other findings:
We had assumed that the boundaries between working time and leisure time and those between the different kinds of work would also be an obstacle in the way of personal development and a humanization of work, their dissolution by computerization an opportunity. This opportunity, though was also experienced as a threat and new boundaries were drawn and hardened. The main activity was to hinder openings. Work should not be taken home; even more important: the private person should not enter the sphere of work. Control of personal information becomes an important factor.
This is the third time where we meet the phenomenon of a growing isolation as a consequence of computerization.

Research on display units should keep in mind that diseases are mainly observed among women. Their numbers in office jobs grew in the last decade by 64% and fell in the last 2 years by 5%, whereas in these 2 years male occupations grew by 9%.
We could not accept the argument that women only work in unqualified lower positions, since we met men in the same jobs as well as discovering that 50% of all dialogue-workers were women. So we examined one more prejudice which could explain female problems with computers: women are hostile to technology as such. An aversion against technology could both explain anxiety and an inability to learn as well as being allergic to display units and a following disease. The result was: there was no practical defence against computers. But there was the idea that women were unable to master it, and that this was observed and accordingly treated by superiors. This was represented by men older that 35 and married women. (Could this hold out hope for the younger male generation and a fight for a future where women are not married?)

What are the demands of computerized office jobs? Our informants agreed that more knowledge and capacities were necessary but they also informed us that there was no such education. This complex also involved gender relations: there were introductory courses but mainly for men. Women tried to learn on the job. Advanced training was not granted. Taking computer handbooks home to learn them by heart was not thought to be any kind of education but a compensation for deficits, involving personal guilt. It was not done by women because of family-responsibilities. But learning by doing is an inadequate form of learning, when applied to work which is structured by a different logic from that in everyday practice. Working with computers needs the ability to recognize the stupidity of the computer and to master its logic from a superior vantage point. Women who learn how to deal with this thing by insufficient introductory courses and some time after their male colleagues already know how to handle it, react with panic. They learn the commands by heart with the consequence, that they work within a prison of not understood but always expected catastrophies.

Following the thread of gender we met the problem that women were specially unsatisfied at the end of a working day. They often complained that they had done practically nothing. They wanted to fill the breaks due to a breakdown of the central computer system with other work.
We had assumed that the specifics of computer work, always to be on the alert, to be very diligent and punctilious, to criticize would be very suited to the

female social character, because they were used to the same demands at home and in childrearing. Since they complained beaause they believed that this work was no work, we had to revise our former idea and learn that women cannot accept the domestic attitude in office work. They think it is wasted time which they could better spend at home, even though they do not acknowledge their own work there either.

Once you include them into your research you meet gender battles everywhere. We met them in the way work was defined (as technical work and therefore male instead of being typing which would be female) and especially in the informal way of male solidarity networks, helping each other with advice whilst excluding women. These networks were practically present but not really consciously known by our informants. - Also overtime hours are a field of gender relations. Whereas our informants of both sexes agreed that their partners would take over domestic duties caused by overtime work, women had not tried this practically. They did not work overtime but had resigned themselves to part-time jobs.

Our short survey on some changes caused by computers in office jobs had shown us a series of incompatibilities, contradictions, paradoxes:
a work which could dissolve the genderspecific division of labour and its hierarchical order, a work wich is equalizing is experienced as a sharpening of a cleavage: male work cultures exclude women; where both sexes are equally present, new divisions of labour are shaped by the staff: women agree to being shifted to the less important tasks, which are less acknowledged: like watering flowers, securing data, making coffee, and going on errands, copying and filing.

On the one hand there is an extension of qualifications which all our informants perceived as necessary, on the other hand little is being done to adequately prepare the workforce, although there are some breaks right now: Computer education is becoming an issue at school. But only boys are extremely interested in it.

Work which ought to increase the general competence of the workers - by competence I mean the intervention into the labour process and an overview over the whole of it - this very work leads to an increase in control from above.

Even the question of the property of the means of production and the product becomes diffuse. Stealing data and software becomes an everyday event. And yet this dissolution of one of the very important columns of our society - the column of property - has the effect of more control.

This arrangement of paradoxes is personally experienced as being torn in contradictions and leads to isolation and anxiety. Both are essential causes for a somatic transformation of cultural incompatibilities. What becomes incompatible are the social relations of production and within them the gender relations(4), the habits, values and finally the identity of workers themselves.

References:

(1) Projektgruppe Automation und Qualifikation (Leitung Frigga Haug), Automationsarbeit - Empirische Untersuchungen,
Volume 1 (Argument-Verlag, Berlin-West 1980)
Volume 2 (Argument-Verlag, Berlin-West 1981)
Volume 3 (Argument-Verlag, Berlin-West 1981)
(2) Projektgruppe Automation und Qualifikation (Leitung Frigga Haug), Zerreißproben - Automation im Arbeiterleben (Argument-Verlag, Berlin-West 1983)
(3) Brosius, Gerd and Frigga Haug, (eds.), Frauen / Männer / Computer (Argument-Verlag, Berlin-West 1986)
(4) Projektgruppe Automation und Qualifikation (Leitung Frigga Haug), Automation im Widerspruch - Ein Handbuch (Argument-Verlag, Berlin-West 1986), chapter 3. (A translation of the book into English is in progress.)

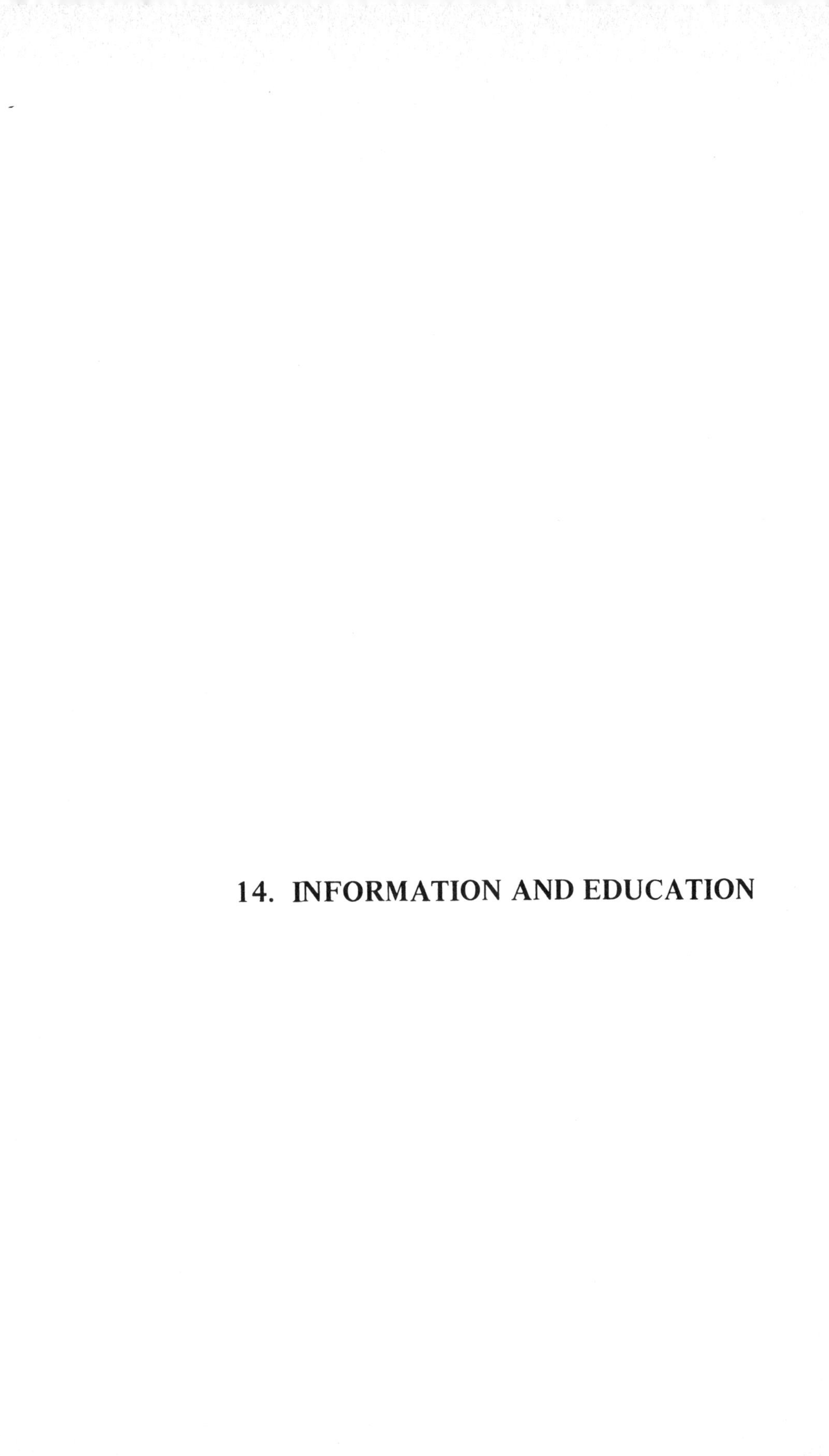

14. INFORMATION AND EDUCATION

WORK WITH DISPLAY UNITS 86
B. Knave and P.-G. Wideback (eds.)

ANALYZING AND IMPROVING VDU WORKING CONDITIONS: WORKERS' EDUCATION

Luc DESNOYERS

Dept. Sci. biologiques, Université du Québec à Montréal C.P. 8888, Succ. "A", Montréal, H3C 3P8 Canada

Computerization has altered working conditions in many ways and new problems have emerged. Confronted with this, trade unions have sought the development of educational workshops intended for workers who are involved in improvement of their working conditions. In such a workshop as described underneath, workers get familiar with the analyzis of visual, postural and mental aspects of VDU work and its effects, and with the evaluation of improvements to be brought to working conditions.

In the middle of the 70s, trade union confederations in Quebec have developped educational programs in occupational safety and health. The workshops offered at this time dealt mostly with fundamentals of occupational health, accident analysis and prevention, functions and responsibilities of occupational health committees etc. The unions developped these workshops with their own personnel and resources, but they requested the participation of occupational health scientists for certain activities.

This was made possible mostly through an agreement that was signed by the Université du Québec à Montréal and the two major trade union confederations, the Confederation of National Trade Unions (CNTU) and the Québec Federation of Labor (QFL) [1]. Through this agreement university professors could, as part of their normal workload, cooperate in the development of courses, mostly on more specialized topics. As we were producing a set of two monographs on Vision and the workplace [2], representatives of a QFL affiliate, the Canadian Union of Public Employees, confronted with the problems of VDU work, asked for our cooperation in the production of an educational workshop on this topic. The workshop was developped with the QFL Education Department. This paper therefore deals with the contents of this course, the educational methods used, as well as with some of the implications of these methods regarding workers' knowledge of work and occupational health.

1. WORKSHOP'S BACKGROUND

The workshop on VDU work is usually offered to groups of about twenty participants, who are generally members of a small number of local unions in a region. The union organizers insist that a fair proportion of participants be workers who use VDUs in the pursuit of their occupational activities. Otherwise, the students are often delegates or members of occupational health committees, although some may have a limited experience of union activity and little or no previous training in occupational health. It is the local unions who select and send members to the workshop and it is understood that participants want to be involved in improving their working conditions.

The workshop is offered by a team of two instructors: one is a scientist from the university, the other is an instructor from the trade union education department. The first instructor deals mostly with scientific and technical aspects, while the second deals mostly with union activities.

The workshop lasts three days. The first two are devoted to analysing working conditions, their effects on health, and identifying means of improving these conditions. The last day is devoted to organizing union activity in order to obtain the necessary improvements.

As far as pedagogical methods are concerned, this workshop is drastically different from lectures. The objectives are not simply to inform workers of what should be good VDU working conditions, in which case, as Lesne [3] has shown, "transmissive" educational means would have been satisfactory. The objective is rather to help each of the workers become a participant in the social process of change that is required to obtain improvements in working conditions. This implies that workers start from their own perception of their work, their health, as well as their perceived relations between work and health; the workshop offers means to better analyse these phenomena and their relations, and to evaluate possible improvements. Finally one third of the workshop is devoted to discussing means of union participation in implementing these improvements. The philosophy underlying these workshops is recognition of the participants' concrete knowledge of VDU work and its effects. Lesne [3] refers to Freire [4] as the author of the model of pedagogical means that have to be used in such circumstances, and Blondin [5] has described how these can be adapted to union education. In short, the role of the educators is first to facilitate the expression of workers' knowledge on work and health and secondly to complement it and to offer means of pursuing the analysis with the help of scientific and technical data and methods. This leads naturally into the identification and evaluation of possible improvements, and it sets a new basis for future union involvement. Therefore pedagogical methods are centered on brief exposés, on group work and discussions rather than straight-forward lecturing. Apart from being better adapted to the goals of the workshop, we believe that these methods are better suited for people who have not necessarily had a long school training or whose schooling dates back to many years and are generally not receptive to lengthy lectures.

The content of the workshop was determined after a long process. In Canada, attention has long been centered on "exposure to" VDU screens and the hazards of ionizing as well as non-ionizing radiations. We felt that this emphasis imposed a quasi toxicological approach to VDU work and health effects. Within this concept, VDUs are perceived as a source of noxious radiation from which one has to be protected by various means of shielding or work-hour limitations. The clusters of miscarriages and birth defects that have been reported exert a considerable impact on workers. However, we felt that there was no solid grounds to link these clusters to radiation, and that there was no solid proof that they could be linked to any working conditions specific to VDU work. Referring to such a toxicological model in the analysis of VDU working conditions seemed to be a dead-end; in our belief, the toxicological model masked the important issues.

The advent of VDUs is but the tip of the iceberg. And the iceberg is computerization of office work, which triggers drastic changes in work content and working conditions. It was therefore felt that we had to refer to a more complete ergonomic model to study the impact of this re-organization of work on activity as well as on health. In this model [6] we include the unusual and at times strenuous reading constraints imposed by the screens in a frequently inadequate luminous environment: they are an important and immediately perceptible part of the new working conditions. We also refer to the frequent postural immobilization imposed by some workstation designs and by the use of unappropriate furniture and equipment; they are also readily perceptible. But the main emphasis is placed on the new type of work activities and conditions brought about by the use and misuse of computers: we include the effects of strict time constraints, of rigid linear procedures, of the new controls exerted on work and workers, of the transformation of work content into activities that are at times highly monotonous and repetitive or on the contrary too complex.

We perceived this new organization of work as stressful and potentially harmful to health and felt that due consideration should be given to these aspects of VDU work.

These considerations led us to plan a workshop in which both the environmental and organizational aspects of VDU work would be analyzed. Pedagogically, this analysis would start from what workers knew of their working conditions and health.

2. THE SESSION

The following section describes the workshop content and methods. We will only consider the activities of the first two days of the workshop in which takes place the scientific and technical analysis of VDU work under the guidance of the scientific instructor.

2.1. Introduction

As soon as participants have taken place around a large rectangular array of tables, they are invited to introduce themselves, stating their names, job title and brief description, employer, union affiliation and experience. They are also invited to comment on their use of a VDU, and to state whether they know of occupational health problems encountered in their workplace.

During this time, the instructors select three or four participants who are performing different jobs with VDUs, v.g. a telephone operator, a data entry operator, a secretary using a word processor etc. These persons are asked to explain freely to participants the work that they perform. Participants are invited to question these workers up to the point where it is felt that everyone has a good understanding of the job being described. Specific questions are asked about working conditions, health status, about changes that the advent of computers has brought to work content and organization. This last aspect is usually well illustrated by the worker's comments.

The instructors then analyse and sum up. They first insist on the diversity of jobs performed with the help of VDUs, classifying them as data entry work, data retrieval or interactive work. Following this, they will propose that the often used concept of a "VDU operator" is a rather poor reference to the complexity of reality; it confines the analysis of work conditions to a quasi-toxicological approach. Therefore, the instructors insist on the necessity to refer not only to environmental conditions of work, but also to work content and organization.

The next step in this summing up is a series of reflexions on the changes in work organization brought about by computerization. Referring to descriptions just put forward by the workers, the instructors make the appropriate parallels to work transformations brought about by taylorism and fordism.

This introduction is then concluded by presenting the model of VDU work that will be the backbone of the analysis to be performed during the session. VDU work is fragmented into three aspects to be covered successively. In the first place oculo-visual constraints are discussed, such as conditions of visibility, sensory and motor functions of the eye and visual fatigue. Postural work is then related to workstation design, to static muscular work and its musculo-skelettal effects. Then mental work is related to work content and organization, to mental workload and stress mechanisms, their symptoms and effects. Each of these three aspects is covered in about half a day.

2.2. Ocular aspects

This topic is first introduced by a brief exposé. The instructor explains the global mechanism of vision. He comments on organic as well as populational limits of the visual apparatus, on the constraints imposed by lighting and by the properties of objects being looked at. He concludes stating the fact that prolonged or intensive visual work may trigger symptoms of visual fatigue.

Participants are then invited to divide into small discussion groups on the subject of eye strain and visual fatigue. Separated in groups of 4-5, they are asked to produce a list of visual fatigue symptoms - if any - that they or their co-workers have felt during a working day; they are also asked to state when, in a day's work, these usually occur.

After ten or fifteen minutes, the groups are brought together, and the instructors call for a report from each group. The list of symptoms thus produced is usually strikingly extensive and diversified and can withstand a comparison with lists printed in relevant textbooks. The instructors then produce and comment published data on eyestrain and VDU work, and compare the list produced by the group to results of different surveys. This is done to show to participants both the efficiency and the limits of the analysis that they have just undertaken. Survey methods may be discussed at this point.

Follows an exposé on the structure and function of the eye and comments on what is known of the basis of eye-strain. The instructor then brings the attention back to constraints imposed upon the visual apparatus by light sources and objects being looked at. Workers are again sent to work in small groups. They are now asked to list problems and complaints that they have, or have heard of about lighting, as well as visibility problems concerning the equipment used in VDU work, i.e. screen, keyboard and source documents.

After fifteen minutes of small group work, the instructor calls for a plenary session and at first collects information about lighting problems. Receiving this information, he classifies problems as relevant to qualitative versus quantitative aspects of lighting. These last ones are considered first. Lighting standards are presented, discussed and criticized; their relevance is discussed by comparisons to personal experience of visibility on a TV screen while in the dark or in full illumination. Advantages of light versus dark screens are considered in reference to illumination levels.

Qualitative aspects of lighting are then dealt with. Good lighting practices are discussed, referring to control of natural lighting, types and arrangements of luminaires, local versus general lighting.

At this point the instructor goes back to questioning the group about the second category of problems they have worked on in the workshop. Collecting the information on visibility problems, he categorizes them under three headings: glare and reflections, source characteristics (size, contrast...) and eye to task distance. This permits an orderly discussion. Glare and reflections are considered in relation to lighting control, and advantages and disadvantages of anti-reflective treatments and filters are discussed. Source characteristics are commented and available recommendations are presented. Discussions on eye to task distance are related to accomodative fatigue; these are considered more fully when analysing workstation design.

This first series of exposés, group-work and discussions has made it possible to consider most aspects of ocular constraints in VDU work. Before considering the contents of the last parts of the session, we would like to comment here on the learning activities and methods used.

2.3. Learning and teaching methods

The above section illustrates that four basic types of activity occur during such workshops. All parts of the workshop start by a **statement** or a definition of the subject or the part of the subject to be considered - for example the area of the "body at work" to be discussed. Follows a session of **small group work** in which participants work at identifying problems encountered, whether these are lists of symptoms or complaints about working conditions, equipment, environment, etc.

The next activity is a **group report** in which problems are brought to the attention of the whole group. Problems are then classified and analyzed. Finally **exposés and discussions** are used to explain problems, mostly by associating constraints and bodily strain; they are of course used as well to point out preventive measures and recommendations.

This four step process is of course not rigidly adhered to. It has however proved quite convenient in planning sessions and in making sure that at every moment, we refer to the basic pedagocical principles mentioned earlier, that is always starting from what workers know of their work, of their working conditions and of their health.

2.4. Postural aspects

The next statement by the instructor sets the ground for the analysis of postural constraints in VDU work. He comments briefly on muscle contraction and its metabolic counterparts. He explains how muscle contraction can be used to move segments of the body as well as to immobilize others: dynamic and static work can both lead to muscle fatigue, which is accompanied by local symptoms. He finally suggests that movements as well as immobility can be imposed by work organization as well as workstation design.

It is with these ideas in mind that workers are invited again to split up into small working groups. They are presented with two requests. The first one is to list symptoms of muscle or articular pains that they or their co-workers have felt working at a VDU. The second is to list relevant problems, if any, in the design of their workstation or equipment.

When the groups have completed their work, they are re-united for a group report. The instructor first collects the information about pain localization. He may, for example, draw a picture of these localizations on a sketch of a human body. The more frequent complaints concern the cervico-brachial area and the back, but there are numerous reports about cold lower extremities and leg discomfort. This sketch is then set aside as the instructor calls for reports on design problems. While dissatisfaction is expressed on aspects of screen, keyboard, table and chair design as well as luminaire or window localization, certain positive features are always brought to the attention of the group by workers who use more recent equipment or operate in an efficiently designed environment.

The analysis and synthesis of all this information is a complex affair. We have found an efficient, although a bit theatrical way to do it. The instructor uses the available furniture to simulate a workstation in the very middle of the room. He sits at it and comments on what are the constraints for head posture in different tasks, with different pieces of equipment and equipment configurations, pointing out more favourable solutions. He demonstrates arm and wrist posture and motions, comments on back and leg problems. This is of course done amidst numerous exchanges and discussions with the participants. Sets of available, up to date recommendations are finally distributed to participants.

2.5. Mental aspects

In the development of this workshop, this section has grown into the most important of all. At first we insisted on analysing cognitive aspects of VDU work in a rather classical approach to mental load. However, the instructors were regularly confronted with much more general preoccupations from workers. Many of these insisted on different aspects of work organization and on the effects that these had on their nervous as well as somatic health. These problems were at times mentioned only after hesitations by workers, who clearly wanted to be careful in linking their personal nervous condition to their working conditions.

It was felt that we needed a general framework, a model that would facilitate such a discussion. The best approximation we found was Selye's model of stress. It has to be realized that the concept of stress is a very familiar one in this country, since Selye did most of his work in Montréal; this has unfortunately not prevented the concept of stress to be submitted to numerous distortions.

This last part of the session then begins with a statement that proposes a definition of stress and of the general adaptation syndrome, referring to Selye's classical three stages. In order not to induce psychological adaptations of the concept, an example of the syndrome is given that has nothing to do with the problems to be discussed. The example given is that of adaptations to hot environments, discussing short term and long term reactions, adaptations, misadaptations and diseases that can happen to people working regularly under such a stressor. The aim here is to confirm that a given stressor may act on many "compartments" of the organism and induce a variety of reactions.

We must insist that, most of the time, at this stage, some of the workers have referred to their health conditions as "being under stress". The instructors have not yet discussed the issue, mentioning that it would be considered later. This is the moment when it is done and a session of group work is organized in which participants are asked to work on two questions. The first one asks for symptoms felt by workers when they consider that they are under the effects of a stressor. The second calls for identification of the stressors in their working conditions.

When participants are finished with this, the instructor calls for a group report on symptoms only. He classifies these in reference to the physiological systems concerned. Most items usually reported refer to the nervous system (feelings of agressivity, tenseness, irritability, anxiety, depression, etc.), to the cardiovascular system (increased heart rate, blood pressure, flushing of the face, etc.) or the digestive system (gastric acidity, cramps, indigestion, intestinal dysfunctions, etc.). The diversity of these reactions is puzzling to many participants and it is not an easy task for the instructor to explain the logic of these reactions.

The exposé that follows tries to explain the general mechanisms of adaptation and misadaptation. It begins by a discussion in which participants are invited to identify all organic changes they have noted when they are submitted to a startle reaction, v.g. a loud noise in a quiet environment. Again these are classified by system and the instructor shows the logic of respiratory, nervous, cardiovascular and muscular changes that prepare the reaction of the organism confronted with danger. Then the instructor explains the effects observed, in animals and man, under chronic exposure to the same type of stimulus, noise. He comments on the unspecific nature of the adaptation syndrome, pointing out that the interindividual variability of dysfunctions that appear in different persons is probalby related to basic and normal structural and functional differences between individuals. Reactions differ, under stress, and the important issue is one of prevention, which calls for identification and elimination of the stressor.

Therefore, the instructor calls for a second group report on the identification of stressors. Experience has shown us that, although these stressors might be quite different from one person to another, from one firm - or one employer to another, some basic categories can be used to classify a large proportion of the factors identified as stressors by participants. These deal mostly with organizational aspects of work and fall into four groups. The first is identified as **informational load**: it includes complaints about the large quantity of information handled during work, and the pressure henceforth created, or it refers to the quality of this information, to its too great diversity, complexity or perceived irrelevance, which contribute to anxiety.

The second group concerns **time constraints.** These might refer to system response time which imposes passive waiting, reported as frustrating. Or they might refer to deadlines dictated by various operations on which the operator has no control and often no information but which impose too rapid a pace.

The third group deals with **control exerted on work and worker.** Computer surveillance reporting on number of phone calls handled per hour, on number of lines typed per day, on number of mistakes or interruptions (etc.) is resented quite viscerally. On the other hand, the fact that many computer programs leave no initiative and no freedom in planning one's work, imposing most of the time rigid linear procedures is also reported as stressful.

The fourth group concerns difficulties in **personal relations.** These refer to misunderstandings or animosity with superiors. But they are most frequently reported by workers whose job is to deal with the public and customers, whose demands often cannot be fulfilled on account of system design or malfunction. In such situations, customers tend to blame the operators for their poor performance; of course, the latter resent the role of scapegoats that is thrust on them.

Workers do report other sources of stress, and noise from telephones, printers and typewriters is frequently mentioned. It is not our purpose here to produce a list of all these stressors, but mostly to illustrate how the mere fact of analysing and classifying these sets the ground for preventive actions to be undertaken. Of course there are no ready-made sets of recommendations that apply in this field. Participants are left with the task to pin-point and analyze specific aspects of work organization which are particularly important in their own working situation and to identify means of improvement. These are only discussed in general terms.

This last discussion concludes the second day of the workshop. The third day, as we mentioned earlier, is taken over by the union instructor. Using identical pedagogical menas, he will help discuss means of improvement to working conditions through information, education, occupational health committee activities and negotiations with the employer.

3. COMMENTS

We have mentioned that, for pedagogical reasons, these workshops are based on workers'knowledge about their work, their health and the relations that they perceive between health and occupation. The expression of this knowledge is sought, and the workshop is a set of activities in which this knowledge is analyzed, completed and at times corrected; the aim is to transform workers' knowledge in such a way that it will be more adequate and more efficient in analysing and improving working conditions.

Little theoretical work has been conducted on workers' knowledge, its content and structure as well as on the transformations that such educational workshops trigger. But the experience gained by instructors tends to confirm some of the findings published on this subject.

Ochanine [7] has produced a series of studies on the structure of knowledge developped by operators. He has developped the concept that operators' knowledge about their work is above all operational. The mental representations that they construct about their own work would be guided and moulded by the strict necessity to concentrate on how to perform a given task. This might be confirmed by observations that, in educational sessions, workers are capable of job descriptions that are extremely rich, detailed and precise, far beyond the contents of any official job descriptions. However, if so structured, this knowledge about work would not be easy to use for other purposes, as for analysis of working conditions and their effects. This characteristic would contribute to explain some of the difficulties encountered by workers when they go from describing their work activity to analysing the environmental or organizational aspects of their working conditions. In such circumstances, instructors receive comments by workers stating that they "never though of it that way"!

On the other hand, workers' perception of their health seems to follow lines similar to those described by Herzlich [8]. This author states that health is generally perceived as the usual functioning of the body when performing in a natural environment; she comments on this equation between nature and health as a Rousseauist approach to health. In this case, diseases are perceived as resulting from alterations to this natural milieu, namely by processes such as infection and intoxication, which are both seen as related to urban life. Intoxication is here described as a rather general process by which agressors, identified mostly as agents that can be detected with the senses (noise, air pollutants), induce slow alterations in body functions and trigger disease in the long term.

Dodier has more recently extended these studies to the perception of health in occupational settings [9]. His findings show that causal associations are perceived with great precision between some given factors in the working environment and some specific alterations of health. However, workers also refer to non-specific alterations which they describe in terms of chronic fatigue, premature ageing, wear and tear of the organism; Dodier classifies these as "loss of biological capital". These effects are caused by work, according to workers. In Dodier's interviews, workers did not identify specific factors or stressors that would induce these alterations but they commented on global effects of the working situation as a whole.

Our observations are generally in agreement with the findings of these sociologists. In matters relating to visual strain and to musculo-skelettal discomfort or pain, causal agents are known or rapidly identified by participants in the sessions. Causal analysis is much more complex in matters relating to unspecific alterations of health appearing in stressful situations. The presentation and description of the general adaptation syndrome is then an efficient tool in this process.

It should be added that some of the workers conceptions about occupational health are tinted with popular beliefs and misconceptions. In Dodier's [9] material, although the author does not comment on this, one can find a limited number of these, and for example the belief that managerial or office work are occupations in which cardio-vascular diseases are more frequent. Statistics do show quite the contrary. The necessity to correct such misconceptions and the complexity of some of the material discussed in the session do illustrate that these have to be conducted by fully trained instructors.

Commenting on one's health problems as well as the risks one is exposed to is not done without some resistance and shyness in certain persons. This is frequently the case in occupational health workshops, and this attitude is generally more pronounced with workers that are exposed to particularly dangerous conditions. In the case of these workers, Dejours and his collaborators [10,

11] have described what they call a trade's defensive ideology ("idéologie défensive de métier"). These occupational psychopathologists submit that risks and health problems are subjects that are tacitly avoided amongst exposed workers. Such a behaviour would contribute to building a barrier against anxiety that build up when one is systematically confronted with the immediate presence of risk in his occupation. It might well be that the resistance of some workers to discuss their occupational health problems could be explained along similar lines, although this cannot be demonstrated for the time beeing.

One must also insist on the limits of the stress model in explaining the health effects of work. On one hand, the mechanism by which physical or chemical components of the working environment trigger unspecific alterations of health is efficiently described by this model. However, it has to be recognized that the extension of the stress model that is performed in trying to explain the unspecific effects or organizational parameters of work (time constraints or abusive controls...) does not rest on very solid grounds. In this area also, occupational psychopathologists [10, 11] are developping models that shed new light on the relations between work organization and psychic functions and dysfunctions. Such an approach may be an efficient complement to the organistic stress model.

Finally, questions must be raised as to the evaluation of such workshops. The relevance of the workshop content is ascertained in evaluative discussions with participants as well as union representatives. There would be no point in trying to measure the "gain in knowledge" by traditional tests or exams: these bear no relation whatsoever with the objectives of the workshop. A behavioral evaluation or a performance evaluation that would try to quantify the actions undertaken after the workshop is also out of the question; such initiatives are submitted to so many parameters of industrial relations that such an evaluation is due to fail.

Therefore we feel that the evaluation process should be one in which we would try and gain better knowledge on what goes on within a workshop. Attempts to better understand and evaluate the structure and content of workers mental representations of work and health have to be undertaken. In the same manner, we have to better understand what transformations happen in the structure and contents of this knowledge, to evaluate the relevance and efficiency of the educational methods and materials that we use. A research program is being conducted on these questions in France [A] and we hope that this project will give us a better insight on workers' education in occupational health.

NOTES

[A] This research program is pursued with ergonomists A. Laville, C. Teiger and F. Daniellou, from the "Laboratoire d'ergonomie et de neurophysiologie du travail" at the Conservatoire national des arts et métiers, in Paris, and M. Guy and J.C. Davidson from the "Institut pour l'Amélioration des Conditions de Travail", also in Paris.

REFERENCES

[1] Protocole d'entente UQAM-CSN-FTQ sur la formation syndicale. Service à la collectivité, Université du Québec à Montréal, 1976.
[2] Desnoyers, L., LeBorgne, D., "Vision et travail". Tome 1: "La protection oculaire". Tome 2: "Les tâches visuelles". Institut de Recherche Appliquée sur le Travail, Montréal, 1982.
[3] Lesne, M. "Travail pédagogique et formation d'adultes". Presses Universitaire de France, Paris, 1977.
[4] Freire, P. "Pédagogie des opprimés". Ed. La Découverte-Maspéro, Paris, 1983.

[5] Blondin, M. "Une formation syndicale faite par les travailleurs eux-mêmes". Revue Internationale d'Action Communautaire 3/43: 73-80, 1980.
[6] Desnoyers, L. "The Physiology of VDT Work". American Public Health Association, Dallas, 1983.
[7] Ochanine, D. "L'image opérative". Dept. d'Ergonomie et d'Ecologie Humaine, Université de Paris I, 1981.
[8] Herzlich, C. "Santé et maladie". Editions de l'Ecole des Hautes Etudes en Sciences Sociales. Paris, 1969.
[9] Dodier, N. "Une construction sociale précaire du biologique. Maladie et vie quotidienne sur le lieu de travail". Thèse de doctorat en Sociologie, Ecole des Hautes Etudes en Sciences Sociales, Paris, 1985.
[10] Dejours, C. "Travail: usure mentale . Essai de psycho-pathologie du travail." Le Centurion, Paris, 1980.
[11] Dejours, C., Veil, C., Wisner, A., editors, "Psychopathologie du travail". Entreprises Modernes d'Edition, Paris, 1985.

WORK WITH DISPLAY UNITS 86
B. Knave and P.-G. Widebäck (eds.)

WORKER EDUCATION AND USER PARTICIPATION IN THE DEVELOPMENT OF PROTECTIVE POLICIES FOR VDT OPERATORS

Robin Baker and Laura Stock

Labor Occupational Health Program, University of California, Berkeley, California, 94720, U.S.A.

1. INTRODUCTION

Worker education is a component of any comprehensive occupational hazard control strategy. Unfortunately, education has been seriously underutilized in efforts to create safe working environments for video display terminal (VDT) operators in the U.S. Most information and training given to workers who use VDTs is so narrow in scope that educational efforts rarely achieve their full potential.

To be effective, education should be designed not only to inform the learner, but also to encourage critical thinking and meaningful action. However, most educational programs aimed at VDT users are corporate based and are designed more to reassure workers than to educate them. For example, a packet of informational factsheets prepared by the American Electronics Association begins with the following overview:

> "VDTs are safe to use and pose no unusual health problems. When properly used, VDTs improve productivity without sacrificing comfort and job satisfaction." (VDTs: What are the Facts? AEA, copyright, 1984.)

Some educational efforts go a bit further, encouraging user participation in a limited fashion. According to the communications director of the Computer and Business Equipment Manufacturer's Association:

> "User training is crucial to an understanding of comfortable VDT work. Unfortunately, employees are not given instructions on how to adjust seating arrangements, nor are they told that failure to have proper arrangements may cause numerous musculoskeletal difficulties." (Occupational Safety and Health Reporter, 11/7/85.)

However, even this educational philosophy is limited in the role it envisions for the workers who are to receive training. According to this view, the purpose of education is to explain to working people what scientists have discovered, what management is doing to protect them, and what workers are expected to do to cooperate with the safety program established by the experts. This approach assumes that decisions regarding the work environment are the exclusive prerogative of management.

In contrast, the Labor Occupational Health Program, a worker education project at the University of California, Berkeley has developed training for VDT operators based on a different view of education. We see the purpose of education as empowering workers to participate actively in discovering unrecognized hazards and in designing control strategies. Since workers are on the "frontline" in VDT workplaces, we explain to them both what scientists do and do not know about the hazards, and we encourage them to share information about their own experiences.

This type of education (which we will term "empowerment" education) is also being pioneered by other union-oriented occupational health programs throughout the U.S. "Empowerment" education assumes that workers have the right to participate in decisions regarding the work environment, and it encourages them to get involved. It facilitates collective worker involvement in finding solutions which can benefit both labor and management, and in shaping public policies for improved health protection.

An empowerment-oriented educational approach is particularly well suited for VDT operators for a number of reasons:

(1) Since VDTs are a relatively new technology, there are many areas of current scientific inquiry which can benefit from VDT user input. Users can provide critical assistance to the scientists who are studying the problem. Without a forum for workers to express their concerns, scientists may not know what hazards to study.

(2) User participation in job and workstation design has been identified as an essential element in overcoming many of the hazards known to be associated with VDTs, such as stress and muscle strain. Worker education is necessary in order for users to participate effectively.

(3) VDT operators are primarily women and consequently often have ingrained cultural conditioning which discourages them from taking an assertive role in calling attention to problems and demanding protection. Education designed for empowerment can help overcome this conditioning.

(4) Social isolation is a common complaint among VDT operators. A good, participatory educational environment can help break down barriers between workers, allowing for dialog, information sharing, and collective action to solve problems.

In this paper, we will describe our own experience with empowerment-type education for VDT operators. We will illustrate how such education has played a role in bringing the health hazards of VDTs to the attention of the American scientific community, allowed individual VDT operators to seek and find solutions to problems in their own workplaces, and encouraged workers to act collectively to demand that VDT hazards be researched and regulated.

CONTRASTING VIEWS OF WORKER EDUCATION

Traditional	Empowerment
° Based on one way communication (expert→users)	° Based on two way communication (expert↔users)
° Explains scientific information only after it is well established	° Explains what science does and does not know about hazards
° Avoids areas of uncertainty	° Seeks worker input in defining hazards
° Explains safety and health programs that have been instituted and seeks compliance	° Empowers workers to participate in determining control strategies
° Assumes decisions regarding work environment are made exclusively by management	° Assumes workers' right to participate in decisions regarding work environment

2. EDUCATION FOR EMPOWERMENT

Our involvement with training VDT operators began in 1975. That year, in conjunction with the California Labor Federation, LOHP sponsored a Northern California Conference on "Women and Occupational Health." Many of the workers attending expressed their concerns about what was then a new technology entering the workplace: VDTs. The stories told by the conference participants were so striking that several follow-up sessions were organized. Participants from a dozen unions met with University experts in an effort to learn more about VDTs.

When they discovered that information on VDT hazards was extremely scarce, these women, along with local and international unions, successfully petitioned NIOSH (the National Institute for Occupational Safety and Health) to do the first U.S. government study of the issue. The NIOSH report, released in 1980, documented and validated the problems expressed by VDT workers and concluded with a series of recommendations that have formed the basis for policy proposals, legislation and contract language throughout the country during the 1980s.

This experience, beginning with the initial conference and culminating with the release of the NIOSH report, established the critical role of VDT operators in calling attention to the health problems associated with VDT use. It also suggested that educational activities can serve as an important catalyst for worker participation.

The original group of concerned workers has since grown into on an-going organization known as the VDT Coalition. It is a network of more than 100 individual VDT workers and a broad range of unions which represent them such as: the Service Employees International Union; American Federation of State, County and Municipal Employees; Communication Workers of America; International Brotherhood of Teamsters; The Newspaper Guild; and International Typographical Union. The Coalition serves as an important inter-union communication system. Additionally, it provides a unique opportunity for unorganized workers to interact with unionists.

The group offers information, technical assistance, and support to hundreds of workers using VDTs. Examples of Coalition activities include: publishing a newsletter called Video Views; co-authoring a model VDT safety bill introduced in the California legislature; providing testimony and research to legislators and press; and helping to design surveys and collect documentation to support demands for changes in individual workplaces.

Information and education have remained central to the Coalition. In addition to sponsoring conferences and presentations (for example, at union meetings), the VDT Coalition has worked with LOHP to design a "train the trainers" program which embodies the model of education as empowerment.

3. TRAIN THE TRAINERS

The "Train the Trainers" program is designed to teach VDT operators to become effective trainers and resource people on VDT safety for their workplaces and/or unions. The program provides participants with both practical information on VDT health and safety and skills in imparting that information to others. After completing the training, participants become members of a peer education "Speakers Bureau" available to provide on-site workshops and assistance in solving VDT-related problems. The goals of this program are:

- to expand the number of VDT resource people available;
- to develop leadership skills in VDT users, many of whom have been denied opportunities to acquire leadership positions and lack confidence in their own abilities to educate and influence others;
- to increase the impact and acceptance of our programs through use of peer educators who have themselves experienced VDT-related problems and therefore have special expertise.

4. PROGRAM DESIGN

Our "Train the Trainers" program is a day-long workshop made up of two parts: a morning session which reviews current research and recommendations about VDT health and safety, and an afternoon session focusing on how to use information and education to promote individual and collective action. Our teaching methodology is consistent with our educational goals in that the methods promote active participation and group problem solving. For example, in developing our morning session, we rejected the standard educational format in which a trainer lectures to a group of students. Instead, our students are provided with written information in advance and, in small groups, prepare short presentations on specific topics (eyestrain, stress, ergonomics, etc.) to deliver to the entire class. Each presentation is followed by a short evaluation in which the presentors are provided feedback on their training skills. The accuracy of each presentation is also reviewed. In this way, information is imparted at the same time that teaching skills are developed.

In the afternoon session, students are presented with sample workplace situations, such as: a non-union pregnant worker concerned about radiation; a union negotiating team proposing health and safety contract language; or a group of workers preparing legislative testimony. Through role playing and group discussion, students develop strategies for addressing the situations. These exercises are designed to prepare participants to become not only educators but also resource people who can help their co-workers develop effective individual and collective strategies for dealing with VDT-related problems.

5. IMPACT OF THE TRAINING PROGRAM

An assessment of our training activities to date revealed the following results:

1. The amount of worksite training and assistance we have been able to offer has greatly increased;

2. Our Speakers' Bureau has given us access to a wide variety of workplaces, as programs are initiated by our trainers in their own worksites;

3. Our workshops have often resulted in specific activities to improve workplace conditions.

The following are two examples of the type of results reported by training participants:

- Member of public employees' union: "After participating in a VDT training I was able to go back and work with my union to develop an agreement with management to do a series of lunch hour meetings in state offices throughout the region, which have recently been automated. Through these meetings, we encouraged people to bring forward their ideas about workstation design. We also won an agreement stipulating that management will work to solve any VDT problems which are brought to their attention."

- A legal secretary in an unorganized office: "A group of us were having problems with stress and eyestrain. When we presented our complaints to our boss he was skeptical that our problems were real. We contacted the VDT Coalition and arranged for a workshop to be held at our office for the secretaries, lawyers and administrative staff. After the presentation, we formed a joint staff-employer committee to look into how VDT working conditions could be improved. Since then we got some document holders and I'm hopeful that if we stick together, we'll be able to get more rest breaks and employer-paid eye exams."

6. CONCLUSION

Scientific discoveries alone will not bring about improvements in workplace conditions and practices. For effective change to take place, workers and their unions must take an active role in seeing that the necessary research is conducted and that study recommendations are implemented. Since the VDT Coalition first started, a nationwide effort has emerged to mobilize social forces toward this end.

User groups, like the VDT Coalition, have been formed in a number of other major U.S. cities. These groups, along with many local and international unions, are beginning to develop and use action-oriented, "empowerment education" techniques similar to LOHP's. These educational efforts not only make information available to VDT users, but also provide them with the skills and support they need in order to take an active role in protecting their health. By facilitating user involvement in the automation process, the Coalition and groups like it will ensure that the great potential of this new technology is realized in a manner designed to serve, rather than harm, working people.

WORK WITH DISPLAY UNITS 86
B. Knave and P.-G. Wideback (eds.)

TRENDS IN U.S. USER POLICIES FOR VDT WORK

Alan F. Westin

Professor of Public Law and Government, Columbia University, 729 International Affairs Building, 117th Street and Amsterdam Avenue, New York, N.Y. 10027, U.S.A., and President, Educational Fund for Individual Rights.

Field studies of U.S. management policies toward ergonomics, health and safety, and work practices involving VDTs in 1982-84 showed weak attention to these issues in 75% of 110 organizations studied. Then, a follow-up study in 1985-86 found that 50-60% of these organizations now had serious and responsive policies in place. The paper discusses the causes and potential future directions of U.S. user policies.

1. INTRODUCTION

This paper reports some of the findings and implications of two field studies of management policies toward VDT work in the United States, the first study conducted in 1982-1984 and the second in 1985-1986. Together, the studies will document the main directions that U.S. users have taken in dealing with ergonomics, health and safety, and work practices aspects of using office systems technology.

2. The 1982-1984 VDT Field Study

2.1 Scope and Methodology

Between April, 1982 and June, 1984, the Educational Fund for Individual Rights conducted a field study of "The Workplace Impact of Using VDTs in the Office." (The Fund is a non-profit research foundation which focuses on new issues of employee rights and technological change at the workplace.) The study examined user practices in the areas of system planning and introduction; job design and work organization; performance measurement and supervision; ergonomics; health and safety policies and communication; employee involvement and/or participation; labor relations issues; and regulatory-legal issues.[1]

The centerpiece of the research was a program of on-site visits conducted during 1982-1983 to 110 organizations implementing office system technology. About sixty per cent of these were business firms, in the insurance, manufacturing, financial services, media, transportation, retail, utility, distribution, energy, and consumer-services industries. About forty per cent were federal, state, and local government agencies and non-profit organizations, such as private universities, hospitals, foundations, religious bodies, and civic groups. At these sites, we conducted open-ended interviews with over 1,100 end-users of VDTs, primarily women at the clerical, secretarial, and lower professional levels, where OA applications were heaviest in 1982-83. We also interviewed over 650 managers and executives involved in OA implementation.

The 110 organizations to which we made on-site visits were not a representative sample of U.S. corporations, government agencies, or non-profits. They were chosen primarily on the basis of their reputations as "advanced" or large-scale users of office systems technology. Many were selected because of a reputation for having "good human resources policies," though this was not a prerequisite for selection. These reputational characteristics were drawn from nominations by vendors, articles in the computer and business press, articles in the personnel and labor relations media, and suggestions from interest groups, OA experts, and academicians. About 10% of the sites were union-represented, about evenly divided between private and government employers.

Most of the interviews with end users were conducted with individual employees, but about 20% took place in small "focus" groups. We used a topic checklist for these interviews, made up of neutrally worded questions designed to minimize prompting or forcing of issues. Our questions asked: how long the employee had been using a VDT; whether she had done this job previously without a VDT; what kind of training for the machine she had received; what personal involvement, if any, she had had in the process of selecting and implementing office systems technology at her job; how the VDT was affecting "her job" and "her work"; whether she had read or heard anything about "VDT issues"; how management supervised and evaluated her performance; what problems, if any, she had encountered using the VDT and whether she had raised any such issues with management; how she saw her future at this organization or elsewhere being affected by her VDT skill; and similar broad inquiries.

We guaranteed employees complete anonymity for their comments, and our interviews were done without supervisors or managers present. As a result, we believe almost all employees were open and candid in their discussion of how they saw VDT uses affecting them, and their responses provided us with valuable reports on the reactions and problems of workers doing intensive VDT work. However, since we did not conduct a representative-sample survey, or use a standardized questionnaire, our interviews do not provide the basis for making statistical statements about national trends, particular industries, or specific occupational groups. Our conclusions should therefore be viewed as exploratory rather than representative, and the rough percentages we report should be treated accordingly.

In addition to the site visits to 110 user organizations, the project made visits to 15 large U.S. vendors of office systems and support equipment; interviewed officials at 40 U.S. labor unions concerned with VDT and OA issues; did a pilot survey and had follow-up meetings with information-system directors in 55 business and government organizations; and interviewed representatives of women's, religious, minority, industry, and user groups concerned with the impact of office technology. Visits were also made to other advanced industrial democracies involved in office automation, specifically, Canada, Britain, France, Switzerland, West Germany, and Sweden.

2.2 Major Findings

The findings of the 1982-1984 study were published in early 1985, in a book directed primarily at managers adopting office system technology and scholars interested in the technology-adoption and technology-impact areas. Westin, Schweder, Baker, and Lehman [1]. In this paper for the Stockholm Conference, we will focus on the study's findings on U.S. user approaches to ergonomics, work practices, and health and safety issues.

2.2.1. Significant Variations in User Practices

Among the organizations visited, we did not find the kind of unitary, deterministic application of office system technology that some social analysts or group spokesmen have asserted to be taking place. Rather, we found significant variations in the design and implementation of VDT work and its management from industry to industry, among individual firms within industries, from division to division, among different local work units and even among specific types of jobs. In addition, there are often significant variations in how supervisors and unit managers are applying top management "OA policies" to the work settings they manage. Such diversities affected both the experiences and attitudes of workers toward the incorporation of VDTs at their workplaces.

2.2.2. Key Role of Human Resources Philosophy

The overall human resources or personnel philosophy of managements at the organizations we visited was the strongest single variable in how the employee relations and quality of work life issues of OA were being perceived and addressed. We found firms with nearly identical types of clerical or professional operations, work force characteristics, lines of business or government activity, and economic circumstances whose policies toward the "people aspects" of office system technology implementation were dramatically different, and were perceived as such by the workers we interviewed. Case studies of such differences were published in the study report.

2.2.3. Positive Employee View of the Technology

Confirming the results of various U.S. national office worker surveys conducted in the 1982-1984 period, a large majority of the employees we interviewed (in the 80-90% range) expressed strongly positive comments about having VDTs to use in their jobs. Specifically, they reported important quantitative and qualitative improvements in their job performance as a result of the new office systems. They were also glad to have VDT skills which they believed would make them more "marketable" for future jobs, both within and outside the firms they were working at. Furthermore, even those workers who did not like the content of their jobs very much, or were upset at the manner in which the new technology was introduced at their workplace, did not attribute the problems to "the machine" as such, but to the way that their management was structuring jobs or work settings around the new technology. Almost all employees interviewed said they would not want to go back to pre-VDT equipment, and would not want to work for an organization that did not provide VDTs to carry out their jobs.

2.2.4. Most VDT Work Not In Satisfactory Ergonomic Conditions

When asked to rate the ergonomic conditions of their intensive VDT operations (jobs in which employees use terminals four hours or more a day), managements in over 90% of the organizations said that a majority of such operations were not yet in "satisfactory" ergonomic conditions. (Satisfactory was defined as three elements being present: an adjustable chair; either an adjustable terminal or adjustable work surface; and a VDT-supportive work environment, in terms of lighting and physical arrangements.) Unsatisfactory ergonomic conditions in the most intensive VDT operations of these firms -- data entry, customer service, and claims-processing functions -- were a source of concern to unit managers and staff groups; however, upgrading such facilities to satisfactory ergonomic conditions had not yet been regarded by top management as a sufficient organizational priority to obtain the necessary funding for improvements, nor had ergonomic standards for such VDT work been developed or promulgated as an organizational objective.

2.2.5. Most Employees Report Physical Discomforts

Majorities of intensive end users, in the 60-75% range, reported the presence of continuing and "significant" physical discomfort. In order of frequency, the problems reported involved vision ("eyestrain"); musculo-skeletal problems (backache, neckache, wrist and elbow pain, etc.); and stress-related symptoms (headache, stomach problems, sleeping problems, etc.). While some employees felt that "nothing could be done" to relieve such discomfort ("it goes with the job..."), most felt that employers could improve ergonomic conditions and work practices to lessen such discomfort, and were looking to their managements to take such actions in the near future.

2.2.6. Employees Seek Communication About Health and Safety

About two out of three employees we interviewed had read or heard about possible long-term, adverse health effects of working with VDTs, especially the issue of reproductive hazards, and said they were "concerned" about these reports. While most of these employees were not sure whether there was scientific evidence to support allegations of such effects, they wanted their employers to provide them with specific information and answer their questions about such health and safety issues. They also felt their immediate supervisors or managers were not knowledgeable or helpful about these issues. (This lack of knowledge and preparedness was also reported by supervisors and managers we interviewed.)

2.2.7. Employees Also Want More Involvement In OA Implementation

Majorities of the employees we interviewed, in the 50-60% range, felt that their employer was not involving employees sufficiently in decisions about office system technology design and implementation, resulting in many unnecessary and costly problems in using new OA systems. Employees felt they had significant positive contributions to make in overall system design, software and screen formats, terminal selection, workstation equipment, and job design. However, they reported that a combination of pressures to get OA systems "up and running" and management doubts that employees could make important contributions and prevented any meaningful employee participation in their organizations. Local union leaders in the unionized organizations we studied reported that they were unable to exercise any role in such OA decisions, because of "management prerogative" doctrines in U.S. labor law.

2.2.8. Major OA Problems at 75% of Sites

Reflecting these employee concerns, we found significant implementation problems and weak employee-technology integration in three out of four organizations studied. What characterized OA applications in these organizations was poor long-range or strategic planning for office system applications, reflecting inadequate top management awareness of VDT issues; overly narrow training, focused on "how to" techniques rather than preparation of employees for dynamic changes in jobs and work relations; inadequate involvement of employees in OA decisions and implementation; lack of attention to ergonomic requirements and inadequate provision of ergonomic equipment and work settings; weak to nonexistent communication with employees on VDT health and safety issues; and lack of organizational attention to new job-design, work-organization, and performance-measurement standards in intensive VDT work, usually reflecting a lack of meaningful participation by personnel or human resources staffs in these matters. Though these problems at 75% of our sites had not produced confrontations or serious employee discontent in the non-union sites, or strikes at union-represented sites, we found most employees to be expectant that employers would address these issues "soon," or else that outside regulation might be necessary.

2.2.9. Excellent Policies at 10% of Sites

In about 10% of the organizations we studied, management policies toward the "people" and "organizational change" aspects of office automation were proceeding very well. This reflected the anticipative style and strong positive-employee-relations philosophy of these organizations, and top management determination that advanced technology should support employee performance and commitment, not jeopardize it. The key characteristics of these organizations were as follows: top management recognition of emerging VDT issues and the need for attentive policies, usually fostered by strong presentations to top management by EDP or human resources staffs; adoption of long-range OA plans that included a priority for "employee impact" issues; creation of a multi-function VDT task force or committee to gather information, assess VDT effects, and propose new VDT-related programs and communications; identification of ergonomic requirements and promulgation of ergonomic standards to be used in upgrade programs; broad communication and training programs for both employees and managers on VDT issues; involvement of employees in VDT planning and implementation matters; and responsible policies for the career-mobility and job-security concerns of employees heavily affected by OA applications, especially women in clerical, secretarial, and para-professional jobs.

2.3 Interpretation and Implications

During what can be seen as the first phase of OA applications in the U.S., roughly between 1975-1981, user organizations concentrated on bringing in new hardware and software systems for office work, and in getting these powerful new tools to work as promised by the vendors. The dominant view was that this was more or less like putting in faster typewriters and better telephones, rather than "transforming" office operations. Though there were some union and activist group protests in this period about "electronic sweatshops," operator discomfort, potential long-term health hazards, loss of jobs, and other "negative effects" of OA, these criticisms did not generate wide public debate or draw much mass media attention. The attention of most managements, employees, and the media was on the positive and innovative aspects of new office technology.

Between 1982-1984, however, just when our field study was conducted, OA entered a new phase in the U.S., the period of "VDT controversy." National office worker surveys, many sponsored by vendors or business groups, showed that majorities of employees, though quite positive about the new tools, reported that they were experiencing the physical discomforts we had documented, were hearing about and were concerned over the long-term health issues, and wanted more communication about and involvement in VDT matters. The mass media now took up "the VDT controversy," usually giving dramatic prominence to the position of critics. "Abuse of technology" and the need for "worker protection" was made a centerpiece of campaigns by U.S. unions to organize office workers in corporate industries moving heavily into office automation, especially banks, insurance companies, and service firms. In addition, beginning about 1983-1984, users were offered well designed ergonomic terminals and work stations as standard equipment, reflecting the judgment of major U.S. vendors that ergonomics was now a feature that users were becoming concerned about and would be willing to pay for. Finally, by 1984, proposals to legislate health and safety, ergonomics, and work-practices standards for employers were introduced and came under consideration in twenty states, sponsored primarily by unions and women's activist groups.

These developments had a powerful effect on VDT vendors and industry groups in the U.S. Recognizing that ergonomic conditions and work practices had become legitimate employee concerns; that charges of potential health hazards needed serious scientific study and dissemination of results showing that such charges were generally unfounded; and that expensive government regulation might be instituted if users did not address these problems directly, a business-led campaign to guide U.S. business and government employers to pay serious attention to VDT policies was mounted in 1984-1986. Since our fieldwork on U.S. user practices was based primarily on 1982-83 activities, and since we were tracking the public "VDT controversy" closely, we undertook a follow-up study in late 1985 and early 1986 to see just how much progress was being made by U.S. users, and of what kind.

3. The 1985-1986 Follow-Up Study of User Practices

3.1. Scope and Methodology

For our follow-up study, we recontacted in late 1985 and early 1986 the 110 user organizations we had previously studied, using a combination of written surveys and telephone contacts. We also undertook extensive field research to produce five in-depth case studies of the organizational factors that produced exemplary user policies.[2] Our preliminary report of the follow-up study is contained in this paper. The full report, case studies, and policy exhibits will be available after January, 1987. (See section 4. below for a description of the full report and ordering information.)

3.2. Characteristics of the 110 Organizations in 1985-86

In addition to the basic characteristics already noted about the 110 organizations studied (60% business, 40% government and non-profit; 10% unionized and 90% non-union, etc.), several additional aspects of these organizations as of 1985-86 deserve notation and are presented in Tables 1-3.

TABLE 1 Workforce Size of Organizations Studied

Less than 1,000 employees	23%
Between 1,000 and 10,000 employees	61%
Over 10,000 employees	16%

TABLE 2 Numbers of VDTs in Use

Less than 250	28%
Between 250 and 5,000	55%
Over 5,000	17%

TABLE 3 Percent of Clerical or Professional Employees Using VDTs Four Hours or More Daily

Under 10%	5%
11-34%	61%
35-59%	17%
60-100%	17%

3.3. Substantial Progress by Users

Table 4 shows that substantial progress was made among our 110 organizations in addressing VDT policy issues in 1985-86.

TABLE 4 Progress on VDT Policies By User Managements, 1982-1986

Activity or Policy on VDTs	% in 1982-84	% in 1985-86
VDT Task Force	14%	61%
Presentation to top management on VDT issues	17%	58%
Ergonomic standard for termnals and workstations	22%	62%
Active employee communications on:		
Health and Safety	14%	58%
Adjustment and comfort	14%	64%
Job design addressed	22%	53%
Used employee participation for:		
Terminal Selection	14%	47%
System/software	8%	35%
Chair/furniture	14%	47%
Job design	6%	29%

As the figures in Table 4 indicate, a majority of these users have recently taken the kinds of policy actions that had been conducted as a unified approach during 1982-84 by only 10% of the organizations studied, and were being done on an ad hoc basis by only another 10-15%. The first four items are especially significant in terms of their potential long-term effects: creating a VDT Task Force (61%); making issue presentations on VDTs to top management (58%); creating and promulgating an ergonomic standard for VDT terminals and workstations (62%); and mounting an active employee communication program on health and safety issues (58%) and adjustment and comfort at the terminal (64%). In addition, 53% report that they have directly addressed issues of job design in VDT applications, to deal with questions of intensity, pacing, and task variety for VDT work.

It is not surprising that somewhat lower figures are reported as far as involving employees in various office automation activities; this reflects the still prevailing conservatism of American managements toward involving largely non-union office workers in decision-making. However, the fact that almost half of these organizations (47%) are involving employees in terminal, chair, and furniture selection represents a significant move in several areas of great importance to employee comfort.

3.4. Expansion of Ergonomic Conditions

We asked managers in these organizations how many of their clerical and professional employees using VDTs four hours or more per day had various ergonomic features at their work sites.

TABLE 5 Ergonomic Feature Currently in Place

Feature Present	Percent of employees having: None	1-34%	35-59%	60-100%
Tilt and swivel screen	0%	29%	11%	60%
Detachable keyboard	6%	0%	6%	88%
Adjustable VDT chair	11%	27%	22%	40%
Adjustable VDT desk	31%	22%	20%	27%

Table 5 shows that ergonomic features in the terminal -- tilt and swivel screens and detachable keyboards -- have been widely adopted in these organizations. Sixty percent of the organizations had tilt and swivel screens and 88% provided detachable keyboards for 60-100% of their intensive end users. Less progress had been made in providing ergonomic chairs for these employees, with only 4 out of 10 of these organizations having such chairs for 60-100% of these employees, and only 27% providing 60-100% of these end users with adjustable desks or workstations.

We then asked each organization what percentage of intensive VDT operators would have such ergonomic features by the end of 1986, under current purchasing and installation programs.

TABLE 6 Ergonomic Feature to be Installed by End of 1986

Feature	Percent of employees to have by end 1986			
	None	1-34%	35-59%	60-100%
Tilt and swivel screen	0%	24%	6%	70%
Detachable keyboard	6%	0%	0%	94%
Adjustable VDT chair	6%	24%	6%	64%
Adjustable VDT desk	31%	24%	0%	45%

Table 6 shows that major steps were under way in these organizations to increase the presence of ergonomic furniture. Adjustable VDT chairs for 60-100% of intensive users would be present in almost two out of three of these organizations (64%) and adjustable desks or workstations would be installed for most intensive users in almost half of the sites (42%). Further installation of ergonomic features in the terminals was also under way, with 70% of these organizations to have tilt and swivel screens and 94% to have detachable keyboards for 60-100% of their intensive end users.

3.5. Sources of New User Policies

Clearly, the upgrading of ergonomic features in terminals and workstations, the providing of extensive employee communications, and the activities of VDT Task Forces involve substantial costs for organizations. In an era of sharp business competition and cutbacks in government budgets, such costs are not lightly or easily undertaken. The obvious question is what explains this shift of leadership policy toward more "employee centered" or "quality-of-work-life oriented" actions for VDT work?

In our follow-up survey, we asked managers in these 110 organizations whether the "public controversy over VDTs" played any part in adoption of their current VDT policies. Almost three out of four (72%) said that the VDT controversy played either a "major" or "contributing" role in their policies; only 28% said that the VDT controversy had played "no role."

In our telephone interviews following up the survey responses, we probed what managers had in mind when they said that the VDT controversy had been a factor in their policymaking. Three elements were cited by most of these managers: (1) that the public controversy threatened to upset many of their employees, and could thereby affect their positive orientation toward VDT work and productivity if the employees believed management was not taking proper measures and dealing with the genuine problems; (2) that the public controversy strengthened the hands of staff groups (in information technology or human resources) in their recommendations to top management that substantial organizational resources should be committed to improving VDT working conditions; and (3) that avoiding what was seen as highly restrictive and expensive VDT legislation, and preventing "electronic sweatshops" from becoming a successful union organizing or bargaining issue, made the adoption of voluntary actions an important priority for these organizations.

Several other reasons were cited by managers for their organization's move to adopt new VDT policies. One manager put this in terms of new information resources. "It was only in 1985 that we obtained understandable presentations of the scientific findings showing that there was no evidence of long-term health hazards from the video display terminal. We also learned that a combination of poor ergonomics, bad job design, close employee monitoring, and fears about job security could produce harmful physical effects and bad stress conditions among our employees using VDTs all day. Once we had these materials in our hands, we were ready to communicate directly with our employees on the health issues. We also understood what we had to do to prevent employee discomfort and stress, and keep good employee morale."

Another manager cited the arrival in 1985-86 of publications and user seminars documenting innovative user practices. "We aren't a company that pioneers in areas such as this. We generally wait to see what the IBM's, Citibank's, or Aetna's do, and how that is working out. If it seems to be responding to a real need, if it is practical in terms of scarce dollars, and if it doesn't create more problems than it solves, then we see how we can install this in our organizational culture. What essentially moved us in 1985 was that there were successful models we could turn to."

3.6. Seminars and Educational Materials for Users

As this manager's comment indicates, 1985-86 was marked in the U.S. by a well-financed and well-coordinated campaign by private-industry associations and government executive agencies to educate their members about VDT issues, and provide them with samples of successful policies to improve VDT working environments. We are aware of over 150 VDT seminars or meetings in 1985-86, attended by representatives from several thousand business, government, and non-profit organizations. Some of these were sponsored by national or state industry associations (in banking, insurance, publishing, etc.); some by state or local chambers of commerce or manufacturers' associations; some by associations of technology or support-equipment manufacturers; some by state or local governments; and others by consulting firms in office automation, ergonomics, or human resources. There were also important academic and university meetings attended by user representatives. Also influential in shaping user policies was a series of VDT seminars sponsored by the Center for Office Technology, a coalition of major industry associations, computer manufacturers, and individual companies organized to promulgate scientific information and support voluntary actions in the use of office systems technology.

3.7. Employee Satisfaction With New User Policies

During the period of our follow-up study, we conducted intensive on-site interviews with employees, supervisors, managers, and executives at five large organizations pursuing strong VDT policies: a bank; a life insurance company; a newspaper; an overnight delivery service; and a federal government agency. In all of these five organizations, there was high employee satisfaction with the ergonomic, employee-communication, and work practices programs being carried out by these managements in 1985-86. In these organizations, the highly positive attitude of employees toward the technology itself was being augmented (rather than undercut) by the employee-relations and quality-of-work-life policies that were dealing with the problematic aspects of intensive VDT work.

What also emerged from our case studies was that these organizations were now moving into a "next set" of VDT people-application issues: job design and work organization choices; development of performance measurement and "fair work standards"; and retraining, career-opportunity, and job-security issues. These organizations were also busy developing managers' guides and supervisor-training materials on how to manage the VDT workplace. Such guides described the use of office systems technology at the particular organization; explained the VDT controversy (its sources, players, and issues); provided a detailed briefing on health and safety, ergonomic, and work practices issues involving VDTs; and outlines techniques for managers to use in responding to employee concerns.

3.8. Interpretation and Implications

As we have emphasized, the 110 organizations we studied in 1982-84 and returned to in 1985-86 are not a representative sample of U.S. organizations using VDTs. If anything, we believe they represent a somewhat more innovation-minded and positive-employee-relations oriented group than the total population of VDT users. That is what made our finding in 1984 that 75% were not addressing the people aspects of office automation effectively such a disturbing conclusion. Now we found that the percentage of these organizations following good user practices in ergonomics, user education, and employee communication has risen into the 50-60% range. Even if this is somewhat higher than the percentage of the total U.S. organizational world doing this, it clearly represents a major move by U.S. users toward responsive and effective VDT policies, and in quite a short period of time.

This raises an important social issue for the future. Will these policies continue to spread in the U.S. user community in the next few years, or have we reached a "natural plateau" of voluntary action? After more than 30 years of studying organizational innovation in the U.S., we see a recurring pattern of innovation and limitation in policy areas involving sensitive employee and labor relations. About 10-15% of organizations seek to be and are early-innovators in human resources policies. They try to anticipate new social trends, technological impacts, and organizational-change requirements, and they are ready to formulate and implement innovative policies that aim to keep the organization ahead of regulatory requirements.

Another group of organizations, in the 30-50% range, depending on the issue, seek to be second-wave actors. They look to see what the early-innovators are doing, and when experience has accumulated as to how the new policies are working, the second-wave organizations take up these programs. Where IBM is a model early-innovator, American Telephone and Telegraph exemplifies the essential second-waver. Second-wavers wait until the bandwagon has been identified, and they like to see an "industry consensus" before they move.

Finally, in about 40-50% of U.S. organizations the management culture and organizational capacities are such that they wait until "the law says that it must be done." Through a combination of inertia, conservatism, and husbanding of resources for traditional priorities, these organizations tend to wait until regulation compels them to act.

If we project from our follow-up study, we can hypothesize that at least 35-45% of U.S. organizations using VDTs have not yet addressed the issues of ergonomics, work practices, employee communication, and employee involvement in a fashion that responds to the growing consensus of leading organizations and experts as to what constitutes responsible employer practices. If the considerable momentum illustrated by our 110 organizations' progress on VDT issues in 1985-86 continues to spread into the 70, 80, and 90 percentiles, because of the stimulating and supportive factors we identified as being present, and if this is roughly representative of the total U.S. user community, this would bring most U.S. employees using VDTs intensively under the mantle of good management policies. It would make regulation and legislation unnecessary, and avoid its limiting impact on organizational innovation.

However, if either a reduction in perceived threats in the external environment or the competition for attention and resources inside organizations leads the 35-45% or more of organizations which have not yet installed good user policies to ignore these issues, the situation in the U.S. could quickly become one in which regulation or legislation directed at setting minimum standards for ergonomics and work practices might take on greater momentum. Once the unreal and insubstantial issues pertaining to good VDT policies are stripped away, that makes what users do about the real and substantial issues all the more significant for millions of workers, and for American society as a whole. Whether the path of expanding voluntary action and no legislation, or a leveling off of user action and a turn to regulatory minimum standards becomes the direction of U.S. national policy in the next decade will be a major issue for both patterns of technological change and social-policy-making in the United States.

4. Report Available in 1987

The Educational Fund for Individual Rights will have available in early 1987 a report of approximately 250 pages based on the field work case studies, and analysis drawn on for this report in Stockholm. The U.S. VDT Report contains:

A. A summary of the 1982-84 original field study of "The Workplace Impact of Using VDTs in the Office."

B. The 1985-86 "Follow-Up Study of User Policies."

C. Five In-Depth Case Studies of VDT policy formulation and implementation by innovative business and government organizations.

D. Ten Profiles of good user practices in business and government organizations, including four joint union-management programs involving ergonomics, work practices, and health and safety protections.

E. A User Policies Appendix, with samples of organizational ergonomics standards, VDT Task Force charters, managers' guides to the VDT environment, end-user booklets on VDTs, employee survey reports, and collective bargaining proposals and contract provisions on VDTs.*

---

* The U.S. VDT Report may be ordered directly from the Educational Fund, with check or money order for $55 (U.S.) made out to: "The Educational Fund." Send to U.S. VDT Report, Educational Fund for Individual Rights, Suite 550, 475 Riverside Drive, New York, N.Y. 10115, U.S.A. The report will be sent by surface mail.

FOOTNOTES

1. The study was supported, in part, by unrestricted grants from the IBM Corporation, Hewlett Packard, NCR, Control Data Business Advisors, Kelly Services, Inc., Haworth, Inc., Northern Telecom, and Optical Coating Laboratories, Inc. The design, conduct, reporting, and interpretation of the study are solely the responsibility of the Educational Fund for Individual Rights and its staff, and not of the study's grantors.

2. The follow-up study was supported by a grant from IBM, with the same independent responsibility of the Fund for the study's conduct and conclusions as specified in note 1.

REFERENCES

[1] Westin, A.F., Schweder, H.A., Baker, M.A. and Lehman, S., The Changing Workplace: A Guide to the People, Organizational, and Regulatory Aspects of Office Technology (White Plains, N.Y. and London, Knowledge Industry Publications, Inc., 1985).

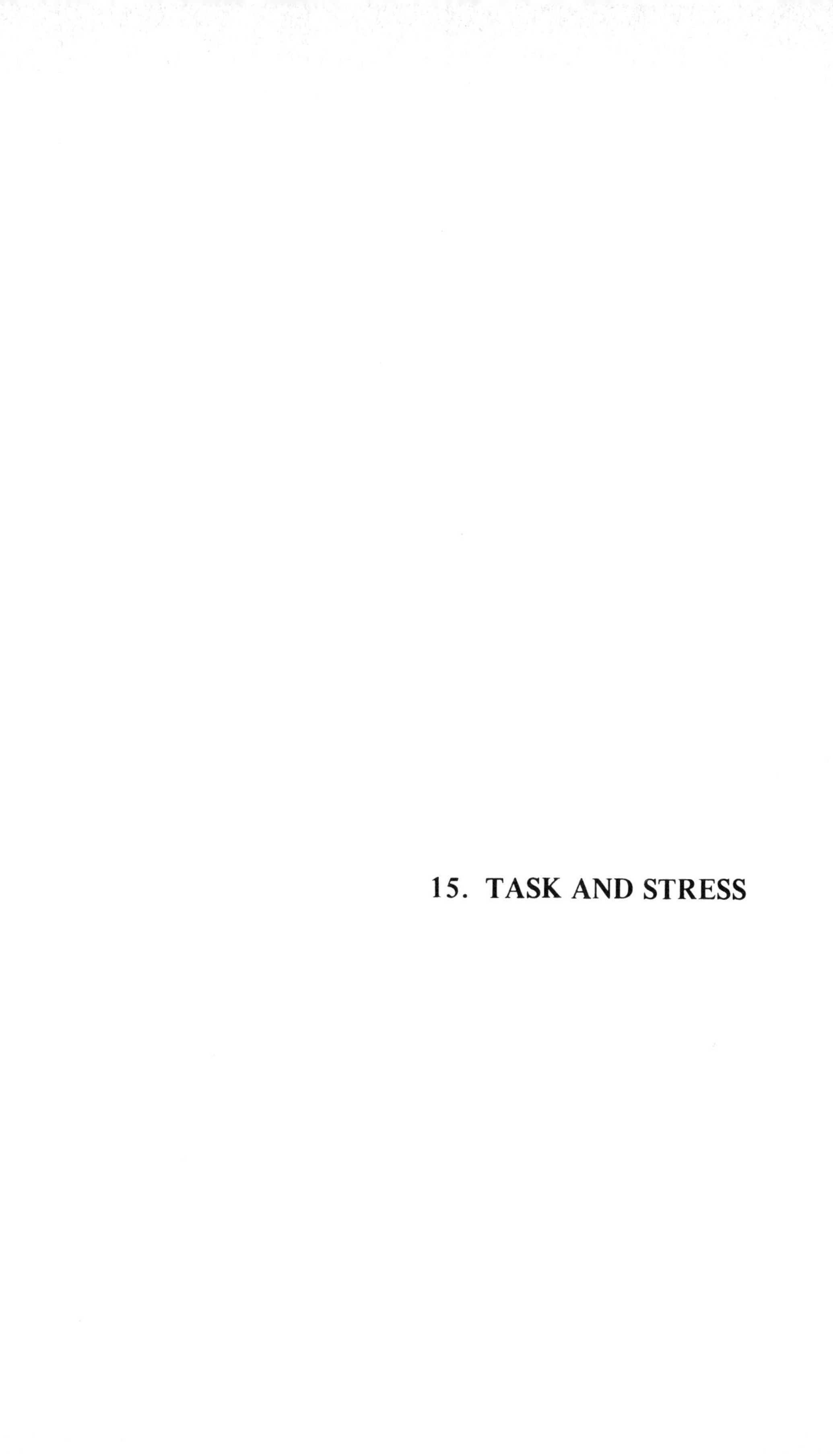

15. TASK AND STRESS

WORK WITH DISPLAY UNITS 86
B. Knave and P.-G. Widebäck (eds.)

Characterization of VDT Work

Sakae Yamamoto*, Kageyu Noro**

* University of Occupational, Environmental Health, Japan
1-1 Iseigaoka Yahatanishiku Kitakyushu, 807, Japan.
** Waseda University, 1-6-1 Nishiwaseda Shinjuku Tokyo,
160, Japan.

1. INTRODUCTION

1.1. Problem of VDT

Many problems in VDT have been pointed out. We can condense these problems into two points. One is operators' health problems and the other is the VDT work, that is, performing work with VDT.

Operators engaged in VDT work have complained of health problems, as follows;

- General eye discomfort (eye strain, burning and irritation, lacrimation and red eyes, blurring or double vision)
- Pains in neck, shoulder, waist, etc.

On the other hand, the problems of VDT work arise from the introduction of the computer systems into work places. These effects are recognized as the variation of handling, operating, and scheduling of work.
Moreover, these effects change the organization of work systems and human relations.

These two types of problems do not exist independently but are closely related. Thus, it is necessary to consider both factors simultaneously, but here we shall take them up separately.

1.2. Health Problems and Coping with Them

Have solutions been found to the foregoing health problems?
No definite solutions have yet been clarified. However, a few results of studies have been noted as follows; operators have complained of feeling physical pain following long hours in a fixed posture. It was found necessary to furnish movable desks and chairs whose height and angle operators could change easily.

Discomfort of the eyes was caused by the physical characteristics of VDT hardware ; for example, the numbers of the scanning lines, flicker, brightness, etc. But the results of the past studies have pointed out that it was necessary to improve the quality of VDT hardware. Cakir et al.[1], Grandjean[2], and others' studies are well known and are interesting. Manufacturers have made considerable progress in improving VDT hardware, such as making improvements in enhancing screen image quality.

1.3. The Problems of VDT Work

In problems relating to VDT work,it is necessary to discuss them from the standpoints of the relationship between operators and the VDT(Computer). In other words,we need to take up the problems connected with the design of human interface. More attention needs to be paid to the design and to improving VDT work. What concrete way is there to solve these problems?

1.4. VDT Work and Its Degree of Freedom

Smith et al. [3] reported that operators engaged in different VDT tasks complained of different matters. Namely, the professional VDT operators did not report levels of job stress as high as those of other VDT operators. The complaints made by the operators vary with the freedom allowed them in their VDT work. This freedom means the degree at which operators are able to control their work pace and work time; that is, the allowance of a work flexibility. The rate of complaints decreases as the freedom in controlling their VDT work increases. If operators have little freedom, they will feel an urge to continue their work and have little allowance for rest. Operators having little freedom also feel being constantly watched by the computer and controlled by the supervisor. This indicates that their freedom is also effect their concentration on the VDT work and the design of the human interface.

The operator's posture is an example of this freedom in work. When the operators' degree of freedom decreases, their rate of fixed posture increases. Indeed, operators enjoying a high degree of freedom in their work complain little. We consider this point to have some relation to the designing of VDT work.

1.5. Types of VDT Work and Its Degree of Freedom

There are many types of VDT work, for example, the data entry, reservation of tickets, retrieval, word processing, etc. There are constraints in every type of VDT work too, so that the degree of freedom in VDT work cannot be discussed in general terms.

We first classify the VDT work according to the typical and fundamental work elements. After this procedure, the VDT work is characterized for each element. This characterization is necessary to reflect the contents of all VDT work. It is also desirable that the characterization of the VDT work is not to be based on a specialized measurement but constructed of a few measurements. The simplified procedure issuitable in order to characterize VDT work, because complicated measurements are not useful for the characterization. VDT work is visual work and the looking, watching or viewing are important factors in VDT work. It is useful to investigate the operators' viewing in VDT work. So we study these characteristics based on the operators' viewing.

Basing our conclusions on this characterization, we will be able to handle the method of decreasing operators' fatigue. The degree of freedom relating to work, such as the work time and the rest allowance should also be taken up.

2. FIXATION TIME

2.1. Work Analysis

VDT work was first analyzed to classify the work types. The method involved dividing work elements and investigating what the operator fixed his eyes on during the assigned task. The working operators were recorded by the video-recorder and the video-tape was played to measure the operator's fixation time on the screen, keyboard and paper document, etc.

2.2. Results of Work Analysis

The operator's fixation time on each work element in the two most popular VDT tasks, retrieval and data entry, was investigated. Observing the VDT work, we divide it into four work elements; that is, the looking at the screen, keyboard, paper documents, etc. From the result, it can be found that these four work elements constitue a large part of VDT work in the fixation time. The percentage of the fixation time on each work element is shown in Figure 1. These results are derived from six subjects.

These two types of tasks were different in work content. This indicated that it was difficult to consider different VDT tasks in a lump. Moreover in VDT work,the quality of the operator, for instance, his experience, has a lot to do with the results. Similar work analysis was conducted to see how experienced and inexperienced operators would perform VDT work. The experienced operators had all had VDT work experience of three or more years. Three experienced operators were investigated, and five in experienced operators were also analyzed. The results shown in Figure 2 were obtained as the operator conducted search tasks.

No marked differences were observed between the experienced and inexperienced operators in searching tasks.

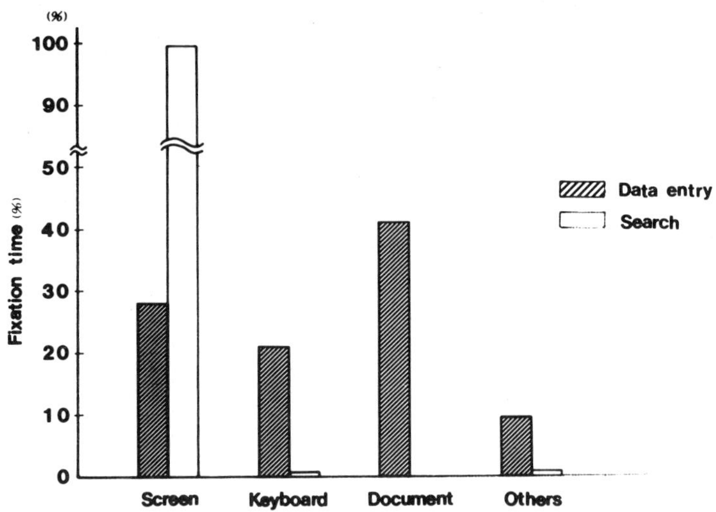

Fig.1. Effect of operators' experience in fixation time during search task and data entry task.

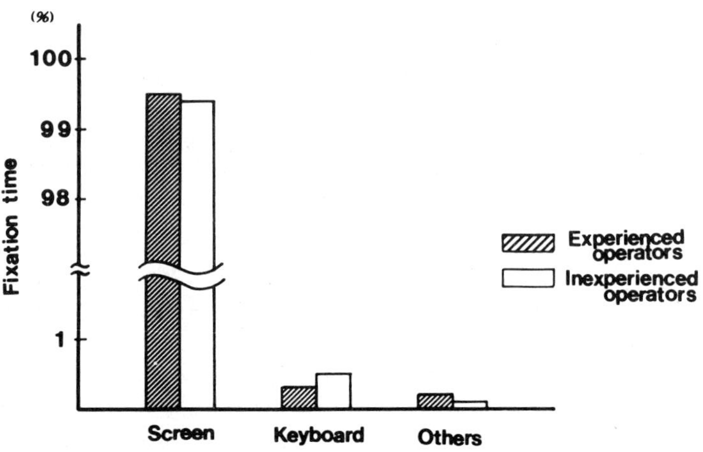

Fig.2. Effect of operators' experience in fixation time during search tasks.

The results of investigation during a data entry task are given in Figure 3.

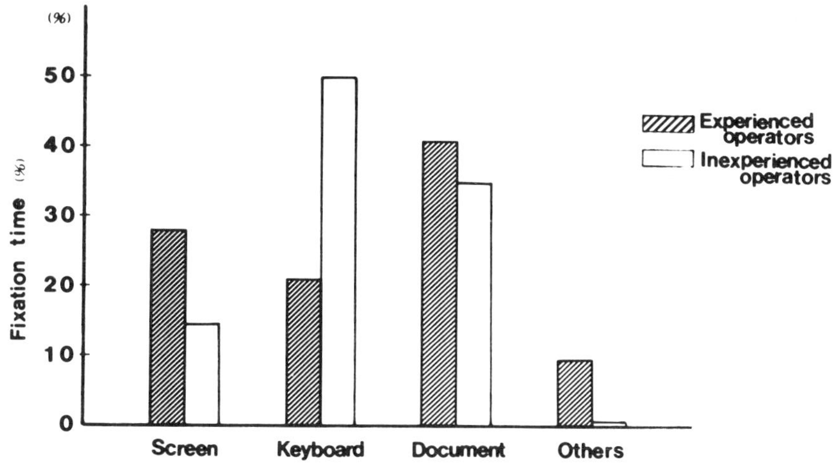

Fig.3. Effect of operators' experience in fixation time during data entry tasks.

In this task, the two groups of operators exhibited significant differences in the fixation time on the screen and keyboard.

If VDT work is reconstructed by means of the fixation time in this way, its characteristics can be revealed and VDT work can be classified by considering the characteristics (aptitude) of the operators.

3. VARIATION OF VISUAL DISTANCE

3.1. The Relation of The Visual Distance and The Posture

Looking at a display closely concerns not only fixation time but also visual distance. The visual distance indicates the distance between the position of the operator' eyes and that of the surface of VDT. This is a very important factor in the degree of freedom of work. The freedom is closely connected with the working posture and concerned with the physical pains, that is, that of the neck, shoulder, waist, etc., because a fixed posture increases such pains and visual fatigue.

Searching for good posture is an important matter in maintaining operators' health. What is good posture? We shall first consider the visual distance. This visual distance gave us a helpful information about operators' posture. It can be measured easily and also gives us a good dimension, that is, the distance. So we investigate the relationship between the degree of freedom of VDT work and the visual distance.

Other factors also could be considered but they are not proper. In addition, the visual distance is also closely related to the size of the displayed characters. If the visual distance is short, we can detect small sized characters, but if the distance is long, we can see only large sized characters. From this, we can see that the visual distance is a very important factor discussing the size of displayed characters.

This visual distance is not the same for each operator, because the visual distance is affected by the following factors, that is, the visual acuity, the body size of the operator, the height of desk and chair, the position of VDT. So it is difficult to make comparisons based on the visual distance in each operator. The visual distance is also not the same for all operators during VDT work. Operators usually change their working posture and visual distance during the whole period of work. The figure 4 shows the variations of visual distance in VDT work.

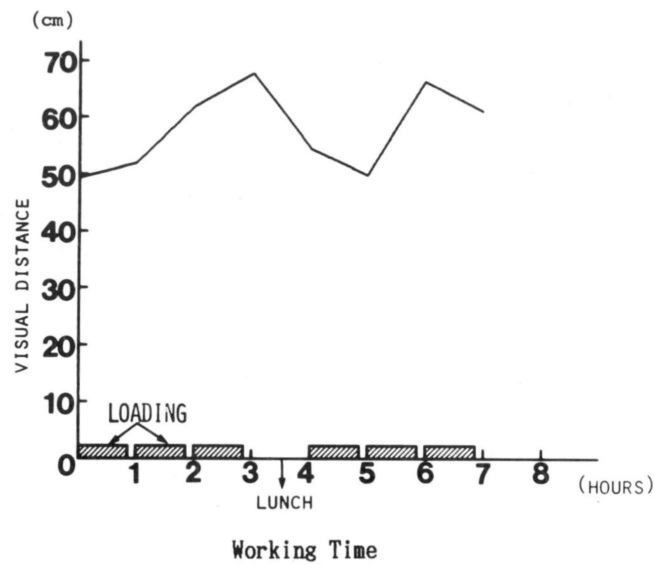

Fig. 4. The variations of visual distance in VDT work

From these results, we can see the need to discuss the variation of the visual distance which reflects the changing posture. So the degree of freedom in work can be considered by investigating this variation.

3.2. Measurement of Visual Distance

We are able to take two ways of measuring the visual distance. One is the exact measurement using photos and calculating the distance in the geometric way.

The other is using the scaler; that is, we measure the operator's visual distance directly by using the scaler. This method cannot measure the exact visual distance but can easily get the visual distance. However, this measurement has been found useful in the field study. There are no statistical differences in the two measurements. So we take the scaler method which is a very easy way to measure the visual distance. We measure the visual distance about 8 times in VDT work.

3.3. Analysis of The Variation of Visual Distance

The standard deviation of the visual distance for each subject was calculated, and after that, the coefficient variation (CV) of the standard deviation was required. We consider this CV will diminish the individual differences in operators. This CV is considered as follows; if the CV is large, operator has much freedom and can make big movements in his posture. If the CV is small, the operator's posture stays put more or less, and this is considered as a case of little freedom.

3.4. CV in VDT Work

We apply this CV to VDT work. We take two types of VDT task and one cross reference task, that is, retrieval VDT task and data entry VDT task, such as VDT tasks, and retrieval hard copy tasks. In hard copy task, the visual distance is measured from the operators' eyes to paper documents. These tasks are loaded for two hours. Subjects were six. The results are shown in Figure 5.

From these results, we can see that the retrieval VDT task has as maller variation of visual distance than the retrieval hard copy task. The variation of data entry type rises in the middle of retrieval VDT and hard copy task.

The VDT and the hard task work are investigated. From the result of variations, VDT task fixed the operators' posture, but the hard copy task had a large variation in their posture. The hard copy task had more freedom than the VDT tasks.

4. CHARACTERIZATION OF VDT WORK

We have considered the two factors that characterized VDT work. The fixation time of the display hardly gave sufficient information about VDT work because this fixation time did not reflect the operators' concentrationon VDT work. It is difficult to distinguish the difference in the act of looking at displays vaguely and that of looking at them with concentration.

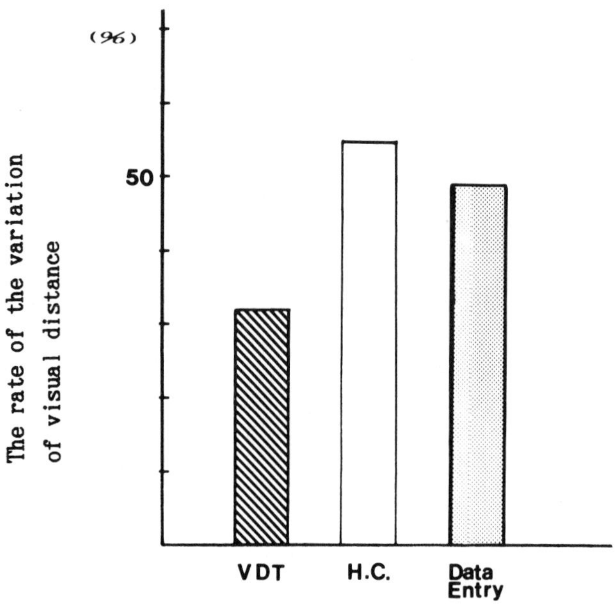

Fig. 5. The variation of a visual distance in VDT, H.C., and Data Entry Task.

Moreover,VDT work has a peculiarity such as the operator's concentration of in the work. This concentration is related to health problems; for example, the operator takes a fixed posture. So we introduced the variation of visual distance. Using this variation and the fixation time, we consider the characterization of many types of VDT work. Using these factors, we consider some eight types of VDT work. These types of VDT work are shown in this table.

Task A and B are retrieval VDT tasks carried out in our laboratory. The difference in the tasks is in the working time; that is, Task of A is performed for two hours, and Task of B for six hours. Tasks of C and D are field studies, and Task of C is Word Processing task and Task of D is Data

Retrieval task. Task of E is a Data Entry type of VDT work. This task is performed in our laboratory. Tasks of F and G are cross reference tasks and Task of F is hard copy task, the data retrieval type. Task G is the usual typing work.

Table 1. The list of the working type

A : Retrieval VDT (2 hr)
B : Retrieval VDT (6 hr)
C : Word Processing (field)
D : Retrieval (field)
E : Data Entry
F : Hard Copy
G : Typing

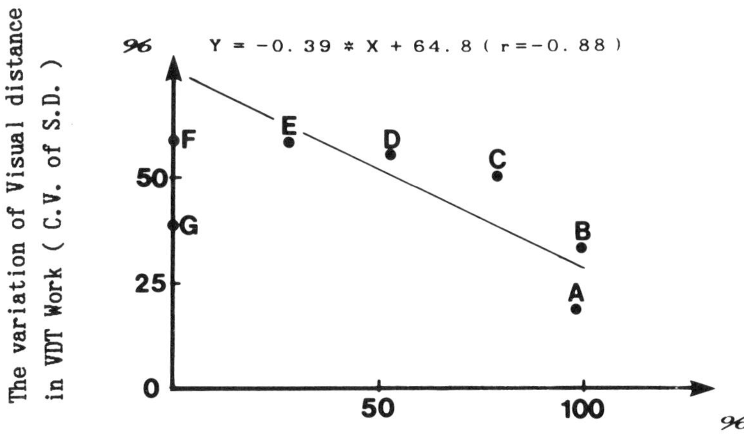

Fig. 6. Characterization of VDT work

The vertical axis indicates CV of S.D. and the horizontal axis indicate fixation time. Tasks of A and B can be found having a high rate of the fixation and low variation of CV. Tasks of C and D have a high rate of fixation time and middle variation of the visual distance. Task of E has a position at a low fixation and middle of the variation of the visula distance.

We note the coefficent of correlation is -0.88 ($p<0.05$) between the variation of the visual distance and the fixation rate in VDT task(except Task of F and G). The linear regression is estimated as

$$Y = -0.39 * X + 64.8.$$

So we can classify the VDT work using this linear regression. We can divide it into three groups, that is, one is Task of A, another is Tasks of B, C, and D, the other is Task of E.

We can find that the group of Tasks of B, C, and D have much freedom and a high rate of the fixation. Task of A has a low variation, that is, low freedom, and has a high rate fixation. This task indicates high concentration in the VDT work. Task of E has a low fixation and a middle variation of visual distance. So Task A and Task E are under the regression line, but it is difficult to consider both tasks as the same type of VDT work.

5. CONCLUSION

From these results, we can find that VDT work is not considered to be all the same work type. We need to classify the VDT work, so the characterization of VDT work is desired. Our proposed method is useful for the characterization. VDT problems should be considered on the basis of these characteristics, for instance, on the health care of operators. However, this is not the only one case. Each type of work requires its own health care.

References

[1] Cakir, A., Hart, D.J.and Stewart, T.F.M.,Visual Display Terminals (John Wiley & Sons, New York, 1983)

[2] Grandjean, E.,Displays,(1980),76

[3] Smith, M.J., Cohen, B.G.F, Stammerjohn, Jr.L.W. and Happ, A., Human Factors, (1981), 401

WORK WITH DISPLAY UNITS 86
B. Knave and P.-G. Widebäck (eds.)

VDT TECHNOLOGY: PSYCHOSOCIAL AND STRESS CONCERNS

Michael J. Smith, Pascale Carayon, and Kathleen Miezio

Department of Industrial Engineering; University of Wisconsin
Madison, WI 53706 USA

Based on the assumption that certain working conditions can create stress, which in turn produces mental strain and psychosomatic diseases, this chapter specifies the most common psychosocial stressors found among VDT operators, as well as distress symptoms and psychosomatic diseases. The review of literature on stress-related effects of VDTs shows that this technology is both directly and indirectly stressful.

Introduction

Over the last few years public interest in the influence of office work on employee health has increased dramatically [1-4]. This interest has been spurred by worker outcries about the adverse health effects of office automation. Complaints of visual dysfunction, muscular aches and pains and psychological disturbances have been the primary problem areas voiced [5-7]. Significant controversy exists in the scientific community as to whether these worker complaints represent serious health problems or are merely minor inconveniences and discomfort issues that will disappear as workers become accustomed to automated working conditions [6]. Much of the controversy concerns the adequacy of current research to address the issue of health risk. This is due to problems with contaminated study populations, poor research designs, and inadequate data analyses which have limited the type and extent of conclusions that can be drawn from current data [6].

Interest in the influences of psychosocial job demands and video display terminal (VDT) operator health has been apparent as early as the late 1970's [8-9]. The question of whether these job demands may also be stressful has also been investigated [10-11]. Recent reviews of the health issues surrounding the use of VDTs [3,12] implicate psychosocial and stress considerations as important issues in the overall impact of VDT technology on worker symptoms and complaints.

In terms of health risk, of particular interest are the reports of mental health problems voiced by office workers in automated environments [3,10,11,13,15]. These studies have shown that office workers in automated jobs suffer from mood disturbances such as nervousness, irritability, fatigue and depression as well as a range of psychosomatic symptoms from muscles spasms to stomach disorders to cardiovascular symptoms. In fact, Haynes [16] has shown that the risk for cardiovascular disease is higher for certain classes of female clerical workers than for non-working women. While these studies have defined a potential mental health risk in office work, they have not been adequate to determine the extent of this risk or the working conditions that may be responsible for adverse mental health outcomes.

While the studies by Smith [10,13-15], Ghiringhelli [18], Elias [19] and Sauter [11] have demonstrated some general mental health effects, they have some limitations. All were cross-sectional surveys of worker attitudes and symptoms, and their main focus was general health symptoms in video display terminal operators and not specifically mental health considerations, which were secondary aspects of the main health concerns. Thus, these studies do not provide the necessary orientation towards mental health considerations nor the focused content to explore the relationships between working conditions and mental health. A further weakness is the reliance on worker perceptions at a single period of time [6]. Changes in employee attitude and mood would be expected based on situational considerations at the time of evaluation, such as experience with the technology used, spousal relationships, the time of year or current workload.

Haynes [16] focused on cardiovascular risks using retrospective data from health records, death certificates and questionnaire surveys given at various time periods to participants in the Framingham Heart Study. While their questionnaire had some items on life stress including aspects about work, the lack of indepth information about the working conditions and job stress factors makes the results useful only in a general sense for highlighting a potential issue of interest.

Stellman [20] has conducted a large scale survey of the effects of video display terminal work on office environmental conditions and other job factors such as job demands and decision latitude. She found that operators that worked at VDTs all day in comparison to those that used it less than full-time or non-users reported greater job demands, postural discomfort, visual health complaints, muscular health complaints and less decision latitude and ability to move around. The suggested implication of this study was that the VDT technology induced discomfort and complaints. However, this study also suffers from some of the same deficiencies as prior studies in that it was a cross-sectional evaluation, and it did not fully define job stressors, job demands, work content and organizational influences that may have been responsible for the observed worker reactions.

A major thesis of our perspective is the belief that constellations of working conditions can cause workers to suffer distress and that extended stressful responses can bring about physical, psychological and behavioral disturbances (see Figure 1). Cooper [21] has proposed a model of how sources of stress at work can produce disease outcomes including mental ill health. This model postulates that various working conditions including intrinsic job features, organizational roles, career considerations, interpersonal relationships and organizational structure and climate coupled with extraorganizational stress sources have direct effects on the individual in terms of symptoms of ill health and behavioral reactions. These effects are mediated by individual characteristics, primarily those related to personality and current psychological states. Prolonged exposure leads to pathological influences such as coronary heart disease and mental ill health.

Cooper [21] provided support for this theory by reviewing an extensive literature on working conditions and stress which defines specific health outcomes that can be related to particular working conditions. For

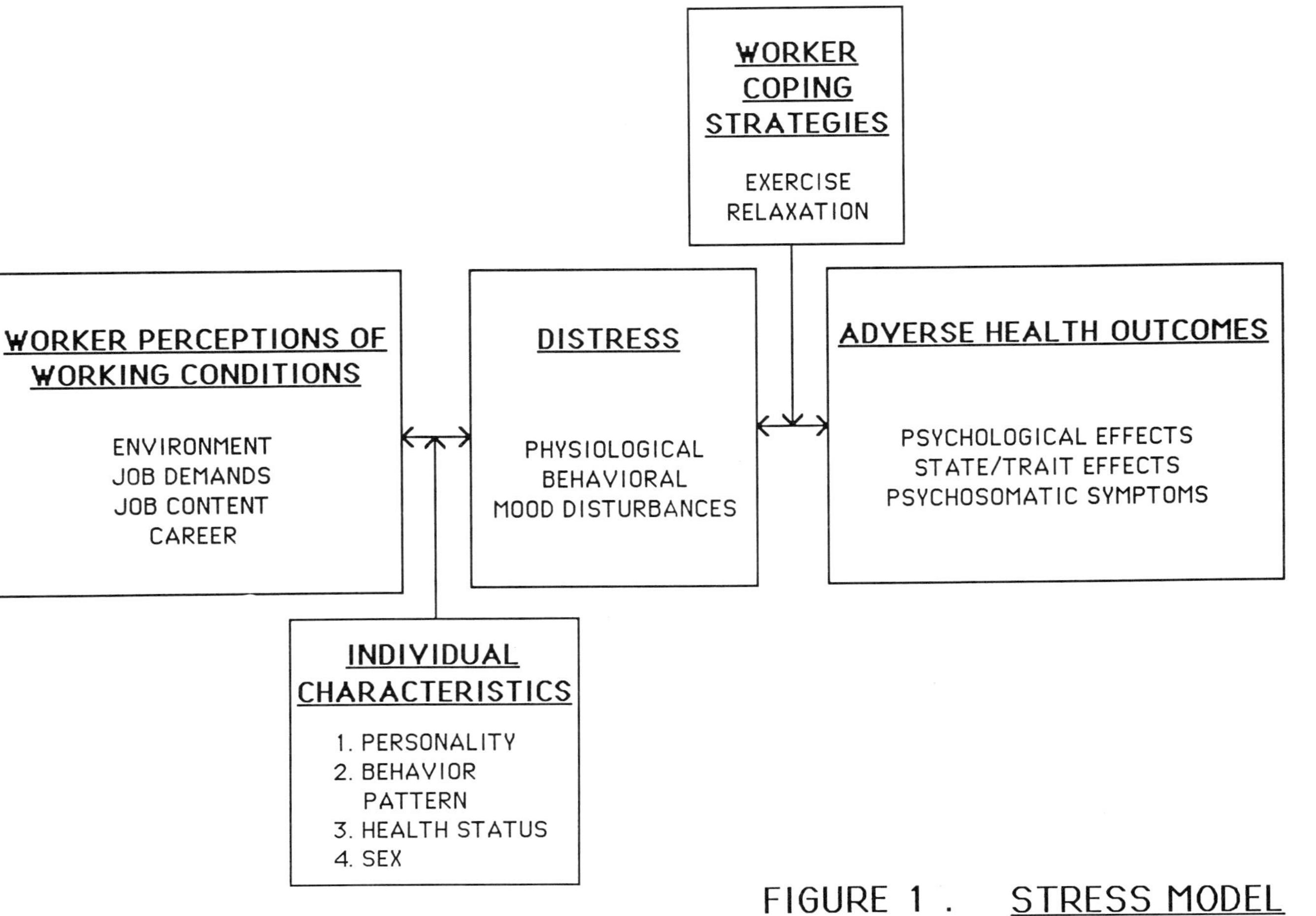

FIGURE 1. STRESS MODEL

instance, shiftwork is clearly related to increased incidence of sleep disorders and gastrointestinal disorders, while machine paced work has been related to mood disturbances [23]. A range of studies have defined how diverse working conditions or combinations of factors have been related to adverse health consequences (see [23] for a review of these studies).

Over the years various theorists have attempted to explain the stress processes that may bring about the health effects of various working conditions. Caplan [24] defined the process as a "misfit" between the individual's perception of the working conditions and the actual conditions, or a misfit between personal needs and the environment's ability to fulfill these needs. This theory suggests that individual perception and interpretation play considerable roles in distress, which eventually can lead to psychological, behavioral and physiological consequences such as job dissatisfaction, anxiety, smoking and elevated blood pressure. Cooper [21] postulated that individual susceptibilities may be important such as anxiety prone persons, Type A behavioral pattern individuals and those with a low tolerance for ambiguity. These people are believed to be at higher risk in responding to adverse working conditions. However, recent research [25-26] suggests that there may not be a strong link between Type A behavior and workplace stress/strain and thus casts doubt on the individual susceptibility theory.

Other theorists such as Lazarus [27] and McGrath [28] have proposed a cognitive process by which individuals evaluate the implications of the working conditions within some individual value framework and that evaluations that produced threat, fear or negative psychological arousal cause distress. Lazarus [27] further extends this conceptualization by proposing that it is the "hassles" of daily living that accumulate over time that are detrimental to mental health.

While all of these theories have postulated an intermediate cognitive process between the working conditions and distress reactions, none have been able to establish firm relationships between particular working conditions, the intermediate cognitive process and specific adverse health effects. Most likely this is due to the highly diverse nature of the influences of stress, as well as mediating characteristics, events or conditions that determine the specific and the prolonged responses to particular working condition(s).

In our chapter a model defined by Levi [29] will be used to examine relationships between VDT work and mental health (see Figure 1). In this model adverse working conditions (as defined by worker perceptions) are postulated to lead to distress that is manifested as physiological, psychological and behavioral responses which can in turn lead to health disorders such as heart disease and mental ill-health if experienced for prolonged time periods on a regular basis. In this model the distress response can be influenced by individual characteristics, coping strategies or social support. Thus the model requires that we define positively and negatively perceived working conditions, individual characteristics of importance, coping strategies employed, social support, distress reactions (physiological, psychological and behavioral) and health status changes.

Within the Levi [29] framework it is necessary to define specific stressors, stressful worker reactions, and moderating factors that can increase or diminish the impact of the workplace conditions. This conceptualization is most appropriate since it keys in on worker perceptions of adverse working conditions and worker reactions to these perceptions. Other approaches have examined influences of working conditions, such as Hackman [30] or Dunham [31] but are more concerned with job satisfaction and motivation than with stress and therefore of less interest here. Employee responses to the adverse working conditions are defined as stress responses. They include measures of mood disturbances such as anxiety and depression [32-33], behavioral reactions such as smoking, drinking, and coping actions, acute physical and psychological health complaints and measures of physiological reactivity (adrenaline and noradrenaline, blood pressure, pulse rate).

Psychosocial Stressors

The major shift in computer automation from a batch process to on-line access has provided a powerful new tool to users. The capability to instantaneously access data, to change data files, to correct errors in software programs has speeded up the access to computing power and has increased efficiency and productivity. What started out as a limited application for computer programmers, scientists, scholars and students has exploded into the work place because of the production benefits, as well as the advent of low cost computers and access devices. While the applications in programming, science and academia have been greeted with enthusiasm, industry applications, mainly in the office sector, have shown mixed responses from workers. For those who express pleasure and delight in use of computerized office automation, the technology typically enhances their capabilities to do their job by serving as a powerful tool under their control. For those not happy with the technology, their jobs often are changed in undesirable ways and the computer seems to exert control over the work process. The reactions of employees to their displeasure is many times reflected in high levels of job stress, stress that can be tied to the way in which the computer technology is used. In the final analysis, it can be said that the change from batch processing to on-line applications of computers has led to changes in the way in which many office jobs are carried out. This may produce job conditions that are stressful. Thus, it is not the computer technology per se that is the basic consideration in job stress, but how it has changed the nature of work through productive improvements in its applications.

The major question that needs to be addressed then is why is computer automated work stressful for some jobs and not as stressful for others? And then, can we determine how to deal with the technology and its associated job changes to eliminate or reduce job stress? To answer these questions, we must examine the nature of the application of the technology.

One of the major benefits of computers from a production standpoint is the ability to automate routine work activities and therefore free workers up for more significant tasks. When we examine the nature of many office jobs it is clear that they are already quite routine and that computers can easily replace workers or so improve the production of workers that fewer are needed to do the work. What then is left for the workers being replaced? Obviously, there is not enough non-routine office work to employ all of them.

In fact, one effect of computerization of the office has been a reduced need for workers. This has not been reflected in employment over the last two decades because of an increase in paper work and the increased shift of the economy of the United States from a manufacturing to a service sector. Thus, there has been an increasing demand for office workers that has far outstretched the lost employment due to increased efficiency because of computer automation. For the time being jobs are not jeopardized, but it is clear that the trends of increasing employment in office jobs cannot continue, and already projections of office employment into the next century indicate a gradual leveling with future decreases in employment [34]. The fear of potential job loss is a major concern for clerical office workers. Smith [13] found that over half of the clerical study subjects that worked on VDTs felt that they would be replaced by the computer within one year, while less than one quarter of their counterparts that did not use computers felt they would be replaced. Unions and clerical workers are fearful of job loss due to computer automation and this is a serious source of job stress [34-35]

The way in which jobs change due to computerization is another major issue related to job stress. For most professional and technical jobs the computer serves as a tool that does not diminish the content of their work. However, for the majority of clerical workers, computer automation can mean more trivial tasks, more redundant activities and less use of skills and thinking processes. The effect is similar to the "Taylorization" of blue collar jobs in the early decades of this century. Interestingly enough, issues of job content are not one of the primary complaints of clerical VDT workers [3,7]. This may occur because even though automation increases the routine nature of the work and simplifies tasks, the prior jobs were not very rich in content either and thus the change does not appear very great to the workers. However, one content area that seems to elicit employee response is boredom. Smith [13] compared a variety of professional and clerical VDT jobs and clerical jobs not using VDTs on job satisfaction and mood dimensions. He found that clerical VDT users reported higher levels of boredom than the professional users and the clerical non-users. Supporting the hypothesis that the nature of clerical work may reflect why job content is not a major stress issue was the finding that clerical non-users reported more boredom than the professionals using VDTs.

Another factor related to content that seems to be a potentially serious job stressor is the issue of control over the work process the ability to make decisions and to exert influence over the job tasks. Karasek [36] and Smith [17] have shown that decision making and control combined with other job demands are significant job stressors with serious psychological and physical health consequences for blue collar workers, particularly those engaged in machine paced work. The same may very well be true for clerical workers using computer automation. Smith [13] found that clerical VDT workers reported less job involvement and less autonomy than professionals who used VDTs or non-user clericals. These same VDT operators reported higher levels of mood disturbances and a greater percentage reported psychosomatic complaints. However, Sauter [11] found that clericals who were non-users reported more mood disturbances than clericals who used VDTs. This may reflect the nature of the clerical jobs more so than the use of the VDT. However, the Sauter [11] study did not include professionals who used VDTs. These seemingly conflicting results may not really be at odds but may demonstrate that for job content and control issues, it is an interaction between the nature of the work and the effects of the automation on the new job that are most critical. Thus, clerical jobs devoid of content to begin with, whether a VDT is used or not, will report more psychosomatic problems than other jobs with a reasonable amount of content. Some jobs are already so devoid of content that the application of computer technology cannot make them that much worse, and in fact may even make them better, even though they are still lacking in meaningful content. It appears that a central aspect of job content is control over the work process which can reduce the stress of even boring jobs.

A factor that is related to the amount of perceived control that workers feel they have over computers is whether or not they are monitored by the computer. In computerized clerical work monitoring typically deals with performance evaluation either in terms of the quantity of work completed and/or the quality of performance. For instance long distance telephone operators are evaluated by the computer in terms of the number of calls they take and the average time to deal with each call. In addition, supervisors listen in on a small percentage of the telephone calls and evaluate the quality of handling the call. This monitoring is unannounced and the operator does not know when it is happening. Monitoring invests significant power in the automation system in controlling the operator's work behavior and performance. Adding to the sense of computer control, in advanced automation systems the computer automatically routes calls to the operator as calls are completed. Thus, the system tends to take on the characteristics of machine pacing. This is an extreme example of monitoring. However, computer technology provides more opportunity to track work performance than previous technologies and the stress of being watched by the machine has been reported as a problem by office VDT workers [13,15].

It may be that monitoring is a problem because it adds to feelings of work pressure by clerical VDT operators. The amount of work processed is sure to increase for clerical VDT operators as this is a main advantage of computer automation. An important question relates to whether this increased number of items processed is an actual increase in workload since the computer automation makes it easier to complete each item and thus reduces the effort necessary for each item. The majority of studies of VDT automation that have examined psychosocial and job design issues [8,9,11,13,14] have found that clerical VDT operators report dissatisfaction with their workload. Smith [13] in comparing professional and clerical VDT users found that the clericals reported higher levels of workload, greater workload dissatisfaction and greater work pressure. It is consistent with ergonomics and stress theory that workers will perceive the automated work as greater even if the same energy expenditure is used since the tasks require more repetitive and more frequent actions which can contribute to chronic trauma, increased fatigue, boredom and greater stress. In fact, the greater number of transactions may be a contributor to the high level of visual and musculoskeletal complaints voiced by VDT operators. Such physical complaints can add to worker perceptions of stress and psychological discomfort.

Another contributor to the perception of increased workload is that more time is spent at the VDT than at non-VDT workstations. Anecdotal evidence from interviews with clerical VDT operators who recently underwent automation indicates they report spending more time at the workstation using the VDT and have more intensive work sessions without a break. Potential reasons for this could be the monitoring of VDT operator performance which can include the time they spend at the VDT, and the increased number of transactions required because of automation which forces them to remain at the VDT longer.

A final aspect of job design and VDT use which also is related to being locked into a workstation at a VDT for long periods of time is isolation from co-workers. Socialization is an important reason that people work and social support has an important moderating effect on stress. Computer technology has the tendency to reduce person to person interaction. Smith [13] indicates that clerical VDT workers reported less peer cohesion and staff support than either computer programmers using VDTs or clerical non-users, while the programmers and clerical non-users did not differ on these dimensions. VDT users also report that computerized monitoring systems can directly impact social contacts on the job [15]. Computerized monitoring systems provide the opportunity for management to fix high output standards. Having to meet these standards, VDT operators may have to reduce their social interactions with co-workers[15]. This suggests that the VDT does not contribute fully to the reduced social effects nor does the clerical work. Again, it appears to be an interaction between the two.

There are hardware and software issues that can contribute to VDT operator feelings of stress. Systems that break down regularly add to feelings of frustration and increase the worker's perception of a lack of control over the work process. When systems are overloaded with operators so that response delays interfere with the timing of work activities, this also can increase frustration and lack of control. Johansson [42] found that delayed response times in the computer system and unpredicted computer breakdowns were associated with higher stress and mental strain. Such problems are exacerbated when performance requirements are not reduced to account for the system breakdowns and slow downs, or when workers are receiving incentive pay for production. Cakir [8] found VDT operators under incentive pay reported more physical and psychological problems than those on hourly wages. Software that does not help the operator recover from mistakes or which is inflexible in accessing files or items in records can also produce frustration. Essentially, these hardware/software concerns need to include human factors considerations of system usability and friendliness to help workers exercise control over the system during normal operations or when recovery from mistakes is needed.

There are a number of environmental conditions that may be of significance in VDT operator stress problems as they tend to contribute to physical health disorders and discomfort such as visual and muscular disturbances and to general feelings of dissatisfaction with work. Such physical stressors tend to wear the worker down and add to the overall stress load [13,38]. Most prominent among employee environmental complaints are glare on VDT screens, poor lighting, unsatisfactory temperature and ventilation problems [5, 39]. Such conditions and others such as poor workstation design reflect a lack of interest and commitment by management in worker comfort and satisfaction and thereby are significant organizational sources of stress.

Organizational factors can also be important in VDT operator stress. Smith [13] found that clerical VDT workers reported greater supervisory control over their activity than the professional VDT users or the clerical non-users, while the clerical non-users reported more supervisory control than the professional VDT users. Again, the nature of the work activity is important since in this case it dictates the extent of contact between workers and supervisors. Thus, the computer technology is not the direct cause of the strained worker/supervisor relationship, but may bring about increased supervision for some jobs that adds to already high levels. Most likely the increased supervision is due to the availability of current information about employee performance and it is the technology that makes this information possible. Furthermore, VDT clericals who are machine-monitored perceive the supervision as heavily emphasizing quantity rather than quality [15]. One of the dangers of current performance information is that it can be used to spur VDT workers on to higher production in a constant fashion. In a monitored environment, even the machine becomes a supervisor. The nature of the supervisory role becomes one of continuous haggling or heckling, or in positive environments one of motivating workers to perform. This adds considerably to worker feelings of work pressure and heavy workload, factors that we have seen can produce job stress [17].

Fear of the unknown may be more stressful than the fear we feel for recognized dangers or problems. The introduction of any kind of automation into the work place can produce fears of the unknown. A number of questions pop into employee conversations which often start rumors. Will the automation affect employment? How will jobs be changed? Will it be hard to learn the new jobs and work with the technology? How much time will workers have to become proficient? Will pay and hours of work be reduced? These and hundreds of other questions will arise and fuel worker fears of the technology. Many employers do not involve employees in the office automation process [3,8,13] and this leads to employee fears. Many of these fears may be unfounded, yet without information, rumors abound and employee fears increase. In light of the fact that computer automation will reduce their clerical workforce, some employers would rather keep information about such effects and others to themselves so as not to work up the employees, often producing the opposite effects.

This leads to another important organizational factor, career concerns of employees. If computer automation is used to simplify and fragment clerical work into "Taylorized" tasks, then the opportunity to advance into high level jobs with more content and greater skill utilization is reduced significantly. To add to this problem, it seems likely that since the major role of supervisors is to monitor workers and provide constant feedback and instruction on job performance, supervisory jobs will be taken over by the computer automation which can do them more efficiently and less personally. Thus, clerical VDT workers will not even have an opportunity to advance into supervisory jobs. The other paths available include parallel jobs at the same pay level using different skills but of the same complexity, or moving into staff support positions that may pay more but require increased education, training and skill acquisition. These latter jobs most likely will also be automated out of the workforce by computers [3]. This leaves only lateral job shifts with no increase in pay, not a very bright prospect for clerical VDT workers and a source of stress.

With prospects for job changes being limited to parallel moves, there is little likelihood of extensive VDT worker training for skill enhancement. In various surveys [3,34] VDT workers have reported that they did not have adequate training in how to use the technology to be able to perform at their best. Many VDT workers report that they acquired their computer skills on-the-job in a trial-and-error fashion, not through formalized training programs. If the current state of training is so poor, it is unlikely that this will improve as career opportunities diminish.

Finally, the physical health and safety hazards associated with VDT use act as job stressors. The physical symptoms of visual and muscular disturbances add to worker fears and concerns. Questions arise. Is the equipment safe? Will I sustain permanent health damage? What about long-term exposure, is it dangerous? To add to the visual and muscular fears is the threat of radiation and reproductive damage. While there is growing evidence that proper workplace design, job and organizational considerations, and administrative actions can substantially reduce the risk of any adverse health effects of VDT work, there is growing concern on the part of unions and workers about the physical risks such as radiation and reproductive effects [3, 40]. As these concerns are aired in the public press, radio and T.V., at union meetings, and at scientific meetings, employees become more and more fearful that their health is at risk. When told that the risk is small, they do not believe it. How can they trust government sources that have in the past shown to be unreliable, or employers who have a vested interest? Can employers, government and scientists be trusted, when public advocacy groups and unions claim that serious problems exist? Whether significant health problems are associated with VDT use or not is not of consequence to stress considerations; employees perceive that they are, and are fearful for their health. They are stressed by this fear.

Distress and Psychosomatic Responses

A number of studies present varieties of health complaints of VDT operators, ranging from psychological and emotional effects to psychosomatic problems. In Finland, Kalimo [41] studied the impact of the VDT technology on tasks involving text preparation. Two hundred and eighteen employees in the preprinting text-preparation section of 12 printing plants were surveyed. Subject were divided into 4 groups on the basis of tasks and technological level of equipment: VDT typesetters (high technological level) and perforator typesetters (medium) on one hand, and VDT photocompositors (high) and proofreaders (low) on the other hand. Using a questionnaire, the researchers assessed employees perceptions of work characteristics along 7 dimensions: challenge, autonomy, role ambiguity, social contacts, supervision, job appreciation and job satisfaction. VDT users reported more challenge and autonomy than non-VDT users. A sub-sample of 99 VDT users participated in individual tests and measurements of daily workload and stress. Fatigue and alertness, rapidity and exactness of visual perception and motor function, and perceived state were measured 1-3 times during a work shift. Both VDT groups - typesetters and photocompositors - reported more challenge and autonomy in their work than the non-VDT group - perforator typesetters and proofreaders. Furthermore non-VDT perforator typesetters were the only one to show an increased level of fatigue during the work shift. Moreover, non-VDT perforator typesetters showed more physiological strain at the end of the work shift than VDT typesetters. That same group of perforator typesetters also differed the three others along the self-rating scales: they reported more fatigue, less competence and a lower level of pleasantness. The results of the study suggest that the computerization of text-preparation tasks can be successfully implemented so that job content is improved and stress and strain reduced.

Other studies which compare VDT and non VDT groups showed different results. In Sweden, Johansson [42] investigated the impact of type of work and amount of VDT work on stress and strain in computerized office work. Ninety-five white-collar workers employed by a large Swedish insurance company using VDTs filled in a questionnaire concerning psychosocial stressors in connection with work at the VDT (response rate: 74%). A psychophysiological study of a smaller group among those who responded to the questionnaire was conducted. Eleven persons with extensive VDT work and ten non-VDT users were studied during regular work, during breakdown of the computer and in their leisure time. Each subject participated for three days, two at work and one weekday off at home. Five times per work day, the subjects made self-ratings of alertness and mood and urine samples were taken - for catecholamine excretion analysis. In addition heart rate and blood pressure were measured. The same data was collected twice at home, with the exception of blood pressure. Results indicate that in the morning the VDT group had a higher adrenaline excretion than the non-VDT group and that this relationship was reversed in the afternoon. The same difference in the pattern during a workday was reflected in fatigue, effort and rush self-ratings. Furthermore, average adrenaline excretion during working hours and later in the evening were higher for VDT group than for the non-VDT group. The self-ratings of mental strain confirmed that tendency. The VDT group carried a persistent negative effect on mental strain after work ended, while the non-VDT group recovered from fatigue after work. In addition, health examinations indicated that the triglyceride content in blood, assumed to be a predictor of cardiovascular disorders, was significantly higher in the VDT group. Questionnaire results indicated that stress and mental strain occured in association with delayed response times in the computer system and unpredicted interruptions of computer operation. An examination of six VDT operators during a computer breakdown showed increased levels of adrenaline, blood pressure and heart rate. During the computer breakdown, these VDT users felt more irritated, tired, rushed and bored, and less calm and relaxed than under normal working conditions. Computer breakdowns were an important source of mental strain for VDT users.

Other studies [8,19] compared different VDT groups and showed that job stressors and thus health complaints varied between different categories of VDT users. Cakir [8] conducted field studies in 30 German companies. One thousand twenty-one office workers took part in this study. A large number of instruments - objective walk-through studies and subjective questionnaires and tests - were used to assess environmental, job-related and individual variables. Results of this large-scale study indicated that VDT workers experienced headaches, back strain and pain, and neck pain, which was higher among workers engaged in highly repetitive activities. Results from the stress questionnaire confirmed that the monotony and repetition of the work resulted in a high degree of stress which was accompanied by an increase in somatic complaints. Most VDT workers felt considerably tense, nervous, rundown, subdued, and tired after work. In many instances, this fatigue persisted for a long time after work so that workers had to spend some of their free time recovering from work.

In France, Elias [19] studied 89 offline data acquisition operators and 81 dialogue operators using a questionnaire and eye movement records. They found significant differences among the two groups. The offline data acquisition group reported more visual strain symptoms and psychological distress: anxiety, 67% vs 38%; irritability, 68% vs 42%; depression, 53% vs 22%; troubled sleep, 45% vs 15%; palpitations, 43% vs 23%; chest pains, 37% vs 20%. The offline operators reported also greater job dissatisfaction (70% vs 28%). The researchers attributed these effects to job content differences between the two groups. In comparison to the dialogue jobs, the data-acquisition jobs were more fragmented and repetitive, involved less freedom and required less training.

Ghiringhelli [18] interviewed seventy-seven VDT operators from two sites to gather subjective opinions about health disorders which were likely induced by VDT work. A control group of 237 female subjects did not use VDTs. The subjects indicated health problems they remembered having before they started to use VDTs and problems they had at the time of the interview. Younger and better educated VDT operators had negative opinions on VDT work, complained of mental discomfort and showed increased anxiety after more than 6 months of work. Ghiringhelli found that mental discomfort was particularly high, with 66% of the VDT operators giving negative opinions on VDTs due mainly to dependence on the machine, lack of meaningfulness in the work, boredom, monotony, anxiety, stress, isolation, mental confusion, or fear of health problems. This led Ghiringhelli to conclude that VDTs could become a symbolic focus of discomfort.

More acute psychosomatic complaints have been found in some studies [43-44]. The North Carolina Occupational Safety and Health Project (NCOSH) and seven locals of the Communications Workers of America (CWA) from throughout North Carolina conducted a survey of office workers employed by telephone companies [43]. A questionnaire on health effects and worker perceptions of working conditions was sent to 2,478 persons. Among the forty percent who responded to the questionnaire, 966 were office workers. They were divided into two groups: VDT users (more than 50% of their work time spent at a VDT) and non-VDT users (less than 50% of their work time spent at a VDT or no use of a VDT). The survey results about health were limited to women employees. VDT users reported higher rates of health problems than non-VDT users in all areas surveyed with the exception of arm and hand pain. In particular, VDT users reported a significantly higher rate of angina (chest pain), a first sign of heart disease, and VDT operators having low control reported the highest rates of angina (16%) of those surveyed. These results were most striking for women 30-39 years olds. A reanalysis of these data was conducted by the National Institute for Occupational Safety and Health [44]. There were 839 persons evaluated who responded to questions on VDT use and chest pain, giving a 34% response rate. Results showed that the frequency of reported "anginal pain" was higher among VDT users than non-users (10.3% versus 4.7%). The data also indicated that the frequency of anginal pain increased both with increasing amount of time spent at a VDT (from 4% among infrequent users to 15.2% among heavy users) and with decreasing job control (from 7.9% for high control jobs to 14% for low control jobs). However the authors point out that the results have two major limitations. First, the response rate of 34% was very low and hence response bias might have been a concern. Second, the questionnaire did not clearly measure anginal pain. The pain might result from problems other than cardiac problems, such as gastrointestinal or musculoskeletal problems.

In the Wisconsin NIOSH study, Sauter [11] surveyed 248 VDT users and 85 non-users. The participants were office workers for the State of Wisconsin and the response rate averaged 92%. The purpose of the study was to investigate the well-being of VDT operators and to identify likely sources of strain. A detailed questionnaire ascertained levels of health, well being, job conditions and working environments. The results of the study indicated that there were no significant differences between users and non-users on scales of job dissatisfaction, affective disturbances or somatic disturbances, except VDT users reported more symptoms of visual or musculo-skeletal strain. The non-VDT users group did report, however, higher levels of depression, tension and a racing pounding heart - all indicators of behavioral autonomic strain. VDT users reported less autonomy, skill underutilization, less supervisory support and more physical environmental problems. The office workers who had less professional jobs had more reported health disturbances and unfavorable working conditions. An analysis of the results indicated that the best predictors of strain related to job design, physical environment and individual characteristics were almost identical for VDT users and non-users.

Finally comparative investigations into the relationship between job stress, health complaints and VDT work conducted by Smith [10,13,45] found a relationship between health complaints and psychological disturbances. A questionnaire survey was distributed to 250 workers at three work sites in one community with an average response rate of 51% for VDT users and 37% for non-users [10]. These questionnaires included measures on job demands, job stressors, psychological stress levels, psychological moods, health complaints and working conditions. Although each site differed in various dimensions, all three sites showed a definite interaction between VDT use, job demands, physical and psychosocial stressors with clerical workers reporting the most health and/or psychological disturbances. This led to the conclusion that job demands, independent of VDT use, were responsible for health complaints and job stress. The results of this study [10] were elaborated in a second report [13]. In the latter report, professional VDT operators (reporters, editors and copy editors] were compared with VDT clericals (data entry, data retrieval, etc.) and non-VDT users. The results indicated that more health problems and psychological distress was reported by the clerical VDT users than the professional VDT users or clerical non-users. The investigators concluded that this difference was due to job demands and job content.

Smith [45] also investigated a work site with 234 computer programmers using VDTs with survey instruments similar to the previous studies [10,13]. The investigation was conducted at the request of the employer and the response rate to the questionnaire was 84%. The VDT users were professional programmers who used the VDT one hour and hard copy one hour alternatively. The results of the investigation showed high levels of respiratory difficulties, visual disorders, psychological problems and stomach disorders among VDT operators. In comparing standard psychological mood state scales with previous studies [10, 13] the VDT programmers demonstrated elevated levels of psychological fatigue and confusion as compared to clericals wh do not use VDU's but were similar to the levels reported by clerical VDT operators. In contrast, the levels of reported anxiety, depression and anger were lower for the programmers than for the other VDT operators from previous studies [10]. A comparison with other VDT users in job satisfaction showed that the programmers demonstrated a higher level of job satisfaction as compared to other VDT users. They also reported less work pressure and work load than other VDT users from previous studies. However, since the programmers reported high job satisfaction levels but low job stress levels, confounded by elevated levels of health complaints, the authors concluded that VDT operator health problems are due, not only to job stress, job dissatisfaction and VDT use, but also to insufficient human factors considerations and that any one of these factors cannot be examined in isolation.

Conclusion

Is VDT technology good or bad regarding stress? Some believe that the technology is neutral and that improper application is at fault for stress problems. Others believe that VDTs are no worse than previous technologies and therefore should be left alone. We feel that VDTs do contribute to stress both directly and indirectly. They contribute indirectly by the way in which they are misapplied in carrying-out various job tasks and by the publicity they generate which feeds worker fears. They contribute directly by the way in which they change the nature of work and the work environment. This is true of all technologies, not just the VDT, but VDTs have qualities that make them particularly stressful. First, they do tasks more effectively and efficiently than prior technology and thus reduce the need for workers. This affects employment, unemployment and worker security. Second, because they are smarter and more flexible in their applications than previous technology, they can be used to deskill jobs to a greater extent than other technologies. These inherent qualities are what makes it possible for uninformed management to develop the stressful working conditions described in this paper. Finally, VDT/computer technology provides capabilities to monitor and track office worker performance never before available to management. While it is uninformed management that misapplies this information, it is the technology capability that makes it possible. Does the VDT cause worker stress? The answer is yes. Can this lead to health disorders? The answer is unclear but suggestive that stress-related disorders are more prevalent in VDT work. Can stress and psychosomatic problems be prevented or controlled? The answer also is yes, if we choose to do so.

References

[1] NIOSH, Potential Health Hazards of Video Display Terminals (National Institute for Occupational Safety and Health, Cincinnati, Ohio, 1981)

[2] OTA (Office of Technology Assessment), Project Proposal on Information and Communications Technologies and the Office (Office of Technology Assessment, United States Congress, Washington, D.C., 1983)

[3] OTA, Automation of America's Offices (Office of Technology Assessment, U.S. Congress, Washington, D.C., 1985)

[4] This volume.

[5] Dainoff, M.J., Occupational Stress factors in visual display terminal operation: A review of empirical research, Behaviour and Information Technology (1982) 1, 141-176.

[6] NAS (National Academy of Sciences), Video Display, Work and Vision (National Academy Press, Washington, D.C., 1983)

[7] Smith, M.J., Health Issues in VDT Work, in: Bennet, J., Case, D., Sandelin, J. and Smith, M.J. (eds.) Visual Display Terminals (Prentice-Hall, Englewood Cliffs, N.J., 1984) pp. 193-228.

[8] Cakir, A., Reuter, H., Von Schmude, L. and Armbruster, A. Untersuchung Zur Anpassung Von Biloschirmarbeitsplaten an die ##?Physiche und Psychische Function. (Bundesminiter fur Arbiet and Sozialondund, Bonn, W. Germany, 1978)

[9] Gunnarsson, E. and Ostberg, O., The Physical and Psychological Working Environment in a Terminal-Based Computer Storage and Retrieval System (National Board of Occupational Safety and Health, Stockholm, 1977)

[10] Smith, M.J., Stammerjohn, L., Cohen, B.G.F. and Lalich, N., Video Display Operator Stress, in Grandjean, E. and Vigliani, E. (eds.), Ergonomic Aspects of Visual Display Terminals (Taylor and Francis, Ltd., London, 1980) pp. 201-210.

[11] Sauter, S.L., Gottlieb, M.S., Rohrer, K.M. and Dodson, V.N., The Well-Being of Video Display Terminal Users (Department of Preventive Medicine, University of Wisconsin, Madison, WI, 1983)

[12] Bergqvist, U.O, Video display terminals and health: A technical and medical appraisal of the state of the art, Scandinavian Journal of Work Environment and Health (1984) 10, pp. 1-87.

[13] Smith, M.J., Cohen, B.G.F., Stammerjohn, L. and Happ, A., An investigation of health complaints and job stress in video display operations, Human Factors (1981) 23, pp. 389-400.

[14] Smith, M.J., Dainoff, M.J., Cohen, B.G.F. and Bierbaum, D.S., Ergonomic Evaluation of VDT Operations at the Woodlawn Building of the Social Security Administration (U.S. Department of Health and Human Services, Publication No. (NIOSH) Heta 82-329, Washington, D.C., 1983)

[15] Smith, M.J., Carayon, P. and Miezio, K., Motivational, Behavioral and Psychological Implications of Electronic Monitoring of Worker Performance (Office of Technology Assessment, U.S. Congress, Washington, D.C., 1986)

[16] Haynes, S., Epidemiological Examination of Cardiovascular Risk in Clerical Workers, in: B.G.F. Cohen, Proceedings of a Conference on Occupational Health Issues Affecting Clerical/Secretarial Personnel. (National Institute for Occupational Safety and Health, Cincinnati, Ohio, 1982)

[17] Smith, M.J., VDT strain: Psychological or physical basis? Proceedings of the Human Factors Society 29th Annual Meeting (1985a) 2, pp. 689-693.

[18] Ghiringhelli, L., Collection of Subjective Opinions on Use of VDUs, in Grandjean, E. and Vigliani, E., (eds.), Ergonomic Aspects of Visual Display Terminals (Taylor and Francis, Ltd., London, England, 1980) pp. 211-218.

[19] Elias, R., Cail, F., Tisserand, M. and Christman, M., Investigations in Operators Working with CRT Display: Relationships Between Task Content and Psychophysiological Alterations, in: Grandjean, E. and Vigliani, E. (eds.) Ergonomic Aspects of Visual Display Terminals (Taylor and Francis, Ltd., London, England, 1980) pp. 227-232.

[20] Stellman, J., A Comparison of Measures of Well-Being Between Full Time, Part-Time VDT Users, Typists and Non-Machine Interactive Clerical Workers (WWDU meeting in Stockholm, Sweden, May 12-15, 1986)

[21] Cooper, C.L. and Marshall, J., Occupational Sources of Stress: A Review of the Literature Relating to Coronary Heart Disease and Mental Ill Health, Journal of Occupational Psychology (1976) 49, pp. 11-28.

[22] Cooper, C. and Smith, M.J. (eds.), Job Stress in Blue Collar Work (John Wiley, London, England, 1985)

[23] Smith, M.J., Occupational Stress in: Salvendy, G. (ed.), Handbook of Ergonomics/Human Factors (John Wiley and Sons, New York, Projected publication in 1986) 70 pages.

[24] Caplan, R., Cobb, S., French, J.R.P., Harrison, R.V. and Pinneau, S.R., Job Demands and Worker Health (U.S. DHEW Publication No. (NIOSH) 75-160, Washington, D.C., 1976)

[25] Mayes, B.T., Sime, W.E. and Ganster, D.C., Convergent Validity of Type A Behavior Pattern Scales and their Ability to Predict Physiological Responsiveness in a Sample of Female Public Employees, Journal of Behavioral Medicine (1984) 7, 83-108.

[26] Chadwick, J.H., Chesney, M.A., Black, G.W., Rosenman, R.H. and Sevelins, G.G., Psychological Job Stress and Coronary Heart Disease, (National Institute for Occupational Safety and Health, Cincinnati, Ohio, 1979)

[27] Lazarus, R.S., Cognitive and Coping Processes in Emotion, in: Monat, A. and Lazarus, R. (eds.) Stress and Coping (Columbia University Press, New York, 1977) pp. 145-158.

[28] McGrath, J.E., Stress and Behavior in Organizations, in: Dunnette, M. (ed.), Handbook in Industrial and Organizational Psychology (Rand McNally, Chicago, IL, 1976) pp. 1353-1395.

[29] Levi, L., Stress and Distress in Response to Psychosocial Stimuli (Pergamon Press, Inc., New York, 1972)

[30] Hackman, J. and Oldham, G., Motivation through the Design of Work: Test of Theory, Organizational Behavior and Human Performance (1976) 16, pp. 250-279.

[31] Dunham, R.B., Smith, F. and Blackburn, R., Validation of the Index of Organizational Reactions with the Job Descriptive Index, the Minnesota Satisfaction Questionnaire and Face Scales, Academy of Management Journal (1977) 20, pp. 402-432.

[32] McNair, D., Lorr, M. and Droppleman, L., Profile of Mood States (Educational and Industrial Testing Service, San Diego, CA, 1971)

[33] Spielberger, C., Gorsuch, R. and Lushene, R., Manual for the State-Trait Inventory (Consulting Psychologist Press, Palo Alto, CA, 1970)

[34] Working Women 9 to 5, 9 to 5 studies trends in office employment, Automated Times (1985) 1(4), 1-6.

[35] AFL-CIO, The Future of Work (American Federation of Labor - Congress of Industrial Organizations, Washington, D.C., 1983)

[36] Karasek, R., Job demands, job decision latitude and mental strain: implications for job design, Administrative Science Quarterly (1979) 24, 285-308.

[37] Westin, A.F., Privacy Issues in the Monitoring of Employee Work on VDTs in the Office Environment: Practices, Interests and Policy Choices (Office of Technology Assessment, U.S. Congress, Washington, D.C., 1985)

[38] Selye, H. The Stress of Life. (McGraw-Hill, New York, 1956)

[39] Stammerjohn, L., Smith, M.J. and Cohen, B.G.F., Evaluation of work station design factors in VDT operations, Human Factors (1981) 23, pp. 401-412.

[40] I.U.D., Conference on Office Automation (Industrial Union Department, American Federation of Labor - Congress of Industrial Organizations, Washington, D.C., 1984)

[41] Kalimo, R. and Leppanen, A., Mental Strain in Computerized and Traditional Text Preparation, in: Salvendy, G. and Smith, M.J. (eds.), Machine Pacing and Occupational Stress (Taylor and Francis, Ltd., London, England, 1981)

[42] Johansson, G. and Aronsson, G., Stress Reactions in Computerized Administrative Work, Journal of Occupational Behavior (1984) 5, pp. 159-181.

[43] North Carolina CWA/NIOSH, Office Workers - Stress Survey Results (North Carolina Occupational Safety and Health Project, NC Communications Workers of America, North Carolina, 1985)

[44] NIOSH, Stress Study: AT&T, Southern Bell and United Telephone - North Carolina (National Institute for Occupational Safety and Health, HETA 85-452-1698, Cincinnati, Ohio, 1986)

[45] Smith, M.J., Cohen, B.G.F., Bierbaum, D.S. and Dainoff, M.J., A Case Study of Human Factors Aspects of Health Complaints and Job Satisfaction in Computer Programmers (National Institute for Occupational Safety and Health, Cincinnati, Ohio, 1982)

WORK WITH DISPLAY UNITS 86
B. Knave and P.-G. Wideback (eds.)

A MODEL FOR EVALUATING STRESS EFFECTS OF WORK WITH DISPLAY UNITS

P.A. HANCOCK and S.M. ROSENBERG

Department of Safety Science and Human Factors Department, Institute of Safety and Systems Management, University of Southern California, Los Angeles, CA 90089, U.S.A.*

With the introduction of new technologies comes stress. In the case of the display unit operator, the action of many of these stresses are at once both subtle and complex. Our impoverished theoretical understanding of stress effects serves to limit designers and managers in their attempts to provide safe, healthy, and productive work environments. The elaboration of a theoretical view of stressor interactions derived from the concepts of comfort and adaptability, as presented in this work, provides an initial direction toward the resolution of this important ergonomic problem.

1. INTRODUCTION

1.1 Preamble

In this paper we take the opportunity to elaborate upon a number of ideas presented in shorter form in our earlier work (Hancock & Rosenberg, 1986). Particularly, we focus upon the more complete descriptive development of an approach to stress and accentuate the application of this position to specific stressors intrinsic to the operation of display units. We present an avenue through which to reconcile the number of disparate stress sources that impact the display unit operator and from these observations derive recommendations for work scheduling, work content, and the constituency of the ambient surround. These suggestions are made as part of an effort to achieve the goals of optimal productivity, with maximal individual comfort and minimal risk to safe and healthy operator functioning. We view these latter aims as mutually inclusive.

1.2 Stress and Technological Innovation

As with the introduction of all new technologies, change in the occupational environment provides a variety of novel stressors that act upon the worker. These result not only from the innovations in task structure and workstation architecture, but also the interaction of these elements with pre-existing propensities toward stress. For the individual who operates a display unit, the environment is replete with potential sources of stress. These range in scale from the micro-level of physical perturbations to the macro-arena of social conflict. From a theoretical perspective how such multi-level and multi-dimensional stressors interact to impact safety, health, performance, and comfort is at present largely unknown.

---

* Address for Correspondence: P.A. Hancock, Department of Safety Science, Institute of Safety and Systems Management, University of Southern California, Los Angeles, CA 90089-0021, U.S.A. Completion of the Paper was made possible through Grant NCC 2-379 from NASA, Ames Research Center. Dr. Michael Vidulich was the Technical Monitor. The views expressed are those of the authors and do not necessarily represent those of the named agency.

1.3 Scope of the Paper

In the present communication, we consider an approach toward understanding the sometimes subtle and often complex interactional effects of discrete stress sources. We base our argument upon a theoretical perspective which has been generated recently (Hancock & Chignell, 1985). Together with the major influential views of stress, the central tenets of this position are elaborated below. We take from this model, information through which those concerned with the design and operation of contemporary workstations may ameliorate potentially harmful impacts of both endogenous and exogenous sources of stress. A single form of stress is considered as an example and potentials for interaction with other identified stressors are elaborated through a generic overview of human-machine cooperation. A brief summary section identifies recommendations and indicates avenues of continuing progress.

2. DEFINITIONS OF STRESS

2.1 Stress and Coping

There have been many attempts to produce a single, ubiquitous, and acceptable definition of the concept of stress. From a behavioral perspective, one of the most influential is the position of Lazarus (Lazarus, 1966). In one of their most recent expositions, Lazarus and Folkman (1984) discuss the historical antecedents of the stress concept. They elucidate the strengths and fallacies of a number of foundational positions. Lazarus and his many colleagues have chosen to emphasize the psychological aspect. Psychological stress is defined in their view as a particular relationship between the person and the environment that is appraised by the person as taxing or exceeding their resources and endangering their well-being.

Contingent upon this definition of stress, an understanding of coping follows as the process through which an individual manages the demands of the person-environment relationship that are appraised as stressful and the emotions they generate. These, almost verbatim, transcriptions of Lazarus's definitions allow some appreciation of the tenor of his work. However, full appreciation may only be had by careful study of original work (Lazarus, 1966; Lazarus & Folkman, 1984). Despite the idiographic perspective which results from the coping proposition, this construct retains considerable importance in the understanding of the influences of stress on those who operate display units.

Defining stress as a percept of the individual leaves open to equivocation what exactly it is in the environment which initiates such response. As such coping as an explanation is difficult to reconcile with system design and operation. Lawful properties and populational standards are at best difficult and at worst impossible to extract from the variety of appraisals that may be made of a common environmental condition. Despite these reservations, coping strategies and procedures are manifest in the activity of display unit operator, and the information available from an assessment of such behavior should not be neglected. Compared with coping, a more traditional approach to the study of stress is derived from physiological considerations which have been most cogently expressed in the work of Selye (1956).

2.2 Non-Specific Response

Founded upon the fundamental regulational aspects of physiological control, Selye was among the first to give direct attention to the specific notion of stress. Based upon his early work and presented in his classic text, Selye (1956) described the unified physiological response to environmental demands (which he called stressors). His general Adaptation Syndrome indicates commonalities of the stress response to diverse and multivariate noxious stimulation. The problem of nomenclature (stress = stressor, strain = stress) has plagued research in this area since, largely because of the dominant role that Selye's work has assumed. Although Selye himself acknowledged this confusion was largely a result of unfamiliarity with English connotation of the terms (Selye, 1979).

It has been observed that stress for biological entities implies a dynamic response in which active measures are taken to counteract perturbing stimulation. This is in contrast to physicalistic representations of stress in which structures are relatively passive in their deformation and subsequent recovery. While this dichotomy is not as clear cut as it initially appears, it is the center of the notion of dynamic stability. Consequently we can follow a direct line from Bernard's (1865) foundational observations through Cannon's (1932) lucid formalization of homeostasis to Selye's outcome view of stress. In his formal definition Selye (1980), concerned primarily with physiological analysis, indicated stress to be the non-specific response of the body to any demand. The integration of this definition into a wider perspective is examined below in our triumverate approach to stress.

2.3 A Trinity of Stress

In our work have advocate a tripartite description as a basis from which to elaborate a theoretical view of stress (Hancock, 1986a; Hancock & Chignell, 1985). This is given in Figure 1.

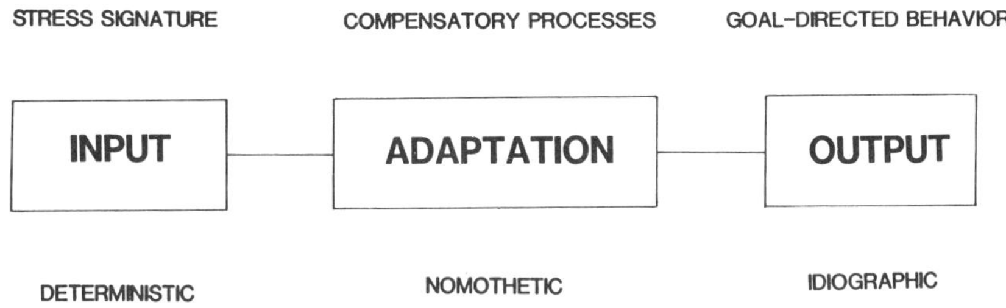

Figure 1. The trinity of stress. Stress is described through three functional loci. The first input locus is the deterministic physical assemblage or signature that composes the time-varying environmental display. The second adaptive locus represents compensatory actions initiated in response to perturbations intrinsic to the input. As strategic solutions to deterministic input are limited by the structural and functional constraints of human response systems, the content of this locus is described probabilistically. However, it presents sufficient consistencies, or nomothetic trends, to allow the specification of law-like properties. The final output locus is the current goal-directed behavior and, as these actions are directly contingent upon individual resolution of perceived current task demands, they are idiographic in nature. The inherent indeterminancy of the final locus sets considerable challenge to the derivation of prediction, which is a necessary condition for an operational model of stress effects.

Generically, stress may be recognized as residing in three descriptive locations. From the above illustration, stress may be recognized as an input, in which case it can be described deterministically as a particular assembly or signature of the physical parameters which compose an environmental display. It is the energy-bound information, which is open to the receptive perceiver, that defines the operational limit of this input with respect to human investigation. While this view can provide detailed information concerning a particular stressful condition, it cannot specify how any individual operator or group of workers might react to the input stress presented. Thus, *in vacuo*, it is a sterile representation and, being unameanable to immediate application has received little attention. However, it is in the more complete specification of the environmental surround that the greatest contemporary gains in stress research may be made.

The second of the three descriptive loci of stress is *adaptation*. This represents actions on behalf of an individual or group of individuals, specifically to counteract the perturbing effects of the input stress array presented. This adaptation may manifest itself through physical, physiological, behavioral (cognitive) or social channels, depending upon the content of the input and the level at which observation is focused. It is important to note that adaptation is the supraordinate set of which behavioral adaptation is paralleled by the coping process as elaborated by Lazarus and explored above.

The final locus is an *output* that represents a pattern of on-going behaviors directed toward the current "task" at hand. This is reminiscent of Selye's non-specific response, in that the aspecificity of physiological response is mirrored in supraordinate behavioral pattern. This locus may be distinguished from adaptation. However, when adaptation is the goal, these loci are coincident. For this reason, the current definition of stress is regarded as a descriptive framework, comprising three co-existing and non-exclusive loci (see also Hancock & Chignell, 1985). It is around this triumvirate framework that the subsequent view of stress and adaptability is erected.

3. STRESS, COMFORT, AND ADAPTABILITY

3.1 Components of the Base Information Axes

In our view of stress, comfort, and adaptability, the *input*, as previously identified, is given is the base axes as represented on Figure 2. They are composed of firstly information rate which is the temporal flow of the display presented. The second axis is information structure, where structure is a non-perjorative term connoting *meaning* as sought by the individual perceiver. As different individuals may seek different meaning amongst a common environmental display, information structure exerts greater control upon behavioral strategy. It should be recognized that the lesser impact of rate does not mean it is an immaleable component of the path selection process, although typically control of rate is dominated by input characteristics.

It is clear that the number of solution paths with respect to any "task", or assembly of "tasks", is constrained by the input presented. With increasing overload, along the two axes, solutions become more stereotypical, until at the highest tolerable levels of input stress, survival defines the single task solution. These base axes are not strictly orthogonal in that at extremes, underload and overload (hypostress and hyperstress) covary. Thus it is often (although not always) the case that low information rate provides intrinsically less meaning to the perceiver and vice versa. This results in a deformation of the base axes at the circumferential periphery of adaptability in Figure 2.

3.2 Composition of the Vertices

Through the vertical axes we have indicated that individuals *seek* to retain an optimum information flow via the available actions that can modify perceived rate and structure. This *seeking* strategy, which can be more readily accomplished through structure compared with the rate axis, can be seen in attentional narrowing to cues of perceived high salience under stressful conditions (Hancock & Dirkin, 1983; Hockey, 1970). It is also present in the load augmentation represented by stimulus hunger and magnification under conditions of sensory and perceptual deprivation where there is a drastic reduction of absolute level and patterning of environmental stimuli, respectively (Zubek, 1964).

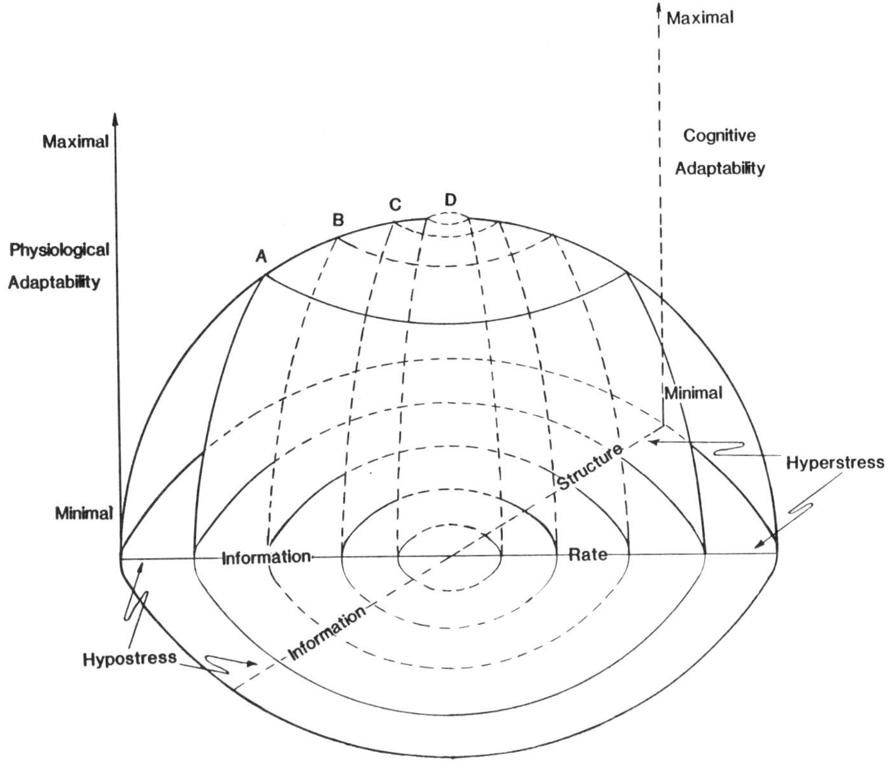

Figure 2. Physiological and cognitive adaptability as functions of hypostress and hyperstress expressed upon axes of Information Rate and Information Structure . Note that in dynamically stable conditions at the topological apices of the four concentric cylinders of the manifold, negative feedback prevails. This is surplanted by positive feedback in regions of dynamic instability, as described by the sides of each of the cylindrical elements. An inverted-U function is preserved, as is expressed uni-dimensionally by the transition points A, B, C, and D which refer to state changes across Physiological, Behavioral (Cognitive), Comfort, and Normative zones respectively. Multiple stressors are represented as summated vectors plotted upon the two-dimensional base. Adaptive reactions, realized through the movement of the overall manifold upon a base plane are initiated to combat perturbing input. This picture preserves the overall inverted-U but in a manner contradictive of the arousal foundation for whose support it has typically been invoked.

3.3 A Topological Representation of Stress and Adaptive Response

Upon the two base axes we have superimposed a topological manifold that expands on our previous formulations (see Hancock & Chignell, 1985). The center of the four sections represents a normative zone. This is a location which implies no necessary adaptive action to remediate input stress. As stress is an almost ubiquitous property of work conditions, residence in this zone is transient and inherently unstable as task and environmental demands rapidly induce transgression of the threshold established. This is surrounded by a comfort zone. The concept of comfort has been variously defined. However, in this work we take the point of comfort violation to represent the cognitive recognition of the failure of the current action of the dynamic adaptive process to counteract the impinging, multivariate input stress matrix. This matrix, for the present purpose, is represented as a summated single vector whose origin is the current location of the individual on the base axes. Vector direction represents the nature of overall stress action, and vector length represents the combined intensity of the input stress experienced. It is upon this vector representation, which is expressed in terms of energy-bound information available to the perceiver, that the action of a number of input stress sources with common paths of physiological mediation, may be combined.

The individual has some degree of freedom with respect to changing the overall location of the manifold on the base. This freedom can be used in adapting to the input stress. However, with progressive increase in the collective severity of the input stress, as measured by the length of the summated vector, the individual sequentially violates comfort, performance, and finally physiological tolerance limits. It is suggested that the dynamic stability as represented by the apex of each cylinder, may be recognized for a negative feedback form of control. Clearly, this form of control underlies successful action in each respective zone. Also the rapid failure as give by the side of each cylinder can be view as an expression of positive feedback. Thus while the transition from success to failure in each zone varies by the level of summated input stress, the strategic adaptive action is replicated at each stage. Also, we would claim that this strategy transcends level of measurement focus where action at differing levels can also be modeled by the manifold presented (see Hancock, 1986; Miller, 1978). In other work we have suggested (Hancock & Chignell, 1985), and continue to explore the application of catastrophe theory to this indicative state transition (see Zeeman, 1977).

At the psychological level we view this seeking strategy, related to attentional resource utilization, as an important behavioral trait in that we expect workers to attempt to optimize their information flow even in the face of considerable underload or overload of input. Initially, this load level is dictated by the information intrinsic to the presented task structure and the physical assemblage of the workstation and ambient environment. It is for this reason for example, that machine-pacing, which rarely approximates the dynamic change in individually freely chosen rate of work (or perceived optimal information flow rate), is of concern to investigators of display work in general (Salvendy, 1981; Salvendy & Smith, 1981).

3.4 Cross-Level Integration of Stress Sources

Although we have suggested that multi-dimensional input can be compacted into a single vector, this synthesis may be particularly difficult when considering different levels of input. We may distinguish physical input such as ionizing radiation, from more physiologically oriented problems such as those associated with muscle fatigue. Behavioral strategies concerned with rest-break and pacing manipulations can be considered qualitatively different form social issues such as multiple operator networking where one operator's actions are contingent upon the response of another. Although we have acknowledged that each level of input impacts the worker as a unified whole, a simple combination across levels cannot be easily accomplished. But whatever the "grain" of environmental information, i.e., whatever specific level it impacts most severely, there are repercussions throughout the other systemic levels of the body. Thus it is possible to assess behavioral stress effects through physiological monitoring and vice versa (Hancock, Meshkati, & Robertson, 1985). The further from the impacted level that a measurement is made, the fainter the echoes of the primary stress and hence the more difficult to record and assess. However it may be through the more precise measurement and assessment of these representations that cross-level integration can be achieved.

4. THE HUMAN-MACHINE INTERFACE AND ITS MILIEU

4.1 A Tabular Representation

Prior to examining the application of this model specifically to display unit operation, we have generated a tabular matrix of the goals, structure, function and adaptive action intrinsic to a generics of human-machine interaction. As given in Table 1 we have distinguish the three contributory elements in human and machine cooperation. Within each of these a supraordinate objective is identified which characterizes the goal of the element itself. Subsuming these objectives are the state constituents and their variation that compose the structures and dynamics of concern. These constituents are divided by their physical and cognitive representations. Derived from these observations are remediants that reduce the stress associated with unacceptable or unbalanced loading. The identification of these symptoms also suggest the expression of concrete solution paths which relate to the model of stress we have presented in the earlier section. Due to the heavy emphasis on interactions, many of the elements in Table 1 impinge directly upon display unit activity which acts as a focal nexus in human-machine action. A single example is drawn through the representation in Table 1, which illustrates stress action concerning display unit work.

4.2 Supra-Ordinate Objectives

It is important to establish the objectives of each component in human-machine interaction as it exists in a functional environment. The simplistic objective of the environment is to provide an envelope within which the human and the system can achieve desired optimal function. It is simplistic in that the boundaries of this envelope are partly contingent upon both the idiographic response of the operator and the subtleties involved in task designation and interface design. In this context the display unit provides not only a focal point of concern but a priori, establishes constraints upon surrounding environmental structure. As a general aim the operator seeks to increase their range of functional self-adaptability. This is achieved through the assimilation of skills and maintainence of systemic fitness represented in both bodily structure and cognitive action. The interface, as instantiated through the display, seeks to retain a functional synchrony between human action and system performance against the fluctuation in environmental and operational variants and in change in task demand. It is therefore the case that the unification of each objective is realized by the adaptive interface as represented in the physical workstation and display configuration.

4.3 Solutions To Stress Loading in Person, Interface, and Environmental Elements

As indicated in Table 1, there are a number of concrete actions that may be undertaken to combat the presence of unwanted input stress. A first line of defense considers control of the ambient surround as a physical strategy and the specification of achieveable task-goals in the cognitive realm. While these actions set the scene for sucessful performance they essentially provide only a frame, or work-envelope, within which more subtle and often complex demands require resolution. The interface with its physical structure and derived cognitive representation is the site of this action. In our work on intelligent interfaces and knowledge-based adaptive machines (Chignell &

TABLE 1. GENERIC OBJECTIVES IN HUMAN-MACHINE INTERACTION: STRUCTURAL AND FUNCTIONAL CONSTRAINTS AND REMEDIANT SOLUTIONS FOR STRESS LOADING.

PERSON

SUPRAORDINATE OBJECTIVE	INCREASE RANGE OF FUNCTIONAL ADAPTABILITY OF HUMAN	
	PHYSICAL	COGNITIVE
ENDOGENOUS STATE CONSTITUENTS	SEX, AGE, SOMATOTYPE	IQ, EDUCATION, TRAINING
ENDOGENOUS STATE VARIATION	PHYSICAL FATIGUE MUSCULOSKELETAL STRAIN	COGNITIVE FATIGUE MENTAL WORKLOAD
REMEDIANTS AND LOADING SOLUTIONS	CARDIOVASCULAR FITNESS NEUROMUSCULAR FITNESS	FITNESS OF CNS PROBLEM-SOLVING SKILLS
SOLUTIONAL EXPRESSION	PHYSICAL SKILLS/FITNESS	COGNITIVE SKILLS/FITNESS

INTERFACE

SUPRAORDINATE OBJECTIVE	FUNCTIONAL SYNCHRONIZATION OF HUMAN, MACHINE AND HUMAN-MACHINE ACTION IN ATTAINING OPTIMAL TASK-SOLUTION PATH	
	PHYSICAL	COGNITIVE
INTERFACE STATE CONSTITUENTS	DISPLAY CONTROL CONFIGURATION	DEMANDED CONCEPTUAL REPRESENTATION
INTERFACE STATE VARIATIONS	MALEABLE STRUCTURE INTERACTION OF CONTROL DISPLAYS	MEDIATED MENTAL MODEL OF TASK
REMEDIANTS AND LOADING SOLUTIONS	ADAPTIVE COGNITIVE TASK OFFLOAD/ONLOAD PHYSICAL ADAPTATION IN REAL TIME (FUNCTIONAL DYNAMIC ANTHROPOMETRY)	
SOLUTIONAL EXPRESSION	PHYSICALLY/COGNITIVELY ADAPTIVE INTERFACES	

ENVIRONMENT

SUPRAORDINATE OBJECTIVE	TO RETAIN AN ACCEPTABLE ENVELOPE WITHIN WHICH BOTH HUMAN AND INTERFACE CAN ACHIEVE DESIRED PHYSICAL/COGNITIVE FUNCTIONING

	PHYSICAL	COGNITIVE
EXOGENOUS STATE CONSTITUENTS	PHYSICAL TASK REQUIREMENT, IMMALEABLE ELEMENTS OF WORK STATION, ENVIROMENTAL STRESSORS	COGNITIVE TASK REQUIREMENTS, SPATIO-TEMPORAL TASK CONSTRAINTS
EXOGENOUS STATE VARIATIONS	DYNAMICS OF OVERALL TASK FLUCTUATION/INTERACTIONS PHYSICAL STRESSORS	DYNAMICS OF TASK CONSTRAINTS
REMEDIANTS AND LOADING SOLUTIONS	ENVIROMENTAL CONTROL E.G. AIR-CONDITIONING	IMPOSITION OF ACHIEVABLE SPATIO-TEMPORAL TASK BOUNDARIES
SOLUTIONAL EXPRESSION	FUNCTIONAL CONTROL OF INPUT STRESS CHARACTERISTICS	STRUCTURED AND OPERATOR COMPATIBLE TASK COMPOSITION

Hancock, 1985; Hancock & Chignell, 1986) we have emphasized the benefit of functionally adaptive interaction, where strategic off-loading and on-loading of the operator maintains an acceptable level of demand. Among others we have advocated the extension of this principal to adaptivity in the physical interface, where the work-station and display unit are dynamically responsive to the changing physical requirements of the operator (see Chignell & Hancock, 1986). While certain, relatively static, adaptations are available (e.g., menu-presentation contingent upon previous address frequency), we forsee a future for the display unit operator in which configuration of both the display and the controls is adaptively synchronized to changes in actual task demand. This principle may be extended into the physical components of the workstation itself.

A final consideration is the capability of the individual operator involved. Individually tolerable workload is contingent upon the functional range of self-adaptability as expressed through superior physical fitness and skill directed toward the task at hand. In many large machine systems, demand already exceeds the greatest range of human adaptive function. Thus augmented aid is not a desired, but a required component of system capability. In the section which follows, we consider the example of pacing as one of the common stressors associated with display unit work.

4.4 The Example of Pacing

There is insufficient space to elaborate upon each of the components expressed in Table 1. Rather, the single example of pacing is drawn through the structure to illustrate the complexity involved. Primarily pacing imposes an invariance in the temporal structure of the information which composes a task and constrains a response within a limited time horizon. There are several ways to interrelate these characteristics where typically operator response generates the cue for cyclical regeneration of demand, or there is recurrence of demand on a rhythmic basis. One common, and not unimportant covariant of paced work is the repetitive structural nature of the demand presented. Eventually, this leads to an appraisal of the task as boring and unmotivating.

As a characteristic of the task, pacing can be placed in the lower third of Table 1 where typically the spatio-temporal constraints and marginal cognitive requirements generate a content underload and response overload (This combination represents a classic configuration for replacement by automation). With the underload in cognitive content and overload on response repetition and presentation, pacing is particularly vulnerable to fatigue effects and generally leaves the individual susceptible to adverse actions which emanate from other forms of input stress. We may train for cognitive overload to provide superior skill and adaptability to this range of demand. Yet, we have perfected few mechanism through which to train for underload. Thus display configuration is of little assistance, although augmentation of cognitive demand e.g., problem-solving elements, and off-load of repetitive response demand can mitigate the stress of pacing. Primarily it is the location of temporal control of task structure beyond the individual and beyond the adaptive interface that reduces the local autonomy so necessary for stress compensation (Karasek, 1979). When fixed input constraints are imposed, they limit the number of task solution paths open to the seeking operator. In doing so, the constraints may also eliminate optimum task solutions paths. As a result of the wide range of human adaptability, adverse effects from these constraints may not become manifest for a considerable period. Yet even a low intensity perturbing input over a long time span can present unsupportable levels of stress.

5. APPLICATION TO THE DISPLAY UNIT OPERATOR

The above represents a brief elaboration of a structured model directed toward the understanding of the relationship of real-world stress conditions and how they impact the health, safety, comfort, and performance of the operator. There is a clear recognition of the variety and complexity of stressors that can impact those who use display units. (Czaja & Helander, 1986; Johanson, 1986). However, without both a descriptive and theoretic framework within which to place such useful information, unifying principles are left to languish and the capability for superior interface design is stifled.

It is possible to take measurements from an existing or proposed display unit workstation and it might be possible to specify _a priori_ what some potential global stress value might be. However, until the operator is exposed to the novel environment this global assessment is of little relative use. For example, some forms of stress are intrinsically antagonistic to other forms, as in the case of exercise opposing the untoward effects of postural cramp. The adaptive worker recognizes these antagonisms and uses such strategies to attempt to retain an optimal condition. The designer needs to facilitate use of these strategies through the physical assembly of the working environment. The manager also can enhance the adaptive capability of the worker by initiating greater control over task structure (Wright, 1986). At the present it is important to emphasize the subtlety, complexity, and numerosity of those input stressors facing individuals who work with display units. Greater use of comfort as a behavioral signal for remedial action can enhance contemporary design but we remain a considerable distance from a full understanding of these important issues, and the capacity for prediction in particular.

6. SUMMARY

The problems of stress facing operators of display units are not easily unraveled. Operators themselves are adaptive with respect to the management and mitigation of the complex and subtle input stresses presented. The violation of individual comfort is a behavioral signal indicative of the presence of a perceived problem. Unchecked, such a problem can supersede behavioral adaptability which is reflected in decreasing performance efficiency. Long-term violation will result in behavioral responses such as burn-out, absenteeism, or re-directed systemic damage manifested through illness. The present work provides a brief overview of a theoretical and descriptive structure through which to comprehend and combat these unwanted stress effects.

ACKNOWLEDGMENT

The authors wish to thank Dr. M.H. Chignell for comments on an earlier draft of the manuscript and Cuong Chu and Binh Trinh for their help in the production of this paper.

REFERENCES

Bernard, C. (1865) The cahier rouge. In: F. Grande and M.B. Visscher (Eds.). Claude Bernard and experimental medicine, Schenkman, Cambridge, MA.

Cannon, W.B. (1932) The wisdom of the body. New York: W.W. Norton.

Chignell, M.H. & Hancock, P.A. (1985) Knowledge-based load leveling and task allocation in human-machine systems. Proceedings of the Annual Conference on Manual Control, 21, 9.1-9.11.

Chignell, M.H. & Hancock, P.A. (1986) Integration of the cognitive and physical aspects of the human-machine interface. Proceedings of the Human Factors Society, Dayton, OH.

Czaja, S.J. & Helander, M.G. (1986) The impact of office automation on organizational structure and office tasks, In: Proceedings of Work with Display Units, 101-104.

Hancock, P.A. (1986) Stress and adaptability. In: G.R.J. Hockey, A.W.K. Gaillard, & M.G.H. Coles. (Eds.). Energetics and human information processing, Martin Nijhoff, Berlin (a).

Hancock, P.A. (1986) On the use of time: The irreplaceable resource. In: O. Brown, Jr, and H. Hendrick (Eds.). Human factors in organizational design and management II, North-Holland: Amsterdam (b).

Hancock, P.A. (1986) Stress, information flow, and adaptability in individuals and collective organizational systems. In: O. Brown, Jr, and H. Hendrick (Eds.). Human factors in organizational design and management II, North-Holland: Amsterdam (c).

Hancock, P.A. & Chignell, M.H. (1985) The principle of maximal adaptability in setting stress tolerance standards. In: R.E. Eberts and C.E. Eberts (Eds.). Trends in Ergonomics/Human Factors II, North-Holland, Amsterdam.

Hancock, P.A. & Chignell, M.H. (1986) Input information requirements for an adaptive human-machine system. Proceedings of the Conference on Psychology in the Department of Defense, 10, 493-498.

Hancock, P.A., & Dirkin, G.R. (1983) Stressor induced attentional narrowing: Implications for design and operation of person-machine systems. Conference Proceedings of the Human Factors Association of Canada, 16, 19-21.

Hancock, P.A., Meshkati, N., & Robertson, M.M. (1985) Physiological reflections of mental workload. Aviation, Space and Environmental Medicine, 56, 1110-1114.

Hancock, P.A. & Rosenberg, S.M. (1986) Application of the concepts of comfort and adaptability in assessing the stress effects of working with display units. In: Proceedings of the Conference on Work With Display Units, 196-200.

Hockey, G.R.J. (1970) Signal probability and spatial location as possible bases for increases selectivity in noise. Quarterly Journal of Experimental Psychology, 22, 37-42.

Johanson, G. (1986) Growth and challenge versus wear and tear of humans in computer mediated work. In: Proceedings of Work with Display Units, 249-251.

Karasek, R.A. (1979) Job demands, job decision latitude, and mental strain: Implications for job redesign. Administrative Science Quarterly, 24, 285-308.

Lazarus, R.S. (1966) Psychological stress and the coping process. New York: McGraw-Hill.

Lazarus, R.S. & Folkman, S. (1984) Stress, appraisal, and coping. New York: Springer.

Miller, J.G. (1978) Living systems. New York: McGraw-Hill.

Selye, H. (1956) The stress of life. New York: McGraw-Hill.

Selye, H. (1979) The stress of my life. New York: Van Nostrand Reinhold.

Selye, H. (1980) Selye's guide to stress research. New York: Van Nostrand Reinhold.

Salvendy, G. (1981) Classification and characteristics of paced work. In: G. Salvendy and M.J. Smith (Eds.). Machine pacing and occupational stress. London: Taylor and Francis.

Salvendy, G. & Smith, M.J. (Eds.) (1981) Machine pacing and occupational stress, London: Taylor and Francis.

Wright, I. (1986) Identification and prevention of work-related mental and psychosomatic disorders among two categories of VDU users Proceedings on Work With Display Units, 308-310.

Zeeman, E.C. (1977) Catastrophe Theory: Selected papers 1972-1977. Addison-Wesley, MA.

Zubek, J.P. (1964) Effects of prolonged sensory and perceptual deprivation. British Medical Bulletin, 20, 38-42.

WORK WITH DISPLAY UNITS 86
B. Knave and P.-G. Wideback (eds.)

GROWTH AND CHALLENGE VS WEAR AND TEAR OF HUMANS IN COMPUTER MEDIATED WORK

Gunn JOHANSSON

Department of Psychology, University of Stockholm,
S-106 91 Stockholm

As wishes, worries, and assuptions about human consequences of electronics in the work place are gradually replaced by empirical knowledge, it becomes possible to identify some of the sources of stress and to eliminate or modify unwanted consequences. A distinction between temporary problems and permanent ones will aid in designing adequate strategies for improvement. Criteria for evaluation of consequences, based on empirical research concerning job stress and health, are suggested. They include consideration of work load as well as autonomy and opportunities for social support.

1. INTRODUCTION

Psychological and social aspects of computer mediated work have been studied and analyzed for at least 10 to 15 years. During this initial phase of large-scale computerization, many of us have been dazzled by the shining novelty of the computer. With fear or hope or with a mixture of both, we have asked questions like "What new jobs will emerge?", "How will computers transform jobs?", "Will the quality of work increase or decrease?" (e.g., 1, 2). These rather vague and tentative questions were parallelled by more specific questions at a microlevel, requiring analyses at the cognitive, perceptual, hormonal, and neural levels (e.g., 3). Although all these perspectives have been necessary, it seems that the glare of the new technology has sometimes made us lose sight of important principles for the construction of good work conditions. As the glare fades, we should again catch sight of criteria for a good work environment and to use them as guidelines in evaluation of computer mediated work just as we use them for more traditional types of work.

Such guidelines can be formulated at varying levels of specificity. For the present purpose, I would like to use the following list which is based on a considerable body of empirical data, a list on which there is wide consensus, and which has formed a basis for recent Scandinavian work environmental legislation (4, 5). The principles state that in order to preserve and improve occupational health and wellbeing we must avoid

- quantitative work overload - too much work in too little time
- qualitative work underload - too simple and unqualified work;

we must also provide possibilities for

- personal control and autonomy
- social support
- professional and personal development

For the evaluation of various conditions in the electronic work place it is also useful to apply a time perspective. That is, we need not only to identify the beneficial and the harmful sides of the new technology, but also to distinguish characteristics and consequences which are likely to be permanent elements of computer mediated work from those which can be assumed to be of a more temporary nature.

Temporary phenomena are those which will disappear by them- selves as time passes, and those which can be altered through deliberate efforts at the technical and organizational levels. These temporary phenomena are likely to affect mainly the first generation of computer users. Beyond those conditions we will find others, which are specific for and characteristic of the new technology. They are the ones which are relatively independent of the process of change, and which can be expected to remain a permanent element in the use of computers.

The evaluation of human consequences of computerization in a time perspective can be structured according to the simplified scheme presented in Figure 1. The next few sections will present examples of positive and negative long-term and short-term consequences.

	POSITIVE CONDITIONS	NEGATIVE CONDITIONS
ASSUMEDLY PERMANENT	SPEED FLEXIBILITY	DEPENDENCE ON TECHNOLOGY "DE-SKILLING" HIGH DEMANDS FOR ATTENTIONS & CONCENTRATION
ASSUMEDLY TEMPORARY	LARGE-SCALE EDUCATION	UNSATISFACTORY DESIGN OF INTERFACE UNSATISFACTORY DESIGN OF SOFTWARE

FIGURE 1.
Evaluative classification of conditions creatd by the application of computer technology.

2. PERMANENT, POSITIVE CONSEQUENCES

The advantage of computer technology most often mentioned by its users is speed.

Table 1 presents ranking lists of major positive and negative consequences of computerized work routines, as experienced by office workers (6). On the average, these workers had used visual display units (VDU) for four years. The emphasis on speed as an advantage and technical disturbances as an important disadvantage is in agreement with data from other investigations.

Table 1. Major advantages and disadvantages of office automation as reported by employees in an insurance company.

Advantages	No. of times mentioned	Disadvantages	No. of times mentioned
Speed	54	Break-downs	26
Eliminates dull work	13	Creates dull work	11
Easy access to information	10	Machine-controlled work pace	5
Makes work simpler	4	Somatic complaints	5
Various	16	Reduces verbal skills	4
		Eliminates interesting work	2
		Various	33

The incredible speed with which large amounts of information can be stored, processed, and retrieved makes it possible for computer systems to carry out routine work in almost no time, work which would otherwise take hours, days, or more. When this capacity is used to enlarge narrow and unqualified jobs, it will certanily reduce qualitative work underload. One of the most wide-spread computer applications, word-processing, is a good example.

Besides speed, the computerś flexibility is an important positive and permanent characteristic. For the well-educated and properly trained person, the personal computer is an extremely flexible and efficient tool. Here lies a great potential for challenge and mental growth. After proper training, the individual worker or groups of workers with or without collaboration with experts, can design and test entirely new procedures for tasks included in their job.

3. TEMPORARY, POSITIVE CONSEQUENCES

As a result of the present technological change, large groups of individuals receive training on the job which will make them better equipped to perform computer mediated work. For many groups this is the first time, or one of few times during their occupational life, that any formal training was invested in them. It will improve their self-image and certainly add to their professional and personal development. But there is a risk that, for some of them, this positive effect will be most noticable during an initial phase of computerization.

4. WHY FOCUS ON NEGATIVE OUTCOMES?

In research on behavioral aspects of the new technology we are sometimes critized for focussing on problems, rather than on improvements. The criticism is highly relevant and legitimate when the purpose is to evaluate consequences of computerization in society at large. However, our present purpose is an evaluation in terms of occupational health and wellbeing, and since the positive impacts do not present a threat, it is natural that they receive less attention. It is important, however, to identify factors which may have a negative impact and to find appropriate remedies. This is simply a matter of work reform strategy and does not exclude serious consideration of positive impacts - for instance their possible role as "buffers" against the unwanted consequences which we try to eliminate.

5. PERMANENT, NEGATIVE CONSEQUENCES

One of the most clear-cut consequences of extensive use of computers will be an increasing dependence on technical systems. This dependence was always a typical element in mechanized industries. It is now spreading to offices, department stores, hotels, and many other work environments. When computer systems are based on communication with one central processing unit, interruption of operation leaves large groups of individuals without a tool which is necessary for the proformance of their work. Telephones or traditional typewriters can be substituted for other ones which will do just as well, but computerized routines do not always have manual alternatives or efficient backup systems. In terms of our criteria for good work conditions this leaves us in a clearly unfavourable situation: individual control over work conditions drops drastically. During break-downs work is also likely to accumulate and result in unacceptable quantitative overload when the system goes up again.

In one of our studies (6) we obtained a clear illustration of the agony and stress experienced in such a situation. We were able to compare mood and stress reactions among data-entry clerks during regular work and during a computer break-down.

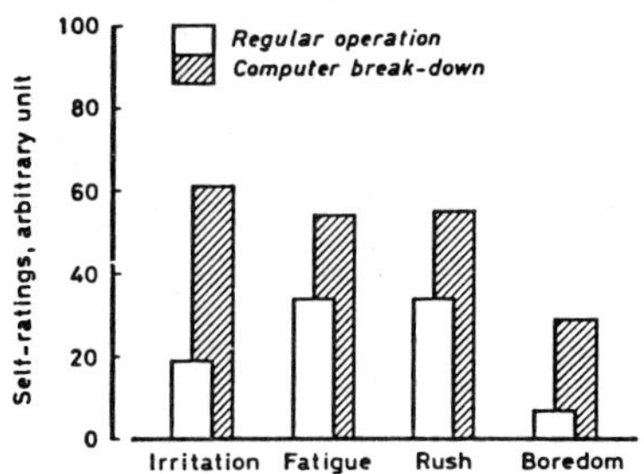

FIGURE 2
Mean self-ratings of mood during a 4-hr computer breakdown and during regular operations at the same time of day. Source: Johansson et al. (6).

Figure 2 shows that feelings of irritation and boredom were much more pronounced during the break-down than during regular operation. At the same time, the excretion of adrenaline, an indicator of the total load on the organism, as well as blood pressure and heart rate increased as compared to ordinary conditions (Figure 3).

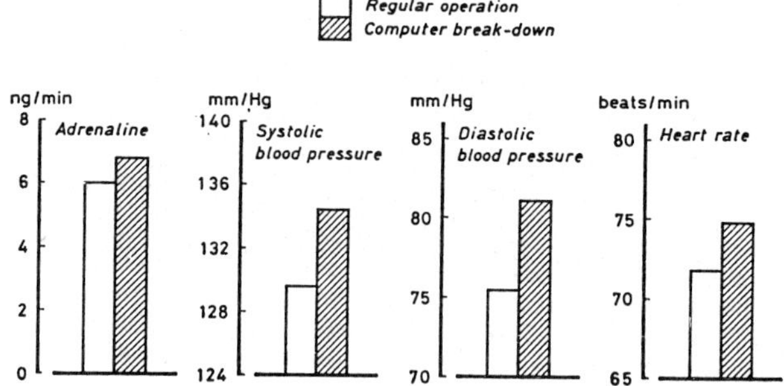

FIGURE 3
Mean urinary excretion of adrenaline, systolic and diastolic blood pressure, and heart rate during a 4-hr computer breakdown and during regular operations at the same time of day. Source: Johansson et al. (6).

Another consequence which seems to remain beyond the initial phase of computer mediated work is a trend towards increased demands for attention, concentration, and endurance (6, 7, 8). These demands have been labeled "intensity qualifications" as opposed to "production qualifications" which are directly associated with the contents of the job, e.g., knowledge of raw materials, product quality, type of goods or services which are produced, etc. This distinction was used by Aronsson (9) in a study of employees in a large electronics manufacturing firms. His results showed that an increase of demands for intensity qualifications was more pronounced for groups at lower levels of the organization than in qualified jobs. There was no corresponding increase in demands for production qualifications.

5.1. De-skilling

One of the items on our list of good work conditions was the provision of possibilities for personal development. This possibility may be directly threatened by the computerś capacity not only to process information but also to make decisions and choices on the basis of the analyses and, finally, initiate changes in a technical system, give instructions to people, etc. This capacity requires that the total responsibility for efficient operation of a man-machine system be divided between humans and machines. There are many examples of an uneven balance here: the responsibility laid down in the computer system often tends to expand at the expense of the human contribution. It seems that the fantastic capacity even of small computers creates a constant temptation among system designers to strive towards maximal automation rather than towards a level of automation which is optimal from a human standpoint.

In tasks such as human monitoring of complex industrial processes it is not unusual that automation result in up to 80% passive monitoring. As a result, qualified and highly trained personnel very seldom gets to use their competence and knowledge. At the same time, elementary psychology of learning tells us that skills and competence which are not used tend to fade away. Therefore, when computers take over decisions and analyses, there is a real risk for "de-skilling".

There are several other factors which may contribute to an impoverishment of qualifications. Let me just mention one: the very abstract nature of computer mediated work. Instead of handling objects, raw materials, goods, or at least paper files, much of the computer mediated work does not include any handling at all - except the handling of the key board.

FIGURE 4
Traditional work station.

Just as an example, compare the two pictures in Figs. 4 and 5, which were used in advertisments for a VDU manufacturer. Let us for the moment disregard that a tidy VDU work place is compared to a very untidy traditional office work place, and that the computer operator is not even considered to need a chair. The difference is still very obvious. In the traditional office, various types of information are associated with colors, with textual characteristics (you can touch paper files, etc.), with a spatial orientation in the room, and even with smells. The VDU work place stores much of this information electronically, odorless, touchless, colorless,and usually in one point in space.

So far, we know very little about the consequences of such "abstraction" for learning and maintenance of competence among adults, but ongoing research will tell us more. From studies of control room operators, we know that the reduc-

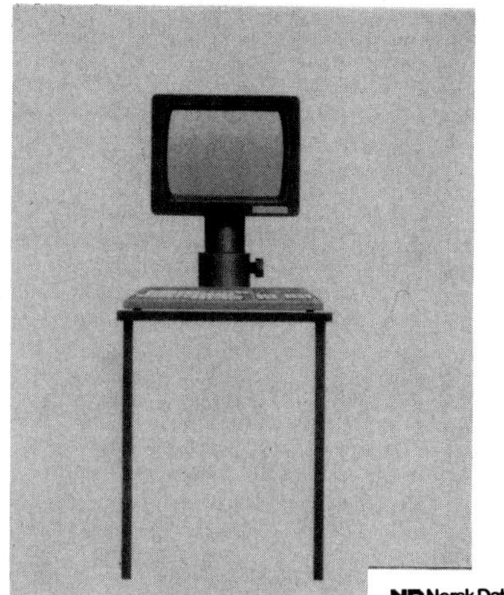

FIGURE 5
Electronic work station.

tion of sensual or sensory knowledge about production processes seems to have negatively affected what is called the process understanding. A likely consequence of a more abstract work situation will be increased feelings of uncertainty, and a subsequent decrease of perceived individual control over the work process. This will have to be compensated for through active involvement of the operator in the production process.

6. TEMPORARY, NEGATIVE CONSEQUENCES

The majority of papers in this session deal with problems which we will be able to influence. The causes of the problems, as we see them today, usually belong to three major areas:

(1) the design of the display unit which poorly matches our visual and locomotor systems,
(2) the design of the software which does not always match the human perceptual and cognitive systems, and
(3) various kinds of work organization which do not match our basic need for variation and task involvement, and which tend to accentuate and concentrate interface and software problems to certain groups of employees.

But in all these areas there should be good possibilities for change towards the guidelines for healthy psychosocial work conditions.

7. CONCLUSIONS

This sketchy overview does not claim to be complete. Its main purpose has been to clarify that among problems caused by the new technology, there are some which should only be tolerated during a period of transition. The widespread eye strain and muscular tension, associated for instance with data entry work, must be eliminated through the development of alternative displays. Frustration over and mental load caused by awkward modes of interaction with the computer must be eliminated through better software design. And monotony, fatigue, and various psychosomatic complaints must be counteracted through job redesign.

But the overview also attempted to clarify that computer technology has other characteristics, such as those resulting in de-skilling, which we will not able to alter. Here we need to develop compensatory strategies. Some of the problems can probably be compensated for through the way in which activities are organized. Continuing education and training - on the job and in the school system - will also play an important role in the compensatory strategies. And - finally - in certain areas, and for certan groups, where compensatory efforts are not sufficient to let growth and challenge outgrow the wear and tear of humans, we also need the sense and courage to choose alternatives to computerized procedures.

ACKNOWLEDGEMENTS

The research reported was supported by the Swedish Work Environment Fund and the National Swedish Board for Technical Development. The preparation of the paper was facilitated by support from the Swedish Concil for Research in the Humanities and Social Sciences.

REFERENCES

(1) Sandberg, Å., (ed.), Computers Dividing Man and Work (Swedish Center for Working Life, Stockholm, 1979).
(2) Kasschau, R.A., Lachman, R. and Laughery, K.R., Information Technology and Psychology. Prospects for the Future (Praeger, New York, 1982)
(3) Salvendy, G., (ed.), Human-Computer Interaction (Elsevier, Amsterdam, 1984)
(4) Gardell, B., International Journal of Health Services 12 (1982) 31.
(5) Levi, L., Frankenhaeuser, M. and Gardell, B., The Characteristics of the work Place and the Nature of its Social Demands, In: Elliott, G.R. and Eisdorfer, C. (eds.), Stress and Human Health (Springer, New York, 1982)
(6) Johansson, G. and Aronsson, G., Journal of Occupational Behaviour 5 (1984) 159
(7) Floru, R., Cail, F. and Elias, R., Ergonomics, 28, 1985, 1455.
(8) U.S. Congress, Office of Technology Assessment. Automation of Americaś Offices, OTA-CIT-287 (U.S. Government Printing Office, Washington, D.C., 1985)
(9) Aronsson, G., Changed Work Qualification Structure in Computer-Mediated Work, National Board of Occupational Safety and Health, 1985:38

WORK WITH DISPLAY UNITS 86
B. Knave and P.-G. Widebäck (eds.)

WORK CONTENT, STRESS AND HEALTH IN COMPUTER-MEDIATED WORK

A seven year follow-up study *

Gunnar ARONSSON

National Board of Occupational Safety and Health, S-171 84 Solna, Sweden

Gunn JOHANSSON

Department of Psychology, University of Stockholm, S-106 91 Stockholm, Sweden

1. INTRODUCTION

1. This study forms part of a long-term program concerning work, stress, and health, which has been carried out in the psychology departments of the University of Stockholm and the Karolinska Institute (for reviews, see e.g., Aronsson, [1], Gardell, [5].

The program, which has gone through various phases with more or less cooperation between the departments, has a multidisciplinary character. Interview and questionnaire data have been combined with measurements of physiological and psychoneurohormonal parameters, with self-ratings of mood and alertness obtained on the job, and with results of clinical health investigations. Single studies have often taken the form of a four-step enterprise. In the initial phase, the researchers interview key persons in the work place(s) concerned: representatives for management, the personnel department, production units, the health care unit, and worker protection committees. A few persons representing prospective participants in the study are also interviewed.

The next step usually is a questionnaire survey directed to a fairly large group and a psychophysiological substudy of a smaller group within the larger sample. Finally, data on health status is obtained through a medical check-up, usually only for the psychophysiological subsample. This general procedure was followed for the studies which are reported on here. The method has been applied in studies of widely varying occupations, such as insurance clerks, bus drivers, sawmill workers, and control room operators.

For the assessment of the individual's reaction to the environment, physiological functions during work are monitored. One of the notions underlying the use of physiological and biochemical techniques in human stress and coping research is that the load which a particular environment places on a person can be determined by measuring the activity of the body's organ systems, which are controlled by the brain and reflect the level of arousal. In our case, the physiological functions include blood pressure and heart rate in addition to the urinary excretion of adrenaline, noradrenaline and cortisol. These hormones can be reliably assessed in urine samples which can be obtained in field settings without interference with the daily routines of the individual. For the interpretation of these physiological parameters it is also necessary to get indications of the individual's experience of the situation. For this purpose the participants give quantitative self-ratings of mood and arousal.

Adrenaline and noradrenaline usually facilitate both mental and physical adjustment to acute environmental demands. However, a growing body of research findings (e.g., Elliott & Eisdorfer, [2]) indicate that frequent or longlasting mobilization of such adaptive reactions may contribute to

* The research reported in this article has been supported by the Swedish Work Environment Fund.

the development of psychosomatic disturbances, among them cardiovascular disease. Recent stress research in the laboratory and in the field has drawn attention to two types of psychosocial conditions at work which tend to be of particular importance for the generation and modulation of stress reactions. Conditions characterized by stimulus overload and underload are both stressful in the sense that they put high demands of the organism's capacity to adapt to environmental conditions. Empirical evidence shows that well-being and performance reach a maximum when the environment offers a moderately intense and moderately varied inflow of stimulation (Frankenhaeuser & Johansson, [4]). Another important aspect of stressful conditions concerns the individual's possibility to exert control over the situation. A lack of control is almost invariably associated with feelings of distress, whereas being in control may prevent a person from experiencing distress. Thus, personal control may act as a buffer which serves to modulate the intensity of the stress reaction and may also decrease the risk of individuals developing disease (e.g., Frankenhaeuser, [3]).

1.1. Studies of computerized administrative work

The data to be reported here were collected in a study of insurance employees in 1977 (Johansson & Aronsson, [6]), and in a follow-up study of the same group seven years later. The study was undertaken in the largest insurance group in the Nordic area, Skandia, a company in which computers were introduced on a large scale and at an early stage in order to rationalize administrative routines and improve client services. In the 1977 study, one of the Group's large officies, where several groups use the computer system, was chosen. Disturbances in computer systems have a bearing on stress, and the risk of disturbances is augmented when VDUs are linked to a central computer by telecommunications. For this reason, a regional office was chosen as the object of the study (and not the head office, where the link to the computer is direct). The office has about 500 employees, and in 1977 there were just over 100 VDUs. In 1984, the number of VDUs had increased to about 180.

The 1977 study was a combination of a psychophysiological substudy for a small group (n = 21) and a questionnaire study for 95 employees. Two subgroups were selected on the basis of the questionnaire data for the second part of the study. One group, a data-entry unit, spent more than 50% (in some cases as much as 90%) of their working hours at the computer terminal; their work was of a routine kind, intellectually undemanding and it was performed at high speed. The control group used the computer no more than 10% of their time. It consisted mainly of typists and secretaries with fairly flexible and variable tasks including social interaction.

The 1977 study reported the following major findings

- During ordinary working conditions with the computer system functioning, the VDU operators, who spent more than 50 percent of their time at VDUs, excreted significantly more adrenaline than the control group.

- The difference in physiological and mental stress between the groups during working hours persisted and increased somewhat after work. This was in line with the fact that the VDU group reported more fatigue after work than the control group (Fig. 1 and 2).

- A temporary breakdown in the computer system elicited significantly elevated blood pressure and adrenaline excretion as well as increased irritation and tension.

- Results of the questionnaire and health examination did not reveal any statistically significant differences between the groups with respect to health status.

- Resting blood pressure levels were higher in the VDU-group than in the control group according to the health examination.

- Triglyceride content in blood, which is assumed to be associated with the development of cardiovascular disorders, was significantly higer in the VDT group.

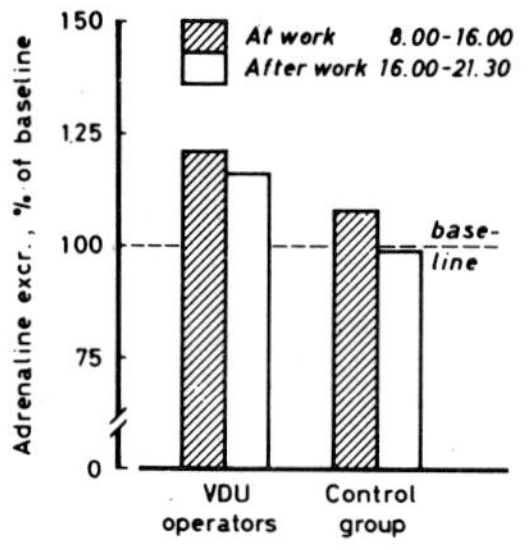

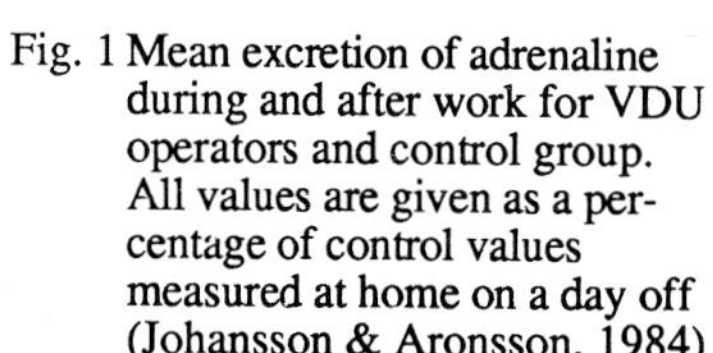
Fig. 1 Mean excretion of adrenaline during and after work for VDU operators and control group. All values are given as a percentage of control values measured at home on a day off (Johansson & Aronsson, 1984)

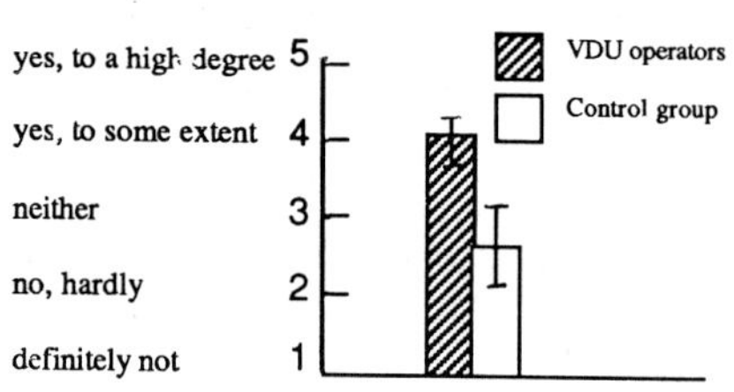

Fig. 2 Mental fatigue after the end of work for a VDU group and a control group (Johansson & Aronsson, 1984

Our recommendations in general and to the company were that stress and strain should be counteracted on the ***technical level***

- by reducing the frequency and duration of breakdowns and
- by reducing response times in the computer system

and on the ***organizational level***

- by redistributing unavoidable and monotonous coding work so that pure data entry work is eliminated
- by organizing work so that the employees are less dependent of the computer system.

The indications of increased acute stress reactions and other problems associated with VDU-work in our 1977 study and the public debate in Sweden about health risks in VDU-work were the main reasons for the 1984 follow up study. An important aim was to trace possible health consequences of long-term exposure to VDT-work.

2. THE FOLLOW-UP QUESTIONNAIRE STUDY

2.1. Subjects and procedure. Dropouts.

The 1984 questionnaire covered background information on age, education etc., questions concerning the content of different jobs, questions about perceived mental strain and well-being and questions covering the person's health status in the past year. Most of the items were copied from the 1977 study but some new questions were formulated concerning VDU-exposure, work content and social contacts.The questions were of the fixed choice type with four or five response alternatives, as a rule.

In the 1977 study, 95 office workers were investigated. In 1984, 71 of them participated again. Among 24 dropouts, 12 had retired with pension (including two with early pension), five had left the company, two were still working for the company but in other towns, one refused to take part, and four gave other reasons for not participating.

Table 1. The changes in amount of VDU-work from 1977 to 1984 among insurance clerks who participated at both studies (n = 71).

Directions of change	Number of operators
increase	23
decrease	25
no change	23
Total	71

2.3. Type and amount of VDU-work 1984

VDU-work was classified into three different categories: data-entry, interactive VDU-work, and word-processing. The operators were asked to estimate the amount of time that they spent performing each type of work. Out of 63 individuals using VDUs, no less than 53 used it for data-entry and 56 for interactive communication. Eleven persons used their terminal for word-processing. These results show that most operators do more than one type of VDU-work. It should be noted, that the majority of the operators doing mainly data-entry work spend less than 20 % of their total work hours at the terminal.

2.4. Changes related to reorganization

During 1982-83, the insurance company was reorganized into divisions. For the majority of the operators in our study this meant that they got a new superior and at least some new workmates. On the average, 35 % got new tasks, and 38 % rated their new tasks as more qualified. It is a complex task to separate the effects of a reorganization from those of a simultaneous computerization. As can be seen from our results so far, there are no systematic relations between the amount of VDU-work in 1984 and the amount of organizational change experienced a couple of years earlier.

2.5. Changes in job demands

The data allowed a direct comparison between 1977 and 1984 with regard to job dimensions. Table 2 presents ratings of job demands and job discretion.

The table demonstrates a significant improvement of possibilities to expand one's tasks with new elements. The operators also report that they better possibilities to alternate between parallel tasks. This is a highly positive finding, since many stress problems in the 1977 study, especially in situations of computer interruptions or breakdowns, were generated by a lack of alternative tasks.

On the social level, there has been an increase in joint problem-solving with colleagues.On the other hand, there is a marked and significant sharpening of perceived time pressure.

Table 2. Mean ratings of job content by workers who participated in the 1977 and the 1984 studies, Ratings were made on a five-point scale where 1 represents "no, never", 3 represents "sometimes" and 5 represents "most of the time". p-values refer to t-tests of differences between occasions.

Job characteristic	Ratings 1977	1984	p
Is your work such that you			
- plan and carry it out independently	4.4	4.4	n.s
- can take independent initiatives	4.1	4.3	n.s
- can discuss solutions to difficult tasks with others	3.5	3.7.	.05
- have a limited number of recurring typical tasks	3.6	3.3	n.s
- continually have to face new matters or learn new tasks	3.7	3.7	n.s
- can expand your tasks with new elements or new content	2.7	2.9	.05
- can alternate between many parallel tasks	3.4	3.7	.07
- have to concentrate and pay attention all day long	3.7	3.7	n.s
- can postpone a task to another day	3.1	3.0	n.s
- work under time pressure	3.4	3.7	.03

2.6. Somatic symptoms, mental fatigue and worry about health problems

On both occasions data were obtained about symptoms that may be associated with mental strain: headache, pain in the shoulder and arms, sour retching/stomach-ache, etc. For the group as a whole, one finds few differences. There is a significant increase in the worry about health hazards on the job and an increase in the use of analgetica. However, various kinds of symptoms and sick leave reamin the same.

3. THE PSYCHOPHYSIOLOGICAL STUDY

3.1. Description of the group. Dropouts.

In the 1977 study, 21 persons took part in the psychobiological sub-study. Six of them had retired during the seven years that had passed, but fourteen were still working in the company. Thirteen of them, agreed to participate in our study .

In 1977, this group consisted of two clearly different categories: VDU operators in data-entry work and secretaries and typists with little or no VDU work at all. In 1984, these groups were no longer distinguishable in the remaning group. Like the rest of the personnel, they had gone through a development in which those who used to have extensive VDU work now had less, and those who used to have no contact with computer systems now had some.

3.2. Results

Our first concern was the 1984 blood pressure levels of the 1977 VDU group. The result show that there are now no systematic differences between those who belonged to the VDT group in 1977 and the others. The previous difference in trigryceride levels between the groups had also vanished.

Since the group no longer represented two clearly different types of work, possible relations between stress hormone levels and "VDU work load" had to be examined in a new manner. For this purpose, the amount and the type of VDU work were combined into an index. The following criteria were rank orderered according to their contribution to VDU work load. Percentage of work hours spent at the terminal, amount of data-entry work, amount of word processing work, and amount of interactive VDU work. The thirteen participants in the substudy were then rank ordered semi-objectively in accordance with their combination of these aspects, and assigned scale numbers identical with their rank. Thus, the highest rank - 13 - was assigned to the person with the highest percentage of work hours at the terminal and with mainly data-entry work, etc.

This VDU work load index was then correlated, by means of rank correlation, with the output of catecholamines. Our preliminary analyses show that the load index is positively related to levels of adrenaline as well as noradrenaline, that the relationship is stronger on a work day than during a day off, and that it is stronger during day-time than during the evening after work.

4. SUMMARY AND CONCLUSIONS

This study concerns a work place that is heavily dependent on computers and VDU-work. The results do not indicate impaired health status for a group of office workers with long-term exposure to VDU-work. It should be emphasized, though, that the analyses are not complete yet. For instance, further analyses of subgroups, classified according to changes in amount and type of VDU-work, are needed.

It can be assumed that the main reason for the positive development with regard to health is to be found in improved work organization. There are two factors of great importance, both of which were emphasized by the results of the 1977 study: the amount of time spent in VDU work and the concentration of routine, monotonous VDU tasks to certain groups.

1) In the follow-up we expected the amount of VDU work to increase over the years, that is, we expected to find even larger groups spending more than half of their work hours in VDU work. In fact, fewer groups are now in that situation. For eight out of nine persons with more than 75 per cent VDU work in 1977, the number of VDU work hours has declined. At the same time, those with no or little VDU-work in 1977 now have more. The change in the amount of VDU work can be described as a movement towards the middle of the scale.

2) According to the 1977 study, the unpredictable breakdowns and disturbances in the computer system were a major problem. It was concluded that they could not be be dealt with by technical means only. Organizational modifications would also be necessary to increase the clerical workers' independence of the computer system. The work analyses of the 1984 study indicate improvements in that aspect. The office workers now report a significant increase in the possibilities of expanding their jobs with new tasks and they also report that they have better possibilities to alternate between parallel tasks. The assumption that computerization is associated with further and undesired work division, is not supported, as far as this work place is concerned. For the group as a whole, the tendency is rather the opposite. Further analyses will be focused on differences between subgroups.

5. REFERENCES

[1] Aronsson, G. Work Content - Autonomy - Stress Reactions. Theories and Field Studies. Doctoral Thesis. In Swedish. (Department of Psychology. University of Stockholm 1985.)

[2] Elliott, G.R. and Eisdorfer, C., Eds., Stress and Human Health. Analysis and Implications of Research. A Study by the Institute of Medicine/National Academy of Sciences.(Springer Publishing Company New York 1982)

[3] Frankenhaeuser, M. Psychoneuroendocrine Approaches to the Study of Emotion as Related to Stress and Coping. In Howe, H.E. and Dienstbier, R.A. (eds). Nebraska Symposium on Motivation, 1978. University of Nebraska press, (Lincoln, 1979) pp 123-161.

[4] Frankenhaeuser, M. and Johansson, G. On the Psychophysiological Consequences of Understimulation and Overstimulation. In L. Levi (Ed.), Society, Stress and Disease, Vol. IV: Working Life. (Oxford University Press, London 1981), pp. 82-89.

[5] Gardell, B. Scandinavian Research on Stress in Working Life. International Journal of Health Services, 12, (1982) pp 31-41.

[6] Johansson, G., Aronsson, G. Stress Reactions in Computerized Administrative Work. Journal of Occupational Behaviour, 5, (1984) pp.159-181.

WORK WITH DISPLAY UNITS 86
B. Knave and P.-G. Widebäck (eds.)

FOCUSING VARIABILITY DURING VISUAL WORK

Leif R. Hedman, Swedish Telecom. Adm., Research Section,
123 86 Farsta, Sweden and

Valdimar Briem, Department of Psychology, Lund University,
223 50 Lund, Sweden.

ABSTRACT

Visual accommodation fluctuates within a certain range for any observer during laser optometer measurements. This "focusing variability" occurs both for accommodation to a visible target and, to a greater extent, in the dark without such a target. In the present optometric study of VDU operators, the amount of focusing variability relative to a visual target was found to be related to a number of factors, but not particularly to work at a VDU. All the factors affecting the focusing variability could be considered as potential stressors for the observers. It is proposed that, given a well controlled, standardized procedure for measuring focusing variability, this measure may function as a useful index whereby sources of difficulty or strain in VDU work situations may be detected.

1. INTRODUCTION

Work with VDUs has in the past been associated with various complaints, some thought to be the result of physical and others of mental factors. Some of these factors are likely to produce decrement in the operators' performance. One of the complaints that have been studied in this context is the eyestrain sometimes reported by VDU operators, particularly changes in the observers' dark focus and the ability to focus on visual targets during or after work with VDUs.

Several investigators (e.g. Leibowitz & Hennessy, 1975; Östberg et al., 1980) have emphasized the advantage of using the laser optometer technique for measuring visual strain in connection with VDU work, as it gives an accurate measurement of accommodation and minimizes the interference with the performance of other tasks. However, there are problems associated with the laser optometer technology. Of these, the purely technical problems are fairly straight-forward, whereas errors introduced by inadequate measurement procedures may go undetected and so reduce the accuracy of the conclusions drawn from the studies.

In our study of VDU operators' visual strain (Hedman & Briem, 1984), we developed a standardized measurement procedure in order to control this source of potential error variance. The procedure is a variation on the "bracketing" technique used by previous laser optometrists, which in turn is a variation on the psychophysical "method of limits". Our procedure (cf. below) made it possible to determine with a greater degree of certainty the amount of variation associated with each of the measures of accommodation obtained. This "focusing variability" (FV) corresponds to the "interval of uncertainty" of classical psychophysics.

The following account gives the principal results obtained from the analyses of this dependent measure (FV) relative to such variables as age of the observer, task, test-session on the day of testing, distance of the visual targets, and presentation order of the targets within a test-session.

2. METHOD

The details of the physical environment of the study, the observers taking part, the procedure, apparatus, and other features of the method used to obtain the data have been presented in our previous report (Hedman & Briem, op. cit.). However, a short resumé of these features is presented here, together with a fuller description of those aspects of the method specifically related to the present dependent measure.

2.1 Observers

These were 29 operators at a telecom enquiry centre, 27 female and 2 male, aged 18 - 54 years. All had normal, corrected or uncorrected, vision.

2.2 Design

The study was done during a period of 6 months, and contained two phases. In the first, the job rotation phase, the operators worked at two information tasks during each work-day, one (VDU) involving the extensive use of VDUs, and another, comparable task (MAN) which did not; there were three two-hour work sessions within a day, each beginning the test-day equally often; accommodation was measured in the dark and in light relative to 4 visual targets at different observation distances before and after the first and after the third work sessions of the day. In phase 2, there were two three-hour sessions involving work at one or the other of the tasks described above, with visual focus tested before the first and after the second work sessions. All conditions were carefully counterbalanced and/or randomized. A third task (MOT), containing a different type of information work, not involving the use of VDUs but in other respects comparable to the other tasks, was included at the end of phase 2. In all, 48 estimates of variability in accommodating to visual targets and 12 related to dark focus were collected from each of the observers.

2.3 Apparatus

This consisted primarily of a Field Laser Optometer (cf. Östberg et al., op. cit.), as well as visual targets at 0.25, 0.5, 1.0 and 6.0 meters' (m) distance from the observer's eyes (corresponding to 4.0 2.0, 1.0, and 0.167 diopters (D)) and a specially programmed microcomputer (cf. below).

2.4 Procedure

The usual "bracketing" technique for measuring accommodation with a laser optometer consists essentially in obtaining the mean of two correct judgements of the apparent movement in the laser speckle pattern visible to the observer. This pattern is seen as superimposed on a visual target in light conditions but in isolation at an indeterminate distance in the dark. The first type of condition results in measures of focusing accuracy, and the second in measures of dark focus.

In order to obtain more accurate estimates of accommodation we developed a standardized bracketing procedure, where we made use of a computer program to calculate the next diopter value to be presented to the observer according to a flexible, predetermined (counterbalanced) schedule. The computer was also used to store the measurement data. Each measure of focusing accuracy or dark focus was derived from a standardized series of at least 8, and at the most

16, laser speckle presentations, and was determined with an accuracy of 0.13 D. A the same time we were able to calculate the FV associated with each accommodation value. This computerized procedure minimized the probability of errors which depend on the experimenter, such as expectations of outcome and failures of memory, as the order of targets and optometer settings for the laser pattern presentations, as well as the measures collected, are managed by the program. The procedure results in a) comparable series for different observers and experimenters, b) more accurate measurements (to the nearest 0.13 D), c) quicker determination of measurement values, and d) the possibility of a subsequent step-by-step analysis of the bracketing sequence for each observer.

3. RESULTS

The results regarding focusing accuracy and dark focus have been described previously (Hedman & Briem, op. cit.). These did not indicate that any visual strain might result specifically from work with VDUs. The analyses (ANOVAs) of the FV corroborate this, but they also reveal significant effects of several others of the independent variables used in the study.

The first variable to influence the FV was the distance of the target on which the observer focused. Thus, least variability was associated with the target at 1 m, but more with targets located nearer or furhter away. This was true for all the tasks in both phases of the study (Figure 1).

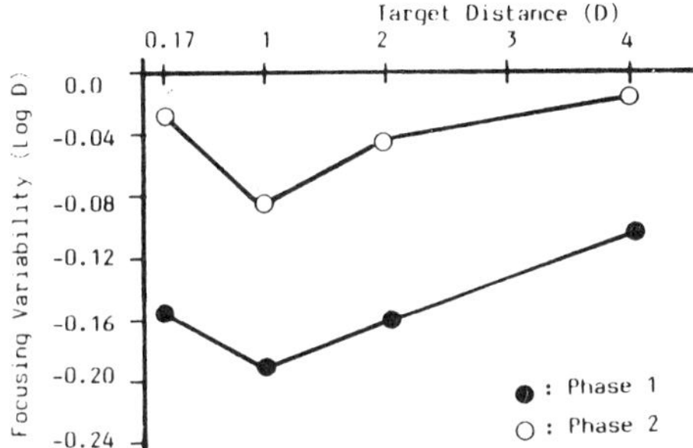

Figure 1. Difference in focusing variability in log diopters relative to the 4 visual targets in Phase 1 (2 tasks; $p < .0001$) and in Phase 2 (3 tasks; $p = .0212$), and between the 2 phases ($p < .0001$).

The second factor to affect the FV was the transition from job rotation to no rotation. This change resulted in a sizeable increase in the variability measured (Figures 1 and 2).

The third factor was the presentation order of the visual targets within a test session, and its effect was shown in an increase in FV throughout a session, but only consistently for the operators over 40 years (Figure 2).

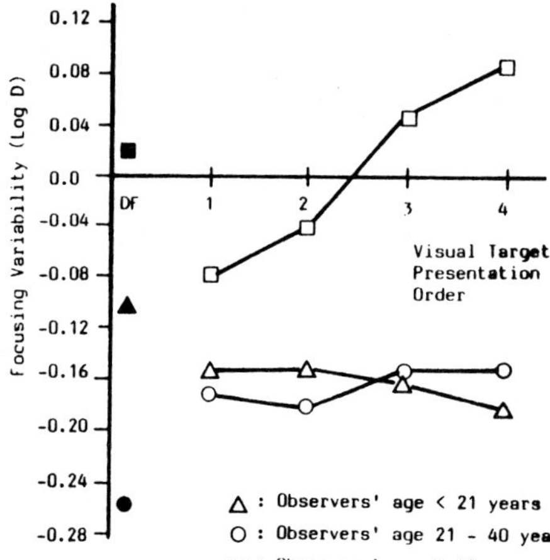

Figure 2. Difference in focusing variability in log diopters for the observers in 3 age groups, relative to the ordinal position of presentation of the targets within a test session (p = .0058 for the interaction).

A fourth effect was seen in the various test-sessions that the operators took part in on the same day. For the tasks VDU and MAN the effect in both phases of the study was a decrease in FV through the test-day, while for the last task in phase 2, MOT, an increase was shown from the morning to the evening test-session (Figure 3).

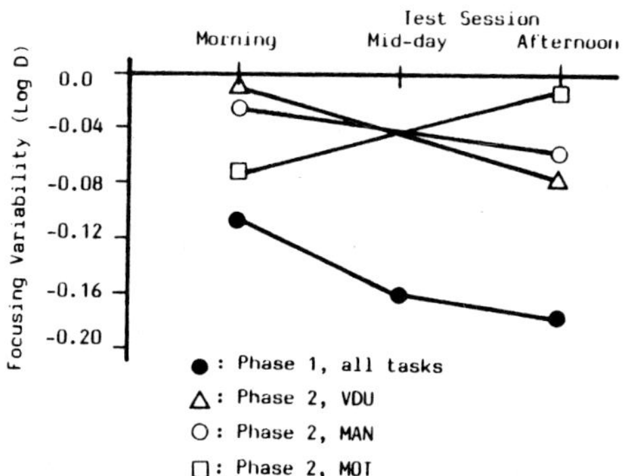

Figure 3. Focusing variability in log diopters measured in Phase 1 (2 tasks, 3 sessions; p = .0038) and in Phase 2 (3 tasks, 2 sessions; p = .0075 for the interaction).

All changes in FV were in connection with the measurement of focusing accuracy, and none were associated with dark focus.

4. DISCUSSION

It is important to note that the FV measured during accommodation to the visual targets was positively related both to variables within the optometric situation itself, viz. the focal distance and the presentation order of the targets, and to variables in the general work situation, viz. change from job rotation to no rotation and the type of task performed on the test-day. The factors are in themselves quite disparate, except in that they may be considered to constitute stressors for the operators, i.e. to increase the level of difficulty or strain present during the time that the tests were conducted. Thus, to begin with, accommodating to certain distances is definitely more difficult than accommodating to others. This was shown previously (Hedman & Briem, 1984) in the measures of focusing accuracy which were fairly accurate at a focal distance of 1 D, but diverged increasingly at greater and smaller distances. A similar, preferred, distance interval of 0.61-0.93 m, within which focusing was most effective, was also reported by Grandjean et.al. (1983). In the present analyses, the FV was smallest at 1 D and greater at other distances where a certain amount of strain associated with attempts at correct focusing may be assumed.

As regards presentation order, we can assume an increasing amount of strain to be associated with repeated visual focusing, particularly for the older observers of whom many would be suffering from some degree of presbyopia, and would, consequently be having some difficulty in accommodating.

Change from job rotation to no rotation is a fairly drastic change in the established work routine, and may have been experienced, by at least some of the observers, as upsetting.

Lastly, increase in FV through a test-day was shown only when the operators worked at the MOT task, a task which was normally not included in their work-day. Therefore, it required considerable readjustment for the operators on that particular day. It had been previously documented (Hedman & Briem, op.cit.) that the operators experienced the MOT task as both "interesting" and "difficult due to high work-load", although, actually, the work-load on these days was not much different from that on other work days. It would be reasonable to suppose that this led to an increase in the general strain level during that day. On the other hand, the FV decreased from morning to evening for the very same operators when they did their customary tasks, VDU and MAN, in phase 2, indicating to us the very opposite to strain on those work days.

While stressors could be detected in connection with accommodating to a visual target, no comparable effects could be detected in connection with the dark focus measurements. However, any such effects may have been obscured by the much greater, general variation associated with focusing in the dark. Simonelli (1979), using a laser optometer and the bracketing method, found that his dark focus measures where surrounded with a "neutral zone" of 0.39 D. This may be compared with the FV in relation to dark focus of 0.79 D which we obtained in the present study. Taylor and McVey (1984) also demonstrated considerable fluctuations in accommodation over time, especially in the absence of a visual target. They showed that the mean in accommodation to stability in the dark was between two and three times greater than that found with a visible target. Thus, both the present results and those of Taylor and McVey indicate that dark focus, due to its instability, has only a limited utility as an index of accommodative strain.

On the basis of the results that we have presented here, we feel justified in concluding that both focusing accuracy relative to visual targets and FV may function as indices of strain resulting from a variety of factors active both in the VDU work situation and the optometer test situation itself. The relation of the present findings to those of other investigators is, however, somewhat unclear at present due to the lack of accordance in the measurement procedures employed in optometric studies. We hope that our results suffice to show the value of using a standardized measurement procedure in studies of this kind.

5. REFERENCES

Grandjean, E., Hünting, W., & Piederman, M., 1983, VDT workstation design: Preferred settings and their effects. Human Factors, 25, 165-175.

Hedman, L.R. & Briem, V, 1984, Short-term changes in eyestrain of VDU users as a function of age. Human Factors, 26, 357-370.

Leibowitz, H.W. & Hennessy, R.T., 1975, The laser optometer and some implications for behavioural research. American Psychologist 30, 349-352.

Simonelli, N.M., 1979, The dark focus of visual accommodation: Its existence, its measurement, its effects. Technical Report, BEL-79-3/AFOSR-7, Behavioral Engineering Laboratory, Las Cruces, New Mexico: New Mexico State University.

Taylor, S.E. & McVey, B.W., 1984, The dynamics of dark focus and accommodation to dark and light character CRT displays. In E. Grandjean (Ed.) Ergonomics and Health in Modern Offices. pp. 248-253. London: Taylor & Francis.

Östberg, O., Powell J., & Blomkvist, A.-C., 1980, Laser optometry in assessment of visual fatigue. Technical report, No. 1 T: 1980, University of Luleå, Sweden.

WORK WITH DISPLAY UNITS 86
B. Knave and P.-G. Widebäck (eds.)

MENTAL FATIGUE OF VDU OPERATORS INDUCED BY MONOTONOUS AND VARIOUS TASKS

Tadeusz MAREK, Czeslaw NOWOROL

The Jagiellonian University
Institute of Psychology
31-007 Cracow, Poland

Mental fatigue is a highly important component of VDU operators work. In order to evaluate alternative solution in man-computer systems design, it is often necessary to measure not only system performance but also human fatigue. The aim of this study is to build models of VDU operators mental fatigue induced by various and monotonous tasks. Thirty five VDU operators were examined. Pupil diameter, CFF, defensive blinking reflex, searching stimulation movements, efficiency of work and self-rating of fatigue were used. Obtained results permited to build two different models of mental fatigue (for various and monotonous tasks). It has been stated that two different types of fatigue are connected with two different mechanisms.

1. PROBLEM

In man-computer interaction mental fatigue becomes an important component of VDU operators' job stress. Modern concepts of mental fatigue are based on the concept of stimulation load which is connected with Hebb's [3] and Leuba's [5] theories of optimal level of arousal. The changes in the level of arousal of VDU operators depend on the type of tasks. In our previous investigation [6,7] it has been stated that several hours of various, complicated tasks cause the increase of arousal level and then (when the task is prolonged) decrease occurs. The monotonous tasks initially cause the decrease of arousal level which then increases and finally decreases again.

Many authors point out that in cases of various and monotonous tasks there are different behaviours aimed to achievement and maintenance of optimal stimulation and cause the optimal level of arousal [2,9]. In the case of various tasks there are defensive behaviours resulting from an extensive arousal level, tending to lower an individual's activity thus primarily decreasing the inflow of stimulation to the system which results in a decrease in the level of arousal. In the case of monotonous tasks, when the level of arousal is low (due to low level of stimulation) there is a need for stimulation. This need for stimulation is connected with behaviours tending to raise the individual's activity (raise the level of stimulation) and, chiefly in this way to increase the arousal level.

This paper deals basically with the problems of bahaviours which determine the regulation of stimulation level and subsequently, the level of arousal of VDU operators who perform various and monotonous tasks. The aim of this study is to build a model of VDU operators mental fatigue induced by various tasks and a model of monotonous mental fatigue induced by monotonous tasks.

2. METHOD

2.1. Subjects

Thirty five operators of VDU were subjects in the study. The operators were 20 - 26 years old. They worked six 50 minute work sessions daily with 15 minute breaks in between. The breaks were investigative sessions. Two kinds of entry data tasks were carried out: 1) various task, which consists of computer program translation (sixteen operators) and 2) monotonous task, which consists of alpha-numeric entry data (nineteen operators). Operators were tested on the morning shift before work and after every fifty minutes (seven investigative sessions).

2.2. Procedure and techniques

Two groups of indicators and indexes were applied. The first group contained three indicators connected with the level of arousal and the mechanisms of regulating the level of stimulation. The second group contained two indexes of the level of performance and the index of self-feeling.

In each investigative session the diameter of the pupil was registered as an indicator of arousal level [1, 4]. As an indicator of defensive behaviours (tending to decrease the stimulation level), the defensive conditioned blinking reflex was measured [8]. As an unconditioned stimulus a strong light flash was applied. The reflex to this was established to a musical tone of middle strength before each operator becam working. The well-established defensive conditioned blinking reflex was tested ten times in every investigative session. The number of conditioned responses per ten times (odds ratio of the blinking reflex) was the indicator. As an indicator of behaviours tending to raise the level of stimulation searching stimulation movements were taken into account [10]. There were movements which were not connected with work. The movements were registered seven times for five minutes: at the beginning of work, and at the end of each 50 minute work session.

As to the second group, the C-ratio (the performance index connected with work) was applied to measure the operators' capacity.

$$C = \frac{\text{number of alpha numeric characters typed per minute}}{\text{number of errors}} \quad \text{or}$$

C = number of alpha numeric characters typed per minute (when number of errors equals zero or one)

The coefficient C was counted for five minutes at the beginning of work, and at the end of each 50 minute work session. As an index of the operators' performance unconnected with work the critical flicker frequency (CFF) was applied. Additionally, in each investigative session was applied self-rating of fatigue, based on the ten centimeters scale streached between two opposite feelings: rested - extremaly tired (subjective index of self-feeling).

3. RESULTS

Obtained data from each investigative session for both groups of indicators and indexes are presented in tables 1, 2, 3 and 4. Tables 1 and 2 present data obtained for: pupil diameter (indicator of the level of arousal), odds ratio of blinking reflex (indicator of defensive behaviours tending to reduce the level of stimulation) and searching stimulation movements (indicator of behaviours tending to raise the level of stimulation) - for various and monotonous tasks respectively.

TABLE 1

The values for the indicators of the arousal level and the two mechanisms of regulating the level of stimulation, for various task (n = 16).

Time of work (min)	Pupil diameter (mm)		Odds ratio of blinking reflex		Searching stimulation movements (per min)	
	Mean	SD	Mean	SD	Mean	SD
0	5.61	0.72	0.22	0.05	1.4	0.05
50	5.76	0.64	0.28	0.07	1.0	0.07
100	6.10	0.91	0.46	0.09	0.6	0.03
150	6.47	0.80	0.70	0.14	0.0	0.00
200	5.63	0.77	0.29	0.09	0.4	0.04
250	5.57	0.94	0.15	0.05	0.0	0.00
300	5.46	0.70	0.11	0.04	0.2	0.06

TABLE 2

The values for the indicators of the arousal level and the two mechanisms of regulating the level of stimulation, for monotonous task (n = 19).

Time of work (min)	Pupil diameter (mm)		Odds ratio of blinking reflex		Searching stimulation movements (per min)	
	Mean	SD	Mean	SD	Mean	SD
0	5.85	0.70	0.20	0.06	2.0	0.07
50	5.79	0.78	0.12	0.07	6.5	0.06
100	5.51	0.90	0.11	0.05	8.6	0.14
150	5.80	0.87	0.07	0.03	12.8	0.22
200	5.75	0.78	0.08	0.04	6.2	0.18
250	5.50	0.96	0.09	0.02	2.8	0.08
300	5.45	0.81	0.07	0.03	0.2	0.01

Tables 3 and 4 show data obtained for: ratio C (the index of performance connected with work), critical flicker frequency (the index of performance unconnected with work) and self-rating of fatigue - for various and monotonous tasks respectively.

TABLE 3

The values for the indexes of the level for two kinds of performances and self-rating of fatigue, for various task (n = 16).

Time of work (min)	Ratio C		CFF (Hz)		Self-rating of fatigue (cm)	
	Mean	SD	Mean	SD	Mean	SD
0	81.2	11.47	40.2	0.96	2.7	0.32
50	92.1	9.20	41.5	1.24	1.2	0.40
100	86.0	6.18	40.0	0.89	2.3	0.36
150	79.3	7.12	39.2	1.04	4.1	0.71
200	70.1	10.14	40.1	0.98	3.5	0.52
250	61.8	8.07	38.5	0.66	6.7	1.96
300	53.5	5.26	38.0	0.73	7.9	1.04

TABLE 4
The values for the indexes of the level for two kinds of performances and self-rating of fatigue, for monotonous task (n = 19).

Time of work (min)	Ratio C		CFF (Hz)		Self-rating of fatigue (cm)	
	Mean	SD	Mean	SD	Mean	SD
0	187.8	12.43	40.5	1.07	2.2	0.37
50	150.9	10.24	39.6	1.30	4.3	0.41
100	133.8	9.32	38.0	0.92	5.6	0.52
150	124.8	10.96	39.8	1.33	3.6	0.48
200	118.5	11.12	38.2	1.12	6.1	0.92
250	112.9	14.06	37.8	0.98	7.1	1.41
300	109.9	9.12	37.8	0.90	7.3	1.23

Two problems arise from our study. The first is: how to change the values of the applied indicators and indexes under various and monotonous tasks due to time. The second is to find out how the level of performance, connected and unconnected with work, and self-feeling depend on the level of arousal and on the two mechanisms of legulation of stimulation level due time various and monotonous tasks.

As to the first problem it was necessary to build mathematical models for changes of each indicators and indexes. Row data (for which the mean values and standard deviations are presented in tables 1, 2, 3 and 4) were the bases for the models building, Regression analysis for repeated measures was applied.

Goodness of fits are statisticly significant ($p \leqslant .05$). Figure 1 presents obtained regression curves for changes in the arousal level which are measured by changes in pupil diameter. The next two figures 2 and 3 show obtained dependencies for two mechanisms regulating the level of stimulation.

As it can be seen in figures 1, 2 and 3 the changes of the three applied basic indicators are quite different under both types of tasks. As pointed out in the first section the level of arousal changes indicated by pupil diameter (figure 1) for various task first increases (increase in pupil diameter = increase of arousal level and vice versa). On the other hand, under monotonous task, the level of arousal first decreases (for about 100 min of work) and then increases (100 - 150 min of work) and finally decreases again. The intensivity of defensive behaviours under various task, increases accordingly to increase of arousal level while, under monotonous task, this intensivity decreases because of the general low level of arousal (see figures 2 and 1). However the number of searching stimulation movements, under various task, decreases all time (because of high level of arousal) and under monotonous task increases in the first 150 minutes of work which is connected with decrease of arousal level (see figures 3 and 1).

Generally for various task the changes in the level of arousal (changes in pupil diameter) are highly correlated with the changes in the odds ratio of blinking reflex which are connected with the behaviours tending to decrease the level of stimulation ($r = .98$, $p \leqslant .05$). In the case of the monotonous task the high curvelinear correlation between the level of arousal (changes in pupil diameter) and the behaviours tending to raise the stimulation level (searching stimulation movements) was found ($r = .81$, $p \leqslant .05$).

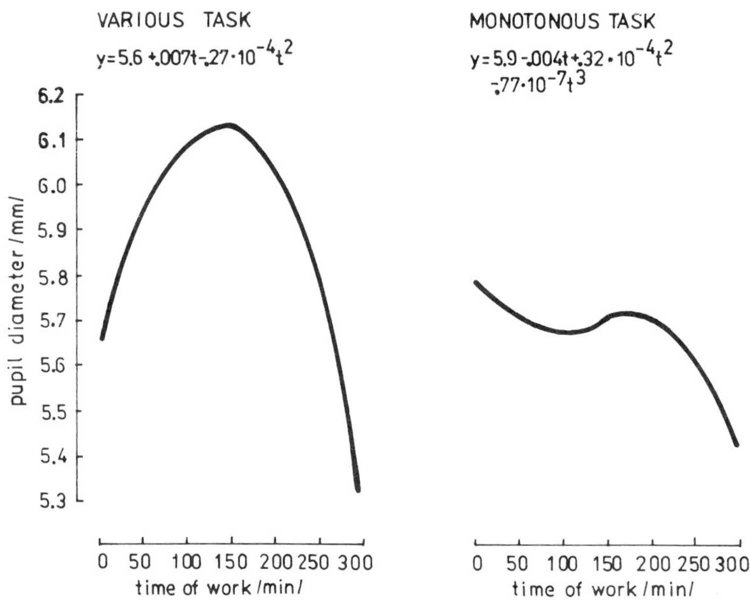

FIGURE 1
The models for the arousal indicator changes: the pupil diameter - y, the work time - t .

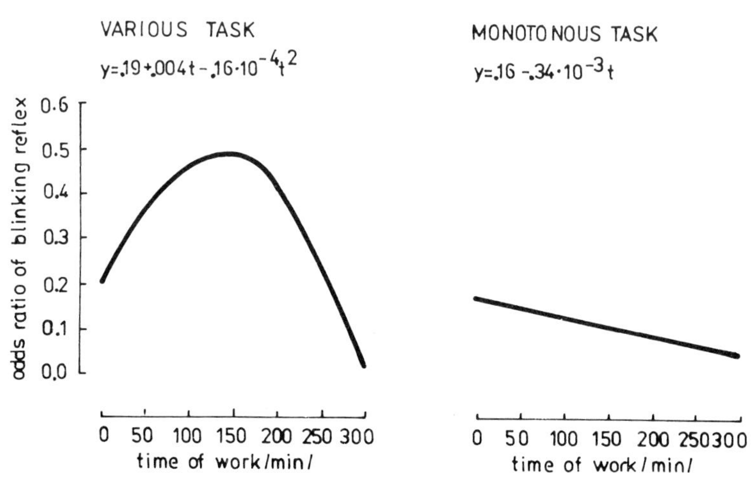

FIGURE 2
The models for the defensive behaviours indicator changes: the odds ratio of blinking reflex - y, the work time - t .

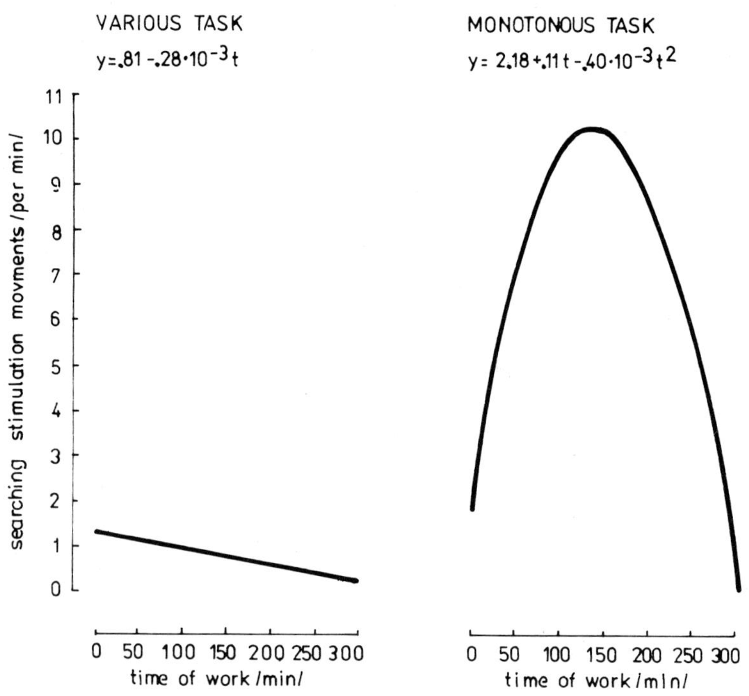

FIGURE 3
The models for the changes of the indicator of the behaviours tending to raise the stimulation level: the searching stimulation movements - y, the work time - t .

Figures 4 and 5 present the regression curves for the performances connected (C ratio) and unconnected (critical flicker frequency - CFF) with work, respectively. Figure 6 presents models for self-feeling index (self-rating of fatigue) .

Obtained models (figures 4, 5 and 6) confirm the previous result (compare figures 1, 2 and 3) . There are very different changes in indexes values stated for various and monotonous tasks. As it can be seen, generally the levels of both performances decrease due to time, but in the case of various task for first fifty minutes increase.

It is very interesting that the changes in the critical flicker frequency and in the self-rating of fatigue in the case of various task are described by the polynomials of the forth degree and in the case of monotonous task by the polynomials of the third degree. In both cases high negative correlations between critical flicker frequency and self-rating were found ($r = -.99$ for various task and $r = -.96$ for monotonous task).

Similarly the correlations between C ratio and self-rating of fatigue are negative, but weaker than those above ($r = -.52$ for various task and $r = -.58$ for monotonous task).

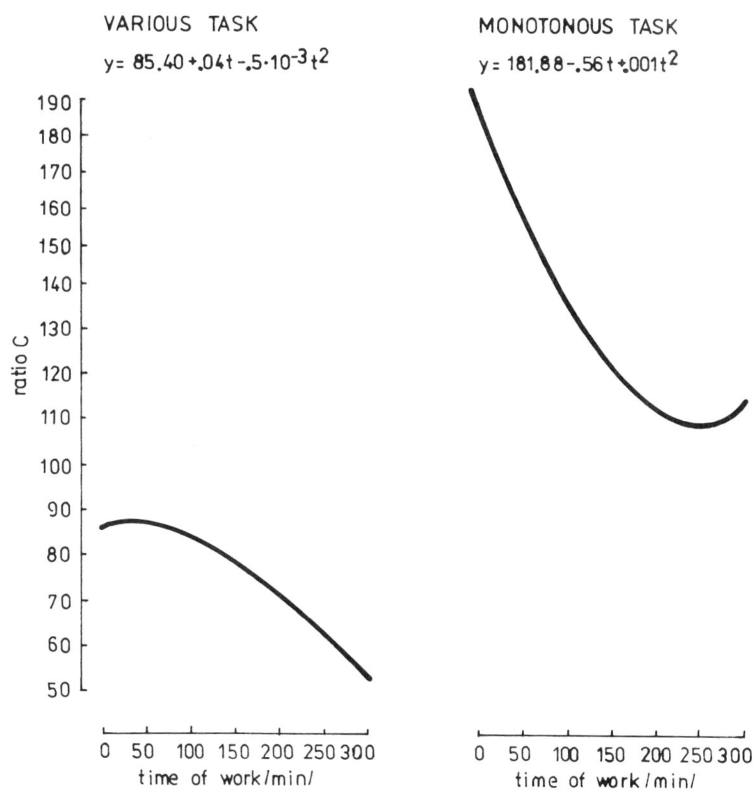

FIGURE 4
The models for the changes of the index of the performance connected with work: the ratio C - y, the work time - t .

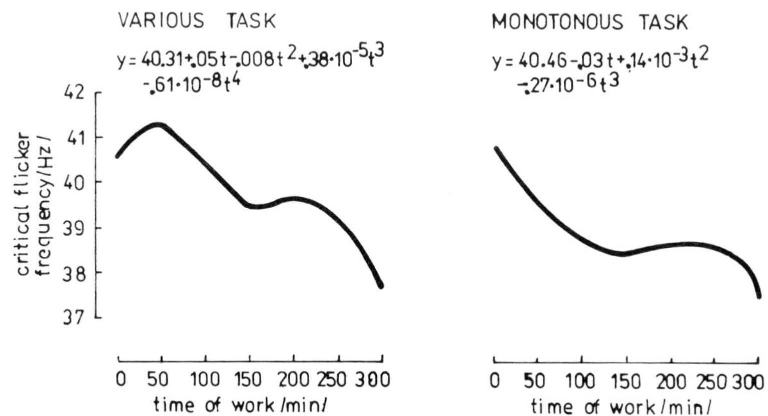

FIGURE 5
The models for the changes of the index of the performance unconnected with work: the CFF - y, the work time - t .

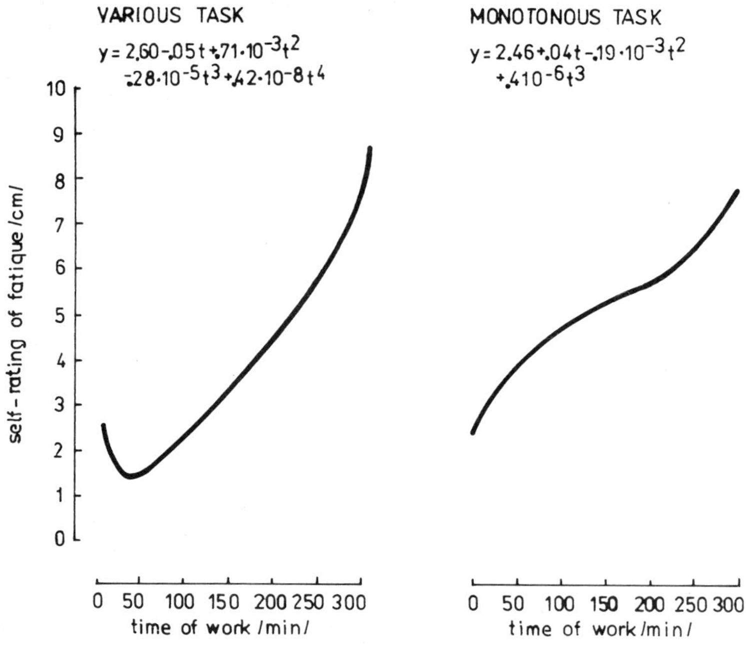

FIGURE 6
The models for the self-feeling index changes: the self-rating of fatigue - y, the work time - t .

For the analysis of the relation between the indicators of arousal and mechanisms of stimulation level regulation and the indexes of performances and self-feeling the partial correlation coefficients were used. The effect of this analysis is shown in tables 5, 6 and 7. The relation between dependend variables (C ratio, CFF and self-rating of fatigue) and independend variables (the indicators of the arousal level and mechanisms of stimulation regulation) are shown as the percent of explained variances, respectively (percent of explained variance = $r^2 \cdot 100\%$).

TABLE 5
Percent of variance explained by the indicator of the arousal level and the indicators of two mechanisms of regulating the level of stimulation for C ratio (the performance connected with work) for various and monotonous tasks ($p \leqslant .05$).

Time of work	Various task			Monotonous task		
	Pupil diameter	Odds ratio of blinking reflex	Searching stimulation movements	Pupil diameter	Odds ratio of blinking reflex	Searching stimulation movements
0	60	0	0	69	0	0
50	66	11	0	69	0	0
100	27	35	0	63	0	10
150	31	42	0	29	0	48
200	43	38	0	41	0	28
250	58	19	0	72	0	0
300	67	0	0	79	0	0

TABLE 6

Percent of variance explained by the indicator of the arousal level and the indicators of two mechanisms of regulating the level of stimulation for CFF (the performance unconnected with work) for various and monotonous tasks ($p \leqslant .05$)

Time of work	Various task			Monotonous task		
	Pupil diameter	Odds ratio of blinking reflex	Searching stimulation movements	Pupil diameter	Odds ratio of blinking reflex	Searching stimulation movements
0	59	0	0	65	0	0
50	72	0	0	71	0	0
100	44	35	0	62	0	9
150	30	41	0	58	0	12
200	38	39	0	59	0	15
250	48	9	0	53	0	19
300	70	0	0	69	0	0

TABLE 7

Percent of variance explained by the indicator of the arousal level and the indicators of two mechanisms of regulating the level of stimulation for self-rating of fatigue, for various and monotonous tasks ($p \leqslant .05$).

Time of work	Various task			Monotonous task		
	Pupil diameter	Odds ratio of blinking reflex	Searching stimulation movements	Pupil diameter	Odds ratio of blinking reflex	Searching stimulation movements
0	52	0	0	50	0	0
50	60	0	0	63	0	0
100	35	13	0	50	0	21
150	44	19	0	48	0	0
200	62	0	0	54	0	0
250	59	0	0	63	0	0
300	64	0	0	68	0	0

As it can be seen from the tables in the case of the various task the variances for all three indexes (dependent variables) are explained only by the indicator of the arousal level (changes in the pupil diameter) and the indicator of behaviours tending to decrease the level of stimulation (odds ratio of blinking reflex) while in the case of the monotonous task all variances are explained only by the indicator of the arousal level and the indicator of behaviours tending to raise the level of stimulation (searching stimulation movements). It is very characteristic that the participation of the odds ratio of blinking reflex (for the various task) and the searching stimulation movements (for the monotonous task) appears and increases in the explained variances when the mechanisms which regulate the level of stimulation reach a high level (see figures 2 and 3), aspecially between 100 and 200 minutes. Generally in the same intervals of time the participation in the explained variances of the arousal level indicator decreases. On the other hand it is relatively higher at the beginning and at the end of work (time intervals 0 - 50 and 250 - 300 minutes, respectively).

In the case of the self-rating of fatigue the percent of explained variances by the odds ratio of blinking reflex (various task) and searching stimulation movements (monotonous task) are on the low levels relative to the C ratio and

CFF (see tables 5, 6 and 7).

4. CONCLUSIONS

We have stated that there are two different mechanisms of VDU operators mental fatigue which are at play. The first is connected with various tasks and the second with monotonous tasks.

As the obtained results show the level of both types of performances (connected and unconnected with work) always depend on the level of arousal. However, in the case of various tasks it depends on the mechanism which tends to decrease the level of stimulation and in the case of monotonous tasks on the mechanism which dends to raise the level. Similar dependences are observed in the case of the self-rating of fatigue in spite of the influence of the mechanisms of the regulation level of stimulation which is weaker.

It is very important to point out that the level of performances (connected and unconnected with work) depends in time curvelinearally on changes in the intensity of the mechanisms of stimulation level regulation and the level of arousal.

Generally the fluctuation of performances depends on the level of arousal as well as on the intensity of mechanisms which regulate the level of stimulation. The intensity of these mechanisms depend in turn on the level of arousal which is connected with the type of task (various or monotonous). It was confirmed that when the level of arousal is high the mechanism tending to raise the stimulation level is at play (see the correlation coefficient between the level of arousal and the behaviours tending to decrease the level of stimulation under various tasks) and when the level of arousal is low the defensive mechanism tending to reduce the stimulation level appears (compare the curvelinear correlation between the level of arousal and the behaviours tending to raise the level of stimulation under monotonous task). Thus, on one hand we can describe the mental fatigue which appears under various task and which depend on the level of arousal and the mechanism tending to reduce the level of stimulation. On the other hand we can describe the monotonous mental fatigue which is connected with monotonous task and depends on the level of arousal and mechanism tending to raise the level of stimulation.

The self-feeling of fatigue depends mainly on the level of arousal. The dependences between self-rating of fatigue and mechanisms of stimulation regulation are less significant. It is interesting that the self-rating of fatigue is highly correlated with the index of performance, unconnected with work (CFF) and much less correlated with the performance index, connected with work (C ratio).

Both types of fatigue lead to the decrease of performance, but in the two different ways.

REFERENCES

[1] Beatty, J., Pupillometric measurement of cognitive workload in complex man-machine systems, in: Proceedings of 12th Annual Conference on Manual Control (NASA TM X-73, 170, 1976) pp.135-143.

[2] Fiske, D.W. and Maddi, S.R., Functions of varied experiences (Homewood, The Dorsey Press, 1967).

[3] Hebb, D.O., Drives and central nervous system, in: Fowler, H., (ed.) Curiosity and exploratory behaviour (Macmillan, New York, 1965).

[4] Kahneman, D. and Beatty, J., Pupil diameter and load on memory, Science 154 (1966) 1583.

[5] Leuba, C., Toward some integration of learning theory, in: Fowler, H., (ed.) Curiosity and exploratory behaviour (Macmillan, New York, 1965).

[6] Marek, T. and Noworol, C., Some remarks on a measure of computer operators workload - changes in pupil reflex, in: Klix, F. and Wandtke, H., (eds.) Man-Computer Interaction Research (North Holland, Amsterdam, 1986) pp.383-389.

[7] Marek, T. and Noworol, C., The influence of under and overstimulation on sitting posture, in: Corlet, E.N., Wilson, J. and Manenica, I., (eds.) Ergonomics of working posture (Taylor and Francis, London, 1986) in print.

[8] McEven, W.K., Secretion of tears and blinking, in: Davson, H. (ed.) The Eye - Muscular Mechanisms (Academic Press, New York, 1962) pp.290-301

[9] Tranel, N., Effects of perceptual isolation in introverts and extraverts, Journal of Psychiatric Research, 1 (1962).

[10] Zuckerman, M., Sensation: Beyond the Optimal Level of Arousal (Hillsdale, New York, 1979).

WORK WITH DISPLAY UNITS 86
B. Knave and P.-G. Wideback (eds.)

DATA ENTRY TASK ON VDU : UNDERLOAD OR OVERLOAD ?

R. FLORU and F. CAIL

Institut National de Recherche et de Sécurité
54501 VANDOEUVRE, FRANCE

This study investigated the psychophysiological changes during a two hours data entry task under three conditions: (a) self-paced continuous work; (b) self-paced but with a rest break after 40 min of work; (c) time pressure elicited by material incentive.
The results showed significantly higher average values for the performances, heart rate, EEG beta index, and lower ones for the eye movement rate and EEG theta index in (b) and (c) versus (a).
The psychophysiological pattern over time clearly indicated that periods of critical imbalance between attentional task demands and cerebral arousal occured in both (a) and (c).
It was concluded that data entry task engendered overloading conditions not only under time pressure but also in self-paced work. The rest break contributed to reduce cerebral compensatory effort.

It is advisable to introduce an active rest break after each 40-50 min of continuous data entry work.

1. INTRODUCTION

1.1. Objective

The objective of this research was to : 1) examine and compare the psychophysiological changes during a data entry task in underloading and overloading conditions; 2) acquire some psychophysiological evidence for suggesting convenient work-rest schedules for data entry operators.

1.2. Background

Many field studies dealing with the impact of video display units (VDUs) use on health complaints indicate that some jobs in which a single task, particularly data entry task, dominates the workday, are associated with frequent visual, musculo-skeletal and nervous strain [1], [2], [3], [4]. Several interacting factors related to the lighting environment, the work station, the psychosocial and organizational requirements contribute to inadequate work conditions. Nevertheless, most authors consider that the major factor contributing to the stress problems and work dissatisfaction is related to the job content and work load.

In data entry task, VDU is used to input data from source documents into the computer system. The task is monotonous and repetitive, and it is often carried out on a full-time basis. It contains many of features characteristic of short-cycled repetitive work [5], [6]. Rigid work procedures, high production standards and constant pressure for performance, usually monitored by the computer contribute to the perception of increased workload [7]. VDU operators who recently underwent automation report spending more time at the work station using VDU and have more intensive session without a break [8].

1.3. Overload, underload and stress

There are many meanings and ambiguities attached to the terms "stress" and "workload", sometimes used interchangeably. McGrath [9] emphasized that stress is the result of an imbalance between (perceived) demand and (perceived) organism's capacity. The mental workload is treated by Welford [10] in terms of the demands made by the task and the capacities the subject brings to meet these demands. Both stress and workload also appeared in a causal relationship. As stated by Cox [11], "a stress state can arise through overload (demands > abilities) or through underload (demands ⩽ abilities)". Accordingly, mental stress can be regarded as a consequence of mental load. Sometimes, the terms stress and strain instead of load and effort are used with nearly the same meaning. The concept of "effort", namely the attentional effort, directly related to physiological activation [12] is relevant to a functional model of mental load.

Johansson and Aronsson [13] show that the adrenaline excretion level of the data entry operators is higher than the control group in the morning and vice versa in the afternoon. The authors note that, because of unforeseeable breakdowns occuring in the computer system, subjects increase the pace early in the day. Hence, the physiological arousal level as well as the mental stress increase under time pressure associated with unpredicted interruptions of system operation.

The data entry work is considered by Johansson [14] as a combination of quantitative overload and qualitative underload. This view is on the lines of the stress hypothesis proposed by Frankenhaeuser. Psychophysiological experiments have demonstrated that the average level of catecholamines excretion was significantly higher in subjects performing either overstimulating or understimulating tasks than in controls. Frankenhaeuser et al. [15] conclude that both understimulation and overstimulation are stressful, and associated with an increase in the overall level of arousal.

From a psychophysiological point of view, the question is whether the overall level of arousal may be taken for a reliable physiological correlate of stress through overload, since arousal may increase with task demands without exceeding the "optimal" state. According to the inverted-U hypothesis, it is generally accepted that mental efficiency may be impaired at a low arousal level as well as a very high one [16]. Yet, it is difficult to conciliate the data showing the decrease in arousal during vigilance or repetitive tasks with those [15] inferring an increase in arousal level in monotonous, understimulating conditions.

Lindsley [17] considers that the activating system of the brain, controlled by sensory and cortical stimulation, works as a homeostat regulating or adjusting input-output relations. Accordingly, one may conceive that in overstimulating as well as in understimulating conditions, homeostatic mechanisms intervene for adjusting the cerebral activation to task demand.

Our hypothesis is that an overload condition may arise when critical imbalance between attentional task demands and required arousal support occurs. The homeostatic mechanisms intervene continuously, but the repeated compensatory efforts may be perceived as stressful. Consequently, it is necessary to take into account the temporal course of the psychophysiological events that could reveal subject's effort to cope with the imbalance between task demands and his operational capacity.

1.4. Work-rest schedules in data entry work

As regards the work-rest schedules for VDU operators, there are some general recommendations (e.g. 15 min after two hours of continuous work), but argument supporting this two hours standard has not been found [18]. After introducing a 15 min rest break in the middle of the morning and of the afternoon session, Zwhalen [19] concludes that they appeared not to be sufficient. For video-coding, Knave [20] considers that "it is not really advisable for workers to spend more than 30-50 min in front of the screen without a break". The NIOSH [21] has recommended a 15 min work-rest break after 2 hours of continuous work for operators under moderate visual demands and/or moderate workload. It was also mentioned that the period of continuous work could be reduced to one hour for operators under high visual demands, high workload and/or those engaged in repetitive work tasks. Certainly, data entry operators belong to the last category, still, as it was remarked by the National Academy of Science [22] "moderate" or "high" workload were not defined by NIOSH.

We may therefore conclude by the available litterature, that we still lack an experimental support for introducing rest time in working hours on visual display terminals.

In order to suggest a suitable work-rest schedule for data entry operators the required step was to chart the course of psychophysiological events over time. This has been done in a previous study [6]. In the present paper, the aim was to test the effects of a rest break on the psychophysiological indices during a data entry task.

2. METHOD

2.1. Work station

An experimental VDU station was built in the laboratory. In order to minimize the factors of constraint not directly related to the task, the ergonomic requirements concerning environmental conditions, display and work place were observed. The VDU system used was a HP 2647A with white caracters on a grey background. The display screen was adjusted for optimal legibility (contrast, lack of glare, reflections or luminance oscillations). All the components of the workplace (supports for VDU, keyboard, wrist-rest, source-document support, chair and backrest) were independently adjustable.

2.2. Task

The task simulated an off-line data entry work at a bank office. It consisted in transferring the numerical data (bank account, customer account and amount) of about thousand cheques to the terminal through the keyboard. The subject filled the display form then pressed the "Return" key for storing the data on a magnetic tape, and a new work cycle begins. Subjects also had the opportunity of correcting errors before storing the data. Because subjects were not trained typists, the graphic control group was modified by assigning them numerical values (see Fig. 1).

2.3. Recordings and data processing

Behavioral (performance, errors) as well as physiological responses [(electroencephalogram (EEG), heart rate (HR) and electrooculogram (EOG)] have been continuously recorded. Performance (correct entries and errors) were recorded on a magnetic tape with a timer set for every 5 min. Bipolar EEG was recorded from silver silver-chloride disc electrodes placed at the O_1 and O_2 positions (according to the Jasper 10-20 system) with a common reference at the vertex (Cz), filled with electrode paste and attached by collodion to the scalp. The EEG was recorded on a Beckman paper polygraph and also fed into a Fast Fourier Analyser through a special (IRIG) output. After artefact rejection and processing, the EEG power spectra for six selected frequency bands (delta: 0.5-3 Hz; theta: 4-7 Hz; alpha: 8-13 Hz; beta 1: 14-20 Hz; beta 2: 21-26 Hz and beta 3: 27-32 Hz), were integrated continuously over epochs of 8 s. The output of each filter was converted into digital form and computed for each 5 min. Bipolar recording of an electrocardiogram was made with skin electrodes attached with adhesive collars on the sternum and below the left breast. The raw electrocardiogram was recorded on the polygraph and the signal was fed into a magnetic tape for off-line computation of the HR. For the EOG recording, two small size skin electrodes were attached with adhesive collars binocularly at the outer canthi, and a third one above the right eyebrow. This arrangement enabled us to distinguish between control-correction eye movement (EM), and short glimpses ending a work cycle. The general behavior of subjects was monitored using a closed-loop TV circuit. Raw performance, errors and corrected performance (errors removed) were computed against time and expressed in units per minute. EEG was processed off-line by computer and the relative amplitude of selected frequency bands were expressed as a percentage of the summated-spectral power. The EM were visually analysed and computed against time.

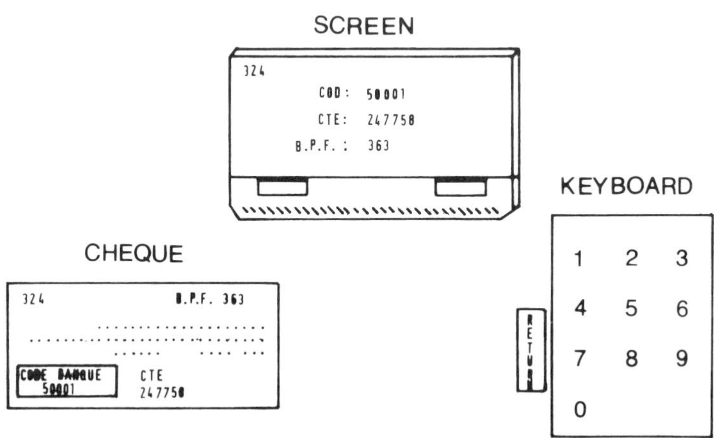

Fig. 1 The data entry task
COD: Bank account; CTE: Customer account; B.P.F.: Amount (in francs). The number in the left corner is the order number of the cheque.

2.4. Procedure

After several training sessions, eight subjects performed the data entry task for two hours under three exprimental conditions: (a) self-paced continuous work (CW); (b) self-paced but with a short (5 min) rest break after 40 min of work (RB); (c) under time pressure elicited by material incentive (TP). The last two conditions were counterbalanced between subjects. In all three conditions, the subjects were instructed to work accurately. In the rest break condition, they were not informed in advance about the pause. During the pause, subjects left the work station and talked with the experimenter. The time pressure condition was equivalent to the incentive-paced situation described by Salvendy [23] since the subjects were financially motivated to produce above the self-paced work.

The location of the rest pause was determined in a former study [6], from the average performance curve of seventeen subjects performing the data entry task at their own pace. Since the maximal decrement of the performance was observed toward the end of the first hour of work, the rest break was given after 40 min of work.

3. RESULTS

3.1. Average psychophysiological levels

Analyses of variance reveal significant differences between conditions for performance ($F=28.14$, $p<.001$); heart rate ($F=12.86$, $p<.001$); eye movement rate ($F=13.55$, $p<.001$); alpha index ($F=4.20$, $p<.05$); beta 1 index ($F=13.55$, $p<.001$; beta 2 index ($F=7.43$, $p<.01$); beta 3 index ($F=6.41$, $p<.01$); df:2,20). The condition x period interaction is not significant.

Fig. 2 shows the average measures obtained in rest break (RB) and time pressure (TP) conditions. Measures obtained during RB and TP conditions have been transformed into percent of corresponding self-paced continuous work (CW) levels.

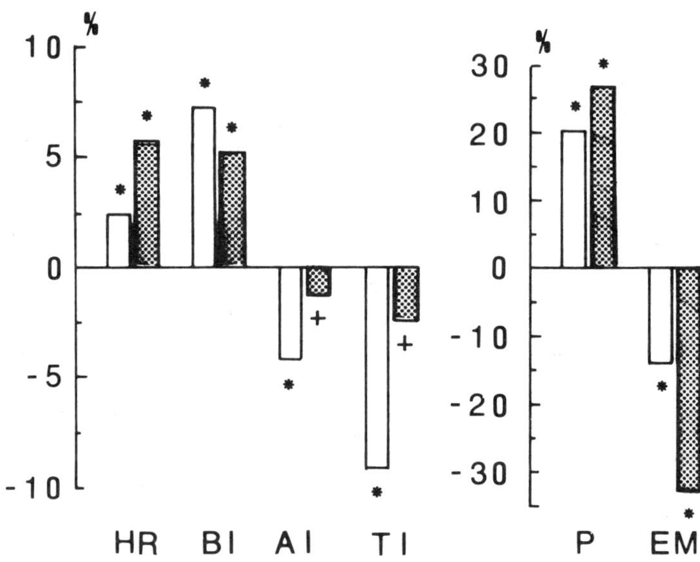

Fig. 2 Data entry task. Mean changes of psychophysiological variables in rest break (RB) and time pressure (TP) conditions.
All values are given as a percentage of the continuous work corresponding measures. White columns: RB; Dotted columns: TP; HR: heart rate; BI: beta 1 index; AI: alpha index; TI: theta index; P: performance; EM: eye movements. (t-test: + $p<.05$; * $p<.01$).

The results appearing in Fig. 2 indicate that, by comparison with the control (CW), in RB and TP, there is a significant increase in performance (Student's t-test=13.56 and 16.26 respectively, $p<.01$), heart rate ($t=3.40$ and 24.40, $p<.01$) and beta index ($t=10.46$ and 8.58, $p<.01$), and a decrease in the alpha index ($t=7.58$, $p<.01$ and 2.18, $p<.05$), theta index ($t=7.58$, $p<.01$ and 2.80, $p<.05$) and in eye movement rate ($t=5.76$ and 13.34, $p<.01$).

As can be noted in Fig. 2, the increase in HR and the decrease in the eye movement rate are more pronounced in TP than in RB condition whereas the beta index increases more in RB than in TP. The differences between average values for HR, BI and EM in RB and TP conditions are significant ($p<.01$).

3.2. Psychophysiological changes over time

Figures 3, 4 and 5 show the average curves of psychophysiological variables during data entry task in CW, RB and TP conditions. The first 15 min were removed from the plotted curves because of large interindividual differences exhibited during this period.

In the CW conditions, the data entry task performance declines progressively reaching a minimal value after 45-60 minutes of work. Then an impressive rebound occurs, followed by some fluctuations around the mean values. The beta index shows rather a parallel trend with the performance (see Fig. 3).

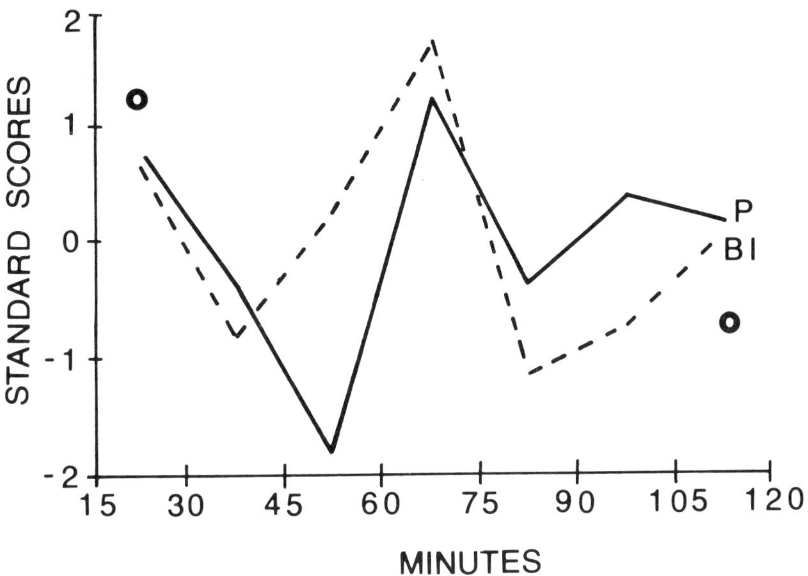

Fig. 3 Temporal course of performance and beta index during self-paced continuous work
P: performance; BI: beta 1 index; circles indicate the average HR level at the beginning and the end of the task.

In the RB condition, performance progressively increases after the pause and is maintained at a high level for the next hour. Beta index increases with performance, then slightly decreases. During the last 15 min both performance and beta index increase (see Fig. 4).

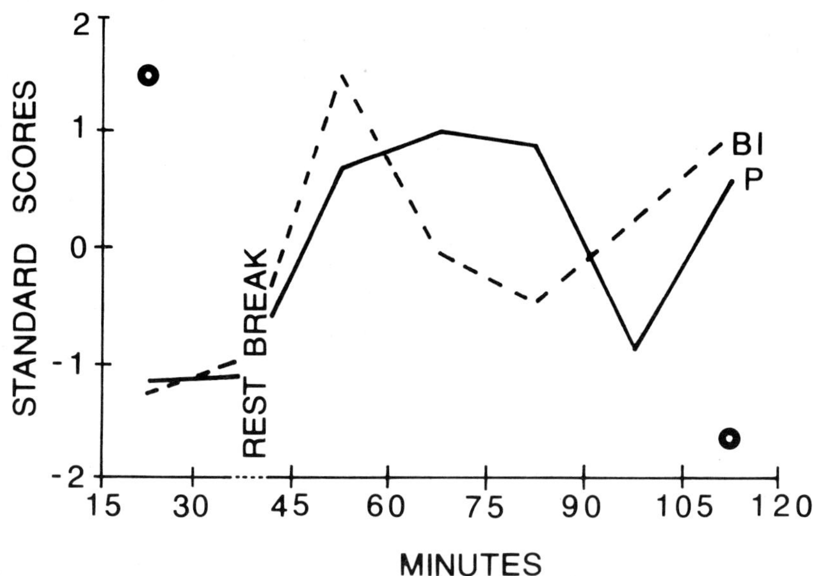

Fig. 4 Psychophysiological changes in rest break condition. A five min pause was given after 40 min of work. (Same legends as in Fig. 3).

As can be noted in Fig. 4, the slight decrease in the beta index (in the middle period of the work) does not affect the relatively steady performance, whereas the peaks of the beta index are associated with enhancements of performance.

In the TP condition, performance and beta index display nearly opposite trends. After 30 min of work, performance increases progressively, then slightly fluctuates, and a dramatic fall occurs at the end of the work (see Fig. 5).

Fig. 5 shows that beta index exhibits a maximal level at the beginning of the task. The decrease in the beta index is associated with an increase in performance. This opposite relationship can also be observed at the end of the task.

In all three conditions (CW, RB and TP) the heart rate declines monotonically from the beginning to the end of the work.

3.3. Persisting effects of the rest break

In order to measure the after-effects of the pause, the mean values of psychophysiological variables scored after the rest break were compared with those obtained in the first 25 min of work. The experimental session was divided into four equal periods, the period before the rest break being considered as a reference. The mean values of each successive (I, II, III) period were then expressed as a percent of the corresponding reference values of different indices for both CW and RB conditions (see Fig. 6).

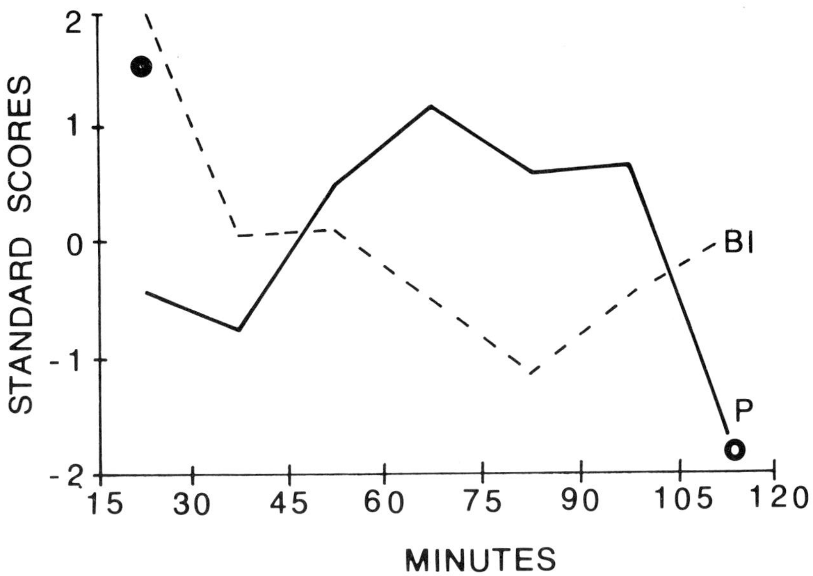

Fig. 5 Psychophysiological changes under time pressure condition.
(Same legends as in Fig. 3).

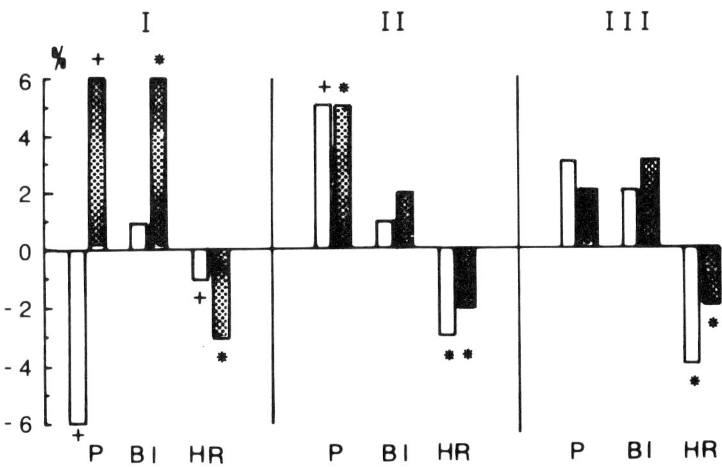

Fig. 6 Comparison between self-paced continuous work (CW) and rest break (RB) conditions
I, II, III: successive 25 min periods after rest break.
White columns: CW; Dotted columns: RB; P: performance; BI: beta 1 index; HR: heart rate. All values are given as a percentage of the corresponding reference values (the first 25 min of work).

By comparison with the reference values, several differences can be observed between CW and RB conditions :

a) During the I-st period, in the RB condition, performance and beta index significantly increase ($t=3.72$, $p<.05$ and $t=4.77$, $p<.01$), and HR significantly decreases ($t=11.14$, $p<.01$).
In the CW condition, performance and HR significantly decrease ($t=2.75$, $p<.05$ and $t=3.62$, $p<.05$).

b) During the II-nd period, in both RB and CW conditions, performance significantly increases ($t=4.80$, $p<.01$ and $t=3.77$, $p<.05$ respectively), and HR decreases ($t=7.90$, and 7.92, $p<.01$).

c) During the III-rd period, in both conditions, performance and beta index values are higher than in the reference period but the differences are not significant. HR still decreases in both conditions.

4. DISCUSSION

The results presented above indicate : a) a clear increase in performance and arousal levels in time pressure and rest break conditions by comparison with the self-paced continuous work; b) a different psychophysiological pattern over time during CW, RB and TP conditions, except for HR that continuously decreases in all conditions.

With regard to the average levels, undoubtely the increase in performance was partly due to learning. This learning effect was already controlled in a previous experiment [24]. It was shown that the increase in performance did not exceed 12% and in beta index 2%, whereas HR slightly decreased from test to restest experiments. In the present study, performance and arousal elevations were much more important than those expected for learning. They can therefore be assigned to the independent variables.

Because in our experiments the average level of arousal increased both in TP and RB conditions, we sought for additional evidence that could support the TP overload hypothesis.

First, psychophysiological changes over time showed that under time pressure, high values in beta index were associated with low performance values and vice versa, whereas in RB, performance enhancements were associated with corresponding shifts in BI.

Secondly, the average HR level was significantly higher in TP than in RB. HR changes were more related to diffuse arousal than those of EEG, that may be interpreted as predominant signs of selective arousal.

Third, the eye movement rate decreased significantly much more in TP than in RB. The important decrease in EM rate under time pressure may be interpreted as a change in information processing strategy. In order to increase the work output, subjects reduce the control of the data on the screen but allocate their attentional ressources on reading and typing. This results in a shortening of the work cycle.

Fourth, significant positive correlation ($r=.56$) between performance and beta index was found in RB. The correlation is negative but not significant in TP.

We may therefore consider that under TP the arousal level exceeds the optimal level, thus impairing the selectivity of responses. Our results agree with those obtained through noradrenaline measure [13].

As one can see, it is rather difficult to infer from only one measure, as for instance the average arousal level, whether a given experimental condition is overloading or underloading. When comparing TP with CW, we may consider that in the first condition, subjects are overloaded since they are overaroused. Indeed, under time pressure subjects were overloaded since the emotional tension added to task demands. Although, we cannot say that in the second condition (CW), subjects are underloaded as they are underaroused. On examining the temporal course of psychophysiological events we found some evidence in support of our work hypothesis. Intermittent periods of overload can be observed in both CW and TP conditions.

Under time pressure, subjects were overaroused from the beginning of the work, then compensatory psychophysiological mechanisms tended to restore a dynamic balance between attentional demands of the task and selective arousal support.

During a self-paced continuous work, arousal decreased progressively with performance but we presume that subjects became overloaded only when the discrepancy between unchanged task demands and arousal support reached a critical, conflicting state. On the same line, Hockey [26] considers that low arousal becomes stressful if an individual is required internally to counteract this state. Thackray hypothesizes that the coupling of an arousal-reducing task characteristic with the opposing requirement for a constant level of alertness makes this combination particularly stressful, and this may result in a considerable effort expenditure and fatigue [25].

In our experiments, the significant EEG arousal and performance rebound observed towards the end of the first hour of work presumably reflected the subject's effort to mobilize his attentional ressources. In real work conditions, this distressing effort is repeated several times a day and, as Knave points out at the Work With Display Units Conference, "5 days a week, 48 weeks a year, year after year..." [27].

We then supposed that an active rest break introduced before the critical state was attained, would restore the arousal level, thus sparing subject's compensatory effort. The comparison before-after rest break (see Fig. 6) confirmed our hypothesis. Continuous monitoring of behavorial and physiological changes during a data entry task on VDU showed that operators spontaneously interrupted their work for several minutes after each 50 min (on average) of work [28]. This observation supports our proposal about rest break location.

5. CONCLUDING REMARKS

This paper has attempted to answer the question whether data entry task may be regarded as underload or overload. In our psychophysiological experiments, both self-paced and under time pressure work appeared to be overloading. In both situations we found evidence that support the overload hypothesis, that is instances where profound discrepancies between task demands and available arousal support occured. These critical states elicited important cerebral compensatory responses tending to readjust the actual arousal potential to the required one. In our view it is misleading to evaluate data entry task as underloading. The term "qualitative underload" concerns the whole job and the underutilisation of skills and capacities but not the intrinsic demands of the task, the work pace and work duration which lead to overload and mental strain.

It is advisable to introduce a rest break after every 40-50 min of continuous work on VDU data entry task. The rest break can spare operator's compensatory effort, although a similar result might be obtained by shifting the users to another non-VDU task. Indeed, a more adequate work-rest schedule does not solve job stress problems of data entry operators. Nevertheless, it may contribute to alleviate their work on VDU.

ACKNOWLEDGMENT

The authors are grateful to J.C. CNOCKAERT for his critical comments on the manuscript.

REFERENCES

[1] Smith, M.J., Cohen, B.G.F., Stammerjohn, L.W.Jr. and Happ, A., An investigation of health complaints and job stress in video display operations, Human Factors 23 (1981) 387-400.
[2] Elias, R., Cail, F., Tisserand, M. and Christman, H., Investigations in operators working with CRT display; relationships between task content and psychophysiological alterations, in: Grandjean, E. and Vigliani, E. (eds.), Ergonomic Aspects of Visual Display Terminals (Taylor & Francis, London, 1980) pp.211-217.
[3] Cohen, B.G.F., Smith, M.J. and Stammerjohn, L.W.Jr., Psychosocial factors contributing to job stress of clerical VDT operators, in : Salvendy, G. and Smith, M.J. (eds.), Machine Pacing and Occupational Stress (Taylor & Francis, London, 1981) pp.337-345.
[4] Johansson, G. and Aronsson, G., Stress reactions in computerized administrative work. Supplement 50 (Department of Psychology, University of Stockholm, Stockholm, 1980)
[5] Mackay, C. and Cox, T., Occupational stress associated with visual display operation, in: Pearce, B. (ed.), Health Hazard of VDTs ? (J. Wiley, New York, 1980) pp.137-143.
[6] Floru, R., Cail, F. and Elias, R., Psychophysiological changes during a VDU repetitive task, Ergonomics 28 (1985) 1455-1468.
[7] Smith, M.J., Stammerjohn, L.W.Jr., Cohen, B.G.F. and Lalich, N.R., Job stress in visual display operations, in: Grandjean, E. and Vigliani, E. (eds.), Ergonomic Aspects of Visual Display Terminals (Taylor & Francis, London, 1980) pp.201-209.
[8] Smith, M.J., Job stress and VDUs: Is the technology a problem ?, Proceedings of the International Scientific Conference: Work With Display Units (Stockholm, 1986) pp.189-195.
[9] McGrath, J.E., A conceptual formulation for research on stress, in: McGrath (ed.), Social and Psychological Factors of Stress (Holt, Rinehart & Winston, New York, 1970) pp. 10-21.
[10] Welford, A.T., Mental work-load as a function of demand, capacity, strategy and skill, Ergonomics 21 (1978) 151-167.
[11] Cox, T., The nature and measurement of stress, Ergonomics 28 (1985) 1155-1164.
[12] Kahneman, D., Attention and Effort (Prentice Hall, New Jersey, 1973)
[13] Johansson, G. and Aronsson, G., Stress reactions in computerized administrative work, Journal of Occupational Behaviour 5 (1984) 159-181.
[14] Johansson, G., Growth and challenge vs wear and tear of humans in computer mediated work, Proceedings of the International Scientific Conference: Work With Display Units (Stockholm, 1986) pp.249-251.
[15] Frankenhaeuser, M., Nordheden, B., Myrsten, A. and Post, B., Psychophysiological reactions to understimulation and overstimulation, Acta Psychologica 35 (1971) 298-308.
[16] Frankenhaeuser, M. and Johansson, G., On the psychophysiological consequences of understimulation and overstimulation, in: Levi, L. (ed.), Society, Stress and Disease (Oxford University Press, Oxford, 1981) IV, pp.82-89.

[17] Lindsley, D.B., Common factors in sensory deprivation, sensory distortion, and sensory overload, in: Solomon, P., Kubzansky, P., Leiderman, J.H., Mendelsohn, J.H. and Wechsler, D. (eds.), Sensory Deprivation (Harvard University Press, Cambridge, 1961) pp.174-194.

[18] Hendricks, D., Kilduff, P., Brooks, P., Marshak, R. and Doyle, B., Human Engineering Guidelines for Management Information System (U.S. Army Human Engineering Laboratory, Maryland, 1981)

[19] Zwahlen, H., Effects of rest break in continuous VDT work on visual and musculoskeletal comfort/discomfort and on performance, in: Salvendy, G. (eds.), Human-Computer Interaction (Elsevier, Amsterdam, 1984) pp.315-319

[20] Knave, B., Work with display units : What we know and want to know, Newsletter 4 (1983) 6-9.

[21] National Institute for Occupational Safety and Health, Potential Health Hazards of Visual Display Terminals, Publication n° 81-129, (DHHS/NIOSH, Washington D.C., 1981)

[22] National Research Council, Video Display Work and Vision (National Academy Press, Washington D.C., 1983)

[23] Salvendy, G., Classification and characteristic of paced work, in: Salvendy, G. and Smith, M.J. (eds.), Machine Pacing and Occupational Stress (Taylor & Francis, London, 1981) pp.5-12.

[24] Cail, F. and Floru, R., Eye movement and task demands, in print

[25] Thackray, R.I., The stress of boredom and monotony: A consideration of the evidence, Psychosomatic Medicine 43 (1981) 165-176.

[26] Hockey, R., Stress and cognitive component of skilled performance, in: Hamilton, V. and Wartburton, D.M. (eds.), Human Stress and Cognition: An Information Process Approach (J. Willey, New York, 1979) 141-177

[27] Knave, B., Presidential address at the WWDU Conference Opening, May 12 (1986)

[28] Lille, F., Le Mire, J.J., Marc, M.E. and Franc, B., Data entry on computer terminal: repetitive work strains on the oculomotor and central nervous system, European Journal of Applied Physiology 53 (1984) 164-168.

WORK WITH DISPLAY UNITS 86
B. Knave and P.-G. Widebäck (eds.)

VIDEOCODING - A HIGHLY MONOTONOUS VDU WORK IN A NEW TECHNIQUE FOR MAIL SORTING

Arne WENNBERG and Margaretha VOSS

Department of Occupational Neuromedicine
Research Department
National Board of Occupationally Safety and Health
S-171 84 Solna, Sweden

Videocoding of letters for mail sorting is a stressfull, monotonous and VDU intensive work. 14 subjects were examined before and after one hour of work, with or without breaks. The following eye functions were measured: refraction, accommodation, convergence and fusion. No changes were found. EEG was recorded during and after work and the amount of drowsiness was judged during three minutes immediately after work. There was no relation between amount of work (= number of coded letters per minute) and drowsiness but the per cent of error (=incorrectly coded letters) increased significantly when the amount of drowsiness was high. In this relation, there was no effect of introducing short breaks during work. The amount of drowsiness in EEG and thus also the amount of incorrectly coded letters showed a clear relation to the amount (=number of hours) of sleep during the night before work.

1. BACKGROUND

A new technique for mail sorting was introduced at the new mail terminal of the Stockholm area in 1983. Postal codes of the letters are scanned by video cameras and sorted automatically, However about 15 % of the letters cannot be sorted automatically because of badly written or lack of postal code. These letters must be coded manually before sorting. This is performed with the aid of a video camera, that displays a picture of the letter on a VDU and the five-digits postal code is written manually from the VDU key board. This work is highly monotonous and to 100 % done against a VDU. The work is also stressfull as it should be continously performed at highest possible speed in periods of 50 minutes without interrupt.

A trained coder can handle up to 70 letters per minute. This is because of the fact that the next-coming letter is displayd on a second screen above the first one. Thus the coder can read and memorize the code of the next letter while still printing the previous one. All coders cannot utilize this facility and in such a case the speed will be lower, around 40 letters per minute.

2. AIMS OF THE STUDY

1. Does video-coding have any influence upon eye functions?
2. Are there any relations between work performance and level of vigilance or wakefulness?
3. If there are such influences or relations - would it be possible to reduce negative effects by reorganizing the VDU videocoding work?

3. MATERIAL AND METHODS

3.1. The subjects

Fourteen subjects (11 women and 3 men) aged 18-60 years were chosen for this study. VDU mail coding was a part of their daily work, thus they were all familiar with the technique. In their daily routine, they all performed video-coding in one period of 50 minutes without break in the morning and a similar period in the afternoon. During the rest of the day they did other types of work without use of VDUs.

3.2. Questionnaire

In the end of each experiment day, the subjects answered the following questions:

(1) *How did you feel before work to-day?* The answer should be given as one of five alternatives: (1) very alert , (2) alert , (3) neutral, (4) tired or (5) very tired.

(2) *How many hours did you sleep last night?* The answer should be given as a number of hours.

(3) *How many hours do you usually sleep in the night?* The answer should be given as a number of hours.

(4) *How was your sleep the last night?* The answer should be given as one of three alternatives: (1) better than usual, (2) as usual or (3) worse than usual.

3.3. Eye function measurements

The following eye functions were measured immediately before and after each period of work:

Accommodation, convergence, fusion at divergence and convergence [1]. The near point of accommodation was determined by a RAF Near Point Ruler (RAF= Royal Air Force). Convergence was studied by determination of the convergence near point with a RAF Near Point Ruler. Fusion was measured with prisms "base out" and "base in", i.e. in the convergent and divergent directions, for far (5 m) and near (0.35 m) distance. The sum of both measurements ("base out" and "base in") constituted the fusion range.

Refraction was measured automatically by using an automatic refractometer (Dioptron II: Coherent Dioptron Ultima Diagnostic Eye Computer) at the same occations and at all short breaks introduced during work (see below).

3.4. Level of vigilance (EEG)

Level of vigilance was measured by EEG recording, which was performed all during the work periods as well as immediately before and after the work periods and during the breaks. The EEG recordings were made with a Siemens-Elema 16 channel EEG machine with electrode positions according to the 10-20 system. The level of vigilance was judged from visual inspection of the EEG and the level of drowsiness were judged according to usual standard [2].

Every subject was examined at two occasions on different days: one morning session and one afternoon session. During each session, two periods of work were performed: one hour without break and one hour with short breaks every quarter: 10 minutes work and 5 minutes rest. During the rest, refraction was measured (usually during 1 minute) as well as 3 minutes EEG with eyes closed.

The EEGs from each work period (1 hr) were compared with those recorded during breaks and after work and presence of signs of drowsiness in the latter were graded in four levels:

- (0) No drowsiness, i.e. constant amount of alpha activity through the whole record.
- (1) Only suspect signs of drowsiness present occasionally, i.e. only few periods of decreased alpha activity, less than 10 seconds each.
- (2) Clear periods of drowsiness, i.e. decrease or absense of alpha activity and slightly or morderately increased amount of theta activity in periods of at least 10 seconds of duration, but totally less than 50 % of the record.
- (3) Longer perod of drowsiness, during more than 50 % of the record.

3.5. Performance

All letters used for coding during these work sessions were video-photographed earlier and stored on disk, from where they were displayed during the experiment. The total number of stored letters was 126 due to limits of the computer capacity. The letters were chosen randomly but of course the same letter was displayed several times, as the total number of letters coded during an one-hour session could be more than 4000.

All operations performed by the coder were recorded and stored by the computer. Thus the number of coded letters per time unit as well as number of errors could be followed continously all during the work session. The time interval between two consecutive key touches was recorded continously as well.

4. RESULTS

4.1. Eye functions

As can bee seen from Figures 1 and 2, none of the eye function parameters changed following work as compared to the conditions immediately before work.

4.2. Performance

Average number of coded letters per minute and per cent errors were as shown in Table I.

Table I. *Average number of coded letters per minute and average per cent errors during the different types of VDU work*

	Morning with breaks	Morning without breaks	Afternoon with breaks	Afternoon without breaks
Letters per minute	47.5	46.0	47.6	45.7
Per cent errors	1.35	1.40	1.67	1.78

In Figure 3, the individual number of letters are shown. Figure 4 shows the individual per cent errors.

4.3. Vigilance and Performance

Table II and III shows the number of letters and per cent errors in relation to level of drowsiness in EEG.

Table II. *Average number of coded letters per minute (number of subjects within brackets)*

Level of drowsiness	Morning with breaks	Morning without breaks	Afternoon with breaks	Afternoon without breaks
0	47.4 (9)	40.7 (6)	50.2 (4)	46.0 (11)
1	27.3 (1)	62.8 (2)	49.5 (7)	43.9 (2)
2	58.9 (4)	66.3 (1)	65.0 (1)	-
3	-	42.9 (1)	50.8 (2)	-

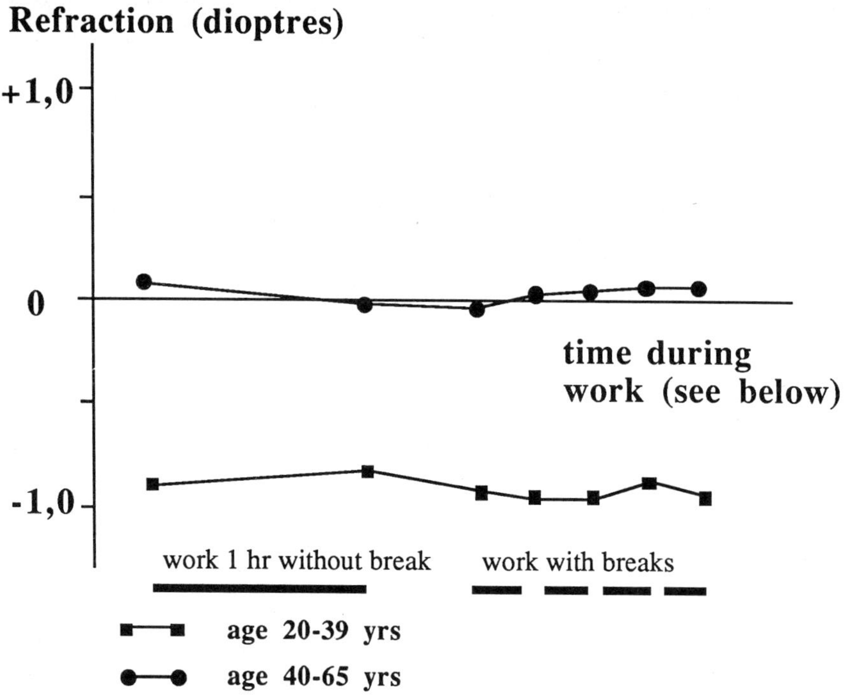

Figure 1. Refraction (mean values) before and after work. Refraction is given as the spherical equivalent, which is the value of the spherical refraction plus half the value of the astigmatic refraction.

Figure 3 shows the individual number of coded letters in relation to the level of drowsiness in EEG and in Figure 4 the individual per cent of errors are shown in a similar plot.

Figures 5 and 6 show the level of drowsiness in the EEG and the percent incorrectly coded letters respectively, as functions of the number of hours of sleep during the preceeding night. Figure 7, finally, shows the relations between per cent miscoded letters during work with and without breaks, respectively.

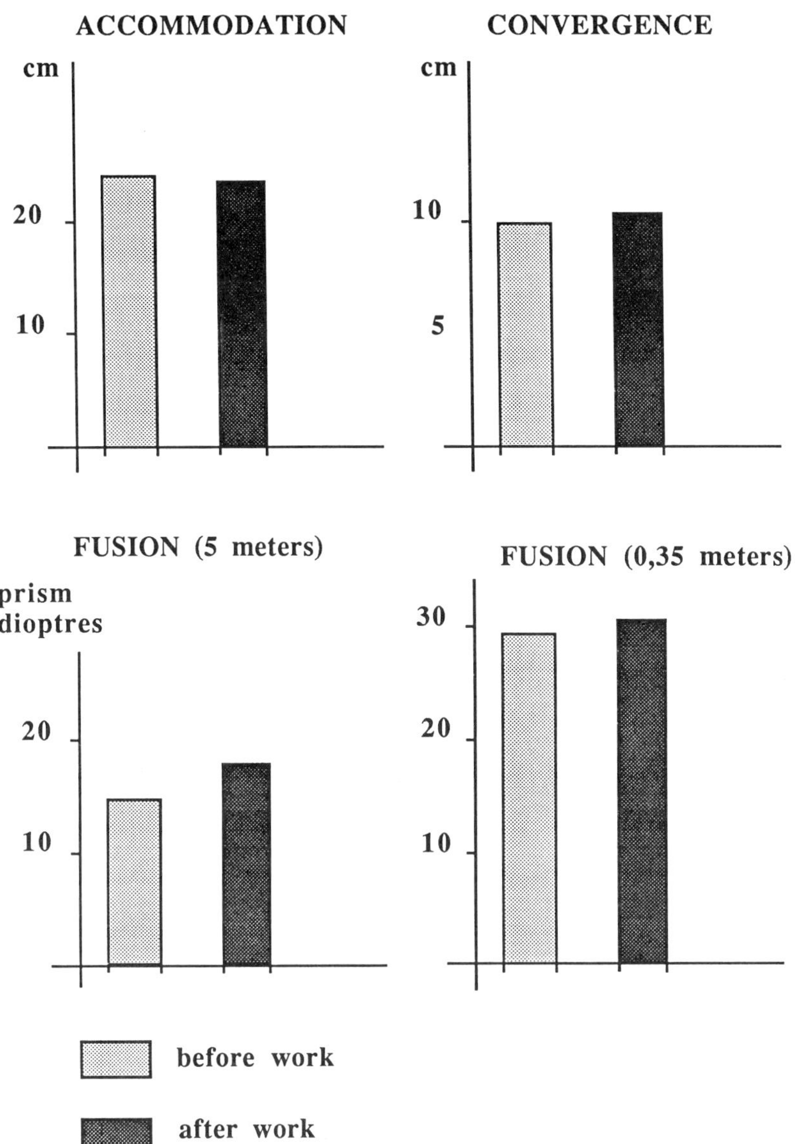

Figure 2. Eye function parameters (mean values) before and after VDU work.

Table III. Average per cent of errors (number of subjects within brackets)

Level of drowsiness	Morning with breaks	Morning without breaks	Afternoon with breaks	Afternoon without breaks
0	0.74 (9)	1.23 (6)	0.94 (4)	1.51 (11)
1	1.94 (1)	0.77 (2)	0.95 (7)	3.91 (2)
2	2.59 (4)	3.37 (1)	1.45 (1)	-
3	-	4.43 (1)	5.73 (2)	-

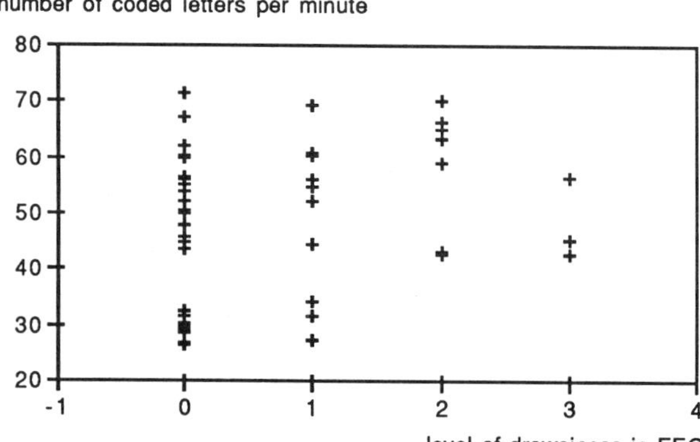

Figure 3. *Number of coded letters per minute in relation to level of drowsiness in the EEG. Each point (+) indicates one subject after one hour of VDU work (with or without breaks).*

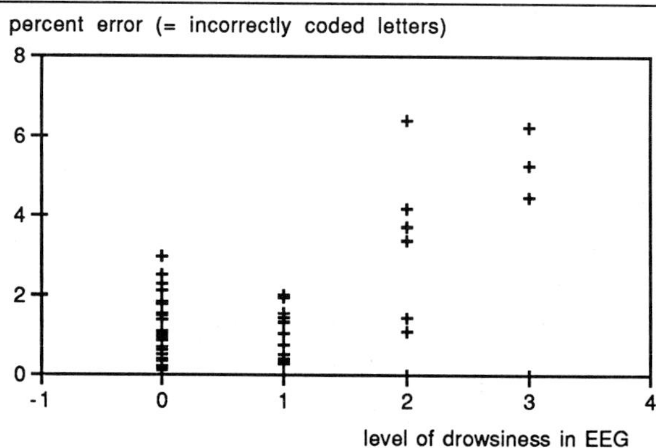

Figure 4. *Per cent incorrectly coded letters in relation to drowsiness in the EEG. Each point (+) indicates one subject after one hour of VDU work (with or without breaks).*

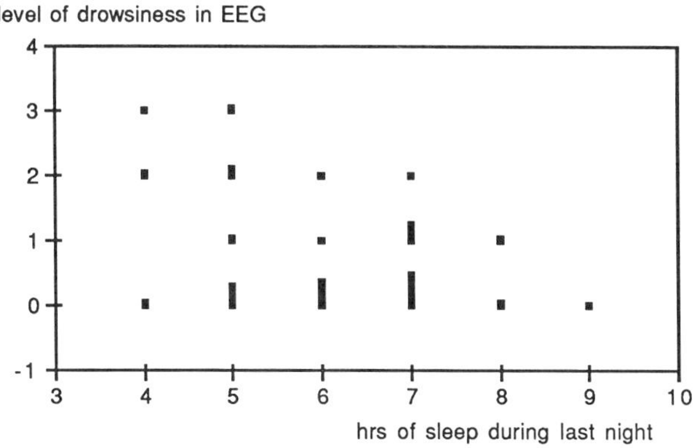

Figure 5. *The level of drowsiness in the EEG in relation to amount of sleep during the night before the experiment. Each point (square) indicates one subject for one day, i.e. all subjects appear on two places in the diagram as the experiments were performed on two separate days. The bars indicates two or more subjects, the hight of the bar relates to the number of subjects.*

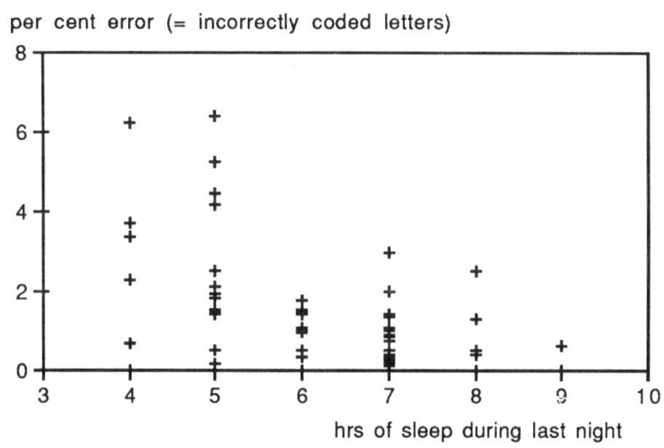

Figure 6. *Per cent incorrectly coded letters in relation to amount of sleep during the night before the experiment. Each point (+) indicates one subject after one hour of work (with or without breaks).*

From the tables and Figures 3-7, the following information can be drawn:

(1) No difference between drowsiness or performance during morning sessions as compared to afternoon sessions (Table I).

(2) A slight tendency to quantitatively higher performance (= higher number of coded letters per minute) during work with breaks as compared to work

without breaks (Table I).

(3) No relation between quantitative performance (= number of coded letters per minute) and level of drowsiness in EEG (Table II and Figure 3).

(3) A tendency to decreased qualitative performance (= higher per cent errors) during work without breaks as compared to work with breaks (Table I and Figure 7) .

(5) Decreased qualitative performance (= higher per cent errors) during work followed by clear signs of drowsiness in EEG as compared to those followed by no or only suspect drowsiness (Table III and Figure 4).

(6) The amount of sleep during the night before work shows a clear correlation with the amount of drowsiness in the EEG as well as the per cent incorrectly coded letters: The less sleep, the more drowsiness and the more mistakes (Figures 5 and 6).

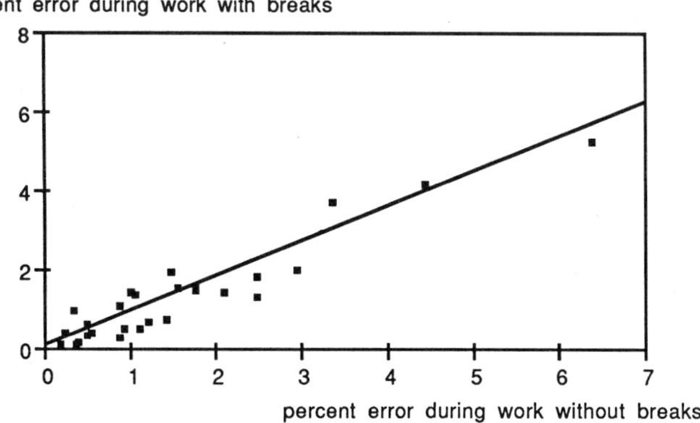

Figure 7. Per cent incorrectly coded letters at VDU work one hour without breaks in relation to work one hour with breaks. The regression line for these two parameters is also calculated and plotted in the diagram.

5. CONCLUSIONS

In several previous studies, VDU work has been related to changes in accommodation and convergence capacity [3,4,5]. However, in a recent study [6] no such effects could be demonstrated and the present results are in agreement with this.

The relations between quantitative and qualitative performance and level of vigilance are not surprising. However, we cannot, on the basis of the present results, demonstrate any influence of the organization of work (i.e. work during one hour without break or with short breaks every quarter) on those conditions. It is reasonable to assume that the presence of drowsiness we found in the EEG were more depending upon individual differences than upon any particular condition at work, as the tendency to drowsiness was found in the same subjects at both occasions of work (morning and afternoon sessions respectively) in spite of the fact that they were performed on different days and thus cannot be explained as an occasional effect. However, the amount of sleep during the night before the work has obviously an effect upon the performance: The less amount of sleep (as reported by the subjects themselves), the more mistakes during VDU coding work. But the total amount of work (i.e. the number of coded letters per minute) was not influenced by the amount of sleep.

Even if the organization of work did not have any effect upon the measured parameters, the subjects found the work with breaks less strenous than the uninterrupted one hour period and they also performed quantitatively slightly better when breaks were introduced. This speaks in favour of introducing short breaks during this type of work, even if the level of vigilance or the quality of work was not influenced thereby.

Further studies on this subject is needed, preferably with subjects in their ordinary work surroundings, and not, as in the present study, in a laboratory milieu.

REFERENCES

[1] Burian, HM., von Noorden GK., Binocular vision and ocular motility. The CV Mosby Company, Saint Louis, MO 1974, pp 203-207.

[2] Roth, B.,The clinical and theoretical importance of EEG rythms corresponding to states of lowered vigilance. Electroenceph. clin. Neurophysiol. 13: 395-399 (1961).

[3] Gunnarsson, E., Söderberg, I., Eye strain resulting from VDT work at the Swedish Telecommunications Administration. App. Egon. 14: 61-69 (1983).

[4] Mourant, R.R., Lakshmanan, R., Chantadisai, R., Visual fatigue and cathode ray tube display terminals. Hum. Factors. 23: 529-540 (1981).

[5] Östberg, O., Accommodation and visual fatigue in display work. Displays July: 81-85 (1980).

[6] Nyman, K.G., Knave, B.G., Voss, M., Work with video display terminals among office employees - IV. Refraction, accommodation, convergence and binocular vision. Scand. J. Work Environ. Health 11: 483-487 (1985).

WORK WITH DISPLAY UNITS 86
B. Knave and P.-G. Widebäck (eds.)

QUALIFIED CAD WORK: AN INTENSIVE CASE STUDY

Leif R. Hedman. Swedish Telecom Adm, Research Section, 123 86 Farsta, Sweden.

ABSTRACT

Fifteen mechanical engineering designers at a medium size machine industrial firm participated in an intensive case study which lasted for a total of 19 months. During this time, the designers were monitored continuously with respect to such variables as work satisfaction, commitment to their work, general stress and eyestrain. Various aspects of the work situation such as physical work conditions, functional characteristics of the CAD system, job content and creative climate were also assessed by the use of questionnaires and interviews. It was found that qualified CAD designers, as compared to a reference group of traditional design workers were committed to their work because of 1) greater opportunity to control their own tasks, 2)somewhat greater trust in their collegues at the department and 3) the feeling that the CAD system had improved the quality of their products. There were, however, no differential effects resulting from general stress, psychosomatic symptoms, eyestrain and degree of work satisfaction.

1 INTRODUCTION

Human factors in computer aided design (CAD) have, as yet, not been explored systematically and work in this field is considerably less advanced than that with the influential factors in more traditional VDU work (Grandjean, 1980). The findings presented so far regarding complaints associated with various CAD tasks differ extensively from one investigation to another (cf. Kjellberg, 1982; Waern, 1985; Wingert, 1983). One way of arriving at more systematic analyses in this area of study is to carry out case studies of relatively small groups of designers, in which physical, organizational and social factors are studied simultaneously during relatively long periods of time.

The present intensive case study is a first attempt to estimate the most important variables contributing to the work quality in a small group of qualified mechanical design engineers. More particularly, the principal aim was to study how CAD users and other designers doing analogous work without the aid of a computer differed with regard to factors such as eyestrain, general stress, work satisfaction and commitment under various conditions of physical work environment, job content and creative climate. Other factors to be considerd were the effects on the designers of factors related to the general information environment and management intervention within the designers' company.

2 METHOD

The present case study was primarily explorative in character. The study spanned a period of 19 months and during the best part of this period the investigator participated as an observer on each work day.

The location of the study was at a medium-sized mechanical industrial firm specializing in the production of short series of high-technology machines. During this period parallel studies of groups of users employing three different, data supported work methods were performed. Detailed results from the whole of the study are presented by Hedman (1986).

2.1 Participants

Fifteen mechanical designers working at the firm on a full-time basis volunteered to take part. All were male, with a mean age of 36 years. Their eye-status and general health were examined at the beginning of the study by an optician and the staff medical officer. On the basis of the nature of their work, the designers were regarded as belonging in two main groups, agroup of ten designers who had received training in CAD work (the 'CAD') and a matched reference group that had not received such training (the 'TRAD'). The CAD group was further subdivided into two groups, each containing 5 designers, called 'CAD-low' and 'CAD-high', respectively; the first group worked with CAD only a small proportion of their work time (0,5-1 hour per day), while the other worked mostly with CAD (6-8 hours per day). The mean age of the designers in the CAD-low, CAD-high and TRAD groups was 33, 39 and 35 years, respectively.

2.2 Design

In addition to the daily observation of the 15 designers, standardized interview data were collected at three test sessions 3, 7 and 14 months after the beginning of the study. At the first test session, data were collected in order to identify important positive and negative work factors, both within the design department and within the company as a whole. The findings from this first session were then used to determine which variables to concentrate on, as well as the kind of measuring instruments to use at the two subsequent test sessions. This design is shown in Table 1.

Table 1. Test sessions and groups tested in the study. The number of designers in each group is shown in parentheses.

Test session	1	2	3
Months after start	3	7	14
Groups tested	CAD (10) TRAD (5)	CAD-high (5) TRAD (5)	CAD-high (5) CAD-low (5) TRAD (5)

The instruments primarily used for collecting data at the test sessions were various semi-structured interviews. During the latter two sessions, latter two sessions, deep-interviews were also employedextensively. Complementary information was collected by the use of various test instruments developed by the author and other investigators. At session 1, 'The Wheel', an attitude test (5 items; Shalit, 1978), was used. At session 2, questionnaires were used for estimation a) influential factors in the work environment, work satisfaction etc (72 items; Rubenowitz, 1984); b) symptoms of negative stress (26 items; Brenner et al, 1983); and c) designers tasks, quality of information and communication within an organization(41 items; Hedman, 1986). At session 3, the following instruments wereused:a) the same as in session 2; b) a new questionnaire for self-judgement of the manner in which the CAD system directly affected the designers' job content and organization, their well-being and the quality of their work (25 items; Hedman, 1986); c) a questionnaire which mapped important CAD system functions for their effectiveness as an aid in the designers' work:

General function, man-machine interface, ease of use and mnemonic and cognitive support (32 items; Hedman, 1986; after Waern, 1985); and c) an instrument to estimate the socio-psychological situation and the creative climate in both the design department and the company as a whole (45 items; Ekvall et al, 1983).

2.3 Procedure

The first session took 1,5-2,5 hours and was carried out in a room adjoining the assembly hall. The length of time for each of the sessions 2 and 3 was approx. 45 minutes. The tests and interviews at the later sessions were administered individually (mostly at home). All the designers participated throughout the study and each served as his own control.

3 RESULTS

The SPSS statistical analysis package was used in the analyses of the results (ANOVAs, Student's t-tests). The results from session 1 show that the factors considered to be most negative in the CAD designers' work were a) the insufficient general information, b) the inferior planning in the company as a whole and c) the insufficient cooperation between the design department and other departments. The most positive characteristics of the design job were considered to be a) stimulating tasks and b) a good spirit of comradeship at the design department. There was no difference between the CAD workers and other designers in these respects.

The results from session 3 regarding the evaluation of the CAD system characteristics by the CAD-high group are shown in Figure 1. These results indicate that the mean values for all indices converged on the medium value. In their respones in other questionnaires (not reported here) the designers judged that the use of the CAD system had resulted directly in better design workmanship ($p<.05$). Furthermore all the CAD designers considerd that the system's technical functioning was good (mean value=3,72) and that the system facilitated their work to a certain degree (mean value= 3,16).

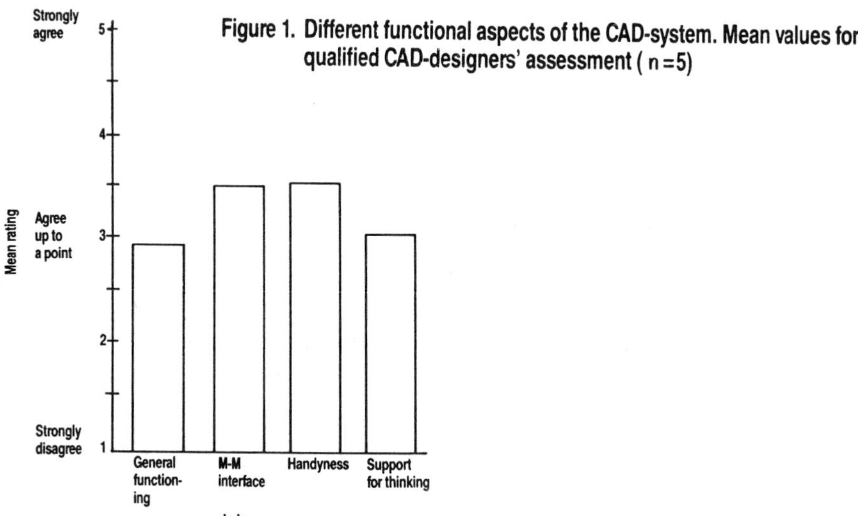

Figure 1. Different functional aspects of the CAD-system. Mean values for qualified CAD-designers' assessment (n =5)

Figure 2 shows that there was a statistically significant difference (p<.05) between the CAD-high and TRAD groups at the last test session in three important respects: The CAD designers judged themselves to a) have greater individual control of their tasks than the TRAD designers judged themselves to have b) be more committed than the TRAD designers and c) have better works manager climate and greater possibilities for individual task control than they had had 7 months earlier. There were no significant differences between the CAD-high and CAD-low groups. Among the factors which are believed to be important prerequisites for high work quality are work solidarity,stimulation from the work and creativity. The indices for all these factors were above medium for all the designers.

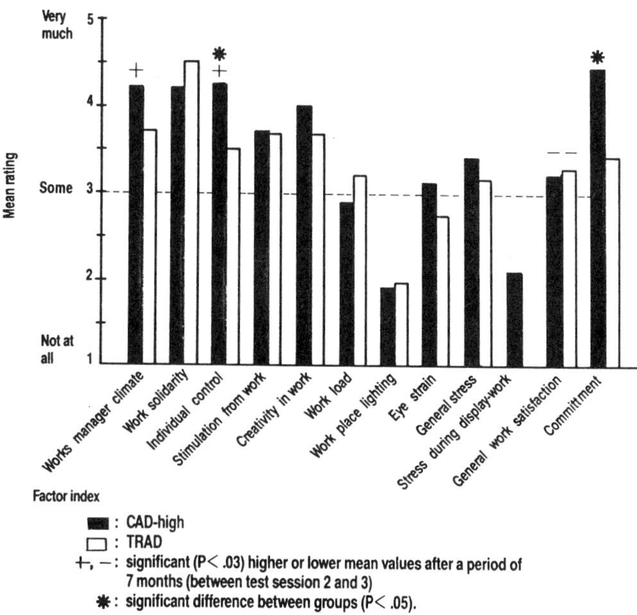

Figure 2. Difference in mean values for six basic characteristics in the CAD work environment and six indices of various effects for the qualified designers in two separate groups, CAD-high (n=5) and TRAD (n=5).

CAD-high and TRAD had both a medium work load as well as, in general, an acceptable physical work enviroment (mean index value=3,70). However, the factor 'work place lighting' had an unexpectedly low mean rating in both groups. Rating indices for several other factors, viz. eyestrain, general stress and work satisfaction, were at about medium levels in both groups. It is also interesting to note that the CAD designers rated the stress during display work as very low and that general work satisfaction was reduced in both the CAD and TRAD groups. One finding not shown in figure 2 was that the mean frequencies of psychosomatic symptoms, i. e. headache , gastric complaints and insomnia during the six months previous to the test were very low for all the designers.

Figure 3 shows the mean ratings for nine indices of creative climate. These were challenge, support for ideas, trust, freedom in the job, dynamism, tension, playfulness, debate and risk-taking.

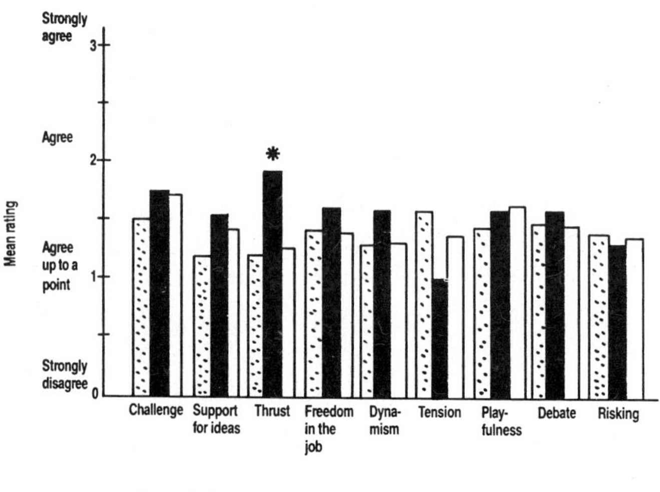

Figure 3. Mean values in the climate indices for all employees (Total, from Hedman, 1986) and for qualified designers (CAD high and TRAD).

The designers described the climate at their department as fairly indifferent, i. e. neither good nor bad and there were no statistically significant differences between the groups in this respect. A similar result was obtained regarding the judgement of all employees at the company of the work climate at the company as a whole. However, there was a strong tendency for the qualified CAD users to judge the 'trust' (e.g.' people do not talk about others behind their backs') in their department to be greater than in the company as a whole (p=.06) and the rating given by the CAD group was somewhat higher than that of the TRAD group in this respect (p=.06).

4 DISCUSSION

One central finding in this study was that the qualified CAD users, as compared to traditional designers were the ones most committed at the end of the study. This can be explained as being the result of a) improvements in the possibilities to control their own work b) somewhat greater trust in the colleques working at their own department and c) the judgement that the CAD system itself had improved the quality of their work. A further explanation along these lines would be that the judged improvement in individual control was not a direct consequence of the CAD-tool itself, but a secondary consequence. They had gained a greater professional competence which gave them a greater freedom of action in relation to their two chief designers, neither of whom were CAD users.

The somewhat higher trust (a tendency) shown by the qualified CAD users in relation to their own group may be seen to be a reflection of other social factors. The designer group as a whole and especially the CAD users, were frequently and for a number of reasons, criticized by some influential employees at other departments. This had the effect that the designers and particularly the CAD users, joined together.

Also, the marked reduction in the designers' work satisfaction may be seen as an effect of social factors outside the immediate CAD work environment. The main sources of this reduced satisfaction as well as the modestly creative climate could then be seen as being the result of a) the increasingly uncertain financial position of the company during the immediately preceding months, a process which had induced a general anxiety among all employees and b) the general insufficient internal communication and lax planning seen by the respondents to exist within the company.

The observed differences between the CAD users and the TRAD designers are not considered to be any selective 'Hawthorne effects' (cf. e. g. Adair, 1984). Although only limited groups of designers had been selected for extended study, all the employees of the company participated in the study and no individuals or groups were openly pointed out as being of special interest. It was subsequenly confirmed in the deep-interviews conducted after the last session that the CAD designers had not perceived themselves as being the object of any special attention during the study (cf. Hedman, 1986).

Another important result was that there were no differential general stress and eyestrain effects between the CAD and TRAD groups. Positive modulation of these factors in the results may have come about by a) perception of medium workload, b) ability to control and plan the work conveniently c) possibility for frequent rests and d) functional system characteristics at acceptable levels.

The finding that the CAD users' perception of their work condition did not differ much from that of their colleques who did not use that system, differs from the results obtained in several other investigations of CAD (cf. Wingert, 1983; Kjellberg, 1982). The present findings indicate that in this case there existed a good possibility for individual control and also that the CAD system function melted naturally into the designers' work process (cf. Waern, 1985).

It is concluded from the results of this study that when one studies the effects of CAD, as well as other work which requires the use of visual display units, it is often appropriate to start with an intensive case study of the group involved. Such as approach is, in the long run, an economical enterprise, since it will assist the investigator in identifying the most important independent and dependent variables to be used in subsequent studies.

ACKNOWLEDGEMENTS

I wish to express my thanks to the employees and trade unions at the company where the study was carried out for their cooperation: the County Government Board in Halland, FOSAM at Lund University and Televerket for their financial support and Drs Brenner, Ekvall, Rubenowitz and Shalit for allowing me to use their test instruments.

REFERENCES

ADAIR, J. G. (1984) The Hawthorne effect: A reconsideration of the methodological artifact. J. Appl. Psychol. 69, 334-345.

BRENNER, S. O & ARNETZ, B. (1983) The effects of job insecurity prior to, during and after notification of job loss. The first three measurements of response to unemployment in a group of workers enrolled in an intervention program. Research Report No 170, Laboratory for Clinical Stress Research, Stockholm, Sweden.

EKVALL, G. ARVONEN, J & WALDENSTRÖM-LINDBLAD, I. (1983) Creative organizational climate:Construction and validation of a measuring instrumentment. Report No 2, The Swedish Council for Management and Organizational Behavior, Stockholm, Sweden.

GRANDJEAN, E. (1980) Ergonomics of VDUs: Review of knowledge. In E. Grandjean and E. Vigliani (Eds.) Ergonomic Aspects of Visual Display Terminals. Pp 1-12. London: Taylor & Francis.

HEDMAN, L. R. (1986) Computer aided design: An intensive case study. Research Report, March 1986 (in swedish). Technology Dept, Swedish Telecommunications Administrations, Farsta, Sweden.

KJELLBERG, T. (1982) Integrated computer aid to support human problem on solving and communication for mechanical producion: A system approach based on product modelling. Doctoral dissertation (in swedish). Dept of Manufacturing Systems, KTH Stockholm.

RUBENOWITZ, S. (1984) Organizational Psychology and Management. Esselte Gothenburg.

SHALIT, B. (1978) Shalit perceptual organization and reduction questionnaire (SPORQ). Report C55021-H6. FOA, Stockholm.

WAERN, K-G. (1985) CAD as a work instrument. Report No 1 HUFACIT, Dept of Psychology, University of Stockholm, Sweden.

WINGERT, B. (1983) Technology induced morphogenesis of skills: The case of CAD. Paper presented at the First European Conference in Computer Applications in Production and Engineering, Amsterdam, April 1983.

WORK WITH DISPLAY UNITS 86
B. Knave and P.-G. Widebäck (eds.)

PROCESS CONTROL SOFTWARE DESIGN: HOW WILL THE OPERATORS WORK?

François DANIELLOU

Laboratoire d'Ergonomie et de Neurophysiologie du Travail
Conservatoire National des Arts et Métiers (*)

Research carried out in cooperation with:
M. BOEL, D. DESMARES, A. LAVILLE and C. TEIGER.

Problems raised by process control software design are presented with reference to research in a chemical plant which involved design engineers, operators and a team of ergonomists.

Continuous process industries are increasingly using computerized systems. These generally comprise a Digital Monitoring and Control System, which manages the control loops, and a computer which performs balance calculations and optimization functions. The interface between the control team and the computer system usually consists of VDUs and keyboards grouped in a control room.

Ergonomic involvement in the design of these devices mainly covers two aspects (DE KEYSER, 1980):

- the physical features of the hardware
- the control software.

The former topic has been widely covered at the conference. This paper will concentrate on the latter, with particular reference to research carried out in a French chemical plant. The technical framework of the research will be presented and basic problems which had to be solved will be indicated, with reference to the theoretical background brought into play by the team of ergonomists. The course of the operation will then be described and the results discussed.

1. TECHNICAL FRAMEWORK OF RESEARCH

The revamping of one plant in a large chemical complex included:

- modification of the process (same raw materials and products but different pressure and temperature conditions)

- the introduction in the control room of a Digital Monitoring and Control System instead of the conventional panels which were used previously.

The production workforce consisted of six shifts of 12 operators.

The involvement of an external team of ergonomists in the software design was requested by the management and the works committee.

It took place one year before start-up of the plant. At this stage, the hardware had already been ordered.

(*) 41 rue Gay-Lussac, 75005 PARIS

2. PROBLEMS TO BE SOLVED

The overall structure of the software resulted from the selected hardware: keyboard functions and rules for dialog had been designed and implemented by the supplier. The main points to be worked out were the division of parameters into screen pages and the page layouts. The problem may be formulated as follows: on the one hand, sensors located throughout the unit provide hundreds of parameters. On the other hand, one screen page can only display forty parameters at a time. How could the data be divided into screen pages?

Previous analyses in similar situations (e.g. BOEL et al, 1984) highlighted the importance of parameter distribution in order to prevent two types of drawback for the operator:

- process variations which are not described on the actual page displayed may be detected later;

- the need to change pages often, while processing a problem, is a strain on short-term memory and vision and may deeply affect the thought process itself, especially during incidents.

The most common approach to the design of screen pages is to assign one page to each main device and the corresponding parameters. This approach leads to underestimation of the following facts:

- most manoeuvres or incidents affect several devices which are interlinked for process reasons or for the sake of energy savings;

- relevant parameters of a device may differ according to the manoeuvre being carried out;

- different overview levels are required to monitor devices in steady state and those which are being operated.

3. AN ERGONOMIC APPROACH TO SOFTWARE DESIGN

To take these aspects into account, the guideline adopted was to work out a list of likely future tasks, group them in classes of task and design one screen page for each class of task. This, of course, implies redundancy between pages.

A distinction has to be made between the tasks which the operators will have to execute in the future plant (i.e. the intermediate targets they have to reach) and the activity they will use to reach these targets. Moreover, tasks are not only the operations specified in procedures (e.g. device start/stop). Many tasks are not specified in work organization: checking the reliability of a device, preventing and handling operation incidents, etc..

The difference between the prescribed work and real work (WISNER et al., 1985) generally involves the under-estimation, by designers and work organizers, of the industrial variability which operators have to deal with: raw materials, sensors and valves may not be assumed to be in a constant state; the operators have to detect their variations and take them into account at all times.

When a new information display system has to be designed for an existing process, the main classes of intervention may be established through an ergonomic analysis of the work done by operators. But in the case reported, some important features of the process itself were modified together with a change in the control system. Operations on the new system could not be observed. They had to be anticipated.

To adapt the structure of displays to the needs of future control activity, an attempt was made first of all to establish a list of future tasks through an analysis of likely causes of variability. This was done by means of a confrontation of operators' and design engineers' mental models (BAINBRIDGE, 1981).

On the one hand, design engineers contributed their knowledge of physico-chemical reactions of the process and of automatic devices planned in the new plant. On the other hand, operators had occupational experience of the variations of raw materials (e.g. their sensitivity to weather conditions), fluctuations of upline and downline conditions, breakdown, jamming or decalibration of devices and so on.

The confrontation was organized by the team of ergonomists on the basis of their knowledge of control activity in similar situations (e.g. BOEL et al., 1984).

4. COURSE OF RESEARCH

Research comprised three stages, each of which was based on six one-day work sessions with the production shifts.

At the start of the first stage, the shifts only had limited training in the main features of the new process. The approach at this stage was to have them explore the detailed drawings of future devices, with particular reference to the possible causes of malfunctions and the main manoeuvres.

As such, a large number of problems were raised by the operators. They were listed and forwarded to the design team which answered by means of a technical note dealing with two aspects:

- some problems required further information to be supplied to the operators
- others indicated difficulties which had been underestimated by designers and required new study.

The second stage

After the first stage, it was possible to establish groups of incidents or manoeuvres. To processs incidents belonging to the same group, operators required roughly the same sets of information and controls. With the help of the shifts, these groups were used to produce synoptic views intended to become screen pages.

Several types may be singled out:

- network synopses displaying the complete circuit of a product, enabling the execution of balance calculations, detection of leaks, etc.
- duty synopses, intended to provide information at shift changeover
- control synopses displaying the parameters and controls required for handling specific incidents.

On the basis of sketches worked out with the shifts, the layout of the synoptic views was designed by the technical team and the ergonomists, with reference to classical rules of information display design (DE KEYSER, 1980, DANIELLOU, 1986) concerning:

- physical features (legibility, choice of colours, etc.)
- connection between information search and action
- parameter grouping
- checkability of displayed values
- homogeneity.

The third stage consisted of a reconstitution, on these synoptic views, of the progress through time of main foreseeable manoeuvres. The views were then corrected and forwarded to the hardware supplier for implementation.

5. DISCUSSION

The work analysis carried out during start-up suggests that the part played by the operators in designing the synopses represented a significant contribution to their training on how to control the new process and handle the new system.

The anticipation of likely future tasks, carried out with the operators and design engineers, had consequences not only on the software but also on the design of production devices, for which alterations have been decided. This suggests that an earlier involvement of operators in the design of future devices might have led to a more efficient and cheaper integration of the elements of variability, of which designers are not always aware.

In process industries, an early introduction of ergonomics in the design process would appear to be an essential part of Project Management (DANIELLOU, 1986).

It is also a challenge for ergonomics itself, since its methods of work analysis have to be developed into means of approaching likely future activity.

REFERENCES

BAINBRIDGE L., 1981
Mathematical equations or processing routines pp 259 - 286
in: RASMUSSEN J., & ROUSE, W.B. (ed) 1981
Human Detection and Diagnosis of System Failures, 716 p.
NATO Conference Series - III - Human factors
Plenum Press, New York

BOEL M., et al., 1984
Elements of Process Control Operators' Reasoning: Activity
Planning and System and Process Response Times pp 1 - 8
in: WHITFIELD D., ed, 1984
Ergonomics Problems in Process Operations, 229 p.
Birmingham Conference 11 - 13 July
Pergamon Press, Oxford

DANIELLOU F., 1986
L'opérateur, la vanne, l'écran : l'ergonomie des salles de contrôle - 442 p.
Collection Outils et Méthodes
ANACT. Montrouge

DE KEYSER V., 1980
Etudes sur la contribution que pourrait apporter l'ergonomie à la conception des systèmes de contrôle et d'alerte dans les industries de transformations.
Commission des Communautés Européennes, Rapports S/79/45 et S/79/545, Brussels and Luxembourg

WISNER A., et al., 1985
Place of work analysis in software design, pp 147-156
in: SALVENDY G., ed, 1985
Human Computer Interaction
Elsevier Science Pub. B.V. Amsterdam.

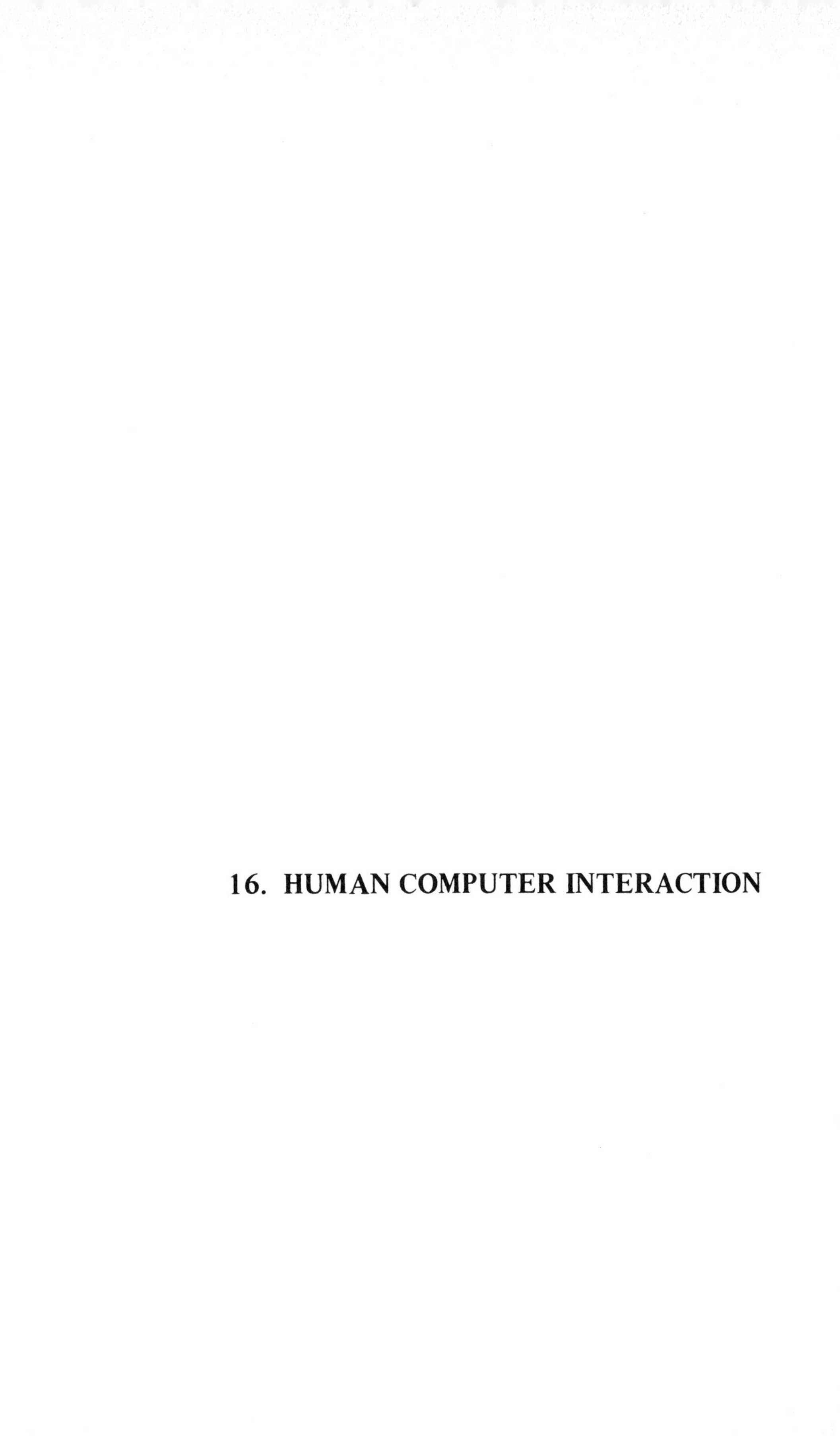

16. HUMAN COMPUTER INTERACTION

WORK WITH DISPLAY UNITS 86
B. Knave and P.-G. Widebäck (eds.)

An Evaluation of Mood Disturbances and Somatic Discomfort Under Slow Computer-Response Time and Incentive-Pay Conditions

LAWRENCE M. SCHLEIFER

Division of Biomedical and Behavioral Science
National Institute For Occupational Safety and Health
Cincinnati, Ohio, USA

This study evaluated the effects of slow computer-response time and incentive pay on mood disturbances and somatic discomfort in a data-entry task. Forty-five subjects worked under either rapid or slow computer-response time. All subjects received a base wage of $5.30 per hour for participating in the study. In addition, incentive pay for keystroke production was awarded to half the subjects in each response-time condition. Self-ratings of mood disturbances and somatic discomfort were taken at regular time intervals over four consecutive workdays. Slow response time generated higher ratings of frustration, impatience, and irritation than did rapid response time. With respect to method of pay, ratings of rush and tension were higher under incentive- than no-incentive-pay conditions.

1. INTRODUCTION

A rather extensive body of research has focused attention on psychosocial and physical strain in computer-mediated work. (See Dainoff [1] and Bergquist [2] for a review of this literature.) While considerable progress has been made in identifying physical working conditions that contribute to visual and musculoskeletal strain in automated office work, the role of complex job-design features and computer-system performance characteristics has been more difficult to delineate. These latter factors are thought to induce psychosocial stress reactions that may have major implications for worker health [3-5].

One aspect of system design that may be a source of stress is slow computer-response time. Johansson and Aronsson [6], for example, found that 63% of the VDT users at an insurance company would not tolerate delays of longer than 5 seconds. "Mental strain" was also found to occur with delayed response time and unscheduled system downtime. In a survey of main-frame users, the Datapro Corporation [7] found that only 56% of 1578 respondents were satisfied with response time. Barber and Lucas [8] reported that user satisfaction dropped during work sessions in a large utility where response time was slow.

Typically, the response time to user inputs or commands increases when a computer system is heavily utilized. Under these conditions, the usual workpace required to perform a given task may be disrupted, and the user may experience considerable frustration and deadline pressure due to lost production time [3].

The work of Lazarus and co-workers [9-10] provides a general framework for understanding the potential stress effects of computer response delays. These investigators have demonstrated the importance of daily hassles in producing symptoms of stress. Daily hassles are annoying, frustrating minor events of everyday life such as misplacing important papers, traffic jams, or repeated telephone interruptions. Based on this stress paradigm, chronic computer delays can be considered a "technological hassle" and may have implications for worker health.

Another potential source of stress in computer-mediated work is the pay regimen or reward system. Computers can be used to monitor keystroke production and administer wage-incentive or piece-rate programs. These alternative pay practices may lead to increased workload and time pressures. Moreover, the worker may be compelled to suppress feelings of tension and fatigue in an effort to earn higher pay.

Levi [11] found among a group of invoicing clerks that self-reported feelings of "rush," "physical discomfort," and "fatigue" increased significantly from salaried to piece-wage conditions; adrenaline and noradrenaline levels were also significantly higher under piece wages. In a series of investigations, Cakir, Hart, and Stewart [12] found that video-display-terminal (VDT) users who performed a data-entry task were more likely to report being "strongly controlled at work" than other types of users such as programmers. It was also reported that VDT typists under piece-work conditions experienced more mood disturbance and "strain" than VDT typists under nonpiece-work conditions.

On the other hand, the use of alternative methods of remuneration have some desirable consequences. Performance incentives may raise productivity and improve worker satisfaction [13]. In addition, incentives may diminish the monotony or chronic under-stimulation that is frequently associated with routine, repetitive office work. Hence, any evaluation of computer-administered pay practices must attend to the possibility of such favorable effects.

The present laboratory study is part of a broad, programmatic research effort directed toward examining stress reactions in computer-mediated work. It was designed to test the hypothesis that slow computer-response time will generate higher levels of mood disturbances than rapid computer-response time among workers performing a data-entry task. Another objective of this study was to evaluate the effects of incentive pay on mood disturbances and somatic discomfort.

2. METHODS

2.1. Subjects

Subjects were 45 female typists (mean age = 28) recruited from a clerical-secretarial agency. All subjects received a comprehensive medical exam and met the following selection criteria: (a) good general health--no heart disease or hypertension; (b) corrected visual acuity of 20:20; (c) no medication except aspirin; (d) not pregnant; and (e) typing speed of at least 45 words per minute with no errors.

2.2. Data-Entry Task

The task performed by the subjects was developed by Dainoff [14], and consisted of entering records at a VDT from paper copy into a computerized data base. Each record contained eleven fields of alphanumeric information from a chemical stock inventory. Data entries were made in response to a series of prompts displayed on a video screen. A sample record follows:

Prompt	Sample entry
Record Number	R100
Part Name	5-Sulfamyl
Stock Number	A320251XL3
Manufacturer	Akro-Mils, Inc.
Street Address	212 Railroad Drive
City, State	Atlanta, GA.
Zip Code	50321
Phone	654-0871
Bin Number	2156
Price	$532.20
Location Code	B3R25S227

Subjects commenced the task by entering the appropriate information next to the "Record Number" prompt and pressing the return or "field termination" key. Data entries were made in a similar manner until the last field of information for a given record (i.e., Location Code) was completed. This task cycle was then repeated for the next record.

2.3. Task Conditions

Subjects performed the data-entry task under one of four randomly-assigned conditions:

Rapid response time (RR)/No-incentive pay (NI). Subjects assigned to this condition received $5.30 per hour for participating in the study. A computer response delay of 350 milliseconds occurred after entering a field of information and striking the return key. During this delay interval, the computer would not accept any data inputs.

Slow response time (SR)/No-incentive pay (NI). Subjects assigned to this condition received $5.30 per hour for participating in the study. Response delays of longer duration than the RR condition were presented. A sample schedule designed to maximize user uncertainty regarding the frequency and duration of the response delays is shown in Figure 1. In Figure 1, "A" intervals consisted of response delays of 350 milliseconds in duration that occurred each time a field of information was completed over a 1-minute period of data entries. "B" intervals consisted of random response delays of 350 milliseconds and delays varying from 3-10 seconds that occurred each time a field of information was completed over a 1-minute period of data entries. The "A" and "B" intervals alternated randomly, but no more than 3 similar intervals were ever presented consecutively.

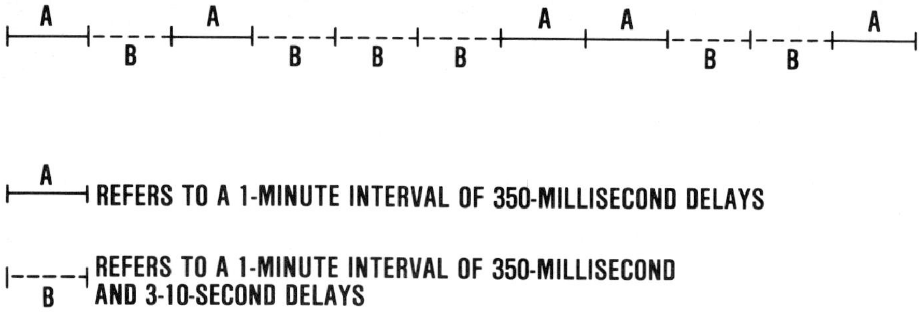

A A A A A
B B B B B B

A REFERS TO A 1-MINUTE INTERVAL OF 350-MILLISECOND DELAYS

B REFERS TO A 1-MINUTE INTERVAL OF 350-MILLISECOND AND 3-10-SECOND DELAYS

FIGURE 1
A sample schedule of response delays under the SR condition.

Rapid response time (RR)/Incentive pay (I). Data entries were made under rapid response-time conditions. Subjects assigned to this condition received a base wage of $5.30 per hour for participating in the study. In addition, subjects were awarded 10 cents for each keystroke per minute above their pre-study baseline, but penalized 5 cents for each error per minute above baseline.

Slow response time (SR)/Incentive pay (I). Data entries were made under slow response-time conditions. Subjects received a base wage of $5.30 per hour for participating in the study. In addition, subjects were awarded 10 cents for each keystroke per minute above their pre-study baseline, but penalized 5 cents for each error per minute above baseline.

2.4. Measures

2.4.1. Mood Disturbances

The scale items and scoring method for the self-evaluation measures of mood disturbances are shown in Table 1. Subjects were instructed to indicate on a continuum from 1 (not at all) to 9 (very much so) the extent to which the scale items for each measure reflected their mood state. Cronbach's alpha coefficients were above .90 for every measure except Impatience (.82).

2.4.2. Somatic Discomfort

The scale items comprising the self-evaluation measures of somatic discomfort shown in Table 1 were developed by Dainoff [14]. The response format for these measures was the same as that used for the measures of mood disturbances. Cronbach's alpha coefficients were above .90 for every measure except Trunk/Legs Discomfort (.72).

TABLE 1

Measures of Mood Disturbances and Somatic Discomfort

Mood Disturbances

Frustration	=	(interrupted + obstructed + impeded + blocked) / 4
Rushed	=	(pressed for time + rushed + hurried) / 3
Impatience	=	(slowed down + impatience) / 2
Irritation	=	(annoyance + aggravation + irritation / 3
Tension	=	(tension + on edge + keyed up) / 3
Fatigue	=	(fatigue + tiredness + weariness + sluggishness / 5

Somatic Discomfort

Visual discomfort	=	(focusing problems + eye irritation + eye fatigue) / 3
Arm/Hands discomfort	=	(arms + wrists + hands or fingers) / 2
Trunk/Legs discomfort	=	(neck, shoulders or upper back + lower back + legs) / 3

2.5. Apparatus

The study was conducted in a simulated, VDT workplace at the Human Performance Laboratories of the National Institute for Occupational Safety and Health. Three VDT workstations were equipped with ergonomic tables and chairs, wrist supports, contrast enhancement filters, and copyholders. Overhead fluorescent lighting fixtures were fitted with diffusing lenses. Ambient illumination levels on the work tables were set at 50 footcandles. All ergonomic adjustments were made on an individual basis in order to maximize physical comfort. A PDP 11/34, real-time computer operating system was used to simulate the task conditions, collect response data, and control the video display terminals.

2.6. Procedure

Following informed consent, the subjects were randomly assigned to one of four task conditions: RR + NI (n = 11), SR + NI (n = 12), RR + I (n = 10), or SR + I (n = 12). The study was conducted over four consecutive days (Days 1, 2, 3, and 4), with each day consisting of a morning and afternoon session (Sessions 1 and 2). Each session was further divided into a pre-session period (Period 0) and three 50-minute work periods (Periods 1, 2, and 3). Self-ratings of mood disturbances and somatic discomfort were taken at the beginning of a session (Period 0) and again at the end of each work period (Period 1, 2, 3). There was a 45-minute lunch break between the morning and afternoon sessions. A 10-minute rest was also taken at the midpoint of the second work period in the morning and afternoon sessions.

The first day of the study was devoted to familiarizing the subjects with the VDT workplace, making appropriate workstation adjustments, and practicing the data-entry task. Baseline measures of mood disturbances and somatic discomfort were established on the second day of the study. During this time subjects performed the data-entry task under RR + NI conditions. At the end of the second day, subjects were informed of their assignment to task conditions. Data entries were made on the third and fourth days of the study under the various response-time and method-of-pay conditions. Subjects assigned to the RR + I or SR + I conditions received feedback regarding the amount of incentive pay earned at the end of each work period after completing their self-ratings of mood disturbances and somatic discomfort.

2.7. Experimental design and data analyses

A mixed-factorial repeated-measure design was employed in which the between factors were Response Time (RR or SR) and Method of Pay (NI or I), and the within factor was Day (2, 3, or 4). Multivariate analyses of variance on repeated measures were performed using General Linear Models [15]. These analyses were carried out primarily to determine whether there were Response Time X Day or Method of Pay X Day interactions, since this demonstrates a change from baseline measures of mood disturbances and somatic discomfort.

Since Day 1 was devoted to subject orientation and task practice, the observations for this day were not included in the data analyses. An initial analysis of the data collected on Day 2 (baseline) indicated that the four groups were statistically equivalent on measures of mood disturbances and somatic discomfort. In addition, the mean age and standard deviation for each group of subjects were highly comparable: RR + NI = 27 (6.0); SR + NI = 26 (5.6); RR + I = 30 (7.9); SR + I = 28 (7.9).

3. RESULTS

3.1. Response Time

Consistent with the study hypothesis, the mean ratings of Frustration and Impatience, which are plotted in Figure 2, were higher for the SR than RR conditions. Multivariate analyses of variance on repeated measures indicated that there was a significant main effect for Response Time on measures of Frustration, $F(1, 41) = 8.32$, $p < .01$; and Impatience, $F(1, 41) = 5.50$, $p < .05$. More importantly, there were significant Response Time X Day interactions on measures of Frustration, $F(2, 40) = 11.05$, $p < .001$; Impatience, $F(2, 40) = 19.73$, $p < .001$; and Irritation, $F(2, 40) = 8.33$, $p < .001$.*

Pair-wise contrasts performed on the within Day factor indicated that, in comparison to Day 2, ratings of Frustration and Impatience were higher for SR than RR on Day 3 and Day 4.

[Day 3: Frustration, $t(41) = 4.49$, $p < .005$, one-tailed test; Impatience, $t(41) = 5.64$, $p < .005$, one-tailed test]

[Day 4: Frustration, $t(41) = 3.26$, $p < .005$, one-tailed test; Impatience, $t(41) = 2.98$, $p < .005$, one-tailed test]

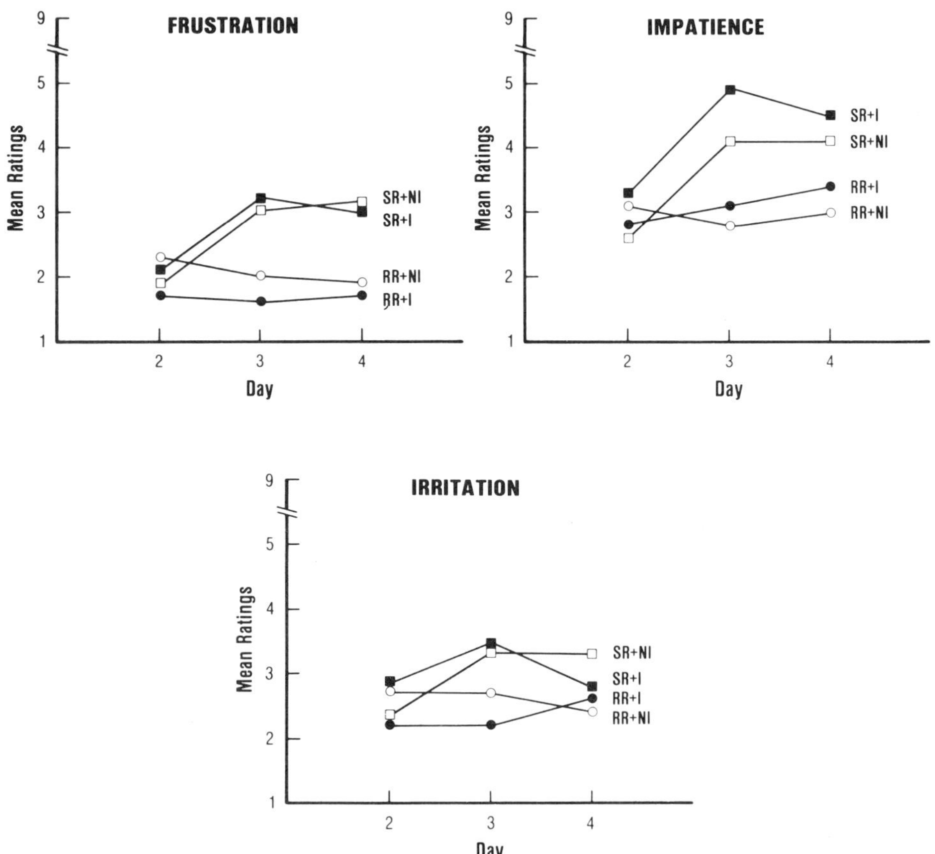

FIGURE 2
Mean ratings of mood disturbances as a function of Day and Group.

Inspection of Figure 2 shows that, in comparison to Day 2, the ratings of Irritation were higher for SR than RR on Day 3 [t (41) = 3.37, $p < .005$, one-tailed test]. The Response Time X Day effect for this measure did not carry over to Day 4. However, there was a significant Response Time X Method of Pay X Day interaction for Irritation, F (1, 41) = 5.06, $p < .05$, indicating that in comparison to Day 2, ratings for this measure were higher for SR + NI than RR + NI on Day 4.

3.2. Method of Pay

The mean ratings across days for measures of Rush, Tension and Fatigue are shown in Figure 3. Multivariate analyses of variance on repeated measures indicated that there was a significant Method of Pay X Day interaction on measures of Rush, F (2, 40) = 9.01, $p < .001$; Tension, F (2, 40) = 4.80, $p < .05$; and Fatigue, F (2, 40) = 3.74, $p < .05$.

Inspection of Figure 3 reveals that the mean ratings across days of Rush and Tension were higher for the I than the NI conditions. With respect to Fatigue, however, the mean ratings across days were lower for the I than NI conditions.

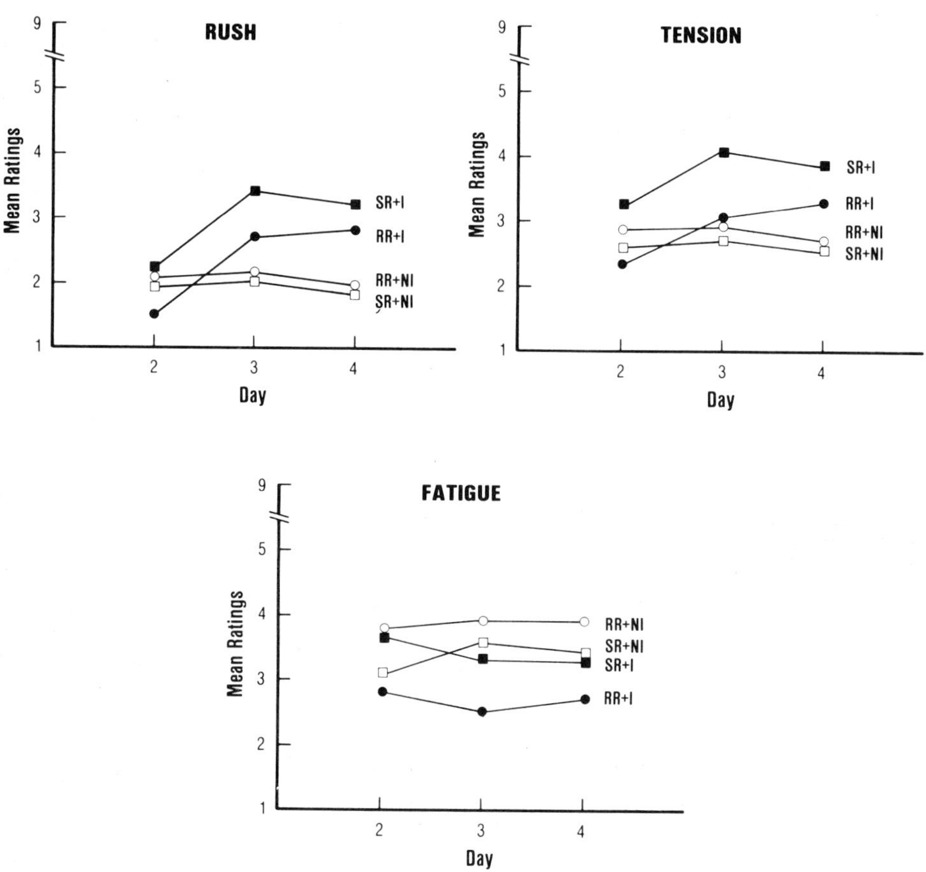

FIGURE 3
Mean ratings of mood disturbances as a function of Day and Group.

Pair-wise contrasts performed on the within Day factor indicated that, in comparison to Day 2, self-ratings of Rush and Tension were higher for I than NI on Day 3 and Day 4.

[Day 3: Rush, $F(1, 41) = 17.60$, $p < .001$;
Tension, $F(1, 41) = 8.59$, $p < .01$]

[Day 4: Rush, $F(1, 41) = 10.65$, $p < .01$;
Tension, $F(1, 41) = 8.55$, $p < .01$]

With respect to Fatigue, the self-ratings, in comparison to Day 2, were lower under I than NI conditions on Day 3 [$F(1, 41) = 7.38$, $p < .01$]. However, the lower ratings of Fatigue did not carry over to Day 4.

4. CONCLUSIONS

Consistent with the study hypothesis, it was found that slow response time generated higher ratings of mood disturbances than did rapid response time. This finding is in general accordance with those of Lazarus and co-workers [9-10] regarding the association of daily hassles with psychological symptoms. Overall, the results of this study indicate that there is a psychological basis for improving computer response time.

With respect to Method of Pay, it was found that ratings of rush and tension were higher under incentive-pay conditions. These results are consistent with those of Levi [11] who obtained an increased sense of rush, and elevated adrenaline and noradrenaline levels under wage-incentive conditions. This kind of psychological activation also may be associated with deleterious behavior patterns (e.g., Type A) [16]. Hence, there is a need for further research on the psychophysiological effects of computer-based incentive-pay systems.

ACKNOWLEDGMENTS

The following individuals deserve recognition for their contribution to various aspects of this study: B. Amick, M. Cady, E. Fullman, R. Ley, R. McFarland, S. Sauter, M. Smith, J. Stevens.

FOOTNOTES

*The potential for multiple comparison errors was not examined. However, the possibility of such errors was minimized by grouping the indicators of mood disturbances and somatic discomfort into two homogeneous subsets of dependent measures. Moreover, the consistent divergence between Response Time and Method of Pay effects on measures of mood disturbances suggests that the probability of multiple comparison errors was relatively low.

REFERENCES

[1] Dainoff, M. J. (1982). Occupational stress factors in visual display terminals. Behavior & Information Technology, 1, 141-176.

[2] Bergquist, U. O. (1984). Video display terminals and health. Scandinavian Journal of Work Environment and Health, 10, (Supplement 2), 1-87.

[3] National Research Council. (1983). Video displays, work, and vision. Washington, D. C.: National Academy Press.

[4] Turner, J. and Karasek, R. (1984). Software ergonomics: effects of of computer application design parameters on operator task performance and health. Ergonomics, 27, (6), 663-690.
[5] U. S. Congress, Office of Technology Assessment. (1985). Automation of America's offices (OTA-CIT-287). Washington, D. C.: U.S. Government Printing Office.
[6] Johansson, G. and Aronsson, G. (1984). Stress reactions in computerized administrative work. Journal of Occupational Behavior, 5, 159-181.
[7] Datapro Corporation. (1983). User ratings of computer systems. Delran, New Jersey: Author.
[8] Barber, R. E. and Lucas, H. C. (1983). System response time, operator productivity, and job satisfaction (CRIS # 31, GBA # 82-11). New York University, New York: Center for Research on Information Systems.
[9] Delongis, A., Coyne, J. C.. Dakof, G., Folkman, S., and Lazarus, R. S. (1982). Relationship of daily hassles, uplifts and major life events to health status. Health Psychology, 1, (2), 119-136.
[10] Kanner, A. D., Coyne, J. C., Schaefer, C. and Lazarus, R. S. (1981). Comparison of two models of stress measurement. Journal of Behavioral Medicine, 4, 1-39.
[11] Levi, L. (1964). The stress of everyday work as reflected in productiveness, subjective feelings, and urinary output of adrenaline and noradrenaline under salaried and piece work conditions. Journal of Psychosomatic Research, 8, 199-202.
[12] Cakir, A., Hart, D. J. and Stewart, T. F. M. (1979). The VDT manual. Darmstadt, West Germany: IFRA.
[13] Katzell, R. A., Yankelovich, D., Fein, M., Ornati, O., and Nash A. (1975). Work, Productivity, and Job Satisfaction. New York: The Psychological Corporation.
[14] Dainoff, M. J., Fraser, L., and Taylor, B. J. (1982). Visual, musculoskeletal and performance differences between good and poor VDT workstations: preliminary findings. In Proceedings of the Human Factors Society 26th Annual Meeting. Seattle, Washington: Human Factors Society.
[15] SAS Institute. (1985). SAS User's Guide: Statistics, Version 5. Cary, North Carolina: Author
[16] Glass, D. (1977). Behavior patterns, stress, and coronary disease. New York: Halstead Press.

WORK WITH DISPLAY UNITS 86
B. Knave and P.-G. Widebäck (eds.)

THE APPLICABILITY OF EYE MOVEMENT ANALYSIS IN THE ERGONOMIC EVALUATION OF HUMAN-COMPUTER INTERACTION

W. Graf, F. Sigl, G. van der Heiden and H. Krueger
Department of Ergonomics and Hygiene, Swiss Federal Institute of Technology, CH-8092 Zürich, Switzerland.

Computer aided eye movement registration was applied for the analysis of human-computer interaction. The mental strain, caused by different tasks was estimated and the difficulty of 10 different tasks could be scaled. The results of the simulation study show a relationship between the subjective assessment of the human-computer interaction by a group of users and the duration of eye fixations as well as the amplitude of eye saccades.

1. INTRODUCTION

The Swiss Federal Railways are introducing VDTs to sell tickets. More than 700 railway operators have to be trained for this new computer system, most of them with no previous computer experience. All possible transactions to sell tickets shall be executed by the same VDT work-station, using 10 different tasks.

Our aim was to build up the VDT work station with regard to software-ergonomical criteria, to enable the users to learn to use each task with minimum difficulty and apply them with maximum efficiency.

The problem we solved can be divided into two phases.

In phase 1 the different masks and the human-computer interaction were built up according to the existing literature as well as from our own experience during the programing phase.
In phase 2 we tried, with the help of field research, to judge the programs according to ergonomic criteria. The judgment was partly done by conventional methods like observing the operator during his work on the VDT, as well as with the help of questionnaires. Furthermore we also used a method which continuously registered the eyemovements to evaluate the human-computer interaction.

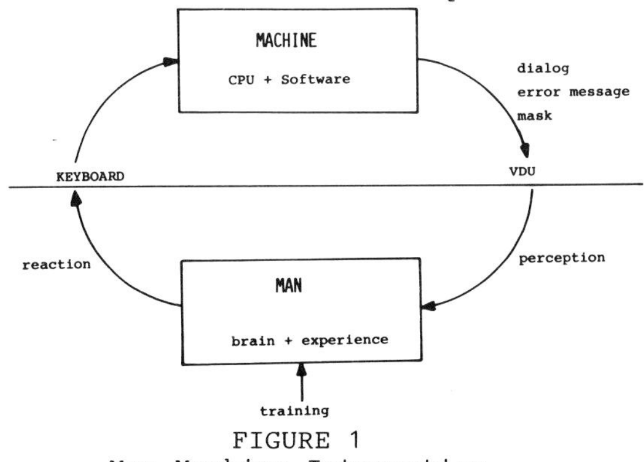

FIGURE 1
Man-Machine Interaction

Figure 1 shows a model of a Man-Machine Interaction. The machine presents it's information on the VDU. The man perceives the information with the eye and after processing the information in the brain, he reacts. By measuring the eyemovements we get information of the perception, which gives us more detailed information about a task than if we measure the reaction only.

In the following part, the evaluation of the eye movement registration is described.

2. METHODS

2.1. Mask design

```
SCHNELL      Verbindungen SCHWEIZ - Schnellzugriff Sortiment 1      Schalter:   07
                                                                    Verkäufer: SLR
01 AARAU         11 'BOWIL         21 CRANS         31 GRINDELWALD   41 KEHRSATZ
02 ADELBODEN     12 BRIENZ         22 DäRLIGEN      32 GROSSHöCHST   42 KERZERS
03 AIGLE         13 BRIG           23 DüDINGEN      33 GüMLIGEN      43 KIESEN
04 BADEN         14 BRUGG AG       24 FAULENSEE     34 GüMMENEN      44 KONOLFINGEN
05 BASEL SBB     15 BRüGG BE       25 FILLISTORF    35 GUNTEN        45 LANGENTHAL
06 BEATENBUCHT   16 BURGISTEIN-    26 FLAMATT       36 HERZOGENBUC   46 LANGNAU
07 BELP          17 BURGDORF       27 FRIBOURG      37 HINDELBANK    47 LAUFEN
08 BERN BüMPLI   18 BUSSWIL        28 FRUTIGEN      38 INS           48 LAUPEN
09 BERN STöCHA   19 CHENENS        29 GENEVE        39 INTERLAKEN    49 LAUSANNE
10 BIEL/BIENNE   20 CHUR           30 GRENCHEN Sü   40 KANDERSTEG    50 LAUTERBRUNN

Bestimmung ...... :                       Gültig 10.09.84 - 09.10.84

Anzahl Ganze .... : 0                     BERN
       Halbe .... : 1                     AARAU


Totalbetrag Fr    14.00                   2. Kl   HR   1/2        Fr    14.00

                                          Hauptauswahl  =   CTRL -EXIT
```

FIGURE 2
Example of a final mask design

Figure 2 shows an example of a final mask design. The window is divided into four parts. On the top of the screen the status information is displayed. The lower left part is the main working area. The upper large window is a lexicon to select the code of the train destinations. The lower right window gives the form of the final version of the ticket. It is the control-field to be used before pushing the print key.

An example of a task : For a ticket to Geneva, the operator has to look for the code (29), then he has to key in the code, as well as the number of tickets etc. and finally he has to push the printing key.

2.2. Some thoughts to the eye-movement analysis

Subjects working with VDT's explore and analyze the VDU contents by repeating saccadic eye movement and fixation. Rayner [1] concluded, that saccade length and fixation duration represent independent aspects of eye behavior. Bouma [2] reported that during saccadic eye movements no information is accepted, all information being accepted during the fixation of eye movement. Witruk [3] reported that parameters of eye movement such as fixation times, fixation points, speed, amplitude and frequency of eye movements are determined globally by the stimulus pattern, but also depend, in many specific ways, on cognitive components of information processing.

Because the eye-movement behaviour depends mainly on the stimulus pattern and on cognitive components of information processing, the complexity of different tasks can be estimated according to the behavior of the eye-movements.

In our experiment, the eye positions were scanned by an Applied Science Laboratory EYE-TRACK 200 and the data stored on a computer.

2.3. Procedure and subjects of the experiment

Subjects:
Six untrained subjects who only got a short instruction and six trained subjects were used for the experiments.

Procedure:
The subjects had to produce several requested tickets in a simulated sale situation. The trained operators had a choice of 10 different tasks, whereas the untrained only had 4. It was possible for the operator to move his eyes between the VDU and the keyboard. The registration of eye movements gave us not only information on the scanning of the mask, but also on the whole human-computer interaction.

3. RESULTS OF EYE MOVEMENT REGISTRATION AND DISCUSSION

3.1. Eye movement performance of trained operators

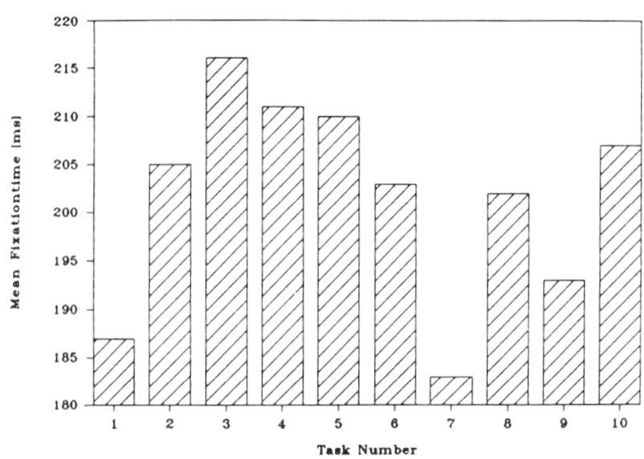

FIGURE 3
Mean fixation times for trained operators

Figure 3 shows the mean fixation times, averaged for trained operators using ten different tasks.

Based on the assumption, that longer fixation times are due to a more difficult stimulus pattern or more difficult cognitive components of information processing, it can be assumed that the tasks with short fixation time (1, 7 and 9) are easy to work with. On the other hand, tasks 3, 4 and 5 result in longer fixationtime. Thus working with this tasks will generally create more mental strain.

3.2. Comparison of trained and untrained operators

Both groups used the same tasks with identical stimulus patterns, that's why we can estimate the influence of cognitive components of information processing. Three tasks are compared.

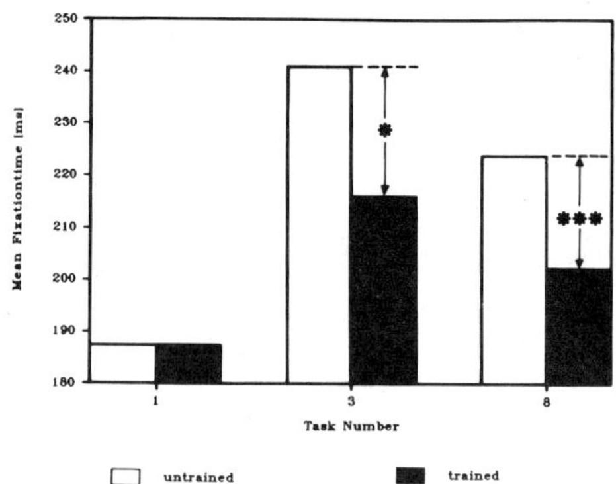

FIGURE 4
Mean fixation time of trained and untrained operators

Figure 4 shows the mean fixation times of trained and untrained operators. Task 1 seems to be very simple, because the fixation time for both groups, trained and untrained, are the same. Task 3 and 8 however show significant differences between these two groups what leads to the assumption, that these tasks are more difficult for untrained operators. We have the same stimulus pattern, but, according to the training, the cognitive component of information processing is faster for trained operators.

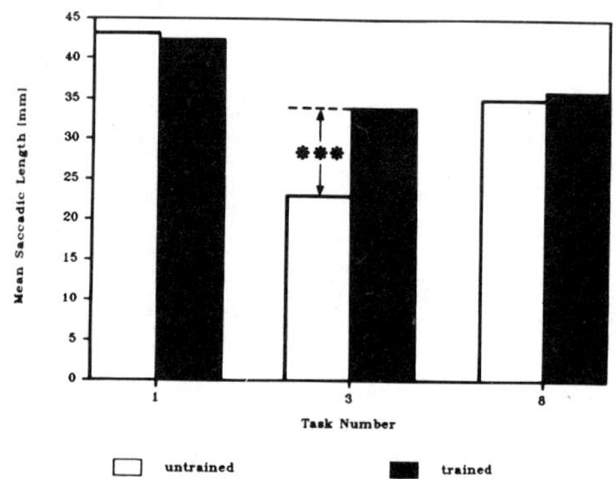

FIGURE 5
Mean saccadic length of trained and untrained operators

The saccadic length depends mainly on the density of the stimulus and on cognitive components. Figure 5 shows, that for task 3, we measured significant smaller saccadic lengths.

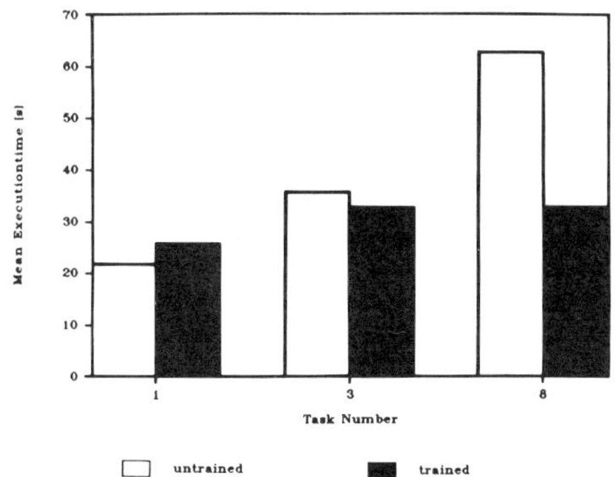

FIGURE 6
Mean execution time of trained and untrained operators

Figure 6 shows, that task 8 resulted in a longer execution time.

By comparing trained and untrained operators, we could see, how cognitive components influence the eye movement parameters.

3.3. A scale of the tasks according to the eye movement results

A scale, which shows the degree of difficulty of the 10 tasks, was prepared according to the measured eye movement parameters from the trained operators.

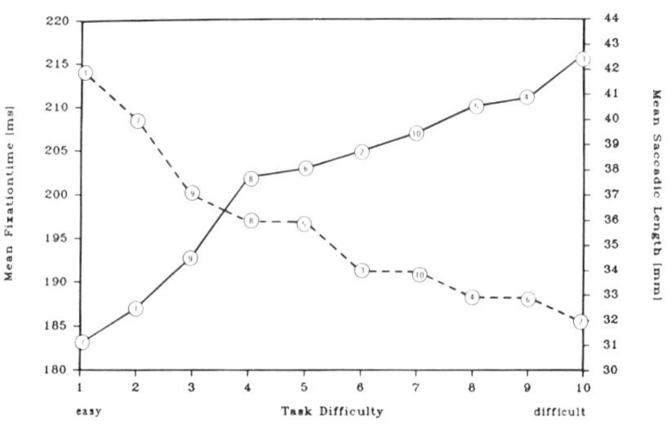

FIGURE 7
A scale of task difficulty according to the eye movement results. The according task numbers are shown in the circle.

Short fixation times as well as long saccadic distances are represented as an easy task. All ten tasks are shown on the graph with increasing difficulty. Short fixation times are represented as easy tasks, whereas long fixation time represent difficult tasks. We did the same with the saccadic length. Long saccadic distances are represented as an easy task, short saccadic distances as a difficult task.

With reference to fixation time as well as saccadic length, the tasks 1, 7, 9 and 8 can be termed as easy (short fixation, long saccadic length). The mental strain seems to be small and the clarity seems to be sufficient. Of special interest are the tasks 2 and 6 as well as 5 and 3. For these tasks, the fixation times and saccadic length are scaled quite different. The results for the tasks 3 and 5 indicate, that a reasonably arranged mask was used, however, it caused a heavy mental load. Task 6 required the operator mainly to enter information by the keyboard, which resulted in very short saccadic distances, because the entered text was continuously visually controlled on the VDT. The results of task 2 could not be explained.

According to the answers on the questionnaires the tasks 1, 2, 8 and 9 were estimated significantly as easy without any exception. Task 10 was rated as very difficult.

4. CONCLUSIONS

With the help of eye-movement registration it was possible to estimate the mental strain caused by the human-computer interaction for different tasks. We got a hint for which tasks the dialog has to be improved or the task has to be trained more intensive. Because the experiment was not performed in the laboratory, it was impossible to clearly establish the factor which influence the saccadic length as well as fixation times for all the difficult tasks. Thus it seems, that the eye-movement registration gives valid information for a global analysis of human-computer interaction, and we hope, that a further improved evaluation of eye-movement data will allow a more differentiated analysis of the human-computer interaction.

REFERENCES

[1] Bouma, H., Visual reading processes and the quality of text displays, in: Grandjean, E. and Vigliani, E., (eds.), Ergonomic Aspects of Visual Display Terminals (Taylor & Francis Ltd, London and Philadelphia, 1980) pp. 101-114.

[2] Rayner, K., Eye movements in reading and information processing, Psychological Bulletin 85 (1978) pp 618-660.

[3] Witruk, E., Eye movements as a process indicator of interindividual differences in cognitive information processing, in: Groner, R. and Fraisse, P., (eds.), Cognition and Eye Movements (North-Holland, Amsterdam, 1982) pp. 194-203.

WORK WITH DISPLAY UNITS 86
B. Knave and P.-G. Widebäck (eds.)

EYE-HEAD-COORDINATION AND INFORMATION UPTAKE DURING TEXTPROCESSING

Andreas G. Fleischer

Bundesanstalt für Arbeitsschutz,
Vogelpothsweg 50-52, D-4600 Dortmund, FRG

1. INTRODUCTION

Skilled text processing comprises a complex interaction of perceiving text, storing perceived characters in the working memory, executing motor actions and cognitive control. At any given moment during typing all of these processes are typically in operation simultaneously (6, 7, 5). The presented paper refers to the skill of touch typing in which the typists employs all fingers and refrains from looking at the keyboard. It has been observed (6) that skilled typists look mainly at the copy and consult the typed text and the keyboard only occasionally. However, during steady keying at a text processor touch typists often scan copy and display in a repetitive way (2). This means that within a single cycle a text string is read from the copy and subsequently the typed characters are checked on the display. This behavioral pattern allows to analyse the input-output relationship between read characters and typed keys with respect to the storage chracteristics of the working memory which are supposed to be affected by mental fatigue.

The reading process has to be generally ahead of the typing process and therefore a working memory has to be postulated to hold the information of a certain number of subsequent characters that have been read from the copy but are not yet typed. This number is called eye-hand-span (5) and provides information about the required load of the working memory to perform fluent typing. Studies of eye movements (1) indicate that irrespective of word boundaries skilled typists look typically about 4 to 8 characters in advance. The application of the preview method (3, 12, 9) allows to manipulate the amount of text the typist can see. The preview at which no further increase of typing speed could be achieved amounts to 8 characters. Forcing it beyond 8 characters produces a deterioration in performance (10), which lead to the assumption that 8 characters represent a limit of working memory load during continuous typing of normal prose. Typists, however, which are forced to alternate between typing and reading and could store up to 46 characters in the working memory (8). These contradictory results lead to the question to what extent working memory load is determined by a fixed limit or by the text structure.

Apart from the working memory the motor buffer plays a major part in providing a continuous typing process, since it allows to restart the reading process before the supply of stored characters has depleted. If the subject is asked to type a word as soon as it appears on the display the typing latency of the first keystroke is about 700 ms (4). Therefore, after the restart of the reading process from the copy this latency, required to store the beginning of the subsequent text string in the working memory and to execute, it should be in a range to be bridged by the motor buffer. If the subject is asked to stop the typing process of a stored string in response to an acoustic stop signal, it still types in average up to 2.8 characters. This number has been considered to represent the average capacity of the motor buffer which normally depletes within 300 ms (5). However, the depletion time of the motor buffer is too short to bridge the typing latency of 700 ms. Therefore, after the restart of the reading process a decrease in typing speed has to be expected.

The visual scanning behavior of copy and display at a textprocessor will be investigated in the presented paper in conjunction with the typed keys in order to estimate working memory and motor buffer load. Touch typists try to type as continuously as possible. This fact allows to study the short term storage strategies on the basis of a spontaneous behavioral pattern and the increase of mental fatigue during the time at work.

2. METHODS

In the experiment presented here, six trained female touch typists, between 20 and 37 years of age, were tested in the morning on 6 subsequent days each. The subjects were experienced in working at workstations with visual display units. Their average typing rate ranges from 3.8 to 5.9 char/s and amounts to an average for all subjects of 4.9 char/s. The daily experimental sessions lasted one hour.

The experimental set-up is schematically illustrated in figure 1. The subjects were asked to read text from a copy on the clipboard and type it on the keyboard. The typed text appeared immediately on the display where it could be checked. Cursor moves, delete options and help functions were available. The subjects had no instructions how to behave but to correct typing errors at once. The presented text has been taken from a sociological report.

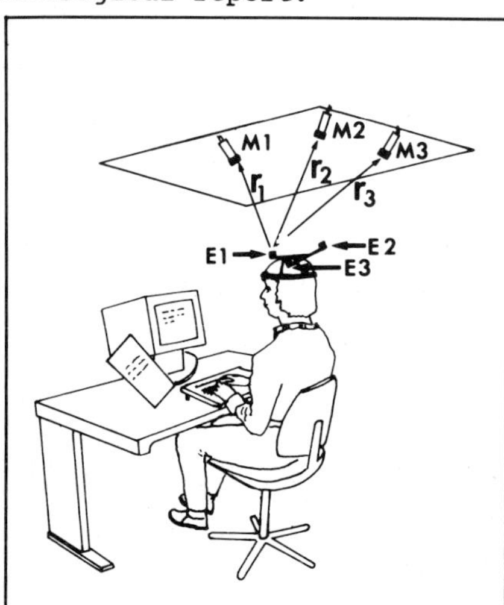

FIGURE 1.
Experimental set-up. The head movements are determined by measuring the transmission time of sequential ultrasonic pulses from three ultrasonic sources E1, E2 and E3, mounted on top of the head, to three microphones M1, M2 and M3 above the workstation. From these data the distances r_1, r_2 and r_3 of the sources from the microphones and the X,Y,Z-coordinates of sources are computed.

In parallel with the typed keys the eye and head movements have been recorded. The head position in space was recorded continuously by means of three ultrasonic sources E1, E2, E3 mounted on top of the head (figure 1). This method is based on the following principle. The spatial coordinates of a moving point are determined by its distances r_1, r_2 and r_3 from three fixed reference points which are obtained by measuring the transmission time of an ultrasonic pulse, for instance, emitted from source E1, to three microphones M1, M2 and M3 arranged above the workstation. The positions of all three ultrasonic sources E1, E2 and E3 were sampled at a rate of 25 Hz. The X,Y,Z-coordinates were calculated off-line with a general purpose computer. Horizontal and vertical eye movements have been recorded by means of the electrooculogram (EOG) applying small electrodes, 11 mm in diameter. The latter requires the application of electrophysiological amplifiers with DC input mode and automatic DC compensation. The head position in space and the EOG has been recorded to gain information about the gaze position. For statistical evaluation of the presented results the standard deviation δ or the standard deviation of the mean s has been plotted in the following figures.

3. RESULTS

At a text processor touch typists read a certain amount of text from the copy on the clipboard and subsequently check the typed characters on the display in a repetitive way. A section, 30s long, of a typical recording obtained from subject S1 during continuously typing text is shown in figure 2.

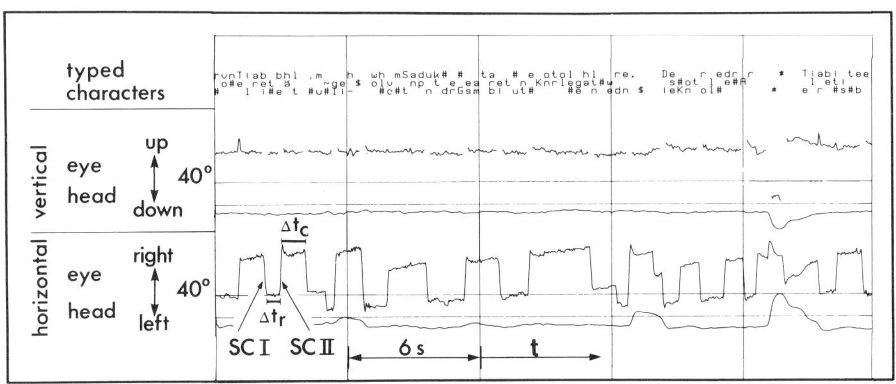

FIGURE 2
Typical behavioural pattern. SCI: saccade from display to copy, SCII: saccade from copy to display, Δt_r: reading time, Δt_c: checking time. In the last section a sequence of detecting and correcting a typing error is shown. Special symbols, #: blank, $: return, *: delete.

In the upper row of figure 2 the typed keys are plotted. Every 120 ms the action on the keyboard has been sampled whether a key has been typed or not. Three subsequent sampling intervals, 120ms long, are presented one beneath the other. This results in a blank space if no character has been typed or in columns of maximal three characters which have to be read vertically in order to reconstruct the typed text. Since the action on all keys has been plotted certain special symbols have to be supplemented which are explained in the corresponding legend. In the second and third row of figure 2 the vertical and horizontal eye and head movements are plotted, respectively. At times the subjects eyes are blinking the plotted trace of the vertical electrooculogram is interrupted. In contrast to the vertical eye movements strong horizontal eye movements have been recorded. In comparison with the horizontal eye movements the corresponding head movements are relatively small. During the reading time Δt_r (figure 2) the subject reads from the copy and during the checking time Δt_c it checks the result of its typing. The following analysis refers to two subsequent types of saccades, SCI from display to copy and SCII from copy to display. The amplitude of the recorded saccades often exceed 40° but corrective saccades could rarely be observed. This fact makes it very likely that the subject memorizes the previous gaze position and is able to reach the target in one step. The large scanning saccades between copy and display represent a complex eye strain. How the gaze position is computed from the recorded eye and head data is given by (2). In the discourse of this presentation the results from subject S1 and S3 will be discussed in detail and they will be complemented by average results from all subjects tested.

The scanning visual behavior between copy and display leads to broad and asymmetrical distributions of the reading and checking time, Δt_r and Δt_c, which vary between 200 ms and 3.5s (figure 3a,b). For each subject the recorded average reading time Δt_r ranges from 890 to 1780 ms (figure 3a) and amounts for all subjects to 1210 ms. The average checking time Δt_c ranges for each subject from 750 to 1350 ms (figure 3b) and amounts for all subjects to 1110 ms.

In order to achieve a continuous transcription process the time required to type a text string which has been read during Δt_r must in average be equal to the sum of Δt_r and Δt_c. Otherwise, if it is smaller, the writing process has to wait until the motor buffer provides new information for the next keystrokes, or if it is larger, the information to be stored in the working memory culminates. Provided, Δt_r is determined by the reading rate v_r (char/s) of an actual text string, these considerations lead to the assumption that the checking time Δt_c depends on the time to type the full text string consisting out of n characters with a typing rate v_t (char/s). This leads to the following equation (1): $\Delta t_c = n\, v_t - \Delta t_r$. The checking time Δt_c is equal to the difference of the required typing time n v_t and the reading time Δt_r. From this hypothesis one can infer that Δt_r and Δt_c should be negatively correlated.

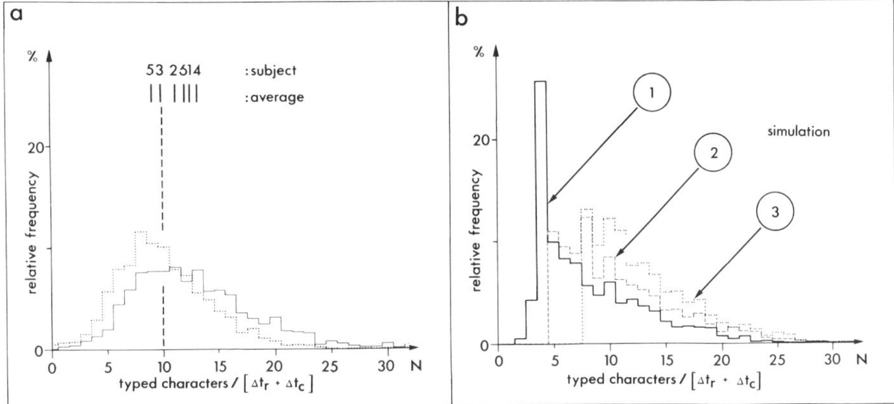

FIGURE 5

a Relative frequency of characters typed during the sum of reading and checking time, $\Delta t_r + \Delta t_c$. **b** Model simulations of the relative frequency of the characters typed during reading and checking time. Different values for high limit HL result in different distributions. HL=2 (curve 1) represents the word length distribution of the original text. Increasing HL (HL=5: curve 2, HL=8: curve 3) leads to a higher percentage of longer text strings.

The working memory allows the reading process to be generally ahead of the typing process. However, analysis of eye movements (1) indicate that typists do not scan the copy word by word and that the eye-hand-span is unrelated to word boundaries. With respect to the behavioral pattern described here saccades SCI and SCII are well defined events and allow to investigate the effect of word structure on the reading and storage process.

In order to test the hypothesis whether the saccades are elicited by reaching word boundaries during the storage process distributions of word delimiters have been computed with the time of the onset of saccade SCI and SCII as reference. For this purpose the time before and after the corresponding reference saccade has been subdivided in intervals, 120 ms long, and the number of word delimiters (blanks) typed within each of these time intervals have been summed. This procedure results in the frequency distribution of typed word delimiters shown in figure 6a,b, obtained from subject S1 and S3. In order to provide statistical criteria for the evaluation of these distributions the same procedure has been performed at randomized reference times on the basis of the typed text. This leads to average $\overline{x}$ (thick horizontal line, figure 6) and standard deviation σ of the delimiter distribution. The 2 σ limits are presented in figure 6.

In order to test this hypothesis by computing the corresponding regression line the large variations of the length of the text strings typed during $\Delta t_r + \Delta t_c$ have to be restricted to a length between 18 and 22 characters. A typical result obtained from subject S1 is shown in figure 4a. For all subjects a significant ($p<0.01$) negative correlation between Δt_r and Δt_c could be obtained. The regression coefficient varies from subject to subject between -0.98 and -0.5. This means that Δt_c is in average shorter than expected from equation (1). This may be caused by the fact that v_t is not constant but shows a decrease after saccade SCI and an increase after SCII and according to equation (1) in comparison with subject S1 the fact that S3 has a higher reading rate should lead to a shorter average reading time $\overline{\Delta t_r}$ and a longer average checking time $\overline{\Delta t_c}$. This assumption is consistent with the obtained results presented in figure 3a, b.

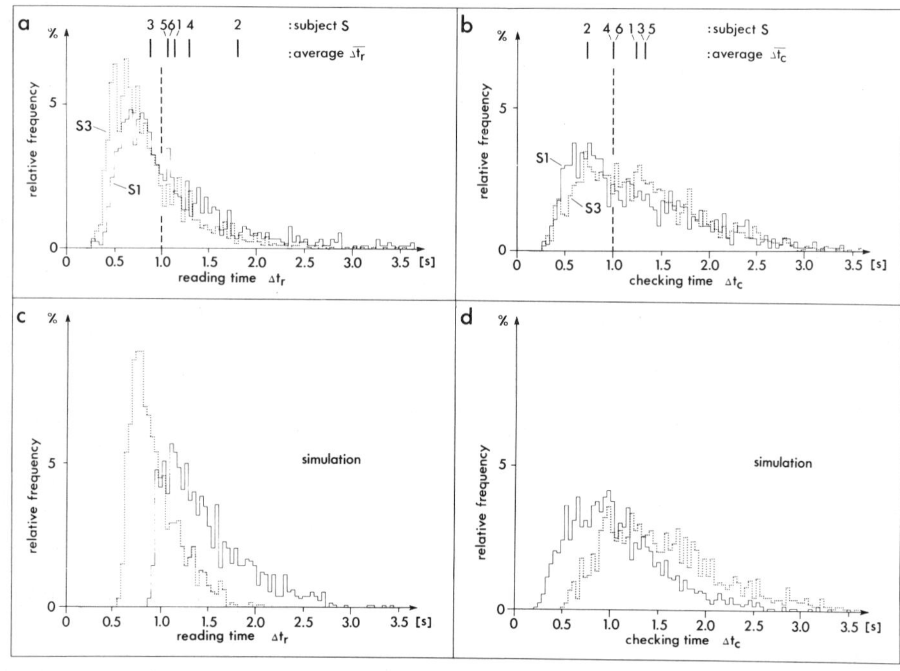

FIGURE 3
Histograms of reading time Δt_r (**a**) and checking time Δt_c (**b**) obtained from subject S1 (solid curve) and S3 (dotted curve). Averages $\overline{\Delta t_r}$ and $\overline{\Delta t_c}$ from each subject are marked by small vertical lines at top of the figures. **c**, **d** Model simulations with reading rate v_r = 11,1 char/s (solid curve) and v_r = 19,2 char/s (dotted curve).

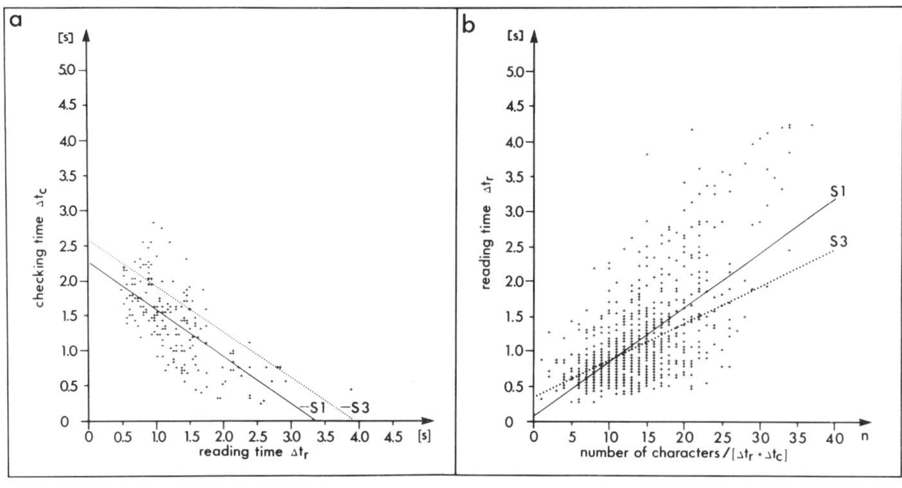

FIGURE 4

a Correlation between reading time Δt_r and checking time Δt_c. The analysed text strings have been restricted from 18 to 22 characters for the presented analysis. **b** Correlation between the number n of characters typed during $\Delta t_r + \Delta t_c$ and the reading time Δt_r. The analysed data from subject S1 and the computed regression lines from subject S1 and S3 are plotted.

The significant negative correlation between Δt_r and Δt_c makes it very likely that the requirements of the information flow are determining the onset of the saccades. Therefore, assuming that the number of characters typed during the sum of Δt_r and Δt_c have to be read during Δt_r, allows to compute the reading rate v_r. From the obtained data a regression coefficient can be computed which represents the reading rate v_r (figure 4b). It amounts to 12.8 char/s for subject S1 (average typing rate v_t = 5.7 char/s) and to 15.4 char/s for subject S3 (v_t = 4.8 char/s). The average reading time per character Δt_{ch} ranges from 55 ms to 124 ms and amounts in average for all subjects to 85 ms. However, considering text strings, 21 characters long, the data obtained from S1 (figure 4b) reveal that the time required to read these text strings varies between 0.44s and 4.2s. This fact makes it very likely that the subject does not necessarily read every text string character by character but that different cues may allow for an immediate detection.

During the time Δt_r the subject reads a certain amount of text from the copy and stores ist in the working memory. Since there is no reason to assume that the stored characters are erased immediately from the working memory after they have been typed, it is possible to estimate the average working memory load wm from the length of the text strings typed during the full period $\Delta t_r + \Delta t_c$. Typical results from subject S1 and S3 are shown in figure 5a. This assumption leads to an average working memory load wm of 11.3 characters for all subjects. However, the histograms show no clear limit of the working memory capacity since up to 30 characters could be stored.

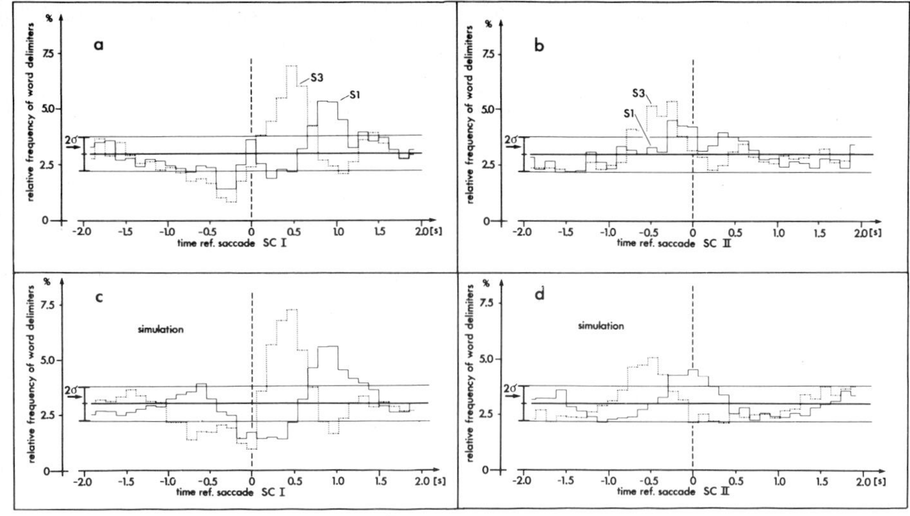

FIGURE 6
Frequency distribution of typed word delimiters with saccade SCI (**a**) and SCII (**b**) as reference. Simulated distributions of word delimiters with saccade SCI (**c**) and SCII (**d**) as reference.

The time of the reference saccades has been marked by dashed vertical lines. The two distributions (figure 6a) referring to SCI show a significant decrease of delimiter frequency before and a strong increase after SCI. The maxima of these distributions occur at +840 ms for subject S1 (solid curve) and at +480 ms for subject S3 (dotted curve). These maxima range from 0 to +840 ms and have an average of +580 ms for all subjects. The highly significant maxima of the distributions after SCI provide clear evidence that the reading and storage process stops at word boundaries. The delay, at which these maxima occur after SCI are determined by the motor buffer load.

In order to verify the presented results the frequency distributions of word delimiters referring to saccade SCII have been analysed. Typical results obtained from subject S1 and S3 are presented in figure 6b. In comparison with figure 6a it becomes clear that the maxima of these distributions are shifted to the left with respect to SCII. This fact makes it likely that saccades SCII are not elicited by reaching a word delimiter. By means of model simulations it will be tested whether the maxima of these distributions before SCII are merely representing the maxima after SCI modified by variations of the reading time.

The process of reading text strings from the copy and subsequently checking the typed keys on the display is determined by strategies to achieve a continuous typing process. The following analytic step deals with the question how well the subjects are able to minimize pauses in writing. The typing latency of about 700 ms between the first keystroke and the time a word appears on the display (4) is supposed to correspond with the time required to type the first character which has been read from the copy after saccade SCI. A continuous typing process can only be achieved by bridging this typing latency by means of the time required to deplete the motor buffer. In order to test this ability the frequency distribution of the typed characters have been computed with time of saccade SCI and SCII as reference.

For this purpose the time before and after the corresponding saccade has been subdivided in intervals, 120 ms long, and the number of keys typed within each of these time intervals have been summed. This procedure results in the frequency distributions of typed keys shown in figure 7a,b, obtained from subject S1 and S3 with saccade SCI and SCII as reference. In order to provide statistical criteria for the evaluation of these distributions the same procedure has been performed at randomized reference times on the basis of the typed text. This leads to the average $\bar{x}$ (thick horizontal line, figure 7a,b) and to the standard deviation σ of the delimiter distribution. The 2 σ limits are presented in figure 7.

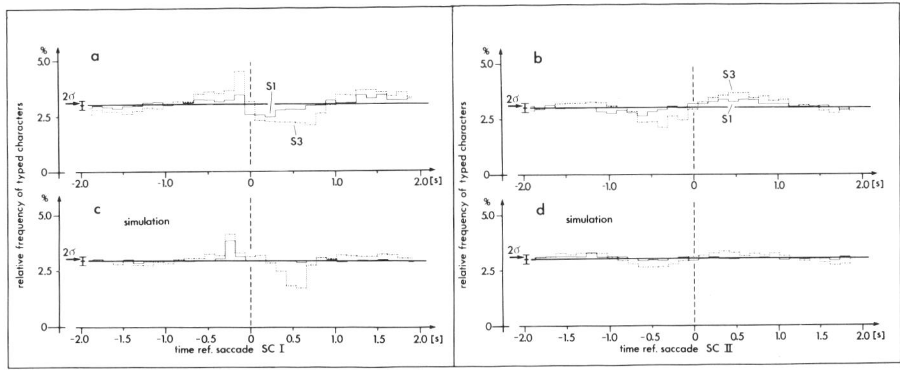

FIGURE 7
Frequency distribution of typed keys with saccade SCI (**a**) and SCII (**b**) as reference. Simulated distributions of typed characters with saccade SCI (**c**) and SCII (**d**) as reference.

The results obtained from subject S1 and S3 show that there is a significant decrease in typing speed after SCI (figure 7a). The amount of this decrease depends on the average load of the motor buffer. Taking the average typing speed into considerations it takes approximately 1 s for S1 and 480 ms for S3 to deplete the motor buffer. Therefore, the decrease in typing speed is larger for S3 than for S1. This result shows that it takes approximately 1 s to overcome the gap in the information flow after SCI and to provide a continuous typing process. Applying the same analytic method but taking SCII as reference revealed that the typing speed increases significantly after the performance of SCII (figure 7b).

4. DISCUSSION

Touch typists working at a text processor scan copy and display in a repetitive manner. In order to provide continuous typing the behavioral pattern, i.e. the reading, typing and checking process, has to be rigidly linked with the state of the information flow. This fact makes it possible to analyse short term storage strategies with respect to the given text structure and to estimate working memory and motor buffer load.
The presented results provide evidence that the reading time and the checking time are determined by the requirements of the

information flow. In general the reading process is faster than the typing process. Therefore, after having stored a certain text string in the working memory the remaining time is used to check the typed keys on the display. The stored text strings are translated character by character into motor programs for the execution of the corresponding finger and hand movements, fed in serial order in the typing motor buffer, typed and finally displayed. These considerations lead to the model presented schematically in figure 8.

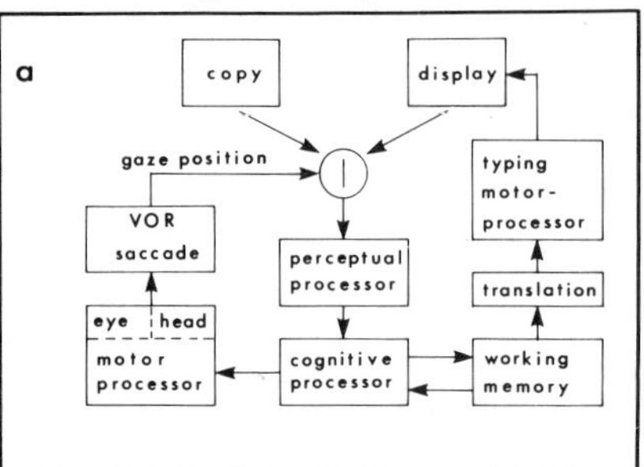

FIGURE 8
Model simulations were performed on the basis of two short term storage buffers, "working memory" and "motor buffer", and of three processes, "read", "translate" and "type".

This model works on the basis of a 40 ms cycle and consists out of three processes, which are "read", "translate" and "type", and two short term storage buffers, which are "working memory" and "motor buffer". First, during the simulations characters of the original text, which has also been used as copy for the subjects, are "read" with a rate v_r. During the reading process a pointer is sequentially shifted from character to character within the text. According to the probability distribution of the characters the number of cycles required to store a single character in the working memory varies. The minimum time to restart the reading process amounts to 280 ms.

The presented analysis revealed that saccade SCI is performed shortly before a word delimiter is typed (figure 6a). This observation leads to the assumption that the storage process is stopped by saccade SCII from copy to display after a word delimiter has been reached during the reading process. Taking into consideration that the working memory load wm has no clear limit (figure 5a), and that the number of words read during Δt_r varies from one to five words, makes clear, that with increasing number of stored characters a limit (HL) will be reached, which causes the reading process to be stopped at the next word delimiter. On the other hand if the stored information has depleted, another limit (LL) has to be introduced which triggers saccade SCI and restarts the reading process. For modeling these assumptions have been realized in the following way (figure 8). The working memory is structered as first-in-first-out buffer with a maximal capacity of 50 characters. The working memory contains a low limit (LL) and high limit (HL). After the text string to be stored reaches HL the reading process stops at the next word delimiter (blank) and saccade SCII from copy to display is elicited. The characters stored in the working memory are fed in the subsequent process by means of pointer P which is shifted along the stored text string. If P reaches LL saccade **SCI from the display to the copy** is elicited and if P has reached the last character of the working memory its contents is erased. This allows to restart the reading process. By means of the translation process the character at the positon of pointer P is fed, statistically delayed between 40 and 160 ms, in the motor buffer, which has a first-in-first-out structure, too. The capacity of the motor buffer can be modified. The typing process delays the output of the motor buffer in steps of 120 ms according to a probability distribution which is similar to the distribution of the interkey times achieved by subjects.

Based on these principles model simulations lead to the distributions of the reading Δt_r and checking time Δt_c shown in figure 3c,d. Simulations performed on the basis of an average reading rate v_r of 19.2 char/s (dotted curves) result in distributions with a shorter Δt_r and a longer Δt_c than simulations on the basis of a lower average reading rate of 11.1 char/s (solid curves). Similar results have been obtained from subject S1 and S3 (figure 3a,b).

The frequency distribution of typed word delimiters referring to saccade SCI shows a significant decrease before and a strong increase after SCI. Model simulations (figure 6c) lead to similar distributions with a decrease of the frequency of word delimiters before and a strong increase after SCI. The solid curve in figure 6c has been simulated by providing an average motor buffer load of 5.7 characters and the dotted curve has been simulated by providing an average motor buffer load of 2.3 charcters. The simulated distributions correspond clearly with the results obtained from subject S1 and S3 and provide an estimation of the average motor buffer load of these subjects. On the basis of these results and taking the average typing speed into consideration it takes for subject S1 1 s and for S3 480 ms to deplete the motor buffer. From the simulated frequency distribution of typed keys (figure 7c) it becomes clear that the smaller motor buffer load of subject S3 leads to a significant decrease of the typing rate shortly after SCI, but that the larger motor buffer load of subject S1 is sufficient to bridge the eye-hand span. This result shows that the postulated timekeeper for achieving a paced regular keying (11) may well be disturbed by small motor buffer load. The average motor buffer load for all subjects amounts to 2.8 characters which closely corresponds with the results described in the literature (5).

Model simulations of the frequency distribution of typed word delimiters referring to SCII (figure 6d) reveal that the significant increase of the frequency of delimiter occurance is caused by the occurance of the maximum after SCI modified by variations of the reading time Δt_r. Model simulations of the frequency distributions of typed keys referring to SCII (figure 7d) show only small variations in typing rate which does not fully correspond with the recorded data presented in figure 7b.

During the transcription process typist achieve an eye-hand-span of up to 8 characters (1). Assuming that the motor buffer stores approximately 3 characters the average working memory load wm can be estimated to 5 characters. On the basis of the results presented here wm is larger and amounts to 11.3 characters and text strings up to 30 characters could be stored (figure 5a). However, these results are not consistent with the average copying span of 30 to 40 characters achieved during the transcription of a more complex text (8).

Working memory load is supposed not to be determined by a fixed capacity limit but by an increasing probability that the reading process is interrupted at the next word delimiter. The similarity between the frequency distributions of typed word delimiters obtained from the original and from the simulated data support this assumption (figure 6a,c). For model simulations the increasing probability to interrupt the reading process has simply been achieved by introducing high limit HL in the working memory. This approach, however, leads to an average working memory load which depends widely on the text structure. The effect of HL becomes evident by considering model simulations. Choosing HL=2 the simulations provides a distribution of the word lengths of the original text (curve 1, figure 5) since the presented text contains no words with less than two characters. The distribution has an average of 8.1 characters and a clear peak at a word length of 4 characters. Raising limit HL to 5 characters results in a distribution (curve 2) with an average of 10.9 characters and raising limit HL to 8 characters results in a distribution (curve 3) with an average of 13.2 characters. These three distributions show that an increase of HL causes an increase of the length of the stored text strings. With respect to these considerations the recorded histograms of the text strings typed during the time $\Delta t_r + \Delta t_c$ (figure 5a) provide evidence that HL is larger for subject S1 than for S3 since longer text strings are stored by S1. A quantitative estimation of HL by comparing the recorded and the simulated histograms is somewhat deteriorated since the recorded data comprise a small percentage of reading and checking sequences with very short text strings (<5 characters, figure 5a) which are not expected from the model simulations. Nevertheless HL could be estimated to 8 characters for subject S1 and to 5 characters for S3. In average the estimation of HL amounts to 6.3 characters for all subjects.

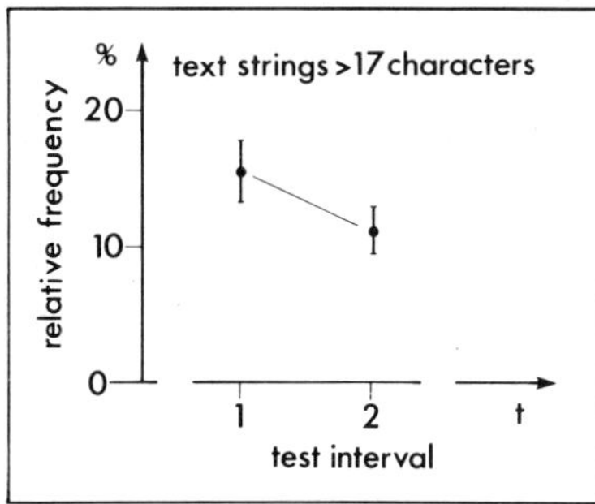

FIGURE 9
Relative frequency and standard deviation of the mean of processed text strings, longer than 17 characters, in relation to the time at work. Test intervals represent the first and second half of the experimental session. Average from all subjects.

The presented considerations support the assumption that working memory load is not determined by a fixed limit but that, after a certain limit HL of working memory load has been exceeded, the reading process is interrupted at the next word delimiter with high probability. Therefore the average working memory load depends widely on HL and on the distribution of the word lengths. In order to test the increase of mental fatigue in terms of the probability to read text strings longer than 17 characters, the relative frequency of the occurance of these text strings has been computed with respect to the time at work (figure 9). The result shows that during the time at work the probability to read long text strings decreases significantly ($p<0.05$). This decrease of average working memory load can be interpreted as an aspect of mental fatigue.

5. CONCLUSIONS

During steady keying at a text processor touch typists scan copy and display in a repetitive way. Within a single cycle a certain text string is read from the copy by the subject and subsequently the remaining time is used to check the typed keys on the display. This behavioral pattern, which represents a complex eye strain, allows to analyse the input-output relationship between read characters and typed keys with respect to the storage characteristics of the working memory. In order to achieve a continuous transcription process the reading time is negatively correlated with the checking time. This allows to investigate the amount of information stored during the reading time. On the basis of model simulaton evidence is provided that working memory load is not determined by a fixed capacity limit but by an increasing probability that the reading process is interrupted at the next word delimiter. The decreasing average working memory load during the time at work represents an aspect of mental fatigue.

REFERENCES

(1) Butsch, R.L.C., Eye movements and the eye-hand-span in typewriting. J. Educat. Psychol. 23 (1932) 104
(2) Fleischer, A.G., Becker, G.,Knabe, K.P. and Rademacher, U., Analyse der Augen- und Kopfbewegungen bei der Textverarbeitung. Z. Arbeitswiss. 38 (1984) 156
(3) Hershman, R.L. and Hillix, W.A., Data processing in typing. Human Factors 7 (1965) 483
(4) Logan, G.D., On the ability to inhibit complex movements: A stop-signal study of typewriting. J. Exp. Psychol.: Human Perception and Performance 8 (1982) 778
(5) Logan, G.D., Time, information, and various spans in typewriting, in: Cooper, W.E. (ed.), Cognitive aspects in skilled typewriting. Springer Verlag (New York, Heidelberg, Berlin, 1983)
(6) Long, J., Visual feedback and skilled keying: Differential effects of masking the printed copy and the keyboard. Ergonomics 19 (1976) 93
(7) Rabitt, P., Detection of errors by skilled typists. Ergonomics 21 (1978) 945
(8) Rothkopf, E.Z., Copying span as a measure of the information burden or written language. J. Verbal Learning and Verbal Behavior 19 (1980) 562
(9) Shaffer, .H., Latency mechanisms in transcription, in: Kornblum, S. (ed.), Attention and performance. London: Academic Press: 1973
(10) Shaffer, L.H., Intention and performance, Psychol. Rev. 83 (1976) 375
(11) Shaffer, L.H., Timing in the motor programming of typing, Quart. J. Exp. Psychol. (1978) 30, 333
(12) Shaffer, L.H. and Hardwick, J., The basis of transcription skill. J. Exp. Psychol. 84 (1970) 424

WORK WITH DISPLAY UNITS 86
B. Knave and P.-G. Wideback (eds.)

EFFECT OF VISUAL PRESENTATION OF DIFFERENT DIALOGUE STRUCTURES ON HUMAN-COMPUTER INTERACTION

Jürgen KASTER and Heino WIDDEL

Forschungsinstitut für Anthropotechnik
Neuenahrer Str. 20
D-5307 Wachtberg-Werthhoven, F.R.G.

A graphical dialogue system was developed as an experimental tool to investigate the effect of different dialogue interfaces on performance of novices interacting with computers. Dialogue structures were varied by realizing three different levels of dialogue transparency. In a three day session each subject of three groups had to perform six tasks twice. The first group, using isolated menus which were presented on a computer terminal, needed the longest task completing times. Subjects of the second group had the best performance values at the first part of the experiment. They were supported by the picture of the whole hierarchical dialogue structure, additionally displayed on a monitor. At the last part of the experiment subjects of the third group were favored. They interacted using a direct manipulation interface, characterized by pull-down menus, which were controlled by a pointing device.

1. INTRODUCTION

The increasing dissemination of information technology as well as the expanding complexity of human-computer systems require optimized, user-friendly interaction techniques. The design of human-computer dialogues is characterized as an interdependent strategy of distinct and well defined development steps connected with a more creative procedure combining the experience and intuition of a designer (THOMAS and CARROLL (1979)). While the second strategy shows a predominance in the design process, at particular levels of design evaluation, analytical and experimental methods can be used. In the field of human factors in computer systems and software engineering the dimension of 'user-perceived quality' (DZIDA et al. (1978)) is attached with highest relevance. It includes a set of subordinated factors, e.g., 'user-friendliness', 'self-descriptiveness', 'transparency'.

2. PROBLEM

Before developing a computer system the designer has to decide what design goal he wants to realize. The goal with highest relevance is user-friendliness, a dialogue aspect, which is determined by multiple characteristics providing a solid starting point in the design of interactive systems. System transparency is a subcategory of this design goal. A designer develops communication partners for users with formal communication behavior (MAASS (1983)), which can be modelled as formal transparency. It can be defined as a well-structured, consistent, and comprehensible appearance of the system for its users. As a result the realization of transparency may support users to build up easily an internal model of the interactive system or relevant parts of it. The approach of the present paper is that a transparent dialogue system makes it easy, especially for occasional and unexperienced users, to create a mental image of the functions, the system can perform for them.

When developing a dialogue system a designer has to analyse the characteristics of the user group the system is addressed to. Thus, dialogue interfaces should be assimilated to mental operations users characteristically are chiefly related to. General knowledge of cognitive human behavior assumes that people build an internal image of the system which is simply structured in the first learning period. Metaphor-based learning is crucial in software psychology and human factors in computer systems (CARROLL and THOMAS (1982)). CARROLL et al. (1980) found that a spatially presented problem obtained better performance and faster solution times than an isomorph but temporal presented problem. Under both conditions the problem solving process was favored by graphically displayed problem structures. Design of dialogue interfaces should integrate such knowledge of cognitive activities.

The user knowledge of a system is represented mentally as a result of interacting with the system. NORMAN (1983) distinguishes this mental model, in human-computer context, from the target system, from the conceptual model of the target system, and from the scientist's conceptualization of the mental model. In contrary to the conceptual model, the mental model is characterized by incompleteness, instability, lack of technical correctness, poor complexity, and a simple structure. Usually, people acquire a level of knowledge of the physical world, which can be expressed in terms of 'naive physics'. Because the user's mental model is functional and referred to the dialogue structure rather than to the internal computer processes, it is possible to design the image, users may form from the system. Obviously, the mental image depends on the succession and the structure of the displayed information, which is determined by the software. Figure 1 illustrates the predominant aspects of this design process being described in detail in WIDDEL and KASTER (1986).

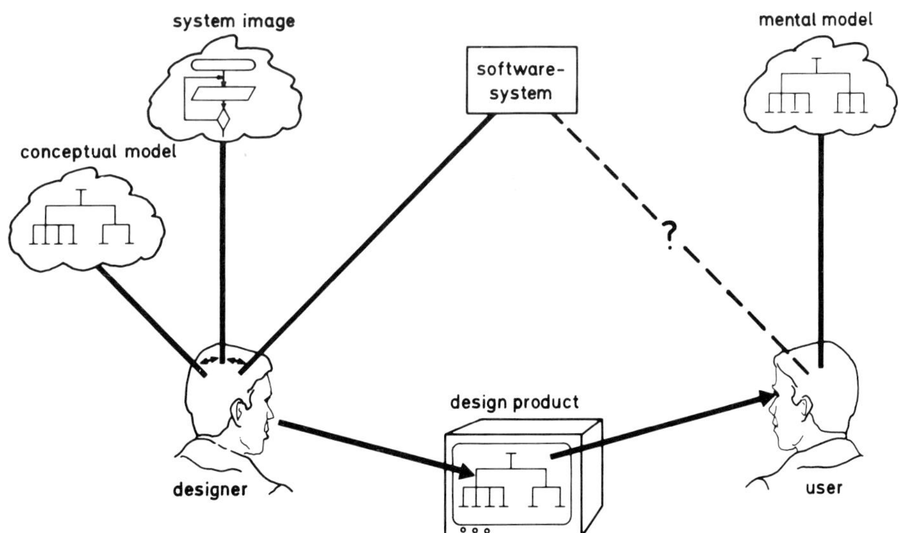

FIGURE 1
Assimilation steps in the process of human-computer interaction

3. EXPERIMENT

In the present paper the results of an experimental investigation are described analyzing ease of use of a computer system by varying its formal transparency on three levels. A graphical editor has been developed to generate color graphic and alpha-numeric data on a TV-monitor. The tasks for the subjects consisted of drawings with different complexity, which had to be performed by using this editor. The system, guaranteeing a highly interactive process, provides facilities to manipulate these synthetic graphical data. A variety of basic functions has been implemented, e.g., picture or picture component generating, data managing, manipulating of picture data bases, being presented in KASTER and WIDDEL (1985).

Objective of a series of experiments was the influence of the visual presentation of dialogue structures on performance and learning behavior of unexperienced computer users. Different dialogue structures were varying formal transparency at three levels. In the first experimental condition isolated menus with alternatives to be selected were presented on a computer terminal. Responses of the subjects had to be given by using a keyboard. In the second condition, additionally, the whole hierarchical menu-structure was displayed as a picture on a second TV-monitor, permanently. Colour coding of the actual user position in the dialogue and the covered path through the dialogue also appears. Both experimental procedures are described in detail in WIDDEL and KASTER (1986).

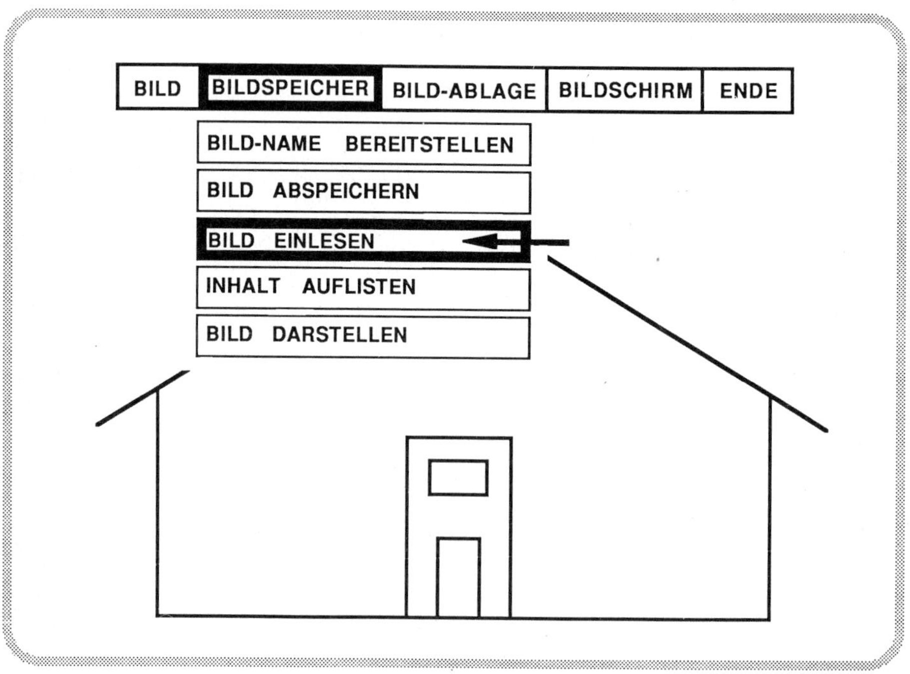

FIGURE 2
Pull-down menus and a task integrated on the same monitor

The characteristics of the third condition was an adaption of these concepts towards newest interaction techniques like 'direct manipulation'. Main menus were displayed permanently at the head of the TV-screen, while menus of lower levels were shown only after the activation of the appropriate main menu (figure 2). This interface design leaves room to integrate the menu system and drawing area on one screen. The usefulness of this integrated dialogue design was compared with the effect of the former described experimental conditions.

Under all conditions an experimental session included the double drawing of six alphanumeric graphics requiring three days for two subjects. The size of the groups was 8 subjects for the first, 6 subjects for the second, and 8 subjects for the third condition. More information about the experiments can be found in WIDDEL and KASTER (1985).

4. RESULTS

The analysis of the experimental data bases on two performance scores. The first score represents the time for completing a task. It is composed of the partitioned decision times subjects needed to select the different menu-alternatives. Such definition of the total time includes purely the interaction activities. The second score to be analyzed represents the frequency of activities, that is the sum of executed decisions for alternative-selections in menus. Statistical analysis makes use of the nonparametric U- and Wilcoxon-tests.

Figure 3 shows the interaction times all groups needed to complete each task twice. The medians of the group values are presented for visual evaluation. A comparison is available between the performance scores of the three groups, separated for each task, as well as the performance scores within each group for the completion of the same task at two trials. In the chart of figure 3 always the two left bars represent the performance of Group I, the two middle bars of Group II, and the two right bars of Group III. The rear bars indicate the time spent to complete the first trial of the task, the front bars indicate the completion time for the second trial of the same task.

Significant differences appear between Group I and Group II for the first trials of tasks 1 and 2 ($p < .01$), for the first trials of tasks 3 and 4, the second trials of tasks 1, 2, 3, and 4 and task 6 ($p < .05$). The differences between Group I and Group III turned out to be significant for most trials on the α-level of 1 %, merely the second trials of tasks 1 and 2 reach a level of significance of 5 %. Groups II and III mainly show insignificant differences with the exception of the first trial of task 1 ($p < .05$) and the second trial of task 5 ($p < .01$). The within group comparisons concerning the first and second trials for each task represent the learning effect of subjects, which is significant in most cases ($p < .01$ resp. $p. < .05$) with the exception of task 4 (Group I), task 1 (Group II), and task 5 (Group III).

The results show that subjects of Group II, using the picture of the hierarchical structure of the dialogue, and subjects of Group III, using the method of pull-down menus, generally needed a smaller amount of time to complete the tasks than subjects of Group I. A comparison of the Groups II and III shows two significant and numerous weak differences with inverse direction corresponding to succession of the trials. Subjects of Group II have shorter times at the initial experimental trials, but longer times at the latter trials than subjects of Group III. A learning effect is evident for all groups with different strength.

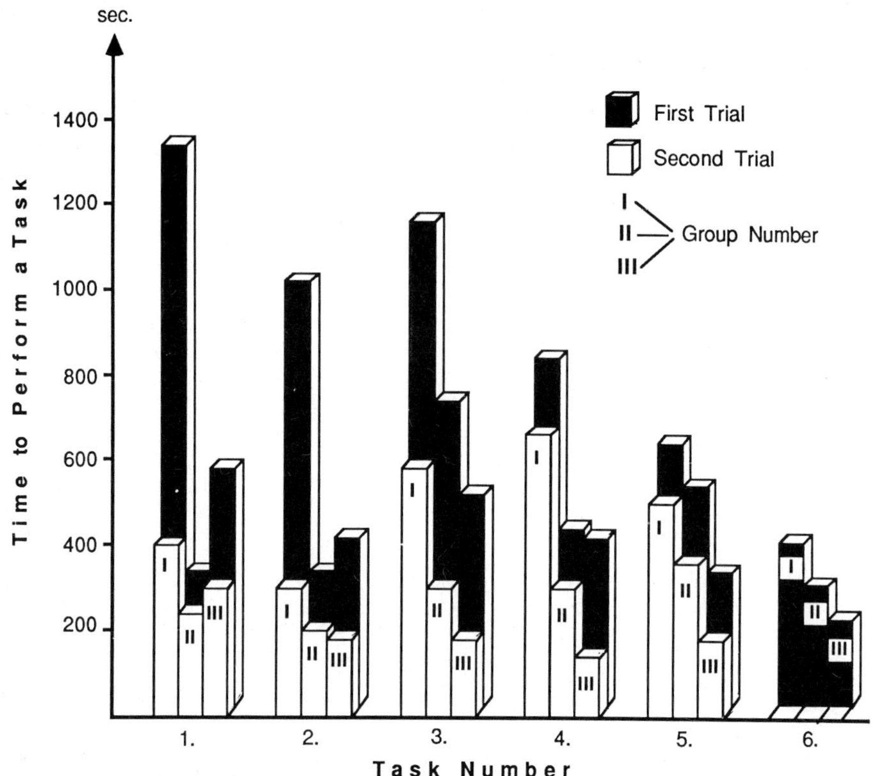

FIGURE 3
Completion times of the groups (medians) for each task at two trials

The frequencies of activities which were executed by the subjects to complete a task are presented in figure 4. They combine the minimum of activities necessary to carry out a task, the deviations from this optimal path, and pure faults. The height of the bars indicate the medians of the activity frequencies of Groups I, II, and III (from left to right for each task). The rear bars represent the frequencies of activities needed for the first trials of the tasks, while the front bars represent the values of the corresponding second trials.

A comparison between the three groups shows only few significant differences. For completion of the tasks 1 and 2 (first trial) and task 4 (first and second trial) Group I needed more actions than Group II ($p < .01$). Group III executed more actions than Group I for the first trial of task 1 ($p < .001$) and the second trials of task 1 and 2 ($p < .05$), but fewer actions for the second trial of task 4 ($p < .001$). Group III indicates more actions than Group II for the first trials of tasks 1 and 2 ($p < .001$) and the second trials of the same tasks ($p < .01$).

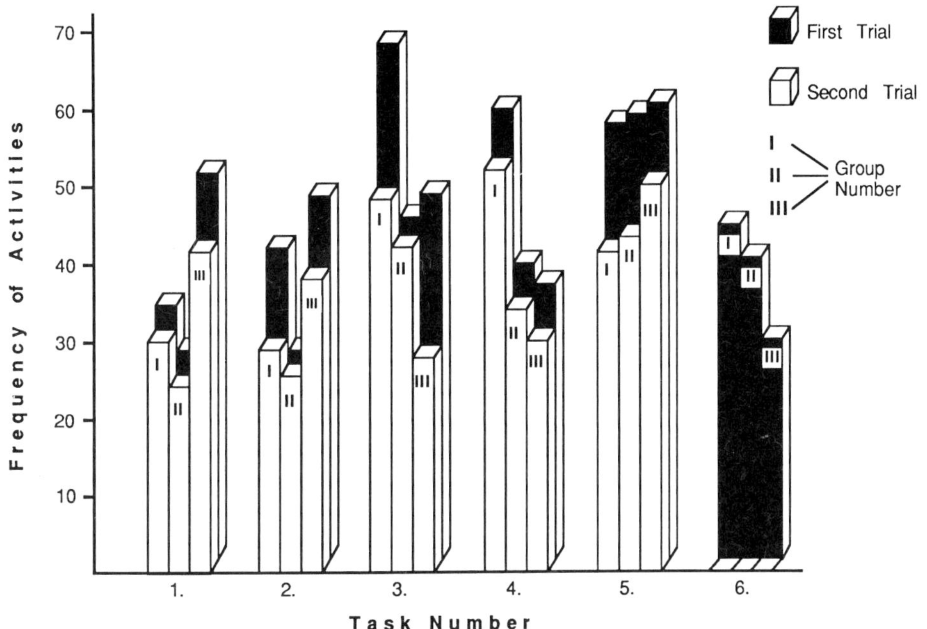

FIGURE 4
Frequencies of activities of the three groups (medians) for each task at two trials

The tendency can be extracted from these data that subjects, supported by the picture of the hierarchical dialogue structure, mostly needed fewer activities to reach the task goal than the subjects of both other groups. Subjects confronted with the dialogue structure represented by pull-down menus had a higher amount of activities at the front part of the experiment with an inversion of this direction at the back part of the experiment, when compared with the subjects who had to run the dialogue with the presentation of isolated menus.

A micro analysis of the findings of different times for the groups to complete the tasks must include pure fault activities as well as less effective navigation through the dialogue system to perform a task. An additional source determining the time variance consists in varying decision times to execute an action, i.e. to choose a system function or select a menu alternative. The discrimination of the first two variables is hardly to realize with the present experimental data, while the identification of the third variable is quite feasible by examining the relationship of the total time to the frequency of actions in each task. The medians of these values are illustrated in successive order of trials for the three groups in figure 5.

In general, Group I has longer decision times for executing an action than Group II and Group III, which has the shortest decision times. With increasing experience Groups II and III show a slightly declining decision duration, over the whole experimental time. Group I has a similar course in the last part of the experiment, but a dramatic decrease of the decision

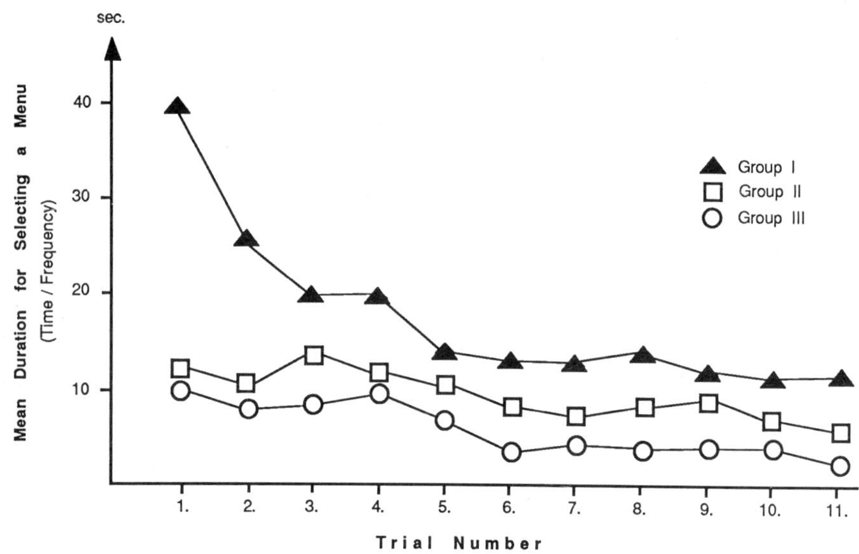

FIGURE 5
Mean decision times (medians) for selecting a menu-alternative

times from the first to the fifth trial. The mean decision durations of Group I and II correspond with their performance times for the tasks while the mean decision durations of Group III do not in the first part of the experiment. For most tasks subjects of Group III needed relatively long times to perform the tasks accompanied by overproportional high frequencies of activities. The relationship of both variables leads to low mean decision times for selecting a menu alternative. An interpretation may be extracted that subjects using the mouse technique combined with pull-down menus tend to act very quickly accepting a high probability to produce faults in unknown situations. On the other side, subjects being supported by the picture of the dialogue structure and confronted with keyboard input tend to act more slowly with less fault probability.

5. DISCUSSION

The previous experiments have shown that a user-friendly, software-ergonomic design of a dialogue can optimize the human computer interaction. A specific category of user-friendliness was realized as transparency of system functions, called formal transparency, which was modelled as a hierarchical menu-structure in one version, and by the method of pull-down menus including the mouse technique in another version.

The hierarchical structure of the dialogue was visualized by presenting it as a picture on a TV monitor. This support facilitates the development of a valid mental model of the user imagining the dialogue structure. The results demonstrate that unexperienced users of the computer system completed the tasks in shorter times, had less fault activities, and navigated more elegant through the dialogue, when the picture of the dialogue structure was presented and integrated in the interaction process. The users were able, after about four trials, to reproduce precisely the hierarchical menu-structure. This indicates that they have internalized the picture as a mentally represented spatial image.

The interaction method of pull-down menus and mouse-technique as a scope of a user-friendly approach seems to represent a very easy input handling. As a consequence this technique provokes a tendency of users for an 'explorative' and trial and error behavior. In poorly defined situations, e.g. when the interaction structure with the computer is unknown to users, they execute a high amount of activities with short decision times. This procedure induces a high rate of fault behavior. When the problem situation becomes clear and experienced users have internalized a proper mental model of the interaction process this method turns out to be more advantageous than the two other versions.

If presenting the isolated textual menus on the computer terminal without integrating the picture of the dialogue structure (Group I), a mental model, merely, could be developed successively by associative connection of the isolated menus. Additionally, it had to be structured to a valid image. This process could run into a distorted and deprivated mental model, restraining the interaction. A testing procedure showed that the users were able to reproduce only very short sequences of the menu-structure; in no case the systematic and hierarchical structure was recognizable and reconstructable by the users. The approach of the interaction performance of the three user groups is based upon the low complexity of the dialogue. After a learning process the execution of activities on skill level is possible which would be impossible in highly complex systems.

The previously investigated procedure of presenting a picture of the dialogue structure can be applied in various forms and fields of human-computer interaction. A picture may serve as an optional element, integrated in the dialogue, which could be activated when the user requests for it. Especially, this should be the case in highly complex systems. There, different menu-hierarchies or sub-hierarchies can be presented by window-technique. Each section of the dialogue the user is navigating through is directly connected with a corresponding picture of the hierarchy to be presented on the display. An additional field of application is training. Displaying the dialogue structure can be integrated as a learning unit for using a computer system and may intensify the understanding of the functional communicating behavior of a dialogue. In the situation of high user experience an integration of this dialogue realization with mouse-driven pull-down menu systems seems to be an optimized design product.

ACKNOWLEDGEMENT

The authors like to express their warmest thanks to Irene for typing this paper in her cultivated and precise working-style; her last act in the institute before giving birth to a little baby.

REFERENCES

CARROLL, J.M., THOMAS, J.C., and MALHOTRA, A., Presentation and representation in design problem-solving, British Journal of Psychology 71 (1980) 143-153.

CARROLL, J.M. and THOMAS, J.C., Metaphor and the cognitive representation of computing systems, IEEE Transactions on Systems, Man, and Cybernetics 12 (1982) 107-116.

DZIDA, W., HERDA, S., and ITZFELD, W.D., User-perceived quality of interactive systems, IEEE Transactions on Software Engineering Vol. SE-4, No. 4 (1978) 270-276.

KASTER, J. and WIDDEL, H., Graphical support for dialogue transparency, in: SHACKEL, B. (ed.), Human-Computer Interaction (North-Holland, Amsterdam, 1985) pp. 329-334.

MAASS, S., Why systems transparency?, in: GREEN, T.R., PAYNE, S.J., and van de VEER, G.C. (eds.), The Psychology of Computer Use (Acacdemic Press, London, 1983) pp. 19-28.

NORMAN, D.A., Some oberservations on mental models, in: GENTNER, D. and STEVENS, A. (eds.), Mental Models (Erlbaum, Hillsdale, N.J., 1983) pp. 7-14.

THOMAS, J.C. and CARROLL, J.M., The psychological study of design, Design Studies 1 (1979) 5-11.

WIDDEL, H. und KASTER, J., Untersuchung zur formalen Transparenz eines Menüsystems, in: BULLINGER, H.-J. (Hrsg.), Software-Ergonomie '85 Mensch-Computer-Interaktion (Teubner, Stuttgart, 1985) pp. 228-238.

WIDDEL, H. and KASTER, J., Transparency of a dialogue through pictorial presentation of the dialogue structure, in: WILLUMEIT, M.-P. (ed.), Human Decision Making and Manual Control (North-Holland, Amsterdam, 1986) pp. 135-143.

WORK WITH DISPLAY UNITS 86
B. Knave and P.-G. Widebäck (eds.)

TOUCH SCREEN, CURSOR KEYS AND MOUSE INTERACTION

Bengt Ahlström and Sören Lenman

National Defence Research Institute
Man and Information Systems (FOA 53)
P.O. Box 1165
S-581 11 LINKÖPING SWEDEN

An experimental comparison between three interaction tools, touch screen, cursor keys and mouse was made. The main objective was to evaluate their effectiveness as cursor positioning devices when choosing a word from a list of words. The results indicated that cursor positioning is fastest when using touch screen and that the difference between cursor keys and mouse is small but the cursor keys seem to be a little faster.

1. INTRODUCTION

New tools for human computer interaction are constantly being introduced. Human factor data is needed concerning both the effectiveness and usage of these tools. What are their advantages and disadvantages and in what situation should they be used?

Experimental comparisons of several input devices for the positioning task can be found in the literature (1,2,3,4,5,6). Different sets of input devices have been compared and different evaluation criteria have been used. Different tools seem to have their advantages in different situations. Thus, there is need for more knowledge about tools for human-computer interaction, especially concerning the effect of task and user variables on the usability of different tools.

The present study addresses this question with respect to touch screen, cursor keys and mouse. The main objective was to evaluate their effectiveness as positioning devices when choosing a word from a list of words, with and without a typing task (subtask) interfering with the positioning task. Furthermore, the sensitive area around the words was varied on two levels: 1 line x 6 columns and 3 lines x 12 columns (Small and large displays). These variables were varied in a 3 x 2 x 2 factorial design. In addition, the patterns of cursor start and stop positions were systematically varied, that is, the effect of distance and type of movement (horizontal, vertical, oblique) from start position to target could be analyzed. The dependent variables were speed, errors and subjective ease of use.

2. METHOD

2.1. Apparatus

A VAX 750 computer system was used to run the experiment. The experimental situations for the three interaction tools were first optimized in pre-studies with respect to ergonomic considerations. An ordinary CRT terminal of VT220 type with positive black and white screen was used. The mechanical mouse and the cursor keys on the keyboard were standard on the terminal. A touchscreen with conductive surface was then mounted in front of the CRT. It should be noted that the mouse used controlled the cursor on an ordinary VDU with 80 x 25 resolution.

2.2. Subjects

Six subjects have so far participated in the experiment. They have some experience in handling conventional keyboards and interaction tools.

2.3. Procedure

The experiment was divided into three parts, one for each tool. The subjects were seated in front of the CRT terminal, and instructed to use the appropriate interaction tool. Some practice was given with each tool and experimental condition. Each trial started with 16 words being presented in a fixed 4 x 4 matrix. The sensitive area for each word was framed. Each word consisted of six random consonants, shown in randomly mixed lower and upper case. The reason for choosing these kinds of "words" was to ensure that the subject's attention was diverted from the positioning task when performing the typing task. The current start position of the cursor was rendered in reverse video and the target position was shown in underscore. The subject's task was to move the cursor from the start position to the stop position, as fast as he could, using the interaction tool in question. In the mouse, condition the positioning was completed by pressing a special key located on the mouse, in the cursor key condition by pressing the carriage return key on the keyboard and in the touch screen condition by just touching the desired position. In the condition without subtask, the trial was completed when the cursor was correctly positioned. In the subtask situation, when the positioning task was completed the cursor jumped to an empty frame under the 4 x 4 matrix. The subject then had to type the "word" correctly, finishing with a carriage return.

The following times were measured:

- Time to position the cursor.
- Time to start typing after positioning the cursor.
- Time to perform the typing task.

Furthermore, the number of errors was measured and after the experiment the subject had to rank the interaction tools with respect to speed, precision and convenience.

3. RESULTS AND DISCUSSION

It is important to mention, that the experimental data has not yet been analyzed to any full extent and that not all subjects have yet been tested. No statistical tests have been performed; findings and conclusions presented in this preliminary report are only based on the appearance of data and consequently some of these may have to be reconsidered. However,all the results presented here have so far held true for all the subjects tested.

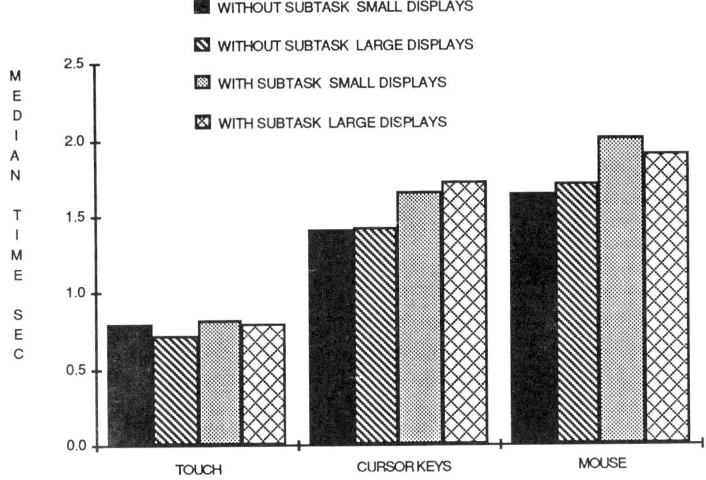

FIG 1: CURSOR POSITIONING TIME FOR ALL CONDITIONS.

Figure 1 shows the cursor positioning times for all conditions. One can see that, in all conditions, cursor positioning is fastest when using the touch screen. The difference between cursor keys and mouse is small, but the cursor keys seem to be a little faster. It should be noted that the measured times also include times for error corrections.

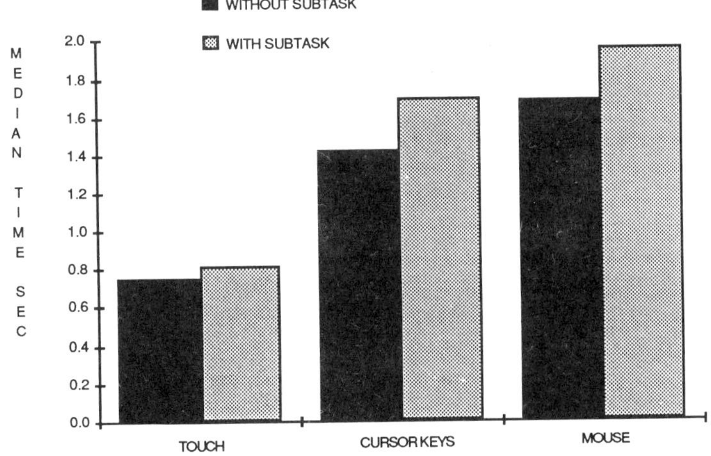

FIG 2: CURSOR POSITIONING TIME WITH AND WITHOUT SUBTASK.

Figure 2 shows cursor positioning times with and without subtask. The most important effect is that the cursor positioning times were longer in the subtask condition. A possible explanation is that in a subtask situation the subject has to readjust between the cursor positioning and the subtask. There seems to be no interaction between subtask condition and interaction device. If this holds true, it means that data from studies without subtask may be valid also in situations with subtask.

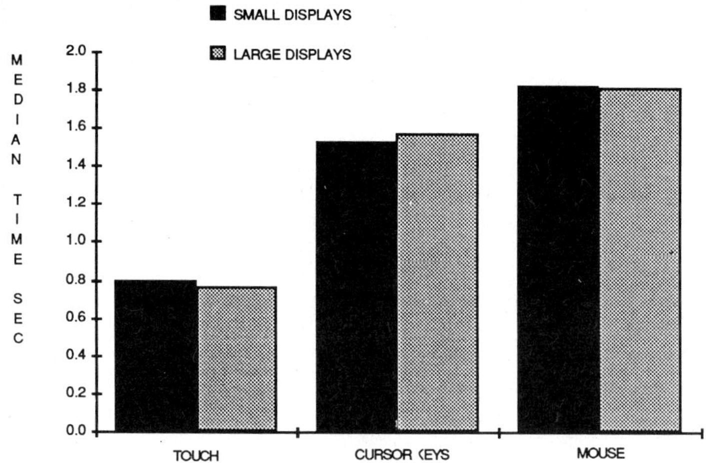

FIG 3: CURSOR POSITIONING TIME WITH SMALL AND LARGE DISPLAYS.

Figure 3 illustrates cursor positioning time for large and small displays. There is virtually no difference, with respect to medians, between the large and small display condition. It should be noted that the measured times also include times for error corrections.

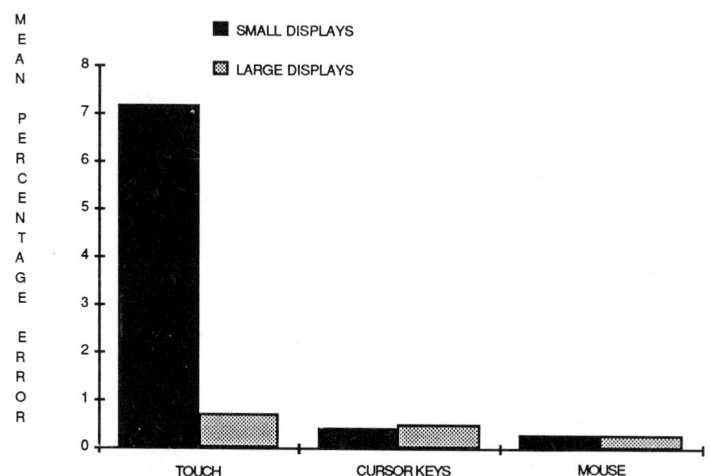

FIG 4: MEAN PERCENTAGE ERROR FOR SMALL AND LARGE DISPLAYS.

Figure 4 shows the percentage error for small and large displays for all positioning tasks. The percentage error was high for touch screen with small display and the error rate for mouse was lower than for touchscreen and cursor keys. This result indicates that for small menu areas, the touch screen has serious drawbacks if an error results in significant consequences.

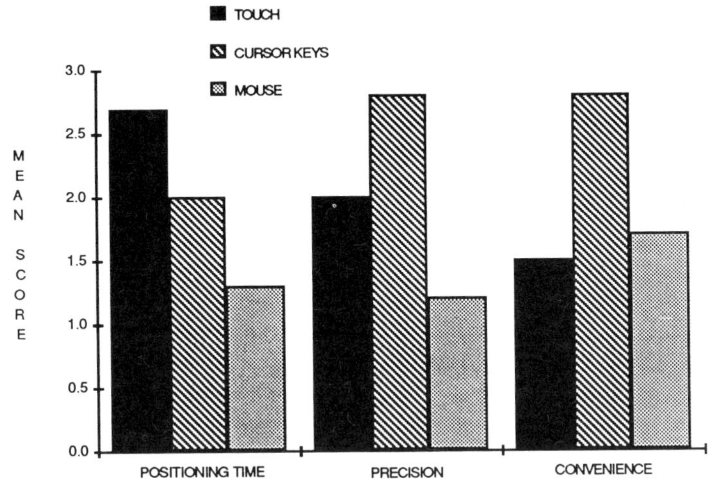

FIG 5: PREFERRED INTERACTION TOOL WITH RESPECT TO POSITIONING TIME, PRECISION AND CONVENIENCE.

Figure 5 shows the preferred tool with respect to positioning time, precision and convenience. Touch was rated best with respect to positioning time and cursor keys with respect to precision and convenience. However, it is important to point out that the repeated lifting of the arm when using the touchscreen can be tiring, especially in continuous tasks. This will be explored in further studies.

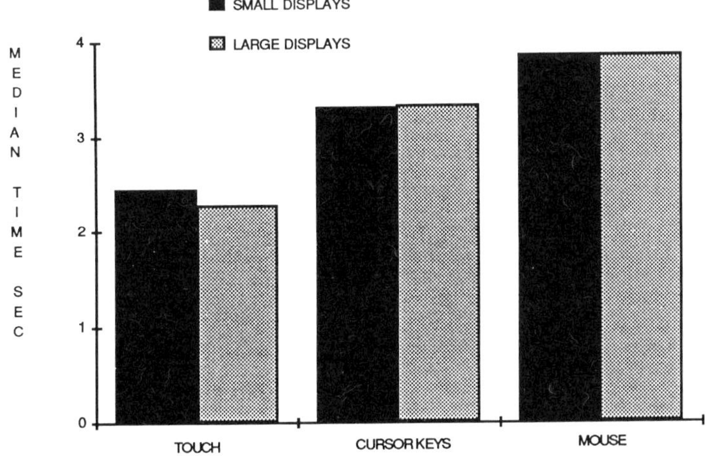

FIG 6: TIME BETWEEN CURSOR POSITIONING AND TYPING TASK.

Figure 6 shows the time between the cursor positioning and the start of the typing task. This time is less when using the touch screen than any of the other tools. There is apparently no difference between small and large displays.

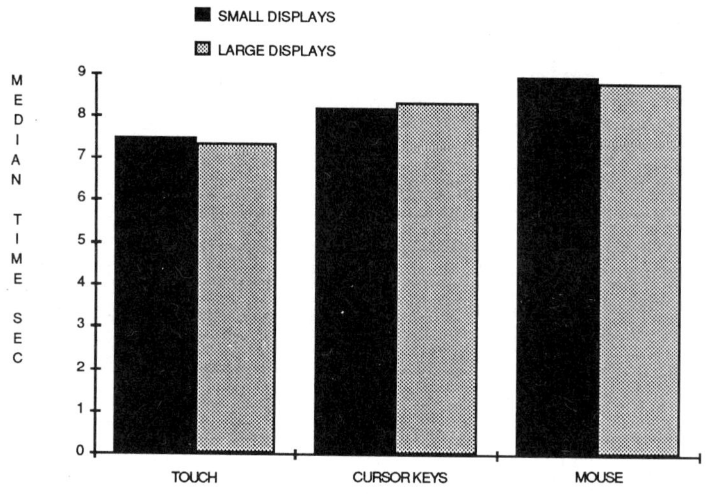

FIG 7: TIME FOR TYPING TASK.

Figure 7 illustrates the time to perform the typing task. It can be seen that typing is faster in the condition with the touch screen. It is not obvious why this effect should appear, and its statistical significance has not yet been studied (which also applies to the other effects). If it holds true, a possible explanation may be that some kind of "mode change" between the positioning task and the typing task in the cursor key and mouse condition is more difficult than when using the touch screen. The effect, then should also appear in the other direction which,judging from figure 2 alone, may be the case. There is virtually no difference between small and large displays.

To summarize:

- Touch screen is a very effective interaction device on ordinary displays irrespective of subtask.

- Touch screen can be used also for small display areas.

- Cursor keys are more effective and user friendly than a mouse in ordinary displays.

- Touch screen has to be systematically evaluated with respect of fatigue (How many positining tasks can you perform without being fatigue).

The full report will be available in October 1986. Until then a control with a different kind of mouse also will be tested, since the implementation used in this experiment might be a little unfair to mouses in general.

REFERENCES

[1] Albert, A.E. "The effect of graphic input devices on performance in cursor positioning task". Proc. Human Factor Soc 26th Annual Meeting Washington/USA. Oct 25-29, 1982, 54-58.

[2] Allen, R.B. "Cognitive Factors in human interaction with computers" Behvaior and information technology 256-278, 1982.

[3] Beaumont, J. G. "Speed of response using keyboard and screen-based microcomputer response media". Int.J. Man-Machine Studies (1985) 23, 61-70.

[4] Card, S.K. English, W., & Burr, B.J. "Evaluation of mouse, rate controlled isometric joystick, step keys and text keys for text selection on a CRT" Ergonomicis 21, 610-613, 1978.

[5] Goodwin, N.C. "Cursor positioning on a electronic display using light-pen, light-gun or keyboard for three basic tasks". Human factors, 17 (1975), 289-295.

[6] Whitfield, D, Ball, R.G., Bird, J.M., "Some comparisons of on-display and off-display touch input devices for interaction with computer generated displays". Ergonomics, 1983, Vol. 26, No. 11, 1033-1053.

WORK WITH DISPLAY UNITS 86
B. Knave and P.-G. Widebäck (eds.)

NAMING ERRORS AND AUTOMATIC ERROR CORRECTION IN HUMAN-COMPUTER INTERACTION

Sören Lenman and Hans Marmolin

National Defence Research Institute Man and Information Systems (FOA 53) P.O. Box 1165 S-581 11 LINKÖPING SWEDEN

A possible use of an automatic spelling corrector in command languages and name entering tasks could be to generate suggestions to the user, rather than standard error messages. This raises questions concerning the design of the user interface. A correction algorithm, was tested in a preliminary experiment where the effects on the user of encountering correct and incorrect suggestions as well as error messages were studied. The classification performance of the spelling corrector is discussed. It is proposed that the effectiveness can be analysed in terms of detection theory. A method of analysis of user interfaces is outlined from the experimental data, based on response latencies and uncertainty analysis. The findings and methods will have to be further tested before any major conclusions can be drawn.

INTRODUCTION

A common obstacle when using command dialogues is their sensitivity even to simple spelling errors. This also can be a problem when searching for a name in a data base. What one would need is an on line spelling corrector, working sufficiently fast to be usable even with rather long lists of commands or names. Of course, such a device would have to compute some arbitrary similarity score between the typed string and all the entries in a list of possible names. This score might provide a basis for ranking the items in the list according to varying degrees of probability. If no perfect match is found, a very simple use of the ranking would be to display the most probable name as a suggestion that the user could accept or reject, eliminating the need to retype if the suggestion was correct. In some applications it might even be possible to accept the most highly ranked item without verification.

This, however, presupposes that the similarity scores somehow reflect the error behaviour of the user, for example by taking into account the probabilities of different kinds of errors. In the ideal case this would guarantee that the comparision between a mistyped string and the target name would gain a higher similarity score than any other comparision in the list of possible names. In practice, however, there always will be a risk of selecting the wrong command or name. To reduce this risk, one can introduce two criteria, or limits. One is an accept limit: input strings that gain a similarity score less than that limit would not be accepted for processing, but would be used to generate a suggestion. The other is a suggest limit: if the highest similarity score found falls below that limit, no suggestion would be generated. Instead a standard action would be taken, for example the display of an error message.

There still will be a risk of errors, however. This risk depends on the quality of the spelling corrector. The question then is: how good must it be to be of any value? What is the effect on the user of encountering suggestions as well as error messages in a command dialogue? What happens if the system at times generates incorrect suggestions? Then there will be three kinds of system responses to a typing error instead of one. There also will be at least two possible user actions: retype or acknowledge. And: is it at all possible to directly accept even slightly mistyped commands or names without forcing the user to verify them? This problem is heavily dependent on the consequences of an error, however, and must be discussed in relation to a specific system or task. Thus, in the work to be presented here the interest has been focused on the first set of questions.

The first step, then, was to develop an algorithm that could classify typing errors into predefined, commonly used categories. The simple classification scheme shown in table 1 was used as a starting point to be further elaborated in the future work.

Table 1. A common classification scheme for typing errors (after Bailey [1])

Category	Correct	Typed
Substitution	ABC	AKC
Transposition	ABC	ACB
Omission	ABC	AC
Insertion	ABC	ABBC

This classification also was used by Pollock & Zamora [2] in their study of spelling errors and spelling correction, and there is a large amount of general error data available, for example [3],[4],[5], relating to a number of factors, such as perceptual and visual similarities, letter position in the name, keyboard layout and so on.

A baseline system for computing similarity scores for this classification scheme was developed. The general idea is to use the error probabilities in reverse, so to say, by applying Bayesian procedures in the computations. For example, a common error should not reduce the similarity score as much as a very uncommon one. In the present implementation, however, the different error classes are only crudely weighed according to their known frequencies of occurence, and only error position in the string is taken into account. The resulting similarity score varies between 0 and 1, where 1 defines a perfect match. The exact workings of the algorithm and the scoring process will be presented elsewhere.

A simple pilot experiment then was designed in order to get a first test of the classification performance of the spelling corrector, to gather some error data and to examine the output of the scoring system. A further aim was to study some effects of encountering different kinds of error messages, as described above, and to generate hypothesises for future work.

METHOD

A simple trancription task was developed. On the screen of an ordinary 24x80 display terminal three framed areas, 1 row * 48 columns in size and with a vertical spacing of 2 rows was displayed. In the upper frame a word to be typed was shown to the subject. In the lower one the letters typed were echoed. Typing of a word was completed by a carriage return. Similarity scores then were computed for the input string against all the words in the list used. If an error was detected a message appeared in the middle frame. Depending on the similarity scores and the experimental condition, the message could be one of three kinds: a standard error message, a correct suggestion or an incorrect suggestion. For example: if the correct word was STOCKHOLM and STOCHOLM was typed, then 'STOCHOLM -- ????' and 'STOCHOLM -- STOCKHOLM?' was the corresponding error message and the correct suggestion, respectively. 'STOCHOLM -- STORHOLM?' would be a possible incorrect suggestion. A correct suggestion could be accepted by the subject by hitting carriage return. On an incorrect suggestion or an error message the word had to be retyped. When a word was correctly entered the terminal bell sounded and a new word was displayed. The time between end of typing and system response was kept constant at 1.7 seconds.

Two factors were varied: the setting of the suggest limit and the quality of the spelling corrector. The variation in suggest limit affects the probability of generating suggestions rather than error messages. In terms of similarity scores it was set at .00, .65 and .80, i. e. "always", "often" and "sometimes". The variation in quality mainly affects the probability of generating incorrect suggestions. This probability was set at .00, .25 and .50. Since the quality of the spelling corrector was fixed and largely unknown, this variation was partly accomplished by using the computer random number generator as well as the computed similarity scores, i.e. incorrect suggestions at times were deliberately generated in response to a typing error. In addition to the nine experimental conditions there also was a control condition where only error messages could come up. Thus, there was total of ten conditions in the experiment.

The experiment was run on a VAX 750 computer system, using a Tandberg TDV2230S display terminal. From an extensive list of names of cities and places in Sweden, 300 names consisting of 10 to 15 letters, were chosen. This rather extreme list of words was chosen to ensure getting a high proportion of typing errors and at the same time making spelling correction easy.The list was used in all the experimental conditions. Two subjects, well trained in the experimental task, were run: a qualified typist and a fair amateur. Both subjects served in all the conditions, given in a different random order. Each condition was preceded by 50 trials of training. The subjects were encouraged to type at, or slightly above their maximum speed. Fast initial reactions to the names and messages presented was also stressed. Response latencies, typing speed and errors were recorded for a hundred trials in each condition for each one of the subjects.

RESULT AND DISCUSSION

As expected, error rates in the experiment were quite high. The typist, at an average speed of 5.9 characters/sec., mistyped 30% of the words and made an average of 1.55 errors/mistyped word. The typing speed of the amateur was 4.9 characters/sec at an error rate of 45% and an average of 1.9 errors/mistyped word. There were no systematic differences between experimental conditions with respect to typing speed.

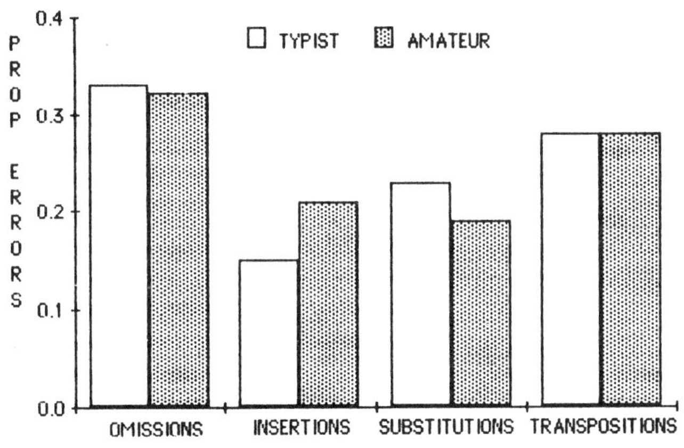

FIG 1. ERROR CLASSIFICATIONS IN THE EXPERIMENT.

The two histograms in fig. 1 show the classifications into error categories made by the spelling corrector during the experiment. One can note the high rate of order errors, and that the typist made relatively more substitution errors than the amateur, who made more insertions. At first glance this does not seem unreasonable. Touch typing at maximum speed should induce order errors. The typist, who does not look at the keyboard, should be at great risk of hitting the wrong key when typing to fast. The amateur, who looks at the keyboard but has less manual dexterity, could be expected to make insertions by hitting two keys at once, especially when using a trigger happy terminal keyboard.

In fig. 2 the error statistics of both subjects are merged and can be compared to the results of the Pollock & Zamora [3] study, based on a very large amount of data . The main differences are the proportion of order errors, and that Pollock & Zamora left multiple errors unclassified. From a strict point of wiew this is the correct thing to do. Many kinds of multiple errors can only be classified into the categories used by adopting some convention. This, rather than the actual errors made, might have caused the high proportion of order errors observed in the experiment. A preliminary inspection shows no such effect, but this will have to be very

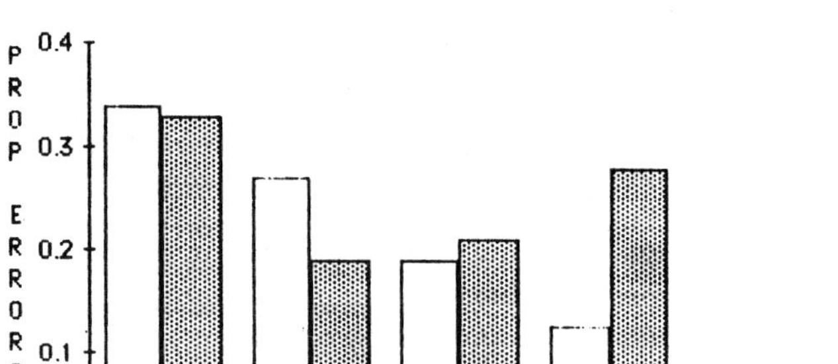

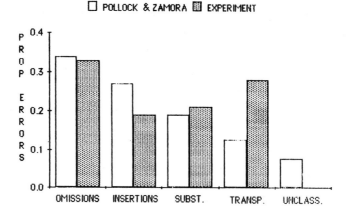

FIG. 2. ERROR CLASSIFICATIONS BY POLLOCK & ZAMORA (2) AND IN THE EXPERIMENT, BOTH SUBJECTS TOGETHER.

carefully analyzed before any conclusions regarding error patterns in general is drawn from classifications made by the present algorithm.

Quite aside from the classification performance, the computed, general similarity scores can be analyzed, and the effectivenes of the algorithm, used as a spelling corrector, can be evaluated. One way to do this is in terms of decision theory or signal detection theory, as described for example by Green&Swets [6]. In fig. 3 the scores computed in the experiment are plotted for both subjects together.

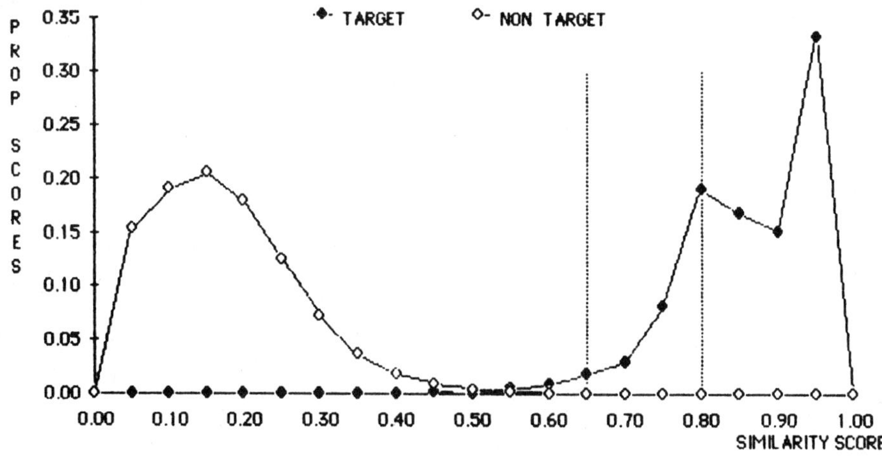

FIG 3: DISTRIBUTION OF SCORES WHEN COMPARING MISTYPED STRINGS AGAINST TARGET AND NON TARGET STRINGS. THE DOTTED LINES REFER TO SUGGEST LIMITS.

The left hand distribution in fig. 3 has been obtained by computing the similarity scores for all the mistyped strings against all the names in the list, except for the target name. In terms of detection theory this corresponds to observations from the noise distribution. The right hand distribution has been obtained by comparing the mistyped strings against their respective target strings. This corresponds to observations drawn from a distribution of signals. In an application, the spelling correction algorithm faces the problem of choosing the correct target name, rejecting all the names in the noise distribution. If the distributions are considered as probability density functions, this always can be done if there is no overlap betweeen them. The greater the overlap, the greater the risk of making an error. Thus, some function of the distance between the distributions can be used as a measure of the quality of the correction algorithm, when used to correct typing errors. The exact appearance of the distributions is of less importance in this context, and will not be discussed here.

In fig. 3 one can see that the spelling corrector used separates the noise and signal distributions quite well. This, however, does not necessarily mean that the algorithm or the scoring system used is a good one. The list of words was deliberately chosen to make correction easy, a necessary prerequisite for the experimental variation. If the words in the list had been very similar, for example, correction would have been much more difficult. Thus, given the algorithm and scoring system, correction performance will vary as a function of the list of words used and the pattern of errors encountered in a specific task. Given some knowledge of error behaviour and the characteristics of the list, however, it might be possible to optimize the scoring system for different lists and different users. Methods for accomplishing this will be explored in the future work. This, then, necessitates the continous gathering of error data.

In addition, if distributions of the kind shown in fig. 3 can be used as probability density functions, the risk of making an error at any given similarity score can be computed. The task of the spelling corrector can be described as choosing one item from a list of length n, where n-1 incorrect choices can be made. Following Green & Birdsall [7] the probability of making an error then is equivalent to the probability that a single drawing from the signal distribution will be larger than the largest of n-1 drawings from the noise distribution. Thus, the length of the list also is an important factor.

The suggest limits .65 and .80, used in the experiment, are marked in fig. 3. According to a crude application of the above mentioned method of computation, the proportion of incorrect suggestions at these limits would have been around .03 and .005 respectively. For the suggest limit of .00 the error rate would have been in the order of .05. Thus, the error rates in the experiment were not very realistic in relation to the list and the subjects used. It must be stressed, though, that these computations are not trivial and that there might be dependencies in the data not taken care of. This has not yet been checked.

The effects of the experimental variations in suggest limit and spelling corrector performance, i.e. the probabilities of error messages and incorrect suggestions, has mainly been evaluated by an analysis of the response latencies. In this analysis both subjects have been treated together and means are used throughout. No statistical tests have been performed. The response latencies when a word was initially shown varied between 0.58 and 0.63 sec between conditions. No systematic differences could be found. This was also true for the associated probability of making a typing error. The latencies to initiate the appropriate action when a message or a suggestion was displayed differed however, as shown if fig. 4.

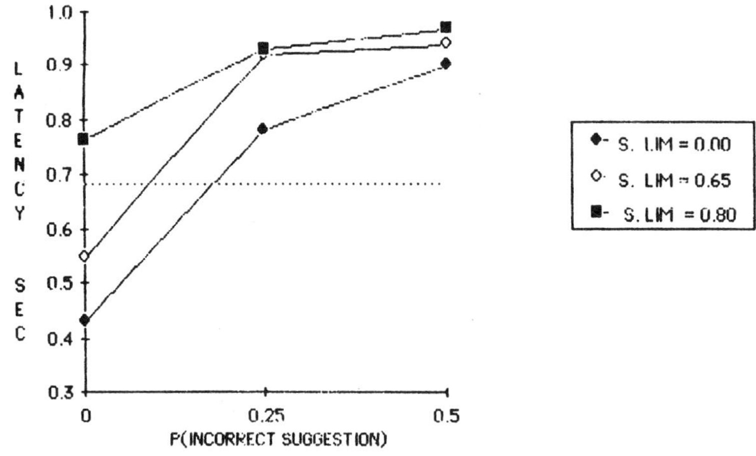

FIG 4. RESPONSE LATENCIES TO ERROR MESSAGES. DOTTED LINE REFERS TO CONTROL CONDITION.

There is a marked increase in reaction times with the probability of incorrect suggestions, the greatest increase taking place at low values. This effect seems to be less, the greater the proportion of error messages. On the other hand, increasing the low-limit also markedly increases the reaction times. This effect, in turn, seems to be less, the higher the percentage of incorrect suggestions. There was a tendency to the same pattern of variation in the associated probability of making a second error in response to error messages and suggestions. However, second errors were very few in number and will not be included in the present analysis.

Taking the effects shown in fig. 3 for granted, there seems to be an inconsistency in the .65 suggest limit condition. This illustrates a general problem with studies of this kind, which also applies to many studies of real systems: the experimental variation is to a great extent in the hands of the subject. In this case, a subject that never makes an error, will not see any difference between experimental conditions at all. Consequently, the data ought to be examined in relation to the variation that the subjects actually experienced.

The actual, relative proportions of error messages, correct and incorrect suggestions can be described as a discrete probability distribution, and the experimental variations as affecting the probabilities of the various outcomes. Then, following Garner [10], a convenient summary measure of the variation is the Shannon measure of average information, or uncertainty.

In fig. 5 the data from fig. 4 is replotted against the average uncertainty, expressed in bits. The maximum possible uncertainty, 1.58 bits, would be reached if the three categories were equally probable. As can be seen, latency seems to be a linear function of uncertainty. This linear relationship is well known from reaction time studies, and is usually explained in terms of an increase in the decision load put upon the subject (Welford, [9]). However, if the present experiment could be described as a standard choice reaction time study, then the control condition ought to be equivalent to the condition where only correct suggestions were given, the uncertainty being 0 bits. This is not the case, as can be seen in fig. 5. Contrary to most reaction

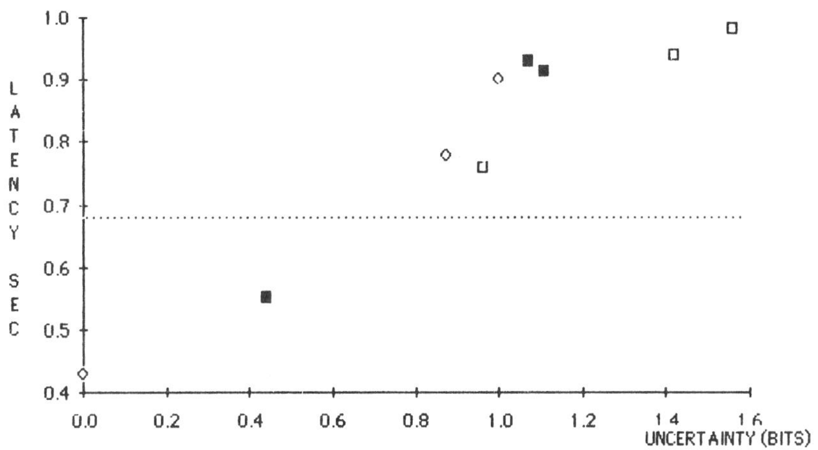

FIG. 5: RESPONSE LATENCY AS A FUNCTION OF UNCERTAINTY. THE CONTROL CONDITION IS MARKED BY THE DOTTED LINE. MAX UNCERTAINTY = 1.58 BITS.

time studies, the responses in this experiment differ in complexity. Correct suggestions could just be acknowledged; on error messages and incorrect suggestions a retype was required. The latencies differ for these responses, being .67, .99 and 1.19 sec for correct reactions to the three kinds of system messages, respectively. In addition, though not shown here, response latencies to correct and incorrect suggestions increase linearly with uncertainty. Latencies to error messages, however, seems to be nearly constant at around 1 sec. in the experimental conditions. This also should be compared to the .68 sec. in the control condition.

The set of relationships hinted at in this superficial data analysis will be further examined in future studies with the aim of developing a general description of user interfaces of the kind described here. The pattern of error probabilities, not taken into account here, then also will be included. Another line of work concerns the design of error messages and the possible use of spelling correction to generate menus in mixed dialogues. In parallell with the experimental work, findings and hypotheses will be tested in real tasks within the context of a C3I system.

REFERENCES

[1] Bailey, R. W. Human Performance Engineering: A Guide For system designers. (New Jersey: Prentice-Hall, 1982) pp. 359 - 386.

[2] Pollock, J.J. & Zamora, A. Automatic Spelling Correction in Scientific and Scholarly Text. Communications of the ACM, 1984, 27(4), pp. 358 - 368.

[3] Pollock, J. J. & Zamora, A. Collection and Characterization of Spelling Errors in Scientific and Scholarly Text. Journal of the American Society for Information Science, 1983,34(1), pp. 51 - 58.

[4] Wing,A.M. & Baddeley, A.D., Spelling errors in Handwriting: A Corpus and a Distributional Analysis. In: Frith, U. (ed.),Cognitive Processes in Spelling. (Academic Press, London,1980) pp. 251 - 273.

[5] Grudin, J.T. Error Patterns in Novice and Skilled Transcription Typing. In: Cooper, W.E.,(ed.),Cognitive Aspects of Skilled Typewriting. (Springer - Verlag, New York, 1983) pp. 121 - 144.

[6] Green, D.M. & Swets, J.A. Signal Detection Theory and Psychophysics (Wiley, New York, 1966)

[7] Green,D.M. and Birdsall,T.G., The Effect of Vocabulary Size on Articulation Score. In: Swets, J.A. (ed.) Signal Detection and Recognition by Human Observers.(Wiley, New York,1964) pp. 609 - 619.

[8] Garner,W.R., Uncertainty and Structure as Psychological Concepts.(Wiley, New York, 1962).

[9] Welford, A.T., Fundamentals of Skill. (Methuen, London, 1968)

WORK WITH DISPLAY UNITS 86
B. Knave and P.-G. Widebäck (eds.)

USER INTERFACE IN NEW PC SOFTWARE

Hans Laestadius

Ericsson Information Systems Sverige AB
161 11 Bromma, Sweden

1. Background

Users of personal computer software are often classified by level of experience (naive or experienced) and by frequency of use (casual or full-time). A single user is however seldom neither-nor but represents a combination of these characteristics for different tasks.

Many software products for personal computers are designed for a certain type of user but do not match the requirements of a "mixed" user. Some users always prefer working by menu selection while others quickly learn to enter commands directly by keys.

2. The software packages

A common user interface (internally named ERGO-FACE), with the approach to support different types of usage, has been implemented in some new PC software packages from Ericsson Information Systems. One is ERGOWORD which contains functions for word processing, document handling and DOS support. Another is SWECURE which is used for encryption and decryption of text and data files (DOS files in PC).

A third package HERMES, used internally for some time, contains functions for PC-PC communication, PC based file servers, and mailing and common storage facilities for PC users connected by various networks.

These software packages are used in standard PC combinations with the screen working in text mode including semi-graphic characters, and a standard PC keyboard used as input medium.

In the following we assume that the keyboard and the screen are the only means for interaction between the user and the software, e.g. the user documentation is left outside.

3. User interface characteristics

The user interacts with this "Ergo-Face" by entering commands from the keyboard. Depending on the situation and the type of command four different types of screen pictures will be presented as "windows".

The screen presents the following basic information when no commands are entered:

Screen	
Status line	Eg. name of document, cursor info
Information window	Eg. a document index or the text within a document file
Message line	Eg. a prompt for next user input

The data entered from the keyboard are inserted at the cursor position in the information window. The four different screen "windows" are overlayed upon the information, and correspond to

- Direct keyboard use
- Keyboard help
- Menu selection
- Help

These screen windows may be combined in many ways depending on user action.

3.1 Direct keyboard use

Besides using the keyboard for typing text, moving the cursor and entering other information the user may also use many direct keys or combination of keys for entering a command (underline on, bold off, new page, search etc).

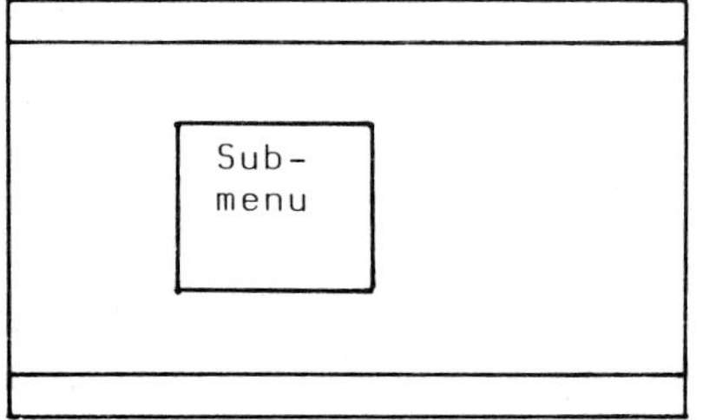

When a direct key command requires one or more parameters a sub-menu (form) is presented.

3.2 Keyboard help

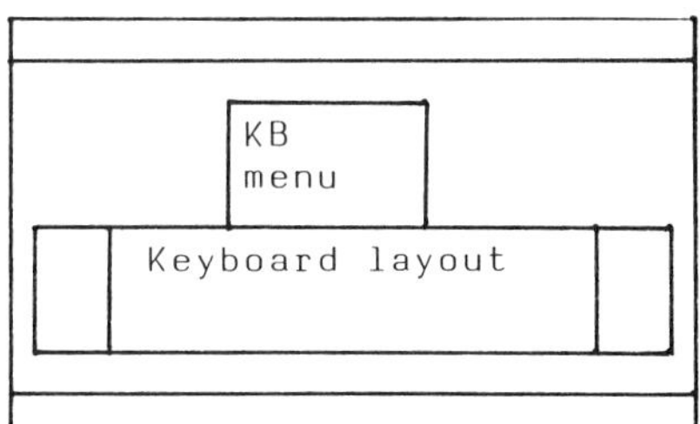

When pressing a special key for keyboard help, a template of the keyboard is presented on the screen, together with a list (menu) of keyboard functions

3.3 Menu selection

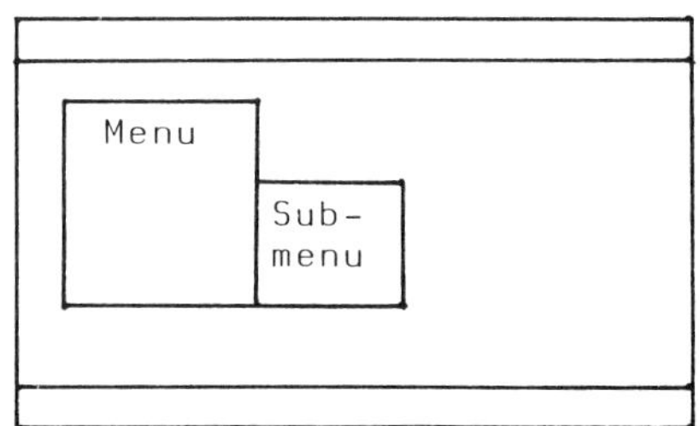

When pressing a special menu key a list of functions is presented in a menu window.

On selection, the function may be executed directly, or after confirmation from the corresponding sub-menu

3.4 Help

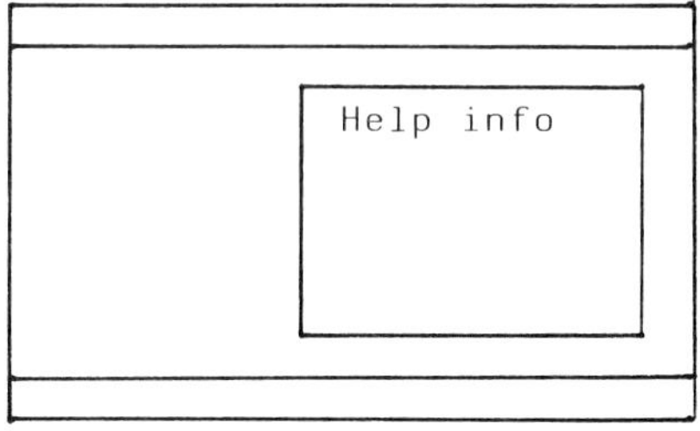

When pressing a special help key a window with help information is presented.

The help information is always related to the selected function or the situation (conceptual help)

4. Classification and reaction of users

Our PC software package ERGOWORD has been used for more than a year and is distributed to more than 2000 users. By interviews and by questions from hundreds of users we have got some feed-back to our design assumptions for the user interface, and how we may classify users and their reactions.

Our users may be classified into four main groups:

Naive/Casual. Little or limited experience of working with personal computers and with word processing software. Uses the software casually.

Experienced/Full-time. The opposite to naive/casual users.

Experienced/Casual. Users with good experience of working with personal computers and word processing software. By using the software only casually this type of user "forgets" and needs repeated training and support from the software.

Naive/Full-time. Users with little initial experience but who gain experience by using the software frequently.

			Preference for each method			
No of users	Type of user	Usage	Key-board	KB help	Menu selec.	Help
40 %	Naive	Casual	Medium	High	High	High
20 %	Naive	Full-time	High	Medium	High	Medium
30 %	Exp.	Casual	High	High	Medium	Medium
10 %	Exp.	Full-time	High	Medium	Low	Low

5. Conclusions

1. Naive/Casual users prefer menu selection and on-line help support for almost all functions.

2. Experienced/Full-time users prefer direct keyboard use and fast selection of functions.

3. Experienced/Casual users often require a mix for the selection of functions, by menu or by direct keyboard use, and an on-line adaptive help support.

4. Naive/Full-time users require **all** these possibilities in order to learn and to work faster, easier and more efficiently.

WORK WITH DISPLAY UNITS 86
B. Knave and P.-G. Widebäck (eds.)

FORMAL SPECIFICATION OF USER INTERFACES: TWO APPLICATION STUDIES

Anker H. Jørgensen[○], Leif C. Nielsen[□] and
Peter H. Carstensen[○]

○ Dansk Datamatik Center, Lundtoftevej 1C,
DK-2800 Lyngby, Denmark

□ CCI-Europe, Søren Nymarksvej 3,
DK-8270 Højbjerg, Denmark

This paper addresses the use of a formal language for specifying user interfaces. Specification is one approach to designing systems "outside in" rather than "inside out", aiming at enhancing the usability of systems. Two studies are reported. In the first the user interface of an existing system, a syntax-directed editor, was described. Working out the description of the system resulted in a very minute and yet very cohererent overall understanding of the system. In the second study the specification language was employed for specifying the user interface of a system early in the design phase. This approach prevented some user difficulties and resulted in a system that was easy to learn. Also it made it possible for the designer to predict half of the user difficulties at the syntactic level of the interaction.

1 INTRODUCTION

One approach to developing more usable interactive software is to design systems "outside in", ie. to start with the user interface as opposed to the "inside out" approach where the data structures and functions are first designed. One "outside in" development strategy is to <u>specify</u> the user interface in a formal specification language. This strategy is investigated in this paper.

As the system is approached "outside in" in specifying the user interface, the designer can be expected to obtain a clearer conception of general levels of the interaction (eg. consistency in use of methaphors) as well as detailed levels (eg. consistency in reaction to syntax errors). Also, this approach could enable the designer to get an overview of the user interface early in the design. This insight could lead to better user interfaces and enable the designer to predict potential user difficulties as well as prevent them.

A number of specification formalisms exist, see Reisner (1984). These address the syntactic and lexical levels of the human-computer interaction. However, few reports of applications exist. In Reisner's study (1981), the user interface of two graphical systems were described in a formal language. Predictions were made as to the usability of the two systems and these were confirmed by user tests. However, the interfaces of the systems were not described during the design, only after implementation.

Recently Browne et al. (1986) investigated the feasibility of the Command Language Grammar (CLG) developed by Moran (1981) for designing an adaptive user interface to a mail system. They found in fact that CLG was a useful tool in that it "opened up" a system for scrutiny at a number of levels of abstraction.

This paper complements the two investigations mentioned above. Two studies are reported. In the first study the interface of an existing system, a syntax-directed editor, was described in a formal language. The results showed that the designer having described the user interface in the formal language had a far more profound understanding of the interface than the designer of the system.

In the second study the language was used early in the design to specify the user interface of a small system. Based on his insights, the designer predicted user difficulties. These were compared to actual user tests. Firstly, the system proved easy to learn and secondly, more than half of the difficulties experienced by the users at the syntactic level of the interaction were predicted by the designer.

2 LANGUAGE FOR USER INTERFACE SPECIFICATION

We employed a specification language described by Bleser & Foley (1982) and in more detail by Bleser (1983). We named the language LUIS: Language for User Interface Specification.

The starting point for the specification language is the demarcation to the levels of the interaction (Foley & van Dam, 1982): conceptual, semantic, syntactic and lexical. The language only comprises the two last levels. The language is defined in a BNF-like notation. Before embarking on the two studies we made some changes to the language for reasons of consistency and applicability. These are not discussed here.

The relationship between the levels of interaction and the parts of a LUIS description is illustrated in figure 1 on the next page.

A LUIS specification of an interface is divided into three parts. The first part, the action/response dialogue, corresponds to the syntactic level. It comprises the sequences of interaction tokens in terms of dialogues, subdialogues, prompts, viewports, etc.

The next part, the type/token list, corresponds to the "upper part" of the lexical level in the interaction. This level defines tokens of the dialogue as either input or output, assigns types to the tokens, and associates tokens with an input or output technique.

The third part, the attribute list, associates the tokens with the physical characteristics of the I/O devices, eg. colour and blink. This level corresponds to the "lower part" of the lexical level, often denoted the physical level of the interaction.

Four-layered model	LUIS specification
Conceptual level	
Semantic level	
Syntactic level	Action/Response Dialog
Lexical level	Type/Token List Attribute List

FIGURE 1
The relationship between the four-layered model of Foley and van Dam and the three parts of a LUIS specification.

We will now give the reader a flavour of the structure of a LUIS description. Figure 2 below presents a brief example.

<u>Action/Response Dialog</u>

```
example_dialog ::= log_in
                   + dialog
                   + stop
log_in         ::= U: PROGRAMNAME
                   + C: CLEAR_SCREEN
```

<u>Type/Token List</u>

```
INPUT TYPE text =
   {PROGRAMNAME  =  keyboard('EXAMPLE')}
```

<u>Attribute List</u>

```
ATTRIBUTES OF keyboard FOR crt_keyboard =
{VIEWPORT = crt_viewport
 COLOR    = green
 BLINK    = off
 REVERSE  = off}
```

FIGURE 2
Excerpt from a LUIS specification

In the action/response dialogue part the syntax of the dialogue is specified. First a log-in part, followed by a dialogue part and terminated with a stop part. These are the major dialogue components. These are in turn specified in subsequent production rules. The log-in part contains an action where the user ("U") indicates a program name, followed by the response from the computer ("C") - clearing of the screen.

In the type/token list the actions and responses are connected to a so-called input/output technique. In the figure the lexeme EXAMPLE is input from the keyboard.

Finally the attributes of the input/output techniques are specified in the attribute list, including color and blink.

3 STUDY 1

In order to gain experience with the language we first tested the feasibility of LUIS by describing the user interface of an existing system: EKKO - a syntax-directed editor (Nørmark, 1984). EKKO supports the programming language Pascal and runs on a PERQ workstation including a graphics screen, pop-up menus, keyboard, and mouse. Thus EKKO has a fairly complicated user interface.

EKKO was studied thoroughly by one of us (referred to as the LUIS designer), who used the system and meticously recorded its behaviour. The recordings were structured into a complete LUIS description of the interface. The description runs to 14 pages and comprises approximately 150 production rules. Thus, given the complexity of the EKKO interface, the description is not overwhelming in terms of volume. This activity also resulted in a list of trouble spots in EKKO including difficulties actually experienced by the LUIS designer as user of the system.

In producing the description, the LUIS designer obtained a very intimate knowledge of the EKKO interface. We wanted to assess the completeness and correctness of this knowledge. We did so by comparing it to other sources of knowledge about the system: a user of EKKO and the designer of EKKO.

A user - a Pascal programmer - was using EKKO for one week. Evidence about the user's conception of the EKKO system was obtained by observation and by three think-aloud sessions followed by interviews. This resulted in a list of 35 difficulties experienced by the user.

The designer of EKKO was also interviewed. The interview addressed general aspects of interface design as well as details of the particular interface. The lists of trouble spots in EKKO served as input to this part of the interview.

3.1. Results of study 1

Thus we had three sources of information about the user interface of EKKO: Firstly, the LUIS description and the knowledge of the LUIS designer, secondly the user difficulties and views, and thirdly the views expressed by the designer. These three sources were compared. Two interesting points emerged.

The EKKO-design had been tackled with a strong view to having a coherent and usable interface. Thus the designer stated: "We were very conscious of the user interface. It's very important in such a system." Indeed, throughout the interview this emphasis on the user interface was clearly apparent. Nevertheless the LUIS designer had a far more detailed and yet coherent view of the system than the designer of EKKO. For example, the LUIS designer was able to pinpoint side effects and inconsistencies that were completely new to the designer.

The second point deals with the difficulties experienced by the Pascal programmer. This programmer had worked with EKKO longer than the LUIS designer. Nevertheless, of the 35 difficulties experienced by the Pascal programmer, only one was "new" to the LUIS designer. Thus, in developing the LUIS description, the LUIS designer had gained such an intimate knowledge of the system that he was familiar with the remaining 34 difficulties. He was for example able to trace the cause of the difficulties immediately to the system.

In terms of using LUIS as a description tool, the LUIS designer found that although LUIS was cumbersome to work with (using paper and pencil), it also served as an excellent aid for creating and manipulating conceptions of the interface. For example, in the action/response dialogue, he could concentrate on this level of the dialog and leave out other aspects, eg., media dependent issues.

In conclusion, LUIS proved to be an excellent means to developing a thorough understanding of a user interface of an existing system. Whether this holds true for design of user interfaces was investigated in the next study.

4 STUDY 2

This study focussed on potential benefits of LUIS in the design of an interactive system. A small system was developed for membership administration in a sports club. The system was running on an IBM PC.

Initially a conceptual design was carried out, carving out the relevant entities, attributes and operations. Typical entities were name, address, etc. and operations were change address, look up a member, etc.

Next a complete specification of the user interface was developed in LUIS. First the action/response dialogue was specified, next the type/token list and finally the attribute list. No considerations were given to the internal structures of the system during this phase. The LUIS specification runs to 7 pages, comprising 40 production rules.

As in the first study, we wanted to assess the utility of the LUIS designer's knowledge about the system being designed. Thus, before embarking upon the implementation, the designer tried to predict potential user difficulties. Eighteen predictions resulted. They addressed all the four levels of the interaction, see fig. 1. Some of these were general, eg. grasping the metaphors built into the system while other were more specific, eg. terminating the function entering a new member. These predictions where based solely upon the LUIS specification of the user interface and done before any coding had taken place.

Next the system was implemented, exactly as specified in the LUIS specification. This means that any new insight of the interface gained from making the predictions were not allowed to be introduced in the actual design.

Following implementation, a user test was run using six fairly computer-naive users in a think-aloud experiment. In each session the user received a short verbal introduction to the system and two pages of documentation. The users were asked to solve ten small tasks, eg. change the address of a member of the sports club. The user-system dialog was logged by the system and the utterances of the user were recorded on audio tape. Practically all the users managed to complete all the tasks in the time allocated. Thus the system was fairly easy to learn.

The protocols from the think-aloud sessions were analyzed and the user difficulties extracted. Only severe difficulties were included, ie., difficulties experienced by more than one user and errors with serious consequences, eg., unintentional deletion of a file. In all 38 user difficulties resulted.

The 38 difficulties were classified in the four levels of the interaction: conceptual, semantic, syntactic, and lexical. This classification needs some comments. There is no clear strategy for classifying the user difficulties, as the boundaries between them are somewhat blurry. However, there are on the other hand clear prototypical examples. These are listed below and can be conceived of as guides for the classification.

Conceptual level: The metaphors used in the system were not grasped by the users.

Semantic level: The users didn´t know what happened when a file was closed, eg., "Does the record disappear?"

Syntactic level: Problems in terminating the insert function.

Lexical level: The users use the wrong backspace key.

4.1. Results of study 2

We will first take the predictions of user difficulties as a starting point. Matching the predictions to the actual difficulties yields the following:

- 10 of the 18 predictions came true, for example termination of the entering function.

- 6 of the predictions did not cause difficulties, for example answering some yes/no questions.

- 2 of the predictions did not come into play in the sessions, for example inserting members in a full file.

Thus quite a large proportion of the predictions came true. This hit rate is quite satisfactory considering how complex the interaction between users and computer systems are.

Now we will take the actual 38 user difficulties as a starting point. Only 10 of these were actually predicted, ie. about one in four. However, if we look at the distribution of these difficulties at the four interaction levels a clear pattern emerges as shown in figure 3 below.

Level	No of user difficulties	Hereof predicted
Conceptual	6	0
Semantic	14	1
Syntactic	12	8
Lexical	6	1
Total	38	10

FIGURE 3
Matching actual user difficulties to predictions

It appears from figure 3 that nearly all the predictions that came true addressed the lower levels of the interaction, in other words the levels addressed by the LUIS language. Thus, at the syntactic level, the designer was able to predict 8 out of 12 actual difficulties.

At the lowest level, the lexical level, many of the user difficulties were caused by limitations in the underlying hardware and software, eg., cursor manipulation and correcting data fields on the screen. These issues are beyond the scope of the LUIS language.

It appears also from figure 3 that practically no user difficulties at the two "highest" levels were predicted. These are also, however, beyond the scope of LUIS.

In summary, developing the system this way forced the designer to carefully consider a large number of issues that in a traditional design might have been overlooked due to focus on the internal structures of the system. Thereby the designer was able to predict more than half of the actual user difficulties at the syntactic level. Given this, there is also every reason to believe that the use of LUIS in the first place has prevented errors. We cannot however, render this assertion probable based on the present data.

5 CONCLUSIONS

These two small-scale studies certainly do not warrant grand conclusions. However, we do believe that the trends reported here are likely to hold generally.

As to the designers' understanding, LUIS undoubtedly supported a thorough, detailed and yet coherent conception of the user interface. A large part of this insight must be ascribed to the mere act of conceptualizing the system from the outside and shaping the conceptions into a formal language - rather than the feasibility of the particular language features of LUIS.

In assessing the benefits of LUIS it should be kept in mind that it only comprises the low levels of the interaction. Often user difficulties are caused by misconceptions at higher levels. However, as our experience demonstrates, there is a marked spin-off in the designers' understanding from the low levels to the higher conceptual levels.

Finally, the lack of computer-based supporting tools should be mentioned. In both studies the need for such tools was urgent: an editor for the specifications, a compiler or interpreter, and a consistency/completeness checker. Clearly, a prerequisite for general application of such formalisms for systems development "outside in" is provision of computer-based tools.

6 ACKNOWLEDGEMENTS

We thank Jakob Nielsen and Kurt Nørmark for providing access to their data from the EKKO user test.

7 REFERENCES

Bleser, T.W. (1983): A formal specification and computer-assisted evaluation of person-computer interface (M.S. Thesis). The George Washington University, School of Engineering and Applied Science. Report GWU-IIST 83-18, Jan. 7, 1983.

Bleser, T.W. & J.D. Foley (1982): Towards Specifying and Evaluating the Human Factors of User-Computer Interfaces. Proc. Human Factors in Computing Systems, Gaithersburg, MD, March 1982, 309-314.

Browne, D.P., B.D. Sharrat and M.A. Norman (1986): The formal specification of adaptive user interfaces using Command Language Grammar. Proc. CHI'86 Human Factors in Computing Systems, Boston, April 1986, 256-260.

Foley, J.D. & A. van Dam (1982): Fundamentals of Interactive Computer Graphics. Reading, Mass.: Addison-Wesley.

Moran, T.P.(1981): The Command Language Grammar: a representation for the user interface of interactive computer systems. Int. J. Man-Machine Studies, 15, 3-50.

Nørmark, K. (1984): The EKKO Editor - User's Guide. Version 1.1, Dept. of Computer Science, University of Århus, Denmark.

Reisner, P. (1981): Formal Grammar and Human Factors Design of an Interactive Graphics System. IEEE Transactions on Software Engineering, SE-7, 229-240.

Reisner, P. (1984): Formal Grammar as a Tool for Analyzing Ease of Use: Some Fundamental Concepts. In J.C. Thomas & M.L. Schneider (eds): Human Factors in Computing Systems. Norwood, NJ: Ablex, 53-78.

WORK WITH DISPLAY UNITS 86
B. Knave and P.-G. Wideback (eds.)

WHERE IS THE ACTION IN HUMAN-COMPUTER INTERACTION?

Thomas MORAN
XEROX PARC
Palo Alto

1. INTRODUCTION

Thomas Moran started by declaring some conclusions he had arrived at by studying the needs of the users:

Systems should be built from simple principles and should be tailorable by the users themselves.
Systems are learnt from colleagues and not from handbooks and onlinehelp. Therefore it is important that the systems are used in a setting which encourages communication between people.

2. HUMAN FACTORS CRITERIA

Experience and research can be summarized in the following Human Factors criteria on computer systems:

Functionality through tailoring of weak representations
Understandibility through simplicity in User Interface design
Learning and trouble management through infrastructure.
Performance through manipulation and displays.
Quality through idea processing.
Sociability through language for communication

3. SUPPORTING COMPLEX INTELLECTUAL TASKS

The problem of most interest to Moran was how to augment users ir performing extensive intellectual tasks that take many months to perform (during which the user builds up a knowledge base about the task). One example could be writing a book.

Moran presented some developmental work, which had the aim to support advanced intellectual work:

Footnote
Thomas Moran was one invited speaker within the topic of Human-Computer Interaction. We can only regret that the hectic atmosphere at the XEROX Palo Alto Research Center, where Thomas Moran works as a research director, did not allow Thomas to present a written version of his talk himself. This is a summary, compiled by Yvonne Waern from summaries provided by Jacob Nielsen, Yvonne Waern, and Marion Wittstock.

3.1. Idea Processing

The goal is to improve the quality of ideas by providing effective representations for generating and evaluating ideas. Problem: People can often not at the early stage separate and structure ideas. Requiring them to do so can risk to encapsulate ideas prematurely. Therefore a system which supports creative thought processes should enable users to jot down ideas during brainstorming without any restrictions. At the same time it should enable them later to relate the ideas to each other and to structure them.

3.2. Multiple Activities

The goal is to support users who are pursuing many activities more or less in parallel . The traditional solution is the multi-windowing technique. However, this technique itself is not without problems. For instance, with many windows simultaneously active, there is not enough display space. A suggested solution is to partition the screen according to activities. You can then imagine that you pass through the screen like you walk through different rooms of a house. Each activity can take place in a separate room, and even be marked (for instance by a particular colour) to be distinguishable from other activities. Then, however, another problem emerges: Is it possible to partition activities cleanly?

3.3. Communication

Whereas the focus of research efforts during the 1960´s-1970´s had been on languages, it switched to considering programming environments, as soon as good languages were available. Nowadays, the need of supporting collaborative teams of computer programmers, is gaining in importance. A solution to the communication needs of programmers consists in giving them a medium to help them communicate their ideas about system development. A simulation of the system to be developed had been found to serve well - even system designers discovered the user-hostile features of the system.

WORK WITH DISPLAY UNITS 86
B. Knave and P.-G. Wideback (eds.)

USER-FRIENDLINESS - FROM SUGAR TO SYMBIOSIS

Yvonne WAERN
Department of Psychology
University of Stockholm
S-106 91 Stockholm
Sweden

The science of human-computer interaction is founded on a need to design computer systems to fit human requirements. To achieve this goal, we must first define "user-friendliness". The definitions indicate that user-friendliness cannot be added to systems design as a final sugar, but must be integrated from the very beginning. Before attempting to prescribe the design of systems, knowledge about human functioning in relation to interactive computer systems must be gathered. The WWDU conference included many good studies concerned both with user performance and user learning. However, the issues are by no means fully understood. Further research is needed to understand the possibility of creating a symbiosis of information processing by combining a human being and a computer program system.

1. WHY IS THE SCIENCE OF HUMAN-COMPUTER INTERACTION NECESSARY?

The science of human-computer interaction is founded on a need to design computer systems to fit human characteristics and requirements. In the advent of interactive computer systems and the invasion of those into the workplaces, it was soon discovered that the programs developed not only missed some of the important functions which were involved in the work they were supposed to perform, but they also forced the users of the programs to unnecessary restrictions and to clumsy ways of performing their tasks. As if this were not enough, these program systems were also difficult to learn, and their documentation was at their best incomplete and inconsistent, at worst incomprehensible. This state of computer programs reflected of course no necessary requirement of the computers themselves, but resulted from a lack of knowledge on the part of the system designers concerning the actual work as well as from a negligence of the importance of human factors in this area.

FOOTNOTE.

It is not possible to follow the new trends in this rapidly developing field only by reading books or articles. Conferences and personal contacts are more important sources of information. Supports for the necessary trips have been obtained from The Swedish Board for Research in the Humanities and Social Sciences, The Swedish Board for Technical Development, and the COST 11-bis and COST 11-ter programs.
I am indebted to Bernard Devine for comments on a first version.

As late as 1969 a reviewer of the field of systems design complained about the lack of concern with human factors issues. (Nickerson 1969). Foresighted human factors experts pointed to the importance of considering the user of the computer systems (Shackel, 1959). However, these isolated ergonomic insights had very little influence on the field before the time had come when computers were more generally used, and when the hardware and software technology were developed as far as to allow the "sugar" of user-friendliness to be put onto the system cake. Often this "sugar" was very ideosyncratic, based upon the taste of the particular user-system designer combination. Creating "user-friendly" systems for many system designers without human factors knowledge was (and still is) very similar to inventing the wheel over and over again for each new road and the carriages that were to pass along it.

The first serious attempts at psychological experimentation in the field of human-computer interaction came during the mid 1970´s. Now, in the 1980´s we see a continued struggle of experts in ergonomics, human factors, cognitive psychology, and linguistics to get beyond the "sugar" concept of user-friendliness. Instead, human factors knowledge should be used in the design of computer systems from the very beginning, in order to allow the electronic and the biological information processing systems to serve each other in an information processing symbiosis.

The problems covered by this emerging science span a broad field, ranging from organizational issues, via learning and performance aspects, into psychophysiological requirements. This is also reflected in the designations given to it. "Human Computer Interaction" is only one of the possible names for the field. "Human Factors in Information Technology" is another, which includes most types of problems involved in trying to fit computers and human beings together. More restricted problems are covered by the designations "Cognitive Ergonomics" or "Software Psychology", where the organizational aspects mostly are excluded, and the learning and performance problems are in focus. Still more focussed are the endeavours covered by the designations "Cognitive Engineering" or "Software Engineering", which mainly concern the problems of designing the interface between the user and the computer system.

At the WWDU conference, the topic of human-computer interaction was distinguished from work organizational issues on the one hand and from visual ergonomics (image quality and vision) on the other. This paper discusses mainly the issues of the cognitive aspects of real time interaction between computer system and user.

2. CRITERIA FOR "USER-FRIENDLY" SYSTEMS

The criteria for "user-friendly" systems can best be presented by quoting Thomas Moran from XEROX, PARC. (1986) In a plenary address at the WWDU conference, he presented the following factors of human-computer interaction:

- Usefulness (functionality)
- Usability (learning, performance, understanding, trouble management, subjective acceptance)

- Productivity (speed, quality of product of using computers)
- Sociability (communicativeness - that is people integration).

These criteria are concerned with the so called "end users" of the computer system. Additional criteria are required to serve the needs of those people who actually work with the development of these computer programs. In addition to the human factors needs of the end user, the needs of the software designer were expressed at the WWDU conference by K-P Faehnrich, who presented the European collaborative project called HUFIT (Human Factors in Information Technology), (Bullinger, Davies, Faehnrich, Schackel & Ziegler, 1986):

- Improved design methods, tools, procedures and guidelines to aid design for usability
- Office analysis and description tools (This could easily be extended to analysis and description of different information processing tasks, for instance including production engineering, decision making, group communication)
- Rapid prototyping and software tailoring tools
- Software architectures for better HCI usability
- Design methods for better documentation, help facilities and user support
- Evaluation methods and product evaluation tools

These criteria can be regarded as mostly belonging to the narrower concept of "cognitive (or software) engineering".

All of these above criteria sound reasonable for describing "user-friendliness" on a general plane. The next problem, however, consists in finding stricter definitions of the terms that will be productive in helping us to measure and understand what is needed. This problem is by no means solved by now, and was also mentioned by K-P. Faehnrich as one of the ongoing activities in the HUFIT project.

The endeavour to define and measure user-friendliness is not an easy one, as evidenced by the ambivalent reactions met when some recommendations were put forward by a distinguished group of German researchers. (see Dzida, 1985). These were formulated in the DIN draft standard No 66234 T8. (1985), and have since been subjected to heavy criticism. Why? The criteria proposed in the draft standard are:

- task appropriateness
- self-explanatoriness
- controllability
- reliability
- error tolerance
- error transparency

The criticism focusses on three main aspects, 1) the vagueness of the dimensions (they are mostly defined through examples), 2) the unrestricted scope of the suggestions (should really all kinds of computer systems comply to these requirements?) and 3) the problems involved in measuring the factors suggested. (see e.g. Hurd, 1986). It was therefore interesting to see an attempt to develop a useable taxonomy of user-friendliness, based upon this draft standard, presented in a paper at the conference. (Pelz & Wittstock, 1986). This study indicates that task appropriateness can be measured objectively (in this particular case in terms of the number of keystrokes required to perform a certain task). The self-explanatoriness criterion is highly related to subjective ratings of learnability. Thus there does not seem to be any reason to critisize the recommendations, where task appropriateness and self-explanatoriness are concerned. These are possible to define and measure. However, the criticism of the unlimited scope still holds. The criteria must be tested in several different situations. (Pelz and Wittstock studied text editors and spreadsheet programs). One further, very promising analysis, aiming at evaluating Computer Aided Instruction in terms of the criteria posed by the DIN draft proposal, was presented at the WWDU conference. (Haack & Mickasch, 1986).

To conclude, we can see that several reasonable criteria of user-friendliness of program systems have been put forward. But the problems of the scope and measurement of these criteria have yet to be solved.

3. SYSTEM FUNCTIONS

One of the most difficult criteria relates to the functionality of a system. Here, the creativity of system designers never seems to end, and sometimes it can be asked, whether or not a certain function really provided what is needed or whether or not it is useful. Some of the new functions under development can however be well motivated. So, for instance, Thomas Moran persuasively presented some seemingly useful functions. (Moran, 1986):

- idea processing, where the goal is to improve the quality of ideas, by providing effective representations for generating and evaluating ideas.
- support for multiple activities through multi-windowing techniques. The problems of such support were pointed out by Moran, who also gave some possible solutions. Other problems and their possible solutions have been discussed by the USCD group (Cypher, 1986, Miyata & Norman, 1986).
- communication, related to the need for a team of system designers to collaborate and intercommunicate regarding the system being designed. One idea worked on in this respect consisted in simulating the system being developed.

Other new functionalities will demand the integration of different systems. User interface management systems to help in the solving of these problems are being developed. An analysis of the issues involved in designing such systems was presented at the conference by Per Carleberg (1986).

New functionalities cannot be suggested without considering the particular task to be performed. An example of such a task analysis, performed for the task of production engineering was discussed at the WWDU conference by Torsten Kjellberg (1986, see also 1982, 1984 and 1985).

To conclude, the question of functionality is related to the tasks to be performed, which requires a careful analysis of the current situation. At the same time functionality questions are related to the ability to see into the future, to predict virtues as well as vices and to create realities out of the crystal ball's dream clouds.

4. STANDARDIZATION ACTIVITIES

The criteria of user-friendliness should ultimately lead to some kinds of guidelines for the design of user-friendly systems. The need for general guidelines or even standards is strong among system designers, end-users and procurers. System designers need guidelines in order to know what characterizes a user-friendly system. Users want systems which at least to some extent are similar, so that they do not have to learn each new system and each new application from the very beginning. Procurement personnel need guidelines as a help in selecting between different available systems. (Hurd, 1986).

Acknowledging these needs, different actions may be taken. Some companies have experienced such a strong need for standardization that they standardize internally, with the motivation that it is better having a nonoptimal standard, than having no standard at all. This strategy has been chosen by i.a. the Swedish Telecommunications Administration (STA), (Eriksson, Andersson & Orring, 1986). Other people are critical to a premature standardization, (cf Hurd, 1986) because of the risk of hampering further development. It is according to them advisable to issue guidelines, which can be used as long as they are useful, but which are not enforced, in order to keep the door open for future technical development. A good example of guidelines of this type is the one issued by Sid Smith (Smith, 1984).

A still more cautious procedure consists in collecting and establishing the knowledge necessary to guide further development. A first step in compiling knowledge which can be useful for systems designers can consist of a "reference model", i.e. a model to which system designers can refer in their design work. A reference model does not contain direct recommendations but rather gives a frame of reference to the requirements posed by the application, the system, the environment and not least by the user. The reference model should also contain possible ways to meet these requirements. The development of relevant requirements and the proposing of possible solutions represent no simple tasks. Intradisciplinary and collaborative efforts are required. One example is a series of workshops, starting at CHI' 85, under the enthusiastic and competent leadership of Gene Lynch and Jon Meads. The first workshop was called "Planning for User Interface Standards", and resulted in a more modest goal, which was pursued at CHI '86, i.e. "User Interface Reference Models". (Lynch & Meads, in press). The workshop will continue at CHI '87.

Many different activities exist, which promise the providing of a solid foundation of human factors knowledge for future recommendations. One recently established group aims at developing at least a draft standard, i.e. the Committee on Software ergonomics and man-machine dialogue, ISO/TC159/SC4/WG5. Another group, within the Human Factors Society in the United States, aims at developing human factors requirements on software. The above mentioned working group on user interface reference models insists on basing its reference model on well established knowledge. European activities sponsored by the ESPRIT program (European Strategic Programme for Research in

Information Technology) have several projects concerned with the collection of human factors knowledge. One is the HUFIT project, mentioned above, another has already resulted in a book (Christie, 1985). Further work is going on, for instance one project aiming at developing a software package of human factors knowledge which can be used by designers of office systems.

To conclude, the issue of standardization within the field of human computer interaction is characterized by a strong need for recommendations, guidelines, and even standardization, coupled to a strong fear that standardization may hamper further, creative development. Much activity is centered towards finding the relevant human factors knowledge. Hereby we approach the research frontier, which will be the topic of the forthcoming paragraphs.

5. USER PERFORMANCE

In order to perform their tasks adequately and quickly, users need systems which are easy to use. User performance, in terms of the time required to perform a particular task, can thus be used as a measurement of the ease of using a particular program. An influential analysis of performance time measurements, made by Card, Moran, & Newell (1983), shows that the time to perform a task in a computer system can be predicted from the number of keystrokes needed to get the task done by the system. This calculation however requires some particular circumstances, i.e. that the analyst knows the user´s method to perform the task (the GOMS model), and that the user is an "expert" in performing the task in the system, i.e. works without errors or hesitation.

This criterion of performance time can be applied in the evaluation of different system implementations. It is important to recognize that the type of question posed will determine the value of the information obtained. Questions of the type: "Are menus better than commands in a human-computer interface?" have resulted in almost as many answers as the number of situations, in which they have been studied. In particular, it has been discovered that the possibility to get a univocal answer to any question depends on a careful analysis of the task to be performed with the system. A form-filling task certainly puts different requirements on the user dialogue than a programming task. A CAD system without graphics is nowadays almost a contradiction, which does not imply that all applications would benefit from graphics.

The prediction of task performance, given a particular program system, is one goal aimed at by the attempts to formalize the knowledge necessary in order to perform a particular task. The GOMS model mentioned above represents one such example, the TAG model represents another. The TAG formalism (task-action grammar) was presented at the WWDU conference by Franz Schiele (Schiele & Green, 1986), and has been worked out in several different papers (Payne & Green, 1986, Green, Schiele and Payne 1986). In contrast to the GOMS model, which can predict performance times, (i.e. represents a performance model), the TAG model intends to formalize the structure of knowledge (a competence model). This can for instance be used to predict errors, which even experts may perform. (Errors are excluded from the GOMS model). (Green, Payne, Gilmore, and Mepham, 1984).

One problem with the recommendation of first specifying the task and then designing the interface to fit the task, is that the system easily gets too specific. In the words of Hutchins, Hollan & Norman: "Beware of the over-specialized system where operations are easy, but little of interest is possible". (op. cit. Norman & Draper, p. 103). Users seldomly have single, specific, tasks to perform. Many tasks which users want to perform are excluded when using a special purpose system. Therefore, it is sometimes necessary to move up at least some steps in generality in specifying the systems in order to provide the desired flexibility. A certain amount of flexibility will also be required on parl of the user.

It can then be asked, how far an expertise ranges, and if the combination of tasks to be performed by different experts is similar enough to warrant a similar general interface solution. Probably not. Instead we must accept that people, even experts, have to learn. They have to learn new applications for old systems, or new systems for old application, or both. Therefore, the criterion of usability in terms of expert performance does not cover all needs in defining user-friendliness. A supplementary measurement of usability for the pre time of rapid technological and conceptual development is "learnability". Let us therefore turn to the issue of user learning.

6. USER LEARNING

It has been argued (Waern, 1986a) and also empirically verified that computer users do not learn systems programs by being told. In particular, they do not read manuals (Carroll, 1985, Scharer, 1983). Instead they learn by doing, whereby they rely upon their own prior extracomputer knowledge.

This particular way of learning implies that a measurement of learnability of a particular system must take the prospective users´ prior knowledge into consideration. It must further consider the support of learning by doing, offered by the system.

We should then collect knowledge about how users of computer systems learn by doing. At the WWDU conference, Jean Marc Robert (Robert, 1986) suggested on basis of observations of users that program systems should support users in understanding what happens, that they must be robust and allow backtracking, and that they should support risk-taking, for instance by immediately saving everything which a user has done. Similar recommendations can be derived from the observations made by in my laboratory (Waern, 1986). In this study the main steps for learning by doing were found to consist in the following cognitive operations: noticing, remembering, interpreting and generalizing. The problems of noticing and remembering are related to the overwhelming amount of information presented in a computer system. A solution to this kind of problems is to let users have access only to selected parts of the system to start with. (e.g. Carroll, 1983).

The issues of interpreting and generalizing are related to how people understand systems, and how they explain why certain things happen. These cognitive activities have in recent research been covered by the concept of "the user´s conceptual model of the system". The model concept is an important one. The user´s possibility to understand a system can be facilitated by the system design itself. A system can work with and present a model which is understandable by the user. This will make it easier to learn than a system which does not present any model or presents an incomprehensible model. The learning advantage of a comprehensible model holds, even if the model may not be functional in the long run (Waern & Rabenius, 1986).

At present, much work is directed towards finding a good model for presenting the idea of a program system. At the WWDU conference, Norbert Streitz showed that providing a desktop metaphor facilitated the learning of file management and editing tasks more than a computer metaphor. (Streitz, Lieser & Wolters, 1986). The performance advantage only persisted over the first trials, however, as was also found in my own study.

The actual content of the model provided is important and much work is needed to elaborate a model which is easy to understand. This has been illustrated by Gerrit van der Veer, who has considered the problem of presenting an existing office automation system to novice users. (van der Veer, 1986). He and his collaborators worked out a rather complex model with pipes and branches which proved to be very useful.

The difficulty to find a good model depends on the task to be performed. For some applications, the task to use a particular program is so different from what users know a priori, that it is difficult to find a model which corresponds to their prior knowledge. This applies for instance to data base search with query languages, which are based on logical concepts. In this context it has been shown by Cecilia Katzeff (1986) that a sophisticated and unfamiliar model (the Venn diagram model) facilitated learning to solve a complex data base search task, whereas a more familiar table model did not. The Venn diagram concerns the structural aspects of the model. That content aspects also are important has been shown by Lena Linde and Monica Bergström (1986). In their study, users who were made familiar with the content of a database performed a database search quicker than those who only were trained in the formal aspects of using tables.

Users´ prior knowledge also shows up in their learnt procedures to finish a task. A theoretical basis has already been established, based on the general idea of transfer, where tasks and prior knowledges are analyzed to predict learning time and learning difficulties. (Polson & Kieras, 1983, Waern, 1983). Several studies have replicated the results from the first preliminary analyses (Ziegler, Hoppe & Faehnrich, 1986, Polson, Muncher, & Engelbeck, 1986, Karat, Boyes, Weisgerber, & Schafer, 1986). Both positive proactive transfer (i.e. increased performance in a new system) and negative proactive transfer (decreased performance in a new system) have been found, depending on the detailed relationships between prior knowledge and the new system to be learnt. Polson et al. (1986) attribute positive transfer to the common elements which exist between the prior knowledge and the system to be learnt. Karat et al. (1986) suggest that the negative transfer found in their study mainly was due to syntactic differences between systems. My own analyses (Waern, 1983, 1986) indicate that interference will occur in all kinds of situations where there is a discrepancy between the actions to be performed in previous knowledge and the new situation. If the previous knowledge contains a similar goal as the new situation and the conditions for actions are similar, the old actions will interfer with the new ones required.

The insights that users do not use manuals and that prior knowledge under some circumstances can hinder rather than help them to learn new systems lead us to consider other possible sources of learning. Several researchers have pointed out that it is important to recognize that learning about computers and computer programs seldomly takes place in splendid isolation. Only when home computers are concerned, users sit alone and ponder over the difficulties encountered. Even then, users often belong to some kind of network where they can get in touch with other users of the same system. In a work organization, contacts between people are natural. At their best such contacts function as one major source of learning for novice users. It is thus important that work is organized (both physically and psychologically) so that users easily can ask for and give help. (Bannon, 1986, Brown, 1986).

7. EFFECTS OF COMPUTERS ON THINKING

Whereas our knowledge of user performance and user learning rests on good empirical basis and sound theoretical concepts, the final topic is characterized by a sparsity of both, which only can be matched by the abundance of speculation. The problem of how computers may affect society and individual users has not yet been formulated in questions which can be answered empirically or theoretically.

A small-scale empirical study which represents one way of delimiting the problem to an empirically manageable one was presented at the WWDU conference by myself. (Waern, El-Khouri, Olofsson, Scherlund, 1986). The idea behind the study was the following: If computers represent something different from other tools which help us perform information processing tasks, it may well be the case that computer studies attract a particular type of person. If the persons attracted further get a particular education, the differences between computer trained people and those who have not been attracted by computer studies will be increased. This in turn may lead to computer systems being developed which are more foreign to a non computer interested user than necessary. The strangeness of a computer system will be further emphasized when particular people work with particular methods. Since computers concern information processing, it is most probable that the differences which will be further developed and emphasized concern information processing skills, for instance logic and problem solving.

The study compared the problem solving approaches used by persons with different educational background. It was found that students with a computational education handled logical and problem solving tasks in a different way than students not having such a background. In particular, students with computer training arrived at a representation of a problem from a given problem text more easily than non computer trained students. Also, computer trained students used more systematic strategies in searching for the solutions. This finding has some implications for the design of user interfaces. First, computer trained persons will probably underestimate the difficulties encountered by "ordinary" people in handling "ordinary" computer systems. Second, non computer trained people may benefit from some training in logics and problem solving in order to manage "ordinary" computer systems.

8. RESEARCH NEEDS FOR THE FUTURE

The research needs for the future are of two kinds: more of the same and something different.

The more of the same need concerns the issues of performance and learning. We have by no means yet all knowledge needed in these respects. In the final chapter in the ESPRIT report on Human Factors of the User-System Interface (Christie, 1986), needs, related to the following issues are stressed:

- the psychophysiological context, where studies at the behavioural, cognitive, affective and physiological (including stress reactions) are wanted.
- the organisational context, particularly when office systems are concerned, including understanding the different needs of different potential users, and developing models of organisations and organisation development.
- functional analysis of office needs.
- evaluation problems.

To this list of needs, concerned with topics to be investigated, I should like to add the topic which was mentioned last above, i.e. the possible effects of computers. The effects can range from wide sociological via narrower psychological to very small-ranged cognitive effects. This topic is included in next year´s INTERACT conference, and can well defend its place in the WWDU conference in Montreal 1989.

Further, a remark related to the methodological approach may be needed. It might seem self-evident that we do not need "blind" trial-and-error investigations comparing one particular system feature to another or one particular organizational form to another. However, much previous research has been concerned with meaningless comparisons. We know that a trial-and-error procedure is too time-consuming to be useful in this area of rapid technical development. Instead empirical investigations must be founded on careful theoretical analyses, which can give grounds for selecting the points where the chances of obtaining useful information are the greatest. We have yet seen too little of theoretically based investigations, mostly due to the fact that the field has been too young. In the future this excuse will not be valid any longer.

For the new directions, the ESPRIT recommendation includes the proposal to work with the development of models of user-system interaction as such. This is an interesting new direction. It is pointed out that "the electronic office system itself is based on information processing technology; the human can be regarded as an information processing system; and the combination of the two makes an information processing system that is a hybrid of a biological and electronic system." (op.cit. Christie, 1986, p

176).

The hybrid idea is of course not exclusively valid for office systems. In all future applications of information technology, the particularities of the combination of human and computer information processing must be considered. This applies to decision making, to production planning. It is valid for the design of mechanical tools and buildings. It must be considered when advanced supervising systems are designed, for traffic supervision as well as in nuclear plants.

We can go further than considering the information processing hybrid. The new possibilities of the combination can be regarded as a symbiosis, where both systems, the electronic and the biological, feed upon each other. Here it is important to consider that a symbiosis can enhance our problem solving capacities as human beings, but also that it can hamper it by draining our competence. Computer systems must be designed to be cognitively compatible with the human mind. Already, advanced so called "expert systems" are being designed with very little consideration of cognitive compatibility. We have to hurry in providing knowledge about human cognition in order to catch up! Come on, Montreal, 1989!

References

Bannon, L. J. Computer-mediated communcation. In: Norman, D.A. & S.W. Draper (Eds.) User centered system design. Hillsdale, New Jersey: Lawrence Erlbaum, 1986, 243-264.

Bannon, L.M. Helping users help each other. In: Norman, D.A. & S.W. Draper (Eds.) User centered system design. Hillsdale, New Jersey: Lawrence Erlbaum, 1986, 243-264.

Brown, J.S. The context of computing. In: Norman, D.A. & S.W. Draper (Eds.) User centered system design. Hillsdale, New Jersey: Lawrence Erlbaum, 1986, 243-264.

Bullinger, H-J., Davies, D.G., Faehnrich, K-P. Schackel, B., and Ziegler, J.E. Research needs and European Collaboration in human-computer interaction. Paper presented at the conference Work With Display Units, Stockholm, 1986.

Card, S., Moran, T.P. & Newell, A. The psychology of human-computer interaction. Hillsdale, New Jersey, Lawrence Erlbaum, 1983.

Carleberg, P. Improved human-computer interface using a user interface management system. Paper presented at the conference Work With Display Units, Stockholm, 1986.

Carroll, J.M. Presentation and form in user-interface architecture. Byte, 1983, 8, 113-122.

Carroll, J.M. Minimalist design for active users. In B. Shackel (Ed.) INTERACT ´84: First conference on human-computer interaction. Amsterdam: North-holland, 1985.

Christie,B. (Ed.) Human factors of the user-system interface. Amsterdam: North-Holland, 1985.

Cypher, A. The structure of users´ activities. In: D.A. Norman & S.W. Draper (Eds). User Centered System Design. Hillsdale, New Jersey: Lawrence Erlbaum, 1986.

DIN 66 234, Teil 8. Bildschirmarbeitsplätze. Grundsätze der Dialoggestaltung. Beuth Verlag, 1985.

Dzida, W. Ergonomische Normen fuer die Dialoggestaltung. In: H.-J. Bullinger (Ed.) Software Ergonomie ´85 - Mensch-Computer-Interaktion. Stuttgart: Teubner Verlag, 1985, 430-444.

Eriksson, E., Andersson, B. & Orring, R. Standardizing the user interface. Paper presented at the conference: Work With Display Units, Stockholm, 1986.

Green, T.R.G., Payne, S.J., Gilmore, D.J., & Mepham, M. Predicting expert slips. INTERACT 84: 1st IFIP conference on Computer Human Factors.

Green, T.R.G., Schiele, F., & Payne, S.J. Formalisable models of user knowledge in HCI. (in preparation).

Haack, J. & Mickasch, H. D. Psychological evaluation of CAI-systems. Paper presented at the conference: Work With Display Units, Stockholm, 1986.

Hurd, J.C. Standardizing the user-machine interface in information-processing systems. Paper presented at the conference: Work With Display Units, Stockholm, 1986.

Karat, J., Boyes, L., Weisgerber, S., & Schafer, C. Transfer between word processing systems. In: M. Mantei & P. Orbeton (Eds.) Human Factors in Computing Systems. CHI ´86 conference proceedings, New York, ACM, 1986.

Katzeff, C. Logical reasoning, models and database query writing. Paper presented at the 21st International Congress of Applied Psychology, Jerusalem, 1986.

Kieras, D.E., & Polson, P.G. An approach to the formal analysis on user complexity. International Journal of Man-Machine Studies, 1985, 22, 365-394.

Kjellberg, T. Some aspects on human factors in CAD. Paper presented at the conference: Work With Display Units, Stockholm, 1986.

Kjellberg, T. Integrated computer aid to support human problem solving and communication for mechanical production. A systems approach based on product modelling. Doctoral dissertation, in Swedish. Department of Manufacturing Systems, The Royal Institute of Technology, Stockholm, 1982.

Kjellberg, T. The integration of CAD/CAM based on product modelling for better human communication. 16th CIRP seminar, Tokyo, 1984.

Kjellberg, T. Use of AI for CAD/CAM. Nicograph, Tokyo, 1985.

Linde, L. & Bergstrm, M. User´s mental image of the content and search principles in a database. Paper presented at the conference: Work With Display Units, Stockholm, 1986.

Lynch, G. & Meads, J. In search of a user interface reference model. Report on the SIGCHI workshop on user interface reference models. SIGCHI bulletin (in press).

Miyata, Y. & Normn, D. Psychological issues in support of multiple activities. In: D.A. Norman & S.W. Draper (Eds). User Centered System Design. Hillsdale, New Jersey: Lawrence Erlbaum, 1986.

Moran, T. P. Where is the action in human-computer interaction? Paper presented at the conference Work With Display Units, Stockholm, 1986.

Nickerson, R.S. Man-Computer Interaction: a challenge for human factors research. IEEE Transactions on Man-Machine Systems, MMS-10 4, 1969, 164 - 180.

Norman, D.A. & Draper, S.W. (Eds.) User centered system design. Hillsdale, New Jersey, Lawrence Erlbaum, 1986.

Payne, S.J. & Green, T.R.G. Task-action grammars: a model of the mental representation of task languages. Submitted to Human Computer Interaction.
Pelz, W.H., & Wittstock, M. Methodological study to develop a taxonomy of userfriendliness for application software. Paper presented at the conference Work With Display Units, Stockholm, 1986.
Polson, P., Muncher, E. & Engelbeck, G. A test of a common elements theory of transfer. In: M. Mantei & P. Orbeton (Eds.) Human Factors in Computing Systems. CHI ´86 conference proceedings, New York, ACM, 1986.
Robert, J.M. Some highlights of learning by exploration. Paper presented at the conference: Work With Display Units, Stockholm, 1986.
Scharer, L.L. User training: Less is more. Datamation, 1983, July, 175-182.
Schiele, F. & Green, T.R.G. Towards task-action grammars for real systems. Paper presented at the conference Work With Display Units, Stockholm, 1986.
Shackel, B. Ergonomics for a computer. Design, 120, 1959, 36-39.
Smith, S., & Mosier, J.N. Design guidelines for user-system interface software. Technical Report ESD-TR-84-190 U.S.A.F. Electronic Systems Division, Hanscom Air Force Base, Massachusetts, 1984.
Streitz, N., Lieser, A. & Wolters, A. User-initiated vs computer-initiated dialogue modes: A comparative analysis of cognitive processes based on differences in user models. Paper presented at the conference: Work With Display Units, Stockholm, 1986.
Waern, Y. Learning computerized tasks. HUFACIT reports, Department of Psychology, University of Stockholm, No.8, 1986 (a).
Waern, Y. Information used and users´ models of a computerized task. Paper presented at the MACINTER meeting, IAAPs 21st International Congress, Jerusalem, 1986 (b).
Waern, Y. Learning computerized tasks as related to prior task knowledge. International Journal of Man-Machine Studies, 1985, 22, 441-445.
Waern, Y., El-Khouri, B., Olofsson, M., & Scherlund, K. Does computer education affect problem solving strategies? Paper presented at the conference: Work With Display Units, Stockholm, 1986.
van der Veer, G.C. Computer systems and human learning. Paper presented at the MACINTER meeting, IAAPs 21st International Congress, Jerusalem, 1986
Ziegler, J.E., Hoppe, H.U., & Fähnrich, K.P. Learning and transfer for text and graphics editing with a direct manipulation interface. In: M. Mantei & P. Orbeton (Eds.) Human Factors in Computing Systems. CHI ´86 conference proceedings, New York, ACM, 1986.

AUTHOR INDEX